MILITARY AIRCRAFT MARKINGS 2025
Stuart R Schofield

Ȼ Crécy

Crécy Publishing Ltd

This 45th edition published by Crécy Publishing Ltd 2025

ISBN 9781800353282

Printed in Turkey by Imak Ofset

Crecy Publishing Ltd
1a Ringway Trading Est
Shadowmoss Rd
Manchester
M22 5LH
Tel +44 (0)161 499 0024
www.crecy.co.uk

FSC
www.fsc.org
MIX
Paper | Supporting
responsible forestry
FSC® C111584

Photo Credits in this edition of Military
Aircraft Markings are:
HJC: Howard Curtis
SRS: Stuart Schofield

Front cover:
The RAF's first Boeing E-7A Wedgetail,
WT001, returns to Birmingham in
October 2024 after being painted at
Southend in the markings of 8 squadron;
the aircraft also has the emblem of
NATO's Airborne Early Warning &
Control Force (NAEW&CF).
© Dave Sturges/AirTeamImages.com

Rear cover:
Top: Firmly established as the
successor to the Hercules in RAF
service, Atlas ZM416 is seen here in
the static park at Farnborough. *HJC*
Middle: PG712, a Dutch-based DH82A
Tiger Moth, normally to be found at
Hilversum airfield close to Amsterdam,
seen here a long way from home at a
Moth fly-in at Belvoir Castle in
Leicestershire. *SRS*
Bottom: When you spot and take
photographs in Switzerland, the stunning
scenery does most of the work for you!
Here EC635 T-353 is seen landing at its
home base at Alpnach. *SRS*

MILITARY AIRCRAFT MARKINGS 2025

CONTENTS

This 46th annual edition of Military Aircraft Markings follows the pattern of previous years and lists in alphabetical and numerical order the aircraft that carry United Kingdom military registrations, and which are normally based, or might be seen, in the UK. It also includes airworthy and current RAF/RN/Army aircraft that are based permanently or temporarily overseas. Aircraft used as targets on MOD ranges to which access is restricted, and UK military aircraft that have been permanently grounded overseas and unlikely to return to Britain, have generally been omitted.

Aircraft in UK military service which carry civil registrations are listed, as are historic aircraft wearing overseas markings which are based in the UK or likely to be seen in the UK. Aircraft belonging to the armed forces or governments of foreign countries are listed, including American military aircraft based in the UK and Europe.

Where an aircraft carries a false registration, this is quoted in italic type and very often these registrations are carried by replicas, which are denoted by <R> after the type. The manufacturer and aircraft type are given, together with recent alternative, previous, secondary or civil identity (shown in round brackets). The operating unit and its based location, along with any known unit and code markings[in square brackets] are given as accurately as possible. Where aircraft carry special or commemorative markings, a $ indicates this.

Up-to-date code changes, for example when aircraft move between units, might not be as printed here because of subsequent events, but codes are regularly updated and sent out in the monthly email updates to the "Military Aircraft Markings" newsgroup accessed through groups.io.

Airframes which will not appear in the next edition because of sale, accident, etc., have their fates, where known, shown in italic type in the locations column.

As is often the case, the only real constant in 2024 was change. Two sizeable wars continue, between Russia and Ukraine, and between Israel and Gaza. Neither shows signs of coming to a logical conclusion, although as I write this we are less than two weeks away from the swearing-in of President Trump for his second term as President of the United States of America, so we will see where that may take us. European support for Ukraine (particularly) continues, with a number of nations having now donated surplus F-16s, as alluded to last year. A flight school (EFTC) has been set up in Fetesti, Romania, utilising ex-Netherlands AF airframes, whilst Norway and Belgium (at least) have also donated aircraft directly to Ukraine. Ironically, these now fall outside the scope of this book! It is always difficult to decide what 'should be in', and the rough rule of thumb that Howard gave me when he handed over the reins in late 2022 as regards what 'makes the cut' is, "Has this been to the UK?", or maybe, "Does this have the potential of coming to the UK?" Obviously the second statement is a lot more subjective than the first! So, I've removed some entries that I don't think belong. I'm sure this may cause some wailing and gnashing of teeth, but there ARE some additions too, which I think fits the remit better.

UK-wise, there have been no F-35B deliveries since the publication of the 2024 edition of this book, with the backlog at the factory at Fort Worth slowly being worked through. Older Typhoons are now at Warton going through the 'Reduce to Produce' (RTP) programme, being stripped for useable parts and the remains scrapped. As ever, the active Typhoon fleet is in a constant state of flux, with jets regularly rotated between the two operational bases at Coningsby and Lossiemouth, and heavier maintenance also undertaken at Coningsby with the TMF.

Army Air Corps aviation continues to build up the AH-64E fleet, with most examples now delivered. Engineering oversight for these helicopters comes from 7 REME at Wattisham, with airframes rotated between the active units both here and at Middle Wallop as required, although a new 'depth' maintenance facility is shortly due to become fully operational at Middle Wallop.

Not a massive amount of change to report in Europe either. F-35 deliveries have begun to trickle in, with Norway almost at full strength, and the Netherlands not too far behind. Belgium also has its first jets on hand, as does Poland, with three airframes recently delivered to the new training facility at Ebbing ANGB/Fort Smith, AR, USA. As already mentioned, any remaining European F-16s have been inducted into the Ukrainian war effort, one way or another, with one airframe already sadly lost while in combat. Spain has signed up for some more Typhoons, ostensibly to replace the mainland-based EF-18M Hornets, in addition to the Typhoons that will directly replace the ex-USN F/A-18As at Gando in the Canary Islands, a process that is due to start in the coming year.

A few changes in the US Air Force – the UK-based F-35s saw no change for much of the year, as the "TR-3" software issues continued. Finally, it was decided that non-updated 'TR-2' jets would be delivered to combat units while the fix was being worked on, so Lakenheath has recently seen the arrival of five jets from Nellis AFB, NV, which at the time of writing retain their 'WA' tailcodes, although the wisdom appears to be that this will not be for much longer. Further Nellis jets are expected at Lakenheath, whilst a number of new-build 'LN'-coded jets have been sighted at Nellis. Elsewhere in the USAF, the KC-10A finally bowed out of service after many years as a "force multiplier". KC-46A deliveries continue, with one-hundred-odd airframes now in service. The KC-135R/T fleet continues, especially with the ANG and AFRC units, and will continue to do so for a number of years yet. Which leaves a brief mention for the B-21 Raider. The first example is test flying, and the USAF is very keen that this is the future of the manned bomber fleet. Once they start to come on stream they will be included in this book, on the assumption that we will get examples visiting the UK at some point. And finally, we need to mention the venerable B-52. The engine upgrade programme is underway, and modified jets will be known as B-52Js. The earliest examples are around ten years older than me and are planned to fly for around another twenty years. I'm interested to see which one outlives which!

The compiler wishes to thank the many people who have taken the trouble to send comments, additions, deletions and other useful information since the publication of the previous edition of Military Aircraft Markings, either directly or through logs online. In particular, the following individuals: John Alexander, Robert Belcher, Lee Botham, Rod Burgess, Mike Bursell, Stu Carr, Ian Carroll, Pete Carter, Mick Crowe, Howard J Curtis, Patrick Dirksen, Matt Ellis, Ian Farquharson, Graham Gaff, Michael Greenway, Kevin Herpe, Anthony Hutchings, Nige Howarth, Dick Johnston, Martin Kaye, Paul van der Linden, "MADFOX", Colin Manville, Steve Martin, Tom McGhee, Paul Moiser, David Moore, Tim Newman, Dave Oliver, Andy Patsalides, Grant Robinson, Ben Sadler, David Stevens, Andrew Stewart, Adrian Stürmer, Martyn Swann, Tony Szulc, David Thompson, Mike Tighe, John Waller, Neil Williams, and any others I may have missed (for which, apologies in advance!)

This 2025 edition has also relied upon the printed publications and/or associated internet web-sites as follows: Air-Britain Information Exchange (AB-IX), Airfields Google Group, 'Air Forces Monthly' magazine, CAA G-INFO Web Site, Coningsby Aviation Site, Delta Reflex, Fighter Control, Humberside Air Review, Joe Baugher's Home Page, Mildenhall and Lakenheath Movements Group (SMAS), Mildenhall-Lakenheath blog, Brian Pickering/'Military Aviation Review', Mil Spotters' Forum, NAMAR Group, Planebase NG, RAF Shawbury Group, Lloyd P Robinson/Aviation Heritage UK, 'Scramble' magazine, Tom McGhee/UK Serials Resource Centre and Mark Ray/Wolverhampton Aviation Group.

Information shown is believed to be correct on 19th January 2025.

From my personal viewpoint, once again I need to offer huge thanks to the 'holy trinity' of Howard Curtis, Graham Gaff and Tom McGhee. Without their input, the content of the book, especially the UK section, would be a tiny shadow of what it currently is. Their constant updates throughout the year allow me to keep things as current as possible, and I thank them hugely for their efforts. A big call out to Kevin Herpe too – as a former "man from the ministry" (Civil Aviation Authority), his regular, detailed UK register updates are particularly useful when updating the UK military section of the book, with a number of warbirds also often featuring.

And as always, huge thanks to my very understanding wife Sam, who is pretty used to the way this works by now. I lock myself away in the office for days and weeks at a time, eventually a book gets produced, and then we go on holiday! 2024 has been an on-and-off year for us both health-wise, so it's gratifying to know I have her unfaltering love and support to help me make this happen, because it would be much more difficult without it.

Finally, may I introduce Dexter. He is a 9-year-old, extremely fluffy, long-haired black cat, who lets Sam and I live in his house. Historically aloof and rarely a lap cat, Dexter decided this winter that he would indeed become one, favouring MY lap at MY desk whilst writing THIS book! As I write this he is next to me, on a storage unit that he has adopted as an acceptable location to spend his sleeping hours, which are most of them nowadays.

Stuart R Schofield, Cheshire, January 2025

Note: The publisher will be pleased to receive comments, corrections and further information for inclusion in subsequent editions of Military Aircraft Markings. Please send your information to Military Aircraft Markings, Crécy Publishing Ltd, 1a Ringway trading Estate, Shadowmoss Road, Manchester M22 5LH.

$	Aircraft in special markings
AAC	Army Air Corps
AACS	Airborne Air Control Squadron
AC	Air Cadets
ACCGS	Air Cadets Central Gliding School
ACS	Air Control Squadron
ACW	Air Control Wing
ADF	Air Defence Force
ADSU	Apache Depth Support Unit
AEF	Air Experience Flight
AESS	Air Engineering & Survival School
AEW	Airborne Early Warning
AFB	Air Force Base
AFD	Air Fleet Department
AFRC	Air Force Reserve Command
AG	Airlift Group
AGA	Academia General del Aire (General Air Academy)
AGS	Air Ground Surveillance
AK	Alaska
AL	Alabama
AMD-BA	Avions Marcel Dassault-Breguet Aviation
AMG	Aircraft Maintenance Group
AM&SU	Aircraft Maintenance & Storage Unit
AMRO	Aircraft Maintenance and Repair Organisation
AMW	Air Mobility Wing
ANG	Air National Guard
AR	Arkansas
ARS	Air Refuelling Squadron
ARW	Air Refuelling Wing
AS	Airlift Squadron/Air Squadron
ATC	Air Training Corps
ATCC	Air Traffic Control Centre
AVDEF	Aviation Defence Service
Avn	Aviation
AW	AgustaWestland/Airlift Wing/Armstrong Whitworth Aircraft
AWC	Air Warfare Centre
BAC	British Aircraft Corporation
BAe	British Aerospace
BAPC	British Aviation Preservation Council (now known as Aviation Heritage UK)
BATUK	British Army Training Unit Kenya
BATUS	British Army Training Unit Suffield
BBMF	Battle of Britain Memorial Flight
BDRF	Battle Damage Repair Flight
BDRT	Battle Damage Repair Training
Be	Beech
Bf	Bayerische Flugzeugwerke
BG	Bomber Group
BGA	British Gliding & Soaring Association
bk	black (squadron colours and markings)
bl	blue (squadron colours and markings)
Blt	Bojová letka (attack squadron)
BP	Boulton & Paul/Boulton Paul
br	brown (squadron colours and markings)
BS	Bomber Squadron
BUPERS SDC	Bureau of Personnel Sea Duty Component
BUTEC	British Underwater Test & Evaluation Centre
B-V	Boeing-Vertol
BW	Bomber Wing
CA	California
CAARP	Co-operative des Ateliers Air de la Région Parisienne
CAC	Commonwealth Aircraft Corporation
CACG	Command and Control Group
CAE	Centro Addastramento Equipaggi (Crew Training Centre)
CASA	Construcciones Aeronautics SA
CATS	Cassidian Aviation Training Services
CC	County Council
CC Air	Competence Centre Air
CCF	Combined Cadet Force/Canadian Car & Foundry Company
CEAM	Centre d'Expertise Aérienne Militaire (Centre of Military Air Expertise)

CEMAST	Centre of Excellence in Engineering & Manufacturing Advanced Skills Training
CEPA	Centre d'Expérimentation Pratique de l'Aéronautique Navale
CFAMI	Centre de Formation Aérienne Militaire Initiale de Salon
CFIA	Centre de Formation Interarmées NH.90
CFS	Central Flying School
CIEH	Centre d'Instruction des Equipages d'Hélicoptères
CHFMU	Commando Helicopter Force Maintenance Unit
CinC	Commander in Chief
CinCLANT	Commander in Chief Atlantic
CLV	Centrum Leteckeho Vycviku (Air Training Centre)
CMU	Central Maintenance Unit
Co	Company
CO	Colorado
COMALAT	Commandement de l'Aviation Légère de l'Armée de Terre
Comp	Composite with
CSP	Capability Sustainment Programme
CT	Connecticut
CV	Chance-Vought
D-BA	Daimler-Benz Aerospace
D-BD	Dassault-Breguet Dornier
D&G	Dumfries and Galloway
DCTT	Defence College of Technical Training
DE	Delaware
DE&S	Defence Equipment and Support
DEFTS	Defence Elementary Flying Training School
DEODS	Defence Explosives Ordnance Disposal School
Det	Detachment
D/F HFAZT	Deutsch/Französisches Heeresfligerausbildungszentrum Tiger
DGA	Délégation Générale de l'Armement
DH	de Havilland
DHC	de Havilland Canada
DMS	Defence Movements School
DS&TL	Defence Science & Technology Laboratory
DSAE	Defence School of Aeronautical Engineering
DSEME	Defence School of Electro-Mechanical Engineering
DSG	Defence Support Group
DSMarE	Defence School of Marine Engineering
Dvlt	Dopravná vrtul'niková letka (Helicopter Transport Squadron)
EA	Escadron Aérien (Air Squadron)
EAAT	Escadrille Avions de l'Armée de Terre
EAC	Ecole de l'Aviation de Chasse (Fighter Aviation School)
EALAT	Ecole de l'Aviation Légère de l'Armée de Terre
EAP	European Aircraft Project
EAT	Ecole de l'Aviation de Transport (Transport Aviation School)
EC	Escadre de Chasse (Fighter Wing)
E-CATS	EADS Cognac Aviation Training Services
ECG	Electronic Combat Group
ECM	Electronic Counter Measures
ECS	Electronic Countermeasures Squadron
EdC	Escadron de Convoyage
EDCA	Escadron de Détection et de Control Aéroportée (Airborne Detection & Control Sqn)
EE	English Electric/Escadrille Electronique
EEA	Escadron Electronique Aéroporté
EFA	Ecole Franco Allemande
EFATT	Escadron Franco-Allemande de Transport Tactique
EFTS	Elementary Flying Training School
EH	Escadron d'Helicoptères (Helicopter Squadron)
EHADT	Escadrille Helicoptères de l'Armée de Terre
EHI	European Helicopter Industries
EKW	Eidgenössiches Konstruktionswerkstätte
el	Eskadra Lotnicza (Air Sqn)
EL	Escadre de Liaison (Liaison Wing)
elt	Eskadra Lotnictwa Taktycznego (Tactical Air Squadron)
eltr	Eskadra Lotnictwa Transportowego (Air Transport Squadron)
EMA	East Midlands Airport
EMB	Ecoles Militaires de Bourges
EMVO	Elementaire Militaire Vlieg Opleiding (Elementary Flying Training)
EoN	Elliot's of Newbury
EPNER	Ecole du Personnel Navigant d'Essais et de Reception

ER	Escadre de Reconnaissance (Reconnaissance Wing)
ERV	Escadron de Ravitaillement en Vol (Aerial Refuelling Squadron)
ERVTS	Escadron de Ravitaillement en Vol et de Transport Stratégique (Air Refuelling and Strategic Transport Squadron]
ES	Escadrille de Servitude
ESAM	Ecole Supérieur d'Application du Matériel
Esc	Escuadron (Squadron)
ESHE	Ecole de Spécialisation sur Hélicoptères Embarqués (School of Specialisation on Embarked Helicopters)
Esk	Eskadrile/Eskadrille (Squadron)
Esq	Esquadra (Squadron)
ET	Escadre de Transport (Transport Wing)
ETED	Escadron de Transformation des Equipages Mirage 2000D
ETO	Escadron de Transition Operationnelle (Operational Transition Squadron)
ETPS	Empire Test Pilots' School
ETR	Escadron de Transformation Rafale
ETS	Engineering Training School/Escadron de Transport Stratégique
ETTL	Escadre de Transport Tactique et Logistique (Tactical and Logistics Transport Wing)
EVAA	Ecole de Voltige de l'Armée de l'Air (French Air Force Aerobatics School)
FAA	Fleet Air Arm (UK)/Federal Aviation Administration (USA)
FACO	Final Assembly & Check Out
FASGW	Future Anti-Surface Guided Weapon
FBS	Flugbereitschaftstaffel (Flight Readiness Squadron)
FBW	Fly-by-wire
FC	Forskokcentralen (Flight Centre)
FE	Further Education
FETC	Fire and Emergency Training Centre
ff	Front fuselage
FG	Fighter Group
FH	Fairchild-Hiller
FI	Falkland Islands
FJWOEU	Fast Jet & Weapons Operational Evaluation Unit
FL	Florida
FLO	Forsvarets Logistikk Organisasjon (Defence Logistics Organisation)
FISt	Fliegerstaffel (Flight Squadron)
Flt	Flight
FMA	Fabrica Militar de Aviones
FMV	Forsvarets Materielwerk (Defence Material Works)
FS	Fighter Squadron
FTS	Flying Training School
FTW	Flying Training Wing
Fw	Focke Wulf
FW	Fighter Wing/FlugWerk/Foster Wickner
FY	Fiscal Year
GA	Georgia
GAF	Government Aircraft Factory
GAL	General Aircraft Ltd
GAM	Groupe Aerien Mixte (Composite Air Group)
GAM/STAT	Groupement Aéromobile/Section Technique de l'Armée de Terre
GASU	Garda Air Support Unit
gd	gold (squadron colours and markings)
GD	General Dynamics
GEA	Gruppo Efficienza Aeromobili (Italian AF)/Gruppo Esplorazione Aeromarittima (GdiF)
GEM	Grupo de Escuelas de Matacán (Matacán Group of Schools)
GI	Ground Instruction/Groupement d'Instruction (Instructional Section)
GMS	Glider Maintenance Section
gn	green (squadron colours and markings)
GRD	Gruppe fur Rustungdienste (Group for Service Preparation)
GT	Grupo de Transporte (Transport Wing)
GTT	Grupo de Transporte de Tropos (Troop Carrier Wing)
gy	grey (squadron colours and markings)
H&HS	Headquarters & Headquarters Squadron
HAF	Historic Aircraft Flight
HAPS	High Altitude Pseudo-Satellite
HavLLv	Hävittäjälentolaivue
HC	Helicopter Combat Support Squadron
HekoP	Helikopteripataljoona (Helicopter Battalion)
HF	Historic Flying Ltd
HI	Hawaii

HK	Helikopterikomppannia (Helicopter Company)
Hkp.Bat	Helikopter Bataljon (Helicopter Battalion)
HMA	Helicopter Maritime Attack
HMS	Her Majesty's Ship
HP	Handley-Page
HQ	Headquarters
HS	Hawker Siddeley
HSG	Hubschraubergeschwader (Helicopter Squadron)
IA	Iowa
IAF	Israeli Air Force
IAP	International Airport
IFTS	International Flying Training School
IL	Illinois
IlmaStk	IlmataiStelukeskus
IN	Indiana
IntHubschr-	Internationales Hubschrauberausbildungszentrum
AusbZ	(International Helicopter Training Centre)
IOW	Isle Of Wight
IWM	Imperial War Museums
JADTEU	Joint Air Delivery Test and Evaluation Unit
JARTS	Joint Aircraft Recovery & Transportation Sqn
JFACTSU	Joint Forward Air Control Training & Standards Unit
JHC	Joint Helicopter Command
JMRC	Joint Multinational Readiness Centre
KHR	Kampfhubschrauberregiment (Combat Helicopter Regiment)
Kridlo	Wing
KS	Kansas
LA	Louisiana
lbvr	letka Bitevnich Vrtulníkú (Attack Helicopter Squadron)
Letka	Squadron
LTDB	Lufttransportdienst des Bundes (Federal Air Transport Services)
LTG	Lufttransportgeschwader (Air Transport Wing)
lTHSSta	leichte Transporthubschrauberstaffel
LTO	Letalska Transportni Oddelek (Air Transport Department)
LtSt	Lufttransport Staffel
LTV	Ling-Temco-Vought
LVG	Luftwaffen Versorgungs Geschwader (Air Force Maintenance Wing)/Luft Verkehrs Gesellschaft
LZO	Letecky Zku ební Odbor (Aviation Test Department)
m	multi-coloured (squadron colours and markings)
MA	Massachusetts
MADG	Marshall Aerospace & Defence Group
MAPK	Mira Anachestisis Pantos Kerou (All Weather Interception Sqn)
MBB	Messerschmitt Bolkow-Blohm
MCAS	Marine Corps Air Station
McD	McDonnell Douglas
MD	Maryland
MDMF	Merlin Depth Maintenance Facility
Med	Medical
MFG	Marine Flieger Geschwader (Naval Air Wing)
MFSU	Merlin Depth Forward Support Unit
MH	Max Holste
MI	Maritime Interdiction/Michigan
MIB	Military Intelligence Battalion
MiG	Mikoyan — Gurevich
MMU	(European) Multinational Multi-Role Tanker Transport Unit
MN	Minnesota
MO	Missouri
Mod	Modified
MOD	Ministry of Defence
MPSU	Multi-Platform Support Unit
MR	Maritime Reconnaissance
MRH	Multi-role Helikopters
M&RU	Marketing & Recruitment Unit
MS	Mississippi/Morane-Saulnier
MT	Montana
MTHR	Mittlerer Transporthubschrauber Regiment (Medium Transport Helicopter Regiment)
MTM	Mira Taktikis Metaforon (Tactical Transport Sqn)
NA	North American

NACDS	Naval Air Command Driving School
NAEW&CF	NATO Airborne Early Warning & Control Force
NAF	Naval Air Facility
NAS	Naval Air Squadron (UK)/Naval Air Station (US)
NATO	North Atlantic Treaty Organisation
NAWC	Naval Air Warfare Center
NAWC-AD	Naval Air Warfare Center Aircraft Division
NBC	Nuclear, Biological and Chemical
ND	North Dakota
NDMA	Norwegian Defence Material Agency
NE	North-East/Nebraska
NFH	NATO Frigate Helicopter
NH	New Hampshire
NI	Northern Ireland
NJ	New Jersey
NM	New Mexico
NV	Nevada
NY	New York
NYARC	North Yorks Aircraft Restoration Centre
OEU	Operational Evaluation Unit
OFMC	Old Flying Machine Company
OGMA	Oficinas Gerais de Material Aeronautico
OH	Ohio
OK	Oklahoma
or	orange (squadron colours and markings)
OSAC	Operational Support Airlift Command
OSBL	Oddelek Sholskih Bojni Letal (Training & Combat School)
OT&E	Operational Test & Evaluation
P2MF	Puma 2 Maintenance Flight
PA	Pennsylvania
PAS	Presidential Airlift Squadron
PAT	Priority Air Transport Detachment
PBN	Pilatus Britten-Norman
PDSH	Puma Depth Support Hub
PLM	Pulk Lotnictwa Mysliwskiego (Fighter Regiment)
pr	purple (squadron colours and markings)
PR	Puerto Rico
r	red (squadron colours and markings)
R	Replica
RAeS	Royal Aeronautical Society
RAF	Royal Aircraft Factory/Royal Air Force
RAFC	Royal Air Force College
RAFM	Royal Air Force Museum
RAFGSA	Royal Air Force Gliding and Soaring Association
RE	Royal Engineers
Regt	Regiment
REME	Royal Electrical & Mechanical Engineers
rf	Rear fuselage
RFA	Royal Fleet Auxiliary
RHC	Régiment d'Helicoptères de Combat (Combat Helicopter Regiment)
RHFS	Régiment d'Helicoptères des Forces Spéciales (Special Forces Helicopter Regiment)
RI	Rhode Island
RJAF	Royal Jordanian Air Force
RM	Royal Marines
RMB	Royal Marines Base
RN	Royal Navy
RNAS	Royal Naval Air Station
RNGSA	Royal Navy Gliding and Soaring Association
RPAS	Remotely Piloted Air System
RQS	Rescue Squadron
R-R	Rolls-Royce
RS	Reid & Sigrist/Reconnaissance Squadron
RSV	Reparto Sperimentale Volo (Experimental Flight School)
RTP	Reduction To Produce
RW	Reconnaissance Wing
SA	Scottish Aviation
SAAB	Svenska Aeroplan Aktieboleg
SAAE	School of Army Aeronautical Engineering
SAC	Strategic Airlift Capability

SAL	Scottish Aviation Limited
SAR	Search and Rescue
Saro	Saunders-Roe
SARTU	Search and Rescue Training Unit
SC	South Carolina
SCW	Strategic Communications Wing
SD	South Dakota
SEPECAT	Société Européenne de Production de l'avion Ecole de Combat et d'Appui Tactique
SES	Science and Engineering Services
SFB	Space Force Base
SFDO	School of Flight Deck Operations
SHAPE	Supreme Headquarters Allied Powers Europe
si	silver (squadron colours and markings)
SKAMG	Sea King Aircraft Maintenance Group
Skv	Skvadron (Squadron)
SLK	Stíhacie Letecké Kridlo (Fighter Air Wing)
slt	stíhací letka (Fighter Squadron)
SLV	School Licht Vliegwezen (Flying School)
Sm	Smaldeel (Squadron)
SNCAN	Société Nationale de Constructions Aéronautiques du Nord
SOG	Special Operations Group
SOS	Special Operations Squadron
SoTT	School of Technical Training
SOW	Special Operations Wing
SPAD	Société Pour les Appareils Deperdussin
SPP	Strojirny Prvni Petilesky
Sqn	Squadron
Sz.D.REB	'Szentgyörgyi Deszö' Harcászati Repülö Bázis
TA	Territorial Army
TAP	Transporten Avio Polk (Air Transport Regiment)
TASF(N)	Tornado Aircraft Servicing Flight (North)
TAZLS	Technische Ausbildungs Zentrum Luftwaffe Süd (TAubZLwSüd, Technical Training Centre South)
TES	Test and Evaluation Squadron
TFC	The Fighter Collection
TGp	Test Groep
TH	Transporthelikopter
TIARA	Tornado Integrated Avionics Research Aircraft
tl	taktická letka (Tactical Squadron)
TLG	Taktisches Luftwaffegeschwader (Air Force Tactical Squadron)
TMU	Typhoon Maintenance Unit
TN	Tennessee
Tr AB	Transport Aviation Brigade
TS	Test Squadron
ts	transportnia speciálni letka (special transport squadron)
TsAGI	Tsentral'ny Aerogidrodinamicheski Instut (Central Aero & Hydrodynamics Institute)
TSF	Tucano Servicing Flight
TsLw	Technische Schule der Luftwaffe (Luftwaffe Technical School)
TST	Tornado Support Team
TTH	Tactical Transport Helicopter
TukiLLv	Tukilentolaivue
TW	Test Wing
TX	Texas
UAS	University Air Squadron
UAV	Unmanned Air Vehicle
Überwg	Überwachungsgeschwader
UK	United Kingdom
US	United States
USAF	United States Air Force
USAFE	United States Air Forces in Europe
USAREUR	US Army Europe
USCGS	US Coast Guard Station
USEUCOM	United States European Command
USMC	United States Marine Corps
USN	United States Navy
USNWTSPM	United States Navy Test Pilots School
USW	University of South Wales
UT	Utah
VA	Virginia

VAAC	Vectored thrust Advanced Aircraft flight Control
VADOR	Vecteur Aéroporté de Désignation, d'Observation et de Reconnaissance (airborne designation, observation and reconnaissance vector)
VFW	Vereinigte Flugtechnische Werke
VGS	Volunteer Gliding Squadron
vlt	výcviková letka (training squadron)
VMGR	Marine Aerial Refuelling/Transport Squadron
VMGRT	Marine Aerial Refuelling/Transport Training Squadron
VQ	Fleet Air Reconnaissance Squadron
VR	Fleet Logistic Support Squadron
vrl	vrtulníková letka (helicopter squadron)
VS	Vickers-Supermarine
w	white (squadron colours and markings)
WA	Washington
WCM	Wildcat Contractor Maintenance
Wg	Wing
WHL	Westland Helicopters Ltd
WI	Wisconsin
WLT	Weapons Loading Training
WMF	Wildcat Maintenance Facility
WR-ALC	Warner Robins Air Logistics Complex
WRS	Weather Reconnaissance Squadron
WS	Westland
WSK	Wytwornia Sprzetu Kominikacyjnego
WST	Wildcat Support Team
WTD	Wehrtechnische Dienstelle (Technical Support Unit)
WV	West Virginia
WW2	World War II
WY	Wyoming
WZM	Wildcat Zonal Maintenance
y	yellow (squadron colours and markings)
zDL	základna Dopravního Letectva (Air Transport Base)
zL	základna Letectva (Air Force Base)
zSL	základna Speciálního Letectva (Training Air Base)
zTL	základna Taktického Letectva (Tactical Air Base)
zVrL	základna Vrtulníkového Letectva (Helicopter Air Base)

A Guide to the Location of Operational Military Bases in the UK

This section is to assist the reader to locate the places in the United Kingdom where operational military aircraft (including helicopters and gliders) are based.

The alphabetical order listing gives each location in relation to its county and to its nearest classified road(s) (*by* means adjoining; *of* means close to), together with its approximate direction and mileage from the centre of a nearby major town or city. Some civil airports are included where active military units are also based, but **excluded** are MoD sites with non-operational aircraft (e.g. *gate guardians*), the bases of privately-owned civil aircraft that wear military markings and museums. For GPS users, Latitude and Longitude are also listed.

User	Base name	County/Region	Location [Lat./long.]	Distance/direction from (town)
Army	Abingdon	Oxfordshire	W by B4017, W of A34 [N51°41'16" W001°18'58"]	5m SSW of Oxford
Army	Aldergrove/Belfast	Co Antrim Airport	W by A26 [N54°39'27" W006°12'578"]	13m W of Belfast
RAF	Barkston Heath	Lincolnshire	W by B6404, S of A153 [N52°57'46" W000°33'38"]	5m NNE of Grantham
RAF	Benson	Oxfordshire	E by A423 [N51°36'55" W001°05'45"]	1m NE of Wallingford
QinetiQ/ RAF	Boscombe Down	Wiltshire	S by A303, W of A338 [N51°09'12" W001°45'04"]	6m N of Salisbury
RAF	Brize Norton	Oxfordshire	W of A4095 [N51°45'00" W001°35'01"]	5m SW of Witney

User	Base name	County/Region	Location [Lat./long.]	Distance/direction from (town)
Marshall	Cambridge Airport/ Teversham	Cambridgeshire	S by A1303 [N52°12'18" E000°10'30"]	2m E of Cambridge
RAF	Coningsby	Lincolnshire	S of A153, W by B1192 [N53°05'35" W000°10'00"]	10m NW of Boston
DCAE	Cosford	Shropshire	W of A41, N of A464 [N52°38'25" W002°18'20"]	9m WNW of Wolverhampton
RAF	Cranwell	Lincolnshire	N by A17, S by B1429 [N53°01'49" W000°29'00"]	5m WNW of Sleaford
RN	Culdrose	Cornwall	E by A3083 [N50°05'08" W005°15'17"]	1m SE of Helston
USAF	Fairford	Gloucestershire	S of A417 [N51°41'01" W001°47'24"]	9m ESE of Cirencester
Standard-Aero	Fleetlands	Hampshire	E by A32 [N50°50'06" W001°10'07"]	2m SE of Fareham
RAF	Halton	Buckinghamshire	N of A4011, S of B4544 [N51°47'28" W000°44'11"]	4m ESE of Aylesbury
RAF	Kenley	Greater London	W of A22 [N51°18'20" W000°05'37"]	1m W of Warlingham
RAF	Kirknewton	Lothian	E by B7031, N by A70 [N55°52'32" W003°24'04"]	8m SW of Edinburgh
USAF	Lakenheath	Suffolk	W by A1065 [N52°24'33" E000°33'40"]	8m W of Thetford
RAF	Leeming	North Yorkshire	E by A1 [N54°17'33" W001°32'07"]	5m SW of Northallerton
Army	Leuchars	Fife	E of A919 [N56°22'28" W002°51'50"]	7m SE of Dundee
RAF	Lossiemouth	Moray	W of B9135, S of B9040 [N57°42'22" W003°20'20"]	4m N of Elgin
RAF	Marham	Norfolk	N by A1122 [N52°38'54" E000°33'02"]	6m W of Swaffham
Army	Middle Wallop	Hampshire	S by A343 [N51°08'35" W001°34'14"]	6m SW of Andover
USAF	Mildenhall	Suffolk	S by A1101 [N52°21'42" E000°29'12"]	9m NNE of Newmarket
RAF	Northolt	Greater London	N by A40 [N51°33'11" W000°25'06"]	3m E of M40 jn 1
RAF	Odiham	Hampshire	E of A32 [N51°14'03" W000°56'34"]	2m S of M3 jn 5
RN	Predannack	Cornwall	W by A3083 [N50°00'07" W005°13'54"]	7m S of Helston
RAF	Scampton	Lincolnshire	W by A15 [N53°18'28" W000°33'04"]	6m N of Lincoln
RAF	Shawbury	Shropshire	W of B5063 [N52°47'53" W002°40'05"]	7m NNE of Shrewsbury
RAF	Syerston	Nottinghamshire	W by A46 [N53°01'22" W000°54'47"]	5m SW of Newark
RAF	Ternhill	Shropshire	SW by A41 [N52°52'24" W002°31'54"]	3m SW of Market Drayton
RAF/Army	Topcliffe	North Yorkshire	E of A167, W of A168 [N54°12'20" W001°22'55"]	3m SW of Thirsk
RAF	Valley	Gwynedd	S of A5 on Anglesey [N53°14'53" W004°32'06"]	5m SE of Holyhead
RAF	Waddington	Lincolnshire	E by A607, W by A15 [N53°09'58" W000°31'26"]	5m S of Lincoln
Army	Wattisham	Suffolk	N of B1078 [N52°07'38" E000°57'21"]	5m SSW of Stowmarket
RAF	Woodvale	Merseyside	W by A565 [N53°34'56" W003°03'24"]	5m SSW of Southport
RAF	Wittering	Cambridgeshire	W by A1, N of A47 [N52°36'52" W000°27'01"]	3m S of Stamford
RN	Yeovilton	Somerset	S by B3151, S of A303 [N51°00'30" W002°38'43"]	5m N of Yeovil

The Committee of Imperial Defence through its Air Committee introduced a standardised system of numbering aircraft in November 1912. The Air Department of the Admiralty was allocated the first batch 1-200 and used these to cover aircraft already in use and those on order. The Army was issued with the next block from 201-800, which included the number 304 which was given to the Cody Biplane now preserved in the Science Museum. By the outbreak of World War I, the Royal Navy was on its second batch of registrations 801-1600 and this system continued with alternating allocations between the Army and Navy until 1916 when number 10000, a Royal Flying Corps BE2C, was reached.

It was decided not to continue with five-digit numbers but instead to start again from 1, prefixing RFC aircraft with the letter A and RNAS aircraft with the prefix N. The RFC allocations commenced with A1 an FE2D and before the end of the year had reached A9999 an Armstrong Whitworth FK8. The next group commenced with B1 and continued in logical sequence through the C, D, E and F prefixes. G was used on a limited basis to identify captured German aircraft, while H was the last block of wartime-ordered aircraft. To avoid confusion I was not used, so the new post-war machines were allocated registrations in the J range. A further minor change was made in the numbering system in August 1929 when it was decided to maintain four numerals after the prefix letter, thus omitting numbers 1 to 999. The new K series therefore commenced at K1000, which was allocated to an AW Atlas.

The Naval N prefix was not used in such a logical way. Blocks of numbers were allocated for specific types of aircraft such as seaplanes or flying boats. By the late 1920s the sequence had largely been used up and a new series using the prefix S was commenced. In 1930 separate naval allocations were stopped and subsequent registrations were issued in the 'military' range which had by this time reached the K series. A further change in the pattern of allocations came in the L range. Commencing with L7272 numbers were issued in blocks with smaller blocks of registrations between not used; these were known as 'broken blocks'. As M had already been used as a suffix for Maintenance Command instructional airframes it was not used as a prefix. Although N had previously been used for naval aircraft it was used again for registrations allocated from 1937.

With the build-up to World War II, the rate of allocations quickly accelerated, and the prefix R was being used when war was declared. The letters O and Q were not allotted, nor was S, which had been used up to S1865 for naval aircraft before integration into the RAF series. By 1940 the registration Z9999 had been reached, as part of a broken block, with the letters U and Y not used to avoid confusion.

The option to recommence registration allocation at A1000 was not taken up; instead, it was decided to use an alphabetical two-letter prefix with three numerals running from 100 to 999. Thus, AA100 was allocated to a Blenheim IV and this two-letter, three-numeral registration system which started in 1940 continues today. The letters C, I, O, Q, U and Y were, with the exception of NC, not used. For various reasons the following letter combinations were not issued: DA, DB, DH, EA, GA to GZ, HA, HT, JE, JH, JJ, KR to KT, MR, NW, NZ, SA to SK, SV, TN, TR and VE. The first post-war registrations issued were in the VP range while the end of the WZs had been reached by the Korean War.

In January 1952 a civil servant at the then Air Ministry penned a memo to his superiors alerting them to the fact that a new military aircraft registration system would soon have to be devised. With allocations accelerating to accommodate a NATO response to the Korean War and a perceived Soviet threat building, he estimated that the end of the ZZs would quickly be reached. However, more than six decades later the allocations are only in the ZKs and at the present rate are unlikely to reach ZZ999 until the end of this century!

Military aircraft registrations are allocated by MOD Head Office and Corporate Services, where the Military Aircraft Register is maintained by the Military Aviation Authority. It should be pointed out that strictly the register places a space before the last three digits of the registration and, contrary to popular opinion, refers to them as 'registrations', not serials.

A change in policy in 2003 resulted in the use of the first 99 digits in the ZK sequence (ZK001 to ZK099), following on from ZJ999. The first of these, ZK001 to ZK004, were allocated to AgustaWestland Merlins. There is also a growing trend for 'out-of-sequence' registration numbers to be issued. At first this was to a manufacturer's prototype or development aircraft. However, following the Boeing C-17 Globemasters leased and subsequently purchased from Boeing (ZZ171-ZZ178), more allocations have been noted.

Since 2002 there has also been a new official policy concerning the use of military registration numbers on some types of UAV. "Where a UAV is of modular construction the nationality and registration mark shall be applied to the fuselage of the vehicle or on the assembly forming the main part of the fuselage. To prevent the high usage of numbers for target drones which are eventually destroyed, a single registration mark (prefix) should be issued relating to the UAV type. The agency or service operating the target drone will be responsible for the identification of each individual UAV covered by that registration mark by adding a suffix." This has resulted in the use of the same registration on a number of UAVs (or RPASs as they are now referred to) and drones with numbers following it - hence the appearance of ZZ420/001 etc. on Banshee drones. Aircraft using this system are denoted in the text by an asterisk (*).

A serial in *italics* denotes that it is not the genuine marking for that airframe.

Serial	Type (code/other identity)	Owner/operator, location or fate	Notes
168	Sopwith Tabloid Scout <R> (G-BFDE)	WW1 Aviation Heritage Trust, Stow Maries, Essex	
304	Cody Biplane (BAPC.62)	Science Museum, South Kensington, London	
471	RAF BE2a <R> (BAPC.321)	Montrose Air Station Heritage Centre, Angus, Scotland	
687	RAF BE2c <R> (G-AWYI/*471*)	Privately owned, Sywell, Northants (wreck)	
687	RAF BE2b <R> (BAPC.181)	RAF Museum, Hendon, Gtr London	
1264	Bristol Scout C <R> (G-FDHB)	Privately owned, Old Warden, Beds	
2345	Vickers FB5 Gunbus <R> (G-ATVP)	RAF Museum, Hendon, Gtr London	
2560	RAF BE2f <R> (F-AZZN)	Privately owned, La Ferté Alais, France	
2699	RAF BE2c	IWM Duxford, Cambs	
2783	RAF BE2b <R> (BAPC.332)	Boscombe Down Aviation Collection, Old Sarum, Wilts	
3066	Caudron GIII (G-AETA/9203M)	RAF Museum, Hendon, Gtr London	
5191	Morane-Saulnier Type N <R> (BAPC.472)	North-East Land, Sea & Air Museums, Usworth, T&W	
5964	DH2 <R> (BAPC.112)	Privately owned, Wickenby, Lincs	
5964	DH2 <R> (G-BFVH)	Privately owned, Wickenby, Lincs	
8359	Short 184 <ff>	FAA Museum, RNAS Yeovilton, Somerset	
9828	Avro 504K <R> (*H1968*/BAPC.42)	Yorkshire Air Museum, Elvington, N. Yorks	
9917	Sopwith Pup (G-EBKY/N5180)	The Shuttleworth Collection, Old Warden, Beds	
9970	RAF BE2c <R> (*6232*/BAPC.41)	Yorkshire Air Museum, Elvington, N. Yorks	
A126	Nieuport 11 <R> (G-CILI)	Privately owned, Sywell, Northants	
A301	Morane BB (frame)	RAF Museum Reserve Collection, Stafford, Staffs	
A653	Sopwith Pup <R> (*A7317*/BAPC.179)	Privately owned, Stow Maries, Essex	
A1452	Vickers FB5 Gunbus <R> (BAPC.234)	Spitfire Spares, Taunton, Somerset	
A1742	Bristol Scout D <R> (BAPC.38)	Aerospace Bristol, Filton, Glos	
A2943	RAF BE2e-1 <R> (G-CJZO)	WW1 Aviation Heritage Trust, Stow Maries, Essex	
A3930	RAF RE8 <R> (ZK-TVC)	RAF Museum, Hendon, Gtr London	
A4850	RAF SE5a <R> (BAPC.176)	Bygone Times Antique Warehouse, Eccleston, Lancs	
A6526	RAF FE2b <R> (BAPC.400)	RAF Museum, Hendon, Gtr London	
A6906	Sherwood Ranger ST (G-CLNZ) [5]	Privately owned, Dudleston Heath, Shropshire	
A7288	Bristol F2b Fighter <R> (BAPC.386)	Aerospace Bristol, Filton, Glos	
A8226	Sopwith 1½ Strutter <R> (G-BIDW)	RAF Museum, Cosford, Shropshire	
A8274	Sopwith 1½ Strutter <R> (BAPC.413)	WW1 Aviation Heritage Trust, Stow Maries, Essex	
A8898	RAF SE5a <R> (F-AZCY)	Privately owned, La Ferté Alais, France	
A8936	Currie Wot (*C3009*/G-BFWD)	Privately owned, Duxford, Cambs	
B595	RAF SE5a <R> (G-BUOD) [W]	Privately owned, Defford, Worcs	
B619	Sopwith 1½ Strutter <R> (BAPC.468)	RAF Manston History Museum, Kent	
B1162	Bristol F2b Fighter (D8096/G-AEPH) [F]	The Shuttleworth Collection, Old Warden, Beds	
B1474	Henry Farman F.20 <R>	WW1 Aviation Heritage Trust, Stow Maries, Essex	
B5539	Sopwith F.1 Camel <R>	Privately owned, Booker, Bucks	
B6401	Sopwith F.1 Camel <R> (G-AWYY/C1701)	FAA Museum, stored Cobham Hall, RNAS Yeovilton, Somerset	
B7270	Sopwith F.1 Camel <R> (G-BFCZ)	Brooklands Museum, Weybridge, Surrey	
B7320	Sopwith F.1 Camel <R> (*D3419*/B5577/BAPC.59) [P]	Montrose Air Station Heritage Centre, Angus, Scotland	
C1096	Memorial Flight SE5a <R> (G-ERFC) [3]	Privately owned, Old Warden, Beds	
C1904	RAF SE5a <R> (G-PFAP) [Z]	Privately owned, Castle Bytham, Lincs	
C3011	Phoenix Currie Super Wot (G-SWOT) [S]	Privately owned, Otherton, Staffs	
C3988	Sopwith 5F.1 Dolphin (BAPC.353) (comp D5329)	RAF Museum, Hendon, Gtr London	
C4451	Avro 504J <R> (BAPC.210)	Solent Sky, Southampton, Hants	
C4918	Bristol M1C <R> (G-BWJM)	The Shuttleworth Collection, Old Warden, Beds	
C4994	Bristol M1C <R> (G-BLWM)	RAF Museum, Cosford, Shropshire	
C5430	RAF SE5a <R> (G-CCXG) [V]	Privately owned, Wrexham, Clwyd, Wales	
C8996	RAF SE5a (G-ECAE/A2-25)	Privately owned, Audley End, Essex	
C9533	RAF SE5a <R> (G-BUWE) [M]	Privately owned, Henstridge, Somerset	
D276	RAF SE5a <R> (BAPC.208) [A]	Prince's Mead Shopping Centre, Farnborough, Hants	
D1851	Sopwith F.1 Camel <R> (G-BZSC) [X]	The Shuttleworth Collection, Old Warden, Beds	

Notes	Serial	Type (code/other identity)	Owner/operator, location or fate
	D3540	RAF SE5a <R> (N125QB) [K]	WW1 Aviation Heritage Trust, Stow Maries, Essex
	D5649	Airco DH9	IWM Duxford, Cambs
	D6447	Sopwith F.1 Camel <R> (BAPC.385)	Privately owned, Knutsford, Cheshire
	D7560	Avro 504K	Science Museum, South Kensington, London
	D8118	Sopwith F.1 Camel <R> (BAPC.567) [T]	Privately owned, Chalford, Glos
	E449	Avro 504K (G-EBJE/9205M)	RAF Museum, Hendon, Gtr London
	E2262	Bristol F2b Fighter <R> (F-AYBF)[A6]	Privately owned, La Ferté Alais, France
	E2466	Bristol F2b Fighter (BAPC.165) [I]	RAF Museum, Hendon, Gtr London
	E2581	Bristol F2b Fighter [13]	IWM Duxford, Cambs
	E2977	Avro 504K (G-EBHB)	Privately owned, Duxford, Cambs
	E3273	Avro 504K (H5199/BK892/ G-ACNB/G-ADEV/3118M)	The Shuttleworth Collection, Old Warden, Beds
	E6655	Sopwith 7F.1 Snipe <R> (BAPC.348) [B]	RAF Museum, Hendon, Gtr London
	E8894	Airco DH9 (G-CDLI)	Aero Vintage, Duxford, Cambs
	F141	RAF SE5a <R> (G-SEVA) [G]	Privately owned, Boscombe Down, Wilts
	F235	RAF SE5a <R> (G-BMDB) [B]	Privately owned, Stow Maries, Essex
	F904	RAF SE5a (G-EBIA)	The Shuttleworth Collection, Old Warden, Beds
	F904	RAF SE5a <R>	South Yorkshire Aircraft Museum, Doncaster, S. Yorks
	F938	RAF SE5a (G-EBIC/9208M)	RAF Museum, Hendon, Gtr London
	F943	RAF SE5a <R> (G-BIHF) [S]	Privately owned, White Waltham, Berks
	F943	RAF SE5a <R> (G-BKDT) [S]	Yorkshire Air Museum, Elvington, N. Yorks
	F1010	Airco DH9A [C]	RAF Museum, Hendon, Gtr London
	F2211	Sopwith 1½ Strutter <R>	Privately owned, East Fortune, Scotland
	F3556	RAF RE8	IWM Duxford, Cambs
	F5447	RAF SE5a <R> (G-BKER) [N]	Privately owned, Bridge of Weir, Scotland
	F5459	RAF SE5a <R> (G-INNY) [Y]	Privately owned, Sywell, Northants
	F5475	RAF SE5a <R> (BAPC.250)	Brooklands Museum, Weybridge, Surrey
	F6314	Sopwith F.1 Camel (9206M) [B]	RAF Museum, Hendon, Gtr London
	F8010	RAF SE5a <R> (G-BDWJ) [Z]	Privately owned, Langar, Somerset
	F8614	Vickers FB27A Vimy IV <R> (G-AWAU)	RAF Museum Reserve Collection, Stafford, Staffs
	J7326	DH53 Humming Bird (G-EBQP)	The Shuttleworth Collection, Old Warden, Beds
	J7904	Gloster Gamecock (BAPC.259) <R>	Jet Age Museum, Gloucestershire Airport, Glos
	J8067	Westland Pterodactyl 1a	Science Museum, South Kensington, London
	J9941	Hawker Hart 2 (G-ABMR)	RAF Museum, Hendon, Gtr London
	K1786	Hawker Tomtit (G-AFTA)	The Shuttleworth Collection, Old Warden, Beds
	K1928	Hawker Fury I <R> (BAPC.362) (build based on wreck of original K1928)	Cambs Fighter & Bomber Society, Little Gransden, Cambs
	K2048	Isaacs Fury II (G-BZNW)	Privately owned, Ledbury, Herefordshire
	K2050	Isaacs Fury II (G-ASCM)	Privately owned, Hinton-in-the-Hedges, Northants
	K2059	Isaacs Fury II (G-PFAR)	Privately owned, Netherthorpe, Derbys
	K2060	Isaacs Fury II (G-BKZM)	Privately owned, stored Limetree, Ireland
	K2065	Isaacs Fury II (G-AYJY/K2046)	Privately owned, Cranwell, Lincs
	K2075	Isaacs Fury II (G-BEER)	Privately owned, Combrook, Warks
	K2227	Bristol 105 Bulldog IIA (G-ABBB)	RAF Museum, Hendon, Gtr London
	K2567	DH82A Tiger Moth (DE306/G-MOTH/7035M)	Privately owned, Audley End, Essex
	K2572	DH82A Tiger Moth (NM129/G-AOZH)	Privately owned, Frensham, Surrey
	K2585	DH82A Tiger Moth II (T6818/G-ANKT)	The Shuttleworth Collection, Old Warden, Beds
	K2587	DH82A Tiger Moth <R> (G-BJAP)	Privately owned, Shobdon, Herefordshire
	K3241	Avro 621 Tutor (K3215/G-AHSA)	The Shuttleworth Collection, Old Warden, Beds
	K3660	Isaacs Fury II (K5673/G-BZAS)	Privately owned, Middlezoy, Somerset
	K3661	Hawker Nimrod II (G-BURZ) [562]	Historic Aircraft Collection Ltd, Duxford, Cambs
	K3731	Isaacs Fury (G-RODI)	Privately owned, RAF Waddington, Lincs
	K4232	Avro 671 Rota I (SE-AZB)	RAF Museum, Hendon, Gtr London
	K4259	DH82A Tiger Moth (G-ANMO) [71]	Privately owned, Headcorn, Kent
	K4556	Boulton & Paul Overstrand <R> (BAPC.358) [F-101]	Norfolk & Suffolk Avn Museum, Flixton, Suffolk
	K4972	Hawker Hart Trainer IIA (1764M)	RAF Museum, Cosford, Shropshire
	K5054	Supermarine Spitfire <R> (BAPC.214)	Tangmere Military Aviation Museum, W. Sussex
	K5054	Supermarine Spitfire <R> (G-BRDV)	Kent Battle of Britain Museum, Hawkinge, Kent
	K5054	Supermarine Spitfire <R> (BAPC.297)	Kent Battle of Britain Museum, Hawkinge, Kent

Serial	Type (code/other identity)	Owner/operator, location or fate	Notes
K5054	Supermarine Spitfire <R>	Southampton Airport, Hants, on display	
K5409	Hawker Hind	*Currently not known*	
K5414	Hawker Hind (G-AENP/BAPC.78)	*Painted as K5533*	
K5462	Hawker Hind	*Currently not known*	
K5533	Hawker Hind (G-AENP/BAPC.78)	The Shuttleworth Collection, Old Warden, Beds	
K5554	Hawker Hind	*Currently not known*	
K5600	Hawker Audax I (G-BVVI/2015M)	Aero Vintage, Westfield, E. Sussex	
K5671	Isaacs Fury I (G-EHMF)	Privately owned, Prestwick, Ayr, Scotland	
K5673	Hawker Fury I <R> (BAPC.249)	Brooklands Museum, Weybridge, Surrey	
K5674	Hawker Fury I (G-CBZP)	Historic Aircraft Collection Ltd, Duxford, Cambs	
K5682	Isaacs Fury II (S1579/G-BBVO) [6]	Privately owned, Felthorpe, Norfolk (wreck)	
K6035	Westland Wallace II (2361M)	RAF Museum, Hendon, Gtr London	
K6618	Hawker Hind	*Currently not known*	
K6833	Hawker Hind	*Currently not known*	
K7271	Hawker Fury II <R> (BAPC.148)	Shropshire Wartime Aircraft Recovery Grp Mus, Sleap, Shropshire	
K7271	Isaacs Fury II <R> (G-CCKV)	Privately owned, Middlezoy, Somerset	
K7985	Gloster Gladiator I (L8032/G-AMRK)	The Shuttleworth Collection, Old Warden, Beds	
K8042	Gloster Gladiator II (8372M)	RAF Museum, Cosford, Shropshire	
K8203	Hawker Demon I (G-BTVE/2292M)	*Sold to USA as N1HD*	
K8303	Isaacs Fury II (G-BWWN) [D]	Privately owned, Turweston, Bucks	
K9942	VS300 Spitfire I (8383M) [SD-D]	RAF Museum, Cosford, Shropshire	
K9998	VS300 Spitfire I (BAPC.431) <R> [QJ-K]	RAF Biggin Hill, Kent, on display	
L1019	VS300 Spitfire I <R> (BAPC.308) [LO-S]	Morayvia, Kinloss, Moray, Scotland	
L1035	VS300 Spitfire I <R> (BAPC.500) [SH-D]	Battle of Britain Bunker, Uxbridge, Middlesex	
L1067	VS300 Spitfire I <R> (BAPC.227) [XT-D]	Edinburgh Airport, Scotland, on display	
L1592	Hawker Hurricane I [KW-Z]	Science Museum, South Kensington, London	
L1639	Hawker Hurricane I <R> (BAPC.402) (complex composite based on numerous donor aircraft)	Cambridge Fighter & Bomber Society, Little Gransden, Cambs	
L1679	Hawker Hurricane I <R> (BAPC.241) [JX-G]	Tangmere Military Aviation Museum, W. Sussex	
L1684	Hawker Hurricane I <R> (BAPC.219)	RAF Northolt, Gtr London, on display	
L2005	Hawker Hurricane I	Hawker Restorations, Elmsett, Suffolk	
L2301	VS Walrus I (G-AIZG)	FAA Museum, RNAS Yeovilton, Somerset	
L2940	Blackburn Skua I	FAA Museum, RNAS Yeovilton, Somerset	
L5343	Fairey Battle I	RAF Museum, Hendon, Gtr London	
L6739	Bristol 149 Bolingbroke IVT (G-BPIV/R3821) [YP-Q]	Blenheim (Duxford) Ltd, Duxford, Cambs	
L6906	Miles M14A Magister I (G-AKKY/T9841/BAPC.44)	Museum of Berkshire Aviation, Woodley, Berks	
L7005	Boulton Paul P82 Defiant I <R> (BAPC.281) [PS-B]	Kent Battle of Britain Museum, Hawkinge, Kent	
L7181	Hawker Hind (G-CBLK)	Aero Vintage, Duxford, Cambs	
L7191	Hawker Hind	*Currently not known*	
L7775	Vickers Wellington B Ic <ff>	Lincolnshire Avn Heritage Centre, E. Kirkby, Lincs	
L8756	Bristol 149 Bolingbroke IVT (RCAF 10001) [XD-E]	RAF Museum, Cosford, Shropshire	
N248	Supermarine S6A (S1596)	Solent Sky, Southampton, Hants	
N500	Sopwith LC-1T Triplane <R> (G-PENY/G-BWRA)	Privately owned, White Waltham, Berks	
N540	Port Victoria PV8 Eastchurch Kitten <R>	Yorkshire Air Museum, Elvington, N. Yorks	
N546	Wight Quadruplane 1 <R> (BAPC.164)	Solent Sky, Southampton, Hants	
N594	Nieuport 11 Scout <R> (G-CLPN) [3982]	Privately owned, Damyns Hall, Gtr London	
N1671	Boulton Paul P82 Defiant I (8370M) [EW-D]	RAF Museum, Cosford, Shropshire	
N1854	Fairey Fulmar II (G-AIBE)	FAA Museum, RNAS Yeovilton, Somerset	
N2078	Sopwith Baby (8214/8215/BAPC.442)	FAA Museum, RNAS Yeovilton, Somerset	
N2532	Hawker Hurricane I <R> (BAPC.272) [GZ-H]	Kent Battle of Britain Museum, Hawkinge, Kent	
N2980	Vickers Wellington Ia [R]	Brooklands Museum, Weybridge, Surrey	
N3200	VS300 Spitfire IA (G-CFGJ) [QV]	The Aircraft Restoration Co, Duxford, Cambs	
N3289	VS300 Spitfire I <R> (BAPC.65) [DW-K]	Kent Battle of Britain Museum, Hawkinge, Kent	
N3290	VS300 Spitfire I <R> [AI-H]	Privately owned, St Mawgan, Cornwall	
N3310	VS361 Spitfire IX <R> (BAPC.393) [AI-A]	Privately owned, Abingdon, Oxon	
N3378	Boulton Paul P82 Defiant I (wreck)	RAF Museum, Cosford, Shropshire	
N3549	DH82A Tiger Moth II (PG645/N3549)	Privately owned, Gamston, Notts	
N3788	Miles M14A Magister I (V1075/G-AKPF)	Privately owned, Old Warden, Beds	

19

Notes	Serial	Type (code/other identity)	Owner/operator, location or fate
	N4389	Fairey Albacore (N4172) [4M]	FAA Museum, stored Cobham Hall, RNAS Yeovilton, Somerset
	N4877	Avro 652A Anson I (G-AMDA) [MK-V]	IWM Duxford, Cambs
	N5137	DH82A Tiger Moth (N6638/G-BNDW)	Caernarfon Air World, Gwynedd, Wales
	N5177	Sopwith 1½ Strutter <R> (BAPC.452)	Privately owned, stored Merstham, Surrey
	N5182	Sopwith Pup <R> (G-APUP/9213M)	RAF Museum, Cosford, Shropshire
	N5195	Sopwith Pup (G-ABOX)	Army Flying Museum, Middle Wallop, Hants
	N5199	Sopwith Pup <R> (G-BZND)	Privately owned, Yarcombe, Devon
	N5459	Sopwith Triplane <R> (BAPC.111)	FAA Museum, stored Cobham Hall, RNAS Yeovilton, Somerset
	N5518	Gloster Sea Gladiator (N5579)	FAA Museum, stored Cobham Hall, RNAS Yeovilton, Somerset
	N5628	Gloster Gladiator II	RAF Museum, Cosford, Shropshire
	N5719	Gloster Gladiator II (G-CBHO)	Privately owned, Dursley, Glos
	N5903	Gloster Gladiator II (N2276/G-GLAD)	The Fighter Collection, Duxford, Cambs
	N5912	Sopwith Triplane (8385M)	RAF Museum, Hendon, Gtr London
	N5914	Gloster Gladiator II (frame)	Jet Age Museum, Gloucestershire Airport, Glos
	N6161	Sopwith Pup (G-ELRT)	Privately owned, Turweston, Bucks
	N6290	Sopwith Triplane <R> (G-BOCK)	The Shuttleworth Collection, Old Warden, Beds
	N6377	Sopwith F.1 Camel <R> (G-BPOB/B2458)	Privately owned, Turweston, Bucks
	N6452	Sopwith Pup <R> (G-BIAU)	FAA Museum, RNAS Yeovilton, Somerset
	N6466	DH82A Tiger Moth (G-ANKZ)	Privately owned, Compton Abbas, Dorset
	N6473	DH82A Tiger Moth (F-GTBO)	Privately owned, Orbigny, France
	N6537	DH82A Tiger Moth (G-AOHY)	Privately owned, Wickenby, Lincs
	N6635	DH82A Tiger Moth (comp G-APAO & G-APAP) [25]	IWM Duxford, Cambs
	N6720	DH82A Tiger Moth (G-BYTN/7014M) [VX]	Privately owned, stored Darley Moor, Derbyshire
	N6797	DH82A Tiger Moth (G-ANEH)	Privately owned, Swyncombe, Oxon
	N6812	Sopwith 2F.1 Camel	IWM London, Lambeth, Gtr London
	N6847	DH82A Tiger Moth (G-APAL)	Privately owned, Langham, Rutland
	N6965	DH82A Tiger Moth (G-AJTW) [FL-J]	Privately owned, Tibenham, Norfolk
	N7033	Noorduyn AT-16 Harvard IIb (FX442)	Kent Battle of Britain Museum, Hawkinge, Kent
	N9181	DH82A Tiger Moth (composite) [5]	Kent Battle of Britain Museum, Hawkinge, Kent
	N9191	DH82A Tiger Moth (G-ALND)	Privately owned, Durley, Hants
	N9192	DH82A Tiger Moth (PG742/G-DHZF) [RCO-N]	Privately owned, Sywell, Northants
	N9328	DH82A Tiger Moth (G-ALWS) [69]	Privately owned, Yeovilton, Somerset
	N9372	DH82A Tiger Moth (G-ANHK)	Privately owned, Breighton, E. Yorks
	N9389	DH82A Tiger Moth (G-ANJA)	Privately owned, stored Seething, Norfolk
	N9399	DH82A Tiger Moth (frame)	South Yorkshire Aircraft Museum, stored Doncaster, S. Yorks
	N9503	DH82A Tiger Moth II (G-ANFP) [39]	Privately owned, Podhořany, Czech Republic
	N9899	Supermarine Southampton I (fuselage)	RAF Museum, Hendon, Gtr London
	P1344	HP52 Hampden I (9175M) [PL-K]	Michael Beetham Conservation Centre, RAFM Cosford, Shropshire
	P2617	Hawker Hurricane I (8373M) [AF-F]	RAF Museum, Hendon, Gtr London
	P2725	Hawker Hurricane I (wreck)	IWM London, Lambeth, Gtr London
	P2725	Hawker Hurricane I <R> (BAPC.68) [TM-B]	Privately owned, Delabole, Cornwall
	P2725	Hawker Hurricane I <R> (Z3427/BAPC.205) [TM-B]	RAF Museum, Hendon, Gtr London
	P2793	Hawker Hurricane I <R> (BAPC.236) [SD-M]	Eden Camp Theme Park, stored Malton, N. Yorks
	P2793	Hawker Hurricane I <R> (BAPC.399) [SD-M]	Eden Camp Theme Park, Malton, N. Yorks
	P2902	Hawker Hurricane I (G-ROBT) [DX-R]	Privately owned, Duxford, Cambs
	P2921	Hawker Hurricane I <R> (BAPC.218) [GZ-L]	RAF Bentley Priory, Gtr London, on display
	P2921	Hawker Hurricane I <R> (BAPC.273) [GZ-L]	Kent Battle of Britain Museum, Hawkinge, Kent
	P2921	Hawker Hurricane I <R> (BAPC.477) [GZ-L]	RAF Biggin Hill, Kent, on display
	P2921	Hawker Sea Hurricane X (AE977/G-CHTK) [GZ-L]	Privately owned, Biggin Hill, Kent
	P2970	Hawker Hurricane I <R> (BAPC.291) [US-X]	Battle of Britain Memorial, Capel le Ferne, Kent
	P3059	Hawker Hurricane I <R> (BAPC.64) [SD-N]	Kent Battle of Britain Museum, Hawkinge, Kent
	P3175	Hawker Hurricane I (wreck)	RAF Museum Reserve Collection, Stafford, Staffs
	P3179	Hawker Hurricane I <ff>	Tangmere Military Aviation Museum, W. Sussex
	P3208	Hawker Hurricane I <R> (BAPC.63/L1592) [SD-T]	Kent Battle of Britain Museum, Hawkinge, Kent
	P3351	Hawker Hurricane IIa (DR393/F-AZXR) [K]	Hawker Restorations, Elmsett, Suffolk (rebuild)
	P3395	Hawker Hurricane IV (KX829)[JX-B]	Thinktank, Birmingham, Warks

Serial	Type (code/other identity)	Owner/operator, location or fate	Notes
P3554	Hawker Hurricane I (composite)	The Air Defence Collection, Salisbury, Wilts	
P3679	Hawker Hurricane I <R> (BAPC.278) [GZ-K]	Kent Battle of Britain Museum, Hawkinge, Kent	
P3708	Hawker Hurricane I (rebuild)	Norfolk & Suffolk Avn Museum, Flixton, Suffolk	
P3717	Hawker Hurricane I (composite) (DR348/G-HITT) [SW-P]	Privately owned, Old Warden, Beds	
P3873	Hawker Hurricane I <R> (BAPC.265) [YO-H]	Yorkshire Air Museum, Elvington, N. Yorks	
P3873	Hawker Hurricane I <R> (BAPC.499) [YO-H]	Battle of Britain Bunker, Uxbridge, Middlesex	
P3901	Hawker Hurricane I <R> (BAPC.475) [RF-E]	Battle of Britain Bunker, Uxbridge, Middlesex	
P3935	Hawker Hurricane IIb(mod) (RCAF 5403/G-HURI) [WX-D] (left side), P2954 [WX-E] (right side)	Privately owned, Duxford, Cambs	
P3966	Hawker Hurricane I (G-LNWZ)	Privately owned, White Waltham, Berks	
P4139	Fairey Swordfish II (HS618) [5H]	FAA Museum, RNAS Yeovilton, Somerset	
P6382	Miles M14A Hawk Trainer 3 (G-AJRS) [C]	The Shuttleworth Collection, Old Warden, Beds	
P7056	Westland Whirlwind Mk.1 (BAPC.373)	Whirlwind Fighter Project, Kent Battle of Britain Trust, Hawkinge, Kent	
P7308	VS300 Spitfire IA (AR213/R9632/G-AIST) [XR-D]	Privately owned, Duxford, Cambs	
P7350	VS329 Spitfire IIa (G-AWIJ) [KL-B]	RAF BBMF, Coningsby, Lincs	
P7370	VS329 Spitfire II <R> (BAPC.410) [ZP-A]	Battle of Britain Experience, Canterbury, Kent	
P7540	VS329 Spitfire IIa [DU-W]	Dumfries & Galloway Avn Mus, Scotland	
P7666	VS329 Spitfire IIa <R> (BAPC.335) [EB-Z]	RAF High Wycombe, Bucks, on display	
P7819	VS329 Spitfire IIa (G-TCHZ)	Privately owned, Exeter, Devon	
P7823	VS329 Spitfire IIa <R> (BAPC.369) [TM-F]	Ulster Aviation Society, Long Kesh, Co. Antrim, NI	
P7913	VS329 Spitfire IIa (wreck)	Privately owned, Biggin Hill, Kent	
P7966	VS329 Spitfire II <R> [D-B]	Manx Aviation & Military Museum, Ronaldsway, IOM	
P8088	VS329 Spitfire IIa (G-CGRM) [NK-K]	Privately owned, Knutsford, Cheshire	
P8140	VS329 Spitfire II <R> (N3317/BAPC.71) [BO-U]	Kent Battle of Britain Museum, Hawkinge, Kent	
P8208	VS329 Spitfire IIb (G-RRFF)	Privately owned, Dursley, Glos	
P8331	VS329 Spitfire IIb (G-KOSC) [RF-M]	Privately owned, Glos	
P8448	VS329 Spitfire II <R> (BAPC.225) [UM-D]	RAF Cranwell, Lincs, on display	
P9337	VS300 Spitfire Ia (G-IADX) <ff>	Privately owned, Manston, Kent	
P9372	VS300 Spitfire I (G-CLIH) [QJ-G](PH-CAM reserved)	Privately owned, Biggin Hill, Kent (to go to Belgium)	
P9373	VS300 Spitfire Ia (G-CFGN)	Privately owned, Duxford, Cambs (rebuild)	
P9398	Supermarine Aircraft Spitfire 26 (G-CEPL) [KL-B]	Privately owned, Rochester, Kent	
P9398	VS300 Spitfire I <R> (N3313/BAPC.69) [KL-B]	Kent Battle of Britain Museum, Hawkinge, Kent	
P9451	VS300 Spitfire I <ff>	Privately owned, Hooton Park, Cheshire	
P9444	VS300 Spitfire Ia [RN-D]	Science Museum, South Kensington, London	
P9637	Supermarine Aircraft Spitfire 26 (G-RORB) [GR-B]	Privately owned, Perth, Scotland	
R1914	Miles M14A Magister (G-AHUJ)	Privately owned, Gloucestershire Airport, Glos	
R4118	Hawker Hurricane I (G-HUPW) [UP-W]	Privately owned, North Moreton, Oxon	
R4229	Hawker Hurricane I <R> (BAPC.334) [GN-J]	Alexandra Park, Windsor, Berks	
R4922	DH82A Tiger Moth II (G-APAO)	Privately owned, Duxford, Cambs	
R4959	DH82A Tiger Moth II (G-ARAZ) [59]	Privately owned, Duxford, Cambs	
R5136	DH82A Tiger Moth II (G-APAP)	Privately owned, Darley Moor, Derbyshire	
R5172	DH82A Tiger Moth II (G-AOIS) [FIJE]	Privately owned, North Denes, Norfolk	
R5246	DH82A Tiger Moth II (G-AMIV) [40]	Privately owned, Podhořany, Czech Republic	
R5868	Avro 683 Lancaster I (7325M) [PO-S]	RAF Museum, Hendon, Gtr London	
R5868	Avro 683 Lancaster I <R> (BAPC.471) [PO-S] <ff>	Avro Heritage Museum, Woodford, Cheshire	
R6599	VS300 Spitfire I <R> (BAPC.539) [DW-J]	Romney Marsh Wartime Collection, Kent	
R6675	VS300 Spitfire I <R> [YT-J]	Battle of Britain Memorial, Capel le Ferne, Kent	
R6690	VS300 Spitfire I <R> (BAPC.254) [PR-A]	Yorkshire Air Museum, Elvington, N. Yorks	
R6775	VS300 Spitfire I <R> (BAPC.299) [YT-J]	Damaged beyond repair, October 2023	
R6904	VS300 Spitfire I <R> [BT-K]	Privately owned, Cornwall	
R6915	VS300 Spitfire I	IWM London, Lambeth, Gtr London	
R7059	VS300 Spitfire I <R> (X4474/BAPC.394) [LY]	IWM Duxford, Cambs	
R9125	Westland Lysander III (8377M)[JR-M]	RAF Museum, Hendon, Gtr London	
R9612	VS300 Spitfire I <R> (G-CGUK)[KL-A]	Privately owned, Duxford, Cambs	
S1287	Fairey Flycatcher <R> (G-BEYB) [5]	FAA Museum, stored Cobham Hall, RNAS Yeovilton, Somerset	
S1581	Hawker Nimrod I (G-BWWK) [573]	The Fighter Collection, Duxford, Cambs	
S1595	Supermarine S6B [1]	Science Museum, South Kensington, London	

Notes	Serial	Type (code/other identity)	Owner/operator, location or fate
	S1615	Isaacs Fury II (G-BMEU)	Privately owned, Tatenhill, Staffs
	T5298	Bristol 156 Beaufighter I (BAPC.398) <ff>	Midland Air Museum, Coventry, Warks
	T5424	DH82A Tiger Moth II (G-AJOA)	Privately owned, Solent Airport, Hants (stored)
	T5854	DH82A Tiger Moth II (G-ANKK)	Privately owned, White Waltham, Berks
	T5879	DH82A Tiger Moth II (G-AXBW) [RUC-W]	Privately owned, Frensham, Surrey (damaged)
	T6296	DH82A Tiger Moth II (8387M)	RAF Museum, Cosford, Shropshire
	T6830	DH82A Tiger Moth (G-ANJI)	Privately owned, Insch, Scotland
	T6953	DH82A Tiger Moth II (G-ANNI)	Privately owned, Solent Airport, Hants
	T6991	DH82A Tiger Moth II (DE694/HB-UPY)	Privately owned, Fasno, Italy
	T7109	DH82A Tiger Moth II (G-AOIM)	Privately owned, Eshott, Northumberland
	T7230	DH82A Tiger Moth II (G-AFVE/SP-YAA)	Privately owned, Mazowiecke, Poland
	T7281	DH82A Tiger Moth II (G-ARTL)	Privately owned, Egton, nr Whitby, N. Yorks
	T7290	DH82A Tiger Moth II (G-ANNK) [14]	Privately owned, Podington, Beds
	T7793	DH82A Tiger Moth II (G-ANKV)	Privately owned, Wickenby, Lincs
	T7794	DH82A Tiger Moth II (G-ASPV)	Privately owned, Bagby, N. Yorks
	T7842	DH82A Tiger Moth II (G-AMTF)	Privately owned, Spanhoe, Northants
	T7909	DH82A Tiger Moth II (G-ANON)	Privately owned, Sherburn-in-Elmet, N. Yorks
	T7997	DH82A Tiger Moth II (NL750/G-AHUF)	Privately owned, Middlezoy, Somerset
	T8191	DH82A Tiger Moth II (G-BWMK)	Privately owned, Henstridge, Somerset
	T9707	Miles M14A Magister I (G-AKKR/8378M/T9708)	RAF Museum, Cosford, Shropshire
	T9738	Miles M14A Magister I (G-AKAT)	Privately owned, Breighton, E. Yorks
	V3388	Airspeed AS10 Oxford I (G-AHTW)	IWM Duxford, Cambs
	V6028	Bristol 149 Bolingbroke IVT (G-MKIV) [GB-D] <rf>	The Aircraft Restoration Co, stored Duxford, Cambs
	V6555	Hawker Hurricane I (BAPC.411/P3144) <R> [DT-A]	Battle of Britain Experience, Canterbury, Kent
	V6748	Hawker Hurricane XII (RCAF 5481/G-ORGI) [PO]	To USA as Z3267/XR-D
	V6799	Hawker Hurricane I <R> (BAPC.72/V7767) [SD-X]	Jet Age Museum, Gloucestershire Airport, Glos
	V7313	Hawker Hurricane I <R> (BAPC.346) [US-F]	Privately owned, North Weald, Essex, on display
	V7350	Hawker Hurricane I <ff>	Romney Marsh Wartime Collection, Kent
	V7467	Hawker Hurricane I <R> (P2954/BAPC.267) [LE-D]	IWM Duxford, Cambs
	V7467	Hawker Hurricane I <R> (BAPC.223) [DU-J]	Hangar 42 Visitors Centre, Blackpool, Lancs
	V7467	Hawker Hurricane I <R> (BAPC.378) [LE-D]	RAF High Wycombe, Bucks, on display
	V7497	Hawker Hurricane I (G-HRLI) [SD-X]	Privately owned, Duxford, Cambs
	V7752	Hawker Hurricane I <R> (V7467/BAPC.288) [ZJ-L]	Lytham Heritage Collection, Blackpool, Lancs
	V9312	Westland Lysander IIIa (G-CCOM) [LX-E]	The Aircraft Restoration Co, Duxford, Cambs
	V9367	Westland Lysander IIIa (V9552/G-AZWT) [MA-B]	The Shuttleworth Collection, Old Warden, Beds
	V9673	Westland Lysander IIIa (V9300/G-LIZY) [MA-J]	IWM Duxford, Cambs
	V9723	Westland Lysander IIIa (V9546/OO-SOT/G-LYZY) [MA-D]	Privately owned, Zaventem, Belgium (restoration)
	V9822	Westland Lysander IIIa <R> (BAPC.371) [MA-E]	Tangmere Military Aviation Museum, W. Sussex
	W1048	HP59 Halifax II (8465M) [TL-S]	RAF Museum, Hendon, Gtr London
	W2068	Avro 652A Anson I (LT773/VH-AZU) [68]	RAF Museum, Hendon, Gtr London
	W3442	VS361 Spitfire IX <R> (PL256/BAPC.325) [FY-D]	Privately owned, Blackpool, Lancs
	W3644	VS349 Spitfire V <R> (BAPC.323) [QV-J]	Privately owned, Lake Fairhaven, Lancs
	W3850	VS349 Spitfire V <R> (BAPC.304) [PR-A]	Privately owned, Knutsford, Cheshire
	W4041	Gloster E28/39	Science Museum, South Kensington, London
	W4041	Gloster E28/39 <R> (BAPC.331)	Jet Age Museum, Gloucestershire Airport, Glos
	W4050	DH98 Mosquito [P]	de Havilland Aircraft Museum, London Colney
	W5856	Fairey Swordfish I (G-BMGC) [4A]	Fly Navy Heritage Trust, Yeovilton, Somerset
	W9385	DH87B Hornet Moth (G-ADND) [YG-L,3]	Privately owned, Oaksey Park, Wiltshire
	X4253	VS300 Spitfire I <R> (BAPC.326) [FY-N]	Hangar 42 Visitors Centre, Blackpool, Lancs
	X4276	VS300 Spitfire I (G-CDGU)	Privately owned, Biggin Hill, Kent
	X4590	VS300 Spitfire I (8384M) [PR-F]	RAF Museum, Hendon, Gtr London
	X4650	VS300 Spitfire I (R9612/G-CGUK) [KL-A]	Privately owned, Duxford, Cambs
	X4683	Jurca MJ10 Spitfire (G-MUTS) [EB-N]	Privately owned, Fishburn, Co. Durham
	X4859	VS300 Spitfire I <R> (BAPC.319) [PQ-N]	Grangemouth Spitfire Memorial Trust, Scotland
	X9407	Percival P.16A Q6 (G-AFFD)	Privately owned, Coventry, Warks (stored)
	X9556	VS Walrus I (W2718/G-RNLI) [S]	The Aircraft Restoration Co, Duxford, Cambs

Serial	Type (code/other identity)	Owner/operator, location or fate	Notes
Z1206	Vickers Wellington IV (fuselage)	Privately owned, Kenilworth, Warks	
Z2033	Fairey Firefly I (G-ASTL) [275/N]	IWM Duxford, Cambs	
Z2315	Hawker Hurricane IIa (BAPC.643) [JU-E]	IWM Duxford, Cambs	
Z2389	Hawker Hurricane IIa [XR-J]	Brooklands Museum, Weybridge, Surrey	
Z5053	Hawker Hurricane IIb (G-BWHA)	Privately owned, Kings Lynn, Norfolk	
Z5207	Hawker Hurricane IIb (G-BYDL)	Privately owned, Aalen, Germany (on rebuild)	
Z7015	Hawker Sea Hurricane Ib (G-BKTH) [7-L]	The Shuttleworth Collection, Old Warden, Beds	
Z7197	Percival P30 Proctor III (G-AKZN/8380M)	RAF Museum Reserve Collection, Stafford, Staffs	
Z7258	DH89A Dragon Rapide (NR786/G-AHGD)	Privately owned, Membury, Wilts (wreck)	
AA810	VS353 Spitfire F IV (G-PRID)	Airframe Assemblies, Sandown, IOW (on rebuild)	
AA937	VS349 Spitfire Vb <R> [AF-O]	IWM, Duxford, Cambs	
AB196	Supermarine Aircraft Spitfire 26 (G-CCGH)	Privately owned, Hawarden, Flintshire, Wales	
AB910	VS349 Spitfire Vb (G-AISU) [SH-F]	RAF BBMF, Coningsby, Lincs	
AD189	VS349 Spitfire Vb (G-CHVJ)	Privately owned, Raglan, Scotland	
AD370	Jurca MJ10 Spitfire (G-CHBW) [PJ-C]	Privately owned, Perranporth, Cornwall	
AD540	VS349 Spitfire Vb (wreck)	Privately owned, on rebuild Twyford, Bucks	
AE436	HP52 Hampden I [PL-J] (parts)	Lincolnshire Avn Heritage Centre, E. Kirkby, Lincs	
AG244	Hawker Hurricane XII (RCAF 5487/G-CBOE)	Privately owned, Aalen, Germany	
AJ841	CCF T-6J Texan (MM33795/G-BJST/KF729)	Privately owned, Duxford, Cambs	
AL246	Grumman Martlet I	FAA Museum, RNAS Yeovilton, Somerset	
AP506	Cierva C30A (G-ACWM) (wreck)	The Helicopter Museum, Weston-super-Mare, Somerset	
AP507	Cierva C30A (G-ACWP) [KX-P]	Science Museum, South Kensington, London	
AR501	VS349 Spitfire LF Vc (G-AWII/AR4474) [DU-E]	The Shuttleworth Collection, Old Warden, Beds	
AV511	EHI-101 Merlin <R> [511]	SFDO, RNAS Culdrose, Cornwall	
AW101	AgustaWestland AW101 Mk.510 (G-17-510)	Leonardo Helicopters, Yeovil, Somerset	
BA377	VS361 Spitfire F IX <R> (EN398/BAPC.377) [UF-J]	Privately owned, Belper, Derbyshire	
BB803	DH82A Tiger Moth (G-ADWJ) [75]	Privately owned, Henstridge, Somerset	
BB807	DH82A Tiger Moth (G-ADWO)	Solent Sky, Southampton, Hants	
BH238	Hawker Hurricane IIb	Privately owned, Rochester, Kent (rebuild)	
BK897	BA Swallow II (G-AFGD)	Privately owned, Shobdon, Herefordshire	
BL614	VS349 Spitfire Vb (4354M) [ZD-F]	RAF Museum, Hendon, Gtr London	
BL655	VS349 Spitfire Vb (wreck)	Lincolnshire Avn Heritage Centre, E. Kirkby, Lincs	
BL688	VS349 Spitfire LF Vb (G-LFVE)	Privately owned, Duxford, Cambs (rebuild)	
BL735	Supermarine Aircraft Spitfire 26 (G-HABT) [BT-A]	Privately owned, Hohenems, Austria	
BL924	VS349 Spitfire Vb <R> (BAPC.242) [AZ-G]	Privately owned, Eshott, Northumberland	
BL927	Supermarine Aircraft Spitfire 26 (G-CGWI) [JH-I]	Privately owned, Perth, Scotland	
BM361	VS349 Spitfire Vb <R> (BAPC.269) [XR-C]	RAF Lakenheath, Suffolk, on display	
BM481	VS349 Spitfire Vb <R> (BAPC.301) [YO-T] (left side) (also as Spitfire F22 PK651/RAO-B right side)	Thornaby Aerodrome Memorial, N. Yorks	
BM539	VS349 Spitfire LF Vb (G-SSVB)	Privately owned, on rebuild Bournemouth, Dorset	
BM597	VS349 Spitfire LF Vb (G-MKVB/5718M) [JH-C]	Historic Aircraft Collection, Duxford	
BN230	Hawker Hurricane IIc (LF751/5466M) [FT-A]	RAF Manston, Kent, Memorial Pavilion	
BN230	Hawker Hurricane I <R> (BAPC.218) [FT-A]	Repainted as P2921/GZ-L	
BP926	VS353 Spitfire PR IV (G-PRIV)	Privately owned, Newport Pagnell, Bucks	
BR954	VS353 Spitfire PR IV <R> (N3194/BAPC.220) [JP-A]	Merlin ERD, Perth, Scotland	
BS239	VS361 Spitfire IX <R> (BAPC.222) [5R-E]	Battle of Britain Bunker, Uxbridge, Middlesex (damaged, stored offsite)	
BS410	VS509 Spitfire T9 (G-TCHI) [PK-A]	Privately owned, Goodwood, W. Sussex	
BS435	VS361 Spitfire IX <R> (BAPC.324) [FY-F]	Hangar 42 Visitors Centre, Blackpool, Lancs	
BW853	Hawker Hurricane XIIa (G-BRKE) (fuselage)	Privately owned, Oxfordshire (restoration)	
DD931	Bristol 152 Beaufort VIII (9131M/BAPC.436) [L]	RAF Museum, Hendon, Gtr London	
DE208	DH82A Tiger Moth II (G-AGYU)	Privately owned, Treswell, Notts	
DE470	DH82A Tiger Moth II (G-ANMY) (frame)	Privately owned, Audley End, Essex (rebuild)	
DE623	DH82A Tiger Moth II (G-ANFI)	Privately owned, Cardiff, Wales	
DE673	DH82A Tiger Moth II (G-ADNZ/6948M)	Privately owned, Tibenham, Norfolk	
DE745	DH82A Tiger Moth II (G-BTOG/NM192)	Privately owned, Audley End, Essex	
DE971	DH82A Tiger Moth II (G-OOSY)	Privately owned, North Denes, Norfolk	
DE974	DH82A Tiger Moth II (G-ANZZ)	Privately owned, Clacton/Duxford	
DE992	DH82A Tiger Moth II (G-AXXV)	Privately owned, White Waltham, Berks (damaged)	

Notes	Serial	Type (code/other identity)	Owner/operator, location or fate
	DF112	DH82A Tiger Moth II (G-ANRM)	Privately owned, Clacton, Essex (on rebuild, Duxford)
	DF128	DH82A Tiger Moth II (G-AOJJ) [RCO-U]	Privately owned, White Waltham, Berks
	DF198	DH82A Tiger Moth II (G-BBRB)	Privately owned, stored West Wickham, Kent
	DG202	Gloster F9/40 (5758M)	RAF Museum, stored Cosford, Shropshire
	DG590	Miles M2H Hawk Major (G-ADMW/8379M)	Montrose Air Station Heritage Centre, Angus, Scotland
	DP872	Fairey Barracuda II <ff>	FAA Museum, Cobham Hall, RNAS Yeovilton, Somerset (restoration)
	DV372	Avro 683 Lancaster I <ff>	IWM London, Lambeth, Gtr London
	DZ313	DH98 Mosquito B IV <R>	Privately owned, Little Rissington, Glos
	EB518	Airspeed AS10 Oxford V	Hangar 42 Visitors Centre, Blackpool, Lancs (rest'n)
	EE416	Gloster Meteor F3 <ff>	Martin Baker Aircraft, Chalgrove, Oxon (fire section)
	EE425	Gloster Meteor F3 <ff>	Jet Age Museum, Gloucestershire Airport, Glos
	EE531	Gloster Meteor F4 (7090M)	Midland Air Museum, Coventry, Warks
	EE549	Gloster Meteor F4 (7008M)	Tangmere Military Aviation Museum, W. Sussex
	EE602	VS349 Spitfire LF Vc (G-IBSY) [DV-V]	Privately owned, Duxford, Cambs
	EF545	VS349 Spitfire LF Vc (G-CDGY)	Biggin Hill Heritage Hangar, Kent (restoration)
	EJ922	Hawker Typhoon Ib <ff>	Privately owned, Uckfield, E. Sussex
	EM720	DH82A Tiger Moth II (G-AXAN) (damaged)	Privately owned, stored Whittlesford, Cambs
	EM726	DH82A Tiger Moth II (G-ANDE) [FY]	Privately owned, Sywell, Northants
	EM840	DH82A Tiger Moth II (G-ANBY)	Privately owned, Hooton Park, Cheshire
	EM973	DH82A Tiger Moth II (T6774/G-ALNA) [OY]	Privately owned, Eggington, Derbyshire
	EN130	Supermarine Aircraft Spitfire 26B (G-ENAA) [FN-A]	Crashed Enstone, Oxon, July 2024
	EN179	VS361 Spitfire F IX (G-TCHO)	Privately owned, Exeter, Devon
	EN223	VS366 Spitfire F XII (G-GXII)	Privately owned, location unknown
	EN224	VS366 Spitfire F XII (G-FXII)	Privately owned, Sywell, Northants
	EN398	VS361 Spitfire F IX <R> (BAPC.541) [JE-J]	RAF Coningsby, Lincs, on display
	EN398	VS361 Spitfire F IX <R> (BAPC.552) [JE-J]	AMSS, Pyle, Bridgend, Wales
	EN398	VS361 Spitfire F IX <R> (BAPC.555) [JE-J]	Spitfire Spares, Taunton, Somerset
	EN398	VS361 Spitfire F IX <R> (BAPC.580) [JE-J]	Secret Spitfires Memorial, Salisbury, Wilts
	EN570	VS361 Spitfire T9 (G-CISP/LN-AOA) [FY-J]	Privately owned, Notodden, Norway
	EN961	Isaacs Spitfire <R> (G-CGIK) [SD-X]	Privately owned, Stoulton, Worcs
	EP120	VS349 Spitfire LF Vb (G-LFVB/5377M/8070M) [AE-A]	The Fighter Collection, Duxford, Cambs
	EP121	VS349 Spitfire LF Vb <R> (BAPC.320) [LO-D]	Montrose Air Station Heritage Centre, Scotland
	EV771	Fairchild UC-61 Argus <R> (BAPC.294)	Thorpe Camp Preservation Group, Tattershall, Lincs
	EX490	NA T-6H Texan (F-AZQK/G-CLCJ) [78]	Privately owned, Enstone, Oxon
	EX976	NA AT-6D Harvard III (FAP 1657)	FAA Museum, RNAS Yeovilton, Somerset
	FE511	Noorduyn AT-16 Harvard IIb (G-CIUW)	Privately owned, White Waltham, Berks
	FE695	Noorduyn AT-16 Harvard IIb (G-BTXI) [94]	Privately owned, Duxford, Cambs
	FE788	CCF Harvard IV (MM54137/G-CTKL)	Privately owned, Biggin Hill, Kent
	FE905	Noorduyn AT-16 Harvard IIb (LN-BNM)	RAF Museum, Hendon, Gtr London
	FJ801	Boeing-Stearman PT-27 Kaydet (N62842/BAPC.375)	Norfolk & Suffolk Avn Museum, Flixton, Suffolk
	FJ821	Boeing-Stearman PT-17 Kaydet (N59731/41-25618)	Privately owned, Enstone, Oxfordshire
	FK338	Fairchild 24W-41 Argus I (G-AJOZ)	Yorkshire Air Museum, Elvington, N. Yorks
	FL517	Douglas C-47A Dakota (N8041B/42-24238) <ff>	Privately owned, Chippenham, Wilts
	FL586	Douglas C-47B Dakota (N99346) [4U-D] (fuselage) (fitted with nose of F-GEFU)	WWII Remembrance Museum, Handcross, W Sussex
	FR886	Piper L-4J Grasshopper (G-BDMS)	Privately owned, Melksham, Wilts
	FS628	Fairchild Argus 2 (43-14601/G-AIZE)	RAF Museum, Cosford, Shropshire
	FS728	Noorduyn AT-16 Harvard IIb (D-FRCP)	Privately owned, Gelnhausen, Germany
	FT118	Noorduyn AT-16 Harvard IIb (G-BZHL) [TM-13]	Privately owned, Hibaldstow, Lincs
	FT323	NA AT-6D Harvard III (FAP 1513/G-CCOY)	Privately owned, France
	FT391	Noorduyn AT-16 Harvard IIb (G-AZBN)	Privately owned, Blackpool, Lancs
	FT466	Beech GB-2 Traveller (N16S)	Privately owned, Goodwood, W. Sussex
	FX322	Noorduyn AT-16 Harvard IIb <ff>	Privately owned, Doncaster, S. Yorks
	FX760	Curtiss P-40N Kittyhawk IV (A29-556/9150M) [GA-?]	RAF Museum, Hendon, Gtr London
	FZ626	Douglas Dakota III (KN566/G-AMPO) [YS-DH]	RAF Brize Norton, Oxon, for display
	GZ100	AgustaWestland AW109SP Grand New (G-ZIOO)	To civil, retired from RAF service December 2024
	HB612	Fairchild Argus II (G-AJSN)	Ulster Aviation Society, Long Kesh, Co. Antrim, NI

Serial	Type (code/other identity)	Owner/operator, location or fate	Notes
HB737	Fairchild Argus III (G-BCBH)	Privately owned, Spanhoe, Northants	
HB751	Fairchild Argus III (G-BCBL)	Privately owned, Breighton, E. Yorks	
HG691	DH89A Dragon Rapide (G-AIYR)	Privately owned, Duxford (damaged)	
HG709	DH89A Dragon Rapide (X7381/F-AZCA) [ZC-A]	Privately owned, La Ferté Alais, France	
HH268	GAL48 Hotspur II (HH379/BAPC.261) [H]	Army Flying Museum, Middle Wallop, Hants	
HJ711	DH98 Mosquito NF II (BAPC.434) [VI-C]	Lincolnshire Avn Heritage Centre, E. Kirkby, Lincs	
HM580	Cierva C-30A (G-ACUU) [KX-K]	IWM Duxford, Cambs	
HS503	Fairey Swordfish IV (BAPC.108)	RAF Museum Reserve Collection, Stafford, Staffs	
HS554	Fairey Swordfish III (G-RNMZ)	Privately owned, White Waltham, Berks	
IR206	Eurofighter Typhoon <R> (BAPC.360) [IR]	RAF M&RU, Bottesford, Leics	
IR808	B-V Chinook <R> (BAPC.361)	RAF M&RU, Bottesford, Leics	
JG241	Supermarine Aircraft Spitfire 26B (G-SMSP) [ZX-J]	Privately owned, Blackbushe, Hants	
JG668	VS502 Spitfire T8 (A58-441/G-CFGA)	Privately owned, Haverfordwest, Pembrokeshire, Wales	
JG891	VS349 Spitfire F Vc (N5TF/G-LFVC) [T-B]	Privately owned, Duxford, Cambs	
JN768	Hawker Tempest V (4887M/G-TMPV)	Privately owned, Sywell, Northants	
JP843	Hawker Typhoon Ib [T] (fuselage)	D-Day Museum, Caen, France	
JV482	Grumman Wildcat V	Ulster Aviation Society, Long Kesh, Co. Antrim, NI	
JV579	Grumman FM-2 Wildcat (N4845V/G-RUMW) [F]	The Fighter Collection, Duxford, Cambs	
KB889	Avro 683 Lancaster B X (G-LANC) [NA-I]	IWM Duxford, Cambs	
KB976	Avro 683 Lancaster B X [LQ] <ff>	Privately owned, Newquay, Cornwall	
KD345	Goodyear FG-1D Corsair (88297/G-FGID) [130-A]	The Fighter Collection, Duxford, Cambs	
KD431	CV Corsair IV [E2-M]	FAA Museum, RNAS Yeovilton, Somerset	
KE209	Grumman Hellcat II	FAA Museum, RNAS Yeovilton, Somerset	
KF183	Noorduyn AT-16 Harvard IIb (G-CORS) [3]	Privately owned, East Midlands, Leics	
KF388	Noorduyn AT-16 Harvard IIb (composite) [15]	Bournemouth Aviation Museum, Dorset	
KF402	NA T-6G Texan (49-3072/G-TEXN) [HT-Y]	Boultbee Flight Academy, Goodwood, W. Sussex	
KF532	Noorduyn AT-16 Harvard IIb <ff>	Sywell Aviation Museum, Northants	
KF650	Noorduyn AT-16 Harvard IIb <ff>	Sywell Aviation Museum, Northants	
KF741	Noorduyn AT-16 Harvard IIb <ff>	Privately owned, Kenilworth, Warks	
KG374	Douglas Dakota III (KP208) [YS-DM]	Merville Barracks, Colchester, Essex, on display	
KG437	Douglas Dakota III (N9050T) <ff>	RAF Museum, Cosford, Shropshire	
KG651	Douglas Dakota III (G-AMHJ)	Metheringham Airfield Visitor Centre, Lincs	
KJ351	Airspeed AS58 Horsa II (TL659/BAPC.80) [23]	Army Flying Museum, Middle Wallop, Hants	
KJ994	Douglas Dakota III (F-AZTE)	Dakota et Cie, La Ferté Alais, France	
KK527	Fairchild 24R Argus III (44-83184/G-RGUS)	Privately owned, Fowlmere, Cambs	
KK995	Sikorsky Hoverfly I (KL110) [E]	RAF Museum, Hendon, Gtr London	
KL216	Republic P-47D Thunderbolt (45-49295/9212M) [RS-L]	RAF Museum, Hendon, Gtr London	
KN353	Douglas Dakota IV (G-AMYJ)	Yorkshire Air Museum, Elvington, N. Yorks	
KN487	Douglas Dakota IV (PH-ALR) [NQ-I]	Preserved Valkenberg AB, Netherlands (Aviodrome loan)	
KN645	Douglas Dakota IV (KG374/8355M)	RAF Museum, Cosford, Shropshire	
KN751	Consolidated Liberator C VI (IAF HE807) [F]	RAF Museum, Hendon, Gtr London	
KP220	Douglas Dakota IV (G-ANAF)	Privately owned, Coventry, Warks	
KZ191	Hawker Hurricane IV (frame only)	Privately owned, East Garston, Berks	
LA198	VS356 Spitfire F21 (7118M) [RAI-G]	Kelvingrove Art Gallery & Museum, Glasgow, Scotland	
LA226	VS356 Spitfire F21 (7119M)	RAF Museum Reserve Collection, Stafford, Staffs	
LA255	VS356 Spitfire F21 (6490M) [JX-U]	RAF Lossiemouth, Moray, Scotland, preserved	
LA543	VS474 Seafire F46 <ff>	The Air Defence Collection, Salisbury, Wilts	
LA546	VS474 Seafire F46 (G-CFZJ)	Privately owned, Colchester, Essex	
LA564	VS474 Seafire F46 (G-FRSX)	Kennet Aviation, stored Old Warden, Beds	
LB264	Taylorcraft Plus D (G-AIXA)	RAF Museum, Hendon, Gtr London	
LB286	Taylorcraft Plus D (EI-AMF/G-ARRK)	Privately owned, Spanhoe, Northants	
LB294	Taylorcraft Plus D (G-AHWJ)	Saywell Heritage Centre, Worthing, W. Sussex	
LB312	Taylorcraft Plus D (HH982/G-AHXE)	Historic Army Aircraft Flight, Middle Wallop, Hants	
LB314	Taylorcraft Plus D (OY-DSZ)	South Yorkshire Aircraft Museum, Doncaster, S. Yorks	
LB352	Taylorcraft Plus D (G-AHCR)	Privately owned, Middlezoy, Somerset	
LB367	Taylorcraft Plus D (G-AHGZ)	Privately owned, Parkend, Glos	
LB369	Taylorcraft Plus D (G-AHHY)	Privately owned, Enstone, Oxon	
LB375	Taylorcraft Plus D (G-AHGW)	Privately owned, Popham , Hants (rebuild)	

Notes	Serial	Type (code/other identity)	Owner/operator, location or fate
	LF363	Hawker Hurricane IIc [RF-J]	RAF BBMF, Coningsby, Lincs
	LF738	Hawker Hurricane IIc (5405M) [UH-A]	RAF Museum, Cosford, Shropshire
	LF789	DH82 Queen Bee (K3584/BAPC.186) [R2-K]	de Havilland Aircraft Museum, London Colney
	LF858	DH82 Queen Bee (G-BLUZ)	Privately owned, Old Warden, Beds
	LS326	Fairey Swordfish II (G-AJVH) [L2]	Fly Navy Heritage Trust, Yeovilton, Somerset
	LS931	Fairey Barracuda II (wreckage)	FAA Museum, stored Cobham Hall, RNAS Yeovilton, Somerset
	LV907	HP59 Halifax III (HR792/BAPC.449) [NP-F] (marked *NP763* [H7-N] on port side)	Yorkshire Air Museum, Elvington, N. Yorks
	LZ551	DH100 Vampire	FAA Museum, RNAS Yeovilton, Somerset
	LZ766	Percival P34 Proctor III (G-ALCK)	IWM Duxford, Cambs
	LZ842	VS361 Spitfire F IX (G-CGZU) [EF-F]	Biggin Hill Heritage Hangar, Biggin Hill, Kent
	LZ844	VS349 Spitfire F Vc [UP-X]	*Currently not known*
	MA764	VS361 Spitfire LF IXe (G-MCDB)	Privately owned, Biggin Hill, Kent
	MB293	VS358 Seafire IIc (G-CFGI)	The Aircraft Restoration Co, Duxford, Cambs
	MF628	Vickers Wellington T10 (9210M)	RAF Museum, Cosford, Shropshire
	MH314	VS361 Spitfire IX <R> (*EN526*/BAPC.221) [SZ-G]	RAF Northolt, Gtr London, on display
	MH367	VS361 Spitfire F IX (G-MHIX) [FL-A]	Ultimate Warbird Flights, Sywell, Northants
	MH415	VS361 Spitfire LF IXb (G-AVDJ) [ZD-E]	*Sold to Belgium, July 2024*
	MH434	VS361 Spitfire LF IXb (G-ASJV) [ZD-B]	The Old Flying Machine Company, Duxford, Cambs
	MH526	Supermarine Aircraft Spitfire 26 (G-CJWW) [LO-D]	Privately owned, Wethersfield, Essex
	MJ306	VS361 Spitfire LF IX (G-HBOX)	Privately owned, location unconfirmed
	MJ444	VS361 Spitfire HF IX (G-LEGD) [KH-D]	Privately owned, Duxford, Cambs
	MJ627	VS509 Spitfire T9 (G-BMSB) [9G-Q]	Privately owned, Biggin Hill, Kent
	MJ772	VS509 Spitfire T9 (G-AVAV/PH-KDH) [GW-A]	Privately owned, Eindhoven, The Netherlands
	MJ832	VS361 Spitfire IX <R> (*L1096*/BAPC.229) [DN-Y]	RAF Digby, Lincs, on display
	MK356	VS361 Spitfire LF IXe (5690M) [QJ-3]	*Destroyed at RAF Coningsby, May 2024*
	MK356	VS361 Spitfire LF IXc <R> [2I-V]	Kent Battle of Britain Museum, Hawkinge, Kent
	MK356	VS361 Spitfire LF IXc <R> (BAPC.298)	Boscombe Down, Wilts (stored)
	MK392	VS361 Spitfire LF IXc <R> (*EN398*/BAPC.184) [JE-J]	Boultbee Flight Academy, Goodwood, W. Sussex
	MK805	VS361 Spitfire IX (BAPC.426) <R> [SH-B]	Simply Spitfires, Oulton Broad, Suffolk
	MK912	VS361 Spitfire LF IXc (G-BRRA) [SH-L]	Privately owned, stored Biggin Hill, Kent
	ML119	VS361 Spitfire LF IXe (G-SDNI)	Biggin Hill Heritage Hangar, Kent (restoration)
	ML135	VS361 Spitfire IX <R> (BAPC.513)	Essex Memorial Spitfire Monument, ON, Canada
	ML295	VS361 Spitfire LF IXb (G-CLXB) [DB-M]	Privately owned, Biggin Hill, Kent
	ML407	VS509 Spitfire T9 (G-LFIX) [OU-V]	Privately owned, Sywell, Northants
	ML407	VS361 Spitfire IX <R> [OU-V]	Castletown D-Day Centre, Portland, Dorset
	ML411	VS361 Spitfire LF IXe (G-CBNU)	Privately owned, Ashford, Kent
	ML417	VS361 Spitfire LF IXe (N2TF) [21-T]	Privately owned, Duxford, Cambs
	ML427	VS361 Spitfire IX (6457M) [HK-A]	Thinktank, Birmingham, Warks
	ML796	Short S25 Sunderland V [NS-F]	IWM Duxford, Cambs
	ML824	Short S25 Sunderland V [NS-Z]	RAF Museum, Hendon, Gtr London
	MN235	Hawker Typhoon Ib [I8-T]	RAF Museum, Hendon, Gtr London
	MP425	Airspeed AS10 Oxford I (G-AITB) [G]	RAF Museum, Hendon, Gtr London
	MS902	Miles M25 Martinet TT1 (TF-SHC)	Museum of Berkshire Aviation, Woodley, Berks
	MS968	Auster AOP5 (G-ALYG)	Privately owned, Old Sarum, Wilts
	MT166	Auster AOP5 (G-BICD)	Privately owned, South Scarle, Notts
	MT182	Auster J/1 Autocrat (G-AJDY)	Privately owned, Eshott, Northumberland (for rebuild)
	MT197	Auster IV (G-ANHS)	Privately owned, Spanhoe, Northants
	MT438	Auster III (G-AREI)	Privately owned, Eggesford, Devon
	MT818	VS502 Spitfire T8 (G-AIDN) [YO-D]	Biggin Hill Heritage Hangar, Kent
	MT928	VS359 Spitfire HF VIIIc (G-BKMI/MV154/*AR654*)[ZX-M]	*Sold to Australia*
	MV293	VS379 Spitfire FR XIVe (G-SPIT) [Z]	Privately owned, Duxford, Cambs
	MW401	Hawker Tempest II (IAF HA604/G-PEST)	Privately owned, stored North Weald, Essex
	MW810	Hawker Tempest II (IAF HA591) <ff>	Privately owned, Bentwaters, Suffolk
	NF314	GEC Phoenix (BAPC.408)	Army, Larkhill, Wilts, on display
	NF370	Fairey Swordfish III [NH-L]	IWM Duxford, Cambs
	NF389	Fairey Swordfish III	Fly Navy Heritage Trust Ltd, Yeovilton, Somerset (restoration)
	NH238	VS361 Spitfire LF IXe (G-MKIX) [D-A]	Privately owned, stored Greenham Common, Berks

Serial	Type (code/other identity)	Owner/operator, location or fate	Notes
NH341	VS509 Spitfire T9 (G-CICK) [DB-E]	Privately owned, Headcorn, Kent	
NJ633	Auster 5D (G-AKXP)	Privately owned, Middlezoy, Somerset	
NJ673	Auster 5D (G-AOCR)	Privately owned, Wisbech, Cambs	
NJ689	Auster AOP5 (G-ALXZ)	Privately owned, Breighton, E. Yorks	
NJ695	Auster AOP5 (G-AJXV)	Privately owned, Boarhunt, Hants	
NJ703	Auster AOP5 (TJ207/G-AKPI) [P]	Privately owned, Wickenby, Lincs	
NJ719	Auster AOP5 (TW385/G-ANFU)	Thorpe Camp Preservation Group, Lincs	
NJ728	Auster AOP5 (G-AIKE)	Privately owned, Sandown, IOW	
NJ889	Auster AOP3 (G-AHLK)	Privately owned, Ledbury, Herefordshire	
NL750	DH82A Tiger Moth II (T7997/G-AOBH)	Privately owned, Middlezoy, Somerset	
NL846	DH82A Tiger Moth I (F-BGEQ)	Brooklands Museum, Weybridge, Surrey (stored offsite)	
NL985	DH82A Tiger Moth I (G-BWIK/7015M)	Privately owned, Oaksey Park, Wilts	
NM138	DH82A Tiger Moth I (G-ANEW) [41]	Privately owned, Henstridge, Somerset	
NM181	DH82A Tiger Moth I (G-AZGZ)	Privately owned, Rush Green, Gtr London	
NP294	Percival P31 Proctor IV	Privately owned, Bridgwater area, Somerset	
NS843	DH98 Mosquito FB.VI <R> (RL249/G-FBVI)	Privately owned, Hastings, E. Sussex	
NV778	Hawker Tempest TT5 (8386M)	RAF Museum, Hendon, Gtr London	
NS710	DH98 Mosquito TT35 (TJ118) <ff>	Victoria and Albert Museum, Knightsbridge, London	
NX534	Auster III (G-BUDL)	Privately owned, Spanhoe, Northants	
NX611	Avro 683 Lancaster B VII (G-ASXX/8375M) [DX-F,LE-H]	Lincolnshire Avn Heritage Centre, E. Kirkby, Lincs	
PA474	Avro 683 Lancaster B I [AR-L,VN-T]	RAF BBMF, Coningsby, Lincs	
PD130	Avro 683 Lancaster B I <R> (fuselage)(BAPC.482)	Boscombe Down Aviation Collection, Old Sarum, Wilts	
PD685	Slingsby T7 Cadet TX1 (BAPC.355)	Tettenhall Transport Heritage Centre, W. Midlands	
PF179	HS Gnat T1 (XR541/8602M)	Bournemouth Aviation Museum, Dorset	
PG657	DH82A Tiger Moth II (G-AGPK)	Privately owned, Clacton, Essex/Duxford, Cambs	
PG712	DH82A Tiger Moth II (PH-CSL) [2]	Privately owned, Middle Zeeland, The Netherlands	
PK519	VS356 Spitfire F22 [G-SPXX]	Privately owned, Newport Pagnell, Bucks	
PK624	VS356 Spitfire F22 (8072M)	The Fighter Collection, Duxford, Cambs	
PK664	VS356 Spitfire F22 (7759M) [V6-B]	Kennet Aviation, Sandown, IOW	
PK683	VS356 Spitfire F24 (7150M)	Solent Sky, Southampton, Hants	
PK724	VS356 Spitfire F24 (7288M)	RAF Museum, Hendon, Gtr London	
PL258	VS361 Spitfire IX (G-NSFS)	Norwegian Spitfire Foundation, Duxford (restoration)	
PL279	VS361 Spitfire IX <R> (N3317/BAPC.268) [ZF-Z] (marked MK464 [Y2-Y] on port side)	Privately owned, Newquay, Cornwall (stored)	
PL788	Supermarine Aircraft Spitfire 26 (G-CIEN)	Privately owned, Perth, Scotland	
PL793	Supermarine Aircraft Spitfire 26 (G-CIXM)	Privately owned, Popham, Hants	
PL904	VS365 Spitfire PR XI <R> (EN343/BAPC.226)	RAF Benson, Oxon, on display	
PL965	VS365 Spitfire PR XI (G-MKXI) [R]	IWM Duxford, Cambs	
PL983	VS365 Spitfire PR XI (G-PRXI)	The Aircraft Restoration Co, Duxford, Cambs	
PM631	VS390 Spitfire PR XIX	RAF BBMF, Coningsby, Lincs	
PM651	VS390 Spitfire PR XIX (7758M) [X]	Michael Beetham Conservation Centre, RAFM Cosford, Shropshire	
PN323	HP Halifax VII <ff>	IWM Duxford, Cambs	
PP566	Fairey Firefly I <rf>	Privately owned, Newton Abbott, Devon	
PP972	VS358 Seafire LF IIIc (G-BUAR) [11-5/N]	Privately owned, Stonesfield, Oxon	
PR005	General Atomics Protector RG1	RAF	
PR006	General Atomics Protector RG1	RAF	
PR007	General Atomics Protector RG1	RAF	
PR009	General Atomics Protector RG1	RAF No 31 Sqn, Waddington, Lincs	
PR010	General Atomics Protector RG1	RAF No 31 Sqn, Waddington, Lincs	
PR478	Supermarine Aircraft Spitfire 26 [S]	Privately owned, Dunkeswell, Devon	
PR533	Hawker Tempest II (MW763/IAF HA586/G-TEMT) [5R-V]	Privately owned, Duxford, Cambs	
PR536	Hawker Tempest II (IAF HA457)[OQ-H]	RAF Museum, Cosford, Shropshire	
PS004	Airbus Zephyr 8B	For MOD	
PS853	VS390 Spitfire PR XIX (G-RRGN) [C]	Rolls-Royce, East Midlands, Leics	
PS890	VS390 Spitfire PR XIX (F-AZJS) [UM-E]	Privately owned, Dijon, France	
PS915	VS390 Spitfire PR XIX (7548M/7711M)	RAF BBMF, Coningsby, Lincs	
PT462	VS509 Spitfire T9 (G-CTIX/N462JC) [SW-A]	Privately owned, Duxford, Cambs	
PT462	VS361 Spitfire IX <R> (BAPC.318) [SW-A]	Privately owned, Moffat, Scotland	
PV144	VS361 Spitfire IX <R> (BAPC.581) [4D-A]	Privately owned, Carlisle, Cumbria	

Notes	Serial	Type (code/other identity)	Owner/operator, location or fate
	PV202	VS509 Spitfire T9 (H-98/W3632/G-CCCA) [5R-H]	Historic Flying Ltd, Duxford, Cambs
	PV303	Supermarine Aircraft Spitfire 26 (G-CCJL) [ON-B]	Privately owned, Enstone, Oxon
	PZ865	Hawker Hurricane IIc (G-AMAU) [ZY-V]	RAF BBMF, Coningsby, Lincs
	RA848	Slingsby T7 Cadet TX1 <ff>	Privately owned, Hooton Park, Cheshire
	RA854	Slingsby T7 Cadet TX1	Yorkshire Air Museum, Elvington, N. Yorks
	RA897	Slingsby T7 Cadet TX1	Newark Air Museum, Winthorpe, Notts
	RA905	Slingsby T7 Cadet TX1 (BGA1143) [BQE]	Trenchard Museum, RAF Halton, Bucks
	RB142	Supermarine Aircraft Spitfire 26 (G-CEFC) [DW-B]	Privately owned, Popham, Hants
	RB159	VS379 Spitfire F XIV <R> [DW-D]	Privately owned, Delabole, Cornwall
	RB396	Hawker Typhoon IB (G-TIFY) [XP-W] (fuselage)	Hawker Typhoon Preservation Group, Duxford
	RD220	Bristol 156 Beaufighter TF X	National Museum of Flight, stored E Fortune, Scotland
	RD253	Bristol 156 Beaufighter TF X (7931M)	RAF Museum, Hendon, Gtr London
	RF398	Avro 694 Lincoln B II (8376M)	RAF Museum, Cosford, Shropshire
	RG333	Miles M38 Messenger IIA (G-AIEK)	Privately owned, Louth, Lincs
	RG904	VS Spitfire <R> (BAPC.333) [BT-K]	RAF Museum, Cosford, Shropshire
	RG907	Miles M25 Martinet <ff> (BAPC.514)	Tettenhall Transport Heritage Centre, W. Midlands
	RH746	Bristol 164 Brigand TF1 (fuselage)	RAF Museum, stored Cosford, Shropshire
	RK838	VS349 Spitfire Vb <R> (BAPC.230/AB550) [GE]	Eden Camp Theme Park, Malton, N. Yorks
	RK855	Supermarine Aircraft Spitfire 26 (G-PIXY) [FT-C]	Privately owned, Henstridge, Somerset
	RK858	VS361 Spitfire IX (G-CGJE)	The Aircraft Restoration Co, Duxford, Cambs
	RK912	VS361 Spitfire LF IX (G-CLCS)	Privately owned, Duxford, Cambs
	RL962	DH89A Dominie II (G-AHED)	South Yorkshire Aircraft Museum, Doncaster, S. Yorks
	RM169	Percival P31 Proctor IV (G-ANVY) [4-47]	Privately owned, Hooton Park, Cheshire
	RM221	Percival P31 Proctor IV (G-ANXR)	Privately owned, Headcorn, Kent
	RM689	VS379 Spitfire F XIV (G-ALGT)	Rolls-Royce, stored East Midlands Airport, Leics
	RM694	VS379 Spitfire F XIV (G-DBKL/6640M)	Biggin Hill Heritage Hangar, Kent (restoration)
	RM927	VS379 Spitfire F XIV (F-AYXX/G-SXIV) [X]	Privately owned, La Ferté Alais, France
	RN201	VS379 Spitfire F XIVe (G-BSKP)	Privately owned, Duxford, Cambs
	RN203	VS379 Spitfire F XIV (G-CLCT)	Privately owned, Duxford, Cambs
	RN218	Isaacs Spitfire <R> (G-BBJI) [N]	Privately owned, Builth Wells, Powys, Wales
	RP001*	AeroVironment RQ-20 Puma AE Micro UAV	Royal Navy
	RP002*	AeroVironment RQ-12 Wasp AE Micro UAV	Royal Navy
	RP003*	AeroVironment Shrike Mk1 Micro UAV	MOD
	RR232	VS361 Spitfire HF IXc (PV181/G-BRSF)	Privately owned, Goodwood, W. Sussex
	RT486	Auster 5 (G-AJGJ)	RAF Manston History Museum, Kent
	RT520	Auster 5 (G-ALYB)	Thorpe Camp Visitor Centre, Tattershall Thorpe, Lincs
	RT578	Auster AOP5 (G-ALNV) (frame)	Privately owned, Dumfries area, Scotland
	RT610	Auster 5A-160 (G-AKWS)	Privately owned, Shobdon, Herefordshire (restoration)
	RW382	VS361 Spitfire LF XVIe (G-PBIX) [WZ-RR]	Privately owned, Sywell, Northants
	RW386	VS361 Spitfire LF XVIe (LN-BSP/6944M) [NG-D]	Privately owned, Angelholm, Sweden
	RW388	VS361 Spitfire LF XVIe (6946M) [U4-U]	Potteries Museum & Art Gallery, Hanley, Staffs
	RX168	VS358 Seafire L IIIc (IAC 157/G-BWEM)	Privately owned, stored Duxford, Cambs
	SL611	VS361 Spitfire LF XVIe (G-SAEA)	Supermarine Aero Engineering, Stoke-on-Trent, Staffs
	SL674	VS361 Spitfire LF IX (8392M) [RAS-H]	RAF Museum Reserve Collection, Stafford, Staffs
	SL721	VS361 Spitfire LF XVIe (OO-XVI) [GE-S]	Privately owned, Brasschaat, Belgium
	SM520	VS509 Spitfire T9 (H-99/G-ILDA) [LO-G]	Boultbee Flight Academy, Goodwood, W. Sussex
	SM639	VS361 Spitfire LF IXe (G-CKYM)	Privately owned, Godalming, Surrey
	SM845	VS361 Spitfire LF XVIIIe (D-FIII) [R]	On rebuild Duxford, Cambs
	SN280	Hawker Tempest V <ff>	South Yorkshire Aircraft Museum, Doncaster, S. Yorks
	SR462	VS377 Seafire F XV (UB415/G-TGVP)	Privately owned, stored Old Warden, Beds
	SR661	Hawker Fury ISS (G-CBEL)	Privately owned, Duxford, Cambs
	SX137	VS384 Seafire F XVII	FAA Museum, RNAS Yeovilton, Somerset
	SX300	VS384 Seafire F XVII (G-RIPH)	Kennet Aviation, stored Old Warden, Beds
	SX336	VS384 Seafire F XVII (G-KASX) [105/VL]	Fly Navy Heritage Trust Ltd, Yeovilton, Somerset
	TA122	DH98 Mosquito FB VI [UP-G]	de Havilland Aircraft Museum, London Colney
	TA634	DH98 Mosquito TT35 (G-AWJV) [8K-K]	de Havilland Aircraft Museum, London Colney
	TA639	DH98 Mosquito TT35 (7806M) [AZ-E]	RAF Museum, Cosford, Shropshire
	TA719	DH98 Mosquito TT35 (G-ASKC) [56]	IWM Duxford, Cambs

Serial	Type (code/other identity)	Owner/operator, location or fate	Notes
TA805	VS361 Spitfire HF IX (G-PMNF) [FX-M]	Privately owned, Biggin Hill, Kent	
TB288	VS361 Spitfire LF IX <R> (MH486/46/BAPC.206) [HT-H]	RAF Museum, Hendon, Gtr London	
TB382	VS361 Spitfire LF XVIe (G-CMSF/X4277/MK673)	Airframe Assemblies, Sandown, IOW	
TB675	VS361 Spitfire LF XVIe (RW393/7293M) [4D-V]	RAF Museum, Hendon, Gtr London	
TB752	VS361 Spitfire LF XVIe (8086M) [KH-Z]	RAF Manston, Kent, Memorial Pavilion	
TB885	VS361 Spitfire LF XVIe (G-CKUE/PH-FVE) [3W-V]	Privately owned, Eindhoven, The Netherlands	
TD248	VS361 Spitfire LF XVIe (G-OXVI/7246M) [CR-S]	Spitfire Ltd, Humberside, Lincs	
TD248	VS361 Spitfire LF XVIe (BAPC.368) [8Q-T] (fuselage)	Norfolk & Suffolk Avn Museum, Flixton, Suffolk	
TD314	VS361 Spitfire LF IX (G-CGYJ) [FX-P]	Privately owned, Duxford, Cambs	
TE184	VS361 Spitfire LF XVIe (G-MXVI/6850M) [DGA]	Privately owned, Biggin Hill	
TE311	VS361 Spitfire LF XVIe (MK178/7241M) [SW-M] (port side),{LN-G} starboard side	RAF BBMF, Coningsby, Lincs	
TE356	VS361 Spitfire LF XVIe (N356TE) [DD-E]	Privately owned, stored Biggin Hill, Kent	
TE462	VS361 Spitfire LF XVIe (7243M)	National Museum of Flight, E Fortune, Scotland	
TE517	VS361 Spitfire LF IXe (G-RYIX) [HL-K]	MSÖ Air & Space Museum, Eskisehir, Turkey	
TE566	VS509 Spitfire T9 (VH-IXT)	Privately owned, Enstone, Oxon (rebuild)	
TG263	Saro SR A1 (G-12-1)	Solent Sky, Southampton, Hants	
TG511	HP67 Hastings T5 (8554M) [511]	RAF Museum, Cosford, Shropshire	
TG517	HP67 Hastings T5 [517]	Newark Air Museum, Winthorpe, Notts	
TG528	HP67 Hastings C1A [528,T]	IWM Duxford, Cambs	
TJ138	DH98 Mosquito B35 (7607M) [VO-L]	RAF Museum, Hendon, Gtr London	
TJ320	Auster AOP5 (G-ANHW, derelict fuselage)	Privately owned, Chichester area, West Sussex	
TJ343	Auster AOP5 (G-AJXC)	Privately owned, White Waltham, Berks	
TJ518	Auster J/1 Autocrat (G-AJIH)	Privately owned, Gloucester, Glos	
TJ534	Auster AOP5 (G-AKSY)	Privately owned, West Tisted, Hants	
TJ569	Auster AOP5 (G-AKOW)	Army Flying Museum, Middle Wallop, Hants	
TJ652	Auster AOP5 (TJ565/G-AMVD)	Privately owned, Hardwick, Norfolk	
TJ672	Auster 5D (G-ANIJ) [TS-D]	Privately owned, Netheravon, Wilts	
TK718	GAL59 Hamilcar I (fuselage)	The Tank Museum, Bovington, Dorset	
TK777	GAL59 Hamilcar I (fuselage)	Army Flying Museum, Middle Wallop, Hants	
TP280	VS394 Spitfire FR XVIIIe (D-FSPT) [VS-Z]	Hangar 10 Collection, Heringsdorf, Germany	
TP298	VS394 Spitfire FR XVIII [UM-T]	Airframe Assemblies, Sandown, IOW	
TS291	Slingsby T7 Cadet TX1 (BGA852)	National Museum of Flight, stored E Fortune, Scotland	
TS798	Avro 685 York C1 (G-AGNV/MW100)	RAF Museum, Cosford, Shropshire	
TW439	Auster AOP5 (G-ANRP)	Privately owned, Breighton, E. Yorks	
TW462	Auster AOP5 (G-AOCP) (frame)	Privately owned, Dumfries area, Scotland	
TW467	Auster AOP5 (G-ANIE)	Privately owned, Hardwick, Suffolk	
TW477	Auster AOP5 (OY-EFI)	Privately owned, Ringsted, Denmark	
TW501	Auster AOP5 (G-ALBJ)	Privately owned, Dunkeswell, Devon	
TW511	Auster AOP5 (G-APAF)	Privately owned, Chisledon, Wilts	
TW519	Auster AOP5 (G-ANHX) [AO-R/V]	Privately owned, Middlezoy, Somerset	
TW536	Auster AOP6 (G-BNGE/7704M)	Privately owned, Popham, Hants	
TW641	Beagle A61 Terrier 2 (G-ATDN)	Privately owned, Biggin Hill, Kent	
TX176	Avro XIX Anson Series 2 (G-AHKX)	The Shuttleworth Collection, Old Warden, Beds	
TX213	Avro 652A Anson C19 (G-AWRS)	North-East Land, Sea & Air Museums, Usworth, T&W	
TX214	Avro 652A Anson C19 (7817M)	RAF Museum, Cosford, Shropshire	
TX226	Avro 652A Anson C19 (7865M)	Montrose Air Station Heritage Centre, Angus, Scotland	
TX235	Avro 652A Anson C19 (frame)	Avro Heritage Museum, Woodford, Cheshire	
TX310	DH89A Dragon Rapide 6 (G-AIDL)	Privately owned, Clacton, Essex/Duxford, Cambs	
TZ164	Isaacs Spitfire (G-ISAC) [01-A]	Privately owned, Hampstead Norreys, Berks	
VF301	DH100 Vampire F1 (7060M) [RAL-G]	Midland Air Museum, Coventry, Warks	
VF512	Auster 6A (G-ARRX) [PF-M]	Privately owned, Popham, Hants	
VF516	Beagle A61 Terrier 2 (G-ASMZ)	Privately owned, Fowlmere, Cambs	
VF519	Auster AOP6 (G-ASYN)	Privately owned, stored Doncaster area, S. Yorks	
VF526	Auster 6A (G-ARXU) [T]	Privately owned, Strubby, Lincs	
VF530	Auster 6A (G-ARGI) (frame)	South Yorkshire Aircraft Museum, stored Doncaster	
VF557	Auster 6A (G-ARHM) [H]	Privately owned, Headcorn, Kent	
VF581	Beagle A61 Terrier 1 (G-ARSL) [G]	National Museum of Scotland, Edinburgh, Scotland	
VF631	Auster AOP6 (G-ASDK)	Privately owned, Hibaldstow, Lincs	
VF635	Auster AOP6 (G-ARGB)	Privately owned, Hooton Park, Cheshire	

Notes	Serial	Type (code/other identity)	Owner/operator, location or fate
	VH127	Fairey Firefly TT4 [200/R]	FAA Museum, stored Cobham Hall, RNAS Yeovilton, Somerset
	VL348	Avro 652A Anson C19 (G-AVVO)	Newark Air Museum, Winthorpe, Notts
	VL349	Avro 652A Anson C19 (N5054/G-AWSA) [V7-Q]	Norfolk & Suffolk Avn Museum, Flixton, Suffolk
	VM325	Avro 652A Anson C19	Privately owned, Carew Cheriton, Pembrokeshire, Wales
	VM360	Avro 652A Anson C19 (G-APHV)	National Museum of Flight, E Fortune, Scotland
	VM659	Slingsby T8 Tutor TX2	Privately owned, stored Ashbourne, Eire
	VM684	Slingsby T8 Tutor TX2 (BGA791)	Privately owned, Knutsford, Cheshire
	VM687	Slingsby T8 Tutor (BGA794)	Privately owned, Saltby, Leics
	VN485	VS356 Spitfire F24 (7326M)	IWM Duxford, Cambs
	VN799	EE Canberra T4 (WJ874/G-CDSX)	Location unknown. Noted for sale 2024
	VP293	Avro 696 Shackleton T4 [X] <ff>	Yorkshire Air Museum, Elvington, N. Yorks
	VP519	Avro 652A Anson C19 (G-AVVR) <ff>	South Yorkshire Aircraft Museum, Doncaster, S. Yorks
	VP952	DH104 Devon C2 (8820M)	RAF Museum, Cosford, Shropshire
	VP955	DH104 Devon C2 (G-DVON)	Privately owned, Dalton, Lancs (restoration)
	VP957	DH104 Devon C2 (8822M) <ff>	No 1137 Sqn ATC, Long Kesh, Co. Antrim, NI
	VP959	DH104 Devon C2 (N959VP)	Privately owned, stored Compton Verney, Warks
	VP967	DH104 Devon C2 (G-KOOL)	Yorkshire Air Museum, Elvington, N. Yorks
	VP975	DH104 Devon C2 [M]	Science Museum, stored Wroughton, Wilts
	VP981	DH104 Devon C2 (G-DHDV)	Aero Legends, Headcorn, Kent/Duxford, Cambs
	VR137	Westland Wyvern TF1	FAA Museum, RNAS Yeovilton, Somerset
	VR192	Percival P40 Prentice T1 (G-APIT)	Romney Marsh Wartime Collection, Kent
	VR249	Percival P40 Prentice T1 (G-APIY) [FA-EL]	Newark Air Museum, Winthorpe, Notts
	VR259	Percival P40 Prentice T1 (G-APJB) [M]	Privately owned, Postling, Kent
	VR930	Hawker Sea Fury FB11 (G-CLNJ/8382M) [110/Q]	Fly Navy Heritage Trust, Yeovilton, Somerset
	VS356	Percival P40 Prentice T1 (G-AOLU)	Privately owned, Fordoun, Aberdeenshire, Scotland
	VS562	Avro 652A Anson T21 (8012M) <ff>	Shannon Aviation Museum, Eire
	VS610	Percival P40 Prentice T1 (G-AOKL)[K-L]	Privately owned, Fordoun, Aberdeenshire, Scotland
	VS618	Percival P40 Prentice T1 (G-AOLK)	RAF Museum Reserve Collection, Stafford, Staffs
	VS623	Percival P40 Prentice T1 (G-AOKZ)[KQ-F]	Midland Air Museum, Coventry, Warks
	VT812	DH100 Vampire F3 (7200M) [N]	RAF Museum, Hendon, Gtr London
	VT935	Boulton Paul P111A (VT769)	Midland Air Museum, Coventry, Warks
	VV106	Supermarine 510 (7175M)	FAA Museum, stored Cobham Hall, RNAS Yeovilton, Somerset
	VV217	DH100 Vampire FB5 (7323M)	de Havilland Aircraft Museum, London Colney (stored offsite)
	VV400	EoN Olympia 2 (BGA1697) [97]	Privately owned, Aston Down, Glos
	VV401	EoN Olympia 2 (BGA1125) [99]	Privately owned, Ringmer, E. Sussex
	VV612	DH112 Venom FB50 (J-1523/G-VENI) <ff>	Shannon Aviation Museum, Eire
	VV901	Avro 652A Anson T21	Yorkshire Air Museum, Elvington, N. Yorks
	VW453	Gloster Meteor T7 (8703M)	Jet Age Museum, Gloucestershire Airport, Glos
	VW957	DH103 Sea Hornet NF21 <rf>	Privately owned, Chelmsford, Essex
	VW993	Beagle A61 Terrier 2 (G-ASCD)	Yorkshire Air Museum, Elvington, N. Yorks
	VX113	Auster AOP6 (G-ARNO) [36]	Privately owned, St. Athan, Glamorgan, Wales (dismantled)
	VX250	DH103 Sea Hornet NF21 [48] <rf>	de Havilland Aircraft Museum, London Colney (stored)
	VX272	Hawker P.1052 (7174M)	FAA Museum, stored Cobham Hall, RNAS Yeovilton, Somerset
	VX275	Slingsby T21B Sedbergh TX1 (BGA572/8884M)	The Helicopter Museum, Weston-Super-Mare, Somerset (restoration off-site)
	VX281	Hawker Sea Fury T20S (G-BCOW) [120/VL]	The Fighter Collection, Reno, NV, USA (wreck)
	VX573	Vickers Valetta C2 (8389M)	RAF Museum, stored Cosford, Shropshire
	VX580	Vickers Valetta C2 [580]	Norfolk & Suffolk Avn Museum, Flixton, Suffolk
	VX595	WS51 Dragonfly HR1	FAA Museum, RNAS Yeovilton, Somerset
	VX653	Hawker Sea Fury FB11 (G-BUCM)	The Fighter Collection, Duxford, Cambs
	VX665	Hawker Sea Fury FB11 <rf>	RN Historic Flight, at BAE Systems Brough, E. Yorks
	VX926	Auster T7 (G-ASKJ)	Privately owned, Gamlingay, Cambs
	VX927	Auster T7 (G-ASYG)	Privately owned, Dubová, Slovakia
	VZ193	DH100 Vampire FB5 <ff>	Privately owned, Warrington, Cheshire
	VZ440	Gloster Meteor F8 (WA984) [X]	Historic Aviation Centre, Fishburn, Co. Durham
	VZ477	Gloster Meteor F8 (7741M) <ff>	Midland Air Museum, Coventry, Warks
	VZ568	Gloster Meteor F8 [C](7261M) <ff>	Privately owned, RAF Halton, Bucks

Serial	Type (code/other identity)	Owner/operator, location or fate	Notes
VZ608	Gloster Meteor FR9	Newark Air Museum, Winthorpe, Notts	
VZ634	Gloster Meteor T7 (8657M)	Newark Air Museum, Winthorpe, Notts	
VZ638	Gloster Meteor T7 (G-JETM) [HF]	Gatwick Aviation Museum, Charlwood, Surrey	
VZ728	RS4 Desford Trainer (G-AGOS)	Newark Air Museum, Winthorpe, Notts	
WA123	DH100 Vampire FB6 (J-1196/*VZ305*/LN-DHY) [6-29]	Norwegian AF Historical Sqn, Rygge, Norway	
WA473	VS Attacker F1 [102/J]	FAA Museum, RNAS Yeovilton, Somerset	
WA576	Bristol 171 Sycamore 3 (G-ALSS/7900M)	Dumfries & Galloway Avn Mus, Dumfries, Scotland	
WA577	Bristol 171 Sycamore 3 (G-ALST/7718M)	Boscombe Down Aviation Collection, Old Sarum, Wilts	
WA630	Gloster Meteor T7 [69] <ff>	Robertsbridge Aviation Society, Newhaven, E. Sussex	
WA634	Gloster Meteor T7/8	Ulster Aviation Society, Long Kesh, Co. Antrim, NI	
WA638	Gloster Meteor T7(mod) (G-JWMA)	Martin-Baker Aircraft, Chalgrove, Oxon	
WA662	Gloster Meteor T7	South Yorkshire Aircraft Museum, Doncaster, S. Yorks	
WB188	Hawker Hunter F3 (7154M)	Tangmere Military Aviation Museum, W. Sussex	
WB188	Hawker Hunter GA11 (XF300/G-BZPC)	Privately owned, Kent	
WB440	Fairey Firefly AS6 <ff>	Privately owned, Newton Abbott, Devon	
WB491	Avro 706 Ashton 2 (TS897/G-AJJW) <ff>	Newark Air Museum, Winthorpe, Notts	
WB549	DHC1 Chipmunk 22A (G-BAPB)	Privately owned, Lidköping, Sweden	
WB555	DHC1 Chipmunk 22 (G-CLKX)	Privately owned, Henstridge, Somerset	
WB560	DHC1 Chipmunk T10 (comp WG403) <ff>	Privately owned, Norwich, Norfolk	
WB565	DHC1 Chipmunk 22 (G-PVET) [X]	Privately owned, Rendcomb, Glos	
WB569	DHC1 Chipmunk 22 (G-BYSJ)	Privately owned, Eshott, Northumberland	
WB571	DHC1 Chipmunk 22 (D-EOSF) [34]	Privately owned, Porta Westfalica, Germany	
WB584	DHC1 Chipmunk T10 (comp WG303/7706M) <ff>	Privately owned, current location unknown	
WB585	DHC1 Chipmunk 22 (G-AOSY) [28]	Privately owned, Audley End, Essex	
WB588	DHC1 Chipmunk 22 (G-AOTD) [D]	Privately owned, Henstridge, Somerset	
WB615	DHC1 Chipmunk 22 (G-BXIA) [E]	Privately owned, Blackpool, Lancs	
WB624	DHC1 Chipmunk T10	Newark Air Museum, Winthorpe, Notts	
WB626	DHC1 Chipmunk T10 [19] <ff>	Trenchard Museum, RAF Halton, Bucks	
WB627	DHC1 Chipmunk T10 (9248M) (fuselage) [N]	Norfolk & Suffolk Avn Museum, Flixton, Suffolk (rest'n)	
WB652	DHC1 Chipmunk 22 (G-CHPY) [V]	*Current status unknown (Cancelled by CAA May 2023)*	
WB654	DHC1 Chipmunk 22 (G-BXGO) [U]	Privately owned, Finmere, Bucks	
WB657	DHC1 Chipmunk T10 (G-RNVR/G-CNVH) [908]	Fly Navy Heritage Trust, Yeovilton, Somerset	
WB670	DHC1 Chipmunk T10 (comp WG303)(8361M)	Privately owned, stored Carlisle, Cumbria	
WB671	DHC1 Chipmunk 22 (G-BWTG) [910]	Privately owned, Teuge, The Netherlands (damaged by fire, July 2024)	
WB685	DHC1 Chipmunk T10 (comp WP969/G-ATHC)	North-East Land, Sea & Air Museums, stored Usworth, T&W	
WB697	DHC1 Chipmunk 22 (OO-PMS/G-BXCT) [95]	Privately owned, Antwerp, Belgium	
WB702	DHC1 Chipmunk 22 (G-AOFE)	Privately owned, Goodwood, W. Sussex	
WB703	DHC1 Chipmunk 22A (G-ARMC)	Privately owned, Booker, Bucks	
WB711	DHC1 Chipmunk 22 (G-APPM)	Privately owned, Sywell, Northants	
WB726	DHC1 Chipmunk 22A (G-AOSK) [E]	Privately owned, Turweston, Bucks	
WB733	DHC1 Chipmunk T10 (comp WG422)	South Yorkshire Aircraft Museum, Doncaster, S. Yorks	
WB763	DHC1 Chipmunk 22 (G-BBMR) [K]	Privately owned, Turweston, Bucks	
WB922	Slingsby T21B Sedbergh TX1 (BGA4366)	Privately owned, Nympsfield, Glos	
WB924	Slingsby T21B Sedbergh TX1 (BGA3901)	*Withdrawn from use, 2017. Current status unknown*	
WB944	Slingsby T21B Sedbergh TX1 (BGA3160)	*Withdrawn from use, 2015. Current status unknown*	
WB945	Slingsby T21B Sedbergh TX1 (BGA1254) [BUW]	Privately owned, stored RAF Halton, Bucks	
WB971	Slingsby T21B Sedbergh TX1 (BGA3324)	Privately owned, Eaglescott, Devon	
WB975	Slingsby T21B Sedbergh TX1 (BGA3288) [FJB]	Privately owned, Atkar, Hungary	
WB980	Slingsby T21B Sedbergh TX1 (BGA3290)	Privately owned, Husbands Bosworth, Leics	
WB981	Slingsby T21B Sedbergh TX1 (BGA3238)	Privately owned, Eaglescott, Devon	
WD286	DHC1 Chipmunk 22 (G-BBND)	Privately owned, Old Warden, Beds	
WD292	DHC1 Chipmunk 22 (G-BCRX)	Privately owned, White Waltham, Berks	
WD293	DHC1 Chipmunk T10 (7645M) <ff>	South Yorkshire Aircraft Museum, Doncaster, S. Yorks	
WD310	DHC1 Chipmunk 22 (G-BWUN) [B]	Privately owned, Jersey, CI	
WD319	DHC1 Chipmunk 22 (F-AYDC)	Privately owned, Vannes-Meucon, France	
WD321	DHC1 Chipmunk 22 (G-BDCC)	Boscombe Down Aviation Collection, Old Sarum, Wilts	
WD325	DHC1 Chipmunk T10 (G-CLWK) [N]	Historic Army Aircraft Flight, Middle Wallop, Hants	

Notes	Serial	Type (code/other identity)	Owner/operator, location or fate
	WD331	DHC1 Chipmunk 22 (G-BXDH)	Privately owned, Farnborough, Hants
	WD355	DHC1 Chipmunk T10 (WD335/G-CBAJ)	Privately owned, Eastleigh, Hants
	WD363	DHC1 Chipmunk 22 (G-BCIH) [5]	Privately owned, Netheravon, Wilts
	WD370	DHC1 Chipmunk T10 <ff>	No 225 Sqn ATC, Brighton, W. Sussex
	WD373	DHC1 Chipmunk 22 (G-BXDI) [12]	Privately owned, Bournemouth, Dorset
	WD377	DHC1 Chipmunk T10 <ff>	Wings Museum, Balcombe, W. Sussex
	WD386	DHC1 Chipmunk T10 (comp WD377)	Ulster Aviation Soc, stored Upper Ballinderry, NI
	WD388	DHC1 Chipmunk 22 (D-EPAK) [68]	Privately owned, Itzehoe, Germany
	WD390	DHC1 Chipmunk 22 (G-BWNK) [68]	Privately owned, Compton Abbas, Dorset
	WD413	Avro 652A Anson T21 (7881M/G-VROE)	Privately owned, Sleap, Shropshire
	WD615	Gloster Meteor TT20 (WD646/8189M) [R]	RAF Manston History Museum, Kent
	WD686	Gloster Meteor NF11	AAC Wattisham museum, Suffolk (restoration)
	WD790	Gloster Meteor NF11 (8743M) <ff>	Boscombe Down Aviation Collection, Old Sarum, Wilts
	WD889	Fairey Firefly AS5 (comp VT809)	Privately owned, Newton Abbot, Devon
	WD935	EE Canberra B2 (8440M) <ff>	South Yorkshire Aircraft Museum, Doncaster, S. Yorks
	WD954	EE Canberra B2 <ff>	Privately owned, St. Columb Major, Cornwall
	WD956	EE Canberra B2 <ff>	RAF Defford Museum, Croome Park, Worcs
	WE113	EE Canberra B2 <ff>	Tangmere Military Aviation Museum, W. Sussex (on loan)
	WE122	EE Canberra TT18 [845] <ff>	Blyth Valley Aviation Collection, Walpole, Suffolk
	WE139	EE Canberra PR3 (8369M)	RAF Museum, Hendon, Gtr London
	WE168	EE Canberra PR3 (8049M) <ff>	Norfolk & Suffolk Avn Museum, Flixton, Suffolk
	WE173	EE Canberra PR3 (8740M) <ff>	Robertsbridge Aviation Society, Mayfield, E. Sussex
	WE188	EE Canberra T4	Solway Aviation Society, Carlisle, Cumbria
	WE191	EE Canberra T4 (Indian AF Q497) <ff>	Stoneykirk Aviation Museum, D&G, Scotland
	WE192	EE Canberra T4 <ff>	Blyth Valley Aviation Collection, Walpole, Suffolk
	WE275	DH112 Venom FB50 (J-1601/G-VIDI)	BAE Systems Hawarden, Fire Section, Flintshire, Wales
	WE536	Auster T7 (G-ARTM)	Privately owned, Hooton Park, Cheshire
	WE558	Auster T7 (frame) (G-ASDL)	East Midlands Airport Aeropark, Leics
	WE569	Auster T7 (G-ASAJ)	Privately owned, Saltford, Somerset
	WE570	Auster T7 (G-ASBU)	Privately owned, Stonehaven, Scotland
	WE591	Auster T7 (F-AZTJ)	Privately owned, Hassfurt, Germany
	WE600	Auster T7 Antarctic (7602M)	Midland Air Museum, Coventry, Warks
	WE724	Hawker Sea Fury FB11 (VX653/G-BUCM) [062]	The Fighter Collection, Duxford, Cambs (rest'n)
	WE982	Slingsby T30B Prefect TX1 (8781M)	RAF Museum, stored Cosford, Shropshire
	WE987	Slingsby T30B Prefect TX1 (BGA2517)	South Yorkshire Aircraft Museum, Doncaster, S. Yorks
	WE990	Slingsby T30B Prefect TX1 (BGA2583)	Privately owned, Tibenham, Norfolk
	WE992	Slingsby T30B Prefect TX1 (BGA2692)	Privately owned, stored Nympsfield, Glos
	WF118	Percival P57 Sea Prince T1 (G-DACA) [569/CU]	Privately owned, Marton Moss, Lancs
	WF122	Percival P57 Sea Prince T1 [575/CU]	Ulster Aviation Society, Long Kesh, Co. Antrim, NI
	WF128	Percival P57 Sea Prince T1 (8611M) [HF-676]	Norfolk & Suffolk Avn Museum, Flixton, Suffolk
	WF145	Hawker Sea Hawk F1 <ff>	Privately owned, Newton Abbot, Devon
	WF219	Hawker Sea Hawk F1 <rf>	FAA Museum, stored Cobham Hall, RNAS Yeovilton, Somerset
	WF225	Hawker Sea Hawk F1 [CU]	RNAS Culdrose, Cornwall, at main gate
	WF259	Hawker Sea Hawk F2 [171/A]	National Museum of Flight, E. Fortune, Scotland
	WF369	Vickers Varsity T1 [F]	Newark Air Museum, Winthorpe, Notts
	WF372	Vickers Varsity T1	Brooklands Museum, Weybridge, Surrey
	WF408	Vickers Varsity T1 (8395M) <ff>	Privately owned, Ashford, Kent
	WF643	Gloster Meteor F8 [F]	Norfolk & Suffolk Avn Museum, Flixton, Suffolk
	WF784	Gloster Meteor T7 (7895M)	South Wales Aviation Museum, St Athan, Glamorgan, Wales
	WF825	Gloster Meteor T7 (8359M)	Montrose Air Station Heritage Centre, Angus, Scotland
	WF911	EE Canberra B2 [CO] <ff>	Ulster Aviation Society, Long Kesh, Co. Antrim, NI
	WF922	EE Canberra PR3	Midland Air Museum, Coventry, Warks
	WG308	DHC1 Chipmunk 22 (G-BYHL) [8]	Privately owned, Averham, Notts
	WG316	DHC1 Chipmunk 22 (G-BCAH) [22]	Privately owned, Gamston, Notts
	WG319	DHC1 Chipmunk T10 <ff>	Privately owned, stored West Raynham, Norfolk
	WG321	DHC1 Chipmunk 22 (G-DHCC) [G]	Privately owned, Wevelgem, Belgium
	WG322	DHC1 Chipmunk 22A (G-ARMF) [H]	Privately owned, Little Gransden, Cambs

Serial	Type (code/other identity)	Owner/operator, location or fate	Notes
WG348	DHC1 Chipmunk 22 (G-BBMV)	Boultbee Flight Academy, Goodwood, W. Sussex	
WG350	DHC1 Chipmunk 22 (G-BPAL)	Privately owned, Portimao, Portugal	
WG362	DHC1 Chipmunk T10 (8437M/8630M/*WX643*) <ff>	No 2523 Sqn ATC, Froghall, Staffs	
WG407	DHC1 Chipmunk 22 (G-BWMX) [67]	Privately owned, Fen End Farm, Cambs	
WG418	DHC1 Chipmunk T10 (8209M/G-ATDY) <ff>	No 1940 Sqn ATC, Levenshulme, Gtr. Manchester	
WG419	DHC1 Chipmunk T10 (8206M)	Sywell Aviation Museum, Sywell, Northants	
WG422	DHC1 Chipmunk 22 (8394M/G-BFAX) [16]	Privately owned, Egginton, Derbys	
WG432	DHC1 Chipmunk T10 [L]	Army Flying Museum, Middle Wallop, Hants	
WG458	DHC1 Chipmunk 22 (N458BG/G-CLLI) [2]	Privately owned, Eshott, Northumberland	
WG465	DHC1 Chipmunk 22 (G-BCEY)	Privately owned, White Waltham, Berks	
WG471	DHC1 Chipmunk T10 (8210M) <ff>	Privately owned, Yateley, Hants	
WG472	DHC1 Chipmunk 22A (G-AOTY)	Privately owned, Cotswold Airport, Glos	
WG477	DHC1 Chipmunk T10 (8362M/G-ATDP) <ff>	Privately owned, Hooton Park, Cheshire	
WG479	DHC1 Chipmunk 22 (F-AZLO/G-CMFC) [F]	Privately owned, Eshott, Northumberland	
WG486	DHC1 Chipmunk T10 [E]	RAF BBMF, Coningsby, Lincs	
WG498	Slingsby T21B Sedbergh TX1 (BGA3245)	Privately owned, Aston Down, Glos	
WG511	Avro 696 Shackleton T4 (fuselage)	Flambards Village Theme Park, Helston, Cornwall	
WG599	Hawker Sea Fury FB11 (G-SEAF) [161/R]	The Fighter Collection, Reno, Nevada, USA	
WG655	Hawker Sea Fury T20 (G-INVN) [910/GN]	Privately owned, Duxford, Cambs (damaged)	
WG719	WS51 Dragonfly HR5 (G-BRMA)	The Helicopter Museum, Weston-super-Mare, Somerset	
WG724	WS51 Dragonfly HR5 [932/LM]	North-East Land, Sea & Air Museums, Usworth, T&W	
WG751	WS51 Dragonfly HR5 [710/GJ]	World Naval Base, Chatham, Kent	
WG760	EE P1A (7755M)	RAF Museum, Cosford, Shropshire	
WG763	EE P1A (7816M)	Boscombe Down Aviation Collection, Old Sarum, Wilts	
WG768	Short SB5 (8005M)	RAF Museum, Cosford, Shropshire	
WG774	BAC 221	Science Museum, at FAA Museum, RNAS Yeovilton	
WG777	Fairey FD2 (7986M)	RAF Museum, Cosford, Shropshire	
WG789	EE Canberra B2/6 <ff>	Norfolk & Suffolk Avn Museum, Flixton, Suffolk	
WH132	Gloster Meteor T7 (7906M) [J]	Privately owned, Hooton Park, Cheshire	
WH166	Gloster Meteor T7 (8052M) [A]	Privately owned, Birlingham, Worcs	
WH291	Gloster Meteor F8	Privately owned, Liverpool Airport, Merseyside	
WH301	Gloster Meteor F8 (7930M) [T]	RAF Museum, Hendon, Gtr London	
WH364	Gloster Meteor F8 (8169M)	Jet Age Museum, Gloucestershire Airport, Glos	
WH453	Gloster Meteor F8	Bentwaters Cold War Museum, Suffolk	
WH646	EE Canberra T17A <ff>	Midland Air Museum, Coventry, Warks	
WH657	EE Canberra B2 <ff>	Romney Marsh Wartime Collection, Kent	
WH725	EE Canberra B2	IWM Duxford, Cambs	
WH739	EE Canberra B2 <ff>	No 2475 Sqn ATC, Ammanford, Carmarthenshire, Wales	
WH740	EE Canberra T17 (8762M) [K]	East Midlands Airport Aeropark, Leics	
WH775	EE Canberra PR7 (8128M/8868M) <ff>	Privately owned, Welshpool, Powys, Wales	
WH779	EE Canberra PR7 <ff>	South Yorkshire Aircraft Museum, Doncaster, S. Yorks	
WH792	EE Canberra PR7 (WH791/8165M/8176M/8187M)	Newark Air Museum, Winthorpe, Notts	
WH798	EE Canberra PR7 (8130M) <ff>	Suffolk Aviation Heritage Centre, Kesgrave, Suffolk	
WH840	EE Canberra T4 (8350M)	Privately owned, Flixton, Suffolk	
WH846	EE Canberra T4	Yorkshire Air Museum, Elvington, N. Yorks	
WH850	EE Canberra T4 <ff>	RAF Marham Aviation Heritage Centre, Norfolk	
WH863	EE Canberra T17 (8693M) <ff>	Newark Air Museum, Winthorpe, Notts	
WH876	EE Canberra B2(mod) <ff>	Boscombe Down Aviation Collection, Old Sarum, Wilts	
WH887	EE Canberra TT18 [847] <ff>	South Yorkshire Aircraft Museum, Doncaster, S. Yorks	
WH903	EE Canberra B2 <ff>	Yorkshire Air Museum, Elvington, N. Yorks	
WH904	EE Canberra T19	Newark Air Museum, Winthorpe, Notts	
WH953	EE Canberra B6(mod) <ff>	Blyth Valley Aviation Collection, Walpole, Suffolk	
WH957	EE Canberra E15 (8869M) <ff>	Lincolnshire Avn Heritage Centre, East Kirkby, Lincs	
WH960	EE Canberra B15 (8344M) <ff>	Rolls-Royce Heritage Trust, Derby, Derbyshire	
WH964	EE Canberra E15 (8870M) <ff>	Privately owned, Lewes, E. Sussex	
WH984	EE Canberra B15 (8101M) <ff>	City of Norwich Aviation Museum, Norfolk	
WH991	WS51 Dragonfly HR3	Yorkshire Helicopter Preservation Group, Elvington	
WJ231	Hawker Sea Fury FB11 (*WE726*) [115/O]	FAA Museum, RNAS Yeovilton, Somerset	
WJ306	Slingsby T21B Sedbergh TX1 (WB957/BGA2720)	Privately owned, Parham Park, W. Sussex	
WJ358	Auster AOP6 (G-ARYD)	Army Flying Museum, Middle Wallop, Hants	

Notes	Serial	Type (code/other identity)	Owner/operator, location or fate
	WJ368	Auster AOP6 (G-ASZX)	Privately owned, Eggesford, Devon
	WJ404	Auster AOP6 (G-ASOI)	Privately owned, Bidford-on-Avon, Warks
	WJ476	Vickers Valetta T3 <ff>	South Yorkshire Aircraft Museum, Doncaster, S. Yorks
	WJ565	EE Canberra T17 (8871M) <ff>	South Yorkshire Aircraft Museum, Doncaster, S. Yorks
	WJ567	EE Canberra B2 <ff>	Privately owned, Houghton, Cambs
	WJ576	EE Canberra T17 <ff>	Tettenhall Transport Heritage Centre, W. Midlands
	WJ633	EE Canberra T17 <ff>	City of Norwich Aviation Museum, Norfolk
	WJ639	EE Canberra TT18 [39]	North-East Land, Sea & Air Museums, Usworth, T&W
	WJ677	EE Canberra B2 <ff>	Privately owned, Redruth, Cornwall
	WJ721	EE Canberra TT18 [21] <ff>	Morayvia, Kinloss, Moray, Scotland
	WJ731	EE Canberra B2T [BK] <ff>	Privately owned, Golders Green, Gtr London
	WJ775	EE Canberra B6 (8581M) <ff>	Privately owned, stored Farnborough, Hants
	WJ865	EE Canberra T4 <ff>	Boscombe Down Aviation Collection, Old Sarum, Wilts
	WJ880	EE Canberra T4 (8491M) <ff>	Dumfries & Galloway Avn Mus, Dumfries, Scotland
	WJ903	Vickers Varsity T1 <ff>	South Yorkshire Aircraft Museum, Doncaster, S. Yorks
	WJ945	Vickers Varsity T1 (G-BEDV)	South Wales Aviation Museum, St Athan, Glamorgan, Wales
	WJ975	EE Canberra T19 <ff>	South Yorkshire Aircraft Museum, Doncaster, S. Yorks
	WJ992	EE Canberra T4 <ff>	South Wales Aviation Museum, St Athan, Glamorgan, Wales
	WK001	Thales Watchkeeper 450 RPAS (4X-USC)	Army 47 Regt Royal Artillery, Larkhill, Wilts
	WK002	Thales Watchkeeper 450 RPAS (4X-USD)	Army 47 Regt Royal Artillery, Larkhill, Wilts
	WK003	Thales Watchkeeper 450 RPAS	Army 47 Regt Royal Artillery, Larkhill, Wilts
	WK004	Thales Watchkeeper 450 RPAS	Army 47 Regt Royal Artillery, Larkhill, Wilts
	WK005	Thales Watchkeeper 450 RPAS	Army 47 Regt Royal Artillery, Larkhill, Wilts
	WK007	Thales Watchkeeper 450 RPAS	Army 47 Regt Royal Artillery, Larkhill, Wilts
	WK008	Thales Watchkeeper 450 RPAS	Army 47 Regt Royal Artillery, Larkhill, Wilts
	WK009	Thales Watchkeeper 450 RPAS	Army 47 Regt Royal Artillery, Larkhill, Wilts
	WK010	Thales Watchkeeper 450 RPAS	Army 47 Regt Royal Artillery, Larkhill, Wilts
	WK011	Thales Watchkeeper 450 RPAS	Army 47 Regt Royal Artillery, Larkhill, Wilts
	WK012	Thales Watchkeeper 450 RPAS	Army 47 Regt Royal Artillery, Larkhill, Wilts
	WK013	Thales Watchkeeper 450 RPAS	Army 47 Regt Royal Artillery, Larkhill, Wilts
	WK014	Thales Watchkeeper 450 RPAS	Army 47 Regt Royal Artillery, Larkhill, Wilts
	WK015	Thales Watchkeeper 450 RPAS	Army 47 Regt Royal Artillery, Larkhill, Wilts
	WK016	Thales Watchkeeper 450 RPAS	Army 47 Regt Royal Artillery, Larkhill, Wilts
	WK017	Thales Watchkeeper 450 RPAS	Army 47 Regt Royal Artillery, Larkhill, Wilts
	WK018	Thales Watchkeeper 450 RPAS	Army 47 Regt Royal Artillery, Larkhill, Wilts
	WK019	Thales Watchkeeper 450 RPAS	Army 47 Regt Royal Artillery, Larkhill, Wilts
	WK020	Thales Watchkeeper 450 RPAS	Army 47 Regt Royal Artillery, Larkhill, Wilts
	WK021	Thales Watchkeeper 450 RPAS	Army 47 Regt Royal Artillery, Larkhill, Wilts
	WK022	Thales Watchkeeper 450 RPAS	Army 47 Regt Royal Artillery, Larkhill, Wilts
	WK023	Thales Watchkeeper 450 RPAS	Army 47 Regt Royal Artillery, Larkhill, Wilts
	WK024	Thales Watchkeeper 450 RPAS	Army 47 Regt Royal Artillery, Larkhill, Wilts
	WK025	Thales Watchkeeper 450 RPAS	Army 47 Regt Royal Artillery, Larkhill, Wilts
	WK026	Thales Watchkeeper 450 RPAS	Army 47 Regt Royal Artillery, Larkhill, Wilts
	WK027	Thales Watchkeeper 450 RPAS	Army 47 Regt Royal Artillery, Larkhill, Wilts
	WK028	Thales Watchkeeper 450 RPAS	Army 47 Regt Royal Artillery, Larkhill, Hants
	WK029	Thales Watchkeeper 450 RPAS	Army 47 Regt Royal Artillery, Larkhill, Wilts
	WK030	Thales Watchkeeper 450 RPAS	Army 47 Regt Royal Artillery, Larkhill, Wilts
	WK032	Thales Watchkeeper 450 RPAS	Army 47 Regt Royal Artillery, Larkhill, Wilts
	WK033	Thales Watchkeeper 450 RPAS	Army 47 Regt Royal Artillery, Larkhill, Wilts
	WK034	Thales Watchkeeper 450 RPAS	Army 47 Regt Royal Artillery, Larkhill, Wilts
	WK035	Thales Watchkeeper 450 RPAS	Army 47 Regt Royal Artillery, Larkhill, Wilts
	WK036	Thales Watchkeeper 450 RPAS	Army 47 Regt Royal Artillery, Larkhill, Wilts
	WK037	Thales Watchkeeper 450 RPAS	Army 47 Regt Royal Artillery, Larkhill, Wilts
	WK038	Thales Watchkeeper 450 RPAS	Army 47 Regt Royal Artillery, Larkhill, Wilts
	WK039	Thales Watchkeeper 450 RPAS	Army 47 Regt Royal Artillery, Larkhill, Wilts
	WK040	Thales Watchkeeper 450 RPAS	Army 47 Regt Royal Artillery, Larkhill, Wilts
	WK041	Thales Watchkeeper 450 RPAS	Army 47 Regt Royal Artillery, Larkhill, Wilts
	WK044	Thales Watchkeeper 450 RPAS	Army 47 Regt Royal Artillery, Larkhill, Wilts
	WK045	Thales Watchkeeper 450 RPAS	Army 47 Regt Royal Artillery, Larkhill, Wilts
	WK046	Thales Watchkeeper 450 RPAS	Army 47 Regt Royal Artillery, Larkhill, Wilts

Serial	Type (code/other identity)	Owner/operator, location or fate	Notes
WK047	Thales Watchkeeper 450 RPAS	Army 47 Regt Royal Artillery, Larkhill, Wilts	
WK048	Thales Watchkeeper 450 RPAS	Army 47 Regt Royal Artillery, Larkhill, Wilts	
WK049	Thales Watchkeeper 450 RPAS	Army 47 Regt Royal Artillery, Larkhill, Wilts	
WK051	Thales Watchkeeper 450 RPAS	Army 47 Regt Royal Artillery, Larkhill, Wilts	
WK052	Thales Watchkeeper 450 RPAS	Army 47 Regt Royal Artillery, Larkhill, Wilts	
WK053	Thales Watchkeeper 450 RPAS	Army 47 Regt Royal Artillery, Larkhill, Wilts	
WK054	Thales Watchkeeper 450 RPAS	Army 47 Regt Royal Artillery, Larkhill, Wilts	
WK060	Thales Watchkeeper 450 RPAS	MOD/Thales, Aberporth, Wales	
WK102	EE Canberra T17 (8780M) <ff>	Privately owned, Welshpool, Powys, Wales	
WK118	EE Canberra TT18 [CQ] <ff>	Avro Heritage Museum, Woodford, Cheshire	
WK122	EE Canberra TT18 <ff>	Lakes Lightnings, Spark Bridge, Cumbria	
WK124	EE Canberra B6 (9093M) <ff>	Stoneykirk Aviation Museum, D&G, Scotland	
WK124	EE Canberra B6 (9093M) <rf>	Dumped former Cornwall Aviation Heritage Centre, Newquay, Cornwall	
WK126	EE Canberra TT18 (N2138J) [843]	South Wales Aviation Museum, St Athan, Glamorgan, Wales (restoration)	
WK127	EE Canberra TT18 (8985M) <ff>	Wings Museum, stored Balcombe, W. Sussex	
WK128	EE Canberra B2 <ff>	South Wales Aviation Museum, St Athan, Glamorgan, Wales	
WK146	EE Canberra B2 <ff>	Gatwick Aviation Museum, Charlwood, Surrey	
WK163	EE Canberra B2/6 (G-BVWC/G-CTTS)	Vulcan To The Sky Trust, Doncaster Sheffield Airport, S. Yorks	
WK198	VS Swift F4 (7428M) (fuselage)	Brooklands Museum, Weybridge, Surrey	
WK275	VS Swift F4	Privately owned, Cumbria	
WK277	VS Swift FR5 (7719M) [N]	Newark Air Museum, Winthorpe, Notts	
WK281	VS Swift FR5 (7712M) [S]	Tangmere Military Aviation Museum, W. Sussex	
WK393	DH112 Venom FB1 <ff>	Privately owned, Lavendon, Bucks	
WK512	DHC1 Chipmunk 22 (G-BXIM) [A]	Privately owned, RAF Halton, Bucks	
WK514	DHC1 Chipmunk 22 (G-BBMO)	Privately owned, Wellesbourne Mountford, Warks	
WK517	DHC1 Chipmunk 22 (G-ULAS) [84]	Privately owned, White Waltham, Berkshire	
WK518	DHC1 Chipmunk T10 [D]	RAF BBMF, Coningsby, Lincs	
WK522	DHC1 Chipmunk 22 (G-BCOU)	Privately owned, Duxford, Cambs	
WK558	DHC1 Chipmunk 22A (G-ARMG) [DH]	Privately owned, RAF Halton, Bucks	
WK562	DHC1 Chipmunk 22 (F-AZUR) [91]	Privately owned, La Baule, France	
WK570	DHC1 Chipmunk T10 (8211M) <ff>	No 424 Sqn ATC, Solent Sky, Southampton, Hants	
WK576	DHC1 Chipmunk T10 (8357M) <ff>	Tettenhall Transport Heritage Centre, W. Midlands	
WK577	DHC1 Chipmunk 22 (G-BCYM)	Privately owned, Oaksey Park, Wilts	
WK584	DHC1 Chipmunk T10 (7556M) <ff>	No 511 Sqn ATC, Ramsey, Cambs	
WK585	DHC1 Chipmunk 22 (9265M/G-BZGA)	Privately owned, Compton Abbas, Dorset	
WK586	DHC1 Chipmunk 22 (G-BXGX) [V]	Privately owned, Shoreham, W. Sussex	
WK590	DHC1 Chipmunk 22 (OO-DHC) [69]	Privately owned, Grimbergen, Belgium	
WK608	DHC1 Chipmunk T10 (G-CLNI) [906,Y]	Fly Navy Heritage Trust, Yeovilton, Somerset	
WK609	DHC1 Chipmunk 22 (G-BXDN) [93]	Privately owned, Booker, Bucks	
WK611	DHC1 Chipmunk 22 (G-ARWB)	Privately owned, Thruxton, Hants	
WK620	DHC1 Chipmunk T10 [T] (fuselage)	Privately owned, Hawarden, Flintshire, Wales	
WK624	DHC1 Chipmunk 22A (G-BWHI)	Privately owned, Blackpool, Lancs	
WK626	DHC1 Chipmunk T10 (8213M) <ff>	South Yorkshire Aircraft Museum, Doncaster, S. Yorks	
WK628	DHC1 Chipmunk 22 (G-BBMW)	Privately owned, Goodwood, W. Sussex	
WK630	DHC1 Chipmunk 22 (G-BXDG)	Privately owned, Felthorpe, Norfolk	
WK633	DHC1 Chipmunk 22 (G-BXEC) [A]	Privately owned, Duxford, Cambs	
WK634	DHC1 Chipmunk T10 (G-CIGE) [902]	Privately owned, Dunkeswell, Devon	
WK635	DHC1 Chipmunk 22 (G-HFRH)	Privately owned, St. Athan, Wales	
WK638	DHC1 Chipmunk 22 (G-BWJZ) (fuselage)	Privately owned, Finningley, N. Yorks	
WK640	DHC1 Chipmunk 22A (G-BWUV) [C]	Yorkshire Air Museum, Elvington, N. Yorks (wreck)	
WK640	OGMA/DHC1 Chipmunk T20 (G-CERD)	Privately owned, St Athan, Wales	
WK642	DHC1 Chipmunk 22 (EI-AFZ) [94]	Privately owned, Kilrush, Eire	
WK654	Gloster Meteor F8 (8092M)	City of Norwich Aviation Museum, Norfolk	
WK800	Gloster Meteor D16 [Z]	Boscombe Down Aviation Collection, Old Sarum, Wilts	
WK864	Gloster Meteor F8 (WL168/7750M) [C]	Yorkshire Air Museum, Elvington, N. Yorks	
WK935	Gloster Meteor Prone Pilot (7869M)	Newark Air Museum, Winthorpe, Notts	
WK991	Gloster Meteor F8 (7825M)	IWM Duxford, Cambs	

Notes	Serial	Type (code/other identity)	Owner/operator, location or fate
	WL131	Gloster Meteor F8 (7751M) <ff>	South Yorkshire Aircraft Museum, Doncaster, S. Yorks
	WL181	Gloster Meteor F8 [X]	North-East Land, Sea & Air Museums, Usworth, T&W
	WL332	Gloster Meteor T7 [888]	Current status unknown (ex-Newquay, Cornwall)
	WL349	Gloster Meteor T7	Repainted as WL462
	WL375	Gloster Meteor T7(mod)	Dumfries & Galloway Avn Mus, Dumfries, Scotland
	WL405	Gloster Meteor T7 <ff>	South Wales Aviation Museum, St Athan, Glamorgan, Wales
	WL419	Gloster Meteor T7(mod) (G-JSMA)	Martin-Baker Aircraft, Chalgrove, Oxon
	WL462	Gloster Meteor T7 (WL349)	Privately owned, Thornwood, Epping, Essex
	WL505	DH100 Vampire FB9 (7705M/G-FBIX)	Privately owned, Mendlesham, Suffolk
	WL626	Vickers Varsity T1 (G-BHDD) [P]	East Midlands Airport Aeropark, Leics
	WL627	Vickers Varsity T1 (8488M) [D] <ff>	Privately owned, Preston, E. Yorkshire
	WL679	Vickers Varsity T1 (9155M)	RAF Museum, Cosford, Shropshire
	WL732	BP P108 Sea Balliol T21	RAF Museum, Cosford, Shropshire
	WL795	Avro 696 Shackleton MR2C (8753M) [T]	Current status unknown (ex-Newquay, Cornwall)
	WL798	Avro 696 Shackleton MR2C (8114M) <ff>	Privately owned, Elgin, Scotland
	WM145	AW Meteor NF11 <ff>	Morayvia, Kinloss, Moray, Scotland
	WM167	AW Meteor NF11 (G-LOSM)	Preserved Bruntingthorpe, Leics
	WM224	AW Meteor TT20 (WM311/8177M)	East Midlands Airport Aeropark, Leics
	WM267	AW Meteor NF11 <ff>	City of Norwich Aviation Museum, Norfolk
	WM292	AW Meteor TT20 [841]	FAA Museum, stored Cobham Hall, RNAS Yeovilton, Somerset
	WM366	AW Meteor NF13 (4X-FNA) (comp VZ462)	Jet Age Museum, Gloucestershire Airport, Glos
	WM367	AW Meteor NF13 <ff>	East Midlands Airport Aeropark, Leics
	WM571	DH112 Sea Venom FAW21 [VL]	Bournemouth Aviation Museum, Dorset (at Bruntingthorpe for restoration)
	WM729	DH113 Vampire NF10 <ff>	de Havilland Aircraft Museum, stored Tilbury, Essex
	WM913	Hawker Sea Hawk FB5 (A2610) [456/J]	Newark Air Museum, Winthorpe, Notts
	WM961	Hawker Sea Hawk FB5 [J]	Caernarfon Air World, Gwynedd, Wales
	WM969	Hawker Sea Hawk FB5 [10/Z]	IWM Duxford, Cambs
	WN105	Hawker Sea Hawk FB3 (WF299/8164M)	East Midlands Airport Aeropark, Leics (rest'n)
	WN108	Hawker Sea Hawk FB5 [033]	Ulster Aviation Society, Long Kesh, Co. Antrim, NI
	WN149	BP P108 Balliol T2 [AT]	Privately owned, North Weald, Essex (restoration)
	WN411	Fairey Gannet AS1 (fuselage)	Current status unknown
	WN493	WS51 Dragonfly HR5	FAA Museum, RNAS Yeovilton, Somerset
	WN499	WS51 Dragonfly HR5	South Yorkshire Aircraft Museum, stored Doncaster
	WN516	BP P108 Balliol T2 <ff>	Tettenhall Transport Heritage Centre, W. Midlands
	WN534	BP P108 Balliol T2 <ff>	Tettenhall Transport Heritage Centre, W. Midlands
	WN890	Hawker Hunter F2 <ff>	Boscombe Down Aviation Collection, Old Sarum, Wilts
	WN904	Hawker Hunter F2 (7544M) [Q] (wears WN921 [S] on starboard side)	Sywell Aviation Museum, Northants
	WN907	Hawker Hunter F2 (7416M) <ff>	Robertsbridge Aviation Society, E. Sussex
	WN957	Hawker Hunter F5 <ff>	Morayvia, Kinloss, Moray, Scotland
	WP185	Hawker Hunter F5 (7583M)	Privately owned, Great Dunmow, Essex
	WP190	Hawker Hunter F5 (7582M/8473M/WP180) [K]	Tangmere Military Aviation Museum, W. Sussex
	WP255	DH113 Vampire NF10 <ff>	South Yorkshire Aircraft Museum, stored Doncaster, S. Yorks
	WP266	EoN AP.5 Primary (BAPC.423)	East Midlands Airport Aeropark, Leics (stored)
	WP269	EoN Eton TX1 (BGA3214)	Privately owned, Little Rissington, Glos
	WP270	EoN Eton TX1 (8598M)	Gliding Heritage Centre, Lasham, Hants
	WP308	Percival P57 Sea Prince T1 (G-GACA) [572/CU]	Gatwick Aviation Museum, Charlwood, Surrey
	WP313	Percival P57 Sea Prince T1 [568/CU]	FAA Museum, stored Cobham Hall, RNAS Yeovilton, Somerset
	WP314	Percival P57 Sea Prince T1 (8634M) [573/CU]	Privately owned, Carlisle Airport, Cumbria
	WP321	Percival P57 Sea Prince T1 (G-BRFC) [750/CU]	South Wales Aviation Museum, St Athan, Glamorgan, Wales
	WP495	WS51 Dragonfly HR5 (G-AJOV) [915/LM]	Morayvia, Kinloss, Moray, Scotland
	WP697	DHC1 Chipmunk 22 (OO-PMS)	Privately owned, Leopoldsburg, Belgium
	WP772	DHC1 Chipmunk T10 [4]	RAF Manston History Museum, Kent

Serial	Type (code/other identity)	Owner/operator, location or fate	Notes
WP784	DHC1 Chipmunk T10 (comp WZ876) [M,RCY-E]	East Midlands Airport Aeropark, Leics	
WP788	DHC1 Chipmunk 22A (G-BCHL)	Privately owned, Sleap, Shropshire	
WP790	DHC1 Chipmunk T10 (G-BBNC) [T]	de Havilland Aircraft Museum, London Colney	
WP795	DHC1 Chipmunk 22 (G-BVZZ)	Privately owned, Netheravon, Wilts	
WP800	DHC1 Chipmunk 22 (G-BCXN) [2]	Privately owned, White Waltham, Berks	
WP803	DHC1 Chipmunk 22 (G-HAPY) [G]	Privately owned, Booker, Bucks	
WP805	DHC1 Chipmunk 22 (G-MAJR) [D]	Privately owned, Solent Airport, Hants	
WP809	DHC1 Chipmunk 22A (G-BVTX) [78]	Privately owned, Leicester, Leics	
WP811	DHC1 Chipmunk 22 (G-BCKN)	Privately owned, Blackpool, Lancs	
WP835	DHC1 Chipmunk 22 (D-ERTY) [N]	Privately owned, Rinteln, Germany	
WP840	DHC1 Chipmunk 22 (F-AZQM) [9]	Privately owned, Reims-Prunay, France	
WP844	DHC1 Chipmunk 22 (G-BWOX) [85]	Privately owned, Adriers, France	
WP848	DHC1 Chipmunk 22 (8342M/G-BFAW)	Privately owned, Old Buckenham, Norfolk	
WP859	DHC1 Chipmunk 22 (G-BXCP) [E] (wreck)	Privately owned, Cam, Glos	
WP860	DHC1 Chipmunk 22 (G-BXDA) <ff>	Privately owned, Glasgow area, Scotland	
WP863	DHC1 Chipmunk T10 (8360M/G-ATJI) <ff>	No 2385 Sqn ATC, Melksham, Wilts	
WP869	DHC1 Chipmunk T10 (8215M) (G-CLXD)	Privately owned, White Waltham, Berks	
WP870	DHC1 Chipmunk 22 (G-BCOI) [12]	Privately owned, Rayne Hall Farm, Essex	
WP872	DHC1 Chipmunk 22 (N198DD/G-IGES)	Privately owned, Audley End, Essex	
WP896	DHC1 Chipmunk 22 (G-BWVY) [M]	Privately owned, RAF Halton, Bucks	
WP901	DHC1 Chipmunk 22 (G-BWNT/OO-WPB) [B]	Privately owned, Seppe, The Netherlands	
WP903	DHC1 Chipmunk 22 (G-BCGC)	Privately owned, Old Warden, Beds	
WP912	DHC1 Chipmunk T10 (8467M)	RAF Museum, Cosford, Shropshire	
WP921	DHC1 Chipmunk T10 (G-ATJJ) <ff>	Privately owned, Brooklands, Surrey	
WP925	DHC1 Chipmunk 22 (G-BXHA) [C]	Privately owned, Biggin Hill, Kent	
WP927	DHC1 Chipmunk T10 (8216M/G-ATJK) <ff>	Privately owned, Graveley, Cambs	
WP928	DHC1 Chipmunk 22 (G-BXGM) [D]	Privately owned, Scotland	
WP929	DHC1 Chipmunk 22 (G-BXCV) [F]	Privately owned, Duxford, Cambs	
WP930	DHC1 Chipmunk 22 (G-BXHF) [J]	Privately owned, Goodwood, W. Sussex	
WP962	DHC1 Chipmunk T10 (9287M) [C]	RAF Museum, Hendon, Gtr London	
WP964	DHC1 Chipmunk T20 (G-HDAE)	Privately owned, Wellesbourne Mountford, Warks	
WP971	DHC1 Chipmunk 22 (G-ATHD)	Privately owned, Turweston, Bucks	
WP973	DHC1 Chipmunk 22 (G-BCPU)	Privately owned, White Waltham, Berks	
WP977	DHC1 Chipmunk 22 (G-BHRD) <ff>	Privately owned, South Molton, Devon	
WP978	DHC1 Chipmunk 22 (7467M) <ff>	Privately owned, Hooton Park, Cheshire	
WP983	DHC1 Chipmunk T10 (G-BXNN) [B]	Privately owned, Eggesford, Devon	
WP984	DHC1 Chipmunk 22 (G-BWTO) [H]	Privately owned, Little Gransden, Cambs	
WR360	DH112 Venom FB50 (J-1626/G-DHSS) <ff>	Privately owned, Maddenstown, Co Kildare, Eire	
WR410	DH112 Venom FB50 (J-1539/G-DHUU)	Shannon Aviation Museum, Eire	
WR421	DH112 Venom FB50 (J-1611/G-DHTT)	Shannon Aviation Museum, Eire	
WR470	DH112 Venom FB50 (J-1542/G-DHVM)	Current status unknown (ex-Bruntingthorpe, Leics)	
WR539	DH112 Venom FB4 (8399M) <ff>	Privately owned, Cantley, Norfolk	
WR960	Avro 696 Shackleton AEW2 (8772M)	Avro Heritage Museum, Woodford, Cheshire	
WR963	Avro 696 Shackleton AEW2 (G-SKTN) [B-M]	Yorkshire Air Museum, Elvington, N. Yorks (rest'n)	
WR971	Avro 696 Shackleton MR3/3 (8119M) [Q] (fuselage)	Morayvia, Kinloss, Moray, Scotland	
WR974	Avro 696 Shackleton MR3/3 (8117M) [K]	South Wales Aviation Museum, St Athan, Glamorgan, Wales	
WR977	Avro 696 Shackleton MR3/3 (8186M) [B]	Newark Air Museum, Winthorpe, Notts	
WR982	Avro 696 Shackleton MR3/3 (8106M) [J]	Gatwick Aviation Museum, Charlwood, Surrey	
WS103	Gloster Meteor T7 [709]	FAA Museum, stored Cobham Hall, RNAS Yeovilton, Somerset	
WS692	Gloster Meteor NF12 (7605M) [C]	Newark Air Museum, Winthorpe, Notts	
WS726	Gloster Meteor NF14 (7960M) [H]	Under restoration, Billericay, Essex	
WS739	Gloster Meteor NF14 (7961M)	Newark Air Museum, Winthorpe, Notts	
WS760	Gloster Meteor NF14 (7964M)	East Midlands Airport Aeropark, Leics, stored	
WS776	Gloster Meteor NF14 (7716M) [K]	Bournemouth Aviation Museum, Dorset	
WS788	Gloster Meteor NF14 (7967M) [Z]	Yorkshire Air Museum, Elvington, N. Yorks	
WS792	Gloster Meteor NF14 (7965M) [K]	Brighouse Bay Caravan Park, Borgue, D&G, Scotland	
WS807	Gloster Meteor NF14 (7973M) [N]	Jet Age Museum, Gloucestershire Airport, Glos	
WS832	Gloster Meteor NF14 [W]	Solway Aviation Society, Carlisle, Cumbria	

Notes	Serial	Type (code/other identity)	Owner/operator, location or fate
	WS838	Gloster Meteor NF14 [D]	Midland Air Museum, Coventry, Warks
	WS840	Gloster Meteor NF14 (7969M) [N] <rf>	Privately owned, Upper Ballinderry, NI
	WS843	Gloster Meteor NF14 (7937M) [J]	RAF Museum, Cosford, Shropshire
	WT001	Boeing E-7A Wedgetail AEW1 (N946BC) [01]	MOD/STS Aviation Services, Birmingham, W. Midlands (conversion)
	WT002	Boeing E-7A Wedgetail AEW1 (N947BC)	MOD/STS Aviation Services, Birmingham, W. Midlands (conversion)
	WT003	Boeing E-7A Wedgetail AEW1 (N576JK)	MOD/STS Aviation Services, Birmingham, W. Midlands (conversion)
	WT121	Douglas Skyraider AEW1 (WT983) [415/CU]	FAA Museum, stored Cobham Hall, RNAS Yeovilton, Somerset
	WT205	EE Canberra B15 <ff>	RAF Manston History Museum, Kent
	WT309	EE Canberra B(I)6 <ff>	Farnborough Air Sciences Trust, Farnborough, Hants
	WT319	EE Canberra B(I)6 <ff>	South Yorkshire Aircraft Museum, Doncaster, S. Yorks
	WT333	EE Canberra B6(mod) (G-BVXC)	Preserved Bruntingthorpe, Leics
	WT339	EE Canberra B(I)8 (8198M)	RAF Barkston Heath Fire Section, Lincs
	WT482	EE Canberra T4 <ff>	Privately owned, location unknown
	WT486	EE Canberra T4 (8102M) <ff>	Privately owned, Westbury, Wilts
	WT507	EE Canberra PR7 (8131M/8548M) [44] <ff>	Privately owned, Dallachy, Moray, Scotland
	WT520	EE Canberra PR7 (8094M/8184M) <ff>	Privately owned, Hooton Park, Cheshire
	WT525	EE Canberra T22 [855] <ff>	South Yorkshire Aircraft Museum, Doncaster, S. Yorks
	WT532	EE Canberra PR7 (8728M/8890M) <ff> [32]	Bournemouth Aviation Museum, Dorset
	WT534	EE Canberra PR7 (8549M) [43] <ff>	Privately owned, Wisbech, Cambs
	WT536	EE Canberra PR7 (8063M) <ff>	South Yorkshire Aircraft Museum, Doncaster, S. Yorks
	WT555	Hawker Hunter F1 (7499M)	Vanguard Haulage, 717 N. Circular Rd, London
	WT569	Hawker Hunter F1 (7491M)	Morayvia, Kinloss, Moray, Scotland
	WT612	Hawker Hunter F1 (7496M)	RAF Henlow, Beds, on display
	WT619	Hawker Hunter F1 (7525M)	Montrose Air Station Heritage Centre, Angus, Scotland
	WT648	Hawker Hunter F1 (7530M) <ff>	Boscombe Down Aviation Collection, Old Sarum, Wilts
	WT651	Hawker Hunter F1 (7532M) [C]	Newark Air Museum, Winthorpe, Notts
	WT660	Hawker Hunter F1 (7421M) [C]	Privately owned, West Raynham, Norfolk
	WT680	Hawker Hunter F1 (7533M) [J]	Privately owned, Holbeach, Lincs
	WT684	Hawker Hunter F1 (7422M) <ff>	Privately owned, Lavendon, Bucks
	WT694	Hawker Hunter F1 (7510M)	Caernarfon Air World, Gwynedd, Wales
	WT711	Hawker Hunter GA11 [833/DD]	Lakes Lightnings, Spark Bridge, Cumbria
	WT722	Hawker Hunter T8C (G-BWGN) [873]	Bournemouth Aviation Museum, Dorset
	WT723	Hawker Hunter PR11 (*XG194*/G-PRII) [692/LM]	Privately owned, Tyseley, Birmingham, W. Midlands
	WT741	Hawker Hunter GA11 [791] <ff>	Privately owned, South Yorks Air Museum, Doncaster, S. Yorks
	WT744	Hawker Hunter GA11 [868/VL]	Privately owned, Braunton, Devon
	WT746	Hawker Hunter F4 (*XF506*/7770M) [A]	Dumfries & Galloway Avn Mus, Dumfries, Scotland
	WT799	Hawker Hunter T8C [879]	Blue Lagoon Diving Centre, Womersley, N. Yorks
	WT804	Hawker Hunter GA11 [831/DD]	Privately owned, Todenham, Glos
	WT806	Hawker Hunter GA11	Preserved Bruntingthorpe, Leics
	WT859	Supermarine 544 <ff>	Boscombe Down Aviation Collection, Old Sarum, Wilts
	WT867	Slingsby T31B Cadet TX3	Privately owned, Eaglescott, Devon
	WT874	Slingsby T31B Cadet TX3 (BGA1255)	Privately owned, Bicester, Oxon
	WT877	Slingsby T31B Cadet TX3	Tettenhall Transport Heritage Centre, W. Midlands
	WT900	Slingsby T31B Cadet TX3 (BGA3272)	Privately owned, Saltby, Leics
	WT905	Slingsby T31B Cadet TX3	Privately owned, Keevil, Wilts
	WT908	Slingsby T31B Cadet TX3 (BGA3487)	Privately owned, Dunstable, Beds
	WT910	Slingsby T31B Cadet TX3 (BGA3953) [HHG]	Privately owned, Llandegla, Denbighshire, Wales
	WT914	Slingsby T31B Cadet TX3 (BGA3194) (fuselage)	East Midlands Airport Aeropark, Leics
	WT933	Bristol 171 Sycamore 3 (G-ALSW/7709M)	Newark Air Museum, Winthorpe, Notts
	WV106	Douglas Skyraider AEW1 [427/C]	FAA Museum, stored Cobham Hall, RNAS Yeovilton, Somerset
	WV198	Sikorsky S55 Whirlwind HAR21 (G-BJWY) [K]	Solway Aviation Society, Carlisle, Cumbria
	WV256	Hawker Hunter GA11 (G-BZPB) [D]	Privately owned, Badwell Green, Suffolk
	WV314	Hawker Hunter F51 (G-9-445/E-424) [B]	South Yorkshire Aircraft Museum, Doncaster, S. Yorks
	WV322	Hawker Hunter T8C (G-BZSE/9096M) [22/VL]	Privately owned, North Weald, Essex

Serial	Type (code/other identity)	Owner/operator, location or fate	Notes
WV332	Hawker Hunter F4 (7673M) <ff>	Tangmere Military Aircraft Museum, W. Sussex	
WV381	Hawker Hunter GA11 [732] <ff>	Morayvia, Kinloss, Moray, Scotland	
WV382	Hawker Hunter GA11 [830]	East Midlands Airport Aeropark, Leics	
WV383	Hawker Hunter T7	Farnborough Air Sciences Trust, Farnborough, Hants	
WV396	Hawker Hunter T8C (9249M)	Tacla Taid Museum, Newborough, Anglesey, Wales	
WV493	Percival P56 Provost T1 (G-BDYG/7696M) [29]	National Museum of Flight, stored E. Fortune, Scotland	
WV499	Percival P56 Provost T1 (G-BZRF/7698M) [P3]	Privately owned, Middlezoy, Somerset	
WV514	Percival P56 Provost T1 (G-BLIW/177) [N-C]	Privately owned, Shoreham, W. Sussex	
WV562	Percival P56 Provost T1 (XF688/7606M) [P-C]	RAF Museum, Cosford, Shropshire	
WV605	Percival P56 Provost T1 [T-B]	Norfolk & Suffolk Avn Museum, Flixton, Suffolk	
WV606	Percival P56 Provost T1 (7622M)[P-B]	Newark Air Museum, Winthorpe, Notts	
WV679	Percival P56 Provost T1 (7615M) [O-J]	Wellesbourne Wartime Museum, Warks	
WV705	Percival P66 Pembroke C1 <ff>	Privately owned, Awbridge, Hants	
WV740	Percival P66 Pembroke C1 (G-BNPH)	Privately owned, St Athan, Wales	
WV746	Percival P66 Pembroke C1 (8938M)	RAF Museum, Cosford, Shropshire	
WV781	Bristol 171 Sycamore HR12 (G-ALTD/7839M) <ff>	Caernarfon Air World, Gwynedd, Wales	
WV783	Bristol 171 Sycamore HR12 (G-ALSP/7841M)	RAF Museum, Hendon, Gtr London	
WV787	EE Canberra B2/8 (8799M)	Newark Air Museum, Winthorpe, Notts	
WV795	Hawker Sea Hawk FGA6 (8151M)	Privately owned, Dunsfold, Surrey	
WV797	Hawker Sea Hawk FGA6 (8155M) [491/J]	Midland Air Museum, Coventry, Warks	
WV798	Hawker Sea Hawk FGA6 [147/E]	Privately owned, North Weald, Essex (restoration)	
WV838	Hawker Sea Hawk FGA6 (182) <ff>	Norfolk & Suffolk Avn Museum, Flixton, Suffolk	
WV856	Hawker Sea Hawk FGA6 (163)	FAA Museum, stored Cobham Hall, RNAS Yeovilton, Somerset	
WV903	Hawker Sea Hawk FGA6 (8153M) [128] <ff>	Stoneykirk Aviation Museum, D&G, Scotland	
WV908	Hawker Sea Hawk FGA6 (8154M/G-CMFB) [188/A]	Fly Navy Heritage Trust, stored RNAS Yeovilton, Somerset	
WV910	Hawker Sea Hawk FGA6 <ff>	Boscombe Down Aviation Collection, Old Sarum, Wilts	
WV911	Hawker Sea Hawk FGA4 [115/C]	RNAS Yeovilton, Fire Section, Somerset	
WW138	DH112 Sea Venom FAW22 [227/Z]	FAA Museum, stored Cobham Hall, RNAS Yeovilton, Somerset	
WW145	DH112 Sea Venom FAW22 [680/LM]	National Museum of Flight, E. Fortune, Scotland	
WW217	DH112 Sea Venom FAW22 [351]	Newark Air Museum, Winthorpe, Notts	
WW388	Percival P56 Provost T1 (7616M)	Privately owned, Bridgwater area, Somerset	
WW442	Percival P56 Provost T1 (7618M)	East Midlands Airport Aeropark, Leics	
WW444	Percival P56 Provost T1 [D]	Privately owned, Brownhills, Staffs	
WW450	Percival P56 Provost T1 (WW421/G-BZRE/7689M)	Bournemouth Aviation Museum, Dorset	
WW453	Percival P56 Provost T1 (G-TMKI)	Privately owned, Bridgwater area, Somerset	
WW654	Hawker Hunter GA11 [834/DD]	Privately owned, Ford, W. Sussex	
WW664	Hawker Hunter F4 <ff>	Privately owned, Thetford, Norfolk	
WX788	DH112 Venom NF3 <ff>	South Yorks Air Museum, stored Doncaster, S. Yorks	
WX853	DH112 Venom NF3 (7443M)	de Havilland Aircraft Mus'm, stored London Colney	
WX905	DH112 Venom NF3 (7458M)	Newark Air Museum, Winthorpe, Notts	
WZ425	DH115 Vampire T11	Privately owned, Birlingham, Worcs	
WZ450	DH115 Vampire T11	Vanguard Storage, Bath, Somerset	
WZ507	DH115 Vampire T11 (G-VTII) [74]	Privately owned, North Weald, Essex	
WZ515	DH115 Vampire T11 [60]	Solway Aviation Society, Carlisle, Cumbria	
WZ518	DH115 Vampire T11 [B]	North-East Land, Sea & Air Museums, Usworth, T&W	
WZ549	DH115 Vampire T11 (8118M) [F]	Ulster Aviation Society, Long Kesh, Co. Antrim, NI	
WZ553	DH115 Vampire T11 (G-DHYY) <ff>	Privately owned, Stockton, Warks	
WZ557	DH115 Vampire T11	Morayvia, Kinloss, Moray, Scotland	
WZ572	DH115 Vampire T11 (8124M) [65] <ff>	Privately owned, Sholing, Hants	
WZ581	DH115 Vampire T11 <ff>	The Vampire Collection, Hemel Hempstead, Herts	
WZ584	Gloster Meteor T7 (WL345, comp with WL360) [54]	Privately owned, Middlezoy, Somerset	
WZ589	DH115 Vampire T11 [19]	Privately owned, Wigmore, Kent	
WZ590	DH115 Vampire T11 [49]	IWM Duxford, Cambs	
WZ662	Auster AOP9 (G-BKVK)	Privately owned, Rawtenstall, Lancs	
WZ679	Auster AOP9 (7863M/XP248/G-CIUX)	Privately owned, Whittlesford, Cambs	
WZ706	Auster AOP9 (7851M/G-BURR)	Privately owned, Spanhoe Lodge, Northants	
WZ711	Auster AOP9/Beagle E3 (G-AVHT)	Privately owned, Messingham, Lincs	

Notes	Serial	Type (code/other identity)	Owner/operator, location or fate
	WZ721	Auster AOP9	Army Flying Museum, Middle Wallop, Hants
	WZ724	Auster AOP9 (7432M) (frame)	Army Flying Museum, Middle Wallop, Hants
	WZ736	Avro 707A (7868M)	Boscombe Down Aviation Collection, Old Sarum, Wilts
	WZ744	Avro 707C (7932M)	Avro Heritage Museum, Woodford, Cheshire
	WZ753	Slingsby T38 Grasshopper TX1	Boscombe Down Aviation Collection, Old Sarum, Wilts
	WZ755	Slingsby T38 Grasshopper TX1 (BGA3481)	Tettenhall Transport Heritage Centre, W. Midlands
	WZ757	Slingsby T38 Grasshopper TX1 (comp XK820)	Privately owned, Saltby, Lincs
	WZ767	Slingsby T38 Grasshopper TX1	North-East Land, Sea & Air Museums, Usworth, T&W
	WZ772	Slingsby T38 Grasshopper TX1	Trenchard Museum, RAF Halton, Bucks
	WZ773	Slingsby T38 Grasshopper TX1	Edinburgh Academy, Edinburgh, Scotland
	WZ784	Slingsby T38 Grasshopper TX1	Privately owned, stored Felixstowe, Kent
	WZ791	Slingsby T38 Grasshopper TX1 (8944M)	RAF Museum, Hendon, Gtr London
	WZ792	Slingsby T38 Grasshopper TX1 (comp WZ784 & WZ824)	Solway Aviation Society, Carlisle, Cumbria
	WZ793	Slingsby T38 Grasshopper TX1	Privately owned, Rufforth, N. Yorks
	WZ796	Slingsby T38 Grasshopper TX1	Privately owned, stored Aston Down, Glos
	WZ797	Slingsby T38 Grasshopper TX1 (BGA3359)	Privately owned, stored Shipdham, Norfolk
	WZ798	Slingsby T38 Grasshopper TX1	Privately owned, Eaglescott, Devon
	WZ818	Slingsby T38 Grasshopper TX1 (BGA4361)	Privately owned, Nympsfield, Glos
	WZ819	Slingsby T38 Grasshopper TX1 (BGA3498) [FSV]	Privately owned, Eaglescott, Devon
	WZ820	Slingsby T38 Grasshopper TX1 <ff>	Sywell Aviation Museum, Northants, stored
	WZ822	Slingsby T38 Grasshopper TX1	South Yorkshire Aircraft Museum, stored Doncaster, S. Yorks
	WZ824	Slingsby T38 Grasshopper TX1	Privately owned, Bridge of Weir, Scotland
	WZ826	Vickers Valiant B(K)1 (XD826/7872M) <ff>	IWM Duxford, Cambs
	WZ828	Slingsby T38 Grasshopper TX1 (BGA4421)	Privately owned, Little Rissington, Glos
	WZ831	Slingsby T38 Grasshopper TX1	Privately owned, stored Aston Down, Glos
	WZ846	DHC1 Chipmunk 22 (G-BCSC/8439M)	No 2427 Sqn ATC, Biggin Hill, Kent
	WZ847	DHC1 Chipmunk 22 (G-CPMK) [F]	Privately owned, Sleap, Shropshire
	WZ869	DHC1 Chipmunk T10 (8019M) <ff> [6]	South Wales Aviation Museum, St Athan, Glamorgan, Wales
	WZ872	DHC1 Chipmunk 22 (G-BZGB) [E]	Privately owned, Spanhoe, Northants
	WZ876	DHC1 Chipmunk 22 (G-BBWN) <ff>	Tangmere Military Aviation Museum, W. Sussex
	WZ877	DHC1 Chipmunk T10 (F-AZLI) [75]	Privately owned, Berck-sur-Mer, France
	WZ879	DHC1 Chipmunk 22 (G-BWUT) [X]	Privately owned, Audley End, Essex
	WZ882	DHC1 Chipmunk 22 (G-BXGP) [K]	Privately owned, Popham, Hants
	XA109	DH115 Sea Vampire T22	Montrose Air Station Heritage Centre, Angus, Scotland
	XA127	DH115 Sea Vampire T22 <ff>	FAA Museum, RNAS Yeovilton, Somerset
	XA177	Auster B.4 <R> (BAPC.645)	Boscombe Down Aviation Collection, Old Sarum, Wilts (rebuild)
	XA129	DH115 Sea Vampire T22	FAA Museum, stored Cobham Hall, RNAS Yeovilton, Somerset
	XA225	Slingsby T38 Grasshopper TX1	Privately owned, Bellarena, NI (stored)
	XA226	Slingsby T38 Grasshopper TX1 (dismantled)	Norfolk & Suffolk Avn Museum, Flixton, Suffolk
	XA228	Slingsby T38 Grasshopper TX1	National Museum of Flight, E. Fortune, Scotland
	XA230	Slingsby T38 Grasshopper TX1 (BGA4098)	Privately owned, Saltby, Leics (dismantled)
	XA231	Slingsby T38 Grasshopper TX1 (8888M)	RAF Manston History Museum, Kent
	XA240	Slingsby T38 Grasshopper TX1 (BGA4556)	Privately owned, Portmoak, Perth & Kinross, Scotland
	XA241	Slingsby T38 Grasshopper TX1	Shuttleworth Collection, stored Old Warden, Beds
	XA243	Slingsby T38 Grasshopper TX1 (8886M)	Privately owned, Gransden Lodge, Cambs
	XA244	Slingsby T38 Grasshopper TX1	Privately owned, Brent Tor, Devon
	XA282	Slingsby T31B Cadet TX3	Caernarfon Air World, Gwynedd, Wales
	XA290	Slingsby T31B Cadet TX3	Privately owned, Portmoak, Perth & Kinross, Scotland
	XA293	Slingsby T31B Cadet TX3 <ff>	South Yorkshire Aircraft Museum, Doncaster, S. Yorks
	XA295	Slingsby T31B Cadet TX3 (BGA3336)	Privately owned, Eaglescott, Devon
	XA302	Slingsby T31B Cadet TX3 (BGA3786)	RAF Museum, Hendon, Gtr London
	XA310	Slingsby T31B Cadet TX3 (BGA4963)	Privately owned, Nympsfield, Glos
	XA312	Slingsby Cadet TX3 (VM791/8876M)	RAF Manston History Museum, Kent
	XA459	Fairey Gannet ECM6 [E]	Solway Aviation Society, Carlisle, Cumbria
	XA460	Fairey Gannet ECM6 [768/BY]	Ulster Aviation Society, Long Kesh, Co. Antrim, NI
	XA466	Fairey Gannet COD4 [777/LM]	FAA Museum, RNAS Yeovilton, Somerset
	XA508	Fairey Gannet T2 [627/GN]	FAA Museum, at Midland Air Museum, Coventry

Serial	Type (code/other identity)	Owner/operator, location or fate	Notes
XA564	Gloster Javelin FAW1 (7464M)	RAF Museum, Cosford, Shropshire	
XA634	Gloster Javelin FAW4 (7641M)	Binbrook Airfield, Lincs, (restoration)	
XA699	Gloster Javelin FAW5 (7809M)	Midland Air Museum, Coventry, Warks	
XA847	EE P1B (8371M)	Privately owned, Stowmarket, Suffolk	
XA862	WS55 Whirlwind HAR1 (G-AMJT) [704] <ff>	South Yorkshire Aircraft Museum, Doncaster, S. Yorks	
XA864	WS55 Whirlwind HAR1	FAA Museum, stored Cobham Hall, RNAS Yeovilton, Somerset	
XA870	WS55 Whirlwind HAR1 [911]	South Yorkshire Aircraft Museum, Doncaster, S. Yorks	
XA880	DH104 Devon C2 (G-BVXR) <ff>	Privately owned, Elstree Studios, Herts	
XA893	Avro 698 Vulcan B1 (8591M) <ff>	RAF Museum, stored Cosford, Shropshire	
XA903	Avro 698 Vulcan B1 <ff>	Stoneykirk Aviation Museum, D&G, Scotland	
XA917	HP80 Victor B1 (7827M) <ff>	Privately owned, Cupar, Fife, Scotland	
XB259	Blackburn B101 Beverley C1 (G-AOAI)	Solway Aviation Society, Carlisle, Cumbria	
XB261	Blackburn B101 Beverley C1 <ff>	Newark Air Museum, Winthorpe, Notts	
XB446	Grumman TBM-3 Avenger ECM6B	FAA Museum, Yeovilton, Somerset	
XB480	Hiller HT1 [537]	FAA Museum, stored Cobham Hall, RNAS Yeovilton, Somerset	
XB812	Canadair CL-13 Sabre F4 (9227M) [U]	RAF Museum, Cosford, Shropshire	
XD145	Saro SR53	Michael Beetham Conservation Centre, RAFM Cosford, Shropshire (stored)	
XD163	WS55 Whirlwind HAR10 (8645M) [X]	The Helicopter Museum, Weston-super-Mare, Somerset	
XD165	WS55 Whirlwind HAR10 (8673M)	Caernarfon Airfield Fire Section, Gwynedd, Wales	
XD215	VS Scimitar F1 <ff>	Privately owned, Cheltenham, Glos	
XD235	VS Scimitar F1 [148] <ff>	Privately owned, Lavendon, Bucks	
XD317	VS Scimitar F1 [112/R]	FAA Museum, RNAS Yeovilton, Somerset	
XD332	VS Scimitar F1 [194/C]	Solent Sky, stored Romsey, Hants	
XD375	DH115 Vampire T11 (7887M)	Privately owned, Elland, W. Yorks	
XD377	DH115 Vampire T11 (8203M) <ff>	Privately owned, Gilberdyke, E. Yorks	
XD425	DH115 Vampire T11 <ff>	Morayvia, Kinloss, Moray, Scotland	
XD434	DH115 Vampire T11 [25]	City of Norwich Aviation Museum, Norfolk	
XD445	DH115 Vampire T11 [51]	Privately owned, Tettenhall, W. Midlands	
XD447	DH115 Vampire T11 [33]	East Midlands Airport Aeropark, Leics	
XD452	DH115 Vampire T11 (7990M) [66] <ff>	Privately owned, Dursley, Glos	
XD506	DH115 Vampire T11 (7983M)	Suffolk Aviation Heritage Centre, Kesgrave, Suffolk	
XD515	DH115 Vampire T11 (7998M/*XM515*)	RAF Museum, stored Cosford, Shropshire	
XD525	DH115 Vampire T11 (7882M) <ff>	Privately owned, Templepatrick, NI	
XD534	DH115 Vampire T11 (comp XD382) [41]	East Midlands Airport Aeropark, Leics	
XD542	DH115 Vampire T11 (7604M) [N]	Privately owned, Patrington, E. Yorks	
XD547	DH115 Vampire T11 (composite) [Z]	Privately owned, Cantley, Norfolk	
XD593	DH115 Vampire T11	Newark Air Museum, Winthorpe, Notts	
XD595	DH115 Vampire T11 <ff>	Privately owned, Kirton in Lindsey, Lincs	
XD596	DH115 Vampire T11 (7939M)	Solent Sky, stored Timsbury, Hants	
XD599	DH115 Vampire T11 [A] <ff>	Sywell Aviation Museum, Northants	
XD601	DH115 Vampire T11 (XE956/G-OBLN)	South Wales Aviation Museum, St Athan, Glamorgan, Wales	
XD616	DH115 Vampire T11 [56] <ff>	*Scrapped Kesgrave, June 2024*	
XD624	DH115 Vampire T11	Privately owned, Hooton Park, Cheshire	
XD626	DH115 Vampire T11 [Q]	Midland Air Museum, stored Coventry, Warks	
XD674	Hunting Jet Provost T1 (7570M)	RAF Museum, Cosford, Shropshire	
XD693	Hunting Jet Provost T1 (XM129/G-AOBU) [Z-Q]	Kennet Aviation, North Weald, Essex	
XD816	Vickers Valiant B(K)1 <ff>	Brooklands Museum, Weybridge, Surrey	
XD818	Vickers Valiant B(K)1 (7894M)	RAF Museum, Cosford, Shropshire	
XD826	Vickers Valiant B(K)1 <ff>	Privately owned, Duxford, Cambs	
XD857	Vickers Valiant B(K)1 <ff>	RAF Marham Aviation Heritage Centre, Norfolk	
XD875	Vickers Valiant B(K)1 <ff>	Morayvia, Kinloss, Moray, Scotland	
XE317	Bristol 171 Sycamore HR14 (G-AMWO)	South Yorkshire Aircraft Museum, Doncaster, S. Yorks	
XE339	Hawker Sea Hawk FGA6 (8156M) [149] <ff>	Privately owned, Glos	
XE339	Hawker Sea Hawk FGA6 (8156M) [E] <rf>	Privately owned, Hooton Park, Cheshire	

Notes	Serial	Type (code/other identity)	Owner/operator, location or fate
	XE340	Hawker Sea Hawk FGA6 [131/Z]	FAA Museum, stored Cobham Hall, RNAS Yeovilton, Somerset
	XE364	Hawker Sea Hawk FGA6 (G-JETH) (comp WM983/XE489) [485/J]	Gatwick Aviation Museum, Charlwood, Surrey
	XE368	Hawker Sea Hawk FGA6 [200/J]	Privately owned, Market Harborough, Leics
	XE521	Fairey Rotodyne Y (parts)	The Helicopter Museum, Weston-super-Mare, Somerset
	XE584	Hawker Hunter FGA9 <ff>	Privately owned, New Brighton, Merseyside
	XE597	Hawker Hunter FGA9 (8874M) <ff>	Privately owned, Bromsgrove, Worcs
	XE620	Hawker Hunter F6A (XE606/8841M) [B]	North-East Land, Sea & Air Museums, Usworth, T&W
	XE624	Hawker Hunter FGA9 (8875M) [G]	Privately owned, Wickenby, Lincs
	XE627	Hawker Hunter F6A [T]	IWM Duxford, Cambs
	XE643	Hawker Hunter FGA9 (8586M) <ff>	No 1137 Sqn ATC, Long Kesh, Co. Antrim, NI
	XE664	Hawker Hunter F4 <ff>	Jet Age Museum, Gloucestershire Airport, Glos
	XE665	Hawker Hunter T8C (G-BWGM)	Privately owned, Cotswold Airport, Glos
	XE668	Hawker Hunter GA11 [832/DD]	Hamburger Hill Paintball, Marksbury, Somerset
	XE670	Hawker Hunter F4 (7762M/8585M) <ff>	RAF Museum, Cosford, Shropshire
	XE683	Hawker Hunter F51 (RDAF E-409) [G]	City of Norwich Aviation Museum, Norfolk
	XE685	Hawker Hunter GA11 (G-GAII) [861/VL]	Privately owned, Wickenby, Lincs
	XE688	Hawker Hunter T72 (XE704/PP-XHH)	Hawker Hunter Aviation, Leeming, N. Yorks
	XE689	Hawker Hunter GA11 (G-BWGK) <ff>	Privately owned, stored Bristol, Glos
	XE707	Hawker Hunter GA11 (N707XE) [865]	Bentwaters Cold War Museum, Suffolk
	XE761	Slingsby T8 Cadet TX1 (BGA804) [BAA]	Privately owned, Little Rissington, Glos
	XE762	Slingsby T8 Cadet TX2 (VM594)	Gliding Heritage Centre, Lasham, Hants
	XE786	Slingsby T31B Cadet TX3 (BGA4033)	Privately owned, Portmoak, Perth and Kinross, Scotland (stored)
	XE793	Slingsby T31B Cadet TX3 (8666M)	Privately owned, Tamworth, Staffs
	XE797	Slingsby T31B Cadet TX3	South Yorkshire Aviation Museum, Doncaster, S. Yorks
	XE799	Slingsby T31B Cadet TX3 (8943M) [R]	Privately owned, stored Riseley, Beds
	XE802	Slingsby T31B Cadet TX3 (BGA5283)	Privately owned, stored Eaglescott, Devon
	XE852	DH115 Vampire T11 [58]	No 2247 Sqn ATC, Hawarden, Flintshire, Wales
	XE855	DH115 Vampire T11 <ff> (wreck)	Midland Air Museum, stored Coventry, Warks
	XE856	DH115 Vampire T11 (G-DUSK) [V]	Bournemouth Aviation Museum, Dorset
	XE874	DH115 Vampire T11 (8582M)	Paintball Commando, Birkin, N. Yorks
	XE897	DH115 Vampire T11 (XD403)	Privately owned, Errol, Tayside, Scotland
	XE921	DH115 Vampire T11 [VR] <ff>	Stoneykirk Aviation Museum, D&G, Scotland
	XE935	DH115 Vampire T11	South Yorkshire Aircraft Museum, Doncaster, S. Yorks
	XE946	DH115 Vampire T11 (7473M) <ff>	RAF Cranwell Aviation Heritage Centre, Lincs
	XE956	DH115 Vampire T11 (G-OBLN)	Repainted as XD601
	XE979	DH115 Vampire T11 [54] <ff>	Privately owned, Cantley, Norfolk
	XE979	DH115 Vampire T11 (fuselage)	Privately owned, Birlingham, Worcs
	XE982	DH115 Vampire T11 (7564M) (fuselage)	Privately owned, Port Talbot, West Glamorgan, Wales
	XE985	DH115 Vampire T11 (WZ476)	Privately owned, New Inn, Torfaen, Wales
	XF113	VS Swift F7 [19] <ff>	Boscombe Down Aviation Collection, Old Sarum, Wilts
	XF114	VS Swift F7 (G-SWIF)	Solent Sky, Southampton, Hants
	XF368	Hawker Hunter F51 (RDAF E-412/XF314)	Brooklands Museum, Weybridge, Surrey
	XF375	Hawker Hunter F6A (8736M/G-BUEZ) [6]	Boscombe Down Aviation Collection, Old Sarum, Wilts
	XF382	Hawker Hunter F6A [15]	Midland Air Museum, Coventry, Warks
	XF383	Hawker Hunter F6 (8706M) <ff>	Gloster Aviation Club, Gloucester, Glos
	XF418	Hawker Hunter F51 (RDAF E-430)	Gatwick Aviation Museum, Charlwood, Surrey
	XF509	Hawker Hunter F6 (8708M)	RAF Manston History Museum, Kent
	XF522	Hawker Hunter F6 <ff>	Trenchard Museum, RAF Halton, Bucks
	XF526	Hawker Hunter F6 (8679M) [78/E]	Historic Aviation Centre, Fishburn, Co. Durham
	XF527	Hawker Hunter F6 (8680M)	RAF Halton, Bucks, on display
	XF545	Percival P56 Provost T1 (7957M) [O-K]	Privately owned, France
	XF597	Percival P56 Provost T1 (G-BKFW) [AH]	Privately owned, Audley End, Essex
	XF603	Percival P56 Provost T1 (G-KAPW)	Shuttleworth Collection, Old Warden, Beds
	XF690	Percival P56 Provost T1 (8041M/G-MOOS)	South Wales Aviation Museum, St Athan, Glamorgan, Wales
	XF708	Avro 716 Shackleton MR3/3 [C]	IWM Duxford, Cambs
	XF785	Bristol 173 (7648M/G-ALBN)	Aerospace Bristol, Filton, Glos
	XF836	Percival P56 Provost T1 (8043M/G-AWRY) [JG]	Privately owned, Middlezoy, Somerset

Serial	Type (code/other identity)	Owner/operator, location or fate	Notes
XF840	Percival P56 Provost T1 <ff>	Tangmere Military Aviation Museum, W. Sussex	
XF926	Bristol 188 (8368M)	RAF Museum, Cosford, Shropshire	
XF940	Hawker Hunter F4 <ff>	Privately owned, Bournemouth, Dorset	
XF994	Hawker Hunter T8C (G-CGHU) [873/VL]	Privately owned, Bruntingthorpe, Leics	
XF995	Hawker Hunter T8B (G-BZSF/9237M) [K]	Stored RAF Scampton, Lincs	
XG154	Hawker Hunter FGA9 (8863M)	RAF Museum, Hendon, Gtr London	
XG160	Hawker Hunter F6A (8831M/G-BWAF) [U]	Bournemouth Aviation Museum, Dorset	
XG164	Hawker Hunter F6 (8681M)	Davidstow Airfield & Cornwall At War Museum, Cornwall	
XG168	Hawker Hunter F6A (XG172/8832M) [10]	City of Norwich Aviation Museum, Norfolk	
XG190	Hawker Hunter F51 (RDAF E-425)	Repainted as RDAF E-425	
XG193	Hawker Hunter FGA9 (XG297) (comp with WT741) <ff>	South Yorkshire Aircraft Museum, Doncaster, S. Yorks	
XG194	Hawker Hunter FGA9 (8839M)	Wattisham Station Heritage Museum, Suffolk	
XG195	Hawker Hunter FGA9 <ff>	Privately owned, Lewes, E. Sussex	
XG196	Hawker Hunter F6A (8702M) [31]	Privately owned, Bentwaters, Suffolk	
XG209	Hawker Hunter F6 (8709M) <ff>	Privately owned, Kingston-on-Thames, Gtr London	
XG210	Hawker Hunter F6	Privately owned, Beck Row, Suffolk	
XG225	Hawker Hunter F6A (8713M)	DSAE Cosford, Shropshire, at main gate	
XG226	Hawker Hunter F6A (8800M) <ff>	RAF Manston History Museum, Kent	
XG254	Hawker Hunter FGA9 (8881M) [A]	Norfolk & Suffolk Avn Museum, Flixton, Suffolk	
XG274	Hawker Hunter F6 (8710M) [71]	Suffolk Aviation Heritage Centre, Kesgrave, Suffolk	
XG290	Hawker Hunter F6 (8711M) <ff>	Boscombe Down Aviation Collection, Old Sarum, Wilts	
XG297	Hawker Hunter FGA9 [Y] <ff>	South Yorkshire Aircraft Museum, Doncaster, S. Yorks	
XG325	EE Lightning F1 <ff>	Privately owned, Thetford, Norfolk	
XG329	EE Lightning F1 (8050M)	Privately owned, Flixton, Suffolk	
XG331	EE Lightning F1 <ff>	Privately owned, Quedgeley, Glos	
XG337	EE Lightning F1 (8056M) [M]	RAF Museum, Cosford, Shropshire	
XG452	Bristol 192 Belvedere HC1 (7997M/G-BRMB)	The Helicopter Museum, Weston-super-Mare, Somerset	
XG454	Bristol 192 Belvedere HC1 (8366M)	The Helicopter Museum, Weston-super-Mare, Somerset	
XG462	Bristol 192 Belvedere HC1 <ff>	The Helicopter Museum, Weston-super-Mare, Somerset	
XG474	Bristol 192 Belvedere HC1 (8367M) [O]	RAF Museum, Hendon, Gtr London	
XG502	Bristol 171 Sycamore HR14	Army Flying Museum, Middle Wallop, Hants	
XG506	Bristol 171 Sycamore HR14 <ff>	Privately owned, South Kirkby, W. Yorkshire	
XG518	Bristol 171 Sycamore HR14 (8009M) [S-E]	Norfolk & Suffolk Avn Museum, Flixton, Suffolk	
XG523	Bristol 171 Sycamore HR14 <ff> [V]	Norfolk & Suffolk Avn Museum, Flixton, Suffolk	
XG545	Bristol 171 Sycamore HR52 (OE-XSY)	Flying Bulls, Salzburg, Austria	
XG574	WS55 Whirlwind HAR3 [752/PO]	FAA Museum, stored Cobham Hall, RNAS Yeovilton, Somerset	
XG588	WS55 Whirlwind HAR3 (G-BAMH/VR-BEP)	East Midlands Airport Aeropark, Leics	
XG592	WS55 Whirlwind HAS7 [54]	Task Force Adventure Park, Cowbridge, S. Glam, Wales	
XG594	WS55 Whirlwind HAS7 [517]	FAA Museum, stored Cobham Hall, RNAS Yeovilton, Somerset	
XG596	WS55 Whirlwind HAS7 [66]	The Helicopter Museum, stored Weston-super-Mare, Somerset	
XG629	DH112 Sea Venom FAW22 [668]	Privately owned, Stone, Staffs	
XG680	DH112 Sea Venom FAW22 [438]	North-East Land, Sea & Air Museums, Usworth, T&W	
XG692	DH112 Sea Venom FAW22 [444/668/LM] (pod)	Morayvia, Kinloss, Moray, Scotland	
XG730	DH112 Sea Venom FAW22	de Havilland Aircraft Museum, London Colney, Herts	
XG736	DH112 Sea Venom FAW22	Privately owned, East Midlands	
XG737	DH112 Sea Venom FAW22 [438] <ff>	East Midlands Airport Aeropark, Leics	
XG743	DH115 Sea Vampire T22 [798/BY]	Historic Aviation Centre, Fishburn, Co. Durham	
XG775	DH115 Sea Vampire T22 <ff>	Jet Age Museum, Gloucestershire Airport, Glos	
XG797	Fairey Gannet ECM6 [277]	IWM Duxford, Cambs	
XG831	Fairey Gannet ECM6 [396]	Davidstow Airfield & Cornwall At War Museum, Cornwall	
XG882	Fairey Gannet T5 (8754M) [771/LM]	Privately owned, Errol, Tayside, Scotland	
XG883	Fairey Gannet T5 [773/BY]	FAA Museum, at Museum of Berkshire Aviation, Woodley, Berks	
XG900	Short SC1	Science Museum, South Kensington, London	
XG905	Short SC1	Ulster Folk & Transport Mus, Holywood, Co. Down, NI	
XH131	EE Canberra PR9	Ulster Aviation Society, Long Kesh, Co. Antrim, NI	
XH134	EE Canberra PR9 (G-OMHD)	Permanently withdrawn from use, November 2024	

Notes	Serial	Type (code/other identity)	Owner/operator, location or fate
	XH135	EE Canberra PR9 <ff>	Preserved, West Raynham, Norfolk
	XH136	EE Canberra PR9 (8782M) [W] <ff>	Romney Marsh Wartime Collection, Kent
	XH165	EE Canberra PR9 <ff>	Blyth Valley Aviation Collection, Walpole, Suffolk
	XH169	EE Canberra PR9	RAF Marham, Norfolk, on display
	XH170	EE Canberra PR9 (8739M)	RAF Wyton, Cambs, on display
	XH171	EE Canberra PR9 (8746M) [U]	RAF Museum, Cosford, Shropshire
	XH174	EE Canberra PR9 <ff>	Privately owned, Devon
	XH175	EE Canberra PR9 <ff>	Privately owned, Bewdley, Worcs
	XH177	EE Canberra PR9 <ff>	Newark Air Museum, Winthorpe, Notts
	XH278	DH115 Vampire T11 (8595M/7866M) [42]	Yorkshire Air Museum, Elvington, N. Yorks
	XH312	DH115 Vampire T11	Outpost Paintball, Higher Kinnerton, Flintshire, Wales
	XH313	DH115 Vampire T11 (G-BZRD) [E]	Tangmere Military Aviation Museum, W. Sussex (rest'n)
	XH318	DH115 Vampire T11 (7761M) [64]	Privately owned, Sholing, Hants
	XH328	DH115 Vampire T11	Privately owned, Cantley, Norfolk
	XH330	DH115 Vampire T11 [73]	Privately owned, Milton Keynes, Bucks
	XH537	Avro 698 Vulcan B2MRR (8749M) <ff>	Bournemouth Aviation Museum, Dorset
	XH558	Avro 698 Vulcan B2 (G-VLCN)	Vulcan To The Sky Trust, Doncaster Sheffield Airport
	XH560	Avro 698 Vulcan K2 <ff>	Privately owned, Neatishead, Norfolk
	XH563	Avro 698 Vulcan B2MRR <ff>	Morayvia, Kinloss, Moray, Scotland
	XH584	EE Canberra T4 (G-27-374) <ff>	South Yorkshire Aircraft Museum, Doncaster, S. Yorks
	XH592	HP80 Victor B1A (8429M) <ff>	Midland Air Museum, Coventry, Warks
	XH648	HP80 Victor K1A	IWM Duxford, Cambs
	XH669	HP80 Victor K2 (9092M) <ff>	Privately owned, Duxford, Cambs
	XH670	HP80 Victor SR2 <ff>	South Wales Aviation Museum, St Athan, Glamorgan, Wales
	XH672	HP80 Victor K2 (9242M)	RAF Museum, Cosford, Shropshire
	XH767	Gloster Javelin FAW9 (7955M) [L]	East Midlands Airport Aeropark, Leics (restoration)
	XH783	Gloster Javelin FAW7 (7798M) <ff>	Privately owned, Catford, Gtr London
	XH837	Gloster Javelin FAW7 (8032M) <ff>	Caernarfon Air World, Gwynedd, Wales
	XH892	Gloster Javelin FAW9R (7982M) [J]	Norfolk & Suffolk Avn Museum, Flixton, Suffolk
	XH897	Gloster Javelin FAW9	IWM Duxford, Cambs
	XH903	Gloster Javelin FAW9 (7938M) [G]	Jet Age Museum, Gloucestershire Airport, Glos
	XH992	Gloster Javelin FAW8 (7829M) [P]	Newark Air Museum, Winthorpe, Notts
	XJ314	RR Thrust Measuring Rig	Science Museum, South Kensington, London
	XJ380	Bristol 171 Sycamore HR14 (8628M)	Morayvia, Kinloss, Moray, Scotland
	XJ389	Fairey Jet Gyrodyne (XD759/G-AJJP)	Museum of Berkshire Aviation, Woodley, Berks
	XJ398	WS55 Whirlwind HAR10 (XD768/G-BDBZ)	South Yorkshire Aircraft Museum, Doncaster, S. Yorks
	XJ407	WS55 Whirlwind HAR10 (N7013H)	Privately owned, North Somercotes, Lincs
	XJ476	DH110 Sea Vixen FAW1 <ff>	Boscombe Down Aviation Collection, Old Sarum, Wilts
	XJ481	DH110 Sea Vixen FAW1 [VL]	FAA Museum, stored Cobham Hall, RNAS Yeovilton, Somerset
	XJ482	DH110 Sea Vixen FAW1 [713/VL]	Norfolk & Suffolk Avn Museum, Flixton, Suffolk
	XJ488	DH110 Sea Vixen FAW1 <ff>	Robertsbridge Aviation Society, Mayfield, E. Sussex
	XJ494	DH110 Sea Vixen FAW2 [121/E]	Preserved Bruntingthorpe, Leics
	XJ560	DH110 Sea Vixen FAW2 (8142M) [302]	Newark Air Museum, Winthorpe, Notts
	XJ565	DH110 Sea Vixen FAW2 [127/E]	de Havilland Aircraft Museum, London Colney, Herts
	XJ571	DH110 Sea Vixen FAW2 (8140M) [242]	Solent Sky, Southampton, Hants
	XJ575	DH110 Sea Vixen FAW2 <ff> [SAH-13]	Wellesbourne Wartime Museum, Warks
	XJ579	DH110 Sea Vixen FAW2 <ff>	Midland Air Museum, stored Coventry, Warks
	XJ580	DH110 Sea Vixen FAW2 [131/E]	Tangmere Military Aviation Museum, W. Sussex
	XJ714	Hawker Hunter FR10 (comp XG226, ET-272, PH-NLH) [B]	East Midlands Airport Aeropark, Leics
	XJ723	WS55 Whirlwind HAR10	Morayvia, Kinloss, Moray, Scotland
	XJ726	WS55 Whirlwind HAR10	Caernarfon Air World, Gwynedd, Wales
	XJ727	WS55 Whirlwind HAR10 (8661M)	Combat Paintball Park, Thetford, Suffolk
	XJ729	WS55 Whirlwind HAR10 (8732M/G-BVGE)	Privately owned, Chard, Somerset
	XJ758	WS55 Whirlwind HAR10 (8464M) <ff>	Privately owned, Welshpool, Powys, Wales
	XJ772	DH115 Vampire T11 [H]	de Havilland Aircraft Museum, London Colney, Herts
	XJ823	Avro 698 Vulcan B2A	Solway Aviation Society, Carlisle, Cumbria
	XJ824	Avro 698 Vulcan B2A	IWM Duxford, Cambs
	XJ917	Bristol 171 Sycamore HR14 [H-S]	North-East Land, Sea & Air Museums, Usworth, T&W

Serial	Type (code/other identity)	Owner/operator, location or fate	Notes
XJ918	Bristol 171 Sycamore HR14 (8190M)	Ulster Aviation Society, Long Kesh, Co. Antrim, NI	
XK416	Auster AOP9 (7855M/G-AYUA)	Privately owned, Widmerpool, Notts	
XK417	Auster AOP9 (G-AVXY)	Privately owned, Messingham, Lincs	
XK418	Auster AOP9 (7976M)	No 1894 Sqn ATC, Swaffham, Norfolk	
XK421	Auster AOP9 (8365M) (comp XP286) (frame)	South Yorkshire Aircraft Museum, stored Doncaster, S. Yorks	
XK488	Blackburn NA39 Buccaneer S1	FAA Museum, stored Cobham Hall, RNAS Yeovilton, Somerset	
XK526	Blackburn NA39 Buccaneer S2 (8648M)	RAF Honington, stored	
XK527	Blackburn NA39 Buccaneer S2D (8818M) <ff>	Privately owned, North Wales	
XK532	Blackburn NA39 Buccaneer S1 (8867M) [632/LM]	Privately owned, Inverness, Scotland	
XK533	Blackburn NA39 Buccaneer S1 <ff>	Stoneykirk Aviation Museum, D&G, Scotland	
XK590	DH115 Vampire T11 [V]	Wellesbourne Wartime Museum, Warks	
XK623	DH115 Vampire T11 (G-VAMP) [56]	Caernarfon Air World, Gwynedd, Wales	
XK624	DH115 Vampire T11 [32]	Norfolk & Suffolk Avn Museum, Flixton, Suffolk	
XK625	DH115 Vampire T11 [14]	Romney Marsh Wartime Collection, Kent	
XK627	DH115 Vampire T11 <ff>	Davidstow Airfield & Cornwall At War Museum, Cornwall	
XK632	DH115 Vampire T11 <ff>	Privately owned, Wickenby, Lincs	
XK637	DH115 Vampire T11 <ff>	Top Gun Flight Simulation Centre, Stalybridge, Gtr Mcr	
XK695	DH106 Comet C2(RC) (G-AMXH/9164M) <ff>	de Havilland Aircraft Museum, London Colney, Herts	
XK699	DH106 Comet C2 (7971M) <ff>	Boscombe Down Aviation Collection, Old Sarum, Wilts	
XK724	Folland Gnat F1 (7715M)	Midland Air Museum, Coventry, Warks	
XK740	Folland Gnat F1 (8396M)	Solent Sky, Southampton, Hants	
XK776	ML Utility 1	Army Flying Museum, Middle Wallop, Hants	
XK789	Slingsby T38 Grasshopper TX1	Midland Air Museum, Coventry, Warks	
XK790	Slingsby T38 Grasshopper TX1	Privately owned, stored Husbands Bosworth, Leics	
XK819	Slingsby T38 Grasshopper TX1	Privately owned, stored Rufforth, N. Yorks	
XK820	Slingsby T38 Grasshopper TX1 (comp WZ754/WZ778)	Privately owned, Bridge of Weir, Renfrew, Scotland	
XK821	Slingsby T38 Grasshopper TX1	Suffolk Aviation Heritage Centre, Kesgrave, Suffolk	
XK885	Percival P66 Pembroke C1 (8452M/N46EA)	Privately owned, Dalton, Lancs (restoration)	
XK895	DH104 Sea Devon C20 (G-SDEV) [19/CU]	South Wales Aviation Museum, St Athan, Glamorgan, Wales	
XK907	WS55 Whirlwind HAS7 <ff>	Midland Air Museum, stored Coventry, Warks	
XK911	WS55 Whirlwind HAS7(mod)	Privately owned, Glastonbury, Somerset	
XK936	WS55 Whirlwind HAS7 [62]	IWM Duxford, Cambs	
XK940	WS55 Whirlwind HAS7 (G-AYXT) [911]	The Helicopter Museum, Weston-super-Mare, Somerset	
XK970	WS55 Whirlwind HAR10 (8789M)	Army, Bramley, Hants (for disposal)	
XL149	Blackburn B101 Beverley C1 (7988M) <ff>	South Yorkshire Aircraft Museum, Doncaster, S. Yorks	
XL160	HP80 Victor K2 (8910M) <ff>	RAF Marham Aviation Heritage Centre, Norfolk	
XL164	HP80 Victor K2 (9215M) <ff>	Bournemouth Aviation Museum, Dorset	
XL190	HP80 Victor K2 (9216M) <ff>	RAF Manston History Museum, Kent	
XL231	HP80 Victor K2	Yorkshire Air Museum, Elvington, N. Yorks	
XL318	Avro 698 Vulcan B2 (8733M)	RAF Museum, Hendon, Gtr London	
XL319	Avro 698 Vulcan B2	North-East Land, Sea & Air Museums, Usworth, T&W	
XL360	Avro 698 Vulcan B2A	Midland Air Museum, Coventry, Warks	
XL388	Avro 698 Vulcan B2 <ff>	South Yorkshire Aircraft Museum, Doncaster, S. Yorks	
XL426	Avro 698 Vulcan B2 (G-VJET)	Vulcan Restoration Trust, Southend, Essex	
XL445	Avro 698 Vulcan K2 (8811M) <ff>	Current location unknown	
XL449	Fairey Gannet AEW3 <ff>	Privately owned, Steventon, Oxon	
XL472	Fairey Gannet AEW3 [044/R]	South Wales Aviation Museum, stored St Athan, Glamorgan, Wales	
XL497	Fairey Gannet AEW3 [041/R]	Dumfries & Galloway Avn Mus, Dumfries, Scotland	
XL500	Fairey Gannet AEW3 (G-KAEW) [CU]	South Wales Aviation Museum, St Athan, Glamorgan, Wales	
XL502	Fairey Gannet AEW3 (8610M/G-BMYP)	Yorkshire Air Museum, Elvington, N. Yorks	
XL503	Fairey Gannet AEW3 [070/E]	FAA Museum, stored Cobham Hall, RNAS Yeovilton, Somerset	
XL563	Hawker Hunter T7 (9218M)	Farnborough Air Sciences Trust, Farnborough, Hants	
XL564	Hawker Hunter T7 <ff>	City of Norwich Aviation Museum, Norfolk	
XL565	Hawker Hunter T7 (parts of WT745) [Y]	Preserved Bruntingthorpe, Leics	

Notes	Serial	Type (code/other identity)	Owner/operator, location or fate
	XL568	Hawker Hunter T7A (9224M) [X]	RAF Museum, Cosford, Shropshire
	XL569	Hawker Hunter T7 (8833M) [85]	East Midlands Airport Aeropark, Leics
XL571	Hawker Hunter T7 (8834M/XL572/G-HNTR) [V]	Yorkshire Air Museum, Elvington, N. Yorks
	XL573	Hawker Hunter T7 (G-BVGH)	South Wales Aviation Museum, St Athan, Glamorgan, Wales
	XL580	Hawker Hunter T8M [723]	FAA Museum, stored Cobham Hall, RNAS Yeovilton, Somerset
	XL586	Hawker Hunter T7 (comp XL578)	Privately owned, Billericay, Essex
	XL587	Hawker Hunter T7 (8807M/G-HPUX)	Privately owned, Arnesby, Leics
	XL591	Hawker Hunter T7	Gatwick Aviation Museum, Charlwood, Surrey
	XL592	Hawker Hunter T7 (8836M) [Y]	Maidenhead Heritage Centre, Berks
	XL609	Hawker Hunter T7 <ff>	Lakes Lightnings, Spark Bridge, Cumbria
	XL621	Hawker Hunter T7 (G-BNCX)	Privately owned, Dunsfold, Surrey
	XL623	Hawker Hunter T7 (8770M)	Privately owned, Dunsfold, Surrey
	XL629	EE Lightning T4	MOD/QinetiQ Boscombe Down, Wilts, at main gate
	XL714	DH82A Tiger Moth II (T6099/G-AOGR)	Privately owned, Boughton, Lincs
	XL736	Saro Skeeter AOP12	The Helicopter Museum stored, Weston-super-Mare, Somerset
XL738	Saro Skeeter AOP12 (XM565/7861M)	Privately owned, Storwood, E. Yorks
	XL739	Saro Skeeter AOP12	Norfolk Tank Museum, Forncett St Peter, Norfolk
	XL762	Saro Skeeter AOP12 (8017M)	National Museum of Flight, stored E. Fortune, Scotland
	XL763	Saro Skeeter AOP12	Privately owned, Storwood, E. Yorks
	XL764	Saro Skeeter AOP12 (7940M) [J]	Newark Air Museum, Winthorpe, Notts
	XL765	Saro Skeeter AOP12	Privately owned, Sandown, IOW
	XL770	Saro Skeeter AOP12 (8046M)	Solent Sky, Southampton, Hants
	XL809	Saro Skeeter AOP12 (G-BLIX)	Privately owned, Wilden, Beds
	XL811	Saro Skeeter AOP12	The Helicopter Museum, Weston-super-Mare, Somerset
	XL812	Saro Skeeter AOP12 (G-SARO)	Historic Army Aircraft Flight, stored Middle Wallop
	XL813	Saro Skeeter AOP12	Army Flying Museum, Middle Wallop, Hants
	XL814	Saro Skeeter AOP12	Army Flying Museum, stored Middle Wallop, Hants
	XL824	Bristol 171 Sycamore HR14 (8021M)	Aerospace Bristol, Filton, Glos
	XL829	Bristol 171 Sycamore HR14	The Helicopter Museum, Weston-super-Mare, Somerset
	XL840	WS55 Whirlwind HAS7	Bawtry Paintball Park, S. Yorks
	XL853	WS55 Whirlwind HAS7 [PO]	FAA Museum, stored Cobham Hall, RNAS Yeovilton, Somerset
	XL875	WS55 Whirlwind HAR9	Privately owned, Scotland
	XL929	Percival P66 Pembroke C1 (G-BNPU)	South Wales Aviation Museum, stored St Athan, Glamorgan, Wales
	XL954	Percival P66 Pembroke C1 (9042M/N4234C/G-BXES)	Privately owned, St. Athan, Glamorgan, Wales
	XL993	SAL Twin Pioneer CC2 (8388M)	RAF Museum, Cosford, Shropshire
	XM135	BAC Lightning F1 [B]	IWM Duxford, Cambs
	XM144	BAC Lightning F1 (8417M) <ff>	Shannon Aviation Museum, Eire (stored)
	XM169	BAC Lightning F1A (8422M) <ff>	Morayvia, Kinloss, Moray, Scotland
	XM172	BAC Lightning F1A (8427M)	Lakes Lightnings, Spark Bridge, Cumbria
	XM173	BAC Lightning F1A (8414M) [A]	Privately owned, Malmesbury, Glos
	XM191	BAC Lightning F1A (7854M/8590M) <ff>	Privately owned, Thorpe Wood, N. Yorks
	XM192	BAC Lightning F1A (8413M) [K]	Thorpe Camp Visitor Centre, Tattershall Thorpe, Lincs
	XM223	DH104 Devon C2 (G-BWWC) [J]	Privately owned, stored Compton Verney, Warks
	XM279	EE Canberra B(I)8 <ff>	Norfolk & Suffolk Avn Museum, Flixton, Suffolk
	XM300	WS58 Wessex HAS1	Privately owned, Nantgarw, Rhondda, Wales
	XM328	WS58 Wessex HAS3 [653/PO]	The Helicopter Museum, Weston-super-Mare, Somerset
	XM330	WS58 Wessex HAS1	The Helicopter Museum, Weston-super-Mare, Somerset
	XM350	Hunting Jet Provost T3A (9036M)	South Yorkshire Aircraft Museum, Doncaster, S. Yorks
	XM351	Hunting Jet Provost T3 (8078M) [Y]	Michael Beetham Conservation Centre, RAFM Cosford, Shropshire (stored outside)
	XM355	Hunting Jet Provost T3 (8229M)	Newcastle Aviation Academy, Tyne and Wear
	XM358	Hunting Jet Provost T3A (8987M) [53]	Privately owned, Newbridge, Powys, Wales
	XM362	Hunting Jet Provost T3 (8230M)	DSAE No 1 SoTT, Cosford, Shropshire
	XM365	Hunting Jet Provost T3A (G-BXBH)	Preserved Bruntingthorpe, Leics
	XM373	Hunting Jet Provost T3 (7726M) [2] <ff>	Yorkshire Air Museum, Elvington, N. Yorks
	XM383	Hunting Jet Provost T3A [90]	Newark Air Museum, Winthorpe, Notts

Serial	Type (code/other identity)	Owner/operator, location or fate	Notes
XM386	Hunting Jet Provost T3 (8076M/69) [08]	STANTA, East Wretham, Norfolk (derelict)	
XM402	Hunting Jet Provost T3 (8055AM) [18]	Morayvia, Kinloss, Moray, Scotland	
XM404	Hunting Jet Provost T3 (8055BM) <ff>	Bournemouth Aviation Museum, Dorset	
XM409	Hunting Jet Provost T3 (8082M) <ff>	Air Scouts, Guernsey Airport, CI	
XM410	Hunting Jet Provost T3 (8054AM)	Privately owned, Erith, Kent	
XM411	Hunting Jet Provost T3 (8434M) <ff>	South Yorkshire Aircraft Museum, Doncaster, S. Yorks	
XM412	Hunting Jet Provost T3A (9011M) [41]	Privately owned, Balado Bridge, Scotland	
XM414	Hunting Jet Provost T3A (8996M) [101]	Ulster Aviation Society, Long Kesh, Co. Antrim, NI	
XM417	Hunting Jet Provost T3A (8054BM) [D] <ff>	Privately owned, Bracknell, Berks	
XM419	Hunting Jet Provost T3A (8990M) [102]	Newcastle Aviation Academy, Tyne and Wear	
XM424	Hunting Jet Provost T3 (G-BWDS)	Privately owned, Dunkeswell, Devon	
XM425	Hunting Jet Provost T3A (8995M) [88]	Privately owned, Longton, Staffs	
XM463	Hunting Jet Provost T3A [38] (dismantled)	Michael Beetham Conservation Centre, RAFM Cosford, Shropshire (stored outside)	
XM468	Hunting Jet Provost T3 (8081M) <ff>	Privately owned, Balcombe, W. Sussex	
XM473	Hunting Jet Provost T3A (8974M/G-TINY)	Privately owned, Wethersfield, Essex	
XM474	Hunting Jet Provost T3 (8121M) <ff>	No 247 Sqn ATC, Ashton-under-Lyne, Gtr Manchester	
XM479	Hunting Jet Provost T3A (G-BVEZ) [U]	Privately owned, Leeds East, N. Yorks	
XM480	Hunting Jet Provost T3 (8080M)	4x4 Car Centre, Chesterfield, Derbyshire	
XM496	Bristol 253 Britannia C1 (EL-WXA) [496]	Britannia Preservation Society, Cotswold Airport, Glos	
XM497	Bristol 175 Britannia 312F (G-AOVF) [497]	RAF Museum, Cosford, Shropshire	
XM529	Saro Skeeter AOP12 (7979M/G-BDNS)	Privately owned, Handforth, Cheshire	
XM553	Saro Skeeter AOP12 (G-AWSV)	Yorkshire Air Museum, Elvington, N. Yorks	
XM555	Saro Skeeter AOP12 (8027M)	North-East Land, Sea & Air Museums, Usworth, T&W	
XM557	Saro Skeeter AOP12 <ff>	The Helicopter Museum, stored Weston-super-Mare, Somerset	
XM564	Saro Skeeter AOP12	The Tank Museum, stored Bovington, Dorset	
XM569	Avro 698 Vulcan B2 <ff>	Jet Age Museum, Gloucestershire Airport, Glos	
XM575	Avro 698 Vulcan B2A (G-BLMC)	East Midlands Airport Aeropark, Leics	
XM594	Avro 698 Vulcan B2	Newark Air Museum, Winthorpe, Notts	
XM597	Avro 698 Vulcan B2	National Museum of Flight, E. Fortune, Scotland	
XM598	Avro 698 Vulcan B2 (8778M)	RAF Museum, Cosford, Shropshire	
XM602	Avro 698 Vulcan B2 (8771M) <ff>	Avro Heritage Museum, Woodford, Cheshire	
XM603	Avro 698 Vulcan B2	Avro Heritage Museum, Woodford, Cheshire	
XM607	Avro 698 Vulcan B2 (8779M)	RAF Waddington, Lincs, on display	
XM612	Avro 698 Vulcan B2	City of Norwich Aviation Museum, Norfolk	
XM651	Saro Skeeter AOP12 (XM561/7980M)	South Yorkshire Aircraft Museum, Doncaster, S. Yorks	
XM652	Avro 698 Vulcan B2 <ff>	Privately owned, Welshpool, Powys, Wales	
XM655	Avro 698 Vulcan B2 (G-VULC)	Privately owned, Wellesbourne Mountford, Warks	
XM685	WS55 Whirlwind HAS7 (G-AYZJ) [513/PO]	Newark Air Museum, Winthorpe, Notts	
XM692	HS Gnat T1 <ff>	Privately owned, Dunkeswell, Devon	
XM693	HS Gnat T1 (7891M)	GE Aviation Hamble, Hants, on display	
XM695	HS Gnat T1 <ff>	Solway Aviation Society, Carlisle, Cumbria	
XM697	HS Gnat T1 (G-NAAT)	Privately owned, Blantyre, S. Lanarkshire, Scotland	
XM708	HS Gnat T1 (8573M)	Privately owned, Lytham St Annes, Lancs	
XM715	HP80 Victor K2	Preserved Bruntingthorpe, Leics	
XM717	HP80 Victor K2 <ff>	RAF Museum, Hendon, Gtr London	
XM819	Lancashire EP9 Prospector (G-APXW)	Army Flying Museum, stored Middle Wallop, Hants	
XM833	WS58 Wessex HAS3	South Wales Aviation Museum, St Athan, Glamorgan, Wales	
XN137	Hunting Jet Provost T3 <ff>	Privately owned, Little Addington, Northants	
XN149	Slingsby T21B (BGA1085/9G-ABD)	Boscombe Down Aviation Collection, Old Sarum, Wilts	
XN156	Slingsby T21B Sedbergh TX1 (BGA3250)	Privately owned, Portmoak, Perth & Kinross, Scotland	
XN157	Slingsby T21B Sedbergh TX1 (BGA3255)	Privately owned, Long Mynd, Shropshire	
XN185	Slingsby T21B Sedbergh TX1 (8942M/BGA4077)	Privately owned, Kirton-in-Lindsey, Lincs (rest'n)	
XN186	Slingsby T21B Sedbergh TX1 (BGA3905) [HFG]	Privately owned, Wattisham, Suffolk	
XN238	Slingsby T31B Cadet TX3 <ff>	Privately owned, Barnstaple, Devon	
XN239	Slingsby T31B Cadet TX3 (8889M) [G]	Privately owned, Bellarena, NI (stored)	
XN246	Slingsby T31B Cadet TX3	Privately owned, stored Riseley, Beds	
XN258	WS55 Whirlwind HAR9 [589/CU]	North-East Land, Sea & Air Museums, Usworth, T&W	
XN304	WS55 Whirlwind HAS7 [WW/B]	Norfolk & Suffolk Avn Museum, Flixton, Suffolk	

Notes	Serial	Type (code/other identity)	Owner/operator, location or fate
	XN332	Saro P531 (G-APNV) [759]	FAA Museum, stored Cobham Hall, RNAS Yeovilton, Somerset
	XN334	Saro P531	FAA Museum, stored Cobham Hall, RNAS Yeovilton, Somerset
	XN344	Saro Skeeter AOP12 (8018M)	Science Museum, South Kensington, London
	XN345	Saro Skeeter AOP12 <ff>	The Helicopter Museum, stored Weston-super-Mare, Somerset
	XN351	Saro Skeeter AOP12 (G-BKSC)	Morayvia, Kinloss, Moray, Scotland
	XN385	WS55 Whirlwind HAS7	Battlezone Paintball, Yarm, N. Yorks
	XN386	WS55 Whirlwind HAR9 [435/ED]	South Yorkshire Aircraft Museum, Doncaster, S. Yorks
	XN412	Auster AOP9 (frame)	Privately owned, Whittlesford, Cambs (rebuild)
	XN437	Auster AOP9 (G-AXWA)	Privately owned, Rush Green, Gtr London
	XN441	Auster AOP9 (G-BGKT)	Privately owned, Week St Mary, Cornwall
	XN458	Hunting Jet Provost T3 (8234M/XN594) [19]	Historic Aviation Centre, Fishburn, Co. Durham
	XN459	Hunting Jet Provost T3A (G-BWOT) [59]	Privately owned, North Weald, Essex
	XN461	Hunting Jet Provost T3A (F-AZMI)	Privately owned, Rouen, France
	XN462	Hunting Jet Provost T3A [17]	FAA Museum, stored Cobham Hall, RNAS Yeovilton, Somerset
	XN466	Hunting Jet Provost T3A [29] <ff>	No 247 Sqn ATC, Ashton-under-Lyne, Gtr Manchester
	XN492	Hunting Jet Provost T3 (8079M) <ff>	East Midlands Airport Aeropark, Leics
	XN494	Hunting Jet Provost T3A (9012M) [43]	Current location unknown (ex-Cornwall Aviation Heritage Centre, Newquay, Cornwall)
	XN495	Hunting Jet Provost T3A (8786M) <ff>	Wings Museum, stored Balcombe, W Sussex
	XN500	Hunting Jet Provost T3A	Norfolk & Suffolk Avn Museum, Flixton, Suffolk
	XN503	Hunting Jet Provost T3 <ff>	North-East Land, Sea & Air Museums, Usworth, T&W
	XN511	Hunting Jet Provost T3 [12] <ff>	South Yorkshire Aircraft Museum, Doncaster, S. Yorks
	XN549	Hunting Jet Provost T3 (8235M) <ff>	Privately owned, Chester, Cheshire
	XN551	Hunting Jet Provost T3A (8984M)	Privately owned, Felton Common, Bristol
	XN554	Hunting Jet Provost T3 (8436M) [K]	Privately owned, Abbotts Ripton, Cambs
	XN573	Hunting Jet Provost T3 [E] <ff>	Newark Air Museum, Winthorpe, Notts
	XN579	Hunting Jet Provost T3A (9137M) [14]	Current location unknown
	XN582	Hunting Jet Provost T3A (8957M) [95]	Yorkshire Air Museum, Elvington, N. Yorks
	XN584	Hunting Jet Provost T3A (9014M) [E]	South Wales Aviation Museum, St Athan, Glamorgan, Wales
	XN586	Hunting Jet Provost T3A (9039M) [91]	Jurby Transport Museum, Isle of Man
	XN589	Hunting Jet Provost T3A (9143M) [46]	Yorkshire Air Museum, Elvington, N. Yorks
	XN597	Hunting Jet Provost T3 (7984M) <ff>	Privately owned, Kent
	XN607	Hunting Jet Provost T3 <ff>	Morayvia, Kinloss, Moray, Scotland
	XN623	Hunting Jet Provost T3 (XN632/8352M)	Privately owned, Birlingham, Worcs
	XN629	Hunting Jet Provost T3A (G-BVEG/G-KNOT) <ff>	Suffolk Aviation Heritage Centre, Kesgrave, Suffolk
	XN634	Hunting Jet Provost T3A <ff>	Lakes Lightnings, Spark Bridge, Cumbria
	XN637	Hunting Jet Provost T3 (G-BKOU) [03]	Privately owned, North Weald, Essex
	XN647	DH110 Sea Vixen FAW2 <ff>	Privately owned, Steventon, Oxon
	XN650	DH110 Sea Vixen FAW2 [456] <ff>	Privately owned, Norfolk
	XN651	DH110 Sea Vixen FAW2 <ff>	Privately owned, Lavendon, Bucks
	XN685	DH110 Sea Vixen FAW2 (8173M) [703/VL]	Midland Air Museum, Coventry, Warks
	XN696	DH110 Sea Vixen FAW2 [751] <ff>	North-East Land, Sea & Air Museums, Usworth, T&W
	XN714	Hunting H126	Michael Beetham Conservation Centre, RAFM Cosford, Shropshire
	XN726	EE Lightning F2A (8545M) <ff>	Boscombe Down Aviation Collection, Old Sarum, Wilts
	XN728	EE Lightning F2A (8546M) <ff>	Privately owned, Binbrook, Lincs
	XN776	EE Lightning F2A (8535M) [C]	National Museum of Flight, E. Fortune, Scotland
	XN795	EE Lightning F2A <ff>	Privately owned, stored Neatishead, Norfolk
	XN819	AW660 Argosy C1 (8205M) <ff>	Newark Air Museum, Winthorpe, Notts
	XN923	HS Buccaneer S1 [13]	Gatwick Aviation Museum, Charlwood, Surrey
	XN928	HS Buccaneer S1 (8179M) <ff>	Privately owned, Gravesend, Kent
	XN957	HS Buccaneer S1 [630/LM]	FAA Museum, RNAS Yeovilton, Somerset
	XN964	HS Buccaneer S1 [630/LM]	Newark Air Museum, Winthorpe, Notts
	XN967	HS Buccaneer S1 [233] <ff>	City of Norwich Aviation Museum, Norfolk
	XN972	HS Buccaneer S1 (8183M/XN962) <ff>	RAF Museum, Cosford, Shropshire
	XN974	HS Buccaneer S2A	Yorkshire Air Museum, Elvington, N. Yorks
	XN981	HS Buccaneer S2B (fuselage)	Privately owned, Errol, Tayside, Scotland

Serial	Type (code/other identity)	Owner/operator, location or fate	Notes
XN983	HS Buccaneer S2B <ff>	Stoneykirk Aviation Museum, D&G, Scotland	
XP142	WS58 Wessex HAS3	FAA Museum, RNAS Yeovilton, Somerset	
XP142	WS58 Wessex HAS3 (A2636/XP110) [55/FL]	DSAE RNAESS, *HMS Sultan*, Gosport, Hants	
XP165	WS Scout AH1	The Helicopter Museum, Weston-super-Mare, Somerset	
XP190	WS Scout AH1	South Yorkshire Aircraft Museum, Doncaster, S. Yorks	
XP191	WS Scout AH1	Privately owned, Prenton, Merseyside	
XP226	Fairey Gannet AEW3	Newark Air Museum, Winthorpe, Notts	
XP241	Auster AOP9 (G-CEHR)	Privately owned, Spanhoe, Northants	
XP242	Auster AOP9 (G-BUCI)	Privately owned, Messingham, Lincs	
XP244	Auster AOP9 (7864M/*M7922*)	Privately owned, Deddington, Oxon	
XP254	Auster AOP11 (G-ASCC)	Privately owned, Whittlesford, Cambs	
XP279	Auster AOP9 (G-BWKK)	Privately owned, stored Winchester, Hants	
XP280	Auster AOP9	Privately owned, stored Leics	
XP281	Auster AOP9	IWM, stored Duxford, Cambs	
XP299	WS55 Whirlwind HAR10 (8726M)	RAF Museum, Hendon, Gtr London	
XP328	WS55 Whirlwind HAR10 (G-BKHC)	Privately owned, North Somercotes, Lincs (wreck)	
XP329	WS55 Whirlwind HAR10 (8791M) [V]	Privately owned, North Somercotes, Lincs (wreck)	
XP330	WS55 Whirlwind HAR10	CAA Fire School, Teesside International Airport	
XP344	WS55 Whirlwind HAR10 (8764M) [H723]	RAF North Luffenham Training Area, Rutland	
XP345	WS55 Whirlwind HAR10 (8792M) [UN]	Yorkshire Helicopter Preservation Group, Doncaster, S. Yorks	
XP346	WS55 Whirlwind HAR10 (8793M)	Privately owned, Hooton Park, Cheshire	
XP350	WS55 Whirlwind HAR10	Privately owned, Bassetts Pole, Staffs	
XP354	WS55 Whirlwind HAR10	Privately owned, Mullingar, Co. Westmeath, Eire	
XP355	WS55 Whirlwind HAR10 (8463M/G-BEBC)	City of Norwich Aviation Museum, Norfolk	
XP360	WS55 Whirlwind HAR10 [V]	Privately owned, Bicton, nr Leominster, Herefordshire	
XP404	WS55 Whirlwind HAR10 (8682M)	The Helicopter Museum, stored Weston-super-Mare, Somerset	
XP411	AW660 Argosy C1 (8442M) [C]	RAF Museum, Cosford, Shropshire	
XP454	Slingsby T38 Grasshopper TX1	Privately owned, Sywell, Northants	
XP459	Slingsby T38 Grasshopper TX1	Privately owned, Wattisham, Suffolk	
XP463	Slingsby T38 Grasshopper TX1 (BGA4372)	Privately owned, Lasham, Hants	
XP488	Slingsby T38 Grasshopper TX1	Privately owned, Sandhill Farm, Oxon	
XP490	Slingsby T38 Grasshopper TX1 (BGA4552)	*Currently not known* (last noted RAF Watton, Norfolk)	
XP492	Slingsby T38 Grasshopper TX1 (BGA3480)	*Currently not known* (noted Aston Down, Glos, Jun 2021)	
XP493	Slingsby T38 Grasshopper TX1	Privately owned, stored Aston Down, Glos	
XP494	Slingsby T38 Grasshopper TX1	Privately owned, stored Tettenhall, W. Midlands	
XP505	HS Gnat T1	Science Museum, stored Wroughton, Wilts	
XP513	HS Gnat T1 (N513X)	Privately owned, North Weald, Essex	
XP516	HS Gnat T1 (8580M) [16]	Farnborough Air Sciences Trust, Farnborough, Hants	
XP540	HS Gnat T1 (8608M) [62]	*Currently not known* (ex-Bruntingthorpe, Leics)	
XP542	HS Gnat T1 (8575M)	No 424 Sqn ATC, Southampton, Hants	
XP556	Hunting Jet Provost T4 (9027M) [B]	RAF Cranwell Aviation Heritage Centre, Lincs	
XP557	Hunting Jet Provost T4 (8494M) [72]	Morayvia, Kinloss, Moray, Scotland	
XP558	Hunting Jet Provost T4 (8627M) <ff>	Stoneykirk Aviation Museum, D&G, Scotland	
XP568	Hunting Jet Provost T4 [85]	East Midlands Airport Aeropark, Leics	
XP573	Hunting Jet Provost T4 (8236M) [19]	Jersey Airport Fire Section, CI	
XP585	Hunting Jet Provost T4 (8407M) [24]	Privately owned, Hawarden, Flintshire, Wales	
XP627	Hunting Jet Provost T4	North-East Land, Sea & Air Museums, Usworth, T&W	
XP629	Hunting Jet Provost T4 (9026M) [P]	Privately owned, Hemswell, Lincs	
XP640	Hunting Jet Provost T4 (8501M) [M]	Yorkshire Air Museum, Elvington, N. Yorks	
XP642	Hunting Jet Provost T4 <ff>	Currently not known (ex-Cornwall Aviation Heritage Centre, Newquay, Cornwall)	
XP672	Hunting Jet Provost T4 (8458M/G-RAFI) [03]	South Wales Aviation Museum, St Athan, Glamorgan, Wales	
XP677	Hunting Jet Provost T4 (8587M) <ff>	Privately owned, Bolton, Lancs	
XP686	Hunting Jet Provost T4 (8401M/8502M) [G]	Current location unknown	
XP693	BAC Lightning F6 (ZU-BEY)	Binbrook Airfield, Lincs, restoration	
XP701	BAC Lightning F3 (8924M) <ff>	Robertsbridge Aviation Society, Mayfield, E. Sussex	
XP703	BAC Lightning F3 <ff>	Currently not known (ex-Bruntingthorpe, Leics)	
XP706	BAC Lightning F3 (8925M)	South Yorkshire Aircraft Museum, Doncaster, S. Yorks	

Notes	Serial	Type (code/other identity)	Owner/operator, location or fate
	XP743	BAC Lightning F3 <ff>	Norfolk & Suffolk Avn Museum, Flixton, Suffolk
	XP745	BAC Lightning F3 (8453M) [H]	Vanguard Self Storage, Bristol, Glos
	XP748	BAC Lightning F53 (ZF583/53-681/306/210)	Solway Aviation Society, Carlisle, Cumbria
	XP757	BAC Lightning F3 <ff>	Privately owned, Boston, Lincs
	XP765	BAC Lightning F6 (XS897) [A]	Lakes Lightnings, RAF Coningsby, Lincs
	XP820	DHC2 Beaver AL1 (G-CICP)	Historic Army Aircraft Flight, Middle Wallop, Hants
	XP821	DHC2 Beaver AL1 [MCO]	Army Flying Museum, Middle Wallop, Hants
	XP822	DHC2 Beaver AL1	Army Flying Museum, Middle Wallop, Hants
	XP831	Hawker P.1127 (8406M)	Science Museum, South Kensington, London
	XP841	Handley-Page HP115	FAA Museum, RNAS Yeovilton, Somerset
	XP847	WS Scout AH1	Army Flying Museum, Middle Wallop, Hants
	XP848	WS Scout AH1	Farnborough Air Sciences Trust, Farnborough, Hants
	XP849	WS Scout AH1 (XP895)	Museum of Berkshire Aviation, Woodley, Berks
	XP853	WS Scout AH1	Privately owned, Sutton, Surrey
	XP854	WS Scout AH1 (7898M/TAD 043)	Mayhem Paintball, Abridge, Essex
	XP855	WS Scout AH1	Privately owned, Arncott, Oxon
	XP883	WS Scout AH1	Privately owned, Wymeswold, Leics
	XP883	WS Scout AH1 (XW281/G-BYNZ) [T]	Privately owned, Dungannon, NI
	XP884	WS Scout AH1 (G-WDST)	Privately owned, Derry City, NI
	XP886	WS Scout AH1	Privately owned, current location unknown
	XP888	WS Scout AH1	Privately owned, Sproughton, Suffolk
	XP890	WS Scout AH1 [G] (fuselage)	Privately owned, Ipswich, Suffolk
	XP899	WS Scout AH1	Boscombe Down Aviation Collection, Old Sarum, Wilts
	XP900	WS Scout AH1	AAC Wattisham, Suffolk, instructional use
	XP902	WS Scout AH1 <ff>	South Yorkshire Aircraft Museum, Doncaster, S. Yorks
	XP905	WS Scout AH1	South Yorkshire Aircraft Museum, stored Doncaster, S. Yorks
	XP907	WS Scout AH1 (G-SROE)	Privately owned, Wattisham, Suffolk
	XP910	WS Scout AH1	Army Flying Museum, Middle Wallop, Hants
	XP924	DH110 Sea Vixen D3 (G-CVIX) [134/E]	Fly Navy Heritage Trust, RNAS Yeovilton, Somerset
	XP925	DH110 Sea Vixen FAW2 [752] <ff>	Stoneykirk Aviation Museum, D&G, Scotland
	XP980	Hawker P.1127	FAA Museum, RNAS Yeovilton, Somerset
	XP984	Hawker P.1127	Brooklands Museum, Weybridge, Surrey
	XR220	BAC TSR2 (7933M)	RAF Museum, Cosford, Shropshire
	XR222	BAC TSR2	IWM Duxford, Cambs
	XR232	Sud Alouette AH2 (F-WEIP)	Army Flying Museum, Middle Wallop, Hants
	XR238	Auster AOP9 (frame)	South Yorkshire Aircraft Museum, Doncaster, S. Yorks (restoration)
	XR239	Auster AOP9	Privately owned, Deddington, Oxon
	XR240	Auster AOP9 (G-BDFH)	Privately owned, Eggesford, Devon
	XR241	Auster AOP9 (G-AXRR)	Privately owned, Eggesford, Devon
	XR244	Auster AOP9 (G-CICR)	Historic Army Aircraft Flight, Middle Wallop, Hants
	XR246	Auster AOP9 (7862M/G-AZBU)	Privately owned, Gaddesby, Leics
	XR267	Auster AOP9 (G-BJXR)	Privately owned, Tatenhill, Staffs
	XR271	Auster AOP9	Privately owned, stored Netheravon, Wilts
	XR346	Northrop Shelduck D1 (comp XW578)	Bournemouth Aviation Museum, Dorset
	XR371	SC5 Belfast C1	RAF Museum, Cosford, Shropshire
	XR379	Sud Alouette AH2 (G-ONTY)	Privately owned, Great Oakley, Notts
	XR447	Northrop Shelduck D1 (wreck)	Morayvia, Kinloss, Moray, Scotland
	XR453	WS55 Whirlwind HAR10 (8873M) [A]	RAF Odiham, Hants, on gate
	XR485	WS55 Whirlwind HAR10 [Q]	Norfolk & Suffolk Avn Museum, Flixton, Suffolk
	XR486	WS55 Whirlwind HCC12 (8727M/G-RWWW)	The Helicopter Museum, Weston-super-Mare, Somerset
	XR498	WS58 Wessex HC2 (9342M)	DSAE Cosford, Shropshire, on display
	XR502	WS58 Wessex HC2 (G-CCUP/N486KA) [Z]	Privately owned, Stonegate, E. Sussex
	XR506	WS58 Wessex HC2 (9343M) [V]	Privately owned, Corley Moor, Warks
	XR516	WS58 Wessex HC2 (9319M) [V]	RAF Shawbury, Shropshire, on display
	XR517	WS58 Wessex HC2 [N]	Ulster Aviation Society, Long Kesh, Co. Antrim, NI
	XR523	WS58 Wessex HC2 [M]	MOD Pembrey Sands Air Weapons Range, GI use
	XR525	WS58 Wessex HC2 [G]	RAF Museum, Cosford, Shropshire
	XR526	WS58 Wessex HC2 (8147M)	The Helicopter Museum, stored Weston-super-Mare, Somerset

Serial	Type (code/other identity)	Owner/operator, location or fate	Notes
XR528	WS58 Wessex HC2	Morayvia, Kinloss, Moray, Scotland	
XR529	WS58 Wessex HC2 (9268M) [E]	Crumlin Road Gaol Experience, Belfast, NI	
XR534	HS Gnat T1 (8578M) [65]	Newark Air Museum, Winthorpe, Notts	
XR537	HS Gnat T1 (8642M/G-NATY)	Privately owned, St Athan, Glamorgan, Wales	
XR538	HS Gnat T1 (8621M/G-RORI) [01]	Privately owned, St Athan, Glamorgan, Wales	
XR540	HS Gnat T1 (XP502/8576M) [2]	Privately owned, Cotswold Airport, Glos	
XR571	HS Gnat T1 (8493M)	Tangmere Military Aircraft Museum, W. Sussex	
XR574	HS Gnat T1 (8631M) [72]	Trenchard Museum, RAF Halton, Bucks	
XR595	WS Scout AH1 (G-BWHU) [M]	Privately owned, Southam, Warks	
XR601	WS Scout AH1	Privately owned, current location unknown	
XR627	WS Scout AH1 [X]	Privately owned, Storwood, E. Yorks	
XR628	WS Scout AH1	Privately owned, Ipswich, Suffolk	
XR629	WS Scout AH1 (fuselage)	Privately owned, Ipswich, Suffolk	
XR635	WS Scout AH1	Midland Air Museum, Coventry, Warks	
XR650	Hunting Jet Provost T4 (8459M) [28]	Boscombe Down Aviation Collection, Old Sarum, Wilts	
XR654	Hunting Jet Provost T4 <ff>	Privately owned, Chester, Cheshire	
XR658	Hunting Jet Provost T4 (8192M)	RAF Manston History Museum, Kent	
XR662	Hunting Jet Provost T4 (8410M) [25]	Privately owned, Gilberdyke, E Yorks	
XR673	Hunting Jet Provost T4 (G-BXLO/9032M) [L]	Privately owned, Gamston, Notts	
XR681	Hunting Jet Provost T4 (8588M) <ff>	Robertsbridge Aviation Society, Mayfield, E, Sussex	
XR700	Hunting Jet Provost T4 (8589M) <ff>	No 1137 Sqn ATC, Long Kesh, Co. Antrim, NI	
XR713	BAC Lightning F3 (8935M) [C]	Preserved Bruntingthorpe, Leics	
	(wears XR718 on starboard side)		
XR718	BAC Lightning F6 (8932M)	Privately owned, Over Dinsdale, N. Yorks	
XR724	BAC Lightning F6 (G-BTSY)	The Lightning Association, Binbrook, Lincs	
XR725	BAC Lightning F6 [BA]	Privately owned, Binbrook, Lincs	
XR726	BAC Lightning F6 <ff>	Privately owned, Harrogate, N. Yorks	
XR728	BAC Lightning F6 [JS]	Currently not known (ex-LPG, Bruntingthorpe, Leics)	
XR747	BAC Lightning F6 <ff>	No 20 Sqn ATC, Bideford, Devon	
XR749	BAC Lightning F3 (8934M) [DA]	Privately owned, Peterhead, Aberdeenshire, Scotland	
XR751	BAC Lightning F3 <ff>	Privately owned, Thorpe Wood, N. Yorks	
XR753	BAC Lightning F6 (8969M) [XI]	RAF Coningsby, Lincs, on display	
XR753	BAC Lightning F53 (ZF578) [A]	Tangmere Military Aviation Museum, W. Sussex	
XR754	BAC Lightning F6 (8972M) <ff>	Privately owned, Upwood, Cambs	
XR755	BAC Lightning F6 [BN]	Privately owned, Callington, Cornwall	
XR757	BAC Lightning F6 <ff>	Newark Air Museum, Winthorpe, Notts	
XR759	BAC Lightning F6 <ff>	Privately owned, North Weald, Essex	
XR770	BAC Lightning F6 [AA]	RAF Manston History Museum, Kent	
XR771	BAC Lightning F6 [BF]	Midland Air Museum, Coventry, Warks	
XR808	BAC VC10 C1K [R] $	RAF Museum, Cosford, Shropshire	
XR810	BAC VC10 C1K <ff>	Privately owned, Crondall, Hants	
XR898	Northrop Shelduck D1 (XT005/BAPC.365)	Boscombe Down Aviation Collection, Old Sarum, Wilts	
XR944	Wallis WA116 (G-ATTB)	Privately owned, Old Buckenham, Norfolk	
XR977	HS Gnat T1 (8640M)	RAF Museum, Hendon, Gtr London	
XR992	HS Gnat T1 (8624M/XS102/G-MOUR)	Heritage Aircraft Trust, North Weald, Essex	
XR993	HS Gnat T1 (8620M/XP534/G-BVPP)	South Wales Aviation Museum, St Athan, Glamorgan, Wales	
XS100	HS Gnat T1 (8561M) <ff>	Privately owned, stored Wimbledon, Gtr London	
XS100	HS Gnat T1 (8561M) <rf>	Privately owned, North Weald, Essex	
XS104	HS Gnat T1 (8604M/G-FRCE)	Privately owned, North Weald, Essex	
XS149	WS58 Wessex HAS3 (661/GL]	Privately owned, Hampshire	
XS176	Hunting Jet Provost T4 (8514M) <ff>	Morayvia, Kinloss, Moray, Scotland	
XS177	Hunting Jet Provost T4 (9044M) [N]	Privately owned, Westbury, Wilts	
XS179	Hunting Jet Provost T4 (8237M) [20]	Secret Nuclear Bunker, Hack Green, Cheshire	
XS180	Hunting Jet Provost T4 (8238M/8338M) [21]	MOD JARTS, Boscombe Down, Wilts	
XS181	Hunting Jet Provost T4 (9033M) <ff>	Privately owned, Lincolnshire area	
XS183	Hunting Jet Provost T4 <ff>	Privately owned, Plymouth, Devon	
XS186	Hunting Jet Provost T4 (8408M) [M]	Stored Fishlake, S. Yorks	
XS209	Hunting Jet Provost T4 (8409M)	Solway Aviation Society, Carlisle, Cumbria	
XS216	Hunting Jet Provost T4 <ff>	South Yorkshire Aircraft Museum, Doncaster, S. Yorks	
XS218	Hunting Jet Provost T4 (8508M) <ff>	No 447 Sqn ATC, Henley-on-Thames, Berks	

Notes	Serial	Type (code/other identity)	Owner/operator, location or fate
	XS228	Hunting Jet Provost T52 (104)	Privately owned, St. Athan, Glamorgan, Wales
	XS231	BAC Jet Provost T5 (G-ATAJ) <ff>	Boscombe Down Aviation Collection, Old Sarum, Wilts
	XS235	DH106 Comet 4C (G-CPDA)	Currently not known (ex-Bruntingthorpe, Leics)
	XS238	Auster AOP9 (TAD 200)	Newark Air Museum, Winthorpe, Notts
	XS416	BAC Lightning T5	Privately owned, Binbrook, Lincs
	XS417	BAC Lightning T5 [DZ]	Newark Air Museum, Winthorpe, Notts
	XS420	BAC Lightning T5	Privately owned, FAST, Farnborough, Hants
	XS421	BAC Lightning T5 <ff>	Privately owned, Coltishall, Norfolk
	XS456	BAC Lightning T5 [DX]	Skegness Water Leisure Park, Lincs
	XS457	BAC Lightning T5 <ff>	Privately owned, Binbrook, Lincs
	XS458	BAC Lightning T5 [T]	T5 Projects, Cranfield, Beds
	XS459	BAC Lightning T5 [AW]	Privately owned, Binbrook, Lincs
	XS481	WS58 Wessex HU5 [VY]	South Yorkshire Aircraft Museum, Doncaster, S. Yorks
	XS482	WS58 Wessex HU5	RAF Manston History Museum, Kent
	XS486	WS58 Wessex HU5 (9272M) [524/CU,F]	The Helicopter Museum, stored Weston-super-Mare, Somerset
	XS488	WS58 Wessex HU5 (9056M) [F]	Submerged, Cromhall Diving Centre, Glos
	XS489	WS58 Wessex HU5 [R]	Privately owned, Westerham, Kent
	XS493	WS58 Wessex HU5	StandardAero, stored Fleetlands, Hants
	XS507	WS58 Wessex HU5	South Wales Aviation Museum, St Athan, Glamorgan, Wales
	XS508	WS58 Wessex HU5	FAA Museum, stored Cobham Hall, RNAS Yeovilton, Somerset
	XS510	WS58 Wessex HU5 [626/PO]	Moravyia, stored Spey Bay, Moray, Scotland
	XS511	WS58 Wessex HU5 [M]	Tangmere Military Aircraft Museum, W. Sussex
	XS513	WS58 Wessex HU5	RNAS Yeovilton Fire Section, Somerset
	XS515	WS58 Wessex HU5 [N]	Army, Keogh Barracks, Aldershot, instructional use
	XS516	WS58 Wessex HU5 [Q]	Privately owned, Redruth, Cornwall
	XS522	WS58 Wessex HU5 [ZL]	Blackball Paintball, Truro, Cornwall
	XS527	WS Wasp HAS1	FAA Museum, stored Cobham Hall, RNAS Yeovilton, Somerset
	XS529	WS Wasp HAS1	Privately owned, Redruth, Cornwall
	XS539	WS Wasp HAS1 [435]	StandardAero, Fleetlands, Hants on display
	XS567	WS Wasp HAS1 [434/E]	IWM Duxford, Cambs
	XS568	WS Wasp HAS1 (A2715) [441]	DSAE, stored *HMS Sultan*, Gosport, Hants
	XS574	Northrop Shelduck D1 <R>	FAA Museum, stored Cobham Hall, RNAS Yeovilton, Somerset
	XS576	DH110 Sea Vixen FAW2 [125/E]	IWM Duxford, Cambs
	XS587	DH110 Sea Vixen FAW(TT)2 (8828M/G-VIXN)	Gatwick Aviation Museum, Charlwood, Surrey
	XS590	DH110 Sea Vixen FAW2 [131/E]	FAA Museum, RNAS Yeovilton, Somerset
	XS639	HS Andover E3A (9241M)	RAF Museum, Cosford, Shropshire
	XS641	HS Andover C1PR (9198M) (fuselage)	Privately owned, Sandbach, Cheshire
	XS643	HS Andover E3A (9278M) <ff>	Privately owned, Bramcote, Notts
	XS646	HS Andover C1(mod) (fuselage)	MOD JARTS, Boscombe Down, Wilts
	XS651	Slingsby T45 Swallow TX1 (BGA1211) [BYB]	Privately owned, Lasham, Hants
	XS652	Slingsby T45 Swallow TX1 (BGA1107)	Privately owned, Chipping, Lancs
	XS674	WS58 Wessex HC2 [R]	Privately owned, Manston, Kent
	XS694	HS Kestrel FGA1 (64-18268)	Wings Museum, stored Balcombe, W. Sussex
	XS695	HS Kestrel FGA1 [5]	RAF Museum, Cosford, Shropshire
	XS709	HS125 Dominie T1 [M]	RAF Museum, Cosford, Shropshire
	XS710	HS125 Dominie T1 (9259M) [O]	RAF Cranwell Fire Section, Lincs
	XS713	HS125 Dominie T1 [C]	Moravyia, Kinloss, Moray, Scotland
	XS726	HS125 Dominie T1 (9273M) [T]	Newark Air Museum, Winthorpe, Notts
	XS727	HS125 Dominie T1 [D]	RAF Cranwell, Lincs, on display
	XS731	HS125 Dominie T1 (N19XY) (fuselage)	Privately owned, Marlborough, Wilts
	XS734	HS125 Dominie T1 (9260M) [N]	Privately owned, location unknown
	XS735	HS125 Dominie T1 (9264M) [R]	South Yorkshire Aircraft Museum, Doncaster, S. Yorks
	XS736	HS125 Dominie T1 [S]	MOD Winterbourne Gunner, Wilts
	XS743	Beagle B206Z	Boscombe Down Aviation Collection, Old Sarum, Wilts
	XS790	HS748 Andover CC2 <ff>	Boscombe Down Aviation Collection, Old Sarum, Wilts
	XS859	Slingsby T45 Swallow TX1 (BGA1136) [859]	Privately owned, stored Felthorpe, Norfolk
	XS863	WS58 Wessex HAS1 [304/R]	IWM Duxford, Cambs

Serial	Type (code/other identity)	Owner/operator, location or fate	Notes
XS865	WS58 Wessex HAS1 (A2694)	Privately owned, Ballygowan, NI	
XS885	WS58 Wessex HAS1 [512/DD]	Delta Force Paintball, Burnley, Lancs	
XS886	WS58 Wessex HAS1 [527/CU]	Privately owned, Ditchling, E. Sussex	
XS887	WS58 Wessex HAS1 [403/FI]	Thorpe Camp Visitor Centre, Tattershall Thorpe, Lincs	
XS898	BAC Lightning F6 <ff>	Privately owned, Lavendon, Bucks	
XS899	BAC Lightning F6 <ff>	Privately owned, Binbrook, Lincs	
XS903	BAC Lightning F6 [BA]	Yorkshire Air Museum, Elvington, N. Yorks	
XS904	BAC Lightning F6 [BQ]	Currently not known (ex-LPG, Bruntingthorpe, Leics)	
XS919	BAC Lightning F6	Privately owned, Wiltshire	
XS921	BAC Lightning F6 <R> (BAPC.357) [BA]	BAE Systems, Samlesbury, Lancs, on display	
XS922	BAC Lightning F6 (8973M) <ff>	Lakes Lightnings, Spark Bridge, Cumbria	
XS923	BAC Lightning F6 <ff>	Privately owned, Welshpool, Powys, Wales	
XS925	BAC Lightning F6 (8961M) [BA]	RAF Museum, Hendon, Gtr London	
XS928	BAC Lightning F6 [AD]	BAE Systems Warton, Lancs, on display	
XS932	BAC Lightning F6 <ff>	Privately owned, Walcott, Lincs	
XS933	BAC Lightning F6 <ff>	Privately owned, Binbrook, Lincs	
XS933	BAC Lightning F53 (ZF594) [BE]	North-East Land, Sea & Air Museums, Usworth, T&W	
XS935	BAC Lightning F53 (53-672/204/ZF580/XR768) [AK]	Privately owned, Binbrook, Lincs	
XS936	BAC Lightning F6	Castle Motors, Liskeard, Cornwall	
XT108	Agusta-Bell 47G-3 Sioux AH1 [U]	Army Flying Museum, Middle Wallop, Hants	
XT123	WS Sioux AH1 (XT827) [D]	Repainted as XT231	
XT131	Agusta-Bell 47G-3 Sioux AH1 (G-CICN) [B]	Historic Army Aircraft Flight, Middle Wallop, Hants	
XT140	Agusta-Bell 47G-3 Sioux AH1	Privately owned, North Weald, Essex (restoration)	
XT147	Agusta-Bell 47G-3 Sioux AH1 (frame only)	Privately owned, Hooton Park, Cheshire	
XT148	Agusta-Bell 47G-3 Sioux AH1	Dumfries & Galloway Avn Mus, Dumfries, Scotland	
XT150	Agusta-Bell 47G-3 Sioux AH1 (7883M) [R]	South Yorkshire Aircraft Museum, Doncaster, S. Yorks (stored)	
XT151	WS Sioux AH1	Army Flying Museum, stored Middle Wallop, Hants	
XT176	WS Sioux AH1 [U]	FAA Museum, stored Cobham Hall, RNAS Yeovilton, Somerset	
XT190	WS Sioux AH1	The Helicopter Museum, Weston-super-Mare, Somerset	
XT200	WS Sioux AH1 [F]	Newark Air Museum, Winthorpe, Notts	
XT208	WS Sioux AH1 (wreck)	Privately owned, Fivemiletown, Co Tyrone, NI	
XT231	WS Sioux AH1 (XT827) [D]	AAC Middle Wallop, Hants, at main gate	
XT236	WS Sioux AH1 (frame only)	Dumfries & Galloway Avn Mus, Dumfries, Scotland	
XT242	WS Sioux AH1 (comp XW179) [12]	South Yorkshire Aircraft Museum, Doncaster, S. Yorks	
XT257	WS58 Wessex HAS3 (8719M)	Bournemouth Aviation Museum, Dorset	
XT277	HS Buccaneer S2A (8853M) <ff>	Privately owned, Welshpool, Powys, Wales	
XT280	HS Buccaneer S2A <ff>	Dumfries & Galloway Avn Mus, Dumfries, Scotland	
XT284	HS Buccaneer S2A (8855M) <ff>	Privately owned, Felixstowe, Suffolk	
XT288	HS Buccaneer S2B (9134M)	National Museum of Flight, E. Fortune, Scotland	
XT420	WS Wasp HAS1 (G-CBUI) [422]	Fly Navy Heritage Trust, RNAS Yeovilton, Somerset	
XT427	WS Wasp HAS1 [606]	FAA Museum, stored Cobham Hall, RNAS Yeovilton, Somerset	
XT431	WS Wasp HAS1 (comp XS463) [462]	Bournemouth Aviation Museum, Dorset	
XT434	WS Wasp HAS1 (G-CGGK) [455]	Fly Navy Heritage Trust, RNAS Yeovilton, Somerset	
XT435	WS Wasp HAS1 (NZ3907/G-RIMM) [426/AR]	Privately owned, North Weald, Essex	
XT437	WS Wasp HAS1 [423]	Boscombe Down Aviation Collection, Old Sarum, Wilts	
XT439	WS Wasp HAS1 [605]	Privately owned, Hemel Hempstead, Herts	
XT443	WS Wasp HAS1 [422/AU]	The Helicopter Museum, Weston-super-Mare, Somerset	
XT453	WS58 Wessex HU5 (A2756) [B/PO]	DSAE, stored HMS Sultan, Gosport, Hants	
XT455	WS58 Wessex HU5 (A2654) [U]	Mayhem Paintball, Abridge, Essex	
XT456	WS58 Wessex HU5 (8941M) [XZ]	Belfast Airport Fire Section, NI	
XT458	WS58 Wessex HU5 (A2768) [P/VL]	RNAS Yeovilton, Somerset, on display	
XT466	WS58 Wessex HU5 (A2617/8921M) [528/CU]	Morayvia, Kinloss, Moray, Scotland	
XT467	WS58 Wessex HU5 (8922M) [BF]	Gunsmoke Paintball, Wickford, Essex	
XT469	WS58 Wessex HU5 (8920M)	Privately owned, Clatterford, Isle of Wight	
XT472	WS58 Wessex HU5 [XC]	The Helicopter Museum, stored Weston-super-Mare, Somerset	
XT480	WS58 Wessex HU5 [468/RG]	Rednal Paintball, Shropshire	
XT482	WS58 Wessex HU5 [ZM/VL]	FAA Museum, RNAS Yeovilton, Somerset	

Notes	Serial	Type (code/other identity)	Owner/operator, location or fate
	XT486	WS58 Wessex HU5 (8919M)	Dumfries & Galloway Avn Mus, Dumfries, Scotland
	XT493	SARO SR.N6 Winchester	Hovercraft Museum, Solent Airport, Hants
	XT550	WS Sioux AH1 [D]	Currently not known
	XT575	Vickers Viscount 837 <ff>	Brooklands Museum, Weybridge, Surrey
	XT581	Northrop Shelduck D1	IWM Duxford, Cambs
	XT581	Northrop Shelduck D1 (BAPC.501)	Muckleburgh Collection, Weybourne, Norfolk
	XT583	Northrop Shelduck D1	Privately owned, stored Netheravon, Wilts
	XT596	McD F-4K Phantom FG1	FAA Museum, RNAS Yeovilton, Somerset
	XT597	McD F-4K Phantom FG1	Privately owned, Cotswold Airport, Glos
	XT601	WS58 Wessex HC2 (9277M) (composite)	RAF Odiham, Hants, BDRT
	XT604	WS58 Wessex HC2	East Midlands Airport Aeropark, Leics
	XT617	WS Scout AH1	Wattisham Station Heritage Museum, Suffolk
	XT621	WS Scout AH1	Privately owned, Colsterworth, Lincs
	XT623	WS Scout AH1	DSAE SAAE, Lyneham, Wilts
	XT626	WS Scout AH1 (G-CIBW) [Q]	Historic Army Aircraft Flight, Middle Wallop, Hants
	XT630	WS Scout AH1 (G-BXRL) [X]	Privately owned, Rough Close, Staffs
	XT631	WS Scout AH1 [D]	Privately owned, Ipswich
	XT633	WS Scout AH1	Bridgwater & Taunton College, Bridgwater, GI use
	XT638	WS Scout AH1 [N]	AAC Middle Wallop, Hants, at main gate
	XT640	WS Scout AH1	Privately owned, South Clifton, Notts
	XT643	WS Scout AH1	STANTA, East Wretham, Norfolk (wreck)
	XT653	Slingsby T45 Swallow TX1 (BGA3469)	Privately owned, Keevil, Wilts
	XT672	WS58 Wessex HC2 [WE]	RAF Stafford, Staffs, on display
	XT681	WS58 Wessex HC2 (9279M) [U] <ff>	Privately owned, stored Oxon
	XT761	WS58 Wessex HU5 (G-WSEX)	Privately owned, Chard, Somerset
	XT762	WS58 Wessex HU5	Hamburger Hill Paintball, Marksbury, Somerset
	XT765	WS58 Wessex HU5 [J]	FAA Museum, RNAS Yeovilton, Somerset
	XT769	WS58 Wessex HU5 [823]	FAA Museum, RNAS Yeovilton, Somerset
	XT771	WS58 Wessex HU5 [620/PO]	Privately owned, stored Chard, Somerset
	XT773	WS58 Wessex HU5 (9123M)	Morayvia, stored Spey Bay, Moray, Scotland
	XT778	WS Wasp HAS1 [430]	FAA Museum, stored Cobham Hall, RNAS Yeovilton, Somerset
	XT780	WS Wasp HAS1 [636]	Fly Navy Heritage Trust, RNAS Yeovilton, Somerset
	XT787	WS Wasp HAS1 (NZ3905/G-KAXT)	Fly Navy Heritage Trust, RNAS Yeovilton, Somerset
	XT788	WS Wasp HAS1 (G-BMIR) [474]	Privately owned, Storwood, E. Yorks
	XT793	WS Wasp HAS1 (G-BZPP) <ff>	South Yorkshire Aircraft Museum, Doncaster, S. Yorks
	XT863	McD F-4K Phantom FG1 <ff>	Privately owned, Northwood, IOW
	XT864	McD F-4K Phantom FG1 (8998M/*XT684*) [007/R]	Ulster Aviation Society, Long Kesh, Co. Antrim, NI
	XT891	McD F-4M Phantom FGR2 (9136M)	RAF Coningsby, Lincs, at main gate
	XT895	McD F-4M Phantom FGR2 <ff> (8171M)	Privately owned, Newburgh, Lancs
	XT903	McD F-4M Phantom FGR2 <ff>	RAF Museum, stored Cosford, Shropshire
	XT905	McD F-4M Phantom FGR2 (9286M) [P]	Privately owned, Cotswold Airport, Glos
	XT907	McD F-4M Phantom FGR2 (9151M) <ff>	Privately owned, Welshpool area, Powys, Wales
	XT914	McD F-4M Phantom FGR2 (9269M) [Z]	Wattisham Station Heritage Museum, Suffolk
	XV104	BAC VC10 C1K <ff>	South Wales Aviation Museum, stored St Athan, Glamorgan, Wales
	XV106	BAC VC10 C1K <ff>	Avro Heritage Museum, Woodford, Cheshire
	XV108	BAC VC10 C1K <ff>	East Midlands Airport Aeropark, Leics
	XV109	BAC VC10 C1K <ff>	South Wales Aviation Museum, stored St Athan, Glamorgan, Wales
	XV122	WS Scout AH1 [D]	Defence Academy of the UK, Shrivenham, Oxon
	XV123	WS Scout AH1 [V]	Vanguard Self Storage, Greenford, Gtr London
	XV124	WS Scout AH1 [W]	Under restoration, Florida, USA
	XV126	WS Scout AH1 (G-SCTA) [50K]	Privately owned, Whepstead, Suffolk
	XV127	WS Scout AH1	Army Flying Museum, Middle Wallop, Hants
	XV130	WS Scout AH1 (G-BWJW) [R]	Royal Engineers Museum, Chatham, Kent
	XV136	WS Scout AH1 [X]	Ulster Aviation Society, Long Kesh, Co. Antrim, NI
	XV137	WS Scout AH1 (G-CRUM)	Privately owned, Chiseldon, Wilts
	XV138	WS Scout AH1 (G-SASM) [S]	Privately owned, North Weald, Essex
	XV139	WS Scout AH1 (comp XP886)	South Yorkshire Aircraft Museum, Doncaster, S. Yorks
	XV141	WS Scout AH1	REME Museum, Lyneham, Wilts

Serial	Type (code/other identity)	Owner/operator, location or fate	Notes
XV148	HS Nimrod MR1(mod) <ff>	Boscombe Down Aviation Collection, Old Sarum, Wilts	
XV161	HS Buccaneer S2B (9117M) <ff>	Currently not known	
XV165	HS Buccaneer S2B <ff>	Privately owned, Ashford, Kent	
XV168	HS Buccaneer S2B [AF]	Yorkshire Air Museum, Elvington, N. Yorks	
XV201	Lockheed C-130K Hercules C1K <ff>	Marshall Aerospace, Cambridge, Cambs	
XV202	Lockheed C-130K Hercules C3 [202]	RAF Museum, Cosford, Shropshire	
XV208	Lockheed C-130K Hercules W2 <ff>	Marshall Aerospace, stored Cambridge, Cambs	
XV226	HS Nimrod MR2	Location not known (ex-preserved Bruntingthorpe, Leics)	
XV229	HS Nimrod MR2 [29] <ff>	RAF Manston History Museum, Kent	
XV231	HS Nimrod MR2 [31]	Aviation Viewing Park, Manchester, Gtr Manchester	
XV232	HS Nimrod MR2 [32]	Privately owned, Coventry, Warks	
XV235	HS Nimrod MR2 [35] <ff>	Avro Heritage Museum, Woodford, Cheshire	
XV240	HS Nimrod MR2 [40] <ff>	Morayvia, Kinloss, Moray, Scotland	
XV241	HS Nimrod MR2 [41] <ff>	National Museum of Flight, E. Fortune, Scotland	
XV244	HS Nimrod MR2 [44]	Morayvia, Kinloss Barracks, Moray, Scotland	
XV249	HS Nimrod R1 $	RAF Museum, Cosford, Shropshire	
XV250	HS Nimrod MR2 [50]	Yorkshire Air Museum, Elvington, N. Yorks	
XV252	HS Nimrod MR2 [52] <ff>	Privately owned, Cullen, Moray, Scotland	
XV254	HS Nimrod MR2 [54] <ff>	South Wales Aviation Museum, St Athan, Glamorgan, Wales	
XV255	HS Nimrod MR2 [55]	City of Norwich Aviation Museum, Norfolk	
XV259	BAe Nimrod AEW3 <ff>	Privately owned, Wales	
XV268	DHC2 Beaver AL1 (G-BVER)	Privately owned, Cumbernauld, Scotland	
XV277	HS P.1127(RAF)	National Museum of Flight, E. Fortune, Scotland	
XV279	HS P.1127(RAF) (8566M)	Harrier Heritage Centre, RAF Wittering, Cambs	
XV280	HS P.1127(RAF) <ff>	South Yorkshire Aviation Museum, Doncaster, S. Yorks	
XV281	HS P.1127(RAF) (BAPC 484)	South Yorkshire Aviation Museum, Doncaster, S. Yorks	
XV304	Lockheed C-130K Hercules C3A	RAF JADTEU, Brize Norton, Oxon, instructional use	
XV328	BAC Lightning T5 <ff>	Currently not known (ex Bruntingthorpe)	
XV333	HS Buccaneer S2B [234/H]	FAA Museum, stored Cobham Hall, RNAS Yeovilton, Somerset	
XV344	HS Buccaneer S2C	QinetiQ Farnborough, Hants, on display	
XV350	HS Buccaneer S2B	East Midlands Airport Aeropark, Leics	
XV352	HS Buccaneer S2B <ff>	RAF Manston History Museum, Kent	
XV359	HS Buccaneer S2B [035/R]	Privately owned, Topsham, Devon	
XV361	HS Buccaneer S2B	Ulster Aviation Society, Long Kesh, Co. Antrim, NI	
XV370	Sikorsky SH-3D (A2682) [260]	DSAE RNAESS, HMS Sultan, Gosport, Hants	
XV371	WS61 Sea King HAS1(DB) [261/DD]	Privately owned, Bristol, Glos	
XV372	WS61 Sea King HAS1	MOD Pembrey Sands Air Weapons Range, Wales, GI use	
XV383	Northrop MQM-57A/3 (fuselage)	Privately owned, Wimborne, Dorset (stored)	
XV401	McD F-4M Phantom FGR2 [I]	Privately owned, Bentwaters, Suffolk	
XV402	McD F-4M Phantom FGR2 <ff>	Privately owned, Kent	
XV406	McD F-4M Phantom FGR2 (9098M) [D]	Solway Aviation Society, Carlisle, Cumbria	
XV408	McD F-4M Phantom FGR2 (9165M) [L]	Tangmere Military Aviation Museum, W. Sussex	
XV415	McD F-4M Phantom FGR2 (9163M) [E]	RAF Boulmer, Northumberland, on display	
XV419	McD F-4M Phantom FGR2 <ff>	Privately owned, Wales	
XV424	McD F-4M Phantom FGR2 (9152M) [I]	RAF Museum, Hendon, Gtr London	
XV426	McD F-4M Phantom FGR2 <ff>	City of Norwich Aviation Museum, Norfolk	
XV460	McD F-4M Phantom FGR2 <ff>	Privately owned, Bentwaters, Suffolk	
XV474	McD F-4M Phantom FGR2 [T]	The Old Flying Machine Company, Duxford, Cambs	
XV490	McD F-4M Phantom FGR2 [R] <ff>	Newark Air Museum, Winthorpe, Notts	
XV497	McD F-4M Phantom FGR2 (9295M) [D]	Norfolk & Suffolk Avn Museum, Flixton, Suffolk	
XV499	McD F-4M Phantom FGR2 <ff>	South Wales Aviation Museum, St Athan, Glamorgan, Wales	
XV581	McD F-4K Phantom FG1 (9070M) <ff>	Privately owned, Syerston, Notts	
XV582	McD F-4K Phantom FG1 (9066M) [M]	South Wales Aviation Museum, St Athan, Glamorgan, Wales	
XV586	McD F-4K Phantom FG1 (9067M) [010-R]	Morayvia, Kinloss, Moray, Scotland	
XV591	McD F-4K Phantom FG1 [013] <ff>	RAF Museum, Cosford, Shropshire	
XV631	WS Wasp HAS1 (fuselage)	Farnborough Air Sciences Trust, stored Farnborough	
XV642	WS61 Sea King HAS2A (A2614) [259]	DSAE, stored HMS Sultan, Gosport, Hants	
XV643	WS61 Sea King HAS6 [262]	DSAE, stored HMS Sultan, Gosport, Hants	

Notes	Serial	Type (code/other identity)	Owner/operator, location or fate
	XV647	WS61 Sea King HU5 (G-CMFN) [28/GJ]	Privately owned, Chard, Somerset
	XV648	WS61 Sea King HU5	Privately owned, Acharacle, Argyll, Scotland
	XV649	WS61 Sea King ASaC7 [180]	DSAE, stored HMS Sultan, Gosport, Hants
	XV651	WS61 Sea King HU5	Current location unknown
	XV653	WS61 Sea King HAS6 (9326M) [63/CU]	DSAE, stored HMS Sultan, Gosport, Hants
	XV654	WS61 Sea King HAS6 [705/DD]	Privately owned, Bristol Events Site, Glos
	XV655	WS61 Sea King HAS6 [270/N]	DSAE RNAESS, HMS Sultan, Gosport, Hants
	XV656	WS61 Sea King ASaC7 [185]	HeliOperations Ltd, stored Somerton, Somerset
	XV657	WS61 Sea King HAS5 (ZA135) [32/DD]	RN, Predannack Fire School, Cornwall
	XV659	WS61 Sea King HAS6 (9324M) [62/CU]	DSAE, stored HMS Sultan, Gosport, Hants
	XV660	WS61 Sea King HAS6 [269/N]	DSAE RNAESS, HMS Sultan, Gosport, Hants
	XV661	WS61 Sea King HU5 [26]	Current location unknown
	XV663	WS61 Sea King HAS6 [18]	FAA Museum, RNAS Yeovilton, Somerset
	XV664	WS61 Sea King ASaC7 [190]	HeliOperations Ltd, stored Somerton, Somerset
	XV665	WS61 Sea King HAS6 [507/CU]	DSAE RNAESS, HMS Sultan, Gosport, Hants
	XV666	WS61 Sea King HU5	HeliOperations Ltd, Portland, Dorset
	XV670	WS61 Sea King HU5 [17]	HeliOperations Ltd, stored Somerton, Somerset
	XV671	WS61 Sea King ASaC7 [183/CU]	HeliOperations Ltd, stored Somerton, Somerset
	XV672	WS61 Sea King ASaC7 [187]	DSAE, stored HMS Sultan, Gosport, Hants
	XV673	WS61 Sea King HU5 [827/CU]	RN Culdrose, Cornwall, on display
	XV674	WS61 Sea King HAS6	Privately owned, Horsham, W. Sussex
	XV675	WS61 Sea King HAS6 [701/PW]	DSAE RNAESS, HMS Sultan, Gosport, Hants
	XV676	WS61 Sea King HC6 [ZE]	DSAE RNAESS, HMS Sultan, Gosport, Hants
	XV677	WS61 Sea King HAS6 [269]	South Yorkshire Aircraft Museum, Doncaster, S. Yorks
	XV696	WS61 Sea King HAS6 [267/L]	SFDO, RNAS Culdrose, Cornwall
	XV697	WS61 Sea King ASaC7 [181/CU]	HeliOperations Ltd, stored Somerton, Somerset
	XV699	WS61 Sea King HU5 [823]	DSAE RNAESS, HMS Sultan, Gosport, Hants
	XV700	WS61 Sea King HC6 [ZC]	DSAE RNAESS, stored HMS Sultan, Gosport, Hants
	XV701	WS61 Sea King HAS6 [268/N,64]	DSAE RNAESS, HMS Sultan, Gosport, Hants
	XV703	WS61 Sea King HC6 [ZD]	DSAE RNAESS, stored HMS Sultan, Gosport, Hants
	XV705	WS61 Sea King HU5 [29]	Privately owned, Stockie Muir, Stirling, Scotland
	XV706	WS61 Sea King HAS6 (9344M) [017/L]	DSAE RNAESS, stored HMS Sultan, Gosport, Hants
	XV707	WS61 Sea King ASaC7 [184]	DSAE RNAESS, stored HMS Sultan, Gosport, Hants
	XV708	WS61 Sea King HAS6 [501/CU]	DSAE RNAESS, stored HMS Sultan, Gosport, Hants
	XV711	WS61 Sea King HAS6 [15/CW]	DSAE, stored HMS Sultan, Gosport, Hants
	XV712	WS61 Sea King HAS6 [66]	IWM Duxford, Cambs
	XV713	WS61 Sea King HAS6 (A2646) [018/L]	DSAE RNAESS, HMS Sultan, Gosport, Hants
	XV714	WS61 Sea King ASaC7 [188]	HeliOperations Ltd, stored Somerton, Somerset
	XV720	WS58 Wessex HC2 (A2701)	Privately owned, Culham, Oxon
	XV722	WS58 Wessex HC2 (8805M) [WH]	Privately owned, Badgers Mount, Kent
	XV725	WS58 Wessex HC2 [C]	Morayvia, stored Spey Bay, Moray, Scotland
	XV726	WS58 Wessex HC2 [J]	Privately owned, Kettering, Northants
	XV728	WS58 Wessex HC2 [A]	Newark Air Museum, Winthorpe, Notts
	XV731	WS58 Wessex HC2 [Y]	Privately owned, Badgers Mount, Kent
	XV732	WS58 Wessex HCC4	RAF Museum, Hendon, Gtr London
	XV733	WS58 Wessex HCC4	The Helicopter Museum, Weston-super-Mare, Somerset
	XV741	HS Harrier GR3 (A2608)	Brooklands Museum, Weybridge, Surrey
	XV744	HS Harrier GR3 (9167M) [3K]	Tangmere Military Aviation Museum, W. Sussex
	XV748	HS Harrier GR3 [B]	Yorkshire Air Museum, Elvington, N. Yorks
	XV751	HS Harrier GR3 [AU]	Gatwick Aviation Museum, Charlwood, Surrey
	XV752	HS Harrier GR3 (9075M) [B]	South Yorkshire Aircraft Museum, Doncaster, S. Yorks
	XV753	HS Harrier GR3 (9078M)	Privately owned, St Athan, Glamorgan, Wales
	XV759	HS Harrier GR3 [O] <ff>	Privately owned, Hitchin, Herts
	XV760	HS Harrier GR3 <ff>	Solent Sky, Southampton, Hants
	XV779	HS Harrier GR3 (8931M) <ff>	Privately owned, Thorpe Wood, N. Yorks
	XV779	HS Harrier GR3 [AP]	Harrier Heritage Centre, RAF Wittering, Cambs
	XV783	HS Harrier GR3 [N]	Privately owned, Corley Moor, Warks
	XV784	HS Harrier GR3 (8909M) <ff>	Boscombe Down Aviation Collection, Old Sarum, Wilts
	XV786	HS Harrier GR3 [123] <ff>	RNAS Culdrose Fire Section, Cornwall
	XV798	HS Harrier GR1(mod) (BAPC 450)	Rolls Royce Heritage Trust, Hucknall, Derbyshire
	XV806	HS Harrier GR3 <ff>	Privately owned, Gateford, Notts
	XV808	HS Harrier GR3 (9076M/A2687) [08/DD]	Privately owned, Chetton, Shropshire

Serial	Type (code/other identity)	Owner/operator, location or fate	Notes
XV810	HS Harrier GR3 (9038M) <ff>	Privately owned, Walcott, Lincs	
XV814	DH106 Comet 4 (G-APDF) <ff>	Privately owned, Chipping Campden, Glos	
XV864	HS Buccaneer S2B (9234M)	RAF Manston History Museum, Kent	
XV865	HS Buccaneer S2B (9226M)	IWM Duxford, Cambs	
XV867	HS Buccaneer S2B <ff>	Morayvia, Kinloss, Moray, Scotland	
XW175	HS Harrier T4(VAAC)	Privately owned, Thorpe Wood, N. Yorks	
XW198	WS Puma HC1	RAF AM&SU, stored Shawbury, Shropshire	
XW199	WS Puma HC2 [A]	RAF No 28 Sqn/No 33 Sqn, Benson, Oxon	
XW202	WS Puma HC1	Army, Strensall Barracks, York	
XW204	WS Puma HC2 [B]	RAF AM&SU, stored Shawbury, Shropshire	
XW208	WS Puma HC1	Newark Air Museum, Winthorpe, Notts	
XW209	WS Puma HC2	RAF AM&SU, stored Shawbury, Shropshire	
XW210	WS Puma HC1 (comp XW215)	RAF AM&SU, stored Shawbury, Shropshire	
XW212	WS Puma HC2 [D]	RAF P2MF, Benson, Oxon	
XW213	WS Puma HC2 [E]	RAF No 230 Sqn, Seria, Brunei	
XW214	WS Puma HC2 [F]	RAF No 28 Sqn/No 33 Sqn, Benson, Oxon	
XW216	WS Puma HC2 (F-ZWDD) [G]	RAF No 84 Sqn, Akrotiri, Cyprus	
XW217	WS Puma HC2 [H]	RAF AM&SU, stored Shawbury, Shropshire	
XW219	WS Puma HC2	RAF, stored Benson, Oxon	
XW220	WS Puma HC2 [K]	RAF No 28 Sqn/No 33 Sqn, Benson, Oxon	
XW222	WS Puma HC1	Ulster Aviation Society, Long Kesh, Co. Antrim, NI	
XW223	WS Puma HC1	RAF AM&SU, stored Shawbury, Shropshire	
XW224	WS Puma HC2 $	RAF No 28 Sqn/No 33 Sqn, Benson, Oxon	
XW225	WS Puma HC1	Army, Beckingham Training Camp, Lincs	
XW226	WS Puma HC1	RAF AM&SU, stored Shawbury, Shropshire	
XW231	WS Puma HC2 [N]	RAF No 230 Sqn, Seria, Brunei	
XW232	WS Puma HC2 (F-ZWDE) [P]	RAF No 84 Sqn, Akrotiri, Cyprus	
XW235	WS Puma HC2 (F-ZWBI) [Q]	RAF No 230 Sqn, Seria, Brunei	
XW236	WS Puma HC1	Fire Dump, RAF Brize Norton, Oxon	
XW237	WS Puma HC2 [R]	RAF P2MF, Benson, Oxon	
XW241	Sud SA330E Puma	Farnborough Air Sciences Trust, Farnborough, Hants	
XW264	HS Harrier T2 <ff>	Privately owned, Ffostrasol area, Ceredigion, Wales	
XW265	HS Harrier T4A (9258M) <ff>	No 2345 Sqn ATC, RAF Leuchars, Fife, Scotland	
XW267	HS Harrier T4 (9263M)	Privately owned, Bentwaters, Suffolk	
XW268	HS Harrier T4N	City of Norwich Aviation Museum, Norfolk	
XW269	HS Harrier T4 [TB]	Caernarfon Air World, Gwynedd, Wales	
XW270	HS Harrier T4 [T]	Coventry University, Warks, instructional use	
XW276	Aérospatiale SA341 Gazelle (F-ZWRI)	Newark Air Museum, Winthorpe, Notts	
XW283	WS Scout AH1 (G-CIMX) [U]	Privately owned, Whepstead – Oak House, Suffolk	
XW289	BAC Jet Provost T5A (G-BVXT/G-JPVA) [73]	RAF St Athan, Glamorgan, Wales, on display	
XW290	BAC Jet Provost T5A (9199M) [41,MA]	Privately owned, Bruntingthorpe, Leics	
XW293	BAC Jet Provost T5 (G-BWCS) [Z]	Privately owned, stored Bournemouth, Dorset	
XW299	BAC Jet Provost T5A (G-CLJW/9146M) [60,MB]	*Sold to Australia, July 2024*	
XW303	BAC Jet Provost T5A (9119M) [127]	RAF Halton, Bucks	
XW304	BAC Jet Provost T5 (9172M) [MD]	Privately owned, Eye, Suffolk	
XW309	BAC Jet Provost T5 (9179M) [V,ME]	Hartlepool College of Further Education, Co. Durham	
XW315	BAC Jet Provost T5A <ff>	Privately owned, Preston, Lancs	
XW320	BAC Jet Provost T5A (9015M) [71]	Privately owned, St. Athan, Glamorgan, Wales	
XW321	BAC Jet Provost T5A (9154M) [62,MH]	Privately owned, Bentwaters, Suffolk	
XW323	BAC Jet Provost T5A (9166M) [86]	RAF Museum, Hendon, Gtr London	
XW324	BAC Jet Provost T5 (G-BWSG) [U]	Privately owned, North Weald, Essex (restoration)	
XW325	BAC Jet Provost T5B (G-BWGF) [E]	Privately owned, St. Athan, Glamorgan, Wales	
XW327	BAC Jet Provost T5A (9130M) [62]	RAF Cosford, at main gate	
XW330	BAC Jet Provost T5A (9195M) [82,MJ]	Privately owned, Sproughton, Suffolk	
XW333	BAC Jet Provost T5A (G-BVTC)	Global Aviation, Humberside, Lincs	
XW353	BAC Jet Provost T5A (9090M) [3]	RAF Cranwell, Lincs, on display	
XW354	BAC Jet Provost T5A (XW355) (G-JPTV) [20] $	*Instructional airframe, Udine - Instituto Tecnico, Italy*	
XW358	BAC Jet Provost T5A (9181M) [59,MK] (fuselage)	Privately owned, Berkshire	
XW360	BAC Jet Provost T5A (9153M) [61,ML]	Privately owned, Thorpe Wood, N. Yorks	
XW363	BAC Jet Provost T5A [36]	Dumfries & Galloway Avn Mus, stored Dumfries, Scotland	
XW364	BAC Jet Provost T5A (9188M) [35,MN]	RAF Halton, Bucks, GI use	

Notes	Serial	Type (code/other identity)	Owner/operator, location or fate
	XW370	BAC Jet Provost T5A (9196M) [72,MP]	Privately owned, location unknown
	XW375	BAC Jet Provost T5A (9149M) [52]	Privately owned, Inverness, Scotland
	XW404	BAC Jet Provost T5A (9049M) [77]	Hartlepool College of Further Education, Co. Durham
	XW405	BAC Jet Provost T5A (9187M)	Hartlepool College of Further Education, Co. Durham
	XW409	BAC Jet Provost T5A (9047M)	Privately owned, Hawarden, Flintshire, Wales
	XW410	BAC Jet Provost T5A (9125M) [80] <ff>	Privately owned, Conington, Cambs
	XW418	BAC Jet Provost T5A (9173M) [MT]	Privately owned, Bentwaters, Suffolk (for sale)
	XW419	BAC Jet Provost T5A (9120M) [125]	Privately owned, Tore, Highland, Scotland
	XW420	BAC Jet Provost T5A (9194M) [83,MU]	South Wales Aviation Museum, St Athan, Glamorgan, Wales
	XW422	BAC Jet Provost T5A (G-BWEB) [3]	Privately owned, Cotswold Airport, Glos
	XW423	BAC Jet Provost T5A (G-BWUW) [14]	Deeside College, Connah's Quay, Flintshire, Wales
	XW430	BAC Jet Provost T5A (9176M) [77,MW]	Privately owned, Arncott, Oxon
	XW432	BAC Jet Provost T5A (9127M) [76,MX]	Privately owned, Thame, Bucks
	XW433	BAC Jet Provost T5A (G-JPRO)	Privately owned, Inverness Airport, Scotland
	XW434	BAC Jet Provost T5A (9091M) [78,MY]	Halfpenny Green Airport, Staffs, on display
	XW436	BAC Jet Provost T5A (9148M) [68]	Privately owned, St Athan, Glamorgan, Wales
	XW530	HS Buccaneer S2B [530]	Privately owned, Cupar, Fife, Scotland
	XW541	HS Buccaneer S2B (8858M) <ff>	Privately owned, Lavendon, Bucks
	XW544	HS Buccaneer S2B (8857M) [O]	The Buccaneer Aviation Group, Cotswold Airport, Glos
	XW547	HS Buccaneer S2B (9095M/9169M) [R]	RAF Museum, Hendon, Gtr London
	XW550	HS Buccaneer S2B <ff>	The Buccaneer Aviation Group, Cotswold Airport, Glos
	XW560	SEPECAT Jaguar S <ff>	Boscombe Down Aviation Collection, Old Sarum, Wilts
	XW563	SEPECAT Jaguar S (XX822/8563M)	County Hall, Norwich, Norfolk, on display
	XW566	SEPECAT Jaguar B	Farnborough Air Sciences Trust, Farnborough, Hants
	XW612	WS Scout AH1 (G-KAXW)	Privately owned, Southam, Warks
	XW616	WS Scout AH1	*Currently not known*
	XW630	HS Harrier GR3	RNAS Yeovilton, Somerset, Fire Section
	XW635	Beagle D5/180 (G-AWSW)	Privately owned, Spanhoe, Northants
	XW664	HS Nimrod R1	East Midlands Airport Aeropark, Leics
	XW666	HS Nimrod R1 <ff>	South Yorkshire Aircraft Museum, Doncaster, S. Yorks
	XW763	HS Harrier GR3 (9002M/9041M) <ff>	Privately owned, Wigston, Leics
	XW768	HS Harrier GR3 (9072M) [N]	Spadeadam Ranges, Cumbria
	XW784	Mitchell-Procter Kittiwake I (G-BBRN)	Privately owned, Bridgwater area, Somerset
	XW795	WS Scout AH1	Privately owned, Fivemiletown, Co Tyrone, NI
	XW796	WS Scout AH1 (wreck)	Privately owned, Sutton, Surrey
	XW838	WS Lynx (TAD009) (boom only from XW838)	RAF Cranwell, Lincs, GI use
	XW839	WS Lynx	The Helicopter Museum, Weston-super-Mare, Somerset
	XW844	WS Gazelle AH1	StandardAero Fleetlands, Hants, preserved
	XW846	WS Gazelle AH1	*Sold as G-CMXM, stored Babcary, Somerset*
	XW847	WS Gazelle AH1	AAC No 7 Regiment Conversion Flt, Middle Wallop, Hants
	XW848	WS Gazelle AH1 [D]	Privately owned, Stapleford Tawney, Essex
	XW849	WS Gazelle AH1	Privately owned, East Hanney, Oxon
	XW851	WS Gazelle AH1 (G-CIEY)	Privately owned, Deighton, N. Yorks
	XW852	WS Gazelle HCC4 (9331M)	RAF AM&SU, stored Shawbury, Shropshire
	XW855	WS Gazelle HCC4	RAF Museum, Hendon, Gtr London
	XW858	WS Gazelle HT3 (G-ONNE) [C]	Privately owned, Steeple Bumstead, Cambs
	XW860	WS Gazelle HT2 (TAD 021)	RAF Honington, Suffolk, GI use
	XW864	WS Gazelle HT2 [54/CU]	FAA Museum, stored Cobham Hall, RNAS Yeovilton, Somerset
	XW865	WS Gazelle AH1	MOD/StandardAero, stored Fleetlands, Hants
	XW870	WS Gazelle HT3 (9299M) [F]	Privately owned, Selby, N. Yorks
	XW888	WS Gazelle AH1 (TAD 017)	Privately owned, East Hanney, Oxon
	XW889	WS Gazelle AH1 (TAD 018)	DSAE No 1 SoTT, Cosford, Shropshire
	XW890	WS Gazelle HT2	RNAS Yeovilton, Somerset, on display
	XW892	WS Gazelle AH1 (G-CGJX/9292M)	Privately owned, Peasemore, Berks
	XW900	WS Gazelle AH1 (TAD 900)	Army, Bramley, Hants
	XW906	WS Gazelle HT3 (G-CMFK) [J]	The Gazelle Squadron Display Team, Garford, Oxon
	XW908	WS Gazelle AH1 [A]	QinetiQ, Boscombe Down, Wilts (spares use)
	XW909	WS Gazelle AH1 (G-HSDL)	Privately owned, Hapton, Lancs
	XW912	WS Gazelle AH1 (TAD 019)	MOD JARTS, Boscombe Down, Wilts
	XW913	WS Gazelle AH1	Privately owned, Stapleford Tawney, Essex

Serial	Type (code/other identity)	Owner/operator, location or fate	Notes
XW917	HS Harrier GR3 (8975M)	NATS Air Traffic Control Centre, Swanwick, Hants	
XW922	HS Harrier GR3 (8885M)	Privately owned, Selby, N. Yorks	
XW923	HS Harrier GR3 (8724M) <ff>	Harrier Heritage Centre, RAF Wittering, Cambs	
XW924	HS Harrier GR3 (9073M) [G]	RAF Coningsby, Lincs, (stored in HAS)	
XW927	HS Harrier T4 <ff>	Privately owned, Doncaster, S. Yorks	
XW934	HS Harrier T4 [Y]	Farnborough Air Sciences Trust, Farnborough, Hants	
XW994	Northrop Chukar D1	FAA Museum, stored Cobham Hall, RNAS Yeovilton, Somerset	
XW999	Northrop Chukar D1	Davidstow Airfield & Cornwall At War Museum, Cornwall	
XX108	SEPECAT Jaguar GR1(mod)	IWM Duxford, Cambs	
XX109	SEPECAT Jaguar GR1 (8918M) [GH]	City of Norwich Aviation Museum, Norfolk	
XX110	SEPECAT Jaguar GR1 (8955M) [EP]	RAF Cosford, Shropshire, on display	
XX110	SEPECAT Jaguar GR1 <R> (BAPC. 169)	DSAE No 1 SoTT, Cosford, Shropshire	
XX112	SEPECAT Jaguar GR3A [EA]	DSAE No 1 SoTT, Cosford, Shropshire	
XX116	SEPECAT Jaguar GR3A [EO] $	Privately owned, Chippenham Lodge, Cambs	
XX117	SEPECAT Jaguar GR3A [ES]	DSAE No 1 SoTT, Cosford, Shropshire	
XX119	SEPECAT Jaguar GR3A (8898M) [AI] $	RAF Lossiemouth, Moray, Scotland, on display	
XX121	SEPECAT Jaguar GR1 [EQ]	Privately owned, Selby, N. Yorks	
XX139	SEPECAT Jaguar T4 [PT]	Privately owned, Sproughton, Suffolk	
XX140	SEPECAT Jaguar T2 (9008M) <ff>	Privately owned, Stockbury, Kent	
XX141	SEPECAT Jaguar T2A (9297M) [T]	DSAE No 1 SoTT, Cosford, Shropshire	
XX144	SEPECAT Jaguar T2A [U]	Privately owned, Sproughton, Suffolk	
XX145	SEPECAT Jaguar T2A	Boscombe Down Aviation Collection, Old Sarum, Wilts	
XX146	SEPECAT Jaguar T4 [GT]	Solway Aviation Museum, Carlisle, Cumbria	
XX153	WS Lynx AH1 (9320M)	Army Flying Museum, Middle Wallop, Hants	
XX154	HS Hawk T1 $	Boscombe Down Aviation Collection, Old Sarum, Wilts	
XX156	HS Hawk T1 [156]	RAF Valley, Gwynedd, Wales, on display	
XX157	HS Hawk T1A [157]	Privately owned, Sproughton, Suffolk	
XX158	HS Hawk T1A [158]	RAF AM&SU, stored Shawbury, Shropshire	
XX159	HS Hawk T1A [159]	RAF AMRO, Valley, Gwynedd, Wales	
XX160	HS Hawk T1 [160]	RAF AM&SU, stored Shawbury, Shropshire	
XX161	HS Hawk T1 [161]	RAF Valley, Gwynedd, Wales, GI use	
XX162	HS Hawk T1 $	RAF AM&SU, stored Shawbury, Shropshire	
XX165	HS Hawk T1 [165] <rf>	MOD JARTS, Boscombe Down, Wilts	
XX167	HS Hawk T1 [167]	RAF AM&SU, stored Shawbury, Shropshire	
XX168	HS Hawk T1 [168]	DSAE No 1 SoTT, Cosford, Shropshire	
XX169	HS Hawk T1W [169]	RAF AM&SU, stored Shawbury, Shropshire	
XX170	HS Hawk T1 [CH]	RAF AM&SU, stored Shawbury, Shropshire	
XX171	HS Hawk T1 [171]	RAF AM&SU, stored Shawbury, Shropshire	
XX172	HS Hawk T1 [172] (fuselage)	QinetiQ Boscombe Down, Wilts, GI use	
XX173	HS Hawk T1 (fuselage)	MOD JARTS, Boscombe Down, Wilts	
XX174	HS Hawk T1 [174]	RAF AM&SU, stored Shawbury, Shropshire	
XX175	HS Hawk T1 [175]	Privately owned, Thorpe Wood, N. Yorks	
XX176	HS Hawk T1W [176]	RAF AM&SU, stored Shawbury, Shropshire	
XX177	HS Hawk T1	RAF, *Red Arrows*, Waddington	
XX178	HS Hawk T1W [178]	DSAE No 1 SoTT, Cosford, Shropshire	
XX181	HS Hawk T1 [181]	DSAE No 1 SoTT, Cosford, Shropshire	
XX184	HS Hawk T1 [CQ]	Sheffield University, S. Yorks, GI use	
XX185	HS Hawk T1 [185]	DSAE No 1 SoTT, Cosford, Shropshire	
XX187	HS Hawk T1A [CO]	RAF AM&SU, stored Shawbury, Shropshire	
XX188	HS Hawk T1A	RAF, *Red Arrows*, Waddington	
XX190	HS Hawk T1A [CN]	RAF AM&SU, stored Shawbury, Shropshire	
XX191	HS Hawk T1A [CC]	RAF AM&SU, stored Shawbury, Shropshire	
XX194	HS Hawk T1A [CP]	RAF AM&SU, stored Shawbury, Shropshire	
XX195	HS Hawk T1W [195]	RAF AM&SU, stored Shawbury, Shropshire	
XX198	HS Hawk T1A [CH]	RAF AM&SU, stored Shawbury, Shropshire	
XX199	HS Hawk T1A [301]	Privately owned, Sproughton, Suffolk	
XX200	HS Hawk T1A [CO] (fuselage)	RAF AM&SU, stored Shawbury, Shropshire	
XX201	HS Hawk T1A [CQ]	RAF AM&SU, stored Shawbury, Shropshire	
XX202	HS Hawk T1A	RAF AMRO, Valley, Gwynedd, Wales	
XX203	HS Hawk T1A [CF]	RAF AM&SU, stored Shawbury, Shropshire	

Notes	Serial	Type (code/other identity)	Owner/operator, location or fate
	XX205	HS Hawk T1A [CK]	RAF AM&SU, stored Shawbury, Shropshire
	XX217	HS Hawk T1A [217]	RAF AM&SU, stored Shawbury, Shropshire
	XX218	HS Hawk T1A [218]	DSAE No 1 SoTT, Cosford, Shropshire
	XX219	HS Hawk T1A	RAF AMRO, Valley, Gwynedd, Wales
	XX220	HS Hawk T1A [220]	*Current location unknown* (Ex-RTP, AMRO, RAF Valley)
	XX221	HS Hawk T1A	RAF AMRO, Valley, Gwynedd, Wales
	XX222	HS Hawk T1A [CI]	RAF AM&SU, stored Shawbury, Shropshire
	XX224	HS Hawk T1 [224]	DSAE No 1 SoTT, Cosford, Shropshire
	XX225	HS Hawk T1 [322]	RAF AM&SU, stored Shawbury, Shropshire
	XX226	HS Hawk T1 [226]	Privately owned, Thorpe Wood, N. Yorks
	XX227	HS Hawk T1 <R> (*XX226*/BAPC.152)	RAF, noted Wickenby, Lincs October 2023
	XX227	HS Hawk T1A	DSAE No 1 SoTT, Cosford, Shropshire
	XX228	HS Hawk T1 [CG]	RAF AM&SU, stored Shawbury, Shropshire
	XX230	HS Hawk T1A [CM]	RAF AM&SU, stored Shawbury, Shropshire
	XX231	HS Hawk T1W [213]	RAF AM&SU, stored Shawbury, Shropshire
	XX232	HS Hawk T1	RAF *Red Arrows*, Waddington, Lincs
	XX234	HS Hawk T1 [234]	RAF AM&SU, stored Shawbury, Shropshire
	XX235	HS Hawk T1 [235]	DSAE No 1 SoTT, Cosford, Shropshire
	XX236	HS Hawk T1W [236]	DSAE No 1 SoTT, Cosford, Shropshire
	XX238	HS Hawk T1 [238]	South Yorkshire Aircraft Museum, Doncaster, S. Yorks
	XX239	HS Hawk T1W	RAF *Red Arrows*, Waddington, Lincs
	XX240	HS Hawk T1 [840/CU]	MOD JARTS, Boscombe Down, Wilts
	XX242	HS Hawk T1	RAF *Red Arrows*, Waddington, Lincs
	XX244	HS Hawk T1	DSAE No 1 SoTT, Cosford, Shropshire
	XX245	HS Hawk T1	RAF *Red Arrows*, Waddington, Lincs
	XX246	HS Hawk T1A [CA]	Privately owned, Sproughton, Suffolk
	XX247	HS Hawk T1A [247]	RAF Woodvale, Merseyside, at main gate
	XX248	HS Hawk T1A [CJ]	RAF AM&SU, stored Shawbury, Shropshire
	XX250	HS Hawk T1W [250]	RAF AM&SU, stored Shawbury, Shropshire
	XX253	HS Hawk T1A	RAF Leeming, N. Yorks, under restoration
	XX254	HS Hawk T1A <R>	Privately owned, Marlow, Bucks
	XX255	HS Hawk T1A [CB]	RAF AM&SU, stored Shawbury, Shropshire
	XX256	HS Hawk T1A [846/CU]	RAF AM&SU, stored Shawbury, Shropshire
	XX258	HS Hawk T1A [CE]	RAF AM&SU, stored Shawbury, Shropshire
	XX260	HS Hawk T1A (Red Arrows c/s)	Ulster Aviation Society, Long Kesh, Co. Antrim, NI
	XX261	HS Hawk T1A [CJ]	RAF AMRO, Valley, Gwynedd, Wales
	XX263	HS Hawk T1A	South Wales Aviation Museum, St Athan, Glamorgan, Wales
	XX264	HS Hawk T1A $	RAF AM&SU, stored Shawbury, Shropshire
	XX265	HS Hawk T1A [CP]	North-East Land, Sea & Air Museums, Usworth, T&W
	XX266	HS Hawk T1A	*RAF Waddington, dumped*
	XX278	HS Hawk T1A	RAF AMRO, Valley, Gwynedd, Wales
	XX280	HS Hawk T1A [280]	RN, preserved RNAS Culdrose, Cornwall
	XX281	HS Hawk T1A	RAF AMRO, Valley, Gwynedd, Wales
	XX283	HS Hawk T1W [283]	DSAE No 1 SoTT, Cosford, Shropshire
	XX284	HS Hawk T1A [CN]	RAF AM&SU, stored Shawbury, Shropshire
	XX285	HS Hawk T1A [CK]	RAF AM&SU, stored Shawbury, Shropshire
	XX286	HS Hawk T1A [286]	Ulster Aviation Society, Long Kesh, Co. Antrim, NI
	XX287	HS Hawk T1A [287]	RAF AM&SU, stored Shawbury, Shropshire
	XX289	HS Hawk T1A [CO]	DSAE No 1 SoTT, Cosford, Shropshire
	XX290	HS Hawk T1W	Privately owned, Thorpe Wood, N Yorks
	XX294	HS Hawk T1	RAF AM&SU, stored Shawbury, Shropshire
	XX295	HS Hawk T1	RAF *Red Arrows*, Waddington, Lincs
	XX296	HS Hawk T1 [296]	RAF AM&SU, stored Shawbury, Shropshire
	XX299	HS Hawk T1W [299]	RAF AM&SU, stored Shawbury, Shropshire
	XX301	HS Hawk T1A $	RAF AM&SU, stored Shawbury, Shropshire
	XX303	HS Hawk T1A [CR]	RAF AM&SU, stored Shawbury, Shropshire
	XX306	HS Hawk T1A (Red Arrows c/s)	Exelby Services, Coneygarth, N. Yorks, on display
	XX307	HS Hawk T1 [307]	Metcalfe Farms, Leyburn, N. Yorks
	XX308	HS Hawk T1	National Museum of Flight, E. Fortune, Scotland
	XX308	HS Hawk T1 <R> (*XX263*/BAPC.171)	RAF M&RU, Bottesford, Leics
	XX309	HS Hawk T1	Caernarfon Air World, Gwynedd, Wales

Serial	Type (code/other identity)	Owner/operator, location or fate	Notes
XX310	HS Hawk T1	RAF *Red Arrows*, Waddington, Lincs	
XX311	HS Hawk T1	RAF *Red Arrows*, Waddington, Lincs	
XX313	HS Hawk T1W [313]	RAF AM&SU, stored Shawbury, Shropshire	
XX314	HS Hawk T1W [314]	RAF AM&SU, stored Shawbury, Shropshire	
XX315	HS Hawk T1A [315]	RAF AM&SU, stored Shawbury, Shropshire	
XX316	HS Hawk T1A [849/CU]	Martin Baker, Chalgrove Airfield, Oxon	
XX317	HS Hawk T1A [CO]	RAF, preserved Leeming, N. Yorks	
XX318	HS Hawk T1A [CG]	Metcalfe Farms, Leyburn, N. Yorks	
XX319	HS Hawk T1A	RAF *Red Arrows*, Waddington, Lincs	
XX320	HS Hawk T1A <ff>	Privately owned, Devonport, Devon	
XX321	HS Hawk T1A	RAF *Red Arrows*, Waddington, Lincs	
XX322	HS Hawk T1A	RAF *Red Arrows*, Waddington, Lincs	
XX323	HS Hawk T1A	RAF *Red Arrows*, Waddington, Lincs	
XX324	HS Hawk T1A [324]	RAF AM&SU, stored Shawbury, Shropshire	
XX325	HS Hawk T1	RAF AMRO, Valley, Gwynedd, Wales, RTP	
XX327	HS Hawk T1	RAF AM&SU, stored Shawbury, Shropshire	
XX329	HS Hawk T1A [844/CU]	MOD JARTS, Boscombe Down, Wilts	
XX330	HS Hawk T1A [330]	RAF AMRO, Valley, Gwynedd, Wales, RTP	
XX331	HS Hawk T1A [331]	RAF AM&SU, stored Shawbury, Shropshire	
XX332	HS Hawk T1A [CD]	Privately owned, Sproughton, Suffolk	
XX335	HS Hawk T1A [335]	DSAE No 1 SoTT, Cosford, Shropshire	
XX337	HS Hawk T1A [CM]	RAF AM&SU, stored Shawbury, Shropshire	
XX338	HS Hawk T1W	RAF AM&SU, stored Shawbury, Shropshire	
XX339	HS Hawk T1A [CL]	RAF AM&SU, stored Shawbury, Shropshire	
XX341	HS Hawk T1 ASTRA	Privately owned, Thorpe Wood, N. Yorks	
XX342	HS Hawk T1 (G-HAWC) [2]	Privately owned, St Athan, Glamorgan, Wales	
XX343	HS Hawk T1 [3] <ff>	Boscombe Down Aviation Collection, Old Sarum, Wilts	
XX345	HS Hawk T1A [CB]	RAF AM&SU, stored Shawbury, Shropshire	
XX346	HS Hawk T1A [CP]	MOD JARTS, Boscombe Down, Wilts	
XX348	HS Hawk T1A [CQ]	RAF AM&SU, stored Shawbury, Shropshire	
XX350	HS Hawk T1A [D] $	RAF AM&SU, stored Shawbury, Shropshire	
XX351	HS Hawk T1A	RAF No 71(IR) Sqn, Wittering, Cambs, GI use	
XX352	HS Hawk T1A <rf>	QinetiQ Farnborough, Hants, on display	
XX372	WS Gazelle AH1 <ff>	*Scrapped*	
XX375	WS Gazelle AH1	*Scrapped*	
XX378	WS Gazelle AH1 <ff>	Privately owned, East Hanney, Oxon (stored)	
XX379	WS Gazelle AH1 [Y]	MOD Boscombe Down, Wilts, GI use	
XX380	WS Gazelle AH1 [A]	AAC Wattisham, Suffolk, on display	
XX381	WS Gazelle AH1	Privately owned, Welbeck, Notts	
XX386	WS Gazelle AH1 (G-UNNS)	Privately owned, Redhill, Surrey	
XX387	WS Gazelle AH1 (TAD 014)	Privately owned, stored Cranfield, Beds	
XX392	WS Gazelle AH1	Army, Bury St Edmunds, Suffolk, recruiting aid	
XX394	WS Gazelle AH1 [X]	Privately owned, Stapleford Tawney, Essex	
XX396	WS Gazelle HT3 (8718M) [N]	Privately owned, Arncott, Oxon	
XX398	WS Gazelle AH1	Privately owned, Stapleford Tawney, Essex	
XX405	WS Gazelle AH1	AAC No 665 Sqn/5 Regt, Aldergrove, NI (stored)	
XX406	WS Gazelle HT3 (G-CBSH) [P]	Privately owned, Peasemore, Berks	
XX411	WS Gazelle AH1 [X]	South Yorkshire Aircraft Museum, Doncaster, S. Yorks	
XX412	WS Gazelle AH1 [B]	DSAE No 1 SoTT, Cosford, Shropshire	
XX414	WS Gazelle AH1 [V]	Privately owned, Biggin Hill, Kent	
XX418	WS Gazelle AH1 <ff>	Privately owned, Andover area, Hants	
XX431	WS Gazelle HT2 (9300M) [43/CU]	Travelling exhibit, *HMS Sultan*, Gosport, Hants	
XX433	WS Gazelle AH1 <rf>	Privately owned, Andover area, Hants	
XX435	WS Gazelle AH1 (fuselage)	QinetiQ, Boscombe Down, Wilts (spares use)	
XX436	WS Gazelle HT2 (G-ZZLE) [39/CU]	Privately owned, East Hanney, Oxon	
XX437	WS Gazelle AH1	Privately owned, Stapleford Tawney, Essex (sold to South Africa)	
XX438	WS Gazelle AH1 [F]	Privately owned, Stapleford Tawney, Essex (stored)	
XX442	WS Gazelle AH1 <ff>	Privately owned, East Hanney, Oxon (stored)	
XX443	WS Gazelle AH1 [Y]	Army, Aldergrove, NI, on display	
XX444	WS Gazelle AH1 {K}	DSAE SAAE, Lyneham, Wilts	
XX447	WS Gazelle AH1 [D1]	Privately owned, Colsterworth, Lincs	

Notes	Serial	Type (code/other identity)	Owner/operator, location or fate
	XX450	WS Gazelle AH1 [D]	Privately owned, Peasemore, Berks
	XX453	WS Gazelle AH1 (G-CMMF)	*Sold to South Africa, March 2024*
XX453		WS Gazelle AH1 (XZ331/G-CLXM) [D]	Privately owned, Peasemore, Berks (restoration)
	XX454	WS Gazelle AH1 (TAD 023)	DSAE SAAE, Lyneham, Wilts
	XX455	WS Gazelle AH1 (G-GRAK)	Privately owned, Stapleford Tawney, Essex
	XX460	WS Gazelle AH1 (G-CMMB)	Privately owned, Deighton, N. Yorks
	XX462	WS Gazelle AH1 [W]	Privately owned, Stapleford Tawney, Essex (stored)
	XX466	HS Hunter T66B/T7 [830] <ff>	Privately owned, Glos
	XX467	HS Hunter T66B/T7 (XL605/G-TVII) [86]	Newark Air Museum, Winthorpe, Notts
	XX477	HP137 Jetstream T1 (G-AXXS/8462M) <ff>	Solway Aviation Society, Carlisle, Cumbria
	XX478	HP137 Jetstream T2 (G-AXXT) [564/CU]	Solihull College, Woodlands Campus, W. Mids
	XX483	SA Jetstream T2 [562] <ff>	Dumfries & Galloway Avn Mus, Dumfries, Scotland
	XX487	SA Jetstream T2 [568/CU]	Int'l Centre for Aerospace Training, Cardiff Airport, Wales
	XX491	SA Jetstream T1 [K]	Northbrook College, Shoreham, W. Sussex, GI use
	XX492	SA Jetstream T1 [A]	Newark Air Museum, Winthorpe, Notts
	XX494	SA Jetstream T1 [B]	East Midlands Airport Aeropark, Leics
	XX495	SA Jetstream T1 [C]	South Yorkshire Aircraft Museum, Doncaster, S. Yorks
	XX496	SA Jetstream T1 [D]	Michael Beetham Conservation Centre, RAFM Cosford, Shropshire (stored outside)
	XX499	SA Jetstream T1 [G]	Privately owned, Wainfleet, Lincs
	XX510	WS Lynx HAS2 [69/DD]	SFDO, RNAS Culdrose, Cornwall
	XX513	SA Bulldog T1 (G-KKKK) [10]	Privately owned, Breighton, E. Yorks
	XX515	SA Bulldog T1 (G-CBBC) [4]	Privately owned, Blackbushe, Hants
	XX518	SA Bulldog T1 (G-UDOG/OO-DOG) [S]	Privately owned, Ursel, Belgium
	XX520	SA Bulldog T1 (9288M) [A]	No 172 Sqn ATC, Haywards Heath, W. Sussex
	XX521	SA Bulldog T1 (G-CBEH) [H]	Privately owned, North Moreton, Oxon
	XX522	SA Bulldog T1 (G-DAWG) [06]	Privately owned, Blackpool, Lancs
	XX524	SA Bulldog T1 (G-DDOG) [04]	Privately owned, Malaga, Spain
	XX528	SA Bulldog T1 (G-BZON) [D]	Privately owned, Earls Colne, Essex
	XX534	SA Bulldog T1 (G-EDAV) [B]	Privately owned, Tollerton, Notts
	XX537	SA Bulldog T1 (G-CBCB) [C]	Privately owned, Turweston, Bucks
	XX538	SA Bulldog T1 (G-TDOG) [O]	Privately owned, Shobdon, Herefordshire
	XX539	SA Bulldog T1	Privately owned, Ashbourne, Derbyshire
	XX546	SA Bulldog T1 (G-WINI) [03]	Privately owned, Conington, Cambs
	XX549	SA Bulldog T1 (G-CBID) [6]	Privately owned, White Waltham, Berkshire
	XX550	SA Bulldog T1 (G-CBBL) [Z]	Privately owned, Abbeyshrule, Eire
	XX551	SA Bulldog T1 (G-BZDP) [E]	Privately owned, Boscombe Down, Wilts
	XX554	SA Bulldog T1 (G-BZMD) [09]	Privately owned, stored Thruxton, Hants
	XX555	SA Bulldog T1 (F-AZKJ)	Privately owned, St Rambert d'Albon, France
	XX557	SA Bulldog T1	*Currently not known (ex-Fort Paull, E. Yorks)*
	XX561	SA Bulldog T1 (G-BZEP) [7]	Privately owned, stored Eggesford, Devon
	XX611	SA Bulldog T1 (G-CBDK) [7]	Privately owned, Cotswold Airport, Glos
	XX612	SA Bulldog T1 (G-BZXC) [A,03]	Privately owned, Prestwick, South Ayrshire, Scotland
XX613		SA Bulldog T1 (XX637/9197M) [A]	Ulster Aviation Society, Long Kesh, Co. Antrim, NI
	XX614	SA Bulldog T1 (G-GGRR) [1]	Privately owned, Gloucestershire Airport, Glos
	XX619	SA Bulldog T1 (G-CBBW) [T]	Privately owned, Coventry, Warks
	XX621	SA Bulldog T1 (G-CBEF) [H]	Privately owned, Little Gransden, Cambs
	XX622	SA Bulldog T1 (G-CBGX) [B]	Privately owned, Dunsfold, Surrey (off-site)
	XX624	SA Bulldog T1 (G-KDOG) [E]	Privately owned, Redhill, Surrey
XX625		SA Bulldog T1 (XX543/G-UWAS) [45]	Privately owned, Tibenham, Norfolk
	XX626	SA Bulldog T1 (G-CDVV/9290M) [W,02]	Privately owned, Sleap, Shropshire
	XX628	SA Bulldog T1 (G-CBFU) [9]	Privately owned, Alkham, Kent
	XX629	SA Bulldog T1 (G-BZXZ)	Privately owned, Turweston, Bucks
	XX630	SA Bulldog T1 (G-SIJW) [5]	Privately owned, Audley End, Essex
	XX631	SA Bulldog T1 (G-BZXS) [W]	Privately owned, Gloucestershire Airport, Glos
	XX634	SA Bulldog T1 [T]	Newark Air Museum, Winthorpe, Notts
	XX636	SA Bulldog T1 (G-CBFP) [Y]	Privately owned, Empingham, Rutland
	XX638	SA Bulldog T1 (G-DOGG)	Privately owned, Thruxton, Hampshire
	XX639	SA Bulldog T1 (F-AZTF) [D]	Privately owned, La Baule, France
	XX654	SA Bulldog T1 [3]	RAF Museum, Cosford, Shropshire
	XX655	SA Bulldog T1 (9294M) [V] <ff>	Privately owned, Bramcote, Warks
	XX656	SA Bulldog T1 [C]	Privately owned, Derbyshire

Serial	Type (code/other identity)	Owner/operator, location or fate	Notes
XX658	SA Bulldog T1 (G-SMAT) [07]	Privately owned, Duxford, Cambs	
XX659	SA Bulldog T1 [E]	Privately owned, Ashbourne, Derbyshire	
XX664	SA Bulldog T1 (F-AZTV) [04]	Privately owned, Pontoise, France	
XX665	SA Bulldog T1 (9289M) [V]	Privately owned, Evesham, Worcs	
XX667	SA Bulldog T1 (G-BZFN) [16]	Privately owned, Ronaldsway, IoM	
XX668	SA Bulldog T1 (G-CBAN) [1]	Privately owned, RNAS Yeovilton, Somerset	
XX669	SA Bulldog T1 (8997M) [B]	South Yorkshire Aircraft Museum, Doncaster, S. Yorks	
XX687	SA Bulldog T1 [F]	Int'l Centre for Aerospace Training, Cardiff Airport, Wales	
XX692	SA Bulldog T1 (G-BZMH) [I]	Privately owned, Wellesbourne Mountford, Warks	
XX693	SA Bulldog T1 (G-BZML) [07]	Privately owned, Elmsett, Suffolk	
XX694	SA Bulldog T1 (G-CBBS) [E]	Privately owned, Turweston, Bucks	
XX695	SA Bulldog T1 (G-CBBT)	Privately owned, Perth, Scotland	
XX698	SA Bulldog T1 (G-BZME) [9]	Privately owned, Sleap, Shropshire	
XX699	SA Bulldog T1 (G-IDID) [F]	Privately owned, Blackbushe, Hants	
XX700	SA Bulldog T1 (G-CBEK) [17]	Privately owned, Thruxton, Hants	
XX702	SA Bulldog T1 (G-CBCR) [π]	Privately owned, Goodwood, W. Sussex	
XX704	SA122 Bulldog (G-BCUV/G-112)	Privately owned, Bournemouth, Dorset	
XX705	SA Bulldog T1 [5]	Privately owned, Thorpe Wood, N. Yorks	
XX707	SA Bulldog T1 (G-CBDS) [4]	Cancelled by the CAA, December 2024	
XX720	SEPECAT Jaguar GR3A [FL]	Privately owned, Stockbury, Kent	
XX722	SEPECAT Jaguar GR1 (9252M) <ff>	Privately owned, St Athan, Glamorgan, Wales	
XX723	SEPECAT Jaguar GR3A [EU]	DSAE No 1 SoTT, Cosford, Shropshire	
XX724	SEPECAT Jaguar GR3A [C]	DSAE No 1 SoTT, Cosford, Shropshire	
XX725	SEPECAT Jaguar GR3A [KC-F,T]	DSAE No 1 SoTT, Cosford, Shropshire	
XX726	SEPECAT Jaguar GR1 (8947M) [EB]	DSAE No 1 SoTT, Cosford, Shropshire	
XX727	SEPECAT Jaguar GR1 (8951M) [ER]	South Wales Aviation Museum, St Athan, Glamorgan, Wales	
XX729	SEPECAT Jaguar GR3A [EL]	DSAE No 1 SoTT, Cosford, Shropshire	
XX734	SEPECAT Jaguar GR1 (8816M)	Boscombe Down Aviation Collection, Old Sarum, Wilts	
XX736	SEPECAT Jaguar GR1 (9110M) <ff>	South Yorkshire Aircraft Museum, Doncaster, S. Yorks	
XX738	SEPECAT Jaguar GR3A [ED]	DSAE No 1 SoTT, Cosford, Shropshire	
XX739	SEPECAT Jaguar GR1 (8902M) [I]	Delta Force Paintball, Birmingham, W. Mids	
XX741	SEPECAT Jaguar GR1A [EJ]	Bentwaters Cold War Museum, Suffolk	
XX743	SEPECAT Jaguar GR1 (8949M) [EG]	Morayvia, Kinloss, Moray, Scotland	
XX744	SEPECAT Jaguar GR1 (9251M)	Mayhem Paintball, Abridge, Essex	
XX745	SEPECAT Jaguar GR1A <ff>	No 1350 Sqn ATC, Fareham, Hants	
XX746	SEPECAT Jaguar GR1 (8895M) [S]	DSAE No 1 SoTT, Cosford, Shropshire	
XX748	SEPECAT Jaguar GR3A [L]	DSAE No 1 SoTT, Cosford, Shropshire	
XX751	SEPECAT Jaguar GR1 (8937M) [10]	Iron Curtain Museum, Alton, Hants	
XX752	SEPECAT Jaguar GR3A [EK]	DSAE No 1 SoTT, Cosford, Shropshire	
XX753	SEPECAT Jaguar GR1 (9087M) <ff>	Newark Air Museum, Winthorpe, Notts	
XX756	SEPECAT Jaguar GR1 (8899M) [W]	DSAE No 1 SoTT, Cosford, Shropshire	
XX761	SEPECAT Jaguar GR1 (8600M) <ff>	Boscombe Down Aviation Collection, Old Sarum, Wilts	
XX763	SEPECAT Jaguar GR1 (9009M) [24]	Bournemouth Aviation Museum, Dorset	
XX764	SEPECAT Jaguar GR1 (9010M) [13]	Privately owned, Enstone, Oxon	
XX765	SEPECAT Jaguar ACT	RAF Museum, Cosford, Shropshire	
XX766	SEPECAT Jaguar GR3A [EF]	DSAE No 1 SoTT, Cosford, Shropshire	
XX767	SEPECAT Jaguar GR3A [Z]	DSAE No 1 SoTT, Cosford, Shropshire	
XX818	SEPECAT Jaguar GR1 (8945M) [DE]	Fire Service training facility, RAF Waddington, Lincs	
XX819	SEPECAT Jaguar GR1 (8923M) [CE]	DSAE No 1 SoTT, Cosford, Shropshire	
XX821	SEPECAT Jaguar GR1 (8896M) [P]	DSAE No 1 SoTT, Cosford, Shropshire	
XX824	SEPECAT Jaguar GR1 (9019M) [AD]	RAF Museum, Hendon, Gtr London	
XX825	SEPECAT Jaguar GR1 (9020M) [BN]	DSAE No 1 SoTT, Cosford, Shropshire	
XX826	SEPECAT Jaguar GR1 (9021M) [34] <ff>	Shannon Aviation Museum, Eire (stored)	
XX829	SEPECAT Jaguar T2A [GZ]	Newark Air Museum, Winthorpe, Notts	
XX830	SEPECAT Jaguar T2 <ff>	City of Norwich Aviation Museum, Norfolk	
XX833	SEPECAT Jaguar T2B	DSAE No 1 SoTT, Cosford, Shropshire	
XX835	SEPECAT Jaguar T4 [P]	DSAE No 1 SoTT, Cosford, Shropshire	
XX836	SEPECAT Jaguar T2A [ER]	Privately owned, Sproughton, Suffolk	
XX837	SEPECAT Jaguar T2 (8978M) [Z]	DSAE No 1 SoTT, Cosford, Shropshire	
XX838	SEPECAT Jaguar T4 [FZ]	Privately owned, Bentwaters, Suffolk (for sale)	
XX840	SEPECAT Jaguar T4 [T]	DSAE No 1 SoTT, Cosford, Shropshire	

Notes	Serial	Type (code/other identity)	Owner/operator, location or fate
	XX841	SEPECAT Jaguar T4 (VH-UXB) [EW]	Privately owned, North Weald, Essex
	XX842	SEPECAT Jaguar T2A [FX]	Privately owned, Bentwaters, Suffolk
	XX845	SEPECAT Jaguar T4 [EV]	South Wales Aviation Museum, St Athan, Glamorgan, Wales
	XX847	SEPECAT Jaguar T4 [EZ]	DSAE No 1 SoTT, Cosford, Shropshire
	XX885	HS Buccaneer S2B (9225M/G-HHAA)	Stored Scampton, Lincs (off-airfield)
	XX888	HS Buccaneer S2B <ff>	South Yorkshire Aircraft Museum, Doncaster, S. Yorks
	XX889	HS Buccaneer S2B [T]	South Wales Aviation Museum, St Athan, Glamorgan, Wales
	XX892	HS Buccaneer S2B <ff>	Privately owned, Lincs
	XX894	HS Buccaneer S2B [020/R]	The Buccaneer Aviation Group, Cotswold Airport, Glos
	XX895	HS Buccaneer S2B <ff>	Thorpe Camp Visitor Centre, Tattershall Thorpe, Lincs
	XX897	HS Buccaneer S2B(mod)	Shannon Aviation Museum, Eire
	XX899	HS Buccaneer S2B <ff>	Newark Air Museum, Winthorpe, Notts
	XX900	HS Buccaneer S2B [900]	Privately owned, Tatenhill, Staffs
	XX901	HS Buccaneer S2B [N]	Yorkshire Air Museum, Elvington, N. Yorks
	XX910	WS Lynx HAS2	The Helicopter Museum, Weston-super-Mare, Somerset
	XX919	BAC 1-11/402AP (PI-C1121) <ff>	Boscombe Down Aviation Collection, Old Sarum, Wilts
	XX946	Panavia Tornado (P02) (8883M) [WT]	RAF Museum, stored Cosford, Shropshire
	XX956	SEPECAT Jaguar GR1 (8950M) [BE]	Morayvia, stored Spey Bay, Moray, Scotland
	XX959	SEPECAT Jaguar GR1 (8953M) [CJ]	DSAE No 1 SoTT, Cosford, Shropshire
	XX962	SEPECAT Jaguar GR1B (9257M) <ff>	RAF Coningsby, Lincs (restoration)
	XX965	SEPECAT Jaguar GR1A (9254M) [C]	DSAE No 1 SoTT, Cosford, Shropshire
	XX967	SEPECAT Jaguar GR1 (9006M) [AC]	Privately owned, Charlwood, Surrey
	XX968	SEPECAT Jaguar GR1 (9007M) [AJ]	DSAE No 1 SoTT, Cosford, Shropshire
	XX969	SEPECAT Jaguar GR1 (8897M) [01]	DSAE No 1 SoTT, Cosford, Shropshire
	XX970	SEPECAT Jaguar GR3A [EH]	DSAE No 1 SoTT, Cosford, Shropshire
	XX975	SEPECAT Jaguar GR1 (8905M) [07]	Montrose Air Station Heritage Centre, Angus, Scotland
	XX976	SEPECAT Jaguar GR1 (8906M) [BD]	DSAE No 1 SoTT, Cosford, Shropshire
	XX977	SEPECAT Jaguar GR1 (9132M) [DL,05] <rf>	Privately owned, Sproughton, Suffolk
	XX979	SEPECAT Jaguar GR1A (9306M) <ff>	RAF Air Defence Radar Museum, Neatishead, Norfolk
	XZ103	SEPECAT Jaguar GR3A [EF]	DSAE No 1 SoTT, Cosford, Shropshire
	XZ104	SEPECAT Jaguar GR3A [FM]	DSAE No 1 SoTT, Cosford, Shropshire
	XZ106	SEPECAT Jaguar GR3A [FR]	RAF Manston History Museum, Kent
	XZ107	SEPECAT Jaguar GR3A [FH]	Privately owned, Selby, N. Yorks
	XZ109	SEPECAT Jaguar GR3A [EN]	DSAE No 1 SoTT, Cosford, Shropshire
	XZ112	SEPECAT Jaguar GR3A [GW]	DSAE No 1 SoTT, Cosford, Shropshire
	XZ113	SEPECAT Jaguar GR3 [A,30]	Morayvia, Kinloss, Moray, Scotland
	XZ114	SEPECAT Jaguar GR3 [EO]	DSAE No 1 SoTT, Cosford, Shropshire
	XZ115	SEPECAT Jaguar GR3 [ER]	DSAE No 1 SoTT, Cosford, Shropshire
	XZ117	SEPECAT Jaguar GR3 [ES]	DSAE No 1 SoTT, Cosford, Shropshire
	XZ119	SEPECAT Jaguar GR1A (9266M) [FG]	National Museum of Flight, E. Fortune, Scotland
	XZ131	HS Harrier GR3 (9174M) <ff>	Privately owned, Wolverhampton, W. Mids
	XZ132	HS Harrier GR3 (9168M) [C]	Privately owned, Gloucestershire Airport, Glos
	XZ133	HS Harrier GR3 [10]	IWM Duxford, Cambs
	XZ138	HS Harrier GR3 (9040M) <ff>	Current location unknown (ex-Scampton Heritage Ctr.)
	XZ146	HS Harrier T4 (9281M) [S]	Harrier Heritage Centre, RAF Wittering, Cambs
	XZ166	WS Lynx HAS2 <ff>	Farnborough Air Sciences Trust, stored Farnborough
	XZ170	WS Lynx AH9	DSEME SAAE, Lyneham, Wilts
	XZ171	WS Lynx AH7	Army, Salisbury Plain, Wilts (derelict)
	XZ172	WS Lynx AH7	DSEME SAAE, Lyneham, Wilts
	XZ173	WS Lynx AH7 [6] <ff>	Privately owned, Weeton, Lancs
	XZ174	WS Lynx AH7 <ff>	Defence School of Policing, Gosport, Hants, GI use
	XZ175	WS Lynx AH7	Privately owned, Wickford, Essex
	XZ177	*Aérospatiale SA341G Gazelle (G-SFTA/XZ345) [T]*	North-East Land, Sea & Air Museums, Usworth, T&W
	XZ177	WS Lynx AH7	Delta Force Paintball, Kegworth, Leics
	XZ178	WS Lynx AH7 <ff>	Bilsthorpe Paintball Park, Notts
	XZ179	WS Lynx AH7 (G-NCKS) [W]	Privately owned, North Weald, Essex
	XZ180	WS Lynx AH7 [C]	DSEME SAAE, Lyneham, Wilts
	XZ181	WS Lynx AH1	AAC Middle Wallop Fire Section, Hants
	XZ184	WS Lynx AH7 [B]	AAC Middle Wallop, Hants, at main gate

Serial	Type (code/other identity)	Owner/operator, location or fate	Notes
XZ187	WS Lynx AH7	FETC, Moreton-in-Marsh, Glos	
XZ188	WS Lynx AH7	Privately owned, North Weald, Essex	
XZ190	WS Lynx AH7 <ff>	Army, Longmoor Camp, Hants, GI use	
XZ191	WS Lynx AH7 [R]	DSEME SAAE, Lyneham, Wilts	
XZ192	WS Lynx AH7 [H]	AAC, stored St Athan, Glamorgan, Wales	
XZ193	WS Lynx AH7 [4] <ff>	Kidderminster Paintball, Worcs	
XZ194	WS Lynx AH7 [V]	IWM Duxford, Cambs	
XZ195	WS Lynx AH7 <ff>	Privately owned, Mildenhall, Suffolk	
XZ196	WS Lynx AH7	Privately owned, Burwell, Cambs	
XZ203	WS Lynx AH7 [F]	Army, Salisbury Plain, Wilts (derelict)	
XZ205	WS Lynx AH7 [239-UA]	Divers Wood Paintball, Crawley, W. Sussex	
XZ207	WS Lynx AH7 <rf>	FETC, Moreton-in-Marsh, Glos	
XZ211	WS Lynx AH7	Bawtry Paintball Park, S. Yorks	
XZ212	WS Lynx AH7 [X]	AAC Middle Wallop Fire Section, Hants	
XZ213	WS Lynx AH1 (TAD 213)	Privately owned, Telford, Shropshire	
XZ214	WS Lynx AH7 <ff>	DSEME SAAE, Lyneham, Wilts	
XZ216	WS Lynx AH7 <ff>	Spadeadam Ranges, Cumbria	
XZ217	WS Lynx AH7	Paintball Park, Guildford, Surrey	
XZ218	WS Lynx AH7	Privately owned, Raigmore Estate, Inverness, Scotland	
XZ219	WS Lynx AH7 <ff>	Army, Bramley, Hants	
XZ220	WS Lynx AH7 <ff>	Privately owned, White Waltham, Berks	
XZ222	WS Lynx AH7	Dumfries & Galloway Avn Mus, Dumfries, Scotland (restoration)	
XZ228	WS Lynx HAS3GMS [313]	FAA Museum, stored Cobham Hall, RNAS Yeovilton, Somerset	
XZ230	WS Lynx HAS3GMS	RNAS Yeovilton, Somerset, GI (Wildcat ground trainer)	
XZ232	WS Lynx HAS3GMS	RelyOn Nutec UK, Aberdeen, Scotland, GI use	
XZ233	WS Lynx HAS3S [696] $	Yorkshire Air Museum, Elvington, N. Yorks	
XZ234	WS Lynx HAS3S [630]	Privately owned, Sproughton, Suffolk	
XZ235	WS Lynx HAS3S(ICE) [630]	Wild Park Derbyshire, Brailsford, Derbys	
XZ236	WS Lynx HMA8 [LST-1]	Privately owned, Woodmancote, W. Sussex	
XZ237	WS Lynx HAS3S [631]	Wild Park Derbyshire, Brailsford, Derbys	
XZ246	WS Lynx HAS3S(ICE) [434/EE]	South Yorkshire Aircraft Museum, Doncaster, S. Yorks	
XZ248	WS Lynx HAS3S	SFDO, RNAS Culdrose, Cornwall	
XZ250	WS Lynx HAS3S [426/PO] $	RN, Portland, Dorset, on display	
XZ255	WS Lynx HMA8SRU [454/DF]	DSEME SAAE, Lyneham, Wilts	
XZ257	WS Lynx HAS3S	RNAS Yeovilton, Somerset, GI (Wildcat ground trainer)	
XZ290	WS Gazelle AH1	MOD/StandardAero, stored Fleetlands, Hants	
XZ292	WS Gazelle AH1	Privately owned, Stapleford Tawney, Essex	
XZ295	WS Gazelle AH1 (G-CLXR)	Privately owned, Peasemore, Berks	
XZ298	WS Gazelle AH1 <ff>	AAC Middle Wallop, Hants, GI use	
XZ300	WS Gazelle AH1	Army, Bramley, Hants	
XZ303	WS Gazelle AH1	Privately owned, Peasemore, Berks	
XZ304	WS Gazelle AH1	Privately owned, Stapleford Tawney, Essex	
XZ305	WS Gazelle AH1 (TAD 020)	DSAE No 1 SoTT, Cosford, Shropshire	
XZ308	WS Gazelle AH1	QinetiQ, Boscombe Down, Wilts (spares use)	
XZ311	WS Gazelle AH1 <ff>	Privately owned, East Hanney, Oxon (stored)	
XZ312	WS Gazelle AH1	RAF Henlow, Beds, instructional use	
XZ313	WS Gazelle AH1	Privately owned, Deighton, N. Yorks	
XZ314	WS Gazelle AH1 [A]	Privately owned, Stapleford Tawney, Essex (stored)	
XZ316	WS Gazelle AH1 [B]	FETC, Moreton-in-Marsh, Glos	
XZ318	WS Gazelle AH1 (fuselage)	Warped Outdoor Activities, Tong, Shropshire	
XZ320	WS Gazelle AH1	*Sold as G-CMXN, stored Babcary, Somerset*	
XZ321	WS Gazelle AH1 (G-CDNS) [D]	Gazelle Squadron Display Team, Babcary (restoration)	
XZ322	WS Gazelle AH1 (G-CMBB/9283M) [N]	Privately owned, Deighton, N. Yorks	
XZ323	WS Gazelle AH1 (G-CLXP) [J]	Privately owned, Peasemore, Berks	
XZ324	WS Gazelle AH1	Privately owned, Stapleford Tawney, Essex	
XZ325	WS Gazelle AH1	Privately owned, N. Yorks area	
XZ326	WS Gazelle AH1	MOD/StandardAero, stored Fleetlands, Hants	
XZ327	WS Gazelle AH1	AAC Middle Wallop, Hants (recruiting aid)	
XZ328	WS Gazelle AH1 [C]	Privately owned, Deighton, N. Yorks	
XZ329	WS Gazelle AH1 (G-BZYD) [J]	Privately owned, Lewes, E. Sussex	

Notes	Serial	Type (code/other identity)	Owner/operator, location or fate
	XZ330	WS Gazelle AH1	Current location unknown
	XZ331	WS Gazelle AH1	Ulster Aviation Society, Long Kesh, Co. Antrim, NI
	XZ333	WS Gazelle AH1	DSAE SAAE, Lyneham, Wilts
	XZ334	WS Gazelle AH1	*Sold as G-CMXO, stored Babcary, Somerset*
	XZ335	WS Gazelle AH1 <ff>	Boscombe Down Aviation Collection, Old Sarum, Wilts
	XZ337	WS Gazelle AH1 [Z]	Privately owned, Freiston, Lincs
	XZ340	WS Gazelle AH1	MOD/StandardAero, stored Fleetlands, Hants
	XZ341	WS Gazelle AH1 (G-CMMA)	Privately owned, Deighton, N. Yorks
	XZ342	WS Gazelle AH1	Current location unknown
	XZ343	WS Gazelle AH1	Privately owned, Deighton, N. Yorks
	XZ344	WS Gazelle AH1 [Y]	Privately owned, Stapleford Tawney, Essex (stored)
	XZ345	WS Gazelle AH1 [M]	DSAE SAAE, Lyneham, Wilts
	XZ346	WS Gazelle AH1	AAC Middle Wallop, at main gate
	XZ356	SEPECAT Jaguar GR3A [FU]	Privately owned, Welshpool, Powys, Wales
	XZ358	SEPECAT Jaguar GR1A (9262M) [L]	DSAE No 1 SoTT, Cosford, Shropshire
	XZ360	SEPECAT Jaguar GR3 [FN]	Teesside International Airport Fire Section, Lincs
	XZ363	SEPECAT Jaguar GR1A <R> (XX824/BAPC.151) [A]	RAF M&RU, Bottesford, Leics
	XZ364	SEPECAT Jaguar GR3A <ff>	Privately owned, Thorpe Wood, N. Yorks
	XZ366	SEPECAT Jaguar GR3A [FC]	Privately owned, Bentwaters, Suffolk
	XZ367	SEPECAT Jaguar GR3 [EE]	DSAE No 1 SoTT, Cosford, Shropshire
	XZ368	SEPECAT Jaguar GR1 (8900M) [E]	DSAE No 1 SoTT, Cosford, Shropshire
	XZ369	SEPECAT Jaguar GR3A [AP]	East Midlands Airport Aeropark, Leics
	XZ370	SEPECAT Jaguar GR1 (9004M) [JB]	DSAE No 1 SoTT, Cosford, Shropshire
	XZ371	SEPECAT Jaguar GR1 (8907M) [AP]	DSAE No 1 SoTT, Cosford, Shropshire
	XZ372	SEPECAT Jaguar GR3 [FV]	Aberdeen Airport Fire Section, Scotland
	XZ374	SEPECAT Jaguar GR1 (9005M) [JC]	RAF Spadeadam, Cumbria, at main gate
	XZ375	SEPECAT Jaguar GR1A (9255M) <ff>	City of Norwich Aviation Museum, Norfolk
	XZ377	SEPECAT Jaguar GR3A [P]	DSAE No 1 SoTT, Cosford, Shropshire
	XZ378	SEPECAT Jaguar GR3A [EP]	Privately owned, Topsham, Devon
	XZ382	SEPECAT Jaguar GR1 (8908M)	Privately owned, Bruntingthorpe, Leics (stored)
	XZ383	SEPECAT Jaguar GR1 (8901M) [AF]	Yorkshire Air Museum, Elvington, N. Yorks
	XZ384	SEPECAT Jaguar GR1 (8954M) [BC]	Privately owned, Coltishall, Norfolk
	XZ385	SEPECAT Jaguar GR3A [FT] <ff>	Privately owned, Biddulph, Staffs
	XZ389	SEPECAT Jaguar GR1 (8946M) [BL]	Ulster Aviation Society, Long Kesh, Co. Antrim, NI
	XZ390	SEPECAT Jaguar GR1 (9003M) [DM]	Dumfries & Galloway Avn Mus, Dumfries, Scotland
	XZ391	SEPECAT Jaguar GR3A [ET]	DSAE No 1 SoTT, Cosford, Shropshire
	XZ392	SEPECAT Jaguar GR3A [EM]	DSAE No 1 SoTT, Cosford, Shropshire
	XZ394	SEPECAT Jaguar GR3	Privately owned, Tattersett, Norfolk
	XZ398	SEPECAT Jaguar GR3A [EQ]	DSAE No 1 SoTT, Cosford, Shropshire
	XZ399	SEPECAT Jaguar GR3A [EJ]	DSAE No 1 SoTT, Cosford, Shropshire
	XZ400	SEPECAT Jaguar GR3A [FQ]	Privately owned, Selby, N. Yorks
	XZ431	HS Buccaneer S2B (9233M) <ff>	South Yorkshire Aircraft Museum, Doncaster, S. Yorks
	XZ440	BAe Sea Harrier FA2 [40/DD]	Privately owned, St Athan, Glamorgan, Wales
	XZ455	BAe Sea Harrier FA2 [001] (wreck)	Privately owned, Thorpe Wood, N. Yorks
	XZ457	BAe Sea Harrier FA2 [104/VL]	Boscombe Down Aviation Collection, Old Sarum, Wilts
	XZ459	BAe Sea Harrier FA2 [25]	Tangmere Military Aviation Museum, W. Sussex
	XZ493	BAe Sea Harrier FRS1 (comp XV760) [001/N]	FAA Museum, RNAS Yeovilton, Somerset
	XZ494	BAe Sea Harrier FA2 [128]	Privately owned, Wedmore, Somerset
	XZ497	BAe Sea Harrier FA2 [126]	Privately owned, Charlwood, Surrey
	XZ499	BAe Sea Harrier FA2 [003]	FAA Museum, RNAS Yeovilton, Somerset
	XZ550	Slingsby T61F Venture T2 (G-BTDA)	Privately owned, Easterton, Moray, Scotland
	XZ559	Slingsby T61F Venture T2 (G-BUEK)	Privately owned, Shipdam, Norfolk
	XZ570	WS61 Sea King HAS5(mod)	Privately owned, preserved Chew Magna, Somerset
	XZ574	WS61 Sea King HAS6	FAA Museum, stored Cobham Hall, RNAS Yeovilton, Somerset
	XZ575	WS61 Sea King HU5	Privately owned, Charlwood, Surrey
	XZ576	WS61 Sea King HAS6	DSAE RNAESS, *HMS Sultan*, Gosport, Hants
	XZ579	WS61 Sea King HAS6 [707/PW]	DSAE RNAESS, stored *HMS Sultan*, Gosport, Hants
	XZ580	WS61 Sea King HC6 [ZB]	DSAE RNAESS, *HMS Sultan*, Gosport, Hants
	XZ581	WS61 Sea King HAS6 [69/CU]	DSAE RNAESS, *HMS Sultan*, Gosport, Hants
	XZ585	WS61 Sea King HAR3 [A]	RAF Museum, Hendon, Gtr London
	XZ586	WS61 Sea King HAR3 [B]	HeliOperations Ltd, stored Somerton, Somerset

Serial	Type (code/other identity)	Owner/operator, location or fate	Notes
XZ587	WS61 Sea King HAR3 [C]	RAF St Mawgan, Cornwall, at main gate	
XZ588	WS61 Sea King HAR3 (G-SEAK)	Privately owned, Chard, Somerset	
XZ589	WS61 Sea King HAR3 [E] $	Privately owned, Scalby, N. Yorks	
XZ590	WS61 Sea King HAR3 [F]	HeliOperations Ltd, stored Somerton, Somerset	
XZ592	WS61 Sea King HAR3 [H]	Morayvia, Kinloss, Moray, Scotland	
XZ594	WS61 Sea King HAR3	HeliOperations Ltd, stored Somerton, Somerset	
XZ595	WS61 Sea King HAR3 [K]	Privately owned, Charlwood, Surrey	
XZ596	WS61 Sea King HAR3 [L]	HeliOperations Ltd, stored Somerton, Somerset	
XZ597	WS61 Sea King HAR3 (G-SKNG) [M]	Privately owned, Chard, Somerset	
XZ605	WS Lynx AH7 [L]	AAC Wattisham, Suffolk, preserved	
XZ606	WS Lynx AH7 [O]	Delta Force Paintball, Maidenhead, Berks	
XZ607	WS Lynx AH7 <ff>	MOD JARTS, Boscombe Down, Wilts	
XZ607	WS Lynx AH7 (comp XZ215)	Spadeadam Ranges, Cumbria	
XZ608	WS Lynx AH7 (fuselage)	Army, stored Old Buckenham, Norfolk (restoration)	
XZ608	WS Lynx AH7 (comp XZ680) [N]	Privately owned, East Grinstead, W. Sussex	
XZ609	WS Lynx AH7 (fuselage)	Army, stored Old Buckenham, Norfolk (restoration)	
XZ611	WS Lynx AH7 <ff>	Bilsthorpe Paintball Park, Notts	
XZ612	WS Lynx AH7	Delta Force Paintball, Bovingdon, Herts	
XZ613	WS Lynx AH7 [F]	Privately owned, Billericay, Essex	
XZ615	WS Lynx AH7 (XZ209) <ff>	MOD JARTS, Boscombe Down, Wilts	
XZ616	WS Lynx AH7 (G-LNKX)	Privately owned, Chard, Somerset	
XZ617	WS Lynx AH7 <ff>	FAA Museum, stored Cobham Hall, RNAS Yeovilton, Somerset	
XZ630	Panavia Tornado (P12) (8976M)	RAF Halton, Bucks, on display	
XZ631	Panavia Tornado (P15)	Yorkshire Air Museum, Elvington, N. Yorks	
XZ642	WS Lynx AH7	AAC, stored Wattisham, Suffolk	
XZ643	WS Lynx AH7 [C]	Culham Paintball, Oxon	
XZ645	WS Lynx AH7	Delta Force Paintball, Romsey, Hants	
XZ646	WS Lynx AH7 <ff>	MOD JARTS, Boscombe Down, Wilts	
XZ646	WS Lynx AH7 (XZ649)	The Helicopter Museum, stored Weston-super-Mare, Somerset	
XZ647	WS Lynx AH7 <ff>	Aberdeen Airport Fire Section, Scotland	
XZ651	WS Lynx AH7 [O]	Army, Pirbright, Surrey, GI use	
XZ652	WS Lynx AH7	IFTC, Teesside International Airport	
XZ653	WS Lynx AH7	AAC, stored Wattisham, Suffolk	
XZ654	WS Lynx AH7	Shannon Aviation Museum, Eire (stored)	
XZ655	WS Lynx AH7 [A/3] <ff>	Privately owned, Werrington, Peterborough, Cambs	
XZ661	WS Lynx AH7 [V]	Army, Bramley, Hants	
XZ664	WS Lynx AH7	R6 Warfighters Paintball, Barby, Warks	
XZ665	WS Lynx AH7	R6 Warfighters Paintball, Barby, Warks	
XZ666	WS Lynx AH7	Ulster Aviation Society, Long Kesh, Co. Antrim, NI	
XZ668	WS Lynx AH7 [UN] <ff>	Privately owned, stored Cranfield, Beds	
XZ670	WS Lynx AH7 [A]	RNAS Yeovilton, Somerset, on display	
XZ671	WS Lynx AH7 <ff>	Leonardo MW, Yeovil, Somerset, instructional use	
XZ672	WS Lynx AH7 <ff>	AAC Middle Wallop, Hants, Fire Section	
XZ673	WS Lynx AH7 [5]	Privately owned, Weeton, Lancs	
XZ674	WS Lynx AH7 [T]	RNAS Yeovilton, Somerset, Fire Section	
XZ675	WS Lynx AH7 [H]	Army Flying Museum, Middle Wallop, Hants	
XZ676	WS Lynx AH7 [N]	Privately owned, Weeton, Lancs	
XZ677	WS Lynx AH7 <ff>	Army, Longmoor Camp, Hants, GI use	
XZ678	WS Lynx AH7 (G-NCKY)	Privately owned, Peasemore, Berks	
XZ679	WS Lynx AH7 [W]	DSEME SAAE, Lyneham, Wilts	
XZ680	WS Lynx AH7 (XZ648)	Privately owned, Mabe Burnthouse, Cornwall	
XZ689	WS Lynx HMA8SRU [314]	Privately owned, Woodmancote, W. Sussex	
XZ690	WS Lynx HMA8SRU [640]	Delta Force Paintball, West Glasgow, Scotland	
XZ691	WS Lynx HMA8SRU [310]	FAA Museum, stored Cobham Hall, RNAS Yeovilton, Somerset	
XZ692	WS Lynx HMA8SRU [764/SN] $	DSAE HMS Sultan, Gosport, Hants, on display	
XZ693	WS Lynx HAS3S [311]	Wild Park Derbyshire, Brailsford, Derbys	
XZ694	WS Lynx HAS3GMS [434]	Privately owned, South Clifton, Notts	
XZ697	WS Lynx HMA8SRU $	MOD/StandardAero, preserved Fleetlands, Hants	
XZ698	WS Lynx HMA8SRU (ZD258) [365]	Privately owned, Blackpool, Lancs	

Notes	Serial	Type (code/other identity)	Owner/operator, location or fate
	XZ699	WS Lynx HAS2	FAA Museum, stored Cobham Hall, RNAS Yeovilton, Somerset
	XZ719	WS Lynx HMA8SRU [64]	RNAS Yeovilton, Somerset, Fire Section
	XZ720	WS Lynx HAS3GMS [410/GC]	FAA Museum, RNAS Yeovilton, Somerset
	XZ721	WS Lynx HAS3GMS [426/GC]	East Midlands Airport Aeropark, Leics
	XZ723	WS Lynx HMA8SRU [672]	Delta Force Paintball, Thornbury, Glos
	XZ725	WS Lynx HMA8SRU [415/MM]	Port Stanley Museum, Falkland Islands (stored)
	XZ726	WS Lynx HMA8SRU [316]	School of Maritime Survival, HMS Raleigh, Plymouth
	XZ727	WS Lynx HAS3S	Battersea Park, London
	XZ728	WS Lynx HMA8 [326/AW]	RNAS Yeovilton, Somerset, on display
	XZ729	WS Lynx HMA8SRU [425/DT]	DSAE RNAESS, HMS Sultan, Gosport, Hants
	XZ731	WS Lynx HMA8SRU [311/VL]	DSAE RNAESS, HMS Sultan, Gosport, Hants
	XZ732	WS Lynx HMA8SRU [315/VL]	DSEME SAAE, Lyneham, Wilts
	XZ735	WS Lynx HAS3GMS [305,404]	Privately owned, Sproughton, Suffolk
	XZ736	WS Lynx HMA8SRU [815]	RN Yeovilton, Somerset, GI use
	XZ791	Northrop Shelduck D1	Davidstow Airfield & Cornwall at War Museum, Cornwall
	XZ795	Northrop Shelduck D1	Army Flying Museum, Middle Wallop, Hants
	XZ921	WS61 Sea King HAS6 [269/N]	Holmside Park, Edmondsley, Co. Durham
	XZ922	WS61 Sea King HC6 [ZA]	DSAE RNAESS, HMS Sultan, Gosport, Hants
	XZ930	WS Gazelle HT3 (A2713) [GJ]	DSAE, HMS Sultan, Gosport, Hants, on display
	XZ932	WS Gazelle HT3 (G-CBJZ) [S]	Privately owned, Hamburg, Germany
	XZ933	WS Gazelle HT3 (XZ936/G-CGJZ)	Privately owned, Peasemore, Berks (restoration)
	XZ934	WS Gazelle HT3 (G-CBSI)	Privately owned, Redhill, Surrey
	XZ935	WS Gazelle HCC4 (G-CMFO)	Privately owned, Peasemore, Berks
	XZ936	WS Gazelle HT3 (G-CLHO) [6]	Privately owned, Peasemore, Berks
	XZ939	WS Gazelle HT3 (G-CLGO)	Privately owned, East Hanney, Oxon
	XZ941	WS Gazelle HT3 (9301M) [B]	DSAE No 1 SoTT, Cosford, Shropshire
	XZ964	BAe Harrier GR3 [D]	Royal Engineers Museum, Chatham, Kent
	XZ966	BAe Harrier GR3 (9221M) [G]	Spadeadam Ranges, Cumbria
	XZ968	BAe Harrier GR3 (9222M) [3G]	Muckleborough Collection, Weybourne, Norfolk
	XZ969	BAe Harrier GR3 [69/DD]	South Wales Aviation Museum, St Athan, Glamorgan, Wales
	XZ971	BAe Harrier GR3 (9219M) [G]	HQ DSDA, Donnington, Shropshire, on display
	XZ987	BAe Harrier GR3 (9185M) [C]	RAF Stafford, Staffs, at main gate
	XZ990	BAe Harrier GR3 <ff>	Currently not known
	XZ990	BAe Harrier GR3 <rf>	RAF Wittering, Cambs, derelict
	XZ991	BAe Harrier GR3 (9162M)	DSAF Cosford, Shropshire, on display
	XZ993	BAe Harrier GR3 (9240M) <ff>	Privately owned, Welshpool area, Powys, Wales
	XZ995	BAe Harrier GR3 (9220M/G-CBGK) [3G]	Privately owned, Dolly's Grove, Co Dublin, Eire
	XZ997	BAe Harrier GR3 (9122M) [V]	RAF Museum, stored Cosford, Shropshire
	ZA101	BAe Hawk 100 (G-HAWK)	Brooklands Museum, Weybridge, Surrey
	ZA105	WS61 Sea King HAR3 [Q]	HeliOperations Ltd, stored Somerton, Somerset
	ZA110	BAe Jetstream T2 (F-BTMI) [563/CU]	Aberdeen Airport Fire Section, Scotland
	ZA111	BAe Jetstream T2 (9Q-CTC) [565/CU]	Scrapped 2021
	ZA126	WS61 Sea King ASaC7 [91]	HeliOperations Ltd, stored Somerton, Somerset
	ZA127	WS61 Sea King HAS6 [509/CU]	Privately owned, Thornhill, Stirlingshire, Scotland
	ZA128	WS61 Sea King HAS6 [010]	DSAE, stored HMS Sultan, Gosport, Hants
	ZA130	WS61 Sea King HU5 [19]	Privately owned, Charlwood, Surrey
	ZA131	WS61 Sea King HAS6 [271/N]	DSAE RNAESS, HMS Sultan, Gosport, Hants
	ZA133	WS61 Sea King HAS6 [831/CU]	DSAE RNAESS, stored HMS Sultan, Gosport, Hants
	ZA135	WS61 Sea King HAS6 [705/CU]	Privately owned, Woodperry, Oxon
	ZA136	WS61 Sea King HAS6 [018] (comp Egyptian 776)	Mayhem Paintball, Abridge, Essex
	ZA137	WS61 Sea King HU5 [20]	HeliOperations Ltd, Portland, Dorset
	ZA148	BAe VC10 K3 (5Y-ADA/N148ZA) [G] <ff>	South Wales Aviation Museum, St Athan, Glamorgan, Wales
	ZA150	BAe VC10 K3 (5H-MOG/N150ZA) [J]	Privately owned, Dunsfold, Surrey
	ZA168	WS61 Sea King HAS6 [830/CU]	DSAE RNAESS, stored HMS Sultan, Gosport, Hants
	ZA169	WS61 Sea King HAS6 [515/CW]	DSAE RNAESS, stored HMS Sultan, Gosport, Hants
	ZA175	BAe Sea Harrier FA2	Norfolk & Suffolk Avn Museum, Flixton, Suffolk
	ZA176	BAe Sea Harrier FA2 [126/R]	Newark Air Museum, Winthorpe, Notts
	ZA180	Diamond Twin Star DA42MPP (G-DOSB)	To G-DOSB

Serial	Type (code/other identity)	Owner/operator, location or fate	Notes
ZA195	BAe Sea Harrier FA2 [710]	South Wales Aviation Museum, St Athan, Glamorgan, Wales	
ZA209	Short MATS-B	Army Flying Museum, stored Middle Wallop, Hants	
ZA220	Short MATS-B (ZA242)	Boscombe Down Aviation Collection, Old Sarum, Wilts	
ZA250	BAe Harrier T52 (G-VTOL)	Brooklands Museum, Weybridge, Surrey	
ZA267	Panavia Tornado ADV (9284M) [FA]	Privately owned, RAF Syerston, Notts	
ZA291	WS61 Sea King HC4 [N]	Holmside Park, Edmondsley, Co. Durham	
ZA298	WS61 Sea King HC4 (G-BJNM) [U/Y]	FAA Museum, RNAS Yeovilton, Somerset	
ZA312	WS61 Sea King HC4 [E]	Privately owned, Charlwood, Surrey	
ZA313	WS61 Sea King HC4 [M]	Privately owned, Holmside Park, Edmondsley, Co. Durham	
ZA314	WS61 Sea King HC4 (G-CMDO) [WT]	Privately owned, Chard, Somerset	
ZA319	Panavia Tornado GR1 (9315M)	Boscombe Down Aviation Collection, Old Sarum, Wilts	
ZA320	Panavia Tornado GR1 (9314M) [CA]	RAF Cosford, Shropshire, on display	
ZA323	Panavia Tornado GR1 [TAZ]	DSAE RNAESS, HMS Sultan, Gosport, Hants	
ZA325	Panavia Tornado GR1 <ff>	RAF Manston History Museum, Kent	
ZA325	Panavia Tornado GR1 [TAX] <rf>	Scrapped St. Athan 2005	
ZA326	Panavia Tornado GR1P	South Wales Aviation Museum, St Athan, Glamorgan, Wales	
ZA327	Panavia Tornado GR1 <ff>	Lakes Lightnings, Spark Bridge, Cumbria	
ZA328	Panavia Tornado GR1	BAE Systems, stored Salmesbury, Lancs	
ZA353	Panavia Tornado GR1 [B-53]	Privately owned, Topsham, Devon	
ZA354	Panavia Tornado GR1	Yorkshire Air Museum, Elvington, N. Yorks	
ZA355	Panavia Tornado GR1 (9310M) [EA]	Privately owned, White Waltham, Berks	
ZA356	Panavia Tornado GR1 <ff>	DSAE No 1 SoTT, Cosford, Shropshire	
ZA357	Panavia Tornado GR1 [TTV]	Privately owned, RAF Syerston, Notts	
ZA359	Panavia Tornado GR1	Privately owned, Thorpe Wood, N. Yorks	
ZA362	Panavia Tornado GR1	Privately owned, New York, Lincs	
ZA398	Panavia Tornado GR4A [087]	RAF, preserved RAF Lossiemouth, Moray, Scotland	
ZA399	Panavia Tornado GR1 (9316M) [AJ-C]	Privately owned, Knutsford, Cheshire	
ZA407	Panavia Tornado GR1 (9336M) [AJ-N]	RAF Marham, Norfolk, fire section	
ZA447	Panavia Tornado GR4 [019]	DSAE No 1 SoTT, Cosford, Shropshire	
ZA450	Panavia Tornado GR1 (9317M) [TH]	DSAE No 1 SoTT, Cosford, Shropshire	
ZA452	Panavia Tornado GR4 [021]	Midland Air Museum, Coventry, Warks	
ZA457	Panavia Tornado GR1 [AJ-J]	RAF Museum, Hendon, Gtr London	
ZA459	Panavia Tornado GR4 [025]	DSAE No 1 SoTT, Cosford, Shropshire	
ZA463	Panavia Tornado GR4 [046]	RAF Lossiemouth, Moray, Scotland, on display	
ZA465	Panavia Tornado GR1 [FF]	IWM Duxford, Cambs	
ZA469	Panavia Tornado GR4 [029]	IWM Duxford, Cambs	
ZA475	Panavia Tornado GR1 (9311M) [AJ-G]	Solway Aviation Society, Carlisle, Cumbria	
ZA549	Panavia Tornado GR4 [041]	BAE Systems Aircraft Maintenance Academy, Humberside, Lincs	
ZA553	Panavia Tornado GR4 [045]	Stored RAF Wittering, Cambs	
ZA556	Panavia Tornado GR4 [047]	Defence Academy of the UK, Shrivenham, Oxon	
ZA556	Panavia Tornado GR1 <R> (ZA368/BAPC.155) [Z]	RAF M&RU, Bottesford, Leics	
ZA560	Panavia Tornado GR4 [EB-Q]	MOD JARTS, Boscombe Down, Wilts	
ZA585	Panavia Tornado GR4 [054]	DSAE No 1 SoTT, Cosford, Shropshire	
ZA587	Panavia Tornado GR4 [055]	RAF Honington, Suffolk, GI use	
ZA607	Panavia Tornado GR4 [EB-X]	MoD Sealand, Flintshire, Wales, on display	
ZA612	Panavia Tornado GR4 [074] $	South Wales Aviation Museum, St Athan, Glamorgan, Wales	
ZA613	Panavia Tornado GR4 [075]	RAF Honington, Suffolk, GI use	
ZA614	Panavia Tornado GR4 $	RAF Marham, Norfolk, at main gate	
ZA630	Slingsby T61F Venture T2 (G-BUGL)	Privately owned, Tibenham, Norfolk	
ZA634	Slingsby T61F Venture T2 (G-BUHA) [C]	Privately owned, Saltby, Leics	
ZA652	Slingsby T61F Venture T2 (G-BUDC)	Cancelled by the CAA, 2023	
ZA656	Slingsby T61F Venture T2 (G-BTWC)	Privately owned, Nympsfield, Glos	
ZA665	Slingsby T61F Venture T2 (G-BVKK)	Privately owned, Saltby, Leics	
ZA670	B-V Chinook HC6A (N37010)	MOD/StandardAero, Fleetlands, Hants	
ZA671	B-V Chinook HC6A (N37011)	RAF No 7 Sqn, Odiham, Hants	
ZA674	B-V Chinook HC6A (N37019)	RAF No 27 Sqn, Odiham, Hants	
ZA675	B-V Chinook HC6A (N37020)	RAF, Operation Shader, Akrotiri, Cyprus	
ZA677	B-V Chinook HC6A (N37022)	RAF No 28 Sqn, Benson, Oxon	

Notes	Serial	Type (code/other identity)	Owner/operator, location or fate
	ZA678	B-V Chinook HC1 (N37023/9229M) [EZ] (wreck)	RAF Odiham, Hants, BDRT
	ZA679	B-V Chinook HC6A (N37025)	RAF No 28 Sqn, Benson, Oxon
	ZA680	B-V Chinook HC6A (N37026)	RAF No 18 Sqn, Odiham, Hants
	ZA682	B-V Chinook HC6A (N37029)	*RAF, Odiham (withdrawn from use)*
	ZA683	B-V Chinook HC6A (N37030)	RAF No 18 Sqn, Odiham, Hants
	ZA684	B-V Chinook HC6A (N37031)	RAF No 28 Sqn, Benson, Oxon
	ZA704	B-V Chinook HC6A (N37033)	RAF No 28 Sqn, Benson, Oxon
	ZA705	B-V Chinook HC6A (N37035)	RAF No 28 Sqn, Benson, Oxon
	ZA707	B-V Chinook HC6A (N37040)	*RAF, Odiham (withdrawn from use)*
	ZA708	B-V Chinook HC6A (N37042)	RAF No 27 Sqn, Odiham, Hants
	ZA710	B-V Chinook HC6A (N37044)	RAF No 18 Sqn, Odiham, Hants
	ZA711	B-V Chinook HC6A (N37046)	RAF No 27 Sqn, Odiham, Hants
	ZA712	B-V Chinook HC6A (N37047)	MOD/StandardAero, Fleetlands, Hants
	ZA713	B-V Chinook HC6A (N37048)	MOD/StandardAero, Fleetlands, Hants (wfu)
	ZA714	B-V Chinook HC6A (N37051)	RAF No 18 Sqn, Odiham, Hants
	ZA717	B-V Chinook HC1 (N37056/9238M) (wreck)	Newark Air Museum, Winthorpe, Notts
	ZA718	B-V Chinook HC6A (N37058) [BN]	RAF Museum, Cosford, Shropshire
	ZA718	WS Lynx AH7 (XZ183) <ff>	MOD JARTS, Boscombe Down, Wilts
	ZA720	B-V Chinook HC6A (N37060)	RAF CMF, Odiham, Hants
	ZA726	WS Gazelle AH1 [F1]	Privately owned, Stapleford Tawney, Essex
	ZA726	WS Gazelle AH1 (XW851/G-CIEY)	Privately owned, Deighton, N. Yorks
	ZA729	WS Gazelle AH1 (cabin)	AAC Wattisham, Suffolk, GI use
	ZA730	WS Gazelle AH1 (G-FUKM) <ff>	Privately owned, Andover area, Hants
	ZA731	WS Gazelle AH1	MOD/StandardAero, stored Fleetlands, Hants
	ZA731	WS Gazelle AH1 (comp XZ313)	Privately owned, Deighton, N. Yorks
	ZA735	WS Gazelle AH1	DSAE SAAE, Lyneham, Wilts
	ZA736	WS Gazelle AH1	MOD/StandardAero, stored Fleetlands, Hants
	ZA737	WS Gazelle AH1	Army Flying Museum, Middle Wallop, Hants
	ZA766	WS Gazelle AH1	MOD/StandardAero, stored Fleetlands, Hants
	ZA769	WS Gazelle AH1 [K]	DSAE SAAE, Lyneham, Wilts
	ZA772	WS Gazelle AH1	MOD/StandardAero, stored Fleetlands, Hants
	ZA773	WS Gazelle AH1 [F]	AAC AM&SU, stored Shawbury, Shropshire
	ZA775	WS Gazelle AH1	*Sold as G-CMXH, stored Babcary, Somerset*
	ZA776	WS Gazelle AH1 [F]	Privately owned, Stapleford Tawney, Essex (stored)
	ZA804	WS Gazelle HT3	Privately owned, Solstice Park, Amesbury, Wilts
	ZA935	WS Puma HC2 [S]	RAF No 230 Sqn, Seria, Brunei
	ZA936	WS Puma HC2 [T]	RAF AM&SU, stored Shawbury, Shropshire
	ZA937	WS Puma HC1	RAF Benson, Oxon, on display
	ZA939	WS Puma HC2 [U]	RAF No 28 Sqn/No 33 Sqn, Benson, Oxon
	ZA940	WS Puma HC2 (F-ZWBZ) [V]	RAF No 84 Sqn, Akrotiri, Cyprus
	ZA947	Douglas Dakota C3	RAF BBMF, Coningsby, Lincs
	ZB131	BAE Systems Hawk Mk.167	RAF Joint Hawk Training Sqn/No 11 Sqn QEAF, Leeming
	ZB132	BAE Systems Hawk Mk.167	RAF Joint Hawk Training Sqn/No 11 Sqn QEAF, Leeming
	ZB133	BAE Systems Hawk Mk.167	RAF Joint Hawk Training Sqn/No 11 Sqn QEAF, Leeming
	ZB134	BAE Systems Hawk Mk.167	RAF Joint Hawk Training Sqn/No 11 Sqn QEAF, Leeming
	ZB135	BAE Systems Hawk Mk.167	RAF Joint Hawk Training Sqn/No 11 Sqn QEAF, Leeming
	ZB136	BAE Systems Hawk Mk.167	RAF Joint Hawk Training Sqn/No 11 Sqn QEAF, Leeming
	ZB137	BAE Systems Hawk Mk.167	RAF Joint Hawk Training Sqn/No 11 Sqn QEAF, Leeming
	ZB138	BAE Systems Hawk Mk.167	RAF Joint Hawk Training Sqn/No 11 Sqn QEAF, Leeming
	ZB139	BAE Systems Hawk Mk.167	RAF Joint Hawk Training Sqn/No 11 Sqn QEAF, Leeming
	ZB500	WS Lynx 800 (G-LYNX/ZA500)	The Helicopter Museum, Weston-super-Mare, Somerset
	ZB506	WS61 Sea King Mk 4X	Privately owned, White Waltham, Berks (dismantled)
	ZB507	WS61 Sea King HC4 [F] (stripped hulk)	Privately owned, Okehampton area, Devon
	ZB601	BAe Harrier T4 (fuselage)	Privately owned, Thorpe Wood, N. Yorks
	ZB603	BAe Harrier T8 [T03/DD]	Privately owned, St Athan, Glamorgan, Wales
	ZB604	BAe Harrier T8 [722]	FAA Museum, stored Cobham Hall, RNAS Yeovilton, Somerset
	ZB615	SEPECAT Jaguar T2A	DSAE No 1 SoTT, Cosford, Shropshire
	ZB625	WS Gazelle HT3 (G-TSTR)	Privately owned, Babcary, Somerset (to Australia)
	ZB627	WS Gazelle HT3 (G-CBSK) [A]	Privately owned, Finmere, Oxon
	ZB646	WS Gazelle HT2 (G-CBGZ) [59/CU]	Privately owned, Suffolk area

Serial	Type (code/other identity)	Owner/operator, location or fate	Notes
ZB647	WS Gazelle HT2 (G-CBSF) [40]	Privately owned, Babcary, Somerset (restoration)	
ZB665	WS Gazelle AH1	MOD/StandardAero, stored Fleetlands, Hants	
ZB668	WS Gazelle AH1 (TAD 015)	DSAE SAAE, Lyneham, Wilts	
ZB669	WS Gazelle AH1	*Sold as G-CMXJ, stored Babcary, Somerset*	
ZB670	WS Gazelle AH1	TA Centre, Taunton, Somerset, on display	
ZB671	WS Gazelle AH1	MOD/StandardAero, stored Fleetlands, Hants	
ZB672	WS Gazelle AH1	Army Training Regiment, Winchester, Hants	
ZB674	WS Gazelle AH1	*Sold as G-CMXP, stored Babcary, Somerset*	
ZB677	WS Gazelle AH1 (G-CMKP)	Privately owned, Deighton, N. Yorks	
ZB678	WS Gazelle AH1	MOD/StandardAero, stored Fleetlands, Hants	
ZB679	WS Gazelle AH1	*Sold as G-CMXK, stored Babcary, Somerset*	
ZB684	WS Gazelle AH1	RAF JADTEU, Brize Norton, Oxon, instructional use	
ZB686	WS Gazelle AH1 <ff>	The Helicopter Museum, Weston-super-Mare, Somerset	
ZB689	WS Gazelle AH1 (HA-LFR/G-CMKT)	Privately owned, Belgium	
ZB690	WS Gazelle AH1	*Sold as G-CMXL, stored Babcary, Somerset*	
ZB691	WS Gazelle AH1 [S]	AAC 7 Regiment Conversion Flt, Middle Wallop, Hants	
ZB692	WS Gazelle AH1 [Y]	Privately owned, Deighton, North Yorks	
ZB693	WS Gazelle AH1	MOD/StandardAero, Fleetlands, Hants	
ZD230	BAC Super VC10 K4 (G-ASGA) <ff>	Privately owned, Crondall, Hants	
ZD240	BAC Super VC10 K4 (G-ASGL) <ff>	Privately owned, Crondall, Hants	
ZD242	BAC Super VC10 K4 (G-ASGP) <ff>	JARTS, Boscombe Down, Wilts	
ZD249	WS Lynx HMA8SRU (XZ698) (comp ZD249) [316]	Delta Force Paintball, Edinburgh, Scotland	
ZD249	WS Lynx HAS3S [635] <ff>	Privately owned, Sproughton, Suffolk	
ZD250	WS Lynx HAS3S [636]	RAF Henlow, Beds, instructional use	
ZD252	WS Lynx HMA8SRU (G-NCKZ) [312/VL]	Privately owned, North Weald, Essex	
ZD254	WS Lynx HAS3S [305/GJ]	DSAE AESS, *HMS Sultan*, Gosport, Hants	
ZD255	WS Lynx HAS3GMS [635]	Bawtry Paintball Park, S Yorks	
ZD257	WS Lynx HMA8SRU [302/VL]	Privately owned, Woodmancote, W. Sussex	
ZD259	WS Lynx HMA8SRU [474/RM]	DSEME DCTT, Lyneham, Wilts	
ZD260	WS Lynx HMA8SRU [313/VL]	DSEME DCTT, Lyneham, Wilts	
ZD261	WS Lynx HMA8SRU [314]	DSEME DCTT, Lyneham, Wilts	
ZD262	WS Lynx HMA8SRU [316]	DSEME SAAE, Lyneham, Wilts	
ZD263	WS Lynx HAS3S [632]	Bawtry Paintball Park, S. Yorks	
ZD264	WS Lynx HAS3GMS [407] (fuselage)	Air Defence Collection, Wilts	
ZD265	WS Lynx HMA8SRU [302]	AAC Middle Wallop, Hants, dumped	
ZD266	WS Lynx HMA8SRU [673]	Privately owned, North Weald, Essex	
ZD267	WS Lynx HMA8 (comp XZ672) [LST-2]	RN, stored St Athan, Wales	
ZD268	WS Lynx HMA8SRU [366/YB]	DSEME SAAE, Lyneham, Wilts	
ZD274	WS Lynx AH7 [M]	Privately owned, Sproughton, Suffolk (for sale)	
ZD276	WS Lynx AH7	Mayhem Paintball, Abridge, Essex	
ZD278	WS Lynx AH7 [F]	Delta Force, Liverpool, Merseyside	
ZD280	WS Lynx AH7	Farnborough Air Sciences Trust, Farnborough, Hants	
ZD281	WS Lynx AH7 [K]	Privately owned, Willenhall, Staffs	
ZD283	WS Lynx AH7 <ff>	Privately owned, Stoke-on-Trent, Staffs	
ZD283	WS Lynx AH7 (ZE379)	Privately owned, Freiston, Lincs	
ZD284	WS Lynx AH7 [K]	Privately owned, Corley Moor, Warks	
ZD285	WS Lynx AH7	Privately owned, Peasemore, Berks	
ZD318	BAe Harrier GR7A	Harrier Heritage Centre, RAF Wittering, Cambs	
ZD433	BAe Harrier GR9A [45A]	FAA Museum, RNAS Yeovilton, Somerset	
ZD461	BAe Harrier GR9A [51A]	IWM London, Lambeth, Gtr London	
ZD462	BAe Harrier GR7 (9302M) [52]	Privately owned, North Weald, Essex	
ZD465	BAe Harrier GR9 [55]	DSAE RNAESS, *HMS Sultan*, Gosport, Hants	
ZD469	BAe Harrier GR7A [59A]	RAF Wittering, Cambs, on display	
ZD476	WS61 Sea King HC4 [WZ]	Privately owned, Charlwood, Surrey	
ZD477	WS61 Sea King HC4 [E]	East Midlands Airport Aeropark, Leics	
ZD478	WS61 Sea King HC4 [J]	Privately owned, Hixon, Staffs	
ZD479	WS61 Sea King HC4 [WQ]	DSAE RNAESS, *HMS Sultan*, Gosport, Hants	
ZD480	WS61 Sea King HC4 [J]	StandardAero, Fleetlands, Hants, on display	
ZD559	WS Lynx AH5X	QinetiQ Apprentice Training School, Boscombe Down	
ZD560	WS Lynx AH7	Leonardo MW, Yeovil, Somerset, on display	
ZD565	WS Lynx HMA8SRU [404/IR]	Delta Force Paintball, Cardiff, Wales	

Notes	Serial	Type (code/other identity)	Owner/operator, location or fate
	ZD566	WS Lynx HMA8SRU [305]	Privately owned, Lizard, Helston, Cornwall
	ZD574	B-V Chinook HC6A (N37077)	RAF CMF, Odiham, Hants
	ZD575	B-V Chinook HC6A (N37078)	MOD/StandardAero, Fleetlands, Hants
	ZD578	BAe Sea Harrier FA2 [000,122]	RNAS Yeovilton, Somerset, at main gate
	ZD579	BAe Sea Harrier FA2 [79/DD]	Privately owned, St Athan, Glamorgan, Wales
	ZD581	BAe Sea Harrier FA2 [124]	Privately owned, Sproughton, Suffolk (for sale)
	ZD582	BAe Sea Harrier FA2 [002/N]	North-East Land, Sea & Air Museums, Usworth, T&W
	ZD607	BAe Sea Harrier FA2	DSDA, Arncott, Oxon, preserved
	ZD610	BAe Sea Harrier FA2 [714,002/N]	Aerospace Bristol, Filton, Glos
	ZD611	BAe Sea Harrier FA2 [001]	RN, Portsmouth Dockyard, Hants, preserved
	ZD612	BAe Sea Harrier FA2 [724]	Privately owned, Topsham, Devon
	ZD613	BAe Sea Harrier FA2 [122/R]	Privately owned, Thorpe Wood, N. Yorks
	ZD614	BAe Sea Harrier FA2 <ff>	Privately owned, Walcott, Lincs
	ZD620	BAe 125 CC3	Bournemouth Aviation Museum, Dorset
	ZD621	BAe 125 CC3	RAF Northolt, Gtr London, on display
	ZD625	WS61 Sea King HC4 [P]	Holmside Park, Edmondsley, Co. Durham
	ZD627	WS61 Sea King HC4 <ff>	South Wales Aviation Museum, stored St Athan, Glamorgan, Wales
	ZD634	WS61 Sea King HAS6 [503]	SFDO, RNAS Culdrose, Cornwall
	ZD636	WS61 Sea King ASaC7 [182/CU]	DSAE, stored HMS Sultan, Gosport, Hants
	ZD637	WS61 Sea King HAS6 [700/PW]	DSAE RNAESS, HMS Sultan, Gosport, Hants
	ZD667	BAe Harrier GR3 (9201M) [U]	Bentwaters Cold War Museum, Suffolk
	ZD703	BAe 125 CC3	Privately owned, Shepton Mallet, Somerset
	ZD704	BAe 125 CC3	MOD JARTS, Boscombe Down, Wilts
	ZD710	Panavia Tornado GR1 <ff>	Privately owned, Lincs
	ZD711	Panavia Tornado GR4 [079]	RAF Honington, Suffolk, GI use
	ZD715	Panavia Tornado GR4 [083]	DSAE No 1 SoTT, Cosford, Shropshire
	ZD744	Panavia Tornado GR4 [092]	Montrose Air Station Heritage Centre, Angus, Scotland
	ZD793	Panavia Tornado GR4 [101]	DSAE No 1 SoTT, Cosford, Shropshire
	ZD849	Panavia Tornado GR4 [110]	DSAE No 1 SoTT, Cosford, Shropshire
	ZD902	Panavia Tornado F2A(TIARA)	To USA, July 2024
	ZD932	Panavia Tornado F2 (comp ZE255) (9308M) (fuselage)	Privately owned, Thorpe Wood, N. Yorks
	ZD936	Panavia Tornado F2 (comp ZE251) <ff>	Boscombe Down Aviation Collection, Old Sarum, Wilts
	ZD938	Panavia Tornado F2 (comp ZE295) <ff>	South Yorkshire Aircraft Museum, Doncaster, S. Yorks
	ZD939	Panavia Tornado F2 (comp ZE292) <ff>	DSAE No 1 SoTT, Cosford, Shropshire, GI use
	ZD980	B-V Chinook HC6A (N37082)	RAF No 18 Sqn, Odiham, Hants
	ZD981	B-V Chinook HC6A (N37083)	RAF, Operation Shader, Akrotiri, Cyprus
	ZD982	B-V Chinook HC6A (N37085)	RAF No 18 Sqn, Odiham, Hants
	ZD983	B-V Chinook HC6A (N37086)	RAF No 27 Sqn, Odiham, Hants
	ZD984	B-V Chinook HC6A (N37088)	MOD/StandardAero, Fleetlands, Hants
	ZD990	BAe Harrier T8 (G-RNTB) [T90/DD]	Privately owned, St Athan, Glamorgan, Wales
	ZD992	BAe Harrier T8 [724]	Privately owned, Knutsford, Cheshire
	ZE165	Panavia Tornado F3 [GE]	Fire Service College, Moreton-in-Marsh, Glos
	ZE168	Panavia Tornado F3 <ff>	Privately owned, Thorpe Wood, N. Yorks
	ZE204	Panavia Tornado F3 [FC]	North-East Land, Sea & Air Museums, Usworth, T&W
	ZE340	Panavia Tornado F3 (ZE758/9298M) [GO]	DSAE No 1 SoTT, Cosford, Shropshire
	ZE352	McD F-4J(UK) Phantom (9086M) <ff>	Privately owned, Newburgh, Lancs
	ZE360	McD F-4J(UK) Phantom (9059M) [O]	Privately owned, Cotswold Airport, Glos
	ZE368	WS61 Sea King HAR3 [R]	Holmside Park, stored Edmondsley, Co. Durham
	ZE369	WS61 Sea King HAR3 [S]	Privately owned, Scalby, N. Yorks
	ZE370	WS61 Sea King HAR3 [T]	Privately owned, Scalby, N. Yorks
	ZE375	WS Lynx AH9A	Privately owned, Sproughton, Suffolk
	ZE376	WS Lynx AH9A	Sheffield University, S. Yorks, GI use
	ZE378	WS Lynx AH7	RAF Cranwell, Lincs, GI use
	ZE380	WS Lynx AH9A	Army, Pirbright, Surrey, GI use
	ZE381	WS Lynx AH7 [X]	DSEME SAAE, Lyneham, Wilts
	ZE395	BAe 125 CC3	Privately owned, Dunsfold, Surrey
	ZE410	Agusta A109A (AE-334)	Army Flying Museum, Middle Wallop, Hants
	ZE412	Agusta A109A	Army, Credenhill, Herefordshire, on display
	ZE413	Agusta A109A	Perth Technical College, Scotland
	ZE418	WS61 Sea King ASaC7 [186]	DSAE, stored HMS Sultan, Gosport, Hants

Serial	Type (code/other identity)	Owner/operator, location or fate	Notes
ZE420	WS61 Sea King ASaC7 [189]	DSAE RNAESS, *HMS Sultan*, Gosport, Hants	
ZE422	WS61 Sea King ASaC7 [192]	HeliOperations Ltd, stored Somerton, Somerset	
ZE425	WS61 Sea King HC4 [WR]	Holmside Park, Edmondsley, Co. Durham	
ZE426	WS61 Sea King HC4 [WX]	DSAE RNAESS, *HMS Sultan*, Gosport, Hants	
ZE428	WS61 Sea King HC4 [H]	Holmside Park, Edmondsley, Co. Durham (damaged)	
ZE432	BAC 1-11/479FU (DQ-FBV) <ff>	Bournemouth Aviation Museum, Dorset	
ZE449	SA330L Puma HC1 (9017M/PA-12)	Army, Whittington Barracks, Lichfield, on display	
ZE477	WS Lynx 3	The Helicopter Museum, Weston-super-Mare, Somerset	
ZE495	Grob G103 Viking T1 (BGA3000) [VA]	RAF No 661 VGS, Kirknewton, W. Lothian, Scotland	
ZE496	Grob G103 Viking T1 (BGA3001) [VB]	RAF No 615 VGS, Kenley, Surrey	
ZE498	Grob G103 Viking T1 (BGA3003) [VC]	RAF, stored Little Rissington, Glos	
ZE499	Grob G103 Viking T1 (BGA3004) [VD]	RAF/Serco GMS, stored Syerston, Notts (dismantled)	
ZE500	Grob G103 Viking T1 (BGA3005) <ff>	Privately owned, Gransden Lodge, Cambs	
ZE502	Grob G103 Viking T1 (BGA3007) [VF]	RAF/Serco GMS, stored Syerston, Notts (dismantled)	
ZE503	Grob G103 Viking T1 (BGA3008) [VG]	RAF, stored Little Rissington, Glos	
ZE504	Grob G103 Viking T1 (BGA3009) [VH]	RAF/Serco GMS, stored Syerston, Notts (dismantled)	
ZE520	Grob G103 Viking T1 (BGA3010) [VJ]	RAF, stored Little Rissington, Glos	
ZE521	Grob G103 Viking T1 (BGA3011) [VK]	RAF CGS/No 644 VGS, Syerston, Notts	
ZE522	Grob G103 Viking T1 (BGA3012) [VL]	RAF No 645 VGS, Topcliffe, N. Yorks	
ZE524	Grob G103 Viking T1 (BGA3014) [VM]	RAF, stored Little Rissington, Glos	
ZE526	Grob G103 Viking T1 (BGA3016) [VN]	RAF CGS/No 644 VGS, Syerston, Notts	
ZE527	Grob G103 Viking T1 (BGA3017) [VP]	RAF No 661 VGS, Kirknewton, W. Lothian, Scotland	
ZE528	Grob G103 Viking T1 (BGA3018) [VQ]	RAF No 622 VGS, Upavon, Wilts	
ZE529	Grob G103 Viking T1 (BGA3019) (comp ZE655) [VR]	RAF No 645 VGS, Topcliffe, N. Yorks	
ZE530	Grob G103 Viking T1 (BGA3020) [VS]	RAF, stored Little Rissington, Glos	
ZE531	Grob G103 Viking T1 (BGA3021) [VT]	RAF, stored Little Rissington, Glos	
ZE532	Grob G103 Viking T1 (BGA3022) [VU]	RAF No 645 VGS, Topcliffe, N. Yorks	
ZE533	Grob G103 Viking T1 (BGA3023) [VV]	RAF, stored Little Rissington, Glos	
ZE550	Grob G103 Viking T1 (BGA3025) [VX] (fuselage)	RAF Syerston, Notts, GI use	
ZE551	Grob G103 Viking T1 (BGA3026) [VY]	RAF No 612 VGS, Little Rissington, Glos	
ZE552	Grob G103 Viking T1 (BGA3027) [VZ]	RAF, stored Little Rissington, Glos	
ZE553	Grob G103 Viking T1 (BGA3028) [WA]	RAF CGS/No 644 VGS, Syerston, Notts	
ZE554	Grob G103 Viking T1 (BGA3029) [WB]	RAF, stored Little Rissington, Glos	
ZE555	Grob G103 Viking T1 (BGA3030) [WC]	RAF No 645 VGS, Topcliffe, N. Yorks	
ZE556	Grob G103 Viking T1 (BGA3031) <ff>	No 308 Sqn ATC, Colchester, Essex	
ZE557	Grob G103 Viking T1 (BGA3032) [WE]	RAF No 612 VGS, Little Rissington, Glos	
ZE558	Grob G103 Viking T1 (BGA3033) [WF]	RAF, stored Little Rissington, Glos	
ZE559	Grob G103 Viking T1 (BGA3034) [WG]	RAF/Serco GMS, stored Syerston, Notts (dismantled)	
ZE560	Grob G103 Viking T1 (BGA3035) [WH]	RAF No 622 VGS, Upavon, Wilts	
ZE561	Grob G103 Viking T1 (BGA3036) [WJ]	RAF, stored Little Rissington, Glos	
ZE562	Grob G103 Viking T1 (BGA3037) [WK]	RAF, stored Little Rissington, Glos	
ZE563	Grob G103 Viking T1 (BGA3038) [WL]	RAF, stored Little Rissington, Glos	
ZE564	Grob G103 Viking T1 (BGA3039) [WN]	RAF No 645 VGS, Topcliffe, N. Yorks	
ZE584	Grob G103 Viking T1 (BGA3040) [WP]	RAF/Serco GMS, Syerston, Notts (dismantled)	
ZE585	Grob G103 Viking T1 (BGA3041) [WQ]	RAF No 611 VGS, Honington, Suffolk	
ZE586	Grob G103 Viking T1 (BGA3042) [WR]	RAF No 612 VGS, Little Rissington, Glos	
ZE587	Grob G103 Viking T1 (BGA3043) [WS]	RAF/Serco GMS, Syerston, Notts (dismantled)	
ZE590	Grob G103 Viking T1 (BGA3046) [WT]	RAF No 615 VGS, Kenley, Surrey	
ZE591	Grob G103 Viking T1 (BGA3047) [WU]	RAF, stored Little Rissington, Glos	
ZE592	Grob G103 Viking T1 (BGA3048) <ff>	RAF, Upavon, Wilts, GI use	
ZE593	Grob G103 Viking T1 (BGA3049) [WW]	RAF, stored Little Rissington, Glos	
ZE594	Grob G103 Viking T1 (BGA3050) [WX]	RAF No 645 VGS, Topcliffe, N. Yorks	
ZE595	Grob G103 Viking T1 (BGA3051) [WY]	RAF No 611 VGS, Honington, Suffolk	
ZE600	Grob G103 Viking T1 (BGA3052) [WZ]	RAF No 626 VGS, Predannack, Cornwall	
ZE601	Grob G103 Viking T1 (BGA3053) [XA]	RAF CGS/No 644 VGS, Syerston, Notts	
ZE602	Grob G103 Viking T1 (BGA3054) [XB]	RAF No 661 VGS, Kirknewton, W. Lothian, Scotland	
ZE603	Grob G103 Viking T1 (BGA3055) [XC]	RAF, stored Little Rissington, Glos	
ZE604	Grob G103 Viking T1 (BGA3056) [XD]	RAF, stored Little Rissington, Glos	
ZE605	Grob G103 Viking T1 (BGA3057) [XE]	RAF No 615 VGS, Kenley, Surrey	
ZE606	Grob G103 Viking T1 (BGA3058) [XF]	RAF, stored Little Rissington, Glos	
ZE607	Grob G103 Viking T1 (BGA3059) [XG]	RAF, stored Little Rissington, Glos	
ZE608	Grob G103 Viking T1 (BGA3060) [XH]	RAF No 615 VGS, Kenley, Surrey	

Notes	Serial	Type (code/other identity)	Owner/operator, location or fate
	ZE609	Grob G103 Viking T1 (BGA3061) [XJ]	RAF No 622 VGS, Upavon, Wilts
	ZE610	Grob G103 Viking T1 (BGA3062) [XK]	RAF, stored Little Rissington, Glos
	ZE611	Grob G103 Viking T1 (BGA3063) [XL]	RAF, stored Little Rissington, Glos
	ZE613	Grob G103 Viking T1 (BGA3065) [XM]	RAF No 622 VGS, Upavon, Wilts
	ZE614	Grob G103 Viking T1 (BGA3066) [XN]	RAF CGS/No 644 VGS, Syerston, Notts
	ZE625	Grob G103 Viking T1 (BGA3067) [XP]	RAF CGS/No 644 VGS, Syerston, Notts
	ZE626	Grob G103 Viking T1 (BGA3068) [XQ]	RAF No 632 VGS, Woodvale, Merseyside
	ZE627	Grob G103 Viking T1 (BGA3069) [XR]	RAF, stored Little Rissington, Glos
	ZE628	Grob G103 Viking T1 (BGA3070) [XS]	RAF CGS/No 644 VGS, Syerston, Notts
	ZE629	Grob G103 Viking T1 (BGA3071) [XT]	RAF No 632 VGS, Woodvale, Merseyside
	ZE630	Grob G103 Viking T1 (BGA3072) [XU]	RAF CGS/No 644 VGS, Syerston, Notts
	ZE631	Grob G103 Viking T1 (BGA3073) [XV]	RAF No 621 VGS/No 637 VGS, Little Rissington, Glos (CAT.4 damage 12/09/2023)
	ZE632	Grob G103 Viking T1 (BGA3074) [XW]	RAF No 615 VGS, Kenley, Surrey
	ZE633	Grob G103 Viking T1 (BGA3075) [XX]	RAF No 645 VGS, Topcliffe, N. Yorks
	ZE636	Grob G103 Viking T1 (BGA3078) [XZ]	RAF CGS/No 644 VGS, Syerston, Notts
	ZE637	Grob G103 Viking T1 (BGA3079) [YA]	RAF CGS/No 644 VGS, Syerston, Notts
	ZE650	Grob G103 Viking T1 (BGA3080) [YB]	RAF No 612 VGS, Little Rissington, Glos
	ZE651	Grob G103 Viking T1 (BGA3081) [YC]	RAF No 611 VGS, Honington, Suffolk
	ZE652	Grob G103 Viking T1 (BGA3082) [YD]	RAF/Serco GMS, Syerston, Notts (damaged)
	ZE653	Grob G103 Viking T1 (BGA3083) [YE]	RAF No 632 VGS, Woodvale, Merseyside
	ZE656	Grob G103 Viking T1 (BGA3086) [YH]	RAF, stored Little Rissington, Glos
	ZE657	Grob G103 Viking T1 (BGA3087) [YJ]	RAF, stored Little Rissington, Glos
	ZE658	Grob G103 Viking T1 (BGA3088) [YK]	RAF CGS/No 644 VGS, Syerston, Notts
	ZE659	Grob G103 Viking T1 <ff>	Privately owned, Lasham, Hants, (converted to simulator)
	ZE677	Grob G103 Viking T1 (BGA3090) [YM]	RAF, stored Little Rissington, Glos
	ZE678	Grob G103 Viking T1 (BGA3091) [YN]	RAF No 622 VGS, Upavon, Wilts
	ZE679	Grob G103 Viking T1 (BGA3092) [YP]	RAF, stored Little Rissington, Glos
	ZE680	Grob G103 Viking T1 (BGA3093) [YQ]	RAF No 626 VGS, Predannack, Cornwall
	ZE681	Grob G103 Viking T1 (BGA3094) <ff>	Privately owned, Frampton Cotterell, Glos, GI use
	ZE682	Grob G103 Viking T1 (BGA3095) [YS]	RAF No 611 VGS, Honington, Suffolk
	ZE683	Grob G103 Viking T1 (BGA3096) [YT]	RAF/Serco GMS, Syerston, Notts (dismantled)
	ZE684	Grob G103 Viking T1 (BGA3097) [YU]	RAF, stored Little Rissington, Glos
	ZE685	Grob G103 Viking T1 (BGA3098) [YV]	RAF CGS/No 644 VGS, Syerston, Notts
	ZE686	Grob G103 Viking T1 (BGA3099) <ff>	Privately owned, Stow Maries, Essex
	ZE690	BAe Sea Harrier FA2 [90/DD]	Privately owned, St Athan, Glamorgan, Wales
	ZE691	BAe Sea Harrier FA2 [710]	Classic Autos, Winsford, Cheshire
	ZE692	BAe Sea Harrier FA2 [92/DD]	Privately owned, St Athan, Glamorgan, Wales
	ZE694	BAe Sea Harrier FA2 [004/N]	Midland Air Museum, Coventry, Warks
	ZE697	BAe Sea Harrier FA2 [006]	Privately owned, Walcott, Norfolk
	ZE698	BAe Sea Harrier FA2 [123]	Privately owned, Charlwood, Surrey
	ZE700	BAe 146 CC2 (G-6-021) (G-CMFY)	South Wales Aviation Museum, St Athan, Glamorgan, Wales
	ZE701	BAe 146 CC2 (G-6-029/G-CMEU)	Duxford Aviation Society, Duxford, Cambs
	ZE707	BAe 146 C3 (OO-TAZ)	Privately owned, Cranfield Airport, Beds
	ZE708	BAe 146 C3 (OO-TAY)	Privately owned, Cranfield Airport, Beds
	ZE760	Panavia Tornado F3 (MM7206) [AP]	RAF Coningsby, Lincs, on display
	ZE788	Panavia Tornado F3 <ff>	Privately owned, Ruthin, Clwyd, Wales
	ZE887	Panavia Tornado F3 [GF] $	RAF Museum, Hendon, Gtr London
	ZE934	Panavia Tornado F3 [TA]	National Museum of Flight, E. Fortune, Scotland
	ZE936	Panavia Tornado F3 <ff>	RAF Air Defence Radar Museum, Neatishead, Norfolk
	ZE965	Panavia Tornado F3 <ff>	Privately owned, Thorpe Wood, N. Yorks
	ZE966	Panavia Tornado F3 [VT]	Tornado Heritage Centre, Hawarden, Flintshire, Wales
	ZE967	Panavia Tornado F3 [UT]	RAF Leuchars, Fife, Scotland, at main gate
	ZF115	WS61 Sea King HC4 [R,WV]	DSAE, stored HMS Sultan, Gosport, Hants
	ZF116	WS61 Sea King HC4 [WP]	Privately owned, White Waltham, Berks
	ZF118	WS61 Sea King HC4 [VO]	RN, preserved Yeovilton, Somerset
	ZF119	WS61 Sea King HC4 [WY]	DSAE RNAESS, HMS Sultan, Gosport, Hants
	ZF121	WS61 Sea King HC4 [T]	Holmside Park, Edmondsley, Co. Durham
	ZF122	WS61 Sea King HC4 (G-CMFM) [V]	Privately owned, Chard, Somerset

Serial	Type (code/other identity)	Owner/operator, location or fate	Notes
ZF135	Shorts Tucano T1 [135]	RAF, stored Linton-on-Ouse, N. Yorks (for disposal)	
ZF139	Shorts Tucano T1 [139]	RAF, stored Linton-on-Ouse, N. Yorks (for disposal)	
ZF140	Shorts Tucano T1 [140] $	RAF, stored Linton-on-Ouse, N. Yorks (for disposal)	
ZF142	Shorts Tucano T1 [142]	RAF, stored Linton-on-Ouse, N. Yorks (for disposal)	
ZF143	Shorts Tucano T1 [143]	RAF, stored Linton-on-Ouse, N. Yorks (for disposal)	
ZF144	Shorts Tucano T1 [144]	RAF, stored Linton-on-Ouse, N. Yorks (for disposal)	
ZF145	Shorts Tucano T1 [145]	RAF, stored Linton-on-Ouse, N. Yorks (for disposal)	
ZF160	Shorts Tucano T1 [160]	Unknown (ex Bentwaters)	
ZF163	Shorts Tucano T1 [163]	RAF AM&SU, stored Shawbury, Shropshire	
ZF167	Shorts Tucano T1 [167]	South Yorkshire Aircraft Museum, Doncaster, S. Yorks (rest'n)	
ZF202	Shorts Tucano T1 [202]	RAF Syerston, Notts, on display	
ZF204	Shorts Tucano T1 [204]	RAF, stored Linton-on-Ouse, N. Yorks (for disposal)	
ZF210	Shorts Tucano T1 [210]	RAF, stored Linton-on-Ouse, N. Yorks (for disposal)	
ZF240	Shorts Tucano T1 [240]	RAF, stored Linton-on-Ouse, N. Yorks (for disposal)	
ZF243	Shorts Tucano T1 [243]	RAF, stored Linton-on-Ouse, N. Yorks (for disposal)	
ZF244	Shorts Tucano T1 [244]	RAF, stored Linton-on-Ouse, N. Yorks (for disposal)	
ZF263	Shorts Tucano T1 [263]	RAF AM&SU, stored Shawbury, Shropshire	
ZF264	Shorts Tucano T1 [264] $	Privately owned, Suffolk area (stored)	
ZF268	Shorts Tucano T1 [268]	Privately owned, Suffolk area (stored)	
ZF269	Shorts Tucano T1 [269]	RAF, stored Linton-on-Ouse, N. Yorks (for disposal)	
ZF286	Shorts Tucano T1 [286]	RAF AM&SU, stored Shawbury, Shropshire	
ZF287	Shorts Tucano T1 [287]	Privately owned, Suffolk area (stored)	
ZF288	Shorts Tucano T1 [288]	RAF AM&SU, stored Shawbury, Shropshire	
ZF290	Shorts Tucano T1 [290] $	RAF, stored Linton-on-Ouse, N. Yorks (for disposal)	
ZF291	Shorts Tucano T1 [291]	Privately owned, Suffolk area (stored)	
ZF293	Shorts Tucano T1 [293] $	Privately owned, Suffolk area (stored)	
ZF295	Shorts Tucano T1 [295] $	Bombardier, Belfast, NI	
ZF315	Shorts Tucano T1 [315]	RAF AM&SU, stored Shawbury, Shropshire	
ZF318	Shorts Tucano T1 [318] $	RAF AM&SU, stored Shawbury, Shropshire	
ZF338	Shorts Tucano T1 [338]	RAF, stored Linton-on-Ouse, N. Yorks (for disposal)	
ZF342	Shorts Tucano T1 [342]	Solent Airport, Hampshire (for onward transport)	
ZF343	Shorts Tucano T1 [343]	RAF, stored Linton-on-Ouse, N. Yorks (for disposal)	
ZF347	Shorts Tucano T1 [347]	RAF, stored Linton-on-Ouse, N. Yorks (for disposal)	
ZF348	Shorts Tucano T1 [348]	RAF, stored Linton-on-Ouse, N. Yorks (for disposal)	
ZF350	Shorts Tucano T1 [350]	RAF AM&SU, stored Shawbury, Shropshire	
ZF355	WS Lynx HAS3S(ICE) (XZ238) [633]	Bournemouth Aviation Museum, Dorset	
ZF372	Shorts Tucano T1 [372]	Newark Air Museum, Winthorpe, Notts (restoration)	
ZF374	Shorts Tucano T1 [374]	Solent Airport, Hampshire (for onward transport)	
ZF376	Shorts Tucano T1 [376]	RAF AM&SU, stored Shawbury, Shropshire	
ZF377	Shorts Tucano T1 [377]	RAF, stored Linton-on-Ouse, N. Yorks (for disposal)	
ZF378	Shorts Tucano T1 [RN-S] $	Ulster Aviation Society, Long Kesh, Co. Antrim, NI	
ZF379	Shorts Tucano T1 [379]	Privately owned, Suffolk area (stored)	
ZF405	Shorts Tucano T1 [405]	RAF AM&SU, stored Shawbury, Shropshire	
ZF406	Shorts Tucano T1 [406]	RAF, stored Linton-on-Ouse, N. Yorks (for disposal)	
ZF407	Shorts Tucano T1 [407]	RAF, stored Linton-on-Ouse, N. Yorks (for disposal)	
ZF408	Shorts Tucano T1 [408]	RAF AM&SU, stored Shawbury, Shropshire	
ZF412	Shorts Tucano T1 [412]	Unknown (ex Bentwaters)	
ZF414	Shorts Tucano T1 [414]	Privately owned, Suffolk area (stored)	
ZF416	Shorts Tucano T1 [416]	Privately owned, Bentwaters, Suffolk (stored)	
ZF417	Shorts Tucano T1 [417]	RAF, stored Linton-on-Ouse, N. Yorks (for disposal)	
ZF418	Shorts Tucano T1 [418]	RAF AM&SU, stored Shawbury, Shropshire	
ZF446	Shorts Tucano T1 [446]	Privately owned, Suffolk area (stored)	
ZF448	Shorts Tucano T1 [448] $	RAF, stored Linton-on-Ouse, N. Yorks (for disposal)	
ZF449	Shorts Tucano T1 [449]	RAF AM&SU, stored Shawbury, Shropshire	
ZF485	Shorts Tucano T1 (G-BULU) [485]	RAF, stored Linton-on-Ouse, N. Yorks (for disposal)	
ZF486	Shorts Tucano T1 [486]	Privately owned, Suffolk area (stored)	
ZF487	Shorts Tucano T1 [487]	RAF AM&SU, stored Shawbury, Shropshire	
ZF488	Shorts Tucano T1 [488]	Yorkshire Air Museum, Elvington, N. Yorks (rest'n)	
ZF489	Shorts Tucano T1 [489]	RAF, stored Linton-on-Ouse, N. Yorks (for disposal)	
ZF490	Shorts Tucano T1 [490]	Privately owned, Suffolk area (stored)	
ZF491	Shorts Tucano T1 [491]	Privately owned, Kent area (stored)	

Notes	Serial	Type (code/other identity)	Owner/operator, location or fate
	ZF492	Shorts Tucano T1 [492]	RAF AM&SU, stored Shawbury, Shropshire
	ZF512	Shorts Tucano T1 [512]	RAF, stored Linton-on-Ouse, N. Yorks (for disposal)
	ZF513	Shorts Tucano T1 [513]	Privately owned, Suffolk area (stored)
	ZF515	Shorts Tucano T1 [515]	RAF, stored Linton-on-Ouse, N. Yorks (for disposal)
	ZF534	BAe EAP	RAF Museum, Cosford, Shropshire
	ZF537	WS Lynx AH9A	AAC, stored Wattisham, Suffolk
	ZF538	WS Lynx AH9A	Unknown location
	ZF539	WS Lynx AH9A	Privately owned, Kessingland, Suffolk
	ZF557	WS Lynx HMA8SRU [426/PD]	Privately owned, Woodmancote, W. Sussex
	ZF558	WS Lynx HMA8SRU [336/WK]	Privately owned, Woodmancote, W. Sussex
	ZF560	WS Lynx HMA8SRU [456]	Privately owned, Woodmancote, W. Sussex
	ZF562	WS Lynx HMA8SRU [353/MB]	Privately owned, Woodmancote, W. Sussex
	ZF563	WS Lynx HMA8SRU [312/VL]	Privately owned, Woodmancote, W. Sussex
	ZF581	BAC Lightning F53 (53-675/206)	Bentwaters Cold War Museum, Suffolk
	ZF582	BAC Lightning F53 (53-676/210/207) <ff>	Bournemouth Aviation Museum, Dorset
	ZF584	BAC Lightning F53 (53-682/307/211)	Dumfries & Galloway Avn Mus, Dumfries, Scotland
	ZF587	BAC Lightning F53 (53-691/215) <ff>	Lashenden Air Warfare Museum, Headcorn, Kent
	ZF587	BAC Lightning F53 (53-691/215) <rf>	Privately owned, Stowmarket, Suffolk
	ZF588	BAC Lightning F53 (53-693/216) [L]	East Midlands Airport Aeropark, Leics
	ZF589	BAC Lightning F53 (53-700/218) <ff>	Privately owned, Charlwood, Surrey
	ZF590	BAC Lightning F53 (53-679/206/1302/220) <ff>	*Current status unknown* (ex-Bruntingthorpe)
	ZF595	BAC Lightning T55 (55-714/212/1317/231) <ff>	Privately owned, North Weald, Essex
	ZF595	BAC Lightning T55 (55-714/212/1317/231) <rf>	Privately owned, Binbrook, Lincs
	ZF596	BAC Lightning T55 (55-715/305/205/220/233) <ff>	Lakes Lightnings, Spark Bridge, Cumbria
	ZF622	Piper PA-31 Navajo Chieftain 350 (N3548Y) (fuselage)	MOD JARTS, Boscombe Down, Wilts
	ZF641	EHI-101 [PP1]	SFDO, RNAS Culdrose, Cornwall
	ZF649	EHI-101 Merlin (A2714) [PP5]	DSAE RNAESS, *HMS Sultan*, Gosport, Hants
	ZG347	Northrop Chukar D2	Davidstow Airfield & Cornwall At War Museum, Cornwall
	ZG477	BAe Harrier GR9 $	RAF Museum, Hendon, Gtr London
	ZG478	BAe Harrier GR9 (fuselage)	Privately owned, Sproughton, Suffolk
	ZG509	BAe Harrier GR7 [80]	Privately owned, Petersfield, Hants
	ZG631	Northrop Chukar D2	Farnborough Air Sciences Trust, Farnborough, Hants
	ZG751	Panavia Tornado F3 (fuselage)	MOD JARTS, Boscombe Down, Wilts
	ZG752	Panavia Tornado GR4 $	RAF Honington, Suffolk, at main gate
	ZG757	Panavia Tornado F2 $ (ZD899)	Privately owned, Chippenham Lodge, Cambs
	ZG771	Panavia Tornado GR4 $	Ulster Aviation Society, Long Kesh, Co. Antrim, NI
	ZG773	Panavia Tornado GR4	Fire Service College, Moreton-in-Marsh, Glos
	ZG817	WS61 Sea King HAS6 [702/PW]	DSAE RNAESS, *HMS Sultan*, Gosport, Hants
	ZG819	WS61 Sea King HAS6 [265/N]	DSAE RNAESS, *HMS Sultan*, Gosport, Hants
	ZG822	WS61 Sea King HC4 [WS]	Privately owned, Wainfleet, Lincs
	ZG875	WS61 Sea King HAS6 [013] <ff>	Privately owned, Market Drayton, Shropshire
	ZG884	WS Lynx AH9A	Privately owned, Bentwaters, Suffolk
	ZG885	WS Lynx AH9A	Privately owned, Clophill, Beds
	ZG886	WS Lynx AH9A (hulk)	Privately owned, White Waltham, Berks
	ZG887	WS Lynx AH9A	Privately owned, Alton Towers, Staffs
	ZG888	WS Lynx AH9A	Privately owned, Chatham, Kent
	ZG889	WS Lynx AH9A	Privately owned, White Waltham, Berks
	ZG914	WS Lynx AH9A	Privately owned, Wainfleet, Lincs
	ZG915	WS Lynx AH9A	Privately owned, Chew Valley, Somerset
	ZG916	WS Lynx AH9A	Fire Service, Aberdeen Airport, Scotland
	ZG917	WS Lynx AH9A $	AAC Middle Wallop, Hants, on display
	ZG918	WS Lynx AH9A	Instructional airframe, AAC Middle Wallop, Hants
	ZG919	WS Lynx AH9A	Privately owned, Bristol area, Glos
	ZG920	WS Lynx AH9A	AAC, stored Wattisham, Suffolk
	ZG921	WS Lynx AH9A	National Army Museum, Chelsea, London
	ZG923	WS Lynx AH9A	Army Bury St Edmunds, Suffolk, GI use
	ZG969	Pilatus PC-9 (HB-HQE)	BAE Systems, Warton, Lancs, GI use
	ZG993	PBN 2T Islander AL1 (G-BOMD)	Army Flying Museum, Middle Wallop, Hants
	ZH139	BAe Harrier GR7 <R> (BAPC.191/*ZD472*) [01]	RAF Exhibition Flight, Cranwell, Lincs
	ZH185	Grob G109B Vigilant T1 [TX]	RAF/Serco, stored Syerston, Notts

Serial	Type (code/other identity)	Owner/operator, location or fate	Notes
ZH200	BAe Hawk 200	Loughborough University, Leics, G.I.	
ZH257	B-V CH-47C Chinook (9217M) (fuselage)	RAF Odiham, Hants, BDRT	
ZH552	Panavia Tornado F3	RAF Leeming, N. Yorks, at main gate	
ZH553	Panavia Tornado F3 [RT]	MOD JARTS, Boscombe Down, Wilts	
ZH580	Westland Super Lynx Mk.95A (FAP 19201)	Leonardo MW, Yeovil, Somerset (upgrade)	
ZH582	Westland Super Lynx Mk.95A (FAP 19203)	Leonardo MW, Yeovil, Somerset (upgrade)	
ZH584	Westland Super Lynx Mk.95A (FAP 19205)	Leonardo MW, Yeovil, Somerset (upgrade)	
ZH588	Eurofighter Typhoon (DA2)	RAF Museum, Hendon, Gtr London	
ZH590	Eurofighter Typhoon (DA4)	DSAE No 1 SoTT, Cosford, Shropshire	
ZH655	BAe Harrier T10 <ff>	Privately owned, Worksop, Notts	
ZH658	BAe Harrier T10 (wreck)	Privately owned, Selby, N. Yorks	
ZH763	BAC 1-11/539GL (G-BGKE) (fuselage)	Solent Sky, Southampton, Hants	
ZH775	B-V Chinook HC6A (N7424J)	RAF, Operation Shader, Akrotiri, Cyprus	
ZH776	B-V Chinook HC6A (N7424L)	RAF No 18 Sqn, Odiham, Hants	
ZH777	B-V Chinook HC6A (N7424M)	RAF No 27 Sqn, Odiham, Hants	
ZH796	BAe Sea Harrier FA2 [001/L]	DSAE No 1 SoTT, stored Cosford, Shropshire	
ZH797	BAe Sea Harrier FA2 [97/DD]	Privately owned, St Athan, Glamorgan, Wales	
ZH798	BAe Sea Harrier FA2 [002/L]	Privately owned, Church Fenton, N. Yorks	
ZH800	BAe Sea Harrier FA2 (ZH800) [123]	Port Stanley Museum, Falkland Islands (stored)	
ZH801	BAe Sea Harrier FA2 (ZH800) [001]	RNAS Yeovilton, Somerset, stored	
ZH802	BAe Sea Harrier FA2 [02/DD]	Privately owned, St Athan, Glamorgan, Wales	
ZH803	BAe Sea Harrier FA2 (G-RNFA) [03/DD]	Privately owned, St Athan, Glamorgan, Wales	
ZH804	BAe Sea Harrier FA2 [003/L]	Privately owned, Thorpe Wood, N. Yorks	
ZH806	BAe Sea Harrier FA2 [007]	Privately owned, Bentwaters, Suffolk	
ZH807	BAe Sea Harrier FA2 <ff>	Privately owned, Thorpe Wood, N. Yorks	
ZH811	BAe Sea Harrier FA2 [002/L]	Privately owned, Chippenham Lodge, Suffolk	
ZH812	BAe Sea Harrier FA2 [005/L]	Privately owned, Bentwaters, Suffolk	
ZH813	BAe Sea Harrier FA2 [13/DD]	Privately owned, St Athan, Glamorgan, Wales	
ZH821	EHI-101 Merlin HM1	Morayvia, Kinloss, Moray, Scotland	
ZH822	EHI-101 Merlin HM1	MOD/Leonardo MW, stored Yeovil, Somerset	
ZH824	EHI-101 Merlin HM2	RN No 824 NAS, Culdrose, Cornwall	
ZH825	EHI-101 Merlin HM1 [583]	MOD/Leonardo MW, stored Yeovil, Somerset	
ZH826	EHI-101 Merlin HM2 [CU]	RN MDMF, Culdrose, Cornwall	
ZH827	EHI-101 Merlin HM2	RN No 820 NAS, Culdrose, Cornwall	
ZH828	EHI-101 Merlin HM2	RN No 820 NAS, Culdrose, Cornwall	
ZH829	EHI-101 Merlin HM2 (Crowsnest)	RN No 824 NAS, Culdrose, Cornwall	
ZH830	EHI-101 Merlin HM1 [88]	DSAE, stored HMS Sultan, Gosport, Hants	
ZH831	EHI-101 Merlin HM2 (Crowsnest)	RN No 820 NAS, Culdrose, Cornwall	
ZH832	EHI-101 Merlin HM2	RN No 814 NAS, Culdrose, Cornwall	
ZH833	EHI-101 Merlin HM2 (Crowsnest) [82]	RN MDMF, Culdrose, Cornwall	
ZH834	EHI-101 Merlin HM2	RN No 820 NAS, Culdrose, Cornwall	
ZH835	EHI-101 Merlin HM2 (Crowsnest)	RN No 820 NAS, Culdrose, Cornwall	
ZH836	EHI-101 Merlin HM2 [80]	RN No 824 NAS, Culdrose, Cornwall	
ZH837	EHI-101 Merlin HM2	RN No 814 NAS, Culdrose, Cornwall	
ZH838	EHI-101 Merlin HM1 [70]	DSAE, stored HMS Sultan, Gosport, Hants	
ZH839	EHI-101 Merlin HM2	RN No 814 NAS, Culdrose, Cornwall	
ZH840	EHI-101 Merlin HM2	RN No 814 NAS, Culdrose, Cornwall	
ZH841	EHI-101 Merlin HM2	RN No 824 NAS, Culdrose, Cornwall	
ZH842	EHI-101 Merlin HM2	RN No 820 NAS, Culdrose, Cornwall	
ZH843	EHI-101 Merlin HM2 (Crowsnest)	RN No 824 NAS, Culdrose, Cornwall	
ZH845	EHI-101 Merlin HM2	RN No 820 NAS, Culdrose, Cornwall	
ZH846	EHI-101 Merlin HM2 (Crowsnest)	RN No 820 NAS, Culdrose, Cornwall	
ZH847	EHI-101 Merlin HM2	RN No 814 NAS, Culdrose, Cornwall	
ZH848	EHI-101 Merlin HM1	DSAE, stored HMS Sultan, Gosport, Hants	
ZH849	EHI-101 Merlin HM1 [67]	DSAE, stored HMS Sultan, Gosport, Hants	
ZH850	EHI-101 Merlin HM2	RN No 814 NAS, Culdrose, Cornwall	
ZH851	EHI-101 Merlin HM2	RN No 820 NAS, Culdrose, Cornwall	
ZH852	EHI-101 Merlin HM1(mod)	DSAE, stored HMS Sultan, Gosport, Hants	
ZH853	EHI-101 Merlin HM2	RN No 820 NAS, Culdrose, Cornwall	
ZH854	EHI-101 Merlin HM2	RN MDMF, Culdrose, Cornwall	
ZH855	EHI-101 Merlin HM1 [68]	DSAE, stored HMS Sultan, Gosport, Hants	
ZH856	EHI-101 Merlin HM2 (Crowsnest)	RN No 820 NAS, Culdrose	

Notes	Serial	Type (code/other identity)	Owner/operator, location or fate
	ZH857	EHI-101 Merlin HM2	RN No 820 NAS, Culdrose
	ZH858	EHI-101 Merlin HM1 [17]	DSAE RNAESS, *HMS Sultan*, Gosport, Hants
	ZH860	EHI-101 Merlin HM2	RN No 814 NAS, Culdrose, Cornwall
	ZH861	EHI-101 Merlin HM2 (Crowsnest)	RN No 814 NAS, Culdrose, Cornwall
	ZH862	EHI-101 Merlin HM2	RN No 824 NAS, Culdrose, Cornwall
	ZH863	EHI-101 Merlin HM1 [80]	DSAE, stored *HMS Sultan*, Gosport, Hants
	ZH864	EHI-101 Merlin HM2 (Crowsnest)	RN No 820 NAS, Culdrose, Cornwall
	ZH865	Lockheed C-130J-30 Hercules C4 (N130JA) [865]	MOD/MADG, stored Cambridge, Cambs
	ZH866	Lockheed C-130J-30 Hercules C4 (N130JE) [866]	MOD/MADG, stored Cambridge, Cambs
	ZH867	Lockheed C-130J-30 Hercules C4 (N130JJ) [867]	MOD/MADG, stored Cambridge, Cambs
	ZH868	Lockheed C-130J-30 Hercules C4 (N130JN) [868]	MOD/MADG, stored Cambridge, Cambs
	ZH869	Lockheed C-130J-30 Hercules C4 (N130JV) [869]	MOD/MADG, stored Cambridge, Cambs
	ZH870	Lockheed C-130J-30 Hercules C4 (N78235) [870]	MOD/MADG, stored Cambridge, Cambs
	ZH871	Lockheed C-130J-30 Hercules C4 (N73238) [871]	MOD/MADG, stored Cambridge, Cambs
	ZH872	Lockheed C-130J-30 Hercules C4 (N4249Y) [872]	MOD/MADG, stored Cambridge, Cambs
	ZH874	Lockheed C-130J-30 Hercules C4 (N41030) [874]	MOD/MADG, stored Cambridge, Cambs
	ZH875	Lockheed C-130J-30 Hercules C4 (N4099R) [875]	MOD/MADG, stored Cambridge, Cambs
	ZH877	Lockheed C-130J-30 Hercules C4 (N4081M) [877]	MOD/MADG, stored Cambridge, Cambs
	ZH878	Lockheed C-130J-30 Hercules C4 (N73232) [878]	MOD/MADG, stored Cambridge, Cambs
	ZH879	Lockheed C-130J-30 Hercules C4 (N4080M) [879]	MOD/MADG, stored Cambridge, Cambs
	ZH883	Lockheed C-130J Hercules C5 (N4242N) [883] $	MADG, Cambridge, for Bangladesh AF as 99-5481
	ZH888	Lockheed C-130J Hercules C5 (N4187) [888]	MOD/MADG, stored Cambridge, Cambs
	ZH889	Lockheed C-130J Hercules C5 (N4099R) [889]	MOD/MADG, stored Cambridge, Cambs
	ZH891	B-V Chinook HC6A (N20075)	RAF, Odiham (withdrawn from use)
	ZH892	B-V Chinook HC6A (N2019V)	*RAF, Odiham (withdrawn from use)*
	ZH893	B-V Chinook HC6A (N2025L)	RAF No 28 Sqn, Benson, Oxon
	ZH894	B-V Chinook HC6A (N2026E)	MOD/StandardAero, Fleetlands, Hants
	ZH895	B-V Chinook HC6A (N2034K)	RAF, Odiham (withdrawn from use)
	ZH896	B-V Chinook HC6A (N2038G)	RAF No 18 Sqn, Odiham, Hants
	ZH897	B-V Chinook HC5 (N2045G)	RAF No 18 Sqn, Odiham, Hants
	ZH898	B-V Chinook HC5 (N2057Q)	MoD/Boeing, Middle Wallop, Hants
	ZH899	B-V Chinook HC5 (N2057R)	RAF No 27 Sqn, Odiham, Hants
	ZH900	B-V Chinook HC5 (N2060H)	RAF No 27 Sqn, Odiham, Hants
	ZH901	B-V Chinook HC5 (N2060M)	MOD/StandardAero, Fleetlands, Hants
	ZH902	B-V Chinook HC5 (N2064W)	RAF No 18 Sqn, Odiham, Hants
	ZH903	B-V Chinook HC5 (N20671)	RAF No 18 Sqn, Odiham, Hants
	ZH904	B-V Chinook HC5 (N2083K)	RAF No 18 Sqn, Odiham, Hants
	ZH961	Westland Super Lynx Mk21A (Brazilian Navy N-4010)	Leonardo MW, Yeovil, Somerset (upgrade)
	ZJ100	BAe Hawk 102D	BAE Systems, Brough, E. Yorks, G.I.
	ZJ117	EHI-101 Merlin HC3 [A]	DSAE RNAESS, *HMS Sultan*, Gosport, Hants
	ZJ118	EHI-101 Merlin HC4 [B]	RN No 845 NAS, Yeovilton, Somerset
	ZJ119	EHI-101 Merlin HC4 [C]	RN No 846 NAS, Yeovilton, Somerset
	ZJ120	EHI-101 Merlin HC4 [D]	RN No 845 NAS, Yeovilton, Somerset
	ZJ121	EHI-101 Merlin HC4 [E]	RN No 845 NAS, Yeovilton, Somerset
	ZJ122	EHI-101 Merlin HC4 [F]	RN No 845 NAS, Yeovilton, Somerset
	ZJ123	EHI-101 Merlin HC4 [G]	RN No 845 NAS, Yeovilton, Somerset
	ZJ124	EHI-101 Merlin HC4 [H]	RN No 845 NAS, Yeovilton, Somerset
	ZJ125	EHI-101 Merlin HC4 [J]	RN No 845 NAS, Yeovilton, Somerset
	ZJ126	EHI-101 Merlin HC4 [K]	RN No 845 NAS, Yeovilton, Somerset
	ZJ127	EHI-101 Merlin HC4 [L]	RN No 845 NAS, Yeovilton, Somerset
	ZJ128	EHI-101 Merlin HC4 [M]	RN No 845 NAS, Yeovilton, Somerset
	ZJ129	EHI-101 Merlin HC4 [N]	RN No 845 NAS, Yeovilton, Somerset
	ZJ130	EHI-101 Merlin HC4 [O]	RN No 845 NAS, Yeovilton, Somerset
	ZJ131	EHI-101 Merlin HC4 [P]	RN No 845 NAS, Yeovilton, Somerset
	ZJ132	EHI-101 Merlin HC4 [Q]	MOD/Leonardo MW, Yeovil, Somerset (depth maint.)
	ZJ133	EHI-101 Merlin HC3 [R]	RAF Brize Norton, Oxon, GI use
	ZJ134	EHI-101 Merlin HC4 [S]	RN No 846 NAS, Yeovilton, Somerset
	ZJ135	EHI-101 Merlin HC4 [T]	*Written off, English Channel, 5th September 2024*
	ZJ136	EHI-101 Merlin HC4 [U]	RN No 845 NAS, Yeovilton, Somerset
	ZJ137	EHI-101 Merlin HC4 [W]	RN No 846 NAS, Yeovilton, Somerset
	ZJ138	EHI-101 Merlin HC3 <ff>	Privately owned, Spey Bay, Moray, Scotland

Serial	Type (code/other identity)	Owner/operator, location or fate	Notes
ZJ165	AS365N-2 Dauphin 2 (G-NTOO)	RN FOST, Newquay, Cornwall	
ZJ171	WAH-64 Apache AH1 (N3266T)	AAC, Middle Wallop (restoration)	
ZJ177	WAH-64 Apache AH1 (stripped cabin)	AAC, instructional airframe, Wattisham, Suffolk	
ZJ189	WAH-64 Apache AH1	DSEME DCTT, Lyneham, Wilts	
ZJ191	WAH-64 Apache AH1	DSEME DCTT, Lyneham, Wilts	
ZJ192	WAH-64 Apache AH1	*AAC, withdrawn from use, Wattisham, Suffolk*	
ZJ197	WAH-64 Apache AH1	*AAC, withdrawn from use, Wattisham, Suffolk*	
ZJ208	WAH-64 Apache AH1	DSEME DCTT, Lyneham, Wilts	
ZJ210	WAH-64 Apache AH1	DSEME DCTT, Lyneham, Wilts	
ZJ211	WAH-64 Apache AH1	*AAC, withdrawn from use, Wattisham, Suffolk*	
ZJ213	WAH-64 Apache AH1	DSEME DCTT, Lyneham, Wilts	
ZJ215	WAH-64 Apache AH1	DSEME DCTT, Lyneham, Wilts	
ZJ220	WAH-64 Apache AH1	*To Australia for GI*	
ZJ221	WAH-64 Apache AH1	DSEME DCTT, Lyneham, Wilts	
ZJ223	WAH-64 Apache AH1	DSEME DCTT, Lyneham, Wilts	
ZJ224	WAH-64 Apache AH1	Army Flying Museum, Middle Wallop, Hants	
ZJ226	WAH-64 Apache AH1	*To Australia for GI*	
ZJ369	GEC Phoenix RPAS	Defence Academy of the UK, Shrivenham, Oxon	
ZJ385	GEC Phoenix RPAS	Muckleburgh Collection, Weybourne, Norfolk	
ZJ449	GEC Phoenix RPAS	REME Museum, Lyneham, Wilts (stored)	
ZJ452	GEC Phoenix RPAS	Science Museum, stored Wroughton, Wilts	
ZJ469	GEC Phoenix RPAS	Bournemouth Aviation Museum, Dorset	
ZJ477	GEC Phoenix RPAS	Boscombe Down Aviation Collection, Old Sarum, Wilts	
ZJ481	Northrop MQM-74C Chukar D2	RNAS Culdrose, Cornwall, preserved	
ZJ493	GAF Jindivik 104AL (A92-814)	RAF Museum Reserve Collection, Stafford, Staffs	
ZJ496	GAF Jindivik 104AL (A92-901)	Farnborough Air Sciences Trust, Farnborough, Hants	
ZJ515	BAE Systems Nimrod MRA4 (XV258) <ff>	Cranfield University, Beds, instructional use	
ZJ620	AgustaWestland Merlin Simulator	RN No 824 NAS, Culdrose, Cornwall	
ZJ621	AgustaWestland Merlin Simulator	RN No 824 NAS, Culdrose, Cornwall	
ZJ622	AgustaWestland Merlin Simulator	RN No 824 NAS, Culdrose, Cornwall	
ZJ623	AgustaWestland Merlin Simulator	RN No 824 NAS, Culdrose, Cornwall	
ZJ624	AgustaWestland Merlin Simulator	RN No 824 NAS, Culdrose, Cornwall	
ZJ625	AgustaWestland Merlin Simulator	RN No 824 NAS, Culdrose, Cornwall	
ZJ626	AgustaWestland Merlin Simulator	RN No 824 NAS, Culdrose, Cornwall	
ZJ699	Eurofighter Typhoon (PT001)	MOD/BAE Systems, stored Warton, Lancs	
ZJ700	Eurofighter Typhoon (PS002)	MOD/BAE Systems, Warton, Lancs	
ZJ748	Meteor Mirach 100/5	Boscombe Down Aviation Collection, Old Sarum	
ZJ765	Meteor Mirach 100/5	QinetiQ Apprentice Training School, Boscombe Down	
ZJ780	AS365N-3 Dauphin AH1 (G-CEXT)	AAC No 658 Sqn, Credenhill, Herefordshire	
ZJ782	AS365N-3 Dauphin AH1 (G-CEXV)	AAC No 658 Sqn, Credenhill, Herefordshire	
ZJ783	AS365N-3 Dauphin AH1 (G-CEXW)	AAC No 658 Sqn, Credenhill, Herefordshire	
ZJ785	AS365N-3 Dauphin AH1 (G-CFFW)	AAC No 658 Sqn, Credenhill, Herefordshire	
ZJ787	AS365N-3 Dauphin AH1 (G-CHNJ)	AAC No 658 Sqn, Credenhill, Herefordshire	
ZJ800	Eurofighter Typhoon T3 [BC]	BAE Systems Aircraft Maintenance Academy, Humberside	
ZJ801	Eurofighter Typhoon T3 [BJ]	BAE Systems, Warton, Lancs (stress testing)	
ZJ807	Eurofighter Typhoon T3 (fuselage)	MOD JARTS, Boscombe Down, Wilts	
ZJ810	Eurofighter Typhoon T3 (fuselage)	MOD JARTS, Boscombe Down, Wilts	
ZJ910	Eurofighter Typhoon FGR4 [DO]	RAF AM&SU, stored Shawbury, Shropshire	
ZJ911	Eurofighter Typhoon FGR4 [QO-Z]	RAF AM&SU, stored Shawbury, Shropshire	
ZJ912	Eurofighter Typhoon FGR4 [912]	RAF AM&SU, stored Shawbury, Shropshire	
ZJ913	Eurofighter Typhoon FGR4 [913,FM-G] $	*GI use, RAF Lossiemouth, Moray, Scotland*	
ZJ914	Eurofighter Typhoon FGR4 $	*To Warton, June 2024 for RTP*	
ZJ915	Eurofighter Typhoon FGR4 [F/'Faith']	RAF No 1435 Flt, Mount Pleasant, FI	
ZJ916	Eurofighter Typhoon FGR4 [916]	RAF Coningsby, Lincs, for GI	
ZJ917	Eurofighter Typhoon FGR4 [917]	*To Warton, October 2024 for RTP*	
ZJ918	Eurofighter Typhoon FGR4	RAF AM&SU, stored Shawbury	
ZJ919	Eurofighter Typhoon FGR4 [919,WS-L]	RAF No 9 Sqn, stored Lossiemouth, Moray, Scotland	
ZJ920	Eurofighter Typhoon FGR4 [H/'Hope']	RAF No 1435 Flt, Mount Pleasant, FI	
ZJ921	Eurofighter Typhoon FGR4 [921]	*To Warton, May 2024 for RTP*	
ZJ922	Eurofighter Typhoon FGR4 [QO-C]	MOD/BAE Systems, Warton, Lancs	
ZJ923	Eurofighter Typhoon FGR4 [923,WS-T]	WLT, RAF Coningsby, Lincs	
ZJ924	Eurofighter Typhoon FGR4 [924,WS-J]	RAF TEF, stored Lossiemouth, Scotland	

Notes	Serial	Type (code/other identity)	Owner/operator, location or fate
	ZJ925	Eurofighter Typhoon FGR4 [DXI] $	RAF AM&SU, stored Shawbury, Shropshire
	ZJ926	Eurofighter Typhoon FGR4 [H]	*To Warton, November 2024 for RTP*
	ZJ927	Eurofighter Typhoon FGR4 [927]	RAF AM&SU, stored Shawbury, Shropshire
	ZJ928	Eurofighter Typhoon FGR4 [C/'Charity']	RAF No 1435 Flt, Mount Pleasant, FI
	ZJ929	Eurofighter Typhoon FGR4 [929]	*Withdrawn from use, Warton, March 2024*
	ZJ930	Eurofighter Typhoon FGR4 [930]	RAF AM&SU, stored Shawbury, Shropshire
	ZJ931	Eurofighter Typhoon FGR4 [931]	RAF TEF, stored Lossiemouth, Scotland
	ZJ932	Eurofighter Typhoon FGR4 [DB]	RAF AM&SU, stored Shawbury, Shropshire
	ZJ933	Eurofighter Typhoon FGR4 [C]	*To Warton, November 2024 for RTP*
	ZJ934	Eurofighter Typhoon FGR4 [934]	RAF AM&SU, stored Shawbury, Shropshire
	ZJ935	Eurofighter Typhoon FGR4 [935,WS-G]	*To Warton, May 2024 for RTP*
	ZJ936	Eurofighter Typhoon FGR4 [QO-C]	RAF AM&SU, stored Shawbury, Shropshire
	ZJ937	Eurofighter Typhoon FGR4 [937]	MOD/BAE Systems, Warton, Lancs
	ZJ938	Eurofighter Typhoon FGR4	MOD/BAE Systems, Warton, Lancs
	ZJ939	Eurofighter Typhoon FGR4 [939, WS-U]	*To Warton, April 2024 for RTP*
	ZJ940	Eurofighter Typhoon FGR4 [DJ666]	RAF, stored Coningsby, Lincs
	ZJ941	Eurofighter Typhoon FGR4 [D]	*To Warton, November 2024 for RTP*
	ZJ942	Eurofighter Typhoon FGR4 [D/'Desperation']	RAF No 1435 Flt, Mount Pleasant, FI
	ZJ944	Eurofighter Typhoon FGR4	RAF TMF, Coningsby, Lincs (stored, pending repair)
	ZJ945	Eurofighter Typhoon FGR4	RAF TMF, stored Coningsby, Lincs
	ZJ946	Eurofighter Typhoon FGR4 [946]	RAF No 9 Sqn, Lossiemouth, Moray, Scotland
	ZJ947	Eurofighter Typhoon FGR4 [947]	RAF TMF, stored Coningsby, Lincs
	ZJ948	Eurofighter Typhoon FGR4	RAF TMF, stored Coningsby, Lincs
	ZJ949	Eurofighter Typhoon FGR4 [949]	RAF No 11 Sqn, Coningsby, Lincs
	ZJ950	Eurofighter Typhoon FGR4 [950]	RAF TEF, Lossiemouth, Scotland
	ZJ951	BAE Systems Advanced Hawk 120D	MOD/BAE Systems, Warton, Lancs (wfu)
	ZJ954	SA330H Puma HC2 (SAAF 144) [W]	RAF No 28 Sqn/No 33 Sqn, Benson, Oxon
	ZJ955	SA330H Puma HC2 (SAAF 148) [X]	RAF No 84 Sqn, Akrotiri, Cyprus
	ZJ956	SA330H Puma HC2 (SAAF 172/F-ZWCC) [Y]	RAF No 28 Sqn/No 33 Sqn, Benson, Oxon
	ZJ957	SA330H Puma HC2 (SAAF 169) [Z]	RAF No 28 Sqn/No 33 Sqn, Benson, Oxon
	ZJ963	Grob G109B Vigilant T1 (D-KMSN) [SL]	RAF, stored Syerston, Notts
	ZJ990	EHI-101 Merlin HC4A (M-501) [AA]	RN No 846 NAS, Yeovilton, Somerset
	ZJ992	EHI-101 Merlin HC4A (M-503) [AB]	RN No 846 NAS, Yeovilton, Somerset
	ZJ994	EHI-101 Merlin HC4A (M-505) [AC]	RN No 846 NAS, Yeovilton, Somerset
	ZJ995	EHI-101 Merlin HC4A (M-506) [AD]	RN No 845 NAS, Yeovilton, Somerset
	ZJ998	EHI-101 Merlin HC4A (M-509) [AE]	RN No 846 NAS, Yeovilton, Somerset
	ZK001	EHI-101 Merlin HC4A (M-511) [AF]	RN No 846 NAS, Yeovilton, Somerset
	ZK010	BAE Systems Hawk T2 [FN]	RAF No 4 FTS/25 Sqn, Valley, Gwynedd, Wales
	ZK011	BAE Systems Hawk T2 [B]	RAF No 4 FTS/4 Sqn, Valley, Gwynedd, Wales
	ZK012	BAE Systems Hawk T2 [C]	RAF No 4 FTS/4 Sqn, Valley, Gwynedd, Wales
	ZK013	BAE Systems Hawk T2 [D]	RAF No 4 FTS/4 Sqn, Valley, Gwynedd, Wales
	ZK014	BAE Systems Hawk T2 [E]	RAF No 4 FTS/4 Sqn, Valley, Gwynedd, Wales
	ZK015	BAE Systems Hawk T2 [F]	RAF No 4 FTS/4 Sqn, Valley, Gwynedd, Wales
	ZK016	BAE Systems Hawk T2 [G]	RAF No 4 FTS/4 Sqn, Valley, Gwynedd, Wales
	ZK017	BAE Systems Hawk T2 [H]	RAF No 4 FTS/4 Sqn, Valley, Gwynedd, Wales
	ZK018	BAE Systems Hawk T2 [I]	RAF No 4 FTS/4 Sqn, Valley, Gwynedd, Wales
	ZK019	BAE Systems Hawk T2 [J]	RAF No 4 FTS/4 Sqn, Valley, Gwynedd, Wales
	ZK020	BAE Systems Hawk T2 [K] $	RAF No 4 FTS/4 Sqn, Valley, Gwynedd, Wales
	ZK021	BAE Systems Hawk T2 [L]	RAF No 4 FTS/4 Sqn, Valley, Gwynedd, Wales
	ZK022	BAE Systems Hawk T2 [M]	RAF No 4 FTS/4 Sqn, Valley, Gwynedd, Wales
	ZK023	BAE Systems Hawk T2 [N]	RAF No 4 FTS/4 Sqn, Valley, Gwynedd, Wales
	ZK024	BAE Systems Hawk T2 [O]	RAF No 4 FTS/4 Sqn, Valley, Gwynedd, Wales
	ZK025	BAE Systems Hawk T2 [FA]	RAF No 4 FTS/25 Sqn, Valley, Gwynedd, Wales
	ZK026	BAE Systems Hawk T2 [FB]	RAF No 4 FTS/25 Sqn, Valley, Gwynedd, Wales
	ZK027	BAE Systems Hawk T2 [FC]	RAF No 4 FTS/25 Sqn, Valley, Gwynedd, Wales
	ZK028	BAE Systems Hawk T2 [FD]	RAF No 4 FTS/25 Sqn, Valley, Gwynedd, Wales
	ZK029	BAE Systems Hawk T2 [FE]	RAF No 4 FTS/25 Sqn, Valley, Gwynedd, Wales
	ZK030	BAE Systems Hawk T2 [FF]	RAF No 4 FTS/25 Sqn, Valley, Gwynedd, Wales
	ZK031	BAE Systems Hawk T2 [FG]	RAF No 4 FTS/25 Sqn, Valley, Gwynedd, Wales
	ZK032	BAE Systems Hawk T2 [FH]	RAF No 4 FTS/25 Sqn, Valley, Gwynedd, Wales
	ZK033	BAE Systems Hawk T2 [FI]	RAF No 4 FTS/25 Sqn, Valley, Gwynedd, Wales

Serial	Type (code/other identity)	Owner/operator, location or fate	Notes
ZK034	BAE Systems Hawk T2 [FJ]	RAF No 4 FTS/25 Sqn, Valley, Gwynedd, Wales	
ZK035	BAE Systems Hawk T2 [FK]	RAF No 4 FTS/25 Sqn, Valley, Gwynedd, Wales	
ZK036	BAE Systems Hawk T2 [FL]	RAF No 4 FTS/25 Sqn, Valley, Gwynedd, Wales	
ZK037	BAE Systems Hawk T2 [FM]	RAF No 4 FTS/25 Sqn, Valley, Gwynedd, Wales	
ZK114	M2370 RPAS	QinetiQ	
ZK150*	Lockheed Martin Desert Hawk 3 RPAS	Army 47 Regt Royal Artillery, Thorney Island	
ZK150	Lockheed Martin Desert Hawk 3 RPAS (ZK150/617)	Imperial War Museum, Lambeth, London	
ZK155*	Honeywell T-Hawk RPAS	Army 32 Regt Royal Artillery, Larkhill, Wilts	
ZK210	BAE Systems Mantis RPAS	MOD/BAE Systems, Warton, Lancs	
ZK300	Eurofighter Typhoon FGR4 [300]	RAF No 2 Sqn, Lossiemouth, Moray, Scotland	
ZK301	Eurofighter Typhoon FGR4 [301]	RAF TEF, Lossiemouth, Scotland	
ZK302	Eurofighter Typhoon FGR4 [302]	RAF No 11 Sqn, Coningsby, Lincs	
ZK303	Eurofighter Typhoon T3 [AX]	MOD/BAE Systems, Warton, Lancs	
ZK304	Eurofighter Typhoon FGR4 [304]	RAF No 1 Sqn, Lossiemouth, Moray, Scotland	
ZK305	Eurofighter Typhoon FGR4 [305]	RAF TMF, Coningsby, Lincs	
ZK306	Eurofighter Typhoon FGR4 [306]	RAF No 11 Sqn, Coningsby, Lincs	
ZK307	Eurofighter Typhoon FGR4 [307]	RAF, Operation Shader, Akrotiri, Cyprus	
ZK308	Eurofighter Typhoon FGR4 [308]	RAF No 2 Sqn, Lossiemouth, Moray, Scotland	
ZK309	Eurofighter Typhoon FGR4 [309]	RAF No 29 Sqn, Coningsby, Lincs	
ZK310	Eurofighter Typhoon FGR4 [310]	RAF No 2 Sqn, Lossiemouth, Moray, Scotland	
ZK311	Eurofighter Typhoon FGR4 [311]	RAF No 29 Sqn, Coningsby, Lincs	
ZK312	Eurofighter Typhoon FGR4 [312]	RAF No 1 Sqn, Lossiemouth, Moray, Scotland	
ZK313	Eurofighter Typhoon FGR4 [313]	RAF TMF, Coningsby, Lincs	
ZK314	Eurofighter Typhoon FGR4 [314]	RAF No 12 Sqn, Coningsby, Lincs	
ZK315	Eurofighter Typhoon FGR4 [315]	RAF AWC/FJWOEU/No 41 Sqn, Coningsby, Lincs	
ZK316	Eurofighter Typhoon FGR4 [316]	*To Warton, June 2024 for RTP*	
ZK317	Eurofighter Typhoon FGR4 [317]	RAF No 1 Sqn, Lossiemouth, Moray, Scotland	
ZK318	Eurofighter Typhoon FGR4 [318]	RAF, Operation Shader, Akrotiri, Cyprus	
ZK319	Eurofighter Typhoon FGR4 [319]	RAF No 29 Sqn, Coningsby, Lincs	
ZK320	Eurofighter Typhoon FGR4 [320]	RAF No 2 Sqn, Lossiemouth, Moray, Scotland	
ZK321	Eurofighter Typhoon FGR4 [321]	RAF No 29 Sqn, Coningsby, Lincs	
ZK322	Eurofighter Typhoon FGR4 [322]	RAF No 1 Sqn, Lossiemouth, Moray, Scotland	
ZK323	Eurofighter Typhoon FGR4 [323]	RAF No 6 Sqn, Lossiemouth, Moray, Scotland	
ZK324	Eurofighter Typhoon FGR4 [324]	RAF No 11 Sqn, Coningsby, Lincs	
ZK325	Eurofighter Typhoon FGR4 [325]	RAF No 29 Sqn, Coningsby, Lincs	
ZK326	Eurofighter Typhoon FGR4 [FB]	RAF, stored Coningsby, Lincs	
ZK327	Eurofighter Typhoon FGR4 [327]	RAF TMF, Coningsby, Lincs	
ZK328	Eurofighter Typhoon FGR4 [328]	RAF No 6 Sqn, Lossiemouth, Moray, Scotland	
ZK329	Eurofighter Typhoon FGR4 [329]	RAF No 29 Sqn, Coningsby, Lincs	
ZK330	Eurofighter Typhoon FGR4 [330]	RAF No 11 Sqn, Coningsby, Lincs	
ZK331	Eurofighter Typhoon FGR4 [331]	RAF TMF, Coningsby, Lincs	
ZK332	Eurofighter Typhoon FGR4 [332/WS-J]	RAF No 2 Sqn, Lossiemouth, Moray, Scotland	
ZK333	Eurofighter Typhoon FGR4 [333]	RAF No 11 Sqn, Coningsby, Lincs	
ZK334	Eurofighter Typhoon FGR4 [334]	RAF, Operation Shader, Akrotiri, Cyprus	
ZK335	Eurofighter Typhoon FGR4 [335]	RAF No 11 Sqn, Coningsby, Lincs	
ZK336	Eurofighter Typhoon FGR4 [336]	RAF No 2 Sqn, Lossiemouth, Moray, Scotland	
ZK337	Eurofighter Typhoon FGR4 [337]	RAF No 1 Sqn, Lossiemouth, Moray, Scotland	
ZK338	Eurofighter Typhoon FGR4 [338]	RAF No 6 Sqn, Lossiemouth, Moray, Scotland	
ZK339	Eurofighter Typhoon FGR4 [339]	RAF AWC/FJWOEU/No 41 Sqn, Coningsby, Lincs	
ZK340	Eurofighter Typhoon FGR4 [340]	RAF No 1 Sqn, Lossiemouth, Moray, Scotland	
ZK341	Eurofighter Typhoon FGR4 [341]	RAF TMF, Coningsby, Lincs	
ZK342	Eurofighter Typhoon FGR4 [342]	RAF, Operation Shader, Akrotiri, Cyprus	
ZK343	Eurofighter Typhoon FGR4 [343]	RAF No 12 Sqn, Coningsby, Lincs	
ZK344	Eurofighter Typhoon FGR4 [344]	RAF No 29 Sqn, Coningsby, Lincs	
ZK345	Eurofighter Typhoon FGR4 [345]	RAF, Operation Shader, Akrotiri, Cyprus	
ZK346	Eurofighter Typhoon FGR4 [346]	RAF No 9 Sqn, Lossiemouth, Moray, Scotland	
ZK347	Eurofighter Typhoon FGR4 [347]	RAF No 1 Sqn, Lossiemouth, Moray, Scotland	
ZK348	Eurofighter Typhoon T2 [348]	RAF TMF, Coningsby, Lincs	
ZK349	Eurofighter Typhoon FGR4 [349]	RAF No 6 Sqn, Lossiemouth, Moray, Scotland	
ZK350	Eurofighter Typhoon FGR4 [350]	RAF No 2 Sqn, Lossiemouth, Moray, Scotland	
ZK351	Eurofighter Typhoon FGR4 [351]	RAF TMF, Coningsby, Lincs	
ZK352*	Eurofighter Typhoon FGR4 [352]	RAF No 2 Sqn, Lossiemouth, Moray, Scotland	

Notes	Serial	Type (code/other identity)	Owner/operator, location or fate
	ZK353	Eurofighter Typhoon FGR4 [353]	RAF No 3 Sqn, Coningsby, Lincs
	ZK354	Eurofighter Typhoon FGR4 [354]	RAF No 29 Sqn, Coningsby, Lincs
	ZK355	Eurofighter Typhoon FGR4	MOD/BAE Systems, Warton, Lancs
	ZK356	Eurofighter Typhoon FGR4	MOD/BAE Systems, Warton, Lancs
	ZK357	Eurofighter Typhoon FGR4 [357, WS-S]	RAF No 9 Sqn, Lossiemouth, Moray, Scotland
	ZK358	Eurofighter Typhoon FGR4 [358]	RAF No 12 Sqn, Coningsby, Lincs
	ZK359	Eurofighter Typhoon FGR4 [359]	RAF No 6 Sqn, Lossiemouth, Moray, Scotland
	ZK360	Eurofighter Typhoon FGR4 [360]	RAF No 6 Sqn, Lossiemouth, Moray, Scotland
	ZK361	Eurofighter Typhoon FGR4 [361]	RAF No 1 Sqn, Lossiemouth, Moray, Scotland
	ZK362	Eurofighter Typhoon FGR4 [362]	RAF No 29 Sqn, Coningsby, Lincs
	ZK363	Eurofighter Typhoon FGR4 [363]	RAF, Operation Shader, Akrotiri, Cyprus
	ZK364	Eurofighter Typhoon FGR4 [364]	RAF No 11 Sqn, Coningsby, Lincs
	ZK365	Eurofighter Typhoon FGR4 [365]	RAF AWC/FJWOEU/No 41 Sqn, Coningsby, Lincs
	ZK366	Eurofighter Typhoon FGR4 [366]	RAF TMF, Coningsby, Lincs
	ZK367	Eurofighter Typhoon FGR4 [367]	RAF AWC/FJWOEU/No 41 Sqn, Coningsby, Lincs
	ZK368	Eurofighter Typhoon FGR4 [368]	RAF No 12 Sqn, Coningsby, Lincs
	ZK369	Eurofighter Typhoon FGR4 [369]	RAF No 6 Sqn, Lossiemouth, Moray, Scotland
	ZK370	Eurofighter Typhoon FGR4 [370]	RAF No 1 Sqn, Lossiemouth, Moray, Scotland
	ZK371	Eurofighter Typhoon FGR4 [371]	RAF No 11 Sqn, Coningsby, Lincs
	ZK372	Eurofighter Typhoon FGR4 [372]	RAF No 2 Sqn, Lossiemouth, Moray, Scotland
	ZK373	Eurofighter Typhoon FGR4 [373]	RAF TMF, Coningsby, Lincs
	ZK374	Eurofighter Typhoon FGR4 [374]	RAF No 29 Sqn, Coningsby, Lincs
	ZK375	Eurofighter Typhoon FGR4 [375]	RAF AWC/FJWOEU/No 41 Sqn, Coningsby, Lincs
	ZK376	Eurofighter Typhoon FGR4 [376]	RAF No 12 Sqn, Coningsby, Lincs
	ZK377	Eurofighter Typhoon FGR4 [377, WS-T]	RAF No 9 Sqn, Lossiemouth, Moray, Scotland
	ZK378	Eurofighter Typhoon FGR4 [378]	RAF No 6 Sqn, Lossiemouth, Moray, Scotland
	ZK379	Eurofighter Typhoon T3 [379]	RAF AWC/FJWOEU/No 41 Sqn, Coningsby, Lincs
	ZK380	Eurofighter Typhoon T3 [380]	RAF No 29 Sqn, Coningsby, Lincs
	ZK381	Eurofighter Typhoon T3 [381]	RAF No 29 Sqn, Coningsby, Lincs
	ZK382	Eurofighter Typhoon T3 [382]	RAF No 29 Sqn, Coningsby, Lincs
	ZK383	Eurofighter Typhoon T3 [383]	RAF No 12 Sqn, Coningsby, Lincs
	ZK424	Eurofighter Typhoon FGR4 [424]	RAF No 29 Sqn, Coningsby, Lincs
	ZK425	Eurofighter Typhoon FGR4 [425]	RAF TMF, Coningsby, Lincs
	ZK426	Eurofighter Typhoon FGR4 [426]	RAF TMF, Coningsby, Lincs
	ZK427	Eurofighter Typhoon FGR4 [427]	RAF No 29 Sqn, Coningsby, Lincs
	ZK428	Eurofighter Typhoon FGR4 [428]	RAF No 9 Sqn, Lossiemouth, Moray, Scotland
	ZK429	Eurofighter Typhoon FGR4 [429]	RAF No 11 Sqn, Coningsby, Lincs
	ZK430	Eurofighter Typhoon FGR4 [430]	RAF, Operation Shader, Akrotiri, Cyprus
	ZK431	Eurofighter Typhoon FGR4 [431]	RAF No 29 Sqn, Coningsby, Lincs
	ZK432	Eurofighter Typhoon FGR4 [432]	RAF No 12 Sqn, Coningsby, Lincs
	ZK433	Eurofighter Typhoon FGR4 [433]	RAF No 6 Sqn, Lossiemouth, Moray, Scotland
	ZK434	Eurofighter Typhoon FGR4 [434]	RAF TMF, Coningsby, Lincs
	ZK435	Eurofighter Typhoon FGR4 [435]	RAF, Operation Shader, Akrotiri, Cyprus
	ZK436	Eurofighter Typhoon FGR4 [436]	RAF No 9 Sqn, Lossiemouth, Moray, Scotland
	ZK437	Eurofighter Typhoon FGR4 [437]	RAF No 11 Sqn, Coningsby, Lincs
	ZK438	Eurofighter Typhoon FGR4 [438]	RAF No 6 Sqn, Lossiemouth, Moray, Scotland
	ZK439	Eurofighter Typhoon FGR4 [439]	RAF No 3 Sqn, Coningsby, Lincs
	ZK531	BAe Hawk T53 (LL-5306)	Humberside Airport, Lincs, on display
	ZK532	BAe Hawk T53 (LL-5315)	MOD/BAE Systems, Samlesbury, Lancs, GI use
	ZK533	BAe Hawk T53 (LL-5317)	MOD/BAE Systems, Samlesbury, Lancs, GI use
	ZK535	BAe Hawk T53 (LL-5320)	BAE Systems Aircraft Maintenance Academy, Humberside
	ZK550	Boeing Chinook HC6 (N701UK)	RAF No 7 Sqn, Odiham, Hants
	ZK551	Boeing Chinook HC6 (N702UK)	RAF No 7 Sqn, Odiham, Hants
	ZK552	Boeing Chinook HC6 (N703UK)	RAF No 7 Sqn, Odiham, Hants
	ZK553	Boeing Chinook HC6 (N700UK)	RAF No 7 Sqn, Odiham, Hants
	ZK554	Boeing Chinook HC6 (N705UK)	RAF No 7 Sqn, Odiham, Hants
	ZK555	Boeing Chinook HC6 (N706UK)	RAF No 7 Sqn, Odiham, Hants
	ZK556	Boeing Chinook HC6 (N707UK)	RAF No 7 Sqn, Odiham, Hants
	ZK557	Boeing Chinook HC6 (N708UK)	RAF, Operation Shader, Akrotiri, Cyprus
	ZK558	Boeing Chinook HC6 (N709UK)	RAF No 7 Sqn, Odiham, Hants
	ZK559	Boeing Chinook HC6 (N710UK)	RAF No 7 Sqn, Odiham, Hants
	ZK560	Boeing Chinook HC6 (N711UK)	RAF No 7 Sqn, Odiham, Hants

Serial	Type (code/other identity)	Owner/operator, location or fate	Notes
ZK561	Boeing Chinook HC6 (N712UK)	RAF No 7 Sqn, Odiham, Hants	
ZK562	Boeing Chinook HC6 (N713UK)	RAF No 7 Sqn, Odiham, Hants	
ZK563	Boeing Chinook HC6 (N714UK)	RAF CMF, Odiham, Hants	
ZM135	Lockheed Martin F-35B Lightning II (168315) [001]	RAF No 17 Sqn, Edwards AFB, CA	
ZM136	Lockheed Martin F-35B Lightning II (168316) [002]	RAF No 17 Sqn, Edwards AFB, CA	
ZM137	Lockheed Martin F-35B Lightning II (168737) [003]	RAF No 207 Sqn, Marham, Norfolk	
ZM138	Lockheed Martin F-35B Lightning II (169170) [004]	RAF No 17 Sqn, Edwards AFB, CA	
ZM139	Lockheed Martin F-35B Lightning II (169298) [005]	RAF No 207 Sqn, Marham, Norfolk	
ZM140	Lockheed Martin F-35B Lightning II (169299) [006]	RAF No 207 Sqn, Marham, Norfolk	
ZM141	Lockheed Martin F-35B Lightning II (169300) [007]	RAF No 207 Sqn, Marham, Norfolk	
ZM142	Lockheed Martin F-35B Lightning II (169301) [008]	RAF No 207 Sqn, Marham, Norfolk	
ZM143	Lockheed Martin F-35B Lightning II (169417) [009]	RAF No 207 Sqn, Marham, Norfolk	
ZM144	Lockheed Martin F-35B Lightning II (169418) [010]	MCAS Cherry Point, SC (maintenance)	
ZM145	Lockheed Martin F-35B Lightning II (169419) [011]	MCAS Cherry Point, SC (maintenance)	
ZM146	Lockheed Martin F-35B Lightning II (169420) [012]	RAF No 207 Sqn, Marham, Norfolk	
ZM147	Lockheed Martin F-35B Lightning II (169421) [013]	RAF No 617 Sqn, Marham, Norfolk	
ZM148	Lockheed Martin F-35B Lightning II (169422) [014]	RAF No 617 Sqn, Marham, Norfolk	
ZM149	Lockheed Martin F-35B Lightning II (169596) [015]	RAF No 617 Sqn, Marham, Norfolk	
ZM150	Lockheed Martin F-35B Lightning II (169597) [016]	RAF No 617 Sqn, Marham, Norfolk	
ZM151	Lockheed Martin F-35B Lightning II (169598) [017]	RAF No 617 Sqn, Marham, Norfolk	
ZM153	Lockheed Martin F-35B Lightning II (169698) [019]	RAF No 617 Sqn, Marham, Norfolk	
ZM154	Lockheed Martin F-35B Lightning II (169699) [020]	RAF No 617 Sqn, Marham, Norfolk	
ZM155	Lockheed Martin F-35B Lightning II (169700) [021]	RAF No 617 Sqn, Marham, Norfolk	
ZM156	Lockheed Martin F-35B Lightning II (169928) [022]	RAF No 207 Sqn, Marham, Norfolk	
ZM157	Lockheed Martin F-35B Lightning II (169929) [023]	RAF No 617 Sqn, Marham, Norfolk	
ZM158	Lockheed Martin F-35B Lightning II (169930) [024]	RAF No 207 Sqn, Marham, Norfolk	
ZM159	Lockheed Martin F-35B Lightning II (169931) [025]	RAF No 617 Sqn, Marham, Norfolk	
ZM160	Lockheed Martin F-35B Lightning II (169932) [026]	RAF No 617 Sqn, Marham, Norfolk	
ZM161	Lockheed Martin F-35B Lightning II (169933) [027]	RAF No 617 Sqn, Marham, Norfolk	
ZM162	Lockheed Martin F-35B Lightning II (170074) [028]	RAF No 617 Sqn, Marham, Norfolk	
ZM163	Lockheed Martin F-35B Lightning II (170075) [029]	RAF No 207 Sqn, Marham, Norfolk	
ZM164	Lockheed Martin F-35B Lightning II (170076) [030]	RAF No 617 Sqn, Marham, Norfolk	
ZM165	Lockheed Martin F-35B Lightning II (170077) [031]	RAF No 17 Sqn, Edwards AFB, CA	
ZM166	Lockheed Martin F-35B Lightning II (170078) [032]	RAF No 617 Sqn, Marham, Norfolk	
ZM167	Lockheed Martin F-35B Lightning II (170079) [033]	RAF No 617 Sqn, Marham, Norfolk	
ZM168	Lockheed Martin F-35B Lightning II (170080) [034]	RAF No 617 Sqn, Marham, Norfolk	
ZM169	Lockheed Martin F-35B Lightning II (170081) [035]	RAF No 207 Sqn, Marham, Norfolk	
ZM170	Lockheed Martin F-35B Lightning II (170535) [036]	RAF No 17 Sqn, NAS Patuxent River, MD	
ZM171	Lockheed Martin F-35B Lightning II (170536) [037]	RAF/LMTAS, Fort Worth, TX	
ZM172	Lockheed Martin F-35B Lightning II	Reservation for RAF/RN	
ZM173	Lockheed Martin F-35B Lightning II	Reservation for RAF/RN	
ZM174	Lockheed Martin F-35B Lightning II	Reservation for RAF/RN	
ZM175	Lockheed Martin F-35B Lightning II	Reservation for RAF/RN	
ZM176	Lockheed Martin F-35B Lightning II	Reservation for RAF/RN	
ZM177	Lockheed Martin F-35B Lightning II	Reservation for RAF/RN	
ZM178	Lockheed Martin F-35B Lightning II	Reservation for RAF/RN	
ZM179	Lockheed Martin F-35B Lightning II	Reservation for RAF/RN	
ZM180	Lockheed Martin F-35B Lightning II	Reservation for RAF/RN	
ZM181	Lockheed Martin F-35B Lightning II	Reservation for RAF/RN	
ZM182	Lockheed Martin F-35B Lightning II	Reservation for RAF/RN	
ZM183	Lockheed Martin F-35B Lightning II	Reservation for RAF/RN	
ZM184	Lockheed Martin F-35B Lightning II	Reservation for RAF/RN	
ZM185	Lockheed Martin F-35B Lightning II	Reservation for RAF/RN	
ZM186	Lockheed Martin F-35B Lightning II	Reservation for RAF/RN	
ZM187	Lockheed Martin F-35B Lightning II	Reservation for RAF/RN	
ZM188	Lockheed Martin F-35B Lightning II	Reservation for RAF/RN	
ZM189	Lockheed Martin F-35B Lightning II	Reservation for RAF/RN	
ZM190	Lockheed Martin F-35B Lightning II	Reservation for RAF/RN	
ZM191	Lockheed Martin F-35B Lightning II	Reservation for RAF/RN	
ZM192	Lockheed Martin F-35B Lightning II	Reservation for RAF/RN	
ZM193	Lockheed Martin F-35B Lightning II	Reservation for RAF/RN	

Notes	Serial	Type (code/other identity)	Owner/operator, location or fate
	ZM194	Lockheed Martin F-35B Lightning II	Reservation for RAF/RN
	ZM195	Lockheed Martin F-35B Lightning II	Reservation for RAF/RN
	ZM196	Lockheed Martin F-35B Lightning II	Reservation for RAF/RN
	ZM197	Lockheed Martin F-35B Lightning II	Reservation for RAF/RN
	ZM198	Lockheed Martin F-35B Lightning II	Reservation for RAF/RN
	ZM199	Lockheed Martin F-35B Lightning II	Reservation for RAF/RN
	ZM200	Lockheed Martin F-35B Lightning II	Reservation for RAF/RN
	ZM300	Grob G120TP-A Prefect T1 (D-ETPJ/G-MFTS) [00]	RAF No 3 FTS/No 57 Sqn, Cranwell/Barkston Heath
	ZM301	Grob G120TP-A Prefect T1 (D-EGUX/G-MEFT) [01]	RAF No 3 FTS/No 57 Sqn, Cranwell/Barkston Heath
	ZM302	Grob G120TP-A Prefect T1 (D-ETPT/G-CJYB) [02]	RAF No 3 FTS/No 57 Sqn, Cranwell/Barkston Heath
	ZM303	Grob G120TP-A Prefect T1 (G-CJYG) [03]	RAF No 3 FTS/No 57 Sqn, Cranwell/Barkston Heath
	ZM304	Grob G120TP-A Prefect T1 (G-CJYH) [04]	RAF No 3 FTS/No 57 Sqn, Cranwell/Barkston Heath
	ZM305	Grob G120TP-A Prefect T1 (G-CJZR) [05]	RAF No 3 FTS/No 57 Sqn, Cranwell/Barkston Heath
	ZM306	Grob G120TP-A Prefect T1 (G-CJZJ) [06]	RAF No 3 FTS/No 57 Sqn, Cranwell/Barkston Heath
	ZM307	Grob G120TP-A Prefect T1 (G-CJZI) [07]	RAF No 3 FTS/No 57 Sqn, Cranwell/Barkston Heath
	ZM308	Grob G120TP-A Prefect T1 (G-CJZF) [08]	RAF No 3 FTS/No 57 Sqn, Cranwell/Barkston Heath
	ZM309	Grob G120TP-A Prefect T1 (G-CKCO) [09]	RAF No 3 FTS/No 57 Sqn, Cranwell/Barkston Heath
	ZM310	Grob G120TP-A Prefect T1 (G-CKCS) [10]	RAF No 3 FTS/No 57 Sqn, Cranwell/Barkston Heath
	ZM311	Grob G120TP-A Prefect T1 (G-CKIA) [11]	RAF No 3 FTS/No 57 Sqn, Cranwell/Barkston Heath
	ZM312	Grob G120TP-A Prefect T1 (G-CKIB) [12]	RAF No 3 FTS/No 57 Sqn, Cranwell/Barkston Heath
	ZM313	Grob G120TP-A Prefect T1 (G-CKIC) [13]	RAF No 3 FTS/No 57 Sqn, Cranwell/Barkston Heath
	ZM314	Grob G120TP-A Prefect T1 (G-CKID) [14]	RAF No 3 FTS/No 57 Sqn, Cranwell/Barkston Heath
	ZM315	Grob G120TP-A Prefect T1 (G-CKIV) [15]	RAF No 3 FTS/No 57 Sqn, Cranwell/Barkston Heath
	ZM316	Grob G120TP-A Prefect T1 (G-CKIW) [16]	RAF No 3 FTS/No 57 Sqn, Cranwell/Barkston Heath
	ZM317	Grob G120TP-A Prefect T1 (G-CKLJ) [17]	RAF No 3 FTS/No 57 Sqn, Cranwell/Barkston Heath
	ZM318	Grob G120TP-A Prefect T1 (G-CKLO) [18]	RAF No 3 FTS/No 57 Sqn, Cranwell/Barkston Heath
	ZM319	Grob G120TP-A Prefect T1 (G-CKRY) [19]	RAF No 3 FTS/No 57 Sqn, Cranwell/Barkston Heath
	ZM320	Grob G120TP-A Prefect T1 (G-CKRP) [20]	RAF No 3 FTS/No 57 Sqn, Cranwell/Barkston Heath
	ZM321	Grob G120TP-A Prefect T1 (G-CKSJ) [21]	RAF No 3 FTS/No 57 Sqn, Cranwell/Barkston Heath
	ZM322	Grob G120TP-A Prefect T1 (G-CKSI) [22]	RAF No 3 FTS/No 57 Sqn, Cranwell/Barkston Heath
	ZM323	Beechcraft T-6C Texan T1 (N2824B/G-TBFT) [323]	Affinity/RAF No 4 FTS/No 72 Sqn, Valley, Wales
	ZM324	Beechcraft T-6C Texan T1 (N2826B/G-CKGO) [324]	Affinity/RAF No 4 FTS/No 72 Sqn, Valley, Wales
	ZM325	Beechcraft T-6C Texan T1 (N2843B/G-CKGP) [325]	Affinity/RAF No 4 FTS/No 72 Sqn, Valley, Wales
	ZM326	Beechcraft T-6C Texan T1 (N2770B/G-CKGW) [326]	Affinity/RAF No 4 FTS/No 72 Sqn, Valley, Wales
	ZM327	Beechcraft T-6C Texan T1 (N2856B/G-CKVL) [327]	Affinity/RAF No 4 FTS/No 72 Sqn, Valley, Wales
	ZM328	Beechcraft T-6C Texan T1 (N2857B/G-CKVN) [328]	Affinity/RAF No 4 FTS/No 72 Sqn, Valley, Wales
	ZM329	Beechcraft T-6C Texan T1 (N2858B/G-CKVO) [329]	Affinity/RAF No 4 FTS/No 72 Sqn, Valley, Wales
	ZM330	Beechcraft T-6C Texan T1 (N2859B/G-CKVR) [330]	Affinity/RAF No 4 FTS/No 72 Sqn, Valley, Wales
	ZM331	Beechcraft T-6C Texan T1 (N2860B/G-CKVS) [331]	Affinity/RAF No 4 FTS/No 72 Sqn, Valley, Wales
	ZM332	Beechcraft T-6C Texan T1 (N2872B/G-CKVU) [332]	Affinity/RAF No 4 FTS/No 72 Sqn, Valley, Wales
	ZM333	Embraer EMB-500 Phenom T1 (PR-PHK/G-MEPT)	Affinity/RAF No 3 FTS/No 45 Sqn, Cranwell, Lincs
	ZM334	Embraer EMB-500 Phenom T1 (PR-ING/G-MEPS)	Affinity/RAF No 3 FTS/No 45 Sqn, Cranwell, Lincs
	ZM335	Embraer EMB-500 Phenom T1 (PR-LTE/G-CJXH)	Affinity/RAF No 3 FTS/No 45 Sqn, Cranwell, Lincs
	ZM336	Embraer EMB-500 Phenom T1 (PR-LTF/G-CKCU)	Affinity/RAF No 3 FTS/No 45 Sqn, Cranwell, Lincs
	ZM337	Embraer EMB-500 Phenom T1 (PR-LTJ/G-CKEF)	Affinity/RAF No 3 FTS/No 45 Sqn, Cranwell, Lincs
	ZM340	Beechcraft T-6C Texan T1 (N2786B/G-CLTZ) [340]	Affinity/RAF No 4 FTS/No 72 Sqn, Valley, Wales
	ZM341	Beechcraft T-6C Texan T1 (N2789B/G-CLUC) [341]	Affinity/RAF No 4 FTS/No 72 Sqn, Valley, Wales
	ZM342	Beechcraft T-6C Texan T1 (N2790B/G-CLUF) [342]	Affinity/RAF No 4 FTS/No 72 Sqn, Valley, Wales
	ZM343	Beechcraft T-6C Texan T1 (N2811B/G-CLUA) [343]	Affinity/RAF No 4 FTS/No 72 Sqn, Valley, Wales
	ZM398	Airbus A400M Atlas Full Flight Simulator	RAF Brize Norton, Oxon
	ZM399	Airbus A400M Atlas Full Flight Simulator	RAF Brize Norton, Oxon
	ZM400	Airbus A400M Atlas C1 (A4M015/EC-405) [400]	RAF, stored Brize Norton, Oxon
	ZM401	Airbus A400M Atlas C1 (A4M016/EC-406) [401]	RAF No 24 Sqn/No 30 Sqn/No 70 Sqn, Brize Norton
	ZM402	Airbus A400M Atlas C1 (A4M017/EC-407) [402]	RAF No 24 Sqn/No 30 Sqn/No 70 Sqn, Brize Norton
	ZM403	Airbus A400M Atlas C1 (A4M020) [403]	RAF, stored Brize Norton, Oxon
	ZM404	Airbus A400M Atlas C1 (A4M021/EC-401) [404]	RAF No 24 Sqn/No 30 Sqn/No 70 Sqn, Brize Norton
	ZM405	Airbus A400M Atlas C1 (A4M024) [405]	RAF No 24 Sqn/No 30 Sqn/No 70 Sqn, Brize Norton
	ZM406	Airbus A400M Atlas C1 (A4M025/EC-405) [406]	RAF, stored Brize Norton, Oxon
	ZM407	Airbus A400M Atlas C1 (A4M026) [407]	RAF, stored Brize Norton, Oxon
	ZM408	Airbus A400M Atlas C1 (A4M027) [408]	RAF No 24 Sqn/No 30 Sqn/No 70 Sqn, Brize Norton
	ZM409	Airbus A400M Atlas C1 (A4M034) [409]	RAF No 24 Sqn/No 30 Sqn/No 70 Sqn, Brize Norton
	ZM410	Airbus A400M Atlas C1 (A4M038) [410]	RAF, stored Brize Norton, Oxon

Serial	Type (code/other identity)	Owner/operator, location or fate	Notes
ZM411	Airbus A400M Atlas C1 (A4M039) [411]	RAF No 24 Sqn/No 30 Sqn/No 70 Sqn, Brize Norton	
ZM412	Airbus A400M Atlas C1 (A4M042) [412]	RAF No 24 Sqn/No 30 Sqn/No 70 Sqn, Brize Norton	
ZM413	Airbus A400M Atlas C1 (A4M045) [413]	RAF No 24 Sqn/No 30 Sqn/No 70 Sqn, Brize Norton	
ZM414	Airbus A400M Atlas C1 (A4M047) [414]	RAF No 24 Sqn/No 30 Sqn/No 70 Sqn, Brize Norton	
ZM415	Airbus A400M Atlas C1 (A4M052) [415]	RAF, stored Brize Norton, Oxon	
ZM416	Airbus A400M Atlas C1 (A4M058) [416]	RAF No 24 Sqn/No 30 Sqn/No 70 Sqn, Brize Norton	
ZM417	Airbus A400M Atlas C1 (A4M060) [417]	RAF No 24 Sqn/No 30 Sqn/No 70 Sqn, Brize Norton	
ZM418	Airbus A400M Atlas C1 (A4M072) [418]	Airbus Defence & Space, Getafe	
ZM419	Airbus A400M Atlas C1 (A4M077) [419]	Airbus Defence & Space, Getafe	
ZM420	Airbus A400M Atlas C1 (A4M056/EC-400) [420]	RAF No 24 Sqn/No 30 Sqn/No 70 Sqn, Brize Norton	
ZM421	Airbus A400M Atlas C1 (A4M129) [421]	RAF No 1312 Flt, Mount Pleasant, Falkland Islands	
ZM496	Airbus H145 Jupiter HT1 (D-HADR/G-CLKI) [96]	RAF No 202 Sqn, Valley, Gwynedd, Wales	
ZM497	Airbus H145 Jupiter HT1 (G-CLKO) [97]	RAF No 202 Sqn, Valley, Gwynedd, Wales	
ZM498	Airbus H145 Jupiter HT1 (G-CLKP) [98]	RAF No 1 FTS, Shawbury, Shropshire	
ZM499	Airbus H145 Jupiter HT1 (D-HADI/G-CLKS) [99]	RAF No 202 Sqn, Valley, Gwynedd, Wales	
ZM500	Airbus H145 Jupiter HT1 (D-HADT/G-CJIV) [00]	RAF No 1 FTS, Shawbury, Shropshire	
ZM501	Airbus H145 Jupiter HT1 (D-HADM/G-CJIZ/G-CKGE) [01]	RAF No 1 FTS, Shawbury, Shropshire	
ZM502	Airbus H145 Jupiter HT1 (D-HADQ/G-CJRW) [02]	RAF No 1 FTS, Shawbury, Shropshire	
ZM...	Airbus H145 Jupiter HC2 (D-HBTD/G-CMXA)	Reservation for RAF	
ZM...	Airbus H145 Jupiter HC2 (D-HADM/G-CMXB)	Reservation for RAF	
ZM504	Airbus H135 Juno HT1 (D-HECZ/G-CJJG) [04]	RAF No 1 FTS, Shawbury, Shropshire	
ZM505	Airbus H135 Juno HT1 (D-HECV/G-CJIW) [05]	RAF No 1 FTS, Shawbury, Shropshire	
ZM506	Airbus H135 Juno HT1 (D-HECW/G-CJIY) [06]	RAF No 1 FTS, Shawbury, Shropshire	
ZM507	Airbus H135 Juno HT1 (D-HECX/G-CJRP) [07]	RAF No 1 FTS, Shawbury, Shropshire	
ZM508	Airbus H135 Juno HT1 (D-HECD/G-CJRY) [08]	RAF No 1 FTS, Shawbury, Shropshire	
ZM509	Airbus H135 Juno HT1 (D-HECB/G-CJTZ) [09]	RAF No 1 FTS, Shawbury, Shropshire	
ZM510	Airbus H135 Juno HT1 (D-HECG/G-CJUA) [10]	RAF No 1 FTS, Shawbury, Shropshire	
ZM511	Airbus H135 Juno HT1 (D-HECJ/G-CJUC) [11]	RAF No 1 FTS, Shawbury, Shropshire	
ZM512	Airbus H135 Juno HT1 (D-HECQ/G-CJXS) [12]	RAF No 1 FTS, Shawbury, Shropshire	
ZM513	Airbus H135 Juno HT1 (D-HECP/G-CJXU) [13]	RAF No 1 FTS, Shawbury, Shropshire	
ZM514	Airbus H135 Juno HT1 (D-HECV/G-CJXV) [14]	RAF No 1 FTS, Shawbury, Shropshire	
ZM515	Airbus H135 Juno HT1 (D-HECT/G-CJSO) [15]	RAF No 1 FTS, Shawbury, Shropshire	
ZM516	Airbus H135 Juno HT1 (D-HECY/G-CJZS) [16]	RAF No 1 FTS, Shawbury, Shropshire	
ZM517	Airbus H135 Juno HT1 (D-HECL/G-CJZT) [17]	RAF No 1 FTS, Shawbury, Shropshire	
ZM518	Airbus H135 Juno HT1 (D-HCBA/G-CKEO) [18]	RAF No 1 FTS, Shawbury, Shropshire	
ZM519	Airbus H135 Juno HT1 (D-HCBC/G-CKEU) [19]	RAF No 1 FTS, Shawbury, Shropshire	
ZM520	Airbus H135 Juno HT1 (D-HCBD/G-CKEW) [20]	RAF No 1 FTS, Shawbury, Shropshire	
ZM521	Airbus H135 Juno HT1 (D-HECJ/G-CKIK) [21]	RAF No 1 FTS, Shawbury, Shropshire	
ZM522	Airbus H135 Juno HT1 (D-HCBB/G-CKIM) [22]	RAF No 1 FTS, Shawbury, Shropshire	
ZM523	Airbus H135 Juno HT1 (D-HECJ/G-CKJW) [23]	RAF No 1 FTS, Shawbury, Shropshire	
ZM524	Airbus H135 Juno HT1 (D-HECK/G-CKJU) [24]	RAF No 1 FTS, Shawbury, Shropshire	
ZM525	Airbus H135 Juno HT1 (D-HECQ/G-CKJX) [25]	RAF No 1 FTS, Shawbury, Shropshire	
ZM526	Airbus H135 Juno HT1 (D-HECU/G-CKOC) [26]	RAF No 1 FTS, Shawbury, Shropshire	
ZM527	Airbus H135 Juno HT1 (D-HECX/G-CKOB) [27]	RAF No 1 FTS, Shawbury, Shropshire	
ZM528	Airbus H135 Juno HT1 (D-HECF/G-CKOA) [28] $	RAF No 1 FTS, Shawbury, Shropshire	
ZM529	Airbus H135 Juno HT1 (D-HECW/G-CKPT) [29]	RAF No 1 FTS, Shawbury, Shropshire	
ZM530	Airbus H135 Juno HT1 (D-HECD/G-CKRA) [30]	RAF No 1 FTS, Shawbury, Shropshire	
ZM531	Airbus H135 Juno HT1 (D-HECA/G-CKSB) [31]	RAF No 1 FTS, Shawbury, Shropshire	
ZM532	Airbus H135 Juno HT1 (D-HECY/G-CKSA) [32]	RAF No 1 FTS, Shawbury, Shropshire	
ZM700	Boeing Apache AH-64E	AAC No 656/664 Sqn/No 4 Regiment, Wattisham, Suffolk	
ZM701	Boeing Apache AH-64E	AAC No 662/663 Sqn/No 3 Regiment, Wattisham, Suffolk	
ZM702	Boeing Apache AH-64E	AAC No 653/673 Sqn/No 7 Regiment, Middle Wallop, Hants	
ZM703	Boeing Apache AH-64E	AAC No 662/663 Sqn/No 3 Regiment, Wattisham, Suffolk	
ZM704	Boeing Apache AH-64E	AAC No 653/673 Sqn/No 7 Regiment, Middle Wallop, Hants	
ZM705	Boeing Apache AH-64E	AAC No 662/663 Sqn/No 3 Regiment, Wattisham, Suffolk	
ZM706	Boeing Apache AH-64E	AAC No 662/663 Sqn/No 3 Regiment, Wattisham, Suffolk	
ZM707	Boeing Apache AH-64E	AAC No 653/673 Sqn/No 7 Regiment, Middle Wallop, Hants	
ZM708	Boeing Apache AH-64E	AAC No 662/663 Sqn/No 3 Regiment, Wattisham, Suffolk	

Notes	Serial	Type (code/other identity)	Owner/operator, location or fate
	ZM709	Boeing Apache AH-64E	AAC No 656/664 Sqn/No 4 Regiment, Wattisham, Suffolk
	ZM710	Boeing Apache AH-64E	AAC No 662/663 Sqn/No 3 Regiment, Wattisham, Suffolk
	ZM711	Boeing Apache AH-64E	AAC No 662/663 Sqn/No 3 Regiment, Wattisham, Suffolk
	ZM712	Boeing Apache AH-64E	AAC No 662/663 Sqn/No 3 Regiment, Wattisham, Suffolk
	ZM713	Boeing Apache AH-64E	MoD/Boeing, Middle Wallop, Hants
	ZM714	Boeing Apache AH-64E	AAC No 664 Sqn/No 4 Regiment, Wattisham, Suffolk
	ZM715	Boeing Apache AH-64E	AAC No 653/673 Sqn/No 7 Regiment, Middle Wallop, Hants
	ZM716	Boeing Apache AH-64E	AAC No 653/673 Sqn/No 7 Regiment, Middle Wallop, Hants
	ZM717	Boeing Apache AH-64E	MoD/Boeing, Middle Wallop, Hants
	ZM718	Boeing Apache AH-64E	AAC No 656/664 Sqn/No 4 Regiment, Wattisham, Suffolk
	ZM719	Boeing Apache AH-64E	AAC No 7 AAB REME, Wattisham, Suffolk
	ZM720	Boeing Apache AH-64E	AAC No 662/663 Sqn/No 3 Regiment, Wattisham, Suffolk
	ZM721	Boeing Apache AH-64E	MOD/QinetiQ, Boscombe Down, Wilts
	ZM722	Boeing Apache AH-64E	AAC No 653/673 Sqn/No 7 Regiment, Middle Wallop, Hants
	ZM723	Boeing Apache AH-64E	AAC No 656/664 Sqn/No 4 Regiment, Wattisham, Suffolk
	ZM724	Boeing Apache AH-64E	AAC No 653/673 Sqn/No 7 Regiment, Middle Wallop, Hants
	ZM725	Boeing Apache AH-64E	AAC No 656/664 Sqn/No 4 Regiment, Wattisham, Suffolk
	ZM726	Boeing Apache AH-64E	AAC No 7 AAB REME, Wattisham, Suffolk
	ZM727	Boeing Apache AH-64E	AAC No 662/663 Sqn/No 3 Regiment, Wattisham, Suffolk
	ZM728	Boeing Apache AH-64E	AAC No 656/664 Sqn/No 4 Regiment, Wattisham, Suffolk
	ZM729	Boeing Apache AH-64E	AAC No 662/663 Sqn/No 3 Regiment, Wattisham, Suffolk
	ZM730	Boeing Apache AH-64E	AAC No 653/673 Sqn/No 7 Regiment, Middle Wallop, Hants
	ZM731	Boeing Apache AH-64E	AAC No 653/673 Sqn/No 7 Regiment, Middle Wallop, Hants
	ZM732	Boeing Apache AH-64E	AAC No 653/673 Sqn/No 7 Regiment, Middle Wallop, Hants
	ZM733	Boeing Apache AH-64E	AAC No 653/673 Sqn/No 7 Regiment, Middle Wallop, Hants
	ZM734	Boeing Apache AH-64E	AAC No 656/664 Sqn/No 4 Regiment, Wattisham, Suffolk
	ZM735	Boeing Apache AH-64E	AAC No 662/663 Sqn/No 3 Regiment, Wattisham, Suffolk
	ZM736	Boeing Apache AH-64E	AAC No 653/673 Sqn/No 7 Regiment, Middle Wallop, Hants
	ZM737	Boeing Apache AH-64E	AAC No 653/673 Sqn/No 7 Regiment, Middle Wallop, Hants
	ZM738	Boeing Apache AH-64E	AAC No 7 AAB REME, Wattisham, Suffolk
	ZM739	Boeing Apache AH-64E	AAC No 7 AAB REME, Wattisham, Suffolk
	ZM740	Boeing Apache AH-64E	AAC No 7 AAB REME, Wattisham, Suffolk
	ZM741	Boeing Apache AH-64E	AAC No 7 AAB REME, Wattisham, Suffolk
	ZM742	Boeing Apache AH-64E	AAC No 7 AAB REME, Wattisham, Suffolk
	ZM743	Boeing Apache AH-64E	AAC No 7 AAB REME, Wattisham, Suffolk
	ZM744	Boeing Apache AH-64E	AAC No 7 AAB REME, Wattisham, Suffolk
	ZM745	Boeing Apache AH-64E	AAC No 7 AAB REME, Wattisham, Suffolk
	ZM746	Boeing Apache AH-64E	AAC No 7 AAB REME, Wattisham, Suffolk
	ZM747	Boeing Apache AH-64E	For AAC
	ZM748	Boeing Apache AH-64E	For AAC
	ZM749	Boeing Apache AH-64E	For AAC
	ZP526	Thales/Schiebel Peregrine RPAS	MoD
	ZP527	Thales/Schiebel Peregrine RPAS	MoD
	ZP801	Boeing P-8A Poseidon MRA1 (169573/N456DS) [01]	RAF No 54 Sqn/No 120 Sqn/No 201 Sqn, Lossiemouth
	ZP802	Boeing P-8A Poseidon MRA1 (169574/N469DS) [02]	RAF No 54 Sqn/No 120 Sqn/No 201 Sqn, Lossiemouth
	ZP803	Boeing P-8A Poseidon MRA1 (169575/N481DS) [03]	RAF No 54 Sqn/No 120 Sqn/No 201 Sqn, Lossiemouth
	ZP804	Boeing P-8A Poseidon MRA1 (169576/N482DS) [04]	RAF No 54 Sqn/No 120 Sqn/No 201 Sqn, Lossiemouth
	ZP805	Boeing P-8A Poseidon MRA1 (169577/N534DS) [05]	RAF No 54 Sqn/No 120 Sqn/No 201 Sqn, Lossiemouth
	ZP806	Boeing P-8A Poseidon MRA1 (169578/N634DS) [06]	RAF No 54 Sqn/No 120 Sqn/No 201 Sqn, Lossiemouth
	ZP807	Boeing P-8A Poseidon MRA1 (169579/N665DS) [07]	RAF No 54 Sqn/No 120 Sqn/No 201 Sqn, Lossiemouth
	ZP808	Boeing P-8A Poseidon MRA1 (169580/N667DS) [08]	RAF No 54 Sqn/No 120 Sqn/No 201 Sqn, Lossiemouth

Serial	Type (code/other identity)	Owner/operator, location or fate	Notes
ZP809	Boeing P-8A Poseidon MRA1 (169581/N673DS) [09]	RAF No 54 Sqn/No 120 Sqn/No 201 Sqn, Lossiemouth	
ZR334	AgustaWestland AW101 Mk.640 (RSAF HMH-1)	Leonardo MW, stored Yeovil, Somerset	
ZR335	AgustaWestland AW101 Mk.640 (RSAF HMH-2)	Leonardo MW, stored Yeovil, Somerset	
ZR342	AgustaWestland AW101 Mk.641 (ZW-4305)	Leonardo MW, stored Yeovil, Somerset	
ZR346	AgustaWestland AW101 Mk.641 (ZW-4309)	Leonardo MW, stored Yeovil, Somerset	
ZR347	AgustaWestland AW101 Mk.641 (ZW-4310)	Leonardo MW, stored Yeovil, for Azerbaijan?	
ZR348	AgustaWestland AW101 Mk.641 (ZW-4311)	Leonardo MW, stored Yeovil, for Azerbaijan?	
ZR349	AgustaWestland AW101 Mk.641 (ZW-4312)	Leonardo MW, stored Yeovil, for Azerbaijan?	
ZR518	Eurofighter Typhoon (MS014)	*To Qatar as QA417, 29th April 2024*	
ZR520	Eurofighter Typhoon (MS016)	*To Qatar as QA419, 29th April 2024*	
ZR521	Eurofighter Typhoon (MS017)	*To Qatar as QA420, 11th November 2024*	
ZR522	Eurofighter Typhoon (MS018)	*To Qatar as QA421, 11th November 2024*	
ZR523	Eurofighter Typhoon (MS019)	BAe Systems, for Qatar as QA422	
ZR524	Eurofighter Typhoon (MS020)	BAe Systems, for Qatar as QA423	
ZS782	WS WG25 Sharpeye (BAPC.451)	The Helicopter Museum, Weston-super-Mare, Somerset	
ZT109	QinetiQ Banshee Jet 80+ RPAS	MOD/QinetiQ, Boscombe Down, Wilts	
ZT800	WS Super Lynx Mk 300	Yeovil College, Somerset, instructional use	
ZZ100	AgustaWestland AW101 Mk.612 (0262)	Leonardo MW, Yeovil, for Norway as 0262	
ZZ171	Boeing C-17A Globemaster III (00-201/N171UK) $	RAF No 99 Sqn, Brize Norton, Oxon	
ZZ172	Boeing C-17A Globemaster III (00-202/N172UK)	RAF No 99 Sqn, Brize Norton, Oxon	
ZZ173	Boeing C-17A Globemaster III (00-203/N173UK)	RAF No 99 Sqn, Brize Norton, Oxon	
ZZ174	Boeing C-17A Globemaster III (00-204/N174UK)	RAF No 99 Sqn, Brize Norton, Oxon	
ZZ175	Boeing C-17A Globemaster III (06-0205/N9500Z)	RAF No 99 Sqn, Brize Norton, Oxon	
ZZ176	Boeing C-17A Globemaster III (08-0206/N9500B)	RAF No 99 Sqn, Brize Norton, Oxon	
ZZ177	Boeing C-17A Globemaster III (09-8207/N9500B)	RAF No 99 Sqn, Brize Norton, Oxon	
ZZ178	Boeing C-17A Globemaster III (12-0208/N9500N)	RAF No 99 Sqn, Brize Norton, Oxon	
ZZ190	Hawker Hunter F58 (J-4066/G-HHAE)	Hawker Hunter Aviation, Leeming, N. Yorks	
ZZ191	Hawker Hunter F58 (J-4058/G-HHAD)	Hawker Hunter Aviation, Leeming, N. Yorks (stored?)	
ZZ194	Hawker Hunter F58 (J-4021/G-HHAC)	Hawker Hunter Aviation, Leeming, N. Yorks (stored?)	
ZZ202	General Atomics Reaper RPAS (07-0117)	RAF No 13 Sqn/No 39 Sqn, Creech AFB, NV, USA	
ZZ203	General Atomics Reaper RPAS (08-0113)	RAF No 13 Sqn/No 39 Sqn, Creech AFB, NV, USA	
ZZ204	General Atomics Reaper RPAS (10-0157)	RAF No 13 Sqn/No 39 Sqn, Creech AFB, NV, USA	
ZZ205	General Atomics Reaper RPAS (10-0157)	RAF, Creech AFB, Nevada, USA (damaged)	
ZZ206	General Atomics Reaper RPAS (12-0707)	RAF No 13 Sqn/No 39 Sqn, Creech AFB, Nevada, USA	
ZZ207	General Atomics Reaper RPAS (12-0708)	RAF No 13 Sqn/No 39 Sqn, Creech AFB, Nevada, USA	
ZZ208	General Atomics Reaper RPAS (12-0709)	RAF No 13 Sqn/No 39 Sqn, Creech AFB, Nevada, USA	
ZZ209	General Atomics Reaper RPAS (12-0710)	RAF No 13 Sqn/No 39 Sqn, Creech AFB, Nevada, USA	
ZZ210	General Atomics Reaper RPAS (12-0711)	RAF No 13 Sqn/No 39 Sqn, Creech AFB, Nevada, USA	
ZZ211	General Atomics Reaper RPAS (12-0712)	RAF No 13 Sqn/No 39 Sqn, Creech AFB, Nevada, USA	
ZZ212	General Atomics Reaper RPAS	RAF No 13 Sqn/No 39 Sqn, Creech AFB, Nevada, USA	
ZZ213	General Atomics Reaper RPAS	RAF No 13 Sqn/No 39 Sqn, Creech AFB, Nevada, USA	
ZZ250	BAE Systems Taranis RPAS	BAE Systems, Warton, Lancs	
ZZ251	BAE Systems HERTI RPAS	BAE Systems, Warton, Lancs	
ZZ252	BAE Systems HERTI RPAS	BAE Systems, Woomera, Australia	
ZZ253	BAE Systems HERTI RPAS	BAE Systems, Woomera, Australia	
ZZ254	BAE Systems HERTI RPAS	BAE Systems, Woomera, Australia	
ZZ330	Airbus A330 Voyager KC2 (MRTT017/EC-337/G-VYGA)	RAF No 10 Sqn/No 101 Sqn, Brize Norton, Oxon	
ZZ331	Airbus A330 Voyager KC2 (MRTT018/EC-331/G-VYGB)	RAF No 10 Sqn/No 101 Sqn, Brize Norton, Oxon	
ZZ332	Airbus A330 Voyager KC3 (MRTT019/EC-330/G-VYGC)	RAF No 10 Sqn/No 101 Sqn, Brize Norton, Oxon	
ZZ333	Airbus A330 Voyager KC3 (MRTT020/EC-337/G-VYGD)	RAF No 10 Sqn/No 101 Sqn, Brize Norton, Oxon	
ZZ334	Airbus A330 Voyager KC3 (MRTT016/EC-335/G-VYGE)	RAF No 10 Sqn/No 101 Sqn, Brize Norton, Oxon	
ZZ335	Airbus A330 Voyager KC3 (MRTT021/EC-338/G-VYGF)	RAF No 10 Sqn/No 101 Sqn, Brize Norton, Oxon	
ZZ336	Airbus A330 Voyager KC3 (MRTT022/EC-333/ G-VYGG) $	RAF No 10 Sqn/No 101 Sqn, Brize Norton, Oxon	
ZZ337	Airbus A330 Voyager KC3 (MRTT023/EC-336/G-VYGH)	RAF No 10 Sqn/No 101 Sqn, Brize Norton, Oxon	
ZZ338	Airbus A330 Voyager KC3 (MRTT024/EC-331/G-VYGI)	RAF No 1312 Flt, Mount Pleasant, Falkland Islands	
ZZ339	Airbus A330-243 (MRTT025/EC-333/G-VYGJ)	Airtanker Ltd, Brize Norton [flies as G-VYGJ]	
ZZ340	Airbus A330-243 (MRTT026/EC-330/G-VYGK)	Airtanker Ltd, Brize Norton [flies as G-VYGM for Jet2]	

Notes	Serial	Type (code/other identity)	Owner/operator, location or fate
	ZZ341	Airbus A330-243 (MRTT027/EC-336/G-VYGL)	Airtanker Ltd, Brize Norton [flies as G-VYGL]
	ZZ342	Airbus A330-243 (MRTT028/EC-332/G-VYGM)	Airtanker Ltd, Brize Norton [flies as G-VYGM for Jet2]
	ZZ343	Airbus A330 Voyager KC2 (MRTT029/EC-331/G-VYGN)	RAF No 10 Sqn/No 101 Sqn, Brize Norton, Oxon
	ZZ375	AgustaWestland AW159 Wildcat HMA2	RN No 825 NAS, Yeovilton, Somerset
	ZZ376	AgustaWestland AW159 Wildcat HMA2	RN No 815 NAS, Yeovilton, Somerset
	ZZ377	AgustaWestland AW159 Wildcat HMA2	MOD/Leonardo MW, Yeovil, Somerset
	ZZ378	AgustaWestland AW159 Wildcat HMA2	RN No 815 NAS, Yeovilton, Somerset
	ZZ379	AgustaWestland AW159 Wildcat HMA2	RN No 825 NAS, Yeovilton, Somerset
	ZZ380	AgustaWestland AW159 Wildcat HMA2	RN No 847 NAS, Yeovilton, Somerset
	ZZ381	AgustaWestland AW159 Wildcat HMA2	RN No 825 NAS, Yeovilton, Somerset
	ZZ382	AgustaWestland AW159 Wildcat AH1	AAC 659/661 Sqn/No 1 Regiment, Yeovilton, Somerset
	ZZ383	AgustaWestland AW159 Wildcat AH1	RN No 847 NAS, Yeovilton, Somerset
	ZZ384	AgustaWestland AW159 Wildcat AH1	AAC 659/661 Sqn/No 1 Regiment, Yeovilton, Somerset
	ZZ385	AgustaWestland AW159 Wildcat AH1	RN No 847 NAS, Yeovilton, Somerset
	ZZ386	AgustaWestland AW159 Wildcat AH1	RN No 847 NAS, Yeovilton, Somerset
	ZZ387	AgustaWestland AW159 Wildcat AH1	RN No 847 NAS, Yeovilton, Somerset
	ZZ388	AgustaWestland AW159 Wildcat AH1	AAC 659/661 Sqn/No 1 Regiment, Yeovilton, Somerset
	ZZ389	AgustaWestland AW159 Wildcat AH1	AAC No 1 Regiment, Yeovilton, Somerset
	ZZ390	AgustaWestland AW159 Wildcat AH1	AAC 659/661 Sqn/No 1 Regiment, Yeovilton, Somerset
	ZZ391	AgustaWestland AW159 Wildcat AH1	AAC 659/661 Sqn/No 1 Regiment, Yeovilton, Somerset
	ZZ392	AgustaWestland AW159 Wildcat AH1	AAC WCM (652 Sqn), Yeovilton, Somerset
	ZZ393	AgustaWestland AW159 Wildcat AH1	AAC WST/WZM, Yeovilton, Somerset
	ZZ394	AgustaWestland AW159 Wildcat AH1	AAC 659/661 Sqn/No 1 Regiment, Yeovilton, Somerset
	ZZ395	AgustaWestland AW159 Wildcat AH1	AAC No 1 Regiment, Yeovilton, Somerset
	ZZ396	AgustaWestland AW159 Wildcat HMA2	RN No 815 NAS, Yeovilton, Somerset
	ZZ397	AgustaWestland AW159 Wildcat HMA2	RN No 815 NAS, Yeovilton, Somerset
	ZZ398	AgustaWestland AW159 Wildcat AH1	AAC WCM (652 Sqn), Yeovilton, Somerset
	ZZ399	AgustaWestland AW159 Wildcat AH1	RN No 847 NAS, Yeovilton, Somerset
	ZZ400	AgustaWestland AW159 Wildcat (TI01)	RNAS Yeovilton, Somerset, GI use
	ZZ401	AgustaWestland AW159 Wildcat (TI02)	RNAS Yeovilton, Somerset, GI use
	ZZ402	AgustaWestland AW159 Wildcat (TI03)	DSAE RNAESS, HMS Sultan, Gosport, Hants
	ZZ403	AgustaWestland AW159 Wildcat AH1	AAC 659/661 Sqn/No 1 Regiment, Yeovilton, Somerset
	ZZ404	AgustaWestland AW159 Wildcat AH1	AAC WCM (652 Sqn), Yeovilton, Somerset
	ZZ405	AgustaWestland AW159 Wildcat AH1	AAC 659/661 Sqn/No 1 Regiment, Yeovilton, Somerset
	ZZ406	AgustaWestland AW159 Wildcat AH1	RN No 847 NAS, Yeovilton, Somerset
	ZZ407	AgustaWestland AW159 Wildcat AH1	AAC WCM (652 Sqn), Yeovilton, Somerset
	ZZ408	AgustaWestland AW159 Wildcat AH1	AAC 659/661 Sqn/No 1 Regiment, Yeovilton, Somerset
	ZZ409	AgustaWestland AW159 Wildcat AH1	AAC WCM (652 Sqn), Yeovilton, Somerset
	ZZ410	AgustaWestland AW159 Wildcat AH1	AAC WCM (652 Sqn), Yeovilton, Somerset
	ZZ413	AgustaWestland AW159 Wildcat HMA2	RN No 825 NAS, Yeovilton, Somerset
	ZZ414	AgustaWestland AW159 Wildcat HMA2	RN No 825 NAS, Yeovilton, Somerset
	ZZ415	AgustaWestland AW159 Wildcat HMA2	RN No 825 NAS, Yeovilton, Somerset
	ZZ416	Hawker Beechcraft Shadow R1+ (G-JENC)	RAF No 14 Sqn/No 54 Sqn, Waddington, Lincs
	ZZ417	Hawker Beechcraft Shadow R1+ (G-NICY)	RAF No 14 Sqn/No 54 Sqn, Waddington, Lincs
	ZZ418	Hawker Beechcraft Shadow R1+ (G-JIMG)	RAF, maintenance, Bournemouth/Hurn, Dorset
	ZZ419	Hawker Beechcraft Shadow R1+ (G-OTCS)	RAF No 14 Sqn/No 54 Sqn, Waddington, Lincs
	ZZ500	Hawker Beechcraft Avenger T1 (G-MFTA)	RN No 750 NAS, Culdrose, Cornwall
	ZZ501	Hawker Beechcraft Avenger T1 (G-MFTB)	RN No 750 NAS, Culdrose, Cornwall
	ZZ502	Hawker Beechcraft Avenger T1 (G-MFTC)	RN No 750 NAS, Culdrose, Cornwall
	ZZ503	Hawker Beechcraft Avenger T1 (G-MFTD)	RN No 750 NAS, Culdrose, Cornwall
	ZZ504	Hawker Beechcraft Shadow R1+ (G-CGUM)	RAF No 14 Sqn/No 54 Sqn, Waddington, Lincs
	ZZ505	Hawker Beechcraft Shadow R2 (G-DAYP)	MOD/Raytheon, Hawarden, Flintshire, Wales (upgrade)
	ZZ506	Hawker Beechcraft Shadow R2 (G-GMAD)	MOD/Raytheon, Hawarden, Flintshire, Wales (upgrade)
	ZZ507	Hawker Beechcraft Shadow R1+ (G-LBSB)	RAF, Operation Shader, Akrotiri, Cyprus
	ZZ510	AgustaWestland AW159 Wildcat AH1	AAC WCM (652 Sqn), Yeovilton, Somerset
	ZZ511	AgustaWestland AW159 Wildcat AH1	AAC WCM (652 Sqn), Yeovilton, Somerset
	ZZ512	AgustaWestland AW159 Wildcat AH1	AAC 659/661 Sqn/No 1 Regiment, Yeovilton, Somerset
	ZZ513	AgustaWestland AW159 Wildcat HMA2	MOD/Leonardo MW, Yeovil, Somerset (FASGW trials)
	ZZ514	AgustaWestland AW159 Wildcat HMA2	RN No 825 NAS, Yeovilton, Somerset
	ZZ515	AgustaWestland AW159 Wildcat HMA2	RN No 825 NAS, Yeovilton, Somerset
	ZZ516	AgustaWestland AW159 Wildcat HMA2	RN No 825 NAS, Yeovilton, Somerset
	ZZ517	AgustaWestland AW159 Wildcat HMA2	RN No 825 NAS, Yeovilton, Somerset

Serial	Type (code/other identity)	Owner/operator, location or fate	Notes
ZZ518	AgustaWestland AW159 Wildcat HMA2	RN No 825 NAS, Yeovilton, Somerset	
ZZ519	AgustaWestland AW159 Wildcat HMA2	RN No 815 NAS, Yeovilton, Somerset	
ZZ520	AgustaWestland AW159 Wildcat AH1	AAC 659/661 Sqn/No 1 Regiment, Yeovilton, Somerset	
ZZ521	AgustaWestland AW159 Wildcat AH1	AAC WCM (652 Sqn), Yeovilton, Somerset	
ZZ522	AgustaWestland AW159 Wildcat HMA2	RN No 815 NAS, Yeovilton, Somerset	
ZZ523	AgustaWestland AW159 Wildcat AH1	AAC WCM (652 Sqn), Yeovilton, Somerset	
ZZ524	AgustaWestland AW159 Wildcat AH1	RN No 847 NAS, Yeovilton, Somerset	
ZZ525	AgustaWestland AW159 Wildcat AH1	RN No 847 NAS, Yeovilton, Somerset	
ZZ526	AgustaWestland AW159 Wildcat AH1	AAC WCM (652 Sqn), Yeovilton, Somerset	
ZZ527	AgustaWestland AW159 Wildcat AH1	AAC 659/661 Sqn/No 1 Regiment, Yeovilton, Somerset	
ZZ528	AgustaWestland AW159 Wildcat HMA2	RN No 825 NAS, Yeovilton, Somerset	
ZZ529	AgustaWestland AW159 Wildcat HMA2	RN No 825 NAS, Yeovilton, Somerset	
ZZ530	AgustaWestland AW159 Wildcat HMA2	AAC WST/WZM, Yeovilton, Somerset	
ZZ531	AgustaWestland AW159 Wildcat HMA2	RN No 825 NAS, Yeovilton, Somerset	
ZZ532	AgustaWestland AW159 Wildcat HMA2	RN No 825 NAS, Yeovilton, Somerset	
ZZ533	AgustaWestland AW159 Wildcat HMA2	RN No 815 NAS, Yeovilton, Somerset	
ZZ534	AgustaWestland AW159 Wildcat HMA2	RN No 825 NAS, Yeovilton, Somerset	
ZZ535	AgustaWestland AW159 Wildcat HMA2	MOD/Leonardo MW, Yeovil, Somerset	
ZZ664	Boeing RC-135W (64-14833)	RAF/Northrop Grumman, Greenville, SC, USA	
ZZ665	Boeing RC-135W (64-14838)	RAF No 51 Sqn, Waddington, Lincs	
ZZ666	Boeing RC-135W (64-14830)	RAF No 51 Sqn, Waddington, Lincs	

ZK341, A Typhoon FGR.4, seen here in the marks of the joint RAF/Qatari 12 sqn, based at RAF Coningsby but seen here at RAF Fairford for RIAT. *HJC*

Notes	Serial	Type (code/other identity)	Owner/operator, location or fate
	C-GFMX	De Havilland Canada DHC-8-315ISR	PAL Aerospace/HM Government, Lydd, Kent
	G-BLNT	PBN 2T Defender R2 (ZG845)	Draken International, Aldergrove, NI
	G-BLNU	PBN 2T Defender R2 (ZG846)	Draken International, Aldergrove, NI
	G-BYUB	Grob G.115E Tutor T1	Babcock/Liverpool UAS/Manchester and Salford Universities AS, Woodvale, Merseyside
	G-BYUC	Grob G.115E Tutor T1	Babcock/No 3 FTS/No 16 Sqn, Cranwell, Lincs
	G-BYUD	Grob G.115E Tutor T1	Babcock/Southern Sailplanes, Membury, Wilts (maint.)
	G-BYUE	Grob G.115E Tutor T1	Babcock/University of Wales AS, St Athan, Wales
	G-BYUF	Grob G.115E Tutor T1	Babcock/Universities of Glasgow & Strathclyde AS, Glasgow, Scotland
	G-BYUH	Grob G.115E Tutor T1	Babcock/University of Birmingham AS, Cosford, Shropshire
	G-BYUI	Grob G.115E Tutor T1	Babcock/University of Birmingham AS, Cosford, Shropshire
	G-BYUJ	Grob G.115E Tutor T1	Babcock/Liverpool UAS/Manchester and Salford Universities AS, Woodvale, Merseyside
	G-BYUK	Grob G.115E Tutor T1	Babcock/Cambridge UAS/East Midlands Universities AS/ University of London AS/No 115 Sqn, Wittering, Cambs
	G-BYUL	Grob G.115E Tutor T1	Babcock/Oxford UAS, Benson, Oxon
	G-BYUM	Grob G.115E Tutor T1	Babcock/Bristol UAS/Southampton UAS, Boscombe Down, Wilts
	G-BYUN	Grob G.115E Tutor T1	Babcock/No 3 FTS/No 16 Sqn, Cranwell, Lincs
	G-BYUO	Grob G.115E Tutor T1	Babcock/Southern Sailplanes, Membury, Wilts (maint.)
	G-BYUR	Grob G.115E Tutor T1	Babcock/Yorkshire Universities AS, Leeming, N. Yorks
	G-BYUS	Grob G.115E Tutor T1	Babcock/Cambridge UAS/East Midlands Universities AS/ University of London AS/No 115 Sqn, Wittering, Cambs
	G-BYUU	Grob G.115E Tutor T1	Babcock/Cambridge UAS/East Midlands Universities AS/ University of London AS/No 115 Sqn, Wittering, Cambs
	G-BYUV	Grob G.115E Tutor T1	Babcock/East of Scotland UAS, Leuchars, Scotland
	G-BYUW	Grob G.115E Tutor T1	Babcock/East of Scotland UAS, Leuchars, Scotland
	G-BYUX	Grob G.115E Tutor T1	Babcock/No 3 FTS/No 16 Sqn, Cranwell, Lincs
	G-BYUY	Grob G.115E Tutor T1	Babcock/Bristol UAS/Southampton UAS, Boscombe Down, Wilts
	G-BYUZ	Grob G.115E Tutor T1	Babcock/University of Birmingham AS, Cosford, Shropshire
	G-BYVA	Grob G.115E Tutor T1	Babcock/Bristol UAS/Southampton UAS, Boscombe Down, Wilts
	G-BYVB	Grob G.115E Tutor T1	Babcock/Cambridge UAS/East Midlands Universities AS/ University of London AS/No 115 Sqn, Wittering, Cambs
	G-BYVC	Grob G.115E Tutor T1	Babcock/Cambridge UAS/East Midlands Universities AS/ University of London AS/No 115 Sqn, Wittering, Cambs
	G-BYVD	Grob G.115E Tutor T1	Babcock/Cambridge UAS/East Midlands Universities AS/ University of London AS/No 115 Sqn, Wittering, Cambs
	G-BYVE	Grob G.115E Tutor T1	Babcock/Southern Sailplanes, Membury, Wilts (maint.)
	G-BYVF	Grob G.115E Tutor T1	Babcock/Liverpool UAS/Manchester and Salford Universities AS, Woodvale, Merseyside
	G-BYVG	Grob G.115E Tutor T1	Babcock/Yorkshire Universities AS, Leeming, N. Yorks
	G-BYVH	Grob G.115E Tutor T1	Babcock/Cambridge UAS/East Midlands Universities AS/ University of London AS/No 115 Sqn, Wittering, Cambs
	G-BYVI	Grob G.115E Tutor T1	Babcock/Cambridge UAS/East Midlands Universities AS/ University of London AS/No 115 Sqn, Wittering, Cambs
	G-BYVK	Grob G.115E Tutor T1	Babcock/University of Wales AS, St Athan, Wales
	G-BYVL	Grob G.115E Tutor T1	Babcock/Southern Sailplanes, Membury, Wilts (maint.)
	G-BYVM	Grob G.115E Tutor T1	Babcock/No 3 FTS/No 16 Sqn, Cranwell, Lincs
	G-BYVO	Grob G.115E Tutor T1	Babcock/Cambridge UAS/East Midlands Universities AS/ University of London AS/No 115 Sqn, Wittering, Cambs
	G-BYVP	Grob G.115E Tutor T1	Babcock/Cambridge UAS/East Midlands Universities AS/ University of London AS/No 115 Sqn, Wittering, Cambs
	G-BYVR	Grob G.115E Tutor T1	Babcock/Yorkshire Universities AS, Leeming, N. Yorks
	G-BYVU	Grob G.115E Tutor T1	Babcock/Bristol UAS/Southampton UAS, Boscombe Down, Wilts
	G-BYVW	Grob G.115E Tutor T1	Babcock/Cambridge UAS/East Midlands Universities AS/ University of London AS/No 115 Sqn, Wittering, Cambs
	G-BYVY	Grob G.115E Tutor T1	Babcock/Liverpool UAS/Manchester and Salford Universities AS, Woodvale, Merseyside

Serial	Type (code/other identity)	Owner/operator, location or fate	Notes
G-BYVZ	Grob G.115E Tutor T1	Babcock/University of Birmingham AS, Cosford, Shropshire	
G-BYWA	Grob G.115E Tutor T1	Babcock/Bristol UAS/Southampton UAS, Boscombe Down, Wilts	
G-BYWB	Grob G.115E Tutor T1	Babcock/Bristol UAS/Southampton UAS, Boscombe Down, Wilts	
G-BYWD	Grob G.115E Tutor T1	Babcock/Oxford UAS, Benson, Oxon	
G-BYWF	Grob G.115E Tutor T1	Babcock/Liverpool UAS/Manchester and Salford Universities AS, Woodvale, Merseyside	
G-BYWG	Grob G.115E Tutor T1	Babcock/East of Scotland UAS, Leuchars, Scotland	
G-BYWH	Grob G.115E Tutor T1	Babcock/Southern Sailplanes, Membury, Wilts (maint.)	
G-BYWI	Grob G.115E Tutor T1	Babcock/Cambridge UAS/East Midlands Universities AS/ University of London AS/No 115 Sqn, Wittering, Cambs	
G-BYWK	Grob G.115E Tutor T1	Babcock/Cambridge UAS/East Midlands Universities AS/ University of London AS/No 115 Sqn, Wittering, Cambs	
G-BYWL	Grob G.115E Tutor T1	Babcock/Bristol UAS/Southampton UAS, Boscombe Down, Wilts	
G-BYWM	Grob G.115E Tutor T1	Babcock/Bristol UAS/Southampton UAS, Boscombe Down, Wilts	
G-BYWO	Grob G.115E Tutor T1	Babcock/Cambridge UAS/East Midlands Universities AS/ University of London AS/No 115 Sqn, Wittering, Cambs	
G-BYWR	Grob G.115E Tutor T1	Babcock/Oxford UAS, Benson, Oxon	
G-BYWS	Grob G.115E Tutor T1	Babcock/University of Birmingham AS, Cosford, Shropshire	
G-BYWU	Grob G.115E Tutor T1	Babcock/Oxford UAS, Benson, Oxon	
G-BYWV	Grob G.115E Tutor T1	Babcock/Yorkshire Universities AS, Leeming, N. Yorks	
G-BYWW	Grob G.115E Tutor T1	Babcock/No 3 FTS/No 16 Sqn, Cranwell, Lincs	
G-BYWX	Grob G.115E Tutor T1	Babcock/University of Birmingham AS, Cosford, Shropshire	
G-BYWY	Grob G.115E Tutor T1	Babcock/Oxford UAS, Benson, Oxon	
G-BYWZ	Grob G.115E Tutor T1	Babcock/Yorkshire Universities AS, Leeming, N. Yorks	
G-BYXA	Grob G.115E Tutor T1	Babcock/Cambridge UAS/East Midlands Universities AS/ University of London AS/No 115 Sqn, Wittering, Cambs	
G-BYXC	Grob G.115E Tutor T1	Babcock/Yorkshire Universities AS, Leeming, N. Yorks	
G-BYXD	Grob G.115E Tutor T1	Babcock/Southern Sailplanes, Membury, Wilts (maint.)	
G-BYXE	Grob G.115E Tutor T1	Babcock/Yorkshire Universities AS, Leeming, N. Yorks	
G-BYXF	Grob G.115E Tutor T1	Babcock/Cambridge UAS/East Midlands Universities AS/ University of London AS/No 115 Sqn, Wittering, Cambs	
G-BYXG	Grob G.115E Tutor T1	Babcock/Bristol UAS/Southampton UAS, Boscombe Down, Wilts	
G-BYXH	Grob G.115E Tutor T1	Babcock/Cambridge UAS/East Midlands Universities AS/ University of London AS/No 115 Sqn, Wittering, Cambs	
G-BYXI	Grob G.115E Tutor T1	Babcock/Oxford UAS, Benson, Oxon	
G-BYXJ	Grob G.115E Tutor T1	Babcock/Cambridge UAS/East Midlands Universities AS/ University of London AS/No 115 Sqn, Wittering, Cambs	
G-BYXK	Grob G.115E Tutor T1	Babcock/Cambridge UAS/East Midlands Universities AS/ University of London AS/No 115 Sqn, Wittering, Cambs	
G-BYXL	Grob G.115E Tutor T1	Babcock/Bristol UAS/Southampton UAS, Boscombe Down, Wilts	
G-BYXM	Grob G.115E Tutor T1	Babcock/Liverpool UAS/Manchester and Salford Universities AS, Woodvale, Merseyside	
G-BYXO	Grob G.115E Tutor T1	Babcock/No 3 FTS/No 16 Sqn, Cranwell, Lincs	
G-BYXP	Grob G.115E Tutor T1	Babcock/Liverpool UAS/Manchester and Salford Universities AS, Woodvale, Merseyside	
G-BYXS	Grob G.115E Tutor T1	Babcock/Bristol UAS/Southampton UAS, Boscombe Down, Wilts	
G-BYXT	Grob G.115E Tutor T1	Babcock/University of Wales AS, St Athan, Wales	
G-BYXX	Grob G.115E Tutor T1	Babcock/Oxford UAS, Benson, Oxon	
G-BYXZ	Grob G.115E Tutor T1	Babcock/Bristol UAS/Southampton UAS, Boscombe Down, Wilts	
G-BYYA	Grob G.115E Tutor T1	Babcock/Universities of Glasgow & Strathclyde AS, Glasgow, Scotland	
G-BYYB	Grob G.115E Tutor T1	Babcock/East of Scotland UAS, Leuchars, Scotland	
G-CGKD	Grob G.115E Tutor T1	Babcock/RN No 727 NAS, Yeovilton, Somerset	
G-CGKE	Grob G.115E Tutor T1	Babcock/RN No 727 NAS, Yeovilton, Somerset	
G-CGKG	Grob G.115E Tutor T1	Babcock/Army Flying Grading, Middle Wallop, Hants	
G-CGKH	Grob G.115E Tutor T1	Babcock/Army Flying Grading, Middle Wallop, Hants	
G-CGKK	Grob G.115E Tutor T1EA	Babcock/Northern Ireland Universities AS, Aldergrove, NI	
G-CGKL	Grob G.115E Tutor T1EA	Babcock/RN No 727 NAS, Yeovilton, Somerset	

Notes	Serial	Type (code/other identity)	Owner/operator, location or fate
	G-CGKN	Grob G.115E Tutor T1EA	Babcock/RN No 727 NAS, Yeovilton, Somerset
	G-CGKP	Grob G.115E Tutor T1EA	Babcock/Northern Ireland Universities AS, Aldergrove, NI
	G-CGKR	Grob G.115E Tutor T1EA	Babcock/RN No 727 NAS, Yeovilton, Somerset
	G-CGKS	Grob G.115E Tutor T1EA	Babcock/Northern Ireland Universities AS, Aldergrove, NI
	G-CGKU	Grob G.115E Tutor T1EA	Babcock/Army Flying Grading, Middle Wallop, Hants
	G-CGKW	Grob G.115E Tutor T1EA	Babcock/Army Flying Grading, Middle Wallop, Hants
	G-DAYP	Hawker Beechcraft Super King Air 350C	MOD/Raytheon, Hawarden, Flintshire, Wales (for conversion to Shadow R2 ZZ505)
	G-DRAK	Canadair Challenger 604 (N420AJ)	Draken International, Bournemouth, Hants
	G-ETPA	Pilatus PC-21 (HB-HYX)	QinetiQ/ETPS, MOD Boscombe Down, Wilts
	G-ETPB	Pilatus PC-21 (HB-HYY)	QinetiQ/ETPS, MOD Boscombe Down, Wilts
	G-ETPC	Grob G.120TP-A (D-ETQI)	QinetiQ/ETPS, MOD Boscombe Down, Wilts
	G-ETPD	Grob G.120TP-A (D-ETIQ)	QinetiQ/ETPS, MOD Boscombe Down, Wilts
	G-ETPÉ	Airbus Helicopters H.125	QinetiQ/ETPS, MOD Boscombe Down, Wilts
	G-ETPF	Airbus Helicopters H.125	QinetiQ/ETPS, MOD Boscombe Down, Wilts
	G-ETPG	Airbus Helicopters H.125	QinetiQ/ETPS, MOD Boscombe Down, Wilts
	G-ETPH	Airbus Helicopters H.125	QinetiQ/ETPS, MOD Boscombe Down, Wilts
	G-ETPI	Agusta A109E Power Elite (G-CFVB/QQ100)	QinetiQ/ETPS, MOD Boscombe Down, Wilts
	G-ETPJ	Agusta A109E Power Elite (G-ESLH/ZE416)	QinetiQ/ETPS, MOD Boscombe Down, Wilts
	G-ETPK	BAe RJ.70ER (G-BVRJ/QQ102)	QinetiQ/ETPS, MOD Boscombe Down, Wilts
	G-ETPL	BAe RJ.100 (G-BZAY/QQ101)	QinetiQ/ETPS, MOD Boscombe Down, Wilts
	G-ETPM	Diamond DA.42M-NG Twin Star (G-LTPA/QQ103)	QinetiQ/ETPS, MOD Boscombe Down, Wilts
	G-ETPN	Agusta A109S Grand (N519CG)	QinetiQ/ETPS, MOD Boscombe Down, Wilts
	G-ETPO	Agusta A109S Grand (XA-ANU)	QinetiQ/ETPS, MOD Boscombe Down, Wilts
	G-ETPP	AgustaWestland AW139 (B-725D)	QinetiQ/ETPS, MOD Boscombe Down, Wilts
	G-ETPR	Hawker Beechcraft Super King Air 350i	QinetiQ/ETPS, MOD Boscombe Down, Wilts
	G-FFRA	Dassault Falcon 20DC (N902FR)	Draken International, Teesside International Airport
	G-FRAD	Dassault Falcon 20E (9M-BDK)	Draken International, Bournemouth, Hants
	G-FRAF	Dassault Falcon 20E (N911FR)	Draken International, Bournemouth, Hants
	G-FRAH	Dassault Falcon 20DC (N900FR)	Draken International, Bournemouth, Hants
	G-FRAI	Dassault Falcon 20E (N901FR)	Draken International, Bournemouth, Hants
	G-FRAJ	Dassault Falcon 20E (N903FR)	Draken International, Bournemouth, Hants
	G-FRAK	Dassault Falcon 20DC (N905FR)	Draken International, Teesside International Airport
	G-FRAL	Dassault Falcon 20DC (N904FR)	Draken International, Teesside International Airport
	G-FRAP	Dassault Falcon 20DC (N908FR)	Draken International, detached King Abdul Aziz AB, KSA
	G-FRAR	Dassault Falcon 20DC (N909FR)	Draken International, Bournemouth, Hants
	G-FRAS	Dassault Falcon 20C (117501)	Draken International, Bournemouth, Hants
	G-FRAT	Dassault Falcon 20C (117502)	Draken International, Teesside International Airport
	G-FRAU	Dassault Falcon 20C (117504)	Draken International, Teesside International Airport
	G-FRAW	Dassault Falcon 20ECM (117507)	Draken International, detached King Abdul Aziz AB, KSA
	G-FRSB	Dassault Falcon 20F (N459SB)	Draken International, Bournemouth, Hants
	G-GBNI	Airbus A.321-251NX (G-POWT)	Titan Airways/UK Government, Stansted, Essex
	G-RNGS	Airbus Helicopters H.145	QinetiQ/BUTEC, Kyle of Lochalsh, Scotland
	G-XATW	Airbus A.321-251NX	Titan Airways/UK Government, Stansted, Essex
	G-ZABH	Dassault Envoy IV CC.1 (Falcon 900LX) (F-WWVF)	MOD/Centreline, No 32(The Royal) Sqn, RAF Northolt
	G-ZAHS	Dassault Envoy IV CC.1 (Falcon 900LX) (F-WWVE)	MOD/Centreline, No 32(The Royal) Sqn, RAF Northolt

In recent years, a number of civilian companies have taken on former military aircraft to operate on private contracts for a number of air forces to provide "Red Air" aggressor training for current military pilots. Many air forces find this a more economical way of providing this kind of training without the large outlay of maintaining their own squadron(s) of aggressor aircraft. The following are likely to be noted in the UK and Western Europe fulfilling this role.

Serial	Type (code/other identity)	Owner/operator, location or fate	Notes
C-FGYL	Douglas A-4N Ayit (IDFAF 329)	Top Aces, Nordholz, Germany	
C-FGYS	Douglas A-4N Ayit (IDFAF 421)	Top Aces, Nordholz, Germany	
C-FGWT	Douglas TA-4J Skyhawk (IDFAF 747) [499]	Top Aces, Nordholz, Germany	
C-FGZD	Douglas A-4N Skyhawk [367]	Top Aces, Nordholz, Germany	
C-FGZE	Douglas A-4N Skyhawk [495]	Top Aces, Nordholz, Germany	
C-FGZH	Douglas A-4N Ayit [534]	Top Aces, Nordholz, Germany	
C-FGZI	Douglas A-4N Ayit (IDFAF 413) [531]	Top Aces, Nordholz, Germany	
C-FGZO	Douglas A-4N Ayit [532]	Top Aces, Nordholz, Germany	
C-FGZS	Douglas A-4N Skyhawk [337]	Top Aces, Nordholz, Germany	
C-FGZT	Douglas A-4N Ayit [542]	Top Aces, Nordholz, Germany	
C-FHTO	DB-D Alpha Jet (41+04) [104]	Top Aces, Nordholz, Germany	
C-GFTO	DB-D Alpha Jet (40+38) [038]	Top Aces, Nordholz, Germany	
C-GITA	DB-D Alpha Jet (40+40) [040]	Top Aces, Nordholz, Germany	
C-GJTA	DB-D Alpha Jet (40+57) [057]	Top Aces, Nordholz, Germany	
C-GLTO	DB-D Alpha Jet (40+69) [069]	Top Aces, Nordholz, Germany	
C-GVTA	DB-D Alpha Jet (40+09) [009]	Top Aces, Nordholz, Germany	
C-GZTO	DB-D Alpha Jet (40+16) [016]	Top Aces, Nordholz, Germany	
G-DKNA	Aero L-159E ALCA (6034/N159EM)	Draken International, Teesside International Airport	
G-DKNB	Aero L-159E ALCA (6019/N264EM)	Draken International, Teesside International Airport	
G-DKNC	Aero L-159E ALCA (6020/N265EM)	Draken International, Teesside International Airport	
G-DKND	Aero L-159E ALCA (6039/N267EM)	Draken International, Teesside International Airport	
G-DKNE	Aero L-159E ALCA (6029/N269EM)	Draken International, Teesside International Airport	
G-DKNF	Aero L-159E ALCA (6030/N259EM)	Draken International, Teesside International Airport	
G-DKNG	Aero L-159E ALCA (6036/N256EM)	Draken International, Teesside International Airport	
G-DKNH	Aero L-159E ALCA (6013/N277EM)	Draken International, Teesside International Airport	
G-DKNI	Aero L-159E ALCA (6040/N262EM)	Draken International, stored Bournemouth, Hants	
G-DKNJ	Aero L-159E ALCA (6007/N257EM)	Draken International, stored Bournemouth, Hants	
G-DKNK	Aero L-159E ALCA (6009/N270EM)	Draken International, Teesside International Airport	
G-DKNL	Aero L-159E ALCA (6024/N274EM)	Draken International, Teesside International Airport	
G-DKNM	Aero L-159E ALCA (6026/N275EM)	Draken International, Teesside International Airport	

NOTE: The Top Aces aircraft frequently detach to RAF Lakenheath, Suffolk.

Draken International (formerly FR Aviation) operates a number of Falcon 20s on military contracts, including G-FRAD, seen here at RIAT 2024 at RAF Fairford. *HJC*

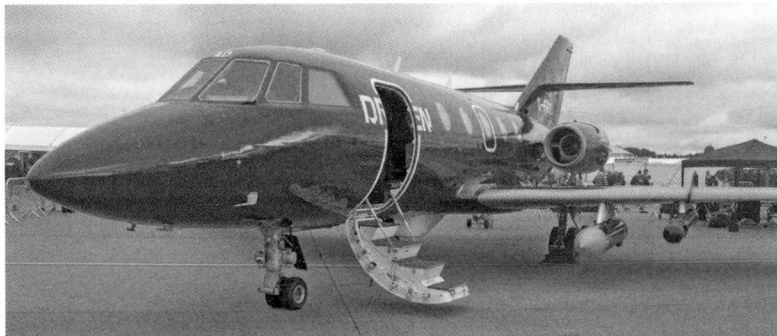

This table gives brief details of the markings worn by aircraft of RAF squadrons. While this may help to identify the operator of a particular machine, it may not always give the true picture. For example, from time to time aircraft are loaned to other units while others wear squadron marks but are actually operated on a pool basis. Squadron badges are usually located on the front fuselage.

Squadron	Type(s) operated	Base(s)	Distinguishing marks & other comments
No 1(F) Sqn	Typhoon FGR4	RAF Lossiemouth	Badge (on tail): A red 1 with yellow wings on a white background, flanked in red. Roundel is flanked by two white chevrons, edged in red.
No 2(AC) Sqn/ II(AC) Sqn	Typhoon FGR4	RAF Lossiemouth	Badge: A wake knot on a white circular background flanked on either side by black and white triangles. Tail fin has a black stripe with white triangles and the badge repeated on it.
No 3(F) Sqn	Typhoon FGR4	RAF Coningsby	Badge: A blue cockatrice on a white circular background flanked by two green bars edged with yellow. Tail fin as a green stripe edged with yellow.
No 4 Sqn/ IV Sqn	Hawk T2	RAF Valley	Badge (on nose): A yellow lightning flash on a red background with IV superimposed. Aircraft carry a yellow lightning flash on a red and black background on the tail and this is repeated in bars either side of the roundel on the fuselage. Part of No 4 FTS.
No 6 Sqn	Typhoon FGR4	RAF Lossiemouth	Badge (on tail): A red, winged can opener on a blue shield, edged in red. The roundel is flanked by a red zigzag on a blue background.
No 7 Sqn	Chinook HC6/HC6A	RAF Odiham	Badge (on tail): A blue badge containing the seven stars of Ursa Major ('The Plough') in yellow.
No 8 Sqn	Wedgetail AEW1	RAF Lossiemouth	Badge (on tail): A grey, sheathed, Arabian dagger. (on order)
No 9 Sqn/ IX Sqn	Typhoon FGR4	RAF Lossiemouth	Badge: A green bat on a black circular background, flanked by yellow and green horizontal stripes. The green bat also appears on the tail, edged in yellow.
No 10 Sqn	Voyager KC2/KC3	RAF Brize Norton	No markings worn.
No 11 Sqn	Typhoon FGR4	RAF Coningsby	Badge (on tail): Two eagles in flight on a white shield. The roundel is flanked by yellow and black triangles.
No 12 Sqn	Typhoon T3/FGR4	RAF Coningsby	Badge (on tail): A fox's head over a Union Flag and Qatari flag. Either side of the roundel are stripes of black, white and green.
No 13 Sqn	Reaper/Protector RG1 (from 2023)	RAF Waddington	No markings worn.
No 14 Sqn	Shadow R1/R1+/R2	RAF Waddington	No markings worn.
No 16 Sqn	Tutor T1	RAF Cranwell	No markings carried. Part of No 1 EFTS.
No 17 Test & Evaluation Sqn	Lightning II	Edwards AFB, USA	No markings worn
No 18(B) Sqn	Chinook HC4/ HC5/HC6/HC6A	RAF Odiham	Badge (on tail): A red winged horse on a black circle. Aircraft pooled with No 27 Sqn.

Squadron	Type(s) operated	Base(s)	Distinguishing marks & other comments
No 22 Sqn	All helicopter types	RAF Benson	No markings worn (aircraft borrowed from other units as needed)
No 24 Sqn/ XXIV Sqn	Atlas C1	RAF Brize Norton	No squadron markings carried. Aircraft pooled with No 30 Sqn, No 47 Sqn and No 70 Sqn.
No 25 Sqn/ XXV Sqn	Hawk T2	RAF Valley	Badge (on tail): A hawk on a gauntlet. Aircraft have XXV on the tail and silver and grey bars either side of the roundel on the fuselage. Part of No 4 FTS. Aircraft are coded F*.
No 27 Sqn	Chinook HC4/ HC5/HC6	RAF Odiham	Badge (on tail): A dark green elephant on a green circle, flanked by green and dark green stripes. Aircraft pooled with No 18 Sqn.
No 28 Sqn	Chinook HC4/ Puma HC2	RAF Benson	Badge: A winged horse above two white crosses on a red shield.
No 29 Sqn	Typhoon T3/FGR4	RAF Coningsby	Badge (on tail): An eagle in flight, preying on a buzzard, with three red Xs across the top. The roundel is flanked by two white bars outlined by a red line, each containing three red Xs.
No 30 Sqn	Atlas C1	RAF Brize Norton	No squadron markings carried. Aircraft pooled with No 24 Sqn and No 47 Sqn.
No 32(The Royal) Sqn	Envoy CC1	RAF Northolt	No squadron markings carried but aircraft carry a distinctive livery with a red stripe, edged in blue along the middle of the fuselage and a red tail.
No 33 Sqn	Puma HC2	RAF Benson	Badge: A stag's head.
No 39 Sqn	Predator/ Reaper	Nellis AFB/ Creech AFB	No markings worn.
No 41 Test & Evaluation Sqn [FJWOEU]	Typhoon T3/FGR4	RAF Coningsby	Badge: A red, double armed cross on the tail with a gold crown above. White and red horizontal bars flanking the roundel on the fuselage.
No 45 Sqn	Phenom T1	RAF Cranwell	The Phenoms carry a black stripe on the tail superimposed with red diamonds. Part of No 3 FTS.
No 51 Sqn	RC-135W	RAF Waddington	Badge (on tail): A red goose in flight.
No 54 Sqn [ISTAR OCU]	Poseidon MRA1/ Shadow R1	RAF Waddington	Based aircraft as required.
No 56 Sqn [ISTAR Test & Evaluation Sqn]	Shadow R1	RAF Waddington	Based aircraft as required.
No 57 Sqn	Prefect T1	RAF Barkston Heath/ RAF Cranwell	No markings carried. Part of No 1 EFTS.
No 70 Sqn Fixed Wing Air Mobility OCU/LXX Sqn	Atlas C1	RAF Brize Norton	No squadron markings usually carried. Aircraft pooled with No 24 Sqn.

Squadron	Type(s) operated	Base(s)	Distinguishing marks & other comments
No 72 Sqn	Texan T1	RAF Valley	Badge: A black swift in flight on a red disk, flanked with blue bars edged with red. Part of No 4 FTS.
No 84 Sqn	Puma HC2	RAF Akrotiri	Badge : A scorpion on a playing card symbol (diamonds, clubs etc).
No 99 Sqn	Globemaster III	RAF Brize Norton	Badge (on tail): A black puma leaping.
No 101 Sqn	Voyager KC2/KC3	RAF Brize Norton	No markings worn.
No 115 Sqn	Tutor T1	Wittering	No markings carried. Part of the CFS.
No 120 Sqn	Poseidon MRA1	Lossiemouth	No markings worn.
No 201 Sqn	Poseidon MRA1	Lossiemouth	No markings worn.
No 202 Sqn	Jupiter HT1	RAF Valley	Badge: A mallard alighting on a white circle.
No 207 Sqn	Lightning II	RAF Marham	No markings worn (some aircraft carry a lightning bolt on the fin, but this does not signify which squadron they belong to)
No 230 Sqn	Puma HC2	RAF Benson	Badge: A tiger in front of a palm tree on a black pentagon.
No 617 Sqn	Lightning II	RAF Marham	No markings worn (some aircraft carry a lightning bolt on the fin, but this does not signify which squadron they belong to)
No 1310 Flt	Chinook HC4	Mount Pleasant, FI	No markings worn
No 1312 Flt	Voyager KC2/KC3	Mount Pleasant, FI	No markings worn
No 1435 Flt	Typhoon FGR4	Mount Pleasant, FI	Badge (on tail): A red Maltese cross on a white circle, flanked by red and white horizontal bars.

ZK024, a 4 FTS Hawk T2, seen here on the runway at RAF Fairford during RIAT 2024. *HJC*

As from 7 September 2015 all UAS flights and AEFs are commanded and managed by No 6 FTS RAF. Some UAS aircraft carry squadron badges and markings, usually on the tail. Squadron crests all consist of a white circle surrounded by a blue circle, topped with a red crown and having a yellow scroll beneath. Each differs by the motto on the scroll, the UAS name running around the blue circle & by the contents at the centre which are described below.
* All AEFs come under the administration of local UASs and these are listed here.

UAS	Base	Marks
Bristol UAS/ No 3 AEF	Boscombe Down	A sailing ship on water.
Cambridge UAS/ No 5 AEF	Wittering	A heraldic lion in front of a red badge. Aircraft pooled with University of London AS.
East Midlands Universities AS/ No 7 AEF	Wittering	A yellow quiver, full of arrows.
East of Scotland UAS/ No 12 AEF	RAF Leuchars	An open book in front of a white diagonal cross edged in blue.
Liverpool UAS	RAF Woodvale	A bird atop an open book, holding a branch in its beak. Aircraft pooled with Manchester and Salford Universities AS
Manchester and Salford Universities AS/ No 10 AEF	RAF Woodvale	A bird of prey with a green snake in its beak. Aircraft pooled with Liverpool UAS
Northern Ireland Universities AS/ No 14 AEF	JHC FS Aldergrove	(Currently not known)
Northumbrian Universities AS/ No 11 AEF	RAF Leeming	A white cross on a blue background.
Oxford UAS/ No 6 AEF	RAF Benson	An open book in front of crossed swords.
Southampton UAS/ No 2 AEF	Boscombe Down	A red stag in front of a stone pillar.
Universities of Glasgow and Strathclyde AS/ No 4 AEF	Glasgow	A bird of prey in flight, holding a branch in its beak, in front of an upright sword.
University of Birmingham AS/ No 8 AEF	DCAE Cosford	A blue griffon with two heads.
University of London AS	Wittering	A globe superimposed over an open book. Aircraft pooled with Cambridge UAS.
University of Wales AS/ No 1 AEF	MOD St Athan	A red Welsh dragon in front of an open book, clasping a sword. Some aircraft have the dragon in front of white and green squares.
Yorkshire Universities AS/ No 9 AEF	RAF Leeming	An open book in front of a Yorkshire rose with leaves.

This table gives brief details of the markings worn by aircraft of FAA squadrons. Squadron badges, when worn, are usually located on the front fuselage. All FAA squadron badges comprise a crown atop a circle edged in gold braid and so the badge details below list only what appears in the circular part.

Squadron	Type(s) operated	Base(s)	Distinguishing marks & other comments
No 700X NAS	RQ-12 Wasp/ RQ-20 Puma/Scan Eagle RM1	RNAS Culdrose	Badge: No markings carried.
No 727 NAS	Tutor T1	RNAS Yeovilton	Badge: The head of Britannia wearing a gold helmet on a background of blue and white waves.
No 744 NAS	Chinook HC6A/ Merlin (Crowsnest)	MOD Boscombe Down	Badge: No details
No 750 NAS	Avenger T1	RNAS Culdrose	Badge: A Greek runner bearing a torch & sword on a background of blue and white waves.
No 809 NAS	Lightning II	RAF Marham	Badge: A Phoenix rising against a light blue background.
No 814 NAS	Merlin HM2	RNAS Culdrose	Badge: A winged tiger mask on a background of dark blue and white waves.
No 815 NAS	Wildcat HMA2	RNAS Yeovilton	Badge: A winged, gold harpoon on a background of blue and white waves.
No 820 NAS	Merlin HM2	RNAS Culdrose	Badge: A flying fish on a background of blue and white waves.
No 824 NAS	Merlin HM2	RNAS Culdrose	Badge: A heron on a background of blue and white waves.
No 825 NAS	Wildcat HMA2	RNAS Yeovilton	Badge: An eagle over a Maltese cross.
No 845 NAS	Merlin HC4	RNAS Yeovilton	Badge: A dragonfly on a background of blue and white waves.
No 846 NAS	Merlin HC4/HC4A	RNAS Yeovilton	Badge: A swordsman riding a winged horse whilst attacking a serpent on a background of blue and white waves.
No 847 NAS	Wildcat AH1	RNAS Yeovilton	Badge (not currently worn): A gold sea lion on a blue background. Aircraft wear ARMY titles.

This new section is aimed at giving a quick reference to the units and types that operate from mainland UK military bases.

Joint Helicopter Command Flying Station (JHCFS) Aldergrove, County Antrim [13m W of Belfast]
Northern Ireland Universities AS/No 14 AEF RAF, operating the Tutor T1.

RAF Barkston Heath, Lincolnshire [5m NNE of Grantham]
No 57 Sqn RAF, operating the Prefect T1 (also at RAF Cranwell)

RAF Benson, Oxfordshire [1m NE of Wallingford]
No 28 Sqn RAF, operating the Chinook HC4 and Puma HC2.
No 33 Sqn RAF, operating the Puma HC2.
No 230 Sqn, operating the Puma HC2.
Oxford UAS/No 6 AEF RAF, operating the Tutor T1EA.

Boscombe Down, Wiltshire [6m N of Salisbury]
Bristol UAS/No 3 AEF RAF, operating the Tutor T1.
Southampton UAS/No 2 AEF RAF, operating the Tutor T1.

RAF Brize Norton, Oxfordshire [5m SW of Witney]
No 10 Sqn RAF, operating the Voyager KC2/KC3.
No 24 Sqn RAF, operating the the Atlas C1.
No 30 Sqn RAF, operating the Atlas C1.
No 70 Sqn RAF, operating the Atlas C1.
No 99 Sqn RAF, operating the Globemaster III.
No 101 Sqn RAF, operating the Voyager KC2/KC3.

RAF Coningsby, Lincolnshire [10m NW of Boston]
No 3(F) Sqn operating the Typhoon FGR4.
No 11 Sqn RAF, operating the Typhoon FGR4.
No 12 Sqn RAF/Qatar Emiri Air Force, operating the Typhoon T3 and FGR4.
No 29 Sqn RAF, operating the Typhoon T3 and FGR4.
No 41 (Test and Evaluation) Sqn RAF, operating the Typhoon T3 and FGR4.
The Battle of Britain Memorial Flight (BBMF) RAF, operating the Chipmunk, Dakota, Hurricane & Spitfire.

DCAE Cosford, Shropshire [9m WNW of Wolverhampton]
University of Birmingham AS/No 8 AEF RAF, operating the Tutor T1.

RAF Cranwell, Lincolnshire [5m WNW of Sleaford]
No 16 Sqn RAF, operating the Tutor T1.
No 45 Sqn RAF, operating the Phenom T1.
No 57 Sqn RAF, operating the Prefect T1 (also at RAF Barkston Heath).

RNAS Culdrose (HMS Seahawk), Cornwall [1m SE of Helston]
No 700X NAS RN, operating the RQ-12 Wasp, RQ-20 Puma and Scan Eagle RM1.
No 750 NAS RN, operating the Avenger T1.
No 814 NAS RN, operating the Merlin HM2.
No 820 NAS RN, operating the Merlin HM2.
No 824 NAS RN, operating the Merlin HM2.

RAF Kenley, Greater London [1m W of Warlingham]
No 615 VGS RAF, operating the Viking T1.

RAF Kirknewton, Lothian [8m SW of Edinburgh]
No 661 VGS RAF, operating the Viking T1.

RAF Leeming, North Yorkshire [5m SW of Northallerton]
Joint RAF/Qatar Emiri Air Force Hawk Training Sqn, operating the Hawk Mk.167.
Northumbrian Universities AS/No 11 AEF RAF, operating the Tutor T1.
Yorkshire Universities AS/No 9 AEF, RAF, flying the Tutor T1.

Leuchars Station, Fife [7m SE of Dundee]
East of Scotland UAS/No 12 AEF RAF, flying the Tutor T1.

RAF Lakenheath, Suffolk [8m W of Thetford]
492nd Fighter Sqn USAF, operating the F-15E Strike Eagle.
493rd Fighter Sqn USAF, operating the F-35A Lightning II.
494th Fighter Sqn USAF, operating the F-15E Strike Eagle.
495th Fighter Sqn USAF, operating the F-35A Lightning II.

RAF Little Rissington, Gloucestershire [5 miles S of Stow-on-the-Wold]
No 621 VGS RAF, operating the Viking T1.
No 637 VGS RAF, operating the Viking T1.

RAF Lossiemouth, Moray [4m N of Elgin]
No 1(F) Sqn RAF, operating the Typhoon FGR4.
No 2(AC) Sqn RAF, operating the Typhoon FGR4.
No 6 Sqn RAF, operating the Typhoon FGR4.
No 9 Sqn RAF, operating the Typhoon FGR4.
No 120 Sqn RAF, operating the Poseidon MRA1.
No 201 Sqn RAF, operating the Poseidon MRA1.

RAF Marham, Norfolk [6m W of Swaffham]
No 207 Sqn RAF/RN, operating the Lightning II.
No 617 Sqn RAF, operating the Lightning II.

AAC Middle Wallop, Hampshire [6m SW of Andover]
AAC No 673 Sqn/No 7 Regiment, operating the AH-64E
Army Flying Grading (AFG) AAC, operating the Tutor T1.

RAF Mildenhall, Suffolk [9m NNE of Newmarket]
7th Special Operations Sqn, operating the CV-22B Osprey.
67th Special Operations Sqn, operating the MC-130J Commando II.
351st Air Refuelling Sqn, operating the KC-135R and KC-135T Stratotanker.

RAF Northolt, Greater London [3m E of M40 junction 1]
No 32 (The Royal) Sqn RAF, operating the Agusta 109SP.

RAF Odiham, Hampshire [2m S of junction 5 of the M3]
No 7 Sqn RAF, operating the Chinook HC6 and HC6A.
No 18(B) Sqn RAF, operating the Chinook HC4, HC5, HC6 and HC6A.
No 27 Sqn RAF, operating the Chinook HC4, HC5 and HC6.

RN Predannack, Cornwall [7m S of Helston]
No 626 VGS RAF, operating the Viking T1.

RAF Shawbury, Shropshire [7m NNE of Shrewsbury]
No 1 FTS RAF, operating the Juno HT1 and Jupiter HT1.

RAF Syerston, Nottinghamshire [5m SW of Newark]
ACCGS/No 644 VGS RAF, operating the Viking T1.

RAF Topcliffe (Alanbrooke Barracks), North Yorkshire [3m SW of Thirsk]
No 645 VGS RAF, operating the Viking T1.

RAF Upavon, Wiltshire [13m N of Salisbury]
No 622 VGS RAF, operating the Viking T1.

RAF Valley, Gwynedd [5m SE of Holyhead]
No 4 Sqn RAF, operating the Hawk T2.
No 25 Sqn RAF, operating the Hawk T2.
No 72 Sqn RAF, operating the Texan T1.
No 202 Sqn RAF, operating the Jupiter HT1.

RAF Waddington, Lincolnshire [5m S of Lincoln]
No 13 Sqn RAF, operating the Reaper.
No 14 Sqn RAF, operating the Shadow.
No 51 Sqn RAF, operating the RC-135W.
No 54 Sqn RAF, operating the Shadow.
No 56 Sqn RAF, operating the Shadow.
The Red Arrows, operating the Hawk T1 and T1A.

Wattisham Airfield, Suffolk [5m SSW of Stowmarket]
653 Sqn/3 Regiment AAC, operating the Apache.
656 Sqn/4 Regiment AAC, operating the Apache.
662 Sqn/3 Regiment AAC, operating the Apache.
663 Sqn/3 Regiment AAC, operating the Apache.
664 Sqn/4 Regiment AAC, operating the Apache.

RAF Wittering, Cambridgeshire [3m S of Stamford]
No 115 Sqn RAF, operating the Tutor T1.
Cambridge UAS/No 5 AEF RAF, operating the Tutor T1.
East Midlands Universities AS/No 7 AEF RAF, operating the Tutor T1.
University of London AS RAF, operating the Tutor T1.

RAF Woodvale, Merseyside [5m SSW of Southport]
Liverpool UAS RAF, operating the Tutor T1.
Manchester & Salford Universities AS/No 10 AEF RAF, operating the Tutor T1.

RNAS Yeovilton (HMS Heron), Somerset [5m N of Yeovil]
652 Sqn AAC/WCM, operating the Wildcat AH1.
659 Sqn/1 Regiment AAC, operating the Wildcat AH1.
661 Sqn/1 Regiment AAC, operating the Wildcat AH1.
No 727 NAS RN, operating the Tutor T1.
No 815 NAS RN, operating the Wildcat HMA2.
No 825 NAS RN, operating the Wildcat HMA2.
No 845 NAS RN, operating the Merlin HC4.
No 846 NAS RN, operating the Merlin HC4 and HC4A.
No 847 NAS RN, operating the Wildcat AH1 for the Royal Marines.

Additionally, although not strictly military bases, the following are listed, for completion:
Glasgow Airport, Renfrewshire [10m W of Glasgow]
Universities of Glasgow & Strathclyde AS/No 4 AEF RAF, operating the Tutor T1EA.

MOD St. Athan, Vale of Glamorgan [8m W of Barry]
University of Wales AS/No 1 AEF RAF, operating the Tutor T1.

This section lists the codes worn by some UK military aircraft and, alongside, the serial of the aircraft currently wearing this code. It should be pointed out that in some cases more than one aircraft wears the same code but the aircraft listed is the one believed to be in service with the unit concerned at the time of going to press. This list will be updated regularly.

Code	Serial	Code	Serial	Code	Serial	Code	Serial
ROYAL AIR FORCE		**Lockheed Martin F-35B**		**WS Puma HC2**		**ROYAL NAVY**	
BAE Hawk T2		**Lightning II**		A	XW199	**EHI-101 Merlin**	
B	ZK011	001	ZM135	B	XW204	A	ZJ117
C	ZK012	002	ZM136	D	XW212	B	ZJ118
D	ZK013	003	ZM137	E	XW213	C	ZJ119
E	ZK014	004	ZM138	F	XW214	D	ZJ120
F	ZK015	005	ZM139	G	XW216	E	ZJ121
G	ZK016	006	ZM140	K	XW220	F	ZJ122
H	ZK017	007	ZM141	N	XW231	G	ZJ123
I	ZK018	008	ZM142	P	XW232	H	ZJ124
J	ZK019	009	ZM143	Q	XW235	J	ZJ125
K	ZK020	010	ZM144	R	XW237	K	ZJ126
L	ZK021	011	ZM145	S	ZA935	L	ZJ127
M	ZK022	012	ZM146	U	ZA939	M	ZJ128
N	ZK023	013	ZM147	V	ZA940	N	ZJ129
O	ZK024	014	ZM148	W	ZJ954	O	ZJ130
FA	ZK025	015	ZM149	X	ZJ955	P	ZJ131
FB	ZK026	016	ZM150	Y	ZJ956	Q	ZJ132
FC	ZK027	017	ZM151	Z	ZJ957	R	ZJ133
FD	ZK028	019	ZM153			S	ZJ134
FE	ZK029	020	ZM154			T	ZJ135
FF	ZK030	021	ZM155			U	ZJ136
FG	ZK031	022	ZM156			W	ZJ137
FH	ZK032	023	ZM157			AA	ZJ990
FI	ZK033	024	ZM158			AB	ZJ992
FJ	ZK034	025	ZM159			AC	ZJ994
FK	ZK035	026	ZM160			AD	ZJ995
FL	ZK036	027	ZM161			AE	ZJ998
FM	ZK037	028	ZM162			AF	ZK001
FN	ZK010	029	ZM163				
		030	ZM164				
		031	ZM165				
Eurofighter Typhoon		032	ZM166				
C	ZJ928	033	ZM167				
D	ZJ942	034	ZM168				
F	ZJ915	035	ZM169				
H	ZJ920	036	ZM170				
AX	ZK303	037	ZM171				
WS-J	ZK332						
WS-S	ZK357						
WS-T	ZK377						

Some *historic, classic and warbird* aircraft carry the markings of overseas air arms and can be seen in the UK, mainly preserved in museums and collections or taking part in air shows.

Serial	Type (code/other identity)	Owner/operator, location or fate	Notes
AFGHANISTAN			
-	Hawker Afghan Hind (K4672/BAPC.82)	RAF Museum, Cosford, Shropshire	
ARGENTINA			
0729	Beech T-34C Turbo Mentor	FAA Museum, stored Cobham Hall, RNAS Yeovilton, Somerset	
0767	Aermacchi MB339A	South Yorkshire Aircraft Museum, Doncaster, S. Yorks	
A-515	FMA IA58 Pucará (ZD485)	RAF Museum, stored Cosford, Shropshire	
A-522	FMA IA58 Pucará (8768M)	FAA Museum, at North-East Land, Sea & Air Museums, Usworth, T&W	
A-528	FMA IA58 Pucará (8769M)	Norfolk & Suffolk Avn Museum, Flixton, Suffolk	
A-533	FMA IA58 Pucará (ZD486) <ff>	South Yorkshire Aircraft Museum, Doncaster, S. Yorks	
A-549	FMA IA58 Pucará (ZD487)	IWM Duxford, Cambs	
AE-331	Agusta A109A (ZE411)	FAA Museum, stored Cobham Hall, RNAS Yeovilton, Somerset	
AE-406	Bell UH-1H Iroquois	South Yorkshire Aircraft Museum, stored Doncaster, S. Yorks	
AE-409	Bell UH-1H Iroquois [656]	Army Flying Museum, Middle Wallop, Hants	
AE-422	Bell UH-1H Iroquois	FAA Museum, stored Cobham Hall, RNAS Yeovilton, Somerset	
AUSTRALIA			
308/K	Hawker Fury ISS (F-AYSF)	Privately owned, la Ferté-Alais, France	
369	Hawker Fury ISS (F-AZXL) [SD]	Privately owned, Avignon-Caumont, France	
A2-4	Supermarine Seagull V (VH-ALB)	RAF Museum Reserve Collection, Stafford, Staffs	
A11-301	Auster J/5G (G-ARKG) [931-NW]	Privately owned, Langham, Rutland	
A16-199	Lockheed Hudson IIIA (G-BEOX) [SF-R]	RAF Museum, Hendon, Gtr London	
A17-48	DH82A Tiger Moth (G-BPHR)	Privately owned, Wanborough, Wilts	
A19-144	Bristol 156 Beaufighter XIc (JM135/A8-324)	The Fighter Collection, Duxford, Cambs	
A23-005	Pilatus PC-9A	Privately owned, St Athan, Wales	
A23-013	Pilatus PC-9A (G-SBST)	Privately owned, St Athan, Wales	
A23-033	Pilatus PC-9A (G-CMJO)	Privately owned, St Athan, Wales	
A23-051	Pilatus PC-9A	Privately owned, St Athan, Wales	
A58-81	VS349 Spitfire LF Vc <R> (G-MKVT)	Privately owned, location unknown	
A58-606	VS509 Spitfire T9 (TE308/G-AWGB) [ZP-W]	Privately owned, Biggin Hill, Kent	
A92-255	GAF Jindivik 102	Privately owned, Thorpe Wood, N Yorks	
A92-466	GAF Jindivik 103A (BAPC.485)	Boscombe Down Aviation Collection, Old Sarum, Wilts	
A92-708	GAF Jindivik 103BL	Newark Air Museum, Winthorpe, Notts	
A92-908	GAF Jindivik 104AL (ZJ503)	Privately owned, Llanbedr, Wales	
N16-114	WS61 Sea King Mk.50A [05]	Privately owned, Horsham, W. Sussex	
N16-125	WS61 Sea King Mk.50A [10]	Privately owned, Horsham, W. Sussex	
N16-238	WS61 Sea King Mk.50A [20]	Privately owned, Horsham, W. Sussex	
N16-239	WS61 Sea King Mk.50A [21]	Privately owned, Horsham, W. Sussex	
N16-918	WS61 Sea King Mk.50B (XZ918) [22]	Privately owned, Horsham, W. Sussex	
WH589	Hawker Fury ISS (F-AZXJ) [115-NW]	*Stored Orlando, FL (dismantled)*	
AUSTRIA			
3F-SX	SAAB S91D Safir (G-EKTP) [04]	Privately owned, Breighton, E. Yorks	
BELGIUM			
A-41	SA318C Alouette II	The Helicopter Museum, Weston-super-Mare	
A-79	SA318C Alouette II (2-LOUD)	Privately owned, Thelwall, Cheshire	
FT-36	Lockheed T-33A Shooting Star	Dumfries & Galloway Avn Mus, Dumfries, Scotland	
H-02	Agusta A109HO (N504TS)	Privately owned, Cotswold Airport, Glos	
H-50	Noorduyn AT-16 Harvard IIb (OO-DAF)	Privately owned, Brasschaat, Belgium	
IF-68	Hawker Hunter F6 <ff>	Privately owned, Boughton South, Norfolk	

Notes	Serial	Type (code/other identity)	Owner/operator, location or fate
	L-44	Piper L-18C Super Cub (OO-SPQ)	Royal Aéro Para Club de Spa, Belgium
	L-47	Piper L-18C Super Cub (OO-SPG)	Aeroclub Brasschaat VZW, Brasschaat, Belgium
	OL-L49	Piper L-18C Super Cub (L-156/OO-LGB)	Aeroclub Brasschaat VZW, Brasschaat, Belgium
	RS-02	Westland Sea King Mk.48 (OO-SEE/G-BDNI)	Privately owned, Chard, Somerset
	RS-04	Westland Sea King Mk.48 (OO-KNG/G-BDNK)	Privately owned, Chard, Somerset
	BOLIVIA		
	FAB-108	BAe RJ.70	Privately owned, stored Southend, Essex
	BRAZIL		
	0931	Cessna T-37C (N3127M)	Wastelands Salvage, Tuamgraney, Eire
	BURKINA FASO		
	BF8431	SIAI-Marchetti SF.260 (G-NRRA) [31]	Privately owned, Lydd, Kent
	CANADA		
	622	Piasecki HUP-3 Retriever (51-16622/N6699D)	The Helicopter Museum, Weston-super-Mare
	920	VS Stranraer (CF-BXO) [Q-N]	RAF Museum, Hendon, Gtr London
	983	NA T-6G Texan (49-2983/F-AZVN) [KF-983]	Privately owned, Beaune-Challenges, France
	3091	NA81 Harvard II (3019/G-CPPM) (fuselage)	Privately owned, stored Enstone, Oxon
	3349	NA64 Yale (G-BYNF)	Privately owned, Old Buckenham, Norfolk
	5084	DH82C Tiger Moth (G-FCTK)	Privately owned, Hailsham, E. Sussex
	7349	Avro Anson II (fuselage)	Privately owned, Hooton Park, Cheshire
	9041	Bristol 149 Bolingbroke IV <ff>	Manx Aviation Museum, Ronaldsway, IOM
	9048	Bristol 149 Bolingbroke IV	Aerospace Bristol, Filton, Glos (rebuild)
	9893	Bristol 149 Bolingbroke IVT <ff> (BAPC.603)	Kent Battle of Britain Museum, Hawkinge, Kent
	9893	Bristol 149 Bolingbroke IVT <rf>	IWM, stored Duxford, Cambs
	9940	Bristol 14g-9 Bolingbroke IVT	National Museum of Flight, E. Fortune, Scotland
	9980	Bristol 149 Bolingbroke IVT (fuselage)	Lincolnshire Avn Heritage Centre, E Kirkby, Lincs (restoration)
	15252	Fairchild PT-19A Cornell (comp 15195)	RAF Museum Reserve Collection, Stafford, Staffs
	16693	Auster J/1N Alpha (PH-CAF/G-BLPG) [693]	Privately owned, Hoogeveen, Netherlands
	17447	McD F-101F Voodoo (56-0312)	Midland Air Museum, Coventry, Warks
	18072	DHC1B-2-S5 Chipmunk (G-FCTY)	Privately owned, Audley End, Essex
	18393	Avro Canada CF-100 Canuck 4B (G-BCYK)	IWM Duxford, Cambs
	18671	DHC1 Chipmunk 22 (WP905/7438M/G-BNZC) [671]	The Shuttleworth Collection, Old Warden, Beds
	20249	Noorduyn AT-16 Harvard IIb (PH-KLU) [XS-249]	Privately owned, Texel, The Netherlands
	21417	Canadair CT-133 Silver Star	Yorkshire Air Museum, Elvington, N. Yorks
	23140	Canadair CL-13A Sabre 5 [AX] <rf>	Midland Air Museum, Coventry, Warks
	23380	Canadair CL-13B Sabre 6 <rf>	Privately owned, Haverigg, Cumbria
	FE992	Noorduyn AT-16 Harvard IIb (G-BDAM) [ER-992]	Privately owned, Duxford, Cambs
	FJ662	Fairchild PT-26 Cornell (G-CRNL) [662]	Privately owned, Wickenby, Lincs
	KN448	Douglas Dakota IV <ff>	Science Museum, South Kensington, London
	CHILE		
	H-255	Aérospatiale SA330H Puma	Ultimate Activity, Faygate, W. Sussex
	CHINA		
	68 r	Nanchang CJ-6A Chujiao (2751219/G-BVVG)	Privately owned, stored Strubby, Lincs
	61367	Nanchang CJ-6A Chujiao (4532009/G-CGHB) [37]	Privately owned, Redhill, Surrey
	CZECH REPUBLIC		
	3677	Letov S-103 (MiG-15bisSB) (613677)	National Museum of Flight, E. Fortune, Scotland
	3794	Letov S-102 (MiG-15) (623794)	Norfolk & Suffolk Avn Museum, Flixton, Suffolk
		(starboard side only, painted in Polish marks as 1972 on port side)	
	9147	Mil Mi-4	The Helicopter Museum, Weston-super-Mare, Somerset
	DENMARK		
	A-011	SAAB A-35XD Draken	Privately owned, Hindley Green, Gtr Manchester
	AR-107	SAAB S-35XD Draken	Newark Air Museum, Winthorpe, Notts
	E-196	SABCA (GD) F-16A MLU Fighting Falcon <ff>	Martin-Baker, Chalgrove, Oxon

Serial	Type (code/other identity)	Owner/operator, location or fate	Notes
E-402	Hawker Hunter F51 (G-9-433)	Paintball Centre, Moorepark, Co. Meath, Eire	
E-419	Hawker Hunter F51 (G-9-441)	North-East Land, Sea & Air Museums, Usworth, T&W	
E-420	Hawker Hunter F51 (G-9-442) <ff>	Privately owned, Walton-on-Thames, Surrey	
E-421	Hawker Hunter F51 (G-9-443)	Brooklands Museum, Weybridge, Surrey	
E-425	Hawker Hunter F51 (XG190/G-9-446)	Solway Aviation Society, Carlisle, Cumbria	
ET-272	Hawker Hunter T53 <ff>	Norfolk & Suffolk Avn Museum, Flixton, Suffolk	
ET-626	SABCA (GD) F-16B MLU Fighting Falcon <ff>	Martin-Baker, Chalgrove, Oxon	
L-866	Consolidated PBY-6A Catalina (8466M)	RAF Museum, Cosford, Shropshire	
P-129	DHC-1 Chipmunk 22 (OY-ATO)	Privately owned, Tonder, Denmark	
P-139	DHC-1 Chipmunk 22 (OY-AVF)	Privately owned, Ringsted, Denmark	
R-756	Lockheed F-104G Starfighter	Midland Air Museum, Coventry, Warks	
S-881	Sikorsky S-55C	The Helicopter Museum, stored Weston-super-Mare, Somerset	
S-882	Sikorsky S-55C	Bristol Activity Centre, Bristol, Glos	
S-886	Sikorsky S-55C	Hamburger Hill Paintball, Marksbury, Somerset	
S-887	Sikorsky S-55C	The Helicopter Museum, stored Weston-super-Mare, Somerset	

EGYPT

Serial	Type (code/other identity)	Owner/operator, location or fate	Notes
771	WS61 Sea King Mk.47 (WA.826)	DSTO Shoeburyness, Essex, GI use	
773	WS61 Sea King Mk.47 (WA.823)	RNAS Yeovilton Fire Section, Somerset	
776	WS61 Sea King Mk.47 (WA.825) <ff> (comp ZA136)	Mayhem Paintball, Aybridge, Essex	
5634	Mikoyan MiG-21UM (0446) <ff>	Lakes Lightnings, Spark Bridge, Cumbria	
7735	Sukhoi Su-7 <ff>	Lakes Lightnings, Spark Bridge, Cumbria	

EIRE and NORTHERN IRELAND

Serial	Type (code/other identity)	Owner/operator, location or fate	Notes
C7	Avro 631 Cadet (EI-AGO)	IAC Museum, Baldonnel	
34	Miles M14A Magister I (N5392)	National Museum of Ireland, Dublin	
141	Avro 652A Anson C19	IAC Museum, Baldonnel	
164	DHC1 Chipmunk T20	Shannon Aviation Museum	
168	DHC1 Chipmunk T20 (EI-HFA)	Irish Historic Flight, Ballyboy	
169	DHC1 Chipmunk 22 (WD305/EI-HFB)	Irish Historic Flight, Ballyboy	
170	DHC1 Chipmunk 22 (WP857/EI-HFC)	Irish Historic Flight, Ballyboy	
172	DHC1 Chipmunk T20	IAC Museum, Baldonnel	
173	DHC1 Chipmunk T20	South-East Aviation Enthusiasts, Dromod	
176	DH104 Dove 4 (VP-YKF)	South-East Aviation Enthusiasts, Waterford	
183	Percival P56 Provost T51	IAC Museum, Baldonnel	
184	Percival P56 Provost T51	South-East Aviation Enthusiasts, Dromod	
187	DH115 Vampire T55	South-East Aviation Enthusiasts, Dromod	
191	DH115 Vampire T55	IAC Museum, Baldonnel	
192	DH115 Vampire T55 <ff>	South-East Aviation Enthusiasts, Dromod	
195	Sud SA316 Alouette III (F-WJDH)	IAC Museum, stored Baldonnel	
198	DH115 Vampire T11 (XE977)	National Museum of Ireland, Dublin	
199	DHC1 Chipmunk T20	IAC Museum, Baldonnel	
202	Sud SA316 Alouette III	Ulster Aviation Society, Long Kesh, NI	
203	Reims-Cessna FR172H	Ulster Aviation Society, Long Kesh, NI	
206	Reims-Cessna FR172H	IAC Museum, Baldonnel	
208	Reims-Cessna FR172H (EI-HFE)	Irish Historic Flight, Ballyboy	
210	Reims-Cessna FR172H	Shannon Aviation Museum	
215	Fouga CM170R Super Magister	IAC Museum, stored Baldonnel	
216	Fouga CM170R Super Magister	Shannon Aviation Museum	
218	Fouga CM170R Super Magister	Ulster Aviation Society, Long Kesh, NI	
219	Fouga CM170R Super Magister	Shannon Aviation Museum	
220	Fouga CM170R Super Magister	Cork University, instructional use	
221	Fouga CM170R Super Magister [79/3-KE]	IAC Museum, stored Baldonnel	
231	SIAI SF-260WE Warrior	Shannon Aviation Museum	
254	PBN-2T Defender 4000 (G-BWPN)	*Stored Solent Airport, Hampshire*	

FINLAND

Serial	Type (code/other identity)	Owner/operator, location or fate	Notes
GA-43	Gloster Gamecock II (G-CGYF)	Privately owned, Dursley, Glos	
GN-101	Folland Gnat F1 (XK741)	Midland Air Museum, Coventry, Warks	
SZ-12	Focke-Wulf Fw44J Stieglitz (D-EXWO/D-EUDT)	Privately owned, Bienenfarm, Germany	

Notes	Serial	Type (code/other identity)	Owner/operator, location or fate
	SZ-35	Focke-Wulf Fw44J Stieglitz (G-EJBB/BB+EJ)	The Shuttleworth Collection, Old Warden, Beds (restoration)
	FRANCE		
	1/4513	Spad XIII <R> (G-BFYO/*S3398*) [1]	American Air Museum, Duxford, Cambs
	02	Mudry CAP.20E (F-AZOE)	Privately owned, la Ferté-Alais, France
	5	MH1521C Broussard (C-GRBL/G-CLLK) [30-QA]	Privately owned, Oaksey Park, Glos
	7	Nord NC854 (G-NORD)	Privately owned, English Bicknor, Glos
	15	Nord 3202 (F-AZIY) [ZIY]	Privately owned, la Ferté-Alais, France
	28	Fouga CM175 Zéphyr [F-AZPF]	Association Zéphyr 28, Nîmes, France
	29	Aerospatiale TB.30 Epsilon (N837MT) (315-VB)	Privately owned, Rosenthal–Field Plössen, Germany
	32	Morane-Saulnier MS760 Paris (F-AZLT)	Armor Aéro Passion, Morlaix, France
	35QR-34	Canadair CT-133 Silver Star (21263/F-AYMD) [QR-34]	Privately owned, La Roche-sur-Yon, France
	37	Nord 3400 (G-ZARA) [MAB]	Privately owned, stored Swaffham, Norfolk
	45	Dassault Mirage IVP [BR]	Yorkshire Air Museum, Elvington, N. Yorks
	59	Breguet Br1050 Alizé (F-AZYI)	Alizé Marine, Nîmes/Garons, France
	63	Aerospatiale TB.30 Epsilon (N815N/F-AYKA) [8]	Privately owned, Elz, Germany
	67	Aerospatiale TB.30 Epsilon (F-AYFM) [315-WJ]	Privately owned, Beaune-Challenges, France
	67	SNCAN 1101 Noralpha (F-GMCY) [CY]	Privately owned, la Ferté-Alais, France
	68	Aerospatiale TB.30 Epsilon (F-AYAB) [315]	Privately owned, Melun-Villaroche, France
	69	Aerospatiale TB.30 Epsilon (F-AYLM) [315-WL]	Privately owned, Biscarosse-Parentis, France
	70	Dassault Mystère IVA [8-NV]	Midland Air Museum, Coventry, Warks
	76	Aerospatiale TB.30 Epsilon (F-AYCL) [315-WS]	Privately owned, Charleville-Mezieres, France
	77	Aerospatiale TB.30 Epsilon (F-AYJB) [315]	Privately owned, Nangis-Les-Loges, France
	78	Nord 3202B-1 (G-BIZK)	Privately owned, Swaffham, Norfolk
	79	Aerospatiale TB.30 Epsilon (F-AYOB)	Privately owned, Melun-Villaroche, France
	79	Dassault Mystère IVA [2-EG]	Norfolk & Suffolk Avn Museum, Flixton, Suffolk
	80	Aerospatiale TB.30 Epsilon (F-HEXA) [06]	Privately owned, Dijon-Longvic, France
	82	Aerospatiale TB.30 Epsilon (F-HBBT)	Privately owned, Pontoise, France
	82	Curtiss H75-C1 Hawk (G-CCVH) [X-881]	The Fighter Collection, Duxford, Cambs
	82	NA T-28D Fennec (F-AZKG)	Privately owned, Strasbourg, France
	83	Dassault Mystère IVA [8-MS]	Newark Air Museum, Winthorpe, Notts
	83	Morane-Saulnier MS733 Alcyon (F-AZKS)	Privately owned, Montlucon, France
	85	Dassault Mystère IVA [8-MV]	Preserved Bruntingthorpe, Leics
	90	Aerospatiale TB.30 Epsilon (F-AYXG) [315-XG]	Privately owned, Toussus-le-Noble, France
	96	Aerospatiale TB.30 Epsilon (F-HKYF) [315-XM]	Privately owned, La Roche-sur-Yon, France
	101	Aerospatiale TB.30 Epsilon (F-HKYH) [315-XR]	Privately owned, La Roche-sur-Yon, France
	104	MH1521M Broussard (F-GHFG) [307-FG]	Privately owned, Montceau-les-Mines, France
	105	Nord N2501F Noratlas (F-AZVM) [62-SI]	Le Noratlas de Provence, Marseille, France
	106	MH1521M Broussard (F-GKJT) [33-JT]	Privately owned, Montceau-les-Mines, France
	108	Aerospatiale TB.30 Epsilon (F-HEXI) [01]	Privately owned, Dijon-Longvic, France
	108	MH1521M Broussard (F-BNEX) [50S9]	Privately owned, Bantheville, France
	108	SO1221 Djinn (FR108) [CDL]	The Helicopter Museum, Weston-super-Mare
	111	Aerospatiale TB.30 Epsilon (F-HEYB) [03]	Privately owned, Dijon-Longvic, France
	113	Aerospatiale TB.30 Epsilon (F-AYYD)	Privately owned, la Ferté-Alais, France
	115	Aerospatiale TB.30 Epsilon (F-HEYF) [04]	Privately owned, Dijon/Longvic, France
	115-237	NA T-6G Harvard IIa (51-15848/F-AZBQ)	Privately owned, la Ferté-Alais, France
	117	Aerospatiale TB.30 Epsilon (F-AYYH) [315-YH]	Privately owned, Toussus-le-Noble, France
	121	Aerospatiale TB.30 Epsilon (F-AYYL)	Privately owned, Pontoise, France
	121	Dassault Mystère IVA [8-MY]	City of Norwich Aviation Museum, Norfolk
	128	Morane-Saulnier MS733 Alcyon (F-BMMY)	Privately owned, St Cyr, France
	129	Aerospatiale TB.30 Epsilon (F-HEYT) [02]	Privately owned, Dijon-Longvic, France
	138	Aerospatiale TB.30 Epsilon (F-AYZC) [315-ZC]	Privately owned, Nogaro, France
	141	Aerospatiale TB.30 Epsilon (F-AYCD)	Privately owned, Epernay, France
	141	Morane-Saulnier MS733 Alcyon (F-AZXU) [VG]	Privately owned, Marmande-Virazeil, France
	143	Aerospatiale TB.30 Epsilon (F-HEZH) [05]	Privately owned, Dijon-Longvic, France
	143	Morane-Saulnier MS733 Alcyon (G-MSAL)	Privately owned, Spanhoe, Northants
	144	Aerospatiale TB.30 Epsilon (F-HKYL) [315-ZI]	Privately owned, Besançon, France
	147	Morane-Saulnier MS733 Alcyon (F-AZRP)	Privately owned, Saint-Yan, France
	149	Aerospatiale TB.30 Epsilon (F-HKYN) [315-ZM]	Privately owned, Dijon-Darois, France
	154	MH1521M Broussard (G-TNUP) [315-SM]	Privately owned, Postling, Kent
	155	Aerospatiale TB.30 Epsilon (F-AYTB) [315-ZR]	Privately owned, Andernos-les-Bains, France

Serial	Type (code/other identity)	Owner/operator, location or fate	Notes
158	Dassault MD312 Flamant (F-AZGE) [12-XA]	Privately owned, Albert/Bray, France	
160	Dassault MD312 Flamant (F-AZDR) [V]	Privately owned, Alençon, France	
170	MH1521M Broussard (F-GDPX)	Patrouille Tranchant, Rennes, France	
189	Dassault MD312 Flamant (F-AZVG) [G]	Ailes Anciennes de Corbas, Lyon/Corbas, France	
208	MH1521C1 Broussard (G-YYYY) [IR]	Privately owned, Eggesford, Devon	
226	Dassault MD312 Flamant (F-AZES) [319-CG]	Privately owned, Montbeliard, France	
237	Dassault MD312 Flamant (F-AZFE) [319-DM]	Privately owned, Alençon, France	
254	Morane-Saulnier MS315 (F-BBZO)	Privately owned, la Ferté-Alais, France	
255	MH1521M Broussard (G-CIGH) [5-ML]	Sold to Germany as D-F...	
260	Dassault MD311 Flamant (F-AZKT) [316-KT]	Privately owned, Albert, France	
261	MH1521M Broussard (F-GIBN) [30-QA]	Privately owned, Walldürn, Germany	
276	Dassault MD311 Flamant (F-AZER) [OA-N]	Privately owned, Alençon, France	
290	Dewoitine D27 (F-AZJD)	Les Casques de Cuir, La Ferté-Alais, France	
315	Fouga CM170R Magister (F-GKYF) [3]	Patrouille Tranchant, Rennes, France	
316	MH1521M Broussard (F-GGKR) [315-SN]	Privately owned, Lognes, France	
318	Dassault Mystère IVA [8-NY]	Dumfries & Galloway Avn Mus, Dumfries, Scotland	
319	Dassault Mystère IVA [8-ND]	Rebel Air Museum, Andrewsfield, Essex	
354	Morane-Saulnier MS315E-D2 (G-BZNK)	Privately owned, Wickenby, Lincs (restoration)	
411	Fouga CM170R Magister (F-AZZD) [2]	Patrouille Tranchant, Rennes, France	
424	Fouga CM170R Magister (F-GJMN) [1]	Patrouille Tranchant, Rennes, France	
455	Fouga CM170R Magister (F-GSYD) [4]	Patrouille Tranchant, Rennes, France	
482	Fouga CM170R Magister (F-HDND) [5]	Patrouille Tranchant, Rennes, France	
538	Dassault Mirage IIIE [3-QH]	Yorkshire Air Museum, Elvington, N. Yorks	
569	Fouga CM170R Magister (F-AZZP)	Privately owned, Le Havre, France	
1101	SNCAN Stampe SV-4B (G-HJSS)	Privately owned, Redhill, Surrey	
1139	SNCAN Stampe SV-4B (G-AYCK)	Privately owned, Dinton – Manor Farm, Wilts	
3615	Aérospatiale SA.342M Gazelle (HA-HSG)	Privately owned, Breighton, E. Yorks	
3815	Piper L-4B Grasshopper (43-815/F-BEGD) [26-R]	Privately owned, France	
24522	Cessna L-19E Bird Dog (F-AYVA)	Privately owned, Chavenay-Villepreux, France	
24541	Cessna L-19E Bird Dog (G-JDOG) [BMG]	Privately owned, Hawarden, Flintshire, Wales	
24545	Cessna L-19E Bird Dog (F-AZTA) [BYA]	Privately owned, Chavenay, France	
24553	Cessna L-19E Bird Dog (F-AYSD) [BIE]	Privately owned, France	
42157	NA F-100D Super Sabre [11-ER]	North-East Land, Sea & Air Museums, Usworth, T&W	
48846	Boeing B-17G Flying Fortress (44-8846/F-AZDX)[DS-M/J]	Association Fortress Volante, La Ferté Alais, France	
54439	Lockheed T-33A Shooting Star (55-4439) [WI]	South Wales Aviation Museum, St Athan, Glamorgan, Wales	
114456	NA T-6G Texan (F-AZCV/51-14456)	Privately owned, Melun-Villaroche, France	
125716	Douglas AD-4N Skyraider (F-AZFN) [22-DG]	Privately owned, Melun, France	
18-1391	Piper L-18C Super Cub (51-15391/G-BHOM) [AO-R]	Privately owned, Shobdon, Herefordshire	
18-5395	Piper L-18C Super Cub (52-2436/G-CUBJ) [CDG]	Privately owned, Old Warden, Beds	
C850	Salmson 2A2 <R>	Barton Aviation Heritage Society, Barton, Gtr Manchester	
F-AYFT	Grumman S-2F Turbo Firecat (Z-ZBET/147559) [15]	Privately owned, Alencon-Valframbert, France	
FR41	Piasecki H-21C	The Helicopter Museum, Weston-super-Mare	
FR150	SO1221 Djinn	Privately owned, Sproughton, Suffolk	
MS824	Morane-Saulnier Type N <R> (G-AWBU)	Privately owned, Turweston, Bucks	
N856	SNCAN NC856 (G-CDWE)	Privately owned, Wickenby, Lincs	
N1977	Nieuport Scout 17/23 <R> (N1723/G-BWMJ) [8]	Privately owned, Old Warden, Beds	
S.3836	SPAD XIII C.1 (F-AZFP) [5]	Privately owned, la Ferté Alais, France	
XC	Piper L-4J Grasshopper (44-80513/G-BSYO)	Privately owned, Postling, Kent	

GERMANY

-	Fieseler Fi103R-IV (V-1) (BAPC.91)	Lashenden Air Warfare Museum, Headcorn, Kent	
-	Fieseler Fi103R-IV (V-1) (BAPC.327)	National Military Museum, Soesterberg, Neth.	
-	Fokker Dr1 Dreidekker <R> (BAPC.88) [102/17]	FAA Museum, stored Cobham Hall, RNAS Yeovilton, Somerset	
-	Messerschmitt Bf109 <R> [<-]	Battle of Britain Experience, Canterbury, Kent	
-	Pilatus P.2-05 (F-AZCC/U-117)	Privately owned, Saint-Rambert d'Albon, France	
<+-	Messerschmitt Bf109 <R> (BAPC.66) [6]	Kent Battle of Britain Museum, Hawkinge, Kent	
I+1	Messerschmitt Bf109 <R> (6357/BAPC.74) [6]	Kent Battle of Britain Museum, Hawkinge, Kent	
White 1	Hispano HA 1.112M1L Buchón (C.4K-111/G-HISP)	Privately owned, Sywell, Northants	

Notes	Serial	Type (code/other identity)	Owner/operator, location or fate
	White 1	Focke-Wulf Fw190 <R> (G-WULF)	Privately owned, Tatenhill, Staffs
	3	SNCAN 1101 Noralpha (G-BAYV) (fuselage)	Privately owned, Bentwaters, Suffolk
	Yellow 3	Hispano HA 1.112M1L Buchón (C.4K-40/D-FDME)	Messerschmitt Stiftung, Manching, Germany
	Red 7	Hispano HA 1.112M1L Buchón (C.4K-75/D-FWME)	Messerschmitt Stiftung, Manching, Germany
	Red 7	Pilatus P.2-06 (F-AZCE/U-152)	Privately owned, la Ferté Alais, France
	Yellow 7	Hispano HA 1.112M1L Buchón (C.4K-99/G-AWHM)	Privately owned, Sywell, Northants
	White 9	Hispano HA 1.112M1L Buchón (C.4K-105/G-AWHH)	Privately owned, Sywell, Northants
	Yellow 10	Hispano HA 1.112M1L Buchón (C.4K-102/G-AWHK)	Historic Flying Ltd, Duxford, Cambs
	Red 11	Hispano HA 1.112K1L Buchón (C.4K-112/G-AWHC)	Privately owned, Sywell, Northants
	Red 12	Messerschmitt Bf109E-4 (D-FEML)	Privately owned, Bonn-Hangelar, Germany
	White 14	Messerschmitt Bf109 <R> (BAPC.67)	Kent Battle of Britain Museum, Hawkinge, Kent
	Yellow 27	Hispano HA 1.112K1L Buchón (D-FMGZ)	Air Fighter Academy, Heringsdorf, Germany
	33/15	Fokker EIII <R> (G-CHAW)	Privately owned, Membury, Wilts
	87	Heinkel He111 <R> <ff>	Privately owned, East Kirkby, Lincs
	105/15	Fokker EIII <R> (G-UDET)	Privately owned, Horsham, W. Sussex
	152/17	Fokker Dr1 Dreidekker <R> (F-AZPQ)	Les Casques de Cuir, la Ferté-Alais, France
	152/17	Fokker Dr1 Dreidekker <R> (G-BVGZ)	Privately owned, Breighton, E. Yorks
	157/18	Fokker D.VIII <R> (BAPC.239)	Norfolk & Suffolk Air Museum, Flixton, Suffolk
	210/16	Fokker EIII (BAPC.56)	Science Museum, South Kensington, London
	403/17	Fokker Dr1 Dreidekker <R> (G-CDXR)	Privately owned, Popham, Hants
	416/15	Fokker EIII <R> (G-GSAL)	Privately owned, South Cave – Mount Airy Farm, E. Yorks
	422/15	Fokker EIII <R> (G-AVJO)	Privately owned, Turweston, Bucks
	422/15	Fokker EIII <R> (G-FOKR)	Privately owned, Eshott, Northumberland
	425/17	Fokker Dr1 Dreidekker <R> (BAPC.133)	Kent Battle of Britain Museum, Hawkinge, Kent
	425/17	Fokker DR.1 Triplane <R> (F-AYDR)	Privately owned, la Ferté Alais, France
	425/17	Fokker Dr1 Dreidekker <R> (G-DREI)	Privately owned, Felthorpe, Norfolk
	477/17	Fokker Dr1 Dreidekker <R> (G-FOKK)	Privately owned, Sywell, Northants
	525/17	Fokker Dr1 Dreidekker <R> (F-AZVD)	Privately owned, Beauvais-Tille, France
	556/17	Fokker Dr1 Dreidekker <R> (G-CFHY)	Privately owned, Tibenham, Norfolk
	626/8	Fokker DVII <R> (N6268)	Privately owned, Booker, Bucks
	764	Mikoyan MiG-21SPS <ff>	Privately owned, Norfolk
	959	Mikoyan MiG-21SPS	Midland Air Museum, Coventry, Warks
	1160	Dornier Do17Z-2	Michael Beetham Conservation Centre, Cosford, Shropshire
	1190	Messerschmitt Bf109E-3 [White 4]	IWM Duxford, Cambs
	1801/18	Bowers Fly Baby 1A (G-BNPV)	Privately owned, Chessington, Gtr London
	1803/18	Bowers Fly Baby 1A (G-BUYU)	Privately owned, Chessington, Gtr London
	3579	Messerschmitt Bf109E-7 (G-CIPB) [White 14]	Privately owned, Biggin Hill, Kent
	4101	Messerschmitt Bf109E-3 (DG200/8477M) [Black 12]	RAF Museum, Hendon, Gtr London
	4400	Fokker DVII <R> (F-AZLM) [18]	Privately owned, la Ferté-Alais, France
	4477	CASA 1.131E Jungmann (G-RETA) [GD+EG]	The Shuttleworth Collection, Old Warden, Beds
	7198/18	LVG CVI (G-AANJ/9239M)	Michael Beetham Conservation Centre, Cosford, Shropshire
	8417/18	Fokker DVII (9207M)	RAF Museum, Hendon, Gtr London
	10639	Messerschmitt Bf109G-2/Trop (8478M/G-USTV) [Black 6]	RAF Museum, Cosford, Shropshire
	12802	Antonov An-2T (D-FOFM)	Historische Flugzeuge, Grossenhain, Germany
	13605	Messerschmitt Bf109G-2 (G-JIMP) [Yellow 12]	Privately owned, Knutsford, Cheshire
	15919	Messerschmitt Bf109G <R> (BAPC.240) [Green 1]	Yorkshire Air Museum, Elvington, N. Yorks
	100143	Focke-Achgelis Fa330A-1 Bachstelze	IWM Duxford, Cambs
	100502	Focke-Achgelis Fa330A-1 Bachstelze	Privately owned, Millom, Cumbria
	100503	Focke-Achgelis Fa330A-1 Bachstelze (8469M)	RAF Museum, Cosford, Shropshire
	100509	Focke-Achgelis Fa330A-1 Bachstelze	Science Museum, stored Wroughton, Wilts
	100545	Focke-Achgelis Fa330A-1 Bachstelze	FAA Museum, RNAS Yeovilton, Somerset
	100549	Focke-Achgelis Fa330A-1 Bachstelze	Lashenden Air Warfare Museum, Headcorn, Kent
	112372	Messerschmitt Me262A-2a (VK893/8482M) [Yellow 4]	RAF Museum, Cosford, Shropshire
	120227	Heinkel He162A-2 Salamander (VN679/8472M) [Red 2]	RAF Museum, Hendon, Gtr London
	120235	Heinkel He162A-1 Salamander (AM.68) [Yellow 6]	IWM Duxford, Cambs
	191316	Messerschmitt Me163B Komet [Yellow 6]	Science Museum, South Kensington, London
	191454	Messerschmitt Me163B Komet <R> (BAPC.271)	The Shuttleworth Collection, Old Warden, Beds
	191461	Messerschmitt Me163B Komet (191614/8481M) [Yellow 14]	RAF Museum, Hendon, Gtr London
	191659	Messerschmitt Me163B Komet (8480M) [Yellow 15]	National Museum of Flight, E. Fortune, Scotland
	280020	Flettner Fl282/B-V20 Kolibri (frame only)	Midland Air Museum, Coventry, Warks

Serial	Type (code/other identity)	Owner/operator, location or fate	Notes
360043	Junkers Ju88R-1 (PJ876/8475M) [D5+EV]	RAF Museum, Cosford, Shropshire	
420430	Messerschmitt Me410A-1/U2 (AM.72/8483M) [3U+CC]	RAF Museum, Cosford, Shropshire	
475081	Fieseler Fi156C-7 Storch (VP546/AM.101/7362M)[GM+AK]	RAF Museum, Cosford, Shropshire	
494083	Junkers Ju87D-3 (8474M) [RI+JK]	RAF Museum, Hendon, Gtr London	
701152	Heinkel He111H-23 (8471M) [NT+SL]	RAF Museum, Hendon, Gtr London	
730301	Messerschmitt Bf110G-4 (AM.34/8479M) [D5+RL]	RAF Museum, Hendon, Gtr London	
733682	Focke-Wulf Fw190A-8/R7 (AM.75/9211M)	RAF Museum, Cosford, Shropshire	
980554	Flug Werk FW190A-8/N (D-FWMV) [1+V]	Meier Motors, Bremgarten, Germany	
2+1	Focke-Wulf Fw190 <R> (G-SYFW) [7334]	Privately owned, Halfpenny Green, Staffs	
20+45	Mikoyan MiG-23BN	Privately owned, Danbury, Essex	
22+35	Lockheed F-104G Starfighter	Current status unknown (ex-Bruntingthorpe)	
2E+RA	Fieseler Fi-156C-3 Storch (F-AZRA)	Amicale J-B Salis, la Ferté-Alais, France	
4+1	Focke-Wulf Fw190 <R> (G-BSLX)	Privately owned, Norwich, Norfolk	
6G+ED	Slepcev Storch (G-BZOB) [5447]	Privately owned, Breighton, E. Yorks	
37+86	McD F-4F Phantom II <ff>	Current status unknown (ex-Bruntingthorpe)	
37+89	McD F-4F Phantom II	Stored Scampton, Lincs (off-airfield)	
58+89	Dornier Do28D-2 Skyservant (D-ICDY)	Privately owned, Uetersen, Germany	
72+59	Dornier UH-1D Iroquois (comp 73+01)	Privately owned, Dunsfold, Surrey	
80+55	MBB Bo.105M (G-HZYI)	Lufthansa Resource Technical Training, Cotswold Airport, Glos	
80+77	MBB Bo.105M	Lufthansa Resource Technical Training, Cotswold Airport, Glos	
81+00	MBB Bo.105M (D-HZYR)	The Helicopter Museum, Weston-super-Mare, Somerset	
96+26	Mil Mi-24D (421)	The Helicopter Museum, Weston-super-Mare, Somerset	
98+14	Sukhoi Su-22M-4	Hawker Hunter Aviation Ltd, stored Scampton, Lincs (offsite)	
99+18	NA OV-10B Bronco (G-ONAA)	Bronco Demo Team, Wevelgem, Belgium	
99+26	NA OV-10B Bronco (G-BZGL)	Bronco Demo Team, Wevelgem, Belgium	
AZ+JU	CASA 352L (T.12B-212/F-AZJU)	Amicale J-B Salis, La Ferté-Alais, France	
BB+103	Canadair CL-13B Sabre 6 (1730/JB+114)	Current status unknown (ex-Bruntingthorpe)	
BF+070	CCF T-6J Texan (G-CHYN)	Privately owned, Dunkeswell, Devon	
BG+KM	Nord 1002 Pingouin (G-ASTG)	Privately owned, Haddon, Cambs	
BU+CC	CASA 1.131E Jungmann (G-BUCC)	Privately owned, Deanland, E. Sussex	
CX+HI	CASA 1.131E Jungmann (E.3B-379/G-CDJU)	Privately owned, Sleap, Shropshire	
D2263	Albatros DVA-1 <R> (ZK-ALB/G-WAHT)	Privately owned, Stow Maries, Essex	
D7343/17	Albatros DVA <R> (ZK-TVD)	RAF Museum, Hendon, Gtr London	
E37/15	Fokker EIII <R> (G-CGJF)	Privately owned, Whepstead, Suffolk	
ES+BH	Messerschmitt Bf108B-2 (D-ESBH)	Messerschmitt Stiftung, Manching, Germany	
F8+CA	Nord 1002 (G-ETME)	Privately owned, White Waltham, Berks	
FI+S	Morane-Saulnier MS505 (G-BIRW)	Privately owned, Duxford, Cambs	
FM+BB	Messerschmitt Bf109G-6 (D-FMBB)	Messerschmitt Stiftung, Manching, Germany	
GK+RR	Nord 1002 (F-AZRR) (painted as Bf108D WN 5126)	Privately owned, la Ferté-Alais, France	
KG+GB	CASA 1.131E Jungmann (E.3B-236/G-BHSL)	Privately owned, Old Warden, Beds	
LF+VO	Jacobs DFS 108-70 (BGA449)	Privately owned, Rufforth, N. Yorks	
LG+01	CASA 1.133L Jungmeister (ES.1-16/G-CIJV)	Privately owned, Sleap, Shropshire	
LG+03	Bücker Bü133C Jungmeister (G-AEZX)	Privately owned, Milden, Suffolk	
NJ+C11	Nord 1002 (G-ATBG)	Privately owned, Duxford, Cambs	
NM+AA	CASA 1.131E Jungmann 1000 (E.3B-367/G-BZJV)	Privately owned, Sleap, Shropshire	
NQ+NR	Klemm Kl35D (D-EQXD)	Quax Flieger, Paderborn, Germany	
NV+KG	Focke-Wulf Fw44J Stieglitz (D-ENAY)	Quax Flieger, Paderborn, Germany	
S4-A07	CASA 1.131E Jungmann (G-BWHP)	Privately owned, Yarcombe, Devon	
SB+UG	Morane-Saulnier MS500 (G-BPHZ)	Historic Aircraft Collection, Duxford, Cambs	
TP+WX	Heliopolis Gomhouria Mk 6 (G-TPWX)	Privately owned, Swanborough, E. Sussex	
VJ+OQ	Messerschmitt Bf110D-0 (3869) <rf>	IWM Duxford, Cambs	
GHANA			
G360	PBN 2T Islander (G-BRSR)	Privately owned, stored Badgers Mount, Leics	
G361	PBN 2T Islander (G-BRPB)	Privately owned, Biggin Hill, Kent	
G363	PBN 2T Islander (G-BRSV)	Privately owned, Cumbernauld, Scotland	

Notes	Serial	Type (code/other identity)	Owner/operator, location or fate
	GREECE		
	26541	Republic F-84F Thunderflash (52-6541) [541]	North-East Land, Sea & Air Museums, Usworth
	49-3424	NA T-6G Texan (G-CMMU)	*Cancelled by the CAA, October 2024*
	HONG KONG		
	HKG-5	SA128 Bulldog (G-BULL)	Privately owned, Cotswold Airport, Glos
	HKG-6	SA128 Bulldog (G-BPCL)	Privately owned, North Weald, Essex
	HKG-11	Slingsby T.67M Firefly 200 (G-LDGU)	Privately owned, stored Tollerton, Notts
	HKG-13	Slingsby T.67M Firefly 200 (G-BXKW)	Privately owned, St Ghislain, Belgium
	HUNGARY		
	125	Aero L-39ZO Albatros (831125/G-JMGP)	Stored, St Athan, Glamorgan, Wales
	335	Mil Mi-24D (3532461715415) (Red 03)	Privately owned, Dunsfold, Surrey
	501	Mikoyan MiG-21PF	IWM Duxford, Cambs
	503	Mikoyan MiG-21SMT (G-BRAM)	RAF Museum, Cosford, Shropshire
	INDIA		
	E296	Hindustan Gnat F1 (G-SLYR)	Privately owned, St Athan, Glamorgan, Wales
	HA561	Hawker Tempest II (MW743)	Privately owned, stored Wickenby, Lincs
	HS683	VS394 Spitfire FR XVIIIe (TZ219)	Privately owned, Sywell, Northants
	INDONESIA		
	LL-5313	BAe Hawk T53	BAE Systems, Brough, E. Yorks, on display
	IRAQ		
	249	Hawker Fury ISS (OO-ISS)	Privately owned, Brasschaat, Belgium
	333	DH115 Vampire T55 <ff>	South Yorkshire Aircraft Museum, stored Doncaster, S. Yorks
	349	Hawker Hunter F51 (E-408/G-9-436/*WT720*/8565M)	Centreprise International, Chineham, Hants
	ISRAEL		
	206	Hughes 500D Lahatoot (G-LEEX)	Privately owned, Sleap, Shropshire
	ITALY		
	MM5701	Fiat CR42 (BT474/8468M) [13-95]	RAF Museum, Hendon, Gtr London
	MM6976	Fiat CR42 (2542/G-CBLS) [85-16]	The Fighter Collection, Duxford, Cambs
	MM53211	Fiat G46-1B (MM52799/BAPC.79) [ZI-4]	Privately owned, Shipdham, Norfolk
	MM53774	Fiat G59-4B (I-MRSV) [181]	Privately owned, Parma, Italy
	MM54099	NA T-6G Texan (G-BRBC) [RR-56]	Privately owned, Chigwell, Essex
	MM54532	SIAI-Marchetti SF.260AM (G-ITAF) [70-42]	Privately owned, Leicester, Leics
	MM80927	Agusta-Bell AB206A-1 JetRanger [CC-49]	The Helicopter Museum, Weston-super-Mare, Somerset
	MM81205	Agusta A109A-2 SEM [GF-128]	The Helicopter Museum, Weston-super-Mare, Somerset
	MM81220	Agusta A109A-2 SEM	Air Service Training, Perth, Scotland
	MM81335	Agusta A109A-2 SEM	Air Service Training, Perth, Scotland
	MM51-15302	Piper L-18C Super Cub (G-BJTP) [E.I.51]	Privately owned, Sleap, Shropshire
	MM52-2392	Piper L-21B Super Cub (G-HELN) [E.I.69]	Privately owned, White Waltham, Berks
	MM54-2372	Piper L-21B Super Cub (I-EIXM) [EI-184]	Privately owned, Foxhall Heath, Suffolk
	PS-45	Agusta A109A (MM80745)	Stored Hixon, Staffs, 2020. Current status?
	PS-48	Agusta A109A (MM80748)	Stored Hixon, Staffs, 2020. Current status?
	PS-49	Agusta A109A (MM80749)	Stored Hixon, Staffs, 2020. Current status?
	PS-59	Agusta A109A (MM80759)	Stored Hixon, Staffs, 2020. Current status?
	PS-64	Agusta A109A (MM81646)	Stored Hixon, Staffs, 2020. Current status?
	JAPAN		
	-	Kawasaki Ki100-1B (16336/8476M/BAPC.83) [24]	RAF Museum, Hendon, Gtr London
	-	Mitsubishi A6M5-52 Zero (196) [BI-05] <ff>	IWM Duxford, Cambs
	-	Yokosuka MXY 7 Ohka II (BAPC.159)	IWM Lambeth, London
	170	NA T-6 Texan Zero (F-AZZM)	Privately owned, la Ferté-Alais, France
	3443	NA T-6 Texan Zero (F-AZRO)	Privately owned, St Rambert d'Albon, France
	5439	Mitsubishi Ki46-III (8484M/BAPC.84)	RAF Museum, Hendon, Gtr London

Serial	Type (code/other identity)	Owner/operator, location or fate	Notes
15-1585	Yokosuka MXY 7 Ohka II (BAPC.58)	Science Museum, stored Cobham Hall, RNAS Yeovilton, Somerset	
I-13	Yokosuka MXY 7 Ohka II (8486M/BAPC.99)	RAF Museum, Hendon, Gtr London	
Y2-176	Mitsubishi A6M3-2 Zero (3685) [76] <rf>	IWM London, Lambeth, London	
KENYA			
115	Dornier Do28D-2 Skyservant (D-IAAI)	Privately owned, stored Hibaldstow	
117	Dornier Do28D-2 Skyservant	Privately owned, stored Hibaldstow	
MALAYSIA			
M25-04	SA102 Bulldog (FM1224) (fuselage)	South Wales Aviation Museum, stored St Athan, Glamorgan, Wales	
MALTA			
AS0022	SA Bulldog T1 (XX709/G-CLJC)	Privately owned, Oxon	
AS0023	SA Bulldog T1 (XX714/G-CLJD)	Privately owned, Oxon	
MEXICO			
52	Mudry CAP-10B (N4238C/EPC-155)	Privately owned, Old Warden, Beds	
MYANMAR			
UB441	VS361 Spitfire IX (ML119/G-SDNI)	Privately owned, Biggin Hill, Kent	
THE NETHERLANDS			
174	Fokker S-11 Instructor (E-31/G-BEPV) [K]	Privately owned, Spanhoe, Northants	
179	Fokker S-11 Instructor (PH-ACG) [K]	Privately owned, Lelystad, The Netherlands	
197	Fokker S-11 Instructor (PH-GRY) [197-K]	KLu Historic Flt, Gilze-Rijen, The Netherlands	
204	Lockheed SP-2H Neptune [V]	RAF Museum, Cosford, Shropshire	
272	Westland SH-14D Lynx	South Wales Aviation Museum, St Athan, Glamorgan, Wales	
A-57	DH82A Tiger Moth (PH-TYG)	KLu Historic Flt, Gilze-Rijen, The Netherlands	
B-64	Noorduyn AT-16 Harvard IIb (PH-LSK)	KLu Historic Flt, Gilze-Rijen, The Netherlands	
B-71	Noorduyn AT-16 Harvard IIb (PH-MLM)	KLu Historic Flt, Gilze-Rijen, The Netherlands	
B-118	Noorduyn AT-16 Harvard IIb (PH-IIB)	KLu Historic Flt, Gilze-Rijen, The Netherlands	
B-182	Noorduyn AT-16 Harvard IIb (PH-TBR)	KLu Historic Flt, Gilze-Rijen, The Netherlands	
E-14	Fokker S-11 Instructor (PH-AFS)	Privately owned, Lelystad, The Netherlands	
E-15	Fokker S-11 Instructor (G-BIYU)	Privately owned, Wassenaar, The Netherlands	
E-20	Fokker S-11 Instructor (PH-GRB)	Privately owned, Gilze-Rijen, The Netherlands	
E-27	Fokker S-11 Instructor (PH-HOL)	Privately owned, Lelystad, The Netherlands	
E-29	Fokker S-11 Instructor (PH-HOK)	Privately owned, Lelystad, The Netherlands	
E-32	Fokker S-11 Instructor (PH-HOI)	Privately owned, Gilze-Rijen, The Netherlands	
E-39	Fokker S-11 Instructor (PH-HOG)	Privately owned, Lelystad, The Netherlands	
G-29	Beech D18S (PH-KHV)	KLu Historic Flt, Gilze-Rijen, The Netherlands	
MK732	VS361 Spitfire LF IXc (8633M/PH-OUQ) [3W-17]	KLu Historic Flt, Gilze-Rijen, The Netherlands	
N-202	Hawker Hunter F6 [10] <ff>	Privately owned, Stockport, Cheshire	
N-250	Hawker Hunter F6 (G-9-185) <ff>	IWM Duxford, Cambs	
N-302	Hawker Hunter T7 (ET-273/G-9-431) <ff>	Privately owned, Coltishall, Norfolk (rest'n)	
N-315	Hawker Hunter T7 (comp XM121)	Privately owned, Netherley, Aberdeenshire	
N-321	Hawker Hunter T8C (XF357/G-BWGL)	Privately owned, Altenrhein, Switzerland	
N5-149	NA B-25J Mitchell (44-29507/HD346/PH-XXV) [232511]	KLu Historic Flt, Gilze-Rijen, The Netherlands	
R-18	Auster III (PH-NGK)	KLu Historic Flt, Gilze-Rijen, The Netherlands	
R-45	Piper L-18C Super Cub (52-2452/G-AXLZ)	Privately owned, Shoreham, W. Sussex (stored)	
R-55	Piper L-18C Super Cub (52-2466/G-BLMI)	Privately owned, Antwerp-Deurne, Belgium	
R-109	Piper L-21B Super Cub (54-2337/PH-GAZ)	KLu Historic Flt, Gilze-Rijen, The Netherlands	
R-122	Piper L-21B Super Cub (54-2412/PH-PPW)	KLu Historic Flt, Gilze-Rijen, The Netherlands	
R-124	Piper L-21B Super Cub (54-2414/PH-APA)	Privately owned, Eindhoven, The Netherlands	
R-137	Piper L-21B Super Cub (54-2427/PH-PSC)	Privately owned, Gilze-Rijen, The Netherlands	
R-151	Piper L-21B Super Cub (54-2441/G-BIYR)	Privately owned, Yarcombe, Devon	
R-156	Piper L-21B Super Cub (54-2446/G-ROVE)	Privately owned, Damyn's Hall, Gtr London	
R-167	Piper L-21B Super Cub (54-2457/G-LION)	Privately owned, Druid, Denbighshire, Wales	
R-170	Piper L-21B Super Cub (52-6222/PH-ENJ)	Privately owned, Seppe, The Netherlands	
R-177	Piper L-21B Super Cub (54-2467/PH-KNR)	KLu Historic Flt, Gilze-Rijen, The Netherlands	
R-181	Piper L-21B Super Cub (54-2471/PH-GAU)	Privately owned, Gilze-Rijen, The Netherlands	

Notes	Serial	Type (code/other identity)	Owner/operator, location or fate
	R-184	Piper L-21B Super Cub (54-2474/G-PCUB)	Privately owned, stored Paddock Wood, Kent
	R-213	Piper L-21A Super Cub (51-15682/PH-RED) (wreck)	Stored Woensdrecht, The Netherlands
	R-345	Piper L-4J Grasshopper (45-4488/PH-UCS)	Privately owned, Hilversum, The Netherlands
	S-9	DHC2 L-20A Beaver (55-4585/PH-DHC)	KLu Historic Flt, Gilze-Rijen, The Netherlands

NETHERLANDS EAST INDIES

| | *S11* | Ryan STM-2 (S-40/N7779) | The Shuttleworth Collection, Old Warden, Beds |

NEW ZEALAND

	NZ3909	WS Wasp HAS1 (XT782/G-CMBE) (comp NZ3901/3904)	Privately owned, Thruxton, Hants
	NZ5911	Bristol 170 Freighter 31M (ZK-EPG)	Aerospace Bristol, stored Filton, Glos
	NZ6300	BAC Strikemaster Mk.80 (G-RNAF)	Privately owned, Hawarden, Flintshire, Wales

NORTH KOREA

| | - | WSK Lim-2 (MiG-15) (01420/G-BMZF) | FAA Museum, RNAS Yeovilton, Somerset |

NORTH VIETNAM

| | 1211 | WSK Lim-5 (MiG-17F) (G-MIGG) | Privately owned, Modlin, Poland |

NORWAY

	145	DH82A Tiger Moth II (DE248/LN-BDM)	Privately owned, Kjeller, Norway
	163	Fairchild PT-19A Cornell (42-83641/LN-BIF)	Privately owned, Kjeller, Norway
	171	DH82A Tiger Moth II (T6168/LN-KAY)	Privately owned, Kjeller, Norway
	599	Canadair CT-133AUP Silver Star Mk.3 (133599/LN-DPS)	Norwegian AF Historical Sqn, Ørland, Norway
	848	Piper L-18C Super Cub (LN-ACL) [FA-N]	Privately owned, Kjeller, Norway
	56321	SAAB S91B Safir (G-BKPY)	Newark Air Museum, Winthorpe, Notts
	PX-M	DH115 Vampire T55 (U-1230/WZ447/LN-DHZ)	Norwegian AF Historical Sqn, Rygge, Norway

OMAN

	417	BAC Strikemaster Mk.80A (G-RSAF)	Privately owned, Hawarden, Flintshire, Wales
	425	BAC Strikemaster Mk.82A (G-SOAF)	Privately owned, Hawarden, Flintshire, Wales
	801	Hawker Hunter T66B <rf>	Privately owned, Hawarden, Flintshire, Wales
	853	Hawker Hunter FR10 (XF426)	RAF Museum, stored Cosford, Shropshire
	XL554	SAL Pioneer CC1 (XL703/8034M)	RAF Museum, stored Cosford, Shropshire

POLAND

	05	WSK SM-2 (Mi-2) (S2-03006)	The Helicopter Museum, Weston-super-Mare
	309	WSK SBLim-2A (MiG-15UTI) <ff>	National Museum of Flight, E. Fortune, Scotland
	458	Mikoyan MiG-23ML (04 red/024003607)	*Repainted as Soviet 44 r*
	1018	WSK-PZL Mielec TS-11 Iskra (1H-1018/G-ISKA)	Preserved Bruntingthorpe, Leics
	1120	WSK Lim-2 (MiG-15bis)	RAF Museum, Cosford, Shropshire
	1706	WSK-PZL Mielec TS-11 Iskra (1H-0408)	Midland Air Museum, Coventry, Warks
	1708	WSK-PZL Mielec TS-11 Iskra bis DF (3H-1625/G-BXVZ) [4]	RAF Manston History Museum, Kent
	1972	Letov S-102 (MiG-15) (623794) (port side only, painted in Czech marks as 3794 on starboard side)	Norfolk & Suffolk Avn Museum, Flixton, Suffolk
	7811	Mikoyan MiG-21MF (96N7811)	Privately owned, Alton, Hants

PORTUGAL

	1350	OGMA/DHC1 Chipmunk T20 (G-CGAO)	Privately owned, Duxford, Cambs
	1365	OGMA/DHC1 Chipmunk T20 (G-DHPM)	Privately owned, Sleap, Shropshire
	1367	OGMA/DHC1 Chipmunk T20 (G-UANO)	Privately owned, Breighton, E. Yorks
	1372	OGMA/DHC1 Chipmunk T20 (HB-TUM)	*Written off, 2009*
	1373	OGMA/DHC1 Chipmunk T20 (G-CBJG)	Privately owned, Winwick, Cambs
	1375	OGMA/DHC1 Chipmunk T20 (F-AZJV)	Privately owned, Valenciennes, France
	1377	DHC1 Chipmunk 22 (WK520/G-BARS)	Privately owned, Yeovilton, Somerset
	1741	CCF T-6J Texan (G-HRVD)	Privately owned, Perigeux, France
	1747	CCF T-6J Texan (53-4619/G-BGPB)	Privately owned, Halfpenny Green, Staffs
	3303	MH1521M Broussard (G-CBGL)	Privately owned, stored Postling, Kent

QATAR

| | QA10 | Hawker Hunter FGA78 | Yorkshire Air Museum, Elvington, N. Yorks |

Serial	Type (code/other identity)	Owner/operator, location or fate	Notes
QA12	Hawker Hunter FGA78 (N-222) <ff>	Privately owned, New Inn, Torfaen, Wales	
QP30	WS Lynx Mk.28 (G-BFDV/TAD013/ZZ003)	FETC, Moreton-in-Marsh, Glos	
QP31	WS Lynx Mk.28 (ZZ004)	Newark Air Museum, Winthorpe, Notts	
QP32	WS Lynx Mk.28 (TAD016/ZZ005) [A]	DSAE SAAE, Lyneham, Wilts, on display	
ROMANIA			
29	LET L-29 Delfin	Privately owned, Skirpenbeck, E. Yorks	
42	LET L-29 Delfin <ff>	Current status unknown	
42	LET L-29 Delfin <rf>	Current status unknown	
47	LET L-29 Delfin <ff>	Top Gun Flight Simulator Centre, Stalybridge, Gtr Manchester	
53	LET L-29 Delfin [66654]	Preserved Bruntingthorpe, Leics	
RUSSIA (& FORMER SOVIET UNION)			
-	Mil Mi-24D (3532464505029)	Midland Air Museum, Coventry, Warks	
00 w	Yakovlev Yak-3M (0470202/G-OLEG)	Privately owned, Sywell, Northants	
1 w	SPP Yak C-11 (171314/G-BZMY)	Privately owned, Alscot Park, Warks	
01 y	Yakovlev Yak-52 (9311709/G-YKSZ/OM-JKK)	Privately owned, White Waltham, Berks	
03 bl	Yakovlev Yak-55M (910103/RA-01274)	Privately owned, Halfpenny Green, Staffs	
03 w	Yakovlev Yak-18A (1160403/G-CEIB)	Privately owned, Breighton, E. Yorks	
03 w	Yakovlev Yak-9UM (0470403/OO-RAW)	Privately owned, Sabadell, Spain	
5 w	Yakovlev Yak-3UA (0470204/D-FYGJ)	Privately owned, Bremgarten, Germany	
5 w	Yakovlev Yak-3UA (F-AZLY)	Privately owned, Yvetot-Baons-le-Comte, France	
6 w	Yakovlev Yak-3UA (127612/F-AZOS)	Privately owned, Melun, France	
07 r	Mil Mi-8P (10618) (618)	The Helicopter Museum, Weston-super-Mare	
07 w	Yakovlev Yak-18M (F-AZFG)	Privately owned, Saint-Rambert d'Albon, France	
07 y	WSK SM-1 (Mi-1) (Polish AF 2007)	The Helicopter Museum, Weston-super-Mare	
07 y	Yakovlev Yak-18M (G-BMJY)	Privately owned, Membury, Berks	
9	SPP Yak C-11 (1701139/G-OYAK)	Privately owned, Little Gransden, Cambs	
9 bk	Polikarpov Po-2 (F-AZDB)	Privately owned, la Ferté-Alais, France	
10 r	Yakovlev Yak-52 (877610/G-YAKE)	Privately owned, Henstridge, Somerset	
14 r	WSK-PZL An-2R (HA-MKE)	Morayvia, Kinloss, Scotland	
15 w	SPP Yak C-11 (170103/D-FYAK)	Classic Aviation Company, Hannover, Germany	
17 w	Bell P-63C Kingcobra (44-4315)	Wings Museum, Balcombe, W. Sussex	
18 r	LET L-29 Delfin (591771/YL-PAF)	Privately owned, Hawarden, Flintshire, Wales	
18 r	Yakovlev Yak-50 (801810/G-BTZB)	Privately owned, Henstridge, Somerset	
20 r	Yakovlev Yak-50 (812003/G-YAAK)	Privately owned, Henstridge, Somerset	
20 w	Lavochkin La-11	The Fighter Collection, stored Duxford, Cambs	
21 w	Yakovlev Yak-3UA (0470203/G-CDBJ)	Privately owned, Folkestone, Kent	
23 y	Bell P-39Q Airacobra (44-2911)	Privately owned, Sussex (also reported at Niagara Falls, NY, USA)	
23 w	Mikoyan MiG-27D (83712515040)	Privately owned, Hawarden, Flintshire, Wales	
26 bl	Yakovlev Yak-52 (9111306/G-BVXK)	Privately owned, White Waltham, Berks	
27 w	Yakovlev Yak-3UTI-PW <R>(9/04623/F-AZIM)	Privately owned, North Weald, Essex	
27 r	Yakovlev Yak-52 (9111307/G-YAKX)	Privately owned, Popham, Hants	
28 w	Polikarpov Po-2 (0094/G-BSSY)	The Shuttleworth Collection, Old Warden, Beds	
33 r	Yakovlev Yak-50 (853206/G-YAKZ)	Privately owned, Henstridge, Somerset	
33 w	Yakovlev Yak-52 (899915/G-YAKH)	Privately owned, White Waltham, Berks	
35 r	Sukhoi Su-17M-3 (25102)	Privately owned, Hawarden, Flintshire, Wales	
36 w	LET/Yak C-11 (171101/G-KYAK)	*To Bremgarten, Germany as D-FMAX*	
36 r	Yakovlev Yak-52 (9111604/G-IUII)	Privately owned, St Athan, Wales	
43 si	Yakovlev Yak-52 (877601/G-BWSV)	Privately owned, North Weald, Essex	
44 r	Mikoyan MiG-23ML (04 red/024003607)	Newark Air Museum, Winthorpe, Notts	
48 w	Yakovlev Yak-3UPW <R> (F-AZZK)	Privately owned, Lelystad, The Netherlands	
49 r	Yakovlev Yak-52 (822305/G-YAKU)	Privately owned, Henstridge, Somerset	
50 gy	Yakovlev Yak-52 (9111415/G-CBRW)	*Sold to Spain, July 2024*	
50 y	Yakovlev Yak-50 (801804/G-EYAK)	Privately owned, Leicester, Leics	
51 r	LET L-29S Delfin (491273/YL-PAC)	Privately owned, Breighton, E. Yorks	
52 bk	Yakovlev Yak-52 (877409/G-FLSH)	Privately owned, stored Newark, Notts (for sale)	
52 w	Yakovlev Yak-52 (9612001/G-CCJK)	Privately owned, White Waltham, Berks	
52 y	Yakovlev Yak-52 (878202/G-BWVR)	Privately owned, stored Eshott, Northumberland	
54 r	Sukhoi Su-17M (69004)	Privately owned, Hawarden, Flintshire, Wales	
61 r	Yakovlev Yak-50 (842710/G-YAKM)	Privately owned, Henstridge, Somerset	

Notes	Serial	Type (code/other identity)	Owner/operator, location or fate
	66 r	Yakovlev Yak-52 (855905/G-YAKN)	Privately owned, Henstridge, Somerset
	71 r	Mikoyan MiG-27K (61912507006)	Newark Air Museum, Winthorpe, Notts
	74 w	Yakovlev Yak-52 (877404/G-OUGH) [JA-74, IV-62]	Privately owned, Swansea, Wales
	86 r	Yakovlev Yak-52 (867212/G-YAKC)	Privately owned, Henstridge, Somerset
	100 bl	Yakovlev Yak-52 (866904/G-YAKI)	Privately owned, Popham, Hants
	526 bk	Mikoyan MiG-29 (2960725887) <ff>	South Wales Aviation Museum, St Athan, Glamorgan, Wales
	1342	Yakovlev Yak-1 (G-BTZD)	Privately owned, Westfield, E. Sussex
	1870710	Ilyushin Il-2 (G-BZVW)	*Sold to the USA, July 2024*
	1878576	Ilyushin Il-2 (G-BZVX)	*Sold to the USA, July 2024*
	PT879	VS361 Spitfire F IX (G-PTIX)	Privately owned, North Weald, Essex
	(RK858)	VS361 Spitfire LF IX (G-CGJE)	The Fighter Collection, Duxford, Cambs
	SAUDI ARABIA		
	1115	BAC Strikemaster Mk.80A (G-STKM)	Global Aviation, Humberside, Lincs
	1129	BAC Strikemaster Mk.80A	Humberside Airport, Lincs, on display
	1133	BAC Strikemaster Mk.80A (G-BESY)	IWM Duxford, Cambs
	53-671	BAC Lightning F53 (203/ZF579)	Gatwick Aviation Museum, Charlwood, Surrey
	53-686	BAC Lightning F53 (G-AWON/201/1305/223/ZF592)	City of Norwich Aviation Museum, Norfolk
	55-713	BAC Lightning T55 (206/1316/235/ZF598) [C]	Midland Air Museum, Coventry, Warks
	SIERRA LEONE		
	SL-01	Westland Commando Mk.2C	South Wales Aviation Museum, St Athan, Glamorgan, Wales
	SINGAPORE		
	311	BAC Strikemaster Mk.84 (G-MXPH)	Privately owned, stored Hawarden, Flintshire, Wales
	323	BAC Strikemaster Mk.81 (N21419)	Privately owned, stored Hawarden, Flintshire Wales
	SOUTH AFRICA		
	91	Westland Wasp HAS1 (pod)	Privately owned, Oaksey Park, Wilts
	92	Westland Wasp HAS1 (G-BYCX)	Privately owned, Dunchurch, Warks
	6130	Lockheed Ventura II (AJ469)	RAF Museum, stored Cosford, Shropshire
	7429	NA AT-6D Harvard III (D-FASS)	Privately owned, Aachen, Germany
	SOUTH ARABIA		
	104	BAC Jet Provost T52A (G-PROV)	Privately owned, North Weald, Essex
	SOUTH VIETNAM		
	24550	Cessna L-19E Bird Dog (G-PDOG) [GP]	Privately owned, Old Warden, Beds
	112471	Cessna L-19G Bird Dog (51-12471/VH-FXY) [DF]	Privately owned, Lydd, Kent
	SPAIN		
	A1+DA	CASA 2.111B (He111H-16) (B.2I-103)	Kent Battle of Britain Museum, Hawkinge, Kent
	C.4K-30	Hispano HA 1.112M1L Buchón [471-26]	Privately owned, Sywell, Northants
	E.3B-143	CASA 1.131E Jungmann (G-JUNG)	Privately owned, Breighton, E. Yorks
	E.3B-153	CASA 1.131E Jungmann (G-BPTS) [781-75]	Privately owned, Egginton, Derbyshire
	E.3B-494	CASA 1.131E Jungmann (G-CDLC) [81-47]	Privately owned, Chiseldon, Wilts
	E.3B-521	CASA 1.131E Jungmann [781-3]	RAF Museum Reserve Collection, Stafford, Staffs
	E.3B-599	CASA 1.131E Jungmann (E.3B-614/G-CGTX) [791-31]	Privately owned, Archerfield, Lothian, Scotland
	E.18-2	Piper PA-31P Navajo 425 [42-71]	High Harthay Outdoor Pursuits, Huntingdon, Cambs
	ES.1-31	Bücker Bü133C Jungmeister (G-RPAX) [35-23]	Privately owned, Breighton, E. Yorks
	T.2B-272	CASA C.352L (G-AFAP)	Kent Battle of Britain Museum, Hawkinge, Kent
	SRI LANKA		
	CT130	Nanchang CJ-6A Chujiao (3151215/G-CJSA)	Privately owned, White Waltham, Berks
	CT180	Nanchang CJ-6A Chujiao (2632016/G-BXZB)	Privately owned, White Waltham, Berks
	SWEDEN		
	-	Thulin A/Bleriot XI (SE-XMC)	*Privately owned, Loberod, Sweden*

Serial	Type (code/other identity)	Owner/operator, location or fate	Notes
087	CFM 01 Tummelisa <R> (SE-XIL)	*Privately owned, Loberod, Sweden*	
5033	Klemm Kl35D (SE-BPT) [78]	*Privately owned, Barkaby, Sweden*	
5060	Klemm Kl35D (SE-BPU) [174]	*Privately owned, Barkaby, Sweden*	
05108	DH60 Moth	Privately owned, Langham, Norfolk	
16028	Noorduyn AT-16ND Harvard IIB (42-12478/SE-FUB) [28]	Swedish Air Force Historic Flt, Såtenäs, Sweden	
16073	Noorduyn AT-16ND Harvard IIB (43-12799/SE-FVU) [73]	Swedish Air Force Historic Flt, Såtenäs, Sweden	
17239	SAAB B 17A (SE-BYH) [7-J]	Flygvapenmuseum, Linköping, Sweden	
29640	SAAB J 29F [20-08]	Midland Air Museum, Coventry, Warks	
29670	SAAB J 29F (SE-DXB) [10-R]	Swedish Air Force Historic Flt, Såtenäs, Sweden	
32028	SAAB 32A Lansen (G-BMSG) <ff>	Privately owned, Willenhall, Staffs	
32542	SAAB J 32B Lansen (SE-RMD) [23]	Swedish Air Force Historic Flt, Såtenäs, Sweden	
32606	SAAB J 32B Lansen (SE-RME) [06]	Swedish Air Force Historic Flt, Såtenäs, Sweden	
32620	SAAB J 32B Lansen (SE-RMF) [20]	Swedish Air Force Historic Flt, Såtenäs, Sweden	
35075	SAAB J 35A Draken [40]	Dumfries & Galloway Aviation Museum, Scotland	
35515	SAAB J 35F Draken [49]	Airborne Systems, Llangeinor, Glamorgan, Wales	
35556	SAAB J 35J Draken (SE-DXR) [56]	Swedish Air Force Historic Flt, Såtenäs, Sweden	
35810	SAAB Sk 35C Draken (SE-DXP) [79]	Swedish Air Force Historic Flt, Såtenäs, Sweden	
37098	SAAB AJSF 37 Viggen (SE-DXN) [52]	Swedish Air Force Historic Flt, Såtenäs, Sweden	
37809	SAAB Sk 37E Viggen (SE-DXO) [61]	Swedish Air Force Historic Flt, Såtenäs, Sweden	
37918	SAAB AJSH 37 Viggen [57]	Newark Air Museum, Winthorpe, Notts	
50042	SAAB S91B Safir (G-CLSP) [72]	Privately owned, Eshott, Northumberland	
60140	SAAB Sk 60E (SE-DXG) [140-5]	Swedish Air Force Historic Flt, Såtenäs, Sweden	
91130	SAAB S91A Safir (SE-BNN) [10-30]	*Privately owned, Barkaby, Sweden*	
SWITZERLAND			
A-10	CASA 1.131E Jungmann (G-BECW)	Privately owned, Postling, Kent	
A-15	CASA 1.131E Jungmann (G-CMSP/HB-UUE)	Privately owned, Henstridge, Somerset	
A-35	Bücker Bü131B Jungmann (G-CLKV)	Privately owned, Henstridge, Somerset	
A-44	CASA 1.131E Jungmann 2000 (G-CIUE)	*Written off, unknown location, August 2024*	
A-57	CASA 1.131E Jungmann (G-BECT)	Privately owned, Deanland, E. Sussex	
A-91	CASA 1.131E Jungmann (F-AYKG)	Privately owned, la Ferté-Alais, France	
A-125	Pilatus P2-05 (G-BLKZ) (fuselage)	Current location unknown (ex-Cornwall Aviation Heritage Museum, Newquay, Cornwall)	
A-806	Pilatus P3-03 (G-BTLL)	Privately owned, Guist, Norfolk	
A-815	Pilatus P3-03 (HB-RCQ)	Privately owned, Locarno, Switzerland	
A-818	Pilatus P3-03 (HB-RCH)	Privately owned, Locarno, Switzerland	
A-829	Pilatus P3-03 (HB-RCJ)	Privately owned, Altenrhein, Switzerland	
A-873	Pilatus P3-03 (OO-RDS)	Privately owned, Brustem, Belgium	
C-509	EKW C-3605 (HB-RDH)	*To Oklahoma City, OK, USA as N56FC*	
C-552	EKW C-3605 (G-DORN)	Privately owned, Little Gransden, Cambs	
C-558	EKW C-3605 (G-CCYZ)	Privately owned, Wickenby, Lincs	
J-143	F+W D-3801 (MS406) (HB-RCF) [7]	Privately owned, Bex, Switzerland	
J-1008	DH100 Vampire FB6	de Havilland Aircraft Museum, London Colney	
J-1169	DH100 Vampire FB6	Privately owned, Henley-on-Thames, Oxon	
J-1172	DH100 Vampire FB6 (8487M)	Morayvia, Kinloss, Scotland	
J-1573	DH112 Venom FB50 (G-VICI) <ff>	Privately owned, Tetbury, Glos	
J-1605	DH112 Venom FB50 (G-BLID)	Gatwick Aviation Museum, Charlwood, Surrey	
J-1632	DH112 Venom FB50 (G-VNOM) <ff>	Privately owned, Lavendon, Bucks	
J-1649	DH112 Venom FB50 <ff>	Privately owned, Tangmere, West Sussex	
J-1704	DH112 Venom FB54	RAF Museum, stored Cosford, Shropshire	
J-1790	DH112 Venom FB54 (G-BLKA/*WR410*)	Historic Aviation Centre, Fishburn, Co. Durham	
J-4110	Hawker Hunter F58A (XF318/G-CJWL)	Hawker Hunter Aviation Ltd, stored Leeming	
J-4201	Hawker Hunter T68 (WV332/HB-RVR)	Privately owned, Altenrhein, Switzerland	
N-322	Hawker Hunter T68 (J-4205/G-EHLW)	*Transferred to USA, July 2024*	
J-4206	Hawker Hunter T68 (HB-RVV)	Fliegermuseum Altenrhein, Switzerland	
U-80	Bücker Bü133D Jungmeister (G-BUKK)	Privately owned, Henstridge, Somerset	
U-88	Bücker Bü133D Jungmeister (G-CMCX)	The Shuttleworth Collection, Old Warden, Beds	
U-95	Bücker Bü133C Jungmeister (G-BVGP)	Privately owned, Turweston, Bucks	
U-99	Bücker Bü133C Jungmeister (G-AXMT)	Privately owned, Breighton, E. Yorks	
U-1215	DH115 Vampire T11 (XE998)	Solent Sky, Southampton, Hants	
V-54	SE3130 Alouette II (2-BVSD)	Privately owned, Glos	

Notes	Serial	Type (code/other identity)	Owner/operator, location or fate
	UNITED ARAB EMIRATES		
	005	Piper PA.44 (G-BHFE)	Privately owned, Shoreham, W. Sussex (stored)
	DU-103	Bell 206B JetRanger II	Privately owned, stored Coney Park, Leeds, W. Yorks
	USA		
	-	Noorduyn AT-16 Harvard IIB (KLu B-168)	American Air Museum, Duxford, Cambs
	14	Boeing-Stearman A75N-1 Kaydet (3486/G-ISDN)	Privately owned, Oaksey Park, Wilts
	18	Agusta-Bell AB204B (MM80279)	MAG36-UK, Manston, Kent
	23	Fairchild PT-23 (N49272) [23]	Privately owned, Sleap, Shropshire
	26	Boeing-Stearman A75N-1 Kaydet (G-BAVO)	Privately owned, Enstone, Oxon
	27	Boeing-Stearman N2S-3 Kaydet (4304/G-CJYK/EI-ABS)	Privately owned, Weston, Dublin, Eire
	28	Boeing-Stearman PT-27 Kaydet (42-15666/G-CKSR)	Privately owned, RAF Woodvale, Merseyside
	29	Boeing-Stearman N2S-3 Kaydet (38140/N73410)	Privately owned, Old Warden, Beds
	29	Boeing-Stearman PT-17 Kaydet (42-17481/N1771B)	Aero Vintage Academy, la Ferté-Alais, France
	31	Boeing-Stearman A75N-1 Kaydet (42-16338/G-KAYD)	Privately owned, Sherburn in Elmet, N. Yorks
	43	Boeing-Stearman PT-13D Kaydet (42-17152/G-CIPE)	Privately owned, Compton Abbas, Dorset
	43	Noorduyn AT-16 Harvard IIB (43-13064/G-AZSC) [SC]	Privately owned, Goodwood, W. Sussex
	44	Boeing-Stearman D75N-1 Kaydet (42-15852/G-LIIZ)	Privately owned, Breighton, E. Yorks
	55	Boeing-Stearman PT-18 Kaydet (40-1991/F-HIZI)	Aero Vintage Academy, la Ferté-Alais, France
	56	NA T-6G Texan (49-3056/F-HLEA)	Aero Vintage Academy, la Ferté-Alais, France
	72	NA SNJ-5 Texan (42-85897/G-NNEE) [JF-72]	DH Heritage Flights Ltd, Compton Abbas, Dorset
	75	Boeing-Stearman E75 Kaydet (42-109026/38438/G-LXXV)	Privately owned, Enstone, Oxon
	85	WAR P-47 Thunderbolt <R> (G-BTBI)	Privately owned, Perth, Scotland
	104	Boeing-Stearman PT-13D Kaydet (42-16931/N4712V) [W]	Privately owned, Hardwick, Norfolk
	107	Boeing-Stearman PT-17 Kaydet (42-16107/N62658)	Privately owned, Popham, Hants
	112	Boeing-Stearman PT-13D Kaydet (42-17397/G-BSWC)	Privately owned, Gloucester, Glos
	131	Boeing-Stearman PT-17 Kaydet (38254/N74677)	Privately owned, Enstone, Oxon
	164	Boeing-Stearman PT-13B Kaydet (41-823/N60320)	Privately owned, Fenland, Lincs
	286	Boeing-Stearman N2S-4 Kaydet (55749/N10053)	Privately owned, Breighton, E. Yorks (stored)
	317	Boeing-Stearman PT-18 Kaydet (41-61042/G-CIJN)	Privately owned, Goodwood, W. Sussex
	349	Boeing-Stearman N2S-2 Kaydet (3572/N2JS) [1349]	Privately owned, Old Warden, Beds
	371	Boeing-Stearman PT-17 Kaydet (41-927/G-CKXY)	Privately owned, Old Warden, Beds
	379	Boeing-Stearman PT-13D Kaydet (42-16865/G-ILLE)	*Sold in the USA, January 2025*
	383	Boeing-Stearman N2S-3 Kaydet (38423/N68941)	Aero Vintage Academy, la Ferté-Alais, France
	399	Boeing-Stearman N2S-5 Kaydet (38495/N67193)	Privately owned, Gelnhausen, Germany
	405	Boeing-Stearman PT-17 Kaydet (40-1885/F-AZSN)	Privately owned, St Rambert d'Albon, France
	411	Boeing-Stearman N2S-4 Kaydet (30010/G-BTFG)	Privately owned, Postling, Kent
	443983	Boeing-Stearman E75 Kaydet (N43YP) [6018]	Privately owned, East Hanney, Oxon
	466	Boeing-Stearman PT-13A Kaydet (37-0089/G-PTBA)	Privately owned, Halfpenny Green, Staffs
	540	Piper L-4H Grasshopper (43-29877/G-BCNX)	Privately owned, Monewden, Suffolk
	560	Bell UH-1H Iroquois (73-22077/G-HUEY)	Privately owned, North Weald, Essex
	578	Boeing-Stearman N2S-5 Kaydet (N1364V)	Privately owned, North Weald, Essex
	578	Boeing-Stearman PT-17 Kaydet (41-8196/N67195)	Privately owned, Abbeyshrule, Eire
	582	Boeing-Stearman PT-17 Kaydet (42-16663/4826/G-CJIN)	Privately owned, Breighton, E. Yorks
	586	Boeing-Stearman N2S-3 Kaydet (07874/N74650)	Privately owned, Seppe, The Netherlands
	628	Beech D17S (44-67761/N18V)	*Repainted as DR628/PB1*
	669	Boeing-Stearman A75N-1 Kaydet (37869/G-CCXA)	Privately owned, Old Buckenham, Norfolk
	671	Boeing-Stearman PT-13D Kaydet (61181/G-CGPY)	Privately owned, Dunkeswell, Devon
	699	Boeing-Stearman N2S-3 Kaydet (38233/G-CCXB)	Privately owned, Goodwood, W. Sussex
	716	Boeing-Stearman PT-13D Kaydet (42-17553/N1731B)	Privately owned, Oaksey Park, Wilts
	718	Boeing-Stearman PT-13D Kaydet (42-17555/N5345N)	Privately owned, Tibenham, Norfolk
	744	Boeing-Stearman A75N-1 Kaydet (42-16532/OO-USN/ D-EMFL)	Privately owned, Tannheim, Germany
	796	Boeing-Stearman PT-13D Kaydet (42-17378/N43SV)	Aero Vintage Academy, la Ferté-Alais, France
	805	Boeing-Stearman PT-17 Kaydet (42-17642/N3922B)	Privately owned, Tibenham, Norfolk
	854	Ryan PT-22 Recruit (41-20854/G-BTBH)	Privately owned, Turweston, Bucks
	855	Ryan PT-22 Recruit (41-15510/N56421)	Privately owned, Sleap, Shropshire
	897	Aeronca 11AC Chief (G-BJEV) [E]	Privately owned, English Bicknor, Glos
	1102	Boeing-Stearman N2S-5 Kaydet (43449/G-AZLE) [102]	DH Heritage Flights Ltd, Compton Abbas, Dorset
	2610	Boeing-Stearman A75 Kaydet (4280/G-FRDM) [408]	Privately owned, Bicester, Oxon
	2909	Naval Aircraft Factory N3N-3 (F-AZNF) [69]	Privately owned, la Ferté-Alais, France
	3397	Boeing-Stearman N2S-3 Kaydet (G-OBEE) [174]	Privately owned, Inverness, Scotland

Serial	Type (code/other identity)	Owner/operator, location or fate	Notes
3583	Piper L-4B Grasshopper (43-0583/G-FINT) [44-D]	Privately owned, Eggesford, Devon	
3681	Piper L-4J Grasshopper (44-80248/G-AXGP)	Privately owned, Bentwaters, Suffolk	
3815	Piper L-4B Grasshopper (43-0815/F-BEGD) [R-26]	Privately owned, France	
3914	Piper L-4B Grasshopper (43-0914/G-BHZU) [72-F]	Privately owned, Sandtoft, Lincs	
4273	Boeing-Stearman PT-13D Kaydet (F-AZJR) [741]	Privately owned, la Ferté-Alais, France	
4406	Naval Aircraft Factory N3N-3 (G-ONAF) [12]	Privately owned, Sandown, IOW	
4445	Naval Aircraft Factory N3N-3 (G-CFXT) [228]	Privately owned, Leeds East, N. Yorks	
6136	Boeing-Stearman A75N-1 Kaydet(42-16136/G-BRUJ/ OM-WAR) [205]	Privately owned, Dubová, Slovakia	
6771	Republic F-84F Thunderstreak (BAF FU-6)	Bentwaters Cold War Museum, Suffolk	
7616	WSK SBLim-2 (MiG-15UTI) (1A01004/N104CJ) [TC-616]	Norwegian AF Historical Sqn, Rygge, Norway	
7797	Aeronca L-16A Grasshopper (47-0797/G-BFAF)	Privately owned, Finmere, Oxon	
8010S	Replica SE5a <R> (PH-WWI/G-CCBN) [19]	Privately owned, White Waltham, Berks	
8242	NA F-86A Sabre (48-0242/N196B) [FU-242]	Midland Air Museum, Coventry, Warks	
01532	Northrop F-5E Tiger II <R> (BAPC.336)	RAF Alconbury, Cambs, on display	
01675	Canadair CL-13B Sabre 6 (F-AYSB) [FU-675]	Privately owned, Avignon-Caumont, France	
02538	Fairchild PT-19A Cornell (N33870)	Privately owned, Mendlesham, Suffolk	
07539	Boeing-Stearman N2S-3 Kaydet (N63590) [143]	Privately owned, Solent Airport, Hants (for sale)	
O-14419	Lockheed T-33A Shooting Star (51-4419)	Midland Air Museum, Coventry, Warks	
O-14781	Cessna L-19A Bird Dog (51-4781/G-VNAM)	Privately owned, Membury, Berks	
15372	Piper L-18C Super Cub (51-15372/N123SA) [372-A]	Privately owned, Crowfield, Suffolk	
15943	NA AT-6D Texan (41-34671/F-AZSC) [TA-943]	Privately owned, Epernay, France	
15979	Hughes OH-6A Cayuse (69-15979)	RAF Mildenhall, Suffolk, instructional use	
15990	Bell AH-1F Hueycobra (70-15990)	Army Flying Museum, Middle Wallop, Hants	
16037	Piper J-3C-65 Cub (G-BSFD)	Privately owned, Sleap, Shropshire	
16171	NA F-86D Sabre (51-6171)	North-East Land, Sea & Air Museums, Usworth, T&W	
16445	Bell AH-1F Hueycobra (69-16445)	Defence Academy of the UK, Shrivenham, Oxon	
16506	Hughes OH-6A Cayuse (67-16506)	The Helicopter Museum, Weston-super-Mare	
16544	NA AT-6A Texan (41-16544/N13FY) [FY]	Privately owned, Hilversum, The Netherlands	
16579	Bell UH-1H Iroquois (66-16579)	The Helicopter Museum, Weston-super-Mare	
16718	Lockheed T-33A Shooting Star (51-6718) [TR-999]	City of Norwich Aviation Museum, Norfolk	
O-16957	Cessna L-19A Bird Dog (N51-16957/N5308G)	Privately owned, Sleap, Shropshire	
17206	NA T-28S Fennec (51-7545/N14113) [TL-206]	Privately owned, Nangis-Les Loges, France	
17692	NA T-28S Fennec (51-7692/G-TROY) [TL-692]	Privately owned, Coventry, Warks	
17962	Lockheed SR-71A Blackbird (61-7962)	American Air Museum, Duxford, Cambs	
18263	Boeing-Stearman PT-17 Kaydet (41-8263/N38940) [822]	Privately owned, Tibenham, Norfolk	
19252	Lockheed T-33A Shooting Star (51-9252)	Bentwaters Cold War Museum, Suffolk	
21300	Cessna O-2A Super Skymaster (67-21300/N590D)	Privately owned, Lelystad, The Netherlands	
21509	Bell UH-1H Iroquois (72-21509/G-UHIH)	Privately owned, Wesham, Lancs	
21605	Bell UH-1H Iroquois (72-21605)	American Air Museum, Duxford, Cambs	
23648	Breda-Nardi NH-500MC (MM81000)	Privately owned, Bristol, Glos	
24535	Kaman HH-43F Huskie (62-4535)	Midland Air Museum, Coventry, Warks	
24568	Cessna L-19E Bird Dog (LN-WNO)	Army Aviation Norway, Kjeller, Norway	
24582	Cessna L-19E Bird Dog (G-VDOG)	Privately owned, Glenrothes, Scotland	
26359	Piper L-21B Super Cub (54-2619/G-BNXM) [32]	Privately owned, Brimpton, Berks	
30274	Piper AE-1 Cub Cruiser (F-AZTY)	Privately owned, Nangis, France	
30861	NA TB-25J Mitchell (44-30861/N9089Z)	Privately owned, Balcombe, W. Sussex	
31145	Piper L-4B Grasshopper (43-1145/G-BBLH) [26-G]	Privately owned, Biggin Hill, Kent	
31952	Aeronca O-58B Defender (G-BRPR)	Privately owned, Solent Airport, Hants	
34037	NA TB-25N Mitchell (44-29366/N9115Z/8838M)	Privately owned, East Kirkby, Lincs	
34064	NA B-25J Mitchell (44-31171/N7614C) [8U]	American Air Museum, Duxford, Cambs	
36922	Titan T-51 Mustang (G-CMPC) [WD-Y]	Privately owned, Benwick, Cambs	
37414	McD F-4C Phantom II (63-7414)	Midland Air Museum, stored Coventry, Warks	
39624	Wag Aero Sport Trainer (EI-GMH) [39-D]	Privately owned, Abbeyshrule, Eire	
41386	Thomas-Morse S4 Scout <R> (G-MJTD)	Privately owned, Lutterworth, Leics	
42165	NA F-100D Super Sabre (54-2165) [VM]	IWM, stored Duxford, Cambs	
42196	NA F-100D Super Sabre (54-2196)	Norfolk & Suffolk Avn Museum, Flixton, Suffolk	
43517	Boeing-Stearman N2S-5 Kaydet (G-NZSS) [227]	Privately owned, Woodchurch, Kent	
46214	Grumman TBM-3E Avenger (69327/CF-KCG) [X-3]	Preserved Wirral Museum, Merseyside	
51970	NA AT-6D Texan (41-33888/D-FURI) [V-970]	Privately owned, Aalen, Germany	
53319	Grumman TBM-3E Avenger (HB-RDG) [19]	Privately owned, Bitburg, Germany	
54433	Lockheed T-33A Shooting Star (55-4433) [TR-433]	Norfolk & Suffolk Avn Museum, Flixton, Suffolk	

Notes	Serial	Type (code/other identity)	Owner/operator, location or fate
	55454	NA OV-10B Bronco (158300/99+24/F-AZKM) [26]	Privately owned, Montelimar, France
	55771	Boeing-Stearman N2S-4 Kaydet (N68427) [427]	Privately owned, Dunkeswell, Devon (damaged)
	56498	Douglas C-54Q Skymaster (N44914)	Privately owned, stored North Weald, Essex
	59620	NA AT-6D Texan (F-AZRD/42-44467) [TA-620]	Privately owned, Lens Benifontaine, France
	60344	Ryan Navion (N4956C)	Privately owned, Earls Colne, Essex
	60689	Boeing B-52D Stratofortress (56-0689)	American Air Museum, Duxford, Cambs
	O-63008	NA F-100D Super Sabre (54-2223) [LT]	Newark Air Museum, Winthorpe, Notts
	63319	NA F-100D Super Sabre (54-2269) [FW-319]	RAF Lakenheath, Suffolk, on display
	66692	Lockheed U-2CT (56-6692)	American Air Museum, Duxford, Cambs
	70270	McD F-101B Voodoo (57-270) (fuselage)	Midland Air Museum, stored Coventry, Warks
	82062	DHC U-6A Beaver (58-2062)	Midland Air Museum, Coventry, Warks
	82127	Cessna 310 (G-APNJ)	Newark Air Museum, Winthorpe, Notts
	85061	NA SNJ-5 Texan (G-OSNJ) [C-124]	Privately owned, Kidlington, Oxon
	90669	NA AT-6C Harvard IIa (42-85886/F-AZBL) [TA-669]	Privately owned, Pouilly, France
	90747	NA AT-6D Texan (F-AZRB) [PA-47]	Privately owned, Blois-le Breuil, France
	91007	Lockheed T-33A Shooting Star (51-9036) [TR-007]	Newark Air Museum, Winthorpe, Notts
	96995	CV F4U-4 Corsair (OE-EAS) [RB-37]	Flying Bulls, Salzburg, Austria
	111836	NA AT-6C Harvard IIa (41-33262/G-TSIX) [JZ-6]	Privately owned, Earls Colne, Oxon
	111989	Cessna L-19A Bird Dog (51-11989/N33600)	Army Flying Museum, Middle Wallop, Hants
	113570	Curtiss P-40E Warhawk (41-13570/OO-WHK/F-AYKH)	Privately owned, Brasschaat, Belgium
	115042	NA T-6G Texan (51-15042/G-BGHU) [TA-042]	Privately owned, Postling, Kent
	115227	NA T-6G Texan (51-15227/G-BKRA)	Privately owned, Shoreham, W. Sussex
	115373	Piper L-18C Super Cub (51-15373/G-AYPM) [A-373]	Privately owned, Popham, Hants
	115629	Piper L-18C Super Cub (51-15629/N7238X)	Privately owned, Tollerton, Notts
	115684	Piper L-21A Super Cub (51-15684/G-BKVM) [849-DC]	Privately owned, Dunkeswell, Devon
	117415	Canadair CT-133 Silver Star (21231/G-BYOY) [TR-415]	RAF Manston History Museum, Kent
	117529	Lockheed T-33A Shooting Star (17473) [TR-529]	Midland Air Museum, Coventry, Warks
	121714	Grumman F8F-2P Bearcat (G-RUMM) [201-B]	The Fighter Collection, Duxford, Cambs
	123716	CV F4U-5NL Corsair (124541/D-FCOR) [19-WF]	Meier Motors, Bremgarten, Germany
	124143	Douglas AD-4NA Skyraider (F-AZDP) [205-RM]	Amicale J-B Salis, la Ferté-Alais, France
	124485	Boeing B-17G Flying Fortress (44-85784/G-BEDF)[DF-A]	B-17 Preservation Ltd, Duxford, Cambs
	124724	CV F4U-5NL Corsair (F-AZEG) [22-NP]	Les Casques de Cuir, La Ferté-Alais, France
	126922	Douglas AD-4NA Skyraider (G-RADR) [503-H]	Kennet Aviation, North Weald, Essex
	133908	NA AT-6D Texan (41-33908/EX935/G-BGOR)	Privately owned, Sywell, Shropshire
	134076	NA AT-6D Texan (41-34671/F-AZSC) [TA-943]	Privately owned, Epernay, France
	138171	NA T-28B Trojan (F-AYBA) [BA-8171/841]	Privately owned, France
	138343	NA T-28B Trojan (F-AYSL) [212]	Privately owned, Nangis-Les-Loges, France
	138352	NA T-28B Trojan (OE-EMM) [TP-642]	Flying Bulls, Salzburg, Austria
	138360	NA T-28B Trojan (F-AYVF) [KB-5]	Privately owned, Persan-Beaumont, France
	140547	NA T-28C Trojan (F-AZHN) [IF-28]	Privately owned, Toussus le Noble, France
	140566	NA T-28C Trojan (N556EB) [252]	Privately owned, la Ferté-Alais, France
	146287	NA T-28C Trojan (F-AZQV) [WS-08]	Privately owned, La Roche-sur-Yon, France
	146289	NA T-28C Trojan (N99153) [2W/FG-289]	Norfolk & Suffolk Avn Museum, Flixton, Suffolk
	150225	WS58 Wessex 60 (G-AWOX) [123]	Privately owned, Lulsgate, Glos
	155529	McD F-4J(UK) Phantom II (ZE359) [AJ-114]	American Air Museum, Duxford, Cambs
	155848	McD F-4S Phantom II [WT-11]	National Museum of Flight, E. Fortune, Scotland
	159233	HS AV-8A Harrier [CG-33]	IWM North, Salford Quays, Gtr Manchester
	162068	McD AV-8B Harrier II (fuselage)	Harrier Heritage Centre, RAF Wittering, Cambs
	162071	McD AV-8B Harrier II (fuselage)	Rolls-Royce, Filton, Glos
	162074	McD AV-8B Harrier II <ff>	Privately owned, Redditch, Worcs
	162730	McD AV-8B Harrier II <ff>	Privately owned, Liverpool, Merseyside(for sale)
	162737	McD AV-8B Harrier II (fuselage) [38]	RAF, Wittering, Cambs
	162958	McD AV-8B Harrier II <ff>	QinetiQ, Farnborough, Hants
	162964	McD AV-8B Harrier II <ff>	Harrier Heritage Centre, RAF Wittering, Cambs
	162964	McD AV-8B Harrier II <rf>	Privately owned, Charlwood, Surrey
	163205	McD AV-8B Harrier II (fuselage)	Privately owned, Thorpe Wood, N. Yorks
	163423	McD AV-8B Harrier II <ff>	QinetiQ, Boscombe Down, Wilts
	163423	McD AV-8B Harrier II	Privately owned, Leeds Castle, Kent
	210766	Douglas C-47B Skytrain (42-100611)(comp K-1) [4U]	Wings Museum, Balcombe, W. Sussex
	217786	Boeing-Stearman PT-17 Kaydet (41-8169/CF-EQS) [25]	American Air Museum, Duxford, Cambs
	224319	Douglas C-47B Skytrain (44-77047/G-AMSN) <ff>	Privately owned, Sussex
	226413	Republic P-47D Thunderbolt (45-49192/N47DD) [UN-Z]	American Air Museum, Duxford, Cambs
	234539	Fairchild PT-19B Cornell (42-34539/N50429) [63]	Flying Bulls, Salzburg, Austria

Serial	Type (code/other identity)	Owner/operator, location or fate	Notes
236657	Piper L-4A Grasshopper (42-36657/G-BGSJ) [72-D]	Privately owned, Henstridge, Somerset	
237123	Waco CG-4A Hadrian <R> (fuselage)	Repainted as 319764	
238133	Boeing B-17G Flying Fortress (44-83735/F-BDRS) [C]	American Air Museum, Duxford, Cambs	
238410	Piper L-4A Grasshopper (42-38410/G-BHPK) [44-A]	Privately owned, Tibenham, Norfolk	
241079	Waco CG-4A Hadrian <R> (BAPC.370)	Dumfries & Galloway Avn Mus, Dumfries, Scotland	
243809	Waco CG-4A Hadrian (BAPC.185)	Army Flying Museum, Middle Wallop, Hants	
252983	Schweizer TG-3A (42-52983/N66630/BGA6084)	Gliding Heritage Centre, Lasham, Hants	
268810	Douglas C-53D (42-68810/F-HVED) [D/T3-003]	Privately owned, Rennes–St. Jaques Aeroport, France	
285068	NA AT-6D Texan (42-85068/G-KAMY)	Privately owned, Old Warden, Beds	
298177	Stinson L-5A Sentinel (42-98177/N6438C) [8-R]	Privately owned, Tibenham, Norfolk	
298381	Stinson L-5A Sentinel (42-98680/G-CMIW)	Privately owned, White Waltham, Berks	
300496	Piper L-4B Grasshopper (F-GHIP) [86-M]	Privately owned, France	
313048	NA AT-6D Texan (44-81506/OO-JOY)	Privately owned, Wevelgem, Belgium	
313142	Douglas C-47A Skytrain (42-93251/F-BLOZ)	Amicale J-B Salis, la Ferté-Alais, France	
314887	Fairchild Argus III (43-14887/G-AJPI)	Privately owned, Eelde, The Netherlands	
315509	Douglas C-47A Skytrain (43-15509/G-BHUB) [W7-S]	American Air Museum, Duxford, Cambs	
315536	Douglas C-47A Skytrain (43-15536/G-BGCG)	Skysport Engineering Ltd, Hatch, Beds	
319764	Waco CG-4A Hadrian (237123/BAPC.157) (fuselage)	Yorkshire Air Museum, Elvington, N. Yorks	
329282	Piper J-3C-65 Cub (43-29282/N46779)	Privately owned, Abbots Bromley, Staffs	
329405	Piper L-4A Grasshopper (43-29405/G-BCOB) [23-A]	Privately owned, Bicester, Oxon	
329417	Piper L-4A Grasshopper (42-38400/G-BDHK)	Privately owned, English Bicknor, Glos	
329471	Piper L-4A Grasshopper (43-29471/G-BGXA) [44-F]	Privately owned, Martley, Worcs	
329594	Piper L-4H Grasshopper (43-29594/G-BROR)	Privately owned, East Winch, Norfolk	
329601	Piper L-4H Grasshopper (43-29601/G-AXHR) [44-D]	Privately owned, Nayland, Suffolk	
329707	Piper L-4H Grasshopper (43-29707/G-BFBY) [44-S]	Privately owned, Old Buckenham, Norfolk	
329854	Piper L-4H Grasshopper (43-29854/G-BMKC) [44-R]	Privately owned, Biggin Hill, Kent	
329934	Piper L-4H Grasshopper (43-29934/G-BCPH) [72-B]	Privately owned, Garford, Oxon	
330238	Piper L-4H Grasshopper (43-30238/G-LIVH) [24-A]	Privately owned, Yarcombe, Devon	
330244	Piper L-4H Grasshopper (43-30244/G-CGIY) [46-C]	Privately owned, Perth, Scotland	
330314	Piper L-4H Grasshopper (43-30314/G-BAET)	Privately owned, Winwick, Cambs	
330372	Piper L-4H Grasshopper (43-30372/G-AISX)	Privately owned, Booker, Bucks	
330426	Piper L-4J Grasshopper (45-4884/N61787) [53-K]	Privately owned, Podington, Beds	
330485	Piper L-4H Grasshopper (43-30485/G-AJES) [44-C]	Privately owned, Shifnal, Shropshire	
379994	Piper J-3L-65 Cub (G-BPUR) [52-J]	Privately owned, Popham, Hants	
411622	NA P-51D Mustang (44-74427/F-AZSB/OE-EFB) [G4-C]	Flying Bulls, Salzburg, Austria	
411631	NA P-51D Mustang (44-73979/472218) [MX-V]	American Air Museum, Duxford, Cambs	
413305	NA P-51D Mustang (44-74391/N351MX) [WR-Z]	Privately owned, Bern, Switzerland	
413317	NA P-51D Mustang (44-74409/N51RT) [VF-B]	RAF Museum, Hendon, Gtr London	
413357	NA P-51D Mustang <R> [B7-R]	Privately owned, Byfleet, Surrey	
413410	NA P-51D Mustang <R> (BAPC.255)	Bottisham Airfield Museum, Cambs	
413521	NA P-51D Mustang (44-13521/G-MRLL) [5Q-B]	Privately owned, Duxford, Cambs	
413578	NA P-51D Mustang (44-74923/PH-JAT) [C5-W]	Privately owned, Lelystad, The Netherlands	
413779	NA P-51D Mustang (44-73877/G-CMDK) [WD-C]	Privately owned, East Midlands Airport, Leics	
413926	Stewart S-51 Mustang (G-CGOI) [E2-S]	Privately owned, Benwick, Cambs	
414237	NA P-51D Mustang (44-73656/N51VL/G-MCSW) [HO-W]	Privately owned, Biggin Hill, Kent	
414419	NA P-51D Mustang (45-11518/G-MSTG/G-CLNV) [23]	Privately owned, la Ferté-Alais, France	
414673	Bonsall Replica Mustang (G-BDWM) [LH-I]	Privately owned, Netherthorpe, Derbyshire	
414907	Titan T-51 Mustang (G-DHYS) [CY-S]	Privately owned, Compton Abbas, Dorset	
415152	CAC Mustang Mk.21 (A68-110/VH-MFT/G-JERK) [QI-T]	Privately owned, Sywell, Northants	
433915	Consolidated PBV-1A Canso A (RCAF 11005/G-PBYA)	Privately owned, Duxford, Cambs	
434602	Douglas A-26B Invader (44-34602/N167B) [B]	Nordic Warbirds, Sandefjord, Sweden	
436021	Piper J-3C-65 Cub (G-BWEZ)	Privately owned, Archerfield, Lothian, Scotland	
436784	Beech G18S (N45CF)	Privately owned, Bressaucourt, Switzerland	
441968	Titan T-51 Mustang (G-FION) [VF-E]	Written off Netherthorpe, Derbyshire, Jan 2024	
442268	Noorduyn AT-16 Harvard IIb (KF568/LN-TEX) [TA-268]	Privately owned, Kjeller, Norway	
454467	Piper L-4J Grasshopper (45-4467/G-BILI) [44-J]	Privately owned, Bicester, Oxon	
454471	Piper L-4J Grasshopper (45-4471/G-AKTH)	Privately owned, Goodwood, W. Sussex	
454537	Piper L-4J Grasshopper (45-4537/G-BFDL) [04-J]	Privately owned, Insch, Aberdeenshire, Scotland (rebuild)	
454630	Piper L-4J Grasshopper (45-4446/G-BDOL) [LI-7]	Privately owned, Bidford-on-Avon, Warks	
461748	Boeing B-29A Superfortress (44-61748/G-BHDK) [Y]	American Air Museum, Duxford, Cambs	

119

Notes	Serial	Type (code/other identity)	Owner/operator, location or fate
	464005	NA P-51D Mustang (44-64005/N51CK) [E9-Z]	Privately owned, Sywell, Northants
	472216	NA P-51D Mustang (44-72216/G-BIXL) [HO-M]	Privately owned, Goodwood, W. Sussex
	472218	Titan T-51 Mustang (G-MUZY) [WZ-I]	Privately owned, Tibenham, Norfolk
	472773	NA P-51D Mustang (44-72773/D-FPSI) [WD-U]	Meier Motors, Bremgarten, Germany
	472922	NA TF-51D Mustang (44-72922/OO-RYL) [L2-W]	Privately owned, Brasschaat, Belgium
	472927	NA P-51D Mustang (44-74453/NL51ZW) [WZ-W]	Privately owned, Bremgarten, Germany
	472934	NA P-51D Mustang (45-11553/G-FSID) [VF-T]	Privately owned, Sywell, Northants
	474008	Jurca MJ77 Gnatsum (G-PSIR) [VF-R]	Privately owned, Fishburn, Co. Durham
	474425	NA P-51D Mustang (44-74425/PH-PSI) [OC-G]	Damaged 30th September 2023, Oostwold, Netherlands
	479712	Piper L-4H Grasshopper (44-79826/G-AHIP) [8-R]	Privately owned, Coleford, Glos
	479744	Piper L-4H Grasshopper (44-79744/G-BGPD) [49-M]	Privately owned, Marsh, Bucks
	479766	Piper L-4H Grasshopper (44-79766/G-BKHG) [63-D]	Privately owned, Duxford, Cambs
	479781	Piper L-4H Grasshopper (44-79781/G-AISS)	Privately owned, Insch, Scotland (restoration)
	479878	Piper L-4H Grasshopper (44-79878/G-BEUI) [57-A]	Privately owned, Roche, Cornwall
	479897	Piper L-4H Grasshopper (44-79897/G-BOXJ) [JD]	Privately owned, Rochester, Kent
	480015	Piper L-4H Grasshopper (44-80015/G-AKIB) [44-M]	Privately owned, Perranporth, Cornwall
	480133	Piper L-4J Grasshopper (44-80133/G-BDCD) [44-B]	Privately owned, Slinfold, W. Sussex
	480173	Piper L-4J Grasshopper (44-80609/G-RRSR) [57-H]	Privately owned, Shotteswell, Warks
	480231	Piper L-4J Grasshopper (44-80231/F-BFMQ) [84-V]	Privately owned, Avignon-Caumont, France
	480321	Piper L-4J Grasshopper (44-80321/G-FRAN) [44-H]	Privately owned, Rayne, Essex
	480361	Piper Cub J-3C-65 (44-80361/EI-BIO) [47-H]	Privately owned, Walshestown, Ireland
	480480	Piper L-4J Grasshopper (44-80480/G-BECN) [44-E]	Privately owned, Audley End, Cambs
	480594	Piper L-4J Grasshopper (G-BEDJ)	Privately owned, Stow Maries, Essex
	480636	Piper L-4J Grasshopper (44-80636/G-AXHP) [58-A]	Privately owned, Great Ponton, Lincs
	480723	Piper L-4J Grasshopper (44-80723/G-BFZB) [E5-J]	Privately owned, Duxford, Cambs
	480752	Piper L-4J Grasshopper (44-80752/G-BCXJ) [39-E]	Privately owned, Melksham, Wilts
	480762	Piper L-4J Grasshopper (44-80762/EI-BBV)	Privately owned, Ballyboy, Eire
	481273	CCF T-6J Harvard IV (20306/G-CJWE) [NG]	Privately owned, Leicester, Leics
	483868	Boeing B-17G Flying Fortress (44-83868/N5237V) [A-N]	RAF Museum, Hendon, Gtr London
	484786	NA F-6D Mustang (44-84786/N51BS) [5M-K]	Privately owned, Ceresara, Italy (damaged)
	493209	NA T-6G Texan (49-3209/G-DDMV/*41*)	Privately owned, Headcorn, Kent
	517749	NA T-28S Fennec (F-AZHR) [749]	Privately owned, Beaune-Challenges, France
	521475	CCF T-6J Harvard IV (F-AZGB/20384)	Privately owned, Pontoise, France
	542454	Piper L-21B Super Cub (54-2454/G-KUBY)	Privately owned, Duxford, Cambs
	549192	Republic P-47D Thunderbolt (45-49192/G-THUN) [F4-J]	Privately owned, Duxford/Sywell
	779465	Hiller UH-12C (N5315V)	Privately owned, Lower Upham, Hants
	2106638	Titan T-51 Mustang (G-CIFD) [E9-R]	Privately owned, Shobdon, Herefordshire
	2100882	Douglas C-47A Skytrain (42-100882/N473DC) [3X-P]	Privately owned, North Weald, Essex
	2100884	Douglas C-47A Skytrain (42-100884/N147DC) [S6-A]	Privately owned, Dunsfold, Surrey
	2105915	Curtiss P-40N Kittyhawk (42-105915/F-AZKU)	France's Flying Warbirds, Melun, France
	03-08003	B-V CH-47F Chinook (comp 83-24121) [DT]	RAF Odiham, Hants, at main gate
	03-33119	General Atomics MQ-1B Predator [CH]	RAF Museum, Hendon, Gtr London
	03-33120	General Atomics MQ-1B Predator [CH]	American Air Museum, Duxford, Cambs
	3-1923	Aeronca O-58B Defender (43-1923/G-BRHP)	Privately owned, Eggesford, Devon
	18-2001	Piper L-18C Super Cub (52-2401/G-BIZV)	Privately owned, Wicklow, Ireland
	22-296	Eberhardt SE5E Replica (G-BLXT)	Privately owned
	37-002	Douglas AD-4NA Skyraider (127002/F-AZHK) [TC]	Privately owned, Avignon-Caumont, France
	39-139	Beech YC-43 Traveler (N295BS)	Duke of Brabant AF, Eindhoven, The Netherlands
	39-285	Curtiss P-40B Warhawk	The Fighter Collection, Duxford, Cambs (wreck)
	39-287	Curtiss P-40B Warhawk	The Fighter Collection, Duxford, Cambs (wreck)
	40-2538	Fairchild PT-19A Cornell (N33870)	*See entry for 02538*
	41-8689	Boeing-Stearman PT-17D Kaydet (G-BIXN) (frame)	Privately owned, Rendcomb, Glos
	41-13557	Curtiss P-40C Warhawk (G-CIIO) [160,10AB]	The Fighter Collection, Duxford, Cambs
	41-19393	Douglas A-20C Havoc (wreck)	Wings Museum, Balcombe, W. Sussex
	41-33275	NA AT-6C Texan (G-BICE) [CE]	Privately owned, Great Oakley, Essex
	41-35253	Martin B-26C Marauder <rf>	Boxted Airfield Museum, Essex
	42-9749	Curtiss TP-40N Kittyhawk (N293FR)	Privately owned, Biggin Hill, Kent
	42-103007	NA P-51C Mustang (wreck)	Lincolnshire Avn Heritage Centre, East Kirkby, Lincs
	42-12417	Noorduyn AT-16 Harvard IIb (KLu. B-163)	Newark Air Museum, Winthorpe, Notts
	42-17335	Boeing-Stearman PT-13D Kaydet (G-EDII)	Privately owned, Great Oakley, Northants
	42-35870	Taylorcraft DCO-65 (G-BWLJ) [129]	Privately owned, Hexham, Northumberland

Serial	Type (code/other identity)	Owner/operator, location or fate	Notes
42-38384	Piper L-4A Grasshopper (G-BHVV)	Privately owned, Old Warden, Beds	
42-46703	Stinson AT-19 Reliant (FK877/N69745)	Privately owned, RNAS Yeovilton, Somerset	
42-58678	Taylorcraft DF-65 (G-BRIY) [IY]	Privately owned, Carlisle, Cumbria	
42-66841	Lockheed P-38H Lightning [153]	Privately owned, stored Sywell, Northants	
42-72343	Douglas C-54B Skymaster <ff>	Privately owned, Southend area, Essex	
42-78044	Aeronca 11AC Chief (G-BRXL)	Privately owned, Andrewsfield, Essex	
42-84555	NA AT-6D Harvard III (FAP.1662/G-ELMH) [EP-H]	Privately owned, Hardwick, Norfolk	
42-93510	Douglas C-47A Skytrain (F-GEFY)[CM] <ff>	Boscombe Down Aviation Collection, Old Sarum, Wilts	
42-109026	Boeing-Stearman E75 Kaydet (38438/G-LXXV)	Repainted as 75	
43-9628	Douglas A-20G Havoc <ff>	Privately owned, Hinckley, Leics	
43-11137	Bell P-63C Kingcobra (wreck)	Wings Museum, Balcombe, W. Sussex	
43-12127	NA AT-6C Harvard IIa (41-33606/F-AZBE) [TA-127]	Privately owned, la Ferté-Alais, France	
43-21664	Douglas A-20G Havoc (wreck)	Wings Museum, Balcombe, W. Sussex	
43-35943	Beech 3N (G-BKRN) [943]	Privately owned, Spanhoe, Northants	
43-36140	NA B-25J Mitchell <ff>	Wings Museum, Balcombe, W. Sussex	
44-4368	Bell P-63C Kingcobra	Wings Museum, Balcombe, W. Sussex	
44-14574	NA P-51D Mustang (fuselage)	East Essex Aviation Museum, Clacton, Essex	
44-30861	NA TB-25J Mitchell (N9089Z)	Wings Museum, Balcombe, W. Sussex	
44-42914	Douglas DC-4 (N31356) <ff>	Privately owned, Burtonwood, Cheshire	
44-51228	Consolidated B-24M Liberator [EC-493]	American Air Museum, Duxford, Cambs	
44-63684	Titan T-51 Mustang (G-CKVJ) [SX-B]	Privately owned, Rochester, Kent	
44-72181	NA P-51D Mustang (N5470V)	Privately owned, Norfolk area (rebuild)	
44-73196	NA P-51D Mustang (G-CITN)	Privately owned, UK (rebuild)	
44-79609	Piper L-4H Grasshopper (G-BHXY) [PR]	Privately owned, Bealbury, Cornwall	
44-79649	Piper L-4H Grasshopper (G-AIIH) [69-K]	Privately owned, Stonesfield, Oxon	
44-80297	Piper Cub J-3C-65 (G-CMIZ)	Privately owned, Booker, Bucks	
44-80594	Piper L-4J Grasshopper (G-BEDJ)	Painted as 480594	
44-80647	Piper L-4J Grasshopper (D-EGAF)	Privately owned, Donauwörth, Germany	
51-7655	NA T-28A Fennec (G-CMNJ) [655]	Privately owned, Sywell, Northants	
51-9036	Lockheed T-33A Shooting Star	Repainted as 91007/TR-007	
51-15319	Piper L-18C Super Cub (G-FUZZ) [A-319]	Privately owned, Elvington, N. Yorks	
51-1555	Piper L-18C Super Cub (G-OSPS/G-CUBT) [A-544]	Privately owned, Hereford, Herefordshire	
54-005	NA F-100D Super Sabre (54-2163) [HA]	Dumfries & Galloway Avn Mus, Dumfries, Scotland	
54-174	NA F-100D Super Sabre (54-2174) [SM]	Midland Air Museum, Coventry, Warks	
54-2445	Piper L-21B Super Cub (G-OTAN) [A-445]	Privately owned, Hawarden, Flintshire, Wales	
54-2447	Piper L-21B Super Cub (G-SCUB)	Privately owned, Anwick, Lincs	
55-138354	NA T-28B Trojan (138354/N1328B) [TL-354]	Privately owned, Zwartberg, Belgium	
63-699	McD F-4C Phantom II (63-7699) [CG]	Midland Air Museum, Coventry, Warks	
64-0553	Lockheed WC-130E Hercules <ff>	RAF Museum, Hendon, Gtr London	
64-17657	Douglas B-26K Counter Invader (N99218) <ff>	Wings Museum, Balcombe, W. Sussex	
65-777	McD F-4C Phantom II (63-7419) [SA]	RAF Lakenheath, Suffolk, on display	
66-374	Helio H.295 Super Courier (G-BAGT) [EO]	Privately owned, Spanhoe, Northants	
67-120	GD F-111E Aardvark (67-0120) [UH]	American Air Museum, Duxford, Cambs	
68-0060	GD F-111E Aardvark <ff>	Dumfries & Galloway Avn Mus, Dumfries, Scotland	
68-8284	Sikorsky MH-53M Pave Low IV	RAF Museum, Cosford, Shropshire	
70-0389	GD F-111E Aardvark (68-0011) [LN]	RAF Lakenheath, Suffolk, on display	
72-1447	GD F-111F Aardvark <ff> (70-2366)	American Air Museum, Duxford, Cambs	
74-0177	GD F-111F Aardvark [LN]	RAF Museum, Cosford, Shropshire	
76-020	McD F-15A Eagle (76-0020) [BT]	American Air Museum, Duxford, Cambs	
76-124	McD F-15B Eagle (76-0124) [LN] [48 FW]	RAF Lakenheath, Suffolk, stored	
77-259	Fairchild A-10A Thunderbolt (77-0259) [AR]	American Air Museum, Duxford, Cambs	
80-219	Fairchild GA-10A Thunderbolt (80-0219) [WR]	Bentwaters Cold War Museum, Suffolk	
80-23476	Sikorsky UH-60A (fuselage)	Privately owned, White Waltham, Berks	
82-23762	B-V CH-47D Chinook <ff>	RAF Benson, Oxon, instructional use	
83-24104	B-V CH-47D Chinook [BN] <ff>	RAF Museum, Hendon, Gtr London	
84-0001	McD F-15C Eagle [LN] bk/y	RAF Lakenheath, Suffolk, GI use	
86-180	McD F-15A Eagle (74-0131) [LN] (starboard side only, painted as 86-169 on port side)	RAF Lakenheath, Suffolk, on display	
86-01677	B-V CH-47D Chinook	RAF, stored Odiham, Hants	
89-00159	B-V CH-47D Chinook	RAF, stored Odiham, Hants	

Notes	Serial	Type (code/other identity)	Owner/operator, location or fate
	108-1601	Stinson 108-1 Voyager (G-CFGE) [H]	Privately owned, Spanhoe, Northants
	146-11042	Wolf W-11 Boredom Fighter (G-BMZX) [7]	Privately owned, Popham, Hants
	146-11083	Wolf W-11 Boredom Fighter (G-BNAI) [5]	Privately owned, Haverfordwest, Wales
	A3-3	NA P-51D Mustang (44-72035/G-SIJJ)	Hangar 11 Collection, North Weald, Essex
	S666	Noorduyn AT-16 Harvard IIb (KF435) [BS]	Maidenhead Heritage Centre, Berks
	X-17	Curtiss P-40F Warhawk (41-19841/G-CGZP)	The Fighter Collection, Duxford, Cambs
	CY-G	Titan T-51 Mustang (G-TSIM)	Privately owned, Shobdon, Herefordshire
	DR628	Beech D17S (44-67761/N18V) [PB1]	Privately owned, Leopoldsburg/Sanicole, Belgium
	DS-1482	Gyrodyne QH-50 DASH	The Helicopter Museum, Weston-super-Mare, Somerset
	NP-22	CV F4U-5NL Corsair (124724/F-AZEG)	Privately owned, la Ferté-Alais, France
	PA50	Curtiss P-36C Hawk (38-0210/G-CIXJ)	The Fighter Collection, Duxford, Cambs
	(RW382)	VS361 Spitfire LF XVIe (G-PBIX) [WZ-RR]	Privately owned, Biggin Hill, Kent
	YUGOSLAVIA		
	30140	Soko P-2 Kraguj (G-RADA) [140]	Privately owned, Fishburn, Co. Durham
	30146	Soko P-2 Kraguj (G-BSXD) [146]	Privately owned, Gamston, Notts
	30149	Soko P-2 Kraguj (G-SOKO) [149]	Privately owned, Perth, Scotland
	51109	Utva-66 (G-CLJX)	Privately owned, Eshott, Northumberland

One of a number of airworthy Flamants to be found in France, this particular example is 260/F-AZKT, based at Albert in the North-West of the country, seen here at la Ferte Alais. *HJC*

Aircraft included in this section include those likely to be seen visiting UK civil and military airfields on transport flights, exchange visits, exercises and for air shows, as well as more comprehensive listings for those countries frequently visited by UK-based enthusiasts. It is not a comprehensive list of *all* aircraft operated by the air arms concerned.

Serial	Type (code/other identity)	Owner/operator, location or fate	Notes
ALBANIA			
TC-ANA	Airbus A.319CJ-115X	*Returned to Turkey as TC-GVC, May 2024*	
ALGERIA			
Ministry of Defence			
7T-VPC	Grumman G.1159C Gulfstream IV-SP (1418)	Ministry of Defence, Boufarik	
7T-VPG	Gulfstream Aerospace Gulfstream V (617)	Ministry of Defence, Boufarik	
7T-VPM	Grumman G.1159C Gulfstream IV-SP (1421)	Ministry of Defence, Boufarik	
7T-VPP	Airbus A.340-541	Ministry of Defence, Boufarik	
7T-VPR	Grumman G.1159C Gulfstream IV-SP (1288)	Ministry of Defence, Boufarik	
7T-VPS	Grumman G.1159C Gulfstream IV-SP (1291)	Ministry of Defence, Boufarik	
Force Aérienne Algérienne (FAA)/Al Quwwat al Jawwiya al Jaza'eriya			
7T-WHA	Lockheed C-130H-30 Hercules (4997)	*Withdrawn from use, Boufarik (damaged 2010)*	
7T-WHB	Lockheed C-130H-30 Hercules (5224)	FAA 2 ETTL, Boufarik	
7T-WHD	Lockheed C-130H-30 Hercules (4987)	FAA 2 ETTL, Boufarik	
7T-WHE	Lockheed C-130H Hercules (4935)	FAA 2 ETTL, Boufarik	
7T-WHF	Lockheed C-130H Hercules (4934)	FAA 2 ETTL, Boufarik	
7T-WHI	Lockheed C-130H Hercules (4930)	FAA 2 ETTL, Boufarik	
7T-WHJ	Lockheed C-130H Hercules (4928)	FAA 2 ETTL, Boufarik	
7T-WHL	Lockheed C-130H-30 Hercules (4989)	FAA 2 ETTL, Boufarik	
7T-WHN	Lockheed C-130H-30 Hercules (4894)	FAA 2 ETTL, Boufarik	
7T-WHO	Lockheed C-130H-30 Hercules (4897)	FAA 2 ETTL, Boufarik	
7T-WHP	Lockheed C-130H-30 Hercules (4921)	FAA 2 ETTL, Boufarik	
7T-WHR	Lockheed C-130H Hercules (4924)	FAA 2 ETTL, Boufarik	
7T-WHS	Lockheed C-130H Hercules (4912)	FAA 2 ETTL, Boufarik	
7T-WHY	Lockheed C-130H Hercules (4913)	FAA 2 ETTL, Boufarik	
7T-WHZ	Lockheed C-130H Hercules (4914)	FAA 2 ETTL, Boufarik	
7T-WIA	Ilyushin Il-76MD	FAA 347 ETS, Boufarik	
7T-WIB	Ilyushin Il-76MD	FAA 347 ETS, Boufarik	
7T-WIC	Ilyushin Il-76MD	FAA 347 ETS, Boufarik	
7T-WID	Ilyushin Il-76TD	FAA 347 ETS, Boufarik	
7T-WIE	Ilyushin Il-76TD	FAA 347 ETS, Boufarik	
7T-WIF	Ilyushin Il-76	FAA 347 ETS, Boufarik	
7T-WIG	Ilyushin Il-76TD	FAA 347 ETS, Boufarik	
7T-WIH	Ilyushin Il-76	FAA 347 ETS, Boufarik	
7T-WIL	Ilyushin Il-76	FAA 347 ETS, Boufarik	
7T-WIM	Ilyushin Il-76TD	FAA 347 ETS, Boufarik	
7T-WIN	Ilyushin Il-76	FAA 347 ETS, Boufarik	
7T-WIP	Ilyushin Il-76TD	FAA 347 ETS, Boufarik	
7T-WIQ	Ilyushin Il-76	FAA 347 ETS, Boufarik	
7T-WIR	Ilyushin Il-76TD	FAA 347 ETS, Boufarik	
7T-WIS	Ilyushin Il-76	FAA 347 ETS, Boufarik	
7T-WIT	Ilyushin Il-76TD	FAA 347 ETS, Boufarik	
7T-WIU	Ilyushin Il-76TD	FAA 347 ETS, Boufarik	
7T-WJA	Lockheed LM.100J Super Hercules (5818/N1382J)	FAA 2 ETTL, Boufarik	
7T-WJB	Lockheed LM.100J Super Hercules (5824/N2382J)	FAA 2 ETTL, Boufarik	
7T-WJC	Lockheed LM.100J Super Hercules (5952/N5104Q)	FAA 2 ETTL, Boufarik	
7T-WJD	Lockheed LM.100J Super Hercules (5954/N5104S)	FAA 2 ETTL, Boufarik	
ANGOLA			
D2-ANG	Bombardier Global Express XRS	Government of Angola, Luanda	
D2-ANH	Bombardier Global Express	Government of Angola, Luanda	
ARGENTINA			
ARG-01	Boeing 757-256	Government of Argentina, Buenos Aires	
ARMENIA			
701	Airbus A.319CJ-132	Government of Armenia, Yerevan	

Notes	Serial	Type (code/other identity)	Owner/operator, location or fate
	AUSTRALIA		
	Royal Australian Air Force (RAAF)		
	A30-001	Boeing E-7A Wedgetail (737-7ES)	RAAF 2 Sqn/41 Wing, Canberra, ACT
	A30-002	Boeing E-7A Wedgetail (737-7ES)	RAAF 2 Sqn/41 Wing, Canberra, ACT
	A30-003	Boeing E-7A Wedgetail (737-7ES)	RAAF 2 Sqn/41 Wing, Canberra, ACT
	A30-004	Boeing E-7A Wedgetail (737-7ES)	RAAF 2 Sqn/41 Wing, Canberra, ACT
	A30-005	Boeing E-7A Wedgetail (737-7ES)	RAAF 2 Sqn/41 Wing, Canberra, ACT
	A30-006	Boeing E-7A Wedgetail (737-7ES)	RAAF 2 Sqn/41 Wing, Canberra, ACT
	A36-001	Boeing 737-7DT	*RAAF, stored Alice Springs, August 2024*
	A36-002	Boeing 737-7DF	*RAAF, stored Alice Springs, August 2024*
	A62-001	Boeing 737MAX 8 BBJ (N786BJ)	RAAF 34 Sqn/84 Wing, Canberra, ACT
	A62-002	Boeing 737MAX 8 BBJ (N787BJ)	RAAF 34 Sqn/84 Wing, Canberra, ACT
	A39-001	Airbus KC-30A (A.330-203 MRTT) (MRTT001)	RAAF 33 Sqn/84 Wing, Amberley, Queensland
	A39-002	Airbus KC-30A (A.330-203 MRTT) (MRTT002)	RAAF 33 Sqn/84 Wing, Amberley, Queensland
	A39-003	Airbus KC-30A (A.330-203 MRTT) (MRTT003)	RAAF 33 Sqn/84 Wing, Amberley, Queensland
	A39-004	Airbus KC-30A (A.330-203 MRTT) (MRTT004)	RAAF 33 Sqn/84 Wing, Amberley, Queensland
	A39-005	Airbus KC-30A (A.330-203 MRTT) (MRTT005)	RAAF 33 Sqn/84 Wing, Amberley, Queensland
	A39-006	Airbus KC-30A (A.330-203 MRTT) (VH-EBH) (MRTT039)	RAAF 33 Sqn/84 Wing, Amberley, Queensland
	A39-007	Airbus KC-30A (A.330-203 MRTT) (VH-EBI) (MRTT040)	RAAF 33 Sqn/84 Wing, Amberley, Queensland
	A41-206	Boeing C-17A Globemaster III (06-0206)	RAAF 36 Sqn/86 Wing, Amberley, Queensland
	A41-207	Boeing C-17A Globemaster III (06-0207)	RAAF 36 Sqn/86 Wing, Amberley, Queensland
	A41-208	Boeing C-17A Globemaster III (06-0208)	RAAF 36 Sqn/86 Wing, Amberley, Queensland
	A41-209	Boeing C-17A Globemaster III (06-0209)	RAAF 36 Sqn/86 Wing, Amberley, Queensland
	A41-210	Boeing C-17A Globemaster III (11-0210)	RAAF 36 Sqn/86 Wing, Amberley, Queensland
	A41-211	Boeing C-17A Globemaster III (12-0211)	RAAF 36 Sqn/86 Wing, Amberley, Queensland
	A41-212	Boeing C-17A Globemaster III (14-0001)	RAAF 36 Sqn/86 Wing, Amberley, Queensland
	A41-213	Boeing C-17A Globemaster III (14-0002)	RAAF 36 Sqn/86 Wing, Amberley, Queensland
	A47-001	Boeing P-8A Poseidon (N940DS)	RAAF 11 Sqn/92 Wing, Edinburgh, South Australia
	A47-002	Boeing P-8A Poseidon (N956DS)	RAAF 11 Sqn/92 Wing, Edinburgh, South Australia
	A47-003	Boeing P-8A Poseidon (N959DS)	RAAF 11 Sqn/92 Wing, Edinburgh, South Australia
	A47-004	Boeing P-8A Poseidon (N974DS)	RAAF 11 Sqn/92 Wing, Edinburgh, South Australia
	A47-005	Boeing P-8A Poseidon (N832DS)	RAAF 11 Sqn/92 Wing, Edinburgh, South Australia
	A47-006	Boeing P-8A Poseidon (N849DS)	RAAF 11 Sqn/92 Wing, Edinburgh, South Australia
	A47-007	Boeing P-8A Poseidon (N862DS)	RAAF 11 Sqn/92 Wing, Edinburgh, South Australia
	A47-008	Boeing P-8A Poseidon (N872DS)	RAAF 11 Sqn/92 Wing, Edinburgh, South Australia
	A47-009	Boeing P-8A Poseidon (N391DS)	RAAF 11 Sqn/92 Wing, Edinburgh, South Australia
	A47-010	Boeing P-8A Poseidon (N397DS)	RAAF 11 Sqn/92 Wing, Edinburgh, South Australia
	A47-011	Boeing P-8A Poseidon (N398DS)	RAAF 11 Sqn/92 Wing, Edinburgh, South Australia
	A47-012	Boeing P-8A Poseidon (N468DS)	RAAF 11 Sqn/92 Wing, Edinburgh, South Australia
	A47-013	Boeing P-8A Poseidon	RAAF (on order)
	A47-014	Boeing P-8A Poseidon	RAAF (on order)
	A47-015	Boeing P-8A Poseidon	RAAF (on order)
	A51-...	Gulfstream Aerospace MC-55A Peregrine (N542GD)	RAAF (on order)
	A51-...	Gulfstream Aerospace MC-55A Peregrine (N540GA)	RAAF (on order)
	A51-...	Gulfstream Aerospace MC-55A Peregrine (N584GA)	RAAF (on order)
	A56-001	Dassault Falcon 7X (F-WWHE)	RAAF 34 Sqn/84 Wing, Canberra, ACT
	A56-002	Dassault Falcon 7X (F-WWHF)	RAAF 34 Sqn/84 Wing, Canberra, ACT
	A56-003	Dassault Falcon 7X (F-WWHK)	RAAF 34 Sqn/84 Wing, Canberra, ACT
	A62-001	Boeing 737MAX-8BBJ (N786BJ)	RAAF 34 Sqn/84 Wing, Canberra, ACT
	A62-002	Boeing 737MAX-8BBJ (N787BJ)	RAAF 34 Sqn/84 Wing, Canberra, ACT
	A97-440	Lockheed C-130J-30 Hercules II	RAAF 37 Sqn/86 Wing, Richmond, NSW
	A97-441	Lockheed C-130J-30 Hercules II	RAAF 37 Sqn/86 Wing, Richmond, NSW
	A97-442	Lockheed C-130J-30 Hercules II	RAAF 37 Sqn/86 Wing, Richmond, NSW
	A97-447	Lockheed C-130J-30 Hercules II	RAAF 37 Sqn/86 Wing, Richmond, NSW
	A97-448	Lockheed C-130J-30 Hercules II	RAAF 37 Sqn/86 Wing, Richmond, NSW
	A97-449	Lockheed C-130J-30 Hercules II	RAAF 37 Sqn/86 Wing, Richmond, NSW
	A97-450	Lockheed C-130J-30 Hercules II	RAAF 37 Sqn/86 Wing, Richmond, NSW
	A97-464	Lockheed C-130J-30 Hercules II	RAAF 37 Sqn/86 Wing, Richmond, NSW
	A97-465	Lockheed C-130J-30 Hercules II	RAAF 37 Sqn/86 Wing, Richmond, NSW
	A97-466	Lockheed C-130J-30 Hercules II	RAAF 37 Sqn/86 Wing, Richmond, NSW
	A97-467	Lockheed C-130J-30 Hercules II	RAAF 37 Sqn/86 Wing, Richmond, NSW
	A97-468	Lockheed C-130J-30 Hercules II	RAAF 37 Sqn/86 Wing, Richmond, NSW

Serial	Type (code/other identity)	Owner/operator, location or fate	Notes

AUSTRIA
Öesterreichische Luftstreitkräfte (OL)

Serial	Type (code/other identity)	Owner/operator, location or fate	Notes
7L-WA	Eurofighter EF.2000 $	OL 1 Staffel/2 Staffel Überwg, Zeltweg	
7L-WB	Eurofighter EF.2000	OL 1 Staffel/2 Staffel Überwg, Zeltweg	
7L-WC	Eurofighter EF.2000 $	OL 1 Staffel/2 Staffel Überwg, Zeltweg	
7L-WD	Eurofighter EF.2000 $	OL 1 Staffel/2 Staffel Überwg, Zeltweg	
7L-WE	Eurofighter EF.2000	OL 1 Staffel/2 Staffel Überwg, Zeltweg	
7L-WF	Eurofighter EF.2000	OL 1 Staffel/2 Staffel Überwg, Zeltweg	
7L-WG	Eurofighter EF.2000	OL 1 Staffel/2 Staffel Überwg, Zeltweg	
7L-WH	Eurofighter EF.2000	OL 1 Staffel/2 Staffel Überwg, Zeltweg	
7L-WI	Eurofighter EF.2000	OL 1 Staffel/2 Staffel Überwg, Zeltweg	
7L-WJ	Eurofighter EF.2000	OL 1 Staffel/2 Staffel Überwg, Zeltweg	
7L-WK	Eurofighter EF.2000	OL 1 Staffel/2 Staffel Überwg, Zeltweg	
7L-WL	Eurofighter EF.2000	OL 1 Staffel/2 Staffel Überwg, Zeltweg	
7L-WM	Eurofighter EF.2000	OL 1 Staffel/2 Staffel Überwg, Zeltweg	
7L-WN	Eurofighter EF.2000	OL 1 Staffel/2 Staffel Überwg, Zeltweg	
7L-WO	Eurofighter EF.2000 $	OL 1 Staffel/2 Staffel Überwg, Zeltweg	
8T-CA	Lockheed C-130K Hercules (XV181)	OL Lufttransportstaffel, Linz	
8T-CB	Lockheed C-130K Hercules (XV291)	OL Lufttransportstaffel, Linz	
8T-CC	Lockheed C-130K Hercules (XV292)	OL Lufttransportstaffel, Linz	

AZERBAIJAN

Serial	Type (code/other identity)	Owner/operator, location or fate	Notes
4K-AI01	Boeing 767-32LER	Government of Azerbaijan, Baku	
4K-AI001	Boeing 777-200LR	Government of Azerbaijan, Baku	
4K-AI06	Gulfstream Aerospace G.550	Government of Azerbaijan, Baku	
4K-AI07	Airbus ACJ320-214X	Government of Azerbaijan, Baku	
4K-AI08	Airbus ACJ340-642X	Government of Azerbaijan, Baku	
4K-AI88	Gulfstream Aerospace G.650	Government of Azerbaijan, Baku	
4K-8888	Airbus A.319-115LR	Government of Azerbaijan, Baku	

BAHRAIN

Serial	Type (code/other identity)	Owner/operator, location or fate	Notes
701	Lockheed C-130J Hercules II	Bahrain Defence Force, Bahrain	
702	Lockheed C-130J Hercules II	Bahrain Defence Force, Bahrain	
A9C-AWL	BAE RJ100	*Withdrawn from use, Norwich, UK*	
A9C-BA	Boeing 727-2M7/W	*Withdrawn from use, Bahrain*	
A9C-BAH	Gulfstream Aerospace G.650	Bahrain Royal Flight, Sakhir	
A9C-BDF	BAE RJ85	Bahrain Defence Force, Bahrain	
A9C-BG	Grumman G.1159 Gulfstream IITT	*Bahrain Royal Flight, stored Bahrain*	
A9C-BHR	Gulfstream Aerospace G.600	Bahrain Royal Flight, Sakhir	
A9C-BRF	BAE RJ.70ER (M-STRY)	Bahrain Royal Flight, Bahrain	
A9C-BRN	Gulfstream Aerospace G.600	Bahrain Royal Flight, Sakhir	
A9C-HAK	Boeing 747-4F6	Bahrain Royal Flight, Sakhir	
A9C-HMH	Boeing 767-4FSER	Bahrain Royal Flight, Sakhir	
A9C-HMK	Boeing 747-4P8	Bahrain Royal Flight, Sakhir	
A9C-HWR	BAE RJ85	Bahrain Defence Force, Bahrain	
A9C-ISA	Boeing 737-86J/W	Bahrain Royal Flight, Bahrain	
A9C-KAS	BAE RJ100 (SE-DSZ)	Bahrain Defence Force, Bahrain	
A9C-SLM	Gulfstream Aerospace G.550	Bahrain Royal Flight, Sakhir	

BANGLADESH
Bānlādēśa Bimāna Byabahāra/Bangladesh Air Force (BAF)

Serial	Type (code/other identity)	Owner/operator, location or fate	Notes
99-5479	Lockheed C-130J Hercules II (S3-AGE/ZH881)	BAF, BAF Base Bashar, Dhaka	
99-5480	Lockheed C-130J Hercules II (S3-AGG/ZH882)	BAF, BAF Base Bashar, Dhaka	
99-5481	Lockheed C-130J Hercules II (S3-AGH/ZH883)	BAF, BAF Base Bashar, Dhaka	
99-5482	Lockheed C-130J Hercules II (S3-AGF/ZH884)	BAF, BAF Base Bashar, Dhaka	
99-5485	Lockheed C-130J Hercules II (S3-AGJ/ZH887)	BAF, BAF Base Bashar, Dhaka	

BELGIUM
Composante Aérienne Belge/Belgische Luchtcomponent/Belgian Air Component (BAC)

Serial	Type (code/other identity)	Owner/operator, location or fate	Notes
CT-01	Airbus Military A.400M	BAC/Luxembourg Armed Forces 20 Smaldeel (15 Wg), Brussels/Melsbroek	
CT-02	Airbus Military A.400M	BAC 20 Smaldeel (15 Wg), Brussels/Melsbroek	

Notes	Serial	Type (code/other identity)	Owner/operator, location or fate
	CT-03	Airbus Military A.400M	BAC 20 Smaldeel, stored Brussels/Melsbroek
	CT-04	Airbus Military A.400M	BAC 20 Smaldeel (15 Wg), Brussels/Melsbroek
	CT-05	Airbus Military A.400M	BAC 20 Smaldeel (15 Wg), Brussels/Melsbroek
	CT-06	Airbus Military A.400M	BAC 20 Smaldeel (15 Wg), Brussels/Melsbroek
	CT-07	Airbus Military A.400M	BAC 20 Smaldeel (15 Wg), Brussels/Melsbroek
	CT-08	Airbus Military A.400M	BAC 20 Smaldeel (15 Wg), Brussels/Melsbroek
	FA-56	SABCA (GD) F-16A MLU Fighting Falcon	BAC 1 Sm/350 Sm (2 Wg), Florennes
	FA-57	SABCA (GD) F-16A MLU Fighting Falcon $	BAC 1 Sm/350 Sm (2 Wg), Florennes
	FA-67	SABCA (GD) F-16A MLU Fighting Falcon	BAC 1 Sm/350 Sm (2 Wg), Florennes
	FA-68	SABCA (GD) F-16A MLU Fighting Falcon	BAC 1 Sm/350 Sm (2 Wg), Florennes
	FA-69	SABCA (GD) F-16A MLU Fighting Falcon	BAC 31 Sm/349 Sm/OCU (10 Wg), Kleine-Brogel
	FA-70	SABCA (GD) F-16A MLU Fighting Falcon	BAC 1 Sm/350 Sm (2 Wg), Florennes
	FA-71	SABCA (GD) F-16A MLU Fighting Falcon	BAB 1 Sm/350 Sm (2 Wg), Florennes
	FA-72	SABCA (GD) F-16A MLU Fighting Falcon	BAC 1 Sm/350 Sm (2 Wg), Florennes
	FA-77	SABCA (GD) F-16A MLU Fighting Falcon	BAC 31 Sm/349 Sm/OCU (10 Wg), Kleine-Brogel
	FA-81	SABCA (GD) F-16A MLU Fighting Falcon	BAC 31 Sm/349 Sm/OCU (10 Wg), Kleine-Brogel
	FA-82	SABCA (GD) F-16A MLU Fighting Falcon	BAC 31 Sm/349 Sm/OCU (10 Wg), Kleine-Brogel
	FA-83	SABCA (GD) F-16A MLU Fighting Falcon	BAC 1 Sm/350 Sm (2 Wg), Florennes
	FA-84	SABCA (GD) F-16A MLU Fighting Falcon	BAC 1 Sm/350 Sm (2 Wg), Florennes
	FA-86	SABCA (GD) F-16A MLU Fighting Falcon	BAC 1 Sm/350 Sm (2 Wg), Florennes
	FA-87	SABCA (GD) F-16A MLU Fighting Falcon $	BAC 31 Sm/349 Sm/OCU (10 Wg), Kleine-Brogel
	FA-89	SABCA (GD) F-16A MLU Fighting Falcon	BAC 31 Sm/349 Sm/OCU (10 Wg), Kleine-Brogel
	FA-91	SABCA (GD) F-16A MLU Fighting Falcon	BAC 1 Sm/350 Sm (2 Wg), Florennes
	FA-92	SABCA (GD) F-16A MLU Fighting Falcon	BAC 1 Sm/350 Sm (2 Wg), Florennes
	FA-94	SABCA (GD) F-16A MLU Fighting Falcon	BAC 1 Sm/350 Sm (2 Wg), Florennes
	FA-95	SABCA (GD) F-16A MLU Fighting Falcon $	BAC, withdrawn from use Kleine-Brogel
	FA-97	SABCA (GD) F-16A MLU Fighting Falcon	BAC 1 Sm/350 Sm (2 Wg), Florennes
	FA-98	SABCA (GD) F-16A MLU Fighting Falcon	BAC 1 Sm/350 Sm (2 Wg), Florennes
	FA-101	SABCA (GD) F-16A MLU Fighting Falcon $	BAC 1 Sm/350 Sm (2 Wg), Florennes
	FA-103	SABCA (GD) F-16A MLU Fighting Falcon	BAC 31 Sm/349 Sm/OCU (10 Wg), Kleine-Brogel
	FA-104	SABCA (GD) F-16A MLU Fighting Falcon	BAC 31 Sm/349 Sm/OCU (10 Wg), Kleine-Brogel
	FA-106	SABCA (GD) F-16A MLU Fighting Falcon	BAC 31 Sm/349 Sm/OCU (10 Wg), Kleine-Brogel
	FA-107	SABCA (GD) F-16A MLU Fighting Falcon	BAC 31 Sm/349 Sm/OCU (10 Wg), Kleine-Brogel
	FA-109	SABCA (GD) F-16A MLU Fighting Falcon	BAC 1 Sm/350 Sm (2 Wg), Florennes
	FA-110	SABCA (GD) F-16A MLU Fighting Falcon	BAC 31 Sm/349 Sm/OCU (10 Wg), Kleine-Brogel
	FA-114	SABCA (GD) F-16A MLU Fighting Falcon	BAC 31 Sm/349 Sm/OCU (10 Wg), Kleine-Brogel
	FA-116	SABCA (GD) F-16A MLU Fighting Falcon $	BAC 31 Sm/349 Sm/OCU (10 Wg), Kleine-Brogel
	FA-117	SABCA (GD) F-16A MLU Fighting Falcon	BAC 1 Sm/350 Sm (2 Wg), Florennes
	FA-118	SABCA (GD) F-16A MLU Fighting Falcon	BAC 1 Sm/350 Sm (2 Wg), Florennes
	FA-119	SABCA (GD) F-16A MLU Fighting Falcon	BAC 31 Sm/349 Sm/OCU (10 Wg), Kleine-Brogel
	FA-121	SABCA (GD) F-16A MLU Fighting Falcon	BAC 1 Sm/350 Sm (2 Wg), Florennes
	FA-123	SABCA (GD) F-16A MLU Fighting Falcon	BAC 31 Sm/349 Sm/OCU (10 Wg), Kleine-Brogel
	FA-124	SABCA (GD) F-16A MLU Fighting Falcon	BAC 31 Sm/349 Sm/OCU (10 Wg), Kleine-Brogel
	FA-126	SABCA (GD) F-16A MLU Fighting Falcon	BAC 31 Sm/349 Sm/OCU (10 Wg), Kleine-Brogel
	FA-127	SABCA (GD) F-16A MLU Fighting Falcon	BAC 31 Sm/349 Sm/OCU (10 Wg), Kleine-Brogel
	FA-129	SABCA (GD) F-16A MLU Fighting Falcon	BAC 1 Sm/350 Sm (2 Wg), Florennes
	FA-131	SABCA (GD) F-16A MLU Fighting Falcon	BAC 31 Sm/349 Sm/OCU (10 Wg), Kleine-Brogel
	FA-132	SABCA (GD) F-16A MLU Fighting Falcon	BAC 31 Sm/349 Sm/OCU (10 Wg), Kleine-Brogel
	FA-133	SABCA (GD) F-16A MLU Fighting Falcon	BAC 1 Sm/350 Sm (2 Wg), Florennes
	FA-134	SABCA (GD) F-16A MLU Fighting Falcon	BAC 31 Sm/349 Sm/OCU (10 Wg), Kleine-Brogel
	FA-135	SABCA (GD) F-16A MLU Fighting Falcon	BAC 1 Sm/350 Sm (2 Wg), Florennes
	FA-136	SABCA (GD) F-16A MLU Fighting Falcon	BAC 31 Sm/349 Sm/OCU (10 Wg), Kleine-Brogel
	FB-14	SABCA (GD) F-16B MLU Fighting Falcon	BAC 1 Sm/350 Sm (2 Wg), Florennes
	FB-15	SABCA (GD) F-16B MLU Fighting Falcon	BAC 31 Sm/349 Sm/OCU (10 Wg), Kleine-Brogel
	FB-17	SABCA (GD) F-16B MLU Fighting Falcon	BAC 31 Sm/349 Sm/OCU (10 Wg), Kleine-Brogel
	FB-20	SABCA (GD) F-16B MLU Fighting Falcon	BAC, Skrydstrup, Denmark (Ukrainian training)
	FB-21	SABCA (GD) F-16B MLU Fighting Falcon	BAC, Skrydstrup, Denmark (Ukrainian training)
	FB-22	SABCA (GD) F-16B MLU Fighting Falcon	BAC, Skrydstrup, Denmark (Ukrainian training)
	FB-23	SABCA (GD) F-16B MLU Fighting Falcon	BAC 31 Sm/349 Sm/OCU (10 Wg), Kleine-Brogel
	FB-24	SABCA (GD) F-16B MLU Fighting Falcon $	BAC, Skrydstrup, Denmark (Ukrainian training)
	FL001	Lockheed Martin F-35A Lightning II	BAC, on order, LMTAS, Fort Worth, TX
	FL002	Lockheed Martin F-35A Lightning II	BAC, 312th FS/56th FW, Luke AFB, AZ

Serial	Type (code/other identity)	Owner/operator, location or fate	Notes
FL003	Lockheed Martin F-35A Lightning II	BAC, 312th FS/56th FW, Luke AFB, AZ	
FL004	Lockheed Martin F-35A Lightning II	BAC, 312th FS/56th FW, Luke AFB, AZ	
FL005	Lockheed Martin F-35A Lightning II	BAC, on order, LMTAS, Fort Worth, TX	
FL006	Lockheed Martin F-35A Lightning II	BAC, 312th FS/56th FW, Luke AFB, AZ	
FL007	Lockheed Martin F-35A Lightning II	BAC, on order, LMTAS, Fort Worth, TX	
FL008	Lockheed Martin F-35A Lightning II	BAC, 312th FS/56th FW, Luke AFB, AZ	
G-01	Cessna 182Q Skylane	BAC Federal Police, Brussels/Melsbroek	
G-04	Cessna 182R Skylane	BAC Federal Police, Brussels/Melsbroek	
G-10	MDH MD.902 Explorer	BAC Federal Police, Brussels/Melsbroek	
G-11	MDH MD.902 Explorer	BAC Federal Police, Brussels/Melsbroek	
G-12	MDH MD.902 Explorer	BAC Federal Police, Brussels/Melsbroek	
G-14	MDH MD.520N	BAC Federal Police, Brussels/Melsbroek	
G-15	MDH MD.520N	BAC Federal Police, Brussels/Melsbroek	
G-16	MDH MD.902 Explorer	BAC Federal Police, Brussels/Melsbroek	
G-17	MDH MD.902 Explorer	BAC Federal Police, Brussels/Melsbroek	
H-21	Agusta A109HA	BAC 17 Smaldeel MRH (1 Wg), Beauvechain	
H-24	Agusta A109HA $	BAC 17 Smaldeel MRH (1 Wg), Beauvechain	
H-26	Agusta A109HA	BAC 17 Smaldeel MRH (1 Wg), Beauvechain	
H-27	Agusta A109HA	BAC 17 Smaldeel MRH (1 Wg), Beauvechain	
H-28	Agusta A109HA	BAC 17 Smaldeel MRH (1 Wg), Beauvechain	
H-29	Agusta A109HA $	BAC 17 Smaldeel MRH (1 Wg), Beauvechain	
H-31	Agusta A109HA	BAC 17 Smaldeel MRH (1 Wg), Beauvechain	
H-35	Agusta A109HA	BAC 17 Smaldeel MRH (1 Wg), Beauvechain	
H-38	Agusta A109HA	BAC 17 Smaldeel MRH (1 Wg), Beauvechain	
H-39	Agusta A109HA	BAC 17 Smaldeel MRH (1 Wg), Beauvechain	
H-42	Agusta A109HA	BAC SLV (1 Wg), Beauvechain	
H-46	Agusta A109HA $	BAC 17 Smaldeel MRH (1 Wg), Beauvechain	
LB-01	Piper L-21B Super Cub	BAC Air Cadets, Florennes/Goetsenhoven/Zoersel	
LB-02	Piper L-21B Super Cub	BAC Air Cadets, Florennes/Goetsenhoven/Zoersel	
LB-03	Piper L-21B Super Cub	BAC Air Cadets, Florennes/Goetsenhoven/Zoersel	
LB-05	Piper L-21B Super Cub	BAC Air Cadets, Florennes/Goetsenhoven/Zoersel	
LB-06	Piper L-21B Super Cub	BAC Air Cadets, Florennes/Goetsenhoven/Zoersel	
RN-01	NH Industries NH.90-NFH	BAC 40 Smaldeel (1 Wg), Koksijde	
RN-02	NH Industries NH.90-NFH	BAC 40 Smaldeel (1 Wg), Koksijde	
RN-03	NH Industries NH.90-NFH	BAC 40 Smaldeel (1 Wg), Koksijde	
RN-04	NH Industries NH.90-NFH	BAC 40 Smaldeel (1 Wg), Koksijde	
RN-05	NH Industries NH.90-TTH	BAC 18 Smaldeel MRH (1 Wg), Beauvechain	
RN-06	NH Industries NH.90-TTH	BAC 18 Smaldeel MRH (1 Wg), Beauvechain	
RN-07	NH Industries NH.90-TTH	BAC 18 Smaldeel MRH (1 Wg), Beauvechain	
RN-08	NH Industries NH.90-TTH	BAC 18 Smaldeel MRH (1 Wg), Beauvechain	
ST-02	SIAI Marchetti SF260M+	BAC 5 Smaldeel/9 Smaldeel, CC Air, Beauvechain	
ST-03	SIAI Marchetti SF260M+	BAC 5 Smaldeel/9 Smaldeel, CC Air, Beauvechain	
ST-04	SIAI Marchetti SF260M+	BAC 5 Smaldeel/9 Smaldeel, CC Air, Beauvechain	
ST-06	SIAI Marchetti SF260M+	BAC *Red Devils*, CC Air, Beauvechain	
ST-12	SIAI Marchetti SF260M+	BAC 5 Smaldeel/9 Smaldeel, CC Air, Beauvechain	
ST-15	SIAI Marchetti SF260M+	BAC *Red Devils*, CC Air, Beauvechain	
ST-16	SIAI Marchetti SF260M+	BAC *Red Devils*, CC Air, Beauvechain	
ST-17	SIAI Marchetti SF260M+	BAC 5 Smaldeel/9 Smaldeel, CC Air, Beauvechain	
ST-18	SIAI Marchetti SF260M+	BAC *Red Devils*, CC Air, Beauvechain	
ST-20	SIAI Marchetti SF260M+	BAC *Red Devils*, CC Air, Beauvechain	
ST-23	SIAI Marchetti SF260M+	BAC *Red Devils*, CC Air, Beauvechain	
ST-24	SIAI Marchetti SF260M+	BAC 5 Smaldeel/9 Smaldeel, CC Air, Beauvechain	
ST-25	SIAI Marchetti SF260M+	BAC *Red Devils*, CC Air, Beauvechain	
ST-30	SIAI Marchetti SF260M+	BAC 5 Smaldeel/9 Smaldeel, CC Air, Beauvechain	
ST-31	SIAI Marchetti SF260M+	BAC *Red Devils*, CC Air, Beauvechain	
ST-32	SIAI Marchetti SF260M+	BAC 5 Smaldeel/9 Smaldeel, CC Air, Beauvechain	
ST-34	SIAI Marchetti SF260M+	BAC *Red Devils*, CC Air, Beauvechain	
ST-36	SIAI Marchetti SF260M+	BAC *Red Devils*, CC Air, Beauvechain	
ST-40	SIAI Marchetti SF260D	BAC 5 Smaldeel/9 Smaldeel, CC Air, Beauvechain	
ST-41	SIAI Marchetti SF260D	BAC 5 Smaldeel/9 Smaldeel, CC Air, Beauvechain	
ST-42	SIAI Marchetti SF260D	BAC 5 Smaldeel/9 Smaldeel, CC Air, Beauvechain	
ST-43	SIAI Marchetti SF260D	BAC 5 Smaldeel/9 Smaldeel, CC Air, Beauvechain	

Notes	Serial	Type (code/other identity)	Owner/operator, location or fate
	ST-44	SIAI Marchetti SF260D	BAC 5 Smaldeel/9 Smaldeel, CC Air, Beauvechain
	ST-45	SIAI Marchetti SF260D	BAC 5 Smaldeel/9 Smaldeel, CC Air, Beauvechain
	ST-46	SIAI Marchetti SF260D	BAC 5 Smaldeel/9 Smaldeel, CC Air, Beauvechain
	ST-47	SIAI Marchetti SF260D	BAC 5 Smaldeel/9 Smaldeel, CC Air, Beauvechain
	ST-48	SIAI Marchetti SF260D	BAC 5 Smaldeel/9 Smaldeel, CC Air, Beauvechain
	OO-FAE	Dassault Falcon 7X	BAC 21 Smaldeel (15 Wg), Brussels/Melsbroek
	OO-LUM	Dassault Falcon 7X	BAC 21 Smaldeel (15 Wg), Brussels/Melsbroek

BOLIVIA
Fuerza Aérea Boliviana

	FAB-001	Dassault Falcon 900X EASy	FAB Escuadron de Ejecutivos, La Paz

BOTSWANA
Botswana Defence Force (BDF)

	OK1	Bombardier Global Express	BDF VIP Sqn, Sir Seretse Kharma IAP, Gaborone
	OM1	Lockheed C-130B Hercules	BDF Z10 Sqn, Thebephatshwa
	OM2	Lockheed C-130B Hercules	BDF Z10 Sqn, Thebephatshwa
	OM3	Lockheed C-130B Hercules	BDF Z10 Sqn, Thebephatshwa
	OM4	Lockheed C-130H Hercules (74-1675)	BDF Z10 Sqn, Thebephatshwa

BRAZIL
Força Aérea Brasileira (FAB)

	2101	Airbus A.319-133CJ (VC-1A)	FAB 1º GT Especial, 1º Esq, Brasilia
	2550	Embraer VC-99A Legacy	FAB 2º GT Especial, 1º Esq, Brasilia
	2560	Embraer VC-99C Legacy	FAB 2º GT Especial, 1º Esq, Brasilia
	2561	Embraer VC-99C Legacy	FAB 2º GT Especial, 1º Esq, Brasilia
	2580	Embraer VC-99B Legacy	FAB 2º GT Especial, 1º Esq, Brasilia
	2581	Embraer VC-99B Legacy	FAB 2º GT Especial, 1º Esq, Brasilia
	2582	Embraer VC-99B Legacy	FAB 2º GT Especial, 1º Esq, Brasilia
	2583	Embraer VC-99B Legacy	FAB 2º GT Especial, 1º Esq, Brasilia
	2584	Embraer VC-99B Legacy	FAB 2º GT Especial, 1º Esq, Brasilia
	2585	Embraer VC-99B Legacy	FAB 2º GT Especial, 1º Esq, Brasilia
	2590	Embraer EMB.190-190IGW (VC-2)	FAB 1º GT Especial, 1º Esq, Brasilia
	2591	Embraer EMB.190-190IGW (VC-2)	FAB 1º GT Especial, 1º Esq, Brasilia
	2852	Embraer KC-390 Millennium (PT-ZNG)	FAB (on order)
	2853	Embraer KC-390 Millennium	FAB 1º GTT, 2º Esq, Galeão
	2854	Embraer KC-390 Millennium	FAB 1º GTT, 2º Esq, Galeão
	2855	Embraer KC-390 Millennium	FAB 1º GTT, 2º Esq, Galeão
	2856	Embraer KC-390 Millennium	FAB 1º GTT, 2º Esq, Galeão
	2857	Embraer KC-390 Millennium	FAB 1º GTT, 2º Esq, Galeão
	2858	Embraer KC-390 Millennium	FAB 1º GTT, 2º Esq, Galeão
	2859	Embraer KC-390 Millennium	FAB 1º GTT, 2º Esq, Galeão
	2860	Embraer KC-390 Millennium	FAB 1º GTT, 2º Esq, Galeão
	2901	Airbus A.330-200	FAB 2º GT, 2º Esq, Galeão (KC-30M conversion)
	2902	Airbus A.330-200	FAB 2º GT, 2º Esq, Galeão (KC-30M conversion)
	6700	Embraer E-99M Guardião	FAB 2º Esq, 6º GAv, Anapolis
	6701	Embraer E-99M Guardião	FAB 2º Esq, 6º GAv, Anapolis
	6702	Embraer E-99M Guardião	FAB 2º Esq, 6º GAv, Anapolis
	6703	Embraer E-99M Guardião	FAB 2º Esq, 6º GAv, Anapolis
	6704	Embraer E-99M Guardião	FAB 2º Esq, 6º GAv, Anapolis
	6750	Embraer R-99	FAB 2º Esq, 6º GAv, Anapolis
	6751	Embraer R-99	FAB 2º Esq, 6º GAv, Anapolis
	6752	Embraer R-99	FAB 2º Esq, 6º GAv, Anapolis

BRUNEI

	V8-BKH	Boeing 747-8LQ	Government of Brunei, Bandar Seri Bergawan
	V8-MHB	Boeing 767-27GER	Government of Brunei, Bandar Seri Bergawan
	V8-OAS	Boeing 787-8 (N508BJ)	Government of Brunei, Bandar Seri Bergawan

BULGARIA
Bulgarsky Voenno-Vazdushni Sily (BVVS)

	020	Pilatus PC.XII/45	BVVS 16.TrAB, Sofia/Vrazhdebna

Serial	Type (code/other identity)	Owner/operator, location or fate	Notes
055	Antonov An-30	BVVS 16.TrAB, Sofia/Vrazhdebna	
071	Aeritalia C-27J Spartan	BVVS 16.TrAB, Sofia/Vrazhdebna	
072	Aeritalia C-27J Spartan	BVVS 16.TrAB, Sofia/Vrazhdebna	
073	Aeritalia C-27J Spartan	BVVS 16.TrAB, Sofia/Vrazhdebna	
Bulgarian Government			
LZ-AOB	Airbus A.319-112	Government of Bulgaria/BH Air, Sofia/Vrazhdebna	
LZ-OOI	Dassault Falcon 2000	Government of Bulgaria/BH Air, Sofia/Vrazhdebna	
BURKINA FASO			
XT-BFA	Boeing 727-282/W	Government of Burkina Faso, Ouagadougou	
CAMEROON			
TJ-AAW	Grumman G.1159A Gulfstream III	*Stored Basel, Switzerland*	
CANADA			
Royal Canadian Air Force (RCAF)			
15001	Airbus CC-150 Polaris (A.310-304) [991]	RCAF 437 Sqn (8 Wing), Trenton	
15002	Airbus CC-150 Polaris (A.310-304F) [992]	RCAF 437 Sqn (8 Wing), Trenton	
15004	Airbus CC-150 Polaris (A.310-304F) [994]	RCAF 437 Sqn (8 Wing), Trenton	
15005	Airbus CC-150 Polaris (A.310-304F) [995]	RCAF 437 Sqn (8 Wing), Trenton	
130332	Lockheed CC-130H(SAR) Hercules	RCAF 426 Sqn (8 Wing), Trenton	
130333	Lockheed CC-130H(SAR) Hercules	RCAF 413 Sqn (14 Wing), Greenwood	
130334	Lockheed CC-130H(SAR) Hercules	RCAF 413 Sqn (14 Wing), Greenwood	
130335	Lockheed CC-130H(SAR) Hercules	RCAF 426 Sqn (8 Wing), Trenton	
130336	Lockheed CC-130H(SAR) Hercules	RCAF 426 Sqn (8 Wing), Trenton	
130337	Lockheed CC-130H(SAR) Hercules	RCAF 426 Sqn (8 Wing), Trenton (damaged 2023)	
130338	Lockheed CC-130H(T) Hercules	RCAF 435 Sqn (17 Wing), Winnipeg	
130339	Lockheed CC-130H(T) Hercules	RCAF 435 Sqn (17 Wing), Winnipeg	
130340	Lockheed CC-130H(T) Hercules	RCAF 435 Sqn (17 Wing), Winnipeg	
130341	Lockheed CC-130H(T) Hercules	RCAF 435 Sqn (17 Wing), Winnipeg	
130343	Lockheed CC-130H-30 Hercules	RCAF 426 Sqn (8 Wing), Trenton	
130344	Lockheed CC-130H-30 Hercules	RCAF 413 Sqn (14 Wing), Greenwood	
130601	Lockheed CC-130J Hercules II	RCAF 436 Sqn (8 Wing), Trenton	
130602	Lockheed CC-130J Hercules II	RCAF 436 Sqn (8 Wing), Trenton	
130603	Lockheed CC-130J Hercules II	RCAF 436 Sqn (8 Wing), Trenton	
130604	Lockheed CC-130J Hercules II	RCAF 436 Sqn (8 Wing), Trenton	
130605	Lockheed CC-130J Hercules II	RCAF 436 Sqn (8 Wing), Trenton	
130606	Lockheed CC-130J Hercules II	RCAF 436 Sqn (8 Wing), Trenton	
130607	Lockheed CC-130J Hercules II	RCAF 436 Sqn (8 Wing), Trenton	
130608	Lockheed CC-130J Hercules II	RCAF 436 Sqn (8 Wing), Trenton	
130609	Lockheed CC-130J Hercules II	RCAF 436 Sqn (8 Wing), Trenton	
130610	Lockheed CC-130J Hercules II	RCAF 436 Sqn (8 Wing), Trenton	
130611	Lockheed CC-130J Hercules II	RCAF 436 Sqn (8 Wing), Trenton	
130612	Lockheed CC-130J Hercules II	RCAF 436 Sqn (8 Wing), Trenton	
130613	Lockheed CC-130J Hercules II	RCAF 436 Sqn (8 Wing), Trenton	
130614	Lockheed CC-130J Hercules II	RCAF 436 Sqn (8 Wing), Trenton	
130615	Lockheed CC-130J Hercules II	RCAF 436 Sqn (8 Wing), Trenton	
130616	Lockheed CC-130J Hercules II	RCAF 436 Sqn (8 Wing), Trenton	
130617	Lockheed CC-130J Hercules II	RCAF 436 Sqn (8 Wing), Trenton	
140101	Lockheed CP-140M Aurora	RCAF 407 Sqn (19 Wing), Comox	
140103	Lockheed CP-140M Aurora	RCAF 407 Sqn (19 Wing), Comox	
140104	Lockheed CP-140M Aurora	RCAF 404 Sqn/405 Sqn (14 Wing), Greenwood	
140105	Lockheed CP-140M Aurora	RCAF 407 Sqn (19 Wing), Comox	
140106	Lockheed CP-140 Aurora	RCAF 407 Sqn (19 Wing), Comox	
140108	Lockheed CP-140M Aurora	RCAF 404 Sqn/405 Sqn (14 Wing), Greenwood	
140110	Lockheed CP-140M Aurora	RCAF 407 Sqn (19 Wing), Comox	
140111	Lockheed CP-140M Aurora	RCAF 404 Sqn/405 Sqn (14 Wing), Greenwood	
140112	Lockheed CP-140M Aurora	RCAF 407 Sqn (19 Wing), Comox	
140113	Lockheed CP-140 Aurora	RCAF 404 Sqn/405 Sqn (14 Wing), Greenwood	
140114	Lockheed CP-140M Aurora	RCAF 407 Sqn (19 Wing), Comox	
140115	Lockheed CP-140M Aurora	RCAF 404 Sqn/405 Sqn (14 Wing), Greenwood	
140116	Lockheed CP-140M Aurora	RCAF 404 Sqn/405 Sqn (14 Wing), Greenwood	

Notes	Serial	Type (code/other identity)	Owner/operator, location or fate
	140117	Lockheed CP-140M Aurora	RCAF 407 Sqn (19 Wing), Comox
	140118	Lockheed CP-140M Aurora	RCAF 407 Sqn (19 Wing), Comox
	142803	De Havilland Canada CT-142	RCAF 402 Sqn (17 Wing), Winnipeg
	142804	De Havilland Canada CT-142	RCAF 402 Sqn (17 Wing), Winnipeg
	142805	De Havilland Canada CT-142	RCAF 402 Sqn (17 Wing), Winnipeg
	142806	De Havilland Canada CT-142	RCAF 402 Sqn (17 Wing), Winnipeg
	144617	Canadair CC-144C Challenger (C-GKGR)	RCAF 412 Sqn (8 Wing), Ottawa
	144618	Canadair CC-144C Challenger (C-GKGS)	RCAF 412 Sqn (8 Wing), Ottawa
	144619	Canadair CC-144D Challenger (C-GRIS)	RCAF 412 Sqn (8 Wing), Ottawa
	144620	Canadair CC-144D Challenger (C-FAMN)	RCAF 412 Sqn (8 Wing), Ottawa
	177701	Boeing CC-177 Globemaster III (07-7701/N9500B)	RCAF 429 Sqn (8 Wing), Trenton
	177702	Boeing CC-177 Globemaster III (07-7702/N9500H)	RCAF 429 Sqn (8 Wing), Trenton
	177703	Boeing CC-177 Globemaster III (07-7703/N9500N)	RCAF 429 Sqn (8 Wing), Trenton
	177704	Boeing CC-177 Globemaster III (07-7704/N9500R)	RCAF 429 Sqn (8 Wing), Trenton
	177705	Boeing CC-177 Globemaster III (14-0004/N273ZD)	RCAF 429 Sqn (8 Wing), Trenton
	330001	Airbus CC-330 Husky (9K-APA)	RCAF (on order)
	330002	Airbus CC-330 Husky (9K-APC)	RCAF 437 Sqn (8 Wing), Trenton
	330003	Airbus CC-330 Husky (9K-APD)	RCAF 437 Sqn (8 Wing), Trenton
	330004	Airbus CC-330 Husky (9K-APB)	RCAF (on order)
	330005	Airbus CC-330 Husky (9K-APE)	RCAF (on order)
	33000.	Airbus CC-330 Husky (F-WWCB)	RCAF (on order)
	CHAD		
	TT-ABD	Boeing 737-74Q	Government of Chad, N'djamena
	CHILE		
	Fuerza Aérea de Chile (FACh)		
	20	Game Composites GB1 GameBird (N259GC)	FACh *Los Halcones*, Santiago
	21	Game Composites GB1 GameBird (N963GC)	FACh *Los Halcones*, Santiago
	22	Game Composites GB1 GameBird (N898GC)	FACh *Los Halcones*, Santiago
	....	Game Composites GB1 GameBird (N146GC)	FACh *Los Halcones*, Santiago
	....	Game Composites GB1 GameBird (N174GC)	FACh *Los Halcones*, Santiago
	....	Game Composites GB1 GameBird (N219GC)	FACh *Los Halcones*, Santiago
	....	Game Composites GB1 GameBird (N228GC)	FACh *Los Halcones*, Santiago
	145	Extra EA-300L [5]	FACh *Los Halcones*, Santiago
	146	Extra EA-300L [4]	FACh *Los Halcones*, Santiago
	147	Extra EA-300L [2]	*Registered as CC-DHN*
	904	Boeing 707-358C Phalcon AEW	FACh, Grupo de Aviación 10, Santiago
	911	Grumman G.1159C Gulfstream IV	FACh, Grupo de Aviación 10, Santiago
	912	Grumman G.1159C Gulfstream IV	FACh, Grupo de Aviación 10, Santiago
	913	Grumman G.1159C Gulfstream IV-SP	FACh, Grupo de Aviación 10, Santiago
	914	Grumman G.1159C Gulfstream IV-SP	FACh, Grupo de Aviación 10, Santiago
	921	Boeing 737-58N	FACh, Grupo de Aviación 10, Santiago
	922	Boeing 737-330	FACh, Grupo de Aviación 10, Santiago
	982	Boeing KC-135E Stratotanker	FACh, Grupo de Aviación 10, Santiago
	983	Boeing KC-135E Stratotanker	FACh, Grupo de Aviación 10, Santiago
	985	Boeing 767-3Y0ER	FACh, Grupo de Aviación 10, Santiago
	991	Lockheed C-130R Hercules	FACh, Grupo de Aviación 10, Santiago
	992	Lockheed C-130R Hercules	FACh, Grupo de Aviación 10, Santiago
	993	Lockheed C-130H Hercules	FACh, Grupo de Aviación 10, Santiago
	994	Lockheed C-130H Hercules	FACh, Grupo de Aviación 10, Santiago
	995	Lockheed C-130H Hercules	FACh, Grupo de Aviación 10, Santiago
	996	Lockheed C-130H Hercules	FACh, Grupo de Aviación 10, Santiago
	999	Lockheed KC-130R Hercules	FACh, Grupo de Aviación 10, Santiago
	1304	Extra EA-300L [3]	FACh *Los Halcones*, Santiago
	1325	Extra EA-300L [1]	*Registered as N9494R*
	COLOMBIA		
	Fuerza Aérea Colombiana (FAC)		
	FAC0001	Boeing 737-74V	FAC Escuadrón de Transporte Especial, Bogotà
	FAC1202	Boeing 767-2J6ER	FAC Escuadrón de Transporte 811, Bogota
	FAC1219	Boeing 737-732/W	FAC Escuadrón de Transporte 811, Bogota

Serial	Type (code/other identity)	Owner/operator, location or fate	Notes
FAC1220	Boeing 737-732/W	FAC Escuadrón de Transporte 811, Bogota	
FAC1222	Boeing 737-732/W	FAC Escuadrón de Transporte 811, Bogota	

CROATIA
Hrvatske Zračne Snage (HZS)

054	Pilatus PC-9M	HZS 392.Eskadrila Aviona/93.Krilo, Zadar	
055	Pilatus PC-9M	HZS 392.Eskadrila Aviona/93.Krilo, Zadar	
056	Pilatus PC-9M	HZS 392.Eskadrila Aviona/93.Krilo, Zadar	
057	Pilatus PC-9M	HZS 392.Eskadrila Aviona/93.Krilo, Zadar	
059	Pilatus PC-9M $	HZS 392.Eskadrila Aviona/93.Krilo, Zadar	
061	Pilatus PC-9M	HZS 392.Eskadrila Aviona/93.Krilo, Zadar	
062	Pilatus PC-9M	HZS 392.Eskadrila Aviona/93.Krilo, Zadar	
063	Pilatus PC-9M	HZS 392.Eskadrila Aviona/93.Krilo, Zadar	
064	Pilatus PC-9M	HZS 392.Eskadrila Aviona/93.Krilo, Zadar	
066	Pilatus PC-9M	HZS 392.Eskadrila Aviona/93.Krilo, Zadar	
067	Pilatus PC-9M	HZS 392.Eskadrila Aviona/93.Krilo, Zadar	
068	Pilatus PC-9M	HZS 392.Eskadrila Aviona/93.Krilo, Zadar	
069	Pilatus PC-9M	HZS 392.Eskadrila Aviona/93.Krilo, Zadar	
070	Pilatus PC-9M	HZS 392.Eskadrila Aviona/93.Krilo, Zadar	
150	Dassault Rafale C (124)	HZS 191.Eskadrila Aviona/91.Krilo, Zagreb	
151	Dassault Rafale C (131)	HZS 191.Eskadrila Aviona/91.Krilo, Zagreb	
152	Dassault Rafale C (141)	HZS 191.Eskadrila Aviona/91.Krilo, Zagreb	
153	Dassault Rafale C (144)	HZS 191.Eskadrila Aviona/91.Krilo, Zagreb	
154	Dassault Rafale C (130)	HZS 191.Eskadrila Aviona/91.Krilo, Zagreb	
155	Dassault Rafale C	HZS 191.Eskadrila Aviona/91.Krilo, Zagreb	
156	Dassault Rafale C	HZS 191.Eskadrila Aviona/91.Krilo, Zagreb	
...	Dassault Rafale C	HZS, on order	
...	Dassault Rafale C	HZS, on order	
...	Dassault Rafale C	HZS, on order	
...	Dassault Rafale C	HZS, on order	
...	Dassault Rafale C	HZS, on order	
170	Dassault Rafale B (318)	HZS 191.Eskadrila Aviona/91.Krilo, Zagreb	
171	Dassault Rafale B (315)	HZS 191.Eskadrila Aviona/91.Krilo, Zagreb	

Government of Croatia

9A-CRO	Canadair CL.601 Challenger	Government of Croatia, Zagreb	

CYPRUS
Government of Cyprus

CAF-001	Embraer ERJ.135BJ Legacy	Government of Cyprus, Paphos	

CZECH REPUBLIC
Vzdušné Síly Armády (Czech Air Force)

0113	Aero L-39C Albatros	Czech AF CLV, Pardubice	
0115	Aero L-39C Albatros	Czech AF CLV, Pardubice	
0441	Aero L-39C Albatros	Czech AF CLV, Pardubice	
0444	Aero L-39C Albatros	Czech AF CLV, Pardubice	
0445	Aero L-39C Albatros	Czech AF CLV, Pardubice	
0448	Aero L-39C Albatros	Czech AF CLV, Pardubice	
0452	CASA C-295M	Czech AF 242.tsl/24.zDL, Praha/Kbely	
0453	CASA C-295M	Czech AF 242.tsl/24.zDL, Praha/Kbely	
0454	CASA C-295M	Czech AF 242.tsl/24.zDL, Praha/Kbely	
0455	CASA C-295M	Czech AF 242.tsl/24.zDL, Praha/Kbely	
0457	Mil Mi-17V-11	Czech AF CLV, Pardubice	
0475	Aero L-39NG Skyfox (7001)	Aero, Vodochody	
0476	Aero L-39NG Skyfox (7004)	Aero, Vodochody	
0477	Aero L-39NG Skyfox [7]	Czech AF CLV, Pardubice	
0478	Aero L-39NG Skyfox [8]	Czech AF CLV, Pardubice	
0481	CASA C-295W	Czech AF 242.tsl/24.zDL, Praha/Kbely	
0482	CASA C-295W	Czech AF 242.tsl/24.zDL, Praha/Kbely	
0486	Bell Helicopter AH-1Z Viper	Czech AF 221.lbvr/22.zL, Náměšt	
0487	Bell Helicopter AH-1Z Viper	Czech AF 221.lbvr/22.zL, Náměšt	
0488	Bell Helicopter AH-1Z Viper	Czech AF 221.lbvr/22.zL, Náměšt	

Notes	Serial	Type (code/other identity)	Owner/operator, location or fate
	0489	Bell Helicopter AH-1Z Viper	Czech AF 221.lbvr/22.zL, Náměšt
	0490	Bell Helicopter UH-1Y Venom	Czech AF 222.vrlt/22.zVrL, Náměšt
	0491	Bell Helicopter UH-1Y Venom	Czech AF 222.vrlt/22.zVrL, Náměšt
	0492	Bell Helicopter UH-1Y Venom	Czech AF 222.vrlt/22.zVrL, Náměšt
	0493	Bell Helicopter UH-1Y Venom	Czech AF 222.vrlt/22.zVrL, Náměšt
	0494	Bell Helicopter UH-1Y Venom	Czech AF 222.vrlt/22.zVrL, Náměšt
	0495	Bell Helicopter UH-1Y Venom	Czech AF 222.vrlt/22.zVrL, Náměšt
	0496	Bell Helicopter UH-1Y Venom	Czech AF 222.vrlt/22.zVrL, Náměšt
	0497	Bell Helicopter UH-1Y Venom	Czech AF 222.vrlt/22.zVrL, Náměšt
	0529	Aero L-39NG Skyfox	Czech AF (on order, at Aero, Vodochody)
	0825	Mil Mi-17	Czech AF CLV, Pardubice
	0832	Mil Mi-17	Czech AF CLV, Pardubice
	0834	Mil Mi-17	Czech AF 243.vrl/24.zDL, Praha/Kbely
	0835	Mil Mi-17	Czech AF CLV, Pardubice
	0839	Mil Mi-17	Czech AF 243.vrl/24.zDL, Praha/Kbely
	0848	Mil Mi-17	Czech AF 243.vrl/24.zDL, Praha/Kbely
	0849	Mil Mi-17	Czech AF 243.vrl/24.zDL, Praha/Kbely
	0850	Mil Mi-17	Czech AF 243.vrl/24.zDL, Praha/Kbely
	0928	LET L-410UVP-T Turbolet	Czech AF CLV, Pardubice
	1525	LET L-410FG Turbolet	Czech AF 242.tsl/24.zDL, Praha/Kbely
	1526	LET L-410FG Turbolet	Czech AF 242.tsl/24.zDL, Praha/Kbely
	2312	LET L-410UVP-E Turbolet	Czech AF 242.tsl/24.zDL, Praha/Kbely
	2601	LET L-410UVP-E Turbolet	Czech AF 242.tsl/24.zDL, Praha/Kbely
	2602	LET L-410UVP-E Turbolet	Czech AF 242.tsl/24.zDL, Praha/Kbely
	2626	Aero L-39NG Skyfox	Aero, stored Vodochody
	2710	LET L-410UVP-E Turbolet	Czech AF 242.tsl/24.zDL, Praha/Kbely
	2801	Airbus A.319CJ-115X	Czech AF 241.dlt/24.zDL, Praha/Kbely
	3085	Airbus A.319CJ-115X	Czech AF 241.dlt/24.zDL, Praha/Kbely
	6028	Aero L-159T-2 ALCA	Czech AF 213.vlt/21.zTL, Cáslav
	6031	Aero L-159T-2 ALCA	Czech AF 213.vlt/21.zTL, Cáslav
	6038	Aero L-159T-2 ALCA	Czech AF 213.vlt/21.zTL, Cáslav
	6046	Aero L-159T-1 ALCA	Czech AF 213.vlt/21.zTL, Cáslav
	6047	Aero L-159T-1 ALCA	Czech AF 213.vlt/21.zTL, Cáslav
	6048	Aero L-159A ALCA	Czech AF 212.tl/21.zTL, Cáslav
	6050	Aero L-159A ALCA	Czech AF 212.tl/21.zTL, Cáslav
	6051	Aero L-159A ALCA	Czech AF 212.tl/21.zTL, Cáslav
	6052	Aero L-159A ALCA	Czech AF 212.tl/21.zTL, Cáslav
	6053	Aero L-159A ALCA	Czech AF 212.tl/21.zTL, Cáslav
	6054	Aero L-159A ALCA	Czech AF 212.tl/21.zTL, Cáslav
	6057	Aero L-159A ALCA	Czech AF 212.tl/21.zTL, Cáslav
	6058	Aero L-159A ALCA	Czech AF 212.tl/21.zTL, Cáslav
	6059	Aero L-159A ALCA	Czech AF 212.tl/21.zTL, Cáslav
	6060	Aero L-159A ALCA	Czech AF 212.tl/21.zTL, Cáslav
	6062	Aero L-159A ALCA	Czech AF 212.tl/21.zTL, Cáslav
	6063	Aero L-159A ALCA	Czech AF 212.tl/21.zTL, Cáslav
	6064	Aero L-159A ALCA	Czech AF 212.tl/21.zTL, Cáslav
	6066	Aero L-159A ALCA	Czech AF 212.tl/21.zTL, Cáslav
	6067	Aero L-159T-1 ALCA	Czech AF 213.vlt/21.zTL, Cáslav
	6070	Aero L-159A ALCA $	Czech AF 212.tl/21.zTL, Cáslav
	6073	Aero L-159T-2X ALCA	Aero, stored Vodochody
	6077	Aero L-159T-1 ALCA	Czech AF 213.vlt/21.zTL, Cáslav
	6078	Aero L-159T-1 ALCA	Czech AF 213.vlt/21.zTL, Cáslav
	9234	SAAB JAS 39C Gripen	Czech AF 211.tl/21.zTL, Cáslav
	9235	SAAB JAS 39C Gripen	Czech AF 211.tl/21.zTL, Cáslav
	9236	SAAB JAS 39C Gripen	Czech AF 211.tl/21.zTL, Cáslav
	9237	SAAB JAS 39C Gripen	Czech AF 211.tl/21.zTL, Cáslav
	9238	SAAB JAS 39C Gripen	Czech AF 211.tl/21.zTL, Cáslav
	9239	SAAB JAS 39C Gripen	Czech AF 211.tl/21.zTL, Cáslav
	9240	SAAB JAS 39C Gripen	Czech AF 211.tl/21.zTL, Cáslav
	9241	SAAB JAS 39C Gripen	Czech AF 211.tl/21.zTL, Cáslav
	9242	SAAB JAS 39C Gripen $	Czech AF 211.tl/21.zTL, Cáslav
	9243	SAAB JAS 39C Gripen	Czech AF 211.tl/21.zTL, Cáslav

Serial	Type (code/other identity)	Owner/operator, location or fate	Notes
9244	SAAB JAS 39C Gripen $	Czech AF 211.tl/21.zTL, Cáslav	
9245	SAAB JAS 39C Gripen	Czech AF 211.tl/21.zTL, Cáslav	
9767	Mil Mi-171Sh	Czech AF 221.lbvr & 222.vrlt/22.zVrL, Náměšt	
9781	Mil Mi-171Sh	Czech AF 221.lbvr & 222.vrlt/22.zVrL, Náměšt	
9799	Mil Mi-171Sh	Czech AF 221.lbvr & 222.vrlt/22.zVrL, Náměšt	
9806	Mil Mi-171Sh	Czech AF 221.lbvr & 222.vrlt/22.zVrL, Náměšt	
9813	Mil Mi-171Sh	Czech AF 221.lbvr & 222.vrlt/22.zVrL, Náměšt	
9819	SAAB JAS 39D Gripen	Czech AF 211.tl/21.zTL, Cáslav	
9820	SAAB JAS 39D Gripen	Czech AF 211.tl/21.zTL, Cáslav	
9825	Mil Mi-171Sh	Czech AF 221.lbvr & 222.vrlt/22.zVrL, Náměšt	
9837	Mil Mi-171Sh	Czech AF 221.lbvr & 222.vrlt/22.zVrL, Náměšt	
9844	Mil Mi-171Sh	Czech AF 221.lbvr & 222.vrlt/22.zVrL, Náměšt	
9868	Mil Mi-171Sh	Czech AF 221.lbvr & 222.vrlt/22.zVrL, Náměšt	
9873	Mil Mi-171Sh	Czech AF 221.lbvr & 222.vrlt/22.zVrL, Náměšt	
9887	Mil Mi-171Sh	Czech AF 221.lbvr & 222.vrlt/22.zVrL, Náměšt	
9892	Mil Mi-171Sh	Czech AF 221.lbvr & 222.vrlt/22.zVrL, Náměšt	
9904	Mil Mi-171Sh	Czech AF 221.lbvr & 222.vrlt/22.zVrL, Náměšt	
9915	Mil Mi-171Sh	Czech AF 221.lbvr & 222.vrlt/22.zVrL, Náměšt	
9926	Mil Mi-171Sh	Czech AF 221.lbvr & 222.vrlt/22.zVrL, Náměšt	
....	Bell Helicopter AH-1Z Viper	Czech AF (on order)	
....	Bell Helicopter AH-1Z Viper	Czech AF (on order)	
....	Bell Helicopter AH-1Z Viper	Czech AF (on order)	
....	Bell Helicopter AH-1Z Viper	Czech AF (on order)	
....	Bell Helicopter AH-1Z Viper	Czech AF (on order)	
....	Bell Helicopter AH-1Z Viper	Czech AF (on order)	
....	Bell Helicopter UH-1Y Venom	Czech AF (on order)	
....	Bell Helicopter UH-1Y Venom	Czech AF (on order)	
....	Bell Helicopter UH-1Y Venom	Czech AF (on order)	
....	Bell Helicopter UH-1Y Venom	Czech AF (on order)	
....	Bombardier Global 5000	Czech AF (on order)	
....	Bombardier Global 5000	Czech AF (on order)	

DEMOCRATIC REPUBLIC OF CONGO

| T7-RDC | Boeing 737-9JAER(BBJ) | Government of Democratic Republic of Congo, Kinshasa | |

DENMARK
Kongelige Danske Flyvevåben (KDF)

B-536	Lockheed C-130J-30 Hercules II	KDF Eskadrille 721, Aalborg	
B-537	Lockheed C-130J-30 Hercules II	KDF Eskadrille 721, Aalborg	
B-538	Lockheed C-130J-30 Hercules II	KDF Eskadrille 721, Aalborg	
B-583	Lockheed C-130J-30 Hercules II	KDF Eskadrille 721, Aalborg	
C-080	Canadair CL.604 Challenger	KDF Eskadrille 721, Aalborg	
C-168	Canadair CL.604 Challenger	KDF Eskadrille 721, Aalborg	
C-172	Canadair CL.604 Challenger	KDF Eskadrille 721, Aalborg	
C-215	Canadair CL.604 Challenger	KDF Eskadrille 721, Aalborg	
E-004	SABCA (GD) F-16A MLU Fighting Falcon	KDF Eskadrille 727/730 (FWS), Skrydstrup	
E-005	SABCA (GD) F-16A MLU Fighting Falcon	KDF Eskadrille 727/730 (FWS), Skrydstrup	
E-006	SABCA (GD) F-16A MLU Fighting Falcon $	KDF Eskadrille 727/730 (FWS), Skrydstrup	
E-007	SABCA (GD) F-16A MLU Fighting Falcon	KDF Eskadrille 727/730 (FWS), Skrydstrup	
E-008	SABCA (GD) F-16A MLU Fighting Falcon	KDF Eskadrille 727/730 (FWS), Skrydstrup	
E-011	GD F-16A MLU Fighting Falcon	KDF Eskadrille 727/730 (FWS), Skrydstrup	
E-016	SABCA (GD) F-16A MLU Fighting Falcon	KDF Eskadrille 727/730 (FWS), Skrydstrup	
E-017	SABCA (GD) F-16A MLU Fighting Falcon	KDF Eskadrille 727/730 (FWS), Skrydstrup	
E-018	SABCA (GD) F-16A MLU Fighting Falcon	KDF Eskadrille 727/730 (FWS), Skrydstrup	
E-024	GD F-16A MLU Fighting Falcon	KDF Eskadrille 727/730 (FWS), Skrydstrup	
E-074	GD F-16A MLU Fighting Falcon	KDF Eskadrille 727/730 (FWS), Skrydstrup	
E-075	GD F-16A MLU Fighting Falcon	KDF Eskadrille 727/730 (FWS), Skrydstrup	
E-107	GD F-16A MLU Fighting Falcon	KDF Eskadrille 727/730 (FWS), Skrydstrup	
E-189	SABCA (GD) F-16A MLU Fighting Falcon	KDF Eskadrille 727/730 (FWS), Skrydstrup	
E-190	SABCA (GD) F-16A MLU Fighting Falcon	KDF Eskadrille 727/730 (FWS), Skrydstrup	
E-191	SABCA (GD) F-16A MLU Fighting Falcon $	KDF Eskadrille 727/730 (FWS), Skrydstrup	

Notes	Serial	Type (code/other identity)	Owner/operator, location or fate
	E-194	SABCA (GD) F-16A MLU Fighting Falcon	KDF Eskadrille 727/730 (FWS), Skrydstrup
	E-596	SABCA (GD) F-16A MLU Fighting Falcon	To Ukraine as 80-3596, August 2024
	E-597	SABCA (GD) F-16A MLU Fighting Falcon	KDF Eskadrille 727/730 (FWS), Skrydstrup
	E-598	SABCA (GD) F-16A MLU Fighting Falcon	KDF Eskadrille 727/730 (FWS), Skrydstrup
	E-599	SABCA (GD) F-16A MLU Fighting Falcon	To Ukraine as 80-3599, August 2024
	E-600	SABCA (GD) F-16A MLU Fighting Falcon	To Ukraine as 80-3600, August 2024 (destroyed 24th August 2024)
	E-601	SABCA (GD) F-16A MLU Fighting Falcon	KDF Eskadrille 727/730 (FWS), Skrydstrup
	E-602	SABCA (GD) F-16A MLU Fighting Falcon	KDF Eskadrille 727/730 (FWS), Skrydstrup
	E-603	SABCA (GD) F-16A MLU Fighting Falcon	To Ukraine as 80-3603, 2024
	E-604	SABCA (GD) F-16A MLU Fighting Falcon	KDF Eskadrille 727/730 (FWS), Skrydstrup
	E-605	SABCA (GD) F-16A MLU Fighting Falcon	KDF Eskadrille 727/730 (FWS), Skrydstrup
	E-606	SABCA (GD) F-16A MLU Fighting Falcon	KDF Eskadrille 727/730 (FWS), Skrydstrup
	E-607	SABCA (GD) F-16A MLU Fighting Falcon	KDF Eskadrille 727/730 (FWS), Skrydstrup
	E-608	SABCA (GD) F-16A MLU Fighting Falcon	KDF Eskadrille 727/730 (FWS), Skrydstrup
	E-609	SABCA (GD) F-16A MLU Fighting Falcon	KDF Eskadrille 727/730 (FWS), Skrydstrup
	E-610	SABCA (GD) F-16A MLU Fighting Falcon	KDF Eskadrille 727/730 (FWS), Skrydstrup
	E-611	SABCA (GD) F-16A MLU Fighting Falcon	KDF Eskadrille 727/730 (FWS), Skrydstrup
	ET-022	Fokker (GD) F-16B MLU Fighting Falcon	KDF Eskadrille 727/730 (FWS), Skrydstrup
	ET-197	Fokker (GD) F-16B MLU Fighting Falcon	KDF Eskadrille 727/730 (FWS), Skrydstrup
	ET-198	Fokker (GD) F-16B MLU Fighting Falcon	KDF Eskadrille 727/730 (FWS), Skrydstrup
	ET-199	Fokker (GD) F-16B MLU Fighting Falcon	KDF Eskadrille 727/730 (FWS), Skrydstrup
	ET-207	SABCA (GD) F-16B MLU Fighting Falcon	KDF Eskadrille 727/730 (FWS), Skrydstrup
	ET-208	SABCA (GD) F-16B MLU Fighting Falcon	KDF Eskadrille 727/730 (FWS), Skrydstrup
	ET-612	SABCA (GD) F-16B MLU Fighting Falcon	KDF Eskadrille 727/730 (FWS), Skrydstrup
	ET-613	SABCA (GD) F-16B MLU Fighting Falcon	KDF Eskadrille 727/730 (FWS), Skrydstrup
	ET-614	SABCA (GD) F-16B MLU Fighting Falcon	KDF Eskadrille 727/730 (FWS), Skrydstrup
	ET-615	SABCA (GD) F-16B MLU Fighting Falcon	KDF Eskadrille 727/730 (FWS), Skrydstrup
	L-001	Lockheed Martin F-35A Lightning II	KDF Eskadrille 727, Skrydstrup
	L-002	Lockheed Martin F-35A Lightning II	KDF Eskadrille 727, Skrydstrup
	L-003	Lockheed Martin F-35A Lightning II	KDF Eskadrille 727, Skrydstrup
	L-004	Lockheed Martin F-35A Lightning II	KDF Eskadrille 727, Skrydstrup
	L-005	Lockheed Martin F-35A Lightning II	KDF Eskadrille 727, Skrydstrup
	L-006	Lockheed Martin F-35A Lightning II	KDF Eskadrille 727, Skrydstrup
	L-007	Lockheed Martin F-35A Lightning II	KDF Eskadrille 727, Skrydstrup
	L-008	Lockheed Martin F-35A Lightning II	KDF Eskadrille 727, Skrydstrup
	L-009	Lockheed Martin F-35A Lightning II	KDF Eskadrille 727, Skrydstrup
	L-010	Lockheed Martin F-35A Lightning II	KDF Eskadrille 727, Skrydstrup
	L-011	Lockheed Martin F-35A Lightning II	KDF Eskadrille 727, Skrydstrup
	L-012	Lockheed Martin F-35A Lightning II	KDF 308th FS/56th FW, Luke AFB, AZ, USA
	L-013	Lockheed Martin F-35A Lightning II	KDF 308th FS/56th FW, Luke AFB, AZ, USA
	L-014	Lockheed Martin F-35A Lightning II	KDF 308th FS/56th FW, Luke AFB, AZ, USA
	L-015	Lockheed Martin F-35A Lightning II	KDF 308th FS/56th FW, Luke AFB, AZ, USA
	L-016	Lockheed Martin F-35A Lightning II	KDF 308th FS/56th FW, Luke AFB, AZ, USA
	L-017	Lockheed Martin F-35A Lightning II	KDF 308th FS/56th FW, Luke AFB, AZ, USA
	L-018	Lockheed Martin F-35A Lightning II	KDF (on order)
	L-019	Lockheed Martin F-35A Lightning II	KDF (on order)
	L-020	Lockheed Martin F-35A Lightning II	KDF (on order)
	L-021	Lockheed Martin F-35A Lightning II	KDF (on order)
	L-022	Lockheed Martin F-35A Lightning II	KDF (on order)
	L-023	Lockheed Martin F-35A Lightning II	KDF (on order)
	L-024	Lockheed Martin F-35A Lightning II	KDF (on order)
	L-025	Lockheed Martin F-35A Lightning II	KDF (on order)
	L-026	Lockheed Martin F-35A Lightning II	KDF (on order)
	L-027	Lockheed Martin F-35A Lightning II	KDF (on order)
	M-502	AgustaWestland EH.101 Mk.512 (ZJ991)	KDF Eskadrille 722, Karup
	M-504	AgustaWestland EH.101 Mk.512 (ZJ993)	KDF Eskadrille 722, Karup
	M-507	AgustaWestland EH.101 Mk.512 (ZJ996)	KDF Eskadrille 722, Karup
	M-508	AgustaWestland EH.101 Mk.512 (ZJ997)	KDF Eskadrille 722, Karup
	M-510	AgustaWestland EH.101 Mk.512 (ZJ999)	KDF Eskadrille 722, Karup
	M-512	AgustaWestland EH.101 Mk.512 (ZK002)	KDF Eskadrille 722, Karup
	M-513	AgustaWestland EH.101 Mk.512 (ZK003)	KDF Eskadrille 722, Karup

Serial	Type (code/other identity)	Owner/operator, location or fate	Notes
M-514	AgustaWestland EH.101 Mk.512 (ZK004)	KDF Eskadrille 722, Karup	
M-515	AgustaWestland EH.101 Mk.512 (ZK160)	KDF Eskadrille 722, Karup	
M-516	AgustaWestland EH.101 Mk.512 (ZK161)	KDF Eskadrille 722, Karup	
M-517	AgustaWestland EH.101 Mk.512 (ZK162)	KDF Eskadrille 722, Karup	
M-518	AgustaWestland EH.101 Mk.512 (ZK163)	KDF Eskadrille 722, Karup	
M-519	AgustaWestland EH.101 Mk.512 (ZK164)	KDF Eskadrille 722, Karup	
M-520	AgustaWestland EH.101 Mk.512 (ZK165)	KDF Eskadrille 722, Karup	
N-971	Sikorsky MH-60R Sea Hawk	KDF Eskadrille 723, Karup	
N-972	Sikorsky MH-60R Sea Hawk	KDF Eskadrille 723, Karup	
N-973	Sikorsky MH-60R Sea Hawk	KDF Eskadrille 723, Karup	
N-974	Sikorsky MH-60R Sea Hawk	KDF Eskadrille 723, Karup	
N-975	Sikorsky MH-60R Sea Hawk	KDF Eskadrille 723, Karup	
N-976	Sikorsky MH-60R Sea Hawk	KDF Eskadrille 723, Karup	
N-977	Sikorsky MH-60R Sea Hawk	KDF Eskadrille 723, Karup	
N-978	Sikorsky MH-60R Sea Hawk	KDF Eskadrille 723, Karup	
N-979	Sikorsky MH-60R Sea Hawk	KDF Eskadrille 723, Karup	
P-234	Aérospatiale AS.550C-2 Fennec	KDF Eskadrille 724, Karup	
P-254	Aérospatiale AS.550C-2 Fennec	KDF Eskadrille 724, Karup	
P-275	Aérospatiale AS.550C-2 Fennec	KDF Eskadrille 724, Karup	
P-276	Aérospatiale AS.550C-2 Fennec	KDF Eskadrille 724, Karup	
P-287	Aérospatiale AS.550C-2 Fennec	KDF Eskadrille 724, Karup	
P-288	Aérospatiale AS.550C-2 Fennec	KDF Eskadrille 724, Karup	
P-319	Aérospatiale AS.550C-2 Fennec	KDF Eskadrille 724, Karup	
P-320	Aérospatiale AS.550C-2 Fennec	KDF Eskadrille 724, Karup	
P-339	Aérospatiale AS.550C-2 Fennec	KDF Eskadrille 724, Karup	
P-352	Aérospatiale AS.550C-2 Fennec	KDF Eskadrille 724, Karup	
P-369	Aérospatiale AS.550C-2 Fennec	KDF Eskadrille 724, Karup	
T-401	SAAB T-17 Supporter	KDF Flyveskolen, Karup	
T-402	SAAB T-17 Supporter	KDF Flyveskolen, Karup	
T-403	SAAB T-17 Supporter	KDF Flyveskolen, Karup	
T-404	SAAB T-17 Supporter	KDF Flyveskolen, Karup	
T-405	SAAB T-17 Supporter	KDF Skrydstrup Station Flight	
T-407	SAAB T-17 Supporter	*Instructional airframe, Karup*	
T-409	SAAB T-17 Supporter	KDF Flyveskolen, Karup	
T-410	SAAB T-17 Supporter	KDF Flyveskolen, Karup	
T-412	SAAB T-17 Supporter	KDF Flyveskolen, Karup	
T-413	SAAB T-17 Supporter	KDF, *Baby Blue Display Team, Skrydstrup*	
T-414	SAAB T-17 Supporter	KDF Eskadrille 721, Aalborg	
T-415	SAAB T-17 Supporter $	KDF, *Baby Blue Display Team, Skrydstrup*	
T-417	SAAB T-17 Supporter	KDF Flyveskolen, Karup	
T-418	SAAB T-17 Supporter	KDF Skrydstrup Station Flight	
T-419	SAAB T-17 Supporter	KDF Flyveskolen, Karup	
T-420	SAAB T-17 Supporter	KDF Skrydstrup Station Flight	
T-421	SAAB T-17 Supporter	KDF, *Baby Blue Display Team, Skrydstrup*	
T-423	SAAB T-17 Supporter	KDF, *Baby Blue Display Team, Skrydstrup*	
T-425	SAAB T-17 Supporter	KDF Flyveskolen, Karup	
T-426	SAAB T-17 Supporter	KDF, *Baby Blue Display Team, Skrydstrup*	
T-427	SAAB T-17 Supporter	KDF Flyveskolen, Karup	
T-428	SAAB T-17 Supporter	KDF, *Baby Blue Display Team, Skrydstrup*	
T-429	SAAB T-17 Supporter	KDF Flyveskolen, Karup	
T-430	SAAB T-17 Supporter	KDF Flyveskolen, Karup	
T-431	SAAB T-17 Supporter	KDF Flyveskolen, Karup	
T-432	SAAB T-17 Supporter	KDF Flyveskolen, Karup	

ECUADOR
Fuerza Aérea Ecuatoriana (FAE)

FAE-051	Embraer ERJ.135 Legacy 600	FAE Escuadrón de Transporte 1114, Quito	
FAE-052	Dassault Falcon 7X	FAE Escuadrón de Transporte 1114, Quito	

EGYPT
Al Quwwat al-Jawwiya il Misriya (Egyptian Air Force)

1331	Ilyushin Il-76MF (SU-BTX)	Egyptian AF 16 Sqn, Cairo West	

Notes	Serial	Type (code/other identity)	Owner/operator, location or fate
	1332	Ilyushin Il-76MF (SU-BTY)	Egyptian AF 16 Sqn, Cairo West
	1271	Lockheed C-130H Hercules (SU-BAB)	Egyptian AF 16 Sqn, Cairo West
	1273	Lockheed C-130H Hercules (SU-BAD)	Egyptian AF 16 Sqn, Cairo West
	1274	Lockheed C-130H Hercules (SU-BAE)	Egyptian AF 16 Sqn, Cairo West
	1275	Lockheed C-130H Hercules (SU-BAF)	Egyptian AF 16 Sqn, Cairo West
	1277	Lockheed C-130H Hercules (SU-BAI)	Egyptian AF 16 Sqn, Cairo West
	1278	Lockheed C-130H Hercules (SU-BAJ)	Egyptian AF 16 Sqn, Cairo West
	1279	Lockheed C-130H Hercules (SU-BAK)	Egyptian AF 16 Sqn, Cairo West
	1280	Lockheed C-130H Hercules (SU-BAL)	Egyptian AF 16 Sqn, Cairo West
	1281	Lockheed C-130H Hercules (SU-BAM)	Egyptian AF 16 Sqn, Cairo West
	1282	Lockheed C-130H Hercules (SU-BAN)	Egyptian AF 16 Sqn, Cairo West (written off?)
	1283	Lockheed C-130H Hercules (SU-BAP)	Egyptian AF 16 Sqn, Cairo West
	1284	Lockheed C-130H Hercules (SU-BAQ)	Egyptian AF 16 Sqn, Cairo West
	1285	Lockheed C-130H Hercules (SU-BAR)	Egyptian AF 16 Sqn, Cairo West
	1286	Lockheed C-130H Hercules (SU-BAS)	Egyptian AF 16 Sqn, Cairo West
	1287	Lockheed C-130H Hercules (SU-BAT)	Egyptian AF 16 Sqn, Cairo West (written off?)
	1288	Lockheed C-130H Hercules (SU-BAU)	Egyptian AF 16 Sqn, Cairo West
	1289	Lockheed C-130H Hercules (SU-BAV)	Egyptian AF 16 Sqn, Cairo West
	1290	Lockheed C-130H Hercules (SU-BEW)	Egyptian AF 16 Sqn, Cairo West
	1291	Lockheed C-130H Hercules (SU-BEX)	Egyptian AF 16 Sqn, Cairo West
	1292	Lockheed C-130H Hercules (SU-BEY)	Egyptian AF 16 Sqn, Cairo West
	1293	Lockheed C-130H-30 Hercules (SU-BKS)	Egyptian AF 16 Sqn, Cairo West
	1294	Lockheed C-130H-30 Hercules (SU-BKT)	Egyptian AF 16 Sqn, Cairo West
	1295	Lockheed C-130H-30 Hercules (SU-BKU)	Egyptian AF 16 Sqn, Cairo West
	1296	Lockheed C-130H Hercules (SU-BPJ)	Egyptian AF 16 Sqn, Cairo West
	1297	Lockheed C-130H Hercules (SU-BPK)	Egyptian AF 16 Sqn, Cairo West
	1298	Lockheed C-130H Hercules (SU-BPL)	Egyptian AF 16 Sqn, Cairo West
	....	Lockheed C-130J Hercules II	Egyptian AF (on order)
	....	Lockheed C-130J Hercules II	Egyptian AF (on order)
Government of Egypt			
	SU-BGM	Grumman G.1159A Gulfstream III	Egyptian AF/Government, Cairo
	SU-BGV	Grumman G.1159A Gulfstream III	Egyptian AF/Government, Cairo
	SU-BNC	Grumman G.1159C Gulfstream IV-SP	Egyptian AF/Government, Cairo
	SU-BND	Grumman G.1159C Gulfstream IV-SP	Egyptian AF/Government, Cairo
	SU-BNO	Grumman G.1159C Gulfstream IV-SP	Egyptian AF/Government, Cairo
	SU-BNP	Grumman G.1159C Gulfstream IV-SP	Egyptian AF/Government, Cairo
	SU-BPE	Gulfstream Aerospace G.400	Egyptian AF/Government, Cairo
	SU-BPF	Gulfstream Aerospace G.400	Egyptian AF/Government, Cairo
	SU-BRF	Cessna 680 Citation Sovereign	Government of Egypt, Cairo
	SU-BRG	Cessna 680 Citation Sovereign	Government of Egypt, Cairo
	SU-BTT	Dassault Falcon 7X (F-WWHP)	Egyptian AF/Government, Cairo
	SU-BTU	Dassault Falcon 7X (F-WWUR)	Egyptian AF/Government, Cairo
	SU-BTV	Dassault Falcon 7X (F-WWUQ)	Egyptian AF/Government, Cairo
	SU-BTW	Dassault Falcon 8X (F-WWVL)	Egyptian AF/Government, Cairo
	SU-EGY	Boeing 747-830	Government of Egypt, Cairo (stored Hamburg)
	SU-GGG	Airbus A.340-211	Government of Egypt, Cairo
EIRE			
An tAerchór/Irish Air Corps (IAC)			
	205	Reims-Cessna FR172H	IAC Baldonnel (wfu)
	215	Fouga CM170R Super Magister	IAC Baldonnel, GI use
	252	Airtech CN.235 MPA Persuader	Airbus Defence & Space, Sevilla (to be preserved)
	253	Airtech CN.235 MPA Persuader	Airbus Defence & Space, Sevilla (to be preserved)
	256	Eurocopter EC135T-1 (G-BZRM)	IAC GASU (No 106 Sqn)/1 Operations Wing, Baldonnel
	258	Gates Learjet 45 (N5009T)	IAC No 102 Sqn/1 Operations Wing, Baldonnel
	260	Pilatus PC-9M (HB-HQS) $	IAC Flying Training School, Baldonnel
	261	Pilatus PC-9M (HB-HQT)	IAC Flying Training School, Baldonnel
	262	Pilatus PC-9M (HB-HQU)	IAC Flying Training School, Baldonnel
	263	Pilatus PC-9M (HB-HQV)	IAC Flying Training School, Baldonnel
	264	Pilatus PC-9M (HB-HQW) $	IAC Flying Training School, Baldonnel
	266	Pilatus PC-9M (HB-HQY) $	IAC Flying Training School, Baldonnel

Serial	Type (code/other identity)	Owner/operator, location or fate	Notes
267	Pilatus PC-9M (HB-HQZ) $	IAC Flying Training School, Baldonnel	
269	Pilatus PC-9M (HB-HXI) $	IAC Flying Training School, Baldonnel	
270	Eurocopter EC135P-2 (D-HECF) $	IAC No 302 Sqn/3 Operations Wing, Baldonnel	
271	Eurocopter EC135P-2 (D-HECB)	IAC No 302 Sqn/3 Operations Wing, Baldonnel	
272	Eurocopter EC135T-2 (G-CECT)	IAC GASU (No 106 Sqn)/1 Operations Wing, Baldonnel	
274	AgustaWestland AW139	IAC No 301 Sqn/3 Operations Wing, Baldonnel	
275	AgustaWestland AW139	IAC No 301 Sqn/3 Operations Wing, Baldonnel	
276	AgustaWestland AW139 $	IAC No 301 Sqn/3 Operations Wing, Baldonnel	
277	AgustaWestland AW139	IAC No 301 Sqn/3 Operations Wing, Baldonnel	
278	AgustaWestland AW139 $	IAC No 301 Sqn/3 Operations Wing, Baldonnel	
279	AgustaWestland AW139	IAC No 301 Sqn/3 Operations Wing, Baldonnel	
280	Pilatus PC.XII/47E (HB-FXT) $	IAC No 102 Sqn/1 Operations Wing, Baldonnel	
281	Pilatus PC.XII/47E Spectre (N280NG) $	IAC No 104 Sqn/1 Operations Wing, Baldonnel	
282	Pilatus PC.XII/47E Spectre (N281NG) $	IAC No 104 Sqn/1 Operations Wing, Baldonnel	
283	Pilatus PC.XII/47E Spectre (N282NG) $	IAC No 104 Sqn/1 Operations Wing, Baldonnel	
284	CASA C-295MPA (EC-010)	IAC No 101 Sqn/1 Operations Wing, Baldonnel	
285	CASA C-295MPA	IAC No 101 Sqn/1 Operations Wing, Baldonnel	
2..	CASA C-295W	IAC (on order)	

EQUATORIAL GUINEA
| 3C-EGE | Boeing 737-7FB(BBJ) | Government of Equatorial Guinea, Malabo | |

ESTONIA
Estonian Air Force
40 y	WSK-PZL An-2T	Estonian AF 1.Eskadrill/Lennugrupp, Ämari	
41 y	Antonov An-2	Estonian AF 1.Eskadrill/Lennugrupp, Ämari	
43 bk	PZL-Mielec M28-05 Skytruck (09-0320)	Estonian AF 1.Eskadrill/Lennugrupp, Ämari	
44 bk	PZL-Mielec M28-05 Skytruck (09-0317)	Estonian AF 1.Eskadrill/Lennugrupp, Ämari	

ESWATINI
| 3DC-SDF | Airbus A.340-213X | Government of Eswatini, Manzini/Sikhupe | |

FINLAND
Suomen Ilmavoimat (Finnish Air Force) & Suomen Maavoimat (Finnish Army)
CC-1	CASA C-295M	Ilmavoimat TukiLLv, Tampere/Pirkkala	
CC-2	CASA C-295M	Ilmavoimat TukiLLv, Tampere/Pirkkala	
CC-3	CASA C-295M	Ilmavoimat TukiLLv, Tampere/Pirkkala	
HN-401	McDonnell Douglas F-18C Hornet	Stored Halli (spares use)	
HN-402	McDonnell Douglas F-18C Hornet	Ilmavoimat HävLLv 11, Roveniemi	
HN-403	McDonnell Douglas F-18C Hornet	Ilmavoimat HävLLv 31, Kuopio/Rissala	
HN-404	McDonnell Douglas F-18C Hornet	Ilmavoimat HävLLv 11, Roveniemi	
HN-405	McDonnell Douglas F-18C Hornet	Ilmavoimat HävLLv 31, Kuopio/Rissala	
HN-406	McDonnell Douglas F-18C Hornet	Ilmavoimat HävLLv 31, Kuopio/Rissala	
HN-407	McDonnell Douglas F-18C Hornet	Ilmavoimat HävLLv 11, Roveniemi	
HN-408	McDonnell Douglas F-18C Hornet	Ilmavoimat HävLLv 31, Kuopio/Rissala	
HN-409	McDonnell Douglas F-18C Hornet	Ilmavoimat HävLLv 11, Roveniemi	
HN-410	McDonnell Douglas F-18C Hornet	Ilmavoimat HävLLv 31, Kuopio/Rissala	
HN-411	McDonnell Douglas F-18C Hornet $	Ilmavoimat HävLLv 11, Roveniemi	
HN-412	McDonnell Douglas F-18C Hornet	Ilmavoimat HävLLv 11, Roveniemi	
HN-414	McDonnell Douglas F-18C Hornet	Ilmavoimat HävLLv 31, Kuopio/Rissala	
HN-415	McDonnell Douglas F-18C Hornet	Ilmavoimat HävLLv 31, Kuopio/Rissala	
HN-416	McDonnell Douglas F-18C Hornet	Ilmavoimat HävLLv 11, Roveniemi	
HN-417	McDonnell Douglas F-18C Hornet	Ilmavoimat HävLLv 11, Roveniemi	
HN-418	McDonnell Douglas F-18C Hornet	Ilmavoimat HävLLv 11, Roveniemi	
HN-419	McDonnell Douglas F-18C Hornet	Ilmavoimat HävLLv 11, Roveniemi	
HN-420	McDonnell Douglas F-18C Hornet	Ilmavoimat HävLLv 31, Kuopio/Rissala	
HN-421	McDonnell Douglas F-18C Hornet	Ilmavoimat HävLLv 11, Roveniemi	
HN-422	McDonnell Douglas F-18C Hornet	Ilmavoimat HävLLv 11, Roveniemi	
HN-423	McDonnell Douglas F-18C Hornet	Ilmavoimat HävLLv 31, Kuopio/Rissala	
HN-424	McDonnell Douglas F-18C Hornet	Ilmavoimat HävLLv 31, Kuopio/Rissala	
HN-425	McDonnell Douglas F-18C Hornet	Ilmavoimat HävLLv 31, Kuopio/Rissala	

Notes	Serial	Type (code/other identity)	Owner/operator, location or fate
	HN-426	McDonnell Douglas F-18C Hornet	Ilmavoimat HävLLv 31, Kuopio/Rissala
	HN-427	McDonnell Douglas F-18C Hornet	Ilmavoimat HävLLv 11, Roveniemi
	HN-428	McDonnell Douglas F-18C Hornet	Ilmavoimat HävLLv 11, Roveniemi
	HN-429	McDonnell Douglas F-18C Hornet	Ilmavoimat HävLLv 11, Roveniemi
	HN-431	McDonnell Douglas F-18C Hornet	Ilmavoimat HävLLv 31, Kuopio/Rissala
	HN-432	McDonnell Douglas F-18C Hornet	Ilmavoimat HävLLv 31, Kuopio/Rissala
	HN-433	McDonnell Douglas F-18C Hornet	Ilmavoimat HävLLv 31, Kuopio/Rissala
	HN-434	McDonnell Douglas F-18C Hornet	Ilmavoimat HävLLv 11, Roveniemi
	HN-435	McDonnell Douglas F-18C Hornet	Ilmavoimat HävLLv 31, Kuopio/Rissala
	HN-436	McDonnell Douglas F-18C Hornet	Ilmavoimat HävLLv 31, Kuopio/Rissala
	HN-437	McDonnell Douglas F-18C Hornet	Ilmavoimat HävLLv 31, Kuopio/Rissala
	HN-438	McDonnell Douglas F-18C Hornet	Ilmavoimat HävLLv 31, Kuopio/Rissala
	HN-439	McDonnell Douglas F-18C Hornet	Ilmavoimat HävLLv 31, Kuopio/Rissala
	HN-440	McDonnell Douglas F-18C Hornet	Ilmavoimat HävLLv 11, Roveniemi
	HN-441	McDonnell Douglas F-18C Hornet	Ilmavoimat HävLLv 11, Roveniemi
	HN-442	McDonnell Douglas F-18C Hornet	Ilmavoimat HävLLv 31, Kuopio/Rissala
	HN-443	McDonnell Douglas F-18C Hornet	Ilmavoimat HävLLv 31, Kuopio/Rissala
	HN-444	McDonnell Douglas F-18C Hornet	Ilmavoimat HävLLv 11, Roveniemi
	HN-445	McDonnell Douglas F-18C Hornet	Ilmavoimat HävLLv 11, Roveniemi
	HN-446	McDonnell Douglas F-18C Hornet	Ilmavoimat HävLLv 11, Roveniemi
	HN-447	McDonnell Douglas F-18C Hornet	Ilmavoimat HävLLv 31, Kuopio/Rissala
	HN-448	McDonnell Douglas F-18C Hornet	Ilmavoimat HävLLv 31, Kuopio/Rissala
	HN-449	McDonnell Douglas F-18C Hornet	Ilmavoimat HävLLv 11, Roveniemi
	HN-450	McDonnell Douglas F-18C Hornet	Ilmavoimat HävLLv 11, Roveniemi
	HN-451	McDonnell Douglas F-18C Hornet	Ilmavoimat HavLLv 31, Kuopio/Rissala
	HN-452	McDonnell Douglas F-18C Hornet	Ilmavoimat HävLLv 11, Roveniemi
	HN-453	McDonnell Douglas F-18C Hornet	Ilmavoimat HävLLv 31, Kuopio/Rissala
	HN-454	McDonnell Douglas F-18C Hornet	Ilmavoimat HävLLv 31, Kuopio/Rissala
	HN-455	McDonnell Douglas F-18C Hornet	Ilmavoimat HävLLv 31, Kuopio/Rissala
	HN-456	McDonnell Douglas F-18C Hornet	Ilmavoimat HävLLv 31, Kuopio/Rissala
	HN-457	McDonnell Douglas F-18C Hornet $	Ilmavoimat HävLLv 11, Roveniemi
	HN-461	McDonnell Douglas F-18D Hornet	Ilmavoimat HävLLv 31, Kuopio/Rissala
	HN-462	McDonnell Douglas F-18D Hornet	Ilmavoimat HävLLv 31, Kuopio/Rissala
	HN-463	McDonnell Douglas F-18D Hornet	Ilmavoimat HävLLv 11, Roveniemi
	HN-464	McDonnell Douglas F-18D Hornet	Ilmavoimat HävLLv 11, Roveniemi
	HN-465	McDonnell Douglas F-18D Hornet	Ilmavoimat HävLLv 11, Roveniemi
	HN-466	McDonnell Douglas F-18D Hornet	Ilmavoimat HävLLv 31, Kuopio/Rissala
	HN-467	McDonnell Douglas F-18D Hornet	Ilmavoimat HävLLv 31, Kuopio/Rissala
	HW-307	BAe Hawk 51	Ilmavoimat HävLLv 41, Jyväskylä/Tikkakoski
	HW-321	BAe Hawk 51	Ilmavoimat HävLLv 41, Jyväskylä/Tikkakoski
	HW-327	BAe Hawk 51	Ilmavoimat HävLLv 41, Jyväskylä/Tikkakoski
	HW-334	BAe Hawk 51	Ilmavoimat HävLLv 41, Jyväskylä/Tikkakoski
	HW-339	BAe Hawk 51	Ilmavoimat HävLLv 41, Jyväskylä/Tikkakoski
	HW-340	BAe Hawk 51 $	Ilmavoimat HävLLv 41, Jyväskylä/Tikkakoski
	HW-341	BAe Hawk 51	Ilmavoimat HävLLv 41, Jyväskylä/Tikkakoski
	HW-343	BAe Hawk 51	Ilmavoimat HävLLv 41, Jyväskylä/Tikkakoski
	HW-344	BAe Hawk 51	Ilmavoimat HävLLv 41, Jyväskylä/Tikkakoski
	HW-345	BAe Hawk 51	Ilmavoimat HävLLv 41, Jyväskylä/Tikkakoski
	HW-348	BAe Hawk 51	Ilmavoimat HävLLv 41, Jyväskylä/Tikkakoski
	HW-349	BAe Hawk 51	Ilmavoimat HävLLv 41, Jyväskylä/Tikkakoski
	HW-350	BAe Hawk 51	Ilmavoimat HävLLv 41, Jyväskylä/Tikkakoski
	HW-351	BAe Hawk 51A	Ilmavoimat HävLLv 41, Jyväskylä/Tikkakoski
	HW-352	BAe Hawk 51A [4]	Ilmavoimat HävLLv 41, Jyväskylä/Tikkakoski
	HW-353	BAe Hawk 51A $	Ilmavoimat HävLLv 41, Jyväskylä/Tikkakoski
	HW-354	BAe Hawk 51A [3]	Ilmavoimat HävLLv 41, Jyväskylä/Tikkakoski
	HW-355	BAe Hawk 51A	Ilmavoimat HävLLv 41, Jyväskylä/Tikkakoski
	HW-356	BAe Hawk 51A	Ilmavoimat HävLLv 41, Jyväskylä/Tikkakoski
	HW-357	BAe Hawk 51A [2]	Ilmavoimat HävLLv 41, Jyväskylä/Tikkakoski
	HW-360	BAe Hawk 66	Ilmavoimat HävLLv 41, Jyväskylä/Tikkakoski
	HW-361	BAe Hawk 66	Ilmavoimat HävLLv 41, Jyväskylä/Tikkakoski
	HW-362	BAe Hawk 66	Ilmavoimat HävLLv 41, Jyväskylä/Tikkakoski
	HW-363	BAe Hawk 66	Ilmavoimat HävLLv 41, Jyväskylä/Tikkakoski

Serial	Type (code/other identity)	Owner/operator, location or fate	Notes
HW-364	BAe Hawk 66	Ilmavoimat HävLLv 41, Jyväskylä/Tikkakoski	
HW-365	BAe Hawk 66	Ilmavoimat HävLLv 41, Jyväskylä/Tikkakoski	
HW-366	BAe Hawk 66	Ilmavoimat HävLLv 41, Jyväskylä/Tikkakoski	
HW-367	BAe Hawk 66	Ilmavoimat HävLLv 41, Jyväskylä/Tikkakoski	
HW-368	BAe Hawk 66	Ilmavoimat HävLLv 41, Jyväskylä/Tikkakoski	
HW-370	BAe Hawk 66	Ilmavoimat HävLLv 41, Jyväskylä/Tikkakoski	
HW-371	BAe Hawk 66	Ilmavoimat HävLLv 41, Jyväskylä/Tikkakoski	
HW-373	BAe Hawk 66	Ilmavoimat HävLLv 41, Jyväskylä/Tikkakoski	
HW-374	BAe Hawk 66	Ilmavoimat HävLLv 41, Jyväskylä/Tikkakoski	
HW-375	BAe Hawk 66	Ilmavoimat HävLLv 41, Jyväskylä/Tikkakoski	
HW-376	BAe Hawk 66	Ilmavoimat HävLLv 41, Jyväskylä/Tikkakoski	
HW-377	BAe Hawk 66	Ilmavoimat HävLLv 41, Jyväskylä/Tikkakoski	
LJ-1	Gates Learjet 35A	Ilmavoimat TukiLLv, Tampere/Pirkkala	
LJ-2	Gates Learjet 35A	Ilmavoimat TukiLLv, Tampere/Pirkkala	
LJ-3	Gates Learjet 35A	Ilmavoimat TukiLLv, Tampere/Pirkkala	
NH-201	NH Industries NH.90-TTH (F-ZWTF)	Eurocopter, Marseille (trials)	
NH-202	NH Industries NH.90-TTH	Maavoimat 1.HK/HekoP, Utti	
NH-203	NH Industries NH.90-TTH	Maavoimat 1.HK/HekoP, Utti	
NH-204	NH Industries NH.90-TTH	Maavoimat 1.HK/HekoP, Utti	
NH-205	NH Industries NH.90-TTH	Maavoimat 1.HK/HekoP, Utti	
NH-206	NH Industries NH.90-TTH	Maavoimat 1.HK/HekoP, Utti	
NH-207	NH Industries NH.90-TTH	Maavoimat 1.HK/HekoP, Utti	
NH-208	NH Industries NH.90-TTH	Maavoimat 1.HK/HekoP, Utti	
NH-209	NH Industries NH.90-TTH	Maavoimat 1.HK/HekoP, Utti	
NH-210	NH Industries NH.90-TTH	Maavoimat 1.HK/HekoP, Utti	
NH-211	NH Industries NH.90-TTH	Maavoimat 1.HK/HekoP, Utti	
NH-212	NH Industries NH.90-TTH	Maavoimat 1.HK/HekoP, Utti	
NH-213	NH Industries NH.90-TTH	Maavoimat 1.HK/HekoP, Utti	
NH-214	NH Industries NH.90-TTH	Maavoimat 1.HK/HekoP, Utti	
NH-215	NH Industries NH.90-TTH	Maavoimat 1.HK/HekoP, Utti	
NH-216	NH Industries NH.90-TTH	Maavoimat 1.HK/HekoP, Utti	
NH-217	NH Industries NH.90-TTH	Maavoimat 1.HK/HekoP, Utti	
NH-218	NH Industries NH.90-TTH	Maavoimat 1.HK/HekoP, Utti	
NH-219	NH Industries NH.90-TTH	Maavoimat 1.HK/HekoP, Utti	
NH-220	NH Industries NH.90-TTH	Maavoimat 1.HK/HekoP, Utti	
NH-221	NH Industries NH.90-TTH	Maavoimat 1.HK/HekoP, Utti	
PI-01	Pilatus PC-12/47E	Ilmavoimat TukiLLv, Tampere/Pirkkala	
PI-02	Pilatus PC-12/47E	Ilmavoimat TukiLLv, Tampere/Pirkkala	
PI-03	Pilatus PC-12/47E	Ilmavoimat TukiLLv, Tampere/Pirkkala	
PI-04	Pilatus PC-12/47E	Ilmavoimat TukiLLv, Tampere/Pirkkala	
PI-05	Pilatus PC-12/47E	Ilmavoimat TukiLLv, Tampere/Pirkkala	
PI-06	Pilatus PC-12/47E	Ilmavoimat TukiLLv, Tampere/Pirkkala	

FRANCE

NB: Due to the way in which French military aircraft serials are issued, this section is sorted by type. Each Armée de l'Air aircraft has its own, fixed registration, in the form F-xxxx, but in general these are only worn on transports, tankers and a handful of other aircraft.

Armée de l'Air et de l'Espace (AA)

240	Airbus A.330-223 (F-RARF)	AA ET 00.060, Evreux/Fauville	
1608	Airbus A.330-243 [F-UJCS] (to become serial 070)	Airbus Defence & Space, Getafe (MRTT conversion)	
1657	Airbus A.330-243 [F-UJCT] (to become serial 071)	AA ERVTS 02.031 *Esterel*, Paris/Charles de Gaulle	
2022	Airbus A.330-243 [F-UJCU]	AA ERVTS 02.031 *Esterel*, Paris/Charles de Gaulle	
041	Airbus A.330-243 MRTT Phénix (MRTT041) [F-UJCG]	AA ERVTS 01.031 *Bretagne*, Istres/Le Tubé	
042	Airbus A.330-243 MRTT Phénix (MRTT042) [F-UJCH]	AA ERVTS 01.031 *Bretagne*, Istres/Le Tubé	
043	Airbus A.330-243 MRTT Phénix (MRTT043) [F-UJCI]	AA ERVTS 01.031 *Bretagne*, Istres/Le Tubé	
044	Airbus A.330-243 MRTT Phénix (MRTT044) [F-UJCJ]	AA ERVTS 02.031 *Esterel*, Istres/Le Tubé	
045	Airbus A.330-243 MRTT Phénix (MRTT045) [F-UJCK]	AA ERVTS 01.031 *Bretagne*, Istres/Le Tubé	
046	Airbus A.330-243 MRTT Phénix (MRTT046) [F-UJCL]	AA ERVTS 02.031 *Esterel*, Istres/Le Tubé	
047	Airbus A.330-243 MRTT Phénix (MRTT047) [F-UJCM]	AA ETP 03.031 *Bretagne*, Istres/Le Tubé	
048	Airbus A.330-243 MRTT Phénix (MRTT048) [F-UJCN]	AA ERVTS 02.031 *Bretagne*, Istres/Le Tubé	
049	Airbus A.330-243 MRTT Phénix (MRTT049) [F-UJCO]	AA ERVTS 02.031 *Bretagne*, Istres/Le Tubé	
067	Airbus A.330-243 MRTT Phénix (MRTT067) [F-UJCP]	AA ERVTS 01.031 *Bretagne*, Istres/Le Tubé	

Notes	Serial	Type (code/other identity)	Owner/operator, location or fate
	068	Airbus A.330-243 MRTT Phénix (MRTT068) [F-UJCQ]	AA ERVTS 02.031 *Bretagne*, Istres/Le Tubé
	069	Airbus A.330-243 MRTT Phénix [MRTT069] [F-UJCR]	AA ERVTS 02.031 *Bretagne*, Istres/Le Tubé
	0007	Airbus Military A.400M [F-RBAA] $	AA ET 01.061 *Touraine*, Orléans/Bricy
	0008	Airbus Military A.400M [F-RBAB]	AA ET 01.061 *Touraine*, Orléans/Bricy
	0010	Airbus Military A.400M [F-RBAC]	AA ET 01.061 *Touraine*, Orléans/Bricy
	0011	Airbus Military A.400M [F-RBAD]	AA, stored Orléans/Bricy
	0012	Airbus Military A.400M [F-RBAE]	AA, noted Clermont-Ferrand Nov 2024 (maint.)
	0014	Airbus Military A.400M [F-RBAF]	AA, stored Orléans/Bricy
	0019	Airbus Military A.400M [F-RBAG]	Airbus Defence & Space, Sevilla
	0031	Airbus Military A.400M [F-RBAH]	AA, noted Clermont-Ferrand Oct 2023 (maint.)
	0033	Airbus Military A.400M [F-RBAI]	AA ET 01.061 *Touraine*, Orléans/Bricy
	0037	Airbus Military A.400M [F-RBAJ]	AA, noted Clermont-Ferrand Dec 2024 (maint.)
	0053	Airbus Military A.400M [F-RBAK]	AA, noted Clermont-Ferrand Dec 2024 (maint.)
	0062	Airbus Military A.400M [F-RBAL] $	AA, noted Clermont-Ferrand 2023 (maint.)
	0065	Airbus Military A.400M [F-RBAM]	Airbus Defence & Space, Sevilla
	0073	Airbus Military A.400M [F-RBAN]	AA ET 01.061 *Touraine*, Orléans/Bricy
	0075	Airbus Military A.400M [F-RBAT]	AA ET 01.061 *Touraine*, Orléans/Bricy
	0089	Airbus Military A.400M [F-RBAO]	AA, stored Orléans
	0095	Airbus Military A.400M [F-RBAP]	Airbus Defence & Space, Getafe
	0102	Airbus Military A.400M [F-RBAQ] $	AA ET 01.061 *Touraine*, Orléans/Bricy
	0110	Airbus Military A.400M [F-RBAR] $	Airbus Defence & Space, Sevilla
	0122	Airbus Military A.400M [F-RBAS]	AA ET 01.061 *Touraine*, Orléans/Bricy
	0127	Airbus Military A.400M [F-RBAU]	AA ET 01.061 *Touraine*, Orléans/Bricy
	0130	Airbus Military A.400M [F-RBAV]	AA ET 01.061 *Touraine*, Orléans/Bricy
	0134	Airbus Military A.400M [F-RBAW]	AA ET 01.061 *Touraine*, Orléans/Bricy
	0137	Airbus Military A.400M [F-RBAX]	AA ET 01.061 *Touraine*, Orléans/Bricy
	0142	Airbus Military A.400M [F-RBAY]	AA (on order)
	0146	Airbus Military A.400M [F-RB..]	AA (on order)
	0153	Airbus Military A.400M [F-RB..]	AA (on order)
	0154	Airbus Military A.400M [F-RB..]	AA (on order)
	...	Airbus Military A.400M [F-RB..]	AA (on order)
	...	Airbus Military A.400M [F-RB..]	AA (on order)
	...	Airbus Military A.400M [F-RB..]	AA (on order)
	...	Airbus Military A.400M [F-RB..]	AA (on order)
	045	Airtech CN-235M-200 [64-IB]	AA ET 01.062 *Vercours*, Evreux/Fauville
	065	Airtech CN-235M-200 [52-IC]	AA ET 00.052 *La Tontouta*, Nouméa
	066	Airtech CN-235M-200 [52-ID]	AA ET 00.052 *La Tontouta*, Nouméa
	071	Airtech CN-235M-200 [64-IE]	AA ET 01.062 *Vercours*, Evreux/Fauville
	072	Airtech CN-235M-200 [64-IF]	AA ET 01.062 *Vercours*, Evreux/Fauville
	105	Airtech CN-235M-200 [82-IG]	AA ET 00.082 *Maine*, Papeete, Tahiti
	107	Airtech CN-235M-200 [82-IH]	AA ET 00.082 *Maine*, Papeete, Tahiti
	111	Airtech CN-235M-200 [64-II]	AA ET 03.062 *Ventoux*, Evreux/Fauville
	114	Airtech CN-235M-200 [64-IJ]	AA ET 01.062 *Vercours*, Evreux/Fauville
	123	Airtech CN-235M-200 [64-IM]	AA ET 01.062 *Vercours*, Evreux/Fauville
	128	Airtech CN-235M-200 [64-IK]	AA ET 01.062 *Vercours*, Evreux/Fauville
	129	Airtech CN-235M-200 [68-IL]	AA ET 00.068 *Antilles*, Fort-de-France
	137	Airtech CN-235M-200 [68-IN]	AA ET 00.068 *Antilles*, Fort-de-France
	141	Airtech CN-235M-200 [68-IO]	AA ET 00.068 *Antilles*, Fort-de-France
	152	Airtech CN-235M-200 [64-IP]	AA ET 01.062 *Vercours*, Evreux/Fauville
	156	Airtech CN-235M-200 [64-IQ]	AA ET 01.062 *Vercours*, Evreux/Fauville
	158	Airtech CN-235M-200 [62-IR]	AA ET 01.062 *Vercours*, Evreux/Fauville
	160	Airtech CN-235M-200 [64-IS]	AA ET 01.062 *Vercours*, Evreux/Fauville
	165	Airtech CN-235M-200 [64-IT]	AA ET 01.062 *Vercours*, Evreux/Fauville
	193	Airtech CN-235M-300 [64-HA]	AA ET 03.062 *Ventoux*, Evreux/Fauville
	194	Airtech CN-235M-300 [64-HB]	AA ET 03.062 *Ventoux*, Evreux/Fauville
	195	Airtech CN-235M-300 [64-HC]	AA ET 03.062 *Ventoux*, Evreux/Fauville
	196	Airtech CN-235M-300 [62-HD]	AA ET 03.062 *Ventoux*, Evreux/Fauville
	197	Airtech CN-235M-300 [64-HE]	AA ET 03.062 *Ventoux*, Evreux/Fauville
	198	Airtech CN-235M-300 [64-HF]	AA ET 00.050 *Réunion*, Saint-Denis, La Réunion
	199	Airtech CN-235M-300 [64-HG]	AA ET 03.062 *Ventoux*, Evreux/Fauville
	200	Airtech CN-235M-300 [62-HH]	AA ET 03.062 *Ventoux*, Evreux/Fauville
	479	Beechcraft King Air 350 VADOR (F-GYEE)	AA (on order)

Serial	Type (code/other identity)	Owner/operator, location or fate	Notes
1018	Beechcraft King Air 350 VADOR (F-WTAO) [F-RACG]	AA ER 04.033 *Périgord*, Cognac/Châteaubernard	
1030	Beechcraft King Air 350 VADOR (F-WTAP) [F-RACH]	AA ER 04.033 *Périgord*, Cognac/Châteaubernard	
470	Boeing C-135FR Stratotanker [31-CA]	*Sold to USA as N604MA, July 2024*	
497	Boeing KC-135RG Stratotanker [31-CM]	AA ERV 04.031 *Sologne*, Istres/Le Tubé	
525	Boeing KC-135RG Stratotanker [31-CN]	AA ERV 04.031 *Sologne*, Istres/Le Tubé	
574	Boeing KC-135RG Stratotanker [31-CP]	AA ERV 04.031 *Sologne*, Istres/Le Tubé	
737	Boeing C-135FR Stratotanker [31-CI]	*Sold to USA as N763MA, July 2024*	
739	Boeing C-135FR Stratotanker [31-CK]	*Sold to USA as N767MA, July 2024*	
740	Boeing C-135FR Stratotanker [31-CL]	*Sold to USA as N781MA, July 2024*	
201	Boeing E-3F Sentry [36-CA]	AA EDCA 00.036, Avord	
202	Boeing E-3F Sentry [36-CB]	AA EDCA 00.036, Avord	
203	Boeing E-3F Sentry [36-CC]	AA EDCA 00.036, Avord	
204	Boeing E-3F Sentry [36-CD] $	AA EDCA 00.036, Avord	
377	CASA 212-300 Aviocar [F-ZAEA]	AA DGA EV, Cazaux & Istres	
E1	D-BD Alpha Jet (PdF c/s)	AA BCRE, recruiting aid	
E4	D-BD Alpha Jet E	AA DGA EV, Cazaux & Istres	
E8	D-BD Alpha Jet E	AA DGA EV, Cazaux & Istres	
E11	D-BD Alpha Jet E [8-UB]	AA	
E12	D-BD Alpha Jet E	AA DGA EV, Cazaux & Istres	
E13	D-BD Alpha Jet E [8-MM]	AA, stored Ambérieu-en-Bugey	
E20	D-BD Alpha Jet E [F-TEMS]	AA *Patrouille de France*, Salon de Provence	
E22	D-BD Alpha Jet E [8-LS] $	AA	
E25	D-BD Alpha Jet E [8-TJ]	AA	
E33	D-BD Alpha Jet E [8-FJ]	AA	
E35	D-BD Alpha Jet E [F-TEMA]	AA *Patrouille de France*, Salon de Provence	
E38	D-BD Alpha Jet E [8-LH]	AA EE 03.008 *Côte d'Or*, Cazaux	
E42	D-BD Alpha Jet E [8-TA]	AA EE 03.008 *Côte d'Or*, Cazaux	
E44	D-BD Alpha Jet E [F-UHRE]	AA *Patrouille de France*, Salon de Provence	
E45	D-BD Alpha Jet E [F-TETF]	AA *Patrouille de France*, Salon de Provence	
E46	D-BD Alpha Jet E	AA	
E48	D-BD Alpha Jet E [F-TEMH]	AA *Patrouille de France*, Salon de Provence	
E53	D-BD Alpha Jet E [102-LI]	AA	
E60	D-BD Alpha Jet E	AA EPNER, Istres/Le Tubé	
E67	D-BD Alpha Jet E [705-TB]	AA	
E68	D-BD Alpha Jet E [8-MO]	AA	
E73	D-BD Alpha Jet E [F-TENE]	AA *Patrouille de France*, Salon de Provence	
E79	D-BD Alpha Jet E [8-NA]	AA	
E80	D-BD Alpha Jet E	AA DGA EV, Cazaux & Istres	
E81	D-BD Alpha Jet E [F-UGFO]	AA *Patrouille de France*, Salon de Provence	
E82	D-BD Alpha Jet E [8-LW]	AA EE 03.008 *Côte d'Or*, Cazaux	
E83	D-BD Alpha Jet E [8-TZ]	AA EE 03.008 *Côte d'Or*, Cazaux	
E87	D-BD Alpha Jet E [F-TELC]	AA *Patrouille de France*, Salon de Provence	
E88	D-BD Alpha Jet E [8-LL]	AA EE 03.008 *Côte d'Or*, Cazaux	
E90	D-BD Alpha Jet E [8-TH]	AA EE 03.008 *Côte d'Or*, Cazaux	
E93	D-BD Alpha Jet E [8-TX]	AA EE 03.008 *Côte d'Or*, Cazaux	
E94	D-BD Alpha Jet E [8-RH]	AA EE 03.008 *Côte d'Or*, Cazaux	
E98	D-BD Alpha Jet E [F-TEMF]	AA *Patrouille de France*, Salon de Provence	
E100	D-BD Alpha Jet E	AA EPNER, Istres/Le Tubé	
E101	D-BD Alpha Jet E	AA	
E102	D-BD Alpha Jet E [8-LM]	AA EE 03.008 *Côte d'Or*, Cazaux	
E105	D-BD Alpha Jet E [F-UGFM]	AA *Patrouille de France*, Salon de Provence	
E107	D-BD Alpha Jet E [8-UD]	AA EE 03.008 *Côte d'Or*, Cazaux	
E108	D-BD Alpha Jet E [8-AF]	AA EE 03.008 *Côte d'Or*, Cazaux	
E109	D-BD Alpha Jet E [8-AG]	AA EE 03.008 *Côte d'Or*, Cazaux	
E112	D-BD Alpha Jet E [F-SDAO]	AA *Patrouille de France*, Salon de Provence	
E113	D-BD Alpha Jet E [F-TETD]	AA *Patrouille de France*, Salon de Provence	
E114	D-BD Alpha Jet E [705-RR]	AA	
E115	D-BD Alpha Jet E [8-MR]	AA	
E116	D-BD Alpha Jet E [8-FN]	AA	
E117	D-BD Alpha Jet E [8-RI]	AA	
E118	D-BD Alpha Jet E [8-LN]	AA	
E119	D-BD Alpha Jet E [F-UGFE]	AA *Patrouille de France*, Salon de Provence	

Notes	Serial	Type (code/other identity)	Owner/operator, location or fate
	E123	D-BD Alpha Jet E [8-RM]	AA EE 03.008 *Côte d'Or*, Cazaux
	E124	D-BD Alpha Jet E [8-RN]	*Instructional airframe, Rochefort–St. Agnant*
	E127	D-BD Alpha Jet E [F-UGFK]	AA *Patrouille de France*, Salon de Provence
	E128	D-BD Alpha Jet E [8-TM]	AA
	E129	D-BD Alpha Jet E [F-TELP]	AA *Patrouille de France*, Salon de Provence
	E130	D-BD Alpha Jet E [8-RP]	AA EE 03.008 *Côte d'Or*, Cazaux
	E131	D-BD Alpha Jet E [8-RO]	AA
	E137	D-BD Alpha Jet E [F-TELJ]	AA *Patrouille de France*, Salon de Provence
	E138	D-BD Alpha Jet E [8-RQ]	AA EE 03.008 *Côte d'Or*, Cazaux
	E139	D-BD Alpha Jet E [F-UGFC]	AA *Patrouille de France*, Salon de Provence
	E141	D-BD Alpha Jet E [8-NF]	AA EE 03.008 *Côte d'Or*, Cazaux
	E142	D-BD Alpha Jet E [8-LO]	AA
	E144	D-BD Alpha Jet E [8-AK]	AA EE 03.008 *Côte d'Or*, Cazaux
	E147	D-BD Alpha Jet E [8-LT]	AA
	E148	D-BD Alpha Jet E [F-TELU]	AA *Patrouille de France*, Salon de Provence
	E149	D-BD Alpha Jet E [8-RS]	AA EE 03.008 *Côte d'Or*, Cazaux
	E151	D-BD Alpha Jet E [8-FD]	AA EE 03.008 *Côte d'Or*, Cazaux
	E152	D-BD Alpha Jet E [F-UHRT]	AA *Patrouille de France*, Salon de Provence
	E153	D-BD Alpha Jet E	AA
	E154	D-BD Alpha Jet E [8-AL]	AA
	E157	D-BD Alpha Jet E [8-UC]	AA
	E158	D-BD Alpha Jet E	AA
	E160	D-BD Alpha Jet E [8-UH]	AA
	E162	D-BD Alpha Jet E [8-RJ]	AA EE 03.008 *Côte d'Or*, Cazaux
	E163	D-BD Alpha Jet E [705-RB]	AA
	E164	D-BD Alpha Jet E [8-RV]	AA EE 03.008 *Côte d'Or*, Cazaux
	E165	D-BD Alpha Jet E [F-TERE]	AA *Patrouille de France*, Salon de Provence
	E166	D-BD Alpha Jet E [705-RW]	AA
	E168	D-BD Alpha Jet E [F-UGFP]	AA *Patrouille de France*, Salon de Provence
	E169	D-BD Alpha Jet E [F-UHRX]	AA *Patrouille de France*, Salon de Provence
	E170	D-BD Alpha Jet E [F-UHRY]	AA *Patrouille de France*, Salon de Provence
	E171	D-BD Alpha Jet E [F-UHRZ]	AA *Patrouille de France*, Salon de Provence
	E173	D-BD Alpha Jet E [8-MA]	AA
	E176	D-BD Alpha Jet E [8-MB]	AA EE 03.008 *Côte d'Or*, Cazaux
	1372	Daher TBM 940 [F-ZCEV,EV]	AA DGA EV, Cazaux & Istres
	1376	Daher TBM 940 [F-ZDGA,GA]	AA DGA EV, Cazaux & Istres
	1381	Daher TBM 940 [F-ZCER,ER]	AA DGA EV, Cazaux & Istres
	1382	Daher TBM 940 [F-ZCPN,PN]	AA DGA EV, Cazaux & Istres
	68	Dassault Falcon 7X (F-RAFA)	AA ET 00.060, Villacoublay/ Vélizy
	86	Dassault Falcon 7X (F-RAFB)	AA ET 00.060, Villacoublay/ Vélizy
	104	Dassault Falcon 20C [CW]	AA DGA EV, stored Cazaux
	288	Dassault Falcon 20E [CV]	AA DGA EV, stored Istres/Le Tubé
	342	Dassault Falcon 20F [CU]	AA DGA EV, stored Cazaux
	2	Dassault Falcon 900 (F-RAFP)	AA ET 00.060, Villacoublay/ Vélizy
	4	Dassault Falcon 900 (F-RAFQ)	AA ET 00.060, Villacoublay/ Vélizy
	231	Dassault Falcon 2000LX (F-RAFC)	AA ET 00.060, Villacoublay/ Vélizy
	237	Dassault Falcon 2000LX (F-RAFD)	AA ET 00.060, Villacoublay/ Vélizy
	523	Dassault Mirage 2000B [3-KJ]	AA EC 02.003 *Champagne*, Nancy/Ochey
	524	Dassault Mirage 2000B [3-OA]	AA EC 02.003 *Champagne*, Nancy/Ochey
	525	Dassault Mirage 2000B [3-AM]	AA EC 02.003 *Champagne*, Nancy/Ochey
	527	Dassault Mirage 2000B [3-OR]	AA EC 02.003 *Champagne*, Nancy/Ochey
	528	Dassault Mirage 2000B [3-KS]	AA EC 02.003 *Champagne*, Nancy/Ochey
	529	Dassault Mirage 2000B [3-OC]	AA EC 02.003 *Champagne*, Nancy/Ochey
	530	Dassault Mirage 2000B [3-OL]	AA EC 02.003 *Champagne*, Nancy/Ochey
	01	Dassault Mirage 2000-5F	AA DGA EV, Istres/Le Tubé
	38	Dassault Mirage 2000-5F [2-EI]	AA GC 01.002 *Cigognes*, Luxeuil/St.Sauveur
	40	Dassault Mirage 2000-5F [2-EX]	AA GC 01.002 *Cigognes*, Luxeuil/St.Sauveur
	41	Dassault Mirage 2000-5F [2-FZ]	AA GC 01.002 *Cigognes*, Luxeuil/St.Sauveur
	42	Dassault Mirage 2000-5F [2-EY]	AA GC 01.002 *Cigognes*, Luxeuil/St.Sauveur
	44	Dassault Mirage 2000-5F [2-EQ]	AA GC 01.002 *Cigognes*, Luxeuil/St.Sauveur
	45	Dassault Mirage 2000-5F [188-EF]	AA EC 03.011 *Corse*, Djibouti
	46	Dassault Mirage 2000-5F [2-EN]	AA GC 01.002 *Cigognes*, Luxeuil/St.Sauveur

Serial	Type (code/other identity)	Owner/operator, location or fate	Notes
47	Dassault Mirage 2000-5F [2-EP]	AA GC 01.002 *Cigognes*, Luxeuil/St.Sauveur	
48	Dassault Mirage 2000-5F [2-EW]	AA GC 01.002 *Cigognes*, Luxeuil/St.Sauveur	
49	Dassault Mirage 2000-5F [2-EA]	AA GC 01.002 *Cigognes*, Luxeuil/St.Sauveur	
51	Dassault Mirage 2000-5F	AA DGA EV, Istres/Le Tubé	
52	Dassault Mirage 2000-5F [2-EH]	AA, stored Luxeuil/St.Sauveur	
54	Dassault Mirage 2000-5F [188-EZ]	AA EC 03.011 *Corse*, Djibouti	
55	Dassault Mirage 2000-5F [2-EU]	AA GC 01.002 *Cigognes*, Luxeuil/St.Sauveur	
56	Dassault Mirage 2000-5F [2-EG]	AA GC 01.002 *Cigognes*, Luxeuil/St.Sauveur	
57	Dassault Mirage 2000-5F [188-ET]	AA EC 03.011 *Corse*, Djibouti	
58	Dassault Mirage 2000-5F [2-EL]	AA GC 01.002 *Cigognes*, Luxeuil/St.Sauveur	
59	Dassault Mirage 2000-5F [2-EV]	AA GC 01.002 *Cigognes*, Luxeuil/St.Sauveur	
61	Dassault Mirage 2000-5F [2-ME]	AA GC 01.002 *Cigognes*, Luxeuil/St.Sauveur	
62	Dassault Mirage 2000-5F [2-ED]	AA GC 01.002 *Cigognes*, Luxeuil/St.Sauveur	
63	Dassault Mirage 2000-5F [2-EM]	AA GC 01.002 *Cigognes*, Luxeuil/St.Sauveur	
64	Dassault Mirage 2000C	AA, stored Cazaux	
65	Dassault Mirage 2000-5F [2-MG]	AA GC 01.002 *Cigognes*, Luxeuil/St.Sauveur	
66	Dassault Mirage 2000-5F [2-EO]	AA GC 01.002 *Cigognes*, Luxeuil/St.Sauveur	
67	Dassault Mirage 2000-5F [2-MH]	AA GC 01.002 *Cigognes*, Luxeuil/St.Sauveur	
71	Dassault Mirage 2000-5F [2-EE]	AA GC 01.002 *Cigognes*, Luxeuil/St.Sauveur	
74	Dassault Mirage 2000-5F [2-MK]	AA GC 01.002 *Cigognes*, Luxeuil/St.Sauveur	
77	Dassault Mirage 2000-5F [188-AX]	AA EC 03.011 *Corse*, Djibouti	
78	Dassault Mirage 2000-5F [2-EC]	AA GC 01.002 *Cigognes*, Luxeuil/St.Sauveur	
601	Dassault Mirage 2000D [3-JG]	AA EC 01.003 *Navarre*, Nancy/Ochey	
602	Dassault Mirage 2000D [3-XJ] $	AA EC 02.003 *Champagne*, Nancy/Ochey	
603	Dassault Mirage 2000D [3-XL]	AA EC 03.003 *Ardennes*, Nancy/Ochey	
604	Dassault Mirage 2000D [3-IP]	AA EC 03.003 *Ardennes*, Nancy	
606	Dassault Mirage 2000D [3-JC]	AA EC 02.003 *Champagne*, Nancy	
607	Dassault Mirage 2000D	AA DGA EV, Istres	
609	Dassault Mirage 2000D [3-IF]	AA EC 01.003 *Navarre*, Nancy/Ochey	
610	Dassault Mirage 2000D [3-XX]	AA EC 03.003 *Ardennes*, Nancy/Ochey	
611	Dassault Mirage 2000D [3-JP]	AA EC 02.003 *Champagne*, Nancy/Ochey	
613	Dassault Mirage 2000D [3-MO]	AA EC 01.003 *Navarre*, Nancy/Ochey	
614	Dassault Mirage 2000D [3-JU]	AA EC 02.003 *Champagne*, Nancy/Ochey	
615	Dassault Mirage 2000D [3-JY]	AA EC 02.003 *Champagne*, Nancy/Ochey	
617	Dassault Mirage 2000D [3-IS]	AA EC 01.003 *Navarre*, Nancy/Ochey	
618	Dassault Mirage 2000D [3-XC]	AA EC 03.003 *Ardennes*, Nancy/Ochey	
620	Dassault Mirage 2000D [3-IU]	AA EC 01.003 *Navarre*, Nancy/Ochey	
622	Dassault Mirage 2000D [3-IL]	AA EC 02.003 *Champagne*, Nancy/Ochey	
624	Dassault Mirage 2000D [3-IT]	AA DGA EV, Istres	
625	Dassault Mirage 2000D [3-XG]	AA EC 03.003 *Ardennes*, Nancy/Ochey	
626	Dassault Mirage 2000D [3-IC]	AA EC 01.003 *Navarre*, Nancy/Ochey	
627	Dassault Mirage 2000D [3-JO]	AA EC 02.003 *Champagne*, Nancy/Ochey	
628	Dassault Mirage 2000D [3-JL]	AA EC 02.003 *Champagne*, Nancy/Ochey	
629	Dassault Mirage 2000D [3-XO]	AA EC 03.003 *Ardennes*, Nancy/Ochey	
630	Dassault Mirage 2000D [3-XD]	AA EC 03.003 *Ardennes*, Nancy/Ochey	
631	Dassault Mirage 2000D [3-IH]	AA EC 01.003 *Navarre*, Nancy/Ochey	
632	Dassault Mirage 2000D [3-XE]	AA EC 01.003 *Navarre*, Nancy/Ochey	
635	Dassault Mirage 2000D [3-AS]	AA EC 03.003 *Navarre*, Nancy/Ochey	
636	Dassault Mirage 2000D [3-JV]	AA EC 00.003, Nancy/Ochey	
637	Dassault Mirage 2000D [3-XQ]	AA EC 03.003 *Champagne*, Nancy/Ochey	
638	Dassault Mirage 2000D [3-IJ]	AA EC 02.003 *Champagne*, Nancy/Ochey	
639	Dassault Mirage 2000D MLU [30-JJ]	AA CEAM/ECE 01.030 *Côte d'Argent*, Mont-de-Marsan	
640	Dassault Mirage 2000D [3-IN]	AA EC 01.003 *Navarre*, Nancy/Ochey	
641	Dassault Mirage 2000D [30-JW]	AA CEAM/ECE 01.030 *Côte d'Argent*, Mont-de-Marsan	
642	Dassault Mirage 2000D [3-IE]	AA EC 02.003 *Champagne*, Nancy/Ochey	
643	Dassault Mirage 2000D [3-JD]	AA EC 03.003 *Champagne*, Nancy/Ochey	
644	Dassault Mirage 2000D	AA DGA EV, Istres/Le Tubé	
645	Dassault Mirage 2000D [3-XP]	AA EC 02.003 *Champagne*, Nancy/Ochey	
646	Dassault Mirage 2000D [30-MQ]	AA CEAM/ECE 01.030 *Côte d'Argent*, Mont-de-Marsan	

Notes	Serial	Type (code/other identity)	Owner/operator, location or fate
	647	Dassault Mirage 2000D [3-IO]	AA EC 01.003 *Navarre*, Nancy/Ochey
	648	Dassault Mirage 2000D [3-XT]	AA EC 03.003 *Ardennes*, Nancy/Ochey
	649	Dassault Mirage 2000D [3-XY]	AA EC 03.003 *Ardennes*, Nancy/Ochey
	650	Dassault Mirage 2000D [3-IA]	AA EC 01.003 *Navarre*, Nancy/Ochey
	652	Dassault Mirage 2000D [3-XN]	AA EC 03.003 *Ardennes*, Nancy/Ochey
	653	Dassault Mirage 2000D [3-AU]	AA EC 02.003 *Champagne*, Nancy/Ochey
	654	Dassault Mirage 2000D [3-ID]	AA EC 01.003 *Navarre*, Nancy/Ochey
	655	Dassault Mirage 2000D [3-LH]	AA EC 03.003 *Ardennes*, Nancy/Ochey
	657	Dassault Mirage 2000D [3-JM]	AA EC 02.003 *Champagne*, Nancy/Ochey
	658	Dassault Mirage 2000D [3-JN]	AA EC 02.003 *Champagne*, Nancy/Ochey
	659	Dassault Mirage 2000D [3-XR]	AA EC 01.003 *Navarre*, Nancy
	660	Dassault Mirage 2000D [30-JF]	AA CEAM/ECE 01.030 *Côte d'Argent*, Mont-de-Marsan
	661	Dassault Mirage 2000D [3-XI]	AA EC 03.003 *Ardennes*, Nancy/Ochey
	662	Dassault Mirage 2000D [3-XA]	AA EC 01.003 *Navarre*, Nancy/Ochey
	664	Dassault Mirage 2000D [3-IW]	AA EC 03.003 *Ardennes*, Nancy/Ochey
	666	Dassault Mirage 2000D [3-IQ]	AA EC 02.003 *Champagne*, Nancy
	668	Dassault Mirage 2000D [3-IG]	AA EC 01.003 *Navarre*, Nancy/Ochey
	670	Dassault Mirage 2000D [3-XF]	AA EC 03.003 *Ardennes*, Nancy/Ochey
	671	Dassault Mirage 2000D [3-XK]	AA EC 03.003 *Ardennes*, Nancy/Ochey
	672	Dassault Mirage 2000D [3-XV]	AA EC 03.003 *Ardennes*, Nancy/Ochey
	673	Dassault Mirage 2000D	AA DGA EV, Istres/Le Tubé
	674	Dassault Mirage 2000D [3-IR]	AA EC 02.003 *Champagne*, Nancy/Ochey
	675	Dassault Mirage 2000D [3-JI]	AA EC 01.003 *Navarre*, Nancy/Ochey
	676	Dassault Mirage 2000D $	AA DGA EV, Istres/Le Tubé
	677	Dassault Mirage 2000D [3-JT]	AA EC 02.003 *Champagne*, Nancy/Ochey
	678	Dassault Mirage 2000D [30-JB]	AA CEAM/ECE 01.030 *Côte d'Argent*, Mont-de-Marsan
	679	Dassault Mirage 2000D [3-JX]	AA EC 02.003 *Navarre*, Nancy/Ochey
	680	Dassault Mirage 2000D [3-XM]	AA EC 03.003 *Ardennes*, Nancy/Ochey
	681	Dassault Mirage 2000D [3-AG]	AA EC 03.003 *Ardennes*, Nancy/Ochey
	682	Dassault Mirage 2000D [3-JR]	AA EC 02.003 *Champagne*, Nancy/Ochey
	683	Dassault Mirage 2000D [3-IV]	AA EC 03.003 *Ardennes*, Nancy/Ochey
	685	Dassault Mirage 2000D [3-XZ]	AA EC 01.003 *Navarre*, Nancy/Ochey
	686	Dassault Mirage 2000D [3-JH]	AA EC 01.003 *Navarre*, Nancy/Ochey
	301	Dassault Rafale B	AA DGA EV, Istres/Le Tube
	302	Dassault Rafale B	AA DGA EV, Istres/Le Tube
	303	Dassault Rafale B [4-EA]	AA ETR 03.004 *Aquitaine*, St Dizier/Robinson
	304	Dassault Rafale B [4-EB]	AA ETR 03.004 *Aquitaine*, St Dizier/Robinson
	307	Dassault Rafale B [4-IA]	AA EC 02.004 *La Fayette*, St Dizier/Robinson
	308	Dassault Rafale B [4-HA]	AA EC 02.004 *La Fayette*, St Dizier/Robinson
	309	Dassault Rafale B [4-HB]	AA EC 02.004 *La Fayette*, St Dizier/Robinson
	310	Dassault Rafale B [4-HC]	AA EC 02.004 *La Fayette*, St Dizier/Robinson
	311	Dassault Rafale B [4-HD]	AA EC 01.004 *Gascogne*, St Dizier/Robinson
	312	Dassault Rafale B [4-HF]	AA EC 01.004 *Gascogne*, St Dizier/Robinson
	313	Dassault Rafale B [4-HI]	AA ETR 03.004 *Aquitaine*, St Dizier/Robinson
	314	Dassault Rafale B [4-HP]	AA EC 01.004 *Gascogne*, St Dizier/Robinson
	317	Dassault Rafale B [4-HO]	AA ETR 03.004 *Aquitaine*, St Dizier/Robinson
	319	Dassault Rafale B [4-HN]	AA EC 01.004 *Gascogne*, St Dizier/Robinson
	320	Dassault Rafale B [4-HV]	AA EC 01.004 *Gascogne*, St Dizier/Robinson
	321	Dassault Rafale B [4-HQ]	AA EC 01.004 *Gascogne*, St Dizier/Robinson
	322	Dassault Rafale B [4-HU]	AA EC 01.004 *Gascogne*, St Dizier/Robinson
	323	Dassault Rafale B [4-HT]	AA EC 01.004 *Gascogne*, St Dizier/Robinson
	324	Dassault Rafale B [4-HW]	AA ETR 03.004 *Aquitaine*, St Dizier/Robinson
	325	Dassault Rafale B [4-HX]	AA ETR 03.004 *Aquitaine*, St Dizier/Robinson
	326	Dassault Rafale B [4-HY]	AA EC 01.004 *Gascogne*, St Dizier/Robinson
	327	Dassault Rafale B [4-HZ]	AA EC 01.004 *Gascogne*, St Dizier/Robinson
	328	Dassault Rafale B [4-IC]	AA EC 01.004 *Gascogne*, St Dizier/Robinson
	329	Dassault Rafale B [4-ID]	AA EC 02.004 *La Fayette*, St Dizier/Robinson
	330	Dassault Rafale B [4-IE]	AA EC 01.004 *Gascogne*, St Dizier/Robinson
	331	Dassault Rafale B [4-IF]	AA EC 02.004 *La Fayette*, St Dizier/Robinson
	332	Dassault Rafale B [4-IG]	AA EC 02.004 *La Fayette*, St Dizier/Robinson

Serial	Type (code/other identity)	Owner/operator, location or fate	Notes
333	Dassault Rafale B [4-IH]	AA ETR 03.004 *Aquitaine*, St Dizier/Robinson	
334	Dassault Rafale B [4-II]	AA EC 02.004 *La Fayette*, St Dizier/Robinson	
335	Dassault Rafale B [4-IJ]	AA EC 01.004 *Gascogne*, St Dizier/Robinson	
336	Dassault Rafale B [4-IK]	AA EC 02.004 *La Fayette*, St Dizier/Robinson	
337	Dassault Rafale B [4-IL]	AA EC 01.004 *Gascogne*, St Dizier/Robinson	
338	Dassault Rafale B [4-IO]	AA EC 02.004 *La Fayette*, St Dizier/Robinson	
339	Dassault Rafale B [4-FF]	AA ETR 03.004 *Aquitaine*, St Dizier/Robinson	
340	Dassault Rafale B [4-FG]	AA EC 01.004 *Gascogne*, St Dizier/Robinson	
341	Dassault Rafale B [4-FH]	AA EC 01.004 *Gascogne*, St Dizier/Robinson	
342	Dassault Rafale B [4-FI]	AA EC 01.004 *Gascogne*, St Dizier/Robinson	
343	Dassault Rafale B [4-FJ]	AA EC 01.004 *Gascogne*, St Dizier/Robinson	
344	Dassault Rafale B [4-FK]	AA EC 01.004 *Gascogne*, St Dizier/Robinson	
345	Dassault Rafale B [4-FL]	AA EC 02.004 *La Fayette*, St Dizier/Robinson	
346	Dassault Rafale B [4-FM]	AA ETR 03.004 *Aquitaine*, St Dizier/Robinson	
347	Dassault Rafale B [4-FN]	AA EC 01.004 *Gascogne*, St Dizier/Robinson	
348	Dassault Rafale B	AA DGA EV, Istres/Le Tube	
349	Dassault Rafale B [4-FP]	AA ETR 03.004 *Aquitaine*, St Dizier/Robinson	
350	Dassault Rafale B [4-FQ]	*Destroyed Meurthe-et-Moselle, France, Aug 2024*	
351	Dassault Rafale B [30-FR]	AA CEAM/ECE 01.030 *Côte d'Argent*, Mont-de-Marsan	
352	Dassault Rafale B [4-FS]	AA EC 02.004 *La Fayette*, St Dizier/Robinson	
353	Dassault Rafale B [4-FT]	AA EC 02.004 *La Fayette*, St Dizier/Robinson	
354	Dassault Rafale B [30-FU]	AA EC 02.030 *Normandie-Niémen*, Mont-de-Marsan	
355	Dassault Rafale B [4-FV]	AA EC 01.004 *Gascogne*, St Dizier/Robinson	
356	Dassault Rafale B [4-FW]	*Destroyed Meurthe-et-Moselle, France, Aug 2024*	
357	Dassault Rafale B [4-FX]	AA EC 02.004 *La Fayette*, St Dizier/Robinson	
358	Dassault Rafale B [4-FY]	AA ETR 03.004 *Aquitaine*, St Dizier/Robinson	
359	Dassault Rafale B [30-FZ]	AA CEAM/ECE 01.030 *Côte d'Argent*, Mont-de-Marsan	
360	Dassault Rafale B [30-SI]	AA CEAM/ECE 01.030 *Côte d'Argent*, Mont-de-Marsan	
361	Dassault Rafale B [30-SJ]	AA CEAM/ECE 01.030 *Côte d'Argent*, Mont-de-Marsan	
362	Dassault Rafale B [30-SK]	AA CEAM/ECE 01.030 *Côte d'Argent*, Mont-de-Marsan	
363	Dassault Rafale B [5-SL]	AA EC 01.005 *Vendée*, Orange/Caritat	
364	Dassault Rafale B [30-SM]	AA EC 02.030 *Normandie-Niémen*, Mont-de-Marsan	
365	Dassault Rafale B [30-SN]	AA CEAM/ECE 01.030 *Côte d'Argent*, Mont-de-Marsan	
366	Dassault Rafale B [30-SO]	AA EC 02.030 *Normandie-Niémen*, Mont-de-Marsan	
367	Dassault Rafale B	AA (on order)	
368	Dassault Rafale B	AA (on order)	
369	Dassault Rafale B	AA (on order)	
101	Dassault Rafale C	AA DGA EV, Istres/Le Tube	
102	Dassault Rafale C [30-EF]	AA EC 02.030 *Normandie-Niémen*, Mont-de-Marsan	
104	Dassault Rafale C [30-HH]	AA EC 03.030 *Lorraine*, Mont-de-Marsan	
105	Dassault Rafale C [30-HE]	AA EC 02.030 *Normandie-Niémen*, Mont-de-Marsan	
106	Dassault Rafale C [30-HG]	AA EC 03.030 *Lorraine*, Mont-de-Marsan	
107	Dassault Rafale C [30-HJ]	AA EC 02.030 *Normandie-Niémen*, Mont-de-Marsan	
108	Dassault Rafale C [30-HS]	AA EC 03.030 *Lorraine*, Mont-de-Marsan	
109	Dassault Rafale C [30-IM]	AA EC 03.030 *Lorraine*, Mont-de-Marsan	
110	Dassault Rafale C [30-IN]	AA EC 03.030 *Lorraine*, Mont-de-Marsan (damaged)	
113	Dassault Rafale C [30-IR]	AA EC 00.030, Mont-de-Marsan	
114	Dassault Rafale C [30-IS]	AA (To Greece?)	
115	Dassault Rafale C [30-IT]	AA EC 03.030 *Lorraine*, Mont-de-Marsan	

Notes	Serial	Type (code/other identity)	Owner/operator, location or fate
	116	Dassault Rafale C [30-IU]	AA EC 02.030 Normandie-Niémen, Mont-de-Marsan
	117	Dassault Rafale C [30-IV]	AA EC 02.030 Normandie-Niémen, Mont-de-Marsan
	119	Dassault Rafale C [30-IX]	AA EC 03.030 Lorraine, Mont-de-Marsan
	121	Dassault Rafale C [30-IZ]	AA EC 03.030 Lorraine, Mont-de-Marsan
	122	Dassault Rafale C [30-GA]	AA CEAM/ECE 01.030 Côte d'Argent, Mont-de-Marsan
	125	Dassault Rafale C [30-GD] $	AA EC 02.030 Normandie-Niémen, Mont-de-Marsan
	126	Dassault Rafale C [30-GE]	AA EC 03.030 Lorraine, Mont-de-Marsan
	127	Dassault Rafale C [30-GF]	AA EC 03.030 Lorraine, Mont-de-Marsan
	129	Dassault Rafale C [30-GH]	AA EC 02.030 Normandie-Niémen, Mont-de-Marsan
	130	Dassault Rafale C [30-GI]	AA EC 02.030 Normandie-Niémen, Mont-de-Marsan
	132	Dassault Rafale C [30-GK]	AA EC 02.030 Normandie-Niémen, Mont-de-Marsan
	133	Dassault Rafale C [30-GL]	AA EC 02.030 Normandie-Niémen, Mont-de-Marsan
	135	Dassault Rafale C [5-GN]	AA EC 01.005 Vendée, Orange/Caritat
	136	Dassault Rafale C [4-GO]	AA ETR 03.004 Aquitaine, St Dizier/Robinson
	138	Dassault Rafale C [30-GQ] $	AA EC 03.030 Lorraine, Mont-de-Marsan
	139	Dassault Rafale C [7-GR]	AA EC 01.007 Provence, Al Dhafra, UAE
	140	Dassault Rafale C [30-GS]	AA EC 03.030 Lorraine, Mont-de-Marsan
	142	Dassault Rafale C [7-GU]	AA EC 01.007 Provence, Al Dhafra, UAE
	145	Dassault Rafale C [30-GX]	AA EC 03.030 Lorraine, Mont-de-Marsan
	146	Dassault Rafale C [4-GY]	AA ETR 03.004 Aquitaine, St Dizier
	147	Dassault Rafale C [7-GZ]	AA EC 01.007 Provence, Al Dhafra, UAE
	148	Dassault Rafale C [7-VA]	AA EC 01.007 Provence, Al Dhafra, UAE
	149	Dassault Rafale C [5-VB]	AA EC 01.005 Vendée, Orange/Caritat
	150	Dassault Rafale C [5-VC] $	AA EC 01.005 Vendée, Orange/Caritat
	151	Dassault Rafale C [30-VD]	AA EC 02.030 Normandie-Niémen, Mont-de-Marsan
	152	Dassault Rafale C [30-VE]	AA EC 02.030 Normandie-Niémen, Mont-de-Marsan
	153	Dassault Rafale C [5-VF]	AA EC 01.005 Vendée, Orange/Caritat
	154	Dassault Rafale C [30-VG]	AA EC 03.030 Lorraine, Mont-de-Marsan
	155	Dassault Rafale C [30-VH]	AA EC 03.030 Lorraine, Mont-de-Marsan
	156	Dassault Rafale C [30-VI]	AA EC 03.030 Lorraine, Mont-de-Marsan
	157	Dassault Rafale C [5-VJ]	AA EC 01.005 Vendée, Orange/Caritat
	158	Dassault Rafale C [5-VK]	AA EC 01.005 Vendée, Orange/Caritat
	159	Dassault Rafale C [5-VL]	AA EC 01.005 Vendée, Orange/Caritat
	160	Dassault Rafale C [30-VM]	AA EC 03.030 Lorraine, Mont-de-Marsan
	161	Dassault Rafale C [30-VN]	AA EC 03.030 Lorraine, Mont-de-Marsan
	162	Dassault Rafale C	AA (on order)
	163	Dassault Rafale C	AA (on order)
	164	Dassault Rafale C	AA (on order)
	165	Dassault Rafale C	AA (on order)
	166	Dassault Rafale C	AA (on order)
	167	Dassault Rafale C	AA (on order)
	168	Dassault Rafale C	AA (on order)
	169	Dassault Rafale C	AA (on order)
	292	DHC-6 Twin Otter 200 [F-RACC]	AA GAM 00.056 Vaucluse, Evreux/Fauville
	298	DHC-6 Twin Otter 200 [F-RACD]	AA GAM 00.056 Vaucluse, Evreux/Fauville
	300	DHC-6 Twin Otter 200 [F-RACE]	AA GAM 00.056 Vaucluse, Evreux/Fauville
	730	DHC-6 Twin Otter 300 [F-RACA]	AA ET 03.061 Poitou, Orléans/Bricy
	745	DHC-6 Twin Otter 300 [F-RACV]	AA ET 03.061 Poitou, Orléans/Bricy
	054	Embraer EMB.121AA Xingu [YX]	AA, stored Avord
	064	Embraer EMB.121AA Xingu [YY]	AA EAT 00.319 Capitaine Dartigues, Avord
	066	Embraer EMB.121AN Xingu [ZA]	AA, stored Avord
	072	Embraer EMB.121AA Xingu [YA]	AA EAT 00.319 Capitaine Dartigues, Avord

Serial	Type (code/other identity)	Owner/operator, location or fate	Notes
075	Embraer EMB.121AA Xingu [YC]	AA, stored Avord	
078	Embraer EMB.121AA Xingu [YE]	AA EAT 00.319 *Capitaine Dartigues*, Avord	
082	Embraer EMB.121AA Xingu [YG]	AA EAT 00.319 *Capitaine Dartigues*, Avord	
083	Embraer EMB.121AN Xingu [ZE]	AA EAT 00.319 *Capitaine Dartigues*, Avord	
084	Embraer EMB.121AA Xingu [YH]	AA EAT 00.319 *Capitaine Dartigues*, Avord	
086	Embraer EMB.121AA Xingu [YI]	AA EAT 00.319 *Capitaine Dartigues*, Avord	
089	Embraer EMB.121AA Xingu [YJ]	AA EAT 00.319 *Capitaine Dartigues*, Avord	
090	Embraer EMB.121AN Xingu [ZF]	AA EAT 00.319 *Capitaine Dartigues*, Avord	
091	Embraer EMB.121AA Xingu [YK]	AA, stored Avord	
092	Embraer EMB.121AA Xingu [YL]	AA EAT 00.319 *Capitaine Dartigues*, Avord	
096	Embraer EMB.121AA Xingu [YN]	AA, stored Avord	
098	Embraer EMB.121AA Xingu [YO]	AA EAT 00.319 *Capitaine Dartigues*, Avord	
099	Embraer EMB.121AA Xingu [YP]	AA EAT 00.319 *Capitaine Dartigues*, Avord	
102	Embraer EMB.121AA Xingu [YS]	AA, stored Avord	
103	Embraer EMB.121AA Xingu [YT]	AA EAT 00.319 *Capitaine Dartigues*, Avord	
105	Embraer EMB.121AA Xingu [YU]	AA EAT 00.319 *Capitaine Dartigues*, Avord	
107	Embraer EMB.121AA Xingu [YV]	AA EAT 00.319 *Capitaine Dartigues*, Avord	
108	Embraer EMB.121AA Xingu [YW]	AA EAT 00.319 *Capitaine Dartigues*, Avord	
2233	Eurocopter AS.332L-1 Super Puma [FY]	AA EH 03.067 *Parisis*, Villacoublay/ Vélizy	
2235	Eurocopter AS.332L-1 Super Puma [FZ]	AA EH 03.067 *Parisis*, Villacoublay/ Vélizy	
2377	Eurocopter AS.332L-1 Super Puma [FU]	AA EH 03.067 *Parisis*, Villacoublay/ Vélizy	
2461	Eurocopter EC.725R2 Caracal [SA]	AA EH 01.067 *Pyrénées*, Cazaux	
2549	Eurocopter EC.725R2 Caracal [SB]	AA EH 01.067 *Pyrénées*, Cazaux	
2552	Eurocopter EC.725R2 Caracal [SE]	AA EH 01.067 *Pyrénées*, Cazaux	
2619	Eurocopter EC.725R2 Caracal [SC]	AA EH 01.067 *Pyrénées*, Cazaux	
2626	Eurocopter EC.725R2 Caracal [SD]	AA EH 01.067 *Pyrénées*, Cazaux	
2741	Eurocopter EC.225LP Caracal [SY]	AA GAM 00.056 *Vaucluse*, Evreux/Fauville	
2752	Eurocopter EC.225LP Caracal [SZ]	AA GAM 00.056 *Vaucluse*, Evreux/Fauville	
2770	Eurocopter EC.725R2 Caracal [SG]	AA EH 01.067 *Pyrénées*, Cazaux	
2772	Eurocopter EC.725R2 Caracal [SH]	AA EH 01.067 *Pyrénées*, Cazaux	
2778	Eurocopter EC.725R2 Caracal [SI]	AA EH 01.067 *Pyrénées*, Cazaux	
2789	Eurocopter EC.725R2 Caracal [SJ]	AA EH 01.067 *Pyrénées*, Cazaux	
2802	Eurocopter EC.725R2 Caracal [SK]	AA EH 01.067 *Pyrénées*, Cazaux	
2897	Eurocopter EC.225LP Caracal [F-ZAJB]	AA DGA EV, Istres/Le Tubé	
2932	Eurocopter EC.225LP Caracal [F-ZAJC]	AA DGA EV, Istres/Le Tubé	
5361	Eurocopter AS.555AN Fennec [UT]	AA EH 01.065 *Alpilles*, Orange/Caritat	
5382	Eurocopter AS.555AN Fennec [UV]	AA EH 01.065 *Alpilles*, Orange/Caritat	
5386	Eurocopter AS.555AN Fennec [UX]	AA EH 01.065 *Alpilles*, Orange/Caritat	
5387	Eurocopter AS.555AN Fennec [UY]	AA EH 03.067 *Parisis*, Villacoublay/ Vélizy	
5390	Eurocopter AS.555AN Fennec [UZ]	AA EH 03.067 *Parisis*, Villacoublay/ Vélizy	
5391	Eurocopter AS.555AN Fennec [VA]	AA EH 01.065 *Alpilles*, Orange/Caritat	
5392	Eurocopter AS.555AN Fennec [VB]	AA EH 01.065 *Alpilles*, Orange/Caritat	
5393	Eurocopter AS.555AN Fennec [VC]	AA EH 01.065 *Alpilles*, Orange/Caritat	
5396	Eurocopter AS.555AN Fennec [VD]	AA EH 01.065 *Alpilles*, Orange/Caritat	
5397	Eurocopter AS.555AN Fennec [VE]	AA EH 01.065 *Alpilles*, Orange/Caritat	
5398	Eurocopter AS.555AN Fennec [VF]	AA EH 01.065 *Alpilles*, Orange/Caritat	
5399	Eurocopter AS.555AN Fennec [VG]	AA EH 01.065 *Alpilles*, Orange/Caritat	
5400	Eurocopter AS.555AN Fennec [VH]	AA EH 03.067 *Parisis*, Villacoublay/ Vélizy	
5412	Eurocopter AS.555AN Fennec [VI]	AA EH 05.067 *Alpilles*, Orange/Caritat	
5427	Eurocopter AS.555AN Fennec [VJ]	AA ET 00.068 *Antilles-Guyane*, Cayenne	
5430	Eurocopter AS.555AN Fennec [VL]	AA EH 03.067 *Parisis*, Villacoublay/ Vélizy	
5431	Eurocopter AS.555AN Fennec [VM]	AA EH 01.065 *Alpilles*, Orange/Caritat	
5441	Eurocopter AS.555AN Fennec [VO]	AA EH 01.065 *Alpilles*, Orange/Caritat	
5444	Eurocopter AS.555AN Fennec [VP]	AA EH 01.065 *Alpilles*, Orange/Caritat	
5445	Eurocopter AS.555AN Fennec [VQ]	AA EH 03.067 *Parisis*, Villacoublay/ Vélizy	
5448	Eurocopter AS.555AN Fennec [VR]	AA EH 01.065 *Alpilles*, Orange/Caritat	
5452	Eurocopter AS.555AN Fennec [VS]	AA EH 01.065 *Alpilles*, Orange/Caritat	
5455	Eurocopter AS.555AN Fennec [VT]	AA EH 01.065 *Alpilles*, Orange/Caritat	
5457	Eurocopter AS.555AN Fennec [VU]	AA ET 00.068 *Antilles-Guyane*, Cayenne	
5458	Eurocopter AS.555AN Fennec [VV]	AA EH 01.065 *Alpilles*, Orange/Caritat	
5466	Eurocopter AS.555AN Fennec [VW]	AA EH 03.067 *Parisis*, Villacoublay/ Vélizy	
5468	Eurocopter AS.555AN Fennec [VX]	AA EH 03.067 *Parisis*, Villacoublay/ Vélizy	

Notes	Serial	Type (code/other identity)	Owner/operator, location or fate
	5490	Eurocopter AS.555AN Fennec [VY]	AA EH 03.067 *Parisis*, Villacoublay/ Vélizy
	5506	Eurocopter AS.555AN Fennec [WA]	AA EH 01.065 *Alpilles*, Orange/Caritat
	5509	Eurocopter AS.555AN Fennec [WB]	AA EH 01.065 *Alpilles*, Orange/Caritat
	5511	Eurocopter AS.555AN Fennec [WC] $	AA EH 03.067 *Parisis*, Villacoublay/ Vélizy
	5516	Eurocopter AS.555AN Fennec [WD]	AA EH 01.065 *Alpilles*, Orange/Caritat
	5520	Eurocopter AS.555AN Fennec [WE]	AA EH 01.065 *Alpilles*, Orange/Caritat
	5523	Eurocopter AS.555AN Fennec [WF]	AA EH 01.065 *Alpilles*, Orange/Caritat
	5526	Eurocopter AS.555AN Fennec [WG]	AA EH 03.067 *Parisis*, Villacoublay/ Vélizy
	5530	Eurocopter AS.555AN Fennec [WH]	AA EH 01.065 *Alpilles*, Orange/Caritat
	5532	Eurocopter AS.555AN Fennec [WI]	AA EH 01.065 *Alpilles*, Orange/Caritat
	5534	Eurocopter AS.555AN Fennec [WJ]	AA EH 03.067 *Parisis*, Villacoublay/ Vélizy
	5536	Eurocopter AS.555AN Fennec [WK]	AA EH 03.067 *Parisis*, Villacoublay/ Vélizy
	5559	Eurocopter AS.555AN Fennec [WL]	AA EH 01.065 *Alpilles*, Orange/Caritat
	04	Extra EA-330SC [F-TGCI]	AA EVAA, Salon de Provence
	05	Extra EA-330SC [F-TGCJ]	AA EVAA, Salon de Provence
	96	Extra EA-330LX [F-TGCK]	AA EVAA, Salon de Provence
	290	Fokker 100 [F-ZAFT]	AA DGA EV, Istres
	400	Fokker 100 [F-ZASN/F-WTBY]	AA DGA EV, Bordeaux
	4588	Lockheed C-130H Hercules [61-PM] $	AA ET 03.061 *Poitou*, Evreux/Fauville
	4589	Lockheed C-130H Hercules [61-PN]	AA ET 03.061 *Poitou*, Evreux/Fauville
	5114	Lockheed C-130H Hercules [61-PA]	AA ET 03.061 *Poitou*, Evreux/Fauville
	5116	Lockheed C-130H Hercules [61-PB]	AA ET 03.061 *Poitou*, Evreux/Fauville
	5119	Lockheed C-130H Hercules [61-PC]	AA ET 03.061 *Poitou*, Evreux/Fauville
	5140	Lockheed C-130H-30 Hercules [61-PD]	AA ET 03.061 *Poitou*, Evreux/Fauville
	5142	Lockheed C-130H-30 Hercules [61-PE]	AA ET 03.061 *Poitou*, Evreux/Fauville
	5144	Lockheed C-130H-30 Hercules [61-PF]	AA ET 03.061 *Poitou*, Evreux/Fauville
	5150	Lockheed C-130H-30 Hercules [61-PG]	AA ET 03.061 *Poitou*, Evreux/Fauville
	5151	Lockheed C-130H-30 Hercules [61-PH]	AA ET 03.061 *Poitou*, Evreux/Fauville
	5152	Lockheed C-130H-30 Hercules [61-PI]	AA ET 03.061 *Poitou*, Evreux/Fauville
	5153	Lockheed C-130H-30 Hercules [61-PJ]	AA ET 03.061 *Poitou*, Evreux/Fauville
	5226	Lockheed C-130H-30 Hercules [61-PK]	AA ET 03.061 *Poitou*, Evreux/Fauville
	5227	Lockheed C-130H-30 Hercules [61-PL]	AA ET 03.061 *Poitou*, Evreux/Fauville
	5836	Lockheed C-130J-30 Hercules II [61-PO]	AA ET 02.061 *Franche-Comté*, Orléans/Bricy
	5847	Lockheed C-130J-30 Hercules II [61-PP]	AA ET 02.061 *Franche-Comté*, Orléans/Bricy
	5874	Lockheed KC-130J Hercules II [61-PQ]	AA ET 02.061 *Franche-Comté*, Orléans/Bricy
	5890	Lockheed KC-130J Hercules II [61-PR]	AA ET 02.061 *Franche-Comté*, Orléans/Bricy
	576	Pilatus PC-7 Turbo Trainer [AF]	AA DGA EV, Cazaux
	578	Pilatus PC-7 Turbo Trainer [AH]	AA EPNER, Istres/Le Tubé
	579	Pilatus PC-7 Turbo Trainer [AI]	AA EPNER, Istres/Le Tubé
	580	Pilatus PC-7 Turbo Trainer [AJ]	AA DGA EV, Cazaux
	01	Pilatus PC-21 (HB-HVA) [709-FC]	AA EAC 00.315, Cognac
	02	Pilatus PC-21 (HB-HVB) [709-FD]	AA EAC 00.315, Cognac
	03	Pilatus PC-21 (HB-HVC/F-ZXAC) [709-FE]	AA EAC 00.315, Cognac
	04	Pilatus PC-21 (HB-HVD) [709-FF]	AA EAC 00.315, Cognac
	05	Pilatus PC-21 (HB-HVE) [709-FG]	AA EAC 00.315, Cognac
	06	Pilatus PC-21 (HB-HVF) [709-FH]	AA EAC 00.315, Cognac
	07	Pilatus PC-21 (HB-HVG) [709-FI]	AA EAC 00.315, Cognac
	08	Pilatus PC-21 (HB-HVH) [709-FJ]	AA EAC 00.315, Cognac
	09	Pilatus PC-21 (HB-HVI) [709-FK]	AA EAC 00.315, Cognac
	10	Pilatus PC-21 (HB-HVJ) [709-FL]	AA EAC 00.315, Cognac
	11	Pilatus PC-21 (HB-HVK) [709-FM]	AA EAC 00.315, Cognac
	12	Pilatus PC-21 (HB-HVL) [709-FN]	AA EAC 00.315, Cognac
	13	Pilatus PC-21 (HB-HVM) [709-FO]	AA EAC 00.315, Cognac
	14	Pilatus PC-21 (HB-HVN) [709-FP]	AA EAC 00.315, Cognac
	15	Pilatus PC-21 (HB-HVO) [709-FQ]	AA EAC 00.315, Cognac
	16	Pilatus PC-21 (HB-HVP) [709-FR]	AA EAC 00.315, Cognac
	17	Pilatus PC-21 (HB-HVQ) [709-FS]	AA EAC 00.315, Cognac
	18	Pilatus PC-21 (HB-HXA) [709-GA]	AA EAC 00.315, Cognac
	19	Pilatus PC-21 (HB-HXB) [709-GB]	AA EAC 00.315, Cognac
	20	Pilatus PC-21 (HB-HXC) [709-GC]	AA EAC 00.315, Cognac
	21	Pilatus PC-21 (HB-HXD) [709-GD]	AA EAC 00.315, Cognac
	22	Pilatus PC-21 (HB-HXE) [709-GE]	AA EAC 00.315, Cognac

Serial	Type (code/other identity)	Owner/operator, location or fate	Notes
23	Pilatus PC-21 (HB-HXF) [709-GF]	AA EAC 00.315, Cognac	
24	Pilatus PC-21 (HB-HXG) [709-GG]	AA EAC 00.315, Cognac	
25	Pilatus PC-21 (HB-HXH) [709-GH]	AA EAC 00.315, Cognac	
26	Pilatus PC-21 (HB-HXI) [709-GI]	AA EAC 00.315, Cognac	
27	Pilatus PC-21	AA (on order)	
28	Pilatus PC-21	AA (on order)	
29	Pilatus PC-21	AA (on order)	
30	Pilatus PC-21	AA (on order)	
33	SOCATA TBM 700A [XA]	AA ET 00.043 *Médoc*, Bordeaux	
35	SOCATA TBM 700A [BW]	*Sold as F-GLAT, 2023*	
77	SOCATA TBM 700A [XD]	AA ET 00.043 *Médoc*, Bordeaux	
78	SOCATA TBM 700A [XE]	AA CEAM, Mont-de-Marsan	
93	SOCATA TBM 700A [XL]	AA ET 00.041 *Verdun*, Villacoublay/ Vélizy	
94	SOCATA TBM 700A [XG]	AA ET 00.041 *Verdun*, Villacoublay/ Vélizy	
95	SOCATA TBM 700A [XH]	AA CEAM, Mont-de-Marsan	
103	SOCATA TBM 700A [XI]	AA ET 00.041 *Verdun*, Villacoublay/ Vélizy	
104	SOCATA TBM 700A [XJ]	AA ET 00.043 *Médoc*, Bordeaux	
105	SOCATA TBM 700A [XK]	AA ET 00.043 *Médoc*, Bordeaux	
110	SOCATA TBM 700A [XP]	AA ET 00.041 *Verdun*, Villacoublay/ Vélizy	
111	SOCATA TBM 700A [XM]	AA ET 00.043 *Médoc*, Bordeaux	
117	SOCATA TBM 700A [XN]	AA ET 00.043 *Médoc*, Bordeaux	
125	SOCATA TBM 700A [XO]	AA ET 00.043 *Médoc*, Bordeaux	
131	SOCATA TBM 700A [XQ]	AA ET 00.041 *Verdun*, Villacoublay/ Vélizy	
146	SOCATA TBM 700A [XR]	AA ET 00.041 *Verdun*, Villacoublay/ Vélizy	
147	SOCATA TBM 700A [XS]	AA ET 00.041 *Verdun*, Villacoublay/ Vélizy	
Aéronautique Navale/Marine (AN)			
008	Airbus Helicopters H.160B (F-WWOA/F-HMRE)	AN 32 Flottille, Lanvéoc/Poulmic	
016	Airbus Helicopters H.160B (F-WWOV/F-HTNS)	AN 32 Flottille, Lanvéoc/Poulmic	
020	Airbus Helicopters H.160B (F-WMXX/F-HQBN)	AN 32 Flottille, Lanvéoc/Poulmic	
024	Airbus Helicopters H.160B (F-WWOG/F-HDBE)	AN 32 Flottille, Lanvéoc/Poulmic	
030	Airbus Helicopters H.160B (F-WWOJ/F-HFYT)	AN 32 Flottille, Lanvéoc/Poulmic	
031	Airbus Helicopters H.160B (F-WJXD/F-HTHC)	AN 32 Flottille, Lanvéoc/Poulmic	
3	Dassault-Breguet Atlantique 2	AN 23 Flottille, Lorient/Lann Bihoué	
4	Dassault-Breguet Atlantique 2	AN 23 Flottille, Lorient/Lann Bihoué	
5	Dassault-Breguet Atlantique 2	AN 21 Flottille, Lorient/Lann Bihoué	
9	Dassault-Breguet Atlantique 2	AN 23 Flottille, Lorient/Lann Bihoué	
11	Dassault-Breguet Atlantique 2	AN 21 Flottille, Lorient/Lann Bihoué	
12	Dassault-Breguet Atlantique 2	AN 21 Flottille, Lorient/Lann Bihoué	
13	Dassault-Breguet Atlantique 2	AN 21 Flottille, Lorient/Lann Bihoué	
15	Dassault-Breguet Atlantique 2	AN 21 Flottille, Lorient/Lann Bihoué	
16	Dassault-Breguet Atlantique 2	AN 23 Flottille, Lorient/Lann Bihoué	
17	Dassault-Breguet Atlantique 2	AN 21 Flottille, Lorient/Lann Bihoué	
18	Dassault-Breguet Atlantique 2	AN 21 Flottille, Lorient/Lann Bihoué	
19	Dassault-Breguet Atlantique 2	AN 23 Flottille, Lorient/Lann Bihoué	
20	Dassault-Breguet Atlantique 2	AN 23 Flottille, Lorient/Lann Bihoué	
21	Dassault-Breguet Atlantique 2	AN 21 Flottille, Lorient/Lann Bihoué	
22	Dassault-Breguet Atlantique 2	AN 21 Flottille, Lorient/Lann Bihoué	
23	Dassault-Breguet Atlantique 2	AN 21 Flottille, Lorient/Lann Bihoué	
24	Dassault-Breguet Atlantique 2	AN 21 Flottille, Lorient/Lann Bihoué	
25	Dassault-Breguet Atlantique 2	AN 21 Flottille, Lorient/Lann Bihoué	
26	Dassault-Breguet Atlantique 2	AN 23 Flottille, Lorient/Lann Bihoué	
27	Dassault-Breguet Atlantique 2	AN 21 Flottille, Lorient/Lann Bihoué	
28	Dassault-Breguet Atlantique 2	AN 23 Flottille, Lorient/Lann Bihoué	
32	Dassault Falcon 10(MER)	AN 57 Escadrille, Landivisiau	
101	Dassault Falcon 10(MER)	AN 57 Escadrille, Landivisiau	
129	Dassault Falcon 10(MER)	AN 57 Escadrille, Landivisiau	
133	Dassault Falcon 10(MER)	AN 57 Escadrille, Landivisiau	
143	Dassault Falcon 10(MER)	AN 57 Escadrille, Landivisiau	
185	Dassault Falcon 10(MER)	AN 57 Escadrille, Landivisiau	
48	Dassault Falcon 20G Guardian	AN 25 Flottille, Papeete & Tontouta	
65	Dassault Falcon 20G Guardian	AN 25 Flottille, Papeete & Tontouta	
72	Dassault Falcon 20G Guardian	AN 25 Flottille, Papeete & Tontouta	

Notes	Serial	Type (code/other identity)	Owner/operator, location or fate
	77	Dassault Falcon 20G Guardian	AN 25 Flottille, Papeete & Tontouta
	80	Dassault Falcon 20G Guardian	AN 25 Flottille, Papeete & Tontouta
	5	Dassault Falcon 50MS SURMAR	AN 24 Flottille, Lorient/Lann Bihoué
	7	Dassault Falcon 50MI SURMAR	AN 24 Flottille, Lorient/Lann Bihoué
	27	Dassault Falcon 50MS SURMAR (F-ZWMM)	AN 24 Flottille, Lorient/Lann Bihoué
	30	Dassault Falcon 50MI SURMAR	AN 24 Flottille, Lorient/Lann Bihoué
	34	Dassault Falcon 50MS SURMAR (F-ZWMT)	AN 24 Flottille, Lorient/Lann Bihoué
	36	Dassault Falcon 50MI SURMAR	AN 24 Flottille, Lorient/Lann Bihoué
	78	Dassault Falcon 50MS SURMAR (F-ZWMO)	AN 24 Flottille, Lorient/Lann Bihoué
	132	Dassault Falcon 50MI SURMAR	AN 24 Flottille, Lorient/Lann Bihoué
	...	Dassault Falcon 2000LXS Albatros (F-WATM)	AN (on order)
	...	Dassault Falcon 2000LXS Albatros	AN (on order)
	...	Dassault Falcon 2000LXS Albatros	AN (on order)
	...	Dassault Falcon 2000LXS Albatros	AN (on order)
	...	Dassault Falcon 2000LXS Albatros	AN (on order)
	...	Dassault Falcon 2000LXS Albatros	AN (on order)
	...	Dassault Falcon 2000LXS Albatros	AN (on order)
	1	Dassault Rafale M	AN DGA EV, Istres
	2	Dassault Rafale M	AN 17 Flottille, Landivisiau
	3	Dassault Rafale M	AN 17 Flottille, Landivisiau
	4	Dassault Rafale M	AN ETR 03.004 *Aquitaine*, St Dizier
	5	Dassault Rafale M	AN 17 Flottille, Landivisiau
	6	Dassault Rafale M	AN 17 Flottille, Landivisiau
	7	Dassault Rafale M $	AN 11 Flottille, Landivisiau
	8	Dassault Rafale M	AN ETR 03.004 *Aquitaine*, St Dizier
	9	Dassault Rafale M	AN 12 Flottille, Landivisiau
	10	Dassault Rafale M	AN 12 Flottille, Landivisiau
	11	Dassault Rafale M	AN 11 Flottille, Landivisiau
	12	Dassault Rafale M	AN ETR 03.004 *Aquitaine*, St Dizier
	13	Dassault Rafale M	AN 11 Flottille, Landivisiau
	14	Dassault Rafale M	AN 11 Flottille, Landivisiau
	15	Dassault Rafale M	AN 11 Flottille, Landivisiau
	16	Dassault Rafale M	AN 12 Flottille, Landivisiau
	17	Dassault Rafale M	AN 12 Flottille, Landivisiau
	19	Dassault Rafale M	AN 11 Flottille, Landivisiau
	20	Dassault Rafale M	AN 17 Flottille, Landivisiau
	21	Dassault Rafale M	AN 12 Flottille, Landivisiau
	23	Dassault Rafale M	AN 12 Flottille, Landivisiau
	26	Dassault Rafale M	AN 12 Flottille, Landivisiau
	27	Dassault Rafale M $	AN ETR 03.004 *Aquitaine*, St Dizier
	28	Dassault Rafale M	AN ETR 03.004 *Aquitaine*, St Dizier
	29	Dassault Rafale M	AN ETR 03.004 *Aquitaine*, St Dizier
	30	Dassault Rafale M	AN CEPA/10 Escadrille, Landivisiau
	31	Dassault Rafale M	AN 11 Flottille, Landivisiau
	32	Dassault Rafale M $	AN 12 Flottille, Landivisiau
	33	Dassault Rafale M	AN ETR 03.004 *Aquitaine*, St Dizier
	34	Dassault Rafale M	AN 11 Flottille, Landivisiau
	35	Dassault Rafale M $	AN 17 Flottille, Landivisiau
	36	Dassault Rafale M	AN 17 Flottille, Landivisiau
	37	Dassault Rafale M $	AN 11 Flottille, Landivisiau
	38	Dassault Rafale M	AN 12 Flottille, Landivisiau
	39	Dassault Rafale M	AN 11 Flottille, Landivisiau
	40	Dassault Rafale M $	AN 17 Flottille, Landivisiau
	41	Dassault Rafale M	AN 12 Flottille, Landivisiau
	42	Dassault Rafale M	AN 11 Flottille, Landivisiau
	43	Dassault Rafale M	AN 11 Flottille, Landivisiau
	44	Dassault Rafale M	AN 11 Flottille, Landivisiau
	45	Dassault Rafale M	AN 11 Flottille, Landivisiau
	46	Dassault Rafale M	AN 11 Flottille, Landivisiau
	47	Dassault Rafale M	AN (on order)
	48	Dassault Rafale M	AN (on order)
	49	Dassault Rafale M	AN (on order)

Serial	Type (code/other identity)	Owner/operator, location or fate	Notes
50	Dassault Rafale M	AN (on order)	
65	Embraer EMB.121AN Xingu	AN 28 Flottille, Hyères	
67	Embraer EMB.121AN Xingu	AN 28 Flottille, Hyères	
68	Embraer EMB.121AN Xingu	AN 28 Flottille, Hyères	
69	Embraer EMB.121AN Xingu	AN 28 Flottille, Hyères	
71	Embraer EMB.121AN Xingu	AN 28 Flottille, Hyères	
74	Embraer EMB.121AN Xingu	AN 28 Flottille, Hyères	
77	Embraer EMB.121AN Xingu	AN 28 Flottille, Hyères	
81	Embraer EMB.121AN Xingu	AN 28 Flottille, Hyères	
85	Embraer EMB.121AN Xingu	AN 28 Flottille, Hyères	
87	Embraer EMB.121AN Xingu	AN 28 Flottille, Hyères	
17	Eurocopter AS.365N Dauphin	AN 35 Flottille, Hyères	
19	Eurocopter AS.365N Dauphin	AN 35 Flottille, Hyères	
24	Eurocopter AS.365N Dauphin	AN 35 Flottille, Hyères	
81	Eurocopter AS.365N Dauphin	AN 35 Flottille, Hyères	
91	Eurocopter AS.365N Dauphin $	AN 35 Flottille, Hyères	
157	Eurocopter AS.365N Dauphin	AN 35 Flottille, Hyères	
313	Eurocopter SA.365F-1 Dauphin II	AN 35 Flottille, Hyères	
318	Eurocopter SA.365F-1 Dauphin II	AN 35 Flottille, Hyères	
322	Eurocopter SA.365F-1 Dauphin II	AN 35 Flottille, Hyères	
355	Eurocopter AS.565MA Panther	AN 36 Flottille, Hyères	
362	Eurocopter AS.565MA Panther	AN 36 Flottille, Hyères	
403	Eurocopter AS.565UA Panther	AN 36 Flottille, Hyères	
436	Eurocopter AS.565MA Panther	AN 36 Flottille, Hyères	
452	Eurocopter AS.565MA Panther	AN 36 Flottille, Hyères	
466	Eurocopter AS.565MA Panther	AN 36 Flottille, Hyères	
486	Eurocopter AS.565MA Panther	AN 36 Flottille, Hyères	
488	Eurocopter AS.565MA Panther	AN 36 Flottille, Hyères	
503	Eurocopter AS.565MA Panther	AN 36 Flottille, Hyères	
505	Eurocopter AS.565SA Panther	AN 36 Flottille, Hyères	
506	Eurocopter AS.565MA Panther	AN 36 Flottille, Hyères	
507	Eurocopter AS.565MA Panther	AN 36 Flottille, Hyères	
511	Eurocopter AS.565MA Panther	AN 36 Flottille, Hyères	
519	Eurocopter AS.565MA Panther	AN 36 Flottille, Hyères	
522	Eurocopter AS.565MA Panther	AN 36 Flottille, Hyères	
524	Eurocopter AS.565MA Panther	AN 36 Flottille, Hyères	
001	Eurocopter AS.365N-3 Dauphin (F-HURX)	AN 34 Flottille, Lanvéoc/Poulmic	
705	Eurocopter AS.365N-3 Dauphin (F-GNYH)	AN 34 Flottille, Lanvéoc/Poulmic	
710	Eurocopter AS.365N-3 Dauphin (F-GTCH)	AN 34 Flottille, Lanvéoc/Poulmic	
724	Eurocopter AS.365N-3 Dauphin (F-GVGV)	AN 34 Flottille, Lanvéoc/Poulmic	
726	Eurocopter AS.365N-3 Dauphin (F-HUZS)	AN (on order)	
745	Eurocopter AS.365N-3 Dauphin (F-HUDT)	AN 35 Flottille, Tahiti	
751	Eurocopter AS.365N-3 Dauphin (F-HABF)	AN (on order)	
756	Eurocopter AS.365N-3 Dauphin (F-GLTB)	AN (on order)	
772	Eurocopter AS.365N-3 Dauphin (F-GNVT)	AN (on order)	
810	Eurocopter AS.365N-3 Dauphin (F-GZAD)	AN (on order)	
879	Eurocopter AS.365N-3 Dauphin (F-HUAJ)	AN (on order)	
884	Eurocopter AS.365N-3 Dauphin (F-HUFZ)	AN (on order)	
...	Eurocopter AS.365N-3 Dauphin	AN (on order)	
6872	Eurocopter AS.365N-3 Dauphin	AN 35 Flottille, Tahiti	
6928	Eurocopter AS.365N-3 Dauphin	AN 35 Flottille, Tahiti	
1	NH Industries NH.90-NFH Caïman (F-ZWTO)	AN 31 Flottille, Hyères	
2	NH Industries NH.90-NFH Caïman	AN CEPA/10 Escadrille, Hyères	
3	NH Industries NH.90-NFH Caïman	AN 33 Flottille, Lanvéoc/Poulmic	
4	NH Industries NH.90-NFH Caïman	AN 33 Flottille, Lanvéoc/Poulmic	
5	NH Industries NH.90-NFH Caïman	AN 33 Flottille, Lanvéoc/Poulmic	
6	NH Industries NH.90-NFH Caïman	AN 31 Flottille, Hyères	
7	NH Industries NH.90-NFH Caïman	AN 33 Flottille, Lanvéoc/Poulmic	
8	NH Industries NH.90-NFH Caïman	AN 33 Flottille, Lanvéoc/Poulmic	
9	NH Industries NH.90-NFH Caïman	AN 31 Flottille, Hyères	
10	NH Industries NH.90-NFH Caïman	AN 33 Flottille, Lanvéoc/Poulmic	
11	NH Industries NH.90-NFH Caïman	AN 33 Flottille, Lanvéoc/Poulmic	

Notes	Serial	Type (code/other identity)	Owner/operator, location or fate
	12	NH Industries NH.90-NFH Caïman	AN 33 Flottille, Lanvéoc/Poulmic
	13	NH Industries NH.90-NFH Caïman	Airbus Helicopters, Marseille, Sep 2024
	14	NH Industries NH.90-NFH Caïman	AN 33 Flottille, Lanvéoc/Poulmic
	15	NH Industries NH.90-NFH Caïman	AN 31 Flottille, Hyères
	16	NH Industries NH.90-NFH Caïman	AN 31 Flottille, Hyères
	17	NH Industries NH.90-NFH Caïman	AN 33 Flottille, Lanvéoc/Poulmic
	18	NH Industries NH.90-NFH Caïman	AN 33 Flottille, Lanvéoc/Poulmic
	19	NH Industries NH.90-NFH Caïman	AN 31 Flottille, Hyères
	20	NH Industries NH.90-NFH Caïman	AN 33 Flottille, Lanvéoc/Poulmic
	21	NH Industries NH.90-NFH Caïman	AN 31 Flottille, Hyères
	22	NH Industries NH.90-NFH Caïman	AN 31 Flottille, Hyères
	23	NH Industries NH.90-NFH Caïman	AN 33 Flottille, Lanvéoc/Poulmic
	24	NH Industries NH.90-NFH Caïman	AN
	25	NH Industries NH.90-NFH Caïman	AN 31 Flottille, Hyères
	26	NH Industries NH.90-NFH Caïman	AN 31 Flottille, Hyères
	27	NH Industries NH.90-NFH Caïman	AN 33 Flottille, Lanvéoc/Poulmic
	1	Northrop Grumman E-2C Hawkeye (165455)	AN 4 Flottille, Lorient/Lann Bihoué
	2	Northrop Grumman E-2C Hawkeye (165456)	AN 4 Flottille, Lorient/Lann Bihoué
	3	Northrop Grumman E-2C Hawkeye (166417)	AN 4 Flottille, Lorient/Lann Bihoué
	Aviation Legére de l'Armée de Terre (ALAT)		
	1006	Aérospatiale SA.330Ba Puma [DAA]	ALAT 3 RHC, Etain
	1036	Aérospatiale SA.330Ba Puma [DAC]	ALAT 3 RHC, Etain
	1037	Aérospatiale SA.330Ba Puma [DAD]	ALAT EALAT, Le Luc
	1049	Aérospatiale SA.330Ba Puma [DAE]	ALAT 5 RHC, Pau
	1055	Aérospatiale SA.330Ba Puma [DAF]	ALAT GIH, Cazaux
	1069	Aérospatiale SA.330Ba Puma [DAG]	ALAT 3 RHC, Etain
	1073	Aérospatiale SA.330Ba Puma [DCF]	ALAT EALAT, Le Luc
	1078	Aérospatiale SA.330Ba Puma [DAH]	ALAT 3 RHC, Etain
	1092	Aérospatiale SA.330Ba Puma [DAI]	ALAT 4 RHFS (GIH), Villacoublay/ Vélizy
	1100	Aérospatiale SA.330Ba Puma [DAJ]	ALAT 3 RHC, Etain
	1102	Aérospatiale SA.330Ba Puma [DAK]	ALAT, stored Romorantin/Pruniers, Jan 2024
	1107	Aérospatiale SA.330Ba Puma [DAL]	ALAT 3 RHC, Etain
	1109	Aérospatiale SA.330Ba Puma [DAM]	ALAT EALAT, Le Luc
	1128	Aérospatiale SA.330Ba Puma [DAN]	ALAT 4 RHFS (GIH), Villacoublay/ Vélizy
	1143	Aérospatiale SA.330Ba Puma [DAO]	ALAT EALAT, Le Luc
	1149	Aérospatiale SA.330Ba Puma [DAP]	ALAT 3 RHC, Etain
	1156	Aérospatiale SA.330Ba Puma [DAQ]	ALAT 3 RHC, Etain
	1173	Aérospatiale SA.330Ba Puma [DAR]	ALAT 4 RHFS (GIH), Villacoublay/ Vélizy
	1176	Aérospatiale SA.330Ba Puma [DAS]	Airbus Helicopters, Marseille, Nov 2024
	1198	Aérospatiale SA.330Ba Puma [DDD]	ALAT
	1211	Aérospatiale SA.330Ba Puma [DAW]	ALAT 4 RHFS (GIH), Villacoublay/ Vélizy
	1214	Aérospatiale SA.330Ba Puma [DAX]	ALAT 3 RHC, Etain
	1217	Aérospatiale SA.330Ba Puma [DAY]	ALAT 3 RHC, Etain
	1219	Aérospatiale SA.330Ba Puma [DAZ]	ALAT 3 RHC, Etain
	1231	Aérospatiale SA.330Ba Puma [DDK]	*ALAT, Latresne, for GI*
	1232	Aérospatiale SA.330Ba Puma [DBA]	ALAT
	1236	Aérospatiale SA.330Ba Puma [DDM]	ALAT EALAT, Le Luc
	1243	Aérospatiale SA.330Ba Puma [DBB]	ALAT 4 RHFS (GIH), Villacoublay/ Vélizy
	1252	Aérospatiale SA.330Ba Puma [DDP]	ALAT EALAT, Le Luc
	1269	Aérospatiale SA.330Ba Puma [DDT]	ALAT 3 RHC, Etain
	1417	Aérospatiale SA.330Ba Puma [DBF]	ALAT 3 RHC, Etain
	1438	Aérospatiale SA.330Ba Puma [DBG]	ALAT
	1447	Aérospatiale SA.330Ba Puma [DDW]	ALAT 3 RHC, Etain
	1451	Aérospatiale SA.330Ba Puma [DBH]	ALAT
	1507	Aérospatiale SA.330Ba Puma [DBI]	ALAT EALAT, Le Luc
	1510	Aérospatiale SA.330Ba Puma [DBJ]	ALAT 3 RHC, Etain
	1512	Aérospatiale SA.330Ba Puma [DBK]	ALAT 4 RHFS (GIH), Villacoublay/ Vélizy
	1519	Aérospatiale SA.330Ba Puma [DBL]	ALAT 4 RHFS (GIH), Villacoublay/ Vélizy
	1617	Aérospatiale SA.330Ba Puma [DBM]	ALAT
	1632	Aérospatiale SA.330Ba Puma [DBN]	ALAT 4 RHFS (GIH), Villacoublay/ Vélizy
	1634	Aérospatiale SA.330Ba Puma [DBO]	ALAT 3 RHC, Etain
	1654	Aérospatiale SA.330Ba Puma [DBP]	ALAT 3 RHC, Etain

Serial	Type (code/other identity)	Owner/operator, location or fate	Notes
1662	Aérospatiale SA.330Ba Puma [DDX]	ALAT EALAT, Le Luc (damaged)	
1663	Aérospatiale SA.330Ba Puma [DBQ]	ALAT 3 RHC, Etain	
5682	Aérospatiale SA.330Ba Puma [DBR]	ALAT 3 RHC, Etain	
3459	Aérospatiale SA.342M-1 Gazelle [GAA]	ALAT 1 RHC, Phalsbourg	
3512	Aérospatiale SA.342M-1 Gazelle [GAC]	ALAT 1 RHC, Phalsbourg	
3530	Aérospatiale SA.342M-1 Gazelle [GAD]	ALAT 4 RHFS, Pau	
3664	Aérospatiale SA.342M-1 Gazelle [GAF]	ALAT EALAT, Le Luc	
3848	Aérospatiale SA.342M-1 Gazelle [GAG]	ALAT 5 RHC, Pau	
3849	Aérospatiale SA.342M-1 Gazelle [GAH]	ALAT 5 RHC, Pau	
3850	Aérospatiale SA.342M-1 Gazelle [GAI]	ALAT EALAT, Le Luc	
3856	Aérospatiale SA.342M-1 Gazelle [GAJ]	ALAT 3 RHC, Etain	
3857	Aérospatiale SA.342M Gazelle [GJK]	ALAT, stored Marseille	
3859	Aérospatiale SA.342M-1 Gazelle [GAK]	ALAT 5 RHC, Pau	
3862	Aérospatiale SA.342M-1 Gazelle [GAL]	ALAT 3 RHC, Etain	
3863	Aérospatiale SA.342M-1 Gazelle [GAM]	ALAT EALAT, Le Luc	
3865	Aérospatiale SA.342M-1 Gazelle [GAN]	ALAT EALAT, Le Luc	
3868	Aérospatiale SA.342M-1 Gazelle [GAO]	ALAT 3 RHC, Etain	
3911	Aérospatiale SA.342M-1 Gazelle [GAP]	ALAT 1 RHC, Phalsbourg	
3921	Aérospatiale SA.342M-1 Gazelle [GAQ]	ALAT EALAT, Le Luc	
3938	Aérospatiale SA.342M-1 Gazelle [GAR]	ALAT EALAT, Le Luc	
3947	Aérospatiale SA.342M-1 Gazelle [GAS]	ALAT 3 RHC, Etain	
3948	Aérospatiale SA.342M-1 Gazelle [GAT]	ALAT 1 RHC, Phalsbourg	
3957	Aérospatiale SA.342M-1 Gazelle [GAU]	ALAT 5 RHC, Pau	
3964	Aérospatiale SA.342M-1 Gazelle [GAV]	ALAT 3 RHC, Etain	
3996	Aérospatiale SA.342M-1 Gazelle [GAW]	ALAT 5 RHC, Pau	
4018	Aérospatiale SA.342M-1 Gazelle [GAX]	ALAT 3 RHC, Etain	
4022	Aérospatiale SA.342M Gazelle [GJQ]	ALAT, stored Marseille	
4026	Aérospatiale SA.342M-1 Gazelle [GBA]	ALAT 1 RHC, Phalsbourg	
4034	Aérospatiale SA.342M-1 Gazelle [GBB]	ALAT 1 RHC, Phalsbourg	
4039	Aérospatiale SA.342M-1 Gazelle [GBC]	ALAT EALAT, Le Luc	
4042	Aérospatiale SA.342M Gazelle [GMB]	ALAT EALAT, Le Luc	
4053	Aérospatiale SA.342M-1 Gazelle [GBE]	ALAT 3 RHC, Etain	
4059	Aérospatiale SA.342M-1 Gazelle [GBF]	ALAT 1 RHC, Phalsbourg	
4061	Aérospatiale SA.342M-1 Gazelle [GBG]	ALAT GAM/STAT, Valence	
4066	Aérospatiale SA.342M-1 Gazelle [GBH]	ALAT 3 RHC, Etain	
4071	Aérospatiale SA.342M Gazelle [GNS]	*ALAT, stored Montauban*	
4072	Aérospatiale SA.342M-1 Gazelle [GBI]	ALAT 3 RHC, Etain	
4079	Aérospatiale SA.342M-1 Gazelle [GMC]	ALAT EALAT, Le Luc	
4083	Aérospatiale SA.342M Gazelle [GNT]	ALAT, stored Marseille	
4084	Aérospatiale SA.342M-1 Gazelle [GBJ]	ALAT 3 RHC, Etain	
4095	Aérospatiale SA.342M-1 Gazelle [GBL]	ALAT	
4109	Aérospatiale SA.342M-1 Gazelle [GBN]	ALAT 3 RHC, Etain	
4114	Aérospatiale SA.342M-1 Gazelle [GBO]	ALAT	
4115	Aérospatiale SA.342M-1 Gazelle [GBP]	ALAT EALAT, Le Luc	
4118	Aérospatiale SA.342M Gazelle [GNV]	ALAT, stored Marseille	
4119	Aérospatiale SA.342M-1 Gazelle [GBQ]	ALAT 1 RHC, Phalsbourg	
4120	Aérospatiale SA.342M-1 Gazelle [GBR]	ALAT EALAT, Le Luc	
4124	Aérospatiale SA.342M-1 Gazelle [GBS]	ALAT 1 RHC, Phalsbourg	
4136	Aérospatiale SA.342M-1 Gazelle [GBT]	ALAT 3 RHC, Etain	
4140	Aérospatiale SA.342M-1 Gazelle [GBU]	ALAT 5 RHC, Pau	
4141	Aérospatiale SA.342M-1 Gazelle [GBV]	ALAT	
4142	Aérospatiale SA.342M-1 Gazelle [GBW]	ALAT 3 RHC, Etain	
4144	Aérospatiale SA.342M-1 Gazelle [GBX]	ALAT 3 RHC, Etain	
4145	Aérospatiale SA.342M-1 Gazelle [GBY] $	ALAT 3 RHC, Etain	
4160	Aérospatiale SA.342M-1 Gazelle [GCC]	ALAT 3 RHC, Etain	
4161	Aérospatiale SA.342M-1 Gazelle [GCD]	ALAT 5 RHC, Pau	
4162	Aérospatiale SA.342M-1 Gazelle [GCE]	ALAT	
4164	Aérospatiale SA.342M-1 Gazelle [GCF]	ALAT	
4168	Aérospatiale SA.342M-1 Gazelle [GCG]	ALAT 5 RHC, Pau	
4175	Aérospatiale SA.342M-1 Gazelle [GCI]	ALAT 1 RHC, Phalsbourg	
4179	Aérospatiale SA.342M-1 Gazelle [GCJ]	ALAT 3 RHC, Etain	
4180	Aérospatiale SA.342M-1 Gazelle [GCK]	ALAT	

Notes	Serial	Type (code/other identity)	Owner/operator, location or fate
	4181	Aérospatiale SA.342M-1 Gazelle [GCL]	ALAT EALAT, Le Luc
	4185	Aérospatiale SA.342M Gazelle [GKD]	ALAT, stored Marseille
	4186	Aérospatiale SA.342M-1 Gazelle [GCM]	ALAT 3 RHC, Etain
	4189	Aérospatiale SA.342M-1 Gazelle [GCN]	ALAT
	4191	Aérospatiale SA.342M-1 Gazelle [GCO]	Airbus Helicopters, Marseille, Jul 2024
	4195	Aérospatiale SA.342M-1 Gazelle [GCP]	ALAT 3 RHC, Etain
	4198	Aérospatiale SA.342M-1 Gazelle [GCQ]	ALAT 3 RHC, Etain
	4205	Aérospatiale SA.342Ma Gazelle [GEA]	ALAT 1 RHC, Phalsbourg
	4206	Aérospatiale SA.342Ma Gazelle [GEB]	ALAT
	4207	Aérospatiale SA.342Ma Gazelle [GEC]	ALAT 3 RHC, Etain
	4208	Aérospatiale SA.342Ma Gazelle [GED]	ALAT GAM/STAT, Valence
	4210	Aérospatiale SA.342Ma Gazelle [GEF]	ALAT
	4211	Aérospatiale SA.342Ma Gazelle [GEG]	ALAT
	4214	Aérospatiale SA.342Ma Gazelle [GEI]	ALAT EALAT, Le Luc
	4215	Aérospatiale SA.342Ma Gazelle [GEJ]	ALAT 4 RHFS, Pau
	4216	Aérospatiale SA.342Ma Gazelle [GEK]	ALAT 1 RHC, Phalsbourg
	4218	Aérospatiale SA.342Ma Gazelle [GEM]	ALAT 3 RHC, Etain
	4219	Aérospatiale SA.342Ma Gazelle [GEN]	ALAT 4 RHFS, Pau
	4220	Aérospatiale SA.342Ma Gazelle [GEO]	ALAT 3 RHC, Etain
	4221	Aérospatiale SA.342Ma Gazelle [GEP]	ALAT 3 RHC, Etain
	4222	Aérospatiale SA.342Ma Gazelle [GEQ]	ALAT EALAT, Le Luc
	4223	Aérospatiale SA.342Ma Gazelle [GER]	ALAT EALAT, Le Luc
	4224	Aérospatiale SA.342Ma Gazelle [GES]	ALAT GAM/STAT, Valence
	4225	Aérospatiale SA.342Ma Gazelle [GET]	ALAT 4 RHFS, Pau
	4226	Aérospatiale SA.342Ma Gazelle [GEU]	ALAT GAM/STAT, Valence
	4227	Aérospatiale SA.342Ma Gazelle [GEV]	ALAT EALAT, Le Luc
	4228	Aérospatiale SA.342Ma Gazelle [GEW]	ALAT 1 RHC, Phalsbourg
	4229	Aérospatiale SA.342Ma Gazelle [GEX]	ALAT 3 RHC, Etain
	4230	Aérospatiale SA.342Ma Gazelle [GEY]	ALAT EALAT, Le Luc
	4232	Aérospatiale SA.342Ma Gazelle [GFA]	ALAT
	4233	Aérospatiale SA.342Ma Gazelle [GFB]	ALAT
	2252	Aérospatiale AS.532UL Cougar [CGA]	ALAT GAM/STAT, Valence
	2266	Aérospatiale AS.532UL Cougar [CGB]	ALAT 5 RHC, Pau
	2267	Aérospatiale AS.532UL Cougar [CGC]	ALAT 4 RHFS, Pau
	2271	Aérospatiale AS.532UL Cougar [CGD]	ALAT 4 RHFS, Pau
	2273	Aérospatiale AS.532UL Cougar [CGF]	ALAT 4 RHFS, Pau
	2282	Aérospatiale AS.532UL Cougar [CGG]	ALAT 4 RHFS, Pau
	2285	Aérospatiale AS.532UL Cougar [CGH]	ALAT 4 RHFS, Pau
	2290	Aérospatiale AS.532UL Cougar [CGI]	ALAT 4 RHFS, Pau
	2293	Aérospatiale AS.532UL Cougar [CGJ]	ALAT 1 RHC, Phalsbourg
	2299	Aérospatiale AS.532UL Cougar [CGK]	ALAT 4 RHFS, Pau
	2300	Aérospatiale AS.532UL Cougar [CGL]	ALAT
	2301	Aérospatiale AS.532UL Cougar [CGM]	ALAT 4 RHFS, Pau
	2303	Aérospatiale AS.532UL Cougar [CGN]	ALAT
	2316	Aérospatiale AS.532UL Cougar [CGO]	ALAT 1 RHC, Phalsbourg
	2323	Aérospatiale AS.532UL Cougar [CGQ]	ALAT 4 RHFS, Pau
	2324	Aérospatiale AS.532UL Cougar [CGR]	ALAT 4 RHFS, Pau
	2325	Aérospatiale AS.532UL Cougar [CGS]	ALAT
	2327	Aérospatiale AS.532UL Cougar [CGT]	ALAT
	2331	Aérospatiale AS.532UL Cougar [CGU]	ALAT
	2342	Aérospatiale AS.532UL Cougar [CHA]	ALAT 5 RHC, Pau
	2369	Aérospatiale AS.532UL Cougar [CHB]	ALAT
	2375	Aérospatiale AS.532UL Cougar [CHC]	ALAT 5 RHC, Pau
	2443	Aérospatiale AS.532UL Cougar [CGW]	ALAT 1 RHC, Phalsbourg
	2446	Aérospatiale AS.532UL Cougar [CGX]	ALAT 5 RHC, Pau
	5471	Eurocopter AS.555UN Fennec [AYA]	ALAT EALAT, Le Luc
	5491	Eurocopter AS.555UN Fennec [AYB]	ALAT EALAT, Le Luc
	5496	Eurocopter AS.555UN Fennec [AYC]	ALAT EALAT, Le Luc
	5503	Eurocopter AS.555UN Fennec [AYD]	ALAT EALAT, Le Luc
	5527	Eurocopter AS.555UN Fennec [AYE]	ALAT EALAT, Le Luc
	5529	Eurocopter AS.555UN Fennec [AYF]	ALAT EALAT, Le Luc
	5537	Eurocopter AS.555UN Fennec [AYG]	ALAT EALAT, Le Luc

Serial	Type (code/other identity)	Owner/operator, location or fate	Notes
5539	Eurocopter AS.555UN Fennec [AYH]	ALAT EALAT, Le Luc	
5541	Eurocopter AS.555UN Fennec [AYI]	ALAT EALAT, Le Luc	
5544	Eurocopter AS.555UN Fennec [AYJ]	ALAT EALAT, Le Luc	
5591	Eurocopter AS.555UN Fennec [AYL]	ALAT EALAT, Le Luc	
5593	Eurocopter AS.555UN Fennec [AYM]	ALAT EALAT, Le Luc	
5599	Eurocopter AS.555UN Fennec [AYN]	ALAT EALAT, Le Luc	
5602	Eurocopter AS.555UN Fennec [AYO]	ALAT EALAT, Le Luc	
5606	Eurocopter AS.555UN Fennec [AYP]	ALAT EALAT, Le Luc	
5608	Eurocopter AS.555UN Fennec [AYQ]	ALAT EALAT, Le Luc	
5610	Eurocopter AS.555UN Fennec [AYR]	ALAT EALAT, Le Luc	
5611	Eurocopter AS.555UN Fennec [AYK]	ALAT EALAT, Le Luc	
2001	Eurocopter EC.665 Tigre HAP [BHH]	ALAT 5 RHC, Pau	
2002	Eurocopter EC.665 Tigre HAP [BHI]	ALAT 5 RHC, Pau	
2003	Eurocopter EC.665 Tigre HAP (F-ZWRM) [BHJ]	ALAT 5 RHC, Pau	
2004	Eurocopter EC.665 Tigre HAD [BHK]	ALAT EALAT, Le Luc	
2006	Eurocopter EC.665 Tigre HAD [BHL]	Airbus Helicopters, Marseille (conversion)	
2009	Eurocopter EC.665 Tigre HAD [BHB]	ALAT EALAT, Le Luc	
2010	Eurocopter EC.665 Tigre HAD [BHA]	ALAT 5 RHC, Pau	
2011	Eurocopter EC.665 Tigre HAD [BHM]	Airbus Helicopters, Marseille (conversion)	
2012	Eurocopter EC.665 Tigre HAP [BHT]	Airbus Helicopters, Marseille (conversion)	
2013	Eurocopter EC.665 Tigre HAP [BHC]	ALAT 5 RHC, Pau	
2015	Eurocopter EC.665 Tigre HAD (F-ZKBO) [BHD]	ALAT 5 RHC, Pau	
2016	Eurocopter EC.665 Tigre HAD [BIA]	Airbus Helicopters, Marseille (conversion)	
2018	Eurocopter EC.665 Tigre HAP [BHF]	ALAT GAM/STAT, Valence	
2019	Eurocopter EC.665 Tigre HAD [BHE]	ALAT EALAT, Le Luc	
2021	Eurocopter EC.665 Tigre HAP [BHN]	ALAT GAM/STAT, Valence	
2022	Eurocopter EC.665 Tigre HAP [BHG]	ALAT 5 RHC, Pau	
2023	Eurocopter EC.665 Tigre HAD [BHP]	ALAT EALAT, Le Luc	
2024	Eurocopter EC.665 Tigre HAD [BHO]	Airbus Helicopters, Marseille (conversion)	
2025	Eurocopter EC.665 Tigre HAP [BHQ]	ALAT 5 RHC, Pau	
2026	Eurocopter EC.665 Tigre HAD (F-ZKBA) [BHR]	ALAT 1 RHC, Phalsbourg	
2027	Eurocopter EC.665 Tigre HAD [BHS]	ALAT 5 RHC, Pau	
2029	Eurocopter EC.665 Tigre HAD [BHV]	ALAT EALAT, Le Luc	
2030	Eurocopter EC.665 Tigre HAP [BHW]	Airbus Helicopters, Marseille (conversion)	
2031	Eurocopter EC.665 Tigre HAP [BHX]	ALAT 4 RHFS, Pau	
2033	Eurocopter EC.665 Tigre HAD [BHZ]	ALAT 1 RHC, Phalsbourg	
2034	Eurocopter EC.665 Tigre HAP [BIB]	ALAT 4 RHFS, Pau	
2035	Eurocopter EC.665 Tigre HAD [BIC]	Airbus Helicopters, Marseille (conversion)	
2037	Eurocopter EC.665 Tigre HAP [BIE] $	ALAT 1 RHC, Phalsbourg	
2038	Eurocopter EC.665 Tigre HAD [BIF]	ALAT 1 RHC, Phalsbourg	
2039	Eurocopter EC.665 Tigre HAD [BIG]	Airbus Helicopters, Marseille (conversion)	
2040	Eurocopter EC.665 Tigre HAP [BIH]	ALAT 4 RHFS, Pau	
2041	Eurocopter EC.665 Tigre HAP [BII]	Airbus Helicopters, Marseille (conversion)	
2042	Eurocopter EC.665 Tigre HAD [BIJ]	Airbus Helicopters, Marseille (conversion)	
2043	Eurocopter EC.665 Tigre HAP [BIK]	ALAT 4 RHFS, Pau	
2044	Eurocopter EC.665 Tigre HAD [BIL]	ALAT EALAT, Le Luc	
2045	Eurocopter EC.665 Tigre HAP [BIM]	ALAT 4 RHFS, Pau	
2046	Eurocopter EC.665 Tigre HAD [BIN]	Airbus Helicopters, Marseille (conversion)	
2047	Eurocopter EC.665 Tigre HAP [BIO]	ALAT (on order)	
6001	Eurocopter EC.665 Tigre HAD [BJA]	ALAT EALAT, Le Luc	
6002	Eurocopter EC.665 Tigre HAD [BJB]	ALAT 5 RHC, Pau	
6003	Eurocopter EC.665 Tigre HAD [BJC]	ALAT EALAT, Le Luc	
6004	Eurocopter EC.665 Tigre HAD [BJD]	ALAT 4 RHFS, Pau	
6005	Eurocopter EC.665 Tigre HAD [BJE] $	ALAT 5 RHC, Pau	
6006	Eurocopter EC.665 Tigre HAD [BJF]	ALAT 1 RHC, Phalsbourg	
6007	Eurocopter EC.665 Tigre HAD [BJG]	ALAT EALAT, Le Luc	
6008	Eurocopter EC.665 Tigre HAD [BJH]	ALAT 1 RHC, Phalsbourg	
6009	Eurocopter EC.665 Tigre HAD [BJI]	ALAT 1 RHC, Phalsbourg	
6010	Eurocopter EC.665 Tigre HAD [BJJ]	ALAT 5 RHC, Pau	
6011	Eurocopter EC.665 Tigre HAD [BJK]	ALAT 1 RHC, Phalsbourg	
6012	Eurocopter EC.665 Tigre HAD [BJL]	ALAT 1 RHC, Phalsbourg	
6013	Eurocopter EC.665 Tigre HAD [BJM]	ALAT EALAT, Le Luc	

Notes	Serial	Type (code/other identity)	Owner/operator, location or fate
	6014	Eurocopter EC.665 Tigre HAD [BJN]	ALAT EALAT, Le Luc
	6015	Eurocopter EC.665 Tigre HAD [BJO]	ALAT 1 RHC, Phalsbourg
	6016	Eurocopter EC.665 Tigre HAD [BJP]	ALAT GAM/STAT, Valence
	6018	Eurocopter EC.665 Tigre HAD [BJR]	ALAT 1 RHC, Phalsbourg
	6019	Eurocopter EC.665 Tigre HAD [BJS]	ALAT 1 RHC, Phalsbourg
	6020	Eurocopter EC.665 Tigre HAD [BJT]	ALAT 1 RHC, Phalsbourg
	6021	Eurocopter EC.665 Tigre HAD [BJU]	ALAT 4 RHFS, Pau
	6022	Eurocopter EC.665 Tigre HAD (F-ZWDM) [BJV]	Airbus Helicopters, Marseille
	6023	Eurocopter EC.665 Tigre HAD [BJW]	ALAT EALAT, Le Luc
	6024	Eurocopter EC.665 Tigre HAD [BJX]	ALAT 1 RHC, Phalsbourg
	6025	Eurocopter EC.665 Tigre HAD [BJY]	ALAT 1 RHC, Phalsbourg
	6026	Eurocopter EC.665 Tigre HAD [BJZ]	Airbus Helicopters, Marseille
	6027	Eurocopter EC.665 Tigre HAD [BKA]	Airbus Helicopters, Marseille
	6028	Eurocopter EC.665 Tigre HAD [BKB]	ALAT 1 RHC, Phalsbourg
	6029	Eurocopter EC.665 Tigre HAD [BKC]	ALAT 1 RHC, Phalsbourg
	6030	Eurocopter EC.665 Tigre HAD [BKD]	ALAT 5 RHC, Pau
	6031	Eurocopter EC.665 Tigre HAD [BKE]	ALAT 5 RHC, Pau
	2611	Eurocopter EC.725AP Caracal [CAA]	ALAT 4 RHFS, Pau
	2628	Eurocopter EC.725AP Caracal [CAB]	ALAT/Airbus Helicopters, Marseille
	2630	Eurocopter EC.725AP Caracal [CAC]	ALAT 4 RHFS, Pau
	2631	Eurocopter EC.725AP Caracal [CAD]	ALAT 4 RHFS, Pau
	2633	Eurocopter EC.725AP Caracal [CAE]	ALAT 4 RHFS, Pau
	2638	Eurocopter EC.725AP Caracal [CAF]	ALAT/Airbus Helicopters, Marseille
	2640	Eurocopter EC.725AP Caracal [CAG]	ALAT
	2642	Eurocopter EC.725AP Caracal [CAH]	ALAT
	1239	NH Industries NH.90-TTH Caïman [EAA]	ALAT EALAT, Le Luc
	1256	NH Industries NH.90-TTH Caïman [EAB]	ALAT EALAT, Le Luc
	1271	NH Industries NH.90-TTH Caïman [EAC]	ALAT EALAT, Le Luc
	1273	NH Industries NH.90-TTH Caïman [EAD]	ALAT 1 RHC, Phalsbourg
	1290	NH Industries NH.90-TTH Caïman [EAE]	ALAT EALAT, Le Luc
	1291	NH Industries NH.90-TTH Caïman [EAF]	ALAT 1 RHC, Phalsbourg
	1292	NH Industries NH.90-TTH Caïman [EAG]	ALAT 1 RHC, Phalsbourg
	1293	NH Industries NH.90-TTH Caïman [EAH]	ALAT EALAT, Le Luc
	1294	NH Industries NH.90-TTH Caïman [EAI]	ALAT 1 RHC, Phalsbourg
	1295	NH Industries NH.90-TTH Caïman [EAJ]	ALAT 1 RHC, Phalsbourg
	1306	NH Industries NH.90-TTH Caïman [EAK]	ALAT
	1307	NH Industries NH.90 TTH Caïman [EAL]	ALAT 1 RHC, Phalsbourg
	1308	NH Industries NH.90-TTH Caïman [EAM]	ALAT/Airbus Helicopters, Marseille
	1309	NH Industries NH.90-TTH Caïman [EAN]	ALAT/Airbus Helicopters, Marseille
	1310	NH Industries NH.90-TTH Caïman [EAO]	ALAT 5 RHC, Pau
	1311	NH Industries NH.90-TTH Caïman [EAP]	ALAT 1 RHC, Phalsbourg
	1312	NH Industries NH.90-TTH Caïman [EAQ]	ALAT 1 RHC, Phalsbourg
	1313	NH Industries NH.90-TTH Caïman [EAR]	ALAT 1 RHC, Phalsbourg
	1332	NH Industries NH.90-TTH Caïman [EAS]	ALAT 1 RHC, Phalsbourg (damaged)
	1333	NH Industries NH.90-TTH Caïman [EAT]	ALAT
	1334	NH Industries NH.90-TTH Caïman [EAU]	ALAT 1 RHC, Phalsbourg
	1335	NH Industries NH.90-TTH Caïman [EAV]	ALAT 1 RHC, Phalsbourg
	1336	NH Industries NH.90-TTH Caïman [EAW]	ALAT
	1337	NH Industries NH.90-TTH Caïman [EAX]	ALAT 1 RHC, Phalsbourg
	1338	NH Industries NH.90-TTH Caïman [EAY]	ALAT 1 RHC, Phalsbourg
	1386	NH Industries NH.90-TTH Caïman [EAZ]	ALAT
	1387	NH Industries NH.90-TTH Caïman [EBC]	ALAT 1 RHC, Phalsbourg
	1390	NH Industries NH.90-TTH Caïman [EBA]	ALAT 1 RHC, Phalsbourg
	1391	NH Industries NH.90-TTH Caïman [EBB]	ALAT 1 RHC, Phalsbourg
	1392	NH Industries NH.90-TTH Caïman [EBD]	ALAT 1 RHC, Phalsbourg
	1401	NH Industries NH.90-TTH Caïman [EBE]	ALAT GAM/STAT, Valence
	1402	NH Industries NH.90-TTH Caïman [EBF]	ALAT 1 RHC, Phalsbourg
	1403	NH Industries NH.90-TTH Caïman [EBG]	ALAT EALAT, Le Luc
	1404	NH Industries NH.90-TTH Caïman [EBH]	ALAT 1 RHC, Phalsbourg
	1405	NH Industries NH.90-TTH Caïman [EBI]	ALAT 5 RHC, Pau
	1427	NH Industries NH.90-TTH Caïman [EBK]	ALAT EALAT, Le Luc
	1428	NH Industries NH.90-TTH Caïman [EBL]	ALAT 5 RHC, Pau

Serial	Type (code/other identity)	Owner/operator, location or fate	Notes
1429	NH Industries NH.90-TTH Caïman [EBM]	ALAT 5 RHC, Pau	
1430	NH Industries NH.90-TTH Caïman [EBO]	ALAT 3 RHC, Etain	
1431	NH Industries NH.90-TTH Caïman [EBP]	ALAT 3 RHC, Etain	
1432	NH Industries NH.90-TTH Caïman [EBJ]	ALAT 5 RHC, Pau	
1433	NH Industries NH.90-TTH Caïman [EBN]	ALAT 5 RHC, Pau	
1441	NH Industries NH.90-TTH Caïman [EBR]	ALAT	
1442	NH Industries NH.90-TTH Caïman [EBQ]	ALAT	
1443	NH Industries NH.90-TTH Caïman [EBS]	ALAT 5 RHC, Pau	
1454	NH Industries NH.90-TTH Caïman [EBT]	ALAT 5 RHC, Pau	
1455	NH Industries NH.90-TTH Caïman [EBU]	ALAT 1 RHC, Phalsbourg	
1456	NH Industries NH.90-TTH Caïman (F-ZKCE) [EBV]	ALAT (on order)	
1457	NH Industries NH.90-TTH Caïman [EBW]	ALAT 5 RHC, Pau	
1458	NH Industries NH.90-TTH Caïman [EBX]	ALAT	
1479	NH Industries NH.90-TTH Caïman (F-ZKBT) [EBY]	ALAT (on order)	
1480	NH Industries NH.90-TTH Caïman (F-ZWBW) [EBZ]	ALAT 3 RHC, Etain	
1481	NH Industries NH.90-TTH Caïman (F-ZKCG) [ECA]	ALAT GAM/STAT, Valence	
1482	NH Industries NH.90-TTH Caïman (F-ZKBC) [ECB] $	ALAT 3 RHC, Etain	
1483	NH Industries NH.90-TTH Caïman (F-ZKBV) [ECC]	ALAT 3 RHC, Etain	
1484	NH Industries NH.90-TTH Caïman (F-ZKBB) [ECD]	ALAT 3 RHC, Etain	
1485	NH Industries NH.90-TTH Caïman (F-ZK..) [ECE]	ALAT 5 RHC, Pau	
1496	NH Industries NH.90-TTH Caïman (F-ZKBA) [ECF]	ALAT (on order)	
1497	NH Industries NH.90-TTH Caïman (F-ZKBW) [ECG]	ALAT GAM/STAT, Valence	
1526	NH Industries NH.90-TTH Caïman (F-ZKBE) [ECH]	ALAT 5 RHC, Pau	
1527	NH Industries NH.90-TTH Caïman (F-ZKBG) [ECI]	ALAT 5 RHC, Pau	
1528	NH Industries NH.90-TTH Caïman (F-ZKBH) [ECJ]	ALAT 5 RHC, Pau	
1529	NH Industries NH.90-TTH Caïman (F-ZKBF) [ECK]	ALAT/Airbus Helicopters, Marseille	
1547	NH Industries NH.90-TTH Caïman (F-ZWBT) [ECL]	ALAT/Airbus Helicopters, Marseille	
1550	NH Industries NH.90-TTH Caïman (F-ZKCJ) [ECM]	ALAT/Airbus Helicopters, Marseille	
887	Pilatus PC-6B/B2-H4 Turbo Porter [MCA]	ALAT 1 GSALAT, Montauban	
888	Pilatus PC-6B/B2-H4 Turbo Porter [MCB]	ALAT 1 GSALAT, Montauban	
889	Pilatus PC-6B/B2-H4 Turbo Porter [MCC]	ALAT 1 GSALAT, Montauban	
890	Pilatus PC-6B/B2-H4 Turbo Porter [MCD]	ALAT 1 GSALAT, Montauban	
891	Pilatus PC-6B/B2-H4 Turbo Porter [MCE]	ALAT 1 GSALAT, Montauban	
80	SOCATA TBM 700A [ABY]	ALAT EAAT, Rennes	
99	SOCATA TBM 700A [ABO]	ALAT EAAT, Rennes	
100	SOCATA TBM 700A [ABP]	ALAT EAAT, Rennes	
115	SOCATA TBM 700A [ABQ]	ALAT EAAT, Rennes	
136	SOCATA TBM 700A [ABR]	ALAT EAAT, Rennes	
139	SOCATA TBM 700A [ABS]	ALAT EAAT, Rennes	
156	SOCATA TBM 700B [ABT]	ALAT EAAT, Rennes	
159	SOCATA TBM 700B [ABU]	ALAT EAAT, Rennes	
160	SOCATA TBM 700B [ABV]	ALAT EAAT, Rennes	

French Government

Note: The main base and maintenance centre for the Sécurité Civile fleet is Nimes, with helicopters placed on "détachements saisonniers" across France through the summer months

JBA	Eurocopter EC.145C-1 (9008)	Gendarmerie	
JBC	Eurocopter EC.145C-1 (9018)	Gendarmerie	
JBD	Eurocopter EC.145C-1 (9019)	Gendarmerie	
JBE	Eurocopter EC.145C-1 (9025)	Gendarmerie	
JBF	Eurocopter EC.145C-2 (9035)	Gendarmerie	
JBG	Eurocopter EC.145C-2 (9036)	Gendarmerie	
JBH	Eurocopter EC.145C-2 (9037)	Gendarmerie	
JBI	Eurocopter EC.145C-2 (9127)	Gendarmerie	
JBJ	Eurocopter EC.145C-2 (9140)	Gendarmerie	
JBK	Eurocopter EC.145C-2 (9162)	Gendarmerie	
JBM	Eurocopter EC.145C-2 (9113)	Gendarmerie	
JBO	Eurocopter EC.145C-2 (9124)	Gendarmerie	
JBR	Eurocopter EC.145C-2 (9169)	Gendarmerie	
JBT	Eurocopter EC.145C-2 (9173)	Gendarmerie	
JBU	Eurocopter EC.145C-2 (9700)	Gendarmerie	
JCB	Aérospatiale AS.350BA Ecureuil (1574)	Gendarmerie	
JCC	Aérospatiale AS.350BA Ecureuil (1916)	Gendarmerie	

Notes	Serial	Type (code/other identity)	Owner/operator, location or fate
	JCD	Aérospatiale AS.350BA Ecureuil (1576)	Gendarmerie
	JCE	Aérospatiale AS.350B-2 Ecureuil (1812)	Gendarmerie
	JCF	Aérospatiale AS.350B-2 Ecureuil (1691)	Gendarmerie
	JCI	Aérospatiale AS.350B-2 Ecureuil (2222)	Gendarmerie
	JCK	Aérospatiale AS.350BA Ecureuil (1953)	Gendarmerie
	JCM	Aérospatiale AS.350BA Ecureuil (1952)	Gendarmerie
	JCN	Aérospatiale AS.350BA Ecureuil (2044)	Gendarmerie
	JCO	Aérospatiale AS.350BA Ecureuil (1917)	Gendarmerie
	JCP	Aérospatiale AS.350BA Ecureuil (2045)	Gendarmerie
	JCQ	Aérospatiale AS.350BA Ecureuil (2057)	Gendarmerie
	JCR	Aérospatiale AS.350BA Ecureuil (2088)	Gendarmerie
	JCS	Aérospatiale AS.350B-2 Ecureuil (1575)	Gendarmerie
	JCT	Aérospatiale AS.350BA Ecureuil (2104)	Gendarmerie
	JCU	Aérospatiale AS.350BA Ecureuil (2117)	Gendarmerie
	JCV	Aérospatiale AS.350BA Ecureuil (2118)	Gendarmerie
	JCW	Aérospatiale AS.350BA Ecureuil (2218)	Gendarmerie
	JCX	Aérospatiale AS.350BA Ecureuil (2219)	Gendarmerie
	JCY	Aérospatiale AS.350BA Ecureuil (2221)	Gendarmerie
	JCZ	Aérospatiale AS.350BA Ecureuil (1467)	Gendarmerie
	JDA	Eurocopter EC.135T-2 (0642)	Gendarmerie
	JDB	Eurocopter EC.135T-2 (0654)	Gendarmerie
	JDC	Eurocopter EC.135T-2 (0717)	Gendarmerie
	JDD	Eurocopter EC.135T-2 (0727)	Gendarmerie
	JDE	Eurocopter EC.135T-2 (0747)	Gendarmerie
	JDF	Eurocopter EC.135T-2 (0757)	Gendarmerie
	JDG	Eurocopter EC.135T-2 (0772)	Gendarmerie
	JDH	Eurocopter EC.135T-2 (0787)	Gendarmerie
	JDI	Eurocopter EC.135T-2 (0797)	Gendarmerie
	JDJ	Eurocopter EC.135T-2 (0806)	Gendarmerie
	JDK	Eurocopter EC.135T-2 (0857)	Gendarmerie
	JDL	Eurocopter EC.135T-2 (0867)	Gendarmerie
	JDM	Eurocopter EC.135T-2 (1055)	Gendarmerie
	JDN	Eurocopter EC.135T-2 (1058)	Gendarmerie
	JDO	Eurocopter EC.135T-2 (1086)	Gendarmerie
	JED	Aérospatiale AS.350B-2 Ecureuil (2096)	Gendarmerie
	JEE	Aérospatiale AS.350B-2 Ecureuil (2423)	Gendarmerie
	JEF	Aérospatiale AS.350B-2 Ecureuil (2225)	Gendarmerie
	F-ZBAD	Aérospatiale AS.355F-2 Twin Ecureuil	Douanes Françaises
	F-ZBEF	Aérospatiale AS.355F-1 Twin Ecureuil	Douanes Françaises
	F-ZBEG	Canadair CL-415 [39]	Sécurité Civile, Nîmes/Garons
	F-ZBEK	Aérospatiale AS.355F-1 Twin Ecureuil	Douanes Françaises
	F-ZBEL	Aérospatiale AS.355F-1 Twin Ecureuil	Douanes Françaises
	F-ZBEU	Canadair CL-415 [42]	Sécurité Civile, Nîmes/Garons
	F-ZBFJ	Beech Super King Air B200 [98]	Sécurité Civile, Nîmes/Garons
	F-ZBFK	Beech Super King Air B200 [96]	Sécurité Civile, Nîmes/Garons
	F-ZBFN	Canadair CL-415 [33]	Sécurité Civile, Nîmes/Garons
	F-ZBFP	Canadair CL-415 [31]	Sécurité Civile, Nîmes/Garons
	F-ZBFS	Canadair CL-415 [32]	Sécurité Civile, Nîmes/Garons
	F-ZBFV	Canadair CL-415 [37]	Sécurité Civile, Nîmes/Garons
	F-ZBFW	Canadair CL-415 [38]	Sécurité Civile, Nîmes/Garons
	F-ZBFX	Canadair CL-415 [34]	Sécurité Civile, Nîmes/Garons
	F-ZBFY	Canadair CL-415 [35]	Sécurité Civile, Nîmes/Garons
	F-ZBGF	Eurocopter EC.135T-2	Douanes Françaises
	F-ZBGG	Eurocopter EC.135T-2	Douanes Françaises
	F-ZBGH	Eurocopter EC.135T-2	Douanes Françaises
	F-ZBGI	Eurocopter EC.135T-2	Douanes Françaises
	F-ZBGJ	Eurocopter EC.135T-2	Douanes Françaises
	F-ZBGK	Hawker Beechcraft King Air B350ER (FL-682)	Douanes Françaises
	F-ZBGL	Hawker Beechcraft King Air B350ER (FL-746)	Douanes Françaises
	F-ZBGM	Hawker Beechcraft King Air B350ER (FL-752)	Douanes Francaises
	F-ZBGN	Hawker Beechcraft King Air B350ER (FL-781)	Douanes Françaises
	F-ZBGO	Hawker Beechcraft King Air B350ER (FL-800)	Douanes Francaises

Serial	Type (code/other identity)	Owner/operator, location or fate	Notes
F-ZBGP	Hawker Beechcraft King Air B350ER (FL-802)	Douanes Francaises	
F-ZBGQ	Hawker Beechcraft King Air B350ER (FL-777)	Douanes Francaises	
F-ZBGR	Hawker Beechcraft King Air B350ER	Douanes Francaises (on order)	
F-ZBMB	Beech Super King Air B200 [97]	Sécurité Civile, Nîmes/Garons	
F-ZBMC	De Havilland Canada DHC-8-Q401MR [73]	Sécurité Civile, Nîmes/Garons	
F-ZBMD	De Havilland Canada DHC-8-Q401MR [74]	Sécurité Civile, Nîmes/Garons	
F-ZBME	Canadair CL-415 [44]	Sécurité Civile, Nîmes/Garons	
F-ZBMF	Canadair CL-415 [45]	Sécurité Civile, Nîmes/Garons	
F-ZBMG	Canadair CL-415 [48]	Sécurité Civile, Nîmes/Garons	
F-ZBMH	De Havilland Canada DHC-8-Q402MR [75]	Sécurité Civile, Nîmes/Garons	
F-ZBMI	De Havilland Canada DHC-8-Q402MR [76]	Sécurité Civile, Nîmes/Garons	
F-ZBMJ	De Havilland Canada DHC-8-Q402MR [77]	Sécurité Civile, Nîmes/Garons	
F-ZBMK	De Havilland Canada DHC-8-Q402MR [78]	Sécurité Civile, Nîmes/Garons	
F-ZBML	De Havilland Canada DHC-8-Q402MR [79]	Sécurité Civile, Nîmes/Garons	
F-ZBMM	De Havilland Canada DHC-8-Q402MR (C-GUKH) [80]	Sécurité Civile, Nîmes/Garons	
F-ZBPA	Eurocopter EC.145C-1	Sécurité Civile	
F-ZBPD	Eurocopter EC.145C-1	Sécurité Civile	
F-ZBPE	Eurocopter EC.145C-1	Sécurité Civile	
F-ZBPF	Eurocopter EC.145C-1	Sécurité Civile	
F-ZBPG	Eurocopter EC.145C-1	Sécurité Civile	
F-ZBPH	Eurocopter EC.145C-1	Sécurité Civile	
F-ZBPI	Eurocopter EC.145C-1	Sécurité Civile	
F-ZBPJ	Eurocopter EC.145C-1	Sécurité Civile	
F-ZBPK	Eurocopter EC.145C-1	Sécurité Civile	
F-ZBPL	Eurocopter EC.145C-1	Sécurité Civile	
F-ZBPM	Eurocopter EC.145C-1	Sécurité Civile	
F-ZBPN	Eurocopter EC.145C-1	Sécurité Civile	
F-ZBPO	Eurocopter EC.145C-1	Sécurité Civile	
F-ZBPP	Eurocopter EC.145C-2	Sécurité Civile	
F-ZBPQ	Eurocopter EC.145C-2	Sécurité Civile	
F-ZBPS	Eurocopter EC.145C-2	Sécurité Civile	
F-ZBPT	Eurocopter EC.145C-2	Sécurité Civile	
F-ZBPU	Eurocopter EC.145C-2	Sécurité Civile	
F-ZBPV	Eurocopter EC.145C-2	Sécurité Civile	
F-ZBPW	Eurocopter EC.145C-2	Sécurité Civile	
F-ZBPX	Eurocopter EC.145C-2	Sécurité Civile	
F-ZBPY	Eurocopter EC.145C-2	Sécurité Civile	
F-ZBQA	Eurocopter EC.145C-2	Sécurité Civile	
F-ZBQB	Eurocopter EC.145C-2	Sécurité Civile	
F-ZBQC	Eurocopter EC.145C-2	Sécurité Civile	
F-ZBQD	Eurocopter EC.145C-2	Sécurité Civile	
F-ZBQE	Eurocopter EC.145C-2	Sécurité Civile	
F-ZBQF	Eurocopter EC.145C-2	Sécurité Civile	
F-ZBQH	Eurocopter EC.145C-2	Sécurité Civile	
F-ZBQI	Eurocopter EC.145C-2	Sécurité Civile	
F-ZBQJ	Eurocopter EC.145C-2	Sécurité Civile	
F-ZBQK	Eurocopter EC.145C-2	Sécurité Civile	
F-ZBQL	Eurocopter EC.145C-2	Sécurité Civile	
F-ZBQM	Airbus H.145D-3	Sécurité Civile	
F-ZBQN	Airbus H.145D-3	Sécurité Civile	
F-ZBQO	Airbus H.145D-3	Sécurité Civile	
F-ZBQP	Airbus H.145D-3	Sécurité Civile	
F-ZBQQ	Airbus H.145D-3	Sécurité Civile	
Civil operated aircraft in military use			
F-GJDB	Dassault Falcon 20C	AVDEF, Nîmes/Garons	
F-GKCI	Cirrus SR.22	CATS/CFAMI 05.312, Salon de Provence	
F-GKCT	Cirrus SR.22	CATS/CFAMI 05.312, Salon de Provence	
F-GPAA	Dassault Falcon 20ECM	AVDEF, Nîmes/Garons	
F-GPAD	Dassault Falcon 20E	AVDEF, Nîmes/Garons	
F-GUKA	Grob G120A-F	CATS/EAC 00.315, Cognac	
F-GUKB	Grob G120A-F	CATS/EAC 00.315, Cognac	
F-GUKC	Grob G120A-F	CATS/EAC 00.315, Cognac	

Notes	Serial	Type (code/other identity)	Owner/operator, location or fate
	F-GUKD	Grob G120A-F	CATS/EAC 00.315, Cognac
	F-GUKE	Grob G120A-F	CATS/EAC 00.315, Cognac
	F-GUKF	Grob G120A-F	CATS/EAC 00.315, Cognac
	F-GUKG	Grob G120A-F	CATS/EAC 00.315, Cognac
	F-GUKH	Grob G120A-F	CATS/EAC 00.315, Cognac
	F-GUKI	Grob G120A-F	CATS/EAC 00.315, Cognac
	F-GUKJ	Grob G120A-F	CATS/EAC 00.315, Cognac
	F-GUKK	Grob G120A-F	CATS/EAC 00.315, Cognac
	F-GUKL	Grob G120A-F	CATS/EAC 00.315, Cognac
	F-GUKM	Grob G120A-F	CATS/EAC 00.315, Cognac
	F-GUKN	Grob G120A-F	CATS/EAC 00.315, Cognac
	F-GUKP	Grob G120A-F	CATS/EAC 00.315, Cognac
	F-GUKR	Grob G120A-F	CATS/EAC 00.315, Cognac
	F-GUKS	Grob G120A-F	CATS/EAC 00.315, Cognac
	F-HAVD	BAE Jetstream 41	AVDEF, Nîmes/Garons
	F-HAVF	BAE Jetstream 41	AVDEF, Nîmes/Garons
	F-HDHN	Eurocopter AS.365N-3 Dauphin	AN 34 Flottille/ESHE, Lanvéoc/Poulmic
	F-HGHN	Eurocopter AS.365N-3 Dauphin	AN 34 Flottille/ESHE, Lanvéoc/Poulmic
	F-HGDU	Cirrus SR.20	AN 50S/AFAE, Lanvéoc/Poulmic
	F-HKCA	Cirrus SR.22	CATS/CFAMI 05.312, Salon de Provence
	F-HKCB	Cirrus SR.20	CATS/CFAMI 05.312, Salon de Provence
	F-HKCC	Cirrus SR.22	CATS/CFAMI 05.312, Salon de Provence
	F-HKCD	Cirrus SR.20	CATS/CFAMI 05.312, Salon de Provence
	F-HKCE	Cirrus SR.20	AN 50S/AFAE, Lanvéoc/Poulmic
	F-HKCF	Cirrus SR.22	CATS/CFAMI 05.312, Salon de Provence
	F-HKCG	Cirrus SR.20	CATS/CFAMI 05.312, Salon de Provence
	F-HKCH	Cirrus SR.20	AN 50S/AFAE, Lanvéoc/Poulmic
	F-HKCI	Cirrus SR.22	CATS/CFAMI 05.312, Salon de Provence
	F-HKCJ	Cirrus SR.20	CATS/CFAMI 05.312, Salon de Provence
	F-HKCK	Cirrus SR.20	AN 50S/AFAE, Lanvéoc/Poulmic
	F-HKCL	Cirrus SR.22	CATS/CFAMI 05.312, Salon de Provence
	F-HKCN	Cirrus SR.20	CATS/CFAMI 05.312, Salon de Provence
	F-HKCO	Cirrus SR.22	CATS/CFAMI 05.312, Salon de Provence
	F-HKCP	Cirrus SR.20	CATS/CFAMI 05.312, Salon de Provence
	F-HKCQ	Cirrus SR.20	CATS/CFAMI 05.312, Salon de Provence
	F-HKCT	Cirrus SR.20	CATS/CFAMI 05.312, Salon de Provence
	F-HKCU	Cirrus SR.20	AN 50S/AFAE, Lanvéoc/Poulmic
	F-HKCV	Cirrus SR.20	CATS/CFAMI 05.312, Salon de Provence
	F-HKCX	Cirrus SR.20	CATS/CFAMI 05.312, Salon de Provence
	F-HKCY	Cirrus SR.22	CATS/CFAMI 05.312, Salon de Provence
	F-HKCZ	Cirrus SR.22	CATS/CFAMI 05.312, Salon de Provence
	F-HNHN	Eurocopter AS.365N-3 Dauphin	AN 34 Flottille/ESHE, Lanvéoc/Poulmic
	F-HOHN	Eurocopter AS.365N-3 Dauphin	AN 34 Flottille/ESHE, Lanvéoc/Poulmic
	F-HYHN	Eurocopter AS.365N-3 Dauphin	AN 34 Flottille/ESHE, Lanvéoc/Poulmic

GABON

	TR-KGM	Gulfstream Aerospace G.650ER	Gabonese Government, Libreville
	TR-KPR	Boeing 777-236	Gabonese Government, stored Basel
	TR-KSP	Grumman G.1159C Gulfstream IV-SP	*Sold as P4-ORJ, November 2024*

GERMANY

Please note that German serials do not officially include the '+' part in them but aircraft wearing German markings are often painted with a cross in the middle, which is why it is included here.

TLG 33, normally based at Buchel, has moved to Norvenich until 2026 whilst Buchel is upgraded to receive the recently ordered F-35, and as a result the base for TLG 33 is shown here as Norvenich. In a similar vein, TLG 71 moved from Wittmund to Laage in January 2022 while major work is undertaken at the former base. This move will last for up to three years and consequently the base for TLG 71 is shown as Laage in this edition.

Luftwaffe, Marineflieger & Heeresfliegertruppe (Heer)

	10+01	Airbus A350-941 (F-WZGL)	Luftwaffe FBS, Köln-Bonn
	10+02	Airbus A350-941 (F-WZHF/D-AKAY)	Luftwaffe FBS, Köln-Bonn
	10+03	Airbus A350-941 (D-AGAF)	Luftwaffe FBS, Köln-Bonn
	14+02	Bombardier Global 5000	Luftwaffe FBS, Köln-Bonn

Serial	Type (code/other identity)	Owner/operator, location or fate	Notes
14+03	Bombardier Global 5000	Luftwaffe FBS, Köln-Bonn	
14+04	Bombardier Global 5000	Luftwaffe FBS, Köln-Bonn	
14+05	Bombardier Global 6000 (C-GDRL)	Luftwaffe FBS, Köln-Bonn	
14+06	Bombardier Global 6000 (C-GEVP)	Luftwaffe FBS, Köln-Bonn	
14+07	Bombardier Global 6000 (C-GEVX)	Luftwaffe FBS, Köln-Bonn	
14+08	Bombardier Global 6000 (D-AEND/N637HN)	Luftwaffe (at Wichita, KS for conversion to PEGASUS SIGINT platform)	
15+01	Airbus A.319CJ-115X	Luftwaffe FBS, Köln-Bonn	
15+02	Airbus A.319CJ-115X	Luftwaffe FBS, Köln-Bonn	
15+03	Airbus A.319CJ-133X (98+11)	Luftwaffe FBS, Köln-Bonn	
15+04	Airbus A.321-231 (D-AISE/98+10)	Luftwaffe FBS, Köln-Bonn	
15+10	Airbus A.321-251NX (D-AVXU)	Luftwaffe FBS, Köln-Bonn	
15+11	Airbus A.321-251NX (D-AYAA)	Luftwaffe FBS, Köln-Bonn	
30+01	Eurofighter EF.2000GT	Luftwaffe TLG 73 *Steinhoff*, Laage	
30+02	Eurofighter EF.2000GT	Luftwaffe TLG 73 *Steinhoff*, Laage	
30+03	Eurofighter EF.2000GT	Luftwaffe TLG 74 *Molders*, Neuburg/Donau	
30+04	Eurofighter EF.2000GT $	Luftwaffe TLG 71 *Richthofen*, Laage	
30+05	Eurofighter EF.2000GT	Luftwaffe TLG 31 *Boelcke*, Nörvenich	
30+06	Eurofighter EF.2000GS	Luftwaffe TLG 71 *Richthofen*, Laage	
30+07	Eurofighter EF.2000GS	Luftwaffe TLG 74 *Molders*, Neuburg/Donau	
30+09	Eurofighter EF.2000GS	Luftwaffe TAubZLwSüd, Kaufbeuren	
30+10	Eurofighter EF.2000GT	Luftwaffe TLG 73 *Steinhoff*, Laage	
30+11	Eurofighter EF.2000GS	Luftwaffe TLG 71 *Richthofen*, Laage	
30+12	Eurofighter EF.2000GS	Luftwaffe TLG 74 *Molders*, Neuburg/Donau	
30+14	Eurofighter EF.2000GT	Luftwaffe TLG 31 *Boelcke*, Nörvenich	
30+15	Eurofighter EF.2000GS	Luftwaffe TLG 74 *Molders*, Neuburg/Donau	
30+17	Eurofighter EF.2000GT	Luftwaffe TLG 73 *Steinhoff*, Laage	
30+20	Eurofighter EF.2000GT	Luftwaffe TLG 73 *Steinhoff*, Laage	
30+22	Eurofighter EF.2000GS	Luftwaffe TLG 71 *Richthofen*, Laage	
30+23	Eurofighter EF.2000GS	*Luftwaffe, Nörvenich, for GI*	
30+24	Eurofighter EF.2000GT	Luftwaffe TLG 73 *Steinhoff*, Laage	
30+25	Eurofighter EF.2000GS	*Luftwaffe, Wittmund, for GI*	
30+28	Eurofighter EF.2000GS	Luftwaffe TLG 74 *Molders*, Neuburg/Donau	
30+29	Eurofighter EF.2000GS	Luftwaffe TLG 71 *Richthofen*, Laage	
30+30	Eurofighter EF.2000GS	Luftwaffe TLG 71 *Richthofen*, Laage	
30+31	Eurofighter EF.2000GT	Luftwaffe TLG 31 *Boelcke*, Nörvenich	
30+32	Eurofighter EF.2000GS	*Luftwaffe, Laage, for GI*	
30+33	Eurofighter EF.2000GS	Luftwaffe TLG 71 *Richthofen*, Laage	
30+35	Eurofighter EF.2000GT	Luftwaffe TLG 73 *Steinhoff*, Laage	
30+38	Eurofighter EF.2000GS	Luftwaffe TLG 73 *Steinhoff*, Laage	
30+40	Eurofighter EF.2000GS	Luftwaffe TLG 71 *Richthofen*, Laage	
30+42	Eurofighter EF.2000GT	Luftwaffe TLG 73 *Steinhoff*, Laage	
30+45	Eurofighter EF.2000GS	Luftwaffe TLG 74 *Molders*, Neuburg/Donau	
30+46	Eurofighter EF.2000GS	Luftwaffe TLG 73 *Steinhoff*, Laage	
30+47	Eurofighter EF.2000GS	Luftwaffe TLG 74 *Molders*, Neuburg/Donau	
30+49	Eurofighter EF.2000GS	Luftwaffe TLG 31 *Boelcke*, Nörvenich	
30+50	Eurofighter EF.2000GS	Luftwaffe TLG 73 *Steinhoff*, Laage	
30+51	Eurofighter EF.2000GS	Luftwaffe TLG 73 *Steinhoff*, Laage	
30+52	Eurofighter EF.2000GS	Luftwaffe TLG 31 *Boelcke*, Nörvenich	
30+53	Eurofighter EF.2000GS	Luftwaffe TLG 74 *Molders*, Neuburg/Donau	
30+54	Eurofighter EF.2000GT	Luftwaffe TLG 31 *Boelcke*, Nörvenich	
30+56	Eurofighter EF.2000GS	Luftwaffe TLG 71 *Richthofen*, Laage	
30+57	Eurofighter EF.2000GS	Luftwaffe TLG 71 *Richthofen*, Laage	
30+58	Eurofighter EF.2000GS	Luftwaffe TLG 71 *Richthofen*, Laage	
30+59	Eurofighter EF.2000GT	Luftwaffe TLG 71 *Richthofen*, Laage	
30+60	Eurofighter EF.2000GS	Luftwaffe TLG 73 *Steinhoff*, Laage	
30+61	Eurofighter EF.2000GS	Luftwaffe TLG 73 *Steinhoff*, Laage	
30+62	Eurofighter EF.2000GS	Luftwaffe TLG 31 *Boelcke*, Nörvenich	
30+63	Eurofighter EF.2000GS	*Luftwaffe TAubZLwSüd, Kaufbeuren*	
30+64	Eurofighter EF.2000GS	Luftwaffe TLG 73 *Steinhoff*, Laage	
30+65	Eurofighter EF.2000GS $	Luftwaffe TLG 31 *Boelcke*, Nörvenich	
30+66	Eurofighter EF.2000GS	Luftwaffe TLG 71 *Richthofen*, Laage	

Notes	Serial	Type (code/other identity)	Owner/operator, location or fate
	30+67	Eurofighter EF.2000GT	Luftwaffe TLG 31 *Boelcke*, Nörvenich
	30+68	Eurofighter EF.2000GS	Luftwaffe TLG 74 *Molders*, Neuburg/Donau
	30+69	Eurofighter EF.2000GS	Luftwaffe TLG 74 *Molders*, Neuburg/Donau
	30+70	Eurofighter EF.2000GS	Luftwaffe TLG 74 *Molders*, Neuburg/Donau
	30+71	Eurofighter EF.2000GT	Luftwaffe TLG 31 *Boelcke*, Nörvenich
	30+72	Eurofighter EF.2000GS	Luftwaffe TLG 74 *Molders*, Neuburg/Donau
	30+73	Eurofighter EF.2000GS $	Luftwaffe TLG 73 *Steinhoff*, Laage
	30+74	Eurofighter EF.2000GS	Luftwaffe TLG 74 *Molders*, Neuburg/Donau
	30+75	Eurofighter EF.2000GS	Luftwaffe TLG 74 *Molders*, Neuburg/Donau
	30+76	Eurofighter EF.2000GS $	Luftwaffe TLG 74 *Molders*, Neuburg/Donau
	30+77	Eurofighter EF.2000GT	Luftwaffe TLG 31 *Boelcke*, Nörvenich
	30+78	Eurofighter EF.2000GS	Luftwaffe TLG 71 *Richthofen*, Laage
	30+79	Eurofighter EF.2000GS	Luftwaffe TLG 73 *Steinhoff*, Laage
	30+80	Eurofighter EF.2000GS	Luftwaffe TLG 74 *Molders*, Neuburg/Donau
	30+81	Eurofighter EF.2000GS	Luftwaffe TLG 74 *Molders*, Neuburg/Donau
	30+82	Eurofighter EF.2000GS	Luftwaffe TLG 71 *Richthofen*, Laage
	30+83	Eurofighter EF.2000GS	Luftwaffe TLG 71 *Richthofen*, Laage
	30+84	Eurofighter EF.2000GT	Luftwaffe TLG 31 *Boelcke*, Nörvenich
	30+85	Eurofighter EF.2000GS	Luftwaffe TLG 71 *Richthofen*, Laage
	30+86	Eurofighter EF.2000GS	Luftwaffe TLG 71 *Richthofen*, Laage
	30+87	Eurofighter EF.2000GS	Luftwaffe TLG 71 *Richthofen*, Laage
	30+88	Eurofighter EF.2000GS	Luftwaffe TLG 71 *Richthofen*, Laage
	30+89	Eurofighter EF.2000GS	Luftwaffe TLG 71 *Richthofen*, Laage
	30+90	Eurofighter EF.2000GS $	Luftwaffe TLG 71 *Richthofen*, Laage
	30+91	Eurofighter EF.2000GS	Luftwaffe TLG 31 *Boelcke*, Nörvenich
	30+92	Eurofighter EF.2000GS	Luftwaffe TLG 71 *Richthofen*, Laage
	30+93	Eurofighter EF.2000GS	Luftwaffe TLG 71 *Richthofen*, Laage
	30+94	Eurofighter EF.2000GS	Luftwaffe TLG 74 *Molders*, Neuburg/Donau
	30+95	Eurofighter EF.2000GT	Luftwaffe TLG 74 *Molders*, Neuburg/Donau
	30+96	Eurofighter EF.2000GS $	Luftwaffe TLG 31 *Boelcke*, Nörvenich
	30+97	Eurofighter EF.2000GS	Luftwaffe TLG 31 *Boelcke*, Nörvenich
	30+98	Eurofighter EF.2000GS	Luftwaffe TLG 71 *Richthofen*, Laage
	30+99	Eurofighter EF.2000GT	Luftwaffe TLG 71 *Richthofen*, Laage
	31+00	Eurofighter EF.2000GS	Luftwaffe TLG 74 *Molders*, Neuburg/Donau
	31+01	Eurofighter EF.2000GS $	Luftwaffe TLG 74 *Molders*, Neuburg/Donau
	31+02	Eurofighter EF.2000GS	Luftwaffe TLG 74 *Molders*, Neuburg/Donau
	31+03	Eurofighter EF.2000GT	Luftwaffe TLG 31 *Boelcke*, Nörvenich
	31+04	Eurofighter EF.2000GS	Luftwaffe TLG 73 *Steinhoff*, Laage
	31+05	Eurofighter EF.2000GS	Luftwaffe TLG 71 *Richthofen*, Laage
	31+06	Eurofighter EF.2000GS	Luftwaffe TLG 74 *Molders*, Neuburg/Donau
	31+07	Eurofighter EF.2000GS	Luftwaffe TLG 71 *Richthofen*, Laage
	31+08	Eurofighter EF.2000GS	Luftwaffe TLG 74 *Molders*, Neuburg/Donau
	31+09	Eurofighter EF.2000GS	Luftwaffe TLG 31 *Boelcke*, Nörvenich
	31+10	Eurofighter EF.2000GS	Luftwaffe TAubZLwSüd, Kaufbeuren
	31+11	Eurofighter EF.2000GS	Luftwaffe TLG 74 *Molders*, Neuburg/Donau
	31+12	Eurofighter EF.2000GS	Luftwaffe TLG 31 *Boelcke*, Nörvenich
	31+13	Eurofighter EF.2000GT	Luftwaffe TLG 74 *Molders*, Neuburg/Donau
	31+14	Eurofighter EF.2000GS	Luftwaffe TLG 73 *Steinhoff*, Laage
	31+15	Eurofighter EF.2000GS	Luftwaffe TLG 74 *Molders*, Neuburg/Donau
	31+16	Eurofighter EF.2000GS	Luftwaffe TLG 31 *Boelcke*, Nörvenich
	31+17	Eurofighter EF.2000GS	Luftwaffe TLG 73 *Steinhoff*, Laage
	31+18	Eurofighter EF.2000GS	Luftwaffe TLG 73 *Steinhoff*, Laage
	31+19	Eurofighter EF.2000GS	Luftwaffe TLG 74 *Molders*, Neuburg/Donau
	31+20	Eurofighter EF.2000GS	Luftwaffe TLG 74 *Molders*, Neuburg/Donau
	31+21	Eurofighter EF.2000GS	Luftwaffe TLG 73 *Steinhoff*, Laage
	31+22	Eurofighter EF.2000GS	Luftwaffe TLG 73 *Steinhoff*, Laage
	31+24	Eurofighter EF.2000GT	Luftwaffe TLG 73 *Steinhoff*, Laage
	31+25	Eurofighter EF.2000GT	Luftwaffe TLG 74 *Molders*, Neuburg/Donau
	31+26	Eurofighter EF.2000GT	Luftwaffe TLG 73 *Steinhoff*, Laage
	31+27	Eurofighter EF.2000GT	Luftwaffe TLG 31 *Boelcke*, Nörvenich
	31+28	Eurofighter EF.2000GT	Luftwaffe TLG 74 *Molders*, Neuburg/Donau
	31+29	Eurofighter EF.2000GS	Luftwaffe TLG 31 *Boelcke*, Nörvenich

Serial	Type (code/other identity)	Owner/operator, location or fate	Notes
31+30	Eurofighter EF.2000GS	Luftwaffe TLG 73 *Steinhoff*, Laage	
31+31	Eurofighter EF.2000GS $	Luftwaffe TLG 31 *Boelcke*, Nörvenich	
31+32	Eurofighter EF.2000GS	Luftwaffe TLG 31 *Boelcke*, Nörvenich	
31+33	Eurofighter EF.2000GS	Luftwaffe TLG 31 *Boelcke*, Nörvenich	
31+34	Eurofighter EF.2000GS	Luftwaffe TLG 31 *Boelcke*, Nörvenich	
31+35	Eurofighter EF.2000GS	Luftwaffe TLG 74 *Molders*, Neuburg/Donau	
31+36	Eurofighter EF.2000GS	Luftwaffe TLG 74 *Molders*, Neuburg/Donau	
31+37	Eurofighter EF.2000GS	Luftwaffe TLG 31 *Boelcke*, Nörvenich	
31+38	Eurofighter EF.2000GS	Luftwaffe TLG 31 *Boelcke*, Nörvenich	
31+39	Eurofighter EF.2000GS	Luftwaffe TLG 73 *Steinhoff*, Laage	
31+40	Eurofighter EF.2000GS	Luftwaffe TLG 31 *Boelcke*, Nörvenich	
31+41	Eurofighter EF.2000GS	Luftwaffe TLG 31 *Boelcke*, Nörvenich	
31+42	Eurofighter EF.2000GS $	Luftwaffe TLG 73 *Steinhoff*, Laage	
31+43	Eurofighter EF.2000GS	Luftwaffe TLG 31 *Boelcke*, Nörvenich	
31+44	Eurofighter EF.2000GS	Luftwaffe TLG 31 *Boelcke*, Nörvenich	
31+45	Eurofighter EF.2000GS $	Luftwaffe TLG 71 *Richthofen*, Laage	
31+46	Eurofighter EF.2000GS	Luftwaffe TLG 31 *Boelcke*, Nörvenich	
31+47	Eurofighter EF.2000GS	Luftwaffe TLG 31 *Boelcke*, Nörvenich	
31+48	Eurofighter EF.2000GS	Luftwaffe TLG 31 *Boelcke*, Nörvenich	
31+49	Eurofighter EF.2000GS	Luftwaffe TLG 31 *Boelcke*, Nörvenich	
31+50	Eurofighter EF.2000GS	Luftwaffe TLG 74 *Molders*, Neuburg/Donau	
31+51	Eurofighter EF.2000GS	Luftwaffe TLG 73 *Steinhoff*, Laage	
31+52	Eurofighter EF.2000GS	Luftwaffe TLG 31 *Boelcke*, Nörvenich	
31+53	Eurofighter EF.2000GS	Luftwaffe TLG 31 *Boelcke*, Nörvenich	
43+25	Panavia Tornado IDS $	Luftwaffe TLG 51 *Immelmann*, Schleswig/Jagel	
43+29	Panavia Tornado IDS(T)	Luftwaffe TLG 51 *Immelmann*, Schleswig/Jagel	
43+38	Panavia Tornado IDS	Luftwaffe TLG 33, Nörvenich	
43+42	Panavia Tornado IDS(T)	Luftwaffe TLG 33, Nörvenich	
43+45	Panavia Tornado IDS(T)	Luftwaffe TLG 51 *Immelmann*, Schleswig/Jagel	
43+46	Panavia Tornado IDS	Luftwaffe TLG 33, Nörvenich	
43+48	Panavia Tornado IDS	Luftwaffe TLG 33, Nörvenich	
43+50	Panavia Tornado IDS	Luftwaffe TLG 33, Nörvenich	
43+54	Panavia Tornado IDS	Luftwaffe TAubZLwSüd, Kaufbeuren	
43+59	Panavia Tornado IDS	Luftwaffe TLG 51 *Immelmann*, Schleswig/Jagel	
43+92	Panavia Tornado IDS(T) $	Luftwaffe TLG 33, Nörvenich	
43+97	Panavia Tornado IDS(T) $	Luftwaffe WTD 61, Manching-Ingolstadt	
43+98	Panavia Tornado IDS	Luftwaffe TLG 33, Nörvenich	
44+06	Panavia Tornado IDS	Luftwaffe TLG 33, Nörvenich	
44+16	Panavia Tornado IDS(T)	Luftwaffe TLG 33, Nörvenich	
44+21	Panavia Tornado IDS	Luftwaffe TLG 51 *Immelmann*, Schleswig/Jagel	
44+23	Panavia Tornado IDS	Luftwaffe TLG 33, Nörvenich	
44+29	Panavia Tornado IDS	Luftwaffe TLG 33, Nörvenich	
44+30	Panavia Tornado IDS	*Luftwaffe TAubZLwSüd, Kaufbeuren*	
44+33	Panavia Tornado IDS	Luftwaffe TLG 33, Nörvenich	
44+34	Panavia Tornado IDS	Luftwaffe TLG 33, Nörvenich	
44+58	Panavia Tornado IDS	Luftwaffe TLG 33, Nörvenich	
44+61	Panavia Tornado IDS $	Luftwaffe TLG 33, Nörvenich	
44+64	Panavia Tornado IDS	Luftwaffe TLG 33, Nörvenich	
44+65	Panavia Tornado IDS	Luftwaffe TLG 51 *Immelmann*, Schleswig/Jagel	
44+69	Panavia Tornado IDS $	Luftwaffe TLG 51 *Immelmann*, Schleswig/Jagel	
44+70	Panavia Tornado IDS	Luftwaffe TLG 33, Nörvenich	
44+72	Panavia Tornado IDS(T)	Luftwaffe TLG 33, Nörvenich	
44+73	Panavia Tornado IDS(T)	Luftwaffe TLG 33, Nörvenich	
44+75	Panavia Tornado IDS(T)	Luftwaffe TLG 51 *Immelmann*, Schleswig/Jagel	
44+78	Panavia Tornado IDS	Luftwaffe TLG 33, Nörvenich	
44+79	Panavia Tornado IDS	Luftwaffe TLG 33, Nörvenich	
44+90	Panavia Tornado IDS	Luftwaffe TLG 33, Nörvenich	
45+00	Panavia Tornado IDS	Luftwaffe TLG 33, Nörvenich	
45+09	Panavia Tornado IDS	Luftwaffe TLG 33, Nörvenich	
45+13	Panavia Tornado IDS(T)	Luftwaffe TLG 51 *Immelmann*, Schleswig/Jagel	
45+14	Panavia Tornado IDS(T)	Luftwaffe TLG 51 *Immelmann*, Schleswig/Jagel	
45+16	Panavia Tornado IDS(T)	Luftwaffe TLG 51 *Immelmann*, Schleswig/Jagel	

Notes	Serial	Type (code/other identity)	Owner/operator, location or fate
	45+19	Panavia Tornado IDS	Luftwaffe TLG 33, Nörvenich
	45+20	Panavia Tornado IDS	Luftwaffe TLG 33, Nörvenich
	45+23	Panavia Tornado IDS	Luftwaffe TLG 51 *Immelmann*, Schleswig/Jagel
	45+28	Panavia Tornado IDS	*Withdrawn from use?*
	45+35	Panavia Tornado IDS	Luftwaffe TLG 33, Nörvenich
	45+39	Panavia Tornado IDS	Luftwaffe TLG 51 *Immelmann*, Schleswig/Jagel
	45+50	Panavia Tornado IDS	Luftwaffe TLG 51 *Immelmann*, Schleswig/Jagel
	45+53	Panavia Tornado IDS	Luftwaffe TAubZLwSüd, Kaufbeuren
	45+57	Panavia Tornado IDS	Luftwaffe TLG 33, Nörvenich
	45+59	Panavia Tornado IDS	Luftwaffe TLG 51 *Immelmann*, Schleswig/Jagel
	45+61	Panavia Tornado IDS(T)	Luftwaffe TLG 51 *Immelmann*, Schleswig/Jagel
	45+66	Panavia Tornado IDS	Luftwaffe TLG 33, Nörvenich
	45+67	Panavia Tornado IDS	Luftwaffe TLG 33, Nörvenich
	45+70	Panavia Tornado IDS(T)	Luftwaffe TLG 51 *Immelmann*, Schleswig/Jagel
	45+71	Panavia Tornado IDS	Luftwaffe TLG 33, Nörvenich
	45+74	Panavia Tornado IDS	Luftwaffe TAubZLwSüd, Kaufbeuren
	45+76	Panavia Tornado IDS	Luftwaffe TLG 33, Nörvenich
	45+77	Panavia Tornado IDS(T)	Luftwaffe TLG 51 *Immelmann*, Schleswig/Jagel
	45+85	Panavia Tornado IDS	Luftwaffe TLG 33, Nörvenich
	45+88	Panavia Tornado IDS	Luftwaffe TLG 33, Nörvenich
	45+92	Panavia Tornado IDS	Luftwaffe TLG 33, Nörvenich
	45+94	Panavia Tornado IDS	Luftwaffe TLG 33, Nörvenich
	46+02	Panavia Tornado IDS	Luftwaffe TLG 33, Nörvenich
	46+05	Panavia Tornado IDS(T)	Luftwaffe TLG 51 *Immelmann*, Schleswig/Jagel
	46+07	Panavia Tornado IDS(T)	Luftwaffe TLG 33, Nörvenich
	46+10	Panavia Tornado IDS	Luftwaffe TLG 33, Nörvenich
	46+11	Panavia Tornado IDS	Luftwaffe TLG 33, Nörvenich
	46+15	Panavia Tornado IDS	Luftwaffe TLG 33, Nörvenich
	46+18	Panavia Tornado IDS	Luftwaffe TLG 33, Nörvenich
	46+21	Panavia Tornado IDS	Luftwaffe TLG 33, Nörvenich
	46+22	Panavia Tornado IDS	Luftwaffe TLG 33, Nörvenich
	46+23	Panavia Tornado ECR	Luftwaffe TLG 51 *Immelmann*, Schleswig/Jagel
	46+24	Panavia Tornado ECR	Luftwaffe TLG 51 *Immelmann*, Schleswig/Jagel
	46+25	Panavia Tornado ECR	Luftwaffe TLG 51 *Immelmann*, Schleswig/Jagel
	46+28	Panavia Tornado ECR	Luftwaffe TLG 51 *Immelmann*, Schleswig/Jagel
	46+32	Panavia Tornado ECR	Luftwaffe TLG 51 *Immelmann*, Schleswig/Jagel
	46+35	Panavia Tornado ECR	Luftwaffe TLG 51 *Immelmann*, Schleswig/Jagel
	46+36	Panavia Tornado ECR	Luftwaffe TLG 51 *Immelmann*, Schleswig/Jagel
	46+38	Panavia Tornado ECR $	Luftwaffe TLG 51 *Immelmann*, Schleswig/Jagel
	46+39	Panavia Tornado ECR	Luftwaffe TAubZLwSüd, Kaufbeuren
	46+40	Panavia Tornado ECR	Luftwaffe TLG 51 *Immelmann*, Schleswig/Jagel
	46+44	Panavia Tornado ECR	Luftwaffe TLG 51 *Immelmann*, Schleswig/Jagel
	46+45	Panavia Tornado ECR	Luftwaffe TLG 51 *Immelmann*, Schleswig/Jagel
	46+46	Panavia Tornado ECR	Luftwaffe TLG 51 *Immelmann*, Schleswig/Jagel
	46+48	Panavia Tornado ECR	Luftwaffe TLG 51 *Immelmann*, Schleswig/Jagel
	46+49	Panavia Tornado ECR	Luftwaffe TLG 51 *Immelmann*, Schleswig/Jagel
	46+50	Panavia Tornado ECR	Luftwaffe TLG 51 *Immelmann*, Schleswig/Jagel
	46+51	Panavia Tornado ECR	Luftwaffe TLG 51 *Immelmann*, Schleswig/Jagel
	46+52	Panavia Tornado ECR $	Luftwaffe TLG 51 *Immelmann*, Schleswig/Jagel
	46+54	Panavia Tornado ECR	Luftwaffe TLG 51 *Immelmann*, Schleswig/Jagel
	46+55	Panavia Tornado ECR	Luftwaffe TLG 51 *Immelmann*, Schleswig/Jagel
	46+56	Panavia Tornado ECR	Luftwaffe TLG 51 *Immelmann*, Schleswig/Jagel
	46+57	Panavia Tornado ECR	Luftwaffe TLG 51 *Immelmann*, Schleswig/Jagel
	54+01	Airbus Military A.400M $	Luftwaffe LTG 62, Wunstorf
	54+02	Airbus Military A.400M	Luftwaffe LTG 62, Wunstorf
	54+03	Airbus Military A.400M	Luftwaffe LTG 62, Wunstorf
	54+04	Airbus Military A.400M	Luftwaffe LTG 62, Wunstorf
	54+05	Airbus Military A.400M	Luftwaffe, stored Wunstorf
	54+06	Airbus Military A.400M	Airbus Defence & Space, Getafe
	54+07	Airbus Military A.400M	Luftwaffe LTG 62, Wunstorf
	54+08	Airbus Military A.400M	Airbus Defence & Space, Sevilla
	54+09	Airbus Military A.400M $	Luftwaffe LTG 62, Wunstorf

Serial	Type (code/other identity)	Owner/operator, location or fate	Notes
54+10	Airbus Military A.400M	Luftwaffe LTG 62, Wunstorf	
54+11	Airbus Military A.400M	Luftwaffe LTG 62, Wunstorf	
54+12	Airbus Military A.400M	Luftwaffe LTG 62, Wunstorf	
54+13	Airbus Military A.400M	Luftwaffe LTG 62, Wunstorf	
54+14	Airbus Military A.400M	Luftwaffe, stored Wunstorf	
54+15	Airbus Military A.400M	Luftwaffe LTG 62, Wunstorf	
54+16	Airbus Military A.400M	Luftwaffe LTG 62, Wunstorf	
54+17	Airbus Military A.400M	Luftwaffe LTG 62 (noted Manching Jan 2024)	
54+18	Airbus Military A.400M	Luftwaffe, stored Wunstorf	
54+19	Airbus Military A.400M $	Luftwaffe LTG 62, Wunstorf	
54+20	Airbus Military A.400M	Luftwaffe LTG 62, Wunstorf	
54+21	Airbus Military A.400M $	Luftwaffe LTG 62 (noted Manching Apr 2024)	
54+22	Airbus Military A.400M	Luftwaffe LTG 62 (noted Manching Aug 2024)	
54+23	Airbus Military A.400M	Luftwaffe LTG 62 (noted Manching Sep 2024)	
54+24	Airbus Military A.400M	Luftwaffe LTG 62, Wunstorf	
54+25	Airbus Military A.400M	Luftwaffe LTG 62 (noted Manching Jul 2024)	
54+26	Airbus Military A.400M	Luftwaffe, stored Wunstorf	
54+27	Airbus Military A.400M	Luftwaffe, stored Wunstorf	
54+28	Airbus Military A.400M	Luftwaffe LTG 62, Wunstorf	
54+29	Airbus Military A.400M	Luftwaffe LTG 62, Wunstorf	
54+30	Airbus Military A.400M	Luftwaffe LTG 62, Wunstorf	
54+31	Airbus Military A.400M	Luftwaffe LTG 62, Wunstorf	
54+32	Airbus Military A.400M	Luftwaffe, stored Wunstorf	
54+33	Airbus Military A.400M	Luftwaffe LTG 62, Wunstorf	
54+34	Airbus Military A.400M	Luftwaffe, stored Wunstorf	
54+35	Airbus Military A.400M	Airbus Defence & Space, Sevilla	
54+36	Airbus Military A.400M	Luftwaffe LTG 62, Wunstorf	
54+37	Airbus Military A.400M	Luftwaffe LTG 62, Wunstorf	
54+38	Airbus Military A.400M	Luftwaffe LTG 62, Wunstorf	
54+39	Airbus Military A.400M	Luftwaffe LTG 62, Wunstorf	
54+40	Airbus Military A.400M	Luftwaffe, stored Wunstorf	
54+41	Airbus Military A.400M	Airbus Defence & Space, Getafe	
54+42	Airbus Military A.400M	Luftwaffe LTG 62, Wunstorf	
54+43	Airbus Military A.400M	Luftwaffe LTG 62, Wunstorf	
54+44	Airbus Military A.400M	Luftwaffe LTG 62, Wunstorf	
54+45	Airbus Military A.400M	Luftwaffe LTG 62, Wunstorf	
54+46	Airbus Military A.400M	Luftwaffe LTG 62, Wunstorf	
54+47	Airbus Military A.400M	Luftwaffe LTG 62, Wunstorf	
54+48	Airbus Military A.400M	Luftwaffe, stored Wunstorf	
54+49	Airbus Military A.400M	Luftwaffe (on order)	
54+50	Airbus Military A.400M	Luftwaffe (on order)	
54+51	Airbus Military A.400M	Luftwaffe (on order)	
54+52	Airbus Military A.400M	Luftwaffe (on order)	
54+53	Airbus Military A.400M	Luftwaffe (on order)	
55+01	Lockheed C-130J-30 Hercules II	Luftwaffe EFATT, Evreux	
55+02	Lockheed C-130J-30 Hercules II	Luftwaffe EFATT, Evreux	
55+03	Lockheed C-130J-30 Hercules II	Luftwaffe EFATT, Evreux	
55+04	Lockheed KC-130J Hercules II	Luftwaffe EFATT, Evreux	
55+05	Lockheed KC-130J Hercules II	Luftwaffe EFATT, Evreux	
55+06	Lockheed KC-130J Hercules II	Luftwaffe EFATT, Evreux	
57+04	Dornier Do.228LM	Marineflieger MFG 3, Nordholz	
57+05	Dornier Do.228NG	Marineflieger MFG 3, Nordholz	
60+03	Lockheed P-3C CUP Orion	*To Portugal as 24812*	
60+04	Lockheed P-3C CUP Orion	*For Portugal as 24813*	
60+05	Lockheed P-3C CUP Orion	*To Portugal as 24814*	
60+06	Lockheed P-3C CUP Orion	*To Portugal as 24815*	
60+07	Lockheed P-3C CUP Orion	*To Portugal as 24816*	
60+08	Lockheed P-3C CUP Orion	*To Portugal as 24817*	
6.+01	Boeing P-8A Poseidon	Marineflieger (on order)	
6.+02	Boeing P-8A Poseidon	Marineflieger (on order)	
6.+03	Boeing P-8A Poseidon	Marineflieger (on order)	
6.+04	Boeing P-8A Poseidon	Marineflieger (on order)	

Notes	Serial	Type (code/other identity)	Owner/operator, location or fate
	6.+05	Boeing P-8A Poseidon	Marineflieger (on order)
	6.+06	Boeing P-8A Poseidon	Marineflieger (on order)
	6.+07	Boeing P-8A Poseidon	Marineflieger (on order)
	6.+08	Boeing P-8A Poseidon	Marineflieger (on order)
	74+01	Eurocopter EC.665 Tiger UHT	Heer KHR 36, Fritzlar
	74+03	Eurocopter EC.665 Tiger UHT	Luftwaffe TsLw 3, Fassberg
	74+04	Eurocopter EC.665 Tiger UHT	*Heer, Fritzlar (spares recovery)*
	74+05	Eurocopter EC.665 Tiger UHT	Luftwaffe TsLw 3, Fassberg
	74+07	Eurocopter EC.665 Tiger UHT	Luftwaffe TsLw 3, Fassberg
	74+08	Eurocopter EC.665 Tiger UHT	*GI, Fritzlar as "SAG74+08"*
	74+10	Eurocopter EC.665 Tiger UHT	Luftwaffe TsLw 3, Fassberg
	74+11	Eurocopter EC.665 Tiger UHT	*Withdrawn from use, Fritzlar*
	74+13	Eurocopter EC.665 Tiger UHT	Luftwaffe TsLw 3, Fassberg
	74+14	Eurocopter EC.665 Tiger UHT	Luftwaffe TsLw 3, Fassberg
	74+15	Eurocopter EC.665 Tiger UHT	Luftwaffe TsLw 3, Fassberg
	74+16	Eurocopter EC.665 Tiger UHT	Heer D/F HFAZT, Le Luc, France
	74+17	Eurocopter EC.665 Tiger UHT	Heer KHR 36, Fritzlar
	74+18	Eurocopter EC.665 Tiger UHT	Heer KHR 36, Fritzlar
	74+19	Eurocopter EC.665 Tiger UHT	Heer KHR 36, Fritzlar
	74+20	Eurocopter EC.665 Tiger UHT	Heer D/F HFAZT, Le Luc, France
	74+21	Eurocopter EC.665 Tiger UHT	Heer KHR 36, Fritzlar
	74+22	Eurocopter EC.665 Tiger UHT	*Heer, Fritzlar (spares recovery)*
	74+23	Eurocopter EC.665 Tiger UHT	Luftwaffe WTD 61, Manching-Ingolstadt
	74+24	Eurocopter EC.665 Tiger UHT	Heer KHR 36, Fritzlar
	74+25	Eurocopter EC.665 Tiger UHT	Heer KHR 36, Fritzlar
	74+26	Eurocopter EC.665 Tiger UHT	Heer KHR 36, Fritzlar
	74+28	Eurocopter EC.665 Tiger UHT	Heer KHR 36, Fritzlar
	74+29	Eurocopter EC.665 Tiger UHT	Heer KHR 36, Fritzlar
	74+30	Eurocopter EC.665 Tiger UHT	Heer KHR 36, Fritzlar
	74+31	Eurocopter EC.665 Tiger UHT	Heer KHR 36, Fritzlar
	74+32	Eurocopter EC.665 Tiger UHT	Heer KHR 36, Fritzlar
	74+34	Eurocopter EC.665 Tiger UHT	Heer KHR 36, Fritzlar
	74+35	Eurocopter EC.665 Tiger UHT	Heer KHR 36, Fritzlar
	74+36	Eurocopter EC.665 Tiger UHT	Heer KHR 36, Fritzlar
	74+37	Eurocopter EC.665 Tiger UHT	Heer D/F HFAZT, Le Luc, France
	74+38	Eurocopter EC.665 Tiger UHT	Heer D/F HFAZT, Le Luc, France
	74+39	Eurocopter EC.665 Tiger UHT	Hoer
	74+40	Eurocopter EC.665 Tiger UHT	Heer KHR 36, Fritzlar
	74+41	Eurocopter EC.665 Tiger UHT	Heer D/F HFAZT, Le Luc, France
	74+42	Eurocopter EC.665 Tiger UHT	Heer KHR 36, Fritzlar
	74+43	Eurocopter EC.665 Tiger UHT	Heer KHR 36, Fritzlar
	74+44	Eurocopter EC.665 Tiger UHT	Luftwaffe TsLw 3, Fassberg
	74+45	Eurocopter EC.665 Tiger UHT	Heer KHR 36, Fritzlar
	74+46	Eurocopter EC.665 Tiger UHT	Heer KHR 36, Fritzlar
	74+47	Eurocopter EC.665 Tiger UHT	Heer KHR 36, Fritzlar
	74+48	Eurocopter EC.665 Tiger UHT	*Written off Viens, France 8th November 2023*
	74+50	Eurocopter EC.665 Tiger UHT	Heer D/F HFAZT, Le Luc, France
	74+51	Eurocopter EC.665 Tiger UHT	Heer D/F HFAZT, Le Luc, France
	74+52	Eurocopter EC.665 Tiger UHT	Heer KHR 36, Fritzlar
	74+53	Eurocopter EC.665 Tiger UHT	Heer KHR 36, Fritzlar
	74+54	Eurocopter EC.665 Tiger UHT	Heer KHR 36, Fritzlar
	74+55	Eurocopter EC.665 Tiger UHT	Heer D/F HFAZT, Le Luc, France
	74+56	Eurocopter EC.665 Tiger UHT	Heer KHR 36, Fritzlar
	74+57	Eurocopter EC.665 Tiger UHT	Heer KHR 36, Fritzlar
	74+58	Eurocopter EC.665 Tiger UHT	Heer KHR 36, Fritzlar
	74+59	Eurocopter EC.665 Tiger UHT	Heer
	74+60	Eurocopter EC.665 Tiger UHT	Heer D/F HFAZT, Le Luc, France
	74+61	Eurocopter EC.665 Tiger UHT	Heer KHR 36, Fritzlar
	74+62	Eurocopter EC.665 Tiger UHT	Heer D/F HFAZT, Le Luc, France
	74+63	Eurocopter EC.665 Tiger UHT	Heer KHR 36, Fritzlar
	74+64	Eurocopter EC.665 Tiger UHT	Heer KHR 36, Fritzlar
	74+65	Eurocopter EC.665 Tiger UHT	Heer KHR 36, Fritzlar

Serial	Type (code/other identity)	Owner/operator, location or fate	Notes
74+66	Eurocopter EC.665 Tiger UHT	Heer D/F HFAZT, Le Luc, France	
74+67	Eurocopter EC.665 Tiger UHT	Heer KHR 36, Fritzlar	
74+68	Eurocopter EC.665 Tiger UHT	Heer D/F HFAZT, Le Luc, France	
74+69	Eurocopter EC.665 Tiger UHT	Heer D/F HFAZT, Le Luc, France	
74+70	Eurocopter EC.665 Tiger UHT	Heer KHR 36, Fritzlar	
76+01	Airbus Helicopters H.145M	Luftwaffe HSG 64, Laupheim	
76+02	Airbus Helicopters H.145M	Luftwaffe HSG 64, Laupheim	
76+03	Airbus Helicopters H.145M	Luftwaffe HSG 64, Laupheim	
76+04	Airbus Helicopters H.145M	Luftwaffe HSG 64, Laupheim	
76+05	Airbus Helicopters H.145M	Luftwaffe HSG 64, Laupheim	
76+06	Airbus Helicopters H.145M	Luftwaffe HSG 64, Laupheim	
76+07	Airbus Helicopters H.145M	Luftwaffe HSG 64, Laupheim	
76+08	Airbus Helicopters H.145M	Luftwaffe HSG 64, Laupheim	
76+09	Airbus Helicopters H.145M	Luftwaffe HSG 64, Laupheim	
76+10	Airbus Helicopters H.145M	Luftwaffe HSG 64, Laupheim	
76+11	Airbus Helicopters H.145M	Luftwaffe HSG 64, Laupheim	
76+12	Airbus Helicopters H.145M	Luftwaffe HSG 64, Laupheim	
76+13	Airbus Helicopters H.145M	Luftwaffe HSG 64, Laupheim	
76+14	Airbus Helicopters H.145M	Luftwaffe HSG 64, Laupheim	
76+15	Airbus Helicopters H.145M	Luftwaffe HSG 64, Laupheim	
76+16	Airbus Helicopters H.145M	Luftwaffe WTD 61, Manching-Ingolstadt	
77+01	Airbus Helicopters H.145M	Heer THR 30, Niederstetten	
77+02	Airbus Helicopters H.145M	Heer THR 30, Niederstetten	
77+03	Airbus Helicopters H.145M	Heer THR 30, Niederstetten	
77+04	Airbus Helicopters H.145M	Heer THR 30, Niederstetten	
77+05	Airbus Helicopters H.145M	Heer THR 30, Niederstetten	
77+06	Airbus Helicopters H.145M	Heer THR 30, Niederstetten	
77+07	Airbus Helicopters H.145M	Heer THR 30, Niederstetten	
77+08	Airbus Helicopters H.145M	Heer THR 30, Niederstetten	
78+04	NH Industries NH.90-TTH (98+94)	Luftwaffe TsLw 3, Fassberg	
78+05	NH Industries NH.90-TTH	Luftwaffe TsLw 3, Fassberg	
78+06	NH Industries NH.90-TTH	Heer IntHubschrAusbZ, Bückeburg	
78+07	NH Industries NH.90-TTH	Heer IntHubschrAusbZ, Bückeburg	
78+08	NH Industries NH.90-TTH	Heer IntHubschrAusbZ, Bückeburg	
78+09	NH Industries NH.90-TTH (98+92)	Heer THR 30, Niederstetten	
78+10	NH Industries NH.90-TTH (98+94)	Heer THR 10, Fassberg	
78+11	NH Industries NH.90-TTH (98+95)	Heer THR 30, Niederstetten	
78+12	NH Industries NH.90-TTH (98+96)	Heer THR 30, Niederstetten	
78+13	NH Industries NH.90-TTH (98+97)	Heer THR 10, Fassberg	
78+14	NH Industries NH.90-TTH	Heer THR 30, Niederstetten	
78+15	NH Industries NH.90-TTH	Heer IntHubschrAusbZ, Bückeburg	
78+16	NH Industries NH.90-TTH	Heer THR 30, Niederstetten	
78+17	NH Industries NH.90-TTH	Heer THR 10, Fassberg	
78+18	NH Industries NH.90-TTH	Heer THR 10, Fassberg	
78+19	NH Industries NH.90-TTH (98+49)	Heer THR 10, Fassberg	
78+20	NH Industries NH.90-TTH (98+52)	Heer THR 10, Fassberg	
78+21	NH Industries NH.90-TTH (98+56)	Heer THR 10, Fassberg	
78+22	NH Industries NH.90-TTH (98+57)	Heer THR 30, Niederstetten	
78+23	NH Industries NH.90-TTH	Heer THR 10, Fassberg	
78+24	NH Industries NH.90-TTH	Heer THR 10, Fassberg	
78+25	NH Industries NH.90-TTH	Heer THR 10, Fassberg	
78+26	NH Industries NH.90-TTH	Heer THR 10, Fassberg	
78+27	NH Industries NH.90-TTH	Heer THR 10, Fassberg	
78+28	NH Industries NH.90-TTH	Heer THR 10, Fassberg	
78+29	NH Industries NH.90-TTH	Heer THR 10, Fassberg	
78+30	NH Industries NH.90-TTH	Heer THR 10, Fassberg	
78+31	NH Industries NH.90-TTH	Heer THR 10, Fassberg	
78+32	NH Industries NH.90-TTH	Heer IntHubschrAusbZ, Bückeburg	
78+33	NH Industries NH.90-TTH	Heer THR 10, Fassberg	
78+34	NH Industries NH.90-TTH	Heer THR 10, Fassberg	
78+35	NH Industries NH.90-TTH	Heer THR 10, Fassberg	
78+36	NH Industries NH.90-TTH	Heer THR 30, Niederstetten	

Notes	Serial	Type (code/other identity)	Owner/operator, location or fate
	78+37	NH Industries NH.90-TTH	Heer THR 30, Niederstetten
	78+38	NH Industries NH.90-TTH	Heer THR 30, Fassberg
	78+39	NH Industries NH.90-TTH	Heer THR 30, Niederstetten
	78+40	NH Industries NH.90-TTH	Heer THR 30, Niederstetten
	79+01	NH Industries NH.90-TTH (98+91)	Heer IntHubschrAusbZ, Bückeburg
	79+02	NH Industries NH.90-TTH (79+09)	Heer THR 10, Fassberg
	79+03	NH Industries NH.90-TTH (79+10)	Heer THR 10, Fassberg
	79+04	NH Industries NH.90-TTH (79+11)	Heer THR 10, Fassberg
	79+05	NH Industries NH.90-TTH (79+12)	Heer THR 10, Fassberg
	79+06	NH Industries NH.90-TTH (79+13)	Heer THR 10, Fassberg
	79+07	NH Industries NH.90-TTH	Heer THR 10, Fassberg
	79+08	NH Industries NH.90-TTH (98+50)	Luftwaffe TsLw 3, Fassberg
	79+09	NH Industries NH.90-TTH	Heer THR 10, Fassberg
	79+10	NH Industries NH.90-TTH	Heer THR 10, Fassberg
	79+11	NH Industries NH.90-TTH	Heer THR 30, Niederstetten
	79+12	NH Industries NH.90-TTH	Heer THR 30, Niederstetten
	79+13	NH Industries NH.90-TTH	Heer THR 30, Niederstetten
	79+14	NH Industries NH.90-TTH	Heer THR 30, Niederstetten
	79+15	NH Industries NH.90-TTH	Heer THR 30, Niederstetten
	79+16	NH Industries NH.90-TTH	Heer THR 30, Niederstetten
	79+17	NH Industries NH.90-TTH	Heer THR 10, Fassberg
	79+18	NH Industries NH.90-TTH	Heer THR 10, Fassberg
	79+19	NH Industries NH.90-TTH	Heer IntHubschrAusbZ, Bückeburg
	79+20	NH Industries NH.90-TTH	Heer IntHubschrAusbZ, Bückeburg
	79+21	NH Industries NH.90-TTH	Heer THR 30, Niederstetten
	79+22	NH Industries NH.90-TTH	Heer IntHubschrAusbZ, Bückeburg
	79+23	NH Industries NH.90-TTH	Heer THR 30, Niederstetten
	79+24	NH Industries NH.90-TTH (79+02/98+93)	Heer THR 10, Fassberg
	79+25	NH Industries NH.90-TTH (79+03/98+97)	Heer THR 10, Fassberg
	79+26	NH Industries NH.90-TTH (79+04/98+99)	Heer THR 30, Niederstetten
	79+27	NH Industries NH.90-TTH (79+05)	Heer THR 10, Fassberg
	79+28	NH Industries NH.90-TTH (79+06)	Heer IntHubschrAusbZ, Bückeburg
	79+29	NH Industries NH.90-TTH (79+07)	Heer IntHubschrAusbZ, Bückeburg
	79+30	NH Industries NH.90-TTH (79+08)	Heer THR 10, Fassberg
	79+31	NH Industries NH.90-TTH	Heer THR 30, Niederstetten
	79+32	NH Industries NH.90-TTH	Heer THR 30, Niederstetten
	79+33	NH Industries NH.90-TTH	Heer THR 10, Fassberg
	79+34	NH Industries NH.90-TTH	Heer THR 10, Fassberg
	79+35	NH Industries NH.90-TTH	Heer THR 10, Fassberg
	79+36	NH Industries NH.90-TTH	Heer IntHubschrAusbZ, Bückeburg
	79+37	NH Industries NH.90-TTH	Heer IntHubschrAusbZ, Bückeburg
	79+38	NH Industries NH.90-TTH	Heer THR 10, Fassberg
	79+39	NH Industries NH.90-TTH	Heer IntHubschrAusbZ, Bückeburg
	79+40	NH Industries NH.90-TTH	Heer IntHubschrAusbZ, Bückeburg
	79+41	NH Industries NH.90-TTH	Heer THR 10, Fassberg
	79+42	NH Industries NH.90-TTH	Heer THR 10, Fassberg
	79+43	NH Industries NH.90-TTH	Heer THR 10, Fassberg
	79+44	NH Industries NH.90-TTH	Heer THR 10, Fassberg
	79+45	NH Industries NH.90-TTH	Heer/Airbus Helicopters, Donauwörth (on order)
	79+46	NH Industries NH.90-TTH	Heer/Airbus Helicopters, Donauwörth (on order)
	79+47	NH Industries NH.90-TTH	Heer (on order?)
	79+48	NH Industries NH.90-TTH	Heer (on order?)
	79+49	NH Industries NH.90-TTH	Heer (on order?)
	79+50	NH Industries NH.90-TTH	Heer (on order?)
	79+51	NH Industries NH.90-NFH Sea Lion (98+51)	Marineflieger MFG 5, Nordholz
	79+52	NH Industries NH.90-NFH Sea Lion (98+56)	Marineflieger MFG 5, Nordholz
	79+53	NH Industries NH.90-NFH Sea Lion (98+40)	Marineflieger MFG 5, Nordholz
	79+54	NH Industries NH.90-NFH Sea Lion (98+41)	Marineflieger MFG 5, Nordholz
	79+55	NH Industries NH.90-NFH Sea Lion (98+50)	Marineflieger MFG 5, Nordholz
	79+56	NH Industries NH.90-NFH Sea Lion	Marineflieger MFG 5, Nordholz
	79+57	NH Industries NH.90-NFH Sea Lion	Marineflieger MFG 5, Nordholz
	79+58	NH Industries NH.90-NFH Sea Lion	Marineflieger MFG 5, Nordholz

Serial	Type (code/other identity)	Owner/operator, location or fate	Notes
79+59	NH Industries NH.90-NFH Sea Lion	Marineflieger MFG 5, Nordholz	
79+60	NH Industries NH.90-NFH Sea Lion	Marineflieger MFG 5, Nordholz	
79+61	NH Industries NH.90-NFH Sea Lion	Marineflieger MFG 5, Nordholz	
79+62	NH Industries NH.90-NFH Sea Lion	Marineflieger MFG 5, Nordholz	
79+63	NH Industries NH.90-NFH Sea Lion	Marineflieger MFG 5, Nordholz	
79+64	NH Industries NH.90-NFH Sea Lion	Marineflieger MFG 5, Nordholz	
79+65	NH Industries NH.90-NFH Sea Lion	Marineflieger MFG 5, Nordholz	
79+66	NH Industries NH.90-NFH Sea Lion	Marineflieger MFG 5, Nordholz	
79+67	NH Industries NH.90-NFH Sea Lion	Marineflieger MFG 5, Nordholz	
79+68	NH Industries NH.90-NFH Sea Lion	Marineflieger MFG 5, Nordholz	
79+70	NH Industries NH.90-MRFH Sea Tiger	Marineflieger/Airbus Helicopters, Donauwörth	
79+71	NH Industries NH.90-MRFH Sea Tiger	Marineflieger/Airbus Helicopters, Donauwörth	
82+01	Eurocopter AS.532U-2 Cougar	Luftwaffe FBS, Berlin-Tegel	
82+02	Eurocopter AS.532U-2 Cougar	Luftwaffe FBS, Berlin-Tegel	
82+03	Eurocopter AS.532U-2 Cougar	Luftwaffe FBS, Berlin-Tegel	
82+51	Eurocopter EC.135P-1	Heer IntHubschrAusbZ, Bückeburg	
82+52	Eurocopter EC.135P-1	Heer IntHubschrAusbZ, Bückeburg	
82+53	Eurocopter EC.135P-1	Heer IntHubschrAusbZ, Bückeburg	
82+54	Eurocopter EC.135P-1	Heer IntHubschrAusbZ, Bückeburg	
82+55	Eurocopter EC.135P-1	Heer IntHubschrAusbZ, Bückeburg	
82+56	Eurocopter EC.135P-1	Heer IntHubschrAusbZ, Bückeburg	
82+57	Eurocopter EC.135P-1	Heer IntHubschrAusbZ, Bückeburg	
82+59	Eurocopter EC.135P-1	Heer IntHubschrAusbZ, Bückeburg	
82+60	Eurocopter EC.135P-1	Heer IntHubschrAusbZ, Bückeburg	
82+61	Eurocopter EC.135P-1	Heer IntHubschrAusbZ, Bückeburg	
82+63	Eurocopter EC.135P-1	Heer IntHubschrAusbZ, Bückeburg	
82+64	Eurocopter EC.135P-1	Heer IntHubschrAusbZ, Bückeburg	
82+65	Eurocopter EC.135P-1	Heer IntHubschrAusbZ, Bückeburg	
83+02	Westland Sea Lynx Mk88A	Marineflieger MFG 5, Nordholz	
83+03	Westland Sea Lynx Mk88A	Marineflieger MFG 5, Nordholz	
83+04	Westland Sea Lynx Mk88A	Marineflieger MFG 5, Nordholz	
83+05	Westland Sea Lynx Mk88A	Marineflieger MFG 5, Nordholz	
83+06	Westland Sea Lynx Mk88A	Marineflieger MFG 5, Nordholz	
83+07	Westland Sea Lynx Mk88A	Marineflieger MFG 5, Nordholz	
83+09	Westland Sea Lynx Mk88A	Marineflieger MFG 5, Nordholz	
83+10	Westland Sea Lynx Mk88A	Marineflieger MFG 5, Nordholz	
83+11	Westland Sea Lynx Mk88A	Marineflieger MFG 5, Nordholz	
83+12	Westland Sea Lynx Mk88A	Marineflieger MFG 5, Nordholz	
83+13	Westland Sea Lynx Mk88A	Marineflieger MFG 5, Nordholz	
83+15	Westland Sea Lynx Mk88A	Marineflieger MFG 5, Nordholz	
83+17	Westland Sea Lynx Mk88A	Marineflieger MFG 5, Nordholz	
83+18	Westland Sea Lynx Mk88A	Marineflieger MFG 5, Nordholz	
83+19	Westland Sea Lynx Mk88A	Marineflieger MFG 5, Nordholz	
83+20	Westland Sea Lynx Mk88A	Marineflieger MFG 5, Nordholz	
83+21	Westland Sea Lynx Mk88A	Marineflieger MFG 5, Nordholz	
83+22	Westland Sea Lynx Mk88A	Marineflieger MFG 5, Nordholz	
83+23	Westland Sea Lynx Mk88A	Marineflieger MFG 5, Nordholz	
83+24	Westland Sea Lynx Mk88A	Marineflieger MFG 5, Nordholz	
83+25	Westland Sea Lynx Mk88A	Marineflieger MFG 5, Nordholz	
83+26	Westland Sea Lynx Mk88A	Marineflieger MFG 5, Nordholz	
84+09	Sikorsky/VFW CH-53G	Luftwaffe TsLw 3, Fassberg	
84+13	Sikorsky/VFW CH-53GA	Luftwaffe HSG 64, Laupheim	
84+14	Sikorsky/VFW CH-53GE	Luftwaffe HSG 64, Laupheim	
84+15	Sikorsky/VFW CH-53GS	Luftwaffe HSG 64, Laupheim	
84+18	Sikorsky/VFW CH-53G	Luftwaffe HSG 64, Laupheim	
84+19	Sikorsky/VFW CH-53G	Luftwaffe TsLw 3, Fassberg	
84+24	Sikorsky/VFW CH-53GA	Luftwaffe HSG 64, Laupheim	
84+25	Sikorsky/VFW CH-53GS	Luftwaffe HSG 64, Laupheim	
84+26	Sikorsky/VFW CH-53GE	Luftwaffe HSG 64, Laupheim	
84+28	Sikorsky/VFW CH-53GA	Luftwaffe WTD 61, Manching-Ingolstadt	
84+29	Sikorsky/VFW CH-53G	Luftwaffe HSG 64, Laupheim	
84+30	Sikorsky/VFW CH-53GS	Luftwaffe HSG 64, Laupheim	

Notes	Serial	Type (code/other identity)	Owner/operator, location or fate
	84+31	Sikorsky/VFW CH-53GA	Luftwaffe HSG 64, Laupheim
	84+32	Sikorsky/VFW CH-53G	Luftwaffe HSG 64, Laupheim
	84+33	Sikorsky/VFW CH-53GA	Luftwaffe TsLw 3, Fassberg
	84+34	Sikorsky/VFW CH-53G	Luftwaffe HSG 64, Laupheim
	84+35	Sikorsky/VFW CH-53GA	Luftwaffe HSG 64, Laupheim
	84+37	Sikorsky/VFW CH-53GA	Luftwaffe HSG 64, Laupheim
	84+38	Sikorsky/VFW CH-53G	Luftwaffe HSG 64, Laupheim
	84+39	Sikorsky/VFW CH-53GA	Luftwaffe HSG 64, Laupheim
	84+42	Sikorsky/VFW CH-53GS	Luftwaffe HSG 64, Laupheim
	84+43	Sikorsky/VFW CH-53GS	Luftwaffe HSG 64, Laupheim
	84+44	Sikorsky/VFW CH-53G	Luftwaffe HSG 64, Laupheim
	84+45	Sikorsky/VFW CH-53GS	Luftwaffe HSG 64, Laupheim
	84+46	Sikorsky/VFW CH-53G	Luftwaffe HSG 64, Laupheim
	84+47	Sikorsky/VFW CH-53GA	Luftwaffe HSG 64, Laupheim
	84+48	Sikorsky/VFW CH-53G	Luftwaffe HSG 64, Laupheim
	84+49	Sikorsky/VFW CH-53GA	Luftwaffe HSG 64, Laupheim
	84+50	Sikorsky/VFW CH-53GA	Luftwaffe HSG 64, Laupheim
	84+51	Sikorsky/VFW CH-53GS	Luftwaffe HSG 64, Laupheim
	84+52	Sikorsky/VFW CH-53GS	Luftwaffe HSG 64, Laupheim
	84+53	Sikorsky/VFW CH-53GE	Luftwaffe HSG 64, Laupheim
	84+54	Sikorsky/VFW CH-53G	Luftwaffe HSG 64, Laupheim
	84+55	Sikorsky/VFW CH-53G	Airbus Helicopters, Donauwörth
	84+57	Sikorsky/VFW CH-53G	Luftwaffe HSG 64, Laupheim
	84+58	Sikorsky/VFW CH-53G	Luftwaffe HSG 64, Laupheim
	84+59	Sikorsky/VFW CH-53GS	Luftwaffe HSG 64, Laupheim
	84+62	Sikorsky/VFW CH-53GS	Luftwaffe HSG 64, Laupheim
	84+63	Sikorsky/VFW CH-53GA	Luftwaffe HSG 64, Laupheim
	84+64	Sikorsky/VFW CH-53GS	Luftwaffe HSG 64, Laupheim
	84+65	Sikorsky/VFW CH-53GA	Luftwaffe HSG 64, Laupheim
	84+66	Sikorsky/VFW CH-53GS	Luftwaffe HSG 64, Laupheim
	84+67	Sikorsky/VFW CH-53GS	Luftwaffe HSG 64, Laupheim
	84+68	Sikorsky/VFW CH-53GS	Luftwaffe HSG 64, Laupheim
	84+70	Sikorsky/VFW CH-53GA	Luftwaffe TsLw 3, Fassberg
	84+71	Sikorsky/VFW CH-53G	Luftwaffe HSG 64, Laupheim
	84+72	Sikorsky/VFW CH-53G	Luftwaffe HSG 64, Laupheim
	84+73	Sikorsky/VFW CH-53GS	Luftwaffe HSG 64, Laupheim
	84+74	Sikorsky/VFW CH-53G	Luftwaffe HSG 64, Laupheim
	84+75	Sikorsky/VFW CH-53G	Luftwaffe HSG 64, Laupheim
	84+76	Sikorsky/VFW CH-53G	Luftwaffe HSG 64, Laupheim
	84+78	Sikorsky/VFW CH-53GS	Luftwaffe TsLw 3, Fassberg
	84+79	Sikorsky/VFW CH-53GS	Luftwaffe HSG 64, Laupheim
	84+82	Sikorsky/VFW CH-53GE	Luftwaffe HSG 64, Laupheim
	84+83	Sikorsky/VFW CH-53G	Luftwaffe TsLw 3, Fassberg
	84+85	Sikorsky/VFW CH-53GS	Luftwaffe HSG 64, Laupheim
	84+86	Sikorsky/VFW CH-53GA	Luftwaffe HSG 64, Laupheim
	84+87	Sikorsky/VFW CH-53GS	Luftwaffe HSG 64, Laupheim
	84+88	Sikorsky/VFW CH-53G	Luftwaffe HSG 64, Laupheim
	84+89	Sikorsky/VFW CH-53GA	Luftwaffe HSG 64, Laupheim
	84+90	Sikorsky/VFW CH-53G	Luftwaffe HSG 64, Laupheim
	84+91	Sikorsky/VFW CH-53GS	Luftwaffe HSG 64, Laupheim
	84+92	Sikorsky/VFW CH-53GS	Luftwaffe HSG 64, Laupheim
	84+94	Sikorsky/VFW CH-53G	Luftwaffe WTD 61, Manching-Ingolstadt
	84+96	Sikorsky/VFW CH-53GE	Luftwaffe HSG 64, Laupheim
	84+97	Sikorsky/VFW CH-53GA	Luftwaffe HSG 64, Laupheim
	84+98	Sikorsky/VFW CH-53GS	Luftwaffe HSG 64, Laupheim
	84+99	Sikorsky/VFW CH-53GA	Luftwaffe HSG 64, Laupheim
	85+00	Sikorsky/VFW CH-53GS	Luftwaffe HSG 64, Laupheim
	85+01	Sikorsky/VFW CH-53GS	Luftwaffe HSG 64, Laupheim
	85+03	Sikorsky/VFW CH-53GA	Luftwaffe HSG 64, Laupheim
	85+04	Sikorsky/VFW CH-53GA	Luftwaffe HSG 64, Laupheim
	85+05	Sikorsky/VFW CH-53GS	Luftwaffe HSG 64, Laupheim
	85+06	Sikorsky/VFW CH-53GA	Luftwaffe HSG 64, Laupheim

Serial	Type (code/other identity)	Owner/operator, location or fate	Notes
85+07	Sikorsky/VFW CH-53GS	Luftwaffe HSG 64, Laupheim	
85+08	Sikorsky/VFW CH-53GS	Luftwaffe HSG 64, Laupheim	
85+10	Sikorsky/VFW CH-53GS	Luftwaffe HSG 64, Laupheim	
85+12	Sikorsky/VFW CH-53GS	Luftwaffe HSG 64, Laupheim	
89+51	Westland Sea King Mk.41	*Withdrawn from use, Nordholz*	
89+54	Westland Sea King Mk.41	*Withdrawn from use, Nordholz*	
89+55	Westland Sea King Mk.41 $	*Preserved Berlin-Gatow Museum, Germany*	
89+56	Westland Sea King Mk.41	HeliOperations Ltd, stored Somerton, Somerset	
89+57	Westland Sea King Mk.41	*Withdrawn from use, Nordholz*	
89+58	Westland Sea King Mk.41 $	HeliOperations Ltd, stored Somerton, Somerset	
89+60	Westland Sea King Mk.41	*Withdrawn from use, Nordholz*	
89+61	Westland Sea King Mk.41	Heli Operations, Portland, Dorset (for Ukraine)	
89+63	Westland Sea King Mk.41	*Withdrawn from use, Nordholz*	
89+64	Westland Sea King Mk.41	Heli Operations, Portland, Dorset (for Ukraine)	
89+65	Westland Sea King Mk.41	*Withdrawn from use, Nordholz*	
89+66	Westland Sea King Mk.41	HeliOperations Ltd, stored Somerton, Somerset	
89+68	Westland Sea King Mk.41	HeliOperations Ltd, stored Somerton, Somerset	
89+69	Westland Sea King Mk.41	*Withdrawn from use, Nordholz*	
89+70	Westland Sea King Mk.41	*Withdrawn from use, Nordholz*	
89+71	Westland Sea King Mk.41	*Withdrawn from use, Nordholz*	
98+03	Eurofighter EF.2000(T) (IPA3)	Luftwaffe WTD 61, Manching-Ingolstadt	
98+07	Eurofighter EF.2000 (IPA7) $	Luftwaffe WTD 61, Manching-Ingolstadt	
98+08	Eurofighter EF.2000GT (IPA8)	Luftwaffe WTD 61, Manching-Ingolstadt	
98+16	Eurocopter EC.665 Tiger UHT	Luftwaffe TsLw 3, Fassberg	
98+18	Eurocopter EC.665 Tiger UHT (74+04)	Airbus Helicopters, Donauwörth	
98+49	Eurocopter EC.665 Tiger UHT (74+49)	Airbus Helicopters, Donauwörth	
98+51	NH Industries NH.90-NFH Sea Lion	*Re-serialled as 78+51*	
98+55	NH Industries NH.90-MRFH Sea Tiger	Airbus Helicopters, Donauwörth	
98+59	Panavia Tornado IDS(T) (43+21) $	Luftwaffe WTD 61, Manching-Ingolstadt	
98+60	Panavia Tornado IDS (43+89)	Luftwaffe WTD 61, Manching-Ingolstadt	
98+77	Panavia Tornado IDS (45+29) $	Luftwaffe WTD 61, Manching-Ingolstadt	
98+79	Panavia Tornado ECR (45+75) $	Luftwaffe WTD 61, Manching-Ingolstadt	
98+90	NH Industries NH.90-TTH	Airbus Helicopters, Donauwörth	
Civil operated aircraft in military use			
D-HABP	Eurocopter EC.135T3	Heer IntHubschrAusbZ, Bückeburg	
D-HABQ	Eurocopter EC.135T3	Heer IntHubschrAusbZ, Bückeburg	
D-HABR	Eurocopter EC.135T3	Heer IntHubschrAusbZ, Bückeburg	
D-HABS	Eurocopter EC.135T3	Heer IntHubschrAusbZ, Bückeburg	
D-HABT	Eurocopter EC.135T3	Heer IntHubschrAusbZ, Bückeburg	
D-HABU	Eurocopter EC.135T3	Heer IntHubschrAusbZ, Bückeburg	
D-HABV	Eurocopter EC.135T3	Heer IntHubschrAusbZ, Bückeburg	
D-HABW	Eurocopter EC.135T3	Heer IntHubschrAusbZ, Bückeburg	
D-HCDL	Eurocopter EC.135P-2+	Marineflieger MFG 5, Nordholz	
D-HDDL	Eurocopter EC.135P-2+	Marineflieger MFG 5, Nordholz	
D-HMFA	Bell 206B Jet Ranger	Heer IntHubschrAusbZ, Bückeburg	
D-HMFB	Bell 206B Jet Ranger	Heer IntHubschrAusbZ, Bückeburg	
D-HMFC	Bell 206B Jet Ranger	Heer IntHubschrAusbZ, Bückeburg	
D-HMFD	Bell 206B Jet Ranger	Heer IntHubschrAusbZ, Bückeburg	
D-HMFE	Bell 206B Jet Ranger	Heer IntHubschrAusbZ, Bückeburg	
D-HMFF	Bell 206B Jet Ranger	Heer IntHubschrAusbZ, Bückeburg	
D-HTMG	Eurocopter EC.135P-2+	Marineflieger MFG 5, Nordholz	

GHANA

| 9G-EXE | Dassault Falcon 900EASy | Ghana Air Force VIP Flight, Accra | |

GREECE

Elliniki Polemiki Aeroporía/Hellenic Air Force (HAF)

001	Lockheed Martin F-16C-52 Fighting Falcon	HAF 335 Mira/116 PM, Áraxos	
002	Lockheed Martin F-16C-52 Fighting Falcon	HAF 336 Mira/116 PM, Áraxos	
003	Lockheed Martin F-16C-52 Fighting Falcon	HAF 335 Mira/116 PM, Áraxos	
004	Lockheed Martin F-16C-52 Fighting Falcon	HAF 336 Mira/116 PM, Áraxos	
005	Lockheed Martin F-16V-72 Fighting Falcon	HAF 343 Mira/115 PM, Souda	

Notes	Serial	Type (code/other identity)	Owner/operator, location or fate
	006	Lockheed Martin F-16V-72 Fighting Falcon	HAF 343 Mira/115 PM, Souda
	007	Lockheed Martin F-16C-52 Fighting Falcon	HAF 335 Mira/116 PM, Áraxos
	008	Lockheed Martin F-16C-52 Fighting Falcon	HAF 336 Mira/116 PM, Áraxos
	009	Lockheed Martin F-16C-52 Fighting Falcon	HAF 335 Mira/116 PM, Áraxos
	010	Lockheed Martin F-16C-52 Fighting Falcon	HAF 336 Mira/116 PM, Áraxos
	011	Lockheed Martin F-16C-52 Fighting Falcon	HAF 335 Mira/116 PM, Áraxos
	012	Lockheed Martin F-16C-52 Fighting Falcon	HAF 336 Mira/116 PM, Áraxos
	013	Lockheed Martin F-16C-52 Fighting Falcon	HAF 335 Mira/116 PM, Áraxos
	014	Lockheed Martin F-16C-52 Fighting Falcon	HAF 336 Mira/116 PM, Áraxos
	015	Lockheed Martin F-16C-52 Fighting Falcon	HAF 335 Mira/116 PM, Áraxos
	016	Lockheed Martin F-16C-52 Fighting Falcon	HAF 336 Mira/116 PM, Áraxos
	017	Lockheed Martin F-16C-52 Fighting Falcon	HAF 335 Mira/116 PM, Áraxos
	018	Lockheed Martin F-16C-52 Fighting Falcon	HAF 336 Mira/116 PM, Áraxos
	019	Lockheed Martin F-16C-52 Fighting Falcon	HAF 335 Mira/116 PM, Áraxos
	020	Lockheed Martin F-16C-52 Fighting Falcon	HAF 336 Mira/116 PM, Áraxos
	021	Lockheed Martin F-16D-52 Fighting Falcon	HAF 335 Mira/116 PM, Áraxos
	022	Lockheed Martin F-16D-52 Fighting Falcon	HAF 336 Mira/116 PM, Áraxos
	023	Lockheed Martin F-16D-52 Fighting Falcon $	HAF 335 Mira/116 PM, Áraxos
	024	Lockheed Martin F-16D-52 Fighting Falcon	HAF 336 Mira/116 PM, Áraxos
	025	Lockheed Martin F-16V Fighting Falcon	HAF 335 Mira/116 PM, Áraxos
	026	Lockheed Martin F-16D-52 Fighting Falcon	HAF 336 Mira/116 PM, Áraxos
	027	Lockheed Martin F-16D-52 Fighting Falcon	HAF 335 Mira/116 PM, Áraxos
	028	Lockheed Martin F-16D-52 Fighting Falcon $	HAF 336 Mira/116 PM, Áraxos
	029	Lockheed Martin F-16D-52 Fighting Falcon	HAF 335 Mira/116 PM, Áraxos
	030	Lockheed Martin F-16D-52 Fighting Falcon	HAF 336 Mira/116 PM, Áraxos
	045	Lockheed Martin F-16C-50 Fighting Falcon	HAF 347 Mira/111 PM, Nea Ankhialos
	046	Lockheed Martin F-16C-50 Fighting Falcon	HAF 341 Mira/111 PM, Nea Ankhialos
	047	Lockheed Martin F-16C-50 Fighting Falcon	HAF 347 Mira/111 PM, Nea Ankhialos
	048	Lockheed Martin F-16C-50 Fighting Falcon	HAF 341 Mira/111 PM, Nea Ankhialos
	049	Lockheed Martin F-16C-50 Fighting Falcon	HAF 347 Mira/111 PM, Nea Ankhialos
	050	Lockheed Martin F-16C-50 Fighting Falcon	HAF 341 Mira/111 PM, Nea Ankhialos
	051	Lockheed Martin F-16C-50 Fighting Falcon	HAF 347 Mira/111 PM, Nea Ankhialos
	052	Lockheed Martin F-16C-50 Fighting Falcon	HAF 341 Mira/111 PM, Nea Ankhialos
	053	Lockheed Martin F-16C-50 Fighting Falcon	HAF 347 Mira/111 PM, Nea Ankhialos
	054	Lockheed Martin F-16C-50 Fighting Falcon	HAF 341 Mira/111 PM, Nea Ankhialos
	055	Lockheed Martin F-16C-50 Fighting Falcon	HAF 347 Mira/111 PM, Nea Ankhialos
	056	Lockheed Martin F-16C-50 Fighting Falcon	HAF 341 Mira/111 PM, Nea Ankhialos
	057	Lockheed Martin F-16C-50 Fighting Falcon	HAF 347 Mira/111 PM, Nea Ankhialos
	058	Lockheed Martin F-16C-50 Fighting Falcon	HAF 341 Mira/111 PM, Nea Ankhialos
	060	Lockheed Martin F-16C-50 Fighting Falcon	HAF 347 Mira/111 PM, Nea Ankhialos
	061	Lockheed Martin F-16C-50 Fighting Falcon	HAF 347 Mira/111 PM, Nea Ankhialos
	062	Lockheed Martin F-16C-50 Fighting Falcon $	HAF 341 Mira/111 PM, Nea Ankhialos
	063	Lockheed Martin F-16C-50 Fighting Falcon	HAF 347 Mira/111 PM, Nea Ankhialos
	064	Lockheed Martin F-16C-50 Fighting Falcon	HAF 341 Mira/111 PM, Nea Ankhialos
	065	Lockheed Martin F-16C-50 Fighting Falcon	HAF 347 Mira/111 PM, Nea Ankhialos
	066	Lockheed Martin F-16C-50 Fighting Falcon	HAF 341 Mira/111 PM, Nea Ankhialos
	067	Lockheed Martin F-16C-50 Fighting Falcon	HAF 347 Mira/111 PM, Nea Ankhialos
	068	Lockheed Martin F-16C-50 Fighting Falcon	HAF 341 Mira/111 PM, Nea Ankhialos
	069	Lockheed Martin F-16C-50 Fighting Falcon	HAF 347 Mira/111 PM, Nea Ankhialos
	070	Lockheed Martin F-16C-50 Fighting Falcon $	HAF 341 Mira/111 PM, Nea Ankhialos
	071	Lockheed Martin F-16C-50 Fighting Falcon	HAF 347 Mira/111 PM, Nea Ankhialos
	072	Lockheed Martin F-16C-50 Fighting Falcon	HAF 341 Mira/111 PM, Nea Ankhialos
	073	Lockheed Martin F-16C-50 Fighting Falcon	HAF 347 Mira/111 PM, Nea Ankhialos
	074	Lockheed Martin F-16C-50 Fighting Falcon	HAF 341 Mira/111 PM, Nea Ankhialos
	075	Lockheed Martin F-16C-50 Fighting Falcon	HAF 347 Mira/111 PM, Nea Ankhialos
	076	Lockheed Martin F-16C-50 Fighting Falcon $	HAF 341 Mira/111 PM, Nea Ankhialos
	077	Lockheed Martin F-16D-50 Fighting Falcon	HAF 341 Mira/111 PM, Nea Ankhialos
	078	Lockheed Martin F-16D-50 Fighting Falcon	HAF 347 Mira/111 PM, Nea Ankhialos
	079	Lockheed Martin F-16D-50 Fighting Falcon	HAF 347 Mira/111 PM, Nea Ankhialos
	080	Lockheed Martin F-16D-50 Fighting Falcon	HAF 341 Mira/111 PM, Nea Ankhialos
	081	Lockheed Martin F-16D-50 Fighting Falcon	HAF 347 Mira/111 PM, Nea Ankhialos
	082	Lockheed Martin F-16D-50 Fighting Falcon	HAF 341 Mira/111 PM, Nea Ankhialos

Serial	Type (code/other identity)	Owner/operator, location or fate	Notes
083	Lockheed Martin F-16D-50 Fighting Falcon	HAF 347 Mira/111 PM, Nea Ankhialos	
110	Lockheed Martin F-16C-30 Fighting Falcon	HAF 330 Mira/111 PM, Nea Ankhialos	
111	Lockheed Martin F-16C-30 Fighting Falcon	HAF 330 Mira/111 PM, Nea Ankhialos	
112	Lockheed Martin F-16C-30 Fighting Falcon	HAF 330 Mira/111 PM, Nea Ankhialos	
113	Lockheed Martin F-16C-30 Fighting Falcon	HAF 330 Mira/111 PM, Nea Ankhialos	
114	Lockheed Martin F-16C-30 Fighting Falcon	HAF 330 Mira/111 PM, Nea Ankhialos	
115	Lockheed Martin F-16C-30 Fighting Falcon	HAF 330 Mira/111 PM, Nea Ankhialos	
116	Lockheed Martin F-16C-30 Fighting Falcon	HAF 330 Mira/111 PM, Nea Ankhialos	
117	Lockheed Martin F-16C-30 Fighting Falcon	HAF 330 Mira/111 PM, Nea Ankhialos	
118	Lockheed Martin F-16C-30 Fighting Falcon	HAF 330 Mira/111 PM, Nea Ankhialos	
119	Lockheed Martin F-16C-30 Fighting Falcon	HAF 330 Mira/111 PM, Nea Ankhialos	
120	Lockheed Martin F-16C-30 Fighting Falcon	HAF 330 Mira/111 PM, Nea Ankhialos	
121	Lockheed Martin F-16C-30 Fighting Falcon	HAF 330 Mira/111 PM, Nea Ankhialos	
122	Lockheed Martin F-16C-30 Fighting Falcon	HAF 330 Mira/111 PM, Nea Ankhialos	
124	Lockheed Martin F-16C-30 Fighting Falcon	HAF 330 Mira/111 PM, Nea Ankhialos	
125	Lockheed Martin F-16C-30 Fighting Falcon	HAF 330 Mira/111 PM, Nea Ankhialos	
126	Lockheed Martin F-16C-30 Fighting Falcon	HAF 330 Mira/111 PM, Nea Ankhialos	
127	Lockheed Martin F-16C-30 Fighting Falcon	HAF 330 Mira/111 PM, Nea Ankhialos	
128	Lockheed Martin F-16C-30 Fighting Falcon	HAF 330 Mira/111 PM, Nea Ankhialos	
129	Lockheed Martin F-16C-30 Fighting Falcon	HAF 330 Mira/111 PM, Nea Ankhialos	
130	Lockheed Martin F-16C-30 Fighting Falcon	HAF 330 Mira/111 PM, Nea Ankhialos	
132	Lockheed Martin F-16C-30 Fighting Falcon	HAF 330 Mira/111 PM, Nea Ankhialos	
133	Lockheed Martin F-16C-30 Fighting Falcon	HAF 330 Mira/111 PM, Nea Ankhialos	
134	Lockheed Martin F-16C-30 Fighting Falcon	HAF 330 Mira/111 PM, Nea Ankhialos	
136	Lockheed Martin F-16C-30 Fighting Falcon	HAF 330 Mira/111 PM, Nea Ankhialos	
138	Lockheed Martin F-16C-30 Fighting Falcon	HAF 330 Mira/111 PM, Nea Ankhialos	
139	Lockheed Martin F-16C-30 Fighting Falcon	HAF 330 Mira/111 PM, Nea Ankhialos	
140	Lockheed Martin F-16C-30 Fighting Falcon	HAF 330 Mira/111 PM, Nea Ankhialos	
141	Lockheed Martin F-16C-30 Fighting Falcon	HAF 330 Mira/111 PM, Nea Ankhialos	
143	Lockheed Martin F-16C-30 Fighting Falcon	HAF 330 Mira/111 PM, Nea Ankhialos	
144	Lockheed Martin F-16D-30 Fighting Falcon	HAF 330 Mira/111 PM, Nea Ankhialos	
145	Lockheed Martin F-16D-30 Fighting Falcon	HAF 330 Mira/111 PM, Nea Ankhialos	
148	Lockheed Martin F-16D-30 Fighting Falcon	HAF 330 Mira/111 PM, Nea Ankhialos	
149	Lockheed Martin F-16D-30 Fighting Falcon	HAF 330 Mira/111 PM, Nea Ankhialos	
273	Dassault Falcon 7X (F-HHED)	HAF 352 MMYP/112 PM, Elefsís	
...	Dassault Rafale EG	HAF 332 MAPK/114 PM, Tanagra (on order)	
...	Dassault Rafale EG	HAF 332 MAPK/114 PM, Tanagra (on order)	
...	Dassault Rafale EG	HAF 332 MAPK/114 PM, Tanagra (on order)	
...	Dassault Rafale EG	HAF 332 MAPK/114 PM, Tanagra (on order)	
...	Dassault Rafale EG	HAF 332 MAPK/114 PM, Tanagra (on order)	
...	Dassault Rafale EG	HAF 332 MAPK/114 PM, Tanagra (on order)	
...	Dassault Rafale EG	HAF 332 MAPK/114 PM, Tanagra (on order)	
...	Dassault Rafale EG	HAF 332 MAPK/114 PM, Tanagra (on order)	
...	Dassault Rafale EG	HAF 332 MAPK/114 PM, Tanagra (on order)	
...	Dassault Rafale EG	HAF 332 MAPK/114 PM, Tanagra (on order)	
...	Dassault Rafale EG	HAF 332 MAPK/114 PM, Tanagra (on order)	
...	Dassault Rafale EG	HAF 332 MAPK/114 PM, Tanagra (on order)	
...	Dassault Rafale EG	HAF 332 MAPK/114 PM, Tanagra (on order)	
374	Embraer ERJ.145H AEW&C (SX-BKO)	HAF 380 Mira/112 PM, Elefsís	
401	Dassault Rafale DG (305)	HAF 332 MAPK/114 PM, Tanagra	
402	Dassault Rafale DG (306)	HAF 332 MAPK/114 PM, Tanagra	
...	Dassault Rafale DG	HAF 332 MAPK/114 PM, Tanagra (on order)	
...	Dassault Rafale DG	HAF 332 MAPK/114 PM, Tanagra (on order)	
410	Dassault Rafale EG (103)	HAF 332 MAPK/114 PM, Tanagra	
411	Dassault Rafale EG (118)	HAF 332 MAPK/114 PM, Tanagra	
412	Dassault Rafale EG (123)	HAF 332 MAPK/114 PM, Tanagra	
413	Dassault Rafale EG (112)	HAF 332 MAPK/114 PM, Tanagra	
414	Dassault Rafale EG (111)	HAF 332 MAPK/114 PM, Tanagra	
415	Dassault Rafale EG (143)	HAF 332 MAPK/114 PM, Tanagra	
416	Dassault Rafale EG (134)	HAF 332 MAPK/114 PM, Tanagra	
417	Dassault Rafale EG (120)	HAF 332 MAPK/114 PM, Tanagra	

Notes	Serial	Type (code/other identity)	Owner/operator, location or fate
	418	Dassault Rafale EG (137)	HAF 332 MAPK/114 PM, Tanagra
	419	Dassault Rafale EG (128)	HAF 332 MAPK/114 PM, Tanagra
	441	Dassault Rafale DG	HAF 332 MAPK/114 PM, Tanagra
	442	Dassault Rafale DG	HAF 332 MAPK/114 PM, Tanagra
	450	Dassault Rafale EG	HAF 332 MAPK/114 PM, Tanagra
	451	Dassault Rafale EG $	HAF 332 MAPK/114 PM, Tanagra
	452	Dassault Rafale EG	HAF 332 MAPK/114 PM, Tanagra
	453	Dassault Rafale EG	HAF 332 MAPK/114 PM, Tanagra
	454	Dassault Rafale EG	HAF 332 MAPK/114 PM, Tanagra
	455	Dassault Rafale EG	HAF 332 MAPK/114 PM, Tanagra
	456	Dassault Rafale EG	HAF 332 MAPK/114 PM, Tanagra
	457	Dassault Rafale EG	HAF 332 MAPK/114 PM, Tanagra
	500	Lockheed Martin F-16C-52 Fighting Falcon	HAF 343 Mira/115 PM, Souda
	501	Lockheed Martin F-16C-52 Fighting Falcon	HAF 337 Mira/110 PM, Larissa
	502	Lockheed Martin F-16C-52 Fighting Falcon	HAF 337 Mira/110 PM, Larissa
	503	Lockheed Martin F-16C-52 Fighting Falcon	HAF 343 Mira/115 PM, Souda
	504	Lockheed Martin F-16C-52 Fighting Falcon	HAF 343 Mira/115 PM, Souda
	505	Lockheed Martin F-16V-72 Fighting Falcon $	HAF 343 Mira/115 PM, Souda
	506	Lockheed Martin F-16C-52 Fighting Falcon	HAF 343 Mira/115 PM, Souda
	507	Lockheed Martin F-16V-72 Fighting Falcon	HAF 343 Mira/115 PM, Souda
	508	Lockheed Martin F-16V-72 Fighting Falcon	HAF 343 Mira/115 PM, Souda
	509	Lockheed Martin F-16V-72 Fighting Falcon	HAF 343 Mira/115 PM, Souda
	510	Lockheed Martin F-16C-52 Fighting Falcon	HAF 343 Mira/115 PM, Souda
	511	Lockheed Martin F-16C-52 Fighting Falcon	HAF 343 Mira/115 PM, Souda
	515	Lockheed Martin F-16C-52 Fighting Falcon	HAF 337 Mira/110 PM, Larissa
	517	Lockheed Martin F-16C-52 Fighting Falcon	HAF 337 Mira/110 PM, Larissa
	518	Lockheed Martin F-16C-52 Fighting Falcon	HAF 340 Mira/115 PM, Souda
	519	Lockheed Martin F-16C-52 Fighting Falcon	HAF 340 Mira/115 PM, Souda
	520	Lockheed Martin F-16C-52 Fighting Falcon	HAF 340 Mira/115 PM, Souda
	521	Lockheed Martin F-16C-52 Fighting Falcon	HAF 340 Mira/115 PM, Souda
	523	Lockheed Martin F-16C-52 Fighting Falcon $	HAF 340 Mira/115 PM, Souda
	524	Lockheed Martin F-16C-52 Fighting Falcon	HAF 337 Mira/110 PM, Larissa
	525	Lockheed Martin F-16C-52 Fighting Falcon	HAF 343 Mira/115 PM, Souda
	526	Lockheed Martin F-16C-52 Fighting Falcon	HAF 340 Mira/115 PM, Souda
	527	Lockheed Martin F-16V-72 Fighting Falcon	HAF 343 Mira/115 PM, Souda
	528	Lockheed Martin F-16C-52 Fighting Falcon	*Crashed off Psathoura, Aegean Sea, 20th Mar 2024*
	529	Lockheed Martin F-16C-52 Fighting Falcon	HAF 343 Mira/115 PM, Souda
	530	Lockheed Martin F-16C-52 Fighting Falcon	HAF 337 Mira/110 PM, Larissa
	531	Lockheed Martin F-16C-52 Fighting Falcon $	HAF 337 Mira/110 PM, Larissa
	532	Lockheed Martin F-16C-52 Fighting Falcon	HAF 337 Mira/110 PM, Larissa
	533	Lockheed Martin F-16C-52 Fighting Falcon	HAF 340 Mira/115 PM, Souda
	534	Lockheed Martin F-16C-52 Fighting Falcon	HAF 340 Mira/115 PM, Souda
	535	Lockheed Martin F-16C-52 Fighting Falcon	HAF 340 Mira/115 PM, Souda
	536	Lockheed Martin F-16C-52 Fighting Falcon	HAF 340 Mira/115 PM, Souda
	537	Lockheed Martin F-16C-52 Fighting Falcon	HAF 340 Mira/115 PM, Souda
	538	Lockheed Martin F-16C-52 Fighting Falcon	HAF 340 Mira/115 PM, Souda
	539	Lockheed Martin F-16C-52 Fighting Falcon	HAF 337 Mira/110 PM, Larissa
	600	Lockheed Martin F-16D-52 Fighting Falcon	HAF 337 Mira/110 PM, Larissa
	601	Lockheed Martin F-16D-52 Fighting Falcon	HAF 340 Mira/115 PM, Souda
	602	Lockheed Martin F-16D-52 Fighting Falcon	HAF 340 Mira/115 PM, Souda
	603	Lockheed Martin F-16D-52 Fighting Falcon	HAF 340 Mira/115 PM, Souda
	605	Lockheed Martin F-16D-52 Fighting Falcon	HAF 340 Mira/115 PM, Souda
	606	Lockheed Martin F-16D-52 Fighting Falcon	HAF 337 Mira/110 PM, Larissa
	607	Lockheed Martin F-16D-52 Fighting Falcon	HAF 343 Mira/115 PM, Souda
	608	Lockheed Martin F-16D-52 Fighting Falcon	HAF 340 Mira/115 PM, Souda
	609	Lockheed Martin F-16D-52 Fighting Falcon	HAF 340 Mira/115 PM, Souda
	610	Lockheed Martin F-16D-52 Fighting Falcon	HAF 340 Mira/115 PM, Souda
	611	Lockheed Martin F-16D-52 Fighting Falcon	HAF 337 Mira/110 PM, Larissa
	612	Lockheed Martin F-16D-52 Fighting Falcon	HAF 337 Mira/110 PM, Larissa
	613	Lockheed Martin F-16D-52 Fighting Falcon	HAF 343 Mira/115 PM, Souda
	614	Lockheed Martin F-16D-52 Fighting Falcon	HAF 343 Mira/115 PM, Souda
	615	Lockheed Martin F-16D-52 Fighting Falcon	HAF 343 Mira/115 PM, Souda

Serial	Type (code/other identity)	Owner/operator, location or fate	Notes
616	Lockheed Martin F-16D-52 Fighting Falcon	HAF 343 Mira/115 PM, Souda	
617	Lockheed Martin F-16D-52 Fighting Falcon	HAF 343 Mira/115 PM, Souda	
618	Lockheed Martin F-16D-52 Fighting Falcon	HAF 343 Mira/115 PM, Souda	
619	Lockheed Martin F-16D-52 Fighting Falcon $	HAF 337 Mira/110 PM, Larissa	
671	Embraer ERJ.145H AEW&C	HAF 380 Mira/112 PM, Elefsís	
678	Gulfstream Aerospace Gulfstream V	HAF 352 MMYP/112 PM, Elefsís	
729	Embraer ERJ.145H AEW&C	HAF 380 Mira/112 PM, Elefsís	
741	Lockheed C-130H Hercules	HAF 356 MTM/112 PM, Elefsís	
742	Lockheed C-130H Hercules	HAF, stored Tanagra	
743	Lockheed C-130H Hercules	HAF, stored Tanagra	
744	Lockheed C-130H Hercules	HAF, stored Tanagra	
745	Lockheed C-130H Hercules $	HAF, stored Tanagra	
746	Lockheed C-130H Hercules	HAF, stored Tanagra	
747	Lockheed C-130H Hercules	HAF 356 MTM/112 PM, Elefsís	
749	Lockheed C-130H Hercules	HAF, stored Tanagra	
751	Lockheed C-130H Hercules	HAF 356 MTM/112 PM, Elefsís	
752	Lockheed C-130H Hercules $	HAF 356 MTM/112 PM, Elefsís	
757	Embraer ERJ.145H AEW&C	HAF 380 Mira/112 PM, Elefsís	
4117	Aeritalia C-27J Spartan $	HAF 354 Mira, Elefsís	
4118	Aeritalia C-27J Spartan	HAF 354 Mira, Elefsís	
4120	Aeritalia C-27J Spartan	HAF 354 Mira, Elefsís	
4121	Aeritalia C-27J Spartan	HAF 354 Mira, Elefsís	
4122	Aeritalia C-27J Spartan	HAF 354 Mira, Elefsís	
4123	Aeritalia C-27J Spartan	HAF 354 Mira, Elefsís	
4124	Aeritalia C-27J Spartan	HAF 354 Mira, Elefsís	
4125	Aeritalia C-27J Spartan	HAF 354 Mira, Elefsís	
145-209	Embraer ERJ.135LR	HAF 352 MMYP/112 PM, Elefsís	

HONDURAS
Fuerza Aérea Hondureña (FAH)/Honduran Air Force

FAH-001	Embraer ERJ.135BJ Legacy 600	FAH, Tegucigalpa	

HUNGARY
Magyar Légierö/Hungarian Air Force

01	Boeing C-17A Globemaster III (08-0001)	NATO SAC, Heavy Airlift Wing, Pápa	
02	Boeing C-17A Globemaster III (08-0002)	NATO SAC, Heavy Airlift Wing, Pápa	
03	Boeing C-17A Globemaster III (08-0003)	NATO SAC, Heavy Airlift Wing, Pápa	
30	SAAB JAS 39C Gripen	Hungarian AF 101 Sz.D.REB, Kecskemét	
31	SAAB JAS 39C Gripen	Hungarian AF 101 Sz.D.REB, Kecskemét	
32	SAAB JAS 39C Gripen	Hungarian AF 101 Sz.D.REB, Kecskemét	
33	SAAB JAS 39C Gripen	Hungarian AF 101 Sz.D.REB, Kecskemét	
34	SAAB JAS 39C Gripen	Hungarian AF 101 Sz.D.REB, Kecskemét	
35	SAAB JAS 39C Gripen	Hungarian AF 101 Sz.D.REB, Kecskemét	
36	SAAB JAS 39C Gripen	Hungarian AF 101 Sz.D.REB, Kecskemét	
37	SAAB JAS 39C Gripen	Hungarian AF 101 Sz.D.REB, Kecskemét	
38	SAAB JAS 39C Gripen	Hungarian AF 101 Sz.D.REB, Kecskemét	
39	SAAB JAS 39C Gripen	Hungarian AF 101 Sz.D.REB, Kecskemét	
40	SAAB JAS 39C Gripen	Hungarian AF 101 Sz.D.REB, Kecskemét	
41	SAAB JAS 39C Gripen	Hungarian AF 101 Sz.D.REB, Kecskemét	
43	SAAB JAS 39D Gripen	Hungarian AF 101 Sz.D.REB, Kecskemét	
44	SAAB JAS 39D Gripen (39842)	Hungarian AF 101 Sz.D.REB, Kecskemét	
604	Airbus A.319-112 (9H-AGM)	Hungarian AF 101 Sz.D.REB, Kecskemét	
605	Airbus A.319-112 (9H-AGN)	Hungarian AF 101 Sz.D.REB, Kecskemét	
606	Dassault Falcon 7X (9H-AGO)	Hungarian AF 101 Sz.D.REB, Kecskemét	
607	Dassault Falcon 7X (HA-LKX)	Hungarian AF 101 Sz.D.REB, Kecskemét	
610	Embraer KC-390 (PT-ZHP)	Hungarian AF 101 Sz.D.REB, Kecskemét	
...	Embraer KC-390	Hungarian AF (on order)	

INDIA
Bharatiya Vayu Sena/Indian Air Force (IAF)

CB-8001	Boeing C-17A Globemaster III (11-0101)	IAF 81 Sqn, Hindon AB	
CB-8002	Boeing C-17A Globemaster III (11-0102)	IAF 81 Sqn, Hindon AB	

Notes	Serial	Type (code/other identity)	Owner/operator, location or fate
	CB-8003	Boeing C-17A Globemaster III (11-0103)	IAF 81 Sqn, Hindon AB
	CB-8004	Boeing C-17A Globemaster III (11-0104)	IAF 81 Sqn, Hindon AB
	CB-8005	Boeing C-17A Globemaster III (11-0105)	IAF 81 Sqn, Hindon AB
	CB-8006	Boeing C-17A Globemaster III (11-0106)	IAF 81 Sqn, Hindon AB
	CB-8007	Boeing C-17A Globemaster III (11-0107)	IAF 81 Sqn, Hindon AB
	CB-8008	Boeing C-17A Globemaster III (11-0108)	IAF 81 Sqn, Hindon AB
	CB-8009	Boeing C-17A Globemaster III (11-0109)	IAF 81 Sqn, Hindon AB
	CB-8010	Boeing C-17A Globemaster III (11-0110)	IAF 81 Sqn, Hindon AB
	CB-8011	Boeing C-17A Globemaster III (14-0003)	IAF 81 Sqn, Hindon AB
	KC-3801	Lockheed C-130J-30 Hercules II	IAF 77 Sqn, Hindon AB
	KC-3802	Lockheed C-130J-30 Hercules II	IAF 77 Sqn, Hindon AB
	KC-3804	Lockheed C-130J-30 Hercules II	IAF 77 Sqn, Hindon AB
	KC-3805	Lockheed C-130J-30 Hercules II	IAF 77 Sqn, Hindon AB
	KC-3806	Lockheed C-130J-30 Hercules II	IAF 77 Sqn, Hindon AB
	KC-3807	Lockheed C-130J-30 Hercules II	IAF 87 Sqn, Arjan Singh AB
	KC-3808	Lockheed C-130J-30 Hercules II	IAF 87 Sqn, Arjan Singh AB
	KC-3809	Lockheed C-130J-30 Hercules II	IAF 87 Sqn, Arjan Singh AB
	KC-3810	Lockheed C-130J-30 Hercules II	IAF 87 Sqn, Arjan Singh AB
	KC-3811	Lockheed C-130J-30 Hercules II	IAF 87 Sqn, Arjan Singh AB
	KC-3812	Lockheed C-130J-30 Hercules II	IAF 87 Sqn, Arjan Singh AB
	KC-3813	Lockheed C-130J-30 Hercules II	IAF 77 Sqn, Hindon AB
Indian Government			
	K-7066	Boeing 777-337ER (VT-ALV)	Indian Government, New Delhi
	K-7067	Boeing 777-337ER (VT-ALW)	Indian Government, New Delhi
INDONESIA			
Indonesian Government			
	A-001	Boeing 737-8U3	Government of Indonesia, Jakarta
IRAQ			
Iraqi Government			
	YI-ASF	Boeing 737-81Z	Government of Iraq, Baghdad
ISRAEL			
Heyl ha'Avir/Israeli Air Force			
	102	Lockheed C-130HI Karnaf	Israeli AF 131 Sqn, Nevatim
	250	Boeing KC-707 Re'em	Israeli AF 120 Sqn, Nevatim
	260	Boeing KC-707 Re'em	Israeli AF 120 Sqn, Nevatim
	264	Boeing KC-707 Re'em	Israeli AF 120 Sqn, Nevatim
	272	Boeing KC-707 Re'em	Israeli AF 120 Sqn, Nevatim
	275	Boeing KC-707 Re'em	Israeli AF 120 Sqn, Nevatim
	290	Boeing KC-707 Re'em	Israeli AF 120 Sqn, Nevatim
	295	Boeing KC-707 Re'em	Israeli AF 120 Sqn, Nevatim
	420	Lockheed KC-130HI Karnaf	Israeli AF 131 Sqn, Nevatim
	427	Lockheed C-130HI Karnaf	Israeli AF 131 Sqn, Nevatim
	428	Lockheed C-130HI Karnaf	Israeli AF 131 Sqn, Nevatim
	435	Lockheed C-130HI Karnaf	Israeli AF 131 Sqn, Nevatim
	436	Lockheed KC-130HI Karnaf	Israeli AF 131 Sqn, Nevatim
	522	Lockheed KC-130HI Karnaf	Israeli AF 131 Sqn, Nevatim
	545	Lockheed KC-130HI Karnaf	Israeli AF 131 Sqn, Nevatim
	661	Lockheed C-130J-30 Shimshon	Israeli AF 103 Sqn, Nevatim
	662	Lockheed C-130J-30 Shimshon	Israeli AF 103 Sqn, Nevatim
	663	Lockheed C-130J-30 Shimshon	Israeli AF 103 Sqn, Nevatim
	665	Lockheed C-130J-30 Shimshon	Israeli AF 103 Sqn, Nevatim
	667	Lockheed C-130J-30 Shimshon	Israeli AF 103 Sqn, Nevatim
	668	Lockheed C-130J-30 Shimshon	Israeli AF 103 Sqn, Nevatim
	669	Lockheed C-130J-30 Shimshon	Israeli AF 103 Sqn, Nevatim
	...	Boeing KC-46A Pegasus	Israeli AF (on order)
	...	Boeing KC-46A Pegasus	Israeli AF (on order)
	...	Boeing KC-46A Pegasus	Israeli AF (on order)
	...	Boeing KC-46A Pegasus	Israeli AF (on order)
	...	Boeing KC-46A Pegasus	Israeli AF (on order)

Serial	Type (code/other identity)	Owner/operator, location or fate	Notes
...	Boeing KC-46A Pegasus	Israeli AF (on order)	
...	Boeing KC-46A Pegasus	Israeli AF (on order)	
...	Boeing KC-46A Pegasus	Israeli AF (on order)	
Israeli Government			
4X-ISR	Boeing 767-338ER	Israeli AF/State of Israel, Tel Aviv	
ITALY			
Aeronautica Militare Italiana (AMI), Aviazione dell'Esercito, Guardia di Finanza (GdiF) & Marina Militare Italiana (MMI)			
CPX614	Eurofighter TF-2000A Typhoon	Alenia, Torino/Caselle	
CPX622	Aermacchi M-346FA	Leonardo, Venegono	
CPX624	Aermacchi T-345A	Leonardo, Venegono	
CPX625	Aermacchi M-346LFFA	Leonardo, Venegono	
MM7004	Panavia A-200C Tornado (IDS (MLU)) [6-55]	AMI GEA 6° Stormo, Ghedi	
MM7006	Panavia A-200C Tornado (IDS (MLU)) [6-31] $	Scrapped Ghedi	
MM7008	Panavia A-200C Tornado (IDS (MLU)) [50-53]	AMI, stored Ghedi	
MM7013	Panavia A-200C Tornado (IDS (MLU)) [6-75]	AMI GEA 6° Stormo, Ghedi	
MM7014	Panavia A-200C Tornado (IDS (MLU)) [6-13]	AMI GEA 6° Stormo, Ghedi	
MM7015	Panavia A-200C Tornado (IDS (MLU)) [6-32]	Scrapped Ghedi	
MM7019	Panavia EA-200B Tornado (ECR) [6-02]	AMI GEA 6° Stormo, Ghedi	
MM7020	Panavia EA-200D Tornado (ECR (MLU)) [6-77]	AMI GEA 6° Stormo, Ghedi	
MM7021	Panavia EA-200B Tornado (ECR) [6-20]	AMI GEA 6° Stormo, Ghedi	
MM7024	Panavia A-200C Tornado (IDS (MLU)) [6-50]	AMI GEA 6° Stormo, Ghedi	
MM7025	Panavia A-200A Tornado (IDS) [6-05]	AMI, stored Ghedi	
MM7029	Panavia A-200A Tornado (IDS) [6-22]	AMI GEA 6° Stormo, Ghedi	
MM7030	Panavia EA-200D Tornado (ECR (MLU)) [6-73]	AMI GEA 6° Stormo, Ghedi	
MM7036	Panavia EA-200D Tornado (ECR MLU) [6-06]	AMI GEA 6° Stormo, Ghedi	
MM7038	Panavia A-200C Tornado (IDS (MLU)) [6-37]	AMI GEA 6° Stormo, Ghedi	
MM7039	Panavia EA-200D Tornado (IDS (MLU)) [6-33]	AMI GEA 6° Stormo, Ghedi	
MM7040	Panavia A-200C Tornado (IDS (MLU)) [6-21]	AMI GEA 6° Stormo, Ghedi	
MM7043	Panavia A-200A Tornado (IDS) [6-25]	Scrapped Ghedi	
MM7044	Panavia A-200C Tornado (IDS (MLU)) [6-76]	AMI GEA 6° Stormo, Ghedi	
MM7047	Panavia EA-200D Tornado (ECR (MLU)) [6-61]	AMI GEA 6° Stormo, Ghedi	
MM7051	Panavia EA-200D Tornado (ECR (MLU)) [6-72] $	AMI GEA 6° Stormo, Ghedi	
MM7052	Panavia EA-200D Tornado (ECR (MLU)) [6-64]	AMI GEA 6° Stormo, Ghedi	
MM7053	Panavia EA-200D Tornado (ECR (MLU)) [6-101]	AMI GEA 6° Stormo, Ghedi	
MM7054	Panavia EA-200D Tornado (ECR (MLU)) [6-100] $	AMI GEA 6° Stormo, Ghedi	
MM7055	Panavia EA-200D Tornado (ECR (MLU)) [6-65]	AMI GEA 6° Stormo, Ghedi	
MM7056	Panavia A-200A Tornado (IDS)	Scrapped Ghedi	
MM7057	Panavia A-200C Tornado (IDS (MLU)) [6-04]	AMI GEA 6° Stormo, Ghedi	
MM7058	Panavia A-200C Tornado (IDS (MLU)) [6-11]	Scrapped Ghedi	
MM7059	Panavia EA-200D Tornado (ECR (MLU)) [6-66] $	AMI GEA 6° Stormo, Ghedi	
MM7062	Panavia EA-200D Tornado (ECR (MLU)) [6-74]	AMI GEA 6° Stormo, Ghedi	
MM7063	Panavia A-200C Tornado (IDS (MLU)) [6-26]	Scrapped Ghedi	
MM7064	Panavia A-200C Tornado (IDS (MLU)) [6-24]	AMI GEA 6° Stormo, Ghedi	
MM7066	Panavia EA-200D Tornado (ECR (MLU)) [6-43]	AMI GEA 6° Stormo, Ghedi	
MM7067	Panavia EA-200D Tornado (ECR (MLU)) [6-41] $	AMI GEA 6° Stormo, Ghedi	
MM7068	Panavia EA-200D Tornado (ECR (MLU)) [6-67]	AMI GEA 6° Stormo, Ghedi	
MM7070	Panavia EA-200D Tornado (ECR (MLU)) [6-71]	AMI GEA 6° Stormo, Ghedi	
MM7073	Panavia EA-200D Tornado (ECR (MLU)) [6-34]	AMI GEA 6° Stormo, Ghedi	
MM7075	Panavia A-200C Tornado (IDS (MLU)) [6-07]	AMI GEA 6° Stormo, Ghedi	
CSX7079	Panavia EA-200D Tornado (ECR (MLU)) [RS-01]	AMI RSV, Pratica di Mare	
MM7081	Panavia EA-200D Tornado (ECR (MLU)) [6-57]	AMI GEA 6° Stormo, Ghedi	
MM7082	Panavia EA-200D Tornado (ECR (MLU)) [6-62]	AMI GEA 6° Stormo, Ghedi	
MM7084	Panavia EA-200D Tornado (ECR (MLU)) [6-03]	AMI GEA 6° Stormo, Ghedi	
CMX7085	Panavia A-200A Tornado (IDS) [36-50]	Alenia, dumped Torino/Caselle	
MM7086	Panavia A-200A Tornado (IDS) [6-60]	AMI GEA 6° Stormo, Ghedi	
MM7114	Aeritalia-EMB A-11B Ghibli (AMX-ACOL) [51-27] $	AMI, withdrawn from use, Istrana	
MM7126	Aeritalia-EMB A-11B Ghibli (AMX-ACOL) [51-61]	AMI, withdrawn from use, Istrana	
MM7129	Aeritalia-EMB A-11B Ghibli (AMX-ACOL) [32-15]	AMI, stored Amendola	
MM7149	Aeritalia-EMB A-11B Ghibli (AMX-ACOL) [51-26]	AMI, withdrawn from use, Istrana	
MM7160	Aeritalia-EMB A-11B Ghibli (AMX-ACOL) [32-10]	AMI, withdrawn from use, Amendola	
MM7161	Aeritalia-EMB A-11B Ghibli (AMX-ACOL) [51-31]	AMI, withdrawn from use, Istrana	

Notes	Serial	Type (code/other identity)	Owner/operator, location or fate
	MM7162	Aeritalia-EMB A-11B Ghibli (AMX-ACOL) [51-33]	*AMI, preserved Piacenza*
	MM7163	Aeritalia-EMB A-11B Ghibli (AMX-ACOL) [51-72] $	*AMI, withdrawn from use, Istrana*
	MM7164	Aeritalia-EMB A-11B Ghibli (AMX-ACOL) [51-40]	*AMI, preserved Viterbo*
	MM7165	Aeritalia-EMB A-11B Ghibli (AMX-ACOL) [32-16]	*AMI, stored Amendola*
	MM7166	Aeritalia-EMB A-11B Ghibli (AMX-ACOL) [51-32]	*AMI, withdrawn from use, Istrana*
	MM7167	Aeritalia-EMB A-11B Ghibli (AMX-ACOL) [51-56]	*AMI, withdrawn from use, Istrana*
	MM7168	Aeritalia-EMB A-11B Ghibli (AMX-ACOL) [51-55]	*AMI, instructional airframe, Grazzanise*
	MM7169	Aeritalia-EMB A-11B Ghibli (AMX-ACOL) [51-66]	*AMI, withdrawn from use, Istrana*
	MM7170	Aeritalia-EMB A-11B Ghibli (AMX-ACOL) [51-30]	*AMI, withdrawn from use, Istrana*
	MM7171	Aeritalia-EMB A-11B Ghibli (AMX-ACOL) [51-52]	*AMI, dumped Istrana*
	MM7172	Aeritalia-EMB A-11B Ghibli (AMX-ACOL) [51-67]	*AMI, withdrawn from use, Istrana*
	MM7174	Aeritalia-EMB A-11B Ghibli (AMX-ACOL) [51-60]	*AMI, withdrawn from use, Istrana*
	MM7175	Aeritalia-EMB A-11B Ghibli (AMX-ACOL) [51-45]	*AMI, withdrawn from use, Istrana*
	MM7176	Aeritalia-EMB A-11B Ghibli (AMX-ACOL) [51-47]	*AMI, withdrawn from use, Istrana*
	MM7177	Aeritalia-EMB A-11B Ghibli (AMX-ACOL) [51-42]	*AMI, withdrawn from use, Istrana*
	MM7180	Aeritalia-EMB A-11B Ghibli (AMX-ACOL) [51-53] $	*AMI, withdrawn from use, Istrana*
	MM7182	Aeritalia-EMB A-11B Ghibli (AMX-ACOL) [51-62]	*AMI, withdrawn from use, Istrana*
	MM7183	Aeritalia-EMB A-11B Ghibli (AMX-ACOL) [51-41]	*AMI, withdrawn from use, Istrana*
	MM7184	Aeritalia-EMB A-11B Ghibli (AMX-ACOL) [51-65]	*AMI, withdrawn from use, Istrana*
	MM7185	Aeritalia-EMB A-11B Ghibli (AMX-ACOL) [51-36]	*AMI, withdrawn from use, Istrana*
	MM7186	Aeritalia-EMB A-11B Ghibli (AMX-ACOL) [51-50]	*AMI, withdrawn from use, Istrana*
	MM7189	Aeritalia-EMB A-11B Ghibli (AMX-ACOL) [51-71]	*AMI, withdrawn from use, Istrana*
	MM7190	Aeritalia-EMB A-11B Ghibli (AMX-ACOL) [51-57]	*AMI, withdrawn from use, Istrana*
	MM7191	Aeritalia-EMB A-11B Ghibli (AMX-ACOL) [51-34]	*AMI, withdrawn from use, Istrana*
	MM7192	Aeritalia-EMB A-11B Ghibli (AMX-ACOL) [51-70]	*AMI, withdrawn from use, Istrana*
	MM7194	Aeritalia-EMB A-11B Ghibli (AMX-ACOL) $	*AMI, withdrawn from use, Istrana*
	MM7196	Aeritalia-EMB A-11B Ghibli (AMX-ACOL) [51-35]	*AMI, withdrawn from use, Istrana*
	MM7197	Aeritalia-EMB A-11B Ghibli (AMX-ACOL) [51-46]	*AMI, preserved Piacenza*
	MM7198	Aeritalia-EMB A-11B Ghibli (AMX-ACOL) [51-44] $	*AMI, withdrawn from use, Istrana*
	MM7199	McDonnell Douglas AV-8B Harrier II+ [1-03]	MMI Gruppo Aerei Imbarcati, Taranto/Grottaglie
	MM7200	McDonnell Douglas AV-8B Harrier II+ [1-04] $	MMI Gruppo Aerei Imbarcati, Taranto/Grottaglie
	MM7201	McDonnell Douglas AV-8B Harrier II+ [1-05]	MMI Gruppo Aerei Imbarcati, Taranto/Grottaglie
	MM7213	McDonnell Douglas AV-8B Harrier II+ [1-07]	MMI Gruppo Aerei Imbarcati, Taranto/Grottaglie
	MM7214	McDonnell Douglas AV-8B Harrier II+ [1-08]	MMI Gruppo Aerei Imbarcati, Taranto/Grottaglie
	MM7215	McDonnell Douglas AV-8B Harrier II+ [1-09]	MMI, stored Taranto/Grottaglie
	MM7217	McDonnell Douglas AV-8B Harrier II+ [1-11]	MMI, stored Taranto/Grottaglie
	MM7218	McDonnell Douglas AV-8B Harrier II+ [1-12]	MMI Gruppo Aerei Imbarcati, Taranto/Grottaglie
	MM7219	McDonnell Douglas AV-8B Harrier II+ [1-13] $	MMI Gruppo Aerei Imbarcati, Taranto/Grottaglie
	MM7220	McDonnell Douglas AV-8B Harrier II+ [1-14]	MMI Gruppo Aerei Imbarcati, Taranto/Grottaglie
	MM7222	McDonnell Douglas AV-8B Harrier II+ [1-16]	MMI Gruppo Aerei Imbarcati, Taranto/Grottaglie
	MM7223	McDonnell Douglas AV-8B Harrier II+ [1-18] $	MMI Gruppo Aerei Imbarcati, Taranto/Grottaglie
	MM7224	McDonnell Douglas AV-8B Harrier II+ [1-19] $	MMI Gruppo Aerei Imbarcati, Taranto/Grottaglie
	MM7235	Eurofighter F-2000A Typhoon [4-13]	AMI 904° GEA/4° Stormo, Grosseto
	MM7270	Eurofighter F-2000A Typhoon [36-04]	AMI 936° GEA/36° Stormo, Gioia del Colle
	MM7271	Eurofighter F-2000A Typhoon [4-15]	AMI 904° GEA/4° Stormo, Grosseto
	MM7272	Eurofighter F-2000A Typhoon [4-18]	AMI 904° GEA/4° Stormo, Grosseto
	MM7273	Eurofighter F-2000A Typhoon [4-10]	AMI 904° GEA/4° Stormo, Grosseto
	MM7274	Eurofighter F-2000A Typhoon [36-06]	AMI 936° GEA/36° Stormo, Gioia del Colle
	MM7275	Eurofighter F-2000A Typhoon [36-05]	AMI 936° GEA/36° Stormo, Gioia del Colle
	MM7276	Eurofighter F-2000A Typhoon [4-4]	AMI 904° GEA/4° Stormo, Grosseto
	MM7277	Eurofighter F-2000A Typhoon [36-14]	AMI 936° GEA/36° Stormo, Gioia del Colle
	MM7279	Eurofighter F-2000A Typhoon [36-07]	AMI 936° GEA/36° Stormo, Gioia del Colle
	MM7280	Eurofighter F-2000A Typhoon [36-30]	AMI 936° GEA/36° Stormo, Gioia del Colle
	MM7281	Eurofighter F-2000A Typhoon [36-03]	AMI 936° GEA/36° Stormo, Gioia del Colle
	MM7282	Eurofighter F-2000A Typhoon [4-8]	AMI 904° GEA/4° Stormo, Grosseto
	MM7284	Eurofighter F-2000A Typhoon [36-15]	AMI 936° GEA/36° Stormo, Gioia del Colle
	MM7285	Eurofighter F-2000A Typhoon [4-16]	AMI 904° GEA/4° Stormo, Grosseto
	MM7286	Eurofighter F-2000A Typhoon [4-1]	AMI 904° GEA/4° Stormo, Grosseto
	MM7287	Eurofighter F-2000A Typhoon [4-3]	AMI 904° GEA/4° Stormo, Grosseto
	MM7288	Eurofighter F-2000A Typhoon [4-40]	AMI 904° GEA/4° Stormo, Grosseto
	MM7289	Eurofighter F-2000A Typhoon [4-5]	AMI 904° GEA/4° Stormo, Grosseto
	MM7290	Eurofighter F-2000A Typhoon [36-22]	AMI 936° GEA/36° Stormo, Gioia del Colle

Serial	Type (code/other identity)	Owner/operator, location or fate	Notes
MM7291	Eurofighter F-2000A Typhoon [4-41]	AMI 904° GEA/4° Stormo, Grosseto	
MM7292	Eurofighter F-2000A Typhoon [4-50]	AMI 904° GEA/4° Stormo, Grosseto	
MM7293	Eurofighter F-2000A Typhoon [37-22]	AMI 18° Gruppo/37° Stormo, Trapani/Birgi	
MM7294	Eurofighter F-2000A Typhoon [4-52]	AMI 904° GEA/4° Stormo, Grosseto	
MM7295	Eurofighter F-2000A Typhoon [51-95]	AMI 132° Gruppo/51° Stormo, Istrana	
MM7296	Eurofighter F-2000A Typhoon [51-96]	AMI 132° Gruppo/51° Stormo, Istrana	
MM7297	Eurofighter F-2000A Typhoon [36-23]	*Crashed Douglas Daly region, Australia, Jul 2024*	
MM7298	Eurofighter F-2000A Typhoon [51-98]	AMI 132° Gruppo/51° Stormo, Istrana	
MM7299	Eurofighter F-2000A Typhoon [51-99]	AMI 132° Gruppo/51° Stormo, Istrana	
MM7300	Eurofighter F-2000A Typhoon [37-40]	AMI 18° Gruppo/37° Stormo, Trapani/Birgi	
MM7301	Eurofighter F-2000A Typhoon [37-11]	AMI 18° Gruppo/37° Stormo, Trapani/Birgi	
MM7302	Eurofighter F-2000A Typhoon [36-10]	AMI 936° GEA/36° Stormo, Gioia del Colle	
MM7303	Eurofighter F-2000A Typhoon [4-53]	AMI 904° GEA/4° Stormo, Grosseto	
MM7304	Eurofighter F-2000A Typhoon [37-04]	AMI 18° Gruppo/37° Stormo, Trapani/Birgi	
CSX7305	Eurofighter F-2000A Typhoon	AMI 311° Gruppo/RSV, Pratica di Mare	
MM7306	Eurofighter F-2000A Typhoon [37-18]	AMI 18° Gruppo/37° Stormo, Trapani/Birgi	
MM7308	Eurofighter F-2000A Typhoon [51-08]	AMI 132° Gruppo/51° Stormo, Istrana	
MM7309	Eurofighter F-2000A Typhoon [51-09]	AMI 132° Gruppo/51° Stormo, Istrana	
MM7310	Eurofighter F-2000A Typhoon [37-09]	AMI 18° Gruppo/37° Stormo, Trapani/Birgi	
MM7311	Eurofighter F-2000A Typhoon [51-11]	AMI 132° Gruppo/51° Stormo, Istrana	
MM7312	Eurofighter F-2000A Typhoon [51-12]	AMI 132° Gruppo/51° Stormo, Istrana	
MM7313	Eurofighter F-2000A Typhoon [51-13]	AMI 132° Gruppo/51° Stormo, Istrana	
MM7314	Eurofighter F-2000A Typhoon [37-19]	AMI 18° Gruppo/37° Stormo, Trapani/Birgi	
MM7315	Eurofighter F-2000A Typhoon [36-46]	AMI 936° GEA/36° Stormo, Gioia del Colle	
MM7316	Eurofighter F-2000A Typhoon [4-42]	AMI 904° GEA/4° Stormo, Grosseto	
MM7317	Eurofighter F-2000A Typhoon [4-43]	AMI 904° GEA/4° Stormo, Grosseto	
MM7318	Eurofighter F-2000A Typhoon [37-35]	AMI 18° Gruppo/37° Stormo, Trapani/Birgi	
MM7319	Eurofighter F-2000A Typhoon [51-19]	AMI 132° Gruppo/51° Stormo, Istrana	
MM7320	Eurofighter F-2000A Typhoon [51-20]	AMI 132° Gruppo/51° Stormo, Istrana	
MM7321	Eurofighter F-2000A Typhoon [36-43]	AMI 936° GEA/36° Stormo, Gioia del Colle	
MM7322	Eurofighter F-2000A Typhoon [36-40]	AMI 936° GEA/36° Stormo, Gioia del Colle	
MM7323	Eurofighter F-2000A Typhoon [51-23]	AMI 132° Gruppo/51° Stormo, Istrana	
MM7324	Eurofighter F-2000A Typhoon [36-41] $	AMI 936° GEA/36° Stormo, Gioia del Colle	
MM7325	Eurofighter F-2000A Typhoon [36-44]	AMI 936° GEA/36° Stormo, Gioia del Colle	
MM7326	Eurofighter F-2000A Typhoon [4-46] $	AMI 904° GEA/4° Stormo, Grosseto	
MM7327	Eurofighter F-2000A Typhoon [36-42]	AMI 936° GEA/36° Stormo, Gioia del Colle	
MM7328	Eurofighter F-2000A Typhoon [37-14]	AMI 18° Gruppo/37° Stormo, Trapani/Birgi	
MM7329	Eurofighter F-2000A Typhoon [36-52]	AMI 936° GEA/36° Stormo, Gioia del Colle	
MM7330	Eurofighter F-2000A Typhoon [37-28]	AMI 18° Gruppo/37° Stormo, Trapani/Birgi	
MM7331	Eurofighter F-2000A Typhoon [36-47]	AMI 936° GEA/36° Stormo, Gioia del Colle	
MM7332	Lockheed Martin F-35A Lightning II [32-01]	AMI 62nd FS/56th FW, Luke AFB, AZ, USA	
MM7333	Lockheed Martin F-35A Lightning II [32-02]	AMI 62nd FS/56th FW, Luke AFB, AZ, USA	
MM7334	Lockheed Martin F-35A Lightning II [32-03]	AMI 62nd FS/56th FW, Luke AFB, AZ, USA	
MM7335	Lockheed Martin F-35A Lightning II [32-04]	AMI 62nd FS/56th FW, Luke AFB, AZ, USA	
MM7336	Lockheed Martin F-35A Lightning II [32-05] $	AMI 13° Gruppo/32° Stormo, Amendola	
MM7337	Lockheed Martin F-35A Lightning II [32-13] $	AMI 62nd FS/56th FW, Luke AFB, AZ, USA	
CSX7338	Eurofighter F-2000A Typhoon [4-60]	AMI 311° Gruppo/RSV, Pratica di Mare (on loan)	
MM7339	Eurofighter F-2000A Typhoon [51-39]	AMI 132° Gruppo/51° Stormo, Istrana	
MM7340	Eurofighter F-2000A Typhoon [4-64]	AMI 904° GEA/4° Stormo, Grosseto	
MM7341	Eurofighter F-2000A Typhoon [4-66]	AMI 904° GEA/4° Stormo, Grosseto	
MM7342	Eurofighter F-2000A Typhoon [4-68]	AMI 904° GEA/4° Stormo, Grosseto	
MM7343	Eurofighter F-2000A Typhoon [51-43]	AMI 132° Gruppo/51° Stormo, Istrana	
MM7344	Eurofighter F-2000A Typhoon [36-51]	AMI 936° GEA/36° Stormo, Gioia del Colle	
MM7345	Eurofighter F-2000A Typhoon [37-45]	AMI 18° Gruppo/37° Stormo, Trapani/Birgi	
MM7346	Eurofighter F-2000A Typhoon [51-46]	AMI 132° Gruppo/51° Stormo, Istrana	
MM7347	Eurofighter F-2000A Typhoon [37-08]	AMI 18° Gruppo/37° Stormo, Trapani/Birgi	
MM7348	Eurofighter F-2000A Typhoon [37-24]	AMI 18° Gruppo/37° Stormo, Trapani/Birgi	
MM7349	Eurofighter F-2000A Typhoon [4-51]	AMI 904° GEA/4° Stormo, Grosseto	
MM7350	Eurofighter F-2000A Typhoon [4-9]	AMI 904° GEA/4° Stormo, Grosseto	
MM7351	Eurofighter F-2000A Typhoon [37-36]	AMI 18° Gruppo/37° Stormo, Trapani/Birgi	
MM7352	Eurofighter F-2000A Typhoon [51-52]	AMI 132° Gruppo/51° Stormo, Istrana	
MM7353	Eurofighter F-2000A Typhoon [36-56]	AMI 936° GEA/36° Stormo, Gioia del Colle	

Notes	Serial	Type (code/other identity)	Owner/operator, location or fate
	MM7354	Eurofighter F-2000A Typhoon [37-54]	AMI 18° Gruppo/37° Stormo, Trapani/Birgi
	MM7355	Eurofighter F-2000A Typhoon [4-67]	AMI 904° GEA/4° Stormo, Grosseto
	MM7356	Eurofighter F-2000A Typhoon [51-56]	AMI 132° Gruppo/51° Stormo, Istrana
	MM7357	Lockheed Martin F-35A Lightning II [32-07]	AMI 62nd FS/56th FW, Luke AFB, AZ, USA
	MM7358	Lockheed Martin F-35A Lightning II [32-08]	AMI 62nd FS/56th FW, Luke AFB, AZ, USA
	MM7359	Lockheed Martin F-35A Lightning II [32-09]	AMI 13° Gruppo/32° Stormo, Amendola
	MM7360	Lockheed Martin F-35A Lightning II [32-10]	AMI 13° Gruppo/32° Stormo, Amendola
	MM7361	Lockheed Martin F-35A Lightning II [32-11]	AMI 13° Gruppo/32° Stormo, Amendola
	MM7362	Lockheed Martin F-35A Lightning II [32-12]	AMI 13° Gruppo/32° Stormo, Amendola
	MM7363	Lockheed Martin F-35A Lightning II [32-06]	AMI 13° Gruppo/32° Stormo, Amendola
	MM7364	Lockheed Martin F-35A Lightning II [32-15]	AMI 13° Gruppo/32° Stormo, Amendola
	MM7365	Lockheed Martin F-35A Lightning II [32-16]	AMI 13° Gruppo/32° Stormo, Amendola
	MM7366	Lockheed Martin F-35A Lightning II [6-01]	AMI 102° Gruppo/6° Stormo, Ghedi
	MM7367	Lockheed Martin F-35A Lightning II [6-02]	AMI 102° Gruppo/6° Stormo, Ghedi
	MM7368	Lockheed Martin F-35A Lightning II [6-03]	AMI 102° Gruppo/6° Stormo, Ghedi
	MM7369	Lockheed Martin F-35A Lightning II [6-04]	AMI 102° Gruppo/6° Stormo, Ghedi
	MM7370	Lockheed Martin F-35A Lightning II [6-05]	AMI 102° Gruppo/6° Stormo, Ghedi
	MM7371	Lockheed Martin F-35A Lightning II [6-06]	AMI 102° Gruppo/6° Stormo, Ghedi
	MM7372	Lockheed Martin F-35A Lightning II [6-07]	AMI 102° Gruppo/6° Stormo, Ghedi
	MM7373	Lockheed Martin F-35A Lightning II [32-19]	AMI 13° Gruppo/32° Stormo, Amendola
	MM7374	Lockheed Martin F-35A Lightning II [32-20]	AMI 13° Gruppo/32° Stormo, Amendola
	MM7375	Lockheed Martin F-35A Lightning II [32-21]	AMI (on order)
	MM7376	Lockheed Martin F-35A Lightning II [32-22]	AMI (on order)
	MM7377	Lockheed Martin F-35A Lightning II	AMI (on order)
	MM7378	Lockheed Martin F-35A Lightning II [32-23]	AMI (on order)
	MM7379	Lockheed Martin F-35A Lightning II [32-24]	AMI (on order)
	MM7451	Lockheed Martin F-35B Lightning II [4-01]	MMI Gruppo Aerei Imbarcarti, Amendola
	MM7452	Lockheed Martin F-35B Lightning II [4-02]	MMI Gruppo Aerei Imbarcarti, Amendola
	MM7453	Lockheed Martin F-35B Lightning II [32-14]	AMI 13° Gruppo/32° Stormo, Amendola
	MM7454	Lockheed Martin F-35B Lightning II [4-03]	MMI Gruppo Aerei Imbarcarti, Amendola
	MM7455	Lockheed Martin F-35B Lightning II [32-18]	AMI 13° Gruppo/32° Stormo, Amendola
	MM7456	Lockheed Martin F-35B Lightning II [4-04]	MMI Gruppo Aerei Imbarcarti, Amendola
	MM7457	Lockheed Martin F-35B Lightning II [4-05]	MMI Gruppo Aerei Imbarcarti, Amendola (on order)
	MM7458	Lockheed Martin F-35B Lightning II [4-06]	MMI Gruppo Aerei Imbarcarti, Amendola (on order)
	MM7...	Lockheed Martin F-35 Lightning II	AMI/MMI (on order)
	MM7...	Lockheed Martin F-35 Lightning II	AMI/MMI (on order)
	MM54456	Aermacchi T-339A (MB339A) [61-10]	*AMI, preserved Lecce*
	MM54457	Aermacchi T-339A (MB339A(MLU)) [61-11]	*AMI, stored Lecce (no tail)*
	MM54458	Aermacchi T-339A (MB339A(MLU)) [61-121]	AMI 214° Gruppo/61° Stormo, Lecce
	MM54465	Aermacchi T-339A (MB339A(MLU)) [61-116]	AMI 214° Gruppo/61° Stormo, Lecce
	MM54468	Aermacchi T-339A (MB339A(MLU)) [61-241]	AMI 214° Gruppo/61° Stormo, Lecce
	MM54473	Aermacchi AT-339A (MB339PAN)	AMI *Frecce Tricolori* (313° Gruppo), Rivolto
	MM54477	Aermacchi AT-339A (MB339PAN)	AMI *Frecce Tricolori* (313° Gruppo), Rivolto
	MM54479	Aermacchi AT-339A (MB339PAN)	AMI *Frecce Tricolori* (313° Gruppo), Rivolto
	MM54480	Aermacchi AT-339A (MB339PAN)	AMI *Frecce Tricolori* (313° Gruppo), Rivolto
	MM54482	Aermacchi AT-339A (MB339PAN)	AMI *Frecce Tricolori* (313° Gruppo), Rivolto
	MM54487	Aermacchi AT-339A (MB339PAN)	AMI *Frecce Tricolori* (313° Gruppo), Rivolto
	MM54488	Aermacchi T-339A (MB339A(MLU)) [61-160]	*AMI, stored Lecce*
	MM54492	Aermacchi T-339A (MB339A(MLU)) [61-36] (no tail)	*AMI, stored Lecce*
	MM54493	Aermacchi T-339A (MB339A(MLU)) [61-37] (no tail)	*AMI, stored Lecce*
	MM54496	Aermacchi T-339A (MB339A(MLU)) [61-42]	*AMI, stored Lecce*
	MM54499	Aermacchi T-339A (MB339A(MLU)) [61-45] (no tail)	*AMI, stored Lecce*
	MM54500	Aermacchi AT-339A (MB339PAN)	AMI *Frecce Tricolori* (313° Gruppo), Rivolto
	MM54504	Aermacchi T-339A (MB339A(MLU)) [61-52]	AMI 214° Gruppo/61° Stormo, Lecce
	MM54505	Aermacchi AT-339A (MB339PAN) (no tail)	*AMI, stored Lecce*
	MM54507	Aermacchi T-339A (MB339A(MLU)) [61-55] (no tail)	*AMI, stored Lecce*
	MM54509	Aermacchi T-339A (MB339A(MLU)) [61-57]	AMI 214° Gruppo/61° Stormo, Lecce
	MM54510	Aermacchi AT-339A (MB339PAN)	AMI *Frecce Tricolori* (313° Gruppo), Rivolto
	MM54511	Aermacchi T-339A (MB339A(MLU)) [61-61]	AMI 214° Gruppo/61° Stormo, Lecce
	MM54512	Aermacchi T-339A (MB339A(MLU)) [61-62]	AMI 214° Gruppo/61° Stormo, Lecce
	MM54514	Aermacchi AT-339A (MB339PAN)	AMI *Frecce Tricolori* (313° Gruppo), Rivolto
	MM54515	Aermacchi T-339A (MB339A(MLU)) [61-65]	AMI 214° Gruppo/61° Stormo, Lecce

Serial	Type (code/other identity)	Owner/operator, location or fate	Notes
MM54516	Aermacchi T-339A (MB339A(MLU)) [61-66]	AMI 214° Gruppo/61° Stormo, Lecce	
MM54517	Aermacchi AT-339A (MB339PAN)	AMI *Frecce Tricolori* (313° Gruppo), Rivolto	
MM54518	Aermacchi AT-339A (MB339PAN)	AMI *Frecce Tricolori* (313° Gruppo), Rivolto	
MM54533	Aermacchi T-339A (MB339A(MLU)) [61-72] (no tail)	*AMI, stored Lecce*	
MM54534	Aermacchi AT-339A (MB339PAN)	AMI *Frecce Tricolori* (313° Gruppo), Rivolto	
MM54535	Aermacchi T-339A (MB339A(MLU)) [61-74]	*AMI, stored Lecce*	
MM54538	Aermacchi AT-339A (MB339PAN)	AMI *Frecce Tricolori* (313° Gruppo), Rivolto	
MM54548	Aermacchi T-339A (MB339A(MLU)) [61-106]	AMI 214° Gruppo/61° Stormo, Lecce	
MM54549	Aermacchi T-339A (MB339A(MLU)) [61-107]	AMI 214° Gruppo/61° Stormo, Lecce	
MM54551	Aermacchi AT-339A (MB339PAN)	AMI *Frecce Tricolori* (313° Gruppo), Rivolto	
MM55002	Panavia TA-200A Tornado (IDS Trainer) [6-52] $	AMI GEA 6° Stormo, Ghedi	
MM55006	Panavia TA-200C Tornado (IDS Trainer (MLU)) [6-15]	AMI GEA 6° Stormo, Ghedi	
MM55007	Panavia TA-200A Tornado (IDS Trainer) [6-56]	AMI GEA 6° Stormo, Ghedi	
MM55008	Panavia TA-200A Tornado (IDS Trainer) [6-45]	AMI GEA 6° Stormo, Ghedi	
MM55009	Panavia TA-200A Tornado (IDS Trainer) [6-44] $	AMI GEA 6° Stormo, Ghedi	
MM55032	McDonnell Douglas TAV-8B Harrier II+ [1-01]	MMI Gruppo Aerei Imbarcarti, Taranto/Grottaglie	
MM55033	McDonnell Douglas TAV-8B Harrier II+ [1-02]	MMI, stored Taranto/Grottaglie	
MM55034	Aeritalia-EMB TA-11B Ghibli (AMX-T-ACOL) [RS-20]	*AMI, withdrawn from use, Pratica di Mare*	
MM55036	Aeritalia-EMB TA-11B Ghibli (AMX-T-ACOL) [32-51]	*AMI, withdrawn from use, Amendola*	
MM55037	Aeritalia-EMB TA-11B Ghibli (AMX-T-ACOL) [51-80]	*AMI, withdrawn from use, Istrana*	
MM55042	Aeritalia-EMB TA-11B Ghibli (AMX-T-ACOL) [32-56]	AMI, dumped Amendola	
MM55043	Aeritalia-EMB TA-11B Ghibli (AMX-T-ACOL) [51-81]	AMI, preserved Piacenza	
MM55044	Aeritalia-EMB TA-11B Ghibli (AMX-T-ACOL) [51-82]$	AMI, preserved Piacenza	
MM55046	Aeritalia-EMB TA-11B Ghibli (AMX-T-ACOL) [32-60]	AMI, dumped Amendola	
MM55047	Aeritalia-EMB TA-11B Ghibli (AMX-T-ACOL) [32-53]	AMI, dumped Amendola	
MM55049	Aeritalia-EMB TA-11B Ghibli (AMX-T-ACOL) [51-83]	*AMI, withdrawn from use, Istrana*	
MM55051	Aeritalia-EMB TA-11B Ghibli (AMX-T-ACOL) [51-84]	*AMI, withdrawn from use, Istrana*	
MM55052	Aermacchi AT-339A (MB339PAN)	AMI *Frecce Tricolori* (313° Gruppo), Rivolto	
MM55053	Aermacchi AT-339A (MB339PAN)	AMI *Frecce Tricolori* (313° Gruppo), Rivolto	
MM55054	Aermacchi AT-339A (MB339PAN)	AMI *Frecce Tricolori* (313° Gruppo), Rivolto	
MM55055	Aermacchi AT-339A (MB339PAN)	AMI *Frecce Tricolori* (313° Gruppo), Rivolto	
MM55058	Aermacchi AT-339A (MB339PAN)	AMI *Frecce Tricolori* (313° Gruppo), Rivolto	
MM55059	Aermacchi AT-339A (MB339PAN)	AMI *Frecce Tricolori* (313° Gruppo), Rivolto	
MM55062	Aermacchi FT-339C (MB339CD) [61-126]	AMI 213° Gruppo/61° Stormo, Lecce	
MM55063	Aermacchi FT-339C (MB339CD) [61-127]	AMI 213° Gruppo/61° Stormo, Lecce	
MM55064	Aermacchi FT-339C (MB339CD) [61-130]	AMI 213° Gruppo/61° Stormo, Lecce	
MM55065	Aermacchi FT-339C (MB339CD) [61-131] $	AMI 213° Gruppo/61° Stormo, Lecce	
MM55066	Aermacchi FT-339C (MB339CD) [61-132]	AMI 213° Gruppo/61° Stormo, Lecce	
MM55067	Aermacchi FT-339C (MB339CD) [61-133]	AMI 213° Gruppo/61° Stormo, Lecce	
MM55068	Aermacchi FT-339C (MB339CD) [61-134]	AMI 213° Gruppo/61° Stormo, Lecce	
MM55069	Aermacchi FT-339C (MB339CD) [61-135]	AMI 213° Gruppo/61° Stormo, Lecce	
MM55070	Aermacchi FT-339C (MB339CD) [61-136]	AMI 213° Gruppo/61° Stormo, Lecce	
MM55072	Aermacchi FT-339C (MB339CD) [61-140]	AMI 213° Gruppo/61° Stormo, Lecce	
MM55073	Aermacchi FT-339C (MB339CD) [61-141]	AMI 213° Gruppo/61° Stormo, Lecce	
MM55074	Aermacchi FT-339C (MB339CD) [61-142]	AMI 213° Gruppo/61° Stormo, Lecce	
MM55075	Aermacchi FT-339C (MB339CD) [61-143]	AMI 213° Gruppo/61° Stormo, Lecce	
MM55076	Aermacchi FT-339C (MB339CD) [61-144]	AMI 213° Gruppo/61° Stormo, Lecce	
MM55077	Aermacchi FT-339C (MB339CD) [61-145]	AMI, stored Venegono (awaiting overhaul)	
MM55078	Aermacchi FT-339C (MB339CD) [61-146]	AMI 213° Gruppo/61° Stormo, Lecce	
MM55079	Aermacchi FT-339C (MB339CD) [61-147]	AMI, stored Venegono (awaiting overhaul)	
MM55080	Aermacchi FT-339C (MB339CD) [61-150]	AMI 213° Gruppo/61° Stormo, Lecce	
MM55081	Aermacchi FT-339C (MB339CD) [61-151]	AMI, stored Venegono (awaiting overhaul)	
MM55082	Aermacchi FT-339C (MB339CD) [61-152]	AMI 213° Gruppo/61° Stormo, Lecce	
MM55084	Aermacchi FT-339C (MB339CD) [61-154]	AMI 213° Gruppo/61° Stormo, Lecce	
MM55085	Aermacchi FT-339C (MB339CD) [61-155]	AMI 213° Gruppo/61° Stormo, Lecce	
MM55086	Aermacchi FT-339C (MB339CD) [61-156]	AMI 213° Gruppo/61° Stormo, Lecce	
MM55087	Aermacchi FT-339C (MB339CD) [61-157]	AMI 213° Gruppo/61° Stormo, Lecce	
MM55088	Aermacchi FT-339C (MB339CD) [61-160]	AMI 213° Gruppo/61° Stormo, Lecce	
MM55089	Aermacchi FT-339C (MB339CD) [61-161]	AMI 213° Gruppo/61° Stormo, Lecce	
MM55090	Aermacchi FT-339C (MB339CD) [61-162]	AMI 213° Gruppo/61° Stormo, Lecce	
MM55091	Aermacchi FT-339C (MB339CD) [61-163]	AMI 213° Gruppo/61° Stormo, Lecce	
MM55092	Eurofighter TF-2000A Typhoon [4-25]	AMI 904° GEA/4° Stormo, Grosseto	

Notes	Serial	Type (code/other identity)	Owner/operator, location or fate
	MM55093	Eurofighter TF-2000A Typhoon [4-31]	AMI 904° GEA/4° Stormo, Grosseto
	MM55094	Eurofighter TF-2000A Typhoon [4-27]	AMI 904° GEA/4° Stormo, Grosseto
	MM55095	Eurofighter TF-2000A Typhoon [4-23]	AMI 904° GEA/4° Stormo, Grosseto
	MM55096	Eurofighter TF-2000A Typhoon [4-30]	AMI 904° GEA/4° Stormo, Grosseto
	MM55097	Eurofighter TF-2000A Typhoon [36-62]	AMI 936° GEA/36° Stormo, Gioia del Colle
	MM55128	Eurofighter TF-2000A Typhoon [36-64]	AMI 936° GEA/36° Stormo, Gioia del Colle
	MM55129	Eurofighter TF-2000A Typhoon [36-63]	AMI 936° GEA/36° Stormo, Gioia del Colle
	MM55130	Eurofighter TF-2000A Typhoon [4-33]	AMI 904° GEA/4° Stormo, Grosseto
	MM55131	Eurofighter TF-2000A Typhoon [4-34]	AMI 904° GEA/4° Stormo, Grosseto
	MM55132	Eurofighter TF-2000A Typhoon [51-32]	AMI 132° Gruppo/51° Stormo, Istrana
	MM55133	Eurofighter TF-2000A Typhoon [51-33]	AMI 132° Gruppo/51° Stormo, Istrana
	MM55144	Aermacchi T-346A Master [61-02]	AMI 212° Gruppo/61° Stormo, Lecce
	MM55145	Aermacchi T-346A Master [61-03]	AMI 212° Gruppo/61° Stormo, Lecce
	MM55152	Aermacchi T-346A Master [61-11]	AMI 212° Gruppo/61° Stormo, Lecce
	MM55153	Aermacchi T-346A Master [61-05]	AMI 212° Gruppo/61° Stormo, Lecce
	MM55154	Aermacchi T-346A Master [61-01]	AMI 212° Gruppo/61° Stormo, Lecce
	MM55155	Aermacchi T-346A Master [61-04]	AMI 212° Gruppo/61° Stormo, Lecce
	MM55168	Eurofighter TF-2000A Typhoon [37-34]	AMI 18° Gruppo/37° Stormo, Trapani/Birgi
	CSX55169	Eurofighter TF-2000A Typhoon	Leonardo, Turin
	MM55213	Aermacchi T-346A Master [61-06]	AMI 212° Gruppo/61° Stormo, Decimomannu
	MM55214	Aermacchi T-346A Master [61-07]	AMI 212° Gruppo/61° Stormo, Decimomannu
	MM55215	Aermacchi T-346A Master [61-10]	AMI 212° Gruppo/61° Stormo, Decimomannu
	MM55216	Aermacchi T-346A Master [61-12]	AMI 212° Gruppo/61° Stormo, Decimomannu
	MM55217	Aermacchi T-346A Master [61-13]	AMI 212° Gruppo/61° Stormo, Decimomannu
	MM55218	Aermacchi T-346A Master [61-14]	AMI 212° Gruppo/61° Stormo, Decimomannu
	MM55219	Aermacchi T-346A Master [61-20]	AMI 212° Gruppo/61° Stormo, Decimomannu
	MM55220	Aermacchi T-346A Master [61-16]	AMI 212° Gruppo/61° Stormo, Decimomannu
	MM55221	Aermacchi T-346A Master [61-15]	AMI 212° Gruppo/61° Stormo, Decimomannu
	MM55222	Aermacchi T-346A Master [61-21]	AMI 212° Gruppo/61° Stormo, Decimomannu
	CSX55223	Aermacchi T-346A Master [61-22]	AMI 212° Gruppo/61° Stormo, Decimomannu
	MM55224	Aermacchi T-346A Master [61-23]	AMI 212° Gruppo/61° Stormo, Decimomannu
	MM55229	Aermacchi T-346A Master [61-24]	AMI 212° Gruppo/61° Stormo, Decimomannu
	MM55230	Aermacchi T-346A Master [61-25]	AMI 212° Gruppo/61° Stormo, Decimomannu
	MM55231	Aermacchi T-346A Master [61-26]	AMI 212° Gruppo/61° Stormo, Decimomannu
	MM55232	Aermacchi T-346A Master [61-27]	AMI 212° Gruppo/61° Stormo, Decimomannu
	CSX55233	Aermacchi T-345A [61-22]	AMI 311° Gruppo/RSV, Pratica di Mare (on loan)
	MM55234	Aermacchi T-345A [61-202]	AMI 214° Gruppo/61° Stormo, Lecce
	MM55235	Aermacchi T-345A [61-203]	AMI 214° Gruppo/61° Stormo, Lecce
	MM55236	Aermacchi T-345A [61-204]	AMI 214° Gruppo/61° Stormo, Lecce
	MM55237	Aermacchi T-345A [61-205]	AMI 214° Gruppo/61° Stormo, Lecce
	MM55239	Aermacchi T-346B Master [61-30]	AMI 212° Gruppo/61° Stormo, Lecce
	MM55240	Aermacchi T-346B Master [61-31]	AMI 212° Gruppo/61° Stormo, Lecce
	MM55241	Aermacchi T-346B Master [61-32]	AMI 212° Gruppo/61° Stormo, Lecce
	MM55242	Aermacchi T-346B Master [61-33]	AMI 212° Gruppo/61° Stormo, Lecce
	MM55248	Aermacchi T-345A [61-206]	AMI 311° Gruppo/RSV, Pratica di Mare
	MM55249	Aermacchi T-345A [61-207]	AMI 311° Gruppo/RSV, Pratica di Mare
	MM55250	Aermacchi T-345A [61-210]	AMI 311° Gruppo/RSV, Pratica di Mare
	MM55251	Aermacchi T-345A	AMI (on order)
	MM55252	Aermacchi T-345A	AMI (on order)
	MM55253	Aermacchi T-345A	AMI (on order)
	MM552..	Aermacchi T-345A	AMI (on order)
	MM62026	Dassault VC-50A (Falcon 50)	*Preserved Milan-Volandia Museum, Italy*
	MM62029	Dassault VC-50A (Falcon 50)	AMI 93° Gruppo/31° Stormo, Roma-Ciampino
	CSX62127	Aeritalia MC-27J Pretorian	Alenia, Turin
	MM62156	Dornier UC-228 (Do.228-212) [E.I.101]	Esercito 28° Gruppo Squadroni, Viterbo
	MM62157	Dornier UC-228 (Do.228-212) [E.I.102]	Esercito 28° Gruppo Squadroni, Viterbo
	MM62158	Dornier UC-228 (Do.228-212) [E.I.103]	Esercito 28° Gruppo Squadroni, Viterbo
	MM62160	Piaggio EC-180A (P-180RM) Avanti	AMI 71° Gruppo/14° Stormo, Pratica di Mare
	MM62161	Piaggio VC-180A (P-180AM) Avanti	AMI 311° Gruppo/RSV, Pratica di Mare
	MM62162	Piaggio EC-180A (P-180RM) Avanti	AMI 71° Gruppo/14° Stormo, Pratica di Mare
	MM62163	Piaggio EC-180A (P-180RM) Avanti	AMI 71° Gruppo/14° Stormo, Pratica di Mare
	MM62164	Piaggio EC-180A (P-180RM) Avanti	AMI 71° Gruppo/14° Stormo, Pratica di Mare

Serial	Type (code/other identity)	Owner/operator, location or fate	Notes
MM62165	Aérospatiale P-42A (ATR.42-400MP) [GF-13]	GdiF GEA, Pratica di Mare	
MM62166	Aérospatiale P-42A (ATR.42-400MP) [GF-14]	GdiF GEA, Pratica di Mare	
MM62167	Piaggio VC-180A (P-180AM) Avanti	Esercito 28° Gruppo Sqd Det, Roma/Ciampino	
MM62168	Piaggio VC-180A (P-180AM) Avanti	Esercito 28° Gruppo Sqd Det, Roma/Ciampino	
MM62169	Piaggio VC-180A (P-180AM) Avanti	Esercito 28° Gruppo Sqd Det, Roma/Ciampino	
MM62170	Aérospatiale P-42A (ATR.42-400MP) [10-01]	Guardia Costiera 3° Nucleo, Pescara	
MM62174	Airbus VC-319A (A.319CJ-115X)	AMI 306° Gruppo/31° Stormo, Roma-Ciampino	
MM62175	Lockheed C-130J Hercules II [46-40]	AMI, stored Pisa	
MM62177	Lockheed C-130J Hercules II [46-42]	AMI 50° Gruppo/46ª Brigata Aerea, Pisa	
MM62178	Lockheed KC-130J Hercules II [46-43]	AMI 50° Gruppo/46ª Brigata Aerea, Pisa	
MM62179	Lockheed C-130J Hercules II [46-44]	AMI 50° Gruppo/46ª Brigata Aerea, Pisa	
MM62180	Lockheed C-130J Hercules II [46-45]	AMI 50° Gruppo/46ª Brigata Aerea, Pisa	
MM62181	Lockheed KC-130J Hercules II [46-46]	AMI 50° Gruppo/46ª Brigata Aerea, Pisa	
MM62182	Lockheed C-130J Hercules II [46-47]	AMI, stored Pisa	
MM62183	Lockheed KC-130J Hercules II [46-48]	AMI, stored Venice	
MM62184	Lockheed C-130J Hercules II [46-49]	AMI, stored Pisa	
MM62185	Lockheed C-130J Hercules II [46-50]	AMI 46ª Brigata Aerea, Pisa	
MM62186	Lockheed C-130J Hercules II [46-51]	AMI 46ª Brigata Aerea, Pisa	
MM62187	Lockheed C-130J-30 Hercules II [46-53]	AMI, stored Pisa	
MM62188	Lockheed C-130J-30 Hercules II [46-54]	AMI, stored Pisa	
MM62189	Lockheed C-130J-30 Hercules II [46-55]	AMI 50° Gruppo/46ª Brigata Aerea, Pisa	
MM62190	Lockheed C-130J-30 Hercules II [46-56]	AMI, stored Pisa	
MM62191	Lockheed C-130J-30 Hercules II [46-57]	AMI 50° Gruppo/46ª Brigata Aerea, Pisa	
MM62192	Lockheed C-130J-30 Hercules II [46-58]	AMI, stored Pisa	
MM62193	Lockheed C-130J-30 Hercules II [46-59]	AMI 46ª Brigata Aerea, Pisa	
MM62194	Lockheed C-130J-30 Hercules II [46-60]	AMI 50° Gruppo/46ª Brigata Aerea, Pisa	
MM62195	Lockheed C-130J-30 Hercules II [46-61]	AMI 50° Gruppo/46ª Brigata Aerea, Pisa	
MM62196	Lockheed C-130J-30 Hercules II [46-62]	AMI 50° Gruppo/46ª Brigata Aerea, Pisa	
MM62199	Piaggio VC-180A (P-180AM) Avanti	AMI CAE Multicrew, Pratica di Mare	
MM62200	Piaggio VC-180A (P-180AM) Avanti	AMI 71° Gruppo/14° Stormo, Pratica di Mare	
MM62201	Piaggio VC-180A (P-180AM) Avanti	AMI CAE Multicrew, Pratica di Mare	
MM62202	Piaggio VC-180A (P-180AM) Avanti	AMI 71° Gruppo/14° Stormo, Pratica di Mare	
MM62203	Piaggio VC-180A (P-180AM) Avanti	AMI CAE Multicrew, Pratica di Mare	
MM62204	Piaggio VC-180A (P-180AM) Avanti	AMI 71° Gruppo/14° Stormo, Pratica di Mare	
MM62205	Piaggio VC-180A (P-180AM) Avanti	AMI CAE Multicrew, Pratica di Mare	
MM62206	Piaggio VC-180A (P-180AM) Avanti	AMI CAE Multicrew, Pratica di Mare	
MM62207	Piaggio VC-180A (P-180AM) Avanti	AMI CAE Multicrew, Pratica di Mare	
MM62208	Aérospatiale P-42B (ATR.42-500MP) [10-02]	Guardia Costiera 2° Nucleo, Catania	
MM62209	Airbus VC-319A (A.319CJ-115X)	AMI 306° Gruppo/31° Stormo, Roma-Ciampino	
MM62210	Dassault VC-900A (Falcon 900EX)	AMI 93° Gruppo/31° Stormo, Roma-Ciampino	
MM62211	Piaggio VC-180A (P-180AM) Avanti [9-02]	MMI 9ª Brigata Aerea, Pratica di Mare	
MM62212	Piaggio VC-180A (P-180AM) Avanti [9-01]	MMI 9ª Brigata Aerea, Pratica di Mare	
MM62213	Piaggio VC-180A (P-180AM) Avanti [9-03]	MMI 9ª Brigata Aerea, Pratica di Mare	
MM62214	Aeritalia C-27J Spartan [46-84]	AMI 46ª Brigata Aerea, Pisa	
MM62215	Aeritalia C-27J Spartan [46-80]	AMI 311° Gruppo/RSV, Pratica di Mare	
MM62217	Aeritalia C-27J Spartan [46-81]	AMI 98° Gruppo/46ª Brigata Aerea, Pisa	
MM62218	Aeritalia C-27J Spartan [46-82]	AMI 98° Gruppo/46ª Brigata Aerea, Pisa	
CSX62219	Aeritalia C-27J Spartan [RS-50] $	AMI 311° Gruppo/RSV, Pratica di Mare	
MM62220	Aeritalia MC-27J Pretorian [46-83]	AMI 98° Gruppo/46ª Brigata Aerea, Pisa	
MM62221	Aeritalia EC-27J JEDI [46-85]	AMI 98° Gruppo/46ª Brigata Aerea, Pisa	
MM62222	Aeritalia C-27J Spartan [46-86]	AMI 98° Gruppo/46ª Brigata Aerea, Pisa	
MM62223	Aeritalia C-27J Spartan [46-88]	AMI 98° Gruppo/46ª Brigata Aerea, Pisa	
MM62224	Aeritalia EC-27J JEDI [46-89]	AMI 98° Gruppo/46ª Brigata Aerea, Pisa	
CSX62225	Aeritalia YEC-27J JEDI [46-90]	Leonardo, Turin	
MM62226	Boeing KC-767A (767-2EYER) [14-01] $	AMI 8° Gruppo/14° Stormo, Pratica di Mare	
MM62227	Boeing KC-767A (767-2EYER) [14-02]	AMI 8° Gruppo/14° Stormo, Pratica di Mare	
MM62228	Boeing KC-767A (767-2EYER) [14-03]	AMI 8° Gruppo/14° Stormo, Pratica di Mare	
MM62229	Boeing KC-767A (767-2EYER) [14-04]	AMI 8° Gruppo/14° Stormo, Pratica di Mare	
MM62230	Aérospatiale P-42B (ATR.42-500MP) [GF-15]	GdiF GEA, Pratica di Mare	
MM62243	Airbus VC-319A (A.319CJ-115X)	AMI 306° Gruppo/31° Stormo, Roma-Ciampino	
MM62244	Dassault VC-900B (Falcon 900EX EASy)	AMI 93° Gruppo/31° Stormo, Roma-Ciampino	
MM62245	Dassault VC-900B (Falcon 900EX EASy)	AMI 93° Gruppo/31° Stormo, Roma-Ciampino	

Notes	Serial	Type (code/other identity)	Owner/operator, location or fate
	MM62248	Piaggio VC-180A (P-180AM) Avanti [GF-18]	GdiF GEA, Pratica di Mare
	MM62249	Piaggio VC-180B (P-180AM) Avanti II [GF-19]	GdiF GEA, Pratica di Mare
	MM62250	Aeritalia C-27J Spartan [46-91]	AMI 98° Gruppo/46ª Brigata Aerea, Pisa
	MM62251	Aérospatiale P-42B (ATR.42-500MP) [GF-16]	GdiF GEA, Pratica di Mare
	MM62270	Aérospatiale P-42B (ATR.42-500MP) [10-03]	Guardia Costiera 2° Nucleo, Catania
	MM62274	Piaggio VC-180B (P-180AM) Avanti II [12-01]	Guardia Costiera 2° Nucleo, Catania
	MM62279	Aérospatiale P-72A Argo (ATR.72-600MP) [41-01]	AMI 88° Gruppo/41° Stormo, Sigonella
	MM62280	Aérospatiale P-72A Argo (ATR.72-600MP) [41-02]	AMI 88° Gruppo/41° Stormo, Sigonella
	MM62281	Aérospatiale P-72A Argo (ATR.72-600MP) [41-04]	AMI 88° Gruppo/41° Stormo, Sigonella
	CSX62282	Aérospatiale P-72A Argo (ATR.72-600MP) [41-05]	(on order)
	MM62286	Piaggio VC-180B (P-180AM) Avanti II	AMI 93° Gruppo/31° Stormo, Roma-Ciampino
	MM62287	Piaggio VC-180B (P-180AM) Avanti II	AMI 93° Gruppo/31° Stormo, Roma-Ciampino
	MM62293	Gulfstream Aerospace E-550A (N849GA) [14-11]	AMI 71° Gruppo/14° Stormo, Pratica di Mare
	MM62298	Aérospatiale P-72A Argo (ATR.72-600MP) [41-03]	AMI 88° Gruppo/41° Stormo, Sigonella
	MM62300	Beechcraft King Air 350ER [14-30]	AMI 71° Gruppo/14° Stormo, Pratica di Mare
	MM62303	Gulfstream Aerospace E-550A (N554GA) [14-12]	AMI 71° Gruppo/14° Stormo, Pratica di Mare
	MM62311	Aérospatiale P-72B (ATR.72-600MP) [GF-20]	GdiF GEA, Pratica di Mare
	MM62315	Aérospatiale P-72B (ATR.72-600MP) [GF-21]	GdiF GEA, Pratica di Mare
	MM62317	Beechcraft King Air 350ER [14-31]	AMI 71° Gruppo/14° Stormo, Pratica di Mare
	MM62321	Aérospatiale P-72B (ATR.72-600MP) [GF-22]	GdiF GEA, Pratica di Mare
	MM62329	Gulfstream Aerospace G550 (N581GA) [14-13]	AMI 71° Gruppo/14° Stormo, Pratica di Mare
	MM62331	Aérospatiale P-72B (ATR.72-600MP) [GF-23]	GdiF GEA, Pratica di Mare
	MM62332	Gulfstream Aerospace G550 (N559GA) [14-14]	AMI 71° Gruppo/14° Stormo, Pratica di Mare
	MM62335	Piaggio P-180 EVO Plus (I-PDVO)	AMI 71° Gruppo/14° Stormo, Pratica di Mare
	MM62336	Piaggio P-180 EVO Plus [14-51]	AMI 71° Gruppo/14° Stormo, Pratica di Mare
	MM62337	Piaggio P-180 EVO Plus [14-52]	AMI 71° Gruppo/14° Stormo, Pratica di Mare
	MM62..	Piaggio P-180 EVO Plus	AMI/MMI (on order)
	MM62..	Piaggio P-180 EVO Plus	AMI/MMI (on order)
	MM62..	Piaggio P-180 EVO Plus	AMI/MMI (on order)
	MM62..	Piaggio P-180 EVO Plus	AMI/MMI (on order)
	MM81796	AgustaWestland HH-139A [15-40]	AMI 83° Gruppo CSAR/15° Stormo, Cervia
	MM81797	AgustaWestland HH-139A [15-41]	AMI 80° Centro CSAR/15° Stormo, Decimomannu
	MM81798	AgustaWestland HH-139A [15-42]	AMI 85° Centro CSAR/15° Stormo, Pratica di Mare
	MM81799	AgustaWestland HH-139A [15-43]	AMI 85° Centro CSAR/15° Stormo, Pratica di Mare
	MM81800	AgustaWestland HH-139A [15-44]	AMI 85° Centro CSAR/15° Stormo, Pratica di Mare
	MM81801	AgustaWestland HH-139A [15-45]	AMI 84° Centro CSAR/15° Stormo, Brindisi
	MM81802	AgustaWestland HH-139A [15-46]	AMI 83° Gruppo CSAR/15° Stormo, Cervia
	MM81803	AgustaWestland HH-139A [15-47]	AMI 85° Centro CSAR/15° Stormo, Pratica di Mare
	MM81804	AgustaWestland HH-139A [15-48]	AMI 85° Centro CSAR/15° Stormo, Pratica di Mare
	MM81805	AgustaWestland HH-139A [15-49]	AMI 82° Centro CSAR/15° Stormo, Trapani/Birgi
	MM81822	AgustaWestland HH-139A [15-50]	AMI 80° Centro CSAR/15° Stormo, Decimomannu
	MM81823	AgustaWestland HH-139A [15-51]	AMI 83° Gruppo CSAR/15° Stormo, Cervia
	MM81824	AgustaWestland HH-139A [15-52]	AMI 80° Centro CSAR/15° Stormo, Decimomannu
	CSX81848	AgustaWestland AW149	Leonardo div. Elicotteri, Vergiate
	MM81864	AgustaWestland HH-101A Caesar (ZR352) [9-01]	AMI 21° Gruppo/9° Stormo, Grazzanise
	MM81865	AgustaWestland HH-101A Caesar (ZR353) [9-02]	AMI 21° Gruppo/9° Stormo, Grazzanise
	MM81866	AgustaWestland HH-101A Caesar (ZR354) [9-03]	AMI 21° Gruppo/9° Stormo, Grazzanise
	MM81867	AgustaWestland HH-101A Caesar (ZR355) [15-04]	AMI 23° Gruppo/15° Stormo, Cervia
	MM81868	AgustaWestland HH-101A Caesar (ZR356) [9-05]	AMI 21° Gruppo/9° Stormo, Grazzanise
	MM81869	AgustaWestland HH-101A Caesar (ZR357) [9-06]	AMI 21° Gruppo/9° Stormo, Grazzanise
	MM81870	AgustaWestland HH-101A Caesar (ZR358) [15-07]	AMI 81° Centro/15° Stormo, Cervia
	MM81871	AgustaWestland HH-101A Caesar (ZR359) [9-10]	AMI 21° Gruppo/9° Stormo, Grazzanise
	MM81872	AgustaWestland HH-101A Caesar (ZR360) [9-11]	AMI 21° Gruppo/9° Stormo, Grazzanise
	MM81873	AgustaWestland HH-101A Caesar (ZR361) [9-12]	AMI 21° Gruppo/9° Stormo, Grazzanise
	MM81874	AgustaWestland HH-101A Caesar (ZR362) [9-13]	AMI 21° Gruppo/9° Stormo, Grazzanise
	MM81875	AgustaWestland HH-101A Caesar (ZR363) [9-14]	AMI 21° Gruppo/9° Stormo, Grazzanise
	CSX81890	AgustaWestland AW149	Leonardo div. Elicotteri, Vergiate
	MM81985	AgustaWestland HH-139B [15-55]	AMI 85° Centro CSAR/15° Stormo, Pratica di Mare
	MM81986	AgustaWestland HH-139A [15-56]	AMI 81° Centro/15° Stormo, Cervia
	MM81989	AgustaWestland HH-139B [15-57]	AMI 81° Centro/15° Stormo, Cervia
	MM81990	AgustaWestland HH-139B [15-60] $	AMI 84° Centro CSAR/15° Stormo, Brindisi
	MM81991	AgustaWestland HH-139B [15-61]	AMI 81° Centro/15° Stormo, Cervia

Serial	Type (code/other identity)	Owner/operator, location or fate	Notes
MM82003	AgustaWestland HH-139B [15-62]	AMI 85° Centro CSAR/15° Stormo, Pratica di Mare	
MM82007	AgustaWestland HH-139B [15-63]	AMI 83° Gruppo CSAR/15° Stormo, Cervia	
MM82011	AgustaWestland HH-139B [15-64]	AMI 81° Centro/15° Stormo, Cervia	
MM82013	AgustaWestland HH-139B [15-65]	AMI 83° Gruppo CSAR/15° Stormo, Cervia	
CSX82017	AgustaWestland HH-139B [15-66]	AMI (on order)	
MM82018	AgustaWestland HH-139B [15-67]	AMI 83° Gruppo CSAR/15° Stormo, Cervia	
MM82023	AgustaWestland HH-139B [15-70]	AMI 85° Centro CSAR/15° Stormo, Pratica di Mare	
MM82026	AgustaWestland HH-139B [15-71] $	AMI 82° Centro CSAR/15° Stormo, Trapani/Birgi	
MM82028	AgustaWestland HH-139B [15-72]	AMI 85° Centro CSAR/15° Stormo, Pratica di Mare	
MM82029	AgustaWestland HH-139B [15-73]	AMI 85° Centro CSAR/15° Stormo, Pratica di Mare	
MM82030	AgustaWestland HH-139B [15-74]	AMI 85° Centro CSAR/15° Stormo, Pratica di Mare	
MM82038	AgustaWestland HH-139B [15-75]	AMI 83° Gruppo CSAR/15° Stormo, Cervia	
MM.....	Gulfstream Aerospace G650ER (N684GA)	AMI (on order)	
MM.....	Gulfstream Aerospace G650ER	AMI (on order)	
MM.....	Gulfstream Aerospace G650ER	AMI (on order)	
MM.....	Gulfstream Aerospace G650ER	AMI (on order)	
MM.....	Gulfstream Aerospace G650ER	AMI (on order)	
Italian Government			
I-ANIG	Gulfstream Aerospace G.600	Italian Government/Soc. CAI, Roma/Ciampino	
I-DIEM	Dassault Falcon 900LX	Italian Government/Soc. CAI, Roma/Ciampino	
I-GATC	Gulfstream Aerospace G.600	Italian Government/Soc. CAI, Roma/Ciampino	
I-NEMO	Dassault Falcon 900LX	Italian Government/Soc. CAI, Roma/Ciampino	

IVORY COAST

Serial	Type (code/other identity)	Owner/operator, location or fate	Notes
TU-VAE	Gulfstream Aerospace G.550	Ivory Coast Government, Abidjan	
TU-VAG	Gulfstream Aerospace G.450 (T7-LIA)	Ivory Coast Government, Abidjan	
TU-VAI	Grumman G.1159C Gulfstream IV-SP	Ivory Coast Government, Abidjan	
TU-VAS	Airbus A.319CJ-133	Ivory Coast Government, Abidjan (noted stored Tucson, AZ, USA, Dec 2024)	

JAPAN
Japan Air Self Defence Force (JASDF)

Serial	Type (code/other identity)	Owner/operator, location or fate	Notes
07-3604	Boeing KC-767J	JASDF 404th Hikotai, Nagoya	
14-3611	Boeing KC-46A (N6018N)	JASDF 405th Hikotai, Yonago-Miho	
24-3612	Boeing KC-46A (N5512S)	JASDF 405th Hikotai, Yonago-Miho	
44-3613	Boeing KC-46A (N2014D/34-3613 ntu)	JASDF 405th Hikotai, Yonago-Miho	
44-3614	Boeing KC-46A (N8287V/34-3614 ntu)	JASDF 405th Hikotai, Yonago-Miho	
54-3615	Boeing KC-46A	JASDF (on order)	
54-3616	Boeing KC-46A	JASDF (on order)	
80-1111	Boeing 777-3SB(ER) (N509BJ)	JASDF 701st Hikotai, Chitose	
80-1112	Boeing 777-3SB(ER) (N511BJ)	JASDF 701st Hikotai, Chitose	
87-3601	Boeing KC-767J	JASDF 404th Hikotai, Nagoya	
87-3602	Boeing KC-767J	JASDF 404th Hikotai, Nagoya	
97-3603	Boeing KC-767J	JASDF 404th Hikotai, Nagoya	

JORDAN
Al Quwwat al Jawwiya al Malakiya al Urduniya/Jordanian Air Force

Serial	Type (code/other identity)	Owner/operator, location or fate	Notes
344	Lockheed C-130H Hercules	Jordanian AF 3 Sqn, Amman/Marka	
345	Lockheed C-130H Hercules $	Jordanian AF 3 Sqn, Amman/Marka	
346	Lockheed C-130H Hercules	Jordanian AF 3 Sqn, Amman/Marka	
347	Lockheed C-130H Hercules $	Jordanian AF 3 Sqn, Amman/Marka	
357	Lockheed C-130H Hercules	Jordanian AF 3 Sqn, Amman/Marka	
358	Lockheed C-130H Hercules	Jordanian AF 3 Sqn, Amman/Marka	
359	Lockheed C-130H Hercules	Jordanian AF 3 Sqn, Amman/Marka	
RJF 01	Extra EA-330LX	Jordanian AF *Royal Jordanian Falcons*, Aqaba	
RJF 02	Extra EA-330LX	*Destroyed Bleid, Belgium, 16th September 2024*	
RJF 03	Extra EA-330LX	Jordanian AF *Royal Jordanian Falcons*, Aqaba	
RJF 04	Extra EA-330LX	Jordanian AF *Royal Jordanian Falcons*, Aqaba	
RJF 05	Extra EA-330LX	Jordanian AF *Royal Jordanian Falcons*, Aqaba	
Jordanian Government			
VQ-BNZ	Gulfstream Aerospace G.650ER (N658GD)	Jordanian Government, Amman/Queen Alia Int'l	
VP-BXS	Gulfstream Aerospace G.700 (N721GD)	Jordanian Government, Amman/Queen Alia Int'l	

Notes	Serial	Type (code/other identity)	Owner/operator, location or fate
	KAZAKHSTAN		
	01 r	CASA C-295M	Kazakhstan ADF 281st Air Transport Sqn, Almaty
	02 r	CASA C-295M	Kazakhstan ADF 281st Air Transport Sqn, Almaty
	03 r	CASA C-295M	Kazakhstan ADF 281st Air Transport Sqn, Almaty
	04 r	CASA C-295M	Kazakhstan ADF 281st Air Transport Sqn, Almaty
	05 r	CASA C-295M	Kazakhstan ADF 281st Air Transport Sqn, Almaty
	06 r	CASA C-295M	Kazakhstan ADF 281st Air Transport Sqn, Almaty
	07 r	Antonov An-72	Kazakhstan ADF 281st Air Transport Sqn, Almaty
	07 r	CASA C-295M	Kazakhstan ADF 281st Air Transport Sqn, Almaty
	08 r	Antonov An-72	Kazakhstan ADF 281st Air Transport Sqn, Almaty
	08 r	CASA C-295M	Kazakhstan ADF 281st Air Transport Sqn, Almaty
	09 r	CASA C-295W	Kazakhstan ADF 281st Air Transport Sqn, Almaty
	21 r	Airbus Military A.400M (A4M139)	Kazakhstan ADF 281st Air Transport Sqn, Almaty
	..	Airbus Military A.400M	Kazakhstan ADF (on order)
	5701	Boeing 757-2M6	Kazakhstan ADF
	65001	Embraer Legacy 650	Kazakhstan Border Guards, Almaty
	UP-A2001	Airbus A.320CJ-214X	Government of Kazakhstan, Astana
	UP-A2101	Airbus A.321CJ-211SL	Government of Kazakhstan, Astana
	UP-A3001	Airbus A.330-223	Government of Kazakhstan, Astana
	UP-T5401	Tupolev Tu-154M	Government of Kazakhstan, Astana
	KENYA		
	KAF 308	Fokker 70ER	Kenyan Government, Nairobi
	KUWAIT		
	Al Quwwat al Jawwiya al Kuwaitiya/Kuwaiti Air Force		
	KAF 326	Lockheed KC-130J Hercules II	Kuwaiti AF 41 Sqn, Kuwait International
	KAF 327	Lockheed KC-130J Hercules II	Kuwaiti AF 41 Sqn, Kuwait International
	KAF 328	Lockheed KC-130J Hercules II	Kuwaiti AF 41 Sqn, Kuwait International
	KAF 342	Boeing C-17A Globemaster III (13-0001)	Kuwaiti AF 41 Sqn, Kuwait International
	KAF 343	Boeing C-17A Globemaster III (13-0002)	Kuwaiti AF 41 Sqn, Kuwait International
	Kuwaiti Government		
	9K-AKD	Airbus A.320-212	Kuwaiti Government, Safat
	9K-GAA	Boeing 747-8JK	Kuwaiti Government, Safat (stored Basel)
	9K-GBA	Airbus A.340-542	Kuwaiti Government, Safat
	9K-GBB	Airbus A.340-542	Kuwaiti Government, Safat
	9K-GCC	Boeing 737-9BQER	Kuwaiti Government, Safat
	9K-GEA	Airbus A.319CJ-115X	Kuwaiti Government, Safat
	9K-GFA	Gulfstream Aerospace G.550	Kuwaiti Government, Safat
	9K-GGA	Gulfstream Aerospace G.650	Kuwaiti Government, Safat
	9K-GGB	Gulfstream Aerospace G.650	Kuwaiti Government, Safat
	9K-GGC	Gulfstream Aerospace G.650	Kuwaiti Government, Safat
	9K-GGD	Gulfstream Aerospace G.650	Kuwaiti Government, Safat
	LIBYA		
	5A-DCN	Dassault Falcon 900EX	Libyan Government, Tripoli
	5A-ONE	Airbus A.340-213	Libyan Government, Tripoli (stored Basel)
	LITHUANIA		
	Karines Oro Pajegos (KOP)		
	01 bl	LET 410UVP Turbolet	KOP Transporto Esk, Siauliai/Zokniai
	02 bl	LET 410UVP Turbolet	KOP Transporto Esk, Siauliai/Zokniai
	06 bl	Aeritalia C-27J Spartan	KOP Transporto Esk, Siauliai/Zokniai
	07 bl	Aeritalia C-27J Spartan	KOP Transporto Esk, Siauliai/Zokniai
	08 bl	Aeritalia C-27J Spartan	KOP Transporto Esk, Siauliai/Zokniai
	26 bl	Mil Mi-8T (09 bl)	KOP Sraigtasparniu Esk, Siauliai/Zokniai
	LUXEMBOURG		
	Note: see also Belgium for A400M		
	NATO		
	LX-N90442	Boeing E-3A Sentry	NATO NAEW&CF, Geilenkirchen, Germany
	LX-N90443	Boeing E-3A Sentry	NATO NAEW&CF, Geilenkirchen, Germany

Serial	Type (code/other identity)	Owner/operator, location or fate	Notes
LX-N90444	Boeing E-3A Sentry	NATO NAEW&CF, Geilenkirchen, Germany	
LX-N90445	Boeing E-3A Sentry	NATO NAEW&CF, Geilenkirchen, Germany	
LX-N90446	Boeing E-3A Sentry	NATO NAEW&CF, Geilenkirchen, Germany	
LX-N90447	Boeing E-3A Sentry	NATO NAEW&CF, Geilenkirchen, Germany	
LX-N90448	Boeing E-3A Sentry	NATO NAEW&CF, Geilenkirchen, Germany	
LX-N90450	Boeing E-3A Sentry $	NATO NAEW&CF, Geilenkirchen, Germany	
LX-N90451	Boeing E-3A Sentry	NATO NAEW&CF, Geilenkirchen, Germany	
LX-N90452	Boeing E-3A Sentry	NATO NAEW&CF, stored Venice, Italy	
LX-N90453	Boeing E-3A Sentry	NATO NAEW&CF, Geilenkirchen, Germany	
LX-N90454	Boeing E-3A Sentry	NATO NAEW&CF, Geilenkirchen, Germany	
LX-N90456	Boeing E-3A Sentry	NATO NAEW&CF, Geilenkirchen, Germany	
LX-N90459	Boeing E-3A Sentry	NATO NAEW&CF, Geilenkirchen, Germany	

MACEDONIA

Serial	Type (code/other identity)	Owner/operator, location or fate	Notes
Z3-MKD	Bombardier Lear 60	Macedonian Government, Skopje	

MALAYSIA
Tentera Udara Diraja Malaysia/Royal Malaysian Air Force (RMAF)

Serial	Type (code/other identity)	Owner/operator, location or fate	Notes
M30-01	Lockheed C-130T Hercules	RMAF 20 Skn, Subang	
M30-02	Lockheed C-130T Hercules	RMAF 20 Skn, Subang	
M30-04	Lockheed C-130H-30 Hercules	RMAF 14 Skn, Labuan	
M30-05	Lockheed C-130H-30 Hercules	RMAF 14 Skn, Labuan	
M30-06	Lockheed C-130H-30 Hercules	RMAF 14 Skn, Labuan	
M30-07	Lockheed KC-130H Hercules	RMAF 20 Skn, Subang	
M30-08	Lockheed KC-130H Hercules	RMAF 20 Skn, Subang	
M30-09	Lockheed C-130H(MP) Hercules	RMAF 20 Skn, Subang	
M30-10	Lockheed C-130H-30 Hercules	RMAF 14 Skn, Labuan	
M30-11	Lockheed C-130H-30 Hercules	RMAF 20 Skn, Subang	
M30-12	Lockheed C-130H-30 Hercules	RMAF 20 Skn, Subang	
M30-14	Lockheed C-130H-30 Hercules	RMAF 14 Skn, Labuan	
M30-15	Lockheed C-130H-30 Hercules	RMAF 20 Skn, Subang	
M30-16	Lockheed C-130H-30 Hercules	RMAF 20 Skn, Subang	
M37-01	Dassault Falcon 900	RMAF 2 Skn, Subang	
M48-02	Bombardier BD.700-1A10 Global Express	RMAF 2 Skn, Subang	
M54-01	Airbus Military A.400M	RMAF 22 Skn, Subang	
M54-02	Airbus Military A.400M	RMAF 22 Skn, Subang	
M54-03	Airbus Military A.400M	RMAF, stored Subang	
M54-04	Airbus Military A.400M	RMAF, stored Subang	
9M-NAA	Airbus A.319CJ-115X	RMAF 2 Skn, Subang	
9M-NAB	Airbus A.320CJ-214	RMAF 2 Skn, Subang	

MALI

Serial	Type (code/other identity)	Owner/operator, location or fate	Notes
TZ-PRM	Boeing 737-7DW	Government of Mali, Bamako	

MAURITANIA

Serial	Type (code/other identity)	Owner/operator, location or fate	Notes
5T-ONE	Boeing 737-7BQ/W(BBJ)	Government of Mauritania, Nouakchott	

MEXICO
Fuerza Aérea Mexicana/Mexican Air Force (FAM), Armada de Mexico/Mexican Navy

Serial	Type (code/other identity)	Owner/operator, location or fate	Notes
3527	Boeing 737-800/W	*To Mexicana as XA-ATM, January 2024*	
3528	Boeing 737-800/W	*To Mexicana as XA-AWM, January 2024*	
ANX-1201	Gulfstream Aerospace G.550	Armada PRIESCAERTRANS, Mexico City	
ANX-1202	Gulfstream Aerospace G.450 (XC-LMF)	Armada Esc Aeronaval 031, Mexico City	

MOROCCO
Al Quwwat al Jawwiya al Malakiya Marakishiya/Force Aérienne Royaume Marocaine/Royal Moroccan Air Force (RMAF) & Moroccan Government

Serial	Type (code/other identity)	Owner/operator, location or fate	Notes
CN-ABP	CAP-232 (28)	RMAF *Marche Verte*, Marrakech/Ménara	
CN-ABQ	CAP-232 (29)	RMAF *Marche Verte*, Marrakech/Ménara	
CN-ABR	CAP-232 (31)	RMAF *Marche Verte*, Marrakech/Ménara	
CN-ABS	CAP-232 (36)	RMAF *Marche Verte*, Marrakech/Ménara	
CN-ABT	CAP-232 (37)	RMAF *Marche Verte*, Marrakech/Ménara	

Notes	Serial	Type (code/other identity)	Owner/operator, location or fate
	CN-ABU	CAP-232 (41)	RMAF *Marche Verte*, Marrakech/Ménara
	CN-ABV	CAP-232 (42)	RMAF *Marche Verte*, Marrakech/Ménara
	CN-ABW	CAP-232 (43)	RMAF *Marche Verte*, Marrakech/Ménara
	CN-ABX	CAP-232 (44)	RMAF *Marche Verte*, Marrakech/Ménara
	CN-ABY	CAP-232 (46)	RMAF *Marche Verte*, Marrakech/Ménara
	CN-ABZ	CAP-232 (47)	RMAF *Marche Verte*, Marrakech/Ménara
	CN-AMA	Airtech CN.235M-100 (023)	RMAF Escadrille de Transport 3, Kenitra
	CN-AMB	Airtech CN.235M-100 (024)	RMAF Escadrille de Transport 3, Kenitra
	CN-AMC	Airtech CN.235M-100 (025)	RMAF Escadrille de Transport 3, Kenitra
	CN-AMD	Airtech CN.235M-100 (026)	RMAF Escadrille de Transport 3, Kenitra
	CN-AME	Airtech CN.235M-100 (027)	RMAF Escadrille de Transport 3, Kenitra
	CN-AMF	Airtech CN.235M-100 (028)	RMAF Escadrille de Transport 3, Kenitra
	CN-AMG	Airtech CN.235M-100 (031)	RMAF Escadrille de Transport 3, Kenitra
	CN-AMN	Aeritalia C-27J Spartan	RMAF Escadrille de Transport 3, Kenitra
	CN-AMO	Aeritalia C-27J Spartan	RMAF Escadrille de Transport 3, Kenitra
	CN-AMP	Aeritalia C-27J Spartan	RMAF Escadrille de Transport 3, Kenitra
	CN-AMQ	Aeritalia C-27J Spartan	RMAF Escadrille de Transport 3, Kenitra
	CN-ANO	Dassault Falcon 50	RMAF VIP Flight, Rabat
	CN-ANU	Grumman G.1159A Gulfstream III	RMAF, Marrakech/Ménara, for GI
	CNA-NV	Cessna 560 Citation V	RMAF VIP Flight, Rabat
	CNA-NW	Cessna 560 Citation V	RMAF VIP Flight, Rabat
	CN-AOA	Lockheed C-130H Hercules (4535)	RMAF Escadrille de Transport 3, Kenitra
	CNA-OC	Lockheed C-130H Hercules (4551)	RMAF Escadrille de Transport 3, Kenitra
	CN-AOD	Lockheed C-130H Hercules (4575)	RMAF Escadrille de Transport 3, Kenitra
	CN-AOE	Lockheed C-130H Hercules (4581)	RMAF Escadrille de Transport 3, Kenitra
	CN-AOF	Lockheed C-130H Hercules (4583)	RMAF Escadrille de Transport 3, Kenitra
	CN-AOG	Lockheed C-130H Hercules (4713)	RMAF Escadrille de Transport 3, Kenitra
	CN-AOI	Lockheed C-130H Hercules (4733)	RMAF Escadrille de Transport 3, Kenitra
	CN-AOJ	Lockheed C-130H Hercules (4738)	RMAF Escadrille de Transport 3, Kenitra
	CN-AOK	Lockheed C-130H Hercules (4739)	RMAF Escadrille de Transport 3, Kenitra
	CN-AOL	Lockheed C-130H Hercules (4742)	RMAF Escadrille de Transport 3, Kenitra
	CN-AOM	Lockheed C-130H Hercules (4875)	RMAF Escadrille de Transport 3, Kenitra
	CN-AON	Lockheed C-130H Hercules (4876)	RMAF Escadrille de Transport 3, Kenitra
	CN-AOO	Lockheed EC-130H Hercules (4877)	RMAF Escadron Electronique, Kenitra
	CN-AOP	Lockheed C-130H Hercules (4888)	RMAF Escadrille de Transport 3, Kenitra
	CN-AOR	Lockheed KC-130H Hercules (4907)	RMAF Escadrille de Transport 3, Kenitra
	CN-AOS	Lockheed KC-130H Hercules (4909)	RMAF Escadrille de Transport 3, Kenitra

Moroccan Government

Notes	Serial	Type (code/other identity)	Owner/operator, location or fate
	CN-MBH	Boeing 747-8Z5 (A6-PFA)	Government of Morocco, Rabat
	CN-MMH	Gulfstream Aerospace G.650 (CN-AMH)	Government of Morocco, Rabat
	CN-MMJ	Cessna 560XLS+ Citation Excel (CN-AMJ)	Government of Morocco, Rabat
	CN-MMK	Cessna 560XLS+ Citation Excel (CN-AMK)	Government of Morocco, Rabat
	CN-MMR	Gulfstream Aerospace G.550 (CN-AMR)	Government of Morocco, Rabat
	CN-MMT	Gulfstream Aerospace G.550 (CN-AMS)	Government of Morocco, Rabat
	CN-MMY	Cessna 560XLS+ Citation Excel (CN-AMY)	Government of Morocco, Rabat
	CN-MSM	BAE RJ100 (CNA-SM)	Government of Morocco, Rabat
	CN-MVI	Boeing 737-8KB	Government of Morocco, Rabat
	CN-RGA	Boeing 747-428	Government of Morocco, Rabat

NAMIBIA

Notes	Serial	Type (code/other identity)	Owner/operator, location or fate
	V5-GON	Dassault Falcon 7X	Government of Namibia, Windhoek/Eros
	V5-NAM	Dassault Falcon 900B	Government of Namibia, Windhoek/Eros

NETHERLANDS
Koninklijke Luchtmacht (KLu)

Notes	Serial	Type (code/other identity)	Owner/operator, location or fate
	D-472	Boeing-Vertol CH-47F Chinook	KLu 298 Sqn, Gilze-Rijen
	D-473	Boeing-Vertol CH-47F Chinook	KLu 298 Sqn, Gilze-Rijen
	D-474	Boeing-Vertol CH-47F Chinook	KLu 302 Sqn, Fort Hood, Texas, USA
	D-475	Boeing-Vertol CH-47F Chinook	KLu 302 Sqn, Fort Hood, Texas, USA
	D-476	Boeing-Vertol CH-47F Chinook	KLu 302 Sqn, Fort Hood, Texas, USA
	D-477	Boeing-Vertol CH-47F Chinook	KLu 302 Sqn, Fort Hood, Texas, USA
	D-478	Boeing-Vertol CH-47F Chinook	KLu 302 Sqn, Fort Hood, Texas, USA

Serial	Type (code/other identity)	Owner/operator, location or fate	Notes
D-479	Boeing-Vertol CH-47F Chinook	KLu 298 Sqn, Gilze-Rijen	
D-480	Boeing-Vertol CH-47F Chinook	KLu 298 Sqn, Gilze-Rijen	
D-481	Boeing-Vertol CH-47F Chinook	KLu 298 Sqn, Gilze-Rijen	
D-482	Boeing-Vertol CH-47F Chinook	KLu 298 Sqn, Gilze-Rijen	
D-483	Boeing-Vertol CH-47F Chinook	KLu 298 Sqn, Gilze-Rijen	
D-484	Boeing-Vertol CH-47F Chinook	KLu 298 Sqn, Gilze-Rijen	
D-485	Boeing-Vertol CH-47F Chinook	KLu 298 Sqn, Gilze-Rijen	
D-601	Boeing-Vertol CH-47F Chinook	KLu 298 Sqn, Gilze-Rijen	
D-602	Boeing-Vertol CH-47F Chinook	KLu 298 Sqn, Gilze-Rijen	
D-603	Boeing-Vertol CH-47F Chinook	KLu 298 Sqn, Gilze-Rijen	
D-604	Boeing-Vertol CH-47F Chinook	KLu 298 Sqn, Gilze-Rijen	
D-605	Boeing-Vertol CH-47F Chinook	KLu 298 Sqn, Gilze-Rijen	
D-606	Boeing-Vertol CH-47F Chinook	KLu 298 Sqn, Gilze-Rijen	
F-001	Lockheed Martin F-35A Lightning II	KLu 308th FS/56th FW, Luke AFB, Arizona, USA	
F-002	Lockheed Martin F-35A Lightning II	KLu 308th FS/56th FW, Luke AFB, Arizona, USA	
F-003	Lockheed Martin F-35A Lightning II	KLu 308th FS/56th FW, Luke AFB, Arizona, USA	
F-004	Lockheed Martin F-35A Lightning II	KLu 308th FS/56th FW, Luke AFB, Arizona, USA	
F-005	Lockheed Martin F-35A Lightning II	KLu 308th FS/56th FW, Luke AFB, Arizona, USA	
F-006	Lockheed Martin F-35A Lightning II	KLu 308th FS/56th FW, Luke AFB, Arizona, USA	
F-007	Lockheed Martin F-35A Lightning II	KLu 308th FS/56th FW, Luke AFB, Arizona, USA	
F-008	Lockheed Martin F-35A Lightning II	KLu 308th FS/56th FW, Luke AFB, Arizona, USA	
F-009	Lockheed Martin F-35A Lightning II	KLu 322 Sqn, Leeuwarden	
F-010	Lockheed Martin F-35A Lightning II	KLu 322 Sqn, Leeuwarden	
F-011	Lockheed Martin F-35A Lightning II	KLu 322 Sqn, Leeuwarden	
F-012	Lockheed Martin F-35A Lightning II	KLu 322 Sqn, Leeuwarden	
F-013	Lockheed Martin F-35A Lightning II	KLu 322 Sqn, Leeuwarden	
F-014	Lockheed Martin F-35A Lightning II	KLu 322 Sqn, Leeuwarden	
F-015	Lockheed Martin F-35A Lightning II	KLu 322 Sqn, Leeuwarden	
F-016	Lockheed Martin F-35A Lightning II	KLu 322 Sqn, Leeuwarden	
F-017	Lockheed Martin F-35A Lightning II	KLu 322 Sqn, Leeuwarden	
F-018	Lockheed Martin F-35A Lightning II	KLu 322 Sqn, Leeuwarden	
F-019	Lockheed Martin F-35A Lightning II	KLu 322 Sqn, Leeuwarden	
F-020	Lockheed Martin F-35A Lightning II	KLu 322 Sqn, Leeuwarden	
F-021	Lockheed Martin F-35A Lightning II	KLu 322 Sqn, Leeuwarden	
F-022	Lockheed Martin F-35A Lightning II	KLu 322 Sqn, Leeuwarden	
F-023	Lockheed Martin F-35A Lightning II	KLu 322 Sqn, Leeuwarden	
F-024	Lockheed Martin F-35A Lightning II	KLu 313 Sqn, Volkel	
F-025	Lockheed Martin F-35A Lightning II	KLu 313 Sqn, Volkel	
F-026	Lockheed Martin F-35A Lightning II	KLu 313 Sqn, Volkel	
F-027	Lockheed Martin F-35A Lightning II	KLu 313 Sqn, Volkel	
F-028	Lockheed Martin F-35A Lightning II $	KLu 313 Sqn, Volkel	
F-029	Lockheed Martin F-35A Lightning II	KLu 313 Sqn, Volkel	
F-030	Lockheed Martin F-35A Lightning II	KLu 313 Sqn, Volkel	
F-031	Lockheed Martin F-35A Lightning II $	KLu 313 Sqn, Volkel	
F-032	Lockheed Martin F-35A Lightning II	KLu 313 Sqn, Volkel	
F-033	Lockheed Martin F-35A Lightning II	KLu 313 Sqn, Volkel	
F-034	Lockheed Martin F-35A Lightning II	KLu 313 Sqn, Volkel	
F-035	Lockheed Martin F-35A Lightning II	KLu 313 Sqn, Volkel	
F-036	Lockheed Martin F-35A Lightning II	KLu 313 Sqn, Volkel	
F-037	Lockheed Martin F-35A Lightning II	KLu 313 Sqn, Volkel	
F-038	Lockheed Martin F-35A Lightning II	KLu 322 Sqn, Leeuwarden	
F-039	Lockheed Martin F-35A Lightning II	KLu 312 Sqn, Volkel (on loan to 322 Sqn)	
F-040	Lockheed Martin F-35A Lightning II	KLu 322 Sqn, Leeuwarden	
F-041	Lockheed Martin F-35A Lightning II	KLu (on order)	
F-042	Lockheed Martin F-35A Lightning II	KLu (on order)	
F-043	Lockheed Martin F-35A Lightning II	KLu (on order)	
F-044	Lockheed Martin F-35A Lightning II	KLu (on order)	
F-045	Lockheed Martin F-35A Lightning II	KLu (on order)	
F-046	Lockheed Martin F-35A Lightning II	KLu (on order)	
F-047	Lockheed Martin F-35A Lightning II	KLu (on order)	
F-048	Lockheed Martin F-35A Lightning II	KLu (on order)	
F-049	Lockheed Martin F-35A Lightning II	KLu (on order)	

Notes	Serial	Type (code/other identity)	Owner/operator, location or fate
	F-050	Lockheed Martin F-35A Lightning II	KLu (on order)
	F-051	Lockheed Martin F-35A Lightnig II	KLu (on order)
	F-052	Lockheed Martin F-35A Lightning II	KLu (on order)
	G-273	Lockheed C-130H-30 Hercules	KLu 336 Sqn, Eindhoven
	G-275	Lockheed C-130H-30 Hercules	KLu 336 Sqn, Eindhoven
	G-781	Lockheed C-130H Hercules	KLu 336 Sqn, Eindhoven
	G-988	Lockheed C-130H Hercules	KLu 336 Sqn, Eindhoven
	J-003	Fokker (GD) F-16AM Fighting Falcon	*To Ukraine, 2024*
	J-004	Fokker (GD) F-16AM Fighting Falcon	KLu, EFTC, Fetesti, Romania
	J-005	Fokker (GD) F-16AM Fighting Falcon	*KLu, stored Volkel (for Ukraine)*
	J-006	Fokker (GD) F-16AM Fighting Falcon	*KLu, stored Volkel (for Ukraine)*
	J-008	Fokker (GD) F-16AM Fighting Falcon	*KLu, stored Volkel (for Ukraine)*
	J-010	Fokker (GD) F-16AM Fighting Falcon	KLu, EFTC, Fetesti, Romania
	J-011	Fokker (GD) F-16AM Fighting Falcon	*KLu, stored Volkel (for Ukraine)*
	J-013	Fokker (GD) F-16AM Fighting Falcon	*KLu, stored Volkel (for Ukraine)*
	J-014	Fokker (GD) F-16AM Fighting Falcon	*To Ukraine, 2024*
	J-015	Fokker (GD) F-16AM Fighting Falcon	*KLu, stored Volkel (for Ukraine)*
	J-016	Fokker (GD) F-16AM Fighting Falcon	*KLu, stored Volkel (for Ukraine)*
	J-017	Fokker (GD) F-16AM Fighting Falcon	*KLu, stored Volkel (for Ukraine)*
	J-018	Fokker (GD) F-16AM Fighting Falcon	KLu, EFTC, Fetesti, Romania
	J-019	Fokker (GD) F-16AM Fighting Falcon	KLu, EFTC, Fetesti, Romania
	J-020	Fokker (GD) F-16AM Fighting Falcon	*KLu, stored Volkel (for Ukraine)*
	J-021	Fokker (GD) F-16AM Fighting Falcon	KLu, EFTC, Fetesti, Romania
	J-055	Fokker (GD) F-16AM Fighting Falcon	*KLu, stored Volkel (for Ukraine)*
	J-060	Fokker (GD) F-16AM Fighting Falcon	*KLu, stored Volkel (for Ukraine)*
	J-062	Fokker (GD) F-16AM Fighting Falcon	*KLu, stored Volkel (for Ukraine)*
	J-064	Fokker (GD) F-16BM Fighting Falcon	KLu, EFTC, Fetesti, Romania
	J-067	Fokker (GD) F-16BM Fighting Falcon	KLu, EFTC, Fetesti, Romania
	J-136	Fokker (GD) F-16AM Fighting Falcon	*KLu, stored Volkel (for Ukraine)*
	J-144	Fokker (GD) F-16AM Fighting Falcon	KLu, EFTC, Fetesti, Romania
	J-146	Fokker (GD) F-16AM Fighting Falcon	*KLu, stored Volkel (for Ukraine)*
	J-197	Fokker (GD) F-16AM Fighting Falcon	*KLu, stored Volkel (for Ukraine)*
	J-201	Fokker (GD) F-16AM Fighting Falcon	KLu, EFTC, Fetesti, Romania
	J-202	Fokker (GD) F-16AM Fighting Falcon	*KLu, Charleroi, Belgium, for GI*
	J-209	Fokker (GD) F-16BM Fighting Falcon	KLu, EFTC, Fetesti, Romania
	J-210	Fokker (GD) F-16BM Fighting Falcon	KLu, EFTC, Fetesti, Romania
	J-366	Fokker (GD) F-16AM Fighting Falcon	KLu, EFTC, Fetesti, Romania
	J-367	Fokker (GD) F-16AM Fighting Falcon	*KLu, stored Volkel (for Ukraine)*
	J-368	Fokker (GD) F-16BM Fighting Falcon	KLu, EFTC, Fetesti, Romania
	J-369	Fokker (GD) F-16BM Fighting Falcon	KLu, EFTC, Fetesti, Romania
	J-508	Fokker (GD) F-16AM Fighting Falcon	*KLu, stored Volkel (for Ukraine)*
	J-509	Fokker (GD) F-16AM Fighting Falcon	KLu, EFTC, Fetesti, Romania
	J-512	Fokker (GD) F-16AM Fighting Falcon	*KLu, stored Volkel (for Ukraine)*
	J-514	Fokker (GD) F-16AM Fighting Falcon	*KLu, stored Volkel (for Ukraine)*
	J-515	Fokker (GD) F-16AM Fighting Falcon	*KLu, stored Volkel (for Ukraine)*
	J-516	Fokker (GD) F-16AM Fighting Falcon	*KLu, stored Volkel (for Ukraine)*
	J-641	Fokker (GD) F-16AM Fighting Falcon	*KLu, stored Volkel (for Ukraine)*
	J-644	Fokker (GD) F-16AM Fighting Falcon	KLu, EFTC, Fetesti, Romania
	J-646	Fokker (GD) F-16AM Fighting Falcon	KLu, EFTC, Fetesti, Romania
	J-882	Fokker (GD) F-16BM Fighting Falcon	KLu, EFTC, Fetesti, Romania
	L-01	Pilatus PC-7 Turbo Trainer	KLu 131 EMVO Sqn, Woensdrecht
	L-02	Pilatus PC-7 Turbo Trainer	KLu 131 EMVO Sqn, Woensdrecht
	L-03	Pilatus PC-7 Turbo Trainer	KLu 131 EMVO Sqn, Woensdrecht
	L-04	Pilatus PC-7 Turbo Trainer $	KLu 131 EMVO Sqn, Woensdrecht
	L-05	Pilatus PC-7 Turbo Trainer	KLu 131 EMVO Sqn, Woensdrecht
	L-06	Pilatus PC-7 Turbo Trainer	KLu 131 EMVO Sqn, Woensdrecht
	L-07	Pilatus PC-7 Turbo Trainer	KLu 131 EMVO Sqn, Woensdrecht
	L-08	Pilatus PC-7 Turbo Trainer	KLu 131 EMVO Sqn, Woensdrecht
	L-09	Pilatus PC-7 Turbo Trainer	KLu 131 EMVO Sqn, Woensdrecht
	L-10	Pilatus PC-7 Turbo Trainer	KLu 131 EMVO Sqn, Woensdrecht
	L-11	Pilatus PC-7 Turbo Trainer	KLu 131 EMVO Sqn, Woensdrecht
	L-12	Pilatus PC-7 Turbo Trainer	KLu 131 EMVO Sqn, Woensdrecht

Serial	Type (code/other identity)	Owner/operator, location or fate	Notes
L-13	Pilatus PC-7 Turbo Trainer	KLu 131 EMVO Sqn, Woensdrecht	
N-088	NH Industries NH.90-NFH	KLu 860 Sqn, De Kooij	
N-102	NH Industries NH.90-NFH	KLu 860 Sqn, De Kooij	
N-110	NH Industries NH.90-NFH	KLu 860 Sqn, De Kooij	
N-164	NH Industries NH.90-NFH	KLu 860 Sqn, De Kooij	
N-175	NH Industries NH.90-NFH	KLu 860 Sqn, De Kooij	
N-195	NH Industries NH.90-NFH	KLu 860 Sqn, De Kooij	
N-227	NH Industries NH.90-NFH	KLu 860 Sqn, De Kooij	
N-228	NH Industries NH.90-NFH	KLu 860 Sqn, De Kooij	
N-233	NH Industries NH.90-NFH	KLu 860 Sqn, De Kooij	
N-234	NH Industries NH.90-NFH	KLu 860 Sqn, De Kooij	
N-258	NH Industries NH.90-NFH	KLu 860 Sqn, De Kooij	
N-277	NH Industries NH.90-NFH	KLu 860 Sqn, De Kooij	
N-316	NH Industries NH.90-NFH	KLu 860 Sqn, De Kooij	
N-317	NH Industries NH.90-NFH	KLu 860 Sqn, De Kooij	
N-318	NH Industries NH.90-NFH	KLu 860 Sqn, De Kooij	
N-319	NH Industries NH.90-NFH	KLu 860 Sqn, De Kooij	
N-325	NH Industries NH.90-NFH	KLu 860 Sqn, De Kooij	
N-326	NH Industries NH.90-NFH	KLu 860 Sqn, De Kooij	
N-327	NH Industries NH.90-NFH	KLu 860 Sqn, De Kooij	
Q-31	MDH AH-64E Apache Guardian	KLu 302 Sqn, Fort *Cavazos*, Texas, USA	
Q-32	MDH AH-64E Apache Guardian	KLu 302 Sqn, Fort *Cavazos*, Texas, USA	
Q-33	MDH AH-64E Apache Guardian	KLu 302 Sqn, Fort *Cavazos*, Texas, USA	
Q-34	MDH AH-64E Apache Guardian	KLu 302 Sqn, Fort *Cavazos*, Texas, USA	
Q-35	MDH AH-64E Apache Guardian	KLu 302 Sqn, Fort *Cavazos*, Texas, USA	
Q-36	MDH AH-64E Apache Guardian	KLu 302 Sqn, Fort *Cavazos*, Texas, USA	
Q-37	MDH AH-64E Apache Guardian	KLu 301 Sqn, Gilze-Rijen	
Q-38	MDH AH-64E Apache Guardian	KLu 301 Sqn, Gilze-Rijen	
Q-39	MDH AH-64E Apache Guardian	KLu 301 Sqn, Gilze-Rijen	
Q-40	MDH AH-64E Apache Guardian	KLu 301 Sqn, Gilze-Rijen	
Q-41	MDH AH-64E Apache Guardian	KLu 301 Sqn, Gilze-Rijen	
Q-42	MDH AH-64E Apache Guardian	KLu 301 Sqn, Gilze-Rijen	
Q-43	MDH AH-64E Apache Guardian	KLu (on order)	
Q-44	MDH AH-64E Apache Guardian	KLu (on order)	
Q-45	MDH AH-64E Apache Guardian	KLu (on order)	
Q-46	MDH AH-64E Apache Guardian	KLu (on order)	
Q-47	MDH AH-64E Apache Guardian	KLu (on order)	
Q-48	MDH AH-64E Apache Guardian	KLu (on order)	
Q-49	MDH AH-64E Apache Guardian	KLu (on order)	
Q-50	MDH AH-64E Apache Guardian	KLu (on order)	
Q-51	MDH AH-64E Apache Guardian	KLu (on order)	
Q-52	MDH AH-64E Apache Guardian	KLu (on order)	
Q-53	MDH AH-64E Apache Guardian	KLu (on order)	
Q-54	MDH AH-64E Apache Guardian	KLu (on order)	
Q-55	MDH AH-64E Apache Guardian	KLu (on order)	
Q-56	MDH AH-64E Apache Guardian	KLu (on order)	
Q-57	MDH AH-64E Apache Guardian	KLu (on order)	
Q-58	MDH AH-64E Apache Guardian	KLu (on order)	
S-419	Eurocopter AS.532U-2 Cougar	KLu 300 Sqn, Gilze-Rijen	
S-440	Eurocopter AS.532U-2 Cougar	KLu 300 Sqn, Gilze-Rijen	
S-441	Eurocopter AS.532U-2 Cougar	KLu 300 Sqn, Gilze-Rijen	
S-442	Eurocopter AS.532U-2 Cougar	KLu 300 Sqn, Gilze-Rijen	
S-444	Eurocopter AS.532U-2 Cougar	KLu 300 Sqn, Gilze-Rijen	
S-445	Eurocopter AS.532U-2 Cougar	KLu 300 Sqn, Gilze-Rijen	
S-447	Eurocopter AS.532U-2 Cougar	KLu 300 Sqn, Gilze-Rijen	
S-453	Eurocopter AS.532U-2 Cougar	KLu 300 Sqn, Gilze-Rijen	
S-454	Eurocopter AS.532U-2 Cougar	KLu 300 Sqn, Gilze-Rijen	
S-456	Eurocopter AS.532U-2 Cougar	KLu 300 Sqn, Gilze-Rijen	
S-458	Eurocopter AS.532U-2 Cougar	KLu 300 Sqn, Gilze-Rijen	
S-459	Eurocopter AS.532U-2 Cougar	KLu 300 Sqn, Gilze-Rijen	
T-054	Airbus A.330-243 MRTT (KC-30) (EC-340/MRTT054)	KLu/MMU, 334 Sqn, Eindhoven	
T-055	Airbus A.330-243 MRTT (KC-30) (EC-336/MRTT055)	KLu/MMU, 334 Sqn, Eindhoven	

Notes	Serial	Type (code/other identity)	Owner/operator, location or fate
	T-056	Airbus A.330-243 MRTT (KC-30) (EC-331/MRTT056)	KLu/MMU, 334 Sqn, Eindhoven
	T-057	Airbus A.330-243 MRTT (KC-30) (EC-337/MRTT057)	KLu/MMU, 334 Sqn, Eindhoven
	T-058	Airbus A.330-243 MRTT (KC-30) (EC-335/MRTT058)	KLu/MMU, 334 Sqn, Eindhoven
	T-059	Airbus A.330-243 MRTT (KC-30) (EC-338/MRTT059)	KLu/MMU, 334 Sqn, Eindhoven
	T-060	Airbus A.330-243 MRTT (KC-30) (EC-340/MRTT060)	KLu/MMU, 334 Sqn, Eindhoven
	T-061	Airbus A.330-243 MRTT (KC-30) (EC-344/MRTT061)	KLu/MMU, 334 Sqn, Eindhoven
	T-062	Airbus A.330-243 MRTT (KC-30) (EC-332/MRTT062)	KLu/MMU (or order)
	V-117	Gulfstream Aerospace G.650ER	KLu 334 Sqn, Eindhoven
	Kustwacht & Netherlands Government		
	PH-CGD	De Havilland Canada DHC-8-102 (C-GCFK)	Kustwacht, Amsterdam/Schiphol
	PH-CGE	De Havilland Canada DHC-8-102 (C-FCGE)	Kustwacht, Amsterdam/Schiphol
	PH-GOV	Boeing 737-700(BBJ) (N513BJ)	Dutch Royal Flight, Amsterdam/Schiphol

NEW ZEALAND
Royal New Zealand Air Force (RNZAF)

Notes	Serial	Type (code/other identity)	Owner/operator, location or fate
	NZ7001	Lockheed C-130H(NZ) Hercules $	*Withdrawn from use, Woodbourne, January 2025*
	NZ7002	Lockheed C-130H(NZ) Hercules	*Withdrawn from use, Woodbourne, January 2025*
	NZ7005	Lockheed C-130H(NZ) Hercules	*Withdrawn from use, Woodbourne, January 2025*
	NZ7571	Boeing 757-2K2	RNZAF 40 Sqn, Whenuapai
	NZ7572	Boeing 757-2K2	RNZAF 40 Sqn, Whenuapai
	NZ4801	Boeing P-8A Poseidon	RNZAF 5 Sqn, Ohakea
	NZ4802	Boeing P-8A Poseidon	RNZAF 5 Sqn, Ohakea
	NZ4803	Boeing P-8A Poseidon	RNZAF 5 Sqn, Ohakea
	NZ4804	Boeing P-8A Poseidon	RNZAF 5 Sqn, Ohakea
	NZ7011	Lockheed C-130J-30 Hercules	RNZAF 40 Sqn, Whenuapai
	NZ7012	Lockheed C-130J-30 Hercules	RNZAF 40 Sqn, Whenuapai
	NZ7013	Lockheed C-130J-30 Hercules	RNZAF 40 Sqn, Whenuapai
	NZ7014	Lockheed C-130J-30 Hercules	RNZAF 40 Sqn, Whenuapai
	NZ7015	Lockheed C-130J-30 Hercules	RNZAF 40 Sqn, Whenuapai

NIGER

Notes	Serial	Type (code/other identity)	Owner/operator, location or fate
	5U-GRN	Boeing 737-75U	Government of Niger, Niamey

NIGERIA
Nigerian Air Force (NAF)

Notes	Serial	Type (code/other identity)	Owner/operator, location or fate
	NAF913	Lockheed C-130H Hercules	NAF 301 HAG, Ikeja
	NAF917	Lockheed C-130H-30 Hercules	NAF, stored Lagos
	NAF918	Lockheed C-130H-30 Hercules	NAF 301 HAG, Ikeja
	NAF962	Cessna 680 Citation Sovereign (5N-EMS)	NAF, Abuja
	Nigerian Government		
	5N-FGA	Airbus ACJ330-243	Federal Government of Nigeria, Abuja
	5N-FGS	Gulfstream Aerospace Gulfstream V	Federal Government of Nigeria, Abuja
	5N-FGT	Boeing 737-7N6 [001]	*Stored Basel, Switzerland (for sale)*
	5N-FGU	Dassault Falcon 7X	Stored Paris-Le Bourget, France
	5N-FGV	Dassault Falcon 7X	Federal Government of Nigeria, Abuja
	5N-FGW	Gulfstream Aerospace G.550	Federal Government of Nigeria, Abuja
	5N-FGZ	Bombardier CL-605	Federal Government of Nigeria, Abuja

NORWAY
Luftforsvaret/Royal Norwegian Air Force (RNoAF)

NOTE:330 Skv maintains SAR detachments at Bodø, Florø, Lakselv/Banak and Rygge

Notes	Serial	Type (code/other identity)	Owner/operator, location or fate
	139	Bell 412HP	RNoAF 339 Skv, Bardufoss
	140	Bell 412HP	RNoAF 339 Skv, Bardufoss
	141	Bell 412HP	RNoAF 339 Skv, Bardufoss
	142	Bell 412HP	RNoAF 339 Skv, Bardufoss
	143	Bell 412HP	RNoAF 339 Skv, Bardufoss
	144	Bell 412HP	RNoAF 339 Skv, Bardufoss
	145	Bell 412HP	RNoAF 339 Skv, Bardufoss
	146	Bell 412HP	RNoAF 339 Skv, Bardufoss
	147	Bell 412HP	RNoAF 339 Skv, Bardufoss
	148	Bell 412HP	RNoAF 339 Skv, Bardufoss
	149	Bell 412HP	RNoAF 339 Skv, Bardufoss

Serial	Type (code/other identity)	Owner/operator, location or fate	Notes
161	Bell 412HP	RNoAF 339 Skv, Bardufoss	
162	Bell 412HP	RNoAF 339 Skv, Bardufoss	
163	Bell 412HP	RNoAF 339 Skv, Bardufoss	
164	Bell 412HP	RNoAF 339 Skv, Bardufoss	
165	Bell 412HP	RNoAF 339 Skv, Bardufoss	
166	Bell 412HP	RNoAF 339 Skv, Bardufoss	
		(damaged January 2024)	
167	Bell 412HP	RNoAF 339 Skv, Bardufoss	
0262	AgustaWestland AW101 Mk.612 (ZZ100)	RNoAF (on order)	
0264	AgustaWestland AW101 Mk.612 (ZZ101)	RNoAF 330 SKV, Sola	
0265	AgustaWestland AW101 Mk.612 (ZZ102)	RNoAF 330 SKV, Sola	
0268	AgustaWestland AW101 Mk.612 (ZZ103)	RNoAF 330 SKV, Sola	
0270	AgustaWestland AW101 Mk.612 (ZZ104)	RNoAF 330 SKV, Sola	
0273	AgustaWestland AW101 Mk.612 (ZZ105)	RNoAF 330 SKV, Sola	
0275	AgustaWestland AW101 Mk.612 (ZZ106)	RNoAF 330 SKV, Sola	
0276	AgustaWestland AW101 Mk.612 (ZZ107)	RNoAF 330 SKV, Sola	
0277	AgustaWestland AW101 Mk.612 (ZZ108)	RNoAF 330 SKV, Sola	
0278	AgustaWestland AW101 Mk.612 (ZZ109)	RNoAF 330 SKV, Sola	
0279	AgustaWestland AW101 Mk.612 (ZZ110)	RNoAF 330 SKV, Sola	
0280	AgustaWestland AW101 Mk.612 (ZZ111)	RNoAF 330 SKV, Sola	
0281	AgustaWestland AW101 Mk.612 (ZZ112)	RNoAF 330 SKV, Sola	
0282	AgustaWestland AW101 Mk.612 (ZZ113)	RNoAF 330 SKV, Sola	
0283	AgustaWestland AW101 Mk.612 (ZZ114)	RNoAF 330 SKV, Sola	
0284	AgustaWestland AW101 Mk.612 (ZZ115)	RNoAF 330 SKV, Sola	
5087	Lockheed Martin F-35A Lightning II	RNoAF 62nd FS/56th FW, Luke AFB, AZ, USA	
5088	Lockheed Martin F-35A Lightning II	RNoAF 62nd FS/56th FW, Luke AFB, AZ, USA	
5110	Lockheed Martin F-35A Lightning II	RNoAF 62nd FS/56th FW, Luke AFB, AZ, USA	
5111	Lockheed Martin F-35A Lightning II	RNoAF 62nd FS/56th FW, Luke AFB, AZ, USA	
5145	Lockheed Martin F-35A Lightning II	RNoAF 62nd FS/56th FW, Luke AFB, AZ, USA	
5146	Lockheed Martin F-35A Lightning II $	RNoAF 62nd FS/56th FW, Luke AFB, AZ, USA	
5147	Lockheed Martin F-35A Lightning II	RNoAF 62nd FS/56th FW, Luke AFB, AZ, USA	
5148	Lockheed Martin F-35A Lightning II	RNoAF 332 Skv, Ørland	
5149	Lockheed Martin F-35A Lightning II	RNoAF 332 Skv, Ørland	
5150	Lockheed Martin F-35A Lightning II	RNoAF 332 Skv, Ørland	
5205	Lockheed Martin F-35A Lightning II	RNoAF 332 Skv, Ørland	
5206	Lockheed Martin F-35A Lightning II	RNoAF 332 Skv, Ørland	
5207	Lockheed Martin F-35A Lightning II	RNoAF 332 Skv, Ørland	
5208	Lockheed Martin F-35A Lightning II	RNoAF 332 Skv, Ørland	
5209	Lockheed Martin F-35A Lightning II	RNoAF 332 Skv, Ørland	
5210	Lockheed Martin F-35A Lightning II	RNoAF 332 Skv, Ørland	
5288	Lockheed Martin F-35A Lightning II	RNoAF 332 Skv, Ørland	
5289	Lockheed Martin F-35A Lightning II	RNoAF 332 Skv, Ørland	
5290	Lockheed Martin F-35A Lightning II	RNoAF 332 Skv, Ørland	
5291	Lockheed Martin F-35A Lightning II	RNoAF 62nd FS/56th FW, Luke AFB, AZ, USA	
5292	Lockheed Martin F-35A Lightning II	RNoAF 62nd FS/56th FW, Luke AFB, AZ, USA	
5293	Lockheed Martin F-35A Lightning II	RNoAF 332 Skv, Ørland	
5384	Lockheed Martin F-35A Lightning II	RNoAF 332 Skv, Ørland	
5385	Lockheed Martin F-35A Lightning II	RNoAF 332 Skv, Ørland	
5386	Lockheed Martin F-35A Lightning II	RNoAF 332 Skv, Ørland	
5387	Lockheed Martin F-35A Lightning II	RNoAF 332 Skv, Ørland	
5388	Lockheed Martin F-35A Lightning II	RNoAF 332 Skv, Ørland	
5389	Lockheed Martin F-35A Lightning II	RNoAF 332 Skv, Ørland	
5501	Lockheed Martin F-35A Lightning II	RNoAF 332 Skv, Ørland	
5502	Lockheed Martin F-35A Lightning II	RNoAF 332 Skv, Ørland	
5503	Lockheed Martin F-35A Lightning II	RNoAF 332 Skv, Ørland	
5504	Lockheed Martin F-35A Lightning II	RNoAF 332 Skv, Ørland	
5505	Lockheed Martin F-35A Lightning II	RNoAF 332 Skv, Ørland	
5506	Lockheed Martin F-35A Lightning II	RNoAF 332 Skv, Ørland	
5664	Lockheed Martin F-35A Lightning II	RNoAF 332 Skv, Ørland	
5665	Lockheed Martin F-35A Lightning II	RNoAF 332 Skv, Ørland	
5666	Lockheed Martin F-35A Lightning II	RNoAF 332 Skv, Ørland	
5667	Lockheed Martin F-35A Lightning II	RNoAF 332 Skv, Ørland	

Notes	Serial	Type (code/other identity)	Owner/operator, location or fate
	5668	Lockheed Martin F-35A Lightning II	RNoAF 332 Skv, Ørland
	5669	Lockheed Martin F-35A Lightning II	RNoAF 332 Skv, Ørland
	5746	Lockheed Martin F-35A Lightning II	RNoAF 332 Skv, Ørland
	5747	Lockheed Martin F-35A Lightning II	RNoAF 332 Skv, Ørland
	5748	Lockheed Martin F-35A Lightning II	RNoAF 332 Skv, Ørland
	5749	Lockheed Martin F-35A Lightning II	RNoAF 332 Skv, Ørland
	5750	Lockheed Martin F-35A Lightning II	RNoAF 332 Skv, Ørland
	5751	Lockheed Martin F-35A Lightning II	RNoAF 332 Skv, Ørland
	5823	Lockheed Martin F-35A Lightning II	RNoAF (on order)
	5824	Lockheed Martin F-35A Lightning II	RNoAF (on order)
	5825	Lockheed Martin F-35A Lightning II	RNoAF (on order)
	5826	Lockheed Martin F-35A Lightning II	RNoAF (on order)
	5827	Lockheed Martin F-35A Lightning II	RNoAF (on order)
	5828	Lockheed Martin F-35A Lightning II	RNoAF (on order)
	5601	Lockheed C-130J-30 Hercules II	RNoAF 335 Skv, Gardermoen
	5607	Lockheed C-130J-30 Hercules II	RNoAF 335 Skv, Gardermoen
	5629	Lockheed C-130J-30 Hercules II	RNoAF 335 Skv, Gardermoen
	5699	Lockheed C-130J-30 Hercules II	RNoAF 335 Skv, Gardermoen
	9582	Boeing P-8A Poseidon (N682DS)	RNoAF 333 Skv, Evenes
	9583	Boeing P-8A Poseidon (N684DS)	RNoAF 333 Skv, Evenes
	9584	Boeing P-8A Poseidon (N685DS)	RNoAF 333 Skv, Evenes
	9585	Boeing P-8A Poseidon (N687DS)	RNoAF 333 Skv, Evenes
	9586	Boeing P-8A Poseidon (N688DS)	RNoAF 333 Skv, Evenes

OMAN
Royal Air Force of Oman (RAFO)

Notes	Serial	Type (code/other identity)	Owner/operator, location or fate
	501	Lockheed C-130H Hercules	RAFO 16 Sqn, Al Musana
	502	Lockheed C-130H Hercules	RAFO 16 Sqn, Al Musana
	503	Lockheed C-130H Hercules	RAFO 16 Sqn, Al Musana
	505	Lockheed C-130J Hercules II	RAFO 16 Sqn, Al Musana
	506	Lockheed C-130J Hercules II	RAFO 16 Sqn, Al Musana
	525	Lockheed C-130J-30 Hercules II	RAFO Royal Flt, Seeb
	554	Airbus A.320CJ-214X	RAFO 4 Sqn, Seeb
	555	Airbus A.320CJ-214X	RAFO 4 Sqn, Seeb
	556	Airbus A.320CJ-214X	RAFO 4 Sqn, Seeb
	557	Grumman G.1159C Gulfstream IV	RAFO 4 Sqn, Seeb
	558	Grumman G.1159C Gulfstream IV	RAFO 4 Sqn, Seeb
	901	CASA C-295M	RAFO 5 Sqn, Salalah
	902	CASA C-295M	RAFO 5 Sqn, Salalah
	903	CASA C-295M	RAFO 5 Sqn, Salalah
	904	CASA C-295M	RAFO 5 Sqn, Salalah
	910	CASA C-295MPA Persuader	RAFO 2 Sqn, Al Musana
	911	CASA C-295MPA Persuader	RAFO 2 Sqn, Al Musana
	912	CASA C-295MPA Persuader	RAFO 2 Sqn, Al Musana
	913	CASA C-295MPA Persuader	RAFO 2 Sqn, Al Musana

Government of Oman

Notes	Serial	Type (code/other identity)	Owner/operator, location or fate
	A4O-AA	Airbus A.320-233	Government of Oman, Seeb
	A4O-AD	Gulfstream Aerospace G.550	Government of Oman, Seeb
	A4O-AE	Gulfstream Aerospace G.550	Government of Oman, Seeb
	A4O-AJ	Airbus A.319-115CJ	Government of Oman, Seeb
	A4O-SO	Boeing 747SP-27	Government of Oman, Seeb
	A4O-HMS	Boeing 747-8H0BBJ	Government of Oman, Seeb
	A4O-OMN	Boeing 747-430	Government of Oman, Seeb

PAKISTAN
Pakistan Air Force (PAF)/Pakistani Army

Notes	Serial	Type (code/other identity)	Owner/operator, location or fate
	4119	Lockheed C-130E Hercules [119]	PAF 21 Sqn, Karachi
	4144	Lockheed L.100 Hercules [144]	PAF 6 Sqn, Islamabad
	4148	Lockheed C-130E Hercules [148]	PAF 6 Sqn, Islamabad
	4153	Lockheed C-130E Hercules [153]	PAF 21 Sqn, Karachi
	4159	Lockheed C-130E Hercules [159]	PAF 21 Sqn, Karachi
	4171	Lockheed C-130E Hercules [171]	PAF 6 Sqn, Islamabad

Serial	Type (code/other identity)	Owner/operator, location or fate	Notes
4177	Lockheed C-130E Hercules [177]	PAF 6 Sqn, Islamabad	
4178	Lockheed C-130E Hercules [178] $	PAF 6 Sqn, Islamabad	
4189	Lockheed C-130E Hercules [189]	PAF 6 Sqn, Islamabad	
4270	Gulfstream Aerospace G.450	Pakistani Army, Rawalpindi	
4282	Lockheed C-130E Hercules [282]	PAF 6 Sqn, Islamabad	
4455	Lockheed C-130H Hercules (CH-01)	PAF 6 Sqn, Islamabad	
4467	Lockheed C-130H Hercules (CH-04)	PAF 6 Sqn, Islamabad	
4470	Lockheed C-130H Hercules (CH-05/N992BA)	PAF 6 Sqn, Islamabad	
4476	Lockheed C-130H Hercules (CH-07/N993BA)	PAF 6 Sqn, Islamabad	
4479	Lockheed C-130H Hercules (CH-09)	PAF 6 Sqn, Islamabad	
4482	Lockheed C-130H Hercules (CH-11)	PAF 6 Sqn, Islamabad	
4483	Lockheed C-130H Hercules (CH-12)	PAF 6 Sqn, Islamabad	
J-754	Cessna 560 Citation VI	PAF 12 VIP Communications Sqn, Islamabad	
J-755	Gulfstream Aerospace G.1159C Gulfstream IV-SP	PAF 12 VIP Communications Sqn, Islamabad	
J-756	Gulfstream Aerospace G.450	PAF 12 VIP Communications Sqn, Islamabad	
J-758	Bombardier Global 6000	PAF 12 VIP Communications Sqn, Islamabad	
Pakistan Government			
PA-9834	Bombardier Global 5000 (AP-XAA)	Government of Pakistan, Dhamial	

PANAMA

| HP-1A | Embraer ERJ.135 Legacy 600 | Governement of Panama, Panama City | |

POLAND

Sily Powietrzne (SP)/Polish Air Force & Lotnictwo Marynarki Wojennej (LMW)/Polish Navy

NOTE: All SU-22 operations that were formerly at Swidwin have now moved to Miroslawiec as Swidwin is prepared for the arrival of the recently ordered F-35As.

NOTE: The 2 Saab 340AEW&C aircraft recently received from Sweden are allocated to 44.BLMW of the Polish Navy at Siemerowice but are operated by the Air Force.

0001	Gulfstream Aerospace G.550 (N547GA)	SP 1.BLTr, Warszawa	
0002	Gulfstream Aerospace G.550 (N554GD)	SP 1.BLTr, Warszawa	
011	CASA C-295M	SP 13.eltr/8.BLTr, Kraków/Balice	
012	CASA C-295M $	SP 13.eltr/8.BLTr, Kraków/Balice	
013	CASA C-295M	SP 13.eltr/8.BLTr, Kraków/Balice	
014	CASA C-295M	SP 13.eltr/8.BLTr, Kraków/Balice	
015	CASA C-295M	SP 13.eltr/8.BLTr, Kraków/Balice	
15	Mikoyan MiG-29UBM	SP 41.elt/22.BLT, Malbork	
016	CASA C-295M	SP 13.eltr/8.BLTr, Kraków/Balice	
017	CASA C-295M $	SP 13.eltr/8.BLTr, Kraków/Balice	
018	CASA C-295M	SP 13.eltr/8.BLTr, Kraków/Balice	
019	PZL 130TC-I Orlik	SP 2.OSzL/42.BLSz, Radom	
020	CASA C-295M	SP 13.eltr/8.BLTr, Kraków/Balice	
020	PZL 130TC-I Orlik	SP 2.OSzL/42.BLSz, Radom	
021	CASA C-295M	SP 13.eltr/8.BLTr, Kraków/Balice	
022	CASA C-295M	SP 13.eltr/8.BLTr, Kraków/Balice	
022	PZL 130TC-I Orlik	SP 2.OSzL/42.BLSz, Radom	
023	CASA C-295M	SP 13.eltr/8.BLTr, Kraków/Balice	
023	PZL 130TC-I Orlik	SP 2.OSzL/42.BLSz, Radom	
024	CASA C-295M	SP 13.eltr/8.BLTr, Kraków/Balice	
024	PZL 130TC-I Orlik	SP 2.OSzL/42.BLSz, Radom	
025	CASA C-295M	SP 13.eltr/8.BLTr, Kraków/Balice	
025	PZL 130TC-I Orlik	SP 2.OSzL/42.BLSz, Radom	
026	CASA C-295M	SP 13.eltr/8.BLTr, Kraków/Balice	
026	PZL 130TC-I Orlik	SP 2.OSzL/42.BLSz, Radom	
027	CASA C-295M	SP 13.eltr/8.BLTr, Kraków/Balice	
28	Mikoyan MiG-29UBM	SP 41.elt/22.BLT, Malbork	
029	PZL 130TC-II Orlik	SP 2.OSzL/42.BLSz, Radom	
030	PZL 130TC-II Orlik	SP 2.OSzL/42.BLSz, Radom	
031	PZL 130TC-II Orlik	SP 2.OSzL/42.BLSz, Radom	
032	PZL 130TC-II Orlik	SP 2.OSzL/42.BLSz, Radom	
035	PZL 130TC-I Orlik	SP 2.OSzL/42.BLSz, Radom	
036	PZL 130TC-I Orlik	SP 2.OSzL/42.BLSz, Radom	
037	PZL 130TC-I Orlik	SP 2.OSzL/42.BLSz, Radom	

Notes	Serial	Type (code/other identity)	Owner/operator, location or fate
	38	Mikoyan MiG-29M	SP 41.elt/22.BLT, Malbork
	038	PZL 130TC-II Orlik	SP 2.OSzL/42.BLSz, Radom
	040	PZL 130TC-II Orlik	SP 2.OSzL/42.BLSz, Radom
	041	PZL 130TC-II Orlik	SP 2.OSzL/42.BLSz, Radom
	42	Mikoyan MiG-29UBM	SP 41.elt/22.BLT, Malbork
	042	PZL 130TC-II Orlik	SP 2.OSzL/42.BLSz, Radom
	043	PZL 130TC-II Orlik	SP 2.OSzL/42.BLSz, Radom (stored)
	044	PZL 130TC-II Orlik	SP 2.OSzL/42.BLSz, Radom
	045	PZL 130TC-I Orlik	SP 2.OSzL/42.BLSz, Radom
	046	PZL 130TC-II Orlik	SP 2.OSzL/42.BLSz, Radom
	047	PZL 130TC-II Orlik	SP 2.OSzL/42.BLSz, Radom
	048	PZL 130TC-II Orlik	SP 2.OSzL/42.BLSz, Radom
	049	PZL 130TC-II Orlik	SP 2.OSzL/42.BLSz, Radom
	050	PZL 130TC-II Orlik	SP 2.OSzL/42.BLSz, Radom
	051	PZL 130TC-II Orlik	SP 2.OSzL/42.BLSz, Radom
	052	PZL 130TC-II Orlik	SP 2.OSzL/42.BLSz, Radom
	54	Mikoyan MiG-29M	SP 41.elt/22.BLT, Malbork
	56	Mikoyan MiG-29M	SP 41.elt/22.BLT, Malbork
	59	Mikoyan MiG-29M	SP 41.elt/22.BLT, Malbork
	65	Mikoyan MiG-29M	SP 41.elt/22.BLT, Malbork
	66	Mikoyan MiG-29M	SP 41.elt/22.BLT, Malbork
	70	Mikoyan MiG-29M	SP 41.elt/22.BLT, Malbork
	77	Mikoyan MiG-29M	SP 41.elt/22.BLT, Malbork
	83	Mikoyan MiG-29M	SP 41.elt/22.BLT, Malbork
	89	Mikoyan MiG-29M	SP 41.elt/22.BLT, Malbork
	92	Mikoyan MiG-29M	SP 41.elt/22.BLT, Malbork
	105	Mikoyan MiG-29M	SP 41.elt/22.BLT, Malbork
	108	Mikoyan MiG-29M	SP 41.elt/22.BLT, Malbork
	0110	Boeing 737-800 (N893BA)	SP 1.BLTr, Warszawa
	111	Mikoyan MiG-29M	SP 41.elt/22.BLT, Malbork
	0111	Boeing 737-800BBJ (N784BJ/F-WTBK)	SP 1.BLTr, Warszawa
	0112	Boeing 737-800BBJ (N785BJ)	SP 1.BLTr, Warszawa
	114	Mikoyan MiG-29M	SP 41.elt/22.BLT, Malbork
	115	Mikoyan MiG-29M	SP 41.elt/22.BLT, Malbork
	0203	PZL M28B-TD Bryza	SP 1.OSzL/41.BLSz, Deblin
	0204	PZL M28B-TD Bryza	SP 1.OSzL/41.BLSz, Deblin
	0205	PZL M28B-TD Bryza	SP 1.OSzL/41.BLSz, Deblin
	0206	PZL M28B-TD Bryza	SP 14.eltr/33.BLTr, Powidz
	0207	PZL M28B-TD Bryza	SP 1.OSzL/41.BLSz, Deblin
	0208	PZL M28B-TD Bryza	SP 14.eltr/33.BLTr, Powidz
	0209	PZL M28B-TD Bryza	SP 1.OSzL/41.BLSz, Deblin
	0210	PZL M28B-TD Bryza	SP 1.OSzL/41.BLSz, Deblin
	0211	PZL M28B-TD Bryza	SP 1.OSzL/41.BLSz, Deblin
	0212	PZL M28B-TD Bryza	SP 1.OSzL/41.BLSz, Deblin
	0213	PZL M28B/PT Bryza	SP 13.eltr/8.BLTr, Kraków/Balice
	0214	PZL M28B/PT Bryza	SP 14.eltr/33.BLTr, Powidz
	0215	PZL M28B/PT Bryza	SP 14.eltr/33.BLTr, Powidz
	0216	PZL M28B/PT Bryza	SP 13.eltr/8.BLTr, Kraków/Balice
	0217	PZL M28B/PT Bryza	SP 13.eltr/8.BLTr, Kraków/Balice
	0218	PZL M28B/PT Bryza	SP 13.eltr/8.BLTr, Kraków/Balice
	0219	PZL M28B/PT Bryza	SP 13.eltr/8.BLTr, Kraków/Balice
	0220	PZL M28B/PT Bryza	SP 13.eltr/8.BLTr, Kraków/Balice
	0221	PZL M28B/PT Bryza	SP 13.eltr/8.BLTr, Kraków/Balice
	0222	PZL M28B/PT Bryza	SP 13.eltr/8.BLTr, Kraków/Balice
	0223	PZL M28B/PT Bryza	SP 13.eltr/8.BLTr, Kraków/Balice
	0224	PZL M28B/PT Bryza	SP 13.eltr/8.BLTr, Kraków/Balice
	0225	PZL M28B/PT Bryza	SP 13.eltr/8.BLTr, Kraków/Balice
	305	Sukhoi Su-22UM-3K	SP 1/2.elt/1.SLT, Miroslawiec
	308	Sukhoi Su-22UM-3K	SP 1/2.elt/1.SLT, Miroslawiec
	310	Sukhoi Su-22UM-3K	SP 1/2.elt/1.SLT, Miroslawiec
	0404	PZL M28B-1E Bryza	LMW 30.el/44.BLMW, Cewice/Siemirowice
	0405	PZL M28B-1E Bryza	LMW 30.el/44.BLMW, Cewice/Siemirowice

Serial	Type (code/other identity)	Owner/operator, location or fate	Notes
508	Sukhoi Su-22UM-3K	SP 1/2.elt/1.SLT, Miroslawiec	
509	Sukhoi Su-22UM-3K	SP 1/2.elt/1.SLT, Miroslawiec	
707	Sukhoi Su-22UM-3K $	SP 1/2.elt/1.SLT, Miroslawiec	
0723	PZL M28B-TD Bryza	LMW 28.el/43.BLMW, Gydnia/Babie Doly	
0810	PZL M28B-1RM Bryza	LMW 30.el/44.BLMW, Cewice/Siemirowice	
1001	Mil Mi-14PL	LMW 29.el/44.BLMW, Darlowo	
1002	Mil Mi-14PL	LMW 29.el/44.BLMW, Darlowo	
1003	Mil Mi-14PL	LMW 29.el/44.BLMW, Darlowo	
1003	PZL M28B-TD Bryza	LMW 28.el/43.BLMW, Gydnia/Babie Doly	
1005	Mil Mi-14PL	LMW 29.el/44.BLMW, Darlowo	
1006	PZL M28B-1R Bryza	LMW 30.el/44.BLMW, Cewice/Siemirowice	
1007	Mil Mi-14PL	LMW 29.el/44.BLMW, Darlowo	
1008	Mil Mi-14PL	LMW 29.el/44.BLMW, Darlowo	
1008	PZL M28B-1R Bryza	LMW 30.el/44.BLMW, Cewice/Siemirowice	
1009	Mil Mi-14PL	LMW 29.el/44.BLMW, Darlowo	
1010	Mil Mi-14PL	LMW 29.el/44.BLMW, Darlowo	
1011	Mil Mi-14PL	LMW 29.el/44.BLMW, Darlowo	
1012	Mil Mi-14PL/R	LMW 29.el/44.BLMW, Darlowo	
1017	PZL M28B-1R Bryza $	LMW 30.el/44.BLMW, Cewice/Siemirowice	
1022	PZL M28B-1R Bryza	LMW 30.el/44.BLMW, Cewice/Siemirowice	
1114	PZL M28B-1R Bryza	LMW 30.el/44.BLMW, Cewice/Siemirowice	
1115	PZL M28B-1R Bryza	LMW 30.el/44.BLMW, Cewice/Siemirowice	
1116	PZL M28B-1R Bryza	LMW 30.el/44.BLMW, Cewice/Siemirowice	
1117	PZL M28B-1 Bryza	LMW 28.el/43.BLMW, Gydnia/Babie Doly	
1118	PZL M28B-1 Bryza	LMW 28.el/43.BLMW, Gydnia/Babie Doly	
1501	Lockheed C-130E Hercules	SP 14.eltr/33.BLTr, Powidz	
1502	Lockheed C-130E Hercules	*SP, wfu Powidz*	
1503	Lockheed C-130E Hercules	*To Deblin Museum, November 2024*	
1504	Lockheed C-130E Hercules	SP 14.eltr/33.BLTr, Powidz	
1505	Lockheed C-130E Hercules $	SP 14.eltr/33.BLTr, Powidz	
....	Lockheed C-130H Hercules (85-0035)	SP 14.eltr/33.BLTr, Powidz	
....	Lockheed C-130H Hercules (85-0036)	SP 14.eltr/33.BLTr, Powidz	
1511	Lockheed C-130H Hercules (91-9511)	SP 14.eltr/33.BLTr, Powidz	
151.	Lockheed C-130H Hercules (89-1182)	SP (on order)	
151.	Lockheed C-130H Hercules (89-1185)	SP (on order)	
151.	Lockheed C-130H Hercules (89-1187)	SP (on order)	
3201	Sukhoi Su-22M-4	SP 1/2.elt/1.SLT, Miroslawiec	
3304	Sukhoi Su-22M-4	SP 1/2.elt/1.SLT, Miroslawiec	
3401	SAAB SF.340AEW&C (100006)	LMW 30.el/44.BLMW, Cewice/Siemirowice	
3402	SAAB SF.340AEW&C (100005)	LMW 30.el/44.BLMW, Cewice/Siemirowice	
3501	Lockheed Martin F-35A Lightning II	SP 57th FS/33rd FW, Ebbing ANGB, AR, USA	
3502	Lockheed Martin F-35A Lightning II	SP 57th FS/33rd FW, Ebbing ANGB, AR, USA	
3503	Lockheed Martin F-35A Lightning II	SP 57th FS/33rd FW, Ebbing ANGB, AR, USA	
....	Lockheed Martin F-35A Lightning II	SP (on order)	
3612	Sukhoi Su-22M-4	SP 1/2.elt/1.SLT, Miroslawiec	
3713	Sukhoi Su-22M-4	SP 1/2.elt/1.SLT, Miroslawiec	
3715	Sukhoi Su-22M-4	SP 1/2.elt/1.SLT, Miroslawiec	
3816	Sukhoi Su-22M-4	SP 1/2.elt/1.SLT, Miroslawiec	
3817	Sukhoi Su-22M-4	SP 1/2.elt/1.SLT, Miroslawiec	
3819	Sukhoi Su-22M-4	SP 1/2.elt/1.SLT, Miroslawiec	
3920	Sukhoi Su-22M-4	SP 1/2.elt/1.SLT, Miroslawiec	
4040	Lockheed Martin F-16C-52 Fighting Falcon	SP 6.elt/31.BLT, Poznan/Krzesiny	
4041	Lockheed Martin F-16C-52 Fighting Falcon	SP 6.elt/31.BLT, Poznan/Krzesiny	
4042	Lockheed Martin F-16C-52 Fighting Falcon	SP 6.elt/31.BLT, Poznan/Krzesiny	
4043	Lockheed Martin F-16C-52 Fighting Falcon	SP 3.elt/31.BLT, Poznan/Krzesiny	
4044	Lockheed Martin F-16C-52 Fighting Falcon	SP 3.elt/31.BLT, Poznan/Krzesiny	
4045	Lockheed Martin F-16C-52 Fighting Falcon	SP 3.elt/31.BLT, Poznan/Krzesiny	
4046	Lockheed Martin F-16C-52 Fighting Falcon	SP 6.elt/31.BLT, Poznan/Krzesiny	
4047	Lockheed Martin F-16C-52 Fighting Falcon	SP 3.elt/31.BLT, Poznan/Krzesiny	
4048	Lockheed Martin F-16C-52 Fighting Falcon	SP 3.elt/31.BLT, Poznan/Krzesiny	
4049	Lockheed Martin F-16C-52 Fighting Falcon	SP 3.elt/31.BLT, Poznan/Krzesiny	
4050	Lockheed Martin F-16C-52 Fighting Falcon $	SP 3.elt/31.BLT, Poznan/Krzesiny	

Notes	Serial	Type (code/other identity)	Owner/operator, location or fate
	4051	Lockheed Martin F-16C-52 Fighting Falcon	SP 3.elt/31.BLT, Poznan/Krzesiny
	4052	Lockheed Martin F-16C-52 Fighting Falcon	SP 6.elt/31.BLT, Poznan/Krzesiny
	4053	Lockheed Martin F-16C-52 Fighting Falcon	SP 6.elt/31.BLT, Poznan/Krzesiny
	4054	Lockheed Martin F-16C-52 Fighting Falcon	SP 6.elt/31.BLT, Poznan/Krzesiny
	4055	Lockheed Martin F-16C-52 Fighting Falcon	SP 6.elt/31.BLT, Poznan/Krzesiny
	4056	Lockheed Martin F-16C-52 Fighting Falcon	SP 6.elt/31.BLT, Poznan/Krzesiny
	4057	Lockheed Martin F-16C-52 Fighting Falcon	SP 6.elt/31.BLT, Poznan/Krzesiny
	4058	Lockheed Martin F-16C-52 Fighting Falcon	SP 6.elt/31.BLT, Poznan/Krzesiny
	4059	Lockheed Martin F-16C-52 Fighting Falcon	SP 6.elt/31.BLT, Poznan/Krzesiny
	4060	Lockheed Martin F-16C-52 Fighting Falcon	SP 3.elt/31.BLT, Poznan/Krzesiny
	4061	Lockheed Martin F-16C-52 Fighting Falcon	SP 3.elt/31.BLT, Poznan/Krzesiny
	4062	Lockheed Martin F-16C-52 Fighting Falcon	SP 6.elt/31.BLT, Poznan/Krzesiny
	4063	Lockheed Martin F-16C-52 Fighting Falcon	SP 10.elt/32.BLT, Lask
	4064	Lockheed Martin F-16C-52 Fighting Falcon	SP 10.elt/32.BLT, Lask
	4065	Lockheed Martin F-16C-52 Fighting Falcon	SP 10.elt/32.BLT, Lask
	4066	Lockheed Martin F-16C-52 Fighting Falcon	SP 10.elt/32.BLT, Lask
	4067	Lockheed Martin F-16C-52 Fighting Falcon	SP 10.elt/32.BLT, Lask
	4068	Lockheed Martin F-16C-52 Fighting Falcon	SP 10.elt/32.BLT, Lask
	4069	Lockheed Martin F-16C-52 Fighting Falcon	SP 10.elt/32.BLT, Lask
	4070	Lockheed Martin F-16C-52 Fighting Falcon	SP 10.elt/32.BLT, Lask
	4071	Lockheed Martin F-16C-52 Fighting Falcon	SP 10.elt/32.BLT, Lask
	4072	Lockheed Martin F-16C-52 Fighting Falcon	SP 10.elt/32.BLT, Lask
	4073	Lockheed Martin F-16C-52 Fighting Falcon	SP 10.elt/32.BLT, Lask
	4074	Lockheed Martin F-16C-52 Fighting Falcon	SP 10.elt/32.BLT, Lask
	4075	Lockheed Martin F-16C-52 Fighting Falcon	SP 10.elt/32.BLT, Lask
	4076	Lockheed Martin F-16D-52 Fighting Falcon	SP 3.elt/31.BLT, Poznan/Krzesiny
	4077	Lockheed Martin F-16D-52 Fighting Falcon	SP 3.elt/31.BLT, Poznan/Krzesiny
	4078	Lockheed Martin F-16D-52 Fighting Falcon	SP 6.elt/31.BLT, Poznan/Krzesiny
	4079	Lockheed Martin F-16D-52 Fighting Falcon	SP 3.elt/31.BLT, Poznan/Krzesiny
	4080	Lockheed Martin F-16D-52 Fighting Falcon	SP 3.elt/31.BLT, Poznan/Krzesiny
	4081	Lockheed Martin F-16D-52 Fighting Falcon	SP 3.elt/31.BLT, Poznan/Krzesiny
	4082	Lockheed Martin F-16D-52 Fighting Falcon	SP 6.elt/31.BLT, Poznan/Krzesiny
	4083	Lockheed Martin F-16D-52 Fighting Falcon	SP 6.elt/31.BLT, Poznan/Krzesiny
	4084	Lockheed Martin F-16D-52 Fighting Falcon	SP 6.elt/31.BLT, Poznan/Krzesiny
	4085	Lockheed Martin F-16D-52 Fighting Falcon	SP 10.elt/32.BLT, Lask
	4086	Lockheed Martin F-16D-52 Fighting Falcon	SP 10.elt/32.BLT, Lask
	4087	Lockheed Martin Г-16D-52 Fighting Falcon	SP 10.elt/32.BLT, Lask
	4101	Mikoyan MiG-29G	SP 41.elt/22.BLT, Malbork
	4104	Mikoyan MiG-29G	SP 41.elt/22.BLT, Malbork
	4105	Mikoyan MiG-29GT	SP 41.elt/22.BLT, Malbork
	4110	Mikoyan MiG-29GT	SP 41.elt/22.BLT, Malbork
	4113	Mikoyan MiG-29G	SP 41.elt/22.BLT, Malbork
	4116	Mikoyan MiG-29G	*Preserved Swidwin, 2024*
	4120	Mikoyan MiG-29G	SP, stored Malbork
	4121	Mikoyan MiG-29G	SP 41.elt/22.BLT, Malbork
	4122	Mikoyan MiG-29G	SP 41.elt/22.BLT, Malbork
	4123	Mikoyan MiG-29GT	SP 41.elt/22.BLT, Malbork
	5001	Korean Aerospace Industries (KAI) FA-50GF	SP 23.BLT, Miñsk Mazowiecki
	5002	Korean Aerospace Industries (KAI) FA-50GF	SP 23.BLT, Miñsk Mazowiecki
	5003	Korean Aerospace Industries (KAI) FA-50GF	SP 23.BLT, Miñsk Mazowiecki
	5004	Korean Aerospace Industries (KAI) FA-50GF	SP 23.BLT, Miñsk Mazowiecki
	5005	Korean Aerospace Industries (KAI) FA-50GF	SP 23.BLT, Miñsk Mazowiecki
	5006	Korean Aerospace Industries (KAI) FA-50GF	SP 23.BLT, Miñsk Mazowiecki
	5007	Korean Aerospace Industries (KAI) FA-50GF	SP 23.BLT, Miñsk Mazowiecki
	5008	Korean Aerospace Industries (KAI) FA-50GF	SP 23.BLT, Miñsk Mazowiecki
	5009	Korean Aerospace Industries (KAI) FA-50GF	SP 23.BLT, Miñsk Mazowiecki
	5010	Korean Aerospace Industries (KAI) FA-50GF	SP 23.BLT, Miñsk Mazowiecki
	5011	Korean Aerospace Industries (KAI) FA-50GF	SP 23.BLT, Miñsk Mazowiecki
	5012	Korean Aerospace Industries (KAI) FA-50GF	SP 23.BLT, Miñsk Mazowiecki
	6201	AgustaWestland AW101 Mk.614 (ZR285)	LMW 29.el/44.BLMW, Darlowo
	6202	AgustaWestland AW101 Mk.614 (ZR286)	LMW 29.el/44.BLMW, Darlowo
	6203	AgustaWestland AW101 Mk.614 (ZR287)	LMW 29.el/44.BLMW, Darlowo

Serial	Type (code/other identity)	Owner/operator, location or fate	Notes
6204	AgustaWestland AW101 Mk.614 (ZR288)	LMW 29.el/44.BLMW, Darlowo	
7701	Aermacchi M-346 Bielik (CSX55209)	SP 48.el/41.BLSz, Deblin	
7702	Aermacchi M-346 Bielik (CSX55210)	SP 48.el/41.BLSz, Deblin	
7703	Aermacchi M-346 Bielik (CSX55211)	SP 48.el/41.BLSz, Deblin	
7704	Aermacchi M-346 Bielik (CSX55212)	SP 48.el/41.BLSz, Deblin	
7705	Aermacchi M-346 Bielik (MT55225)	SP 48.el/41.BLSz, Deblin	
7706	Aermacchi M-346 Bielik (MT55226)	SP 48.el/41.BLSz, Deblin	
7707	Aermacchi M-346 Bielik (MT55227)	SP 48.el/41.BLSz, Deblin	
7708	Aermacchi M-346 Bielik (MT55228)	SP 48.el/41.BLSz, Deblin	
7709	Aermacchi M-346 Bielik (CSX55238)	SP 48.el/41.BLSz, Deblin	
7710	Aermacchi M-346 Bielik (CSX55245)	SP 48.el/41.BLSz, Deblin	
7711	Aermacchi M-346 Bielik (CSX55246)	SP 48.el/41.BLSz, Deblin	
7712	Aermacchi M-346 Bielik (CSX55247)	SP 48.el/41.BLSz, Deblin	
7713	Aermacchi M-346 Bielik (CSX55271)	SP 48.el/41.BLSz, Deblin	
7714	Aermacchi M-346 Bielik (CSX55272)	*Written off Gdynia AB, Poland, 12th July 2024*	
7715	Aermacchi M-346 Bielik (CSX55275)	SP 48.el/41.BLSz, Deblin	
7716	Aermacchi M-346 Bielik (CSX55276)	SP 48.el/41.BLSz, Deblin	
8101	Sukhoi Su-22M-4	SP 1/2.elt/1.SLT, Miroslawiec	
8205	Sukhoi Su-22M-4	SP 1/2.elt/1.SLT, Miroslawiec	
8309	Sukhoi Su-22M-4	SP 1/2.elt/1.SLT, Miroslawiec	
Straz Graniczna (Polish Border Guard)			
SN-50YG	PZL M20 Mewa	Straz Graniczna, Gdansk/Rebiechowo	
SN-60YG	PZL M28-05 Skytruck	Straz Graniczna, Gdansk/Rebiechowo	
SN-61YG	LET L-410UVP-E Turbolet	Straz Graniczna, Gdansk/Rebiechowo	
SN-62YG	LET L-410UVP-E Turbolet	Straz Graniczna, Gdansk/Rebiechowo	
......	LET L-410UVP-E20 Turbolet (OK-AMH)	Straz Graniczna, Gdansk/Rebiechowo	
......	LET L-410UVP-E20 Turbolet (OK-AMI)	Straz Graniczna, Gdansk/Rebiechowo	
Polish Government			
SP-LIG	Embraer EMB.175-200LR	Polish Government, Warszawa	
SP-LIH	Embraer EMB.175-200LR	Polish Government, Warszawa	

PORTUGAL

Serial	Type (code/other identity)	Owner/operator, location or fate	Notes
Força Aérea Portuguesa (FAP)/Marinha			
11401	Aérospatiale TB-30 Epsilon	FAP Esq 101, Beja	
11402	Aérospatiale TB-30 Epsilon $	FAP Esq 101, Beja	
11403	Aérospatiale TB-30 Epsilon	FAP Esq 101, Beja	
11404	Aérospatiale TB-30 Epsilon	FAP Esq 101, Beja	
11405	Aérospatiale TB-30 Epsilon	FAP Esq 101, Beja	
11406	Aérospatiale TB-30 Epsilon	FAP Esq 101, Beja	
11407	Aérospatiale TB-30 Epsilon	FAP Esq 101, Beja	
11411	Aérospatiale TB-30 Epsilon	FAP Esq 101, Beja	
11413	Aérospatiale TB-30 Epsilon	FAP Esq 101, Beja	
11417	Aérospatiale TB-30 Epsilon	FAP Esq 101, Beja	
11418	Aérospatiale TB-30 Epsilon	FAP Esq 101, Beja	
14807	Lockheed P-3C CUP+ Orion	FAP, stored Beja	
14808	Lockheed P-3C CUP+ Orion $	FAP Esq 601, Beja	
14809	Lockheed P-3C CUP+ Orion	FAP Esq 601, Beja	
14810	Lockheed P-3C CUP+ Orion	FAP Esq 601, Beja	
14811	Lockheed P-3C CUP+ Orion	FAP, stored Beja	
15101	Lockheed Martin F-16A MLU Fighting Falcon $	FAP Esq 201/Esq 301, Monte Real	
15102	Lockheed Martin F-16A MLU Fighting Falcon	FAP Esq 201/Esq 301, Monte Real	
15103	Lockheed Martin F-16A MLU Fighting Falcon $	FAP Esq 201/Esq 301, Monte Real	
15104	Lockheed Martin F-16A MLU Fighting Falcon	FAP Esq 201/Esq 301, Monte Real	
15105	Lockheed Martin F-16A MLU Fighting Falcon	FAP Esq 201/Esq 301, Monte Real	
15106	Lockheed Martin F-16A MLU Fighting Falcon $	FAP Esq 201/Esq 301, Monte Real	
15107	Lockheed Martin F-16A MLU Fighting Falcon	FAP Esq 201/Esq 301, Monte Real	
15108	Lockheed Martin F-16A MLU Fighting Falcon	FAP Esq 201/Esq 301, Monte Real	
15109	Lockheed Martin F-16A MLU Fighting Falcon	FAP Esq 201/Esq 301, Monte Real	
15110	Lockheed Martin F-16A MLU Fighting Falcon	FAP Esq 201/Esq 301, Monte Real	
15112	Lockheed Martin F-16A MLU Fighting Falcon	FAP Esq 201/Esq 301, Monte Real	
15113	Lockheed Martin F-16A MLU Fighting Falcon	FAP Esq 201/Esq 301, Monte Real	
15114	Lockheed Martin F-16A MLU Fighting Falcon	FAP Esq 201/Esq 301, Monte Real	

Notes	Serial	Type (code/other identity)	Owner/operator, location or fate
	15115	Lockheed Martin F-16A MLU Fighting Falcon $	FAP Esq 201/Esq 301, Monte Real
	15116	Lockheed Martin F-16A MLU Fighting Falcon $	FAP Esq 201/Esq 301, Monte Real
	15117	Lockheed Martin F-16A MLU Fighting Falcon	FAP Esq 201/Esq 301, Monte Real
	15118	Lockheed Martin F-16B MLU Fighting Falcon	FAP Esq 201/Esq 301, Monte Real
	15119	Lockheed Martin F-16B MLU Fighting Falcon	FAP Esq 201/Esq 301, Monte Real
	15120	Lockheed Martin F-16B MLU Fighting Falcon	FAP Esq 201/Esq 301, Monte Real
	15131	Lockheed Martin F-16A MLU Fighting Falcon	FAP Esq 201/Esq 301, Monte Real
	15133	Lockheed Martin F-16A MLU Fighting Falcon	FAP Esq 201/Esq 301, Monte Real
	15136	Lockheed Martin F-16A MLU Fighting Falcon	FAP Esq 201/Esq 301, Monte Real
	15142	Lockheed Martin F-16A MLU Fighting Falcon	FAP Esq 201/Esq 301, Monte Real
	15143	Lockheed Martin F-16A MLU Fighting Falcon	FAP Esq 201/Esq 301, Monte Real
	15144	Lockheed Martin F-16B MLU Fighting Falcon	FAP Esq 201/Esq 301, Monte Real
	15145	Lockheed Martin F-16A MLU Fighting Falcon	FAP (on order)
	15146	Lockheed Martin F-16A MLU Fighting Falcon	FAP (on order)
	15147	Lockheed Martin F-16A MLU Fighting Falcon	FAP (on order)
	16701	CASA C-295M	FAP Esq 502, Lisbon/Montijo & Lajes
	16702	CASA C-295M	FAP, stored Beja
	16703	CASA C-295M	FAP Esq 502, Lisbon/Montijo & Lajes
	16704	CASA C-295M	FAP Esq 502, Lisbon/Montijo & Lajes
	16705	CASA C-295M	FAP Esq 502, Lisbon/Montijo & Lajes
	16706	CASA C-295M	Airbus Defence & Space, Sevilla
	16707	CASA C-295M	FAP Esq 502, Lisbon/Montijo & Lajes
	16708	CASA C-295MPA	FAP Esq 502, Lisbon/Montijo & Lajes
	16709	CASA C-295MPA	FAP Esq 502, Lisbon/Montijo & Lajes
	16710	CASA C-295MPA	FAP Esq 502, Lisbon/Montijo & Lajes
	16711	CASA C-295MPA	FAP Esq 502, Lisbon/Montijo & Lajes
	16712	CASA C-295MPA	FAP Esq 502, Lisbon/Montijo & Lajes
	16801	Lockheed C-130H-30 Hercules	FAP Esq 501, Lisbon/Montijo
	16802	Lockheed C-130H-30 Hercules	FAP, stored Lisbon/Montijo
	16803	Lockheed C-130H Hercules	FAP Esq 501, Lisbon/Montijo
	16805	Lockheed C-130H Hercules	FAP Esq 501, Lisbon/Montijo
	16806	Lockheed C-130H-30 Hercules $	FAP Esq 501, Lisbon/Montijo
	17401	Dassault Falcon 50	FAP Esq 504, Lisbon/Montijo
	17402	Dassault Falcon 50	FAP Esq 504, Lisbon/Montijo
	17403	Dassault Falcon 50	FAP Esq 504, Lisbon/Montijo
	19201	Westland Super Lynx Mk.95A (ZH580)	Leonardo MW, Yeovil, UK (update)
	19202	Westland Super Lynx Mk.95A (ZH581)	Marina Esq de Helicopteros, Lisbon/Montijo
	19203	Westland Super Lynx Mk.95A (ZH582)	Leonardo MW, Yeovil, UK (update)
	19204	Westland Super Lynx Mk.95A (ZH583)	Marina Esq de Helicopteros, Lisbon/Montijo
	19205	Westland Super Lynx Mk.95A (ZH584)	Marina Esq de Helicopteros, Lisbon/Montijo
	19601	EHI EH-101 Mk.514	FAP Esq 751, Lisbon/Montijo
	19602	EHI EH-101 Mk.514	FAP Esq 751, Lisbon/Montijo
	19603	EHI EH-101 Mk.514	FAP Esq 751, Lisbon/Montijo
	19604	EHI EH-101 Mk.514	FAP Esq 751, Lisbon/Montijo
	19605	EHI EH-101 Mk.514	FAP Esq 751, Lisbon/Montijo
	19606	EHI EH-101 Mk.514	FAP Esq 751, Lisbon/Montijo
	19607	EHI EH-101 Mk.515	FAP Esq 751, Lisbon/Montijo
	19608	EHI EH-101 Mk.515	FAP Esq 751, Lisbon/Montijo
	19609	EHI EH-101 Mk.516	FAP Esq 751, Lisbon/Montijo
	19610	EHI EH-101 Mk.516	FAP Esq 751, Lisbon/Montijo
	19611	EHI EH-101 Mk.516	FAP Esq 751, Lisbon/Montijo
	19612	EHI EH-101 Mk.516	FAP, stored Lisbon/Montijo (damaged)
	24812	Lockheed P-3C CUP Orion (60+03)	FAP, Beja (for spares)
	24813	Lockheed P-3C CUP Orion (60+04)	FAP, Beja (for spares)
	24814	Lockheed P-3C CUP Orion (60+05)	FAP, Beja (for spares)
	24815	Lockheed P-3C CUP Orion (60+06)	FAP, Beja (for spares)
	24816	Lockheed P-3C CUP Orion (60+07)	FAP, Beja (for spares)
	24817	Lockheed P-3C CUP Orion (60+08)	FAP, Beja (for spares)
	26901	Embraer KC-390 (PT-ZDK)	FAP Esq 506, Beja
	26902	Embraer KC-390 (PT-ZDH)	FAP Esq 506, Beja
	26903	Embraer KC-390	FAP (on order)
	26904	Embraer KC-390	FAP (on order)

Serial	Type (code/other identity)	Owner/operator, location or fate	Notes
26905	Embraer KC-390	FAP (on order)	
29701	AgustaWestland AW119 Koala	FAP Esq 552, Beja	
29702	AgustaWestland AW119 Koala	FAP Esq 552, Beja	
29703	AgustaWestland AW119 Koala	FAP Esq 552, Beja	
29704	AgustaWestland AW119 Koala	FAP Esq 552, Beja	
29705	AgustaWestland AW119 Koala	FAP Esq 552, Beja	
29706	AgustaWestland AW119 Koala	FAP Esq 552, Beja (detachment at Ovar)	
29707	AgustaWestland AW119 Koala	FAP Esq 552, Beja (detachment at Ovar)	
29801	Sikorsky UH-60A Black Hawk (87-24669)	FAP Esq 551, Ovar	
29802	Sikorsky UH-60A Black Hawk (87-24666)	FAP Esq 551, Ovar	
29803	Sikorsky UH-60A Black Hawk (87-24599)	FAP Esq 551, Ovar	

QATAR
Qatar Emiri Air Force (QEAF)

Serial	Type (code/other identity)	Owner/operator, location or fate	Notes
211	Lockheed C-130J-30 Hercules II (08-0211) [MAH]	QEAF 12 Transport Sqn, Al-Udeid	
212	Lockheed C-130J-30 Hercules II (08-0212) [MAI]	QEAF 12 Transport Sqn, Al-Udeid	
213	Lockheed C-130J-30 Hercules II (08-0213) [MAJ]	QEAF 12 Transport Sqn, Al-Udeid	
214	Lockheed C-130J-30 Hercules II (08-0214) [MAK]	QEAF 12 Transport Sqn, Al-Udeid	
MAA	Boeing C-17A Globemaster III (08-0201)	QEAF 12 Transport Sqn, Al-Udeid	
MAB	Boeing C-17A Globemaster III (08-0202)	QEAF 12 Transport Sqn, Al-Udeid	
MAC	Boeing C-17A Globemaster III (12-0203)	QEAF 12 Transport Sqn, Al-Udeid	
MAE	Boeing C-17A Globemaster III (12-0204)	QEAF 12 Transport Sqn, Al-Udeid	
MAM	Boeing C-17A Globemaster III (14-0005)	QEAF 12 Transport Sqn, Al-Udeid	
MAN	Boeing C-17A Globemaster III (14-0006)	QEAF 12 Transport Sqn, Al-Udeid	
MAO	Boeing C-17A Globemaster III (14-0009)	QEAF 12 Transport Sqn, Al-Udeid	
MAP	Boeing C-17A Globemaster III (14-0010)	QEAF 12 Transport Sqn, Al-Udeid	
MAX	Dassault Falcon 2000LXS (F-WWJR)	QEAF, Doha	
QA397	Pilatus PC-24	QEAF, Doha	

Qatari Government

Serial	Type (code/other identity)	Owner/operator, location or fate	Notes
A7-AAG	Airbus A.320-232	Qatari Amiri Flight, Doha	
A7-AAH	Airbus A.340-313X	Qatari Amiri Flight, Doha	
A7-HBJ	Boeing 747-8KB	Sold as P4-HBJ, December 2023	
A7-HHE	Boeing 747-8KB	Qatari Amiri Flight, Doha	
A7-HHF	Boeing 747-8Z5	Qatari Amiri Flight, Doha	
A7-HHH	Airbus A.340-541	Qatari Amiri Flight, Doha	
A7-HHJ	Airbus A.319CJ-133	Qatari Amiri Flight, Doha	
A7-HHK	Airbus A.340-211	Qatari Amiri Flight, Doha	
A7-HHM	Airbus A.330-203	Qatari Amiri Flight, Doha	
A7-HJJ	Airbus A.330-202	Qatari Amiri Flight, Doha	
A7-MBK	Airbus A.320-232CJ	Qatari Amiri Flight, Doha	
A7-MED	Airbus A.319CJ-133	Qatari Amiri Flight, Doha	
A7-MHH	Airbus A.319CJ-115	Qatari Amiri Flight, Doha	

ROMANIA
Fortele Aeriene Romania (FAR)

Serial	Type (code/other identity)	Owner/operator, location or fate	Notes
2701	Alenia C-27J Spartan	FAR Escadrilla 902, Bucharest/Otopeni	
2702	Alenia C-27J Spartan	FAR Escadrilla 902, Bucharest/Otopeni	
2703	Alenia C-27J Spartan	FAR Escadrilla 902, Bucharest/Otopeni	
2704	Alenia C-27J Spartan	FAR Escadrilla 902, Bucharest/Otopeni	
2705	Alenia C-27J Spartan	FAR Escadrilla 902, Bucharest/Otopeni	
2706	Alenia C-27J Spartan	FAR Escadrilla 902, Bucharest/Otopeni	
2707	Alenia C-27J Spartan	FAR Escadrilla 902, Bucharest/Otopeni	
5930	Lockheed C-130B Hercules	FAR Escadrilla 901, Bucharest/Otopeni	
6166	Lockheed C-130H Hercules	FAR Escadrilla 901, Bucharest/Otopeni	
6191	Lockheed C-130H Hercules	FAR, stored Bucharest/Otopeni	
7432	Lockheed C-130H Hercules (74-2132)	FAR Escadrilla 901, Bucharest/Otopeni	
9142	Lockheed C-130H-2 Hercules (91-9142)	FAR Escadrilla 901, Bucharest/Otopeni	
9143	Lockheed C-130H-2 Hercules (91-9143)	FAR Escadrilla 901, Bucharest/Otopeni	

RUSSIA
Voenno-Vozdushniye Sily Rossioki Federatsii (VVS) (Russian Air Force)/Russian Government

Serial	Type (code/other identity)	Owner/operator, location or fate	Notes
595 w	Sukhoi Su-27P(LL) (36911037511)	VVS, Gromov Research Institute, Zhukovsky	

Notes	Serial	Type (code/other identity)	Owner/operator, location or fate
	597 bl	Sukhoi Su-30LL (96310102005)	VVS, Gromov Research Institute, Zhukhovsky
	598 r	Sukhoi Su-27P(LL) (36911037820)	VVS, Gromov Research Institute, Zhukhovsky
	RA-09007	Dassault Falcon 7X	Rossiya Special Flight Det, Moscow/Vnukovo
	RA-09090	Dassault Falcon 7X	Rossiya Special Flight Det, Moscow/Vnukovo
	RA-26226	Antonov An-30	VVS (Open Skies), Moscow/Kubinka
	RA-30078	Antonov An-30	VVS (Open Skies), Moscow/Kubinka
	RA-64057	Tupolev Tu-204-300	Rossiya Special Flight Det, Moscow/Vnukovo
	RA-64058	Tupolev Tu-204-300	Rossiya Special Flight Det, Moscow/Vnukovo
	RA-64059	Tupolev Tu-204-300	Rossiya Special Flight Det, Moscow/Vnukovo
	RA-64504	Tupolev Tu-214	Rossiya, stored Kazan Borisoglebskoe
	RA-64505	Tupolev Tu-214	Rossiya, stored Moscow/Vnukovo
	RA-64506	Tupolev Tu-214	Rossiya Special Flight Det, Moscow/Vnukovo
	RA-64515	Tupolev Tu-214SR	Rossiya, stored Kazan Borisoglebskoe
	RA-64516	Tupolev Tu-214SR	Rossiya Special Flight Det, Moscow/Vnukovo
	RA-64517	Tupolev Tu-214PU	Rossiya Special Flight Det, Moscow/Vnukovo
	RA-64520	Tupolev Tu-214PU	Rossiya Special Flight Det, Moscow/Vnukovo
	RA-64521	Tupolev Tu-214	Rossiya Special Flight Det, Ulyanovsk
	RA-64522	Tupolev Tu-214SUS	Rossiya Special Flight Det, Moscow/Vnukovo
	RA-64524	Tupolev Tu-214SUS	Rossiya Special Flight Det, Moscow/Vnukovo
	RA-64526	Tupolev Tu-214SR	Rossiya Special Flight Det, Moscow/Vnukovo
	RA-64527	Tupolev Tu-214SR	Rossiya Special Flight Det, Moscow/Vnukovo
	RA-64528	Tupolev Tu-214SR	Rossiya Special Flight Det, Moscow/Vnukovo
	RA-64531	Tupolev Tu-214PU	Rossiya Special Flight Det, Moscow/Vnukovo
	RA-64532	Tupolev Tu-214PU	Rossiya Special Flight Det, Moscow/Vnukovo
	RA-64533	Tupolev Tu-214PU	Rossiya Special Flight Det, Moscow/Vnukovo
	RA-65905	Tupolev Tu-134AK-3	Rossiya Special Flight Det, Moscow/Vnukovo
	RA-65911	Tupolev Tu-134AK-3	Rossiya Special Flight Det, Moscow/Vnukovo
	RA-73025	Airbus A.319-115CJ	Rossiya Special Flight Det, Moscow/Vnukovo
	RA-73026	Airbus A.319-115CJ	Rossiya Special Flight Det, Moscow/Vnukovo
	RA-82010	Antonov An-124-100	VVS 224th Transport Regiment, Seshcha/Bryansk
	RA-82013	Antonov An-124-100	VVS 224th Transport Regiment, Seshcha/Bryansk
	RA-82014	Antonov An-124-100	VVS 224th Transport Regiment, Seshcha/Bryansk
	RA-82030	Antonov An-124-100	VVS 224th Transport Regiment, Seshcha/Bryansk
	RA-82035	Antonov An-124-100	VVS 224th Transport Regiment, Seshcha/Bryansk
	RA-82037	Antonov An-124-100	VVS 224th Transport Regiment, Seshcha/Bryansk
	RA-82038	Antonov An-124-100	VVS 224th Transport Regiment, Seshcha/Bryansk
	RA-82039	Antonov An-124-100	VVS 224th Transport Regiment, Seshcha/Bryansk
	RA-85041	Tupolev Tu-154M	VVS 6991 AvB, Chalovskiy
	RA-85042	Tupolev Tu-154M	VVS 6991 AvB, Chalovskiy
	RA-85155	Tupolev Tu-154M	VVS 8 oae, Chalovskiy
	RA-96012	Ilyushin Il-96-300PU	*Stored, Moscow/Vnukovo*
	RA-96014	Ilyushin Il-96-300	Rossiya Special Flight Det, Moscow/Vnukovo
	RA-96016	Ilyushin Il-96-300PU	Rossiya Special Flight Det, Moscow/Vnukovo
	RA-96017	Ilyushin Il-96-300S	Rossiya Special Flight Det, Moscow/Vnukovo
	RA-96018	Ilyushin Il-96-300	Rossiya Special Flight Det, Moscow/Vnukovo
	RA-96019	Ilyushin Il-96-300PU	Rossiya Special Flight Det, Moscow/Vnukovo
	RA-96020	Ilyushin Il-96-300PU	Rossiya Special Flight Det, Moscow/Vnukovo
	RA-96021	Ilyushin Il-96-300PU	Rossiya Special Flight Det, Moscow/Vnukovo
	RA-96022	Ilyushin Il-96-300PU	Rossiya Special Flight Det, Moscow/Vnukovo
	RA-96023	Ilyushin Il-96-300PU	Rossiya Special Flight Det, Moscow/Vnukovo
	RA-96024	Ilyushin Il-96-300PU	Rossiya Special Flight Det, Moscow/Vnukovo
	RA-96025	Ilyushin Il-96-300PU	Rossiya Special Flight Det, Moscow/Vnukovo
	RA-96102	Ilyushin Il-96-400VPU	Rossiya Special Flight Det, Moscow/Vnukovo
	RA-96104	Ilyushin Il-96-400VPU	Rossiya Special Flight Det, Moscow/Vnukovo
	RF-36052	Antonov An-30B (87 bk)	VVS (Open Skies), Moscow/Kubinka
	RF-64519	Tupolev Tu-214ON	VVS (Open Skies), Moscow/Kubinka
	RF-82011	Antonov An-124-100	VVS 224th Transport Regiment, Seshcha/Bryansk
	RF-82032	Antonov An-124-100	VVS 224th Transport Regiment, Seshcha/Bryansk
	RF-82034	Antonov An-124-100	VVS 224th Transport Regiment, Seshcha/Bryansk
	RF-82041	Antonov An-124-100	VVS 224th Transport Regiment, Seshcha/Bryansk
	RF-85655	Tupolev Tu-154M-LK1	VVS (Open Skies), Moscow/Kubinka

Serial	Type (code/other identity)	Owner/operator, location or fate	Notes
SAUDI ARABIA			
Al Quwwat al Jawwiya as Sa'udiya/Royal Saudi Air Force (RSAF) & Saudi Government			
111	Lockheed VC-130H Hercules	RSAF 1 Sqn, Riyadh	
112	Lockheed VC-130H Hercules	RSAF 1 Sqn, Riyadh	
464	Lockheed C-130H Hercules	RSAF 4 Sqn, Jeddah	
465	Lockheed C-130H Hercules	RSAF 4 Sqn, Jeddah	
466	Lockheed C-130H Hercules	RSAF 4 Sqn, Jeddah	
467	Lockheed C-130H Hercules	RSAF 4 Sqn, Jeddah	
468	Lockheed C-130H Hercules	RSAF 4 Sqn, Jeddah	
472	Lockheed C-130H Hercules	RSAF 4 Sqn, Jeddah	
473	Lockheed C-130H Hercules	RSAF 4 Sqn, Jeddah	
474	Lockheed C-130H Hercules	RSAF 4 Sqn, Jeddah	
475	Lockheed C-130H Hercules	RSAF 4 Sqn, Jeddah	
477	Lockheed C-130H Hercules	RSAF 4 Sqn, Jeddah	
478	Lockheed C-130H Hercules	RSAF 4 Sqn, Jeddah	
482	Lockheed C-130H Hercules	RSAF 4 Sqn, Jeddah	
483	Lockheed C-130H Hercules	RSAF 4 Sqn, Jeddah	
484	Lockheed C-130H Hercules	RSAF 4 Sqn, Jeddah	
485	Lockheed C-130H Hercules	RSAF 4 Sqn, Jeddah	
486	Lockheed C-130H Hercules	RSAF 4 Sqn, Jeddah	
1601	Lockheed C-130H Hercules	RSAF 16 Sqn, Jeddah	
1602	Lockheed C-130H Hercules	RSAF 16 Sqn, Jeddah	
1604	Lockheed C-130H Hercules	RSAF 16 Sqn, Jeddah	
1605	Lockheed C-130H Hercules	RSAF 16 Sqn, Jeddah	
1615	Lockheed C-130H Hercules	RSAF 16 Sqn, Jeddah	
1622	Lockheed C-130H-30 Hercules	RSAF 16 Sqn, Jeddah	
1623	Lockheed C-130H Hercules	RSAF 16 Sqn, Jeddah	
1624	Lockheed C-130H Hercules	RSAF 16 Sqn, Jeddah	
1625	Lockheed C-130H Hercules	RSAF 16 Sqn, Jeddah	
1626	Lockheed C-130H Hercules	RSAF 16 Sqn, Jeddah	
1627	Lockheed C-130H Hercules	RSAF 16 Sqn, Jeddah	
1628	Lockheed C-130H Hercules	RSAF 16 Sqn, Jeddah	
1629	Lockheed C-130H Hercules	RSAF 16 Sqn, Jeddah	
1630	Lockheed C-130H-30 Hercules	RSAF 16 Sqn, Jeddah	
1631	Lockheed C-130H-30 Hercules	RSAF 16 Sqn, Jeddah	
1632	Lockheed C-130H Hercules	RSAF 16 Sqn, Jeddah	
1801	Boeing E-3A Sentry	RSAF 18 Sqn, Al Kharj	
1802	Boeing E-3A Sentry	RSAF 18 Sqn, Al Kharj	
1803	Boeing E-3A Sentry	RSAF 18 Sqn, Al Kharj	
1804	Boeing E-3A Sentry	RSAF 18 Sqn, Al Kharj	
1805	Boeing E-3A Sentry	RSAF 18 Sqn, Al Kharj	
1901	Boeing RE-3A (1817)	RSAF 19 Sqn, Al Kharj	
1902	Boeing RE-3B	*RSAF, wfu Riyadh, Saudi Arabia*	
2301	Boeing KE-3A Sentry (1811)	RSAF 23 Sqn, Al Kharj	
2302	Boeing KE-3A Sentry (1812)	RSAF 23 Sqn, Al Kharj	
2303	Boeing KE-3A Sentry (1813)	RSAF 23 Sqn, Al Kharj	
2304	Boeing KE-3A Sentry (1814)	RSAF 23 Sqn, Al Kharj	
2305	Boeing KE-3A Sentry (1815)	RSAF 23 Sqn, Al Kharj	
2306	Boeing KE-3A Sentry (1816)	RSAF 23 Sqn, Al Kharj	
2307	Boeing KE-3A Sentry (1818)	RSAF 23 Sqn, Al Kharj	
2401	Airbus A.330-203 MRTT	RSAF 24 Sqn, Al Kharj	
2402	Airbus A.330-203 MRTT $	RSAF 24 Sqn, Al Kharj	
2403	Airbus A.330-203 MRTT $	RSAF 24 Sqn, Al Kharj	
2404	Airbus A.330-203 MRTT	RSAF 24 Sqn, Al Kharj	
2405	Airbus A.330-203 MRTT $	RSAF 24 Sqn, Al Kharj	
2406	Airbus A.330-203 MRTT $	RSAF 24 Sqn, Al Kharj	
2407	Airbus A.330-203 MRTT (F-WWYR/EC-353)	RSAF (on order), stored Getafe, Spain	
3201	Lockheed KC-130H Hercules	RSAF 32 Sqn, Al Kharj	
3202	Lockheed KC-130H Hercules	RSAF 32 Sqn, Al Kharj	
3203	Lockheed KC-130H Hercules	RSAF 32 Sqn, Al Kharj	
3204	Lockheed KC-130H Hercules	RSAF 32 Sqn, Al Kharj	
3205	Lockheed KC-130H Hercules	RSAF 32 Sqn, Al Kharj	

Notes	Serial	Type (code/other identity)	Owner/operator, location or fate
	3206	Lockheed KC-130H Hercules	RSAF 32 Sqn, Al Kharj
	3207	Lockheed KC-130H Hercules	RSAF 32 Sqn, Al Kharj
	3208	Lockheed KC-130J Hercules II	RSAF 32 Sqn, Al Kharj
	3209	Lockheed KC-130J Hercules II	RSAF 32 Sqn, Al Kharj
	8805	BAe Hawk 65A	RSAF 88 Sqn, *Saudi Hawks*, Tabuk
	8806	BAe Hawk 65A	RSAF 88 Sqn, *Saudi Hawks*, Tabuk
	8807	BAe Hawk 65	RSAF 88 Sqn, *Saudi Hawks*, Tabuk
	8808	BAe Hawk 65	RSAF 88 Sqn, *Saudi Hawks*, Tabuk
	8810	BAe Hawk 65	RSAF 88 Sqn, *Saudi Hawks*, Tabuk
	8811	BAe Hawk 65A	RSAF 88 Sqn, *Saudi Hawks*, Tabuk
	8812	BAe Hawk 65A	RSAF 88 Sqn, *Saudi Hawks*, Tabuk
	8813	BAe Hawk 65	RSAF 88 Sqn, *Saudi Hawks*, Tabuk
	8814	BAe Hawk 65	RSAF 88 Sqn, *Saudi Hawks*, Tabuk
	8816	BAe Hawk 65A	RSAF 88 Sqn, *Saudi Hawks*, Tabuk
	8817	BAe Hawk 65A	RSAF 88 Sqn, *Saudi Hawks*, Tabuk
	8818	BAe Hawk 65A	RSAF 88 Sqn, *Saudi Hawks*, Tabuk
	8819	BAe Hawk 65A	RSAF 88 Sqn, *Saudi Hawks*, Tabuk
	8820	BAe Hawk 65A	RSAF 88 Sqn, *Saudi Hawks*, Tabuk
	8821	BAe Hawk 65A	RSAF 88 Sqn, *Saudi Hawks*, Tabuk
	HZ-101	Boeing 737-7DP	RSAF 1 Sqn, Riyadh
	HZ-102	Boeing 737-8DP	RSAF 1 Sqn, Riyadh
	HZ-103	Grumman G.1159C Gulfstream IV	RSAF 1 Sqn, Riyadh
	HZ-104	Grumman G.1159C Gulfstream IV-SP (HZ-MS4)	RSAF 1 Sqn, Riyadh
	HZ-117	Lockheed L.100-30 Hercules	RSAF 1 Sqn, Riyadh
	HZ-124	Airbus A.340-211	RSAF 1 Sqn, Riyadh
	HZ-128	Lockheed L.100-30 Hercules	RSAF 1 Sqn, Riyadh
	HZ-129	Lockheed L.100-30 Hercules	RSAF 1 Sqn, Riyadh
	HZ-132	Lockheed L.100-30 Hercules	RSAF 1 Sqn, Riyadh
	HZ-HM1	Boeing 747-468	Saudi Royal Flight, Jeddah
	HZ-HMED	Boeing 757-23A	Saudi Royal Flight, Riyadh
	HZ-MS2	Lockheed C-130H Hercules	Saudi Armed Forces Medical Services, Riyadh
	HZ-MS4A	Gulfstream Aerospace G.450	Saudi Armed Forces Medical Services, Riyadh
	HZ-MS4B	Gulfstream Aerospace G.450	Saudi Armed Forces Medical Services, Riyadh
	HZ-MS4C	Gulfstream Aerospace G.450	Saudi Armed Forces Medical Services, Riyadh
	HZ-MS5A	Gulfstream Aerospace Gulfstream V	Saudi Armed Forces Medical Services, Riyadh
	HZ-MS5B	Gulfstream Aerospace Gulfstream V	Saudi Armed Forces Medical Services, Riyadh
	HZ-MS6	Lockheed L.100-30 Hercules	Saudi Armed Forces Medical Services, Riyadh
	HZ-MS7	Lockheed C-130H Hercules	Saudi Armed Forces Medical Services, Riyadh
	HZ-MS9	Lockheed L.100-30 Hercules	Saudi Armed Forces Medical Services, Riyadh
	SENEGAL		
	6V-SEN	Airbus A.320CJ-251NX	Government of Senegal, Dakar
	SERBIA		
	Ratno vazduhoplovstvo i protivvazduhoplovna odbrana Vojske Srbije/Serbian Air Force and Air Defence		
	29501	CASA C-295MW	Serbian Air Force and Air Defence, Batajnica
	29502	CASA C-295MW	Serbian Air Force and Air Defence, Batajnica
	YU-BNA	Dassault Falcon 50	Government of Serbia, Belgrade
	YU-SRB	Embraer ERJ.135BJ Legacy 600	Government of Serbia, Belgrade
	SINGAPORE		
	Republic of Singapore Air Force (RSAF)		
	720	Lockheed KC-130B Hercules	RSAF 122 Sqn, Paya Labar
	721	Lockheed KC-130B Hercules	RSAF 122 Sqn, Paya Labar
	724	Lockheed KC-130B Hercules	RSAF 122 Sqn, Paya Labar
	725	Lockheed KC-130B Hercules	RSAF 122 Sqn, Paya Labar
	730	Lockheed C-130H Hercules	RSAF 122 Sqn, Paya Labar
	731	Lockheed KC-130H Hercules	RSAF 122 Sqn, Paya Labar
	732	Lockheed C-130H Hercules	RSAF 122 Sqn, Paya Labar
	733	Lockheed KC-130H Hercules	RSAF 122 Sqn, Paya Labar
	734	Lockheed KC-130H Hercules	RSAF 122 Sqn, Paya Labar
	735	Lockheed C-130H Hercules	RSAF 122 Sqn, Paya Labar

Serial	Type (code/other identity)	Owner/operator, location or fate	Notes
760	Airbus A.330-203 MRTT (EC-333/MRTT033) [60]	RSAF 112 Sqn, Changi	
761	Airbus A.330-203 MRTT (EC-332/MRTT034) $ [61]	RSAF 112 Sqn, Changi	
762	Airbus A.330-203 MRTT (EC-336/MRTT035) [62]	RSAF 112 Sqn, Changi	
763	Airbus A.330-203 MRTT (EC-337/MRTT036) [63]	RSAF 112 Sqn, Changi	
764	Airbus A.330-203 MRTT (EC-335/MRTT037) [64]	RSAF 112 Sqn, Changi	
765	Airbus A.330-203 MRTT (EC-332/MRTT038) [65]	RSAF 112 Sqn, Changi	

SLOVAKIA
Slovenské Vojenske Letectvo (SVL)

Serial	Type (code/other identity)	Owner/operator, location or fate	Notes
0808	Mil Mi-17	SVL 2.Dvlt/Vrtulnikové Letcecké Kridlo, Prešov	
0820	Mil Mi-17	SVL 2.Dvlt/Vrtulnikové Letcecké Kridlo, Prešov	
0823	Mil Mi-17M	SVL 2.Dvlt/Vrtulnikové Letcecké Kridlo, Prešov	
0826	Mil Mi-17	SVL 2.Dvlt/Vrtulnikové Letcecké Kridlo, Prešov	
0827	Mil Mi-17	SVL 2.Dvlt/Vrtulnikové Letcecké Kridlo, Prešov	
0841	Mil Mi-17	SVL 2.Dvlt/Vrtulnikové Letcecké Kridlo, Prešov	
0845	Mil Mi-17	SVL 2.Dvlt/Vrtulnikové Letcecké Kridlo, Prešov	
0846	Mil Mi-17	SVL 2.Dvlt/Vrtulnikové Letcecké Kridlo, Prešov	
1001	Lockheed Martin F-16V Fighting Falcon (20-4001)	SVL 2.vlt/Zmiešané Letecké Kridlo, Sliač	
1002	Lockheed Martin F-16V Fighting Falcon (20-4002)	SVL 2.vlt/Zmiešané Letecké Kridlo, Sliač	
1003	Lockheed Martin F-16V Fighting Falcon (20-4003)	SVL 2.vlt/Zmiešané Letecké Kridlo, Sliač	
1004	Lockheed Martin F-16V Fighting Falcon (20-4004)	SVL 2.vlt/Zmiešané Letecké Kridlo, Sliač	
1005	Lockheed Martin F-16V Fighting Falcon (20-4005)	SVL (on order)	
1006	Lockheed Martin F-16V Fighting Falcon (20-4006)	SVL (on order)	
1007	Lockheed Martin F-16V Fighting Falcon (20-4007)	SVL (on order)	
1008	Lockheed Martin F-16V Fighting Falcon (20-4008)	SVL (on order)	
1009	Lockheed Martin F-16V Fighting Falcon (20-4009)	SVL (on order)	
1010	Lockheed Martin F-16V Fighting Falcon (20-4010)	SVL (on order)	
1011	Lockheed Martin F-16V Fighting Falcon (20-4011)	SVL (on order)	
1012	Lockheed Martin F-16V Fighting Falcon (20-4012)	SVL (on order)	
1101	Lockheed Martin F-16V Fighting Falcon (20-4013)	SVL (on order)	
1102	Lockheed Martin F-16V Fighting Falcon (20-4014)	SVL (on order)	
1521	LET L-410FG Turbolet	SVL 1.Dopravná Letka/Dopravné Kridlo, Malacky	
1931	Aeritalia C-27J Spartan (CSX62302)	SVL 1.Dopravná Letka/Dopravné Kridlo, Malacky	
1962	Aeritalia C-27J Spartan (CSX62306)	SVL 1.Dopravná Letka/Dopravné Kridlo, Malacky	
2311	LET L-410UVP Turbolet	SVL 1.Dopravná Letka/Dopravné Kridlo, Malacky	
2421	LET L-410UVP Turbolet	SVL 1.Dopravná Letka/Dopravné Kridlo, Malacky	
2718	LET L-401UVP-E Turbolet	SVL 1.Dopravná Letka/Dopravné Kridlo, Malacky	
2721	LET L-401UVP-E Turbolet	SVL 1.Dopravná Letka/Dopravné Kridlo, Malacky	
2818	LET L-401UVP-20 Turbolet	SVL 1.Dopravná Letka/Dopravné Kridlo, Malacky	
2901	LET L-401UVP-20 Turbolet	SVL 1.Dopravná Letka/Dopravné Kridlo, Malacky	
4701	Aero L-39ZAM Albatros	SVL 2.vlt/Zmiešané Letecké Kridlo, Sliač	
4703	Aero L-39ZAM Albatros	SVL 2.vlt/Zmiešané Letecké Kridlo, Sliač	
4707	Aero L-39ZAM Albatros	SVL 2.vlt/Zmiešané Letecké Kridlo, Sliač	
5251	Aero L-39CM Albatros	SVL 2.vlt/Zmiešané Letecké Kridlo, Sliač	
5252	Aero L-39CM Albatros	SVL 2.vlt/Zmiešané Letecké Kridlo, Sliač	
5253	Aero L-39CM Albatros	SVL 2.vlt/Zmiešané Letecké Kridlo, Sliač	
5254	Aero L-39CM Albatros	SVL 2.vlt/Zmiešané Letecké Kridlo, Sliač	
5301	Aero L-39CM Albatros $	SVL 2.vlt/Zmiešané Letecké Kridlo, Sliač	
5302	Aero L-39CM Albatros	SVL 2.vlt/Zmiešané Letecké Kridlo, Sliač	
7445	Sikorsky UH-60M Black Hawk	SVL 1.vlt/Vrtulnikové Letecké Kridlo, Prešov	
7446	Sikorsky UH-60M Black Hawk	SVL 1.vlt/Vrtulnikové Letecké Kridlo, Prešov	
7447	Sikorsky UH-60M Black Hawk	SVL 1.vlt/Vrtulnikové Letecké Kridlo, Prešov	
7448	Sikorsky UH-60M Black Hawk	SVL 1.vlt/Vrtulnikové Letecké Kridlo, Prešov	
7449	Sikorsky UH-60M Black Hawk	SVL 1.vlt/Vrtulnikové Letecké Kridlo, Prešov	
7639	Sikorsky UH-60M Black Hawk	SVL 1.vlt/Vrtulnikové Letecké Kridlo, Prešov	
7640	Sikorsky UH-60M Black Hawk	SVL 1.vlt/Vrtulnikové Letecké Kridlo, Prešov	
7641	Sikorsky UH-60M Black Hawk	SVL 1.vlt/Vrtulnikové Letecké Kridlo, Prešov	
7642	Sikorsky UH-60M Black Hawk	SVL 1.vlt/Vrtulnikové Letecké Kridlo, Prešov	

Slovak Government

Serial	Type (code/other identity)	Owner/operator, location or fate	Notes
OM-BYA	Airbus A.319-115	Slovak Government, Bratislava/Ivanka	
OM-BYB	Fokker 100	Slovak Government, Bratislava/Ivanka	
OM-BYC	Fokker 100	Slovak Government, Bratislava/Ivanka	

Notes	Serial	Type (code/other identity)	Owner/operator, location or fate
	OM-BYK	Airbus A.319-115XCJ	Slovak Government, Bratislava/Ivanka

SLOVENIA
Slovenska Vojska (SV)/Slovenian Armed Forces

	L1-01	Dassault Falcon 2000EX	Government of Slovenia, Ljubljana/Brnik
	L2-01	Alenia C-27J Spartan	SV 152 Letalska Eskadrilja, Ljubljana/Brnik
	L2-02	Alenia C-27J Spartan	SV 152 Letalska Eskadrilja, Ljubljana/Brnik
	L4-01	LET 410UVP-E Turbolet	SV 107 Letalska Baza, Cerklje ob Krki
	L9-61	Pilatus PC-9M	SV Letalska Šola, Cerklje ob Krki
	L9-62	Pilatus PC-9M	SV Letalska Šola, Cerklje ob Krki
	L9-63	Pilatus PC-9M	SV Letalska Šola, Cerklje ob Krki
	L9-64	Pilatus PC-9M	SV Letalska Šola, Cerklje ob Krki
	L9-65	Pilatus PC-9M	SV Letalska Šola, Cerklje ob Krki
	L9-66	Pilatus PC-9M	SV Letalska Šola, Cerklje ob Krki
	L9-67	Pilatus PC-9M	SV Letalska Šola, Cerklje ob Krki
	L9-68	Pilatus PC-9M	SV Letalska Šola, Cerklje ob Krki
	L9-69	Pilatus PC-9M	SV Letalska Šola, Cerklje ob Krki

SOUTH AFRICA
Suid Afrikaanse Lugmag/South African Air Force (SAAF)

	401	Lockheed C-130BZ Hercules	SAAF 28 Sqn, Waterkloof
	402	Lockheed C-130BZ Hercules	*SAAF, stored Waterkloof*
	405	Lockheed C-130BZ Hercules $	SAAF 28 Sqn, Waterkloof
	406	Lockheed C-130BZ Hercules	SAAF 28 Sqn, Waterkloof
	409	Lockheed C-130BZ Hercules	SAAF 28 Sqn, Waterkloof
	ZS-NAN	Dassault Falcon 900	SAAF 21 Sqn, Waterkloof
	ZS-RSA	Boeing 737-7ED	SAAF 21 Sqn, Waterkloof

SOUTH KOREA
Han Guk Gong Gun/Republic of Korea Air Force

	18-001	Airbus KC-330 Cygnus (MRTT050)	RoKAF 261 Air Tanker Sqn/5 Tactical Air Transport Wing, Gimhae
	19-002	Airbus KC-330 Cygnus (MRTT051)	RoKAF 261 Air Tanker Sqn/5 Tactical Air Transport Wing, Gimhae
	19-003	Airbus KC-330 Cygnus (MRTT052)	RoKAF 261 Air Tanker Sqn/5 Tactical Air Transport Wing, Gimhae
	19-004	Airbus KC-330 Cygnus (MRTT053)	RoKAF 261 Air Tanker Sqn/5 Tactical Air Transport Wing, Gimhae
	22001	Boeing 747-8I (HL7643)	RoKAF 257 Special Flight Squadron, Seongmu

SPAIN
Arma Aérea de l'Armada Española, Ejército del Aire (EdA)/Spanish Air Force & Guardia Civil

	C.15-13	McDonnell Douglas EF-18M Hornet [12-01]	EdA 121 Esc/122 Esc/Ala 12, Madrid/Torrejón
	C.15-14	McDonnell Douglas EF-18M Hornet [15-01]	EdA 151 Esc/152 Esc/153 Esc/Ala 15, Zaragoza
	C.15-15	McDonnell Douglas EF-18M Hornet [15-02] $	EdA 151 Esc/152 Esc/153 Esc/Ala 15, Zaragoza
	C.15-16	McDonnell Douglas EF-18M Hornet [15-03]	EdA 151 Esc/152 Esc/153 Esc/Ala 15, Zaragoza
	C.15-18	McDonnell Douglas EF-18M Hornet [15-05]	EdA 151 Esc/152 Esc/153 Esc/Ala 15, Zaragoza
	C.15-21	McDonnell Douglas EF-18M Hornet [15-08] $	EdA 151 Esc/152 Esc/153 Esc/Ala 15, Zaragoza
	C.15-22	McDonnell Douglas EF-18M Hornet [15-09]	EdA 151 Esc/152 Esc/153 Esc/Ala 15, Zaragoza
	C.15-23	McDonnell Douglas EF-18M Hornet [15-10]	EdA 151 Esc/152 Esc/153 Esc/Ala 15, Zaragoza
	C.15-24	McDonnell Douglas EF-18M Hornet [15-11]	EdA 151 Esc/152 Esc/153 Esc/Ala 15, Zaragoza
	C.15-25	McDonnell Douglas EF-18M Hornet [15-12]	*Written off 20th May 2023, Zaragoza, Spain*
	C.15-26	McDonnell Douglas EF-18M Hornet [15-13]	EdA 151 Esc/152 Esc/153 Esc/Ala 15, Zaragoza
	C.15-27	McDonnell Douglas EF-18M Hornet [15-14]	EdA 151 Esc/152 Esc/153 Esc/Ala 15, Zaragoza
	C.15-28	McDonnell Douglas EF-18M Hornet [15-15] $	EdA 151 Esc/152 Esc/153 Esc/Ala 15, Zaragoza
	C.15-29	McDonnell Douglas EF-18M Hornet [15-16]	EdA 151 Esc/152 Esc/153 Esc/Ala 15, Zaragoza
	C.15-30	McDonnell Douglas EF-18M Hornet [15-17]	EdA 151 Esc/152 Esc/153 Esc/Ala 15, Zaragoza
	C.15-31	McDonnell Douglas EF-18M Hornet [15-18]	EdA 151 Esc/152 Esc/153 Esc/Ala 15, Zaragoza
	C.15-32	McDonnell Douglas EF-18M Hornet [15-19]	EdA 151 Esc/152 Esc/153 Esc/Ala 15, Zaragoza
	C.15-33	McDonnell Douglas EF-18M Hornet [15-20]	EdA 151 Esc/152 Esc/153 Esc/Ala 15, Zaragoza
	C.15-34	McDonnell Douglas EF-18M Hornet [12-50]	EdA 121 Esc/122 Esc/Ala 12, Madrid/Torrejón
	C.15-35	McDonnell Douglas EF-18M Hornet [15-22]	EdA 151 Esc/152 Esc/153 Esc/Ala 15, Zaragoza

Serial	Type (code/other identity)	Owner/operator, location or fate	Notes
C.15-36	McDonnell Douglas EF-18M Hornet [15-23]	EdA 151 Esc/152 Esc/153 Esc/Ala 15, Zaragoza	
C.15-37	McDonnell Douglas EF-18M Hornet [15-24]	EdA 151 Esc/152 Esc/153 Esc/Ala 15, Zaragoza	
C.15-38	McDonnell Douglas EF-18M Hornet [15-25]	EdA 151 Esc/152 Esc/153 Esc/Ala 15, Zaragoza	
C.15-39	McDonnell Douglas EF-18M Hornet [15-26]	EdA 151 Esc/152 Esc/153 Esc/Ala 15, Zaragoza	
C.15-40	McDonnell Douglas EF-18M Hornet [15-27]	EdA 151 Esc/152 Esc/153 Esc/Ala 15, Zaragoza	
C.15-41	McDonnell Douglas EF-18M Hornet [15-28]	EdA 151 Esc/152 Esc/153 Esc/Ala 15, Zaragoza	
C.15-43	McDonnell Douglas EF-18M Hornet [15-30]	EdA 151 Esc/152 Esc/153 Esc/Ala 15, Zaragoza	
C.15-44	McDonnell Douglas EF-18M Hornet [12-02]	EdA 121 Esc/122 Esc/Ala 12, Madrid/Torrejón	
C.15-45	McDonnell Douglas EF-18M Hornet [12-03]	EdA 121 Esc/122 Esc/Ala 12, Madrid/Torrejón	
C.15-46	McDonnell Douglas EF-18M Hornet [12-04]	EdA 121 Esc/122 Esc/Ala 12, Madrid/Torrejón	
C.15-47	McDonnell Douglas EF-18M Hornet [15-31]	EdA 151 Esc/152 Esc/153 Esc/Ala 15, Zaragoza	
C.15-48	McDonnell Douglas EF-18M Hornet [12-06]	EdA 121 Esc/122 Esc/Ala 12, Madrid/Torrejón	
C.15-49	McDonnell Douglas EF-18M Hornet [12-07]	EdA 121 Esc/122 Esc/Ala 12, Madrid/Torrejón	
C.15-50	McDonnell Douglas EF-18M Hornet [12-08]	EdA 121 Esc/122 Esc/Ala 12, Madrid/Torrejón	
C.15-51	McDonnell Douglas EF-18M Hornet [12-09]	EdA 121 Esc/122 Esc/Ala 12, Madrid/Torrejón	
C.15-53	McDonnell Douglas EF-18M Hornet [12-11]	EdA 121 Esc/122 Esc/Ala 12, Madrid/Torrejón	
C.15-54	McDonnell Douglas EF-18M Hornet [12-12]	EdA 121 Esc/122 Esc/Ala 12, Madrid/Torrejón	
C.15-55	McDonnell Douglas EF-18M Hornet [12-13]	EdA 121 Esc/122 Esc/Ala 12, Madrid/Torrejón	
C.15-56	McDonnell Douglas EF-18M Hornet [12-14]	EdA 121 Esc/122 Esc/Ala 12, Madrid/Torrejón	
C.15-57	McDonnell Douglas EF-18M Hornet [12-15]	EdA 121 Esc/122 Esc/Ala 12, Madrid/Torrejón	
C.15-59	McDonnell Douglas EF-18M Hornet [12-17]	EdA 121 Esc/122 Esc/Ala 12, Madrid/Torrejón	
C.15-60	McDonnell Douglas EF-18M Hornet [12-18]	EdA 121 Esc/122 Esc/Ala 12, Madrid/Torrejón	
C.15-61	McDonnell Douglas EF-18M Hornet [12-19]	EdA 121 Esc/122 Esc/Ala 12, Madrid/Torrejón	
C.15-62	McDonnell Douglas EF-18M Hornet [12-20]	EdA 121 Esc/122 Esc/Ala 12, Madrid/Torrejón	
C.15-64	McDonnell Douglas EF-18M Hornet [15-34]	EdA 151 Esc/152 Esc/153 Esc/Ala 15, Zaragoza	
C.15-65	McDonnell Douglas EF-18M Hornet [12-23]	EdA 121 Esc/122 Esc/Ala 12, Madrid/Torrejón	
C.15-66	McDonnell Douglas EF-18M Hornet [12-24]	*Written off 4th October 2024, Teruel, Spain*	
C.15-67	McDonnell Douglas EF-18M Hornet [15-33]	EdA 151 Esc/152 Esc/153 Esc/Ala 15, Zaragoza	
C.15-68	McDonnell Douglas EF-18M Hornet [12-26]	EdA 121 Esc/122 Esc/Ala 12, Madrid/Torrejón	
C.15-69	McDonnell Douglas EF-18M Hornet [12-27]	EdA 121 Esc/122 Esc/Ala 12, Madrid/Torrejón	
C.15-70	McDonnell Douglas EF-18M Hornet [12-28]	EdA 121 Esc/122 Esc/Ala 12, Madrid/Torrejón	
C.15-72	McDonnell Douglas F-18M Hornet [12-30]	EdA 121 Esc/122 Esc/Ala 12, Madrid/Torrejón	
C.15-73	McDonnell Douglas F/A-18A+ Hornet [46-01] $	EdA 462 Esc/Ala 46, Gando, Gran Canaria	
C.15-75	McDonnell Douglas F/A-18A+ Hornet [46-03]	EdA 462 Esc/Ala 46, Gando, Gran Canaria	
C.15-77	McDonnell Douglas F/A-18A+ Hornet [46-05]	EdA 462 Esc/Ala 46, Gando, Gran Canaria	
C.15-79	McDonnell Douglas F/A-18A+ Hornet [46-07]	EdA 462 Esc/Ala 46, Gando, Gran Canaria	
C.15-80	McDonnell Douglas F/A-18A+ Hornet [46-08]	EdA 462 Esc/Ala 46, Gando, Gran Canaria	
C.15-81	McDonnell Douglas F/A-18A+ Hornet [46-09]	EdA 462 Esc/Ala 46, Gando, Gran Canaria	
C.15-82	McDonnell Douglas F/A-18A+ Hornet [46-10]	EdA 462 Esc/Ala 46, Gando, Gran Canaria	
C.15-83	McDonnell Douglas F/A-18A+ Hornet [46-11]	EdA 462 Esc/Ala 46, Gando, Gran Canaria	
C.15-85	McDonnell Douglas F/A-18A+ Hornet [46-13]	EdA 462 Esc/Ala 46, Gando, Gran Canaria	
C.15-86	McDonnell Douglas F/A-18A+ Hornet [46-14]	EdA 462 Esc/Ala 46, Gando, Gran Canaria	
C.15-88	McDonnell Douglas F/A-18A+ Hornet [46-16] $	EdA 462 Esc/Ala 46, Gando, Gran Canaria	
C.15-89	McDonnell Douglas F/A-18A+ Hornet [46-17]	EdA 462 Esc/Ala 46, Gando, Gran Canaria	
C.15-90	McDonnell Douglas F/A-18A+ Hornet [46-18]	EdA 462 Esc/Ala 46, Gando, Gran Canaria	
C.15-92	McDonnell Douglas F/A-18A+ Hornet [46-20]	EdA 462 Esc/Ala 46, Gando, Gran Canaria	
C.15-93	McDonnell Douglas F/A-18A+ Hornet [46-21]	EdA 462 Esc/Ala 46, Gando, Gran Canaria	
C.15-94	McDonnell Douglas F/A-18A+ Hornet [46-22]	EdA 462 Esc/Ala 46, Gando, Gran Canaria	
C.15-95	McDonnell Douglas F/A-18A+ Hornet [46-23]	EdA 462 Esc/Ala 46, Gando, Gran Canaria	
C.15-96	McDonnell Douglas F/A-18A+ Hornet [46-24]	EdA 462 Esc/Ala 46, Gando, Gran Canaria	
CE.15-01	McDonnell Douglas EF-18BM Hornet [15-70]	EdA 151 Esc/152 Esc/153 Esc/Ala 15, Zaragoza	
CE.15-02	McDonnell Douglas EF-18BM Hornet [15-71]	EdA 151 Esc/152 Esc/153 Esc/Ala 15, Zaragoza	
CE.15-03	McDonnell Douglas EF-18BM Hornet [15-72]	EdA 151 Esc/152 Esc/153 Esc/Ala 15, Zaragoza	
CE.15-04	McDonnell Douglas EF-18BM Hornet [15-73]	EdA 151 Esc/152 Esc/153 Esc/Ala 15, Zaragoza	
CE.15-05	McDonnell Douglas EF-18BM Hornet [15-74]	*EdA, wfu Zaragoza, Spain*	
CE.15-06	McDonnell Douglas EF-18BM Hornet [15-75]	EdA 151 Esc/152 Esc/153 Esc/Ala 15, Zaragoza	
CE.15-07	McDonnell Douglas EF-18BM Hornet [15-76]	EdA 151 Esc/152 Esc/153 Esc/Ala 15, Zaragoza	
CE.15-08	McDonnell Douglas EF-18BM Hornet [12-71]	EdA 121 Esc/122 Esc/Ala 12, Madrid/Torrejón	
CE.15-09	McDonnell Douglas EF-18BM Hornet [15-77]	EdA 151 Esc/152 Esc/153 Esc/Ala 15, Zaragoza	
CE.15-10	McDonnell Douglas EF-18BM Hornet [12-73]	EdA 121 Esc/122 Esc/Ala 12, Madrid/Torrejón	
CE.15-11	McDonnell Douglas EF-18BM Hornet [12-74]	EdA 121 Esc/122 Esc/Ala 12, Madrid/Torrejón	
CE.15-12	McDonnell Douglas EF-18BM Hornet [12-75]	EdA 121 Esc/122 Esc/Ala 12, Madrid/Torrejón	

Notes	Serial	Type (code/other identity)	Owner/operator, location or fate
	C.16-20	Eurofighter EF.2000 Tifón [11-91]	Airbus Defence & Space, Getafe
	C.16-21	Eurofighter EF.2000 Tifón [11-21]	EdA 111 Esc/113 Esc/Ala 11, Sevilla/Morón
	C.16-22	Eurofighter EF.2000 Tifón [11-22]	EdA 111 Esc/113 Esc/Ala 11, Sevilla/Morón
	C.16-23	Eurofighter EF.2000 Tifón [11-23]	EdA 111 Esc/113 Esc/Ala 11, Sevilla/Morón
	C.16-24	Eurofighter EF.2000 Tifón [11-24]	EdA 111 Esc/113 Esc/Ala 11, Sevilla/Morón
	C.16-25	Eurofighter EF.2000 Tifón [11-25]	EdA 111 Esc/113 Esc/Ala 11, Sevilla/Morón
	C.16-26	Eurofighter EF.2000 Tifón [11-26]	EdA 111 Esc/113 Esc/Ala 11, Sevilla/Morón
	C.16-27	Eurofighter EF.2000 Tifón [11-27]	EdA 111 Esc/113 Esc/Ala 11, Sevilla/Morón
	C.16-28	Eurofighter EF.2000 Tifón [11-28]	EdA 111 Esc/113 Esc/Ala 11, Sevilla/Morón
	C.16-29	Eurofighter EF.2000 Tifón [11-29]	EdA 111 Esc/113 Esc/Ala 11, Sevilla/Morón
	C.16-30	Eurofighter EF.2000 Tifón [11-30]	EdA 111 Esc/113 Esc/Ala 11, Sevilla/Morón
	C.16-31	Eurofighter EF.2000 Tifón [14-31] $	EdA 142 Esc/Ala 14, Albacete/Los Llanos
	C.16-32	Eurofighter EF.2000 Tifón [11-32]	EdA 111 Esc/113 Esc/Ala 11, Sevilla/Morón
	C.16-33	Eurofighter EF.2000 Tifón [11-33]	EdA 111 Esc/113 Esc/Ala 11, Sevilla/Morón
	C.16-35	Eurofighter EF.2000 Tifón [11-35]	EdA 111 Esc/113 Esc/Ala 11, Sevilla/Morón
	C.16-36	Eurofighter EF.2000 Tifón [14-36]	EdA 142 Esc/Ala 14, Albacete/Los Llanos
	C.16-37	Eurofighter EF.2000 Tifón [14-37]	EdA 142 Esc/Ala 14, Albacete/Los Llanos
	C.16-38	Eurofighter EF.2000 Tifón [11-38]	EdA 111 Esc/113 Esc/Ala 11, Sevilla/Morón
	C.16-39	Eurofighter EF.2000 Tifón [14-39]	EdA 142 Esc/Ala 14, Albacete/Los Llanos
	C.16-40	Eurofighter EF.2000 Tifón [11-40]	EdA 111 Esc/113 Esc/Ala 11, Sevilla/Morón
	C.16-41	Eurofighter EF.2000 Tifón [11-41]	EdA 111 Esc/113 Esc/Ala 11, Sevilla/Morón
	C.16-42	Eurofighter EF.2000 Tifón [11-42]	EdA 111 Esc/113 Esc/Ala 11, Sevilla/Morón
	C.16-43	Eurofighter EF.2000 Tifón [11-43]	EdA 111 Esc/113 Esc/Ala 11, Sevilla/Morón
	C.16-44	Eurofighter EF.2000 Tifón [14-44]	EdA 142 Esc/Ala 14, Albacete/Los Llanos
	C.16-45	Eurofighter EF.2000 Tifón [11-45]	EdA 111 Esc/113 Esc/Ala 11, Sevilla/Morón
	C.16-46	Eurofighter EF.2000 Tifón [11-46]	EdA 111 Esc/113 Esc/Ala 11, Sevilla/Morón
	C.16-47	Eurofighter EF.2000 Tifón [14-47]	EdA 142 Esc/Ala 14, Albacete/Los Llanos
	C.16-48	Eurofighter EF.2000 Tifón [11-48]	EdA 111 Esc/113 Esc/Ala 11, Sevilla/Morón
	C.16-49	Eurofighter EF.2000 Tifón [14-49]	EdA 142 Esc/Ala 14, Albacete/Los Llanos
	C.16-50	Eurofighter EF.2000 Tifón [14-14]	EdA 142 Esc/Ala 14, Albacete/Los Llanos
	C.16-51	Eurofighter EF.2000 Tifón [11-51]	EdA 111 Esc/113 Esc/Ala 11, Sevilla/Morón
	C.16-52	Eurofighter EF.2000 Tifón (C.16-10001) [11-52]	EdA 111 Esc/113 Esc/Ala 11, Sevilla/Morón
	C.16-53	Eurofighter EF.2000 Tifón (C.16-10002) [11-53]	EdA 111 Esc/113 Esc/Ala 11, Sevilla/Morón
	C.16-54	Eurofighter EF.2000 Tifón (C.16-10003) [11-54]	EdA 111 Esc/113 Esc/Ala 11, Sevilla/Morón
	C.16-55	Eurofighter EF.2000 Tifón (C.16-10004) [11-55]	EdA 111 Esc/113 Esc/Ala 11, Sevilla/Morón
	C.16-56	Eurofighter EF.2000 Tifón (10007) [11-56]	EdA 111 Esc/113 Esc/Ala 11, Sevilla/Morón
	C.16-57	Eurofighter EF.2000 Tifón (10012) [11-57]	EdA 111 Esc/113 Esc/Ala 11, Sevilla/Morón
	C.16-58	Eurofighter EF.2000 Tifón (10019) [14-58]	EdA 142 Esc/Ala 14, Albacete/Los Llanos
	C.16-59	Eurofighter EF.2000 Tifón (10020) [14-59] $	EdA 142 Esc/Ala 14, Albacete/Los Llanos
	C.16-60	Eurofighter EF.2000 Tifón (10040) [14-60]	EdA 142 Esc/Ala 14, Albacete/Los Llanos
	C.16-61	Eurofighter EF.2000 Tifón (10046) [14-61]	EdA 142 Esc/Ala 14, Albacete/Los Llanos
	C.16-62	Eurofighter EF.2000 Tifón (10047) [14-62]	EdA 142 Esc/Ala 14, Albacete/Los Llanos
	C.16-63	Eurofighter EF.2000 Tifón (10048) [11-63]	EdA 111 Esc/113 Esc/Ala 11, Sevilla/Morón
	C.16-64	Eurofighter EF.2000 Tifón (10053) [14-64]	EdA 142 Esc/Ala 14, Albacete/Los Llanos
	C.16-65	Eurofighter EF.2000 Tifón (10054) [14-65]	EdA 142 Esc/Ala 14, Albacete/Los Llanos
	C.16-66	Eurofighter EF.2000 Tifón (10064) [14-66] $	EdA 142 Esc/Ala 14, Albacete/Los Llanos
	C.16-67	Eurofighter EF.2000 Tifón (10090) [14-67]	EdA 142 Esc/Ala 14, Albacete/Los Llanos
	C.16-68	Eurofighter EF.2000 Tifón (10091) [14-68]	EdA 142 Esc/Ala 14, Albacete/Los Llanos
	C.16-70	Eurofighter EF.2000 Tifón (10145) [14-28]	Airbus Defence & Space, Getafe
	C.16-71	Eurofighter EF.2000 Tifón (10146) [14-71]	EdA 142 Esc/Ala 14, Albacete/Los Llanos
	C.16-72	Eurofighter EF.2000 Tifón (10147) [14-72]	EdA 142 Esc/Ala 14, Albacete/Los Llanos
	C.16-73	Eurofighter EF.2000 Tifón (10155) [14-73] $	EdA 142 Esc/Ala 14, Albacete/Los Llanos
	C.16-74	Eurofighter EF.2000 Tifón (10202) [14-74]	EdA 142 Esc/Ala 14, Albacete/Los Llanos
	C.16-75	Eurofighter EF.2000 Tifón (10205) [14-75]	EdA 142 Esc/Ala 14, Albacete/Los Llanos
	C.16-76	Eurofighter EF.2000 Tifón (10215) [14-76]	EdA 142 Esc/Ala 14, Albacete/Los Llanos
	C.16-77	Eurofighter EF.2000 Tifón (10234) [14-77]	EdA 142 Esc/Ala 14, Albacete/Los Llanos
	C.16-78	Eurofighter EF.2000 Tifón (10235) [14-78]	EdA 142 Esc/Ala 14, Albacete/Los Llanos
	CE.16-01	Eurofighter EF.2000(T) Tifón [11-01]	EdA 111 Esc/113 Esc/Ala 11, Sevilla/Morón
	CE.16-02	Eurofighter EF.2000(T) Tifón [11-02]	EdA 111 Esc/113 Esc/Ala 11, Sevilla/Morón
	CE.16-03	Eurofighter EF.2000(T) Tifón [11-03]	EdA 111 Esc/113 Esc/Ala 11, Sevilla/Morón
	CE.16-04	Eurofighter EF.2000(T) Tifón [11-04]	EdA 111 Esc/113 Esc/Ala 11, Sevilla/Morón
	CE.16-05	Eurofighter EF.2000(T) Tifón [11-05]	EdA 111 Esc/113 Esc/Ala 11, Sevilla/Morón

Serial	Type (code/other identity)	Owner/operator, location or fate	Notes
CE.16-06	Eurofighter EF.2000(T) Tifón [11-06]	EdA 111 Esc/113 Esc/Ala 11, Sevilla/Morón	
CE.16-07	Eurofighter EF.2000(T) Tifón [11-07]	EdA 111 Esc/113 Esc/Ala 11, Sevilla/Morón	
CE.16-09	Eurofighter EF.2000(T) Tifón [11-09]	EdA 111 Esc/113 Esc/Ala 11, Sevilla/Morón	
CE.16-10	Eurofighter EF.2000(T) Tifón [11-10]	Airbus Defence & Space, Getafe	
CE.16-11	Eurofighter EF.2000(T) Tifón [14-11]	EdA 142 Esc/Ala 14, Albacete/Los Llanos	
CE.16-12	Eurofighter EF.2000(T) Tifón (10000) [11-12]	EdA 111 Esc/113 Esc/Ala 11, Sevilla/Morón	
CE.16-13	Eurofighter EF.2000(T) Tifón (10005) [11-13]	EdA 111 Esc/113 Esc/Ala 11, Sevilla/Morón	
CE.16-14	Eurofighter EF.2000(T) Tifón (10015) [11-14]	EdA 111 Esc/113 Esc/Ala 11, Sevilla/Morón	
D.4-01	Airtech CN.235M-100(MPA) (T.19B-12) [37-01]	EdA 801 Esc/Ala 49, Palma/Son San Juan	
D.4-02	Airtech CN.235M-100(MPA) (T.19B-09) [37-02]	EdA 801 Esc/Ala 49, Palma/Son San Juan	
D.4-03	Airtech CN.235M-100(MPA) (T.19B-10) [37-03]	EdA 801 Esc/Ala 49, Palma/Son San Juan	
D.4-04	Airtech CN.235M-100(MPA) (T.19B-08) [37-04]	EdA 801 Esc/Ala 49, Palma/Son San Juan	
D.4-05	Airtech CN.235M-100(MPA) (T.19B-06) [37-05]	EdA 801 Esc/Ala 49, Palma/Son San Juan	
D.4-06	Airtech CN.235M-100(MPA) (T.19B-05) [37-06]	EdA 801 Esc/Ala 49, Palma/Son San Juan	
D.4-07	Airtech CN.235M-100(MPA) (T.19B-15)	EdA 803 Esc/Ala 48, Madrid/Getafe	
D.4-08	Airtech CN.235M-100(MPA) (T.19B-14) [37-08]	EdA 802 Esc/Ala 46, Gran Canaria	
DT.05-01	Beechcraft King Air 350 (10224) [09-601]	Guardia Civil Servicio Aéreo, Madrid/Torrejón	
E.25-05	CASA 101EB Aviojet [79-05]	Preserved Universidad Politécnica de Madrid	
E.25-06	CASA 101EB Aviojet [79-06]	EdA 794 Esc/AGA, Murcia/San Javier	
E.25-08	CASA 101EB Aviojet [79-08]	EdA Patrulla Aguila/AGA, Murcia/San Javier	
E.25-11	CASA 101EB Aviojet [79-11]	EdA 794 Esc/AGA, Murcia/San Javier	
E.25-12	CASA 101EB Aviojet [79-12]	EdA Patrulla Aguila/AGA, Murcia/San Javier	
E.25-13	CASA 101EB Aviojet [79-13]	EdA Patrulla Aguila/AGA, Murcia/San Javier	
E.25-21	CASA 101EB Aviojet [79-21]	EdA 794 Esc/AGA, Murcia/San Javier	
E.25-24	CASA 101EB Aviojet [79-24]	EdA, stored Albacete	
E.25-25	CASA 101EB Aviojet [79-25]	EdA Patrulla Aguila/AGA, Murcia/San Javier	
E.25-27	CASA 101EB Aviojet [79-27]	EdA Patrulla Aguila/AGA, Murcia/San Javier	
E.25-28	CASA 101EB Aviojet [79-28]	EdA Patrulla Aguila/AGA, Murcia/San Javier	
E.25-31	CASA 101EB Aviojet [79-31]	EdA Patrulla Aguila/AGA, Murcia/San Javier	
E.25-33	CASA 101EB Aviojet [74-02]	GEM, Salamanca/Matacán	
E.25-34	CASA 101EB Aviojet [74-44]	EdA 794 Esc/AGA, Murcia/San Javier	
E.25-35	CASA 101EB Aviojet [54-20] $	EdA 541 Esc/CLAEX/Grupo 54, Madrid/Torrejón	
E.25-37	CASA 101EB Aviojet [794-37]	EdA Patrulla Aguila/AGA, Murcia/San Javier	
E.25-38	CASA 101EB Aviojet [79-38]	EdA Patrulla Aguila/AGA, Murcia/San Javier	
E.25-40	CASA 101EB Aviojet [794-40]	EdA Patrulla Aguila/AGA, Murcia/San Javier	
E.25-43	CASA 101EB Aviojet [74-43]	EdA, stored Albacete	
E.25-44	CASA 101EB Aviojet [79-44]	EdA 794 Esc/AGA, Murcia/San Javier	
E.25-51	CASA 101EB Aviojet [74-07]	EdA 741 Esc/GEM, Salamanca/Matacán	
E.25-52	CASA 101EB Aviojet [794-52]	EdA 794 Esc, Murcia/San Javier	
E.25-53	CASA 101EB Aviojet [74-09]	EdA 794 Esc, Murcia/San Javier	
E.25-54	CASA 101EB Aviojet [79-35]	EdA GEM, Salamanca/Matacán	
E.25-55	CASA 101EB Aviojet [54-21]	EdA 541 Esc/CLAEX/Grupo 54, Madrid/Torrejón	
E.25-56	CASA 101EB Aviojet [74-11]	EdA 794 Esc/AGA, Murcia/San Javier	
E.25-57	CASA 101EB Aviojet [793-57]	EdA 794 Esc/AGA, Murcia/San Javier	
E.25-59	CASA 101EB Aviojet [74-13]	EdA 794 Esc/AGA, Murcia/San Javier	
E.25-61	CASA 101EB Aviojet [54-22]	EdA 794 Esc/AGA, Murcia/San Javier	
E.25-62	CASA 101EB Aviojet [79-17]	EdA 794 Esc/AGA, Murcia/San Javier	
E.25-63	CASA 101EB Aviojet [74-17]	EdA Patrulla Aguila/AGA, Murcia/San Javier	
E.25-66	CASA 101EB Aviojet [74-20]	EdA 794 Esc/AGA, Murcia/San Javier	
E.25-67	CASA 101EB Aviojet [74-21]	EdA GEM, Salamanca/Matacán	
E.25-68	CASA 101EB Aviojet [741-68]	EdA Patrulla Aguila/AGA, Murcia/San Javier	
E.25-69	CASA 101EB Aviojet [79-97]	EdA Patrulla Aguila/AGA, Murcia/San Javier	
E.25-71	CASA 101EB Aviojet [74-25]	EdA 794 Esc/AGA, Murcia/San Javier	
E.25-72	CASA 101EB Aviojet [74-26]	EdA GEM, Salamanca/Matacán	
E.25-73	CASA 101EB Aviojet [79-98]	EdA 794 Esc/AGA, Murcia/San Javier	
E.25-74	CASA 101EB Aviojet [74-28]	EdA GEM, Salamanca/Matacán	
E.25-76	CASA 101EB Aviojet [74-30]	EdA 794 Esc/AGA, Murcia/San Javier	
E.25-78	CASA 101EB Aviojet [79-02]	EdA Patrulla Aguila/AGA, Murcia/San Javier	
E.25-79	CASA 101EB Aviojet [79-39]	EdA 794 Esc/AGA, Murcia/San Javier	
E.25-80	CASA 101EB Aviojet [79-03]	EdA 794 Esc/AGA, Murcia/San Javier	
E.25-81	CASA 101EB Aviojet [793-81]	EdA 794 Esc/AGA, Murcia/San Javier	
E.25-83	CASA 101EB Aviojet [74-35]	EdA, stored Albacete	

Notes	Serial	Type (code/other identity)	Owner/operator, location or fate
	E.25-84	CASA 101EB Aviojet [79-04]	EdA 794 Esc/AGA, Murcia/San Javier
	E.25-86	CASA 101EB Aviojet [79-32]	EdA 794 Esc/AGA, Murcia/San Javier
	E.25-87	CASA 101EB Aviojet [79-29]	*EdA, stored Albacete*
	E.25-88	CASA 101EB Aviojet [74-39]	*EdA, stored Albacete*
	HD.29-16	NH Industries NH.90-TTH (10227) [803-16]	EdA 803 Esc/Ala 48, Cuatro Vientos
	HD.29-17	NH Industries NH.90-TTH (10236) [803-17]	EdA 803 Esc/Ala 48, Cuatro Vientos
	HD.29-18	NH Industries NH.90-TTH (10237) [803-18]	EdA 803 Esc/Ala 48, Cuatro Vientos
	HD.29-19	NH Industries NH.90-TTH (10238) [803-19]	EdA 803 Esc/Ala 48, Cuatro Vientos
	HD.29-20	NH Industries NH.90-TTH (10263) [803-20]	EdA 803 Esc/Ala 48, Cuatro Vientos
	HD.29-21	NH Industries NH.90-TTH (10264) [803-21]	EdA 803 Esc/Ala 48, Cuatro Vientos
	HD.29-23	NH Industries NH.90-TTH (10304) [803-23]	EdA 803 Esc/Ala 48, Cuatro Vientos
	HE.25-01	Eurocopter EC.120B Colibri [782-01]	EdA *Patrulla Aspa*/Ala 78, Granada/Armilla
	HE.25-02	Eurocopter EC.120B Colibri [782-02]	EdA *Patrulla Aspa*/Ala 78, Granada/Armilla
	HE.25-03	Eurocopter EC.120B Colibri [782-03]	EdA *Patrulla Aspa*/Ala 78, Granada/Armilla
	HE.25-4	Eurocopter EC.120B Colibri [782-04]	EdA *Patrulla Aspa*/Ala 78, Granada/Armilla
	HE.25-6	Eurocopter EC.120B Colibri [78-25]	EdA 541 Esc/CLAEX/Grupo 54, Madrid/Torrejón
	HE.25-07	Eurocopter EC.120B Colibri [782-07]	EdA *Patrulla Aspa*/Ala 78, Granada/Armilla
	HE.25-8	Eurocopter EC.120B Colibri [782-08]	EdA *Patrulla Aspa*/Ala 78, Granada/Armilla
	HE.25-09	Eurocopter EC.120B Colibri [782-09]	EdA *Patrulla Aspa*/Ala 78, Granada/Armilla
	HE.25-10	Eurocopter EC.120B Colibri [78-29]	EdA 782 Esc/Ala 78, Granada/Armilla
	HE.25-11	Eurocopter EC.120B Colibri [782-11]	EdA 782 Esc/Ala 78, Granada/Armilla
	HE.25-12	Eurocopter EC.120B Colibri [782-12]	EdA *Patrulla Aspa*/Ala 78, Granada/Armilla
	HE.25-13	Eurocopter EC.120B Colibri [782-13]	EdA *Patrulla Aspa*/Ala 78, Granada/Armilla
	HE.25-14	Eurocopter EC.120B Colibri [782-14]	EdA *Patrulla Aspa*/Ala 78, Granada/Armilla
	HE.25-15	Eurocopter EC.120B Colibri [782-15]	EdA *Patrulla Aspa*/Ala 78, Granada/Armilla
	HT.29-39	NH Industries NH.90-TTH (10345) [01-1401]	Armada 14 Esc, Rota
	HT.29-40	NH Industries NH.90-MSPT (10346) [01-1402]	Armada 14 Esc, Rota
	HT.29-41	NH Industries NH.90-MSPT (10347) [01-1403]	Armada (on order)
	HT.29-42	NH Industries NH.90-MSPT	Armada (on order)
	HT.29-43	NH Industries NH.90-MSPT	Armada (on order)
	P.3M-08	Lockheed P-3M Orion [22-31]	*EdA, stored Sevilla/Morón*
	P.3M-09	Lockheed P-3M Orion [22-32]	*EdA, stored Sevilla/Morón*
	P.3M-12	Lockheed P-3M Orion [22-35]	*EdA, stored Sevilla/San Pablo*
	T.12B-49	CASA 212A Aviocar [72-49]	EdA 721 Esc, Murcia/Alcantarilla
	T.12B-62	CASA 212A Aviocar (D.3A-2) [72-62]	*EdA, stored Cuatro Vientos*
	T.12B-63	CASA 212A Aviocar [72-63]	EdA 721 Esc, Murcia/Alcantarilla
	T.12B-65	CASA 212A Aviocar [72-65]	EdA 721 Esc, Murcia/Alcantarilla
	T.12B-66	CASA 212A Aviocar [72-66]	EdA 721 Esc, Murcia/Alcantarilla
	T.12B-67	CASA 212A Aviocar [72-12]	EdA 721 Esc, Murcia/Alcantarilla
	T.12B-69	CASA 212A Aviocar [72-69]	EdA 721 Esc, Murcia/Alcantarilla
	T.12B-70	CASA 212A Aviocar [72-70]	EdA 721 Esc, Murcia/Alcantarilla
	T.12B-71	CASA 212A Aviocar [72-71] $	EdA 721 Esc, Murcia/Alcantarilla
	T.12D-74	CASA 212-200 Aviocar [54-11]	*EdA, stored Sevilla/San Pablo*
	T.12D-75	CASA 212-200 Aviocar [47-14]	*EdA, stored Cuatro Vientos*
	T.18-1	Dassault Falcon 900 [45-40]	EdA 451 Esc/Grupo 45, Madrid/Torrejón
	T.18-2	Dassault Falcon 900 [45-41]	EdA 451 Esc/Grupo 45, Madrid/Torrejón
	T.18-3	Dassault Falcon 900B [45-03]	EdA 451 Esc/Grupo 45, Madrid/Torrejón
	T.18-4	Dassault Falcon 900B [45-04]	EdA 451 Esc/Grupo 45, Madrid/Torrejón
	T.18-5	Dassault Falcon 900B [45-05]	EdA 451 Esc/Grupo 45, Madrid/Torrejón
	T.19A-02	Airtech CN.235M-10 [403-02]	*EdA, stored Cuatro Vientos*
	T.19B-07	Airtech CN.235M-100 [744-07]	EdA 744 Esc/GEM, Salamanca/Matacán
	T.19B-11	Airtech CN.235M-100 [744-11]	EdA 744 Esc/GEM, Salamanca/Matacán
	T.19B-13	Airtech CN.235M-100 [74-13]	EdA 744 Esc/GEM, Salamanca/Matacán
	T.19B-16	Airtech CN.235M-100 [74-16]	EdA 744 Esc/GEM, Salamanca/Matacán
	T.19B-17	Airtech CN.235M-100 [744-17]	EdA 744 Esc/GEM, Salamanca/Matacán
	T.19B-18	Airtech CN.235M-100 [74-18]	EdA 744 Esc/GEM, Salamanca/Matacán
	T.19B-19	Airtech CN.235M-100 [744-19]	EdA 744 Esc/GEM, Salamanca/Matacán
	T.19B-20	Airtech CN.235M-100 [744-20]	EdA, Torrejon, for GI
	T.19B-21	Airtech CN.235M VIGMA [09-501]	Guardia Civil Servicio Aéreo, Gran Canaria
	T.19B-22	Airtech CN.235M VIGMA [09-502]	Guardia Civil Servicio Aéreo, Gran Canaria
	TR.20-01	Cessna 560 Citation VI [403-11]	EdA 403 Esc, Madrid/Getafe
	TR.20-02	Cessna 560 Citation VI [403-12]	EdA 403 Esc, Madrid/Getafe

Serial	Type (code/other identity)	Owner/operator, location or fate	Notes
TR.20-03	Cessna 560 Citation VI [403-21]	EdA 403 Esc, Madrid/Getafe	
T.21-01	CASA C-295M [35-01]	EdA 353 Esc/Ala 35, Madrid/Getafe	
T.21-02	CASA C-295M [35-02] $	EdA 353 Esc/Ala 35, Madrid/Getafe	
T.21-03	CASA C-295M [35-03]	EdA 353 Esc/Ala 35, Madrid/Getafe	
T.21-04	CASA C-295M [35-04]	Airbus Defence & Space, Sevilla	
T.21-05	CASA C-295M [35-05]	EdA 353 Esc/Ala 35, Madrid/Getafe	
T.21-06	CASA C-295M [35-06]	EdA 353 Esc/Ala 35, Madrid/Getafe	
T.21-07	CASA C-295M [35-07]	EdA 353 Esc/Ala 35, Madrid/Getafe	
T.21-08	CASA C-295M [35-08] $	EdA 353 Esc/Ala 35, Madrid/Getafe	
T.21-09	CASA C-295M [35-09]	EdA 353 Esc/Ala 35, Madrid/Getafe	
T.21-11	CASA C-295M [35-11]	EdA 353 Esc/Ala 35, Madrid/Getafe	
T.21-12	CASA C-295M [35-12]	EdA 353 Esc/Ala 35, Madrid/Getafe	
T.21-13	CASA C-295M [35-13]	EdA 353 Esc/Ala 35, Madrid/Getafe	
T.22-1	Airbus A.310-304 [451-01]	EdA 451 Esc/Grupo 45, Madrid/Torrejón	
T.22-2	Airbus A.310-304 [451-02]	EdA 451 Esc/Grupo 45, Madrid/Torrejón	
T.23-01	Airbus Military A.400M (10074) [31-21]	EdA/Airbus Defence & Space, Sevilla	
TK.23-02	Airbus Military A.400M (10075) [31-22]	EdA/Airbus Defence & Space, Sevilla	
TK.23-03	Airbus Military A.400M (10076) [31-23]	EdA/Airbus Defence & Space, Sevilla	
T.23-04	Airbus Military A.400M (10174) [31-24]	EdA 311 Esc/312 Esc/Ala 31, Zaragoza	
T.23-05	Airbus Military A.400M (10206) [31-25]	EdA 311 Esc/312 Esc/Ala 31, Zaragoza	
T.23-06	Airbus Military A.400M (10207) [31-26]	EdA 311 Esc/312 Esc/Ala 31, Zaragoza	
TK.23-07	Airbus Military A.400M (10208) [31-27]	EdA 311 Esc/312 Esc/Ala 31, Zaragoza	
T.23-08	Airbus Military A.400M (10217) [31-28]	EdA 311 Esc/312 Esc/Ala 31, Zaragoza	
TK.23-09	Airbus Military A.400M (10218) [31-29]	EdA/Airbus Defence & Space, Sevilla	
T.23-10	Airbus Military A.400M (10219) [31-30]	EdA 311 Esc/312 Esc/Ala 31, Zaragoza	
T.23-11	Airbus Military A.400M (10220) [31-31]	EdA 311 Esc/312 Esc/Ala 31, Zaragoza	
T.23-12	Airbus Military A.400M (10221) [31-32]	EdA/Airbus Defence & Space, Sevilla	
T.23-13	Airbus Military A.400M (10222) [31-33]	EdA 311 Esc/312 Esc/Ala 31, Zaragoza	
TK.23-14	Airbus Military A.400M (10223) [31-34] $	EdA 311 Esc/312 Esc/Ala 31, Zaragoza	
T.24-01	Airbus A.330-202 (10273) [452-01]	EdA 451 Esc/Grupo 45, Madrid/Torrejón	
T.24-02	Airbus A.330-202 MRTT (10274) [452-02]	Airbus Defence & Space, Getafe (MRTT conversion)	
TK.24-03	Airbus A.330-202 MRTT (10275) (MRTT073) [452-03]	Airbus Defence & Space, Getafe (MRTT conversion)	
TX.21-14	CASA C-295W (10332) [541-14]	EdA 541 Esc/CLAEX/INTA, Grupo 54, Madrid/Torrejón	
U.20-2	Cessna 550 Citation II [01-406]	Armada 4 Esc, Rota	
U.20-3	Cessna 550 Citation II [01-407]	Armada 4 Esc, Rota	
U.21-01	Cessna 650 Citation VII [01-408]	Armada 4 Esc, Rota	
UD.13-20	Canadair CL-215T [43-20]	EdA 431 Esc/Grupo 43, Madrid/Torrejón	
UD.13-21	Canadair CL-215T [43-21]	EdA 431 Esc/Grupo 43, Madrid/Torrejón	
UD.13-22	Canadair CL-215T [43-22]	EdA 431 Esc/Grupo 43, Madrid/Torrejón	
UD.13T-23	Canadair CL-215T [43-23]	EdA 431 Esc/Grupo 43, Madrid/Torrejón	
UD.13T-24	Canadair CL-215T [43-24]	EdA 431 Esc/Grupo 43, Madrid/Torrejón	
UD.13-25	Canadair CL-215T [43-25]	EdA 431 Esc/Grupo 43, Madrid/Torrejón	
UD.13T-26	Canadair CL-215T [43-26]	EdA 431 Esc/Grupo 43, Madrid/Torrejón	
UD.13-27	Canadair CL-215T [43-27]	EdA 431 Esc/Grupo 43, Madrid/Torrejón	
UD.13T-28	Canadair CL-215T [43-28]	EdA 431 Esc/Grupo 43, Madrid/Torrejón	
UD.13-30	Canadair CL-215T [43-30]	EdA 431 Esc/Grupo 43, Madrid/Torrejón	
UD.14-01	Canadair CL-415T [43-31]	EdA 431 Esc/Grupo 43, Madrid/Torrejón	
UD.14-02	Canadair CL-415T [43-32]	EdA 431 Esc/Grupo 43, Madrid/Torrejón	
UD.14-03	Canadair CL-415T [43-33]	EdA 431 Esc/Grupo 43, Madrid/Torrejón	
UD.14-04	Canadair CL-415T [43-34]	EdA 431 Esc/Grupo 43, Madrid/Torrejón	
VA.1B-24	McDonnell Douglas EAV-8B+ Matador [01-914]	Armada 9 Esc, Rota	
VA.1B-26	McDonnell Douglas EAV-8B+ Matador [01-916]	Armada 9 Esc, Rota	
VA.1B-27	McDonnell Douglas EAV-8B+ Matador [01-917]	Armada 9 Esc, Rota	
VA.1B-29	McDonnell Douglas EAV-8B+ Matador [01-919]	Armada 9 Esc, Rota	
VA.1B-30	McDonnell Douglas EAV-8B+ Matador [01-920]	Armada 9 Esc, Rota	
VA.1B-35	McDonnell Douglas EAV-8B+ Matador [01-923]	Armada 9 Esc, Rota	
VA.1B-36	McDonnell Douglas EAV-8B+ Matador [01-924]	Armada 9 Esc, Rota	
VA.1B-37	McDonnell Douglas EAV-8B+ Matador [01-925]	Armada 9 Esc, Rota	
VA.1B-38	McDonnell Douglas EAV-8B+ Matador [01-926]	Armada 9 Esc, Rota	
VA.1B-39	McDonnell Douglas EAV-8B+ Matador [01-927]	Armada 9 Esc, Rota	
VA.1B-40	McDonnell Douglas EAV-8B+ Matador (10266) [01-999]	Armada 9 Esc, Rota	

Notes	Serial	Type (code/other identity)	Owner/operator, location or fate
	SUDAN		
	ST-PSA	Dassault Falcon 900B	Sudanese Government, Khartoum
	ST-PSR	Dassault Falcon 50	Sudanese Government, Khartoum
	SWEDEN		
	Försvarsmakten/Swedish Armed Forces: Försvarsmaktens Helikopterflottilj (Hkpflj)/Armed Forces Helicopter Wing & Svenska Flygvapnet/Swedish Air Force		
	35-075	Gates Learjet 35A (Tp.104) (SE-DHP)	Flygvapnet FMV, Linköping/Malmen
	35-195	Gates Learjet 35A (Tp.104) (SE-DHO)	Flygvapnet FMV, Linköping/Malmen
	39-6	SAAB JAS 39C Gripen [6]	SAAB, Linköping/Malmen
	39-7	SAAB JAS 39NG Gripen	SAAB, Linköping/Malmen
	39-8	SAAB JAS 39E Gripen	SAAB, Linköping/Malmen
	39-9	SAAB JAS 39E Gripen	SAAB, Linköping/Malmen
	39-10	SAAB JAS 39E Gripen	SAAB, Linköping/Malmen
	39208	SAAB JAS 39C Gripen [208]	Flygvapnet Flottiljer 17, Ronneby/Kallinge
	39209	SAAB JAS 39C Gripen [209]	Flygvapnet Flottiljer 7, Såtenäs
	39210	SAAB JAS 39C Gripen [210]	Flygvapnet Flottiljer 17, Ronneby/Kallinge
	39211	SAAB JAS 39C Gripen [211]	Flygvapnet Flottiljer 17, Ronneby/Kallinge
	39212	SAAB JAS 39C Gripen [212]	Flygvapnet Flottiljer 21, Luleå/Kallax
	39213	SAAB JAS 39C Gripen [213]	Flygvapnet Flottiljer 7, Såtenäs
	39214	SAAB JAS 39C Gripen [214]	Flygvapnet Flottiljer 7, Såtenäs
	39215	SAAB JAS 39C Gripen [215]	Flygvapnet Flottiljer 7, Såtenäs
	39216	SAAB JAS 39C Gripen [216]	Flygvapnet Flottiljer 17, Ronneby/Kallinge
	39217	SAAB JAS 39C Gripen [217]	Flygvapnet Flottiljer 21, Luleå/Kallax
	39218	SAAB JAS 39C Gripen [218]	Flygvapnet Flottiljer 17, Ronneby/Kallinge
	39219	SAAB JAS 39C Gripen [219]	Flygvapnet Flottiljer 21, Luleå/Kallax
	39220	SAAB JAS 39C Gripen [220]	Flygvapnet Flottiljer 7, Såtenäs
	39221	SAAB JAS 39C Gripen [221]	Flygvapnet Flottiljer 17, Ronneby/Kallinge
	39222	SAAB JAS 39C Gripen [222]	Flygvapnet Flottiljer 17, Ronneby/Kallinge
	39223	SAAB JAS 39C Gripen [223]	Flygvapnet Flottiljer 21, Luleå/Kallax
	39224	SAAB JAS 39C Gripen [224]	Flygvapnet Flottiljer 17, Ronneby/Kallinge
	39225	SAAB JAS 39C Gripen [225]	Flygvapnet Flottiljer 7, Såtenäs
	39226	SAAB JAS 39C Gripen [226]	Flygvapnet Flottiljer 7, Såtenäs
	39227	SAAB JAS 39C Gripen [227]	Flygvapnet Flottiljer 7, Såtenäs
	39228	SAAB JAS 39C Gripen [228]	Flygvapnet Flottiljer 17, Ronneby/Kallinge
	39229	SAAB JAS 39C Gripen [229]	Flygvapnet Flottiljer 21, Luleå/Kallax
	39230	SAAB JAS 39C Gripen [230]	Flygvapnet Flottiljer 17, Ronneby/Kallinge
	39231	SAAB JAS 39C Gripen [231]	Flygvapnet Flottiljer 7, Såtenäs
	39232	SAAB JAS 39C Gripen [232]	Flygvapnet Flottiljer 17, Ronneby/Kallinge
	39233	SAAB JAS 39C Gripen [233]	Flygvapnet Flottiljer 17, Ronneby/Kallinge
	39246	SAAB JAS 39C Gripen [246]	Flygvapnet Flottiljer 17, Ronneby/Kallinge
	39247	SAAB JAS 39C Gripen [247]	Flygvapnet Flottiljer 17, Ronneby/Kallinge
	39248	SAAB JAS 39C Gripen [248]	Flygvapnet Flottiljer 21, Luleå/Kallax
	39249	SAAB JAS 39C Gripen [249]	Flygvapnet Flottiljer 21, Luleå/Kallax
	39250	SAAB JAS 39C Gripen [250]	Flygvapnet FC, Linköping/Malmen
	39251	SAAB JAS 39C Gripen [251]	Flygvapnet FC, Linköping/Malmen
	39253	SAAB JAS 39C Gripen [253]	Flygvapnet Flottiljer 7, Såtenäs
	39254	SAAB JAS 39C Gripen [254]	Flygvapnet Flottiljer 17, Ronneby/Kallinge
	39255	SAAB JAS 39C Gripen [255]	Flygvapnet Flottiljer 17, Ronneby/Kallinge
	39256	SAAB JAS 39C Gripen [256]	Flygvapnet Flottiljer 17, Ronneby/Kallinge
	39257	SAAB JAS 39C Gripen [257]	Flygvapnet Flottiljer 21, Luleå/Kallax
	39258	SAAB JAS 39C Gripen [258]	Flygvapnet Flottiljer 21, Luleå/Kallax
	39260	SAAB JAS 39C Gripen [260]	Flygvapnet Flottiljer 21, Luleå/Kallax
	39261	SAAB JAS 39C Gripen [261]	Flygvapnet Flottiljer 21, Luleå/Kallax
	39262	SAAB JAS 39C Gripen [262]	Flygvapnet Flottiljer 17, Ronneby/Kallinge
	39263	SAAB JAS 39C Gripen [263]	Flygvapnet Flottiljer 21, Luleå/Kallax
	39264	SAAB JAS 39C Gripen [264]	Flygvapnet Flottiljer 17, Ronneby/Kallinge
	39265	SAAB JAS 39C Gripen [265]	Flygvapnet Flottiljer 21, Luleå/Kallax
	39266	SAAB JAS 39C Gripen [266]	Flygvapnet Flottiljer 7, Såtenäs
	39267	SAAB JAS 39C Gripen [267]	Flygvapnet Flottiljer 21, Luleå/Kallax
	39268	SAAB JAS 39C Gripen [268]	Flygvapnet Flottiljer 7, Såtenäs
	39269	SAAB JAS 39C Gripen [269]	Flygvapnet Flottiljer 17, Ronneby/Kallinge

Serial	Type (code/other identity)	Owner/operator, location or fate	Notes
39270	SAAB JAS 39C Gripen [270]	Flygvapnet Flottiljer 17, Ronneby/Kallinge	
39271	SAAB JAS 39C Gripen [271]	Flygvapnet Flottiljer 21, Luleå/Kallax	
39272	SAAB JAS 39C Gripen [272]	Flygvapnet Flottiljer 7, Såtenäs	
39273	SAAB JAS 39C Gripen [273]	Flygvapnet Flottiljer 17, Ronneby/Kallinge	
39274	SAAB JAS 39C Gripen [274]	Flygvapnet Flottiljer 21, Luleå/Kallax	
39275	SAAB JAS 39C Gripen [275]	Flygvapnet Flottiljer 7, Såtenäs	
39276	SAAB JAS 39C Gripen [276]	SAAB, Linköping/Malmen	
39277	SAAB JAS 39C Gripen [277]	Flygvapnet Flottiljer 7, Såtenäs	
39278	SAAB JAS 39C Gripen [278]	Flygvapnet Flottiljer 17, Ronneby/Kallinge	
39279	SAAB JAS 39C Gripen [279]	Flygvapnet Flottiljer 21, Luleå/Kallax	
39280	SAAB JAS 39C Gripen [280]	Flygvapnet Flottiljer 21, Luleå/Kallax	
39281	SAAB JAS 39C Gripen [281]	Flygvapnet Flottiljer 17, Ronneby/Kallinge	
39282	SAAB JAS 39C Gripen [282]	Flygvapnet Flottiljer 7, Såtenäs	
39283	SAAB JAS 39C Gripen [283]	Flygvapnet Flottiljer 21, Luleå/Kallax	
39284	SAAB JAS 39C Gripen [284]	Flygvapnet Flottiljer 17, Ronneby/Kallinge	
39285	SAAB JAS 39C Gripen [285]	Flygvapnet Flottiljer 21, Luleå/Kallax	
39286	SAAB JAS 39C Gripen [286]	Flygvapnet Flottiljer 21, Luleå/Kallax	
39287	SAAB JAS 39C Gripen [287]	Flygvapnet Flottiljer 17, Ronneby/Kallinge	
39288	SAAB JAS 39C Gripen [288]	Flygvapnet Flottiljer 21, Luleå/Kallax	
39289	SAAB JAS 39C Gripen [289]	Flygvapnet Flottiljer 7, Såtenäs	
39290	SAAB JAS 39C Gripen [290]	Flygvapnet Flottiljer 21, Luleå/Kallax	
39291	SAAB JAS 39C Gripen [291]	Flygvapnet Flottiljer 7, Såtenäs	
39292	SAAB JAS 39C Gripen [292]	Flygvapnet Flottiljer 17, Ronneby/Kallinge	
39293	SAAB JAS 39C Gripen [293]	Flygvapnet Flottiljer 7, Såtenäs	
39294	SAAB JAS 39C Gripen [294]	Flygvapnet Flottiljer 17, Ronneby/Kallinge	
39815	SAAB JAS 39D Gripen [815]	Flygvapnet Flottiljer 7, Såtenäs	
39816	SAAB JAS 39D Gripen [816]	Flygvapnet Flottiljer 7, Såtenäs	
39817	SAAB JAS 39D Gripen [817]	Flygvapnet Flottiljer 17, Ronneby/Kallinge	
39821	SAAB JAS 39D Gripen [821]	Flygvapnet Flottiljer 7, Såtenäs	
39822	SAAB JAS 39D Gripen [822]	Flygvapnet Flottiljer 21, Luleå/Kallax	
39823	SAAB JAS 39D Gripen [823]	Flygvapnet Flottiljer 21, Luleå/Kallax	
39824	SAAB JAS 39D Gripen [824]	Flygvapnet Flottiljer 21, Luleå/Kallax	
39825	SAAB JAS 39D Gripen [825]	Flygvapnet Flottiljer 7, Såtenäs	
39826	SAAB JAS 39D Gripen [826]	Flygvapnet Flottiljer 17, Ronneby/Kallinge	
39827	SAAB JAS 39D Gripen [827]	Flygvapnet Flottiljer 7, Såtenäs	
39829	SAAB JAS 39D Gripen [829]	Flygvapnet Flottiljer 17, Ronneby/Kallinge	
39830	SAAB JAS 39D Gripen [830]	Flygvapnet Flottiljer 7, Såtenäs	
39831	SAAB JAS 39D Gripen [831]	Flygvapnet Flottiljer 17, Ronneby/Kallinge	
39832	SAAB JAS 39D Gripen [832]	SAAB, Linköping/Malmen	
39833	SAAB JAS 39D Gripen [833]	Flygvapnet Flottiljer 21, Luleå/Kallax	
39834	SAAB JAS 39D Gripen [834]	Flygvapnet Flottiljer 7, Såtenäs	
39835	SAAB JAS 39D Gripen [835]	Flygvapnet Flottiljer 7, Såtenäs	
39836	SAAB JAS 39D Gripen [836]	Flygvapnet Flottiljer 17, Ronneby/Kallinge	
39837	SAAB JAS 39D Gripen [837]	Flygvapnet Flottiljer 21, Luleå/Kallax	
39838	SAAB JAS 39D Gripen [838]	SAAB, Linköping/Malmen	
39839	SAAB JAS 39D Gripen [839]	Flygvapnet Flottiljer 7, Såtenäs	
39840	SAAB JAS 39D Gripen [840]	Flygvapnet Flottiljer 21, Luleå/Kallax	
39841	SAAB JAS 39D Gripen [841]	Flygvapnet Flottiljer 7, Såtenäs	
39....	SAAB JAS 39E Gripen	SAAB, Linköping/Malmen	
396002	SAAB JAS 39E Gripen	SAAB, Linköping/Malmen	
396003	SAAB JAS 39E Gripen	SAAB, Linköping/Malmen	
396004	SAAB JAS 39E Gripen	Flygvapnet FMV, Linköping/Malmen	
396005	SAAB JAS 39E Gripen	Flygvapnet FMV, Linköping/Malmen	
396006	SAAB JAS 39E Gripen	Flygvapnet (on order)	
396007	SAAB JAS 39E Gripen	Flygvapnet (on order)	
396008	SAAB JAS 39E Gripen	Flygvapnet (on order)	
396009	SAAB JAS 39E Gripen	Flygvapnet (on order)	
396010	SAAB JAS 39E Gripen	Flygvapnet (on order)	
396011	SAAB JAS 39E Gripen	SAAB, Linköping/Malmen	
396012	SAAB JAS 39E Gripen	SAAB, Linköping/Malmen	
84002	Lockheed C-130H Hercules (Tp.84) [842]	Flygvapnet TSFE, Såtenäs	
84004	Lockheed C-130H Hercules (Tp.84) [844]	Flygvapnet TSFE, Såtenäs	

Notes	Serial	Type (code/other identity)	Owner/operator, location or fate
	84005	Lockheed C-130H Hercules (Tp.84) [845]	Flygvapnet TSFE, Såtenäs
	84006	Lockheed C-130H Hercules (Tp.84) [846]	Flygvapnet TSFE, Såtenäs
	84007	Lockheed C-130H Hercules (Tp.84) [847]	Flygvapnet TSFE, Såtenäs
	84008	Lockheed C-130H Hercules (Tp.84) [848]	Flygvapnet TSFE, Såtenäs
	100001	SAAB SF.340 (OS.100) [001]	Flygvapnet TSFE, Linköping/Malmen
	100003	SAAB SF.340AEW&C (S.100D Argus) [003]	Flygvapnet TSFE, Linköping/Malmen
	100004	SAAB SF.340AEW&C (S.100D Argus) [004]	Flygvapnet TSFE, Linköping/Malmen
	100008	SAAB SF.340 (Tp.100C) [008]	Flygvapnet TSFE, Linköping/Malmen
	102002	Grumman G.1159C Gulfstream IV (S.102B Korpen)[022]	Flygvapnet TSFE, Linköping/Malmen
	102003	Grumman G.1159C Gulfstream IV (S.102B Korpen)[023]	Flygvapnet TSFE, Linköping/Malmen
	102004	Grumman G.1159C Gulfstream IV-SP (Tp.102C)	Flygvapnet TSFE, Linköping/Malmen
	102005	Gulfstream Aerospace G.550 (Tp.102D)	Flygvapnet TSFE, Linköping/Malmen
	106111	Bombardier Global 6000 (C-GZVH)	Flygvapnet, Linköping/Malmen
	......	Bombardier Global 6000	Flygvapnet (on order)
	......	Bombardier Global 6000	Flygvapnet (on order)
	142044	NH Industries NH.90-TTH (Hkp.14B) (141044) [44]	Hkpflj 3.HkpSkv, Ronneby/Kallinge
	142045	NH Industries NH.90-TTH (Hkp.14B) (141045) [45]	Hkpflj 1.HkpSkv, Luleå/Kallax
	144048	NH Industries NH.90-TTH (Hkp.14D) (141048) [48]	*Reserialled as 145048*
	144049	NH Industries NH.90-TTH (Hkp.14D) (141049) [49]	*Reserialled as 145049*
	144051	NH Industries NH.90-TTH (Hkp.14D) (141051) [51]	Hkpflj 1.HkpSkv, Luleå/Kallax
	145048	NH Industries NH.90-TTH (Hkp.14E) (141048) [48]	Hkpflj 1.HkpSkv, Luleå/Kallax
	145049	NH Industries NH.90-TTH (Hkp.14E) (141049) [49]	Hkpflj 1.HkpSkv, Luleå/Kallax
	145052	NH Industries NH.90-TTH (Hkp.14E) (141052) [52]	Hkpflj 1.HkpSkv, Luleå/Kallax
	145053	NH Industries NH.90-TTH (Hkp.14F) (144053) [53]	Hkpflj 1.HkpSkv, Luleå/Kallax
	146042	NH Industries NH.90-TTH (Hkp.14F) (142042) [42]	Hkpflj 1.HkpSkv, Luleå/Kallax
	146043	NH Industries NH.90-TTH (Hkp.14F) (141043) [43]	**Airbus, Marignane, France**
	146046	NH Industries NH.90-TTH (Hkp.14F) (145046) [46]	Hkpflj 1.HkpSkv, Luleå/Kallax
	146047	NH Industries NH.90-TTH (Hkp.14F) (145047) [47]	Hkpflj 1.HkpSkv, Luleå/Kallax
	146050	NH Industries NH.90-TTH (Hkp.14F) (145050) [50]	Hkpflj 1.HkpSkv, Luleå/Kallax
	146054	NH Industries NH.90-TTH (Hkp.14F) (144054) [54]	Hkpflj 1.HkpSkv, Luleå/Kallax
	146055	NH Industries NH.90-SAR (Hkp.14F) (142055) [55]	Hkpflj 3.HkpSkv, Ronneby/Kallinge
	146056	NH Industries NH.90-SAR (Hkp.14F) (145056) [56]	Hkpflj 3.HkpSkv, Ronneby/Kallinge
	146057	NH Industries NH.90-SAR (Hkp.14F) (145057) [57]	Hkpflj 3.HkpSkv, Ronneby/Kallinge
	146058	NH Industries NH.90-SAR (Hkp.14F) (145058) [58]	Hkpflj 3.HkpSkv, Ronneby/Kallinge
	146059	NH Industries NH.90-SAR (Hkp.14F) (145059) [59]	Hkpflj 3.HkpSkv, Ronneby/Kallinge
	151751	Agusta A109LUH Power (Hkp.15A) [21]	Hkpflj 2.HkpSkv, Linköping/Malmen
	151752	Agusta A109LUH Power (Hkp.15A) [22]	Hkpflj 2.HkpSkv, Linköping/Malmen
	151753	Agusta A109LUH Power (Hkp.15A) [23]	Hkpflj 2.HkpSkv, Linköping/Malmen
	151754	Agusta A109LUH Power (Hkp.15A) [24]	Hkpflj 2.HkpSkv, Linköping/Malmen
	151755	Agusta A109LUH Power (Hkp.15A) [25]	Hkpflj 2.HkpSkv, Linköping/Malmen
	151756	Agusta A109LUH Power (Hkp.15A) [26]	Hkpflj 2.HkpSkv, Linköping/Malmen
	151757	Agusta A109LUH Power (Hkp.15A) [27]	Hkpflj 2.HkpSkv, Linköping/Malmen
	151758	Agusta A109LUH Power (Hkp.15A) [28]	Hkpflj 2.HkpSkv, Linköping/Malmen
	151759	Agusta A109LUH Power (Hkp.15A) [29]	Hkpflj 2.HkpSkv, Linköping/Malmen
	151761	Agusta A109LUH Power (Hkp.15A) [31]	Hkpflj 2.HkpSkv, Linköping/Malmen
	151762	Agusta A109LUH Power (Hkp.15A) [32]	Hkpflj 2.HkpSkv, Linköping/Malmen
	151764	Agusta A109LUH Power (Hkp.15A) [34]	Hkpflj 2.HkpSkv, Linköping/Malmen
	152760	Agusta A109LUH Power (Hkp.15B) [30]	Hkpflj 3.HkpSkv, Ronneby/Kallinge
	152763	Agusta A109LUH Power (Hkp.15B) [33]	Hkpflj 3.HkpSkv, Ronneby/Kallinge
	152765	Agusta A109LUH Power (Hkp.15B) [35]	Hkpflj 3.HkpSkv, Ronneby/Kallinge
	152766	Agusta A109LUH Power (Hkp.15B) [36]	Hkpflj 3.HkpSkv, Ronneby/Kallinge
	152767	Agusta A109LUH Power (Hkp.15B) [37]	Hkpflj 3.HkpSkv, Ronneby/Kallinge
	152768	Agusta A109LUH Power (Hkp.15B) [38]	Hkpflj 3.HkpSkv, Ronneby/Kallinge
	152769	Agusta A109LUH Power (Hkp.15B) [39]	Hkpflj 3.HkpSkv, Ronneby/Kallinge
	152770	Agusta A109LUH Power (Hkp.15B) [40]	Hkpflj 3.HkpSkv, Ronneby/Kallinge
	161226	Sikorsky UH-60M Black Hawk (Hkp.16A) [01]	Hkpflj 2.HkpSkv, Linköping/Malmen
	161227	Sikorsky UH-60M Black Hawk (Hkp.16A) [02]	Hkpflj 2.HkpSkv, Linköping/Malmen
	161228	Sikorsky UH-60M Black Hawk (Hkp.16A) [03]	Hkpflj 2.HkpSkv, Linköping/Malmen
	161229	Sikorsky UH-60M Black Hawk (Hkp.16A) [04]	Hkpflj 2.HkpSkv, Linköping/Malmen
	161230	Sikorsky UH-60M Black Hawk (Hkp.16A) [05]	Hkpflj 2.HkpSkv, Linköping/Malmen
	161231	Sikorsky UH-60M Black Hawk (Hkp.16A) [06]	Hkpflj 2.HkpSkv, Linköping/Malmen
	161232	Sikorsky UH-60M Black Hawk (Hkp.16A) [07]	Hkpflj 2.HkpSkv, Linköping/Malmen

Serial	Type (code/other identity)	Owner/operator, location or fate	Notes
161233	Sikorsky UH-60M Black Hawk (Hkp.16A) [08]	Hkpflj 2.HkpSkv, Linköping/Malmen	
161234	Sikorsky UH-60M Black Hawk (Hkp.16A) [09]	Hkpflj 2.HkpSkv, Linköping/Malmen	
161235	Sikorsky UH-60M Black Hawk (Hkp.16A) [10]	Hkpflj 2.HkpSkv, Linköping/Malmen	
161236	Sikorsky UH-60M Black Hawk (Hkp.16A) [11]	Hkpflj 2.HkpSkv, Linköping/Malmen	
161237	Sikorsky UH-60M Black Hawk (Hkp.16A) [12]	Hkpflj 2.HkpSkv, Linköping/Malmen	
161238	Sikorsky UH-60M Black Hawk (Hkp.16A) [13]	Hkpflj 2.HkpSkv, Linköping/Malmen	
161239	Sikorsky UH-60M Black Hawk (Hkp.16A) [14]	Hkpflj 2.HkpSkv, Linköping/Malmen	
161240	Sikorsky UH-60M Black Hawk (Hkp.16A) [15]	Hkpflj 2.HkpSkv, Linköping/Malmen	

Kustbevakning/Swedish Coast Guard

SE-MAA	Bombardier DHC-8Q-311MPA [501]	Kustbevakning, Nykoping	
SE-MAB	Bombardier DHC-8Q-311MPA [502]	Kustbevakning, Nykoping	
SE-MAC	Bombardier DHC-8Q-311MPA [503]	Kustbevakning, Nykoping	

SWITZERLAND

Schweizer Luftwaffe/Swiss Air Force

(Most aircraft are pooled centrally. Some carry unit badges but these rarely indicate actual operators.)

A-101	Pilatus PC-21	Swiss AF Pilotenschule, Emmen	
A-102	Pilatus PC-21	Swiss AF Pilotenschule, Emmen	
A-103	Pilatus PC-21	Swiss AF Pilotenschule, Emmen	
A-104	Pilatus PC-21	Swiss AF Pilotenschule, Emmen	
A-106	Pilatus PC-21	Swiss AF Pilotenschule, Emmen	
A-107	Pilatus PC-21	Swiss AF Pilotenschule, Emmen	
A-108	Pilatus PC-21	Swiss AF Pilotenschule, Emmen	
A-912	Pilatus NCPC-7 Turbo Trainer	Swiss AF Instrumentenflugstaffel 14, Emmen	
A-913	Pilatus NCPC-7 Turbo Trainer	Swiss AF Instrumentenflugstaffel 14, Emmen	
A-914	Pilatus NCPC-7 Turbo Trainer	Swiss AF Instrumentenflugstaffel 14, Emmen	
A-915	Pilatus NCPC-7 Turbo Trainer	Swiss AF Instrumentenflugstaffel 14, Emmen	
A-916	Pilatus NCPC-7 Turbo Trainer	Swiss AF Instrumentenflugstaffel 14, Emmen	
A-917	Pilatus NCPC-7 Turbo Trainer	Swiss AF Instrumentenflugstaffel 14, Emmen	
A-918	Pilatus NCPC-7 Turbo Trainer	Swiss AF Instrumentenflugstaffel 14, Emmen	
A-919	Pilatus NCPC-7 Turbo Trainer	Swiss AF Instrumentenflugstaffel 14, Emmen	
A-922	Pilatus NCPC-7 Turbo Trainer	Swiss AF Instrumentenflugstaffel 14, Emmen	
A-923	Pilatus NCPC-7 Turbo Trainer	Swiss AF Instrumentenflugstaffel 14, Emmen	
A-924	Pilatus NCPC-7 Turbo Trainer	Swiss AF Instrumentenflugstaffel 14, Emmen	
A-925	Pilatus NCPC-7 Turbo Trainer	Swiss AF Instrumentenflugstaffel 14, Emmen	
A-926	Pilatus NCPC-7 Turbo Trainer	Swiss AF Instrumentenflugstaffel 14, Emmen	
A-927	Pilatus NCPC-7 Turbo Trainer	Swiss AF Instrumentenflugstaffel 14, Emmen	
A-928	Pilatus NCPC-7 Turbo Trainer	Swiss AF Instrumentenflugstaffel 14, Emmen	
A-929	Pilatus NCPC-7 Turbo Trainer	Swiss AF Instrumentenflugstaffel 14, Emmen	
A-930	Pilatus NCPC-7 Turbo Trainer	Swiss AF Instrumentenflugstaffel 14, Emmen	
A-931	Pilatus NCPC-7 Turbo Trainer	Swiss AF Instrumentenflugstaffel 14, Emmen	
A-932	Pilatus NCPC-7 Turbo Trainer	Swiss AF Instrumentenflugstaffel 14, Emmen	
A-933	Pilatus NCPC-7 Turbo Trainer	Swiss AF Instrumentenflugstaffel 14, Emmen	
A-934	Pilatus NCPC-7 Turbo Trainer	Swiss AF Instrumentenflugstaffel 14, Emmen	
A-935	Pilatus NCPC-7 Turbo Trainer	Swiss AF Instrumentenflugstaffel 14, Emmen	
A-936	Pilatus NCPC-7 Turbo Trainer	Swiss AF Instrumentenflugstaffel 14, Emmen	
A-938	Pilatus NCPC-7 Turbo Trainer	Swiss AF Instrumentenflugstaffel 14, Emmen	
A-939	Pilatus NCPC-7 Turbo Trainer	Swiss AF Instrumentenflugstaffel 14, Emmen	
A-940	Pilatus NCPC-7 Turbo Trainer	Swiss AF Instrumentenflugstaffel 14, Emmen	
A-941	Pilatus NCPC-7 Turbo Trainer	Swiss AF Instrumentenflugstaffel 14, Emmen	
J-3044	Northrop F-5E Tiger II	Swiss AF, wfu Stans-Buochs, Switzerland	
J-3070	Northrop F-5E Tiger II	Swiss AF FISt 6 & 19, Payerne	
J-3077	Northrop F-5E Tiger II	Swiss AF FISt 6 & 19, Payerne	
J-3080	Northrop F-5E Tiger II	Swiss AF Patrouille Suisse, Emmen	
J-3081	Northrop F-5E Tiger II	Swiss AF Patrouille Suisse, Emmen	
J-3082	Northrop F-5E Tiger II	Swiss AF Patrouille Suisse, Emmen	
J-3083	Northrop F-5E Tiger II	Swiss AF Patrouille Suisse, Emmen	
J-3084	Northrop F-5E Tiger II	Swiss AF Patrouille Suisse, Emmen	
J-3085	Northrop F-5E Tiger II	Swiss AF Patrouille Suisse, Emmen	
J-3087	Northrop F-5E Tiger II	Swiss AF Patrouille Suisse, Emmen	
J-3088	Northrop F-5E Tiger II	Swiss AF Patrouille Suisse, Emmen	
J-3090	Northrop F-5E Tiger II	Swiss AF Patrouille Suisse, Emmen	

Notes	Serial	Type (code/other identity)	Owner/operator, location or fate
	J-3091	Northrop F-5E Tiger II	Swiss AF *Patrouille Suisse*, Emmen
	J-3093	Northrop F-5E Tiger II	Swiss AF FISt 6 & 19, Payerne
	J-3095	Northrop F-5E Tiger II	Swiss AF FISt 6 & 19, Payerne
	J-3097	Northrop F-5E Tiger II	*Swiss AF, wfu Stans-Buochs, Switzerland*
	J-3201	Northrop F-5F Tiger II	Swiss AF FISt 6 & 19, Payerne
	J-3203	Northrop F-5F Tiger II	Swiss AF FISt 6 & 19, Payerne
	J-3210	Northrop F-5F Tiger II	Swiss AF FISt 6 & 19, Payerne
	J-3212	Northrop F-5F Tiger II	Swiss AF FISt 6 & 19, Payerne
	J-5001	McDonnell Douglas F/A-18C Hornet	Swiss AF FISt 11, Meiringen/FISt 17 & 18 Payerne
	J-5002	McDonnell Douglas F/A-18C Hornet	Swiss AF FISt 11, Meiringen/FISt 17 & 18 Payerne
	J-5003	McDonnell Douglas F/A-18C Hornet	Swiss AF FISt 11, Meiringen/FISt 17 & 18 Payerne
	J-5004	McDonnell Douglas F/A-18C Hornet	Swiss AF FISt 11, Meiringen/FISt 17 & 18 Payerne
	J-5005	McDonnell Douglas F/A-18C Hornet	Swiss AF FISt 11, Meiringen/FISt 17 & 18 Payerne
	J-5006	McDonnell Douglas F/A-18C Hornet	Swiss AF FISt 11, Meiringen/FISt 17 & 18 Payerne
	J-5007	McDonnell Douglas F/A-18C Hornet	Swiss AF FISt 11, Meiringen/FISt 17 & 18 Payerne
	J-5008	McDonnell Douglas F/A-18C Hornet	Swiss AF FISt 11, Meiringen/FISt 17 & 18 Payerne
	J-5009	McDonnell Douglas F/A-18C Hornet	Swiss AF FISt 11, Meiringen/FISt 17 & 18 Payerne
	J-5010	McDonnell Douglas F/A-18C Hornet	Swiss AF FISt 11, Meiringen/FISt 17 & 18 Payerne
	J-5011	McDonnell Douglas F/A-18C Hornet $	Swiss AF FISt 11, Meiringen/FISt 17 & 18 Payerne
	J-5012	McDonnell Douglas F/A-18C Hornet	Swiss AF FISt 11, Meiringen/FISt 17 & 18 Payerne
	J-5013	McDonnell Douglas F/A-18C Hornet	Swiss AF FISt 11, Meiringen/FISt 17 & 18 Payerne
	J-5014	McDonnell Douglas F/A-18C Hornet	Swiss AF FISt 11, Meiringen/FISt 17 & 18 Payerne
	J-5015	McDonnell Douglas F/A-18C Hornet	Swiss AF FISt 11, Meiringen/FISt 17 & 18 Payerne
	J-5016	McDonnell Douglas F/A-18C Hornet	Swiss AF FISt 11, Meiringen/FISt 17 & 18 Payerne
	J-5017	McDonnell Douglas F/A-18C Hornet $	Swiss AF FISt 11, Meiringen/FISt 17 & 18 Payerne
	J-5018	McDonnell Douglas F/A-18C Hornet $	Swiss AF FISt 11, Meiringen/FISt 17 & 18 Payerne
	J-5019	McDonnell Douglas F/A-18C Hornet	Swiss AF FISt 11, Meiringen/FISt 17 & 18 Payerne
	J-5020	McDonnell Douglas F/A-18C Hornet	Swiss AF FISt 11, Meiringen/FISt 17 & 18 Payerne
	J-5021	McDonnell Douglas F/A-18C Hornet	Swiss AF FISt 11, Meiringen/FISt 17 & 18 Payerne
	J-5023	McDonnell Douglas F/A-18C Hornet	Swiss AF FISt 11, Meiringen/FISt 17 & 18 Payerne
	J-5024	McDonnell Douglas F/A-18C Hornet	Swiss AF FISt 11, Meiringen/FISt 17 & 18 Payerne
	J-5025	McDonnell Douglas F/A-18C Hornet	Swiss AF FISt 11, Meiringen/FISt 17 & 18 Payerne
	J-5026	McDonnell Douglas F/A-18C Hornet	Swiss AF FISt 11, Meiringen/FISt 17 & 18 Payerne
	J-5232	McDonnell Douglas F/A-18D Hornet	Swiss AF FISt 11, Meiringen/FISt 17 & 18 Payerne
	J-5233	McDonnell Douglas F/A-18D Hornet	Swiss AF FISt 11, Meiringen/FISt 17 & 18 Payerne
	J-5234	McDonnell Douglas F/A-18D Hornet	Swiss AF FISt 11, Meiringen/FISt 17 & 18 Payerne
	J-5236	McDonnell Douglas F/A-18D Hornet	Swiss AF FISt 11, Meiringen/FISt 17 & 18 Payerne
	J-5238	McDonnell Douglas F/A-18D Hornet	Swiss AF FISt 11, Meiringen/FISt 17 & 18 Payerne
	R-711	Aurora Flight Services Centaur OPA	Armasuisse, Emmen
	T-311	Aérospatiale AS.332M-1 Super Puma (TH 06)	Swiss AF LtSt 6 & 8, Alpnach/ LtSt 3 & 4, Dübendorf/LtSt 1 & 5, Payerne
	T-312	Aérospatiale AS.332M-1 Super Puma (TH 06)	Swiss AF LtSt 6 & 8, Alpnach/ LtSt 3 & 4, Dübendorf/LtSt 1 & 5, Payerne
	T-313	Aérospatiale AS.332M-1 Super Puma (TH 06)	Swiss AF LtSt 6 & 8, Alpnach/ LtSt 3 & 4, Dübendorf/LtSt 1 & 5, Payerne
	T-314	Aérospatiale AS.332M-1 Super Puma (TH 06)	Swiss AF LtSt 6 & 8, Alpnach/ LtSt 3 & 4, Dübendorf/LtSt 1 & 5, Payerne
	T-315	Aérospatiale AS.332M-1 Super Puma (TH 06)	Swiss AF LtSt 6 & 8, Alpnach/ LtSt 3 & 4, Dübendorf/LtSt 1 & 5, Payerne
	T-316	Aérospatiale AS.332M-1 Super Puma (TH 06)	Swiss AF LtSt 6 & 8, Alpnach/ LtSt 3 & 4, Dübendorf/LtSt 1 & 5, Payerne
	T-317	Aérospatiale AS.332M-1 Super Puma (TH 06)	Swiss AF LtSt 6 & 8, Alpnach/ LtSt 3 & 4, Dübendorf/LtSt 1 & 5, Payerne
	T-318	Aérospatiale AS.332M-1 Super Puma (TH 06)	Swiss AF LtSt 6 & 8, Alpnach/ LtSt 3 & 4, Dübendorf/LtSt 1 & 5, Payerne
	T-319	Aérospatiale AS.332M-1 Super Puma (TH 06)	Swiss AF LtSt 6 & 8, Alpnach/ LtSt 3 & 4, Dübendorf/LtSt 1 & 5, Payerne
	T-320	Aérospatiale AS.332M-1 Super Puma (TH 06)	Swiss AF LtSt 6 & 8, Alpnach/ LtSt 3 & 4, Dübendorf/LtSt 1 & 5, Payerne
	T-321	Aérospatiale AS.332M-1 Super Puma (TH 06)	Swiss AF LtSt 6 & 8, Alpnach/ LtSt 3 & 4, Dübendorf/LtSt 1 & 5, Payerne

K2065, an Isaacs Fury, seen here in 2023 at an event at the former RAF Abingdon in Oxfordshire. *HJC*

Spitfire "R7059" is an imposter for a couple of reasons! Firstly, the serial is one allocated to an aircraft that crashed following an engine fire in Scotland in 1943, but more importantly, this is a replica, not the real thing! *HJC*

Beech Traveller FT466/N16S, quite a rarity on the UK airshow circuit, based at Goodwood but on this occasion seen at Sywell. *HJC*

JV579/G-RUMW is a Grumman Wildcat belonging to the Fighter Collection at Duxford airfield, seen here at Sywell. *HJC*

Twin-seat Spitfire T.9 NH341 seen here at Compton Abbas airfield, Dorset. *HJC*

Spitfire PR.XIX PS890/F-AZJS, seen here at the French airfield of la Ferte Alais. The Spitfire is based further South in Dijon. *HJC*

The small, but ever-growing museum at Hurn Airport, Bournemouth, has a number of projects underway to be put on display. One of these is Sea Venom WM571. *HJC*

One of a very limited number of DHC Beavers to be found in the UK, XP822 guards the entrance to the Army Flying Museum at AAC Middle Wallop in Hampshire. *HJC*

Yellow-painted Auster AOP.9 XR241, based at Eggesford in Devon but seen here at the former RAF airfield at Abingdon in Oxfordshire. *HJC*

Beagle XS743 is found in the ever-growing Boscombe Down Aviation Collection at Old Sarum airfield. *HJC*

Scout AH.1 XV138 is seen here displaying at an event at the former RAF Abingdon. *HJC*

Former Royal Navy Sea King HU5 ZA137 is seen here at Farnborough in 2024. *HJC*

Qatari Hawk Mk.167 ZB137, based at RAF Leeming, is seen here taking off from RAF Fairford at RIAT 2024. *HJC*

Chinook HC.6A ZD982 is seen here displaying at Farnborough. *HJC*

RAF F-35B Lightning II M163 seen here at RIAT 2024 at RAF Fairford. *HJC*

RAF Poseidon ZP805 seen flying over Farnborough. *HJC*

QinetiQ operates a varied fleet from its base at Boscombe Down in Wiltshire, including PC-21 G-ETPB seen here at RIAT 2024. *HJC*

QinetiQ Beech King Air 350 G-ETPR is seen here at RIAT 2024 at RAF Fairford. *HJC*

Sleap, Shropshire based L-18C MM51-15302/G-BJTP is seen here at Middle Wallop. *HJC*

An unusual aircraft in the UK, this Ryan Navion is registered N4956C and is marked as US Army example 60344. *HJC*

Canadian CC-130J-30 Hercules II 130605 seen here at RIAT at RAF Fairford. *HJC*

One of the last times we saw operational European F-16s in the UK was when E-190 from the Royal Danish Air Force flew at Farnborough in 2024. *HJC*

Germany has always taken to painting its frontline fighters and bombers in striking schemes, and here we see Tornado IDS 43+07 commemorating 50 years of the Tornado project, seen here in the static park at RIAT 2024. *HJC*

German Air Force A400M 54+23 is seen here about to land at RAF Fairford during RIAT 2024. *HJC*

Italy also likes to paint its aircraft in special colour schemes! Here we see Typhoon CSX7352, on loan from 36 Stormo to the RSV, at RIAT 2023 at RAF Fairford. *HJC*

A type gaining popularity in Europe as several nations have purchased it, KC-390 26902 is one of 2 so far delivered to Portugal, with more on the way, seen here at Fairford. *HJC*

Still going strong, here we see Spanish EAV-8B Matador VA.1B-38 on the runway at RAF Fairford. *HJC*

One of the rarer types to be found at la Ferte Alais was this specially marked Swiss F/A-18C, J-5017. *HJC*

There are two squadrons operating the recently delivered F-35A at RAF Lakenheath. Here 20-5573, belonging to the 495th FS, is seen about to land back at home base. *HJC*

KC-46A 20-46079 is part of a fleet of around 100 aircraft currently in service, seen here at RIAT 2024. *HJC*

A rarity in the RIAT static, here we see U-2S 80-1096. *HJC*

Spangdahlem, Germany based F-16DM 91-0472, seen here at RIAT 2024. *HJC*

Serial	Type (code/other identity)	Owner/operator, location or fate	Notes
T-322	Aérospatiale AS.332M-1 Super Puma (TH 06)	Swiss AF LtSt 6 & 8, Alpnach/	
		LtSt 3 & 4, Dübendorf/LtSt 1 & 5, Payerne	
T-323	Aérospatiale AS.332M-1 Super Puma (TH 06)	Swiss AF LtSt 6 & 8, Alpnach/	
		LtSt 3 & 4, Dübendorf/LtSt 1 & 5, Payerne	
T-324	Aérospatiale AS.332M-1 Super Puma (TH 06)	Swiss AF LtSt 6 & 8, Alpnach/	
		LtSt 3 & 4, Dübendorf/LtSt 1 & 5, Payerne	
T-325	Aérospatiale AS.332M-1 Super Puma (TH 06)	Swiss AF LtSt 6 & 8, Alpnach/	
		LtSt 3 & 4, Dübendorf/LtSt 1 & 5, Payerne	
T-331	Aérospatiale AS.532UL Super Puma (TH 98)	Swiss AF LtSt 6 & 8, Alpnach/	
		LtSt 3 & 4, Dübendorf/LtSt 1 & 5, Payerne	
T-332	Aérospatiale AS.532UL Super Puma (TH 98)	Swiss AF LtSt 6 & 8, Alpnach/	
		LtSt 3 & 4, Dübendorf/LtSt 1 & 5, Payerne	
T-333	Aérospatiale AS.532UL Super Puma (TH 98)	Swiss AF LtSt 6 & 8, Alpnach/	
		LtSt 3 & 4, Dübendorf/LtSt 1 & 5, Payerne	
T-334	Aérospatiale AS.532UL Super Puma (TH 98)	Swiss AF LtSt 6 & 8, Alpnach/	
		LtSt 3 & 4, Dübendorf/LtSt 1 & 5, Payerne	
T-335	Aérospatiale AS.532UL Super Puma (TH 98)	Swiss AF LtSt 6 & 8, Alpnach/	
		LtSt 3 & 4, Dübendorf/LtSt 1 & 5, Payerne	
T-336	Aérospatiale AS.532UL Super Puma (TH 98)	Swiss AF LtSt 6 & 8, Alpnach/	
		LtSt 3 & 4, Dübendorf/LtSt 1 & 5, Payerne	
T-337	Aérospatiale AS.532UL Super Puma (TH 98)	Swiss AF LtSt 6 & 8, Alpnach/	
		LtSt 3 & 4, Dübendorf/LtSt 1 & 5, Payerne	
T-339	Aérospatiale AS.532UL Super Puma (TH 98)	Swiss AF LtSt 6 & 8, Alpnach/	
		LtSt 3 & 4, Dübendorf/LtSt 1 & 5, Payerne	
T-340	Aérospatiale AS.532UL Super Puma (TH 98)	Swiss AF LtSt 6 & 8, Alpnach/	
		LtSt 3 & 4, Dübendorf/LtSt 1 & 5, Payerne	
T-342	Aérospatiale AS.532UL Super Puma (TH 98)	Swiss AF LtSt 6 & 8, Alpnach/	
		LtSt 3 & 4, Dübendorf/LtSt 1 & 5, Payerne	
T-351	Eurocopter EC.135P-2	Swiss AF LTDB, Dübendorf	
T-352	Eurocopter EC.135P-2	Swiss AF LTDB, Dübendorf	
T-353	Eurocopter EC.635P-2+	Swiss AF LtSt 6 & 8, Alpnach/	
		LtSt 3 & 4, Dübendorf/LtSt 1 & 5, Payerne	
T-354	Eurocopter EC.635P-2+	Swiss AF LtSt 6 & 8, Alpnach/	
		LtSt 3 & 4, Dübendorf/LtSt 1 & 5, Payerne	
T-355	Eurocopter EC.635P-2+	Swiss AF LtSt 6 & 8, Alpnach/	
		LtSt 3 & 4, Dübendorf/LtSt 1 & 5, Payerne	
T-356	Eurocopter EC.635P-2+	Swiss AF LtSt 6 & 8, Alpnach/	
		LtSt 3 & 4, Dübendorf/LtSt 1 & 5, Payerne	
T-357	Eurocopter EC.635P-2+	Swiss AF LtSt 6 & 8, Alpnach/	
		LtSt 3 & 4, Dübendorf/LtSt 1 & 5, Payerne	
T-358	Eurocopter EC.635P-2+	Swiss AF LtSt 6 & 8, Alpnach/	
		LtSt 3 & 4, Dübendorf/LtSt 1 & 5, Payerne	
T-359	Eurocopter EC.635P-2+	Swiss AF LtSt 6 & 8, Alpnach/	
		LtSt 3 & 4, Dübendorf/LtSt 1 & 5, Payerne	
T-360	Eurocopter EC.635P-2+	Swiss AF LtSt 6 & 8, Alpnach/	
		LtSt 3 & 4, Dübendorf/LtSt 1 & 5, Payerne	
T-361	Eurocopter EC.635P-2+	Swiss AF LtSt 6 & 8, Alpnach/	
		LtSt 3 & 4, Dübendorf/LtSt 1 & 5, Payerne	
T-362	Eurocopter EC.635P-2+	Swiss AF LtSt 6 & 8, Alpnach/	
		LtSt 3 & 4, Dübendorf/LtSt 1 & 5, Payerne	
T-363	Eurocopter EC.635P-2+	Swiss AF LtSt 6 & 8, Alpnach/	
		LtSt 3 & 4, Dübendorf/LtSt 1 & 5, Payerne	
T-364	Eurocopter EC.635P-2+	Swiss AF LtSt 6 & 8, Alpnach/	
		LtSt 3 & 4, Dübendorf/LtSt 1 & 5, Payerne	
T-365	Eurocopter EC.635P-2+	Swiss AF LtSt 6 & 8, Alpnach/	
		LtSt 3 & 4, Dübendorf/LtSt 1 & 5, Payerne	
T-366	Eurocopter EC.635P-2+	Swiss AF LtSt 6 & 8, Alpnach/	
		LtSt 3 & 4, Dübendorf/LtSt 1 & 5, Payerne	
T-367	Eurocopter EC.635P-2+	*Written off Alpnachstad, Switzerland, 6th Nov 2024*	
T-368	Eurocopter EC.635P-2+	Swiss AF LtSt 6 & 8, Alpnach/	
		LtSt 3 & 4, Dübendorf/LtSt 1 & 5, Payerne	

Notes	Serial	Type (code/other identity)	Owner/operator, location or fate
	T-369	Eurocopter EC.635P-2+	Swiss AF LtSt 6 & 8, Alpnach/ LtSt 3 & 4, Dübendorf/LtSt 1 & 5, Payerne
	T-370	Eurocopter EC.635P-2+	Swiss AF LtSt 6 & 8, Alpnach/ LtSt 3 & 4, Dübendorf/LtSt 1 & 5, Payerne
	T-721	Beechcraft King Air 350C	Swiss AF LTDB, Dübendorf
	T-751	Bombardier Challenger 604 (HB-JRB)	Swiss AF LTDB, Dübendorf
	T-752	Bombardier Challenger 604 (HB-JRC)	Swiss AF LTDB, Dübendorf
	T-784	Cessna 560XL Citation Excel	Swiss AF LTDB, Bern/Belp
	T-785	Dassault Falcon 900EX EASy II	Swiss AF LTDB, Bern/Belp
	T-787	Bombardier Global 7500	Swiss AF LTDB, Bern/Belp
	V-612	Pilatus PC-6B/B2-H2 Turbo Porter	Swiss AF LtSt 7, Emmen
	V-613	Pilatus PC-6B/B2-H2 Turbo Porter	Swiss AF LtSt 7, Emmen
	V-614	Pilatus PC-6B/B2-H2 Turbo Porter	Swiss AF LtSt 7, Emmen
	V-616	Pilatus PC-6B/B2-H2 Turbo Porter	Swiss AF LtSt 7, Emmen
	V-617	Pilatus PC-6B/B2-H2 Turbo Porter	Swiss AF LtSt 7, Emmen
	V-618	Pilatus PC-6B/B2-H2 Turbo Porter	Swiss AF LtSt 7, Emmen
	V-619	Pilatus PC-6B/B2-H2 Turbo Porter	Swiss AF LtSt 7, Emmen
	V-620	Pilatus PC-6B/B2-H2 Turbo Porter	Swiss AF LtSt 7, Emmen
	V-622	Pilatus PC-6B/B2-H2 Turbo Porter $	Swiss AF LtSt 7, Emmen
	V-623	Pilatus PC-6B/B2-H2 Turbo Porter	Swiss AF LtSt 7, Emmen
	V-631	Pilatus PC-6B/B2-H2 Turbo Porter	Swiss AF LtSt 7, Emmen
	V-632	Pilatus PC-6B/B2-H2 Turbo Porter	Swiss AF LtSt 7, Emmen
	V-633	Pilatus PC-6B/B2-H2 Turbo Porter	Swiss AF LtSt 7, Emmen
	V-634	Pilatus PC-6B/B2-H2 Turbo Porter	Swiss AF LtSt 7, Emmen
	V-635	Pilatus PC-6B/B2-H2 Turbo Porter	Swiss AF LtSt 7, Emmen

Swiss Government

	HB-FOG	Pilatus PC-12/45	Armasuisse, Emmen

SYRIA

	YK-ASC	Dassault Falcon 900	Government of Syria, Damascus

TAJIKISTAN

	EY-001	Boeing 787-8BBJ	Government of Tajikistan, Dushanbe

TANZANIA

	5H-ONE	Gulfstream Aerospace G.700 (N715GA)	Tanzanian Government, Dar-es-Salaam
	5H-ONE	Gulfstream Aerospace G.550	Re-registered as 5H-ONF, July 2024
	5H-ONF	Gulfstream Aerospace G.550 (5H-ONE)	Tanzanian Government, Dar-es-Salaam

THAILAND

	L18-1/59	Sukhoi SSJ100-95LR Superjet [60206]	Royal Thai AF 602 Sqn/6 Wing, Bangkok/ Don Muang
	L18-2/59	Sukhoi SSJ100-95LR Superjet [60207]	Royal Thai AF 602 Sqn/6 Wing, Bangkok/ Don Muang
	L18-3/61	Sukhoi SSJ100-95LR Superjet [60208]	Royal Thai AF 602 Sqn/6 Wing, Bangkok/ Don Muang
	HS-CMV	Boeing 737-4Z6 (BL11Kh.MVK-01/38) [11-111, 90401]	Royal Thai AF 904 Sqn/6 Wing, Bangkok/ Don Muang
	HS-HMK	Boeing 737-8Z6 (BL11k.VPR-03/59) [99-904, 90410]	Royal Thai AF 904 Sqn/6 Wing, Bangkok/ Don Muang
	HS-HRH	Boeing 737-448 (BL11Kh.MVK-02/47) [99-999, 90409]	Royal Thai AF 904 Sqn/6 Wing, Bangkok/ Don Muang
	HS-MVS	Boeing 737-8Z6 (BL11k.VPR-04/50) [99-904, 90411]	Royal Thai AF 904 Sqn/6 Wing, Bangkok/ Don Muang
	HS-TYR	Airbus A.319CJ-133 (L15-1/47) [60202]	Royal Thai AF 602 Sqn/6 Wing, Bangkok/ Don Muang
	HS-TYT	Airbus A.320CJ-214 (L15k-1/58) [60203]	Royal Thai AF 602 Sqn/6 Wing, Bangkok/ Don Muang
	HS-TYV	Airbus A.340-541 (BL19-1/59) [60204]	Royal Thai AF 602 Sqn/6 Wing, Bangkok/ Don Muang
	HS-TYW	Airbus A.320CJ-214X (L15k-2/63) [60205]	Royal Thai AF 602 Sqn/6 Wing, Bangkok/ Don Muang

Serial	Type (code/other identity)	Owner/operator, location or fate	Notes

TUNISIA
Tunisian Air Force/Al Quwwat al-Jawwiya al-Jamahiriyah At'Tunisia & Tunisian Government

Serial	Type (code/other identity)	Owner/operator, location or fate	Notes
Z21012	Lockheed C-130H Hercules (TS-MTB)	Tunisian AF 21 Sqn, Bizerte/Sidi Ahmed	
Z21013	Lockheed C-130H Hercules (TS-MTM)	Tunisian AF 21 Sqn, Bizerte/Sidi Ahmed	
Z21014	Lockheed C-130H Hercules (TS-MTN)	Tunisian AF 21 Sqn, Bizerte/Sidi Ahmed	
Z21015	Lockheed C-130H Hercules (89-1055/TS-MT0)	Tunisian AF 21 Sqn, Bizerte/Sidi Ahmed	
Z21121	Lockheed C-130J-30 Hercules II (TS-MTK)	Tunisian AF 11 Sqn, Tunis	
Z21122	Lockheed C-130J-30 Hercules II (TS-MTL)	Tunisian AF 11 Sqn, Tunis	
TS-IOO	Boeing 737-7HJ	Government of Tunisia, Tunis	

TURKEY
Türk Hava Kuvvetleri (THK)/Turkish Air Force & Turkish Government

Serial	Type (code/other identity)	Owner/operator, location or fate	Notes
004	Cessna 650 Citation VII	THK 212 Filo/11 HUAÜK, Ankara/Etimesgut	
005	Cessna 650 Citation VII	THK 212 Filo/11 HUAÜK, Ankara/Etimesgut	
3023	Canadair NF-5A-2000 Freedom Fighter	THK 134 Filo, *Turkish Stars*/3 AJEÜ, Konya	
3025	Canadair NF-5A-2000 Freedom Fighter	THK 134 Filo, *Turkish Stars*/3 AJEÜ, Konya	
3032	Canadair NF-5A-2000 Freedom Fighter	THK 134 Filo, *Turkish Stars*/3 AJEÜ, Konya	
3036	Canadair NF-5A-2000 Freedom Fighter	THK 134 Filo, *Turkish Stars*/3 AJEÜ, Konya	
3046	Canadair NF-5A-2000 Freedom Fighter	THK 134 Filo, *Turkish Stars*/3 AJEÜ, Konya	
3048	Canadair NF-5A-2000 Freedom Fighter	THK 134 Filo, *Turkish Stars*/3 AJEÜ, Konya	
3049	Canadair NF-5A-2000 Freedom Fighter	THK 134 Filo, *Turkish Stars*/3 AJEÜ, Konya	
3052	Canadair NF-5A-2000 Freedom Fighter	THK 134 Filo, *Turkish Stars*/3 AJEÜ, Konya	
3072	Canadair NF-5A-2000 Freedom Fighter	THK 134 Filo, *Turkish Stars*/3 AJEÜ, Konya	
4001	Canadair NF-5B-2000 Freedom Fighter	THK 134 Filo, *Turkish Stars*/3 AJEÜ, Konya	
4005	Canadair NF-5B-2000 Freedom Fighter	THK 134 Filo, *Turkish Stars*/3 AJEÜ, Konya	
4009	Canadair NF-5B-2000 Freedom Fighter	THK 134 Filo, *Turkish Stars*/3 AJEÜ, Konya	
4013	Canadair NF-5B-2000 Freedom Fighter	THK 134 Filo, *Turkish Stars*/3 AJEÜ, Konya	
4020	Canadair NF-5B-2000 Freedom Fighter	THK 134 Filo, *Turkish Stars*/3 AJEÜ, Konya	
4021	Canadair NF-5B-2000 Freedom Fighter	THK 134 Filo, *Turkish Stars*/3 AJEÜ, Konya	
4026	Canadair NF-5B-2000 Freedom Fighter	THK 134 Filo, *Turkish Stars*/3 AJEÜ, Konya	
57-2609	Boeing KC-135R Stratotanker	THK 101 Filo/10 TÜK, Incirlik	
58-0110	Boeing KC-135R Stratotanker	THK 101 Filo/10 TÜK, Incirlik	
60-0325	Boeing KC-135R Stratotanker	THK 101 Filo/10 TÜK, Incirlik	
60-0326	Boeing KC-135R Stratotanker	THK 101 Filo/10 TÜK, Incirlik	
62-3539	Boeing KC-135R Stratotanker	THK 101 Filo/10 TÜK, Incirlik	
62-3563	Boeing KC-135R Stratotanker	THK 101 Filo/10 TÜK, Incirlik	
62-3567	Boeing KC-135R Stratotanker	THK 101 Filo/10 TÜK, Incirlik	
63-13186	Lockheed C-130E Hercules	THK 222 Filo/12 HUAÜ, Erklet	
63-13187	Lockheed C-130E Hercules $	THK 222 Filo/12 HUAÜ, Erklet	
63-13188	Lockheed C-130E Hercules	THK 222 Filo/12 HUAÜ, Erklet	
63-13189	Lockheed C-130E Hercules $	THK 222 Filo/12 HUAÜ, Erklet	
67-0455	Lockheed C-130E Hercules	THK 222 Filo/12 HUAÜ, Erklet	
68-1606	Lockheed C-130E Hercules	THK 222 Filo/12 HUAÜ, Erklet	
68-1608	Lockheed C-130E Hercules	THK 222 Filo/12 HUAÜ, Erklet	
68-1609	Lockheed C-130E Hercules	THK 222 Filo/12 HUAÜ, Erklet	
70-01610	Lockheed C-130E Hercules	THK 222 Filo/12 HUAÜ, Erklet	
70-1947	Lockheed C-130E Hercules	THK 222 Filo/12 HUAÜ, Erklet	
71-01468	Lockheed C-130E Hercules	THK 222 Filo/12 HUAÜ, Erklet	
73-0991	Lockheed C-130E Hercules $	THK 222 Filo/12 HUAÜ, Erklet	
86-0066	TUSAS (GD) F-16C-30 Fighting Falcon	THK 113 Filo/1 AJÜ, Eskisehir	
86-0069	TUSAS (GD) F-16C-30 Fighting Falcon	THK 132 Filo/3 AJEÜ, Konya	
86-0070	TUSAS (GD) F-16C-30 Fighting Falcon	THK 132 Filo/3 AJEÜ, Konya	
86-0071	TUSAS (GD) F-16C-30 Fighting Falcon	THK 132 Filo/3 AJEÜ, Konya	
86-0072	TUSAS (GD) F-16C-30 Fighting Falcon	THK 132 Filo/3 AJEÜ, Konya	
86-0192	TUSAS (GD) F-16D-30 Fighting Falcon	THK 113 Filo/1 AJÜ, Eskisehir	
86-0193	TUSAS (GD) F-16D-30 Fighting Falcon	THK 132 Filo/3 AJEÜ, Konya	
86-0194	TUSAS (GD) F-16D-30 Fighting Falcon	THK	
86-0195	TUSAS (GD) F-16D-30 Fighting Falcon	THK 132 Filo/3 AJEÜ, Konya	
86-0196	TUSAS (GD) F-16D-30 Fighting Falcon	THK 132 Filo/3 AJEÜ, Konya	
87-0002	TUSAS (GD) F-16D-30 Fighting Falcon	THK 113 Filo/1 AJÜ, Eskisehir	
87-0003	TUSAS (GD) F-16D-30 Fighting Falcon	THK 113 Filo/1 AJÜ, Eskisehir	
87-0009	TUSAS (GD) F-16C-30 Fighting Falcon	THK 113 Filo/1 AJÜ, Eskisehir	

Notes	Serial	Type (code/other identity)	Owner/operator, location or fate
	87-0010	TUSAS (GD) F-16C-30 Fighting Falcon	THK 113 Filo/1 AJÜ, Eskisehir
	87-0011	TUSAS (GD) F-16C-30 Fighting Falcon	THK 113 Filo/1 AJÜ, Eskisehir
	87-0013	TUSAS (GD) F-16C-30 Fighting Falcon	THK 132 Filo/3 AJEÜ, Konya
	87-0014	TUSAS (GD) F-16C-30 Fighting Falcon	THK 113 Filo/1 AJÜ, Eskisehir
	87-0015	TUSAS (GD) F-16C-30 Fighting Falcon	THK 113 Filo/1 AJÜ, Eskisehir
	87-0016	TUSAS (GD) F-16C-30 Fighting Falcon	THK 132 Filo/3 AJEÜ, Konya
	87-0018	TUSAS (GD) F-16C-30 Fighting Falcon	THK 113 Filo/1 AJÜ, Eskisehir
	87-0019	TUSAS (GD) F-16C-30 Fighting Falcon	THK 132 Filo/3 AJEÜ, Konya
	87-0020	TUSAS (GD) F-16C-30 Fighting Falcon	THK 152 Filo/10 TÜK, Incirlik
	87-0021	TUSAS (GD) F-16C-30 Fighting Falcon	THK 132 Filo/3 AJEÜ, Konya
	88-0013	TUSAS (GD) F-16D-30 Fighting Falcon	THK 152 Filo/10 TÜK, Incirlik
	88-0014	TUSAS (GD) F-16D-40 Fighting Falcon	THK 132 Filo/3 AJEÜ, Konya
	88-0015	TUSAS (GD) F-16D-40 Fighting Falcon	THK 192 Filo/9 AJÜ, Balikesir
	88-0019	TUSAS (GD) F-16C-30 Fighting Falcon	THK 113 Filo/1 AJÜ, Eskisehir
	88-0020	TUSAS (GD) F-16C-30 Fighting Falcon	THK 132 Filo/3 AJEÜ, Konya
	88-0021	TUSAS (GD) F-16C-30 Fighting Falcon $	THK 132 Filo/3 AJEÜ, Konya
	88-0024	TUSAS (GD) F-16C-30 Fighting Falcon $	THK 132 Filo/3 AJEÜ, Konya
	88-0025	TUSAS (GD) F-16C-30 Fighting Falcon	THK 132 Filo/3 AJEÜ, Konya
	88-0026	TUSAS (GD) F-16C-30 Fighting Falcon $	THK 132 Filo/3 AJEÜ, Konya
	88-0027	TUSAS (GD) F-16C-30 Fighting Falcon	THK 152 Filo/10 TÜK, Incirlik
	88-0028	TUSAS (GD) F-16C-30 Fighting Falcon	THK 192 Filo/9 AJÜ, Balikesir
	88-0029	TUSAS (GD) F-16C-30 Fighting Falcon $	THK 132 Filo/3 AJEÜ, Konya
	88-0030	TUSAS (GD) F-16C-30 Fighting Falcon	THK 152 Filo/10 TÜK, Incirlik
	88-0031	TUSAS (GD) F-16C-30 Fighting Falcon	THK 113 Filo/1 AJÜ, Eskisehir
	88-0032	TUSAS (GD) F-16C-30 Fighting Falcon $	THK 132 Filo/3 AJEÜ, Konya
	88-0033	TUSAS (GD) F-16C-40 Fighting Falcon	THK 152 Filo/10 TÜK, Incirlik
	88-0034	TUSAS (GD) F-16C-40 Fighting Falcon	THK 192 Filo/9 AJÜ, Balikesir
	88-0035	TUSAS (GD) F-16C-40 Fighting Falcon	THK 152 Filo/10 TÜK, Incirlik
	88-0036	TUSAS (GD) F-16C-40 Fighting Falcon	THK 151 Filo/5 AJÜ, Merzifon
	88-0037	TUSAS (GD) F-16C-40 Fighting Falcon	THK 132 Filo/3 AJEÜ, Konya
	89-0022	TUSAS (GD) F-16C-40 Fighting Falcon	THK
	89-0023	TUSAS (GD) F-16C-40 Fighting Falcon	THK 192 Filo/9 AJÜ, Balikesir
	89-0024	TUSAS (GD) F-16C-40 Fighting Falcon	THK 113 Filo/1 AJÜ, Eskisehir
	89-0025	TUSAS (GD) F-16C-40 Fighting Falcon	THK 192 Filo/9 AJÜ, Balikesir
	89-0026	TUSAS (GD) F-16C-40 Fighting Falcon	THK 151 Filo/5 AJÜ, Merzifon
	89-0027	TUSAS (GD) F-16C-40 Fighting Falcon	THK 152 Filo/10 TÜK, Incirlik
	89-0028	TUSAS (GD) F-16C-40 Fighting Falcon	THK 132 Filo/3 AJEÜ, Konya
	89-0030	TUSAS (GD) F-16C-40 Fighting Falcon	THK 152 Filo/10 TÜK, Incirlik
	89-0031	TUSAS (GD) F-16C-40 Fighting Falcon	THK 162 Filo/6 AJÜ, Bandirma
	89-0034	TUSAS (GD) F-16C-40 Fighting Falcon	THK 161 Filo/6 AJÜ, Bandirma
	89-0035	TUSAS (GD) F-16C-40 Fighting Falcon	THK 152 Filo/10 TÜK, Incirlik
	89-0036	TUSAS (GD) F-16C-40 Fighting Falcon	THK 161 Filo/6 AJÜ, Bandirma
	89-0037	TUSAS (GD) F-16C-40 Fighting Falcon	THK 161 Filo/6 AJÜ, Bandirma
	89-0038	TUSAS (GD) F-16C-40 Fighting Falcon	THK 161 Filo/6 AJÜ, Bandirma
	89-0039	TUSAS (GD) F-16C-40 Fighting Falcon	THK 152 Filo/10 TÜK, Incirlik
	89-0040	TUSAS (GD) F-16C-40 Fighting Falcon	THK 113 Filo/1 AJÜ, Eskisehir
	89-0041	TUSAS (GD) F-16C-40 Fighting Falcon	THK 152 Filo/10 TÜK, Incirlik
	89-0042	TUSAS (GD) F-16D-40 Fighting Falcon	THK 113 Filo/1 AJÜ, Eskisehir
	89-0043	TUSAS (GD) F-16D-40 Fighting Falcon	THK 151 Filo/5 AJÜ, Merzifon
	89-0044	TUSAS (GD) F-16D-40 Fighting Falcon	THK 152 Filo/10 TÜK, Incirlik
	89-0045	TUSAS (GD) F-16D-40 Fighting Falcon	THK 161 Filo/6 AJÜ, Bandirma
	90-0004	TUSAS (GD) F-16C-40 Fighting Falcon	THK 152 Filo/10 TÜK, Incirlik
	90-0005	TUSAS (GD) F-16C-40 Fighting Falcon	THK 161 Filo/6 AJÜ, Bandirma
	90-0006	TUSAS (GD) F-16C-40 Fighting Falcon	THK 113 Filo/1 AJÜ, Eskisehir
	90-0007	TUSAS (GD) F-16C-40 Fighting Falcon	THK 132 Filo/3 AJEÜ, Konya
	90-0008	TUSAS (GD) F-16C-40 Fighting Falcon	THK 152 Filo/10 TÜK, Incirlik
	90-0009	TUSAS (GD) F-16C-40 Fighting Falcon	THK 152 Filo/10 TÜK, Incirlik
	90-0010	TUSAS (GD) F-16C-40 Fighting Falcon	THK 132 Filo/3 AJEÜ, Konya
	90-0011	TUSAS (GD) F-16C-40 Fighting Falcon	THK 152 Filo/10 TÜK, Incirlik
	90-0012	TUSAS (GD) F-16C-40 Fighting Falcon	THK 151 Filo/5 AJÜ, Merzifon
	90-0013	TUSAS (GD) F-16C-40 Fighting Falcon	THK 182 Filo/8 AJÜ, Diyarbakir
	90-0014	TUSAS (GD) F-16C-40 Fighting Falcon	THK 152 Filo/10 TÜK, Incirlik

Serial	Type (code/other identity)	Owner/operator, location or fate	Notes
90-0016	TUSAS (GD) F-16C-40 Fighting Falcon	THK 182 Filo/8 AJÜ, Diyarbakir	
90-0017	TUSAS (GD) F-16C-40 Fighting Falcon	THK 192 Filo/9 AJÜ, Balikesir	
90-0018	TUSAS (GD) F-16C-40 Fighting Falcon	THK 161 Filo/6 AJÜ, Bandirma	
90-0019	TUSAS (GD) F-16C-40 Fighting Falcon	THK 161 Filo/6 AJÜ, Bandirma	
90-0020	TUSAS (GD) F-16C-40 Fighting Falcon	THK 161 Filo/6 AJÜ, Bandirma	
90-0021	TUSAS (GD) F-16C-40 Fighting Falcon	THK 401 Filo/1 AJÜ, Eskisehir	
90-0022	TUSAS (GD) F-16D-40 Fighting Falcon	THK 182 Filo/8 AJÜ, Diyarbakir	
90-0023	TUSAS (GD) F-16D-40 Fighting Falcon	THK 152 Filo/10 TÜK, Incirlik	
90-0024	TUSAS (GD) F-16D-40 Fighting Falcon	THK 182 Filo/8 AJÜ, Diyarbakir	
91-003	Grumman G.1159C Gulfstream IV	THK 212 Filo/11 HUAÜK, Ankara/Etimesgut	
91-0001	TUSAS (GD) F-16C-40 Fighting Falcon	THK 162 Filo/6 AJÜ, Bandirma	
91-0002	TUSAS (GD) F-16C-40 Fighting Falcon	THK 401 Filo/1 AJÜ, Eskisehir	
91-0003	TUSAS (GD) F-16C-40 Fighting Falcon	THK 161 Filo/6 AJÜ, Bandirma	
91-0004	TUSAS (GD) F-16C-40 Fighting Falcon	THK 182 Filo/8 AJÜ, Diyarbakir	
91-0005	TUSAS (GD) F-16C-40 Fighting Falcon	THK 182 Filo/8 AJÜ, Diyarbakir	
91-0006	TUSAS (GD) F-16C-40 Fighting Falcon	THK 161 Filo/6 AJÜ, Bandirma	
91-0007	TUSAS (GD) F-16C-40 Fighting Falcon	THK 161 Filo/6 AJÜ, Bandirma	
91-0008	TUSAS (GD) F-16C-40 Fighting Falcon	THK 151 Filo/5 AJÜ, Merzifon	
91-0010	TUSAS (GD) F-16C-40 Fighting Falcon	THK 162 Filo/6 AJÜ, Bandirma	
91-0011	TUSAS (GD) F-16C-40 Fighting Falcon	THK 152 Filo/10 TÜK, Incirlik	
91-0012	TUSAS (GD) F-16C-40 Fighting Falcon	THK 182 Filo/8 AJÜ, Diyarbakir	
91-0014	TUSAS (GD) F-16C-40 Fighting Falcon	THK	
91-0015	TUSAS (GD) F-16C-40 Fighting Falcon	THK 401 Filo/1 AJÜ, Eskisehir	
91-0016	TUSAS (GD) F-16C-40 Fighting Falcon	THK 182 Filo/8 AJÜ, Diyarbakir	
91-0017	TUSAS (GD) F-16C-40 Fighting Falcon	THK 113 Filo/1 AJÜ, Eskisehir	
91-0018	TUSAS (GD) F-16C-40 Fighting Falcon	THK 192 Filo/9 AJÜ, Balikesir	
91-0020	TUSAS (GD) F-16C-40 Fighting Falcon	THK 161 Filo/6 AJÜ, Bandirma	
91-0022	TUSAS (GD) F-16D-40 Fighting Falcon	THK 151 Filo/5 AJÜ, Merzifon	
91-0024	TUSAS (GD) F-16D-40 Fighting Falcon	THK 132 Filo/3 AJEÜ, Konya	
92-0001	TUSAS (GD) F-16C-40 Fighting Falcon	THK 132 Filo/3 AJEÜ, Konya	
92-0002	TUSAS (GD) F-16C-40 Fighting Falcon	THK 182 Filo/8 AJÜ, Diyarbakir	
92-0003	TUSAS (GD) F-16C-40 Fighting Falcon	THK 192 Filo/9 AJÜ, Balikesir	
92-0004	TUSAS (GD) F-16C-40 Fighting Falcon	THK 162 Filo/6 AJÜ, Bandirma	
92-0005	TUSAS (GD) F-16C-40 Fighting Falcon	THK 152 Filo/10 TÜK, Incirlik	
92-0006	TUSAS (GD) F-16C-40 Fighting Falcon	THK 182 Filo/8 AJÜ, Diyarbakir	
92-0007	TUSAS (GD) F-16C-40 Fighting Falcon	THK 192 Filo/9 AJÜ, Balikesir	
92-0008	TUSAS (GD) F-16C-40 Fighting Falcon	THK 162 Filo/6 AJÜ, Bandirma	
92-0010	TUSAS (GD) F-16C-40 Fighting Falcon	THK 151 Filo/5 AJÜ, Merzifon	
92-0011	TUSAS (GD) F-16C-40 Fighting Falcon	THK 182 Filo/8 AJÜ, Diyarbakir	
92-0012	TUSAS (GD) F-16C-40 Fighting Falcon	THK 113 Filo/1 AJÜ, Eskisehir	
92-0013	TUSAS (GD) F-16C-40 Fighting Falcon	THK 152 Filo/10 TÜK, Incirlik	
92-0014	TUSAS (GD) F-16C-40 Fighting Falcon	THK 192 Filo/9 AJÜ, Balikesir	
92-0015	TUSAS (GD) F-16C-40 Fighting Falcon	THK 161 Filo/6 AJÜ, Bandirma	
92-0016	TUSAS (GD) F-16C-40 Fighting Falcon	THK 161 Filo/6 AJÜ, Bandirma	
92-0017	TUSAS (GD) F-16C-40 Fighting Falcon	THK 151 Filo/5 AJÜ, Merzifon	
92-0018	TUSAS (GD) F-16C-40 Fighting Falcon	THK 113 Filo/1 AJÜ, Eskisehir	
92-0019	TUSAS (GD) F-16C-40 Fighting Falcon	THK 181 Filo/8 AJÜ, Diyarbakir	
92-0020	TUSAS (GD) F-16C-40 Fighting Falcon	THK 181 Filo/8 AJÜ, Diyarbakir	
92-0021	TUSAS (GD) F-16C-40 Fighting Falcon	THK 192 Filo/9 AJÜ, Balikesir	
92-0022	TUSAS (GD) F-16D-40 Fighting Falcon	THK 152 Filo/10 TÜK, Incirlik	
92-0023	TUSAS (GD) F-16D-40 Fighting Falcon	THK 132 Filo/3 AJEÜ, Konya	
92-0024	TUSAS (GD) F-16D-40 Fighting Falcon	THK 113 Filo/1 AJÜ, Eskisehir	
93-0001	TUSAS (GD) F-16C-40 Fighting Falcon	THK 401 Filo/1 AJÜ, Eskisehir	
93-0003	TUSAS (GD) F-16C-40 Fighting Falcon	THK 151 Filo/5 AJÜ, Merzifon	
93-0004	TUSAS (GD) F-16C-40 Fighting Falcon	THK 181 Filo/8 AJÜ, Diyarbakir	
93-0005	TUSAS (GD) F-16C-40 Fighting Falcon	THK 182 Filo/8 AJÜ, Diyarbakir	
93-0006	TUSAS (GD) F-16C-40 Fighting Falcon	THK 152 Filo/10 TÜK, Incirlik	
93-0007	TUSAS (GD) F-16C-40 Fighting Falcon	THK 182 Filo/8 AJÜ, Diyarbakir	
93-0008	TUSAS (GD) F-16C-40 Fighting Falcon	THK 132 Filo/3 AJEÜ, Konya	
93-0009	TUSAS (GD) F-16C-40 Fighting Falcon	THK 182 Filo/8 AJÜ, Diyarbakir	
93-0011	TUSAS (GD) F-16C-40 Fighting Falcon	THK 181 Filo/8 AJÜ, Diyarbakir	
93-0012	TUSAS (GD) F-16C-40 Fighting Falcon	THK 181 Filo/8 AJÜ, Diyarbakir	

Notes	Serial	Type (code/other identity)	Owner/operator, location or fate
	93-0013	TUSAS (GD) F-16C-40 Fighting Falcon	THK 181 Filo/8 AJÜ, Diyarbakir
	93-0658	TUSAS (GD) F-16C-50 Fighting Falcon	THK 132 Filo/3 AJEÜ, Konya
	93-0659	TUSAS (GD) F-16C-50 Fighting Falcon	THK 192 Filo/9 AJÜ, Balikesir
	93-0660	TUSAS (GD) F-16C-50 Fighting Falcon	THK 152 Filo/10 TÜK, Incirlik
	93-0661	TUSAS (GD) F-16C-50 Fighting Falcon	THK 132 Filo/3 AJEÜ, Konya
	93-0663	TUSAS (GD) F-16C-50 Fighting Falcon	THK 191 Filo/9 AJÜ, Balikesir
	93-0664	TUSAS (GD) F-16C-50 Fighting Falcon	THK 132 Filo/3 AJEÜ, Konya
	93-0665	TUSAS (GD) F-16C-50 Fighting Falcon	THK 193 Filo/9 AJÜ, Balikesir
	93-0667	TUSAS (GD) F-16C-50 Fighting Falcon	THK 151 Filo/5 AJÜ, Merzifon
	93-0668	TUSAS (GD) F-16C-50 Fighting Falcon	THK 151 Filo/5 AJÜ, Merzifon
	93-0669	TUSAS (GD) F-16C-50 Fighting Falcon	THK 192 Filo/9 AJÜ, Balikesir
	93-0670	TUSAS (GD) F-16C-50 Fighting Falcon	THK 193 Filo/9 AJÜ, Balikesir
	93-0671	TUSAS (GD) F-16C-50 Fighting Falcon	THK 161 Filo/6 AJÜ, Bandirma
	93-0672	TUSAS (GD) F-16C-50 Fighting Falcon	THK 193 Filo/9 AJÜ, Balikesir
	93-0673	TUSAS (GD) F-16C-50 Fighting Falcon	THK 132 Filo/3 AJEÜ, Konya
	93-0674	TUSAS (GD) F-16C-50 Fighting Falcon	THK 132 Filo/3 AJEÜ, Konya
	93-0675	TUSAS (GD) F-16C-50 Fighting Falcon	THK 191 Filo/9 AJÜ, Balikesir
	93-0676	TUSAS (GD) F-16C-50 Fighting Falcon	THK 192 Filo/9 AJÜ, Balikesir
	93-0677	TUSAS (GD) F-16C-50 Fighting Falcon	THK 151 Filo/5 AJÜ, Merzifon
	93-0678	TUSAS (GD) F-16C-50 Fighting Falcon	THK 191 Filo/9 AJÜ, Balikesir
	93-0679	TUSAS (GD) F-16C-50 Fighting Falcon	THK 191 Filo/9 AJÜ, Balikesir
	93-0680	TUSAS (GD) F-16C-50 Fighting Falcon	THK 193 Filo/9 AJÜ, Balikesir
	93-0681	TUSAS (GD) F-16C-50 Fighting Falcon	THK 191 Filo/9 AJÜ, Balikesir
	93-0682	TUSAS (GD) F-16C-50 Fighting Falcon	THK 193 Filo/9 AJÜ, Balikesir
	93-0683	TUSAS (GD) F-16C-50 Fighting Falcon	THK 193 Filo/9 AJÜ, Balikesir
	93-0684	TUSAS (GD) F-16C-50 Fighting Falcon	THK 191 Filo/9 AJÜ, Balikesir
	93-0685	TUSAS (GD) F-16C-50 Fighting Falcon $	THK 192 Filo/9 AJÜ, Balikesir
	93-0687	TUSAS (GD) F-16C-50 Fighting Falcon	THK 132 Filo/3 AJEÜ, Konya
	93-0689	TUSAS (GD) F-16C-50 Fighting Falcon	THK 193 Filo/9 AJÜ, Balikesir
	93-0690	TUSAS (GD) F-16C-50 Fighting Falcon	THK 191 Filo/9 AJÜ, Balikesir
	93-0691	TUSAS (GD) F-16D-50 Fighting Falcon	THK 192 Filo/9 AJÜ, Balikesir
	93-0692	TUSAS (GD) F-16D-50 Fighting Falcon	THK 193 Filo/9 AJÜ, Balikesir
	93-0693	TUSAS (GD) F-16D-50 Fighting Falcon	THK 152 Filo/10 TÜK, Incirlik
	93-0694	TUSAS (GD) F-16D-50 Fighting Falcon	THK 151 Filo/5 AJÜ, Merzifon
	93-0695	TUSAS (GD) F-16D-50 Fighting Falcon	THK 193 Filo/9 AJÜ, Balikesir
	93-0696	TUSAS (GD) F-16D-50 Fighting Falcon	THK 151 Filo/5 AJÜ, Balikesir
	94-0071	TUSAS (GD) F-16C-50 Fighting Falcon	THK 191 Filo/9 AJÜ, Balikesir
	94-0072	TUSAS (GD) F-16C-50 Fighting Falcon	THK 151 Filo/5 AJÜ, Merzifon
	94-0073	TUSAS (GD) F-16C-50 Fighting Falcon	THK 151 Filo/5 AJÜ, Merzifon
	94-0074	TUSAS (GD) F-16C-50 Fighting Falcon	THK 193 Filo/9 AJÜ, Balikesir
	94-0075	TUSAS (GD) F-16C-50 Fighting Falcon	THK 151 Filo/5 AJÜ, Merzifon
	94-0076	TUSAS (GD) F-16C-50 Fighting Falcon	THK 151 Filo/5 AJÜ, Merzifon
	94-0077	TUSAS (GD) F-16C-50 Fighting Falcon	THK 193 Filo/9 AJÜ, Balikesir
	94-0078	TUSAS (GD) F-16C-50 Fighting Falcon	THK 191 Filo/9 AJÜ, Balikesir
	94-0080	TUSAS (GD) F-16C-50 Fighting Falcon	THK 193 Filo/9 AJÜ, Balikesir
	94-0082	TUSAS (GD) F-16C-50 Fighting Falcon	THK 151 Filo/5 AJÜ, Merzifon
	94-0083	TUSAS (GD) F-16C-50 Fighting Falcon	THK 193 Filo/9 AJÜ, Balikesir
	94-0084	TUSAS (GD) F-16C-50 Fighting Falcon	THK 191 Filo/9 AJÜ, Balikesir
	94-0085	TUSAS (GD) F-16C-50 Fighting Falcon	THK 192 Filo/9 AJÜ, Balikesir
	94-0086	TUSAS (GD) F-16C-50 Fighting Falcon	THK 193 Filo/9 AJÜ, Balikesir
	94-0088	TUSAS (GD) F-16C-50 Fighting Falcon $	THK 151 Filo/5 AJÜ, Merzifon
	94-0089	TUSAS (GD) F-16C-50 Fighting Falcon	THK 151 Filo/5 AJÜ, Merzifon
	94-0090	TUSAS (GD) F-16C-50 Fighting Falcon	THK 193 Filo/9 AJÜ, Balikesir
	94-0091	TUSAS (GD) F-16C-50 Fighting Falcon	THK 132 Filo/3 AJEÜ, Konya
	94-0092	TUSAS (GD) F-16C-50 Fighting Falcon	THK 132 Filo/3 AJEÜ, Konya
	94-0093	TUSAS (GD) F-16C-50 Fighting Falcon	THK 191 Filo/9 AJÜ, Balikesir
	94-0094	TUSAS (GD) F-16C-50 Fighting Falcon	THK
	94-0095	TUSAS (GD) F-16C-50 Fighting Falcon	THK 192 Filo/9 AJÜ, Balikesir
	94-0096	TUSAS (GD) F-16C-50 Fighting Falcon	THK 193 Filo/9 AJÜ, Balikesir
	94-0105	TUSAS (GD) F-16D-50 Fighting Falcon	THK 192 Filo/9 AJÜ, Balikesir
	94-0106	TUSAS (GD) F-16D-50 Fighting Falcon	THK 401 Filo/1 AJÜ, Eskisehir
	94-0108	TUSAS (GD) F-16D-50 Fighting Falcon	THK 193 Filo/9 AJÜ, Balikesir

Serial	Type (code/other identity)	Owner/operator, location or fate	Notes
94-0109	TUSAS (GD) F-16D-50 Fighting Falcon	THK 193 Filo/9 AJÜ, Balikesir	
94-0110	TUSAS (GD) F-16D-50 Fighting Falcon	THK 191 Filo/9 AJÜ, Balikesir	
94-1557	TUSAS (GD) F-16D-50 Fighting Falcon	THK 192 Filo/9 AJÜ, Balikesir	
94-1558	TUSAS (GD) F-16D-50 Fighting Falcon	THK 132 Filo/3 AJEÜ, Konya	
94-1559	TUSAS (GD) F-16D-50 Fighting Falcon	THK 152 Filo/10 TÜK, Incirlik	
94-1560	TUSAS (GD) F-16D-50 Fighting Falcon	THK 113 Filo/1 AJÜ, Eskisehir	
94-1561	TUSAS (GD) F-16D-50 Fighting Falcon	THK 192 Filo/9 AJÜ, Balikesir	
94-1562	TUSAS (GD) F-16D-50 Fighting Falcon	THK 193 Filo/9 AJÜ, Balikesir	
94-1563	TUSAS (GD) F-16D-50 Fighting Falcon	THK 193 Filo/9 AJÜ, Balikesir	
94-1564	TUSAS (GD) F-16D-50 Fighting Falcon	THK 193 Filo/9 AJÜ, Balikesir	
07-1001	TUSAS (GD) F-16C-50 Fighting Falcon	THK 161 Filo/6 AJÜ, Bandirma	
07-1002	TUSAS (GD) F-16C-50 Fighting Falcon	THK 181 Filo/8 AJÜ, Diyarbakir	
07-1003	TUSAS (GD) F-16C-50 Fighting Falcon	THK 181 Filo/8 AJÜ, Diyarbakir	
07-1004	TUSAS (GD) F-16C-50 Fighting Falcon	THK 161 Filo/6 AJÜ, Bandirma	
07-1005	TUSAS (GD) F-16C-50 Fighting Falcon	THK 181 Filo/8 AJÜ, Diyarbakir	
07-1006	TUSAS (GD) F-16C-50 Fighting Falcon	THK 161 Filo/6 AJÜ, Bandirma	
07-1007	TUSAS (GD) F-16C-50 Fighting Falcon	THK 161 Filo/6 AJÜ, Bandirma	
07-1008	TUSAS (GD) F-16C-50 Fighting Falcon	THK	
07-1009	TUSAS (GD) F-16C-50 Fighting Falcon	THK 152 Filo/10 TÜK, Incirlik	
07-1010	TUSAS (GD) F-16C-50 Fighting Falcon	THK 152 Filo/10 TÜK, Incirlik	
07-1011	TUSAS (GD) F-16C-50 Fighting Falcon	THK 181 Filo/8 AJÜ, Diyarbakir	
07-1012	TUSAS (GD) F-16C-50 Fighting Falcon	THK 161 Filo/6 AJÜ, Bandirma	
07-1013	TUSAS (GD) F-16C-50 Fighting Falcon	THK 181 Filo/8 AJÜ, Diyarbakir	
07-1014	TUSAS (GD) F-16C-50 Fighting Falcon	THK 161 Filo/6 AJÜ, Bandirma	
07-1015	TUSAS (GD) F-16D-50 Fighting Falcon	THK 161 Filo/6 AJÜ, Bandirma	
07-1016	TUSAS (GD) F-16D-50 Fighting Falcon	THK 181 Filo/8 AJÜ, Diyarbakir	
07-1017	TUSAS (GD) F-16D-50 Fighting Falcon	THK 161 Filo/6 AJÜ, Diyarbakir	
07-1018	TUSAS (GD) F-16D-50 Fighting Falcon	THK 161 Filo/6 AJÜ, Bandirma	
07-1019	TUSAS (GD) F-16D-50 Fighting Falcon	THK 161 Filo/6 AJÜ, Bandirma	
07-1020	TUSAS (GD) F-16D-50 Fighting Falcon	THK 181 Filo/8 AJÜ, Diyarbakir	
07-1021	TUSAS (GD) F-16D-50 Fighting Falcon	THK 181 Filo/8 AJÜ, Diyarbakir	
07-1022	TUSAS (GD) F-16D-50 Fighting Falcon	THK 161 Filo/6 AJÜ, Bandirma	
07-1023	TUSAS (GD) F-16D-50 Fighting Falcon	THK 161 Filo/6 AJÜ, Bandirma	
07-1024	TUSAS (GD) F-16D-50 Fighting Falcon	THK 181 Filo/8 AJÜ, Diyarbakir	
07-1025	TUSAS (GD) F-16D-50 Fighting Falcon	THK 181 Filo/8 AJÜ, Diyarbakir	
07-1026	TUSAS (GD) F-16D-50 Fighting Falcon	THK 181 Filo/8 AJÜ, Diyarbakir	
07-1027	TUSAS (GD) F-16D-50 Fighting Falcon	THK 161 Filo/6 AJÜ, Bandirma	
07-1028	TUSAS (GD) F-16D-50 Fighting Falcon	THK 161 Filo/6 AJÜ, Bandirma	
07-1029	TUSAS (GD) F-16D-50 Fighting Falcon	THK 161 Filo/6 AJÜ, Bandirma	
07-1030	TUSAS (GD) F-16D-50 Fighting Falcon	THK 181 Filo/8 AJÜ, Diyarbakir	
09-001	Gulfstream Aerospace G.550	THK 212 Filo/11 HUAÜK, Ankara/Etimesgut	
13-001	Boeing 737-7FS AEW&C (E-7T)	THK 131 Filo/3 AJEÜ, Konya	
13-002	Boeing 737-7FS AEW&C (E-7T)	THK 131 Filo/3 AJEÜ, Konya	
13-003	Boeing 737-7FS AEW&C (E-7T)	THK 131 Filo/3 AJEÜ, Konya	
13-004	Boeing 737-7FS AEW&C (E-7T)	THK 131 Filo/3 AJEÜ, Konya	
13-0009	Airbus Military A.400M	THK 221 Filo/12 HUAÜ, Erkilet	
14-0013	Airbus Military A.400M	THK 221 Filo/12 HUAÜ, Erkilet	
14-0028	Airbus Military A.400M	THK, stored Erkilet	
15-0051	Airbus Military A.400M	THK 221 Filo/12 HUAÜ, Erkilet	
16-0055	Airbus Military A.400M	THK 221 Filo/12 HUAÜ, Erkilet	
17-0078	Airbus Military A.400M	THK 221 Filo/12 HUAÜ, Erkilet	
17-0080	Airbus Military A.400M	THK 221 Filo/12 HUAÜ, Erkilet	
18-0093	Airbus Military A.400M (17-0095)	THK 221 Filo/12 HUAÜ, Erkilet	
18-0094	Airbus Military A.400M (17-0096)	THK 221 Filo/12 HUAÜ, Erkilet	
21-0118	Airbus Military A.400M	THK 221 Filo/12 HUAÜ, Erkilet	
......	Bombardier Global 6000 (TC-SJA)	TAI, Akinci (ELINT conversion for THK)	
......	Bombardier Global 6000 (TC-SJB)	TAI, Akinci (ELINT conversion for THK)	
......	Bombardier Global 6000 (TC-SJC)	TAI, Akinci (ELINT conversion for THK)	
......	Bombardier Global 6000 (TC-SJD)	TAI, Akinci (ELINT conversion for THK)	
Government of Turkey			
TC-ANK	Airbus A.318-112 (VQ-BDD)	Government of Turkey, Ankara	
TC-ATA	Gulfstream Aerospace G.550	Government of Turkey, Ankara	

Notes	Serial	Type (code/other identity)	Owner/operator, location or fate
	TC-CAN	Airbus A.340-541 (TC-TRK)	Government of Turkey, Ankara
	TC-CBK	Gulfstream Aerospace G.550	Government of Turkey, Ankara
	TC-DAP	Gulfstream Aerospace G.550	Government of Turkey, Ankara
	TC-GAP	Gulfstream Aerospace G.450	Government of Turkey, Ankara
	TC-GVC	Airbus A.319CJ-115X	Government of Turkey, Ankara
	TC-IST	Airbus A.319CJ-133	Government of Turkey, Ankara
	TC-TRK	Boeing 747-8ZV (VQ-BSK)	Government of Turkey, Ankara
	TC-TUR	Airbus A.330-243	Government of Turkey, Ankara
	TURKMENISTAN		
	EZ-A007	Boeing 737-7GL (N1786B)	Government of Turkmenistan, Ashgabat
	EZ-A700	Boeing 737-700(BBJ) (N6065Y)	Government of Turkmenistan, Ashgabat
	EZ-A777	Boeing 777-22KLR	Government of Turkmenistan, Ashgabat
	EZ-B021	BAe 1000B	*Preserved Ashgabat, Turkmenistan*
	EZ-B022	Canadair Challenger 605	Government of Turkmenistan, Ashgabat
	EZ-B023	Canadair Challenger 605	Government of Turkmenistan, Ashgabat
	EZ-B024	Canadair Challenger 870CS	Government of Turkmenistan, Ashgabat
	UGANDA		
	5X-UGF	Gulfstream Aerospace G.550	Government of Uganda, Entebbe
	UKRAINE		
	Ukrainian Air Force		
	NOTE: Due to the continuing conflict in Ukraine, it is not currently possible to verify the continued status of the air force aircraft, so these have been omitted until the picture becomes clearer.		
	Government of Ukraine		
	UR-ABA	Airbus A.319CJ-115X	Government of Ukraine, Krakow, Poland
	UNITED ARAB EMIRATES		
	United Arab Emirates Air Force (UAEAF)		
	311	Lockheed L.100-30 Hercules (A6-QFY)	UAEAF 4 Sqn/Transport Wing, Abu Dhabi
	312	Lockheed C-130H-30 Hercules	UAEAF 4 Sqn/Transport Wing, Abu Dhabi
	1211	Lockheed C-130H Hercules	UAEAF 4 Sqn/Transport Wing, Abu Dhabi
	1213	Lockheed C-130H Hercules	UAEAF 4 Sqn/Transport Wing, Abu Dhabi
	1214	Lockheed C-130H Hercules	UAEAF 4 Sqn/Transport Wing, Abu Dhabi
	1215	Lockheed L.100-30 Hercules	UAEAF 4 Sqn/Transport Wing, Abu Dhabi
	1216	Lockheed L.100-30 Hercules	UAEAF 4 Sqn/Transport Wing, Abu Dhabi
	1217	Lockheed L.100-30 Hercules	UAEAF 4 Sqn/Transport Wing, Abu Dhabi
	1223	Boeing C-17A Globemaster III (10-0401)	UAEAF Heavy Transport Sqn, Abu Dhabi
	1224	Boeing C-17A Globemaster III (10-0402)	UAEAF Heavy Transport Sqn, Abu Dhabi
	1225	Boeing C-17A Globemaster III (10-0403)	UAEAF Heavy Transport Sqn, Abu Dhabi
	1226	Boeing C-17A Globemaster III (10-0404)	UAEAF Heavy Transport Sqn, Abu Dhabi
	1227	Boeing C-17A Globemaster III (10-0405)	UAEAF Heavy Transport Sqn, Abu Dhabi
	1228	Boeing C-17A Globemaster III (10-0406)	UAEAF Heavy Transport Sqn, Abu Dhabi
	1229	Boeing C-17A Globemaster III (14-0007)	UAEAF Heavy Transport Sqn, Abu Dhabi
	1230	Boeing C-17A Globemaster III (14-0008)	UAEAF Heavy Transport Sqn, Abu Dhabi
	1300	Airbus A.330-243 MRTT (EC-339)	UAEAF MRTT Sqn, Al Ain
	1301	Airbus A.330-243 MRTT (EC-334)	UAEAF MRTT Sqn, Al Ain
	1302	Airbus A.330-243 MRTT (EC-332)	UAEAF MRTT Sqn, Al Ain
	1303	Airbus A.330-243 MRTT (EC-345)	UAEAF MRTT Sqn, Al Ain
	1304	Airbus A.330-243 MRTT (EC-346)	UAEAF (on order)
	1305	Airbus A.330-243 MRTT	UAEAF (on order)
	1325	Bombardier Global 6000	UAEAF 10 Sqn, Dubai/Minhad
	1326	Bombardier Global 6000	UAEAF 10 Sqn, Dubai/Minhad
	1340	Bombardier Global 6000	UAEAF 10 Sqn, Dubai/Minhad
	1341	Bombardier Global 6000	UAEAF 10 Sqn, Dubai/Minhad
	1342	Bombardier Global 6000	UAEAF 10 Sqn, Dubai/Minhad
	13..	Bombardier Global 6500 (SE-RMS)	UAEAF 10 Sqn, Dubai/Minhad
	13..	Bombardier Global 6500 (SE-RMV)	UAEAF 10 Sqn, Dubai/Minhad
	1350	Bombardier Challenger 650 (T7-AQL)	UAEAF
	1351	Bombardier Challenger 650 (T7-AQA)	UAEAF
	1999	AgustaWestland AW.139	*UAEAF, Stansted, UK (Summer 2024)*

Serial	Type (code/other identity)	Owner/operator, location or fate	Notes
Government of the UAE			
A6-ALN	Boeing 777-2ANER	Amiri Flight, Abu Dhabi	
A6-AUH	Boeing 737-8EX	Amiri Flight, Abu Dhabi	
A6-COM	Boeing 747-433	Dubai Air Wing	
A6-DLM	Airbus A.320-232	*Sold as VP-COU, 2024*	
A6-FZZ	Boeing 737-8KN	Dubai Air Wing	
A6-GGP	Boeing 747-412F	Dubai Air Wing	
A6-HEH	Boeing 737-8AJ	Dubai Air Wing	
A6-HHH(2)	Boeing 777-29MLR	Dubai Air Wing	
A6-HHH(1)	Grumman G.1159C Gulfstream IV	Stored Stuttgart, AR, USA	
A6-HMM	Gulfstream Aerospace G.650ER (A6-HHH)	*Sold as T7-DXB, 2024*	
A6-HMS	Airbus A.320-232	Governement of Fujairah	
A6-HRM	Boeing 747-422	Dubai Air Wing	
A6-HRS	Boeing 737-7F0	Dubai Air Wing	
A6-MMM	Boeing 747-422	Dubai Air Wing	
A6-MRM	Boeing 737-8EC	Dubai Air Wing	
A6-MRS	Boeing 737-8EO	Dubai Air Wing	
A6-PFC	Boeing 787-8	Amiri Flight, Abu Dhabi	
A6-PFE	Boeing 787-9	Amiri Flight, Abu Dhabi	
A6-PFG	Boeing 787-9	Amiri Flight, stored Moses Lake, WA, USA	
A6-PFH	Boeing 787-9	Amiri Flight, stored Moses Lake, WA, USA	
A6-PFK	Boeing 777-3F6ER	Amiri Flight, Abu Dhabi	
A6-SHJ	Airbus A.320-232X	Ruler of Sharjah Air Wing	
A6-SIL	Boeing 777-35RER	Amiri Flight, Abu Dhabi	
A6-YST	Boeing 737-8SA	Dubai Air Wing	
DU-141	AgustaWestland AW.139	Dubai Air Wing, Stansted, UK (Summer 2024)	
DU-142	AgustaWestland AW.139	Dubai Air Wing, Stansted, UK (Summer 2024)	
P4-HHH	Boeing 777-29MLR	*Re-registered as A6-HHH, January 2024*	
UZBEKISTAN			
UK001	Boeing 787-8	Government of Uzbekistan, Tashkent	

Italian HH-101 MM81871, seen here in the static park at RIAT. *HJC*

This section lists the codes worn by some overseas air forces and, alongside, the serial of the aircraft currently wearing this code. This list will be updated as new information becomes available.

NOTE: TThere has been much discussion recently regarding the French "civil" registration attached to each French Air Force aircraft. In reality, this is the fixed radio callsign assigned to each aircraft, but is also a registration that may, or may not, be carried on the aircraft. The Alpha Jets of the Patrouille de France display the registration on the inside of the nosewheel door, and some of the larger transports (A400M's, for example) also carry details on the airframe. The 2 letters of an aircraft code will also correspond to the "last 2" of the allocated registration (for example, Mirage 2000-5F 77, coded "2-AX", is also allocated registration F-SDAX). Where known I will record the registrations on the following pages. Since it has been pointed out that the codes on the PdF Alpha Jets are only stickers, which can easily be removed and re-applied, I have no longer included these codes in the listings.

FRANCE		8-RN	E124 (F-UHRN)	2-EC	78 (F-UGEC)	3-JP	611 (F-UGJP)
FRENCH AIR FORCE		8-RO	E131 (F-UHRO)	2-ED	62 (F-UGED)	3-JR	682 (F-UGJR)
D-BD Alpha Jet E		8-RP	E130 (F-TERP)	2-EE	71 (F-UGEE)	3-JT	677 (F-UGJT)
[PDF]	E20 (F-TEMS)	8-RQ	E138 (F-UHRQ)	2-EG	56 (F-UGEG)	3-JU	614 (F-UGJU)
[PDF]	E35 (F-TEMA)	8-RS	E149 (F-UHRS)	2-EH	52 (F-UGEH)	3-JV	636 (F-UGJV)
[PDF]	E44 (F-UHRE)	8-RV	E164 (F-UHRV)	2-EI	38 (F-UGEI)	3-JX	679 (F-UGJX)
[PDF]	E45 (F-TETF)	8-TA	E42 (F-TETA)	2-EL	58 (F-UGEL)	3-JY	615 (F-UGJY)
[PDF]	E48 (F-TEMH)	8-TH	E90 (F-TETH)	2-EM	63 (F-UGEM)	3-KJ	523 (F-UGKJ)
[PDF]	E73 (F-TENE)	8-TJ	E25 (F-TETJ)	2-EN	46 (F-UGEN)	3-KS	528 (F-UGKS)
[PDF]	E81 (F-UGFO)	8-TM	E128 (F-TETM)	2-EO	66 (F-UGEO)	3-LH	655 (F-UHLH)
[PDF]	E87 (F-TELC)	8-TX	E93 (F-TETX)	2-EP	47 (F-UGEP)	3-MO	613 (F-UHMO)
[PDF]	E98 (F-TEMF)	8-TZ	E83 (F-TETZ)	2-EQ	44 (F-UGEQ)	3-OA	524 (F-UGOA)
[PDF]	E105 (F-UGFM)	8-UB	E11 (F-TEUB)	2-EU	55 (F-UGEU)	3-OC	529 (F-UGOC)
[PDF]	E112 (F-SDAO)	8-UC	E157 (F-TEUC)	2-EV	59 (F-UGEV)	3-OL	530 (F-UGOL)
[PDF]	E113 (F-TETD)	8-UD	E107 (F-TEUD)	2-EW	48 (F-UGEW)	3-OR	527 (F-UGOR)
[PDF]	E119 (F-UGFE)	8-UH	E160 (F-TEUH)	2-EX	40 (F-UGEX)	3-XA	662 (F-UGXA)
[PDF]	E127 (F-UGFK)	102-LI	E53 (F-TELI)	2-EY	42 (F-UGEY)	3-XC	618 (F-UGXC)
[PDF]	E129 (F-TELP)	705-RB	E163 (F-TERB)	2-FZ	41 (F-UGFZ)	3-XD	630 (F-UGXD)
[PDF]	E137 (F-TELJ)	705-RR	E114 (F-TERR)	2-ME	61 (F-UHME)	3-XE	632 (F-UGXE)
[PDF]	E139 (F-UGFC)	705-RW	E166 (F-UHRW)	2-MG	65 (F-UHMG)	3-XF	670 (F-UGXF)
[PDF]	E148 (F-TELU)	705-RZ	E171 (F-UHRZ)	2-MH	67 (F-UHMH)	3-XG	625 (F-UGXG)
[PDF]	E152 (F-UHRT)	705-TB	E67 (F-TETB)	2-MK	74 (F-UHMK)	3-XI	661 (F-UGXI)
[PDF]	E168 (F-UGFP)	F-RCAF	E108 8-AF	3-AG	681 (F-SDAG)	3-XJ	602 (F-UGXJ)
[PDF]	E169 (F-UHRX)	F-RCAG	E109 8-AG	3-AM	525 (F-SDAM)	3-XK	671 (F-UGXK)
[PDF]	E170 (F-UHRY)	F-RCAI	E117 8-AI	3-AS	635 (F-RCAS)	3-XL	603 (F-UGXL)
[PDF]	E171 [F-UHRZ]	F-RCAK	E144 8-AK	3-AU	653 (F-RCAU)	3-XM	680 (F-UGXM)
8-AF	E108 (F-RCAF)	F-RCAL	E154 8-AL	3-IA	650 (F-UGIA)	3-XN	652 (F-UGXN)
8-AG	E109 (F-RCAG)	F-SDAO	E112 [PDF]	3-IC	626 (F-UGIC)	3-XO	629 (F-UGXO)
8-AI	E117 (F-RCAI)	F-TELC	E87 [PDF]	3-ID	654 (F-UGID)	3-XP	645 (F-UGXP)
8-AK	E144 (F-RCAK)	F-TELJ	E137 [PDF]	3-IE	642 (F-UGIE)	3-XQ	637 (F-UGXQ)
8-AL	E154 (F-RCAL)	F-TELP	E129 [PDF]	3-IF	609 (F-UGIF)	3-XR	659 (F-UGXR)
8-FD	E151 (F-UGFD)	F-TELU	E148 [PDF]	3-IG	668 (F-UGIG)	3-XT	648 (F-UGXT)
8-FJ	E33 (F-UGFJ)	F-TEMA	E35 [PDF]	3-IH	631 (F-UGIH)	3-XV	672 (F-UGXV)
8-FN	E116 (F-UGFN)	F-TEMF	E98 [PDF]	3-IJ	638 (F-UGIJ)	3-XX	610 (F-UGXX)
8-LH	E38 (F-TELH)	F-TEMH	E48 [PDF]	3-IL	622 (F-UGIL)	3-XY	649 (F-UGXY)
8-LL	E88 (F-TELL)	F-TEMS	E20 [PDF]	3-IN	640 (F-UGIN)	3-XZ	685 (F-UGXZ)
8-LM	E102 (F-TELM)	F-TENE	E73 [PDF]	3-IO	647 (F-UGIO)	30-JB	678 (F-UGJB)
8-LN	E118 (F-TELN)	F-TETD	E113 [PDF]	3-IP	604 (F-UGIP)	30-JF	660 (F-UGJF)
8-LO	E142 (F-TELO)	F-TETF	E45 [PDF]	3-IQ	666 (F-UGIQ)	30-JJ	639 (F-UGJJ)
8-LS	E22 (F-TELS)	F-TEUB	E11 8-UB	3-IR	674 (F-UGIR)	30-JW	641 (F-UGJW)
8-LT	E147 (F-TELT)	F-UGFC	E139 [PDF]	3-IS	617 (F-UGIS)	30-MQ	646 (F-UHMQ)
8-LW	E82 (F-TELW)	F-UGFD	E151 8-FD	3-IT	624 (F-UGIT)	188-AX	77 (F-SDAX)
8-MA	E173 (F-UHMA)	F-UGFE	E119 [PDF]	3-IU	620 (F-UGIU)	188-EF	45 (F-UGEF)
8-MB	E176 (F-UHMB)	F-UGFK	E127 [PDF]	3-IV	683 (F-UGIV)	188-ET	57 (F-UGET)
8-MM	E13 (F-TEMM)	F-UGFM	E105 [PDF]	3-IW	664 (F-UGIW)	188-EZ	54 (F-UGEZ)
8-MO	E68 (F-TEMO)	F-UGFO	E81 [PDF]	3-JC	606 (F-UGJC)	**Dassault Rafale**	
8-MR	E115 (F-UHMR)	F-UGFP	E168 [PDF]	3-JD	643 (F-UGJD)	4-EA	303 (F-SDEA)
8-NA	E79 (F-TENA)	F-UHRE	E44 [PDF]	3-JG	601 (F-UGJG)	4-EB	304 (F-SDEB)
8-NF	E141 (F-TENF)	F-UHRT	E152 [PDF]	3-JH	686 (F-UGJH)	4-FF	339 (F-UHFF)
8-RE	E165 (F-TERE)	F-UHRX	E169 [PDF]	3-JI	675 (F-UGJI)	4-FG	340 (F-UHFG)
8-RH	E94 (F-TERH)	F-UHRY	E170 [PDF]	3-JL	628 (F-UGJL)	4-FH	341 (F-UHFH)
8-RI	E117 (F-RCAI)	F-UHRZ	E171 [PDF]	3-JM	657 (F-UGJM)	4-FI	342 (F-UHFI)
8-RJ	E162 (F-TERJ)	**Dassault Mirage 2000**		3-JN	658 (F-UGJN)	4-FJ	343 (F-UHFJ)
8-RM	E123 (F-UHRM)	2-EA	49 (F-UGEA)	3-JO	627 (F-UGJO)	4-FK	344 (F-UHFK)

Code	Reg	Code	Reg	Code	Reg	Code	Reg
4-FL	345 (F-UHFL)	30-GH	129 (F-UHGH)	709 GI	26 (F-RBGI)	GAP	3911 (F-MGAP)
4-FM	346 (F-UHFL)	30-GI	130 (F-UHGI)	**FRENCH ARMY**		GAQ	3921 (F-MGAQ)
4-FN	347 (F-UHFN)	30-GK	132 (F-UHGK)	**SA.330 Puma**		GAR	3938 (F-MGAR)
4-FP	349 (F-UHFP)	30-GL	133 (F-UHGL)	DAA	1006 (F-MDAA)	GAS	3947 (F-MGAS)
4-FQ	350 (F-UHFQ)	30-GQ	138 (F-UHGQ)	DAC	1036 (F-MDAC)	GAT	3948 (F-MGAT)
4-FS	352 (F-UHFS)	30-GS	140 (F-UHGS)	DAD	1037 (F-MDAD)	GAU	3957 (F-MGAU)
4-FT	353 (F-UHFT)	30-GX	145 (F-UHGX)	DAE	1049 (F-MDAE)	GAV	3964 (F-MGAV)
4-FV	355 (F-UHFV)	30-HE	105 (F-UHHE)	DAF	1055 (F-MDAF)	GAW	3996 (F-MGAW)
4-FW	356 (F-UHFW)	30-HG	106 (F-UHHG)	DAG	1069 (F-MDAG)	GAX	4018 (F-MGAX)
4-FX	357 (F-UHFX)	30-HH	104 (F-UHHH)	DAH	1078 (F-MDAH)	GBA	4026 (F-MGBA)
4-FY	358 (F-UHFY)	30-HJ	107 (F-UHHJ)	DAI	1092 (F-MDAI)	GBB	4034 (F-MGBB)
4-GO	136 (F-UGHO)	30-HS	108 (F-UHHS)	DAJ	1100 (F-MDAJ)	GBC	4039 (F-MGBC)
4-GY	146 (F-UHGZ)	30-IM	109 (F-UHIM)	DAK	1102 (F-MDAK)	GBE	4053 (F-MGBE)
4-HA	308 (F-UHHA)	30-IN	110 (F-UHIN)	DAL	1107 (F-MDAL)	GBF	4059 (F-MGBF)
4-HB	309 (F-UHHB)	30-IR	113 (F-UHIR)	DAM	1109 (F-MDAM)	GBG	4061 (F-MGBG)
4-HC	310 (F-UHHC)	30-IS	114 (F-UHIS)	DAN	1128 (F-MDAN)	GBH	4066 (F-MGBH)
4-HD	311 (F-UHHD)	30-IT	115 (F-UHIT)	DAO	1143 (F-MDAO)	GBI	4072 (F-MGBI)
4-HF	312 (F-UHHF)	30-IU	116 (F-UHIU)	DAP	1149 (F-MDAP)	GBJ	4084 (F-MGBJ)
4-HI	313 (F-UHHI)	30-IV	117 (F-UHIV)	DAQ	1156 (F-MDAQ)	GBL	4095 (F-MGBL)
4-HN	319 (F-UHHN)	30-IX	119 (F-UHIX)	DAR	1173 (F-MDAR)	GBN	4109 (F-MGBN)
4-HO	317 (F-UHHO)	30-IZ	121 (F-UHIZ)	DAS	1176 (F-MDAS)	GBO	4114 (F-MGBO)
4-HP	314 (F-UHHP)	30-SI	360 (	DAW	1211 (F-MDAW)	GBP	4115 (F-MGBP)
4-HQ	321 (F-UHHQ)	30-SJ	361 (	DAX	1214 (F-MDAX)	GBQ	4119 (F-MGBQ)
4-HT	323 (F-UHHT)	30-SK	362 (	DAY	1217 (F-MDAY)	GBR	4120 (F-MGBR)
4-HU	322 (F-UHHU)	30-SM	364 (	DAZ	1219 (F-MDAZ)	GBS	4124 (F-MGBS)
4-HV	320 (F-UHHV)	30-SN	365 (	DBA	1232 (F-MDBA)	GBT	4136 (F-MGBT)
4-HW	324 (F-UHHW)	30-SO	366 (	DBB	1243 (F-MDBB)	GBU	4140 (F-MGBU)
4-HX	325 (F-UHHX)	30-VD	151 (F-UHVD)	DBF	1417 (F-MDBF)	GBV	4141 (F-MGBV)
4-HY	326 (F-UHHY)	30-VE	152 (F-UHVE)	DBG	1438 (F-MDBG)	GBW	4142 (F-MGBW)
4-HZ	327 (F-UHHZ)	30-VG	154 (F-UHVG)	DBH	1451 (F-MDBH)	GBX	4144 (F-MGBX)
4-IA	307 (F-UHIA)	30-VH	155 (F-UHVH)	DBI	1507 (F-MDBI)	GBY	4145 (F-MGBY)
4-IC	328 (F-UHIC)	30-VI	156 (F-UHVI)	DBJ	1510 (F-MDBJ)	GCC	4160 (F-MGCC)
4-ID	329 (F-UHID)	30-VM	160 (F-UHVM)	DBK	1512 (F-MDBK)	GCD	4161 (F-MGCD)
4-IE	330 (F-UHIE)	30-VN	161 (F-UHVN)	DBL	1519 (F-MDBL)	GCE	4162 (F-MGCE)
4-IF	331 (F-UHIF)	**Pilatus PC-21**		DBM	1617 (F-MDBM)	GCF	4164 (F-MGCF)
4-IG	332 (F-UHIG)	(NB: These codes do not have		DBN	1632 (F-MDBN)	GCG	4168 (F-MGCG)
4-IH	333 (F-UHIH)	hyphens)		DBO	1634 (F-MDBO)	GCI	4175 (F-MGCI)
4-II	334 (F-UHII)	709 FC	01 (F-RBFC)	DBP	1654 (F-MDBP)	GCJ	4179 (F-MGCJ)
4-IJ	335 (F-UHIJ)	709 FD	02 (F-RBFD)	DBQ	1663 (F-MDBQ)	GCK	4180 (F-MGCK)
4-IK	336 (F-UHIK)	709 FE	03 (F-RBFE)	DBR	5682 (F-MDBR)	GCL	4181 (F-MGCL)
4-IL	337 (F-UHIL)	709 FF	04 (F-RBFF)	DCF	1073 (F-MDCF)	GCM	4186 (F-MGCM)
4-IO	338 (F-UHIO)	709 FG	05 (F-RBFG)	DDD	1198 (F-MDDD)	GCN	4189 (F-MGCN)
5-GN	135 (F-UHGN)	709 FH	06 (F-RBFH)	DDK	1231 (F-MDDK)	GCO	4191 (F-MGCO)
5-SL	363 (	709 FI	07 (F-RBFI)	DDM	1236 (F-MDDM)	GCP	4195 (F-MGCP)
5-VB	149 (F-UHVB)	709 FJ	08 (F-RBFJ)	DDP	1252 (F-MDDP)	GCQ	4198 (F-MGCQ)
5-VC	150 (F-UHVC)	709 FK	09 (F-RBFK)	DDT	1269 (F-MDDT)	GEA	4205 (F-MGEA)
5-VF	153 (F-UHVF)	709 FL	10 (F-RBFL)	DDW	1447 (F-MDDT)	GEB	4206 (F-MGEB)
5-VJ	157 (F-UHVJ)	709 FM	11 (F-RBFM)	DDX	1662 (F-MDDX)	GEC	4207 (F-MGEC)
5-VK	158 (F-UHVK)	709 FN	12 (F-RBFN)	**SA.342 Gazelle**		GED	4208 (F-MGED)
5-VL	159 (F-UHVL)	709 FO	13 (F-RBFO)	GAA	3459 (F-MGAA)	GEF	4210 (F-MGEF)
7-GR	139 (F-UHGR)	709 FP	14 (F-RBFP)	GAC	3512 (F-MGAC)	GEG	4211 (F-MGEG)
7-GU	142 (F-UHGU)	709 FQ	15 (F-RBFQ)	GAD	3530 (F-MGAD)	GEI	4214 (F-MGEI)
7-GZ	147 (F-UHGZ)	709 FR	16 (F-RBFR)	GAF	3664 (F-MGAF)	GEJ	4215 (F-MGEJ)
7-VA	148 (F-UHVA)	709 FS	17 (F-RBFS)	GAG	3848 (F-MGAG)	GEK	4216 (F-MGEK)
30-EF	102 (F-SDEF)	709 GA	18 (F-RBGA)	GAH	3849 (F-MGAH)	GEL	4217 (F-MGEL)
30-FR	351 (F-UHFR)	709 GB	19 (F-RBGB)	GAI	3850 (F-MGAI)	GEM	4218 (F-MGEM)
30-FU	354 (F-UHFU)	709 GC	20 (F-RBGC)	GAJ	3856 (F-MGAJ)	GEN	4219 (F-MGEN)
30-FZ	359 (F-UHFZ)	709 GD	21 (F-RBGD)	GAK	3859 (F-MGAK)	GEO	4220 (F-MGEO)
30-GA	122 (F-UHGA)	709 GE	22 (F-RBGE)	GAL	3862 (F-MGAL)	GEP	4221 (F-MGEP)
30-GD	125 (F-UHGD)	709 GF	23 (F-RBGF)	GAM	3863 (F-MGAM)	GEQ	4222 (F-MGEQ)
30-GE	126 (F-UHGE)	709 GG	24 (F-RBGG)	GAN	3865 (F-MGAN)	GER	4223 (F-MGER)
30-GF	127 (F-UHGF)	709 GH	25 (F-RBGH)	GAO	3868 (F-MGAO)	GES	4224 (F-MGES)

Code	Serial
GET	4225 (F-MGET)
GEU	4226 (F-MGEU)
GEV	4227 (F-MGEV)
GEW	4228 (F-MGEW)
GEX	4229 (F-MGEX)
GEY	4230 (F-MGEY)
GFA	4232 (F-MGFA)
GFB	4233 (F-MGFB)
GJC	3511 (F-MGJC)
GJK	3857 (F-MGJK)
GJN	3929 (F-MGJN)
GJQ	4022 (F-MGJQ)
GKA	4176 (F-MGKA)
GKD	4185 (F-MGKD)
GMA	3567
GMB	4042
GMC	4079
GMK	4201
GND	3617
GNS	4071
GNT	4083
GNV	4118

AS.532UL/EC.725AP Cougar

Code	Serial
CAA	2611 (F-MCAA)
CAB	2628 (F-MCAB)
CAC	2630 (F-MCAC)
CAD	2631 (F-MCAD)
CAE	2633 (F-MCAE)
CAF	2638 (F-MCAF)
CAG	2640 (F-MCAG)
CAH	2642 (F-MCAH)
CGA	2252 (F-MGCA)
CGB	2266 (F-MGCB)
CGC	2267 (F-MGCC)
CGD	2271 (F-MGCD)
CGF	2273 (F-MGCF)
CGG	2282 (F-MGCG)
CGH	2285 (F-MGCH)
CGI	2290 (F-MGCI)
CGJ	2292 (F-MGCJ)
CGK	2299 (F-MGCK)
CGL	2300 (F-MGCL)
CGM	2301 (F-MGCM)
CGN	2303 (F-MGCN)
CGO	2316 (F-MGCO)
CGQ	2323 (F-MGCQ)
CGR	2324 (F-MGCR)
CGS	2325 (F-MGCS)
CGT	2327 (F-MGCT)
CGU	2331 (F-MGCU)
CGW	2443 (F-MGCW)
CGX	2446 (F-MGCX)
CHA	2342 (F-MCHA)
CHB	2369 (F-MCHB)
CHC	2375 (F-MCHC)

EC.665 Tigre

Code	Serial
BHA	2010 (F-MBHA)
BHB	2009 (F-MBHB)
BHC	2013 (F-MBHC)
BHD	2015 (F-MBHD)
BHE	2019 (F-MBHE)
BHF	2018 (F-MBHF)
BHG	2022 (F-MBHG)
BHH	2001 (F-MBHH)
BHI	2002 (F-MBHI)
BHJ	2003 (F-MBHJ)
BHK	2004 (F-MBHK)
BHL	2006 (F-MBHL)
BHM	2011 (F-MBHM)
BHN	2021 (F-MBHN)
BHO	2024 (F-MBHO)
BHP	2023 (F-MBHP)
BHQ	2025 (F-MBHQ)
BHR	2026 (F-MBHR)
BHS	2027 (F-MBHS)
BHT	2012 (F-MBHT)
BHV	2029 (F-MBHV)
BHW	2030 (F-MBHW)
BHX	2031 (F-MBHX)
BHZ	2033 (F-MBHZ)
BIA	2016 (F-MBIA)
BIB	2034 (F-MBIB)
BIC	2035 (F-MBIC)
BIE	2037 (F-MBIE)
BIF	2038 (F-MBIF)
BIG	2039 (F-MBIG)
BIH	2040 (F-MBIH)
BII	2041 (F-MBII)
BIJ	2042 (F-MBIJ)
BIK	2043 (F-MBIK)
BIL	2044 (F-MBIL)
BIM	2045 (F-MBIM)
BIN	2046 (F-MBIN)
BIO	2047 (F-MBIO)
BJA	6001 (F-MBJA)
BJB	6002 (F-MBJB)
BJC	6003 (F-MBJC)
BJD	6004 (F-MBJD)
BJE	6005 (F-MBJE)
BJF	6006 (F-MBJF)
BJG	6007 (F-MBJG)
BJH	6008 (F-MBJH)
BJI	6009 (F-MBJI)
BJJ	6010 (F-MBJJ)
BJK	6011 (F-MBJK)
BJL	6012 (F-MBJL)
BJM	6013 (F-MBJM)
BJN	6014 (F-MBJN)
BJO	6015 (F-MBJO)
BJP	6016 (F-MBJP)
BJR	6018 (F-MBJR)
BJS	6019 (F-MBJS)
BJT	6020 (F-MJBT)
BJU	6021 (F-MBJU)
BJV	6022 (F-MBJV)
BJW	6023 (F-MBJW)
BJX	6024 (F-MBJX)
BJY	6025 (F-MBJY)
BJZ	6026 (F-MBJZ)
BKA	6027 (F-MBKA)
BKB	6028 (F-MBKB)
BKC	6029 (F-MBKC)
BKD	6030 (F-MBKD)
BKE	6031 (F-MBKE)

NH.90-TTH

Code	Serial
EAA	1239 (F-MEAA)
EAB	1256 (F-MEAB)
EAC	1271 (F-MEAC)
EAD	1273 (F-MEAD)
EAE	1290 (F-MEAE)
EAF	1291 (F-MEAF)
EAG	1292 (F-MEAG)
EAH	1293 (F-MEAH)
EAI	1294 (F-MEAI)
EAJ	1295 (F-MEAJ)
EAK	1306 (F-MEAK)
EAL	1307 (F-MEAL)
EAM	1308 (F-MEAM)
EAN	1309 (F-MEAN)
EAO	1310 (F-MEAO)
EAP	1311 (F-MEAP)
EAQ	1312 (F-MEAQ)
EAR	1313 (F-MEAR)
EAS	1332 (F-MEAS)
EAT	1333 (F-MEAT)
EAU	1334 (F-MEAU)
EAV	1335 (F-MEAV)
EAW	1336 (F-MEAW)
EAX	1337 (F-MEAX)
EAY	1338 (F-MEAY)
EAZ	1386 (F-MEAZ)
EBA	1390 (F-MEBA)
EBB	1391 (F-MEBB)
EBC	1387 (F-MEBC)
EBD	1392 (F-MEBD)
EBE	1401 (F-MEBE)
EBF	1402 (F-MEBF)
EBG	1403 (F-MEBG)
EBH	1404 (F-MEBH)
EBI	1405 (F-MEBI)
EBJ	1432 (F-MEBJ)
EBK	1427 (F-MEBK)
EBL	1428 (F-MEBL)
EBM	1429 (F-MEBM)
EBN	1433 (F-MEBN)
EBO	1430 (F-MEBO)
EBP	1431 (F-MEBP)
EBQ	1442 (F-MEBQ)
EBR	1441 (F-MEBR)
EBS	1443 (F-MEBS)
EBT	1454 (F-MEBT)
EBU	1455 (F-MEBU)
EBV	1456 (F-MEBV)
EBW	1457 (F-MEBW)
EBX	1458 (F-MEBX)
EBY	1479 (F-MEBY)
EBZ	1480 (F-MEBZ)
ECA	1481 (F-MECA)
ECB	1482 (F-MECB)
ECC	1483 (F-MECC)
ECD	1484 (F-MECD)
ECE	1485 (F-MECE)
ECF	1496 (F-MECF)
ECG	1497 (F-MECG)
ECH	1526 (F-MECH)
ECI	1527 (F-MECI)
ECJ	1528 (F-MECJ)
ECK	1529 (F-MECK)
ECL	1547 (F-MECL)
ECM	1550 (F-MECM)

ITALY

Aermacchi MB339

Code	Serial
61-52	MM54504
61-57	MM54509
61-61	MM54511
61-62	MM54512
61-65	MM54515
61-66	MM54516
61-106	MM54548
61-107	MM54549
61-116	MM54465
61-121	MM54458
61-126	MM55062
61-127	MM55063
61-130	MM55064
61-131	MM55065
61-132	MM55066
61-133	MM55067
61-134	MM55068
61-135	MM55069
61-136	MM55070
61-140	MM55072
61-141	MM55073
61-142	MM55074
61-143	MM55075
61-145	MM55077
61-146	MM55078
61-147	MM55079
61-150	MM55080
61-151	MM55081
61-152	MM55082
61-154	MM55084
61-155	MM55085
61-156	MM55086
61-157	MM55087
61-160	MM55088
61-161	MM55089
61-162	MM55090
61-163	MM55091
61-241	MM54468

Aermacchi T-345A

Code	Serial
61-202	MM55234
61-203	MM55235
61-204	MM55236
61-205	MM55237
61-206	MM55248
61-207	MM55249
61-210	MM55250

**Aermacchi T-346A/B(*)
Master**

Code	Serial
61-01	MM55154
61-02	MM55144
61-03	MM55145
61-04	MM55155
61-05	MM55153
61-06	MM55213
61-07	MM55214

Code	Serial		Code	Serial		Code	Serial		Code	Serial
61-10	MM55215		36-30	MM7280		6-06	MM7371		6-72	MM7051
61-11	MM55152		36-40	MM7322		6-07	MM7372		6-73	MM7030
61-12	MM55216		36-41	MM7324		32-01	MM7332		6-74	MM7062
61-13	MM55217		36-42	MM7327		32-02	MM7333		6-75	MM7013
61-14	MM55218		36-43	MM7321		32-03	MM7334		6-76	MM7044
61-15	MM55221		36-44	MM7325		32-04	MM7335		6-77	MM7020
61-16	MM55220		36-46	MM7315		32-05	MM7336		6-100	MM7054
61-20	MM55219		36-47	MM7331		32-06	MM7363		6-101	MM7053
61-21	MM55222		36-51	MM7344		32-07	MM7357		50-53	MM7008
61-22	MM55223		36-52	MM7329		32-08	MM7358		RS-01	CSX7079
61-23	MM55224		36-56	MM7353		32-09	MM7359			
61-24	MM55229		36-62	MM55097		32-10	MM7360		**SPAIN**	
61-25	MM55230		36-63	MM55129		32-11	MM7361		**Airtech CN.235**	
61-26	MM55231		36-64	MM55128		32-12	MM7362		37-01	D.4-01
61-27	MM55232		37-04	MM7304		32-13	MM7337		37-02	D.4-02
61-30	MM55239*		37-08	MM7347		32-14	MM7453		37-03	D.4-03
61-31	MM55240*		37-09	MM7310		32-15	MM7364		37-04	D.4-04
61-32	MM55241*		37-11	MM7301		32-16	MM7365		37-05	D.4-05
61-33	MM55242*		37-14	MM7328		32-18	MM7455		37-06	D.4-06
Eurofighter Typhoon			37-18	MM7306		32-19	MM7373		37-08	D.4-08
4-1	MM7286		37-19	MM7314		32-20	MM7374		74-13	T.19B-13
4-3	MM7287		37-22	MM7293		32-21	MM7375		74-16	T.19B-16
4-4	MM7276		37-24	MM7348		32-22	MM7376		74-18	T.19B-18
4-5	MM7289		37-28	MM7330		32-23	MM7378		403-02	T.19A-02
4-8	MM7282		37-34	MM55168		32-34	MM7379		744-07	T.19B-07
4-9	MM7350		37-35	MM7318		**Panavia Tornado**			744-11	T.19B-11
4-10	MM7273		37-36	MM7351		6-02	MM7019		744-17	T.19B-17
4-13	MM7235		37-40	MM7300		6-03	MM7084		744-19	T.19B-19
4-15	MM7271		37-45	MM7345		6-04	MM7057		744-20	T.19B-20
4-16	MM7285		37-54	MM7354		6-05	MM7025		**CASA 101EB Aviojet**	
4-18	MM7272		51-08	MM7308		6-06	MM7036		54-20	E.25-35
4-23	MM55095		51-09	MM7309		6-07	MM7075		54-21	E.25-55
4-25	MM55092		51-11	MM7311		6-11	MM7058		54-22	E.25-61
4-27	MM55094		51-12	MM7312		6-13	MM7014		74-02	E.25-33
4-30	MM55096		51-13	MM7313		6-15	MM55006		74-07	E.25-51
4-31	MM55093		51-19	MM7319		6-20	MM7021		74-09	E.25-53
4-33	MM55130		51-20	MM7320		6-21	MM7040		74-11	E.25-56
4-34	MM55131		51-23	MM7323		6-22	MM7029		74-13	E.25-59
4-40	MM7288		51-32	MM55132		6-24	MM7064		74-17	E.25-63
4-41	MM7291		51-33	MM55133		6-25	MM7043		74-20	E.25-66
4-42	MM7316		51-39	MM7339		6-26	MM7063		74-21	E.25-67
4-43	MM7317		51-43	MM7343		6-32	MM7015		74-25	E.25-71
4-46	MM7326		51-46	MM7346		6-33	MM7039		74-26	E.25-72
4-50	MM7292		51-52	MM7352		6-34	MM7073		74-28	E.25-74
4-51	MM7349		51-56	MM7356		6-37	MM7038		74-30	E.25-76
4-52	MM7294		51-95	MM7295		6-41	MM7067		74-35	E.25-83
4-53	MM7303		51-96	MM7296		6-43	MM7066		74-39	E.25-88
4-60	MM7338		51-98	MM7298		6-44	MM55009		74-43	E.25-43
4-64	MM7340		51-99	MM7299		6-45	MM55008		74-44	E.25-34
4-66	MM7341		**Lockheed Martin F-35A/**			6-50	MM7024		79-02	E.25-78
4-67	MM7355		**F-35B Lightning II**			6-52	MM55002		79-03	E.25-80
4-68	MM7342		4-01	MM7451		6-55	MM7004		79-04	E.25-84
36-03	MM7281		4-02	MM7452		6-56	MM55007		79-05	E.25-05
36-04	MM7270		4-03	MM7454		6-57	MM7081		79-06	E.25-06
36-05	MM7275		4-04	MM7456		6-60	MM7086		79-08	E.25-08
36-06	MM7274		4-05	MM7457		6-61	MM7047		79-11	E.25-11
36-07	MM7279		4-06	MM7458		6-62	MM7082		79-12	E.25-12
36-10	MM7302		6-01	MM7366		6-64	MM7052		79-13	E.25-13
36-14	MM7277		6-02	MM7367		6-65	MM7055		79-17	E.25-62
36-15	MM7284		6-03	MM7368		6-66	MM7059		79-21	E.25-21
36-22	MM7290		6-04	MM7369		6-67	MM7068		79-24	E.25-24
36-23	MM7297		6-05	MM7370		6-71	MM7070		79-25	E.25-25

Code	Serial	Code	Serial	Code	Serial	Code	Serial
79-27	E.25-27	11-28	C.16-28	12-12	C.15-54	46-11	C.15-83
79-28	E.25-28	11-29	C.16-29	12-13	C.15-55	46-13	C.15-85
79-29	E.25-87	11-30	C.16-30	12-14	C.15-56	46-14	C.15-86
79-31	E.25-31	11-32	C.16-32	12-15	C.15-57	46-16	C.15-88
79-32	E.25-86	11-33	C.16-33	12-17	C.15-59	46-17	C.15-89
79-35	E.25-54	11-35	C.16-35	12-18	C.15-60	46-18	C.15-90
79-38	E.25-38	11-38	C.16-38	12-19	C.15-61	46-20	C.15-92
79-39	E.25-79	11-40	C.16-40	12-20	C.15-62	46-21	C.15-93
79-44	E.25-44	11-41	C.16-41	12-23	C.15-65	46-22	C.15-94
79-97	E.25-69	11-42	C.16-42	12-24	C.15-66	46-23	C.15-95
79-98	E.25-73	11-43	C.16-43	12-26	C.15-68	46-24	C.15-96
741-68	E.25-68	11-45	C.16-45	12-27	C.15-69		
793-57	E.25-57	11-46	C.16-46	12-28	C.15-70		
793-81	E.25-81	11-48	C.16-48	12-30	C.15-72		
794-37	E.25-37	11-51	C.16-51	12-50	C.15-34		
794-40	E.25-40	11-52	C.16-52	12-71	CE.15-08		
794-52	E.25-52	11-53	C.16-53	12-73	CE.15-10		
CASA 212 Aviocar		11-54	C.16-54	12-74	CE.15-11		
47-14	T.12D-75	11-55	C.16-55	12-75	CE.15-12		
54-11	T.12D-74	11-56	C.16-56	15-01	C.15-14		
72-12	T.12B-67	11-57	C.16-57	15-02	C.15-15		
72-49	T.12B-49	11-63	C.16-63	15-03	C.15-16		
72-62	T.12B-62	11-91	C.16-20	15-05	C.15-18		
72-63	T.12B-63	14-11	CE.16-11	15-08	C.15-21		
72-65	T.12B-65	14-14	C.16-50	15-09	C.15-22		
72-66	T.12B-66	14-28	C.16-70	15-10	C.15-23		
72-69	T.12B-69	14-31	C.16-31	15-11	C.15-24		
72-70	T.12B-70	14-36	C.16-36	15-12	C.15-25		
72-71	T.12B-71	14-37	C.16-37	15-13	C.15-26		
CASA C-295M		14-39	C.16-39	15-14	C.15-27		
35-01	T.21-01	14-44	C.16-44	15-15	C.15-28		
35-02	T.21-02	14-47	C.16-47	15-16	C.15-29		
35-03	T.21-03	14-49	C.16-49	15-17	C.15-30		
35-04	T.21-04	14-58	C.16-58	15-18	C.15-31		
35-05	T.21-05	14-59	C.16-59	15-19	C.15-32		
35-06	T.21-06	14-60	C.16-60	15-20	C.15-33		
35-07	T.21-07	14 61	C.16-61	15-22	C.15-35		
35-08	T.21-08	14-62	C.16-62	15-23	C.15-36		
35-09	T.21-09	14-64	C.16-64	15-24	C.15-37		
35-11	T.21-11	14-65	C.16-65	15-25	C.15-38		
35-12	T.21-12	14-66	C.16-66	15-26	C.15-39		
35-13	T.21-13	14-67	C.16-67	15-27	C.15-40		
Eurofighter Tifón		14-68	C.16-68	15-28	C.15-41		
11-01	CE.16-01	14-71	C.16-71	15-30	C.15-43		
11-02	CE.16-02	14-72	C.16-72	15-31	C.15-47		
11-03	CE.16-03	14-73	C.16-73	15-33	C.15-67		
11-04	CE.16-04	14-74	C.16-74	15-34	C.15-64		
11-05	CE.16-05	14-75	C.16-75	15-70	CE.15-01		
11-06	CE.16-06	14-76	C.16-76	15-71	CE.15-02		
11-07	CE.16-07	14-77	C.16-77	15-72	CE.15-03		
11-09	CE.16-09	14-78	C.16-78	15-73	CE.15-04		
11-10	CE.16-10	**McDonnell-Douglas**		15-74	CE.15-05		
11-12	CE.16-12	**F/A-18A+/EF-18M Hornet**		15-75	CE.15-06		
11-13	CE.16-13	12-01	C.15-13	15-76	CE.15-07		
11-14	CE.16-14	12-02	C.15-44	15-77	CE.15-09		
11-21	C.16-21	12-03	C.15-45	46-01	C.15-73		
11-22	C.16-22	12-04	C.15-46	46-03	C.15-75		
11-23	C.16-23	12-06	C.15-48	46-05	C.15-77		
11-24	C.16-24	12-07	C.15-49	46-07	C.15-79		
11-25	C.16-25	12-08	C.15-50	46-08	C.15-80		
11-26	C.16-26	12-09	C.15-51	46-09	C.15-81		
11-27	C.16-27	12-11	C.15-53	46-10	C.15-82		

US MILITARY AIRCRAFT MARKINGS

All USAF and US Army aircraft have been allocated a fiscal year (FY) number since 1921. Individual aircraft are given a serial according to the fiscal year in which they are ordered (It should be remembered that the USAF FY starts in the October of the previous calendar year). The numbers commence at 0001 and are prefixed with the year of allocation. For example, KC-135R Stratotanker 58-0001 was the first aircraft ordered in FY58. The fiscal year (FY) serial is carried on the technical data block which is usually stencilled on the left-hand side of the aircraft just below the cockpit. The number displayed on the fin is a corruption of the FY serial, so for the above example we would expect to see 80001 on the fin. Most tactical aircraft carry the fiscal year in small figures followed by the last three or four digits of the serial in large figures. Recent developments have seen transport aircraft (primarily) operating with NO serial information painted on the aircraft at all, a trend that hopefully will die out before too long! In view of this, I haven't attempted to catalogue which airframes are anonymous at this time.

US Army serials have been allocated in a similar way to USAF serials although in recent years an additional zero has been added so that all US Army serials now have the two-figure fiscal year part followed by five digits.

USN and USMC serials follow a straightforward numerical sequence which commenced, for the present series, with the allocation of 00001 to an SB2C Helldiver by the Bureau of Aeronautics in 1940. Numbers in the 170000 series are presently being issued. They are usually carried in full on the rear fuselage of the aircraft.

US Coast Guard serials began with the allocation of the serial 1 to a Loening OL-5 in 1927

UK-BASED USAF AIRCRAFT

The following aircraft are normally based in the UK. They are listed in numerical order of type with individual aircraft in serial number order, as depicted on the aircraft. Where it is possible to identify the allocation of aircraft to individual squadrons by means of colours carried on fin or cockpit edge, this is also provided.

Serial	Type (code/other identity)	Owner/operator, location or fate	Notes
McDonnell Douglas F-15E Strike Eagle			
91-0301	McD F-15E Strike Eagle [LN] bl/w	USAF 492nd FS/48th FW, RAF Lakenheath	
91-0302	McD F-15E Strike Eagle [LN]	USAF 492nd FS/48th FW, RAF Lakenheath	
91-0303	McD F-15E Strike Eagle [LN] bl/w	USAF, on rework, WR-ALC, OK	
91-0306	McD F-15E Strike Eagle [LN] bl/w	USAF 492nd FS/48th FW, RAF Lakenheath	
91-0307	McD F-15E Strike Eagle [LN] bl/w	USAF, on rework, WR-ALC, OK	
91-0308	McD F-15E Strike Eagle [LN] bl/w	USAF 492nd FS/48th FW, RAF Lakenheath	
91-0309	McD F-15E Strike Eagle [LN] r/w	USAF, on rework, WR-ALC, OK	
91-0310	McD F-15E Strike Eagle [LN]	USAF 494th FS/48th FW, RAF Lakenheath	
91-0311	McD F-15E Strike Eagle [LN] r/w	USAF 494th FS/48th FW, RAF Lakenheath	
91-0312	McD F-15E Strike Eagle [LN] m [48 OG]	USAF 492nd FS/48th FW, RAF Lakenheath	
91-0313	McD F-15E Strike Eagle [LN]	USAF 494th FS/48th FW, RAF Lakenheath	
91-0314	McD F-15E Strike Eagle [LN] r/w [494 FS]	USAF, on rework, WR-ALC, OK	
91-0315	McD F-15E Strike Eagle [LN]	USAF 492nd FS/48th FW, RAF Lakenheath	
91-0316	McD F-15E Strike Eagle [LN] bl/w	USAF 492nd FS/48th FW, RAF Lakenheath	
91-0317	McD F-15E Strike Eagle [LN]	USAF 492nd FS/48th FW, RAF Lakenheath	
91-0318	McD F-15E Strike Eagle [LN] bl/w	USAF 492nd FS/48th FW, RAF Lakenheath	
91-0320	McD F-15E Strike Eagle [LN] r/w	USAF, on rework, WR-ALC, OK	
91-0321	McD F-15E Strike Eagle [LN] bl/w	USAF, on rework, WR-ALC, OK	
91-0324	McD F-15E Strike Eagle [LN] r/w	USAF 494th FS/48th FW, RAF Lakenheath	
91-0326	McD F-15E Strike Eagle [LN] r/w	USAF, EPAWSS mods, Kelly AFB, TX	
91-0327	McD F-15E Strike Eagle [LN] bl/w	USAF 492nd FS/48th FW, RAF Lakenheath	
91-0329	McD F-15E Strike Eagle [LN]	USAF 492nd FS/48th FW, RAF Lakenheath	
91-0331	McD F-15E Strike Eagle [LN]	USAF 492nd FS/48th FW, RAF Lakenheath	
91-0332	McD F-15E Strike Eagle [LN]	USAF 492nd FS/48th FW, RAF Lakenheath	
91-0334	McD F-15E Strike Eagle [LN] r/w	USAF 494th FS/48th FW, RAF Lakenheath	
91-0335	McD F-15E Strike Eagle [LN] r/w	USAF 494th FS/48th FW, RAF Lakenheath	
91-0602	McD F-15E Strike Eagle [LN] r/w	USAF 494th FS/48th FW, RAF Lakenheath	
91-0603	McD F-15E Strike Eagle [LN] r/w	USAF 494th FS/48th FW, RAF Lakenheath	
91-0604	McD F-15E Strike Eagle [LN] r/w	USAF 494th FS/48th FW, RAF Lakenheath	
91-0605	McD F-15E Strike Eagle [LN]	USAF 492nd FS/48th FW, RAF Lakenheath	
92-0364	McD F-15E Strike Eagle [LN] r/w [494 FS]	USAF 494th FS/48th FW, RAF Lakenheath	
96-0201	McD F-15E Strike Eagle [LN] m [48 FW]	USAF 494th FS/48th FW, RAF Lakenheath	
96-0202	McD F-15E Strike Eagle [LN] bl/w	USAF 492nd FS/48th FW, RAF Lakenheath	
96-0204	McD F-15E Strike Eagle [LN]	USAF 494th FS/48th FW, RAF Lakenheath	
96-0205	McD F-15E Strike Eagle [LN] bl/w	USAF 492nd FS/48th FW, RAF Lakenheath	
97-0218	McD F-15E Strike Eagle [LN] bl/w	USAF 492nd FS/48th FW, RAF Lakenheath	
97-0219	McD F-15E Strike Eagle [LN] bl/w	USAF 492nd FS/48th FW, RAF Lakenheath	
97-0220	McD F-15E Strike Eagle [LN] bl/w	USAF 492nd FS/48th FW, RAF Lakenheath	

Notes	Serial	Type (code/other identity)	Owner/operator, location or fate
	97-0221	McD F-15E Strike Eagle [LN] bl/w [492 FS]	USAF 492nd FS/48th FW, RAF Lakenheath
	97-0222	McD F-15E Strike Eagle [LN] bl/w	USAF 492nd FS/48th FW, RAF Lakenheath
	98-0131	McD F-15E Strike Eagle [LN] bl/w	USAF 492nd FS/48th FW, RAF Lakenheath
	98-0133	McD F-15E Strike Eagle [LN] bl/w	USAF, EPAWSS mods, Kelly AFB, TX
	98-0134	McD F-15E Strike Eagle [LN] bl/w	USAF 492nd FS/48th FW, RAF Lakenheath
	98-0135	McD F-15E Strike Eagle [LN] bl/w	USAF 492nd FS/48th FW, RAF Lakenheath
	00-3000	McD F-15E Strike Eagle [LN]	USAF 494th FS/48th FW, RAF Lakenheath
	00-3001	McD F-15E Strike Eagle [LN]	USAF 494th FS/48th FW, RAF Lakenheath
	00-3002	McD F-15E Strike Eagle [LN] r/w	USAF 494th FS/48th FW, RAF Lakenheath
	00-3003	McD F-15E Strike Eagle [LN] r/w	USAF 494th FS/48th FW, RAF Lakenheath
	00-3004	McD F-15E Strike Eagle [LN] r/w	USAF, on rework, WR-ALC, OK
	01-2000	McD F-15E Strike Eagle [LN] r/w	USAF, on rework, WR-ALC, OK
	01-2001	McD F-15E Strike Eagle [LN] r/w	USAF 494th FS/48th FW, RAF Lakenheath
	01-2002	McD F-15E Strike Eagle [LN] r/w	USAF 494th FS/48th FW, RAF Lakenheath
	01-2003	McD F-15E Strike Eagle [LN] r/w	USAF, on rework, WR-ALC, OK
	01-2004	McD F-15E Strike Eagle [LN] m [48 FW]	USAF 494th FS/48th FW, RAF Lakenheath
Bell-Boeing CV-22B Osprey			
	08-0048	Bell-Boeing CV-22B Osprey	USAF 7th SOS/352nd SOW, RAF Mildenhall
	08-0049	Bell-Boeing CV-22B Osprey	USAF 7th SOS/352nd SOW, RAF Mildenhall
	08-0050	Bell-Boeing CV-22B Osprey	USAF 7th SOS/352nd SOW, RAF Mildenhall
	09-0042	Bell-Boeing CV-22B Osprey	USAF 7th SOS/352nd SOW, RAF Mildenhall
	10-0053	Bell-Boeing CV-22B Osprey	USAF 7th SOS/352nd SOW, RAF Mildenhall
	11-0057	Bell-Boeing CV-22B Osprey	USAF 7th SOS/352nd SOW, RAF Mildenhall
	11-0058	Bell-Boeing CV-22B Osprey	USAF 7th SOS/352nd SOW, RAF Mildenhall
	11-0061	Bell-Boeing CV-22B Osprey	USAF 7th SOS/352nd SOW, RAF Mildenhall
	16-0076	Bell-Boeing CV-22B Osprey	USAF 7th SOS/352nd SOW, RAF Mildenhall
Lockheed Martin F-35A Lightning II			
	19-5473	Lockheed Martin F-35A Lightning II [LN]	USAF 495th FS/48th FW, RAF Lakenheath
	19-5474	Lockheed Martin F-35A Lightning II [LN]	USAF 495th FS/48th FW, RAF Lakenheath
	19-5475	Lockheed Martin F-35A Lightning II [LN]	USAF 495th FS/48th FW, RAF Lakenheath
	19-5476	Lockheed Martin F-35A Lightning II [LN]	USAF 495th FS/48th FW, RAF Lakenheath
	19-5484	Lockheed Martin F-35A Lightning II [LN] [48 FW]	USAF 495th FS/48th FW, RAF Lakenheath
	19-5485	Lockheed Martin F-35A Lightning II [LN] [48 OG]	USAF 495th FS/48th FW, RAF Lakenheath
	19-5486	Lockheed Martin F-35A Lightning II [LN]	USAF 495th FS/48th FW, RAF Lakenheath
	19-5493	Lockheed Martin F-35A Lightning II [LN] [493 FS]	USAF 493rd FS/48th FW, RAF Lakenheath
	19-5495	Lockheed Martin F-35A Lightning II [LN] [495 FS]	USAF 495th FS/48th FW, RAF Lakenheath
	20-5570	Lockheed Martin F-35A Lightning II [LN]	USAF 495th FS/48th FW, RAF Lakenheath
	20-5571	Lockheed Martin F-35A Lightning II [LN]	USAF 495th FS/48th FW, RAF Lakenheath
	20-5572	Lockheed Martin F-35A Lightning II [LN]	USAF 495th FS/48th FW, RAF Lakenheath
	20-5573	Lockheed Martin F-35A Lightning II [LN]	USAF 495th FS/48th FW, RAF Lakenheath
	20-5574	Lockheed Martin F-35A Lightning II [LN]	USAF 495th FS/48th FW, RAF Lakenheath
	20-5580	Lockheed Martin F-35A Lightning II [LN]	USAF 495th FS/48th FW, RAF Lakenheath
	20-5581	Lockheed Martin F-35A Lightning II [LN]	USAF 495th FS/48th FW, RAF Lakenheath
	20-5582	Lockheed Martin F-35A Lightning II [LN]	USAF 495th FS/48th FW, RAF Lakenheath
	20-5583	Lockheed Martin F-35A Lightning II [LN]	USAF 495th FS/48th FW, RAF Lakenheath
	20-5588	Lockheed Martin F-35A Lightning II [LN]	USAF 495th FS/48th FW, RAF Lakenheath
	20-5589	Lockheed Martin F-35A Lightning II [LN]	USAF 495th FS/48th FW, RAF Lakenheath
	20-5590	Lockheed Martin F-35A Lightning II [LN]	USAF 495th FS/48th FW, RAF Lakenheath
	20-5594	Lockheed Martin F-35A Lightning II [LN]	USAF 493rd FS/48th FW, RAF Lakenheath
	20-5595	Lockheed Martin F-35A Lightning II [LN]	USAF 493rd FS/48th FW, RAF Lakenheath
	20-5596	Lockheed Martin F-35A Lightning II [LN]	USAF 493rd FS/48th FW, RAF Lakenheath
	20-5598	Lockheed Martin F-35A Lightning II [LN]	USAF 493rd FS/48th FW, RAF Lakenheath
	20-5599	Lockheed Martin F-35A Lightning II [LN]	USAF 493rd FS/48th FW, RAF Lakenheath
	20-5600	Lockheed Martin F-35A Lightning II [LN]	USAF 495th FS/48th FW, RAF Lakenheath
	20-5601	Lockheed Martin F-35A Lightning II [LN]	USAF 495th FS/48th FW, RAF Lakenheath
	20-5602	Lockheed Martin F-35A Lightning II [LN]	USAF 495th FS/48th FW, RAF Lakenheath
	20-5603	Lockheed Martin F-35A Lightning II [LN]	USAF 495th FS/48th FW, RAF Lakenheath
	20-5604	Lockheed Martin F-35A Lightning II [LN]	USAF 495th FS/48th FW, RAF Lakenheath
	20-5613	Lockheed Martin F-35A Lightning II [LN]	USAF 493rd FS/48th FW, RAF Lakenheath
	20-5614	Lockheed Martin F-35A Lightning II [LN]	USAF 493rd FS/48th FW, RAF Lakenheath
	20-5615	Lockheed Martin F-35A Lightning II [LN]	USAF 495th FS/48th FW, RAF Lakenheath
	20-5616	Lockheed Martin F-35A Lightning II [LN]	USAF 493rd FS/48th FW, RAF Lakenheath

Serial	Type (code/other identity)	Owner/operator, location or fate	Notes
20-5617	Lockheed Martin F-35A Lightning II [LN]	USAF 493rd FS/48th FW, RAF Lakenheath	
20-5618	Lockheed Martin F-35A Lightning II [LN]	USAF 495th FS/48th FW, RAF Lakenheath	
22-5682	Lockheed Martin F-35A Lightning II [LN]	USAF 493rd FS/48th FW, RAF Lakenheath	
22-5683	Lockheed Martin F-35A Lightning II [LN]	USAF 493rd FS/48th FW, RAF Lakenheath	
22-5684	Lockheed Martin F-35A Lightning II [LN]	USAF 493rd FS/48th FW, RAF Lakenheath	
22-5685	Lockheed Martin F-35A Lightning II [LN]	USAF 493rd FS/48th FW, RAF Lakenheath	
22-5690	Lockheed Martin F-35A Lightning II [LN]	USAF 493rd FS/48th FW, RAF Lakenheath (on loan to 6th WPS/57th Wg, Nellis AFB, NV)	
22-5691	Lockheed Martin F-35A Lightning II [LN]	USAF 493rd FS/48th FW, RAF Lakenheath (on loan to 6th WPS/57th Wg, Nellis AFB, NV)	
22-5703	Lockheed Martin F-35A Lightning II [LN]	USAF 493rd FS/48th FW, RAF Lakenheath (on loan to 6th WPS/57th Wg, Nellis AFB, NV)	
22-5704	Lockheed Martin F-35A Lightning II [LN]	USAF 493rd FS/48th FW, RAF Lakenheath (on loan to 6th WPS/57th Wg, Nellis AFB, NV)	
22-5705	Lockheed Martin F-35A Lightning II [LN]	USAF 493rd FS/48th FW, RAF Lakenheath (on loan to 6th WPS/57th Wg, Nellis AFB, NV)	
22-5710	Lockheed Martin F-35A Lightning II [LN]	USAF 493rd FS/48th FW, RAF Lakenheath (on loan to 6th WPS/57th Wg, Nellis AFB, NV)	
22-5711	Lockheed Martin F-35A Lightning II [LN]	USAF 493rd FS/48th FW, RAF Lakenheath (on loan to 6th WPS/57th Wg, Nellis AFB, NV)	
22-5712	Lockheed Martin F-35A Lightning II [LN]	USAF 493rd FS/48th FW, RAF Lakenheath (on loan to 6th WPS/57th Wg, Nellis AFB, NV)	
22-5714	Lockheed Martin F-35A Lightning II [LN]	USAF 493rd FS/48th FW, RAF Lakenheath (on loan to 6th WPS/57th Wg, Nellis AFB, NV)	
22-5718	Lockheed Martin F-35A Lightning II [LN]	USAF 493rd FS/48th FW, RAF Lakenheath (on order)	
22-5719	Lockheed Martin F-35A Lightning II [LN]	USAF 493rd FS/48th FW, RAF Lakenheath (on order)	
22-5720	Lockheed Martin F-35A Lightning II [LN]	USAF 493rd FS/48th FW, RAF Lakenheath (on order)	
22-5721	Lockheed Martin F-35A Lightning II [LN]	USAF 493rd FS/48th FW, RAF Lakenheath (on order)	

Lockheed MC-130J Commando II

Serial	Type (code/other identity)	Owner/operator, location or fate	Notes
09-5713	Lockheed MC-130J Commando II	USAF 67th SOS/352nd SOW, RAF Mildenhall	
09-6207	Lockheed MC-130J Commando II	USAF 67th SOS/352nd SOW, RAF Mildenhall	
12-5759	Lockheed MC-130J Commando II	USAF 67th SOS/352nd SOW, RAF Mildenhall	
13-5776	Lockheed MC-130J Commando II	USAF 67th SOS/352nd SOW, RAF Mildenhall	
13-5778	Lockheed MC-130J Commando II	USAF 67th SOS/352nd SOW, RAF Mildenhall	
14-5805	Lockheed MC-130J Commando II	*Returned to the USA, 2024*	
16-5839	Lockheed MC-130J Commando II	USAF 67th SOS/352nd SOW, RAF Mildenhall	
20-5937	Lockheed MC-130J Commando II	USAF 67th SOS/352nd SOW, RAF Mildenhall	
20-5941	Lockheed MC-130J Commando II	USAF 67th SOS/352nd SOW, RAF Mildenhall	

Boeing KC-135R Stratotanker/Boeing KC-135T Stratotanker

Serial	Type (code/other identity)	Owner/operator, location or fate	Notes
57-2605	Boeing KC-135R Stratotanker [D] *r/w/bl*	USAF 351st ARS/100th ARW, RAF Mildenhall	
58-0095	Boeing KC-135R Stratotanker [D] *r/w/bl*	USAF 351st ARS/100th ARW, RAF Mildenhall	
58-0100	Boeing KC-135R Stratotanker [D] *r/w/bl*	USAF 351st ARS/100th ARW, RAF Mildenhall	
58-0125	Boeing KC-135T Stratotanker [D] *r/w/bl*	USAF 351st ARS/100th ARW, RAF Mildenhall	
59-1464	Boeing KC-135T Stratotanker [D] *r/w/bl*	USAF 351st ARS/100th ARW, RAF Mildenhall	
59-1470	Boeing KC-135T Stratotanker [D] *r/w/bl*	USAF 351st ARS/100th ARW, RAF Mildenhall	
59-1475	Boeing KC-135T Stratotanker [D] *r/w/bl*	USAF 351st ARS/100th ARW, RAF Mildenhall	
59-1511	Boeing KC-135R Stratotanker [D] *r/w/bl*	USAF 351st ARS/100th ARW, RAF Mildenhall	
60-0324	Boeing KC-135R Stratotanker [D] *r/w/bl*	USAF 351st ARS/100th ARW, RAF Mildenhall	
60-0333	Boeing KC-135R Stratotanker [D] *r/w/bl*	USAF 351st ARS/100th ARW, RAF Mildenhall	
60-0335	Boeing KC-135T Stratotanker [D] *r/w/bl*	To OK-ALC, Tinker, OK for rework Jul 2024	
60-0353	Boeing KC-135R Stratotanker [D] *r/w/bl*	USAF 351st ARS/100th ARW, RAF Mildenhall	
60-0355	Boeing KC-135R Stratotanker [D] *r/w/bl*	USAF 351st ARS/100th ARW, RAF Mildenhall	
61-0315	Boeing KC-135R Stratotanker [D] *r/w/bl*	USAF 351st ARS/100th ARW, RAF Mildenhall	
62-3540	Boeing KC-135R Stratotanker [D] *r/w/bl*	To OK-ALC, Tinker, OK for rework Jan 2025	
63-8008	Boeing KC-135R Stratotanker [D] *r/w/bl*	USAF 351st ARS/100th ARW, RAF Mildenhall	
63-8878	Boeing KC-135R Stratotanker [D] *r/w/bl*	USAF 351st ARS/100th ARW, RAF Mildenhall	

Dornier C-146A Wolfhound

Serial	Type (code/other identity)	Owner/operator, location or fate	Notes
10-3077	Dornier C-146A Wolfhound (N577EF)	USAF 67th SOS/352nd SOW, RAF Mildenhall	

These aircraft are normally based in Western Europe with the USAFE. They are shown in numerical order of type designation, with individual aircraft in serial number order as carried on the aircraft. Fiscal year (FY) details are also provided if necessary. The unit allocation and operating bases are given for most aircraft.

Notes	Serial	Type (code/other identity)	Owner/operator, location or fate
	Beech C-12 Huron		
	83-0499	Beech C-12D Huron	USAF US Embassy Flight, Taszár, Hungary
	Lockheed (GD) F-16CM/F-16DM Fighting Falcon		
	87-0350	Lockheed (GD) F-16CM-40 Fighting Falcon [AV] $	USAF 555th FS/31st FW, Aviano, Italy
	87-0351	Lockheed (GD) F-16CM-40 Fighting Falcon [AV] gn/y	USAF 555th FS/31st FW, Aviano, Italy
	87-0355	Lockheed (GD) F-16CM-40 Fighting Falcon [AV] pr/w	USAF 510th FS/31st FW, Aviano, Italy
	87-0359	Lockheed (GD) F-16CM-40 Fighting Falcon [AV] gn/y	USAF 555th FS/31st FW, Aviano, Italy
	88-0413	Lockheed (GD) F-16CM-40 Fighting Falcon [AV] pr/w	USAF 510th FS/31st FW, Aviano, Italy
	88-0425	Lockheed (GD) F-16CM-40 Fighting Falcon [AV] gn/y	USAF 555th FS/31st FW, Aviano, Italy
	88-0435	Lockheed (GD) F-16CM-40 Fighting Falcon [AV] gn/y	USAF 555th FS/31st FW, Aviano, Italy
	88-0443	Lockheed (GD) F-16CM-40 Fighting Falcon [AV] pr/w	USAF 510th FS/31st FW, Aviano, Italy
	88-0444	Lockheed (GD) F-16CM-40 Fighting Falcon [AV] pr/w	USAF 510th FS/31st FW, Aviano, Italy
	88-0446	Lockheed (GD) F-16CM-40 Fighting Falcon [AV] gn/y	USAF 555th FS/31st FW, Aviano, Italy
	88-0460	Lockheed (GD) F-16CM-40 Fighting Falcon [AV] gn/y	USAF 555th FS/31st FW, Aviano, Italy
	88-0462	Lockheed (GD) F-16CM-40 Fighting Falcon [AV] pr/w	USAF 510th FS/31st FW, Aviano, Italy
	88-0491	Lockheed (GD) F-16CM-40 Fighting Falcon [AV] pr/w	USAF 510th FS/31st FW, Aviano, Italy
	88-0516	Lockheed (GD) F-16CM-40 Fighting Falcon [AV] pr/w	USAF 510th FS/31st FW, Aviano, Italy
	88-0521	Lockheed (GD) F-16CM-40 Fighting Falcon [AV] pr/w	USAF 510th FS/31st FW, Aviano, Italy
	88-0525	Lockheed (GD) F-16CM-40 Fighting Falcon [AV] pr/w	USAF 510th FS/31st FW, Aviano, Italy
	88-0526	Lockheed (GD) F-16CM-40 Fighting Falcon [AV] gn/y	USAF 555th FS/31st FW, Aviano, Italy
	88-0532	Lockheed (GD) F-16CM-40 Fighting Falcon [AV] gn/y	USAF 555th FS/31st FW, Aviano, Italy
	88-0535	Lockheed (GD) F-16CM-40 Fighting Falcon [AV] $	USAF 555th FS/31st FW, Aviano, Italy
	88-0541	Lockheed (GD) F-16CM-40 Fighting Falcon [AV] pr/w	USAF 510th FS/31st FW, Aviano, Italy
	89-2001	Lockheed (GD) F-16CM-40 Fighting Falcon [AV] gn/y	USAF 555th FS/31st FW, Aviano, Italy
	89-2008	Lockheed (GD) F-16CM-40 Fighting Falcon [AV] pr/w	USAF 510th FS/31st FW, Aviano, Italy
	89-2009	Lockheed (GD) F-16CM-40 Fighting Falcon [AV][31 FW]	USAF 510th FS/31st FW, Aviano, Italy
	89-2011	Lockheed (GD) F-16CM-40 Fighting Falcon [AV] pr/w	USAF 510th FS/31st FW, Aviano, Italy
	89-2016	Lockheed (GD) F-16CM-40 Fighting Falcon [AV] gn/y	USAF 555th FS/31st FW, Aviano, Italy
	89-2018	Lockheed (GD) F-16CM-40 Fighting Falcon [AV] pr/w	USAF 510th FS/31st FW, Aviano, Italy
	89-2023	Lockheed (GD) F-16CM-40 Fighting Falcon [AV] gn/y	USAF 555th FS/31st FW, Aviano, Italy
	89-2024	Lockheed (GD) F-16CM-40 Fighting Falcon [AV] gn/y	USAF 555th FS/31st FW, Aviano, Italy
	89-2026	Lockheed (GD) F-16CM-40 Fighting Falcon [AV] pr/w	USAF 510th FS/31st FW, Aviano, Italy
	89-2029	Lockheed (GD) F-16CM-40 Fighting Falcon [AV] pr/w	USAF 510th FS/31st FW, Aviano, Italy
	89-2030	Lockheed (GD) F-16CM-40 Fighting Falcon [AV] pr/w [510 FS] $	USAF 510th FS/31st FW, Aviano, Italy
	89-2035	Lockheed (GD) F-16CM-40 Fighting Falcon [AV] gn/y	USAF 555th FS/31st FW, Aviano, Italy
	89-2038	Lockheed (GD) F-16CM-40 Fighting Falcon [AV] pr/w	USAF 510th FS/31st FW, Aviano, Italy
	89-2039	Lockheed (GD) F-16CM-40 Fighting Falcon [AV] gn/y	USAF 555th FS/31st FW, Aviano, Italy
	89-2041	Lockheed (GD) F-16CM-40 Fighting Falcon [AV] gn/y	USAF 555th FS/31st FW, Aviano, Italy
	89-2044	Lockheed (GD) F-16CM-40 Fighting Falcon [AV] gn/y	USAF 555th FS/31st FW, Aviano, Italy
	89-2046	Lockheed (GD) F-16CM-40 Fighting Falcon [AV] $	USAF 555th FS/31st FW, Aviano, Italy
	89-2047	Lockheed (GD) F-16CM-40 Fighting Falcon [AV] pr/w	USAF 510th FS/31st FW, Aviano, Italy
	89-2049	Lockheed (GD) F-16CM-40 Fighting Falcon [AV] pr/w	USAF 510th FS/31st FW, Aviano, Italy
	89-2057	Lockheed (GD) F-16CM-40 Fighting Falcon [AV] pr/w	USAF 510th FS/31st FW, Aviano, Italy
	89-2068	Lockheed (GD) F-16CM-40 Fighting Falcon [AV] gn/y	USAF 555th FS/31st FW, Aviano, Italy
	89-2096	Lockheed (GD) F-16CM-40 Fighting Falcon [AV]	USAF 510th FS/31st FW, Aviano, Italy
	89-2102	Lockheed (GD) F-16CM-40 Fighting Falcon [AV]	USAF 510th FS/31st FW, Aviano, Italy
	89-2118	Lockheed (GD) F-16CM-40 Fighting Falcon [AV] gn/y	USAF 555th FS/31st FW, Aviano, Italy
	89-2137	Lockheed (GD) F-16CM-40 Fighting Falcon [AV] m [31 OG]	USAF 555th FS/31st FW, Aviano, Italy
	89-2152	Lockheed (GD) F-16CM-40 Fighting Falcon [AV] gn/y	USAF 555th FS/31st FW, Aviano, Italy
	89-2178	Lockheed (GD) F-16DM-40 Fighting Falcon [AV] pr/w	USAF 510th FS/31st FW, Aviano, Italy
	90-0709	Lockheed (GD) F-16CM-40 Fighting Falcon [AV]	USAF 510th FS/31st FW, Aviano, Italy
	90-0772	Lockheed (GD) F-16CM-40 Fighting Falcon [AV] gn/y	USAF 555th FS/31st FW, Aviano, Italy
	90-0773	Lockheed (GD) F-16CM-40 Fighting Falcon [AV] gn/y	USAF 555th FS/31st FW, Aviano, Italy
	90-0777	Lockheed (GD) F-16DM-40 Fighting Falcon [AV] pr/w	*Returned to USA, 2024*
	90-0800	Lockheed (GD) F-16DM-40 Fighting Falcon [AV] gn/y	USAF 555th FS/31st FW, Aviano, Italy

Serial	Type (code/other identity)	Owner/operator, location or fate	Notes
90-0813	Lockheed (GD) F-16CM-50 Fighting Falcon [SP] r/w	USAF 480th FS/52nd FW, Spangdahlem, Germany	
90-0818	Lockheed (GD) F-16CM-50 Fighting Falcon [SP] r/w	USAF 480th FS/52nd FW, Spangdahlem, Germany	
90-0827	Lockheed (GD) F-16CM-50 Fighting Falcon [SP] r/w	USAF 480th FS/52nd FW, Spangdahlem, Germany	
90-0828	Lockheed (GD) F-16CM-50 Fighting Falcon [SP] r/w	USAF 480th FS/52nd FW, Spangdahlem, Germany	
90-0829	Lockheed (GD) F-16CM-50 Fighting Falcon [SP] r/w [52 OG]	USAF 480th FS/52nd FW, Spangdahlem, Germany	
90-0833	Lockheed (GD) F-16CM-50 Fighting Falcon [SP] r/w	USAF 480th FS/52nd FW, Spangdahlem, Germany	
91-0338	Lockheed (GD) F-16CM-50 Fighting Falcon [SP] r/w	USAF 480th FS/52nd FW, Spangdahlem, Germany	
91-0342	Lockheed (GD) F-16CM-50 Fighting Falcon [SP] r/w	USAF 480th FS/52nd FW, Spangdahlem, Germany	
91-0343	Lockheed (GD) F-16CM-50 Fighting Falcon [SP] r/w	USAF 480th FS/52nd FW, Spangdahlem, Germany	
91-0344	Lockheed (GD) F-16CM-50 Fighting Falcon [SP] r/w	USAF 480th FS/52nd FW, Spangdahlem, Germany	
91-0351	Lockheed (GD) F-16CM-50 Fighting Falcon [SP] r/w	USAF 480th FS/52nd FW, Spangdahlem, Germany	
91-0352	Lockheed (GD) F-16CM-50 Fighting Falcon [SP] m [52 FW]	USAF 480th FS/52nd FW, Spangdahlem, Germany	
91-0358	Lockheed (GD) F-16CM-50 Fighting Falcon [SP] r/w	USAF 480th FS/52nd FW, Spangdahlem, Germany	
91-0360	Lockheed (GD) F-16CM-50 Fighting Falcon [SP] r/w	USAF 480th FS/52nd FW, Spangdahlem, Germany	
91-0361	Lockheed (GD) F-16CM-50 Fighting Falcon [SP] r/w	USAF 480th FS/52nd FW, Spangdahlem, Germany	
91-0402	Lockheed (GD) F-16CM-50 Fighting Falcon [SP] r/w	USAF 480th FS/52nd FW, Spangdahlem, Germany	
91-0403	Lockheed (GD) F-16CM-50 Fighting Falcon [SP] r/w	USAF 480th FS/52nd FW, Spangdahlem, Germany	
91-0407	Lockheed (GD) F-16CM-50 Fighting Falcon [SP] r/w	USAF 480th FS/52nd FW, Spangdahlem, Germany	
91-0412	Lockheed (GD) F-16CM-50 Fighting Falcon [SP] r/w	USAF 480th FS/52nd FW, Spangdahlem, Germany	
91-0416	Lockheed (GD) F-16CM-50 Fighting Falcon [SP] r/w	USAF 480th FS/52nd FW, Spangdahlem, Germany	
91-0417	Lockheed (GD) F-16CM-50 Fighting Falcon [SP] r/w	USAF 480th FS/52nd FW, Spangdahlem, Germany	
91-0418	Lockheed (GD) F-16CM-50 Fighting Falcon [SP] $	USAF 480th FS/52nd FW, Spangdahlem, Germany	
91-0472	Lockheed (GD) F-16DM-50 Fighting Falcon [SP] r/w	USAF 480th FS/52nd FW, Spangdahlem, Germany	
91-0481	Lockheed (GD) F-16DM-50 Fighting Falcon [SP] r/w	USAF 480th FS/52nd FW, Spangdahlem, Germany	
92-3918	Lockheed (GD) F-16CM-50 Fighting Falcon [SP] r/w	USAF 480th FS/52nd FW, Spangdahlem, Germany	
96-0080	Lockheed (GD) F-16CM-50 Fighting Falcon [SP] r/w $ [480 FS]	USAF 480th FS/52nd FW, Spangdahlem, Germany	
96-0083	Lockheed (GD) F-16CM-50 Fighting Falcon [SP] r/w $	USAF 480th FS/52nd FW, Spangdahlem, Germany	

Gates C-21A

84-0083	Gates C-21A Learjet	USAF 76th AS/86th AW, Ramstein, Germany	
84-0085	Gates C-21A Learjet	USAF 76th AS/86th AW, Ramstein, Germany	
84-0087	Gates C-21A Learjet	USAF 76th AS/86th AW, Ramstein, Germany	
84-0096	Gates C-21A Learjet	USAF 76th AS/86th AW, Ramstein, Germany	
84-0126	Gates C-21A Learjet	USAF 76th AS/86th AW, Ramstein, Germany	

Notes	Serial	Type (code/other identity)	Owner/operator, location or fate
	Gulfstream Aerospace C-37A Gulfstream V		
	01-0029	Gulfstream Aerospace C-37A Gulfstream V	USAF 309th AS/86th AW, Chièvres, Belgium
	01-0030	Gulfstream Aerospace C-37A Gulfstream V	USAF 76th AS/86th AW, Ramstein, Germany
	01-0076	Gulfstream Aerospace C-37A Gulfstream V	USAF 76th AS/86th AW, Ramstein, Germany
	Sikorsky HH-60G Pave Hawk		
	87-26007	Sikorsky HH-60G Pave Hawk [AV]	USAF 56th RQS/31st FW, Aviano, Italy
	88-26114	Sikorsky HH-60G Pave Hawk	*To 309th AMARG, July 2024*
	89-26205	Sikorsky HH-60G Pave Hawk [AV]	USAF 56th RQS/31st FW, Aviano, Italy
	89-26208	Sikorsky HH-60G Pave Hawk [AV]	*Returned to the USA, 2024*
	92-26471	Sikorsky HH-60G Pave Hawk [AV]	USAF 56th RQS/31st FW, Aviano, Italy
	97-26774	Sikorsky HH-60G Pave Hawk [AV]	USAF 56th RQS/31st FW, Aviano, Italy
	Sikorsky HH-60W Super Jolly II		
	19-14494	Sikorsky HH-60W Super Jolly II	USAF 56th RQS/31st FW, Aviano, Italy
	..-.....	Sikorsky HH-60W Super Jolly II	USAF 56th RQS/31st FW, Aviano, Italy
	..-.....	Sikorsky HH-60W Super Jolly II	USAF 56th RQS/31st FW, Aviano, Italy
	..-.....	Sikorsky HH-60W Super Jolly II	USAF 56th RQS/31st FW, Aviano, Italy
	..-.....	Sikorsky HH-60W Super Jolly II	USAF 56th RQS/31st FW, Aviano, Italy
	..-.....	Sikorsky HH-60W Super Jolly II	USAF 56th RQS/31st FW, Aviano, Italy
	Lockheed C-130J-30 Hercules II		
	04-3142	Lockheed C-130J-30 Hercules II [RS] *bl/w*	USAF 37th AS/86th AW, Ramstein, Germany
	06-4631	Lockheed C-130J-30 Hercules II [RS] *bl/w*	USAF 37th AS/86th AW, Ramstein, Germany
	07-4635	Lockheed C-130J-30 Hercules II [RS] *bl/w*	USAF 37th AS/86th AW, Ramstein, Germany
	07-8608	Lockheed C-130J-30 Hercules II [RS] *bl/w* $	*Returned to USA, 2024*
	07-8609	Lockheed C-130J-30 Hercules II [RS] *bl/w*	USAF 37th AS/86th AW, Ramstein, Germany
	07-8614	Lockheed C-130J-30 Hercules II [RS] *bl/w*	USAF 37th AS/86th AW, Ramstein, Germany
	08-3176	Lockheed C-130J-30 Hercules II [RS] *bl/w*	USAF 37th AS/86th AW, Ramstein, Germany
	08-5683	Lockheed C-130J-30 Hercules II [RS] *bl/w*	USAF 37th AS/86th AW, Ramstein, Germany
	08-8601	Lockheed C-130J-30 Hercules II [RS] *bl/w* [86 AW]	USAF 37th AS/86th AW, Ramstein, Germany
	08-8602	Lockheed C-130J-30 Hercules II [RS] *bl/w* [86 OG]	USAF 37th AS/86th AW, Ramstein, Germany
	11-5736	Lockheed C-130J-30 Hercules II [RS] *bl/w* $	Stored Ramstein AB (damaged)
	11-5738	Lockheed C-130J-30 Hercules II [RS] *bl/w*	USAF 37th AS/86th AW, Ramstein, Germany
	11-5740	Lockheed C-130J-30 Hercules II [RS] *bl/w* $	USAF 37th AS/86th AW, Ramstein, Germany
	15-5822	Lockheed C-130J-30 Hercules II [RS] *bl/w*	USAF 37th AS/86th AW, Ramstein, Germany
	15-5831	Lockheed C-130J-30 Hercules II [RS] *bl/w*	USAF 37th AS/86th AW, Ramstein, Germany
	16-5840	Lockheed C-130J-30 Hercules II [RS] *bl/w* $	USAF 37th AS/86th AW, Ramstein, Germany
	16-5856	Lockheed C-130J-30 Hercules II [RS] *bl/w*	USAF 37th AS/86th AW, Ramstein, Germany
	16-5883	Lockheed C-130J-30 Hercules II [RS] *bl/w*	USAF 37th AS/86th AW, Ramstein, Germany

Notes	Serial	Type (code/other identity)	Owner/operator, location or fate
	Fairchild C-26D		
	900528	Fairchild C-26D	USN NAF Sigonella, Italy
	900530	Fairchild C-26D	USN NAF Sigonella, Italy
	900531	Fairchild C-26D	USN NAF Naples, Italy
	910502	Fairchild C-26D	USN NAF Naples, Italy

Serial	Type (code/other identity)	Owner/operator, location or fate	Notes
Beech C-12 Huron			
84-00156	Beech C-12U-3 Huron	US Army E/1-214th AVN, Wiesbaden, Germany	
84-00157	Beech C-12U-3 Huron	US Army E/1-214th AVN, Wiesbaden, Germany	
84-00162	Beech C-12U-3 Huron	US Army E/1-214th AVN, Wiesbaden, Germany	
84-00165	Beech C-12U-3 Huron	US Army E/1-214th AVN, Wiesbaden, Germany	
Cessna UC-35A Citation V			
95-00123	Cessna UC-35A Citation V	US Army E/1-214th AVN, Wiesbaden, Germany	
96-00107	Cessna UC-35A Citation V	US Army E/1-214th AVN, Wiesbaden, Germany	
97-00102	Cessna UC-35A Citation V	US Army E/1-214th AVN, Wiesbaden, Germany	
97-00105	Cessna UC-35A Citation V	US Army E/1-214th AVN, Wiesbaden, Germany	
99-00102	Cessna UC-35A Citation V	US Army E/1-214th AVN, Wiesbaden, Germany	
Boeing-Vertol CH-47F Chinook			
13-08132	Boeing-Vertol CH-47F Chinook	US Army B/1-214th AVN, Ansbach, Germany	
13-08133	Boeing-Vertol CH-47F Chinook	US Army B/1-214th AVN, Ansbach, Germany	
13-08134	Boeing-Vertol CH-47F Chinook	US Army B/1-214th AVN, Ansbach, Germany	
13-08135	Boeing-Vertol CH-47F Chinook	*Returned to the USA, 2024*	
13-08432	Boeing-Vertol CH-47F Chinook	US Army B/1-214th AVN, Ansbach, Germany	
13-08434	Boeing-Vertol CH-47F Chinook	US Army B/1-214th AVN, Ansbach, Germany	
13-08435	Boeing-Vertol CH-47F Chinook	US Army B/1-214th AVN, Ansbach, Germany	
13-08436	Boeing-Vertol CH-47F Chinook	US Army B/1-214th AVN, Ansbach, Germany	
13-08437	Boeing-Vertol CH-47F Chinook	US Army B/1-214th AVN, Ansbach, Germany	
14-08162	Boeing-Vertol CH-47F Chinook	US Army B/1-214th AVN, Ansbach, Germany	
15-08176	Boeing-Vertol CH-47F Chinook	US Army B/1-214th AVN, Ansbach, Germany	
15-08178	Boeing-Vertol CH-47F Chinook	US Army B/1-214th AVN, Ansbach, Germany	
Sikorsky H-60 Black Hawk			
91-26319	Sikorsky UH-60V Black Hawk	US Army A/1-214th AVN, Wiesbaden, Germany	
92-26459	Sikorsky UH-60V Black Hawk	US Army A/1-214th AVN, Wiesbaden, Germany	
93-26499	Sikorsky UH-60V Black Hawk	US Army A/1-214th AVN, Wiesbaden, Germany	
94-26566	Sikorsky UH-60V Black Hawk	US Army A/1-214th AVN, Wiesbaden, Germany	
95-26609	Sikorsky UH-60V Black Hawk	US Army A/1-214th AVN, Wiesbaden, Germany	
95-26620	Sikorsky UH-60V Black Hawk	US Army A/1-214th AVN, Wiesbaden, Germany	
96-26666	Sikorsky UH-60V Black Hawk	US Army A/1-214th AVN, Wiesbaden, Germany	
98-26824	Sikorsky UH-60V Black Hawk	US Army A/1-214th AVN, Wiesbaden, Germany	
04-27012	Sikorsky UH-60V Black Hawk	US Army A/1-214th AVN, Wiesbaden, Germany	
04-27014	Sikorsky UH-60V Black Hawk	US Army A/1-214th AVN, Wiesbaden, Germany	
10-20245	Sikorsky UH-60M Black Hawk	*Returned to the USA, 2024*	
15-20742	Sikorsky UH-60M Black Hawk	*Returned to the USA, 2024*	
15-20743	Sikorsky UH-60M Black Hawk	*Returned to the USA, 2024*	
15-20754	Sikorsky UH-60M Black Hawk	*Returned to the USA, 2023*	
20-21128	Sikorsky HH-60M Black Hawk	US Army C/1-214th AVN, Grafenwöhr, Germany	
20-21129	Sikorsky HH-60M Black Hawk	US Army C/1-214th AVN, Grafenwöhr, Germany	
20-21130	Sikorsky HH-60M Black Hawk	US Army C/1-214th AVN, Grafenwöhr, Germany	
20-21131	Sikorsky HH-60M Black Hawk	US Army C/1-214th AVN, Grafenwöhr, Germany	
20-21132	Sikorsky HH-60M Black Hawk	US Army C/1-214th AVN, Grafenwöhr, Germany	
20-21133	Sikorsky HH-60M Black Hawk	US Army C/1-214th AVN, Grafenwöhr, Germany	
21-21200	Sikorsky HH-60M Black Hawk	US Army C/1-214th AVN, Grafenwöhr, Germany	
MDH AH-64D Apache			
08-07049	MDH AH-64D Apache	*Returned to the USA, 2023*	
08-07051	MDH AH-64D Apache	*Returned to the USA, 2023*	
09-05580	MDH AH-64D Apache	*Returned to the USA, 2023*	
09-05581	MDH AH-64D Apache	*Returned to the USA, 2023*	
09-05587	MDH AH-64D Apache	*Returned to the USA, 2023*	
09-05589	MDH AH-64D Apache	*Returned to the USA, 2023*	
09-05591	MDH AH-64D Apache	*Returned to the USA, 2023*	
09-05596	MDH AH-64D Apache	*Returned to the USA, 2023*	
09-05597	MDH AH-64D Apache	*Returned to the USA, 2023*	

Notes	Serial	Type (code/other identity)	Owner/operator, location or fate
	Boeing AH-64E Apache Guardian		
	21-03424	Boeing AH-64E Apache Guardian	US Army 1-3rd AVN, Ansbach, Germany
	21-03429	Boeing AH-64E Apache Guardian	US Army 1-3rd AVN, Ansbach, Germany
	21-03434	Boeing AH-64E Apache Guardian	US Army 1-3rd AVN, Ansbach, Germany
	22-03456	Boeing AH-64E Apache Guardian	US Army 1-3rd AVN, Ansbach, Germany
	22-03462	Boeing AH-64E Apache Guardian	US Army 1-3rd AVN, Ansbach, Germany
	22-03463	Boeing AH-64E Apache Guardian	US Army 1-3rd AVN, Ansbach, Germany
	22-03465	Boeing AH-64E Apache Guardian	US Army 1-3rd AVN, Ansbach, Germany
	22-03466	Boeing AH-64E Apache Guardian	US Army 1-3rd AVN, Ansbach, Germany
	22-03467	Boeing AH-64E Apache Guardian	US Army 1-3rd AVN, Ansbach, Germany
	22-03471	Boeing AH-64E Apache Guardian	US Army 1-3rd AVN, Ansbach, Germany
	22-03472	Boeing AH-64E Apache Guardian	US Army 1-3rd AVN, Ansbach, Germany
	22-03473	Boeing AH-64E Apache Guardian	US Army 1-3rd AVN, Ansbach, Germany
	Eurocopter UH-72A Lakota		
	07-72029	Eurocopter UH-72A Lakota	US Army JMRC, Hohenfels, Germany
	09-72097	Eurocopter UH-72A Lakota	US Army JMRC, Hohenfels, Germany
	09-72098	Eurocopter UH-72A Lakota	US Army JMRC, Hohenfels, Germany
	09-72100	Eurocopter UH-72A Lakota	US Army JMRC, Hohenfels, Germany
	09-72105	Eurocopter UH-72A Lakota	US Army JMRC, Hohenfels, Germany
	09-72106	Eurocopter UH-72A Lakota	US Army JMRC, Hohenfels, Germany
	09-72107	Eurocopter UH-72A Lakota	US Army JMRC, Hohenfels, Germany
	09-72108	Eurocopter UH-72A Lakota	US Army JMRC, Hohenfels, Germany

US-BASED USAF AIRCRAFT

The following aircraft are normally based in the USA but are likely to be seen visiting the UK from time to time. The presentation is in numerical order of the type, commencing with the **B-1B** and concluding with the **C-146A**. The aircraft are listed in numerical progression by Fiscal Year (FY). Where possible, operating units and markings carried are noted. Where base-code letter information is carried on the aircrafts' tails, this is detailed with the squadron/base data; for example, 7th Wing's B-1B 86-0105 carries the letters DY on its tail, thus identifying the Wing's home base as Dyess AFB, Texas.

Notes	Serial	Type (code/other identity)	Owner/operator, location or fate
	Rockwell B-1B Lancer		
	NOTE: The active B-1B fleet from Ellsworth AFB have moved to Grand Forks AFB for a period of 10 months, starting in December 2024, whilst Ellsworth undergoes infrastructure work to ready the base for the arrival of the first B-21 Raider bombers.		
	85-0059	Rockwell B-1B Lancer [DY] *bl/w*	USAF 28th BS/7th BW, Dyess AFB, TX
	85-0060	Rockwell B-1B Lancer [EL] *bk/r* $	USAF 34th BS/28th BW, Ellsworth AFB, SD
	85-0061	Rockwell B-1B Lancer [DY] *bl/w*	USAF 28th BS/7th BW, Dyess AFB, TX
	85-0064	Rockwell B-1B Lancer [DY]	USAF 9th BS/7th BW, Dyess AFB, TX
	85-0068	Rockwell B-1B Lancer [ED] *bl/w*	USAF 419th FLTS/412th TW, Edwards AFB
	85-0069	Rockwell B-1B Lancer [EL] *bk/r*	USAF 34th BS/28th BW, Ellsworth AFB, SD
	85-0072	Rockwell B-1B Lancer [EL] *bk/r*	USAF 34th BS/28th BW, Ellsworth AFB, SD
	85-0073	Rockwell B-1B Lancer [DY] *bl/w* [7 OG]	USAF 28th BS/7th BW, Dyess AFB, TX
	85-0075	Rockwell B-1B Lancer [ED] *bl/w*	USAF 419th FLTS/412th TW, Edwards AFB
	85-0079	Rockwell B-1B Lancer [DY]	USAF 7th BW, Dyess AFB, TX
	85-0084	Rockwell B-1B Lancer [EL] *bk/r*	USAF 34th BS/28th BW, Ellsworth AFB, SD
	85-0088	Rockwell B-1B Lancer [DY] *bk/w*	USAF 9th BS/7th BW, Dyess AFB, TX
	86-0094	Rockwell B-1B Lancer [EL] *bk/y* $	USAF 37th BS/28th BW, Ellsworth AFB, SD
	86-0095	Rockwell B-1B Lancer [EL] *bk/r*	USAF 34th BS/28th BW, Ellsworth AFB, SD
	86-0097	Rockwell B-1B Lancer [DY] *bk/w* [9 BS]	USAF 9th BS/7th BW, Dyess AFB, TX
	86-0098	Rockwell B-1B Lancer [DY] *bl/w*	USAF 28th BS/7th BW, Dyess AFB, TX
	86-0102	Rockwell B-1B Lancer [EL] *bk/y*	USAF 37th BS/28th BW, Ellsworth AFB, SD
	86-0103	Rockwell B-1B Lancer [DY] *bk/w*	USAF 9th BS/7th BW, Dyess AFB, TX
	86-0104	Rockwell B-1B Lancer [EL] *bk/y*	USAF 37th BS/28th BW, Ellsworth AFB, SD
	86-0105	Rockwell B-1B Lancer [DY] *bl/w*	USAF 28th BS/7th BW, Dyess AFB, TX
	86-0107	Rockwell B-1B Lancer [DY] *bl/w*	USAF 28th BS/7th BW, Dyess AFB, TX
	86-0108	Rockwell B-1B Lancer [EL] *bk/y*	USAF 37th BS/28th BW, Ellsworth AFB, SD
	86-0110	Rockwell B-1B Lancer [DY] *bk/w*	USAF 9th BS/7th BW, Dyess AFB, TX

Serial	Type (code/other identity)	Owner/operator, location or fate	Notes
86-0111	Rockwell B-1B Lancer [EL] bk/r	USAF 34th BS/28th BW, Ellsworth AFB, SD	
86-0112	Rockwell B-1B Lancer [DY] bl/w	USAF 28th BS/7th BW, Dyess AFB, TX	
86-0113	Rockwell B-1B Lancer [EL] bk/y	USAF 37th BS/28th BW, Ellsworth AFB, SD	
86-0115	Rockwell B-1B Lancer [EL] bk/r	USAF 34th BS/28th BW, Ellsworth AFB, SD	
86-0117	Rockwell B-1B Lancer [DY] [7 BW]	USAF 7th BW, Dyess AFB, TX	
86-0119	Rockwell B-1B Lancer [DY] bl/w	USAF 28th BS/7th BW, Dyess AFB, TX	
86-0120	Rockwell B-1B Lancer [EL] bk/y	USAF 37th BS/28th BW, Ellsworth AFB, SD	
86-0121	Rockwell B-1B Lancer [EL] bk/y	USAF 37th BS/28th BW, Ellsworth AFB, SD	
86-0122	Rockwell B-1B Lancer [DY] bk/w [337 TES/CC]	USAF 9th BS/7th BW, Dyess AFB, TX	
86-0124	Rockwell B-1B Lancer [DY] bk/w	USAF 9th BS/7th BW, Dyess AFB, TX	
86-0125	Rockwell B-1B Lancer [DY] bl/w	USAF 9th BS/7th BW, Dyess AFB, TX	
86-0126	Rockwell B-1B Lancer [DY] bl/w	Withdrawn from use, Palmdale, CA	
86-0127	Rockwell B-1B Lancer [DY] bk/w	USAF 9th BS/7th BW, Dyess AFB, TX	
86-0129	Rockwell B-1B Lancer [EL] bk/r [28 BW]	USAF 34th BS/28th BW, Ellsworth AFB, SD	
86-0134	Rockwell B-1B Lancer [EL] bk/r [34 BS]	USAF 34th BS/28th BW, Ellsworth AFB, SD	
86-0135	Rockwell B-1B Lancer [OT] r/gy [53 WG/337 CC]	USAF 337th TES/53rd Wg, Dyess AFB, TX	
86-0136	Rockwell B-1B Lancer [DY] bl/w	USAF 28th BS/7th BW, Dyess AFB, TX	
86-0137	Rockwell B-1B Lancer [EL] bk/y [37 BS]	USAF 37th BS/28th BW, Ellsworth AFB, SD	
86-0138	Rockwell B-1B Lancer [EL] bk/y	USAF 37th BS/28th BW, Ellsworth AFB, SD	
86-0139	Rockwell B-1B Lancer [EL] bl/y [34 BS]	USAF 34th BS/28th BW, Ellsworth AFB, SD	
86-0140	Rockwell B-1B Lancer [DY] bk/r [345 BS/CC]	USAF 28th BS/7th BW, Dyess AFB, TX	

Northrop B-2 Spirit
(Names are given below. Each begins *Spirit of ...*)

82-1066	Northrop B-2 Spirit [WM] America	USAF 509th BW, Whiteman AFB, MO	
82-1067	Northrop B-2 Spirit [WM] Arizona	USAF 509th BW, Whiteman AFB, MO	
82-1068	Northrop B-2 Spirit [WM] New York	Withdrawn from use, Whiteman AFB, MO (damaged)	
82-1069	Northrop B-2 Spirit [WM] Indiana	USAF 509th BW, Whiteman AFB, MO	
82-1070	Northrop B-2 Spirit [WM] Ohio	USAF 509th BW, Whiteman AFB, MO	
82-1071	Northrop B-2 Spirit [WM] Mississippi	USAF 509th BW, Whiteman AFB, MO	
88-0328	Northrop B-2 Spirit [WM] Texas	USAF 509th BW, Whiteman AFB, MO	
88-0329	Northrop B-2 Spirit [WM] Missouri	USAF 509th BW, Whiteman AFB, MO	
88-0330	Northrop B-2 Spirit [WM] California	USAF 509th BW, Whiteman AFB, MO	
88-0331	Northrop B-2 Spirit [WM] South Carolina	USAF 509th BW, Whiteman AFB, MO	
88-0332	Northrop B-2 Spirit [WM] Washington	USAF 509th BW, Whiteman AFB, MO	
89-0128	Northrop B-2 Spirit [WM] Nebraska	USAF 509th BW, Whiteman AFB, MO	
89-0129	Northrop B-2 Spirit [WM] Georgia	USAF/LMTAS, Palmdale, CA (repairs)	
90-0040	Northrop B-2 Spirit [WM] Alaska	USAF 509th BW, Whiteman AFB, MO	
90-0041	Northrop B-2 Spirit [WM] Hawaii	USAF 509th BW, Whiteman AFB, MO	
92-0700	Northrop B-2 Spirit [WM] Florida	USAF 509th BW, Whiteman AFB, MO	
93-1085	Northrop B-2 Spirit [ED] Oklahoma	USAF 419th FLTS/412th TW, Edwards AFB, CA	
93-1086	Northrop B-2 Spirit [WM] Kitty Hawk	USAF 509th BW, Whiteman AFB, MO	
93-1087	Northrop B-2 Spirit [ED] Pennsylvania	USAF 419th FLTS/412th TW, Edwards AFB, CA	
93-1088	Northrop B-2 Spirit [WM] Louisiana	USAF 509th BW, Whiteman AFB, MO	

Lockheed U-2S Dragon Lady

68-10329	Lockheed U-2S	USAF 9th RW, Beale AFB, CA	
68-10331	Lockheed U-2S [BB]	USAF 9th RW, Beale AFB, CA	
68-10336	Lockheed U-2S [BB]	USAF 9th RW, Beale AFB, CA	
68-10337	Lockheed U-2S [BB]	USAF 9th RW, Beale AFB, CA	
80-1064	Lockheed TU-2S [BB]	USAF 9th RW, Beale AFB, CA	
80-1065	Lockheed TU-2S [BB]	Withdrawn from use, Beale AFB, CA	
80-1066	Lockheed U-2S [BB]	USAF 9th RW, Beale AFB, CA	
80-1067	Lockheed U-2S [BB]	USAF 9th RW, Beale AFB, CA	
80-1069	Lockheed U-2S [BB]	USAF 9th RW, Beale AFB, CA	
80-1070	Lockheed U-2S [BB]	USAF 9th RW, Beale AFB, CA	
80-1071	Lockheed U-2S [BB]	USAF 9th RW, Beale AFB, CA	
80-1073	Lockheed U-2S [BB]	USAF 9th RW, Beale AFB, CA	
80-1074	Lockheed U-2S [BB]	USAF 9th RW, Beale AFB, CA	
80-1076	Lockheed U-2S [BB]	USAF 9th RW, Beale AFB, CA	
80-1077	Lockheed U-2S [BB]	USAF 9th RW, Beale AFB, CA	

Notes	Serial	Type (code/other identity)	Owner/operator, location or fate
	80-1078	Lockheed TU-2S [BB]	USAF 9th RW, Beale AFB, CA
	80-1079	Lockheed U-2S [BB]	USAF 9th RW, Beale AFB, CA
	80-1080	Lockheed U-2S	USAF 9th RW, Beale AFB, CA
	80-1081	Lockheed U-2S [BB]	USAF 9th RW, Beale AFB, CA
	80-1083	Lockheed U-2S [BB]	USAF 9th RW, Beale AFB, CA
	80-1084	Lockheed U-2S [BB]	USAF 9th RW, Beale AFB, CA
	80-1085	Lockheed U-2S [BB]	*Withdrawn from use, Beale AFB, CA*
	80-1086	Lockheed U-2S [BB]	USAF 9th RW, Beale AFB, CA
	80-1087	Lockheed U-2S [BB]	USAF 9th RW, Beale AFB, CA
	80-1089	Lockheed U-2S [BB]	*Damaged Al Dhafra, UAE, 2017*
	80-1090	Lockheed U-2S [BB]	USAF 9th RW, Beale AFB, CA
	80-1091	Lockheed TU-2S [BB]	USAF 9th RW, Beale AFB, CA
	80-1092	Lockheed U-2S [BB]	USAF 9th RW, Beale AFB, CA
	80-1093	Lockheed U-2S [BB]	USAF 9th RW, Beale AFB, CA
	80-1094	Lockheed U-2S [BB]	USAF 9th RW, Beale AFB, CA
	80-1096	Lockheed U-2S [BB]	USAF 9th RW, Beale AFB, CA
	80-1099	Lockheed U-2S [BB]	USAF/LMTAS, Palmdale, CA (rebuild)

Boeing E-3 Sentry

Notes	Serial	Type (code/other identity)	Owner/operator, location or fate
	71-1407	Boeing E-3B Sentry [OK] *w*	USAF 960th AACS/552nd ACW, Tinker AFB, OK
	75-0556	Boeing E-3G Sentry [OK] *bl/bk*	USAF 552nd ACW, Tinker AFB, OK
	75-0558	Boeing E-3G Sentry [OK] *r*	USAF 964th AACS/552nd ACW, Tinker AFB, OK
	76-1604	Boeing E-3G Sentry [OK] *r*	USAF 964th ACCS/552nd ACW, Tinker AFB, OK
	76-1605	Boeing E-3G Sentry [OK] *r*	USAF 964th AACS/552nd ACW, Tinker AFB, OK
	76-1607	Boeing E-3G Sentry [OK] *w*	USAF 960th AACS/552nd ACW, Tinker AFB, OK
	77-0351	Boeing E-3G Sentry [OK] *r*	USAF 964th AACS/552nd ACW, Tinker AFB, OK
	77-0352	Boeing E-3B Sentry [ZZ] *or*	*To 309th AMARG, September 2024*
	77-0356	Boeing E-3G Sentry [OK] *w*	USAF 960th AACS/552nd ACW, Tinker AFB, OK
	78-0577	Boeing E-3G Sentry [OK] *r*	USAF 964th AACS/552nd ACW, Tinker AFB, OK
	78-0578	Boeing E-3G Sentry [OK] *w/y/r*	USAF 964th AACS/552nd ACW, Tinker AFB, OK
	79-0001	Boeing E-3G Sentry [OK] *m* [552 ACW]	USAF 552nd ACW, Tinker AFB, OK
	79-0002	Boeing E-3G Sentry [OK] *r*	USAF 964th AACS/552nd ACW, Tinker AFB, OK
	80-0137	Boeing E-3C Sentry [OK] *w*	USAF 960th AACS/552nd ACW, Tinker AFB, OK
	80-0138	Boeing E-3G Sentry [OK] *r*	USAF 964th AACS/552nd ACW, Tinker AFB, OK
	81-0004	Boeing E-3G Sentry [AK] *gn*	USAF 962nd AACS/3rd Wg, Elmendorf, AK
	81-0005	Boeing E-3G Sentry [ZZ] *or*	USAF 961st AACS/18th Wg, Kadena AB, Japan
	82-0006	Boeing E-3G Sentry [OK] *r*	USAF 964th AACS/552nd ACW, Tinker AFB, OK
	82-0007	Boeing E-3G Sentry [ZZ] *or*	USAF 961st AACS/18th Wg, Kadena AB, Japan

Boeing E-4

Notes	Serial	Type (code/other identity)	Owner/operator, location or fate
	73-1676	Boeing E-4B	USAF 1st ACCS/595th CACG, Offutt AFB, NE
	73-1677	Boeing E-4B	USAF 1st ACCS/595th CACG, Offutt AFB, NE
	74-0787	Boeing E-4B	USAF 1st ACCS/595th CACG, Offutt AFB, NE
	75-0125	Boeing E-4B	USAF 1st ACCS/595th CACG, Offutt AFB, NE
	......	Boeing 747-8B5 (HL7630)	Sierra Nevada Corporation, Dayton, OH (for conversion to E-4C SAOC)
	......	Boeing 747-8B5 (HL7631)	Sierra Nevada Corporation, Dayton, OH (for conversion to E-4C SAOC)

Lockheed C-5M Super Galaxy

Notes	Serial	Type (code/other identity)	Owner/operator, location or fate
	68-0213	Lockheed C-5M Super Galaxy *w/bk*	USAF 22nd AS/60th AMW, Travis AFB, CA
	68-0216	Lockheed C-5M Super Galaxy *w/bk*	USAF 22nd AS/60th AMW, Travis AFB, CA
	69-0024	Lockheed C-5M Super Galaxy *bl/y*	USAF 9th AS/436th AW, Dover AFB, DE
	83-1285	Lockheed C-5M Super Galaxy *bl/y*	USAF 9th AS/436th AW, Dover AFB, DE
	84-0060	Lockheed C-5M Super Galaxy *w/bk*	USAF 22nd AS/60th AMW, Travis AFB, CA
	84-0061	Lockheed C-5M Super Galaxy *bl/y*	USAF 9th AS/436th AW, Dover AFB, DE
	84-0062	Lockheed C-5M Super Galaxy *w/bk*	USAF 22nd AS/60th AMW, Travis AFB, CA
	85-0001	Lockheed C-5M Super Galaxy *bl/y*	USAF 9th AS/436th AW, Dover AFB, DE
	85-0002	Lockheed C-5M Super Galaxy *bl/y*	USAF 9th AS/436th AW, Dover AFB, DE
	85-0003	Lockheed C-5M Super Galaxy *bl/y*	USAF 9th AS/436th AW, Dover AFB, DE
	85-0004	Lockheed C-5M Super Galaxy *bl/y*	USAF 9th AS/436th AW, Dover AFB, DE
	85-0005	Lockheed C-5M Super Galaxy *bl/y*	USAF 9th AS/436th AW, Dover AFB, DE

Serial	Type (code/other identity)	Owner/operator, location or fate	Notes
85-0006	Lockheed C-5M Super Galaxy r/w/bl	USAF 68th AS/433rd AW AFRC, Kelly AFB, TX	
85-0007	Lockheed C-5M Super Galaxy bl/y	USAF 9th AS/436th AW, Dover AFB, DE	
85-0008	Lockheed C-5M Super Galaxy bl/y	USAF 9th AS/436th AW, Dover AFB, DE	
85-0009	Lockheed C-5M Super Galaxy r/w/bl	USAF 68th AS/433rd AW AFRC, Kelly AFB, TX	
85-0010	Lockheed C-5M Super Galaxy w/bk	USAF 22nd AS/60th AMW, Travis AFB, CA	
86-0011	Lockheed C-5M Super Galaxy w/bk	USAF 22nd AS/60th AMW, Travis AFB, CA	
86-0012	Lockheed C-5M Super Galaxy bl/r	USAF 337th AS/439th AW, Westover ARB, MA	
86-0013	Lockheed C-5M Super Galaxy r/w/bl	USAF 68th AS/433rd AW AFRC, Kelly AFB, TX	
86-0014	Lockheed C-5M Super Galaxy bl/r	USAF 337th AS/439th AW, Westover ARB, MA	
86-0015	Lockheed C-5M Super Galaxy r/w/bl	USAF 68th AS/433rd AW AFRC, Kelly AFB, TX	
86-0016	Lockheed C-5M Super Galaxy w/bk	USAF 22nd AS/60th AMW, Travis AFB, CA	
86-0017	Lockheed C-5M Super Galaxy bl/y	USAF 9th AS/436th AW, Dover AFB, DE	
86-0018	Lockheed C-5M Super Galaxy r/w/bl	USAF 68th AS/433rd AW AFRC, Kelly AFB, TX	
86-0019	Lockheed C-5M Super Galaxy r/w/bl	USAF 68th AS/433rd AW AFRC, Kelly AFB, TX	
86-0020	Lockheed C-5M Super Galaxy bl/y	USAF 9th AS/436th AW, Dover AFB, DE	
86-0021	Lockheed C-5M Super Galaxy bl/y	USAF 9th AS/436th AW, Dover AFB, DE	
86-0022	Lockheed C-5M Super Galaxy w/bk	USAF 22nd AS/60th AMW, Travis AFB, CA	
86-0023	Lockheed C-5M Super Galaxy w/bk	USAF 22nd AS/60th AMW, Travis AFB, CA	
86-0024	Lockheed C-5M Super Galaxy w/bk	USAF 22nd AS/60th AMW, Travis AFB, CA	
86-0025	Lockheed C-5M Super Galaxy bl/y	USAF 9th AS/436th AW, Dover AFB, DE	
86-0026	Lockheed C-5M Super Galaxy w/bk	USAF 22nd AS/60th AMW, Travis AFB, CA	
87-0027	Lockheed C-5M Super Galaxy	USAF 337th AS/439th AW, Westover ARB, MA	
87-0028	Lockheed C-5M Super Galaxy w/bk	USAF 22nd AS/60th AMW, Travis AFB, CA	
87-0029	Lockheed C-5M Super Galaxy w/bk	USAF 22nd AS/60th AMW, Travis AFB, CA	
87-0030	Lockheed C-5M Super Galaxy w/bk	USAF 22nd AS/60th AMW, Travis AFB, CA	
87-0031	Lockheed C-5M Super Galaxy bl/r	USAF 337th AS/439th AW, Westover ARB, MA	
87-0032	Lockheed C-5M Super Galaxy w/bk	USAF 22nd AS/60th AMW, Travis AFB, CA	
87-0033	Lockheed C-5M Super Galaxy r/w/bl	USAF 68th AS/433rd AW AFRC, Kelly AFB, TX	
87-0034	Lockheed C-5M Super Galaxy w/bk	USAF 22nd AS/60th AMW, Travis AFB, CA	
87-0035	Lockheed C-5M Super Galaxy bl/y	USAF 9th AS/436th AW, Dover AFB, DE	
87-0036	Lockheed C-5M Super Galaxy bl/y	USAF 9th AS/436th AW, Dover AFB, DE	
87-0037	Lockheed C-5M Super Galaxy bl/r	USAF 337th AS/439th AW, Westover ARB, MA	
87-0038	Lockheed C-5M Super Galaxy r/w/bl	USAF 68th AS/433rd AW AFRC, Kelly AFB, TX	
87-0039	Lockheed C-5M Super Galaxy bl/r	USAF 337th AS/439th AW, Westover ARB, MA	
87-0040	Lockheed C-5M Super Galaxy bl/y	USAF 9th AS/436th AW, Dover AFB, DE	
87-0041	Lockheed C-5M Super Galaxy bl/r	USAF 337th AS/439th AW, Westover ARB, MA	
87-0042	Lockheed C-5M Super Galaxy w/bk	USAF 22nd AS/60th AMW, Travis AFB, CA	
87-0043	Lockheed C-5M Super Galaxy bl/r	USAF 337th AS/439th AW, Westover ARB, MA	
87-0044	Lockheed C-5M Super Galaxy w/bk	USAF 22nd AS/60th AMW, Travis AFB, CA	
87-0045	Lockheed C-5M Super Galaxy bl/y	USAF 9th AS/436th AW, Dover AFB, DE	

McDonnell Douglas KC-10A Extender

Serial	Type (code/other identity)	Owner/operator, location or fate	Notes
79-1948	McDonnell Douglas KC-10A Extender w/bk	To 309th AMARG, 26th September 2024	
82-0193	McDonnell Douglas KC-10A Extender w/bk	To 309th AMARG, 11th April 2024	
83-0078	McDonnell Douglas KC-10A Extender w/bk	To 309th AMARG, 18th June 2024	
84-0186	McDonnell Douglas KC-10A Extender	To 309th AMARG, 21st December 2023	
84-0191	McDonnell Douglas KC-10A Extender w/bk	To USAF Museum, Wright-Patterson AFB, OH	
85-0029	McDonnell Douglas KC-10A Extender w/bk	To 309th AMARG, 9th May 2024	
85-0033	McDonnell Douglas KC-10A Extender w/bk	To 309th AMARG, 27th June 2024	
86-0027	McDonnell Douglas KC-10A Extender	To 309th AMARG, 2nd May 2024	
86-0030	McDonnell Douglas KC-10A Extender w/bk	To 309th AMARG, 11th June 2024	
86-0031	McDonnell Douglas KC-10A Extender w/bk	To 309th AMARG, 5th September 2024	
86-0032	McDonnell Douglas KC-10A Extender	To 309th AMARG, 7th March 2024	
86-0033	McDonnell Douglas KC-10A Extender w/bk	To 309th AMARG, 23rd May 2024	
86-0038	McDonnell Douglas KC-10A Extender w/bk	To 309th AMARG, 22nd August 2024	
87-0119	McDonnell Douglas KC-10A Extender w/bk	To 309th AMARG, 1st August 2024	

Bombardier E-11A Global Express

Serial	Type (code/other identity)	Owner/operator, location or fate	Notes
11-9001	Bombardier E-11A Global Express	USAF 430th EECS/653rd ELSG, Hanscom, MA	
11-9355	Bombardier E-11A Global Express	USAF 430th EECS/653rd ELSG, Hanscom, MA	
12-9506	Bombardier E-11A Global Express	USAF 430th EECS/653rd ELSG, Hanscom, MA	
21-9045	Bombardier E-11A Global Express	USAF 430th EECS/653rd ELSG, Hanscom, MA	

US-BASED USAF AIRCRAFT

Notes	Serial	Type (code/other identity)	Owner/operator, location or fate
	22-9046	Bombardier E-11A Global Express	USAF 18th ACCS/319th RW, Robins AFB, GA
	22-9047	Bombardier E-11A Global Express	USAF 18th ACCS/319th RW, Robins AFB, GA
	McDonnell Douglas F-15E Strike Eagle		
	86-0184	McD F-15E Strike Eagle [ET] *bk/wh*	USAF 40th FLTS/96th TW, Eglin AFB, FL
	86-0185	McD F-15E Strike Eagle [ET] *bk/wh*	USAF 40th FLTS/96th TW, Eglin AFB, FL
	86-0186	McD F-15E Strike Eagle [SJ] *bl*	USAF 334th FS/4th FW, Seymour-Johnson AFB, NC
	86-0187	McD F-15E Strike Eagle [SJ] *gn*	USAF 335th FS/4th FW, Seymour-Johnson AFB, NC
	86-0188	McD F-15E Strike Eagle [ET] *bk/wh*	USAF 40th FLTS/96th TW, Eglin AFB, FL
	86-0189	McD F-15E Strike Eagle [SJ] *bl*	USAF 334th FS/4th FW, Seymour-Johnson AFB, NC
	86-0190	McD F-15E Strike Eagle [SJ]	USAF 333rd FS/4th FW, Seymour-Johnson AFB, NC
	87-0169	McD F-15E Strike Eagle [MO] *r/y*	USAF 389th FS/366th FW, Mountain Home AFB, ID
	87-0170	McD F-15E Strike Eagle [MO] *r/y*	USAF 389th FS/366th FW, Mountain Home AFB, ID
	87-0171	McD F-15E Strike Eagle [SJ] *gn*	USAF 335th FS/4th FW, Seymour-Johnson AFB, NC
	87-0173	McD F-15E Strike Eagle [MO] *r/y*	USAF 389th FS/366th FW, Mountain Home AFB, ID
	87-0174	McD F-15E Strike Eagle [SJ] *gn*	USAF 335th FS/4th FW, Seymour-Johnson AFB, NC
	87-0175	McD F-15E Strike Eagle [SJ] *gn*	USAF 335th FS/4th FW, Seymour-Johnson AFB, NC
	87-0176	McD F-15E Strike Eagle [SJ] *y*	USAF 336th FS/4th FW, Seymour-Johnson AFB, NC
	87-0177	McD F-15E Strike Eagle [SJ] *y*	USAF 336th FS/4th FW, Seymour-Johnson AFB, NC
	87-0178	McD F-15E Strike Eagle [SJ] *bl*	USAF 334th FS/4th FW, Seymour-Johnson AFB, NC
	87-0179	McD F-15E Strike Eagle [SJ] *r*	USAF 333rd FS/4th FW, Seymour-Johnson AFB, NC
	87-0180	McD F-15E Strike Eagle [ET] *bk/wh*	USAF 40th FLTS/96th TW, Eglin AFB, FL
	87-0181	McD F-15E Strike Eagle [SJ] *gn*	USAF 335th FS/4th FW, Seymour-Johnson AFB, NC
	87-0182	McD F-15E Strike Eagle [MO] *r/y*	USAF 389th FS/366th FW, Mountain Home AFB, ID
	87-0183	McD F-15E Strike Eagle [MO] *r/y*	USAF 389th FS/366th FW, Mountain Home AFB, ID
	87-0184	McD F-15E Strike Eagle [SJ] *bl*	USAF 334th FS/4th FW, Seymour-Johnson AFB, NC
	87-0185	McD F-15E Strike Eagle [SJ] *r*	USAF 333rd FS/4th FW, Seymour-Johnson AFB, NC
	87-0187	McD F-15E Strike Eagle [SJ] *r*	USAF 333rd FS/4th FW, Seymour-Johnson AFB, NC
	87-0188	McD F-15E Strike Eagle [SJ] *r*	USAF 333rd FS/4th FW, Seymour-Johnson AFB, NC
	87-0189	McD F-15E Strike Eagle [SJ] *r $*	USAF 333rd FS/4th FW, Seymour-Johnson AFB, NC
	87-0190	McD F-15E Strike Eagle [SJ]	USAF 4th FW, Seymour-Johnson AFB, NC
	87-0191	McD F-15E Strike Eagle [SJ] *r*	USAF 333rd FS/4th FW, Seymour-Johnson AFB, NC
	87-0192	McD F-15E Strike Eagle [SJ] *gn*	USAF 335th FS/4th FW, Seymour-Johnson AFB, NC
	87-0193	McD F-15E Strike Eagle [SJ] *gn*	USAF 335th FS/4th FW, Seymour-Johnson AFB, NC
	87-0194	McD F-15E Strike Eagle [SJ]	USAF 335th FS/4th FW, Seymour-Johnson AFB, NC

Serial	Type (code/other identity)	Owner/operator, location or fate	Notes
87-0195	McD F-15E Strike Eagle [SJ] y	USAF 336th FS/4th FW, Seymour-Johnson AFB, NC	
87-0196	McD F-15E Strike Eagle [SJ] y	USAF 336th FS/4th FW, Seymour-Johnson AFB, NC	
87-0197	McD F-15E Strike Eagle [SJ] bl	USAF 334th FS/4th FW, Seymour-Johnson AFB, NC	
87-0198	McD F-15E Strike Eagle [MO] r/y	USAF 389th FS/366th FW, Mountain Home AFB, ID	
87-0199	McD F-15E Strike Eagle [SJ] r	USAF 333rd FS/4th FW, Seymour-Johnson AFB, NC	
87-0200	McD F-15E Strike Eagle [SJ] bl $ [334 FS]	USAF 334th FS/4th FW, Seymour-Johnson AFB, NC	
87-0201	McD F-15E Strike Eagle [MO] r/y	USAF 389th FS/366th FW, Mountain Home AFB, ID	
87-0202	McD F-15E Strike Eagle [MO] r/y	USAF 389th FS/366th FW, Mountain Home AFB, ID	
87-0204	McD F-15E Strike Eagle [MO] r/y [366 OG]	USAF 389th FS/366th FW, Mountain Home AFB, ID	
87-0205	McD F-15E Strike Eagle [SJ] bl	USAF 334th FS/4th FW, Seymour-Johnson AFB, NC	
87-0206	McD F-15E Strike Eagle [SJ] y	USAF 336th FS/4th FW, Seymour-Johnson AFB, NC	
87-0207	McD F-15E Strike Eagle [MO] r/y	USAF 389th FS/366th FW, Mountain Home AFB, ID	
87-0208	McD F-15E Strike Eagle [MO] r/y	USAF 389th FS/366th FW, Mountain Home AFB, ID	
87-0209	McD F-15E Strike Eagle [MO] r/y	USAF 389th FS/366th FW, Mountain Home AFB, ID	
87-0210	McD F-15E Strike Eagle [MO] r/y	USAF 389th FS/366th FW, Mountain Home AFB, ID	
88-1667	McD F-15E Strike Eagle [MO] r/y	USAF 389th FS/366th FW, Mountain Home AFB, ID	
88-1668	McD F-15E Strike Eagle [SJ] bl	USAF 334th FS/4th FW, Seymour-Johnson AFB, NC	
88-1669	McD F-15E Strike Eagle [SJ] y [336 FS]	USAF 336th FS/4th FW, Seymour-Johnson AFB, NC	
88-1670	McD F-15E Strike Eagle [SJ] gn	USAF 335th FS/4th FW, Seymour-Johnson AFB, NC	
88-1671	McD F-15E Strike Eagle [SJ] y	USAF 336th FS/4th FW, Seymour-Johnson AFB, NC	
88-1672	McD F-15E Strike Eagle [SJ] bl	USAF 334th FS/4th FW, Seymour-Johnson AFB, NC	
88-1673	McD F-15E Strike Eagle [SJ] flag $ [336 FS]	USAF 336th FS/4th FW, Seymour-Johnson AFB, NC	
88-1674	McD F-15E Strike Eagle [SJ] r	USAF 333rd FS/4th FW, Seymour-Johnson AFB, NC	
88-1675	McD F-15E Strike Eagle [SJ] y	USAF 336th FS/4th FW, Seymour-Johnson AFB, NC	
88-1676	McD F-15E Strike Eagle [SJ] gn	USAF 335th FS/4th FW, Seymour-Johnson AFB, NC	
88-1677	McD F-15E Strike Eagle [SJ] r	USAF 333rd FS/4th FW, Seymour-Johnson AFB, NC	
88-1678	McD F-15E Strike Eagle [MO] r/y	USAF 389th FS/366th FW, Mountain Home AFB, ID	
88-1679	McD F-15E Strike Eagle [SJ] bl	USAF 334th FS/4th FW, Seymour-Johnson AFB, NC	
88-1680	McD F-15E Strike Eagle [SJ] y	USAF 336th FS/4th FW, Seymour-Johnson AFB, NC	
88-1681	McD F-15E Strike Eagle [OT] bk/wh	USAF 85th TES/53rd Wg, Eglin AFB, FL	
88-1682	McD F-15E Strike Eagle [SJ] gn	USAF 335th FS/4th FW, Seymour-Johnson AFB, AFB, NC	

Notes	Serial	Type (code/other identity)	Owner/operator, location or fate
	88-1683	McD F-15E Strike Eagle [SJ] r	USAF 333rd FS/4th FW, Seymour-Johnson AFB, NC
	88-1684	McD F-15E Strike Eagle [SJ] gn	USAF 335th FS/4th FW, Seymour-Johnson AFB, NC
	88-1685	McD F-15E Strike Eagle [SJ] r	USAF 333rd FS/4th FW, Seymour-Johnson AFB, NC
	88-1686	McD F-15E Strike Eagle [SJ] bl	USAF 334th FS/4th FW, Seymour-Johnson AFB, NC
	88-1687	McD F-15E Strike Eagle [SJ] r	USAF 333rd FS/4th FW, Seymour-Johnson AFB, NC
	88-1688	McD F-15E Strike Eagle [SJ] y	USAF 336th FS/4th FW, Seymour-Johnson AFB, NC
	88-1690	McD F-15E Strike Eagle [SJ] bl	USAF 334th FS/4th FW, Seymour-Johnson AFB, NC
	88-1691	McD F-15E Strike Eagle [SJ] bl	USAF 334th FS/4th FW, Seymour-Johnson AFB, NC
	88-1693	McD F-15E Strike Eagle [SJ] r	USAF 333rd FS/4th FW, Seymour-Johnson AFB, NC
	88-1695	McD F-15E Strike Eagle [SJ] gn	USAF 335th FS/4th FW, Seymour-Johnson AFB, NC
	88-1696	McD F-15E Strike Eagle [SJ] r	USAF 333rd FS/4th FW, Seymour-Johnson AFB, NC
	88-1697	McD F-15E Strike Eagle [MO] r/y	USAF 389th FS/366th FW, Mountain Home AFB, ID
	88-1698	McD F-15E Strike Eagle [SJ] bl	USAF 334th FS/4th FW, Seymour-Johnson AFB, NC
	88-1699	McD F-15E Strike Eagle [MO] r/y	USAF 389th FS/366th FW, Mountain Home AFB, ID
	88-1700	McD F-15E Strike Eagle [SJ] y	USAF 336th FS/4th FW, Seymour-Johnson AFB, NC
	88-1702	McD F-15E Strike Eagle [SJ] mlt [4 FW]	USAF 4th FW, Seymour-Johnson AFB, NC
	88-1703	McD F-15E Strike Eagle [SJ] gn	USAF 335th FS/4th FW, Seymour-Johnson AFB, NC
	88-1704	McD F-15E Strike Eagle [SJ] bl [334 FS]	USAF 334th FS/4th FW, Seymour-Johnson AFB, NC
	88-1705	McD F-15E Strike Eagle [MO] r/y [389 FS]	USAF 389th FS/366th FW, Mountain Home AFB, ID
	88-1706	McD F-15E Strike Eagle [SJ] y	USAF 336th FS/4th FW, Seymour-Johnson AFB, NC
	88-1707	McD F-15E Strike Eagle [MO] r/y	USAF 389th FS/366th FW, Mountain Home AFB, ID
	88-1708	McD F-15E Strike Eagle [SJ] gn	USAF 335th FS/4th FW, Seymour-Johnson AFB, NC
	89-0471	McD F-15E Strike Eagle [SJ] gn	USAF 335th FS/4th FW, Seymour-Johnson AFB, NC
	89-0472	McD F-15E Strike Eagle [SJ] r	USAF 333rd FS/4th FW, Seymour-Johnson AFB, NC
	89-0473	McD F-15E Strike Eagle [SJ] r	USAF 333rd FS/4th FW, Seymour-Johnson AFB, NC
	89-0474	McD F-15E Strike Eagle [SJ] y	USAF 336th FS/4th FW, Seymour-Johnson AFB, NC
	89-0475	McD F-15E Strike Eagle [SJ] bl	USAF 334th FS/4th FW, Seymour-Johnson AFB, NC
	89-0476	McD F-15E Strike Eagle [SJ] gn	USAF 335th FS/4th FW, Seymour-Johnson AFB, NC
	89-0477	McD F-15E Strike Eagle [SJ] gn	USAF 335th FS/4th FW, Seymour-Johnson AFB, NC
	89-0478	McD F-15E Strike Eagle [SJ] gn	USAF 335th FS/4th FW, Seymour-Johnson AFB, NC
	89-0480	McD F-15E Strike Eagle [SJ] r	USAF 333rd FS/4th FW, Seymour-Johnson AFB, NC

Serial	Type (code/other identity)	Owner/operator, location or fate	Notes
89-0481	McD F-15E Strike Eagle [SJ] *bl*	USAF 334th FS/4th FW, Seymour-Johnson AFB, NC	
89-0482	McD F-15E Strike Eagle [SJ] *r*	USAF 333rd FS/4th FW, Seymour-Johnson AFB, NC	
89-0483	McD F-15E Strike Eagle [SJ] *y*	USAF 336th FS/4th FW, Seymour-Johnson AFB, NC	
89-0484	McD F-15E Strike Eagle [SJ] *r*	USAF 333rd FS/4th FW, Seymour-Johnson AFB, NC	
89-0485	McD F-15E Strike Eagle [SJ] *gn*	USAF 335th FS/4th FW, Seymour-Johnson AFB, NC	
89-0486	McD F-15E Strike Eagle [SJ] *y*	USAF 336th FS/4th FW, Seymour-Johnson AFB, NC	
89-0487	McD F-15E Strike Eagle [SJ] *gn*	USAF 335th FS/4th FW, Seymour-Johnson AFB, NC	
89-0488	McD F-15E Strike Eagle [SJ] *bl*	USAF 334th FS/4th FW, Seymour-Johnson AFB, NC	
89-0489	McD F-15E Strike Eagle [SJ] *y*	USAF 336th FS/4th FW, Seymour-Johnson AFB, NC	
89-0490	McD F-15E Strike Eagle [SJ]	USAF 336th FS/4th FW, Seymour-Johnson AFB, NC	
89-0492	McD F-15E Strike Eagle [SJ] *y* [4 OG]	USAF 336th FS/4th FW, Seymour-Johnson AFB, NC	
89-0493	McD F-15E Strike Eagle [SJ]	USAF 4th FW, Seymour-Johnson AFB, NC	
89-0494	McD F-15E Strike Eagle [SJ] *y*	USAF 336th FS/4th FW, Seymour-Johnson AFB, NC	
89-0495	McD F-15E Strike Eagle [SJ]	USAF 335th FS/4th FW, Seymour-Johnson AFB, NC	
89-0496	McD F-15E Strike Eagle [SJ]	USAF 336th FS/4th FW, Seymour-Johnson AFB, NC	
89-0498	McD F-15E Strike Eagle [SJ] *gn*	USAF 335th FS/4th FW, Seymour-Johnson AFB, NC	
89-0499	McD F-15E Strike Eagle [SJ] *bl*	USAF 334th FS/4th FW, Seymour-Johnson AFB, NC	
89-0500	McD F-15E Strike Eagle [SJ] *bl*	USAF 334th FS/4th FW, Seymour-Johnson AFB, NC	
89-0501	McD F-15E Strike Eagle [SJ] *y*	USAF 336th FS/4th FW, Seymour-Johnson AFB, NC	
89-0502	McD F-15E Strike Eagle [SJ] *gn*	USAF 335th FS/4th FW, Seymour-Johnson AFB, NC	
89-0503	McD F-15E Strike Eagle [SJ] gn	USAF 335th FS/4th FW, Seymour-Johnson AFB, NC	
89-0505	McD F-15E Strike Eagle [SJ] *y*	USAF 336th FS/4th FW, Seymour-Johnson AFB, NC	
89-0506	McD F-15E Strike Eagle [MO] *r/y*	USAF 389th FS/366th FW, Mountain Home AFB, ID	
90-0227	McD F-15E Strike Eagle [MO] *r/y*	USAF 389th FS/366th FW, Mountain Home AFB, ID	
90-0228	McD F-15E Strike Eagle [SJ] *r*	USAF 333rd FS/4th FW, Seymour-Johnson AFB, NC	
90-0229	McD F-15E Strike Eagle [SJ] *r*	USAF 333rd FS/4th FW, Seymour-Johnson AFB, NC	
90-0230	McD F-15E Strike Eagle [SJ] *y*	USAF 336th FS/4th FW, Seymour-Johnson AFB, NC	
90-0232	McD F-15E Strike Eagle [SJ] *gn*	USAF 335th FS/4th FW, Seymour-Johnson AFB, NC	
90-0233	McD F-15E Strike Eagle [MO] *tig* {391 FS]	USAF 391st FS/366th Wg, Mountain Home AFB, ID	
90-0234	McD F-15E Strike Eagle [MO] *tig*	USAF 391st FS/366th Wg, Mountain Home AFB, ID	
90-0236	McD F-15E Strike Eagle [MO] *tig*	USAF 391st FS/366th Wg, Mountain Home AFB, ID	

Notes	Serial	Type (code/other identity)	Owner/operator, location or fate
	90-0237	McD F-15E Strike Eagle [MO] *tig*	USAF 391st FS/366th Wg, Mountain Home AFB, ID
	90-0238	McD F-15E Strike Eagle [MO] *tig*	USAF 391st FS/366th Wg, Mountain Home AFB, ID
	90-0239	McD F-15E Strike Eagle [WA] *bk/y*	USAF 17th WPS/57th Wg, Nellis AFB, NV
	90-0240	McD F-15E Strike Eagle [MO] *tig*	USAF 391st FS/366th Wg, Mountain Home AFB, ID
	90-0241	McD F-15E Strike Eagle [MO] *tig*	USAF 391st FS/366th Wg, Mountain Home AFB, ID
	90-0242	McD F-15E Strike Eagle [MO] *tig*	USAF 391st FS/366th Wg, Mountain Home AFB, ID
	90-0243	McD F-15E Strike Eagle [MO] *tig*	USAF 391st FS/366th Wg, Mountain Home AFB, ID
	90-0244	McD F-15E Strike Eagle [MO] *tig*	USAF 391st FS/366th Wg, Mountain Home AFB, ID
	90-0245	McD F-15E Strike Eagle [MO] *tig*	USAF 391st FS/366th Wg, Mountain Home AFB, ID
	90-0246	McD F-15E Strike Eagle [MO] *tig*	USAF 391st FS/366th Wg, Mountain Home AFB, ID
	90-0247	McD F-15E Strike Eagle [MO] *tig*	USAF 391st FS/366th Wg, Mountain Home AFB, ID
	90-0248	McD F-15E Strike Eagle [MO] *tig*	USAF 391st FS/366th Wg, Mountain Home AFB, ID
	90-0249	McD F-15E Strike Eagle [MO] *tig*	USAF 391st FS/366th Wg, Mountain Home AFB, ID
	90-0250	McD F-15E Strike Eagle [MO] *tig*	USAF 391st FS/366th Wg, Mountain Home AFB, ID
	90-0251	McD F-15E Strike Eagle [WA] *bk/y*	USAF 17th WPS/57th Wg, Nellis AFB, NV
	90-0252	McD F-15E Strike Eagle [ET] *bk/wh*	USAF 40th FLTS/96th TW, Eglin AFB, FL
	90-0253	McD F-15E Strike Eagle [MO] *tig*	USAF 391st FS/366th Wg, Mountain Home AFB, ID
	90-0255	McD F-15E Strike Eagle [MO] *tig*	USAF 391st FS/366th Wg, Mountain Home AFB, ID
	90-0256	McD F-15E Strike Eagle [ET] *bk/wh*	USAF 40th FLTS/96th TW, Eglin AFB, FL
	90-0257	McD F-15E Strike Eagle [WA] *bk/y* [57 FW]	USAF 17th WPS/57th Wg, Nellis AFB, NV
	90-0258	McD F-15E Strike Eagle [OT] *bk/gn*	USAF 422nd TES/53rd Wg, Nellis AFB, NV
	90-0259	McD F-15E Strike Eagle [WA] *bk/y*	USAF 17th WPS/57th Wg, Nellis AFB, NV
	90-0260	McD F-15E Strike Eagle [WA] *bk/y*	USAF 17th WPS/57th Wg, Nellis AFB, NV
	90-0261	McD F-15E Strike Eagle [WA] *bk/y* [17 WPS]	USAF 17th WPS/57th Wg, Nellis AFB, NV
	90-0262	McD F-15E Strike Eagle [WA] *bk/y*	USAF 17th WPS/57th Wg, Nellis AFB, NV
	91-0300	McD F-15E Strike Eagle [MO] *tig*	USAF 391st FS/366th Wg, Mountain Home AFB, ID
	91-0305	McD F-15E Strike Eagle [WA] *bk/y*	USAF 17th WPS/57th Wg, Nellis AFB, NV
	91-0319	McD F-15E Strike Eagle [MO] *tig*	USAF 391st FS/366th Wg, Mountain Home AFB, ID
	91-0322	McD F-15E Strike Eagle [OT] *bk/gn*	USAF 422nd TES/53rd Wg, Nellis AFB, NV
	91-0323	McD F-15E Strike Eagle [MO] *tig*	USAF 391st FS/366th Wg, Mountain Home AFB, ID
	91-0325	McD F-15E Strike Eagle [OT] *bk/gn*	USAF 422nd TES/53rd Wg, Nellis AFB, NV
	91-0328	McD F-15E Strike Eagle [WA] *bk/y*	USAF 17th WPS/57th Wg, Nellis AFB, NV
	91-0330	McD F-15E Strike Eagle [MO] *tig*	USAF 391st FS/366th Wg, Mountain Home AFB, ID
	91-0333	McD F-15E Strike Eagle [MO] *tig*	USAF 391st FS/366th Wg, Mountain Home AFB, ID
	91-0600	McD F-15E Strike Eagle [MO] *tig*	USAF 391st FS/366th Wg, Mountain Home AFB, ID
	91-0601	McD F-15E Strike Eagle [WA] *bk/y*	USAF 17th WPS/57th Wg, Nellis AFB, NV
	92-0365	McD F-15E Strike Eagle [OT] *bk/gn*	USAF 422nd TES/53rd Wg, Nellis AFB, NV
	92-0366	McD F-15E Strike Eagle [MO] *tig*	USAF 391st FS/366th Wg, Mountain Home AFB, ID
	96-0200	McD F-15E Strike Eagle [OT] *bk/gn*	USAF 422nd TES/53rd Wg, Nellis AFB, NV
	97-0217	McD F-15E Strike Eagle [OT] *bk/gn*	USAF 422nd TES/53rd Wg, Nellis AFB, NV

Serial	Type (code/other identity)	Owner/operator, location or fate	Notes
98-0132	McD F-15E Strike Eagle [ET] *bk/wh*	USAF 40th FLTS/96th TW, Eglin AFB, FL	
Boeing C-17A Globemaster III			
88-0265	Boeing C-17A Globemaster III *gn*	USAF 62nd AW, McChord AFB, WA	
88-0266	Boeing C-17A Globemaster III *y/bl*	USAF 437th AW, Charleston AFB, SC	
89-1189	Boeing C-17A Globemaster III *bk/y*	USAF 758th AS/911th AW AFRC, Greater Pittsburgh, PA	
89-1190	Boeing C-17A Globemaster III *r/w*	USAF 167th AS/167th AW, Martinsburg, WV ANG	
89-1191	Boeing C-17A Globemaster III *bl*	USAF 137th AS/105th AW, Stewart AFB, NY ANG	
89-1192	Boeing C-17A Globemaster III *y/bl*	USAF 437th AW, Charleston AFB, SC	
90-0532	Boeing C-17A Globemaster III *bk*	USAF 156th AS/145th AW, Charlotte-Douglas, NC ANG	
90-0533	Boeing C-17A Globemaster III [HH] *r/y*	USAF 535th AS/15th Wg, Hickam AFB, HI	
90-0534	Boeing C-17A Globemaster III *y/bl*	USAF 437th AW, Charleston AFB, SC	
90-0535	Boeing C-17A Globemaster III *r/w*	USAF 89th AS/445th AW AFRC, Wright-Patterson AFB, OH	
92-3291	Boeing C-17A Globemaster III *r/w*	USAF 155th AS/164th AW, Memphis, TN ANG	
92-3292	Boeing C-17A Globemaster III *bk/y*	USAF 758th AS/911th AW AFRC, Greater Pittsburgh, PA	
92-3293	Boeing C-17A Globemaster III *bk*	USAF 156th AS/145th AW, Charlotte-Douglas, NC ANG	
92-3294	Boeing C-17A Globemaster III *bk*	USAF 156th AS/145th AW, Charlotte-Douglas, NC ANG	
93-0599	Boeing C-17A Globemaster III[AK] *bl/y*	USAF 144th AS/176th Wg, Elmendorf AFB, AK ANG	
93-0600	Boeing C-17A Globemaster III *r/w*	USAF 155th AS/164th AW, Memphis, TN ANG	
93-0601	Boeing C-17A Globemaster III *bk/y*	USAF 758th AS/911th AW AFRC, Greater Pittsburgh, PA	
93-0602	Boeing C-17A Globemaster III *bk* $	USAF 156th AS/145th AW, Charlotte-Douglas, NC ANG	
93-0603	Boeing C-17A Globemaster III *r/w*	USAF 89th AS/445th AW AFRC, Wright-Patterson AFB, OH	
93-0604	Boeing C-17A Globemaster III *r/w*	USAF 89th AS/445th AW AFRC, Wright-Patterson AFB, OH	
94-0065	Boeing C-17A Globemaster III *r/w*	USAF 155th AS/164th AW, Memphis, TN ANG	
94-0066	Boeing C-17A Globemaster III *gn*	USAF 62nd AW, McChord AFB, WA	
94-0067	Boeing C-17A Globemaster III *bl*	USAF 137th AS/105th AW, Stewart AFB, NY ANG	
94-0068	Boeing C-17A Globemaster III *or/y*	USAF 729th AS/452nd AMW AFRC, March ARB, CA	
94-0069	Boeing C-17A Globemaster III *r/w*	USAF 167th AS/167th AW, Martinsburg, WV ANG	
94-0070	Boeing C-17A Globemaster III *r/w*	USAF 167th AS/167th AW, Martinsburg, WV ANG	
95-0102	Boeing C-17A Globemaster III *y/bl*	USAF 437th AW, Charleston AFB, SC	
95-0103	Boeing C-17A Globemaster III *gn*	USAF 62nd AW, McChord AFB, WA	
95-0104	Boeing C-17A Globemaster III *gn*	USAF 62nd AW, McChord AFB, WA	
95-0105	Boeing C-17A Globemaster III *bl*	USAF 137th AS/105th AW, Stewart AFB, NY ANG	
95-0106	Boeing C-17A Globemaster III *gn*	USAF 62nd AW, McChord AFB, WA	
95-0107	Boeing C-17A Globemaster III *y/bl*	USAF 437th AW, Charleston AFB, SC	
96-0001	Boeing C-17A Globemaster III *bk/y*	USAF 758th AS/911th AW AFRC, Greater Pittsburgh, PA	
96-0002	Boeing C-17A Globemaster III *y/bl*	USAF 437th AW, Charleston AFB, SC	
96-0003	Boeing C-17A Globemaster III *gn*	USAF 62nd AW, McChord AFB, WA	
96-0004	Boeing C-17A Globemaster III *r/y*	USAF 58th AS/97th AMW, Altus AFB, OK	
96-0005	Boeing C-17A Globemaster III *bl*	USAF 137th AS/105th AW, Stewart AFB, NY ANG	
96-0006	Boeing C-17A Globemaster III *r/w*	USAF 167th AS/167th AW, Martinsburg, WV ANG	
96-0007	Boeing C-17A Globemaster III *bl/gd*	USAF 183rd AS/172nd AW, Jackson Int'l Airport, MS ANG	
96-0008	Boeing C-17A Globemaster III *r/y*	USAF 58th AS/97th AMW, Altus AFB, OK	
97-0041	Boeing C-17A Globemaster III *y/bl*	USAF 437th AW, Charleston AFB, SC	
97-0042	Boeing C-17A Globemaster III *r/w*	USAF 155th AS/164th AW, Memphis, TN ANG	
97-0043	Boeing C-17A Globemaster III *or/y*	USAF 729th AS/452nd AMW AFRC, March ARB, CA	
97-0044	Boeing C-17A Globemaster III *r/w*	USAF 89th AS/445th AW AFRC, Wright-Patterson AFB, OH	

Notes	Serial	Type (code/other identity)	Owner/operator, location or fate
	97-0045	Boeing C-17A Globemaster III *bl*	USAF 137th AS/105th AW, Stewart AFB, NY ANG
	97-0046	Boeing C-17A Globemaster III *y/bl*	USAF 437th AW, Charleston AFB, SC
	97-0047	Boeing C-17A Globemaster III *y/bl*	USAF 437th AW, Charleston AFB, SC
	97-0048	Boeing C-17A Globemaster III *r/w*	USAF 89th AS/445th AW AFRC, Wright-Patterson AFB, OH
	98-0049	Boeing C-17A Globemaster III *r/y*	USAF 58th AS/97th AMW, Altus AFB, OK
	98-0050	Boeing C-17A Globemaster III *r/y*	USAF 58th AS/97th AMW, Altus AFB, OK
	98-0051	Boeing C-17A Globemaster III [AK] *bl/y* [517 AS]	USAF 144th AS/176th Wg, Elmendorf AFB, AK ANG
	98-0052	Boeing C-17A Globemaster III *gn*	USAF 62nd AW, McChord AFB, WA
	98-0053	Boeing C-17A Globemaster III *gn*	USAF 62nd AW, McChord AFB, WA
	98-0054	Boeing C-17A Globemaster III *y/bl*	USAF 437th AW, Charleston AFB, SC
	98-0055	Boeing C-17A Globemaster III *r/y* [58 AS]	USAF 58th AS/97th AMW, Altus AFB, OK
	98-0056	Boeing C-17A Globemaster III [AK] *bl/y*	USAF 144th AS/176th Wg, Elmendorf AFB, AK ANG
	98-0057	Boeing C-17A Globemaster III *bl*	USAF 137th AS/105th AW, Stewart AFB, NY ANG
	99-0058	Boeing C-17A Globemaster III *gn*	USAF 62nd AW, McChord AFB, WA
	99-0059	Boeing C-17A Globemaster III *gn*	USAF 62nd AW, McChord AFB, WA
	99-0060	Boeing C-17A Globemaster III *gn*	USAF 62nd AW, McChord AFB, WA
	99-0061	Boeing C-17A Globemaster III *r/y*	USAF 58th AS/97th AMW, Altus AFB, OK
	99-0062	Boeing C-17A Globemaster III *y/bl*	USAF 437th AW, Charleston AFB, SC
	99-0063	Boeing C-17A Globemaster III *r/y*	USAF 58th AS/97th AMW, Altus AFB, OK
	99-0064	Boeing C-17A Globemaster III *r/y*	USAF 58th AS/97th AMW, Altus AFB, OK
	99-0165	Boeing C-17A Globemaster III *r/w*	USAF 89th AS/445th AW AFRC, Wright-Patterson AFB, OH
	99-0166	Boeing C-17A Globemaster III *gn*	USAF 62nd AW, McChord AFB, WA
	99-0167	Boeing C-17A Globemaster III [AK] *bl/y*	USAF 144th AS/176th Wg, Elmendorf AFB, AK ANG
	99-0168	Boeing C-17A Globemaster III [AK] *bl/y*	USAF 144th AS/176th Wg, Elmendorf AFB, AK ANG
	99-0169	Boeing C-17A Globemaster III *y/bl*	USAF 437th AW, Charleston AFB, SC
	99-0170	Boeing C-17A Globemaster III *r/y*	USAF 58th AS/97th AMW, Altus AFB, OK
	00-0171	Boeing C-17A Globemaster III [AK] *bl/y*	USAF 144th AS/176th Wg, Elmendorf AFB, AK ANG
	00-0172	Boeing C-17A Globemaster III *bk*	USAF 156th AS/145th AW, Charlotte-Douglas, NC ANG
	00-0174	Boeing C-17A Globemaster III [AK] *bl/y*	USAF 144th AS/176th Wg, Elmendorf AFB, AK ANG
	00-0175	Boeing C-17A Globemaster III *bl*	USAF 6th AS/305th AMW, McGuire AFB, NJ
	00-0176	Boeing C-17A Globemaster III *r/w*	USAF 155th AS/164th AW, Memphis, TN ANG
	00-0177	Boeing C-17A Globemaster III *bl*	USAF 137th AS/105th AW, Stewart AFB, NY ANG
	00-0178	Boeing C-17A Globemaster III *r/w*	USAF 89th AS/445th AW AFRC, Wright-Patterson AFB, OH
	00-0179	Boeing C-17A Globemaster III *r/y*	USAF 58th AS/97th AMW, Altus AFB, OK
	00-0180	Boeing C-17A Globemaster III *bk/y*	USAF 758th AS/911th AW AFRC, Greater Pittsburgh, PA
	00-0181	Boeing C-17A Globemaster III *r/w*	USAF 167th AS/167th AW, Martinsburg, WV ANG
	00-0182	Boeing C-17A Globemaster III *r/w*	USAF 167th AS/167th AW, Martinsburg, WV ANG
	00-0183	Boeing C-17A Globemaster III *bk*	USAF 156th AS/145th AW, Charlotte-Douglas, NC ANG
	00-0184	Boeing C-17A Globemaster III *bk/y*	USAF 758th AS/911th AW AFRC, Greater Pittsburgh, PA
	00-0185	Boeing C-17A Globemaster III [AK] *bl/y*	USAF 144th AS/176th Wg, Elmendorf AFB, AK ANG
	01-0186	Boeing C-17A Globemaster III *bl/y*	USAF 3rd AS/436th AW, Dover AFB, DE
	01-0187	Boeing C-17A Globemaster III *gn*	USAF 62nd AW, McChord AFB, WA
	01-0188	Boeing C-17A Globemaster III *bl*	USAF 137th AS/105th AW, Stewart AFB, NY ANG
	01-0189	Boeing C-17A Globemaster III *r/w*	USAF 155th AS/164th AW, Memphis, TN ANG
	01-0190	Boeing C-17A Globemaster III *r/y*	USAF 58th AS/97th AMW, Altus AFB, OK
	01-0191	Boeing C-17A Globemaster III *bl/y*	USAF 3rd AS/436th AW, Dover AFB, DE
	01-0192	Boeing C-17A Globemaster III *bl*	USAF 137th AS/105th AW, Stewart AFB, NY ANG
	01-0193	Boeing C-17A Globemaster III *y/bl*	USAF 437th AW, Charleston AFB, SC

Serial	Type (code/other identity)	Owner/operator, location or fate	Notes
01-0194	Boeing C-17A Globemaster III r/w	USAF 89th AS/445th AW AFRC, Wright-Patterson AFB, OH	
01-0195	Boeing C-17A Globemaster III r/y	USAF 58th AS/97th AMW, Altus AFB, OK	
01-0196	Boeing C-17A Globemaster III r/w	USAF 167th AS/167th AW, Martinsburg, WV ANG	
01-0197	Boeing C-17A Globemaster III bk	USAF 156th AS/145th AW, Charlotte-Douglas, NC ANG	
02-1098	Boeing C-17A Globemaster III bl	USAF 6th AS/305th AMW, McGuire AFB, NJ	
02-1099	Boeing C-17A Globemaster III bk/y	USAF 758th AS/911th AW AFRC, Greater Pittsburgh, PA	
02-1100	Boeing C-17A Globemaster III r/w	USAF 155th AS/164th AW, Memphis, TN ANG	
02-1101	Boeing C-17A Globemaster III bk/y	USAF 758th AS/911th AW AFRC, Greater Pittsburgh, PA	
02-1102	Boeing C-17A Globemaster III r/y	USAF 58th AS/97th AMW, Altus AFB, OK	
02-1103	Boeing C-17A Globemaster III r/y	USAF 58th AS/97th AMW, Altus AFB, OK	
02-1104	Boeing C-17A Globemaster III r/y [97 OG]	USAF 58th AS/97th AMW, Altus AFB, OK	
02-1105	Boeing C-17A Globemaster III gn	USAF 62nd AW, McChord AFB, WA	
02-1106	Boeing C-17A Globemaster III gn	USAF 62nd AW, McChord AFB, WA	
02-1107	Boeing C-17A Globemaster III bk	USAF 156th AS/145th AW, Charlotte-Douglas, NC ANG	
02-1108	Boeing C-17A Globemaster III gn	USAF 62nd AW, McChord AFB, WA	
02-1109	Boeing C-17A Globemaster III gn	USAF 62nd AW, McChord AFB, WA	
02-1110	Boeing C-17A Globemaster III gn	USAF 62nd AW, McChord AFB, WA	
02-1111	Boeing C-17A Globemaster III gn	USAF 62nd AW, McChord AFB, WA	
02-1112	Boeing C-17A Globemaster III bl/gd	USAF 183rd AS/172nd AW, Jackson Int'l Airport, MS ANG	
03-3113	Boeing C-17A Globemaster III bl/gd	USAF 183rd AS/172nd AW, Jackson Int'l Airport, MS ANG	
03-3114	Boeing C-17A Globemaster III bl/gd	USAF 183rd AS/172nd AW, Jackson Int'l Airport, MS ANG	
03-3115	Boeing C-17A Globemaster III bl/gd	USAF 183rd AS/172nd AW, Jackson Int'l Airport, MS ANG	
03-3116	Boeing C-17A Globemaster III bl/gd	USAF 183rd AS/172nd AW, Jackson Int'l Airport, MS ANG	
03-3117	Boeing C-17A Globemaster III bl/gd	USAF 183rd AS/172nd AW, Jackson Int'l Airport, MS ANG	
03-3118	Boeing C-17A Globemaster III bl/gd	USAF 183rd AS/172nd AW, Jackson Int'l Airport, MS ANG	
03-3119	Boeing C-17A Globemaster III bl/gd	USAF 183rd AS/172nd AW, Jackson Int'l Airport, MS ANG	
03-3120	Boeing C-17A Globemaster III gn	USAF 62nd AW, McChord AFB, WA	
03-3121	Boeing C-17A Globemaster III [ED]	USAF 418th FLTS/412th TW, Edwards AFB, CA	
03-3122	Boeing C-17A Globemaster III y/bl	USAF 437th AW, Charleston AFB, SC	
03-3123	Boeing C-17A Globemaster III r/w	USAF 167th AS/167th AW, Martinsburg, WV ANG	
03-3124	Boeing C-17A Globemaster III y/bl	USAF 437th AW, Charleston AFB, SC	
03-3125	Boeing C-17A Globemaster III bl	USAF 6th AS/305th AMW, McGuire AFB, NJ	
03-3126	Boeing C-17A Globemaster III bl	USAF 6th AS/305th AMW, McGuire AFB, NJ	
03-3127	Boeing C-17A Globemaster III gn	USAF 62nd AW, McChord AFB, WA	
04-4128	Boeing C-17A Globemaster III bl	USAF 6th AS/305th AMW, McGuire AFB, NJ	
04-4129	Boeing C-17A Globemaster III gn	USAF 62nd AW, McChord AFB, WA	
04-4130	Boeing C-17A Globemaster III bl	USAF 6th AS/305th AMW, McGuire AFB, NJ	
04-4131	Boeing C-17A Globemaster III bl	USAF 6th AS/305th AMW, McGuire AFB, NJ	
04-4132	Boeing C-17A Globemaster III bl	USAF 6th AS/305th AMW, McGuire AFB, NJ	
04-4133	Boeing C-17A Globemaster III bl	USAF 6th AS/305th AMW, McGuire AFB, NJ	
04-4134	Boeing C-17A Globemaster III bl	USAF 6th AS/305th AMW, McGuire AFB, NJ	
04-4135	Boeing C-17A Globemaster III r/y	USAF 58th AS/97th AMW, Altus AFB, OK	
04-4136	Boeing C-17A Globemaster III bl	USAF 6th AS/305th AMW, McGuire AFB, NJ	
04-4137	Boeing C-17A Globemaster III bl	USAF 6th AS/305th AMW, McGuire AFB, NJ	
04-4138	Boeing C-17A Globemaster III or/y	USAF 729th AS/452nd AMW AFRC, March ARB, CA	
05-5139	Boeing C-17A Globemaster III or/y	USAF 729th AS/452nd AMW AFRC, March ARB, CA	
05-5140	Boeing C-17A Globemaster III or/y	USAF 729th AS/452nd AMW AFRC, March ARB, CA	
05-5141	Boeing C-17A Globemaster III or/y	USAF 729th AS/452nd AMW AFRC, March ARB, CA	
05-5142	Boeing C-17A Globemaster III or/y	USAF 729th AS/452nd AMW AFRC, March ARB, CA	

Notes	Serial	Type (code/other identity)	Owner/operator, location or fate
	05-5143	Boeing C-17A Globemaster III	USAF 729th AS/452nd AMW AFRC, March ARB,
	CA05-5144	Boeing C-17A Globemaster III *or/y*	USAF 729th AS/452nd AMW AFRC, March ARB, CA
	05-5145	Boeing C-17A Globemaster III *or/y*	USAF 729th AS/452nd AMW AFRC, March ARB, CA
	05-5146	Boeing C-17A Globemaster III [HH] *r/y*	USAF 535th AS/15th Wg, Hickam AFB, HI
	05-5147	Boeing C-17A Globemaster III [HH] *r/y*	USAF 535th AS/15th Wg, Hickam AFB, HI
	05-5148	Boeing C-17A Globemaster III [HH] *r/y*	USAF 535th AS/15th Wg, Hickam AFB, HI
	05-5149	Boeing C-17A Globemaster III [HH] *r/y*	USAF 535th AS/15th Wg, Hickam AFB, HI
	05-5150	Boeing C-17A Globemaster III [HH] *r/y*	USAF 535th AS/15th Wg, Hickam AFB, HI
	05-5151	Boeing C-17A Globemaster III [HH] *r/y*	USAF 535th AS/15th Wg, Hickam AFB, HI
	05-5152	Boeing C-17A Globemaster III [HH] *r/y*	USAF 535th AS/15th Wg, Hickam AFB, HI
	05-5153	Boeing C-17A Globemaster III [HH] *r/y]*	USAF 535th AS/15th Wg, Hickam AFB, HI
	06-6154	Boeing C-17A Globemaster III *w/bk*	USAF 21st AS/60th AMW, Travis AFB, CA
	06-6155	Boeing C-17A Globemaster III *w/bk*	USAF 21st AS/60th AMW, Travis AFB, CA
	06-6156	Boeing C-17A Globemaster III *w/bk*	USAF 21st AS/60th AMW, Travis AFB, CA
	06-6157	Boeing C-17A Globemaster III *w/bk*	USAF 21st AS/60th AMW, Travis AFB, CA
	06-6158	Boeing C-17A Globemaster III *w/bk*	USAF 21st AS/60th AMW, Travis AFB, CA
	06-6159	Boeing C-17A Globemaster III *w/bk*	USAF 21st AS/60th AMW, Travis AFB, CA
	06-6160	Boeing C-17A Globemaster III *w/bk*	USAF 21st AS/60th AMW, Travis AFB, CA
	06-6161	Boeing C-17A Globemaster III *w/bk*	USAF 21st AS/60th AMW, Travis AFB, CA
	06-6162	Boeing C-17A Globemaster III *w/bk*	USAF 21st AS/60th AMW, Travis AFB, CA
	06-6163	Boeing C-17A Globemaster III *w/bk*	USAF 21st AS/60th AMW, Travis AFB, CA
	06-6164	Boeing C-17A Globemaster III *w/bk*	USAF 21st AS/60th AMW, Travis AFB, CA
	06-6165	Boeing C-17A Globemaster III *bl/y*	USAF 3rd AS/436th AW, Dover AFB, DE
	06-6166	Boeing C-17A Globemaster III *bl/y*	USAF 3rd AS/436th AW, Dover AFB, DE
	06-6167	Boeing C-17A Globemaster III *bl/y*	USAF 3rd AS/436th AW, Dover AFB, DE
	06-6168	Boeing C-17A Globemaster III *bl/y*	USAF 3rd AS/436th AW, Dover AFB, DE
	07-7169	Boeing C-17A Globemaster III *bl/y*	USAF 3rd AS/436th AW, Dover AFB, DE
	07-7170	Boeing C-17A Globemaster III *bl/y*	USAF 3rd AS/436th AW, Dover AFB, DE
	07-7171	Boeing C-17A Globemaster III *bl*	USAF 6th AS/305th AMW, McGuire AFB, NJ
	07-7172	Boeing C-17A Globemaster III *w/bk*	USAF 21st AS/60th AMW, Travis AFB, CA
	07-7173	Boeing C-17A Globemaster III *bl/y*	USAF 3rd AS/436th AW, Dover AFB, DE
	07-7174	Boeing C-17A Globemaster III *bl/y*	USAF 3rd AS/436th AW, Dover AFB, DE
	07-7175	Boeing C-17A Globemaster III *bl/y*	USAF 3rd AS/436th AW, Dover AFB, DE
	07-7176	Boeing C-17A Globemaster III *bl/y*	USAF 3rd AS/436th AW, Dover AFB, DE
	07-7177	Boeing C-17A Globemaster III *bl/y*	USAF 3rd AS/436th AW, Dover AFB, DE
	07-7178	Boeing C-17A Globemaster III *y/bl*	USAF 437th AW, Charleston AFB, SC
	07-7179	Boeing C-17A Globemaster III *w/bk*	USAF 21st AS/60th AMW, Travis AFB, CA
	07-7180	Boeing C-17A Globemaster III *y/bl*	USAF 437th AW, Charleston AFB, SC
	07-7181	Boeing C-17A Globemaster III *y/bl*	USAF 437th AW, Charleston AFB, SC
	07-7182	Boeing C-17A Globemaster III *y/bl*	USAF 437th AW, Charleston AFB, SC
	07-7183	Boeing C-17A Globemaster III *y/bl*	USAF 437th AW, Charleston AFB, SC
	07-7184	Boeing C-17A Globemaster III *y/bl*	USAF 437th AW, Charleston AFB, SC
	07-7185	Boeing C-17A Globemaster III *y/bl*	USAF 437th AW, Charleston AFB, SC
	07-7186	Boeing C-17A Globemaster III *y/bl*	USAF 437th AW, Charleston AFB, SC
	07-7187	Boeing C-17A Globemaster III *y/bl*	USAF 437th AW, Charleston AFB, SC
	07-7188	Boeing C-17A Globemaster III *y/bl*	USAF 437th AW, Charleston AFB, SC
	07-7189	Boeing C-17A Globemaster III *y/bl*	USAF 437th AW, Charleston AFB, SC
	08-8190	Boeing C-17A Globemaster III *y/bl*	USAF 437th AW, Charleston AFB, SC
	08-8191	Boeing C-17A Globemaster III *y/bl*	USAF 437th AW, Charleston AFB, SC
	08-8192	Boeing C-17A Globemaster III *gn*	USAF 62nd AW, McChord AFB, WA
	08-8193	Boeing C-17A Globemaster III *gn*	USAF 62nd AW, McChord AFB, WA
	08-8194	Boeing C-17A Globemaster III *gn*	USAF 62nd AW, McChord AFB, WA
	08-8195	Boeing C-17A Globemaster III *gn*	USAF 62nd AW, McChord AFB, WA
	08-8196	Boeing C-17A Globemaster III *gn*	USAF 62nd AW, McChord AFB, WA
	08-8197	Boeing C-17A Globemaster III *gn*	USAF 62nd AW, McChord AFB, WA
	08-8198	Boeing C-17A Globemaster III *y/bl*	USAF 437th AW, Charleston AFB, SC
	08-8199	Boeing C-17A Globemaster III *gn*	USAF 62nd AW, McChord AFB, WA
	08-8200	Boeing C-17A Globemaster III *gn*	USAF 62nd AW, McChord AFB, WA
	08-8201	Boeing C-17A Globemaster III *gn*	USAF 62nd AW, McChord AFB, WA
	08-8202	Boeing C-17A Globemaster III *gn*	USAF 62nd AW, McChord AFB, WA
	08-8203	Boeing C-17A Globemaster III *gn*	USAF 62nd AW, McChord AFB, WA
	08-8204	Boeing C-17A Globemaster III *y/bl*	USAF 437th AW, Charleston AFB, SC

Serial	Type (code/other identity)	Owner/operator, location or fate	Notes
09-9205	Boeing C-17A Globemaster III y/bl	USAF 437th AW, Charleston AFB, SC	
09-9206	Boeing C-17A Globemaster III y/bl	USAF 437th AW, Charleston AFB, SC	
09-9207	Boeing C-17A Globemaster III y/bl	USAF 437th AW, Charleston AFB, SC	
09-9208	Boeing C-17A Globemaster III y/bl	USAF 437th AW, Charleston AFB, SC	
09-9209	Boeing C-17A Globemaster III gn	USAF 62nd AW, McChord AFB, WA	
09-9210	Boeing C-17A Globemaster III gn	USAF 62nd AW, McChord AFB, WA	
09-9211	Boeing C-17A Globemaster III gn	USAF 62nd AW, McChord AFB, WA	
09-9212	Boeing C-17A Globemaster III y/bl	USAF 437th AW, Charleston AFB, SC	
10-0213	Boeing C-17A Globemaster III y/bl	USAF 437th AW, Charleston AFB, SC	
10-0214	Boeing C-17A Globemaster III y/bl	USAF 437th AW, Charleston AFB, SC	
10-0215	Boeing C-17A Globemaster III y/bl	USAF 437th AW, Charleston AFB, SC	
10-0216	Boeing C-17A Globemaster III gn	USAF 62nd AW, McChord AFB, WA	
10-0217	Boeing C-17A Globemaster III gn	USAF 62nd AW, McChord AFB, WA	
10-0218	Boeing C-17A Globemaster III gn	USAF 62nd AW, McChord AFB, WA	
10-0219	Boeing C-17A Globemaster III gn	USAF 62nd AW, McChord AFB, WA	
10-0220	Boeing C-17A Globemaster III gn	USAF 62nd AW, McChord AFB, WA	
10-0221	Boeing C-17A Globemaster III y/bl	USAF 437th AW, Charleston AFB, SC	
10-0222	Boeing C-17A Globemaster III y/bl	USAF 437th AW, Charleston AFB, SC	
10-0223	Boeing C-17A Globemaster III y/bl	Stored Kelly Field, TX (damaged)	
	Lockheed Martin F-22A Raptor		
91-4004	Lockheed Martin F-22A Raptor [ED]	USAF 411th FLTS/412th TW, Edwards AFB, CA	
91-4006	Lockheed Martin F-22A Raptor [ED]	USAF 411th FLTS/412th TW, Edwards AFB, CA	
91-4007	Lockheed Martin F-22A Raptor [ED]	USAF 411th FLTS/412th TW, Edwards AFB, CA	
91-4009	Lockheed Martin F-22A Raptor [ED]	USAF 411th FLTS/412th TW, Edwards AFB, CA	
99-4010	Lockheed Martin F-22A Raptor [OT] [422 TES]	USAF 422nd TES/53rd Wg, Nellis AFB, NV	
99-4011	Lockheed Martin F-22A Raptor [WA]	USAF 433rd WPS/57th Wg, Nellis AFB, NV	
00-4012	Lockheed Martin F-22A Raptor [FF]	USAF 71st FS/1st FW, Langley AFB, VA	
00-4015	Lockheed Martin F-22A Raptor [FF]	USAF 71st FS/1st FW, Langley AFB, VA	
00-4016	Lockheed Martin F-22A Raptor [FF]	USAF 71st FS/1st FW, Langley AFB, VA	
00-4017	Lockheed Martin F-22A Raptor [FF]	USAF 71st FS/1st FW, Langley AFB, VA	
01-4018	Lockheed Martin F-22A Raptor [TY]	USAF 43rd FS/325th FW, Eglin AFB, FL	
01-4019	Lockheed Martin F-22A Raptor [FF]	USAF 71st FS/1st FW, Langley AFB, VA	
01-4020	Lockheed Martin F-22A Raptor [TY]	USAF 43rd FS/325th FW, Eglin AFB, FL	
01-4021	Lockheed Martin F-22A Raptor [FF]	USAF 71st FS/1st FW, Langley AFB, VA	
01-4023	Lockheed Martin F-22A Raptor [TY]	USAF 43rd FS/325th FW, Eglin AFB, FL	
01-4024	Lockheed Martin F-22A Raptor [FF]	USAF 1st FW, Langley AFB, VA	
01-4025	Lockheed Martin F-22A Raptor [FF]	USAF 1st FW, Langley AFB, VA	
01-4026	Lockheed Martin F-22A Raptor [TY]	USAF 43rd FS/325th FW, Eglin AFB, FL	
01-4027	Lockheed Martin F-22A Raptor [TY]	USAF 43rd FS/325th FW, Eglin AFB, FL	
02-4028	Lockheed Martin F-22A Raptor [FF]	USAF 71st FS/1st FW, Langley AFB, VA	
02-4029	Lockheed Martin F-22A Raptor [FF] [71FS]	USAF 71st FS/1st FW, Langley AFB, VA	
02-4030	Lockheed Martin F-22A Raptor [FF]	USAF 71st FS/1st FW, Langley AFB, VA	
02-4031	Lockheed Martin F-22A Raptor [FF]	USAF 71st FS/1st FW, Langley AFB, VA	
02-4032	Lockheed Martin F-22A Raptor [FF]	USAF 71st FS/1st FW, Langley AFB, VA	
02-4033	Lockheed Martin F-22A Raptor [FF]	USAF 71st FS/1st FW, Langley AFB, VA	
02-4034	Lockheed Martin F-22A Raptor [FF]	USAF 71st FS/1st FW, Langley AFB, VA	
02-4035	Lockheed Martin F-22A Raptor [FF]	USAF 71st FS/1st FW, Langley AFB, VA	
02-4036	Lockheed Martin F-22A Raptor [FF]	USAF 1st FW, Langley AFB, VA	
02-4037	Lockheed Martin F-22A Raptor [FF]	USAF 1st FW, Langley AFB, VA	
02-4038	Lockheed Martin F-22A Raptor [TY]	USAF 43rd FS/325th FW, Eglin AFB, FL	
02-4039	Lockheed Martin F-22A Raptor [FF]	USAF 71st FS/1st FW, Langley AFB, VA	
02-4040	Lockheed Martin F-22A Raptor [FF]	USAF 71st FS/1st FW, Langley AFB, VA	
03-4041	Lockheed Martin F-22A Raptor [TY]	USAF 43rd FS/325th FW, Eglin AFB, FL	
03-4042	Lockheed Martin F-22A Raptor [FF]	USAF 71st FS/1st FW, Langley AFB, VA	
03-4043	Lockheed Martin F-22A Raptor [FF]	USAF 71st FS/1st FW, Langley AFB, VA	
03-4044	Lockheed Martin F-22A Raptor [TY]	USAF 43rd FS/325th FW, Eglin AFB, FL	
03-4045	Lockheed Martin F-22A Raptor [HH]	USAF 199th FS/154th Wg, Hickam AFB, HI ANG	
03-4046	Lockheed Martin F-22A Raptor [HH] [199 FS]	USAF 199th FS/154th Wg, Hickam AFB, HI ANG	
03-4047	Lockheed Martin F-22A Raptor [HH]	USAF 199th FS/154th Wg, Hickam AFB, HI ANG	
03-4048	Lockheed Martin F-22A Raptor [HH]	USAF 199th FS/154th Wg, Hickam AFB, HI ANG	
03-4049	Lockheed Martin F-22A Raptor [HH]	USAF 199th FS/154th Wg, Hickam AFB, HI ANG	

Notes	Serial	Type (code/other identity)	Owner/operator, location or fate
	03-4050	Lockheed Martin F-22A Raptor [HH]	USAF 199th FS/154th Wg, Hickam AFB, HI ANG
	03-4051	Lockheed Martin F-22A Raptor [HH]	USAF 199th FS/154th Wg, Hickam AFB, HI ANG
	03-4052	Lockheed Martin F-22A Raptor [HH]	USAF 199th FS/154th Wg, Hickam AFB, HI ANG
	03-4053	Lockheed Martin F-22A Raptor [HH]	USAF 199th FS/154th Wg, Hickam AFB, HI ANG
	03-4054	Lockheed Martin F-22A Raptor [HH] [154 WG]	USAF 199th FS/154th Wg, Hickam AFB, HI ANG
	03-4055	Lockheed Martin F-22A Raptor [HH]	USAF 199th FS/154th Wg, Hickam AFB, HI ANG
	03-4056	Lockheed Martin F-22A Raptor [HH]	USAF 199th FS/154th Wg, Hickam AFB, HI ANG
	03-4057	Lockheed Martin F-22A Raptor [HH]	USAF 199th FS/154th Wg, Hickam AFB, HI ANG
	03-4058	Lockheed Martin F-22A Raptor [HH]	USAF 199th FS/154th Wg, Hickam AFB, HI ANG
	03-4059	Lockheed Martin F-22A Raptor [HH]	USAF 199th FS/154th Wg, Hickam AFB, HI ANG
	03-4060	Lockheed Martin F-22A Raptor [HH]	USAF 199th FS/154th Wg, Hickam AFB, HI ANG
	03-4061	Lockheed Martin F-22A Raptor [HH]	USAF 199th FS/154th Wg, Hickam AFB, HI ANG
	04-4062	Lockheed Martin F-22A Raptor [HH]	USAF 199th FS/154th Wg, Hickam AFB, HI ANG
	04-4063	Lockheed Martin F-22A Raptor [HH]	USAF 199th FS/154th Wg, Hickam AFB, HI ANG
	04-4064	Lockheed Martin F-22A Raptor [HH]	USAF 199th FS/154th Wg, Hickam AFB, HI ANG
	04-4065	Lockheed Martin F-22A Raptor [OT]	USAF 422nd TES/53rd Wg, Nellis AFB, NV
	04-4066	Lockheed Martin F-22A Raptor [OT]	USAF 422nd TES/53rd Wg, Nellis AFB, NV
	04-4067	Lockheed Martin F-22A Raptor [FF]	USAF 149th FS/192nd FW/1st FW, Langley AFB, VA ANG
	04-4068	Lockheed Martin F-22A Raptor [OT]	USAF 422nd TES/53rd Wg, Nellis AFB, NV
	04-4069	Lockheed Martin F-22A Raptor [OT] [USAF WC]	USAF 422nd TES/53rd Wg, Nellis AFB, NV
	04-4070	Lockheed Martin F-22A Raptor [WA]	USAF 433rd WPS/57th Wg, Nellis AFB, NV
	04-4071	Lockheed Martin F-22A Raptor [WA]	USAF 433rd WPS/57th Wg, Nellis AFB, NV
	04-4072	Lockheed Martin F-22A Raptor [OT]	USAF 422nd TES/53rd Wg, Nellis AFB, NV
	04-4073	Lockheed Martin F-22A Raptor [OT]	USAF 422nd TES/53rd Wg, Nellis AFB, NV
	04-4074	Lockheed Martin F-22A Raptor [AK]	USAF 90th FS/3rd Wg, Elmendorf AFB, AK
	04-4075	Lockheed Martin F-22A Raptor [AK]	USAF 90th FS/3rd Wg, Elmendorf AFB, AK
	04-4076	Lockheed Martin F-22A Raptor [FF]	USAF 27th FS/1st FW, Langley AFB, VA
	04-4077	Lockheed Martin F-22A Raptor [AK]	USAF 525th FS/3rd Wg, Elmendorf AFB, AK
	04-4078	Lockheed Martin F-22A Raptor [FF]	USAF 27th FS/1st FW, Langley AFB, VA
	04-4079	Lockheed Martin F-22A Raptor [HH]	USAF 199th FS/154th Wg, Hickam AFB, HI ANG
	04-4080	Lockheed Martin F-22A Raptor [HH]	USAF 199th FS/154th Wg, Hickam AFB, HI ANG
	04-4082	Lockheed Martin F-22A Raptor [FF] [149 FS]	USAF 149th FS/192nd FW/1st FW, Langley AFB, VA ANG
	04-4083	Lockheed Martin F-22A Raptor [AK]	USAF 3rd Wg, Elmendorf AFB, AK
	05-4081	Lockheed Martin F-22A Raptor (04-4081) [HH]	USAF 199th FS/154th Wg, Hickam AFB, HI ANG
	05-4084	Lockheed Martin F-22A Raptor [HH]	USAF 199th FS/154th Wg, Hickam AFB, HI ANG
	05-4085	Lockheed Martin F-22A Raptor [FF]	USAF 94th FS/1st FW, Langley AFB, VA
	05-4086	Lockheed Martin F-22A Raptor [AK]	USAF 90th FS/3rd Wg, Elmendorf AFB, AK
	05-4087	Lockheed Martin F-22A Raptor [AK]	USAF 90th FS/3rd Wg, Elmendorf AFB, AK
	05-4088	Lockheed Martin F-22A Raptor [AK]	USAF 90th FS/3rd Wg, Elmendorf AFB, AK
	05-4089	Lockheed Martin F-22A Raptor [FF]	USAF 149th FS/192nd Wg/1st FW, Langley AFB, VA ANG
	05-4090	Lockheed Martin F-22A Raptor [AK] [90 FS]	USAF 90th FS/3rd Wg, Elmendorf AFB, AK
	05-4091	Lockheed Martin F-22A Raptor [FF]	USAF 27th FS/1st FW, Langley AFB, VA
	05-4092	Lockheed Martin F-22A Raptor [AK]	USAF 525th FS/3rd Wg, Elmendorf AFB, AK
	05-4093	Lockheed Martin F-22A Raptor [HH]	USAF 199th FS/154th Wg, Hickam AFB, HI ANG
	05-4094	Lockheed Martin F-22A Raptor [AK]	USAF 525th FS/3rd Wg, Elmendorf AFB, AK
	05-4095	Lockheed Martin F-22A Raptor [FF]	USAF 27th FS/1st FW, Langley AFB, VA
	05-4096	Lockheed Martin F-22A Raptor [WA] [USAF WS]	USAF 433rd WPS/57th Wg, Nellis AFB, NV
	05-4097	Lockheed Martin F-22A Raptor [FF]	USAF 95th FS/1st FW, Langley AFB, VA
	05-4098	Lockheed Martin F-22A Raptor [HH]	USAF 199th FS/154th Wg, Hickam AFB, HI ANG
	05-4099	Lockheed Martin F-22A Raptor [FF]	USAF 94th FS/1st FW, Langley AFB, VA
	05-4100	Lockheed Martin F-22A Raptor [FF]	USAF 27th FS/1st FW, Langley AFB, VA
	05-4101	Lockheed Martin F-22A Raptor [AK]	USAF 3rd Wg, Elmendorf AFB, AK
	05-4102	Lockheed Martin F-22A Raptor [AK] [302 FS]	USAF 302nd FS/477th FG AFRC/3rd Wg, Elmendorf AFB, AK
	05-4103	Lockheed Martin F-22A Raptor [AK] [3 Wg]	USAF 90th FS/3rd Wg, Elmendorf AFB, AK
	05-4104	Lockheed Martin F-22A Raptor [FF]	USAF 27th FS/1st FW, Langley AFB, VA
	05-4105	Lockheed Martin F-22A Raptor [HH]	USAF 199th FS/154th Wg, Hickam AFB, HI ANG
	05-4106	Lockheed Martin F-22A Raptor [AK]	USAF 525th FS/3rd Wg, Elmendorf AFB, AK
	05-4107	Lockheed Martin F-22A Raptor [FF]	USAF 95th FS/1st FW, Langley AFB, VA

Serial	Type (code/other identity)	Owner/operator, location or fate	Notes
06-4108	Lockheed Martin F-22A Raptor [AK]	USAF 525th FS/3rd Wg, Elmendorf AFB, AK	
06-4109	Lockheed Martin F-22A Raptor [WA]	USAF 433rd WPS/57th Wg, Nellis AFB, NV	
06-4110	Lockheed Martin F-22A Raptor [AK] [11 AF]	USAF 90th FS/3rd Wg, Elmendorf AFB, AK	
06-4111	Lockheed Martin F-22A Raptor [OT]	USAF 422nd TES/53rd Wg, Nellis AFB, NV	
06-4112	Lockheed Martin F-22A Raptor [AK]	USAF 525th FS/3rd Wg, Elmendorf AFB, AK	
06-4113	Lockheed Martin F-22A Raptor [AK] [3 OG]	USAF 525th FS/3rd Wg, Elmendorf AFB, AK	
06-4114	Lockheed Martin F-22A Raptor [AK]	USAF 525th FS/3rd Wg, Elmendorf AFB, AK	
06-4115	Lockheed Martin F-22A Raptor [AK]	USAF 525th FS/3rd Wg, Elmendorf AFB, AK	
06-4116	Lockheed Martin F-22A Raptor [WA] [433 WPS]	USAF 433rd WPS/57th Wg, Nellis AFB, NV	
06-4117	Lockheed Martin F-22A Raptor [AK]	USAF 525th FS/3rd Wg, Elmendorf AFB, AK	
06-4118	Lockheed Martin F-22A Raptor [AK]	USAF 525th FS/3rd Wg, Elmendorf AFB, AK	
06-4119	Lockheed Martin F-22A Raptor [AK]	USAF 525th FS/3rd Wg, Elmendorf AFB, AK	
06-4120	Lockheed Martin F-22A Raptor [OT]	USAF 422nd TES/53rd Wg, Nellis AFB, NV	
06-4121	Lockheed Martin F-22A Raptor [AK]	USAF 525th FS/3rd Wg, Elmendorf AFB, AK	
06-4122	Lockheed Martin F-22A Raptor [AK]	USAF 525th FS/3rd Wg, Elmendorf AFB, AK	
06-4123	Lockheed Martin F-22A Raptor [AK]	USAF 525th FS/3rd Wg, Elmendorf AFB, AK	
06-4124	Lockheed Martin F-22A Raptor [OT]	USAF 422nd TES/53rd Wg, Nellis AFB, NV	
06-4126	Lockheed Martin F-22A Raptor [AK]	USAF 525th FS/3rd Wg, Elmendorf AFB, AK	
06-4127	Lockheed Martin F-22A Raptor [AK]	USAF 525th FS/3rd Wg, Elmendorf AFB, AK	
06-4128	Lockheed Martin F-22A Raptor [OT]	USAF 422nd TES/53rd Wg, Nellis AFB, NV	
06-4129	Lockheed Martin F-22A Raptor [AK]	USAF 525th FS/3rd Wg, Elmendorf AFB, AK	
06-4130	Lockheed Martin F-22A Raptor [AK]	USAF 525th FS/3rd Wg, Elmendorf AFB, AK	
07-4131	Lockheed Martin F-22A Raptor [AK]	USAF 525th FS/3rd Wg, Elmendorf AFB, AK	
07-4132	Lockheed Martin F-22A Raptor [ED] [411 FLTS]	USAF 411th FLTS/412th TW, Edwards AFB, CA	
07-4133	Lockheed Martin F-22A Raptor [AK]	USAF 525th FS/3rd Wg, Elmendorf AFB, AK	
07-4134	Lockheed Martin F-22A Raptor [AK]	USAF 525th FS/3rd Wg, Elmendorf AFB, AK	
07-4135	Lockheed Martin F-22A Raptor [AK]	USAF 90th FS/3rd Wg, Elmendorf AFB, AK	
07-4136	Lockheed Martin F-22A Raptor [AK]	USAF 90th FS/3rd Wg, Elmendorf AFB, AK	
07-4137	Lockheed Martin F-22A Raptor [AK]	USAF 90th FS/3rd Wg, Elmendorf AFB, AK	
07-4138	Lockheed Martin F-22A Raptor [AK]	USAF 90th FS/3rd Wg, Elmendorf AFB, AK	
07-4139	Lockheed Martin F-22A Raptor [AK]	USAF 90th FS/3rd Wg, Elmendorf AFB, AK	
07-4140	Lockheed Martin F-22A Raptor [AK]	USAF 90th FS/3rd Wg, Elmendorf AFB, AK	
07-4141	Lockheed Martin F-22A Raptor [AK]	USAF 90th FS/3rd Wg, Elmendorf AFB, AK	
07-4142	Lockheed Martin F-22A Raptor [AK]	USAF 90th FS/3rd Wg, Elmendorf AFB, AK	
07-4143	Lockheed Martin F-22A Raptor [AK]	USAF 90th FS/3rd Wg, Elmendorf AFB, AK	
07-4144	Lockheed Martin F-22A Raptor [AK]	USAF 90th FS/3rd Wg, Elmendorf AFB, AK	
07-4145	Lockheed Martin F-22A Raptor [AK]	USAF 90th FS/3rd Wg, Elmendorf AFB, AK	
07-4146	Lockheed Martin F-22A Raptor [AK]	USAF 90th FS/3rd Wg, Elmendorf AFB, AK	
07-4147	Lockheed Martin F-22A Raptor [AK] [477 FG]	USAF 90th FS/3rd Wg, Elmendorf AFB, AK	
07-4148	Lockheed Martin F-22A Raptor [AK]	USAF 90th FS/3rd Wg, Elmendorf AFB, AK	
07-4149	Lockheed Martin F-22A Raptor [AK]	USAF 90th FS/3rd Wg, Elmendorf AFB, AK	
07-4150	Lockheed Martin F-22A Raptor [AK]	USAF 90th FS/3rd Wg, Elmendorf AFB, AK	
07-4151	Lockheed Martin F-22A Raptor [AK]	USAF 90th FS/3rd Wg, Elmendorf AFB, AK	
08-4152	Lockheed Martin F-22A Raptor [FF]	USAF 94th FS/1st FW, Langley AFB, VA	
08-4153	Lockheed Martin F-22A Raptor [FF]	USAF 27th FS/1st FW, Langley AFB, VA	
08-4154	Lockheed Martin F-22A Raptor [FF]	USAF 27th FS/1st FW, Langley AFB, VA	
08-4155	Lockheed Martin F-22A Raptor [FF]	USAF 149th FS/192nd Wg/1st FW, Langley AFB, VA ANG	
08-4156	Lockheed Martin F-22A Raptor [FF]	USAF 94th FS/1st FW, Langley AFB, VA	
08-4157	Lockheed Martin F-22A Raptor [FF]	USAF 27th FS/1st FW, Langley AFB, VA	
08-4158	Lockheed Martin F-22A Raptor [FF]	USAF 27th FS/1st FW, Langley AFB, VA	
08-4159	Lockheed Martin F-22A Raptor [FF]	USAF 27th FS/1st FW, Langley AFB, VA	
08-4160	Lockheed Martin F-22A Raptor [FF]	USAF 94th FS/1st FW, Langley AFB, VA	
08-4161	Lockheed Martin F-22A Raptor [FF]	USAF 27th FS/1st FW, Langley AFB, VA	
08-4162	Lockheed Martin F-22A Raptor [FF] [1 FW]	USAF 94th FS/1st FW, Langley AFB, VA	
08-4163	Lockheed Martin F-22A Raptor [FF]	USAF 27th FS/1st FW, Langley AFB, VA	
08-4164	Lockheed Martin F-22A Raptor [FF]	USAF 27th FS/1st FW, Langley AFB, VA	
08-4165	Lockheed Martin F-22A Raptor [FF]	USAF 27th FS/1st FW, Langley AFB, VA	
08-4166	Lockheed Martin F-22A Raptor [FF]	USAF 94th FS/1st FW, Langley AFB, VA	
08-4167	Lockheed Martin F-22A Raptor [FF]	USAF 149th FS/192nd Wg/1st FW, Langley AFB, VA ANG	
08-4168	Lockheed Martin F-22A Raptor [FF]	USAF 94th FS/1st FW, Langley AFB, VA	

Notes	Serial	Type (code/other identity)	Owner/operator, location or fate
	08-4169	Lockheed Martin F-22A Raptor [FF]	USAF 94th FS/1st FW, Langley AFB, VA
	08-4170	Lockheed Martin F-22A Raptor [FF]	USAF 27th FS/1st FW, Langley AFB, VA
	08-4171	Lockheed Martin F-22A Raptor [FF]	USAF 94th FS/1st FW, Langley AFB, VA
	09-4172	Lockheed Martin F-22A Raptor [FF] [27 FS]	USAF 27th FS/1st FW, Langley AFB, VA
	09-4173	Lockheed Martin F-22A Raptor [FF]	USAF 94th FS/1st FW, Langley AFB, VA
	09-4174	Lockheed Martin F-22A Raptor [FF]	USAF 27th FS/1st FW, Langley AFB, VA
	09-4175	Lockheed Martin F-22A Raptor [FF]	USAF 94th FS/1st FW, Langley AFB, VA
	09-4176	Lockheed Martin F-22A Raptor [FF]	USAF 27th FS/1st FW, Langley AFB, VA
	09-4177	Lockheed Martin F-22A Raptor [FF]	USAF 149th FS/192nd Wg/1st FW, Langley AFB, VA ANG
	09-4178	Lockheed Martin F-22A Raptor [FF]	USAF 27th FS/1st FW, Langley AFB, VA
	09-4179	Lockheed Martin F-22A Raptor [FF]	USAF 94th FS/1st FW, Langley AFB, VA
	09-4180	Lockheed Martin F-22A Raptor [FF]	USAF 27th FS/1st FW, Langley AFB, VA
	09-4181	Lockheed Martin F-22A Raptor [FF]	USAF 94th FS/1st FW, Langley AFB, VA
	09-4182	Lockheed Martin F-22A Raptor [FF]	USAF 27th FS/1st FW, Langley AFB, VA
	09-4183	Lockheed Martin F-22A Raptor [FF]	USAF 94th FS/1st FW, Langley AFB, VA
	09-4184	Lockheed Martin F-22A Raptor [FF]	USAF 27th FS/1st FW, Langley AFB, VA
	09-4185	Lockheed Martin F-22A Raptor [FF] [1 OG]	USAF 27th FS/1st FW, Langley AFB, VA
	09-4186	Lockheed Martin F-22A Raptor [FF]	USAF 27th FS/1st FW, Langley AFB, VA
	09-4187	Lockheed Martin F-22A Raptor [FF]	USAF 94th FS/1st FW, Langley AFB, VA
	09-4188	Lockheed Martin F-22A Raptor [OT]	USAF 422nd TES/53rd Wg, Nellis AFB, NV
	09-4189	Lockheed Martin F-22A Raptor [FF]	USAF 27th FS/1st FW, Langley AFB, VA
	09-4190	Lockheed Martin F-22A Raptor [AK]	USAF 90th FS/3rd Wg, Elmendorf AFB, AK
	09-4191	Lockheed Martin F-22A Raptor [FF]	USAF 149th FS/192nd Wg/1st FW, Langley AFB, VA ANG
	10-4192	Lockheed Martin F-22A Raptor [FF] [192 WG]	USAF 149th FS/192nd Wg/1st FW, Langley AFB, VA ANG
	10-4193	Lockheed Martin F-22A Raptor [AK] [3 WG]	USAF 90th FS/3rd Wg, Elmendorf AFB, AK
	10-4194	Lockheed Martin F-22A Raptor [FF] [94 FS]	USAF 94th FS/1st FW, Langley AFB, VA
	10-4195	Lockheed Martin F-22A Raptor [AK] [525 FS]	USAF 525th FS/3rd Wg, Elmendorf AFB, AK

Boeing VC-25A/VC-25B

	Serial	Type (code/other identity)	Owner/operator, location or fate
	82-8000	Boeing VC-25A	USAF PAS/89th AW, Andrews AFB, MD
	92-9000	Boeing VC-25A	USAF PAS/89th AW, Andrews AFB, MD
	N894BA	Boeing VC-25B	USAF (on order, stored Kelly Field, TX)
	N895BA	Boeing VC-25B	USAF (on order, stored Kelly Field, TX)

Pilatus U-28A Draco

	Serial	Type (code/other identity)	Owner/operator, location or fate
	01-0415	Pilatus U-28A Draco (N415PB)	USAF 318th SOS/27th SOW, Cannon AFB, NM
	04-0688	Pilatus U-28A Draco (N707KH)	USAF 319th SOS/1st SOW, Hurlburt Field, FL
	05-0409	Pilatus U-28A Draco (N922RG)	USAF 34th SOS/1st SOW, Hurlburt Field, FL
	05-0419	Pilatus U-28A Draco (N419WA)	USAF 319th SOS/1st SOW, Hurlburt Field, FL
	05-0424	Pilatus U-28A Draco (N424PB)	USAF 318th SOS/27th SOW, Cannon AFB, NM
	05-0446	Pilatus U-28A Draco (N131JN)	USAF 318th SOS/27th SOW, Cannon AFB, NM
	05-0447	Pilatus U-28A Draco (N447PC)	USAF 319th SOS/1st SOW, Hurlburt Field, FL
	05-0482	Pilatus U-28A Draco (N482WA)	USAF 319th SOS/1st SOW, Hurlburt Field, FL
	05-0556	Pilatus U-28A Draco (N556HL)	USAF 318th SOS/27th SOW, Cannon AFB, NM
	05-0573	Pilatus U-28A Draco (N666GT)	USAF 319th SOS/1st SOW, Hurlburt Field, FL
	05-0597	Pilatus U-28A Draco (N597CH)	USAF 318th SOS/27th SOW, Cannon AFB, NM
	06-0692	Pilatus U-28A Draco (N692BC)	USAF 318th SOS/27th SOW, Cannon AFB, NM
	06-0740	Pilatus U-28A Draco (N740AF)	USAF 319th SOS/1st SOW, Hurlburt Field, FL
	07-0488	Pilatus U-28A Draco (N56EZ)	USAF 319th SOS/1st SOW, Hurlburt Field, FL
	07-0691	Pilatus U-28A Draco (N691PC)	USAF 318th SOS/27th SOW, Cannon AFB, NM
	07-0711	Pilatus U-28A Draco (N711PN)	USAF 319th SOS/1st SOW, Hurlburt Field, FL
	07-0712	Pilatus U-28A Draco (N609TW)	USAF 319th SOS/1st SOW, Hurlburt Field, FL
	07-0777	Pilatus U-28A Draco (N72DZ)	USAF 319th SOS/1st SOW, Hurlburt Field, FL
	07-0779	Pilatus U-28A Draco (N779PC)	USAF 318th SOS/27th SOW, Cannon AFB, NM
	07-0793	Pilatus U-28A Draco (N96MV)	USAF 318th SOS/27th SOW, Cannon AFB, NM
	07-0808	Pilatus U-28A Draco (N531MP)	USAF 318th SOS/27th SOW, Cannon AFB, NM
	07-0821	Pilatus U-28A Draco (N821PE)	USAF 319th SOS/1st SOW, Hurlburt Field, FL
	07-0829	Pilatus U-28A Draco (N829PE)	USAF 319th SOS/1st SOW, Hurlburt Field, FL
	07-0838	Pilatus U-28A Draco (N838PE)	USAF 319th SOS/1st SOW, Hurlburt Field, FL

Serial	Type (code/other identity)	Owner/operator, location or fate	Notes
07-0840	Pilatus U-28A Draco (N840PE)	USAF 319th SOS/1st SOW, Hurlburt Field, FL	
08-0519	Pilatus U-28A Draco (N519PC)	USAF 319th SOS/1st SOW, Hurlburt Field, FL	
08-0581	Pilatus U-28A Draco (N581PC)	*Preserved Cannon AFB, May 2024*	
08-0646	Pilatus U-28A Draco (N875RJ)	USAF 319th SOS/1st SOW, Hurlburt Field, FL	
08-0700	Pilatus U-28A Draco (N600KP)	USAF 319th SOS/1st SOW, Hurlburt Field, FL	
08-0718	Pilatus U-28A Draco (N824BK)	USAF 319th SOS/1st SOW, Hurlburt Field, FL	
08-0790	Pilatus U-28A Draco (N757ED)	USAF 319th SOS/1st SOW, Hurlburt Field, FL	
08-0809	Pilatus U-28A Draco (N36EG)	USAF 319th SOS/1st SOW, Hurlburt Field, FL	
08-0822	Pilatus U-28A Draco (N822BM)	USAF 319th SOS/1st SOW, Hurlburt Field, FL	
08-0835	Pilatus U-28A Draco (N100MS)	USAF 318th SOS/27th SOW, Cannon AFB, NM	
08-0850	Pilatus U-28A Draco (N850CB)	USAF 319th SOS/1st SOW, Hurlburt Field, FL	

Boeing C-32
NOTE: There is evidence to suggest that the serials 25001 and 96143 have been used by more than one airframe.

Serial	Type (code/other identity)	Owner/operator, location or fate	Notes
98-0001	Boeing C-32A	USAF 1st AS/89th AW, Andrews AFB, MD	
98-0002	Boeing C-32A	USAF 1st AS/89th AW, Andrews AFB, MD	
99-0003	Boeing C-32A	USAF 1st AS/89th AW, Andrews AFB, MD	
99-0004	Boeing C-32A	USAF 1st AS/89th AW, Andrews AFB, MD	
99-6143	Boeing C-32B	USAF 486th FLTS/46th TW, Eglin AFB, FL	
00-9001	Boeing C-32B	USAF 150th SOS/108th Wg, McGuire AFB, NJ ANG	
02-4452	Boeing C-32B	USAF 150th SOS/108th Wg, McGuire AFB, NJ ANG	
02-5001	Boeing C-32B	USAF 486th FLTS/46th TW, Eglin AFB, FL	
09-0015	Boeing C-32A	USAF 1st AS/89th AW, Andrews AFB, MD	
09-0016	Boeing C-32A	USAF 1st AS/89th AW, Andrews AFB, MD	
09-0017	Boeing C-32A	USAF 1st AS/89th AW, Andrews AFB, MD	
19-0018	Boeing C-32A	USAF 1st AS/89th AW, Andrews AFB, MD	

Lockheed Martin F-35A Lightning II

Serial	Type (code/other identity)	Owner/operator, location or fate	Notes
07-0744	Lockheed Martin F-35A Lightning II [ED] [461 FLTS]	USAF 461st FLTS/412th TW, Edwards AFB, CA	
07-0745	Lockheed Martin F-35A Lightning II [ED]	USAF 461st FLTS/412th TW, Edwards AFB, CA	
08-0746	Lockheed Martin F-35A Lightning II [EG]	USAF 58th FS/33rd FW, Eglin AFB, FL	
08-0747	Lockheed Martin F-35A Lightning II [EG]	USAF 58th FS/33rd FW, Eglin AFB, FL	
08-0748	Lockheed Martin F-35A Lightning II [EG]	USAF 58th FS/33rd FW, Eglin AFB, FL	
08-0749	Lockheed Martin F-35A Lightning II [EG]	USAF 58th FS/33rd FW, Eglin AFB, FL	
08-0750	Lockheed Martin F-35A Lightning II [EG]	USAF 58th FS/33rd FW, Eglin AFB, FL	
08-0751	Lockheed Martin F-35A Lightning II [EG]	USAF 58th FS/33rd FW, Eglin AFB, FL	
09-5001	Lockheed Martin F-35A Lightning II [EG]	USAF 58th FS/33rd FW, Eglin AFB, FL	
09-5002	Lockheed Martin F-35A Lightning II [EG]	USAF 58th FS/33rd FW, Eglin AFB, FL	
09-5003	Lockheed Martin F-35A Lightning II [EG]	USAF 58th FS/33rd FW, Eglin AFB, FL	
09-5004	Lockheed Martin F-35A Lightning II [LF]	USAF 61st FS/56th FW, Luke AFB, AZ	
09-5005	Lockheed Martin F-35A Lightning II [LF]	USAF 61st FS/56th FW, Luke AFB, AZ	
09-5006	Lockheed Martin F-35A Lightning II [LF]	USAF 61st FS/56th FW, Luke AFB, AZ	
09-5007	Lockheed Martin F-35A Lightning II [LF]	USAF 61st FS/56th FW, Luke AFB, AZ	
10-5009	Lockheed Martin F-35A Lightning II [LF]	USAF 61st FS/56th FW, Luke AFB, AZ	
10-5010	Lockheed Martin F-35A Lightning II [LF] [310 FS]	USAF 310th FS/56th FW, Luke AFB, AZ	
10-5011	Lockheed Martin F-35A Lightning II [LF]	USAF 61st FS/56th FW, Luke AFB, AZ	
10-5012	Lockheed Martin F-35A Lightning II [OT]	USAF 422nd TES/53rd TEG, Nellis AFB, NV	
10-5013	Lockheed Martin F-35A Lightning II [EG]	USAF 58th FS/33rd FW, Eglin AFB, FL	
10-5014	Lockheed Martin F-35A Lightning II [EG]	USAF 58th FS/33rd FW, Eglin AFB, FL	
10-5016	Lockheed Martin F-35A Lightning II [EG]	USAF 58th FS/33rd FW, Eglin AFB, FL	
10-5017	Lockheed Martin F-35A Lightning II [EG]	USAF 58th FS/33rd FW, Eglin AFB, FL	
10-5018	Lockheed Martin F-35A Lightning II [EG]	USAF 58th FS/33rd FW, Eglin AFB, FL	
11-5020	Lockheed Martin F-35A Lightning II [WA] [57 OG/CC]	USAF 65th AGRS/57th Wg, Nellis AFB, NV	
11-5021	Lockheed Martin F-35A Lightning II [WA] [65 AGRS]	USAF 65th AGRS/57th Wg, Nellis AFB, NV	
11-5022	Lockheed Martin F-35A Lightning II [EG]	USAF 58th FS/33rd FW, Eglin AFB, FL	
11-5023	Lockheed Martin F-35A Lightning II [EG]	USAF 58th FS/33rd FW, Eglin AFB, FL	
11-5024	Lockheed Martin F-35A Lightning II [EG]	USAF 58th FS/33rd FW, Eglin AFB, FL	
11-5025	Lockheed Martin F-35A Lightning II [EG]	USAF 58th FS/33rd FW, Eglin AFB, FL	
11-5026	Lockheed Martin F-35A Lightning II [EG]	USAF 58th FS/33rd FW, Eglin AFB, FL	
11-5027	Lockheed Martin F-35A Lightning II [EG]	USAF 58th FS/33rd FW, Eglin AFB, FL	

Notes	Serial	Type (code/other identity)	Owner/operator, location or fate
	11-5028	Lockheed Martin F-35A Lightning II [EG]	USAF 58th FS/33rd FW, Eglin AFB, FL
	11-5029	Lockheed Martin F-35A Lightning II [EG]	USAF 58th FS/33rd FW, Eglin AFB, FL
	11-5030	Lockheed Martin F-35A Lightning II [LF] [61 FS]	USAF 61st FS/56th FW, Luke AFB, AZ
	11-5031	Lockheed Martin F-35A Lightning II [LF]	USAF 63rd FS/56th FW, Luke AFB, AZ
	11-5032	Lockheed Martin F-35A Lightning II [EG]	USAF 58th FS/33rd FW, Eglin AFB, FL
	11-5033	Lockheed Martin F-35A Lightning II [EG] [33 FW]	USAF 58th FS/33rd FW, Eglin AFB, FL
	11-5034	Lockheed Martin F-35A Lightning II [EG]	USAF 58th FS/33rd FW, Eglin AFB, FL
	11-5035	Lockheed Martin F-35A Lightning II [LF]	USAF 63rd FS/56th FW, Luke AFB, AZ
	11-5036	Lockheed Martin F-35A Lightning II [LF]	USAF 61st FS/56th FW, Luke AFB, AZ
	11-5037	Lockheed Martin F-35A Lightning II [LF]	USAF 63rd FS/56th FW, Luke AFB, AZ
	11-5038	Lockheed Martin F-35A Lightning II [LF]	USAF 63rd FS/56th FW, Luke AFB, AZ
	11-5039	Lockheed Martin F-35A Lightning II [LF]	USAF 63rd FS/56th FW, Luke AFB, AZ
	11-5040	Lockheed Martin F-35A Lightning II [LF]	USAF 63rd FS/56th FW, Luke AFB, AZ
	11-5041	Lockheed Martin F-35A Lightning II [LF]	USAF 63rd FS/56th FW, Luke AFB, AZ
	12-5042	Lockheed Martin F-35A Lightning II [LF]	USAF 61st FS/56th FW, Luke AFB, AZ
	12-5043	Lockheed Martin F-35A Lightning II [LF]	USAF 61st FS/56th FW, Luke AFB, AZ
	12-5044	Lockheed Martin F-35A Lightning II [LF] [944 FW]	USAF 52nd FS/944th FW AFRC, Luke AFB, AZ
	12-5045	Lockheed Martin F-35A Lightning II [LF]	USAF 308th FS/56th FW, Luke AFB, AZ
	12-5046	Lockheed Martin F-35A Lightning II [LF]	USAF 63rd FS/56th FW, Luke AFB, AZ
	12-5047	Lockheed Martin F-35A Lightning II [LF]	USAF 61st FS/56th FW, Luke AFB, AZ
	12-5048	Lockheed Martin F-35A Lightning II [LF]	USAF 61st FS/56th FW, Luke AFB, AZ
	12-5049	Lockheed Martin F-35A Lightning II [LF]	USAF 63rd FS/56th FW, Luke AFB, AZ
	12-5050	Lockheed Martin F-35A Lightning II [LF]	USAF 308th FS/56th FW, Luke AFB, AZ
	12-5051	Lockheed Martin F-35A Lightning II [LF]	USAF 56th FW, Luke AFB, AZ
	12-5054	Lockheed Martin F-35A Lightning II [LF]	USAF 61st FS/56th FW, Luke AFB, AZ
	12-5055	Lockheed Martin F-35A Lightning II [LF]	USAF 61st FS/56th FW, Luke AFB, AZ
	12-5056	Lockheed Martin F-35A Lightning II [LF] [56 FW]	USAF 61st FS/56th FW, Luke AFB, AZ
	12-5057	Lockheed Martin F-35A Lightning II [LF]	USAF 61st FS/56th FW, Luke AFB, AZ
	12-5058	Lockheed Martin F-35A Lightning II [LF]	USAF 62nd FS/56th FW, Luke AFB, AZ
	12-5059	Lockheed Martin F-35A Lightning II [LF]	USAF 63rd FS/56th FW, Luke AFB, AZ
	13-5065	Lockheed Martin F-35A Lightning II [LF]	USAF 62nd FS/56th FW, Luke AFB, AZ
	13-5066	Lockheed Martin F-35A Lightning II [LF]	USAF 308th FS/56th FW, Luke AFB, AZ
	13-5067	Lockheed Martin F-35A Lightning II [LF]	USAF 308th FS/56th FW, Luke AFB, AZ
	13-5068	Lockheed Martin F-35A Lightning II [LF] [62 FS]	USAF 62nd FS/56th FW, Luke AFB, AZ
	13-5069	Lockheed Martin F-35A Lightning II [LF]	USAF 308th FS/56th FW, Luke AFB, AZ
	13-5070	Lockheed Martin F-35A Lightning II [LF]	USAF 308th FS/56th FW, Luke AFB, AZ
	13-5071	Lockheed Martin F-35A Lightning II [LF]	USAF 62nd FS/56th FW, Luke AFB, AZ
	13-5072	Lockheed Martin F-35A Lightning II [LF]	USAF 308th FS/56th FW, Luke AFB, AZ
	13-5073	Lockheed Martin F-35A Lightning II [EG]	USAF 33rd FW, Eglin AFB, FL
	13-5074	Lockheed Martin F-35A Lightning II [OT]	USAF 422nd TES/53rd TEG, Nellis AFB, NV
	13-5075	Lockheed Martin F-35A Lightning II [LF]	USAF 308th FS/56th FW, Luke AFB, AZ
	13-5076	Lockheed Martin F-35A Lightning II [LF]	USAF 62nd FS/56th FW, Luke AFB, AZ
	13-5077	Lockheed Martin F-35A Lightning II [LF]	USAF 308th FS/56th FW, Luke AFB, AZ
	13-5078	Lockheed Martin F-35A Lightning II [LF]	USAF 63rd FS/56th FW, Luke AFB, AZ
	13-5079	Lockheed Martin F-35A Lightning II [LF]	USAF 63rd FS/56th FW, Luke AFB, AZ
	13-5080	Lockheed Martin F-35A Lightning II [LF]	USAF 308th FS/56th FW, Luke AFB, AZ
	13-5081	Lockheed Martin F-35A Lightning II [LF]	USAF 308th FS/56th FW, Luke AFB, AZ
	13-5082	Lockheed Martin F-35A Lightning II [LF]	USAF 308th FS/56th FW, Luke AFB, AZ
	13-5083	Lockheed Martin F-35A Lightning II [LF]	USAF 308th FS/56th FW, Luke AFB, AZ
	14-5089	Lockheed Martin F-35A Lightning II [WA]	USAF 6th WPS/57th Wg, Nellis AFB, NV
	14-5090	Lockheed Martin F-35A Lightning II [LF]	USAF 63rd FS/56th FW, Luke AFB, AZ
	14-5091	Lockheed Martin F-35A Lightning II [LF]	USAF 63rd FS/56th FW, Luke AFB, AZ
	14-5092	Lockheed Martin F-35A Lightning II [LF]	USAF 62nd FS/56th FW, Luke AFB, AZ
	14-5093	Lockheed Martin F-35A Lightning II [LF]	USAF 310th FS/56th FW, Luke AFB, AZ
	14-5094	Lockheed Martin F-35A Lightning II [LF]	USAF 61st FS/56th FW, Luke AFB, AZ
	14-5095	Lockheed Martin F-35A Lightning II [LF]	USAF 62nd FS/56th FW, Luke AFB, AZ
	14-5096	Lockheed Martin F-35A Lightning II [LF]	USAF 61st FS/56th FW, Luke AFB, AZ
	14-5097	Lockheed Martin F-35A Lightning II [LF]	USAF 56th FW, Luke AFB, AZ
	14-5098	Lockheed Martin F-35A Lightning II [EG]	USAF 58th FS/33rd FW, Eglin AFB, FL
	14-5099	Lockheed Martin F-35A Lightning II [EG]	USAF 60th FS/33rd FW, Eglin AFB, FL
	14-5100	Lockheed Martin F-35A Lightning II [EG]	USAF 33rd FW, Eglin AFB, FL
	14-5101	Lockheed Martin F-35A Lightning II [EG]	USAF 60th FS/33rd FW, Eglin AFB, FL

Serial	Type (code/other identity)	Owner/operator, location or fate	Notes
14-5102	Lockheed Martin F-35A Lightning II [EG]	USAF 60th FS/33rd FW, Eglin AFB, FL	
14-5103	Lockheed Martin F-35A Lightning II [LF] [56 OG]	USAF 62nd FS/56th FW, Luke AFB, AZ	
14-5104	Lockheed Martin F-35A Lightning II [LF]	USAF 63rd FS/56th FW, Luke AFB, AZ	
14-5105	Lockheed Martin F-35A Lightning II [EG]	USAF 58th FS/33rd FW, Eglin AFB, FL	
14-5106	Lockheed Martin F-35A Lightning II [LF]	USAF 310th FS/56th FW, Luke AFB, AZ	
14-5107	Lockheed Martin F-35A Lightning II [LF]	USAF 62nd FS/56th FW, Luke AFB, AZ	
15-5118	Lockheed Martin F-35A Lightning II [OT]	USAF 422nd TES/53rd TEG, Nellis AFB, NV	
15-5119	Lockheed Martin F-35A Lightning II [EG]	USAF 60th FS/33rd FW, Eglin AFB, FL	
15-5120	Lockheed Martin F-35A Lightning II [LF] [63 FS]	USAF 63rd FS/56th FW, Luke AFB, AZ	
15-5121	Lockheed Martin F-35A Lightning II []	USAF	
15-5122	Lockheed Martin F-35A Lightning II [EG]	USAF 60th FS/33rd FW, Eglin AFB, FL	
15-5123	Lockheed Martin F-35A Lightning II [LF]	USAF 310th FS/56th FW, Luke AFB, AZ	
15-5124	Lockheed Martin F-35A Lightning II [EG]	USAF 60th FS/33rd FW, Eglin AFB, FL	
15-5125	Lockheed Martin F-35A Lightning II [LF] [52 FS]	USAF 52nd FS/944th FW AFRC, Luke AFB, AZ	
15-5126	Lockheed Martin F-35A Lightning II [EG]	USAF 60th FS/33rd FW, Eglin AFB, FL	
15-5127	Lockheed Martin F-35A Lightning II [LF]	USAF 63rd FS/56th FW, Luke AFB, AZ	
15-5128	Lockheed Martin F-35A Lightning II [EG]	USAF 60th FS/33rd FW, Eglin AFB, FL	
15-5129	Lockheed Martin F-35A Lightning II [LF]	USAF 63rd FS/56th FW, Luke AFB, AZ	
15-5130	Lockheed Martin F-35A Lightning II [EG]	USAF 33rd FW, Eglin AFB, FL	
15-5131	Lockheed Martin F-35A Lightning II [EG]	USAF 60th FS/33rd FW, Eglin AFB, FL	
15-5132	Lockheed Martin F-35A Lightning II [EG]	USAF 60th FS/33rd FW, Eglin AFB, FL	
15-5133	Lockheed Martin F-35A Lightning II [EG] [33 OG]	USAF 60th FS/33rd FW, Eglin AFB, FL	
15-5134	Lockheed Martin F-35A Lightning II [EG]	USAF 60th FS/33rd FW, Eglin AFB, FL	
15-5135	Lockheed Martin F-35A Lightning II [LF]	USAF 63rd FS/56th FW, Luke AFB, AZ	
15-5136	Lockheed Martin F-35A Lightning II [LF]	USAF 62nd FS/56th FW, Luke AFB, AZ	
15-5137	Lockheed Martin F-35A Lightning II [EG]	USAF 60th FS/33rd FW, Eglin AFB, FL	
15-5138	Lockheed Martin F-35A Lightning II [EG]	USAF 60th FS/33rd FW, Eglin AFB, FL	
15-5139	Lockheed Martin F-35A Lightning II [LF]	USAF 56th FW, Luke AFB, AZ	
15-5140	Lockheed Martin F-35A Lightning II [EG]	USAF 58th FS/33rd FW, Eglin AFB, FL	
15-5141	Lockheed Martin F-35A Lightning II [WA]	USAF 6th WPS/57th Wg, Nellis AFB, NV	
15-5142	Lockheed Martin F-35A Lightning II [EG]	USAF 33rd FW, Eglin AFB, FL	
15-5143	Lockheed Martin F-35A Lightning II [EG]	USAF 58th FS/33rd FW, Eglin AFB, FL	
15-5160	Lockheed Martin F-35A Lightning II [WA]	USAF 6th WPS/57th Wg, Nellis AFB, NV	
15-5161	Lockheed Martin F-35A Lightning II [LF] [61 FS]	USAF 61st FS/56th FW, Luke AFB, AZ	
15-5162	Lockheed Martin F-35A Lightning II [HL] [62 FS]	USAF 62nd FS/56th FW, Luke AFB, AZ	
15-5163	Lockheed Martin F-35A Lightning II [HL] [63 FS]	USAF 63rd FS/56th FW, Luke AFB, AZ	
15-5164	Lockheed Martin F-35A Lightning II [LF]	USAF 63rd FS/56th FW, Luke AFB, AZ	
15-5165	Lockheed Martin F-35A Lightning II [HL]	USAF 4th FS/388th FW, Hill AFB, UT	
15-5166	Lockheed Martin F-35A Lightning II [LF]	USAF 63rd FS/56th FW, Luke AFB, AZ	
15-5167	Lockheed Martin F-35A Lightning II [WA]	USAF 6th WPS/57th Wg, Nellis AFB, NV	
15-5168	Lockheed Martin F-35A Lightning II [WA]	USAF 6th WPS/57th Wg, Nellis AFB, NV	
15-5169	Lockheed Martin F-35A Lightning II [LF] [69 FS]	USAF 69th FS/944th FW AFRC, Luke AFB, AZ	
15-5170	Lockheed Martin F-35A Lightning II [HL]	USAF 34th FS/388th FW, Hill AFB, UT	
15-5171	Lockheed Martin F-35A Lightning II [LF]	USAF 63rd FS/56th FW, Luke AFB, AZ	
15-5172	Lockheed Martin F-35A Lightning II [HL]	USAF 34th FS/388th FW, Hill AFB, UT	
15-5173	Lockheed Martin F-35A Lightning II [LF]	USAF 56th FW, Luke AFB, AZ	
15-5174	Lockheed Martin F-35A Lightning II [LF]	USAF 310th FS/56th FW, Luke AFB, AZ	
15-5175	Lockheed Martin F-35A Lightning II [LF]	USAF 56th FW, Luke AFB, AZ	
15-5176	Lockheed Martin F-35A Lightning II [LF]	USAF 56th FW, Luke AFB, AZ	
15-5177	Lockheed Martin F-35A Lightning II [LF]	USAF 63rd FS/56th FW, Luke AFB, AZ	
15-5178	Lockheed Martin F-35A Lightning II [HL]	USAF 34th FS/388th FW, Hill AFB, UT	
15-5179	Lockheed Martin F-35A Lightning II [LF]	USAF 63rd FS/56th FW, Luke AFB, AZ	
15-5180	Lockheed Martin F-35A Lightning II [LF]	USAF 308th FS/56th FW, Luke AFB, AZ	
15-5181	Lockheed Martin F-35A Lightning II [LF]	USAF 62nd FS/56th FW, Luke AFB, AZ	
15-5182	Lockheed Martin F-35A Lightning II [LF]	USAF 62nd FS/56th FW, Luke AFB, AZ	
15-5183	Lockheed Martin F-35A Lightning II [HL]	USAF 421st FS/388th FW, Hill AFB, UT	
15-5184	Lockheed Martin F-35A Lightning II [LF]	USAF 56th FW, Luke AFB, AZ	
15-5185	Lockheed Martin F-35A Lightning II [LF]	USAF 63rd FS/56th FW, Luke AFB, AZ	
15-5186	Lockheed Martin F-35A Lightning II [LF]	USAF 56th FW, Luke AFB, AZ	
15-5187	Lockheed Martin F-35A Lightning II [HL]	USAF 34th FS/388th FW, Hill AFB, UT	
15-5188	Lockheed Martin F-35A Lightning II [EG]	USAF 60th FS/33rd FW, Eglin AFB, FL	
15-5189	Lockheed Martin F-35A Lightning II [LF] [308 FS]	USAF 308th FS/56th FW, Luke AFB, AZ	

Notes	Serial	Type (code/other identity)	Owner/operator, location or fate
	15-5190	Lockheed Martin F-35A Lightning II [LF]	USAF 63rd FS/56th FW, Luke AFB, AZ
	15-5191	Lockheed Martin F-35A Lightning II [LF]	USAF 63rd FS/56th FW, Luke AFB, AZ
	15-5192	Lockheed Martin F-35A Lightning II [HL]	USAF 4th FS/388th FW, Hill AFB, UT
	15-5193	Lockheed Martin F-35A Lightning II [LF]	USAF 63rd FS/56th FW, Luke AFB, AZ
	15-5194	Lockheed Martin F-35A Lightning II [HL]	USAF 4th FS/388th FW, Hill AFB, UT
	15-5195	Lockheed Martin F-35A Lightning II [LF]	USAF 56th FW, Luke AFB, AZ
	15-5196	Lockheed Martin F-35A Lightning II [LF]	USAF 308th FS/56th FW, Luke AFB, AZ
	15-5198	Lockheed Martin F-35A Lightning II [LF]	USAF 63rd FS/56th FW, Luke AFB, AZ
	15-5199	Lockheed Martin F-35A Lightning II [EG]	USAF 60th FS/33rd FW, Eglin AFB, FL
	15-5200	Lockheed Martin F-35A Lightning II [HL]	USAF 421st FS/388th FW, Hill AFB, UT
	15-5201	Lockheed Martin F-35A Lightning II [HL]	USAF 421st FS/388th FW, Hill AFB, UT
	15-5202	Lockheed Martin F-35A Lightning II [EG]	USAF 58th FS/33rd FW, Eglin AFB, FL
	15-5203	Lockheed Martin F-35A Lightning II [HL]	USAF 421st FS/388th FW, Hill AFB, UT
	17-5237	Lockheed Martin F-35A Lightning II [HL]	USAF 34th FS/388th FW, Hill AFB, UT
	17-5238	Lockheed Martin F-35A Lightning II [HL]	USAF 421st FS/388th FW, Hill AFB, UT
	17-5239	Lockheed Martin F-35A Lightning II [HL]	USAF 421st FS/388th FW, Hill AFB, UT
	17-5240	Lockheed Martin F-35A Lightning II [ED]	USAF 461st FLTS/412th TW, Edwards AFB, CA
	17-5241	Lockheed Martin F-35A Lightning II [OT]	USAF 422nd TES/53rd TEG, Nellis AFB, NV
	17-5242	Lockheed Martin F-35A Lightning II [ED]	USAF 461st FLTS/412th TW, Edwards AFB, CA
	17-5243	Lockheed Martin F-35A Lightning II [HL]	USAF 4th FS/388th FW, Hill AFB, UT
	17-5244	Lockheed Martin F-35A Lightning II [OT]	USAF 422nd TES/53rd TEG, Nellis AFB, NV
	17-5245	Lockheed Martin F-35A Lightning II [HL]	USAF 4th FS/388th FW, Hill AFB, UT
	17-5246	Lockheed Martin F-35A Lightning II [WA] [6 WPS]	USAF 6th WPS/57th Wg, Nellis AFB, NV
	17-5247	Lockheed Martin F-35A Lightning II [HL]	USAF 421st FS/388th FW, Hill AFB, UT
	17-5248	Lockheed Martin F-35A Lightning II [HL]	USAF 421st FS/388th FW, Hill AFB, UT
	17-5249	Lockheed Martin F-35A Lightning II [OT]	USAF 422nd TES/53rd TEG, Nellis AFB, NV
	17-5250	Lockheed Martin F-35A Lightning II [WA]	USAF 6th WPS/57th Wg, Nellis AFB, NV
	17-5251	Lockheed Martin F-35A Lightning II [HL]	USAF 4th FS/388th FW, Hill AFB, UT
	17-5252	Lockheed Martin F-35A Lightning II [HL]	USAF 4th FS/388th FW, Hill AFB, UT
	17-5253	Lockheed Martin F-35A Lightning II [HL]	USAF 4th FS/388th FW, Hill AFB, UT
	17-5254	Lockheed Martin F-35A Lightning II [HL]	USAF 34th FS/388th FW, Hill AFB, UT
	17-5255	Lockheed Martin F-35A Lightning II [HL]	USAF 34th FS/388th FW, Hill AFB, UT
	17-5256	Lockheed Martin F-35A Lightning II [HL]	USAF 34th FS/388th FW, Hill AFB, UT
	17-5257	Lockheed Martin F-35A Lightning II [HL]	USAF 34th FS/388th FW, Hill AFB, UT
	17-5258	Lockheed Martin F-35A Lightning II [HL]	USAF 34th FS/388th FW, Hill AFB, UT
	17-5259	Lockheed Martin F-35A Lightning II [HL]	USAF 34th FS/388th FW, Hill AFB, UT
	17-5260	Lockheed Martin F-35A Lightning II [HL]	USAF 34th FS/388th FW, Hill AFB, UT
	17-5261	Lockheed Martin F-35A Lightning II [HL]	USAF 34th FS/388th FW, Hill AFB, UT
	17-5262	Lockheed Martin F-35A Lightning II [HL]	USAF 34th FS/388th FW, Hill AFB, UT
	17-5263	Lockheed Martin F-35A Lightning II [HL]	USAF 34th FS/388th FW, Hill AFB, UT
	17-5264	Lockheed Martin F-35A Lightning II [HL]	USAF 421st FS/388th FW, Hill AFB, UT
	17-5265	Lockheed Martin F-35A Lightning II [VT] [158 FW]	USAF 134th FS/158th FW, Burlington, VT ANG
	17-5266	Lockheed Martin F-35A Lightning II [VT]	USAF 134th FS/158th FW, Burlington, VT ANG
	17-5267	Lockheed Martin F-35A Lightning II [OT] [USAFWC]	USAF 422nd TES/53rd TEG, Nellis AFB, NV
	17-5268	Lockheed Martin F-35A Lightning II [HL]	USAF 421st FS/388th FW, Hill AFB, UT
	17-5269	Lockheed Martin F-35A Lightning II (composite with nose from 10-5015)	Ogden ALC, Hill AFB, UT (rebuild)
	17-5270	Lockheed Martin F-35A Lightning II [HL]	USAF 4th FS/388th FW, Hill AFB, UT
	17-5271	Lockheed Martin F-35A Lightning II [OT]	USAF 422nd TES/53rd TEG, Nellis AFB, NV
	17-5272	Lockheed Martin F-35A Lightning II [WA]	USAF 6th WPS/57th Wg, Nellis AFB, NV
	17-5273	Lockheed Martin F-35A Lightning II [HL]	USAF 421st FS/388th FW, Hill AFB, UT
	17-5274	Lockheed Martin F-35A Lightning II [WA]	USAF 6th WPS/57th Wg, Nellis AFB, NV
	17-5275	Lockheed Martin F-35A Lightning II [WA]	USAF 6th WPS/57th Wg, Nellis AFB, NV
	17-5276	Lockheed Martin F-35A Lightning II [HL]	USAF 421st FS/388th FW, Hill AFB, UT
	17-5277	Lockheed Martin F-35A Lightning II [VT]	USAF 134th FS/158th FW, Burlington, VT ANG
	17-5278	Lockheed Martin F-35A Lightning II [VT]	USAF 134th FS/158th FW, Burlington, VT ANG
	17-5279	Lockheed Martin F-35A Lightning II [VT]	USAF 134th FS/158th FW, Burlington, VT ANG
	17-5280	Lockheed Martin F-35A Lightning II [VT]	USAF 134th FS/158th FW, Burlington, VT ANG
	17-5281	Lockheed Martin F-35A Lightning II [HL]	USAF 421st FS/388th FW, Hill AFB, UT
	17-5282	Lockheed Martin F-35A Lightning II [HL] [419 OG]	USAF 466th FS/388th FW, Hill AFB, UT
	17-5283	Lockheed Martin F-35A Lightning II [WA]	USAF 6th WPS/57th Wg, Nellis AFB, NV
	17-5284	Lockheed Martin F-35A Lightning II [VT]	USAF 134th FS/158th FW, Burlington, VT ANG

Serial	Type (code/other identity)	Owner/operator, location or fate	Notes
18-0001	Lockheed Martin F-35A Lightning II	USAF, stored Luke AFB, AZ (ex THK order)	
18-0002	Lockheed Martin F-35A Lightning II	USAF, stored Luke AFB, AZ (ex THK order)	
18-0003	Lockheed Martin F-35A Lightning II	USAF, stored Luke AFB, AZ (ex THK order)	
18-0004	Lockheed Martin F-35A Lightning II	USAF, stored Luke AFB, AZ (ex THK order)	
18-0005	Lockheed Martin F-35A Lightning II	USAF, stored Fort Worth, TX (ex THK order)	
18-0006	Lockheed Martin F-35A Lightning II	USAF, stored Fort Worth, TX (ex THK order)	
18-5336	Lockheed Martin F-35A Lightning II [VT]	USAF 134th FS/158th FW, Burlington, VT ANG	
18-5337	Lockheed Martin F-35A Lightning II [VT]	USAF 134th FS/158th FW, Burlington, VT ANG	
18-5338	Lockheed Martin F-35A Lightning II [VT]	USAF 134th FS/158th FW, Burlington, VT ANG	
18-5339	Lockheed Martin F-35A Lightning II [VT]	USAF 134th FS/158th FW, Burlington, VT ANG	
18-5340	Lockheed Martin F-35A Lightning II [VT]	USAF 134th FS/158th FW, Burlington, VT ANG	
18-5341	Lockheed Martin F-35A Lightning II [VT]	USAF 134th FS/158th FW, Burlington, VT ANG	
18-5342	Lockheed Martin F-35A Lightning II [TY]	USAF 325th FW, Tyndall AFB, FL	
18-5343	Lockheed Martin F-35A Lightning II [VT]	USAF 134th FS/158th FW, Burlington, VT ANG	
18-5344	Lockheed Martin F-35A Lightning II [VT]	USAF 134th FS/158th FW, Burlington, VT ANG	
18-5345	Lockheed Martin F-35A Lightning II [AK] [354 OG]	USAF 356th FS/354th FW, Eielson AFB, AK	
18-5346	Lockheed Martin F-35A Lightning II [AK]	USAF 356th FS/354th FW, Eielson AFB, AK	
18-5347	Lockheed Martin F-35A Lightning II [AK]	USAF 356th FS/354th FW, Eielson AFB, AK	
18-5348	Lockheed Martin F-35A Lightning II [WA]	USAF 6th WPS/57th Wg, Nellis AFB, NV	
18-5349	Lockheed Martin F-35A Lightning II [VT]	USAF 134th FS/158th FW, Burlington, VT ANG	
18-5350	Lockheed Martin F-35A Lightning II [AK]	USAF 356th FS/354th FW, Eielson AFB, AK	
18-5351	Lockheed Martin F-35A Lightning II [AK]	USAF 356th FS/354th FW, Eielson AFB, AK	
18-5352	Lockheed Martin F-35A Lightning II [AK]	USAF 356th FS/354th FW, Eielson AFB, AK	
18-5353	Lockheed Martin F-35A Lightning II [WA]	USAF 6th WPS/57th Wg, Nellis AFB, NV	
18-5354	Lockheed Martin F-35A Lightning II [AK]	USAF 356th FS/354th FW, Eielson AFB, AK	
18-5355	Lockheed Martin F-35A Lightning II [AK] [355 FS]	USAF 355th FS/354th FW, Eielson AFB, AK	
18-5356	Lockheed Martin F-35A Lightning II [AK] [356 FS]	USAF 356th FS/354th FW, Eielson AFB, AK	
18-5357	Lockheed Martin F-35A Lightning II [WA]	USAF 6th WPS/57th Wg, Nellis AFB, NV	
18-5358	Lockheed Martin F-35A Lightning II [VT]	USAF 134th FS/158th FW, Burlington, VT ANG	
18-5359	Lockheed Martin F-35A Lightning II [VT]	USAF 134th FS/158th FW, Burlington, VT ANG	
18-5360	Lockheed Martin F-35A Lightning II [VT]	USAF 134th FS/158th FW, Burlington, VT ANG	
18-5361	Lockheed Martin F-35A Lightning II [VT]	USAF 134th FS/158th FW, Burlington, VT ANG	
18-5362	Lockheed Martin F-35A Lightning II [WA]	USAF 6th WPS/57th Wg, Nellis AFB, NV	
18-5363	Lockheed Martin F-35A Lightning II [HL]	USAF 421st FS/388th FW, Hill AFB, UT	
18-5364	Lockheed Martin F-35A Lightning II [AK]	USAF 356th FS/354th FW, Eielson AFB, AK	
18-5365	Lockheed Martin F-35A Lightning II [AK]	USAF 356th FS/354th FW, Eielson AFB, AK	
18-5366	Lockheed Martin F-35A Lightning II [AK]	USAF 356th FS/354th FW, Eielson AFB, AK	
18-5367	Lockheed Martin F-35A Lightning II [AK]	USAF 356th FS/354th FW, Eielson AFB, AK	
18-5368	Lockheed Martin F-35A Lightning II [HL]	USAF 421st FS/388th FW, Hill AFB, UT	
18-5369	Lockheed Martin F-35A Lightning II [AK]	USAF 356th FS/354th FW, Eielson AFB, AK	
18-5370	Lockheed Martin F-35A Lightning II [AK]	USAF 356th FS/354th FW, Eielson AFB, AK	
18-5371	Lockheed Martin F-35A Lightning II [AK]	USAF 356th FS/354th FW, Eielson AFB, AK	
18-5372	Lockheed Martin F-35A Lightning II [AK]	USAF 356th FS/354th FW, Eielson AFB, AK	
18-5373	Lockheed Martin F-35A Lightning II [AK]	USAF 356th FS/354th FW, Eielson AFB, AK	
18-5374	Lockheed Martin F-35A Lightning II [WA]	USAF 6th WPS/57th Wg, Nellis AFB, NV	
18-5375	Lockheed Martin F-35A Lightning II [AK]	USAF 356th FS/354th FW, Eielson AFB, AK	
18-5376	Lockheed Martin F-35A Lightning II [AK]	USAF 356th FS/354th FW, Eielson AFB, AK	
18-5377	Lockheed Martin F-35A Lightning II [AK]	USAF 356th FS/354th FW, Eielson AFB, AK	
18-5378	Lockheed Martin F-35A Lightning II [AK]	USAF 356th FS/354th FW, Eielson AFB, AK	
18-5379	Lockheed Martin F-35A Lightning II [AK]	USAF 356th FS/354th FW, Eielson AFB, AK	
18-5380	Lockheed Martin F-35A Lightning II [AK]	USAF 356th FS/354th FW, Eielson AFB, AK	
18-5381	Lockheed Martin F-35A Lightning II [AK]	USAF 356th FS/354th FW, Eielson AFB, AK	
18-5413	Lockheed Martin F-35A Lightning II [WI]	USAF 176th FS/115th FW, Madison, WI ANG	
18-5414	Lockheed Martin F-35A Lightning II [AL]	USAF 100th FS/187th FW, Dannelly Field, AL ANG	
18-5415	Lockheed Martin F-35A Lightning II [LF]	USAF 63rd FS/56th FW, Luke AFB, AZ	
18-5416	Lockheed Martin F-35A Lightning II [TY] [325 OG]	USAF 95th FS/325th FW, Tyndall AFB, FL	
18-5417	Lockheed Martin F-35A Lightning II [WI]	USAF 176th FS/115th FW, Madison, WI ANG	
18-5418	Lockheed Martin F-35A Lightning II [LF]	USAF 62nd FS/56th FW, Luke AFB, AZ	
18-5419	Lockheed Martin F-35A Lightning II [LF]	USAF 308th FS/56th FW, Luke AFB, AZ	
18-5420	Lockheed Martin F-35A Lightning II [AL]$	USAF 100th FS/187th FW, Dannelly Field, AL ANG	
18-5445	Lockheed Martin F-35A Lightning II [HL] [388 FW]	USAF 421st FS/388th FW, Hill AFB, UT	
18-5446	Lockheed Martin F-35A Lightning II [HL]	USAF 421st FS/388th FW, Hill AFB, UT	

Notes	Serial	Type (code/other identity)	Owner/operator, location or fate
	18-5447	Lockheed Martin F-35A Lightning II [WA]	USAF 6th WPS/57th Wg, Nellis AFB, NV
	18-5448	Lockheed Martin F-35A Lightning II [OT]	USAF 422nd TES/53rd TEG, Nellis AFB, NV
	18-5449	Lockheed Martin F-35A Lightning II [OT]	USAF 422nd TES/53rd TEG, Nellis AFB, NV
	18-5450	Lockheed Martin F-35A Lightning II [AK]	USAF 355th FS/354th FW, Eielson AFB, AK
	18-5451	Lockheed Martin F-35A Lightning II [AK]	USAF 355th FS/354th FW, Eielson AFB, AK
	18-5452	Lockheed Martin F-35A Lightning II [HL]	USAF 34th FS/388th FW, Hill AFB, UT
	18-5453	Lockheed Martin F-35A Lightning II [HL]	USAF 34th FS/388th FW, Hill AFB, UT
	18-5454	Lockheed Martin F-35A Lightning II [HL]	USAF 421st FS/388th FW, Hill AFB, UT
	18-5455	Lockheed Martin F-35A Lightning II [HL]	USAF 34th FS/388th FW, Hill AFB, UT
	18-5456	Lockheed Martin F-35A Lightning II [HL]	USAF 34th FS/388th FW, Hill AFB, UT
	18-5457	Lockheed Martin F-35A Lightning II [AK]	USAF 355th FS/354th FW, Eielson AFB, AK
	18-5458	Lockheed Martin F-35A Lightning II [AK]	USAF 355th FS/354th FW, Eielson AFB, AK
	18-5459	Lockheed Martin F-35A Lightning II [AK]	USAF 355th FS/354th FW, Eielson AFB, AK
	19-5460	Lockheed Martin F-35A Lightning II [AK]	USAF 355th FS/354th FW, Eielson AFB, AK
	19-5461	Lockheed Martin F-35A Lightning II [AK]	USAF 355th FS/354th FW, Eielson AFB, AK
	19-5462	Lockheed Martin F-35A Lightning II [AK]	USAF 355th FS/354th FW, Eielson AFB, AK
	19-5463	Lockheed Martin F-35A Lightning II [AK]	USAF 355th FS/354th FW, Eielson AFB, AK
	19-5464	Lockheed Martin F-35A Lightning II [AK]	USAF 355th FS/354th FW, Eielson AFB, AK
	19-5465	Lockheed Martin F-35A Lightning II [AK]	USAF 355th FS/354th FW, Eielson AFB, AK
	19-5466	Lockheed Martin F-35A Lightning II [AK]	USAF 355th FS/354th FW, Eielson AFB, AK
	19-5467	Lockheed Martin F-35A Lightning II [AK]	USAF 355th FS/354th FW, Eielson AFB, AK
	19-5468	Lockheed Martin F-35A Lightning II [AK]	USAF 355th FS/354th FW, Eielson AFB, AK
	19-5469	Lockheed Martin F-35A Lightning II [AK]	USAF 355th FS/354th FW, Eielson AFB, AK
	19-5470	Lockheed Martin F-35A Lightning II [AK]	USAF 355th FS/354th FW, Eielson AFB, AK
	19-5471	Lockheed Martin F-35A Lightning II [HL]	USAF 34th FS/388th FW, Hill AFB, UT
	19-5472	Lockheed Martin F-35A Lightning II [OT]	USAF 422nd TES/53rd TEG, Nellis AFB, NV
	19-5477	Lockheed Martin F-35A Lightning II [HL]	USAF 4th FS/388th FW, Hill AFB, UT
	19-5478	Lockheed Martin F-35A Lightning II [HL]	USAF 34th FS/388th FW, Hill AFB, UT
	19-5479	Lockheed Martin F-35A Lightning II [AK]	USAF 355th FS/354th FW, Eielson AFB, AK
	19-5480	Lockheed Martin F-35A Lightning II [AK]	USAF 355th FS/354th FW, Eielson AFB, AK
	19-5481	Lockheed Martin F-35A Lightning II [AK]	USAF 355th FS/354th FW, Eielson AFB, AK
	19-5482	Lockheed Martin F-35A Lightning II [AK]	USAF 355th FS/354th FW, Eielson AFB, AK
	19-5483	Lockheed Martin F-35A Lightning II [HL]	USAF 34th FS/388th FW, Hill AFB, UT
	19-5487	Lockheed Martin F-35A Lightning II [WA]	USAF 6th WPS/57th Wg, Nellis AFB, NV
	19-5488	Lockheed Martin F-35A Lightning II [HL] [388 FW]	USAF 421st FS/388th FW, Hill AFB, UT
	19-5489	Lockheed Martin F-35A Lightning II [WA]	USAF 6th WPS/57th Wg, Nellis AFB, NV
	19-5490	Lockheed Martin F-35A Lightning II [AK]	USAF 355th FS/354th FW, Eielson AFB, AK
	19-5491	Lockheed Martin F-35A Lightning II [AK]	USAF 355th FS/354th FW, Eielson AFB, AK
	19-5492	Lockheed Martin F-35A Lightning II [AK]	USAF 355th FS/354th FW, Eielson AFB, AK
	19-5494	Lockheed Martin F-35A Lightning II [AK]	USAF 355th FS/354th FW, Eielson AFB, AK
	19-5496	Lockheed Martin F-35A Lightning II [AK]	USAF 355th FS/354th FW, Eielson AFB, AK
	19-5497	Lockheed Martin F-35A Lightning II [WA]	USAF 6th WPS/57th Wg, Nellis AFB, NV (on loan to 493rd FS/48th FW)
	19-5534	Lockheed Martin F-35A Lightning II [AK]	USAF 355th FS/354th FW, Eielson AFB, AK
	19-5535	Lockheed Martin F-35A Lightning II [AK]	USAF 355th FS/354th FW, Eielson AFB, AK
	19-5536	Lockheed Martin F-35A Lightning II [AK]	USAF 355th FS/354th FW, Eielson AFB, AK
	19-5537	Lockheed Martin F-35A Lightning II [AK]	USAF 355th FS/354th FW, Eielson AFB, AK
	19-5538	Lockheed Martin F-35A Lightning II [HL]	USAF 4th FS/388th FW, Hill AFB, UT
	19-5539	Lockheed Martin F-35A Lightning II [HL]	USAF 34th FS/388th FW, Hill AFB, UT
	19-5540	Lockheed Martin F-35A Lightning II [HL]	USAF 34th FS/388th FW, Hill AFB, UT
	19-5541	Lockheed Martin F-35A Lightning II [HL]	USAF 34th FS/388th FW, Hill AFB, UT
	20-5566	Lockheed Martin F-35A Lightning II [HL] [466 FS]	USAF 466th FS/388th FW, Hill AFB, UT
	20-5567	Lockheed Martin F-35A Lightning II [HL]	USAF 421st FS/388th FW, Hill AFB, UT
	20-5568	Lockheed Martin F-35A Lightning II [HL]	USAF 34th FS/388th FW, Hill AFB, UT
	20-5569	Lockheed Martin F-35A Lightning II [HL]	USAF 421st FS/388th FW, Hill AFB, UT
	20-5575	Lockheed Martin F-35A Lightning II [WA]	USAF 6th WPS/57th Wg, Nellis AFB, NV (on loan to 493rd FS/48th FW)
	20-5576	Lockheed Martin F-35A Lightning II [WA]	USAF 6th WPS/57th Wg, Nellis AFB, NV (on loan to 493rd FS/48th FW)
	20-5577	Lockheed Martin F-35A Lightning II [ED]	USAF 461st FLTS/412th TW, Edwards AFB, CA
	20-5578	Lockheed Martin F-35A Lightning II [ED]	USAF 461st FLTS/412th TW, Edwards AFB, CA
	20-5579	Lockheed Martin F-35A Lightning II [HL]	USAF 4th FS/388th FW, Hill AFB, UT

Serial	Type (code/other identity)	Owner/operator, location or fate	Notes
20-5584	Lockheed Martin F-35A Lightning II [HL]	USAF 4th FS/388th FW, Hill AFB, UT	
20-5585	Lockheed Martin F-35A Lightning II [HL]	USAF 421st FS/388th FW, Hill AFB, UT	
20-5586	Lockheed Martin F-35A Lightning II [HL]	USAF 421st FS/388th FW, Hill AFB, UT	
20-5587	Lockheed Martin F-35A Lightning II [WA]	USAF 6th WPS/57th Wg, Nellis AFB, NV	
		(on loan to 493rd FS/48th FW)	
20-5591	Lockheed Martin F-35A Lightning II [WA]	USAF 6th WPS/57th Wg, Nellis AFB, NV	
20-5592	Lockheed Martin F-35A Lightning II [OT]	USAF 422nd TES/53rd TEG, Nellis AFB, NV	
20-5593	Lockheed Martin F-35A Lightning II [WA]	USAF 6th WPS/57th Wg, Nellis AFB, NV	
20-5597	Lockheed Martin F-35A Lightning II [WA]	USAF 6th WPS/57th Wg, Nellis AFB, NV	
		(on loan to 493rd FS/48th FW)	
20-5605	Lockheed Martin F-35A Lightning II [OT]	USAF 422nd TES/53rd TEG, Nellis AFB, NV	
20-5606	Lockheed Martin F-35A Lightning II [OT]	USAF 422nd TES/53rd TEG, Nellis AFB, NV	
20-5607	Lockheed Martin F-35A Lightning II [HL]	USAF 4th FS/388th FW, Hill AFB, UT	
20-5608	Lockheed Martin F-35A Lightning II [WA] [USAF WS]	USAF 6th WPS/57th Wg, Nellis AFB, NV	
20-5609	Lockheed Martin F-35A Lightning II [HL]	USAF 421st FS/388th FW, Hill AFB, UT	
20-5610	Lockheed Martin F-35A Lightning II [HL]	USAF 34th FS/388th FW, Hill AFB, UT	
20-5611	Lockheed Martin F-35A Lightning II [HL]	USAF 421st FS/388th FW, Hill AFB, UT	
20-5612	Lockheed Martin F-35A Lightning II [WA]	USAF 6th WPS/57th Wg, Nellis AFB, NV	
20-5619	Lockheed Martin F-35A Lightning II [HL]	USAF 421st FS/388th FW, Hill AFB, UT	
20-5620	Lockheed Martin F-35A Lightning II [WI]	USAF 176th FS/115th FW, Madison, WI ANG	
20-5621	Lockheed Martin F-35A Lightning II [WI] [115 OG]	USAF 176th FS/115th FW, Madison, WI ANG	
20-5622	Lockheed Martin F-35A Lightning II [HL]	USAF 34th FS/388th FW, Hill AFB, UT	
20-5623	Lockheed Martin F-35A Lightning II [HL]	USAF 4th FS/388th FW, Hill AFB, UT	
20-5624	Lockheed Martin F-35A Lightning II [HL]	USAF 4th FS/388th FW, Hill AFB, UT	
20-5625	Lockheed Martin F-35A Lightning II [HL]	USAF 421st FS/388th FW, Hill AFB, UT	
20-5626	Lockheed Martin F-35A Lightning II [TY] [325 FW]	USAF 95th FS/325th FW, Tyndall AFB, FL	
20-5627	Lockheed Martin F-35A Lightning II [TY] [95 FS]	USAF 95th FS/325th FW, Tyndall AFB, FL	
20-5628	Lockheed Martin F-35A Lightning II [AL]	USAF 100th FS/187th FW, Dannelly Field, AL ANG	
20-5629	Lockheed Martin F-35A Lightning II [WI]	USAF 176th FS/115th FW, Madison, WI ANG	
22-5686	Lockheed Martin F-35A Lightning II [HL]	USAF 4th FS/388th FW, Hill AFB, UT	
22-5687	Lockheed Martin F-35A Lightning II [WI] [176 FS]	USAF 176th FS/115th FW, Madison, WI ANG	
22-5688	Lockheed Martin F-35A Lightning II [HL]	USAF 421st FS/388th FW, Hill AFB, UT (on loan to 457th FS/301st FW)	
22-5689	Lockheed Martin F-35A Lightning II [HL]	USAF 421st FS/388th FW, Hill AFB, UT (on loan to 457th FS/301st FW)	
22-5690	Lockheed Martin F-35A Lightning II [LN]	USAF 493rd FS/48th FW (on loan to 6th WPS/57th Wg, Nellis AFB, NV)	
22-5691	Lockheed Martin F-35A Lightning II [LN]	USAF 493rd FS/48th FW (on loan to 6th WPS/57th Wg, Nellis AFB, NV)	
22-5692	Lockheed Martin F-35A Lightning II [HL]	USAF 421st FS/388th FW, Hill AFB, UT	
22-5693	Lockheed Martin F-35A Lightning II [WI]	USAF 176th FS/115th FW, Madison, WI ANG	
22-5694	Lockheed Martin F-35A Lightning II [HL]	USAF 388th FW, Hill AFB, UT	
22-5695	Lockheed Martin F-35A Lightning II [WI]	USAF 176th FS/115th FW, Madison, WI ANG (on order, with LM)	
22-5696	Lockheed Martin F-35A Lightning II [WI] $	USAF 176th FS/115th FW, Madison, WI ANG (onorder, with LM)	
22-5697	Lockheed Martin F-35A Lightning II [WI]	USAF 176th FS/115th FW, Madison, WI ANG	
22-5698	Lockheed Martin F-35A Lightning II [HL]	USAF 421st FS/388th FW, Hill AFB, UT (on order, with LM)	
22-5699	Lockheed Martin F-35A Lightning II [WI]	USAF 176th FS/115th FW, Madison, WI ANG	
22-5700	Lockheed Martin F-35A Lightning II [TY]	USAF 95th FS/325th FW, Tyndall AFB, FL (on order, with LM)	
22-5701	Lockheed Martin F-35A Lightning II [TY]	USAF 95th FS/325th FW, Tyndall AFB, FL (on order, with LM)	
22-5702	Lockheed Martin F-35A Lightning II [WI]	USAF 176th FS/115th FW, Madison, WI ANG	
22-5703	Lockheed Martin F-35A Lightning II [LN]	USAF 493rd FS/48th FW (on loan to 6th WPS/57th Wg, Nellis AFB, NV)	
22-5704	Lockheed Martin F-35A Lightning II [LN]	USAF 493rd FS/48th FW (on loan to 6th WPS/57th Wg, Nellis AFB, NV)	
22-5705	Lockheed Martin F-35A Lightning II [LN]	USAF 493rd FS/48th FW (on loan to 6th WPS/57th Wg, Nellis AFB, NV)	
22-5706	Lockheed Martin F-35A Lightning II [WI]	USAF 176th FS/115th FW, Madison, WI ANG	

Notes	Serial	Type (code/other identity)	Owner/operator, location or fate
	22-5707	Lockheed Martin F-35A Lightning II [WI]	USAF 176th FS/115th FW, Madison, WI ANG
	22-5708	Lockheed Martin F-35A Lightning II [TY]	USAF 95th FS/325th FW, Tyndall AFB, FL
	22-5709	Lockheed Martin F-35A Lightning II [HL]	USAF 421st FS/388th FW, Hill AFB, UT (on loan to 457th FS/301st FW)
	22-5710	Lockheed Martin F-35A Lightning II [LN]	USAF 493rd FS/48th FW (on loan to 6th WPS/57th Wg, Nellis AFB, NV)
	22-5711	Lockheed Martin F-35A Lightning II [LN]	USAF 493rd FS/48th FW (on loan to 6th WPS/57th Wg, Nellis AFB, NV)
	22-5712	Lockheed Martin F-35A Lightning II [LN]	USAF 493rd FS/48th FW (on loan to 6th WPS/57th Wg, Nellis AFB, NV)
	22-5713	Lockheed Martin F-35A Lightning II [ED]	USAF 461st FLTS/412th TW, Edwards AFB, CA (on order, with LM)
	22-5714	Lockheed Martin F-35A Lightning II [LN]	USAF 493rd FS/48th FW (on loan to 6th WPS/57th Wg, Nellis AFB, NV)
	22-5715	Lockheed Martin F-35A Lightning II [HL]	USAF 421st FS/388th FW, Hill AFB, UT (on loan to 457th FS/301st FW)
	22-5716	Lockheed Martin F-35A Lightning II [AL]	USAF 100th FS/187th FW, Dannelly Field, AL ANG (on order, with LM)
	22-5717	Lockheed Martin F-35A Lightning II [OT]	USAF 422nd TES/53rd TEG, Nellis AFB, NV (on order, with LM)
	22-5722	Lockheed Martin F-35A Lightning II [HL]	USAF 34th FS/388th FW, Hill AFB, UT (on order, with LM)
	22-5723	Lockheed Martin F-35A Lightning II [TY]	USAF 95th FS/325th FW, Tyndall AFB, FL (on order, with LM)
	22-5724	Lockheed Martin F-35A Lightning II [OT]	USAF 422nd TES/53rd TEG, Nellis AFB, NV
	22-5725	Lockheed Martin F-35A Lightning II [WI]	USAF 176th FS/115th FW, Madison, WI ANG
	22-5726	Lockheed Martin F-35A Lightning II [AL]	USAF 100th FS/187th FW, Dannelly Field, AL ANG
	22-5727	Lockheed Martin F-35A Lightning II [AL]	USAF 100th FS/187th FW, Dannelly Field, AL (on order, with LM)
	22-5728	Lockheed Martin F-35A Lightning II [AL]	USAF 100th FS/187th FW, Dannelly Field, AL ANG (on order, with LM)
	22-5729	Lockheed Martin F-35A Lightning II [AL]	USAF 100th FS/187th FW, Dannelly Field, AL ANG
	22-5778	Lockheed Martin F-35A Lightning II	USAF (on order, with LM)
	22-5779	Lockheed Martin F-35A Lightning II	USAF (on order, with LM)
	22-5780	Lockheed Martin F-35A Lightning II	USAF (on order, with LM)
	22-5781	Lockheed Martin F-35A Lightning II	USAF (on order, with LM)
	22-5782	Lockheed Martin F-35A Lightning II [TY]	USAF 95th FS/325th FW, Tyndall AFB, FL (on order, with LM)
	22-5783	Lockheed Martin F-35A Lightning II	USAF (on order, with LM)
	22-5784	Lockheed Martin F-35A Lightning II	USAF (on order, with LM)
	22-5785	Lockheed Martin F-35A Lightning II [AL]	USAF 100th FS/187th FW, Dannelly Field, AL ANG (on order, with LM)
	22-5786	Lockheed Martin F-35A Lightning II [TX]	USAF 457th FS/301st FW AFRC, NAS Fort Worth JRB, TX
	22-5787	Lockheed Martin F-35A Lightning II [TX]	USAF 457th FS/301st FW AFRC, NAS Fort Worth JRB, TX
	22-5788	Lockheed Martin F-35A Lightning II [TY]	USAF 95th FS/325th FW, Tyndall AFB, FL (on order, with LM)
	22-5789	Lockheed Martin F-35A Lightning II [TX]	USAF 457th FS/301st FW AFRC, NAS Fort Worth JRB, TX
	22-5790	Lockheed Martin F-35A Lightning II [ED]	USAF 461st FLTS/412th TW, Edwards AFB, CA (on order, with LM)
	22-5791	Lockheed Martin F-35A Lightning II [TX]	USAF 457th FS/301st FW AFRC, NAS Fort Worth JRB, TX
	22-5792	Lockheed Martin F-35A Lightning II [TX]	USAF 457th FS/301st FW AFRC, NAS Fort Worth JRB, TX (on order, with LM)
	22-5793	Lockheed Martin F-35A Lightning II [TY]	USAF 95th FS/325th FW, Tyndall AFB, FL (on order, with LM)
	22-5794	Lockheed Martin F-35A Lightning II	USAF (on order)
	22-5795	Lockheed Martin F-35A Lightning II	USAF (on order)
	22-5796	Lockheed Martin F-35A Lightning II	USAF (on order)
	22-5797	Lockheed Martin F-35A Lightning II	USAF (on order)

Serial	Type (code/other identity)	Owner/operator, location or fate	Notes
22-5798	Lockheed Martin F-35A Lightning II	USAF (on order)	
22-5799	Lockheed Martin F-35A Lightning II	USAF (on order)	
22-5800	Lockheed Martin F-35A Lightning II	USAF (on order)	
22-5801	Lockheed Martin F-35A Lightning II	USAF (on order)	
22-5802	Lockheed Martin F-35A Lightning II	USAF (on order)	
22-5803	Lockheed Martin F-35A Lightning II	USAF (on order)	
22-5804	Lockheed Martin F-35A Lightning II	USAF (on order)	
22-5805	Lockheed Martin F-35A Lightning II	USAF (on order)	
22-5806	Lockheed Martin F-35A Lightning II	USAF (on order)	
22-5807	Lockheed Martin F-35A Lightning II	USAF (on order)	
22-5808	Lockheed Martin F-35A Lightning II	USAF (on order)	
22-5809	Lockheed Martin F-35A Lightning II	USAF (on order)	
22-5810	Lockheed Martin F-35A Lightning II	USAF (on order)	
22-5811	Lockheed Martin F-35A Lightning II	USAF (on order)	
22-5812	Lockheed Martin F-35A Lightning II	USAF (on order)	
22-5813	Lockheed Martin F-35A Lightning II	USAF (on order)	
22-5814	Lockheed Martin F-35A Lightning II	USAF (on order)	
22-5946	Lockheed Martin F-35A Lightning II [HL]	USAF 388th FW, Hill AFB, UT	
22-5947	Lockheed Martin F-35A Lightning II [AL]	USAF 100th FS/187th FW, Dannelly Field, AL ANG (on order, with LM)	
22-5948	Lockheed Martin F-35A Lightning II [HL]	USAF 34th FS/388th FW, Hill AFB, UT (on order, with LM)	
22-5949	Lockheed Martin F-35A Lightning II [TY]	USAF 95th FS/325th FW, Tyndall AFB, FL	
22-5950	Lockheed Martin F-35A Lightning II [WI]	USAF 176th FS/115th FW, Madison, WI ANG (on order, with LM)	
22-5951	Lockheed Martin F-35A Lightning II [TY]	USAF 95th FS/325th FW, Tyndall AFB, FL (on order, with LM)	
22-5952	Lockheed Martin F-35A Lightning II [AL]	USAF 100th FS/187th FW, Dannelly Field, AL ANG	
22-5953	Lockheed Martin F-35A Lightning II [WI]	USAF 176th FS/115th FW, Madison, WI ANG	
22-5954	Lockheed Martin F-35A Lightning II [WI]	USAF 176th FS/115th FW, Madison, WI ANG	
22-5955	Lockheed Martin F-35A Lightning II [WI]	USAF 176th FS/115th FW, Madison, WI ANG	
22-5956	Lockheed Martin F-35A Lightning II [TY]	USAF 95th FS/325th FW, Tyndall AFB, FL	

Gulfstream Aerospace C-37 Gulfstream V

97-0400	Gulfstream Aerospace C-37A Gulfstream V	USAF 99th AS/89th AW, Andrews AFB, MD	
97-0401	Gulfstream Aerospace C-37A Gulfstream V	USAF 99th AS/89th AW, Andrews AFB, MD	
97-01944	Gulfstream Aerospace C-37A Gulfstream V [1944]	US Army OSAC/PAT, Andrews AFB, MD	
99-0402	Gulfstream Aerospace C-37A Gulfstream V	USAF 99th AS/89th AW, Andrews AFB, MD	
99-0404	Gulfstream Aerospace C-37A Gulfstream V	USAF 99th AS/89th AW, Andrews AFB, MD	
01-0028	Gulfstream Aerospace C-37A Gulfstream V	USAF 99th AS/89th AW, Andrews AFB, MD	
01-0065	Gulfstream Aerospace C-37A Gulfstream V	USAF 65th AS/15th Wg, Hickam AFB, HI	
02-01863	Gulfstream Aerospace C-37A Gulfstream V [1863]	US Army OSAC/PAT, Andrews AFB, MD	
04-01778	Gulfstream Aerospace C-37A Gulfstream V [1778]	US Army OSAC/PAT, Andrews AFB, MD	
06-0500	Gulfstream Aerospace C-37B Gulfstream V	USAF 99th AS/89th AW, Andrews AFB, MD	
09-0525	Gulfstream Aerospace C-37B Gulfstream V	USAF 99th AS/89th AW, Andrews AFB, MD	
11-0550	Gulfstream Aerospace C-37B Gulfstream V	USAF 99th AS/89th AW, Andrews AFB, MD	
18-1942	Gulfstream Aerospace C-37B Gulfstream V [1942]	USAF 99th AS/89th AW, Andrews AFB, MD	
18-1947	Gulfstream Aerospace C-37B Gulfstream V [1947]	USAF 99th AS/89th AW, Andrews AFB, MD	
20-1941	Gulfstream Aerospace C-37B Gulfstream V	USAF 99th AS/89th AW, Andrews AFB, MD	
20-1949	Gulfstream Aerospace C-37B Gulfstream V	USAF 99th AS/89th AW, Andrews AFB, MD	

Gulfstream Aerospace EA-37B Compass Call II

17-5567	Gulfstream Aerospace EA-37B Compass Call [DM] (N967GA)	USAF 55th ECG, Davis-Monthan AFB, AZ	
17-5579	Gulfstream Aerospace EA-37B Compass Call [DM] (N579GA)	USAF 55th ECG, Davis-Monthan AFB, AZ	
19-1587	Gulfstream Aerospace EA-37B Compass Call [DM] (N562GA)	USAF 55th ECG, Davis-Monthan AFB, AZ	
19-5591	Gulfstream Aerospace EA-37B Compass Call [DM] (N591GA)	USAF 55th ECG, Davis-Monthan AFB, AZ	
20-2344	Gulfstream Aerospace EA-37B Compass Call [DM] (N512GA)	USAF 55th ECG, Davis-Monthan AFB, AZ	

Notes	Serial	Type (code/other identity)	Owner/operator, location or fate
..-....		Gulfstream Aerospace EA-37B Compass Call (N518GA)	USAF/L3 Harris(on order)
..-....		Gulfstream Aerospace EA-37B Compass Call (N522GD)	USAF/L3 Harris(on order)
..-....		Gulfstream Aerospace EA-37B Compass Call (N529GA)	USAF/L3 Harris(on order)
..-....		Gulfstream Aerospace EA-37B Compass Call (N530G)	USAF/L3 Harris(on order)
..-....		Gulfstream Aerospace EA-37B Compass Call (N531GA)	USAF/L3 Harris(on order)
Boeing C-40			
01-0015		Boeing C-40B (N378BJ)	USAF 65th AS/15th Wg, Hickam AFB, HI
01-0040		Boeing C-40B (N371BJ)	USAF 1st AS/89th AW, Andrews AFB, MD
01-0041		Boeing C-40B (N374BC)	USAF 1st AS/89th AW, Andrews AFB, MD
02-0042		Boeing C-40B (N237BA)	USAF 1st AS/89th AW, Andrews AFB, MD
02-0201		Boeing C-40C (N752BC)	USAF 201st AS/113th FW DC ANG, Andrews AFB, MD
02-0202		Boeing C-40C (N754BC)	USAF 201st AS/113th FW DC ANG, Andrews AFB, MD
02-0203		Boeing C-40C (N236BA)	USAF 201st AS/113th FW DC ANG, Andrews AFB, MD
05-0730		Boeing C-40C (N365BJ)	USAF 73rd AS/932nd AW AFRC, Scott AFB, IL
05-0932		Boeing C-40C (N366BJ)	USAF 73rd AS/932nd AW AFRC, Scott AFB, IL
05-4613		Boeing C-40C (N368BJ)	USAF 73rd AS/932nd AW AFRC, Scott AFB, IL
09-0540		Boeing C-40C (N736JS)	USAF 73rd AS/932nd AW AFRC, Scott AFB, IL
Boeing 767-2C/KC-46A Pegasus			
11-46001		Boeing KC-46A Pegasus (N461FT)	Boeing, Everett, for USAF
11-46002		Boeing KC-46A Pegasus (N464KC)	Boeing, Seattle, for USAF
11-46003		Boeing KC-46A Pegasus (N463FT)	Boeing, Everett, for USAF
11-46004		Boeing KC-46A Pegasus (N462KC)	Boeing, Seattle, for USAF
11-46057		Boeing KC-46A Pegasus (N2013S/19-46057)	USAF 305th AMW, McGuire AFB, NJ
11-46058		Boeing KC-46A Pegasus (N5107Q/19-46058)	USAF 77th ARS/916th ARW AFRC, Seymour Johnson AFB, NC
11-46059		Boeing KC-46A Pegasus (N5020K/19-46059)	USAF 56th ARS/97th AMW, Altus AFB, OK
11-46060		Boeing KC-46A Pegasus (N2013Z/19-46060)	USAF 305th AMW, McGuire AFB, NJ
15-46005		Boeing KC-46A Pegasus (N842BA)	*See entry for 19-46005*
15-46006		Boeing KC-46A Pegasus (N884BA)	*See entry for 19-46006*
15-46008		Boeing KC-46A Pegasus	*See entry for 19-46008*
15-46009		Boeing KC-46A Pegasus (N50217)	USAF 344th ARS/22nd ARW, McConnell AFB, KS
15-46010		Boeing KC-46A Pegasus (N2007L)	*See entry for 19-46010*
15-46011		Boeing KC-46A Pegasus (N6009F)	USAF 77th ARS/916th ARW AFRC, Seymour Johnson AFB, NC
15-46066		Boeing KC-46A Pegasus (N2014H/19-46066)	USAF 77th ARS/916th ARW AFRC, Seymour Johnson AFB, NC
15-46067		Boeing KC-46A Pegasus (N1785B/19-46067)	USAF 344th ARS/22nd ARW, McConnell AFB, KS
15-46068		Boeing KC-46A Pegasus (N1794B/19-46068)	USAF 77th ARS/916th ARW AFRC, Seymour Johnson AFB, NC
15-46069		Boeing KC-46A Pegasus (N5014K/19-46069)	USAF 305th AMW, McGuire AFB, NJ
15-46070		Boeing KC-46A Pegasus (N5020K/19-46070)	USAF 305th AMW, McGuire AFB, NJ
16-46012		Boeing KC-46A Pegasus (N1785B)	USAF 56th ARS/97th AMW, Altus AFB, OK
16-46013		Boeing KC-46A Pegasus (N5023Q) *bl/w*	USAF 133rd ARS/157th ARW, Pease ANGB, NH ANG
16-46014		Boeing KC-46A Pegasus (N5573S)	USAF 77th ARS/916th ARW AFRC, Seymour Johnson AFB, NC
16-46015		Boeing KC-46A Pegasus (N6009F) *bl/w*	USAF 133rd ARS/157th ARW, Pease ANGB, NH ANG
16-46016		Boeing KC-46A Pegasus (N6018N)	USAF 56th ARS/97th AMW, Altus AFB, OK
16-46017		Boeing KC-46A Pegasus (N5573S)	USAF 344th ARS/22nd ARW, McConnell AFB, KS
16-46018		Boeing KC-46A Pegasus (N5514J) *bl/w*	USAF 133rd ARS/157th ARW, Pease ANGB, NH ANG
16-46019		Boeing KC-46A Pegasus (N5514K) *bl/w*	USAF 133rd ARS/157th ARW, Pease ANGB, NH ANG
16-46020		Boeing KC-46A Pegasus (N5514V) *bl/w*	USAF 133rd ARS/157th ARW, Pease ANGB, NH ANG
16-46021		Boeing KC-46A Pegasus (N5514X)	USAF 2nd ARS/305th AMW, McGuire AFB, NJ

Serial	Type (code/other identity)	Owner/operator, location or fate	Notes
16-46022	Boeing KC-46A Pegasus (N5573S)	USAF 344th ARS/22nd ARW, McConnell AFB, KS	
16-46023	Boeing KC-46A Pegasus (N6018N)	USAF 344th ARS/22nd ARW, McConnell AFB, KS	
17-46024	Boeing KC-46A Pegasus (N5514J)	USAF 77th ARS/916th ARW AFRC, Seymour Johnson AFB, NC	
17-46025	Boeing KC-46A Pegasus (N5017V)	USAF 344th ARS/22nd ARW, McConnell AFB, KS	
17-46026	Boeing KC-46A Pegasus (N6018N)	USAF 344th ARS/22nd ARW, McConnell AFB, KS	
17-46027	Boeing KC-46A Pegasus (N5014K)	USAF 344th ARS/22nd ARW, McConnell AFB, KS	
17-46028	Boeing KC-46A Pegasus (N55141)	USAF 344th ARS/22nd ARW, McConnell AFB, KS	
17-46029	Boeing KC-46A Pegasus (N55141) *bl/w*	USAF 133rd ARS/157th ARW, Pease ANGB, NH ANG	
17-46030	Boeing KC-46A Pegasus (N6009F)	USAF 344th ARS/22nd ARW, McConnell AFB, KS	
17-46031	Boeing KC-46A Pegasus (N5513X)	USAF 344th ARS/22nd ARW, McConnell AFB, KS	
17-46032	Boeing KC-46A Pegasus (N5016R)	USAF 344th ARS/22nd ARW, McConnell AFB, KS	
17-46033	Boeing KC-46A Pegasus (N5016R)	USAF 344th ARS/22nd ARW, McConnell AFB, KS	
17-46034	Boeing KC-46A Pegasus (N5017Q) $	USAF 133rd ARS/157th ARW, Pease ANGB, NH ANG	
17-46035	Boeing KC-46A Pegasus (N5017V)	USAF 344th ARS/22nd ARW, McConnell AFB, KS	
17-46036	Boeing KC-46A Pegasus (N5017V)	USAF 344th ARS/22nd ARW, McConnell AFB, KS	
17-46037	Boeing KC-46A Pegasus (N5511Y)	USAF 344th ARS/22nd ARW, McConnell AFB, KS	
17-46038	Boeing KC-46A Pegasus (N5020K)	USAF 344th ARS/22nd ARW, McConnell AFB, KS	
18-46039	Boeing KC-46A Pegasus (N1785B)	USAF 344th ARS/22nd ARW, McConnell AFB, KS	
18-46040	Boeing KC-46A Pegasus (N6018N)	USAF 56th ARS/97th AMW, Altus AFB, OK	
18-46041	Boeing KC-46A Pegasus (N50217)	USAF 418th FLTS/412th TW, Edwards AFB, CA	
18-46042	Boeing KC-46A Pegasus (N5512A)	USAF 344th ARS/22nd ARW, McConnell AFB, KS	
18-46043	Boeing KC-46A Pegasus (N1785B)	USAF 56th ARS/97th AMW, Altus AFB, OK	
18-46044	Boeing KC-46A Pegasus (N5511V)	USAF 344th ARS/22nd ARW, McConnell AFB, KS	
18-46045	Boeing KC-46A Pegasus (N1794B)	USAF 56th ARS/97th AMW, Altus AFB, OK	
18-46046	Boeing KC-46A Pegasus (N55077)	USAF 418th FLTS/412th TW, Edwards AFB, CA	
18-46047	Boeing KC-46A Pegasus (N5016R) *bl/w*	USAF 133rd ARS/157th ARW, Pease ANGB, NH ANG	
18-46048	Boeing KC-46A Pegasus (N1794B)	USAF 56th ARS/97th AMW, Altus AFB, OK	
18-46049	Boeing KC-46A Pegasus (N5510E)	USAF 344th ARS/22nd ARW, McConnell AFB, KS	
18-46050	Boeing KC-46A Pegasus (N5511Z) *bl/w*	USAF 133rd ARS/157th ARW, Pease ANGB, NH ANG	
18-46051	Boeing KC-46A Pegasus (N6018N) *bl/w*	USAF 133rd ARS/157th ARW, Pease ANGB, NH ANG	
18-46052	Boeing KC-46A Pegasus (N55077)	USAF 77th ARS/916th ARW AFRC, Seymour Johnson AFB, NC	
18-46053	Boeing KC-46A Pegasus (N1785B) *bl/w*	USAF 133rd ARS/157th ARW, Pease ANGB, NH ANG	
18-46054	Boeing KC-46A Pegasus (N50254) *bl/w*	USAF 133rd ARS/157th ARW, Pease ANGB, NH ANG	
18-46055	Boeing KC-46A Pegasus (N50281)	USAF 77th ARS/916th ARW AFRC, Seymour Johnson AFB, NC	
18-46056	Boeing KC-46A Pegasus (N5514K)	USAF 344th ARS/22nd ARW, McConnell AFB, KS	
19-46005	Boeing KC-46A Pegasus (N842BA/15-46005)	Boeing, Everett, for USAF	
19-46006	Boeing KC-46A Pegasus (N884BA/15-46006)	Boeing, Everett, for USAF	
19-46007	Boeing KC-46A Pegasus (N2015U/15-46007)	USAF 305th AMW, McGuire AFB, NJ	
19-46008	Boeing KC-46A Pegasus (15-46008)	Boeing, Everett, for USAF	
19-46010	Boeing KC-46A Pegasus (N2007L/15-46010)	USAF 305th AMW, McGuire AFB, NJ	
19-46061	Boeing KC-46A Pegasus (N20144)	USAF 305th AMW, McGuire AFB, NJ	
19-46062	Boeing KC-46A Pegasus (N2011A)	USAF 77th ARS/916th ARW AFRC, Seymour Johnson AFB, NC	
19-46063	Boeing KC-46A Pegasus (N2011E)	USAF 305th AMW, McGuire AFB, NJ	
19-46064	Boeing KC-46A Pegasus (N20129)	USAF 305th AMW, McGuire AFB, NJ	
19-46065	Boeing KC-46A Pegasus (N20140)	USAF 77th ARS/916th ARW AFRC, Seymour Johnson AFB, NC	
19-46071	Boeing KC-46A Pegasus (N461FT)	USAF 305th AMW, McGuire AFB, NJ	
20-46072	Boeing KC-46A Pegasus (N50281)	USAF 305th AMW, McGuire AFB, NJ	
20-46073	Boeing KC-46A Pegasus (N55061)	USAF 305th AMW, McGuire AFB, NJ	
20-46074	Boeing KC-46A Pegasus (N8570Z)	USAF 305th AMW, McGuire AFB, NJ	
20-46075	Boeing KC-46A Pegasus (N2014K)	USAF 344th ARS/22nd ARW, McConnell AFB, KS	

Notes	Serial	Type (code/other identity)	Owner/operator, location or fate
	20-46076	Boeing KC-46A Pegasus (N1974B)	USAF 344th ARS/22nd ARW, McConnell AFB, KS
	20-46077	Boeing KC-46A Pegasus (N1006F)	USAF 77th ARS/916th ARW AFRC, Seymour Johnson AFB, NC
	20-46078	Boeing KC-46A Pegasus (N2013F)	USAF 60th AMW, Travis AFB, CA
	20-46079	Boeing KC-46A Pegasus (N8570X)	USAF 305th AMW, McGuire AFB, NJ
	20-46080	Boeing KC-46A Pegasus (N8297V)	USAF 305th AMW, McGuire AFB, NJ
	20-46081	Boeing KC-46A Pegasus (N2013M)	USAF 60th AMW, Travis AFB, CA
	20-46082	Boeing KC-46A Pegasus (N8296V)	USAF 305th AMW, McGuire AFB, NJ
	20-46083	Boeing KC-46A Pegasus (N8295V)	USAF 60th AMW, Travis AFB, CA
	21-46084	Boeing KC-46A Pegasus (N8571B)	USAF 60th AMW, Travis AFB, CA
	21-46085	Boeing KC-46A Pegasus (N8570Z)	USAF 60th AMW, Travis AFB, CA
	21-46086	Boeing KC-46A Pegasus (N8571C)	USAF 60th AMW, Travis AFB, CA
	21-46087	Boeing KC-46A Pegasus (N8571F)	USAF 305th AMW, McGuire AFB, NJ
	21-46088	Boeing KC-46A Pegasus (N8297V)	USAF 305th AMW, McGuire AFB, NJ
	21-46089	Boeing KC-46A Pegasus (N1003M)	USAF 305th AMW, McGuire AFB, NJ
	21-46090	Boeing KC-46A Pegasus (N8286V)	USAF 305th AMW, McGuire AFB, NJ
	21-46091	Boeing KC-46A Pegasus (N8296V)	USAF 305th AMW, McGuire AFB, NJ
	21-46092	Boeing KC-46A Pegasus (N8570X)	USAF 305th AMW, McGuire AFB, NJ
	21-46093	Boeing KC-46A Pegasus (N8296V)	USAF 305th AMW, McGuire AFB, NJ
	21-46094	Boeing KC-46A Pegasus (N8570Y)	USAF 60th AMW, Travis AFB, CA
	21-46095	Boeing KC-46A Pegasus (N8571F)	USAF 60th AMW, Travis AFB, CA
	21-46096	Boeing KC-46A Pegasus (N8570Z)	USAF 60th AMW, Travis AFB, CA
	21-46097	Boeing KC-46A Pegasus (N5514X)	USAF (on order)
	21-46098	Boeing KC-46A Pegasus (N8295V)	USAF (on order)
	21-46099	Boeing KC-46A Pegasus (N8296V)	USAF (on order)
	22-46100	Boeing KC-46A Pegasus (N8297V)	USAF (on order)
	22-46101	Boeing KC-46A Pegasus	USAF (on order)
	22-46102	Boeing KC-46A Pegasus	USAF (on order)
	22-46103	Boeing KC-46A Pegasus	USAF (on order)
	22-46104	Boeing KC-46A Pegasus	USAF (on order)
	22-46105	Boeing KC-46A Pegasus	USAF (on order)
	22-46106	Boeing KC-46A Pegasus	USAF (on order)
	22-46107	Boeing KC-46A Pegasus	USAF (on order)
	22-46108	Boeing KC-46A Pegasus	USAF (on order)
	22-46109	Boeing KC-46A Pegasus	USAF (on order)
	23-46110	Boeing KC-46A Pegasus	USAF (on order)
	Boeing B-52H Stratofortress		
	60-0001	Boeing B-52H Stratofortress [LA] *gn*	USAF 96th BS/2nd BW, Barksdale AFB, LA
	60-0002	Boeing B-52H Stratofortress [LA] *gn* [2 BW]	USAF 96th BS/2nd BW, Barksdale AFB, LA
	60-0003	Boeing B-52H Stratofortress [BD] *or/bl*	USAF 93rd BS/307th BW AFRC, Barksdale AFB, LA
	60-0004	Boeing B-52H Stratofortress [MT] *r/y*	USAF 23rd BS/5th BW, Minot AFB, ND
	60-0005	Boeing B-52H Stratofortress [MT] *m* [5 BW]	USAF 23rd BS/5th BW, Minot AFB, ND
	60-0007	Boeing B-52H Stratofortress [MT] *r/y*	USAF 23rd BS/5th BW, Minot AFB, ND
	60-0008	Boeing B-52H Stratofortress [LA] *bl* [8th AF]	USAF 20th BS/2nd BW, Barksdale AFB, LA
	60-0009	Boeing B-52H Stratofortress [MT] *y/bk* [69 BS]	USAF 69th BS/5th BW, Minot AFB, ND
	60-0011	Boeing B-52H Stratofortress [BD] *or/bl* [11 BS]	USAF 93rd BS/307th BW AFRC, Barksdale AFB, LA
	60-0012	Boeing B-52H Stratofortress [MT] *y/bk*	USAF 69th BS/5th BW, Minot AFB, ND
	60-0013	Boeing B-52H Stratofortress [LA] *bl*	USAF 20th BS/2nd BW, Barksdale AFB, LA
	60-0015	Boeing B-52H Stratofortress [BD] *or/bl*	USAF 93rd BS/307th BW AFRC, Barksdale AFB, LA
	60-0017	Boeing B-52H Stratofortress [MT] *y/bk*	USAF 69th BS/5th BW, Minot AFB, ND
	60-0018	Boeing B-52H Stratofortress [MT] *y/bk*	USAF 69th BS/5th BW, Minot AFB, ND
	60-0021	Boeing B-52H Stratofortress [LA] *r*	USAF 96th BS/2nd BW, Barksdale AFB, LA
	60-0022	Boeing B-52H Stratofortress [LA] *r*	USAF 96th BS/2nd BW, Barksdale AFB, LA
	60-0023	Boeing B-52H Stratofortress [LA] *r*	USAF 96th BS/2nd BW, Barksdale AFB, LA

Serial	Type (code/other identity)	Owner/operator, location or fate	Notes
60-0024	Boeing B-52H Stratofortress [LA] bl	USAF 20th BS/2nd BW, Barksdale AFB, LA	
60-0025	Boeing B-52H Stratofortress [LA] bl	USAF 20th BS/2nd BW, Barksdale AFB, LA	
60-0026	Boeing B-52H Stratofortress [MT] r/y	USAF 23rd BS/5th BW, Minot AFB, ND	
60-0028	Boeing B-52H Stratofortress [LA] r	USAF 96th BS/2nd BW, Barksdale AFB, LA	
60-0029	Boeing B-52H Stratofortress [MT] r/y	USAF 23rd BS/5th BW, Minot AFB, ND	
60-0031	Boeing B-52H Stratofortress [OT] or/w	USAF 49th TES/53rd TEG, Barksdale AFB, LA	
60-0032	Boeing B-52H Stratofortress [LA] r	USAF 96th BS/2nd BW, Barksdale AFB, LA	
60-0033	Boeing B-52H Stratofortress [MT] y/bk	USAF 69th BS/5th BW, Minot AFB, ND	
60-0034	Boeing B-52H Stratofortress [MT] r/y	USAF 23rd BS/5th BW, Minot AFB, ND	
60-0035	Boeing B-52H Stratofortress [BD] or/bl	USAF 93rd BS/307th BW AFRC, Barksdale AFB, LA	
60-0036	Boeing B-52H Stratofortress [ED]	USAF 419th FLTS/412th TW, Edwards AFB, CA	
60-0037	Boeing B-52H Stratofortress [MT] y/bk	USAF 69th BS/5th BW, Minot AFB, ND	
60-0038	Boeing B-52H Stratofortress [BD] or/bl	USAF 93rd BS/307th BW AFRC, Barksdale AFB, LA	
60-0041	Boeing B-52H Stratofortress [BD] or/bl	USAF 93rd BS/307th BW AFRC, Barksdale AFB, LA	
60-0042	Boeing B-52H Stratofortress [BD] or/bl	USAF 93rd BS/307th BW AFRC, Barksdale AFB, LA	
60-0044	Boeing B-52H Stratofortress [MT] r/y	USAF 23rd BS/5th BW, Minot AFB, ND	
60-0045	Boeing B-52H Stratofortress [BD] or/bl [307 OG]	USAF 93rd BS/307th BW AFRC, Barksdale AFB, LA	
60-0048	Boeing B-52H Stratofortress [LA] r	USAF 96th BS/2nd BW, Barksdale AFB, LA	
60-0050	Boeing B-52H Stratofortress [ED]	USAF 419th FLTS/412th TW, Edwards AFB, CA	
60-0051	Boeing B-52H Stratofortress [BD] or/bl	USAF 93rd BS/307th BW AFRC, Barksdale AFB, LA	
60-0052	Boeing B-52H Stratofortress [LA] r	USAF 96th BS/2nd BW, Barksdale AFB, LA	
60-0054	Boeing B-52H Stratofortress [LA] bl	USAF 20th BS/2nd BW, Barksdale AFB, LA	
60-0055	Boeing B-52H Stratofortress [MT] r/y [5 OG]	USAF 23rd BS/5th BW, Minot AFB, ND	
60-0056	Boeing B-52H Stratofortress [MT] r/y	USAF 23rd BS/5th BW, Minot AFB, ND	
60-0057	Boeing B-52H Stratofortress [BD] or/bl [340 BS]	USAF 93rd BS/307th BW AFRC, Barksdale AFB, LA	
60-0058	Boeing B-52H Stratofortress [LA] bl	USAF 20th BS/2nd BW, Barksdale AFB, LA	
60-0059	Boeing B-52H Stratofortress [LA] r [96 BS]	USAF 96th BS/2nd BW, Barksdale AFB, LA	
60-0060	Boeing B-52H Stratofortress [MT] r/y	USAF 23rd BS/5th BW, Minot AFB, ND	
60-0061	Boeing B-52H Stratofortress [BD] or/bl [307 BW]	USAF 93rd BS/307th BW AFRC, Barksdale AFB, LA	
60-0062	Boeing B-52H Stratofortress [LA] r	USAF 96th BS/2nd BW, Barksdale AFB, LA	
61-0001	Boeing B-52H Stratofortress [MT] y/bk	USAF 69th BS/5th BW, Minot AFB, ND	
61-0002	Boeing B-52H Stratofortress [LA] bl [2 OG]	USAF 20th BS/2nd BW, Barksdale AFB, LA	
61-0003	Boeing B-52H Stratofortress [MT] y/bk	USAF 69th BS/5th BW, Minot AFB, ND	
61-0004	Boeing B-52H Stratofortress [LA] bl	USAF 20th BS/2nd BW, Barksdale AFB, LA	
61-0005	Boeing B-52H Stratofortress [MT] y/bk [5 BW]	USAF 69th BS/5th BW, Minot AFB, ND	
61-0006	Boeing B-52H Stratofortress [LA] r	USAF 96th BS/2nd BW, Barksdale AFB, LA	
61-0007	Boeing B-52H Stratofortress [MT] y/bk	USAF 69th BS/5th BW, Minot AFB, ND	
61-0008	Boeing B-52H Stratofortress [BD] or/bl	USAF 93rd BS/307th BW AFRC, Barksdale AFB, LA	
61-0010	Boeing B-52H Stratofortress [LA] or/bl [343 BS]	USAF 343rd BS/307th BW AFRC, Barksdale AFB, LA	
61-0011	Boeing B-52H Stratofortress [BD] or/bl	USAF 93rd BS/307th BW AFRC, Barksdale AFB, LA	
61-0012	Boeing B-52H Stratofortress [LA] r	USAF 96th BS/2nd BW, Barksdale AFB, LA	
61-0013	Boeing B-52H Stratofortress [LA] bl	USAF 20th BS/2nd BW, Barksdale AFB, LA	
61-0014	Boeing B-52H Stratofortress [OT]	USAF 49th TES/53rd TEG, Edwards AFB, CA	
61-0015	Boeing B-52H Stratofortress [LA] r	USAF 96th BS/2nd BW, Barksdale AFB, LA	
61-0016	Boeing B-52H Stratofortress [LA] bl	USAF 20th BS/2nd BW, Barksdale AFB, LA	
61-0017	Boeing B-52H Stratofortress [BD] or/bl	USAF 93rd BS/307th BW AFRC, Barksdale AFB, LA	
61-0018	Boeing B-52H Stratofortress [MT] y/bk	USAF 69th BS/5th BW, Minot AFB, ND	
61-0019	Boeing B-52H Stratofortress [LA] bl	USAF 20th BS/2nd BW, Barksdale AFB, LA	
61-0020	Boeing B-52H Stratofortress [LA] bl [20 BS]	USAF 20th BS/2nd BW, Barksdale AFB, LA	
61-0021	Boeing B-52H Stratofortress [BD] [343 BS]	USAF 93rd BS/307th BW AFRC, Barksdale AFB, LA	
61-0028	Boeing B-52H Stratofortress [OT] [49 TES] $	USAF 49th TES/53rd TEG, Barksdale AFB, LA	
61-0029	Boeing B-52H Stratofortress [BD] or/bl [93 BS]	USAF 93rd BS/307th BW AFRC, Barksdale AFB, LA	

Notes	Serial	Type (code/other identity)	Owner/operator, location or fate
	61-0031	Boeing B-52H Stratofortress [BD] or/bl	USAF 93rd BS/307th BW AFRC, Barksdale AFB, LA
	61-0032	Boeing B-52H Stratofortress [MT] r/y	USAF 23rd BS/5th BW, Minot AFB, ND
	61-0034	Boeing B-52H Stratofortress [MT] r/y	USAF 23rd BS/5th BW, Minot AFB, ND
	61-0035	Boeing B-52H Stratofortress [MT] r/y	USAF 23rd BS/5th BW, Minot AFB, ND
	61-0036	Boeing B-52H Stratofortress [LA] r	USAF 96th BS/2nd BW, Barksdale AFB, LA
	61-0038	Boeing B-52H Stratofortress [BD] or/bl	USAF 93rd BS/307th BW AFRC, Barksdale AFB, LA
	61-0039	Boeing B-52H Stratofortress [MT] y/bk	USAF 69th BS/5th BW, Minot AFB, ND
	61-0040	Boeing B-52H Stratofortress [MT] r/y	USAF 23rd BS/5th BW, Minot AFB, ND
	Lockheed C-130 Hercules		
	65-0967	Lockheed EC-130H Compass Call [DM]	*To 309th AMARG, 11th June 2024*
	65-0974	Lockheed HC-130P Combat King	*Current status unknown*
	73-1581	Lockheed EC-130H Compass Call [DM] $	USAF 43rd ECS/55th ECG, Davis-Monthan AFB, AZ
	73-1583	Lockheed EC-130H Compass Call [DM] r	*To 309th AMARG, 8th August 2024*
	73-1586	Lockheed EC-130H Compass Call [DM]	USAF 43rd ECS/55th ECG, Davis-Monthan AFB, AZ
	73-1590	Lockheed EC-130H Compass Call [DM]	USAF 43rd ECS/55th ECG, Davis-Monthan AFB, AZ
	73-1594	Lockheed EC-130H Compass Call [DM]	USAF 43rd ECS/55th ECG, Davis-Monthan AFB, AZ
	73-1595	Lockheed EC-130H Compass Call [DM]	*To 309th AMARG, 25th September 2024*
	73-3300	Lockheed LC-130H Hercules	USAF 139th AS/109th AW, Schenectady, NY ANG
	74-1685	Lockheed C-130H Hercules y/bk	USAF 118th AS/103rd AW, Bradley ANGB, CT ANG
	74-1692	Lockheed C-130H Hercules r/bk	USAF 164th AS/179th AW, Mansfield, OH ANG
	74-2069	Lockheed C-130H Hercules y/bk	USAF 118th AS/103rd AW, Bradley ANGB, CT ANG
	76-3301	Lockheed LC-130H Hercules	USAF 139th AS/109th AW, Schenectady, NY ANG
	76-3302	Lockheed LC-130H Hercules	USAF 139th AS/109th AW, Schenectady, NY ANG
	81-0629	Lockheed C-130H-2 Hercules r/w $	USAF 154th TS/189th AW, Little Rock, AR ANG
	83-0489	Lockheed C-130H-2 Hercules	USAF 139th AS/109th AW, Schenectady, NY ANG
	83-0490	Lockheed LC-130H Hercules	USAF 139th AS/109th AW, Schenectady, NY ANG
	83-0491	Lockheed LC-130H Hercules	USAF 139th AS/109th AW, Schenectady, NY ANG
	83-0492	Lockheed LC-130H Hercules	USAF 139th AS/109th AW, Schenectady, NY ANG
	83-0493	Lockheed LC-130H Hercules	USAF 139th AS/109th AW, Schenectady, NY ANG
	84-0206	Lockheed C-130H-2 Hercules bl/bk	USAF 142nd AS/166th AW, New Castle County, DE ANG
	84-0207	Lockheed C-130H-2 Hercules	USAF 164th AS/179th AW, Mansfield, OH ANG
	84-0208	Lockheed C-130H-2 Hercules	USAF 139th AS/109th AW, Schenectady, NY ANG
	84-0209	Lockheed C-130H-2 Hercules	USAF 142nd AS/166th AW, New Castle County, DE ANG
	84-0210	Lockheed C-130H-2 Hercules	USAF 118th AS/103rd AW, Bradley ANGB, CT ANG
	84-0212	Lockheed C-130H-2 Hercules bl/bk	*Instructional airframe, Sheppard AFB, TX*
	84-0213	Lockheed C-130H-2 Hercules bl/bk	*Instructional airframe, Sheppard AFB, TX*
	85-1363	Lockheed C-130H-2 Hercules r/w	USAF 154th TS/189th AW, Little Rock, AR ANG
	85-1364	Lockheed C-130H-2 Hercules r/w	USAF 154th TS/189th AW, Little Rock, AR ANG
	85-1365	Lockheed C-130H-2 Hercules r/w	USAF 154th TS/189th AW, Little Rock, AR ANG
	85-1366	Lockheed C-130H-2 Hercules r/w	USAF 154th TS/189th AW, Little Rock, AR ANG
	85-1367	Lockheed C-130H-2 Hercules r/w	USAF 154th TS/189th AW, Little Rock, AR ANG
	86-0419	Lockheed C-130H-2 Hercules r/bk	USAF 164th AS/179th AW, Mansfield, OH ANG
	87-9281	Lockheed C-130H-2 Hercules r/bk	USAF 164th AS/179th AW, Mansfield, OH ANG
	87-9283	Lockheed C-130H-2 Hercules r/bk	USAF 164th AS/179th AW, Mansfield, OH ANG
	87-9285	Lockheed C-130H-2 Hercules r/bk	USAF 164th AS/179th AW, Mansfield, OH ANG
	88-1304	Lockheed AC-130W Stinger II	USAF, stored Cannon AFB, NM
	88-1308	Lockheed AC-130W Stinger II	USAF, stored Cannon AFB, NM
	88-4405	Lockheed C-130H-2 Hercules r/bk	USAF 164th AS/179th AW, Mansfield, OH ANG
	89-1055	Lockheed C-130H-2 Hercules	USAF 186th AS/120th AW, Great Falls, MT ANG
	89-1181	Lockheed C-130H-2 Hercules r/w	USAF 154th TS/189th AW, Little Rock, AR ANG
	89-1182	Lockheed C-130H-2 Hercules r/w	*To Poland as 1512?, 2024*
	89-1183	Lockheed C-130H-2 Hercules r/w	USAF 154th TS/189th AW, Little Rock, AR ANG
	89-1184	Lockheed C-130H-2 Hercules r/w $	*Withdrawn from use Little Rock, AR, 2023*
	89-1185	Lockheed C-130H-2 Hercules r/w	*To Poland as 1513?, 2024*

Serial	Type (code/other identity)	Owner/operator, location or fate	Notes
89-1186	Lockheed C-130H-2 Hercules *r/w*	*Withdrawn from use Little Rock, AR, 2023*	
89-1187	Lockheed C-130H-2 Hercules *bl/w*	*To Poland as 1514?, 2024*	
89-9102	Lockheed C-130H-2 Hercules *r/w*	USAF 154th TS/189th AW, Little Rock, AR ANG	
89-9103	Lockheed C-130H-2 Hercules *bl/w*	*Instructional airframe, McGuire AFB, NJ*	
89-9104	Lockheed C-130H-2 Hercules *bl/r*	USAF 757th AS/910th AW AFRC, Youngstown ARS, OH	
89-9105	Lockheed C-130H-2 Hercules *bl/r*	USAF 757th AS/910th AW AFRC, Youngstown ARS, OH	
89-9106	Lockheed C-130H-2 Hercules *bl/r*	USAF 757th AS/910th AW AFRC, Youngstown ARS, OH	
90-1057	Lockheed C-130H-2 Hercules	USAF 142nd AS/166th AW, New Castle County, DE ANG	
90-1791	Lockheed C-130H-2 Hercules	USAF 180th AS/139th AW, Rosencrans Memorial, MO ANG	
90-1792	Lockheed C-130H-2 Hercules	USAF 180th AS/139th AW, Rosencrans Memorial, MO ANG	
90-1793	Lockheed C-130H-2 Hercules	USAF 180th AS/139th AW, Rosencrans Memorial, MO ANG	
90-1794	Lockheed C-130H-2 Hercules	USAF 180th AS/139th AW, Rosencrans Memorial, MO ANG	
90-1795	Lockheed C-130H-2 Hercules	USAF 180th AS/139th AW, Rosencrans Memorial, MO ANG	
90-1796	Lockheed C-130H-2 Hercules	USAF 180th AS/139th AW, Rosencrans Memorial, MO ANG	
90-1797	Lockheed C-130H-2 Hercules	USAF 180th AS/139th AW, Rosencrans Memorial, MO ANG	
90-1798	Lockheed C-130H-2 Hercules	USAF 180th AS/139th AW, Rosencrans Memorial, MO ANG	
90-9107	Lockheed C-130H-2 Hercules *bl/r*	USAF 757th AS/910th AW AFRC, Youngstown ARS, OH	
90-9108	Lockheed C-130H-2 Hercules *bl/r*	USAF 757th AS/910th AW AFRC, Youngstown ARS, OH	
91-1231	Lockheed C-130H-2 Hercules *bl/bk*	USAF 142nd AS/166th AW, New Castle County, DE ANG	
91-1232	Lockheed C-130H-2 Hercules *bl/bk*	USAF 142nd AS/166th AW, New Castle County, DE ANG	
91-1233	Lockheed C-130H-2 Hercules *bl/bk*	USAF 142nd AS/166th AW, New Castle County, DE ANG	
91-1234	Lockheed C-130H-2 Hercules *bl/bk*	USAF 142nd AS/166th AW, New Castle County, DE ANG	
91-1235	Lockheed C-130H-2 Hercules *bl/bk*	USAF 142nd AS/166th AW, New Castle County, DE ANG	
91-1236	Lockheed C-130H-2 Hercules *bl/bk*	USAF 142nd AS/166th AW, New Castle County, DE ANG	
91-1237	Lockheed C-130H-2 Hercules *bl/bk*	USAF 142nd AS/166th AW, New Castle County, DE ANG	
91-1238	Lockheed C-130H-2 Hercules *bl/bk*	USAF 142nd AS/166th AW, New Castle County, DE ANG	
91-1652	Lockheed C-130H-2 Hercules	USAF 180th AS/139th AW, Rosencrans Memorial, MO ANG	
91-1653	Lockheed C-130H-2 Hercules	USAF 180th AS/139th AW, Rosencrans Memorial, MO ANG	
92-0547	Lockheed C-130H-2 Hercules *bl/w*	USAF 192nd AS/152nd AW, Reno, NV ANG	
92-0548	Lockheed C-130H-2 Hercules *bl/w*	USAF 192nd AS/152nd AW, Reno, NV ANG	
92-0549	Lockheed C-130H-2 Hercules *bl/w*	USAF 192nd AS/152nd AW, Reno, NV ANG	
92-0550	Lockheed C-130H-2 Hercules *bl/bk*	USAF 700th AS/94th AW AFRC, Dobbins ARB, GA	
92-0551	Lockheed C-130H-2 Hercules *bl/bk*	USAF 700th AS/94th AW AFRC, Dobbins ARB, GA	
92-0552	Lockheed C-130H-2 Hercules *bl/bk*	USAF 700th AS/94th AW AFRC, Dobbins ARB, GA	
92-0553	Lockheed C-130H-2 Hercules *bl/w*	USAF 192nd AS/152nd AW, Reno, NV ANG	
92-0554	Lockheed C-130H-2 Hercules *bl/w*	USAF 192nd AS/152nd AW, Reno, NV ANG	
92-1094	Lockheed LC-130H Hercules	USAF 139th AS/109th AW, Schenectady, NY ANG	
92-1095	Lockheed LC-130H Hercules	USAF 139th AS/109th AW, Schenectady, NY ANG	

Notes	Serial	Type (code/other identity)	Owner/operator, location or fate
	92-1451	Lockheed C-130H-3 Hercules *or/bk*	USAF 169th AS/182nd AW, Peoria, IL ANG
	92-1452	Lockheed C-130H-3 Hercules *or/bk*	USAF 169th AS/182nd AW, Peoria, IL ANG
	92-1453	Lockheed C-130H-3 Hercules	USAF 118th AS/103rd AW, Bradley ANGB, CT ANG
	92-1454	Lockheed C-130H-3 Hercules	USAF 186th AS/120th AW, Great Falls, MT ANG
	92-1531	Lockheed C-130H-3 Hercules *y/bk*	USAF 187th AS/153rd AW, Cheyenne, WY ANG
	92-1532	Lockheed C-130H-3 Hercules *y/bk*	USAF 187th AS/153rd AW, Cheyenne, WY ANG
	92-1533	Lockheed C-130H-3 Hercules *y/bk*	USAF 187th AS/153rd AW, Cheyenne, WY ANG
	92-1534	Lockheed C-130H-3 Hercules *y/bk*	USAF 187th AS/153rd AW, Cheyenne, WY ANG
	92-1535	Lockheed C-130H-3 Hercules *y/bk*	USAF 187th AS/153rd AW, Cheyenne, WY ANG
	92-1536	Lockheed C-130H-3 Hercules *y/bk*	USAF 187th AS/153rd AW, Cheyenne, WY ANG
	92-1537	Lockheed C-130H-3 Hercules *y/bk*	USAF 187th AS/153rd AW, Cheyenne, WY ANG
	92-1538	Lockheed C-130H-3 Hercules *y/bk*	USAF 187th AS/153rd AW, Cheyenne, WY ANG
	92-3021	Lockheed C-130H-2 Hercules *bl/r*	USAF 757th AS/910th AW AFRC, Youngstown ARS, OH
	92-3022	Lockheed C-130H-2 Hercules *bl/r*	USAF 757th AS/910th AW AFRC, Youngstown ARS, OH
	92-3023	Lockheed C-130H-2 Hercules *bl/r*	USAF 757th AS/910th AW AFRC, Youngstown ARS, OH
	92-3024	Lockheed C-130H-2 Hercules *bl/r*	USAF 757th AS/910th AW AFRC, Youngstown ARS, OH
	92-3281	Lockheed C-130H-3 Hercules *pr/w*	USAF 96th AS/934th AW AFRC, Minneapolis/ St Paul, MN
	92-3282	Lockheed C-130H-3 Hercules *pr/w*	USAF 96th AS/934th AW AFRC, Minneapolis/ St Paul, MN
	92-3283	Lockheed C-130H-3 Hercules *pr/w*	USAF 96th AS/934th AW AFRC, Minneapolis/ St Paul, MN
	92-3284	Lockheed C-130H-3 Hercules *pr/w* $	USAF 96th AS/934th AW AFRC, Minneapolis/ St Paul, MN
	92-3285	Lockheed C-130H-3 Hercules *pr/w*	USAF 96th AS/934th AW AFRC, Minneapolis/ St Paul, MN
	92-3286	Lockheed C-130H-3 Hercules *pr/w*	USAF 96th AS/934th AW AFRC, Minneapolis/ St Paul, MN
	92-3287	Lockheed C-130H-3 Hercules *pr/w*	USAF 96th AS/934th AW AFRC, Minneapolis/ St Paul, MN
	92-3288	Lockheed C-130H-3 Hercules *pr/w*	USAF 96th AS/934th AW AFRC, Minneapolis/ St Paul, MN
	93-1036	Lockheed C-130H-3 Hercules *bl/bk*	USAF 700th AS/94th AW AFRC, Dobbins ARB, GA
	93-1037	Lockheed C-130H-3 Hercules *bl/bk*	USAF 700th AS/94th AW AFRC, Dobbins ARB, GA
	93-1038	Lockheed C-130H-3 Hercules *bl/bk*	USAF 700th AS/94th AW AFRC, Dobbins ARB, GA
	93-1039	Lockheed C-130H-3 Hercules *bl/bk*	USAF 700th AS/94th AW AFRC, Dobbins ARB, GA
	93-1040	Lockheed C-130H-3 Hercules *bl/bk*	USAF 700th AS/94th AW AFRC, Dobbins ARB, GA
	93-1041	Lockheed C-130H-3 Hercules *pr/w*	USAF 731st AS/302nd AW AFRC, Peterson AFB, CO
	93-1096	Lockheed LC-130H Hercules	USAF 139th AS/109th AW, Schenectady, NY ANG
	93-1455	Lockheed C-130H-3 Hercules	USAF 186th AS/120th AW, Great Falls, MT ANG
	93-1456	Lockheed C-130H-3 Hercules $	USAF 118th AS/103rd AW, Bradley ANGB, CT ANG
	93-1457	Lockheed C-130H-3 Hercules *y/bk*	USAF 118th AS/103rd AW, Bradley ANGB, CT ANG
	93-1459	Lockheed C-130H-3 Hercules *y/bk*	USAF 118th AS/103rd AW, Bradley ANGB, CT ANG
	93-1561	Lockheed C-130H-3 Hercules *r/bk*	USAF 158th AS/165th AW, Savannah, GA ANG
	93-1562	Lockheed C-130H-3 Hercules	USAF 142nd AS/166th AW, New Castle County, DE ANG
	93-1563	Lockheed C-130H-3 Hercules *r/bk*	USAF 158th AS/165th AW, Savannah, GA ANG
	93-2041	Lockheed C-130H-3 Hercules *or/bk*	USAF 169th AS/182nd AW, Peoria, IL ANG
	93-2042	Lockheed C-130H-3 Hercules *or/bk*	USAF 169th AS/182nd AW, Peoria, IL ANG
	93-7311	Lockheed C-130H-3 Hercules *bl/w*	USAF 192nd AS/152nd AW, Reno, NV ANG
	93-7312	Lockheed C-130H-3 Hercules *or/bk*	USAF 169th AS/182nd AW, Peoria, IL ANG
	93-7313	Lockheed C-130H-3 Hercules *bl/w*	USAF 192nd AS/152nd AW, Reno, NV ANG
	93-7314	Lockheed C-130H-3 Hercules *bl/w*	USAF 192nd AS/152nd AW, Reno, NV ANG
	94-6701	Lockheed C-130H-3 Hercules *or/bk*	USAF 169th AS/182nd AW, Peoria, IL ANG

Serial	Type (code/other identity)	Owner/operator, location or fate	Notes
94-6702	Lockheed C-130H-3 Hercules *or/bk*	USAF 169th AS/182nd AW, Peoria, IL ANG	
94-6703	Lockheed C-130H-3 Hercules *or/bk*	USAF 169th AS/182nd AW, Peoria, IL ANG	
94-6705	Lockheed C-130H-3 Hercules *r/bk*	USAF 158th AS/165th AW, Savannah, GA ANG	
94-6707	Lockheed C-130H-3 Hercules *r/bk*	USAF 158th AS/165th AW, Savannah, GA ANG	
94-6708	Lockheed C-130H-3 Hercules *r/bk*	USAF 158th AS/165th AW, Savannah, GA ANG	
94-7310	Lockheed C-130H-3 Hercules *pr/w*	USAF 731st AS/302nd AW AFRC, Peterson AFB, CO	
94-7315	Lockheed C-130H-3 Hercules *pr/w*	USAF 731st AS/302nd AW AFRC, Peterson AFB, CO	
94-7316	Lockheed C-130H-3 Hercules *pr/w*	USAF 731st AS/302nd AW AFRC, Peterson AFB, CO	
94-7317	Lockheed C-130H-3 Hercules *pr/w*	USAF 731st AS/302nd AW AFRC, Peterson AFB, CO	
94-7318	Lockheed C-130H-3 Hercules *pr/w*	USAF 731st AS/302nd AW AFRC, Peterson AFB, CO	
94-7319	Lockheed C-130H-3 Hercules *pr/w*	USAF 731st AS/302nd AW AFRC, Peterson AFB, CO	
94-7320	Lockheed C-130H-3 Hercules *pr/w*	USAF 731st AS/302nd AW AFRC, Peterson AFB, CO	
94-7321	Lockheed C-130H-3 Hercules *r/bk*	USAF 158th AS/165th AW, Savannah, GA ANG	
94-8151	Lockheed C-130J Hercules II *bl/bk*	USAF 62nd AS/314th AW, Little Rock AFB, AR	
94-8152	Lockheed C-130J Hercules II *r/bk*	USAF 815th AS/403rd AW AFRC, Keesler AFB, MS	
95-1001	Lockheed C-130H-3 Hercules *pr/bk*	USAF 109th AS/133rd AW, Minneapolis, MN ANG	
95-1002	Lockheed C-130H-3 Hercules *pr/bk*	USAF 109th AS/133rd AW, Minneapolis, MN ANG	
95-6709	Lockheed C-130H-3 Hercules	USAF 186th AS/120th AW, Great Falls, MT ANG	
95-6710	Lockheed C-130H-3 Hercules *y/bk*	USAF 118th AS/103rd AW, Bradley ANGB, CT ANG	
95-6711	Lockheed C-130H-3 Hercules	USAF 186th AS/120th AW, Great Falls, MT ANG	
95-6712	Lockheed C-130H-3 Hercules *y/bk*	USAF 118th AS/103rd AW, Bradley ANGB, CT ANG	
96-1003	Lockheed C-130H-3 Hercules *pr/bk*	USAF 109th AS/133rd AW, Minneapolis, MN ANG	
96-1004	Lockheed C-130H-3 Hercules *pr/bk*	USAF 109th AS/133rd AW, Minneapolis, MN ANG	
96-1005	Lockheed C-130H-3 Hercules *pr/bk*	USAF 109th AS/133rd AW, Minneapolis, MN ANG	
96-1006	Lockheed C-130H-3 Hercules *pr/bk*	USAF 109th AS/133rd AW, Minneapolis, MN ANG	
96-1007	Lockheed C-130H-3 Hercules *pr/bk*	USAF 109th AS/133rd AW, Minneapolis, MN ANG	
96-1008	Lockheed C-130H-3 Hercules *pr/bk*	USAF 109th AS/133rd AW, Minneapolis, MN ANG	
96-5300	Lockheed WC-130J Hercules II	USAF 53rd WRS/403rd AW AFRC, Keesler AFB, MS	
96-5301	Lockheed WC-130J Hercules II	USAF 53rd WRS/403rd AW AFRC, Keesler AFB, MS	
96-5302	Lockheed WC-130J Hercules II	USAF 53rd WRS/403rd AW AFRC, Keesler AFB, MS	
96-7322	Lockheed C-130H-3 Hercules *y/bk*	USAF 118th AS/103rd AW, Bradley ANGB, CT ANG	
96-7323	Lockheed C-130H-3 Hercules	USAF 186th AS/120th AW, Great Falls, MT ANG	
96-7324	Lockheed C-130H-3 Hercules	USAF 186th AS/120th AW, Great Falls, MT ANG	
96-7325	Lockheed C-130H-3 Hercules	USAF 186th AS/120th AW, Great Falls, MT ANG	
96-8153	Lockheed C-130J Hercules II	USAF 154th TS, 189th AW, Little Rock, AR ANG	
97-1351	Lockheed C-130J Hercules II	USAF 48th AS/314th AW, Little Rock AFB, AR	
97-1352	Lockheed C-130J Hercules II	USAF 48th AS/314th AW, Little Rock AFB, AR	
97-1353	Lockheed C-130J Hercules II *r/bk*	USAF 815th AS/403rd AW AFRC, Keesler AFB, MS	
97-1354	Lockheed C-130J Hercules II	USAF 48th AS/314th AW, Little Rock AFB, AR	
97-1931	Lockheed EC-130J Commando Solo III	USAF	
97-5303	Lockheed WC-130J Hercules II	USAF 53rd WRS/403rd AW AFRC, Keesler AFB, MS	
97-5304	Lockheed WC-130J Hercules II	USAF 53rd WRS/403rd AW AFRC, Keesler AFB, MS	
97-5305	Lockheed WC-130J Hercules II	USAF 53rd WRS/403rd AW AFRC, Keesler AFB, MS	
97-5306	Lockheed WC-130J Hercules II	USAF 53rd WRS/403rd AW AFRC, Keesler AFB, MS	
98-1355	Lockheed C-130J Hercules II *bl/bk*	USAF 62nd AS/314th AW, Little Rock AFB, AR	
98-1356	Lockheed C-130J Hercules II *bl/bk*	USAF 62nd AS/314th AW, Little Rock AFB, AR	
98-1357	Lockheed C-130J Hercules II *bl/bk*	USAF 62nd AS/314th AW, Little Rock AFB, AR	
98-1358	Lockheed C-130J Hercules II *bl/bk*	USAF 62nd AS/314th AW, Little Rock AFB, AR	
98-5307	Lockheed WC-130J Hercules II	USAF 53rd WRS/403rd AW AFRC, Keesler AFB, MS	
98-5308	Lockheed WC-130J Hercules II	USAF 53rd WRS/403rd AW AFRC, Keesler AFB, MS	
99-1431	Lockheed C-130J-30 Hercules II *r/bk*	USAF 143rd AS/143rd AW, Quonset, RI ANG	
99-1432	Lockheed C-130J-30 Hercules II *r/bk*	USAF 143rd AS/143rd AW, Quonset, RI ANG	

Notes	Serial	Type (code/other identity)	Owner/operator, location or fate
	99-1433	Lockheed C-130J-30 Hercules II *r/bk*	USAF 143rd AS/143rd AW, Quonset, RI ANG
	99-1933	Lockheed C-130J Hercules II	USAF 154th TS, 189th AW, Little Rock, AR ANG
	99-5309	Lockheed WC-130J Hercules II	USAF 53rd WRS/403rd AW AFRC, Keesler AFB, MS
	01-1461	Lockheed C-130J-30 Hercules II *gn/bk*	USAF 115th AS/146th AW, Channel Islands ANGS, CA ANG
	01-1462	Lockheed C-130J-30 Hercules II *gn/bk*	USAF 115th AS/146th AW, Channel Islands ANGS, CA ANG
	01-1935	Lockheed EC-130J Commando Solo III	USAF
	02-0314	Lockheed C-130J-30 Hercules II *si/bk*	USAF 41st AS/19th AW Little Rock AFB, AR
	02-1434	Lockheed C-130J-30 Hercules II *r/bk*	USAF 143rd AS/143rd AW, Quonset, RI ANG
	02-1463	Lockheed C-130J Hercules II *gn/bk*	USAF 115th AS/146th AW, Channel Islands ANGS, CA ANG
	02-1464	Lockheed C-130J Hercules II *gn/bk*	USAF 115th AS/146th AW, Channel Islands ANGS, CA ANG
	02-8155	Lockheed C-130J-30 Hercules II *r/bk*	USAF 815th AS/403rd AW AFRC, Keesler AFB, MS
	03-8154	Lockheed C-130J-30 Hercules II	USAF 417th FLTS, 96th TW, Eglin AFB, FL
	04-3143	Lockheed C-130J-30 Hercules II	USAF 39th AS/317th AW, Dyess AFB, TX
	04-8153	Lockheed C-130J-30 Hercules II *r/bk*	USAF 815th AS/403rd AW AFRC, Keesler AFB, MS
	05-1435	Lockheed C-130J-30 Hercules II *r/bk*	USAF 143rd AS/143rd AW, Quonset, RI ANG
	05-1436	Lockheed C-130J-30 Hercules II *r/bk*	USAF 143rd AS/143rd AW, Quonset, RI ANG
	05-1465	Lockheed C-130J-30 Hercules II *gn/bk*	USAF 115th AS/146th AW, Channel Islands ANGS, CA ANG
	05-1466	Lockheed C-130J-30 Hercules II *gn/bk*	USAF 115th AS/146th AW, Channel Islands ANGS, CA ANG
	05-3145	Lockheed C-130J-30 Hercules II *si/bk*	USAF 41st AS/19th AW Little Rock AFB, AR
	05-3146	Lockheed C-130J-30 Hercules II *gn/bk*	USAF 61st AS/19th AW Little Rock AFB, AR
	05-3147	Lockheed C-130J-30 Hercules II *gn/bk*	USAF 61st AS/19th AW Little Rock AFB, AR
	05-8152	Lockheed C-130J-30 Hercules II *r/bk*	USAF 815th AS/403rd AW AFRC, Keesler AFB, MS
	05-8156	Lockheed C-130J-30 Hercules II *r/bk*	USAF 815th AS/403rd AW AFRC, Keesler AFB, MS
	05-8157	Lockheed C-130J-30 Hercules II *r/bk*	USAF 815th AS/403rd AW AFRC, Keesler AFB, MS
	05-8158	Lockheed C-130J-30 Hercules II *r/bk*	USAF 815th AS/403rd AW AFRC, Keesler AFB, MS
	06-1437	Lockheed C-130J-30 Hercules II *r/bk*	USAF 143rd AS/143rd AW, Quonset, RI ANG
	06-1438	Lockheed C-130J-30 Hercules II *r/bk*	USAF 143rd AS/143rd AW, Quonset, RI ANG
	06-1467	Lockheed C-130J-30 Hercules II *r/bk*	USAF 115th AS/146th AW, Channel Islands ANGS, CA ANG
	06-3171	Lockheed C-130J-30 Hercules II *bl*	USAF 40th AS/317th AW, Dyess AFB, TX
	06-4632	Lockheed C-130J-30 Hercules II *si/bk*	USAF 41st AS/19th AW Little Rock AFB, AR
	06-4633	Lockheed C-130J-30 Hercules II [YJ] *r*	USAF 36th AS/374th AW, Yokota AB, Japan
	06-4634	Lockheed C-130J-30 Hercules II *si/bk*	USAF 41st AS/19th AW Little Rock AFB, AR
	06-8159	Lockheed C-130J Hercules II *r/bk*	USAF 815th AS/403rd AW AFRC, Keesler AFB, MS
	06-8610	Lockheed C-130J-30 Hercules II [YJ] *r*	USAF 36th AS/374th AW, Yokota AB, Japan
	06-8611	Lockheed C-130J-30 Hercules II	USAF 317th AW, Dyess AFB, TX
	06-8612	Lockheed C-130J-30 Hercules II *gn/bk*	USAF 61st AS/19th AW Little Rock AFB, AR
	07-1468	Lockheed C-130J-30 Hercules II *gn/bk*	USAF 115th AS/146th AW, Channel Islands ANGS, CA ANG
	07-3170	Lockheed C-130J-30 Hercules II *bl*	USAF 40th AS/317th AW, Dyess AFB, TX
	07-4636	Lockheed C-130J-30 Hercules II *si/bk*	USAF 41st AS/19th AW Little Rock AFB, AR
	07-4637	Lockheed C-130J-30 Hercules II *si/bk*	USAF 41st AS/19th AW Little Rock AFB, AR
	07-4638	Lockheed C-130J-30 Hercules II	USAF 317th AW, Dyess AFB, TX
	07-4639	Lockheed C-130J-30 Hercules II	USAF 48th AS/314th AW, Little Rock AFB, AR
	07-8608	Lockheed C-130J-30 Hercules II	Stored Alexandria, LA (Damaged?)
	07-8613	Lockheed C-130J-30 Hercules II *si/bk*	USAF 41st AS/19th AW Little Rock AFB, AR
	07-46310	Lockheed C-130J-30 Hercules II *si/bk*	USAF 41st AS/19th AW Little Rock AFB, AR
	07-46311	Lockheed C-130J-30 Hercules II *si/bk*	USAF 41st AS/19th AW Little Rock AFB, AR
	07-46312	Lockheed C-130J-30 Hercules II *gn/bk*	USAF 61st AS/19th AW Little Rock AFB, AR
	08-3172	Lockheed C-130J-30 Hercules II *bl*	USAF 40th AS/317th AW, Dyess AFB, TX
	08-3173	Lockheed C-130J-30 Hercules II *bl*	USAF 40th AS/317th AW, Dyess AFB, TX
	08-3175	Lockheed C-130J-30 Hercules II *bl*	USAF 40th AS/317th AW, Dyess AFB, TX
	08-3177	Lockheed C-130J-30 Hercules II [YJ] *r*	USAF 36th AS/374th AW, Yokota AB, Japan
	08-3178	Lockheed C-130J-30 Hercules II	USAF 40th AS/317th AW, Dyess AFB, TX
	08-3179	Lockheed C-130J-30 Hercules II	USAF 39th AS/317th AW, Dyess AFB, TX
	08-5675	Lockheed C-130J-30 Hercules II	USAF 317th AW, Dyess AFB, TX

Serial	Type (code/other identity)	Owner/operator, location or fate	Notes
08-5678	Lockheed C-130J-30 Hercules II	USAF 40th AS/317th AW, Dyess AFB, TX	
08-5679	Lockheed C-130J-30 Hercules II bl/bk	USAF 62nd AS/314th AW, Little Rock AFB, AR	
08-5684	Lockheed C-130J-30 Hercules II si/bk	USAF 41st AS/19th AW Little Rock AFB, AR	
08-5685	Lockheed C-130J-30 Hercules II	USAF 314th AW, Little Rock AFB, AR	
08-5686	Lockheed C-130J-30 Hercules II	USAF 317th AW, Dyess AFB, TX	
08-5691	Lockheed C-130J-30 Hercules II	USAF 39th AS/317th AW, Dyess AFB, TX	
08-5692	Lockheed C-130J-30 Hercules II [YJ] r	USAF 36th AS/374th AW, Yokota AB, Japan	
08-5693	Lockheed C-130J-30 Hercules II si/bk	USAF 41st AS/19th AW Little Rock AFB, AR	
08-5697	Lockheed MC-130J Commando II	USAF 19th SOS/492nd SOW, Hurlburt Field, FL	
08-5705	Lockheed C-130J-30 Hercules II $	USAF 41st AS/19th AW Little Rock AFB, AR	
08-5708	Lockheed HC-130J Combat King II [FT]	USAF 71st RQS/347th RQG, Moody AFB, GA	
08-5712	Lockheed C-130J-30 Hercules II	USAF 317th AW, Dyess AFB, TX	
08-5715	Lockheed C-130J-30 Hercules II	USAF 317th AW, Dyess AFB, TX	
08-5724	Lockheed C-130J-30 Hercules II	USAF 317th AW, Dyess AFB, TX	
08-5726	Lockheed C-130J-30 Hercules II	USAF 317th AW, Dyess AFB, TX	
08-6201	Lockheed MC-130J Commando II	USAF 9th SOS/27th SOW, Cannon AFB, NM	
08-6202	Lockheed MC-130J Commando II	USAF 1st SOS/353rd SOG, Kadena AB, Japan	
08-6203	Lockheed MC-130J Commando II	USAF 415th SOS/58th SOW, Kirtland AFB, NM	
08-6204	Lockheed MC-130J Commando II	USAF 9th SOS/27th SOW, Cannon AFB, NM	
08-6205	Lockheed MC-130J Commando II	USAF 15th SOS/1st SOW, Hurlburt Field, FL	
08-6206	Lockheed MC-130J Commando II	USAF 193rd SOS/193rd SOW, Harrisburg, PA ANG	
08-8603	Lockheed C-130J-30 Hercules II	USAF 317th AW, Dyess AFB, TX	
08-8604	Lockheed C-130J-30 Hercules II [YJ] r	USAF 36th AS/374th AW, Yokota AB, Japan	
08-8605	Lockheed C-130J-30 Hercules II [YJ] r	USAF 36th AS/374th AW, Yokota AB, Japan	
08-8606	Lockheed C-130J-30 Hercules II $	USAF 19th AW, Little Rock AFB, AR	
08-8607	Lockheed C-130J-30 Hercules II	USAF 317th AW, Dyess AFB, TX	
09-0108	Lockheed HC-130J Combat King II [OT]	USAF 418th TES/412nd TW, Davis-Monthan AFB, AZ	
09-0109	Lockheed HC-130J Combat King II [FT]	USAF 79th RQS/563rd RQG, Davis-Monthan AFB, AZ	
09-5706	Lockheed HC-130J Combat King II	USAF 415th SOS/58th SOW, Kirtland AFB, NM	
09-5707	Lockheed HC-130J Combat King II [DM]	USAF 79th RQS/563rd RQG, Davis-Monthan AFB, AZ	
09-5709	Lockheed HC-130J Combat King II [DM]	USAF 79th RQS/563rd RQG, Davis-Monthan AFB, AZ	
09-5711	Lockheed MC-130J Commando II	USAF 9th SOS/27th SOW, Cannon AFB, NM	
09-6208	Lockheed MC-130J Commando II	USAF 415th SOS/58th SOW, Kirtland AFB, NM	
09-6209	Lockheed MC-130J Commando II	USAF 9th SOS/27th SOW, Cannon AFB, NM	
09-6210	Lockheed MC-130J Commando II	USAF 9th SOS/27th SOW, Cannon AFB, NM	
10-5700	Lockheed C-130J-30 Hercules II gn/bk	USAF 61st AS/19th AW Little Rock AFB, AR	
10-5701	Lockheed C-130J-30 Hercules II	USAF 39th AS/317th AW, Dyess AFB, TX	
10-5714	Lockheed MC-130J Commando II	USAF 1st SOS/353rd SOG, Kadena AB, Japan	
10-5716	Lockheed HC-130J Combat King II [DM]	USAF 79th RQS/563rd RQG, Davis-Monthan AFB, AZ	
10-5717	Lockheed HC-130J Combat King II [FT]	USAF 71st RQS/347th RQG, Moody AFB, GA	
10-5728	Lockheed C-130J-30 Hercules II bl/bk	USAF 62nd AS/314th AW, Little Rock AFB, AR	
10-5771	Lockheed C-130J-30 Hercules II gn/bk	USAF 61st AS/19th AW Little Rock AFB, AR	
11-5719	Lockheed HC-130J Combat King II [DM]	USAF 79th RQS/563rd RQG, Davis-Monthan AFB, AZ	
11-5725	Lockheed HC-130J Combat King II [FT]	USAF 71st RQS/347th RQG, Moody AFB, GA	
11-5727	Lockheed HC-130J Combat King II [FT]	USAF 71st RQS/347th RQG, Moody AFB, GA	
11-5729	Lockheed MC-130J Commando II	USAF 9th SOS/27th SOW, Cannon AFB, NM	
11-5731	Lockheed MC-130J Commando II	USAF 9th SOS/27th SOW, Cannon AFB, NM	
11-5732	Lockheed C-130J-30 Hercules II	USAF 317th AW, Dyess AFB, TX	
11-5733	Lockheed MC-130J Commando II	USAF 9th SOS/27th SOW, Cannon AFB, NM	
11-5734	Lockheed C-130J-30 Hercules II gn/bk	USAF 61st AS/19th AW Little Rock AFB, AR	
11-5735	Lockheed AC-130J Ghostrider	USAF 4th SOS/1st SOW, Hurlburt Field, FL	
11-5737	Lockheed MC-130J Commando II	USAF 1st SOS/353rd SOG, Kadena AB, Japan	
11-5745	Lockheed C-130J-30 Hercules II si/bk	USAF 41st AS/19th AW Little Rock AFB, AR	
11-5748	Lockheed C-130J-30 Hercules II	USAF 317th AW, Dyess AFB, TX	
11-5752	Lockheed C-130J-30 Hercules II si/bk	USAF 41st AS/19th AW Little Rock AFB, AR	

Notes	Serial	Type (code/other identity)	Owner/operator, location or fate
	11-5765	Lockheed HC-130J Combat King II [FT]	USAF 71st RQS/347th RQG, Moody AFB, GA
	12-5753	Lockheed AC-130J Ghostrider	USAF 73rd SOS/1st SOW, Hurlburt Field, FL
	12-5755	Lockheed HC-130J Combat King II	USAF 415th SOS/58th SOW, Kirtland AFB, NM
	12-5756	Lockheed C-130J-30 Hercules II *gn/bk*	USAF 61st AS/19th AW Little Rock AFB, AR
	12-5757	Lockheed MC-130J Commando II	USAF 9th SOS/27th SOW, Cannon AFB, NM
	12-5760	Lockheed MC-130J Commando II	USAF 15th SOS/1st SOW, Hurlburt Field, FL
	12-5761	Lockheed MC-130J Commando II	USAF 1st SOS/353rd SOG, Kadena AB, Japan
	12-5762	Lockheed MC-130J Commando II	USAF 1st SOS/353rd SOG, Kadena AB, Japan
	12-5763	Lockheed MC-130J Commando II	USAF 1st SOS/353rd SOG, Kadena AB, Japan
	12-5768	Lockheed HC-130J Combat King II [FT]	USAF 71st RQS/347th RQG, Moody AFB, GA
	12-5769	Lockheed HC-130J Combat King II [DM]	USAF 79th RQS/563rd RQG, Davis-Monthan AFB, AZ
	12-5772	Lockheed AC-130J Ghostrider	USAF 73rd SOS/1st SOW, Hurlburt Field, FL
	12-5773	Lockheed HC-130J Combat King II [FT]	USAF 71st RQS/347th RQG, Moody AFB, GA
	13-5770	Lockheed MC-130J Commando II	USAF 9th SOS/27th SOW, Cannon AFB, NM
	13-5775	Lockheed MC-130J Commando II	USAF 9th SOS/27th SOW, Cannon AFB, NM
	13-5777	Lockheed MC-130J Commando II	USAF 9th SOS/27th SOW, Cannon AFB, NM
	13-5782	Lockheed HC-130J Combat King II [DM]	USAF 79th RQS/563rd RQG, Davis-Monthan AFB, AZ
	13-5783	Lockheed AC-130J Ghostrider	USAF 73rd SOS/1st SOW, Hurlburt Field, FL
	13-5784	Lockheed C-130J-30 Hercules II *gn/bk*	USAF 61st AS/19th AW Little Rock AFB, AR
	13-5785	Lockheed HC-130J Combat King II [FT]	USAF 71st RQS/347th RQG, Moody AFB, GA
	13-5786	Lockheed MC-130J Commando II	USAF 1st SOS/353rd SOG, Kadena AB, Japan
	13-5790	Lockheed HC-130J Combat King II [FT]	USAF 71st RQS/347th RQG, Moody AFB, GA
	14-5787	Lockheed AC-130J Ghostrider	USAF 73rd SOS/1st SOW, Hurlburt Field, FL
	14-5788	Lockheed C-130J-30 Hercules II *si/bk*	USAF 41st AS/19th AW Little Rock AFB, AR
	14-5789	Lockheed AC-130J Ghostrider	USAF 73rd SOS/1st SOW, Hurlburt Field, FL
	14-5791	Lockheed C-130J-30 Hercules II *y/bk*	USAF 41st AS/19th AW Little Rock AFB, AR
	14-5793	Lockheed MC-130J Commando II	USAF 1st SOS/353rd SOG, Kadena AB, Japan
	14-5795	Lockheed MC-130J Commando II	USAF 9th SOS/27th SOW, Cannon AFB, NM
	14-5796	Lockheed C-130J-30 Hercules II *gn/bk*	USAF 61st AS/19th AW Little Rock AFB, AR
	14-5797	Lockheed AC-130J Ghostrider	USAF 4th SOS/1st SOW, Hurlburt Field, FL
	14-5800	Lockheed MC-130J Commando II	USAF 9th SOS/27th SOW, Cannon AFB, NM
	14-5802	Lockheed C-130J-30 Hercules II *bl/bk* $	USAF 62nd AS/314th AW, Little Rock AFB, AR
	14-5803	Lockheed AC-130J Ghostrider	USAF 73rd SOS/1st SOW, Hurlburt Field, FL
	14-5804	Lockheed C-130J-30 Hercules II *y*	USAF 48th AS/314th AW, Little Rock AFB, AR
	14-5805	Lockheed MC-130J Commando II	USAF 415th SOS/58th SOW, Kirtland AFB, NM
	14-5807	Lockheed C-130J-30 Hercules II [YJ] *r* [374 AW]	USAF 36th AS/374th AW, Yokota AB, Japan
	14-5809	Lockheed AC-130J Ghostrider	USAF 73rd SOS/1st SOW, Hurlburt Field, FL
	14-5815	Lockheed HC-130J Combat King II [AK]	USAF 211th RQS/176th Wg, Elmendorf AFB, AK ANG
	14-5864	Lockheed HC-130J Combat King II [CA]	USAF 130th RQS/129th RQW, Moffett Field CA ANG
	15-5810	Lockheed C-130J-30 Hercules II [YJ] *r* [374 OG]	USAF 36th AS/374th AW, Yokota AB, Japan
	15-5811	Lockheed AC-130J Ghostrider	USAF 73rd SOS/1st SOW, Hurlburt Field, FL
	15-5813	Lockheed C-130J-30 Hercules II [YJ] *r* [36 AS]	USAF 36th AS/374th AW, Yokota AB, Japan
	15-5817	Lockheed C-130J-30 Hercules II [YJ] *r*	USAF 36th AS/374th AW, Yokota AB, Japan
	15-5825	Lockheed AC-130J Ghostrider	USAF 73rd SOS/1st SOW, Hurlburt Field, FL
	15-5826	Lockheed C-130J-30 Hercules II	USAF 40th AS/317th AW, Dyess AFB, TX
	15-5827	Lockheed HC-130J Combat King II [AK]	USAF 211th RQS/176th Wg, Elmendorf AFB, AK ANG
	15-5828	Lockheed C-130J-30 Hercules II *gn/bk*	USAF 61st AS/19th AW Little Rock AFB, AR
	15-5829	Lockheed HC-130J Combat King II [AK]	USAF 211th RQS/176th Wg, Elmendorf AFB, AK ANG
	15-5832	Lockheed HC-130J Combat King II [AK]	USAF 211th RQS/176th Wg, Elmendorf AFB, AK ANG
	15-5842	Lockheed HC-130J Combat King II [CA]	USAF 130th RQS/129th RQW, Moffett Field CA ANG

Serial	Type (code/other identity)	Owner/operator, location or fate	Notes
15-5893	Lockheed C-130J-30 Hercules II *bl/w*	USAF 165th AS/123rd AW, Standiford Field, KY ANG	
16-5833	Lockheed C-130J-30 Hercules II [YJ] *r* [5 AF]	USAF 36th AS/374th AW, Yokota AB, Japan	
16-5834	Lockheed C-130J-30 Hercules II	USAF 40th AS/317th AW, Dyess AFB, TX	
16-5835	Lockheed AC-130J Ghostrider	USAF 73rd SOS/1st SOW, Hurlburt Field, FL	
16-5837	Lockheed AC-130J Ghostrider	USAF 4th SOS/1st SOW, Hurlburt Field, FL	
16-5838	Lockheed C-130J-30 Hercules II [YJ] *r*	USAF 36th AS/374th AW, Yokota AB, Japan	
16-5839	Lockheed MC-130J Commando II	USAF 415th SOS/58th SOW, Kirtland AFB, NM	
16-5841	Lockheed C-130J-30 Hercules II [YJ] *r*	USAF 36th AS/374th AW, Yokota AB, Japan	
16-5843	Lockheed C-130J-30 Hercules II [YJ] *r*	USAF 36th AS/374th AW, Yokota AB, Japan	
16-5844	Lockheed AC-130J Ghostrider	USAF 4th SOS/1st SOW, Hurlburt Field, FL	
16-5846	Lockheed AC-130J Ghostrider	USAF 4th SOS/1st SOW, Hurlburt Field, FL	
16-5849	Lockheed C-130J-30 Hercules II *pr/y*	USAF 130th AS/130th AW, Yeager Int'l, Charleston, WV ANG	
16-5850	Lockheed MC-130J Commando II	USAF 9th SOS/27th SOW, Cannon AFB, NM	
16-5851	Lockheed C-130J-30 Hercules II *bl/bk*	USAF 181st AS/136th AW, NAS Dallas, TX ANG	
16-5852	Lockheed AC-130J Ghostrider	USAF 4th SOS/1st SOW, Hurlburt Field, FL	
16-5853	Lockheed C-130J-30 Hercules II	USAF 40th AS/317th AW, Dyess AFB, TX	
16-5855	Lockheed C-130J-30 Hercules II *bl/bk*	USAF 181st AS/136th AW, NAS Dallas, TX ANG	
16-5857	Lockheed HC-130J Combat King II [CA]	USAF 130th RQS/129th RQW, Moffett Field CA ANG	
16-5858	Lockheed HC-130J Combat King II [CA]	USAF 130th RQS/129th RQW, Moffett Field CA ANG	
16-5859	Lockheed C-130J-30 Hercules II *w/bl*	USAF 165th AS/123rd AW, Standiford Field, KY ANG	
16-5861	Lockheed AC-130J Ghostrider	USAF 4th SOS/1st SOW, Hurlburt Field, FL	
16-5862	Lockheed MC-130J Commando II	USAF 9th SOS/27th SOW, Cannon AFB, NM	
16-5863	Lockheed HC-130J Combat King II [LI]	USAF 102nd RQS/106th RQW, Suffolk Field, NY ANG	
16-5873	Lockheed HC-130J Combat King II [LI]	USAF 102nd RQS/106th RQW, Suffolk Field, NY ANG	
16-5880	Lockheed C-130J-30 Hercules II *bl*	USAF 40th AS/317th AW, Dyess AFB, TX	
16-5895	Lockheed HC-130J Combat King II [FL]	USAF 39th RQS/920th RQW AFRC, Patrick SFB, FL	
17-5865	Lockheed C-130J-30 Hercules II *bl/w*	USAF 165th AS/123rd AW, Standiford Field, KY ANG	
17-5867	Lockheed C-130J-30 Hercules II *bl/bk*	USAF 181st AS/136th AW, NAS Dallas, TX ANG	
17-5869	Lockheed AC-130J Ghostrider	USAF 4th SOS/1st SOW, Hurlburt Field, FL	
17-5870	Lockheed HC-130J Combat King II [LI]	USAF 102nd RQS/106th RQW, Suffolk Field, NY ANG	
17-5872	Lockheed AC-130J Ghostrider	USAF 4th SOS/1st SOW, Hurlburt Field, FL	
17-5875	Lockheed MC-130J Commando II	USAF 415th SOS/58th SOW, Kirtland AFB, NM	
17-5876	Lockheed MC-130J Commando II	USAF 415th SOS/58th SOW, Kirtland AFB, NM	
17-5877	Lockheed AC-130J Ghostrider	USAF 4th SOS/1st SOW, Hurlburt Field, FL	
17-5878	Lockheed MC-130J Commando II	USAF 9th SOS/27th SOW, Cannon AFB, NM	
17-5892	Lockheed HC-130J Combat King II [FL]	USAF 39th RQS/920th RQW AFRC, Patrick SFB, FL	
17-5897	Lockheed C-130J-30 Hercules II *pr/y*	USAF 130th AS/130th AW, Yeager Int'l, Charleston, WV ANG	
17-5898	Lockheed HC-130J Combat King II [FL]	USAF 39th RQS/920th RQW AFRC, Patrick SFB, FL	
17-5900	Lockheed C-130J-30 Hercules II *bl/bk*	USAF 181st AS/136th AW, NAS Dallas, TX ANG	
17-5901	Lockheed HC-130J Combat King II [FL]	USAF 39th RQS/920th RQW AFRC, Patrick SFB, FL	
17-5902	Lockheed HC-130J Combat King II [FL]	USAF 39th RQS/920th RQW AFRC, Patrick SFB, FL	
17-5903	Lockheed MC-130J Commando II	USAF 9th SOS/27th SOW, Cannon AFB, NM	
17-5904	Lockheed C-130J-30 Hercules II *bl/bk*	USAF 181st AS/136th AW, NAS Dallas, TX ANG	
18-5879	Lockheed HC-130J Combat King II [LI]	USAF 102nd RQS/106th RQW, Suffolk Field, NY ANG	
18-5882	Lockheed AC-130J Ghostrider	USAF 4th SOS/1st SOW, Hurlburt Field, FL	
18-5884	Lockheed MC-130J Commando II	USAF 9th SOS/27th SOW, Cannon AFB, NM	
18-5886	Lockheed AC-130J Ghostrider	USAF 4th SOS/1st SOW, Hurlburt Field, FL	
18-5888	Lockheed AC-130J Ghostrider	USAF 17th SOS/27th SOW, Cannon AFB, NM	
18-5891	Lockheed AC-130J Ghostrider	USAF 17th SOS/27th SOW, Cannon AFB, NM	
18-5905	Lockheed AC-130J Ghostrider	USAF 17th SOS/27th SOW, Cannon AFB, NM	
18-5906	Lockheed HC-130J Combat King II [FL]	USAF 39th RQS/920th RQW AFRC, Patrick SFB, FL	
18-5908	Lockheed C-130J-30 Hercules II *pr/y*	USAF 130th AS/130th AW, Yeager Int'l, Charleston, WV ANG	

Notes	Serial	Type (code/other identity)	Owner/operator, location or fate
	18-5910	Lockheed MC-130J Commando II	USAF 9th SOS/27th SOW, Cannon AFB, NM
	18-5911	Lockheed C-130J-30 Hercules II *bl/bk*	USAF 181st AS/136th AW, NAS Dallas, TX ANG
	18-5913	Lockheed AC-130J Ghostrider	USAF 17th SOS/27th SOW, Cannon AFB, NM
	18-5914	Lockheed C-130J-30 Hercules II *pr/y*	USAF 130th AS/130th AW, Yeager Int'l, Charleston, WV ANG
	18-5916	Lockheed AC-130J Ghostrider	USAF 17th SOS/27th SOW, Cannon AFB, NM
	18-5917	Lockheed C-130J-30 Hercules II *pr/y*	USAF 130th AS/130th AW, Yeager Int'l, Charleston, WV ANG
	18-5919	Lockheed C-130J-30 Hercules II *w/bl*	USAF 165th AS/123rd AW, Standiford Field, KY ANG
	18-5920	Lockheed AC-130J Ghostrider	USAF 4th SOS/1st SOW, Hurlburt Field, FL
	18-5921	Lockheed C-130J-30 Hercules II *w/bl*	USAF 165th AS/123rd AW, Standiford Field, KY ANG
	19-5922	Lockheed AC-130J Ghostrider	USAF 4th SOS/1st SOW, Hurlburt Field, FL
	19-5924	Lockheed MC-130J Commando II	USAF 19th SOS/492nd SOW, Hurlburt Field, FL
	19-5926	Lockheed AC-130J Ghostrider	USAF 17th SOS/27th SOW, Cannon AFB, NM
	19-5927	Lockheed C-130J-30 Hercules II *bl/bk*	USAF 181st AS/136th AW, NAS Dallas, TX ANG
	19-5928	Lockheed C-130J-30 Hercules II *pr/y*	USAF 130th AS/130th AW, Yeager Int'l, Charleston, WV ANG
	19-5932	Lockheed C-130J-30 Hercules II *w/bl*	USAF 165th AS/123rd AW, Standiford Field, KY ANG
	19-5934	Lockheed C-130J-30 Hercules II *pr/y*	USAF 130th AS/130th AW, Yeager Int'l, Charleston, WV ANG
	19-5936	Lockheed C-130J-30 Hercules II *bl/bk*	USAF 181st AS/136th AW, NAS Dallas, TX ANG
	19-5940	Lockheed C-130J-30 Hercules II *pr/y*	USAF 130th AS/130th AW, Yeager Int'l, Charleston, WV ANG
	19-5942	Lockheed C-130J-30 Hercules II w/bl	USAF 165th AS/123rd AW, Standiford Field, KY ANG
	19-5945	Lockheed C-130J-30 Hercules II *w/bl*	USAF 165th AS/123rd AW, Standiford Field, KY ANG
	19-5947	Lockheed HC-130J Combat King II [DM]	USAF 79th RQS/563rd RQG, Davis-Monthan AFB, AZ
	19-5948	Lockheed HC-130J Combat King II [MY]	USAF 71st RQS/347th RQG, Moody AFB, GA
	19-5950	Lockheed MC-130J Commando II	USAF 9th SOS/27th SOW, Cannon AFB, NM
	19-5953	Lockheed MC-130J Commando II	USAF 9th SOS/27th SOW, Cannon AFB, NM
	19-5957	Lockheed MC-130J Commando II	LMTAS, Marietta, GA
	20-5931	Lockheed MC-130J Commando II	USAF 415th SOS/58th SOW, Kirtland AFB, NM
	20-5933	Lockheed MC-130J Commando II	USAF 9th SOS/27th SOW, Cannon AFB, NM
	20-5935	Lockheed MC-130J Commando II	USAF 9th SOS/27th SOW, Cannon AFB, NM
	20-5939	Lockheed MC-130J Commando II	USAF 1st SOS/353rd SOG, Kadena AB, Japan
	20-5943	Lockheed MC-130J Commando II	USAF 9th SOS/27th SOW, Cannon AFB, NM
	20-5946	Lockheed MC-130J Hercules II	USAF 9th SOS/27th SOW, Cannon AFB, NM
	20-5961	Lockheed MC-130J Commando II	USAF 1st SOS/353rd SOG, Kadena AB, Japan
	20-5975	Lockheed C-130J-30 Hercules II	USAF 158th AS/165th AW, Savannah, GA ANG
	20-5980	Lockheed C-130J-30 Hercules II	USAF 158th AS/165th AW, Savannah, GA ANG
	20-5982	Lockheed C-130J-30 Hercules II	USAF 757th AS/910th AW AFRC, Youngstown ARS, OH
	20-5991	Lockheed C-130J-30 Hercules II	USAF 757th AS/910th AW AFRC, Youngstown ARS, OH
	21-5965	Lockheed MC-130J Commando II	USAF 193rd SOS/193rd SOW, Harrisburg, PA ANG
	21-5973	Lockheed MC-130J Commando II	USAF 193rd SOS/193rd SOW, Harrisburg, PA ANG
	21-5976	Lockheed MC-130J Commando II	USAF 9th SOS/27th SOW, Cannon AFB, NM
	21-5981	Lockheed MC-130J Commando II	USAF 9th SOS/27th SOW, Cannon AFB, NM
	21-5996	Lockheed C-130J-30 Hercules II	USAF 158th AS/165th AW, Savannah, GA ANG
	21-5998	Lockheed C-130J-30 Hercules II	LMTAS, Marietta, GA
	22-5985	Lockheed MC-130J Commando II	LMTAS, Marietta, GA
	22-5989	Lockheed MC-130J Commando II	USAF 193rd SOS/193rd SOW, Harrisburg, PA ANG
	22-5993	Lockheed MC-130J Commando II	LMTAS, Marietta, GA
	22-5994	Lockheed MC-130J Commando II	LMTAS, Marietta, GA
	22-5994	Lockheed MC-130J Commando II	USAF 415th SOS/58th SOW, Kirtland AFB, NM

Serial	Type (code/other identity)	Owner/operator, location or fate	Notes
Boeing C-135			
57-1419	Boeing KC-135R Stratotanker	USAF 197th ARS/161st ARW, Phoenix, AZ ANG	
57-1427	Boeing KC-135R Stratotanker bl/y	USAF 117th ARS/190th ARW, Forbes Field, KS ANG	
57-1428	Boeing KC-135R Stratotanker w/or	USAF 151st ARS/134th ARW, Knoxville, TN ANG	
57-1430	Boeing KC-135R Stratotanker [ZZ] or/bk	USAF 909th ARS/18th Wg, Kadena AB, Japan	
57-1432	Boeing KC-135R Stratotanker bl/bk	USAF 191st ARS/151st ARW, Salt Lake City, UT ANG	
57-1435	Boeing KC-135R Stratotanker bl/bk	USAF 191st ARS/151st ARW, Salt Lake City, UT ANG	
57-1436	Boeing KC-135R Stratotanker w/or	USAF 151st ARS/134th ARW, Knoxville, TN ANG	
57-1437	Boeing KC-135R Stratotanker	USAF 116th ARS/141st ARW, Fairchild AFB, WA ANG	
57-1439	Boeing KC-135R Stratotanker	USAF 92nd ARW, Fairchild AFB, WA	
57-1440	Boeing KC-135R Stratotanker	USAF 92nd ARW, Fairchild AFB, WA	
57-1441	Boeing KC-135R Stratotanker y/bk	USAF 174th ARS/185th ARW, Sioux City, IA ANG	
57-1451	Boeing KC-135R Stratotanker w/or	USAF 151st ARS/134th ARW, Knoxville, TN ANG	
57-1453	Boeing KC-135R Stratotanker w/r	USAF 106th ARS/117th ARW, Birmingham, AL ANG	
57-1454	Boeing KC-135R Stratotanker	USAF 92nd ARW, Fairchild AFB, WA	
57-1456	Boeing KC-135R Stratotanker y/bk	USAF 756th ARS/459th ARW AFRC, Andrews AFB, MD	
57-1459	Boeing KC-135R Stratotanker or/y	USAF 336th ARS/452nd AMW AFRC, March ARB, CA	
57-1461	Boeing KC-135R Stratotanker r/w	USAF 173rd ARS/155th ARW, Lincoln, NE ANG	
57-1462	Boeing KC-135R Stratotanker	USAF 153rd ARS/186th ARW, Meridian, MS ANG	
57-1468	Boeing KC-135R Stratotanker or/y	USAF 336th ARS/452nd AMW AFRC, March ARB, CA	
57-1469	Boeing KC-135R Stratotanker $	USAF 197th ARS/161st ARW, Phoenix, AZ ANG	
57-1472	Boeing KC-135R Stratotanker bl	USAF 72nd ARS/434th ARW AFRC, Grissom AFB, IN	
57-1473	Boeing KC-135R Stratotanker w/r	USAF 106th ARS/117th ARW, Birmingham, AL ANG	
57-1479	Boeing KC-135R Stratotanker y/bk	USAF 756th ARS/459th ARW AFRC, Andrews AFB, MD	
57-1483	Boeing KC-135R Stratotanker	USAF 92nd ARW, Fairchild AFB, WA	
57-1486	Boeing KC-135R Stratotanker	USAF 153rd ARS/186th ARW, Meridian, MS ANG	
57-1487	Boeing KC-135R Stratotanker y/bk	USAF 756th ARS/459th ARW AFRC, Andrews AFB, MD	
57-1488	Boeing KC-135R Stratotanker	USAF 92nd ARW, Fairchild AFB, WA	
57-1493	Boeing KC-135R Stratotanker y/bl	USAF 6th ARW, MacDill AFB, FL	
57-1499	Boeing KC-135R Stratotanker bl/bk	USAF 191st ARS/151st ARW, Salt Lake City, UT ANG	
57-1502	Boeing KC-135R Stratotanker	USAF 6th ARW, MacDill AFB, FL	
57-1506	Boeing KC-135R Stratotanker [AK] bl/y	USAF 168th ARS/168th ARW, Eielson AFB, AK ANG	
57-1508	Boeing KC-135R Stratotanker	USAF 6th ARW, MacDill AFB, FL	
57-1512	Boeing KC-135R Stratotanker y/bk	USAF 756th ARS/459th ARW AFRC, Andrews AFB, MD	
57-1514	Boeing KC-135R Stratotanker w/bl	USAF 126th ARS/128th ARW, Mitchell Field, WI ANG	
57-2597	Boeing KC-135R Stratotanker w/or	USAF 151st ARS/134th ARW, Knoxville, TN ANG	
57-2598	Boeing KC-135R Stratotanker or/y	USAF 336th ARS/452nd AMW AFRC, March ARB, CA	
57-2599	Boeing KC-135R Stratotanker r/bk	USAF 314th ARS/940th ARW, Beale AFB, CA	
57-2603	Boeing KC-135R Stratotanker or/y	USAF 336th ARS/452nd AMW AFRC, March ARB, CA	
58-0001	Boeing KC-135R Stratotanker	USAF 6th ARW, MacDill AFB, FL	
58-0004	Boeing KC-135R Stratotanker w/r	USAF 106th ARS/117th ARW, Birmingham, AL ANG	
58-0010	Boeing KC-135R Stratotanker	USAF 92nd ARW, Fairchild AFB, WA	
58-0011	Boeing KC-135R(RT) Stratotanker	USAF 22nd ARW, McConnell AFB, KS	
58-0015	Boeing KC-135R Stratotanker bl/y	USAF 465th ARS/507th ARW AFRC, Tinker AFB, OK	
58-0016	Boeing KC-135R Stratotanker	USAF 92nd ARW, Fairchild AFB, WA	

Notes	Serial	Type (code/other identity)	Owner/operator, location or fate
	58-0018	Boeing KC-135R(RT) Stratotanker	USAF 22nd ARW, McConnell AFB, KS
	58-0021	Boeing KC-135R Stratotanker *w/gn*	USAF 132nd ARS/101st ARW, Bangor, ME ANG
	58-0023	Boeing KC-135R Stratotanker *y/bl*	USAF 6th ARW, MacDill AFB, FL
	58-0027	Boeing KC-135R Stratotanker *bl/bk*	USAF 191st ARS/151st ARW, Salt Lake City, UT ANG
	58-0030	Boeing KC-135R Stratotanker *w/gn*	USAF 132nd ARS/101st ARW, Bangor, ME ANG
	58-0034	Boeing KC-135R Stratotanker *y/r*	USAF 54th ARS/97th AMW, Altus AFB, OK
	58-0035	Boeing KC-135R Stratotanker	USAF 92nd ARW, Fairchild AFB, WA
	58-0036	Boeing KC-135R Stratotanker	USAF 92nd ARW, Fairchild AFB, WA
	58-0038	Boeing KC-135R Stratotanker	USAF 328th ARS/914th ARW AFRC, Niagara Falls, NY
	58-0042	Boeing KC-135T Stratotanker	USAF 22nd ARW, McConnell AFB, KS
	58-0045	Boeing KC-135T Stratotanker	USAF 171st ARW, Greater Pittsburgh, PA ANG
	58-0046	Boeing KC-135R Stratotanker *y/r*	USAF 54th ARS/97th AMW, Altus AFB, OK
	58-0047	Boeing KC-135T Stratotanker	USAF 22nd ARW, McConnell AFB, KS
	58-0049	Boeing KC-135T Stratotanker *bk/y*	USAF 171st ARS/127th Wg, Selfridge ANGB, MI ANG
	58-0050	Boeing KC-135T Stratotanker	USAF 92nd ARW, Fairchild AFB, WA
	58-0051	Boeing KC-135R Stratotanker *bl/y*	USAF 465th ARS/507th ARW AFRC, Tinker AFB, OK
	58-0052	Boeing KC-135R Stratotanker *or/y*	USAF 336th ARS/452nd AMW AFRC, March ARB, CA
	58-0054	Boeing KC-135T Stratotanker *y/bk*	USAF 171st ARW, Greater Pittsburgh, PA ANG
	58-0055	Boeing KC-135T Stratotanker *y/bk*	USAF 171st ARW, Greater Pittsburgh, PA ANG
	58-0056	Boeing KC-135R Stratotanker [HH] *y/bk*	USAF 203rd ARS/15th Wg, Hickam AFB, HI ANG
	58-0057	Boeing KC-135R Stratotanker *y/bk*	USAF 174th ARS/185th ARW, Sioux City, IA ANG
	58-0059	Boeing KC-135R Stratotanker *bl/y*	USAF 117th ARS/190th ARW, Forbes Field, KS ANG
	58-0060	Boeing KC-135T Stratotanker *y/bk*	USAF 171st ARW, Greater Pittsburgh, PA ANG
	58-0061	Boeing KC-135T Stratotanker	USAF 22nd ARW, McConnell AFB, KS
	58-0062	Boeing KC-135T Stratotanker *bk/y*	USAF 171st ARS/127th Wg, Selfridge ANGB, MI ANG
	58-0063	Boeing KC-135R Stratotanker	USAF 328th ARS/914th ARW AFRC, Niagara Falls, NY
	58-0065	Boeing KC-135T Stratotanker	USAF 22nd ARW, McConnell AFB, KS
	58-0066	Boeing KC-135R Stratotanker *w/r*	USAF 6th ARW, MacDill AFB, FL
	58-0069	Boeing KC-135R Stratotanker *y/bl*	USAF 6th ARW, MacDill AFB, FL
	58-0071	Boeing KC-135T Stratotanker *y/bl*	USAF 6th ARW, MacDill AFB, FL
	58-0072	Boeing KC-135T Stratotanker *y/bk*	USAF 171st ARW, Greater Pittsburgh, PA ANG
	58-0073	Boeing KC-135R Stratotanker *w/r*	USAF 106th ARS/117th ARW, Birmingham, AL ANG
	58-0074	Boeing KC-135T Stratotanker *y/bk*	USAF 171st ARW, Greater Pittsburgh, PA ANG
	58-0075	Boeing KC-135R Stratotanker *y/bk*	USAF 756th ARS/459th ARW AFRC, Andrews AFB, MD
	58-0076	Boeing KC-135R Stratotanker *r/w*	USAF 74th ARS/434th ARW AFRC, Grissom AFB, IN
	58-0077	Boeing KC-135T Stratotanker *y/bk*	USAF 171st ARW, Greater Pittsburgh, PA ANG
	58-0079	Boeing KC-135R Stratotanker	USAF 153rd ARS/186th ARW, Meridian, MS ANG
	58-0083	Boeing KC-135R Stratotanker *r/w*	USAF 166th ARS/121st ARW, Rickenbacker ANGB, OH ANG
	58-0084	Boeing KC-135T Stratotanker *y/bk*	USAF 171st ARW, Greater Pittsburgh, PA ANG
	58-0085	Boeing KC-135R Stratotanker *or/y*	USAF 336th ARS/452nd AMW AFRC, March ARB, CA
	58-0086	Boeing KC-135T Stratotanker [ZZ] *or/bk*	USAF 909th ARS/18th Wg, Kadena AB, Japan
	58-0088	Boeing KC-135T Stratotanker *bk/y*	USAF 171st ARS/127th Wg, Selfridge ANGB, MI ANG
	58-0089	Boeing KC-135T Stratotanker	USAF 92nd ARW, Fairchild AFB, WA
	58-0092	Boeing KC-135R Stratotanker	USAF 92nd ARW, Fairchild AFB, WA
	58-0093	Boeing KC-135R Stratotanker [ZZ] *or/bk*	USAF 909th ARS/18th Wg, Kadena AB, Japan
	58-0094	Boeing KC-135T Stratotanker *y/bl*	USAF 6th ARW, MacDill AFB, FL
	58-0098	Boeing KC-135R Stratotanker *w/gn $*	USAF 132nd ARS/101st ARW, Bangor, ME ANG
	58-0099	Boeing KC-135T Stratotanker *y/bk*	USAF 171st ARW, Greater Pittsburgh, PA ANG

Serial	Type (code/other identity)	Owner/operator, location or fate	Notes
58-0102	Boeing KC-135R Stratotanker *bl/y*	USAF 465th ARS/507th ARW AFRC, Tinker AFB, OK	
58-0103	Boeing KC-135T Stratotanker	USAF 6th ARW, MacDill AFB, FL	
58-0104	Boeing KC-135R Stratotanker *w/bl*	USAF 108th ARS/126th ARW, Scott AFB, IL ANG	
58-0106	Boeing KC-135R Stratotanker *w/r*	USAF 106th ARS/117th ARW, Birmingham, AL ANG	
58-0107	Boeing KC-135R Stratotanker *w/gn*	USAF 132nd ARS/101st ARW, Bangor, ME ANG	
58-0109	Boeing KC-135R Stratotanker *y/bk*	USAF 174th ARS/185th ARW, Sioux City, IA ANG	
58-0112	Boeing KC-135T Stratotanker *y/bk*	USAF 171st ARW, Greater Pittsburgh, PA ANG	
58-0113	Boeing KC-135R Stratotanker	USAF 92nd ARW, Fairchild AFB, WA	
58-0117	Boeing KC-135T Stratotanker *y/bk*	USAF 171st ARW, Greater Pittsburgh, PA ANG	
58-0118	Boeing KC-135R Stratotanker	USAF 92nd ARW, Fairchild AFB, WA	
58-0119	Boeing KC-135R Stratotanker *w/or*	USAF 151st ARS/134th ARW, Knoxville, TN ANG	
58-0120	Boeing KC-135R Stratotanker	USAF 153rd ARS/186th ARW, Meridian, MS ANG	
58-0121	Boeing KC-135R Stratotanker *bl/y*	USAF 465th ARS/507th ARW AFRC, Tinker AFB, OK	
58-0122	Boeing KC-135R Stratotanker *bl/y*	USAF 117th ARS/190th ARW, Forbes Field, KS ANG	
58-0123	Boeing KC-135R Stratotanker *y/r*	USAF 54th ARS/97th AMW, Altus AFB, OK	
58-0124	Boeing KC-135R(RT) Stratotanker	USAF 22nd ARW, McConnell AFB, KS	
58-0128	Boeing KC-135R Stratotanker	USAF 92nd ARW, Fairchild AFB, WA	
58-0129	Boeing KC-135T Stratotanker *bk/y*	USAF 171st ARS/127th Wg, Selfridge ANGB, MI ANG	
59-1444	Boeing KC-135R Stratotanker	USAF 166th ARS/121st ARW, Rickenbacker ANGB, OH ANG	
59-1446	Boeing KC-135R Stratotanker *w/gn*	USAF 132nd ARS/101st ARW, Bangor, ME ANG	
59-1448	Boeing KC-135R Stratotanker	USAF 153rd ARS/186th ARW, Meridian, MS ANG	
59-1450	Boeing KC-135R Stratotanker	USAF 197th ARS/161st ARW, Phoenix, AZ ANG	
59-1453	Boeing KC-135R Stratotanker	USAF 153rd ARS/186th ARW, Meridian, MS ANG	
59-1455	Boeing KC-135R Stratotanker [HH] *y/bk*	USAF 203rd ARS/15th Wg, Hickam AFB, HI ANG	
59-1458	Boeing KC-135R Stratotanker *r/w*	USAF 166th ARS/121st ARW, Rickenbacker ANGB, OH ANG	
59-1459	Boeing KC-135R Stratotanker *y/bk*	USAF 6th ARW, MacDill AFB, FL	
59-1460	Boeing KC-135T Stratotanker *y/bk*	USAF 171st ARW, Greater Pittsburgh, PA ANG	
59-1461	Boeing KC-135R Stratotanker *w/bl*	USAF 126th ARS/128th ARW, Mitchell Field, WI ANG	
59-1462	Boeing KC-135T Stratotanker	USAF 92nd ARW, Fairchild AFB, WA	
59-1463	Boeing KC-135R Stratotanker *r/w*	USAF 173rd ARS/155th ARW, Lincoln, NE ANG	
59-1466	Boeing KC-135R Stratotanker *w/bl*	USAF 108th ARS/126th ARW, Scott AFB, IL ANG	
59-1467	Boeing KC-135T Stratotanker *y/bk*	USAF 171st ARW, Greater Pittsburgh, PA ANG	
59-1468	Boeing KC-135T Stratotanker *y/bk*	USAF 171st ARW, Greater Pittsburgh, PA ANG	
59-1469	Boeing KC-135R Stratotanker *y/bk*	USAF 756th ARS/459th ARW AFRC, Andrews AFB, MD	
59-1471	Boeing KC-135T Stratotanker $	USAF 116th ARS/141st ARW, Fairchild AFB, WA ANG	
59-1472	Boeing KC-135R Stratotanker	USAF 328th ARS/914th ARW AFRC, Niagara Falls, NY	
59-1474	Boeing KC-135T Stratotanker *bk/y*	USAF 171st ARS/127th Wg, Selfridge ANGB, MI ANG	
59-1476	Boeing KC-135R Stratotanker	USAF 92nd ARW, Fairchild AFB, WA	
59-1478	Boeing KC-135R Stratotanker *w/or*	USAF 151st ARS/134th ARW, Knoxville, TN ANG	
59-1480	Boeing KC-135T Stratotanker	USAF 92nd ARW, Fairchild AFB, WA	
59-1482	Boeing KC-135R Stratotanker	USAF 328th ARS/914th ARW AFRC, Niagara Falls NY	
59-1483	Boeing KC-135R Stratotanker *r/w*	USAF 166th ARS/121st ARW, Rickenbacker ANGB, OH ANG	
59-1486	Boeing KC-135R Stratotanker	USAF 92nd ARW, Fairchild AFB, WA	
59-1488	Boeing KC-135R Stratotanker *w/gn*	USAF 132nd ARS/101st ARW, Bangor, ME ANG	
59-1492	Boeing KC-135R Stratotanker	USAF 909th ARS/18th Wg, Kadena AB, Japan	
59-1495	Boeing KC-135R Stratotanker *r/w* $	USAF 173rd ARS/155th ARW, Lincoln, NE ANG	
59-1498	Boeing KC-135R Stratotanker *w/gn*	USAF 132nd ARS/101st ARW, Bangor, ME ANG	
59-1499	Boeing KC-135R Stratotanker [HH] *y/bk*	USAF 203rd ARS/15th Wg, Hickam AFB, HI ANG	
59-1500	Boeing KC-135R Stratotanker *w/bl*	USAF 108th ARS/126th ARW, Scott AFB, IL ANG	
59-1501	Boeing KC-135R Stratotanker *y/r*	USAF 54th ARS/97th AMW, Altus AFB, OK	

Notes	Serial	Type (code/other identity)	Owner/operator, location or fate
	59-1502	Boeing KC-135R Stratotanker [ZZ] or/bk	USAF 909th ARS/18th Wg, Kadena AB, Japan
	59-1504	Boeing KC-135T Stratotanker y/bk	USAF 171st ARW, Greater Pittsburgh, PA ANG
	59-1505	Boeing KC-135R Stratotanker w/or	USAF 151st ARS/134th ARW, Knoxville, TN ANG
	59-1506	Boeing KC-135R Stratotanker y/bk	USAF 174th ARS/185th ARW, Sioux City, IA ANG
	59-1507	Boeing KC-135R Stratotanker bl/y	USAF 117th ARS/190th ARW, Forbes Field, KS ANG
	59-1508	Boeing KC-135R Stratotanker	USAF 92nd ARW, Fairchild AFB, WA
	59-1509	Boeing KC-135R Stratotanker w/or	USAF 151st ARS/134th ARW, Knoxville, TN ANG
	59-1510	Boeing KC-135T Stratotanker [ZZ] or/bk	USAF 909th ARS/18th Wg, Kadena AB, Japan
	59-1512	Boeing KC-135T Stratotanker bk/y	USAF 171st ARS/127th Wg, Selfridge ANGB, MI ANG
	59-1513	Boeing KC-135T Stratotanker	USAF 909th ARS/18th Wg, Kadena AB, Japan
	59-1515	Boeing KC-135R Stratotanker	USAF 92nd ARW, Fairchild AFB, WA
	59-1516	Boeing KC-135R Stratotanker w/bl	USAF 126th ARS/128th ARW, Mitchell Field, WI ANG
	59-1517	Boeing KC-135R Stratotanker w/or	USAF 151st ARS/134th ARW, Knoxville, TN ANG
	59-1519	Boeing KC-135R Stratotanker y/bk	USAF 174th ARS/185th ARW, Sioux City, IA ANG
	59-1520	Boeing KC-135T Stratotanker	USAF 92nd ARW, Fairchild AFB, WA
	59-1521	Boeing KC-135R Stratotanker [AK] bl/y	USAF 168th ARS/168th ARW, Eielson AFB, AK ANG
	59-1522	Boeing KC-135R Stratotanker w/bl	USAF 108th ARS/126th ARW, Scott AFB, IL ANG
	60-0313	Boeing KC-135R Stratotanker	USAF 22nd ARW, McConnell AFB, KS
	60-0314	Boeing KC-135R Stratotanker r/w	USAF 74th ARS/434th ARW AFRC, Grissom AFB, IN
	60-0315	Boeing KC-135R Stratotanker w/bl	USAF 126th ARS/128th ARW, Mitchell Field, WI ANG
	60-0316	Boeing KC-135R Stratotanker bl/bk	USAF 191st ARS/151st ARW, Salt Lake City, UT ANG
	60-0318	Boeing KC-135R Stratotanker	USAF 92nd ARW, Fairchild AFB, WA
	60-0320	Boeing KC-135R Stratotanker	USAF 92nd ARW, Fairchild AFB, WA
	60-0322	Boeing KC-135R Stratotanker bl	USAF 72nd ARS/434th ARW AFRC, Grissom AFB, IN
	60-0323	Boeing KC-135R Stratotanker r/bk	USAF 314th ARS/940th ARW, Beale AFB, CA
	60-0328	Boeing KC-135R Stratotanker	USAF 92nd ARW, Fairchild AFB, WA
	60-0331	Boeing KC-135R Stratotanker	USAF 6th ARW, MacDill AFB, FL
	60-0332	Boeing KC-135R Stratotanker [AK] bl/y	USAF 168th ARS/168th ARW, Eielson AFB, AK ANG
	60-0334	Boeing KC-135R Stratotanker [AK] bl/y	USAF 168th ARS/168th ARW, Eielson AFB, AK ANG
	60-0336	Boeing KC-135T Stratotanker y/bl	USAF 6th ARW, MacDill AFB, FL
	60-0337	Boeing KC-135T Stratotanker	USAF 92nd ARW, Fairchild AFB, WA
	60-0339	Boeing KC-135T Stratotanker [ZZ] or/bk	USAF 909th ARS/18th Wg, Kadena AB, Japan
	60-0341	Boeing KC-135R Stratotanker	USAF 153rd ARS/186th ARW, Meridian, MS ANG
	60-0342	Boeing KC-135T Stratotanker	USAF 92nd ARW, Fairchild AFB, WA
	60-0343	Boeing KC-135T Stratotanker	USAF 22nd ARW, McConnell AFB, KS (damaged May 2024)
	60-0345	Boeing KC-135T Stratotanker bk/y $	USAF 171st ARS/127th Wg, Selfridge ANGB, MI ANG
	60-0346	Boeing KC-135T Stratotanker bk/y	USAF 171st ARS/127th Wg, Selfridge ANGB, MI ANG
	60-0347	Boeing KC-135R Stratotanker r/w	USAF 166th ARS/121st ARW, Rickenbacker ANGB, OH ANG
	60-0348	Boeing KC-135R Stratotanker y/r	USAF 54th ARS/97th AMW, Altus AFB, OK
	60-0349	Boeing KC-135R Stratotanker bl/y	USAF 465th ARS/507th ARW AFRC, Tinker AFB, OK
	60-0350	Boeing KC-135R Stratotanker y/r	USAF 54th ARS/97th AMW, Altus AFB, OK
	60-0351	Boeing KC-135R Stratotanker y/r [97 OG]	USAF 54th ARS/97th AMW, Altus AFB, OK
	60-0356	Boeing KC-135R(RT) Stratotanker	USAF 22nd ARW, McConnell AFB, KS
	60-0357	Boeing KC-135R(RT) Stratotanker	USAF 22nd ARW, McConnell AFB, KS
	60-0358	Boeing KC-135R Stratotanker w/bl	USAF 108th ARS/126th ARW, Scott AFB, IL ANG
	60-0359	Boeing KC-135R Stratotanker	USAF 328th ARS/914th ARW AFRC, Niagara Falls, NY

Serial	Type (code/other identity)	Owner/operator, location or fate	Notes
60-0360	Boeing KC-135R Stratotanker y/bl	USAF 6th ARW, MacDill AFB, FL	
60-0362	Boeing KC-135R(RT) Stratotanker	USAF 22nd ARW, McConnell AFB, KS	
60-0363	Boeing KC-135R Stratotanker bl	USAF 72nd ARS/434th ARW AFRC, Grissom AFB, IN	
60-0364	Boeing KC-135R Stratotanker r/w	USAF 74th ARS/434th ARW AFRC, Grissom AFB, IN	
60-0365	Boeing KC-135R Stratotanker bl/y	USAF 117th ARS/190th ARW, Forbes Field, KS ANG	
60-0366	Boeing KC-135R Stratotanker	USAF 132nd ARS/101st ARW, Bangor, ME ANG	
60-0367	Boeing KC-135R Stratotanker r/w	USAF 166th ARS/121st ARW, Rickenbacker ANGB, OH ANG	
61-0264	Boeing KC-135R Stratotanker r/w	USAF 166th ARS/121st ARW, Rickenbacker ANGB, OH ANG	
61-0266	Boeing KC-135R Stratotanker bl/y	USAF 117th ARS/190th ARW, Forbes Field, KS ANG	
61-0267	Boeing KC-135R Stratotanker	USAF 92nd ARW, Fairchild AFB, WA	
61-0272	Boeing KC-135R Stratotanker r/w	USAF 74th ARS/434th ARW AFRC, Grissom AFB, IN	
61-0275	Boeing KC-135R Stratotanker $	USAF 191st ARS/151st ARW, Salt Lake City, UT ANG	
61-0276	Boeing KC-135R Stratotanker r/w	USAF 173rd ARS/155th ARW, Lincoln, NE ANG	
61-0277	Boeing KC-135R Stratotanker bl/y	USAF 117th ARS/190th ARW, Forbes Field, KS ANG	
61-0280	Boeing KC-135R Stratotanker or/y	USAF 336th ARS/452nd AMW AFRC, March ARB, CA	
61-0284	Boeing KC-135R Stratotanker	USAF 197th ARS/161st ARW, Phoenix, AZ ANG	
61-0288	Boeing KC-135R Stratotanker [AK] bl/y	USAF 168th ARS/168th ARW, Eielson AFB, AK ANG	
61-0290	Boeing KC-135R Stratotanker [HH] y/bk	USAF 203rd ARS/15th Wg, Hickam AFB, HI ANG	
61-0292	Boeing KC-135R Stratotanker bl/y	USAF 117th ARS/190th ARW, Forbes Field, KS ANG	
61-0293	Boeing KC-135R(RT) Stratotanker	USAF 22nd ARW, McConnell AFB, KS	
61-0294	Boeing KC-135R Stratotanker	USAF 92nd ARW, Fairchild AFB, WA	
61-0295	Boeing KC-135R Stratotanker	USAF 6th ARW, MacDill AFB, FL	
61-0298	Boeing KC-135R Stratotanker w/bl	USAF 126th ARS/128th ARW, Mitchell Field, WI ANG	
61-0299	Boeing KC-135R Stratotanker or/y	USAF 336th ARS/452nd AMW AFRC, March ARB, CA	
61-0300	Boeing KC-135R Stratotanker w/bl	USAF 108th ARS/126th ARW, Scott AFB, IL ANG	
61-0305	Boeing KC-135R Stratotanker y/r	USAF 54th ARS/97th ARW, Altus AFB, OK	
61-0307	Boeing KC-135R Stratotanker y/bk	USAF 756th ARS/459th ARW AFRC, Andrews AFB, MD	
61-0308	Boeing KC-135R Stratotanker	USAF 92nd ARW, Fairchild AFB, WA	
61-0309	Boeing KC-135R Stratotanker w/bl	USAF 126th ARS/128th ARW, Mitchell Field, WI ANG	
61-0310	Boeing KC-135R Stratotanker w/bl	USAF 126th ARS/128th ARW, Mitchell Field, WI ANG	
61-0311	Boeing KC-135R Stratotanker	USAF 92nd ARW, Fairchild AFB, WA	
61-0313	Boeing KC-135R Stratotanker	USAF 92nd ARW, Fairchild AFB, WA	
61-0314	Boeing KC-135R Stratotanker y/bl	USAF 6th ARW, MacDill AFB, FL	
61-0317	Boeing KC-135R Stratotanker	USAF 197th ARS/161st ARW, Phoenix, AZ ANG	
61-0318	Boeing KC-135R Stratotanker w/r	USAF 106th ARS/117th ARW, Birmingham, AL ANG	
61-0320	Boeing KC-135NK Stratotanker [ED]	USAF 418th FLTS/412th TW, Edwards AFB, CA	
61-0321	Boeing KC-135R Stratotanker y/bl	USAF 6th ARW, MacDill AFB, FL	
61-0323	Boeing KC-135R Stratotanker	USAF 92nd ARW, Fairchild AFB, WA	
61-0324	Boeing KC-135R Stratotanker or/y	USAF 336th ARS/452nd AMW AFRC, March ARB, CA	
61-2662	Boeing RC-135S Cobra Ball [OF] bk	USAF 45th RS/55th Wg, Offutt AFB, NE	
61-2663	Boeing RC-135S Cobra Ball [OF] bk	USAF 45th RS/55th Wg, Offutt AFB, NE	
62-3498	Boeing KC-135R Stratotanker y/bl	USAF 6th ARW, MacDill AFB, FL	
62-3499	Boeing KC-135R Stratotanker	USAF 92nd ARW, Fairchild AFB, WA	

Notes	Serial	Type (code/other identity)	Owner/operator, location or fate
	62-3500	Boeing KC-135R Stratotanker	USAF 197th ARS/161st ARW, Phoenix, AZ ANG
	62-3502	Boeing KC-135R Stratotanker	USAF 92nd ARW, Fairchild AFB, WA
	62-3503	Boeing KC-135R Stratotanker bl/y	USAF 108th ARS/126th ARW, Scott AFB, IL ANG
	62-3505	Boeing KC-135R Stratotanker y/r	USAF 54th ARS/97th AMW, Altus AFB, OK
	62-3506	Boeing KC-135R Stratotanker bl/y	USAF 117th ARS/190th ARW, Forbes Field, KS ANG
	62-3507	Boeing KC-135R Stratotanker or/y	USAF 336th ARS/452nd AMW AFRC, March ARB, CA
	62-3508	Boeing KC-135R Stratotanker r $	USAF 141st ARS/108th Wg, McGuire AFB, NJ ANG
	62-3509	Boeing KC-135R Stratotanker	USAF 92nd ARW, Fairchild AFB, WA
	62-3510	Boeing KC-135R Stratotanker r/w	USAF 74th ARS/434th ARW AFRC, Grissom AFB, IN
	62-3511	Boeing KC-135R Stratotanker r/w	USAF 166th ARS/121st ARW, Rickenbacker ANGB, OH ANG
	62-3512	Boeing KC-135R Stratotanker w/bl	USAF 126th ARS/128th ARW, Mitchell Field, WI ANG
	62-3513	Boeing KC-135R Stratotanker w/gn	USAF 132nd ARS/101st ARW, Bangor, ME ANG
	62-3514	Boeing KC-135R Stratotanker bl/bk	USAF 191st ARS/151st ARW, Salt Lake City, UT ANG
	62-3515	Boeing KC-135R Stratotanker w/bl	USAF 108th ARS/126th ARW, Scott AFB, IL ANG
	62-3516	Boeing KC-135R Stratotanker $	USAF 197th ARS/161st ARW, Phoenix, AZ ANG
	62-3517	Boeing KC-135R Stratotanker y/bl	USAF 6th ARW, MacDill AFB, FL
	62-3518	Boeing KC-135R Stratotanker bl	USAF 72nd ARS/434th ARW AFRC, Grissom AFB, IN
	62-3519	Boeing KC-135R Stratotanker [ZZ] or/bk	USAF 909th ARS/18th Wg, Kadena AB, Japan
	62-3521	Boeing KC-135R Stratotanker bl	USAF 72nd ARS/434th ARW AFRC, Grissom AFB, IN
	62-3523	Boeing KC-135R Stratotanker	USAF 22nd ARW, McConnell AFB, KS
	62-3524	Boeing KC-135R Stratotanker [AK] bl/y	USAF 168th ARS/168th ARW, Eielson AFB, AK ANG
	62-3526	Boeing KC-135R Stratotanker r/w	USAF 173rd ARS/155th ARW, Lincoln, NE ANG
	62-3528	Boeing KC-135R Stratotanker	USAF 54th ARS/97th AMW, Altus AFB, OK
	62-3531	Boeing KC-135R Stratotanker r/w	USAF 166th ARS/121st ARW, Rickenbacker ANGB, OH ANG
	62-3533	Boeing KC-135R Stratotanker	USAF 328th ARS/914th ARW AFRC, Niagara Falls NY
	62-3534	Boeing KC-135R Stratotanker	USAF 22nd ARW, McConnell AFB, KS
	62-3537	Boeing KC-135R Stratotanker	USAF 92nd ARW, Fairchild AFB, WA
	62-3538	Boeing KC-135R Stratotanker y/r	USAF 54th ARS/97th AMW, Altus AFB, OK
	62-3541	Boeing KC-135R Stratotanker	USAF 92nd ARW, Fairchild AFB, WA
	62-3542	Boeing KC-135R Stratotanker r/bk	USAF 314th ARS/940th ARW, Beale AFB, CA
	62-3543	Boeing KC-135R Stratotanker y/bk	USAF 756th ARS/459th ARW AFRC, Andrews AFB, MD
	62-3544	Boeing KC-135R Stratotanker r $	USAF 141st ARS/108th Wg, McGuire AFB, NJ ANG
	62-3547	Boeing KC-135R Stratotanker bl/y	USAF 117th ARS/190th ARW, Forbes Field, KS ANG
	62-3549	Boeing KC-135R Stratotanker y/bk	USAF 174th ARS/185th ARW, Sioux City, IA ANG
	62-3550	Boeing KC-135R Stratotanker	USAF 197th ARS/161st ARW, Phoenix, AZ ANG
	62-3551	Boeing KC-135R Stratotanker	USAF 92nd ARW, Fairchild AFB, WA
	62-3552	Boeing KC-135R Stratotanker	USAF 6th ARW, MacDill AFB, FL
	62-3553	Boeing KC-135R Stratotanker	USAF 92nd ARW, Fairchild AFB, WA
	62-3554	Boeing KC-135R Stratotanker	USAF 22nd ARW, McConnell AFB, KS
	62-3556	Boeing KC-135R Stratotanker y/bk	USAF 756th ARS/459th ARW AFRC, Andrews AFB, MD
	62-3557	Boeing KC-135R Stratotanker	USAF 328th ARS/914th ARW AFRC, Niagara Falls, NY
	62-3558	Boeing KC-135R Stratotanker or/y	USAF 336th ARS/452nd AMW AFRC, March ARB, CA
	62-3559	Boeing KC-135R Stratotanker [ZZ] or/bk	USAF 909th ARS/18th Wg, Kadena AB, Japan
	62-3561	Boeing KC-135R Stratotanker	USAF 92nd ARW, Fairchild AFB, WA

Serial	Type (code/other identity)	Owner/operator, location or fate	Notes
62-3562	Boeing KC-135R Stratotanker	USAF 92nd ARW, Fairchild AFB, WA	
62-3564	Boeing KC-135R Stratotanker	USAF 6th ARW, MacDill AFB, FL	
62-3565	Boeing KC-135R Stratotanker *bl*	USAF 72nd ARS/434th ARW AFRC, Grissom AFB, IN	
62-3566	Boeing KC-135R Stratotanker *y/bk*	USAF 174th ARS/185th ARW, Sioux City, IA ANG	
62-3568	Boeing KC-135R Stratotanker	USAF 336th ARS/452nd AMW AFRC, March ARB, CA	
62-3569	Boeing KC-135R Stratotanker	USAF 22nd ARW, McConnell AFB, KS	
62-3571	Boeing KC-135R Stratotanker [AK] *bl/y*	USAF 168th ARS/168th ARW, Eielson AFB, AK ANG	
62-3573	Boeing KC-135R Stratotanker	USAF 6th ARW, MacDill AFB, FL	
62-3575	Boeing KC-135R Stratotanker	USAF 92nd ARW, Fairchild AFB, WA	
62-3576	Boeing KC-135R Stratotanker *w/bl*	USAF 108th ARS/126th ARW, Scott AFB, IL ANG	
62-3577	Boeing KC-135R Stratotanker	USAF 92nd ARW, Fairchild AFB, WA	
62-3578	Boeing KC-135R Stratotanker *r*	USAF 141st ARS/108th Wg, McGuire AFB, NJ ANG	
62-3580	Boeing KC-135R Stratotanker	USAF 328th ARS/914th ARW AFRC, Niagara Falls, NY	
62-4125	Boeing RC-135W Rivet Joint [OF] *bl*	USAF 38th RS/55th Wg, Offutt AFB, NE	
62-4126	Boeing RC-135W Rivet Joint [OF] *bl*	USAF 38th RS/55th Wg, Offutt AFB, NE	
62-4127	Boeing TC-135W [OF] *bl*	USAF 38th RS/55th Wg, Offutt AFB, NE	
62-4128	Boeing RC-135S Cobra Ball [OF] *bk*	USAF 45th RS/55th Wg, Offutt AFB, NE	
62-4129	Boeing TC-135W [OF] *bl*	USAF 343rd RS/55th Wg, Offutt AFB, NE	
62-4130	Boeing RC-135W Rivet Joint [OF] *bl*	USAF 38th RS/55th Wg, Offutt AFB, NE	
62-4131	Boeing RC-135W Rivet Joint [OF] *bl*	USAF 38th RS/55th Wg, Offutt AFB, NE	
62-4132	Boeing RC-135W Rivet Joint [OF] *bl*	USAF 38th RS/55th Wg, Offutt AFB, NE	
62-4133	Boeing TC-135W [OF] *bk*	USAF, *Greenville Majors, TX – For conversion to an NC-135W "Big Safari"*	
62-4134	Boeing RC-135W Rivet Joint [OF] *bl*	USAF 38th RS/55th Wg, Offutt AFB, NE	
62-4135	Boeing RC-135W Rivet Joint [OF] *bl*	USAF 38th RS/55th Wg, Offutt AFB, NE	
62-4138	Boeing RC-135W Rivet Joint [OF] *bl*	USAF 38th RS/55th Wg, Offutt AFB, NE	
62-4139	Boeing RC-135W Rivet Joint [OF] *bl*	USAF 38th RS/55th Wg, Offutt AFB, NE	
63-7976	Boeing KC-135R Stratotanker *y/bl*	USAF 6th ARW, MacDill AFB, FL	
63-7977	Boeing KC-135R Stratotanker *y/r*	USAF 54th ARS/97th AMW, Altus AFB, OK	
63-7978	Boeing KC-135R Stratotanker *r/w*	USAF 54th ARS/97th AMW, Altus AFB, OK	
63-7979	Boeing KC-135R Stratotanker *y/bl*	USAF 6th ARW, MacDill AFB, FL	
63-7981	Boeing KC-135R Stratotanker *w/bl*	USAF 108th ARS/126th ARW, Scott AFB, IL ANG	
63-7982	Boeing KC-135R Stratotanker [ZZ] *or/bk*	USAF 909th ARS/18th Wg, Kadena AB, Japan	
63-7984	Boeing KC-135R Stratotanker *w/r*	USAF 106th ARS/117th ARW, Birmingham, AL ANG	
63-7985	Boeing KC-135R Stratotanker *bl/y*	USAF 465th ARS/507th ARW AFRC, Tinker AFB, OK	
63-7987	Boeing KC-135R Stratotanker *y/r*	USAF 54th ARS/97th AMW, Altus AFB, OK	
63-7988	Boeing KC-135R Stratotanker *r/w*	USAF 173rd ARS/155th ARW, Lincoln, NE ANG	
63-7991	Boeing KC-135R Stratotanker *r/w*	USAF 173rd ARS/155th ARW, Lincoln, NE ANG	
63-7992	Boeing KC-135R Stratotanker	USAF 153rd ARS/186th ARW, Meridian, MS ANG	
63-7993	Boeing KC-135R Stratotanker *m*	USAF 166th ARS/121st ARW, Rickenbacker ANGB, OH ANG	
63-7995	Boeing KC-135R Stratotanker	USAF 22nd ARW, McConnell AFB, KS	
63-7996	Boeing KC-135R Stratotanker	USAF 72nd ARS/434th ARW AFRC, Grissom AFB, IN	
63-7997	Boeing KC-135R Stratotanker	USAF 92nd ARW, Fairchild AFB, WA	
63-8000	Boeing KC-135R Stratotanker	USAF 92nd ARW, Fairchild AFB, WA	
63-8002	Boeing KC-135R Stratotanker	USAF 22nd ARW, McConnell AFB, KS	
63-8003	Boeing KC-135R Stratotanker *or/bk* $	USAF 141st ARS/108th Wg, McGuire AFB, NJ ANG	
63-8004	Boeing KC-135R Stratotanker *bl/y*	USAF 117th ARS/190th ARW, Forbes Field, KS ANG	
63-8006	Boeing KC-135R Stratotanker *r/w*	USAF 54th ARS/97th AMW, Altus AFB, OK	
63-8007	Boeing KC-135R Stratotanker *w/r*	USAF 106th ARS/117th ARW, Birmingham, AL ANG	
63-8011	Boeing KC-135R Stratotanker *y/r* [54 ARS]	USAF 54th ARS/97th AMW, Altus AFB, OK	
63-8012	Boeing KC-135R Stratotanker	USAF 314th ARS/940th ARW, Beale AFB, CA	
63-8013	Boeing KC-135R Stratotanker *r/w*	USAF 166th ARS/121st ARW, Rickenbacker ANGB, OH ANG	
63-8015	Boeing KC-135R Stratotanker [AK] *bl/y*	USAF 168th ARS/168th ARW, Eielson AFB, AK ANG	

Notes	Serial	Type (code/other identity)	Owner/operator, location or fate
	63-8017	Boeing KC-135R Stratotanker	USAF 328th ARS/914th ARW AFRC, Niagara Falls NY
	63-8018	Boeing KC-135R Stratotanker *r/w*	USAF 173rd ARS/155th ARW, Lincoln, NE ANG
	63-8019	Boeing KC-135R Stratotanker	USAF 92nd ARW, Fairchild AFB, WA
	63-8020	Boeing KC-135R Stratotanker	USAF 6th ARW, MacDill AFB, FL
	63-8021	Boeing KC-135R Stratotanker	USAF 92nd ARW, Fairchild AFB, WA
	63-8022	Boeing KC-135R Stratotanker	USAF 92nd ARW, Fairchild AFB, WA
	63-8023	Boeing KC-135R Stratotanker *w/bl*	USAF 126th ARS/128th ARW, Mitchell Field, WI ANG
	63-8024	Boeing KC-135R Stratotanker *or/y*	USAF 336th ARS/452nd AMW AFRC, March ARB, CA
	63-8025	Boeing KC-135R Stratotanker	USAF 92nd ARW, Fairchild AFB, WA
	63-8026	Boeing KC-135R Stratotanker *bl/bk*	USAF 191st ARS/151st ARW, Salt Lake City, UT ANG
	63-8027	Boeing KC-135R Stratotanker *r/w*	USAF 173rd ARS/155th ARW, Lincoln, NE ANG
	63-8028	Boeing KC-135R Stratotanker [AK] *bl/y*	USAF 168th ARS/168th ARW, Eielson AFB, AK ANG
	63-8029	Boeing KC-135R Stratotanker *r $*	USAF 141st ARS/108th Wg, McGuire AFB,NJ ANG
	63-8030	Boeing KC-135R Stratotanker [HH] *y/bk*	USAF 203rd ARS/15th Wg, Hickam AFB, HI ANG
	63-8031	Boeing KC-135R Stratotanker	USAF 92nd ARW, Fairchild AFB, WA
	63-8032	Boeing KC-135R Stratotanker *bl*	USAF 72nd ARS/434th ARW AFRC, Grissom AFB, IN
	63-8033	Boeing KC-135R Stratotanker *y/r*	USAF 54th ARS/97th AMW, Altus AFB, OK
	63-8034	Boeing KC-135R Stratotanker	USAF 92nd ARW, Fairchild AFB, WA
	63-8035	Boeing KC-135R Stratotanker *w/r*	USAF 106th ARS/117th ARW, Birmingham, AL ANG
	63-8036	Boeing KC-135R Stratotanker	USAF 197th ARS/161st ARW, Phoenix, AZ ANG
	63-8038	Boeing KC-135R Stratotanker [HH] *y/bk*	USAF 203rd ARS/15th Wg, Hickam AFB, HI ANG
	63-8039	Boeing KC-135R Stratotanker *bl/y*	USAF 465th ARS/507th ARW AFRC, Tinker AFB, OK
	63-8040	Boeing KC-135R Stratotanker	USAF 108th ARS/126th ARW, Scott AFB, IL ANG
	63-8041	Boeing KC-135R Stratotanker *bl*	USAF 72nd ARS/434th ARW AFRC, Grissom AFB, IN
	63-8043	Boeing KC-135R Stratotanker [AK] *bl/y*	USAF 168th ARS/168th ARW, Eielson AFB, AK ANG
	63-8044	Boeing KC-135R Stratotanker [NF]	USAF 328th ARS/914th ARW AFRC, Niagara Falls, NY
	63-8045	Boeing KC-135R Stratotanker	USAF 92nd ARW, Fairchild AFB, WA
	63-8871	Boeing KC-135R Stratotanker	USAF 92nd ARW, Fairchild AFB, WA
	63-8872	Boeing KC-135R Stratotanker *w/gn*	USAF 132nd ARS/101st ARW, Bangor, ME ANG
	63-8873	Boeing KC-135R Stratotanker *w/gn*	USAF 132nd ARS/101st ARW, Bangor, ME ANG
	63-8874	Boeing KC-135R Stratotanker	USAF 92nd ARW, Fairchild AFB, WA
	63-8875	Boeing KC-135R Stratotanker *bl/y*	USAF 117th ARS/190th ARW, Forbes Field, KS ANG
	63-8876	Boeing KC-135R Stratotanker [AK] *bl/y*	USAF 168th ARS/168th ARW, Eielson AFB, AK ANG
	63-8879	Boeing KC-135R Stratotanker	USAF 6th ARW, MacDill AFB, FL
	63-8880	Boeing KC-135R Stratotanker [HH] *y/bk*	USAF 203rd ARS/15th Wg, Hickam AFB, HI ANG
	63-8881	Boeing KC-135R Stratotanker	*McConnell AFB, KS, for GI*
	63-8883	Boeing KC-135R Stratotanker *y/bk*	USAF 203rd ARS/15th Wg, Hickam AFB, HI ANG
	63-8884	Boeing KC-135R Stratotanker *y/bl*	USAF 6th ARW, MacDill AFB, FL
	63-8885	Boeing KC-135R Stratotanker *y/bl*	USAF 6th ARW, MacDill AFB, FL
	63-8887	Boeing KC-135R Stratotanker *y/bl*	USAF 6th ARW, MacDill AFB, FL
	63-8888	Boeing KC-135R Stratotanker	USAF 92nd ARW, Fairchild AFB, WA
	63-9792	Boeing RC-135V Rivet Joint [OF] *bl*	USAF 38th RS/55th Wg, Offutt AFB, NE
	64-14828	Boeing KC-135R Stratotanker *bl/bk*	USAF 191st ARS/151st ARW, Salt Lake City, UT ANG
	64-14829	Boeing WC-135R Constant Phoenix *bk*	USAF 45th RS/55th Wg, Offutt AFB, NE
	64-14831	Boeing WC-135R Constant Phoenix *bk*	USAF 45th RS/55th Wg, Offutt AFB, NE
	64-14832	Boeing KC-135R Stratotanker *w/or*	USAF 151st ARS/134th ARW, Knoxville, TN ANG
	64-14834	Boeing KC-135R Stratotanker *r/w*	USAF 74th ARS/434th ARW AFRC, Grissom AFB, IN
	64-14835	Boeing KC-135R Stratotanker *or/y*	USAF 336th ARS/452nd AMW AFRC, March ARB, CA

Serial	Type (code/other identity)	Owner/operator, location or fate	Notes
64-14836	Boeing WC-135R Constant Phoenix *bk*	USAF 45th RS/55th Wg, Offutt AFB, NE	
64-14837	Boeing KC-135R Stratotanker	USAF 92nd ARW, Fairchild AFB, WA	
64-14839	Boeing KC-135R Stratotanker *w/bl*	USAF 108th ARS/126th ARW, Scott AFB, IL ANG	
64-14840	Boeing KC-135R Stratotanker *r/w*	USAF 166th ARS/121st ARW, Rickenbacker ANGB, OH ANG	
64-14841	Boeing RC-135V Rivet Joint [OF] *bl*	USAF 38th RS/55th Wg, Offutt AFB, NE	
64-14842	Boeing RC-135V Rivet Joint [OF] *bl*	USAF 38th RS/55th Wg, Offutt AFB, NE	
64-14843	Boeing RC-135V Rivet Joint [OF] *bl*	USAF 38th RS/55th Wg, Offutt AFB, NE	
64-14844	Boeing RC-135V Rivet Joint [OF] *r*	USAF 38th RS/55th Wg, Offutt AFB, NE	
64-14845	Boeing RC-135V Rivet Joint [OF] *bl*	USAF 38th RS/55th Wg, Offutt AFB, NE	
64-14846	Boeing RC-135V Rivet Joint [OF] *bl*	USAF 38th RS/55th Wg, Offutt AFB, NE	
64-14847	Boeing RC-135U Combat Sent [OF] *bk*	USAF 45th RS/55th Wg, Offutt AFB, NE	
64-14848	Boeing RC-135V Rivet Joint [OF] *bl*	USAF 38th RS/55th Wg, Offutt AFB, NE	
64-14849	Boeing RC-135U Combat Sent [OF] *bk*	USAF 45th RS/55th Wg, Offutt AFB, NE	

Dornier C-146A Wolfhound

NOTE: There have also been reports that 3058, 3091, 3093 and 3106 MAY be FY05, 07 and 09 respectively

95-3058	Dornier C-146A Wolfhound (N570EF)	USAF 524th SOS/492nd SOW, Duke Field, FL	
97-3091	Dornier C-146A Wolfhound (N391EF)	USAF 524th SOS/492nd SOW, Duke Field, FL	
97-3093	Dornier C-146A Wolfhound (N545EF)	USAF 524th SOS/492nd SOW, Duke Field, FL	
99-3106	Dornier C-146A Wolfhound (N525EF)	USAF 524th SOS/492nd SOW, Duke Field, FL	
10-3026	Dornier C-146A Wolfhound (N929EF)	USAF 524th SOS/492nd SOW, Duke Field, FL	
10-3068	Dornier C-146A Wolfhound (N565EF)	USAF 524th SOS/492nd SOW, Duke Field, FL	
10-3077	Dornier C-146A Wolfhound (N577EF)	*Transferred to 67th SOS/352nd SOW, RAF Mildenhall, UK*	
11-3013	Dornier C-146A Wolfhound (N645HM)	USAF 524th SOS/492nd SOW, Duke Field, FL	
11-3016	Dornier C-146A Wolfhound (N941EF)	USAF 524th SOS/492nd SOW, Duke Field, FL	
11-3031	Dornier C-146A Wolfhound (N975EF)	USAF 524th SOS/492nd SOW, Duke Field, FL	
11-3075	Dornier C-146A Wolfhound (N953EF)	USAF 524th SOS/492nd SOW, Duke Field, FL	
11-3097	Dornier C-146A Wolfhound (N307EF)	USAF 524th SOS/492nd SOW, Duke Field, FL	
11-3104	Dornier C-146A Wolfhound (N907EF)	USAF 524th SOS/492nd SOW, Duke Field, FL	
12-3040	Dornier C-146A Wolfhound (N340LS)	USAF 524th SOS/492nd SOW, Duke Field, FL	
12-3047	Dornier C-146A Wolfhound (N347EF)	USAF 524th SOS/492nd SOW, Duke Field, FL	
12-3050	Dornier C-146A Wolfhound (N355EF)	USAF 524th SOS/492nd SOW, Duke Field, FL	
12-3060	Dornier C-146A Wolfhound (N360EF)	USAF 524th SOS/492nd SOW, Duke Field, FL	
12-3085	Dornier C-146A Wolfhound (N385EF)	USAF 524th SOS/492nd SOW, Duke Field, FL	
15-3086	Dornier C-146A Wolfhound (N328ST)	USAF 524th SOS/492nd SOW, Duke Field, FL	
16-3020	Dornier C-146A Wolfhound (N524AW)	USAF 524th SOS/492nd SOW, Duke Field, FL	
16-3025	Dornier C-146A Wolfhound (N250BG)	USAF 524th SOS/492nd SOW, Duke Field, FL	

CASA C235/C295W

NOTE: "30501" and "70601" are 2 of 3 airframes nominally operated by "L-3 Communications", comprising N281MH, N320FC and N523NB, tie-up order currently unknown.

96-6042	CASA CN235-300	USAF, 427th SOS, Pope AFB, NC	
96-6043	CASA CN235-300MPA (N835CE)	USAF, 427th SOS, Pope AFB, NC	
96-6044	CASA CN235-300MPA (N506KM)	USAF, 427th SOS, Pope AFB, NC	
96-6045	CASA CN235-300MPA (N383EC)	USAF, 427th SOS, Pope AFB, NC	
96-6046	CASA CN235-300 (N825FA)	USAF, 427th SOS, Pope AFB, NC	
96-6049	CASA CN235-100 (N385RS)	USAF, 427th SOS, Pope AFB, NC	
"30501"	CASA C295W	USAF, 427th SOS, Pope AFB, NC	
"70601"	CASA C295W	USAF, 427th SOS, Pope AFB, NC	
.....	CASA C295W	USAF, 427th SOS, Pope AFB, NC	

Notes	Serial	Type (code/other identity)	Owner/operator, location or fate
	Lockheed P-3 Orion		
	150521	Lockheed NP-3D Orion [341]	USN VX-30, NAS Point Mugu, CA
	156511	Lockheed EP-3E ARIES II [511]	*Preserved Pima Air and Space Museum, Tucson, AZ*
	156517	Lockheed EP-3E ARIES II [517]	*To 309th AMARG, 29th October 2024*
	156528	Lockheed EP-3E ARIES II [528]	*To 309th AMARG, 5th February 2024*
	156529	Lockheed EP-3E ARIES II [529]	*To 309th AMARG, 23rd October 2024*
	157316	Lockheed EP-3E ARIES II [316]	*To 309th AMARG, 24th April 2024*
	157318	Lockheed EP-3E ARIES II [318]	*To 309th AMARG, 24th April 2024*
	157325	Lockheed EP-3E ARIES II [325]	*To 309th AMARG, 23rd January 2023*
	157326	Lockheed EP-3E ARIES II [326]	*SOC, Greenville, SC*
	158570	Lockheed P-3C-IIIR Orion [RL-570]	USN VXS-1, Patuxent River, MD
	158912	Lockheed NP-3C Orion [RL-912]	USN VXS-1, Patuxent River, MD
	158934	Lockheed P-3C AIP+ Orion [302]	USN VX-30, NAS Point Mugu, CA
	159887	Lockheed EP-3E ARIES II [887]	*To 309th AMARG, 6th November 2024*
	159893	Lockheed EP-3E ARIES II [893]	*Current status unknown*
	160293	Lockheed P-3C BMUP Orion [BH-301]	USN VX-30, NAS Point Mugu, CA
	160610	Lockheed P-3C AIP+ Orion [610]	*To 309th AMARG, 9th February 2023*
	161405	Lockheed P-3C BMUP+ Orion [405]	*To 309th AMARG, 28th August 2024*
	161410	Lockheed EP-3E ARIES II [410]	*To 309th AMARG, 19th December 2024*
	161414	Lockheed P-3C BMUP+ Orion [414]	*To 309th AMARG, 9th December 2024*
	161588	Lockheed P-3C BMUP+ Orion [588]	*Current status unknown*
	161590	Lockheed P-3C BMUP+ Orion [590]	*Transferred to NASA for spares*
	162318	Lockheed P-3C AIP+ Orion [318]	*Preserved Moffett Field, CA*
	162777	Lockheed P-3C AIP+ Orion [777]	*Current status unknown*
	162999	Lockheed P-3C AIP+ Orion [BH-300]	USN VX-30, NAS Point Mugu, CA
	163001	Lockheed P-3C AIP+ Orion [001]	*To 309th AMARG, 25th July 2022*
	163291	Lockheed P-3C AIP+ Orion [304]	USN VX-30, NAS Point Mugu, CA
	163294	Lockheed P-3C AIP+ Orion [303]	USN, wfu NAS Point Mugu, CA
	163295	Lockheed P-3C AIP+ Orion [295]	USN, wfu Waco, TX
	Boeing E-6B Mercury		
	162782	Boeing E-6B Mercury	USN VQ-3/SCW-1, Tinker AFB, OK
	162783	Boeing E-6B Mercury	USN VX-20, Patuxent River, MD
	162784	Boeing E-6B Mercury	USN VQ-3/SCW-1, Tinker AFB, OK
	163918	Boeing E-6B Mercury	USN VQ-4/SCW-1, Tinker AFB, OK
	163919	Boeing E-6B Mercury	USN VQ-3/SCW-1, Tinker AFB, OK
	163920	Boeing E-6B Mercury	USN VX-20, Patuxent River, MD
	164386	Boeing E-6B Mercury	USN VQ-4/SCW-1, Tinker AFB, OK
	164387	Boeing E-6B Mercury	USN VX-20, Patuxent River, MD
	164388	Boeing E-6B Mercury	USN VQ-4/SCW-1, Tinker AFB, OK
	164404	Boeing E-6B Mercury	USN VQ-4/SCW-1, Tinker AFB, OK
	164405	Boeing E-6B Mercury	USN VQ-3/SCW-1, Tinker AFB, OK
	164406	Boeing E-6B Mercury	USN VQ-4/SCW-1, Tinker AFB, OK
	164407	Boeing E-6B Mercury	USN VQ-4/SCW-1, Tinker AFB, OK
	164408	Boeing E-6B Mercury	USN VQ-4/SCW-1, Tinker AFB, OK
	164409	Boeing E-6B Mercury	USN VQ-3/SCW-1, Tinker AFB, OK
	164410	Boeing E-6B Mercury	USN VX-20, Patuxent River, MD
	Boeing P-8A Poseidon		
	167951	Boeing P-8A Poseidon (N541BA) [951]	USN VX-20, Patuxent River, MD
	167952	Boeing P-8A Poseidon (N398DS) [952]	USN BUPERS SDC, Dallas/Love Field, TX
	167953	Boeing P-8A Poseidon (N441BA) [953]	USN VX-20, Patuxent River, MD
	167954	Boeing P-8A Poseidon (N397DS) [954]	USN VX-20, Patuxent River, MD
	167955	Boeing P-8A Poseidon (N328DS) [955]	USN VX-1, NAS Patuxent River, MD
	167956	Boeing P-8A Poseidon (N391DS) [JA-956]	USN VX-1, NAS Patuxent River, MD
	168428	Boeing P-8A Poseidon (N392DS) [LL-428]	USN VP-30, NAS Jacksonville, FL
	168429	Boeing P-8A Poseidon (N397DS) [429]	USN VP-45, NAS Jacksonville, FL
	168430	Boeing P-8A Poseidon (N398DS) [LC-430]	USN VP-8, NAS Jacksonville, FL
	168431	Boeing P-8A Poseidon (N507DS) [YB-431]	USN VP-1, NAS Whidbey Island, WA
	168432	Boeing P-8A Poseidon (N516DS) [LC-432]	USN VP-8, NAS Jacksonville, FL
	168433	Boeing P-8A Poseidon (N530DS) [433]	USN VP-30, NAS Jacksonville, FL

Serial	Type (code/other identity)	Owner/operator, location or fate	Notes
168434	Boeing P-8A Poseidon (N532DS) [LL-434]	USN VP-30, NAS Jacksonville, FL	
168435	Boeing P-8A Poseidon (N533DS) [LL-435]	USN VP-30, NAS Jacksonville, FL	
168436	Boeing P-8A Poseidon (N536DS) [LF-436]	USN VP-16, NAS Jacksonville, FL	
168437	Boeing P-8A Poseidon (N537DS) [LL-437]	USN VP-30, NAS Jacksonville, FL	
168438	Boeing P-8A Poseidon (N327DS) [438] $	USN VPU-2, NAS Jacksonville, FL	
168439	Boeing P-8A Poseidon (N539DS) [QE-439]	USN VP-40, NAS Whidbey Island, WA	
168440	Boeing P-8A Poseidon (N708DS) [LD-440]	USN VP-10, NAS Jacksonville, FL	
168754	Boeing P-8A Poseidon (N736DS) [LK-754]	USN VP-26, NAS Jacksonville, FL	
168755	Boeing P-8A Poseidon (N740DS) [YD-755]	USN VP-4, NAS Whidbey Island, WA	
168756	Boeing P-8A Poseidon (N753DS) [LF-756]	USN VP-16, NAS Jacksonville, FL	
168757	Boeing P-8A Poseidon (N755DS) [YB-757]	USN VP-1, NAS Whidbey Island, WA	
168758	Boeing P-8A Poseidon (N758DS) [RD-758]	USN VP-47, NAS Whidbey Island, WA	
168759	Boeing P-8A Poseidon (N762DS) [759]	USN VP-16, NAS Jacksonville, FL	
168760	Boeing P-8A Poseidon (N768DS) [RD-760]	USN VP-47, NAS Whidbey Island, WA	
168761	Boeing P-8A Poseidon (N771DS) [LK-761]	USN VP-26, NAS Jacksonville, FL	
168762	Boeing P-8A Poseidon (N780DS) [YB-762]	USN VP-1, NAS Whidbey Island, WA	
168763	Boeing P-8A Poseidon (N781DS) [LK-763]	USN VP-26, NAS Jacksonville, FL	
168764	Boeing P-8A Poseidon (N783DS) [LL-764]	USN VP-30, NAS Jacksonville, FL	
168848	Boeing P-8A Poseidon (N784DS) [LD-848]	USN VP-10, NAS Jacksonville, FL	
168849	Boeing P-8A Poseidon (N785DS) [RC-849]	USN VP-46, NAS Whidbey Island, WA	
168850	Boeing P-8A Poseidon (N789DS) [PD-850]	USN VP-9, NAS Whidbey Island, WA	
168851	Boeing P-8A Poseidon (N790DS) [QE-851]	USN VP-40, NAS Whidbey Island, WA	
168852	Boeing P-8A Poseidon (N715DS) [PD-852]	USN VP-9, NAS Whidbey Island, WA	
168853	Boeing P-8A Poseidon (N717DS) [RD-853]	USN VP-47, NAS Whidbey Island, WA	
168854	Boeing P-8A Poseidon (N722DS) (as 169564,168441, 169441)	USN VPU-2, NAS Jacksonville, FL	
168855	Boeing P-8A Poseidon (N729DS) [LN-855]	USN VP-45, NAS Jacksonville, FL	
168856	Boeing P-8A Poseidon (N805DS) [RC-856]	USN VP-46, NAS Whidbey Island, WA	
168857	Boeing P-8A Poseidon (N590DS) [LK-857]	USN VP-26, NAS Jacksonville, FL	
168858	Boeing P-8A Poseidon (N591DS) [RC-858]	USN VP-46, NAS Jacksonville, FL	
168859	Boeing P-8A Poseidon (N592DS) [YB-859] $	USN VP-1, NAS Whidbey Island, WA	
168860	Boeing P-8A Poseidon (N593DS) [LL-860]	USN VP-30, NAS Jacksonville, FL	
168996	Boeing P-8A Poseidon (N595DS) [LK-996]	USN VP-26, NAS Jacksonville, FL	
168997	Boeing P-8A Poseidon (N597DS) [PD-997]	USN VP-9, NAS Whidbey Island, WA	
168998	Boeing P-8A Poseidon (N598DS) [998]	USN VP-16, NAS Jacksonville, FL	
168999	Boeing P-8A Poseidon (N910DS) [012] (as 168012, 169012)	USN VPU-2, NAS Jacksonville, FL	
169000	Boeing P-8A Poseidon (N914DS) [LF-000]	USN VP-16, NAS Jacksonville, FL	
169001	Boeing P-8A Poseidon (N931DS) [RC-001]	USN VP-46, NAS Whidbey Island, WA	
169002	Boeing P-8A Poseidon (N934DS) [RC-002]	USN VP-46, NAS Whidbey Island, WA	
169003	Boeing P-8A Poseidon (N935DS) [PD-003]	USN VP-9, NAS Whidbey Island, WA	
169004	Boeing P-8A Poseidon (N936DS) [PD-004]	USN VP-9, NAS Whidbey Island, WA	
169005	Boeing P-8A Poseidon (N941DS) [PD-005]	USN VP-9, NAS Whidbey Island, WA	
169006	Boeing P-8A Poseidon (N942DS) [LL-006]	USN VP-30, NAS Jacksonville, FL	
169007	Boeing P-8A Poseidon (N943DS) [007]	USN BUPERS SDC, Dallas/Love Field, TX	
169008	Boeing P-8A Poseidon (N944DS) [008]	USN VP-4, NAS Whidbey Island, WA	
169009	Boeing P-8A Poseidon (N949DS) [YD-009]	USN VP-4, NAS Whidbey Island, WA	
169010	Boeing P-8A Poseidon (N957DS) [LA-010]	USN VP-5, NAS Jacksonville, FL	
169011	Boeing P-8A Poseidon (N958DS) [LL-011]	USN VP-30, NAS Jacksonville, FL	
169324	Boeing P-8A Poseidon (N960DS) [PD-324]	USN VP-9, NAS Whidbey Island, WA	
169325	Boeing P-8A Poseidon (N962DS) [325]	USN VP-4, NAS Whidbey Island, WA	
169326	Boeing P-8A Poseidon (N969DS) [LL-326]	USN VP-30, NAS Jacksonville, FL	
169327	Boeing P-8A Poseidon (N963DS) [384] (as 168348, 169384)	USN VPU-2, NAS Jacksonville, FL	
169328	Boeing P-8A Poseidon (N964DS) [QE-328]	USN VP-40, NAS Whidbey Island, WA	
169329	Boeing P-8A Poseidon (N968DS) [329]	USN VP-4, NAS Whidbey Island, WA	
169330	Boeing P-8A Poseidon (N843DS) [330]	USN VP-30, NAS Jacksonville, FL	
169331	Boeing P-8A Poseidon (N852DS) [QE-331]	USN VP-40, NAS Whidbey Island, WA	
169332	Boeing P-8A Poseidon (N848DS) [YB-332]	USN VP-1, NAS Whidbey Island, WA	
169333	Boeing P-8A Poseidon (N838DS) [333]	USN VX-1, NAS Patuxent River, MD	
169334	Boeing P-8A Poseidon (N839DS) [LL-334]	USN VP-30, NAS Jacksonville, FL	
169335	Boeing P-8A Poseidon (N854DS) [LK-335]	USN VP-26, NAS Jacksonville, FL	

Notes	Serial	Type (code/other identity)	Owner/operator, location or fate
	169336	Boeing P-8A Poseidon (N857DS) [LC-336]	USN VP-8, NAS Jacksonville, FL
	169337	Boeing P-8A Poseidon (N858DS) [YB-337]	USN VP-1, NAS Whidbey Island, WA
	169338	Boeing P-8A Poseidon (N860DS) [323] (as 169323)	USN VPU-2, NAS Jacksonville, FL
	169339	Boeing P-8A Poseidon (N863DS) [RC-339]	USN VP-46, NAS Whidbey Island, WA
	169340	Boeing P-8A Poseidon (N864DS) [LA-340]	USN VP-5, NAS Jacksonville, FL
	169341	Boeing P-8A Poseidon (N869DS) [341]	USN BUPERS SDC, Dallas/Love Field, TX
	169342	Boeing P-8A Poseidon (N874DS) [LL-342]	USN VP-30, NAS Jacksonville, FL
	169343	Boeing P-8A Poseidon (N873DS) [YB-343]	USN VP-1, NAS Whidbey Island, WA
	169344	Boeing P-8A Poseidon (N304DS) [RC-344]	USN VP-46, NAS Whidbey Island, WA
	169345	Boeing P-8A Poseidon (N308DS) [QE-345]	USN VP-40, NAS Whidbey Island, WA
	169346	Boeing P-8A Poseidon (N318DS) [YD-346]	USN VP-4, NAS Whidbey Island, WA
	169347	Boeing P-8A Poseidon (N322DS) [YB-347]	USN VP-1, NAS Whidbey Island, WA
	169348	Boeing P-8A Poseidon (N323DS) [348]	USN VP-40, NAS Whidbey Island, WA
	169349	Boeing P-8A Poseidon (N328DS) [QE-349]	USN VP-40, NAS Whidbey Island, WA
	169426	Boeing P-8A Poseidon (N332DS) [426]	USN BUPERS SDC, Dallas/Love Field, TX
	169542	Boeing P-8A Poseidon (N348DS) [YD-542]	USN VP-4, NAS Whidbey Island, WA
	169543	Boeing P-8A Poseidon (N347DS) [YB-543]	USN VP-1, NAS Whidbey Island, WA
	169544	Boeing P-8A Poseidon (N360DS) [PD-544]	USN VP-9, NAS Whidbey Island, WA
	169545	Boeing P-8A Poseidon (N364DS) [LL-545]	USN VP-30, NAS Jacksonville, FL
	169546	Boeing P-8A Poseidon (N368DS) [RD-546]	USN VP-47, NAS Whidbey Island, WA
	169547	Boeing P-8A Poseidon (N374DS) [PD-547]	USN VP-9, NAS Whidbey Island, WA
	169548	Boeing P-8A Poseidon (N383DS) [LN-548]	USN VP-45, NAS Jacksonville, FL
	169549	Boeing P-8A Poseidon (N392DS) [549]	USN VP-10, NAS Jacksonville, FL
	169550	Boeing P-8A Poseidon (N410DS) [LC-550]	USN VP-8, NAS Jacksonville, FL
	169551	Boeing P-8A Poseidon (N438DS) [LA-551]	USN VP-5, NAS Jacksonville, FL
	169552	Boeing P-8A Poseidon (N459DS) [LL-552]	USN VP-30, NAS Jacksonville, FL
	169553	Boeing P-8A Poseidon (N486DS) [553]	USN
	169554	Boeing P-8A Poseidon (N489DS) [LK-554]	USN VP-26, NAS Jacksonville, FL
	169555	Boeing P-8A Poseidon (N508DS) [LT-555]	USN VP-62, NAS Jacksonville, FL
	169556	Boeing P-8A Poseidon (N512DS) [LC-556]	USN VP-8, NAS Jacksonville, FL
	169557	Boeing P-8A Poseidon (N480DS) [PJ-557]	USN VP-69, NAS Whidbey Island, WA
	169558	Boeing P-8A Poseidon (N516DS) [PJ-558]	USN VP-69, NAS Whidbey Island, WA
	169559	Boeing P-8A Poseidon (N532DS) [LF-559]	USN VP-16, NAS Jacksonville, FL
	169560	Boeing P-8A Poseidon (N530DS) [LC-560]	USN VP-8, NAS Jacksonville, FL
	169561	Boeing P-8A Poseidon (N487DS) [YD-561]	*Damaged Kaneohe Bay, HI, 20th November 2023*
	169562	Boeing P-8A Poseidon (N483DS) [QE-562]	USN VP-40, NAS Whidbey Island, WA
	169563	Boeing P-8A Poseidon (N533DS) [LD-563]	USN VP-10, NAS Jacksonville, FL
	169564	Boeing P-8A Poseidon (N533DS) [LT-564]	USN VP-62, NAS Jacksonville, FL
	169565	Boeing P-8A Poseidon (N601DS) [RD-565]	USN VP-47, NAS Whidbey Island, WA
	169566	Boeing P-8A Poseidon (N602DS) [RD-566]	USN VP-47, NAS Whidbey Island, WA
	169567	Boeing P-8A Poseidon (N603DS) [567]	USN BUPERS SDC, Dallas/Love Field, TX
	169568	Boeing P-8A Poseidon (N604DS) [LC-568]	USN VP-8, NAS Jacksonville, FL
	169569	Boeing P-8A Poseidon (N610DS) [LA-569]	USN VP-5, NAS Jacksonville, FL
	169570	Boeing P-8A Poseidon (N612DS) [LL-570]	USN VP-30, NAS Jacksonville, FL
	169571	Boeing P-8A Poseidon (N619DS) [LF-571]	USN VP-16, NAS Jacksonville, FL
	169572	Boeing P-8A Poseidon (N631DS) [LC-572]	USN VP-8, NAS Jacksonville, FL
	170013	Boeing P-8A Poseidon (N689DS) [PJ-013]	USN VP-69, NAS Whidbey Island, WA
	170014	Boeing P-8A Poseidon (N780DS) [LN-014]	USN VP-45, NAS Jacksonville, FL
	170015	Boeing P-8A Poseidon (N781DS) [015]	USN VP-30, NAS Jacksonville, FL
	170016	Boeing P-8A Poseidon (N782DS) [016]	USN BUPERS SDC, Dallas/Love Field, TX
	170017	Boeing P-8A Poseidon (N783DS) [017]	USN VP-5, NAS Jacksonville, FL
	170018	Boeing P-8A Poseidon (N785DS) [018]	USN VX-1, NAS Patuxent River, MD
	170268	Boeing P-8A Poseidon (N827DS) [LA-268]	USN VP-5, NAS Jacksonville, FL
	170269	Boeing P-8A Poseidon (N831DS) [LT-269]	USN VP-62, NAS Jacksonville, FL
	170476	Boeing P-8A Poseidon (N587DS) [LT-476]	USN VP-62, NAS Jacksonville, FL
	170477	Boeing P-8A Poseidon (N795DS) [477]	USN VX-1, NAS Patuxent River, MD
	170478	Boeing P-8A Poseidon (N840DS) [LL-478]	USN VP-30, NAS Jacksonville, FL
	170479	Boeing P-8A Poseidon (N846DS) [479]	USN (on order)
	170480	Boeing P-8A Poseidon (N847DS) [480]	USN (on order)
	170481	Boeing P-8A Poseidon (N853DS) [481]	USN (on order)
	170482	Boeing P-8A Poseidon (N878DS)	USN (on order)
	170483	Boeing P-8A Poseidon (N879DS)	USN (on order)

Serial	Type (code/other identity)	Owner/operator, location or fate	Notes
170484	Boeing P-8A Poseidon (N890DS)	USN (on order)	
170485	Boeing P-8A Poseidon (N868DS)	USN (on order)	
170486	Boeing P-8A Poseidon (N876DS)	USN (on order)	

As mentioned in the listings, the following false markings have been noted on VPU-2 P-8A Poseidons: *168012, 168441, 169012, 169323, 168384, 169384, 169441* and *169564*.

Boeing F/A-18E/F Super Hornet/EA-18G Growler

Serial	Type (code/other identity)	Owner/operator, location or fate	Notes
165167	Boeing F/A-18E Super Hornet [SD-213]	USN VX-23, NAS Patuxent River, MD	
165533	Boeing F/A-18E Super Hornet [DD]	USN VX-31, NAWS China Lake, CA	
165534	Boeing F/A-18E Super Hornet	USN *Blue Angels,* NAS Pensacola, FL	
165535	Boeing F/A-18E Super Hornet	USN, FRC Cecil Field (for Blue Angels)	
165536	Boeing F/A-18E Super Hornet	USN *Blue Angels,* NAS Pensacola, FL	
165537	Boeing F/A-18E Super Hornet [SD-100]	USN VX-23, NAS Patuxent River, MD	
165538	Boeing F/A-18E Super Hornet	USN *Blue Angels,* NAS Pensacola, FL	
165539	Boeing F/A-18E Super Hornet	USN *Blue Angels,* NAS Pensacola, FL	
165540	Boeing F/A-18E Super Hornet	USN *Blue Angels,* NAS Pensacola, FL	
165541	Boeing F/A-18F Super Hornet [00]	USN TPS, NAS Patuxent River, MD	
165542	Boeing F/A-18F Super Hornet [01]	USN TPS, NAS Patuxent River, MD	
165543	Boeing F/A-18F Super Hornet [SD-220]	USN VX-23, NAS Patuxent River, MD	
165544	Boeing F/A-18F Super Hornet [02]	USN TPS, NAS Patuxent River, MD	
165660	Boeing F/A-18E Super Hornet [DD-204]	USN VX-31, NAWS China Lake, CA	
165661	Boeing F/A-18E Super Hornet	USN *Blue Angels,* NAS Pensacola, FL	
165663	Boeing F/A-18E Super Hornet	USN *Blue Angels,* NAS Pensacola, FL	
165664	Boeing F/A-18E Super Hornet	USN *Blue Angels,* NAS Pensacola, FL	
165665	Boeing F/A-18E Super Hornet	USN *Blue Angels,* NAS Pensacola, FL	
165666	Boeing F/A-18E Super Hornet	USN *Blue Angels,* NAS Pensacola, FL	
165667	Boeing F/A-18E Super Hornet	USN *Blue Angels,* NAS Pensacola, FL	
165668	Boeing F/A-18F Super Hornet [201]	USN VX-31, NAWS China Lake, CA	
165669	Boeing F/A-18F Super Hornet [DD-214]	USN VX-31, NAWS China Lake, CA	
165671	Boeing F/A-18F Super Hornet [NJ-102]	USN VFA-122, NAS Lemoore, CA	
165673	Boeing F/A-18F Super Hornet	USN *Blue Angels,* NAS Pensacola, FL	
165675	Boeing F/A-18F Super Hornet [NJ-103]	USN VFA-122, NAS Lemoore, CA	
165677	Boeing F/A-18F Super Hornet [NJ-122]	USN VFA-122, NAS Lemoore, CA	
165679	Boeing F/A-18F Super Hornet	USN *Blue Angels,* NAS Pensacola, FL	
165779	Boeing F/A-18E Super Hornet [SD-101]	USN VX-23, NAS Patuxent River, MD	
165780	Boeing F/A-18E Super Hornet [XE-100]	USN VX-9, NAWS China Lake, CA	
165781	Boeing F/A-18E Super Hornet [00]	USN VFC-12, NAS Oceana, VA	
165782	Boeing F/A-18E Super Hornet	USN *Blue Angels,* NAS Pensacola, FL	
165783	Boeing F/A-18E Super Hornet [12]	USN VFC-12, NAS Oceana, VA	
165784	Boeing F/A-18E Super Hornet [01]	USN VFC-12, NAS Oceana, VA	
165786	Boeing F/A-18E Super Hornet [02]	USN VFC-12, NAS Oceana, VA	
165787	Boeing F/A-18E Super Hornet [AJ-100]	USN VFA-37, NAS Oceana, VA	
165788	Boeing F/A-18E Super Hornet [08]	USN VFC-12, NAS Oceana, VA	
165789	Boeing F/A-18E Super Hornet [03]	USN VFC-12, NAS Oceana, VA	
165790	Boeing F/A-18E Super Hornet	USN	
165792	Boeing F/A-18E Super Hornet [07]	USN VFC-12, NAS Oceana, VA	
165793	Boeing F/A-18F Super Hornet [DD-215]	USN VX-31, NAWS China Lake, CA	
165794	Boeing F/A-18F Super Hornet [NJ-104]	USN VFA-122, NAS Lemoore, CA	
165795	Boeing F/A-18F Super Hornet [101]	USN NAWDC, NAS Fallon, NV	
165796	Boeing F/A-18F Super Hornet [100]	USN NAWDC, NAS Fallon, NV	
165797	Boeing F/A-18F Super Hornet [AD-211]	USN VFA-106, NAS Oceana, VA	
165798	Boeing F/A-18F Super Hornet [00]	USN NAWDC, NAS Fallon, NV	
165799	Boeing F/A-18F Super Hornet [AD-214]	USN VFA-106, NAS Oceana, VA	
165800	Boeing F/A-18F Super Hornet	USN *Blue Angels,* NAS Pensacola, FL	
165801	Boeing F/A-18F Super Hornet [SD-223]	USN VX-23, NAS Patuxent River, MD	
165802	Boeing F/A-18F Super Hornet [NJ-100]	USN VFA-122, NAS Lemoore, CA	
165803	Boeing F/A-18F Super Hornet [AD-215]	USN VFA-106, NAS Oceana, VA	
165804	Boeing F/A-18F Super Hornet [AD-222]	USN VFA-106, NAS Oceana, VA	
165805	Boeing F/A-18F Super Hornet	USN *Blue Angels,* NAS Pensacola, FL	
165806	Boeing F/A-18F Super Hornet [AD-220]	USN VFA-106, NAS Oceana, VA	
165807	Boeing F/A-18F Super Hornet [NJ-106]	USN VFA-122, NAS Lemoore, CA	
165808	Boeing F/A-18F Super Hornet [20]	USN VFC-12, NAS Oceana, VA	

Notes	Serial	Type (code/other identity)	Owner/operator, location or fate
	165860	Boeing F/A-18E Super Hornet [NJ-206]	USN VFA-122, NAS Lemoore, CA
	165861	Boeing F/A-18E Super Hornet [AD-103]	USN VFA-106, NAS Oceana, VA
	165862	Boeing F/A-18E Super Hornet [AB-406]	USN VFA-81, NAS Oceana, VA
	165864	Boeing F/A-18E Super Hornet [NJ-213]	USN VFA-122, NAS Lemoore, CA
	165866	Boeing F/A-18E Super Hornet [AD-116]	USN VFA-37, NAS Oceana, VA
	165867	Boeing F/A-18E Super Hornet [05]	USN VFC-12, NAS Oceana, VA
	165868	Boeing F/A-18E Super Hornet [06]	USN VFC-12, NAS Oceana, VA
	165869	Boeing F/A-18E Super Hornet [NJ-212]	USN VFA-122, NAS Lemoore, CA
	165870	Boeing F/A-18E Super Hornet [AG-411]	USN VFA-103, NAS Oceana, VA
	165871	Boeing F/A-18E Super Hornet [AB-402]	USN VFA-81, NAS Oceana, VA
	165872	Boeing F/A-18E Super Hornet [AD-120]	USN VFA-106, NAS Oceana, VA
	165873	Boeing F/A-18E Super Hornet	USN
	165874	Boeing F/A-18E Super Hornet [NJ-225]	USN VFA-122, NAS Lemoore, CA
	165875	Boeing F/A-18F Super Hornet [AD-122]	USN VFA-106, NAS Oceana, VA
	165876	Boeing F/A-18F Super Hornet [AD-242]	USN VFA-106, NAS Oceana, VA
	165878	Boeing F/A-18F Super Hornet [NJ-107]	USN VFA-122, NAS Lemoore, CA
	165879	Boeing F/A-18F Super Hornet	USN
	165880	Boeing F/A-18F Super Hornet [AD-240]	USN VFA-106, NAS Oceana, VA
	165882	Boeing F/A-18F Super Hornet [AD-251]	USN VFA-106, NAS Oceana, VA
	165883	Boeing F/A-18F Super Hornet [AD-243]	USN VFA-106, NAS Oceana, VA
	165884	Boeing F/A-18F Super Hornet	USN
	165885	Boeing F/A-18F Super Hornet	USN *Blue Angels,* NAS Pensacola, FL
	165886	Boeing F/A-18F Super Hornet [NJ-110]	USN VFA-122, NAS Lemoore, CA
	165887	Boeing F/A-18F Super Hornet [AD-206]	USN VFA-106, NAS Oceana, VA
	165890	Boeing F/A-18F Super Hornet [21]	USN VFC-12, NAS Oceana, VA
	165891	Boeing F/A-18F Super Hornet [NJ-141]	USN VFA-122, NAS Lemoore, CA
	165892	Boeing F/A-18F Super Hornet [AD-245]	USN VFA-106, NAS Oceana, VA
	165893	Boeing F/A-18F Super Hornet [NJ-142]	USN VFA-122, NAS Lemoore, CA
	165894	Boeing F/A-18F Super Hornet [AD-246]	USN VFA-106, NAS Oceana, VA
	165896	Boeing F/A-18E Super Hornet [04]	USN VFC-12, NAS Oceana, VA
	165897	Boeing F/A-18E Super Hornet [AJ-300]	USN VFA-31, NAS Oceana, VA
	165898	Boeing F/A-18E Super Hornet	USN
	165899	Boeing F/A-18E Super Hornet	USN
	165901	Boeing F/A-18E Super Hornet	USN
	165902	Boeing F/A-18E Super Hornet [NJ-210]	USN VFA-122, NAS Lemoore, CA
	165903	Boeing F/A-18E Super Hornet	USN
	165907	Boeing F/A-18E Super Hornet	USN
	165909	Boeing F/A-18E Super Hornet [AD-113]	USN VFA-106, NAS Oceana, VA
	165910	Boeing F/A-18F Super Hornet [22]	USN VFC-12, NAS Oceana, VA
	165911	Boeing F/A-18F Super Hornet [NJ-127]	USN VFA-122, NAS Lemoore, CA
	165912	Boeing F/A-18F Super Hornet [AD-204]	USN VFA-106, NAS Oceana, VA
	165913	Boeing F/A-18F Super Hornet [AD-227]	USN VFA-106, NAS Oceana, VA
	165914	Boeing F/A-18F Super Hornet [NJ-126]	USN VFA-122, NAS Lemoore, CA
	165915	Boeing F/A-18F Super Hornet [NJ-116]	USN VFA-122, NAS Lemoore, CA
	165916	Boeing F/A-18F Super Hornet [NJ-112]	USN VFA-122, NAS Lemoore, CA
	165917	Boeing F/A-18F Super Hornet [AD-205]	USN VFA-106, NAS Oceana, VA
	165918	Boeing F/A-18F Super Hornet [NJ-117]	USN VFA-122, NAS Lemoore, CA
	165919	Boeing F/A-18F Super Hornet [NJ-113]	USN VFA-122, NAS Lemoore, CA
	165920	Boeing F/A-18F Super Hornet [NJ-124]	USN VFA-122, NAS Lemoore, CA
	165921	Boeing F/A-18F Super Hornet [NJ-153]	USN VFA-122, NAS Lemoore, CA
	165922	Boeing F/A-18F Super Hornet [NJ-101]	USN VFA-122, NAS Lemoore, CA
	165923	Boeing F/A-18F Super Hornet [NJ-164]	USN VFA-122, NAS Lemoore, CA
	165924	Boeing F/A-18F Super Hornet [NJ-115]	USN VFA-122, NAS Lemoore, CA
	165925	Boeing F/A-18F Super Hornet [NJ-154]	USN VFA-122, NAS Lemoore, CA
	165926	Boeing F/A-18F Super Hornet [NJ-122]	USN VFA-122, NAS Lemoore, CA
	165927	Boeing F/A-18F Super Hornet [NJ-127]	USN VFA-122, NAS Lemoore, CA
	165928	Boeing F/A-18F Super Hornet [NJ-125]	USN VFA-122, NAS Lemoore, CA
	165929	Boeing F/A-18F Super Hornet [NJ-123]	USN VFA-122, NAS Lemoore, CA
	165930	Boeing F/A-18F Super Hornet [NJ-117]	USN VFA-122, NAS Lemoore, CA
	165931	Boeing F/A-18F Super Hornet [AD-225]	USN VFA-106, NAS Oceana, VA
	165932	Boeing F/A-18F Super Hornet [SD-122]	USN VX-23, NAS Patuxent River, MD
	165934	Boeing F/A-18F Super Hornet [AD-226]	USN VFA-106, NAS Oceana, VA

Serial	Type (code/other identity)	Owner/operator, location or fate	Notes
166420	Boeing F/A-18E Super Hornet	USN	
166421	Boeing F/A-18E Super Hornet [SD-102]	USN VX-23, NAS Patuxent River, MD	
166422	Boeing F/A-18E Super Hornet [AD-122]	USN VFA-106, NAS Oceana, VA	
166423	Boeing F/A-18E Super Hornet [AC-201]	USN VFA-83, NAS Oceana, VA	
166424	Boeing F/A-18E Super Hornet [NJ-200]	USN VFA-122, NAS Lemoore, CA	
166425	Boeing F/A-18E Super Hornet	USN	
166427	Boeing F/A-18E Super Hornet [NJ-217]	USN VFA-122, NAS Lemoore, CA	
166428	Boeing F/A-18E Super Hornet	USN	
166429	Boeing F/A-18E Super Hornet	USN	
166430	Boeing F/A-18E Super Hornet	USN	
166431	Boeing F/A-18E Super Hornet	USN	
166432	Boeing F/A-18E Super Hornet [XE-147]	USN VX-9, NAWS China Lake, CA	
166433	Boeing F/A-18E Super Hornet [NJ-221]	USN VFA-122, NAS Lemoore, CA	
166434	Boeing F/A-18E Super Hornet [AC-206]	USN VFA-83, NAS Oceana, VA	
166436	Boeing F/A-18E Super Hornet	USN	
166437	Boeing F/A-18E Super Hornet [NH-415]	USN VFA-87, NAS Oceana, VA	
166438	Boeing F/A-18E Super Hornet	USN	
166439	Boeing F/A-18E Super Hornet [AC-204]	USN VFA-83, NAS Oceana, VA	
166440	Boeing F/A-18E Super Hornet [NJ-220]	USN VFA-122, NAS Lemoore, CA	
166441	Boeing F/A-18E Super Hornet	USN	
166442	Boeing F/A-18E Super Hornet [NA-404]	USN VFA-146, NAS Lemoore, CA	
166443	Boeing F/A-18E Super Hornet [NA-405]	USN VFA-146, NAS Lemoore, CA	
166444	Boeing F/A-18E Super Hornet [NA-406]	USN VFA-146, NAS Lemoore, CA	
166445	Boeing F/A-18E Super Hornet [NA-407]	USN VFA-146, NAS Lemoore, CA	
166447	Boeing F/A-18E Super Hornet	USN	
166448	Boeing F/A-18E Super Hornet [AC-202]	USN VFA-83, NAS Oceana, VA	
166449	Boeing F/A-18F Super Hornet [SD-121]	USN VX-23, NAS Patuxent River, MD	
166450	Boeing F/A-18F Super Hornet [DD-217]	USN VX-31, NAWS China Lake, CA	
166451	Boeing F/A-18F Super Hornet [DD-218]	USN VX-31, NAWS China Lake, CA	
166452	Boeing F/A-18F Super Hornet [NA-113]	USN VFA-22, NAS Lemoore, CA	
166453	Boeing F/A-18F Super Hornet [AD-264]	USN VFA-106, NAS Oceana, VA	
166454	Boeing F/A-18F Super Hornet [AD-255]	USN VFA-106, NAS Oceana, VA	
166455	Boeing F/A-18F Super Hornet [NJ-137]	USN VFA-122, NAS Lemoore, CA	
166456	Boeing F/A-18F Super Hornet [AD-231]	USN VFA-106, NAS Oceana, VA	
166457	Boeing F/A-18F Super Hornet [NJ-143]	USN VFA-122, NAS Lemoore, CA	
166458	Boeing F/A-18F Super Hornet [AB-100]	USN VFA-11, NAS Oceana, VA	
166460	Boeing F/A-18F Super Hornet [AG-206]	USN VFA-103, NAS Oceana, VA	
166462	Boeing F/A-18F Super Hornet [AD-237]	USN VFA-106, NAS Oceana, VA	
166463	Boeing F/A-18F Super Hornet [NJ-133]	USN VFA-122, NAS Lemoore, CA	
166464	Boeing F/A-18F Super Hornet [NJ-135]	USN VFA-122, NAS Lemoore, CA	
166465	Boeing F/A-18F Super Hornet [AD-261]	USN VFA-106, NAS Oceana, VA	
166466	Boeing F/A-18F Super Hornet [NJ-130]	USN VFA-122, NAS Lemoore, CA	
166467	Boeing F/A-18F Super Hornet [AD-247]	USN VFA-106, NAS Oceana, VA	
166598	Boeing F/A-18E Super Hornet	USN	
166599	Boeing F/A-18E Super Hornet [AC-203]	USN VFA-83, NAS Oceana, VA	
166600	Boeing F/A-18E Super Hornet [AJ-305]	USN VFA-31, NAS Oceana, VA	
166601	Boeing F/A-18E Super Hornet [AD-133]	USN VFA-106, NAS Oceana, VA	
166602	Boeing F/A-18E Super Hornet [AC-412]	USN VFA-105, NAS Oceana, VA	
166604	Boeing F/A-18E Super Hornet	USN	
166605	Boeing F/A-18E Super Hornet [AD-106]	USN VFA-106, NAS Oceana, VA	
166606	Boeing F/A-18E Super Hornet [AJ-306]	USN VFA-31, NAS Oceana, VA	
166607	Boeing F/A-18E Super Hornet [AJ-111]	USN VFA-37, NAS Oceana, VA	
166608	Boeing F/A-18E Super Hornet [AB-302]	USN VFA-81, NAS Oceana, VA	
166609	Boeing F/A-18E Super Hornet [AJ-103]	USN VFA-37, NAS Oceana, VA	
166610	Boeing F/A-18F Super Hornet [AD-210]	USN VFA-106, NAS Oceana, VA	
166611	Boeing F/A-18F Super Hornet [NJ-120]	USN VFA-122, NAS Lemoore, CA	
166612	Boeing F/A-18F Super Hornet [AD-266]	USN VFA-106, NAS Oceana, VA	
166613	Boeing F/A-18F Super Hornet [AD-260]	USN VFA-106, NAS Oceana, VA	
166614	Boeing F/A-18F Super Hornet [NJ-121]	USN VFA-122, NAS Lemoore, CA	
166615	Boeing F/A-18F Super Hornet [AG-201]	USN VFA-103, NAS Oceana, VA	
166617	Boeing F/A-18F Super Hornet [NJ-105]	USN VFA-122, NAS Lemoore, CA	
166618	Boeing F/A-18F Super Hornet [AD-250]	USN VFA-106, NAS Oceana, VA	

US-BASED USN/USMC AIRCRAFT

Notes	Serial	Type (code/other identity)	Owner/operator, location or fate
	166619	Boeing F/A-18F Super Hornet [AD-267]	USN VFA-106, NAS Oceana, VA
	166620	Boeing F/A-18F Super Hornet [AJ-206]	USN VFA-213, NAS Oceana, VA
	166621	Boeing F/A-18F Super Hornet [NJ-136]	USN VFA-122, NAS Lemoore, CA
	166622	Boeing F/A-18F Super Hornet [AD-265]	USN VFA-106, NAS Oceana, VA
	166623	Boeing F/A-18F Super Hornet [AC-110]	USN VFA-32, NAS Oceana, VA
	166624	Boeing F/A-18F Super Hornet [AC-107]	USN VFA-32, NAS Oceana, VA
	166625	Boeing F/A-18F Super Hornet [AJ-202]	USN VFA-213, NAS Oceana, VA
	166626	Boeing F/A-18F Super Hornet [AJ-210]	USN VFA-213, NAS Oceana, VA
	166627	Boeing F/A-18F Super Hornet [AJ-212]	USN VFA-213, NAS Oceana, VA
	166628	Boeing F/A-18F Super Hornet {AC-100]	USN VFA-32, NAS Oceana, VA
	166629	Boeing F/A-18F Super Hornet [AD-235]	USN VFA-106, NAS Oceana, VA
	166630	Boeing F/A-18F Super Hornet [NJ-132]	USN VFA-122, NAS Lemoore, CA
	166631	Boeing F/A-18F Super Hornet [AJ-211]	USN VFA-213, NAS Oceana, VA
	166633	Boeing F/A-18F Super Hornet [AB-107]	USN VFA-11, NAS Oceana, VA
	166634	Boeing F/A-18F Super Hornet [AB-102]	USN VFA-11, NAS Oceana, VA
	166635	Boeing F/A-18F Super Hornet [DD-213]	USN VX-31, NAWS China Lake, CA
	166636	Boeing F/A-18F Super Hornet [AB-103]	USN VFA-11, NAS Oceana, VA
	166638	Boeing F/A-18F Super Hornet [AJ-232]	USN VFA-213, NAS Oceana, VA
	166639	Boeing F/A-18F Super Hornet [AD-253]	USN VFA-106, NAS Oceana, VA
	166640	Boeing F/A-18F Super Hornet [AB-104]	USN VFA-11, NAS Oceana, VA
	166641	Boeing NEA-18G Growler [SD-521]	USN VX-23, NAS Patuxent River, MD
	166642	Boeing NEA-18G Growler [DD-500]	USN VX-31, NAWS China Lake, CA
	166643	Boeing F/A-18E Super Hornet [NJ-243]	USN VFA-122, NAS Lemoore, CA
	166644	Boeing F/A-18E Super Hornet [NA-400]	USN VFA-146, NAS Lemoore, CA
	166646	Boeing F/A-18E Super Hornet [AD-110]	USN VFA-106, NAS Oceana, VA
	166647	Boeing F/A-18E Super Hornet [AG-212]	USN VFA-103, NAS Oceana, VA
	166648	Boeing F/A-18E Super Hornet [AD-101]	USN VFA-106, NAS Oceana, VA
	166649	Boeing F/A-18E Super Hornet [AG-210]	USN VFA-103, NAS Oceana, VA
	166650	Boeing F/A-18E Super Hornet [AC-200]	USN VFA-83, NAS Oceana, VA
	166651	Boeing F/A-18E Super Hornet [AG-201]	USN VFA-83, NAS Oceana, VA
	166652	Boeing F/A-18E Super Hornet [AD-114]	USN VFA-106, NAS Oceana, VA
	166653	Boeing F/A-18E Super Hornet [AJ-331]	USN VFA-31, NAS Oceana, VA
	166654	Boeing F/A-18E Super Hornet [AD-106]	USN VFA-106, NAS Oceana, VA
	166655	Boeing F/A-18E Super Hornet [AC-306]	USN VFA-131, NAS Oceana, VA
	166657	Boeing F/A-18E Super Hornet [AD-115]	USN VFA-106, NAS Oceana, VA
	166658	Boeing F/A-18F Super Hornet [AB-105]	USN VFA-11, NAS Oceana, VA
	166659	Boeing F/A-18F Super Hornet [NG-111]	USN VFA-41, NAS Oceana, VA
	166660	Boeing F/A-18F Super Hornet [AD-233]	USN VFA-106, NAS Oceana, VA
	166661	Boeing F/A-18F Super Hornet [NG-106]	USN VFA-41, NAS Oceana, VA
	166662	Boeing F/A-18F Super Hornet [AJ-201]	USN VFA-213, NAS Oceana, VA
	166663	Boeing F/A-18F Super Hornet [AD-230]	USN VFA-106, NAS Oceana, VA
	166664	Boeing F/A-18F Super Hornet [AJ-205]	USN VFA-213, NAS Oceana, VA
	166665	Boeing F/A-18F Super Hornet [AD-250]	USN VFA-106, NAS Oceana, VA
	166666	Boeing F/A-18F Super Hornet [NJ-166]	USN VFA-122, NAS Lemoore, CA
	166667	Boeing F/A-18F Super Hornet [NH-101]	USN VFA-154, NAS Lemoore, CA
	166668	Boeing F/A-18F Super Hornet	USN
	166669	Boeing F/A-18F Super Hornet [AB-106]	USN VFA-11, NAS Oceana, VA
	166670	Boeing F/A-18F Super Hornet [AD-262]	USN VFA-106, NAS Oceana, VA
	166671	Boeing F/A-18F Super Hornet	USN
	166672	Boeing F/A-18F Super Hornet	USN
	166673	Boeing F/A-18F Super Hornet [XE-1] $	USN VX-9, NAWS China Lake, CA
	166674	Boeing F/A-18F Super Hornet [AD-234]	USN VFA-106, NAS Oceana, VA
	166675	Boeing F/A-18F Super Hornet	USN
	166676	Boeing F/A-18F Super Hornet [NA-107]	USN VFA-22, NAS Lemoore, CA
	166677	Boeing F/A-18F Super Hornet [AG-102]	USN VFA-103, NAS Oceana, VA
	166678	Boeing F/A-18F Super Hornet [AD-263]	USN VFA-106, NAS Oceana, VA
	166679	Boeing F/A-18F Super Hornet [AD-256]	USN VFA-106, NAS Oceana, VA
	166680	Boeing F/A-18F Super Hornet [NE-101]	USN VFA-2, NAS Lemoore, CA
	166681	Boeing F/A-18F Super Hornet [AD-223]	USN VFA-106, NAS Oceana, VA
	166682	Boeing F/A-18F Super Hornet [AJ-204]	USN VFA-213, NAS Oceana, VA
	166684	Boeing F/A-18F Super Hornet [AD-236]	USN VFA-106, NAS Oceana, VA
	166775	Boeing F/A-18E Super Hornet [AC-207]	USN VFA-83, NAS Oceana, VA

Serial	Type (code/other identity)	Owner/operator, location or fate	Notes
166776	Boeing F/A-18E Super Hornet [AB-406]	USN VFA-81, NAS Oceana, VA	
166777	Boeing F/A-18E Super Hornet [AB-307]	USN VFA-81, NAS Oceana, VA	
166778	Boeing F/A-18E Super Hornet [AJ-302]	USN VFA-31, NAS Oceana, VA	
166779	Boeing F/A-18E Super Hornet	USN	
166780	Boeing F/A-18E Super Hornet	USN	
166781	Boeing F/A-18E Super Hornet [AD-107]	USN VFA-106, NAS Oceana, VA	
166782	Boeing F/A-18E Super Hornet [NA-410]	USN VFA-146, NAS Lemoore, CA	
166783	Boeing F/A-18E Super Hornet [AB-403]	USN VFA-81, NAS Oceana, VA	
166784	Boeing F/A-18E Super Hornet [AJ-310]	USN VFA-31, NAS Oceana, VA	
166785	Boeing F/A-18E Super Hornet [AG-114]	USN VFA-105, NAS Oceana, VA	
166786	Boeing F/A-18E Super Hornet [AJ-312]	USN VFA-31, NAS Oceana, VA	
166787	Boeing F/A-18E Super Hornet	USN	
166788	Boeing F/A-18E Super Hornet [AB-210]	USN VFA-143, NAS Oceana, VA	
166789	Boeing F/A-18E Super Hornet [AG-311]	USN VFA-83, NAS Oceana, VA	
166790	Boeing F/A-18F Super Hornet [NJ-111]	USN VFA-122, NAS Lemoore, CA	
166791	Boeing F/A-18F Super Hornet [XE-260]	USN VX-9, NAWS China Lake, CA	
166792	Boeing F/A-18F Super Hornet [AD-254]	USN VFA-106, NAS Oceana, VA	
166793	Boeing F/A-18F Super Hornet [AJ-203]	USN VFA-213, NAS Oceana, VA	
166796	Boeing F/A-18F Super Hornet [NE-112]	USN VFA-2, NAS Lemoore, CA	
166797	Boeing F/A-18F Super Hornet [NF-101]	USN VFA-102, MCAS Iwakuni, Japan	
166799	Boeing F/A-18F Super Hornet [NJ-170]	USN VFA-122, NAS Lemoore, CA	
166800	Boeing F/A-18F Super Hornet [NE-107]	USN VFA-2, NAS Lemoore, CA	
166802	Boeing F/A-18F Super Hornet [AG-204]	USN VFA-103, NAS Oceana, VA	
166803	Boeing F/A-18F Super Hornet	USN	
166804	Boeing F/A-18F Super Hornet [NE-100]	USN VFA-2, NAS Lemoore, CA	
166805	Boeing F/A-18F Super Hornet [AD-232]	USN VFA-106, NAS Oceana, VA	
166806	Boeing F/A-18F Super Hornet [NE-105]	USN VFA-2, NAS Lemoore, CA	
166808	Boeing F/A-18F Super Hornet [NJ-167]	USN VFA-122, NAS Lemoore, CA	
166809	Boeing F/A-18F Super Hornet [AD-244]	USN VFA-106, NAS Oceana, VA	
166810	Boeing F/A-18F Super Hornet [NJ-171]	USN VFA-122, NAS Lemoore, CA	
166811	Boeing F/A-18F Super Hornet [NE-111]	USN VFA-2, NAS Lemoore, CA	
166812	Boeing F/A-18F Super Hornet [AG-103]	USN VFA-103, NAS Oceana, VA	
166815	Boeing F/A-18F Super Hornet [AC-102]	USN VFA-32, NAS Oceana, VA	
166816	Boeing F/A-18F Super Hornet [AD-252]	USN VFA-106, NAS Oceana, VA	
166817	Boeing F/A-18E Super Hornet [AB-400]	USN VFA-136, NAS Lemoore, CA	
166818	Boeing F/A-18E Super Hornet [AB-401]	USN VFA-136, NAS Lemoore, CA	
166819	Boeing F/A-18E Super Hornet [AG-205]	USN VFA-83, NAS Oceana, VA	
166820	Boeing F/A-18E Super Hornet [AB-402]	USN VFA-136, NAS Lemoore, CA	
166821	Boeing F/A-18E Super Hornet [AB-403]	USN VFA-136, NAS Lemoore, CA	
166822	Boeing F/A-18E Super Hornet [NJ-201]	USN VFA-122, NAS Lemoore, CA	
166823	Boeing F/A-18E Super Hornet [AB-404]	USN VFA-136, NAS Lemoore, CA	
166824	Boeing F/A-18E Super Hornet [AB-405]	USN VFA-136, NAS Lemoore, CA	
166825	Boeing F/A-18E Super Hornet [AB-406]	USN VFA-136, NAS Lemoore, CA	
166826	Boeing F/A-18E Super Hornet [AB-407]	USN VFA-136, NAS Lemoore, CA	
166827	Boeing F/A-18E Super Hornet [AB-410]	USN VFA-136, NAS Lemoore, CA	
166828	Boeing F/A-18E Super Hornet [NG-400]	USN VFA-151, NAS Lemoore, CA	
166829	Boeing F/A-18E Super Hornet [AB-411]	USN VFA-136, NAS Lemoore, CA	
166830	Boeing F/A-18E Super Hornet [NA-312]	USN VFA-137, NAS Lemoore, CA	
166832	Boeing F/A-18E Super Hornet [AD-245]	USN VFA-106, NAS Oceana, VA	
166833	Boeing F/A-18E Super Hornet [AC-411]	USN VFA-105, NAS Oceana, VA	
166834	Boeing F/A-18E Super Hornet [AJ-105]	USN VFA-37, NAS Oceana, VA	
166835	Boeing F/A-18E Super Hornet [AC-413]	USN VFA-105, NAS Oceana, VA	
166836	Boeing F/A-18E Super Hornet [AJ-106]	USN VFA-37, NAS Oceana, VA	
166837	Boeing F/A-18E Super Hornet [AJ-300]	USN VFA-31, NAS Oceana, VA	
166838	Boeing F/A-18E Super Hornet [AJ-303]	USN VFA-31, NAS Oceana, VA	
166839	Boeing F/A-18E Super Hornet [AJ-304]	USN VFA-31, NAS Oceana, VA	
166840	Boeing F/A-18E Super Hornet [AJ-307]	USN VFA-31, NAS Oceana, VA	
166841	Boeing F/A-18E Super Hornet [NF-302]	USN VFA-115, MCAS Iwakuni, Japan	
166842	Boeing F/A-18F Super Hornet	USN	
166843	Boeing F/A-18F Super Hornet [DD-223]	USN VX-31, NAWS China Lake, CA	
166844	Boeing F/A-18F Super Hornet [AD-254]	USN VFA-106, NAS Oceana, VA	
166845	Boeing F/A-18F Super Hornet [NH-110]	USN VFA-154, NAS Lemoore, CA	

Notes	Serial	Type (code/other identity)	Owner/operator, location or fate
	166846	Boeing F/A-18F Super Hornet [NG-103]	USN VFA-41, NAS Lemoore, CA
	166847	Boeing F/A-18F Super Hornet [NG-104]	USN VFA-41, NAS Lemoore, CA
	166848	Boeing F/A-18F Super Hornet [NJ-173]	USN VFA-122, NAS Lemoore, CA
	166849	Boeing F/A-18F Super Hornet [NJ-131]	USN VFA-122, NAS Lemoore, CA
	166850	Boeing F/A-18F Super Hornet [NJ-174]	USN VFA-122, NAS Lemoore, CA
	166851	Boeing F/A-18F Super Hornet [NG-110]	USN VFA-41, NAS Lemoore, CA
	166853	Boeing F/A-18F Super Hornet [NG-112]	USN VFA-41, NAS Lemoore, CA
	166854	Boeing F/A-18F Super Hornet [NG-113]	USN VFA-41, NAS Lemoore, CA
	166855	Boeing EA-18G Growler [XE-500]	USN VX-9, NAWS China Lake, CA
	166857	Boeing EA-18G Growler [XE-502]	USN VX-9, NAWS China Lake, CA
	166858	Boeing EA-18G Growler [NL-540]	USN VAQ-132, NAS Whidbey Island, WA
	166859	Boeing F/A-18E Super Hornet [NF-300]	USN VFA-115, MCAS Iwakuni, Japan
	166860	Boeing F/A-18E Super Hornet [NF-301]	USN VFA-115, MCAS Iwakuni, Japan
	166861	Boeing F/A-18E Super Hornet [110]	USN NAWDC, NAS Fallon, NV
	166862	Boeing F/A-18E Super Hornet [NF-303]	USN VFA-115, MCAS Iwakuni, Japan
	166863	Boeing F/A-18E Super Hornet {NF-304]	USN VFA-115, MCAS Iwakuni, Japan
	166864	Boeing F/A-18E Super Hornet {NF-305]	USN VFA-115, MCAS Iwakuni, Japan
	166865	Boeing F/A-18E Super Hornet [NF-306]	USN VFA-115, MCAS Iwakuni, Japan
	166866	Boeing F/A-18E Super Hornet {NF-307]	USN VFA-115, MCAS Iwakuni, Japan
	166867	Boeing F/A-18E Super Hornet [AJ-107]	USN VFA-37, NAS Oceana, VA
	166868	Boeing F/A-18E Super Hornet [NF-411]	USN VFA-195, MCAS Iwakuni, Japan
	166869	Boeing F/A-18E Super Hornet [NF-311]	USN VFA-115, MCAS Iwakuni, Japan
	166870	Boeing F/A-18E Super Hornet	USN
	166871	Boeing F/A-18E Super Hornet [DD-200]	USN VX-31, NAWS China Lake, CA
	166872	Boeing F/A-18E Super Hornet [AJ-301]	USN VFA-31, NAS Oceana, VA
	166873	Boeing F/A-18F Super Hornet [NA-111]	USN VFA-22, NAS Lemoore, CA
	166874	Boeing F/A-18F Super Hornet [NE-104]	USN VFA-2, NAS Lemoore, CA
	166875	Boeing F/A-18F Super Hornet [NF-100]	USN VFA-102, MCAS Iwakuni, Japan
	166876	Boeing F/A-18F Super Hornet [NG-100]	USN VFA-41, NAS Lemoore, CA
	166877	Boeing F/A-18F Super Hornet [NE-103]	USN VFA-146, NAS Lemoore, CA
	166879	Boeing F/A-18F Super Hornet [AG-205]	USN VFA-103, NAS Oceana, VA
	166880	Boeing F/A-18F Super Hornet	USN
	166881	Boeing F/A-18F Super Hornet [AC-132]	USN VFA-32, NAS Oceana, VA
	166882	Boeing F/A-18F Super Hornet [NH-111]	USN VFA-154, NAS Lemoore, CA
	166883	Boeing F/A-18F Super Hornet [113]	USN
	166884	Boeing F/A-18F Super Hornet [AG-106]	USN VFA-103, NAS Oceana, VA
	166885	Boeing F/A-18F Super Hornet [AC-106]	USN VFA-32, NAS Oceana, VA
	166886	Boeing F/A-18F Super Hornet [NJ-172]	USN VFA-122, NAS Lemoore, CA
	166887	Boeing F/A-18F Super Hornet [NF-110]	USN VFA-102, MCAS Iwakuni, Japan
	166889	Boeing F/A-18F Super Hornet [AG-107]	USN VFA-103, NAS Oceana, VA
	166890	Boeing F/A-18F Super Hornet [NF-102]	USN VFA-102, MCAS Iwakuni, Japan
	166891	Boeing F/A-18F Super Hornet [NG-110]	USN VFA-25, NAS Lemoore, CA
	166892	Boeing F/A-18F Super Hornet [NF-116]	USN VFA-102, MCAS Iwakuni, Japan
	166893	Boeing EA-18G Growler [AC-504]	USN VAQ-130, NAS Whidbey Island, WA
	166894	Boeing EA-18G Growler [NJ-556]	USN VAQ-129, NAS Whidbey Island, WA
	166895	Boeing EA-18G Growler [NJ-525]	USN VAQ-129, NAS Whidbey Island, WA
	166896	Boeing EA-18G Growler [AF-500]	USN VAQ-209, NAS Whidbey Island, WA
	166897	Boeing EA-18G Growler [NE-507]	USN VAQ-136, NAS Whidbey Island, WA
	166898	Boeing EA-18G Growler [501]	USN NAWDC, NAS Fallon, NV
	166899	Boeing EA-18G Growler [AF-501]	USN VAQ-209, NAS Whidbey Island, WA
	166900	Boeing EA-18G Growler [NL-514]	USN VAQ-138, NAS Whidbey Island, WA
	166901	Boeing F/A-18E Super Hornet [NF-400]	USN VFA-195, MCAS Iwakuni, Japan
	166902	Boeing F/A-18E Super Hornet [NF-401]	USN VFA-195, MCAS Iwakuni, Japan
	166903	Boeing F/A-18E Super Hornet [NF-402]	USN VFA-195, MCAS Iwakuni, Japan
	166904	Boeing F/A-18E Super Hornet [AJ-110]	USN VFA-37, NAS Oceana, VA
	166905	Boeing F/A-18E Super Hornet [AB-205]	USN VFA-143, NAS Oceana, VA
	166906	Boeing F/A-18E Super Hornet [AB-206]	USN VFA-143, NAS Oceana, VA
	166907	Boeing F/A-18E Super Hornet [NF-404]	USN VFA-195, MCAS Iwakuni, Japan
	166908	Boeing F/A-18E Super Hornet [NF-405]	USN VFA-195, MCAS Iwakuni, Japan
	166909	Boeing F/A-18E Super Hornet [NF-406]	USN VFA-195, MCAS Iwakuni, Japan
	166910	Boeing F/A-18E Super Hornet [NF-407]	USN VFA-195, MCAS Iwakuni, Japan
	166911	Boeing F/A-18E Super Hornet	USN

Serial	Type (code/other identity)	Owner/operator, location or fate	Notes
166912	Boeing F/A-18E Super Hornet [NF-411]	USN VFA-195, MCAS Iwakuni, Japan	
166913	Boeing F/A-18E Super Hornet [NF-412]	USN VFA-195, MCAS Iwakuni, Japan	
166914	Boeing F/A-18E Super Hornet [NF-410]	USN VFA-195, MCAS Iwakuni, Japan	
166915	Boeing F/A-18F Super Hornet	USN	
166916	Boeing F/A-18F Super Hornet	USN	
166917	Boeing F/A-18F Super Hornet [AD-205]	USN VFA-106, NAS Lemoore, CA	
166918	Boeing F/A-18F Super Hornet [NF-103]	USN VFA-102, MCAS Iwakuni, Japan	
166919	Boeing F/A-18F Super Hornet	USN	
166920	Boeing F/A-18F Super Hornet [NF-105]	USN VFA-102, MCAS Iwakuni, Japan	
166921	Boeing F/A-18F Super Hornet [NF-106]	USN VFA-102, MCAS Iwakuni, Japan	
166922	Boeing F/A-18F Super Hornet [NF-107]	USN VFA-102, MCAS Iwakuni, Japan	
166923	Boeing F/A-18F Super Hornet [NF-104]	USN VFA-102, MCAS Iwakuni, Japan	
166924	Boeing F/A-18F Super Hornet [NF-111]	USN VFA-102, MCAS Iwakuni, Japan	
166925	Boeing F/A-18F Super Hornet [XE-230]	USN VX-9, NAWS China Lake, CA	
166926	Boeing F/A-18F Super Hornet [AD-257]	USN VFA-106, NAS Lemoore, CA	
166927	Boeing F/A-18F Super Hornet [XE-231]	USN VX-9 China Lake, CA	
166928	Boeing EA-18G Growler [NE-500]	USN VAQ-136, NAS Whidbey Island, WA	
166929	Boeing EA-18G Growler [NL-541]	USN VAQ-132, NAS Whidbey Island, WA	
166930	Boeing EA-18G Growler [NJ-543]	USN VAQ-129, NAS Whidbey Island, WA	
166931	Boeing EA-18G Growler [AB-500]	USN VAQ-144, NAS Whidbey Island, WA	
166932	Boeing EA-18G Growler [NL-542]	USN VAQ-132, NAS Whidbey Island, WA	
166933	Boeing EA-18G Growler	USN	
166934	Boeing EA-18G Growler [NJ-521]	USN VAQ-129, NAS Whidbey Island, WA	
166935	Boeing EA-18G Growler [NE-506]	USN VAQ-136, NAS Whidbey Island, WA	
166936	Boeing EA-18G Growler [NL-513]	USN VAQ-138, NAS Whidbey Island, WA	
166937	Boeing EA-18G Growler [NJ-531]	USN VAQ-129, NAS Whidbey Island, WA	
166938	Boeing EA-18G Growler [NL-551]	USN VAQ-131, NAS Whidbey Island, WA	
166939	Boeing EA-18G Growler [NF-501]	USN VAQ-141, MCAS Iwakuni, Japan	
166940	Boeing EA-18G Growler [504]	USN NAWDC, NAS Fallon, NV	
166941	Boeing EA-18G Growler [NJ-555]	USN VAQ-129, NAS Whidbey Island, WA	
166942	Boeing EA-18G Growler [NL-550]	USN VAQ-131, NAS Whidbey Island, WA	
166943	Boeing EA-18G Growler [AJ-500]	USN VAQ-142, NAS Whidbey Island, WA	
166944	Boeing EA-18G Growler [NF-502]	USN VAQ-141, NAS Whidbey Island, WA	
166945	Boeing EA-18G Growler [NL-534]	USN VAQ-134, NAS Whidbey Island, WA	
166946	Boeing EA-18G Growler [NL-533]	USN VAQ-134, NAS Whidbey Island, WA	
166947	Boeing F/A-18E Super Hornet [AB-300]	USN VFA-81, NAS Oceana, VA	
166948	Boeing F/A-18E Super Hornet [NG-206]	USN VFA-14, NAS Lemoore, CA	
166949	Boeing F/A-18E Super Hornet [AB-311]	USN VFA-81, NAS Oceana, VA	
166950	Boeing F/A-18E Super Hornet [AB-303]	USN VFA-81, NAS Oceana, VA	
166951	Boeing F/A-18E Super Hornet [AB-301]	USN VFA-81, NAS Lemoore, CA	
166952	Boeing F/A-18E Super Hornet [AJ-302]	USN VFA-31, NAS Oceana, VA	
166953	Boeing F/A-18E Super Hornet [AG-303]	USN VFA-86, NAS Lemoore, CA	
166954	Boeing F/A-18E Super Hornet [NG-202]	USN VFA-14, NAS Lemoore, CA	
166955	Boeing F/A-18E Super Hornet [AB-306]	USN VFA-81, NAS Oceana, VA	
166956	Boeing F/A-18E Super Hornet [AB-310]	USN VFA-81, NAS Oceana, VA	
166957	Boeing F/A-18E Super Hornet [XE-111]	USN VX-9, NAWS China Lake, CA	
166958	Boeing F/A-18E Super Hornet [AB-304]	USN VFA-81, NAS Lemoore, CA	
166959	Boeing F/A-18E Super Hornet [AB-214]	USN VFA-143, NAS Oceana, VA	
166960	Boeing F/A-18E Super Hornet [NH-201]	USN VFA-211, NAS Oceana, VA	
166961	Boeing F/A-18F Super Hornet [NA-100]	USN VFA-22, NAS Lemoore, CA	
166962	Boeing F/A-18F Super Hornet [NE-106]	USN VFA-2, NAS Lemoore, CA	
166963	Boeing F/A-18F Super Hornet [NA-110]	USN VFA-22, NAS Lemoore, CA	
166964	Boeing F/A-18F Super Hornet [XE-433]	USN VX-9, NAWS China Lake, CA	
166965	Boeing F/A-18F Super Hornet [NA-103]	USN VFA-22, NAS Lemoore, CA	
166967	Boeing F/A-18F Super Hornet [NE-112]	USN VFA-2, NAS Lemoore, CA	
166968	Boeing F/A-18F Super Hornet [DD-225]	USN VX-31, NAWS China Lake, CA	
166969	Boeing F/A-18F Super Hornet [SD-123]	USN VX-23, NAS Patuxent River, MD	
166970	Boeing F/A-18F Super Hornet [NA-105]	USN VFA-22, NAS Lemoore, CA	
166971	Boeing F/A-18F Super Hornet [NA-106]	USN VFA-22, NAS Lemoore, CA	
166972	Boeing F/A-18F Super Hornet [NE-110]	USN VFA-2, NAS Lemoore, CA	
166973	Boeing F/A-18F Super Hornet [NA-102]	USN VFA-22, NAS Lemoore, CA	
166974	Boeing F/A-18F Super Hornet [NF-113]	USN VFA-102, MCAS Iwakuni, Japan	

US-BASED USN/USMC AIRCRAFT

Notes	Serial	Type (code/other identity)	Owner/operator, location or fate
	166975	Boeing F/A-18F Super Hornet [NA-101]	USN VFA-22, NAS Lemoore, CA
	166977	Boeing F/A-18F Super Hornet [NA-104]	USN VFA-22, NAS Lemoore, CA
	166978	Boeing F/A-18F Super Hornet [AG-113]	USN VFA-32, NAS Oceana, VA
	166979	Boeing F/A-18F Super Hornet [NE-101]	USN VFA-2, NAS Lemoore, CA
	166980	Boeing F/A-18F Super Hornet [XE-222]	USN VX-9, NAWS China Lake, CA
	166981	Boeing F/A-18F Super Hornet	USN
	166982	Boeing F/A-18F Super Hornet [NJ-147]	USN VFA-122, NAS Lemoore, CA
	168250	Boeing EA-18G Growler [NJ-527]	USN VAQ-129, NAS Whidbey Island, WA
	168251	Boeing EA-18G Growler [AF-502]	USN VAQ-209, NAS Whidbey Island, WA
	168252	Boeing EA-18G Growler [NJ-540]	USN VAQ-129, NAS Whidbey Island, WA
	168253	Boeing EA-18G Growler [AG-501]	USN VAQ-140, NAS Whidbey Island, WA
	168254	Boeing EA-18G Growler [NG-501]	USN VAQ-133, NAS Whidbey Island, WA
	168255	Boeing EA-18G Growler [NL-510]	USN VAQ-138, NAS Whidbey Island, WA
	168256	Boeing EA-18G Growler [NA-500]	USN VAQ-139, NAS Whidbey Island, WA
	168257	Boeing EA-18G Growler [NJ-520]	USN VAQ-129, NAS Whidbey Island, WA
	168258	Boeing EA-18G Growler [AB-501]	USN VAQ-144, NAS Whidbey Island, WA
	168259	Boeing EA-18G Growler [NL-534]	USN VAQ-134, NAS Whidbey Island, WA
	168260	Boeing EA-18G Growler [NA-504]	USN VAQ-139, NAS Whidbey Island, WA
	168261	Boeing EA-18G Growler [NL-511]	USN VAQ-138, NAS Whidbey Island, WA
	168262	Boeing EA-18G Growler [NL-516]	USN VAQ-129, NAS Whidbey Island, WA
	168263	Boeing EA-18G Growler [AG-501]	USN VAQ-140, NAS Whidbey Island, WA
	168264	Boeing EA-18G Growler [NL-552]	USN VAQ-131, NAS Whidbey Island, WA
	168265	Boeing EA-18G Growler [NL-525]	USN VAQ-135, NAS Whidbey Island, WA
	168266	Boeing EA-18G Growler [NH-500]	USN VAQ-137, NAS Whidbey Island, WA
	168267	Boeing EA-18G Growler [NH-500]	USN VAQ-137, NAS Whidbey Island, WA
	168268	Boeing EA-18G Growler [AC-500]	USN VAQ-130, NAS Whidbey Island, WA
	168269	Boeing EA-18G Growler [NJ-515]	USN VAQ-129, NAS Whidbey Island, WA
	168270	Boeing EA-18G Growler [505]	USN NAWDC, NAS Fallon, NV
	168271	Boeing EA-18G Growler [AJ-503]	USN VAQ-142, NAS Whidbey Island, WA
	168272	Boeing EA-18G Growler [NG-506]	USN VAQ-133, NAS Whidbey Island, WA
	168273	Boeing EA-18G Growler [NH-502]	USN VAQ-137, NAS Whidbey Island, WA
	168274	Boeing EA-18G Growler [500]	USN NAWDC, NAS Fallon, NV
	168353	Boeing F/A-18E Super Hornet [NG-210]	USN VFA-14, NAS Lemoore, CA
	168354	Boeing F/A-18E Super Hornet [AB-201]	USN VFA-143, NAS Oceana, VA
	168355	Boeing F/A-18E Super Hornet [AB-200]	USN VFA-143, NAS Oceana, VA
	168356	Boeing F/A-18E Super Hornet [AB-211]	USN VFA-143, NAS Oceana, VA
	168357	Boeing F/A-18E Super Hornet [AB-212]	USN VFA-143, NAS Oceana, VA
	168358	Boeing F/A-18E Super Hornet [NH-203]	USN VFA-211, NAS Oceana, VA
	168359	Boeing F/A-18E Super Hornet [NH-204]	USN VFA-211, NAS Oceana, VA
	168360	Boeing F/A-18E Super Hornet [AJ-311]	USN VFA-31, NAS Oceana, VA
	168361	Boeing F/A-18E Super Hornet [AB-412]	USN VFA-81, NAS Oceana, VA
	168362	Boeing F/A-18E Super Hornet [NF-403]	USN VFA-195, MCAS Iwakuni, Japan
	168363	Boeing F/A-18E Super Hornet [NF-200]	USN VFA-27, MCAS Iwakuni, Japan
	168364	Boeing F/A-18E Super Hornet [NF-202]	USN VFA-27, MCAS Iwakuni, Japan
	168365	Boeing F/A-18E Super Hornet [NF-203]	USN VFA-27, MCAS Iwakuni, Japan
	168366	Boeing F/A-18E Super Hornet [NF-204]	USN VFA-27, MCAS Iwakuni, Japan
	168367	Boeing F/A-18E Super Hornet [NF-205]	USN VFA-27, MCAS Iwakuni, Japan
	168368	Boeing F/A-18E Super Hornet [NF-206]	USN VFA-27, MCAS Iwakuni, Japan
	168369	Boeing F/A-18E Super Hornet [NF-407]	USN VFA-195, MCAS Iwakuni, Japan
	168370	Boeing F/A-18F Super Hornet [DD-227]	USN VX-31, NAWS China Lake, CA
	168372	Boeing EA-18G Growler [NA-501]	USN VAQ-139, NAS Whidbey Island, WA
	168373	Boeing EA-18G Growler [NL-552]	USN VAQ-131, NAS Whidbey Island, WA
	168374	Boeing EA-18G Growler [NF-503]	USN VAQ-141, MCAS Iwakuni, Japan
	168375	Boeing EA-18G Growler [NJ-512]	USN VAQ-129, NAS Whidbey Island, WA
	168376	Boeing EA-18G Growler [NJ-551]	USN VAQ-129, NAS Whidbey Island, WA
	168377	Boeing EA-18G Growler [NF-504]	USN VAQ-141, MCAS Iwakuni, Japan
	168378	Boeing EA-18G Growler [NJ-573]	USN VAQ-129, NAS Whidbey Island, WA
	168379	Boeing EA-18G Growler [NJ-524]	USN VAQ-129, NAS Whidbey Island, WA
	168380	Boeing EA-18G Growler [NL-532]	USN VAQ-134, NAS Whidbey Island, WA
	168381	Boeing EA-18G Growler [NL-543]	USN VAQ-134, NAS Whidbey Island, WA
	168382	Boeing EA-18G Growler [NG-503]	USN VAQ-133, NAS Whidbey Island, WA
	168383	Boeing EA-18G Growler [AB-502]	USN VAQ-144, NAS Whidbey Island, WA

Serial	Type (code/other identity)	Owner/operator, location or fate	Notes
168384	Boeing EA-18G Growler [XE-500]	USN VX-9, NAWS China Lake, CA	
168385	Boeing EA-18G Growler [AJ-502]	USN VAQ-142, NAS Whidbey Island, WA	
168386	Boeing EA-18G Growler [NG-504]	USN VAQ-133, NAS Whidbey Island, WA	
168387	Boeing EA-18G Growler [NL-554]	USN VAQ-131, NAS Whidbey Island, WA	
168388	Boeing EA-18G Growler [NL-524]	USN VAQ-135, NAS Whidbey Island, WA	
168389	Boeing EA-18G Growler [AF-503]	USN VAQ-209, NAS Whidbey Island, WA	
168390	Boeing EA-18G Growler [NJ-526]	USN VAQ-129, NAS Whidbey Island, WA	
168391	Boeing EA-18G Growler [AG-504]	USN VAQ-140, NAS Whidbey Island, WA	
168392	Boeing EA-18G Growler [AJ-500]	USN VAQ-142, NAS Whidbey Island, WA	
168463	Boeing F/A-18E Super Hornet [NF-210]	USN VFA-27, MCAS Iwakuni, Japan	
168464	Boeing F/A-18E Super Hornet [NF-211]	USN VFA-27, MCAS Iwakuni, Japan	
168465	Boeing F/A-18E Super Hornet [NF-212]	USN VFA-27, MCAS Iwakuni, Japan	
168466	Boeing F/A-18E Super Hornet [NF-201]	USN VFA-27, MCAS Iwakuni, Japan	
168467	Boeing F/A-18E Super Hornet [NF-207]	USN VFA-27, MCAS Iwakuni, Japan	
168468	Boeing F/A-18E Super Hornet [NG-214]	USN VFA-14, NAS Lemoore, CA	
168469	Boeing F/A-18E Super Hornet [AJ-405]	USN VFA-87, NAS Oceana, VA	
168470	Boeing F/A-18E Super Hornet [AJ-407]	USN VFA-87, NAS Oceana, VA	
168472	Boeing F/A-18E Super Hornet [NG-402]	USN VFA-151, NAS Lemoore, CA	
168473	Boeing F/A-18E Super Hornet [NG-403]	USN VFA-151, NAS Lemoore, CA	
168474	Boeing F/A-18E Super Hornet [NG-404]	USN VFA-151, NAS Lemoore, CA	
168475	Boeing F/A-18E Super Hornet [NG-405]	USN VFA-151, NAS Lemoore, CA	
168476	Boeing F/A-18E Super Hornet [NG-406]	USN VFA-151, NAS Lemoore, CA	
168477	Boeing F/A-18E Super Hornet [NG-407]	USN VFA-151, NAS Lemoore, CA	
168478	Boeing F/A-18E Super Hornet [NG-410]	USN VFA-151, NAS Lemoore, CA	
168479	Boeing F/A-18E Super Hornet [NG-411]	USN VFA-151, NAS Lemoore, CA	
168480	Boeing F/A-18E Super Hornet [NG-401]	USN VFA-151, NAS Lemoore, CA	
168481	Boeing F/A-18E Super Hornet [NG-201]	USN VFA-14, NAS Lemoore, CA	
168482	Boeing F/A-18E Super Hornet [NG-211]	USN VFA-14, NAS Lemoore, CA	
168483	Boeing F/A-18E Super Hornet [NG-212]	USN VFA-14, NAS Lemoore, CA	
168484	Boeing F/A-18E Super Hornet [NG-213]	USN VFA-14, NAS Lemoore, CA	
168485	Boeing F/A-18F Super Hornet [AC-101]	USN VFA-32, NAS Oceana, VA	
168486	Boeing F/A-18F Super Hornet [AB-110]	USN VFA-11, NAS Oceana, VA	
168487	Boeing F/A-18F Super Hornet [AB-11]	USN VFA-11, NAS Oceana, VA	
168488	Boeing F/A-18F Super Hornet [NE-102]	USN VFA-2, NAS Lemoore, CA	
168489	Boeing F/A-18F Super Hornet [NE-104]	USN VFA-2, NAS Lemoore, CA	
168490	Boeing F/A-18F Super Hornet [AC-112]	USN VFA-32, NAS Oceana, VA	
168491	Boeing F/A-18F Super Hornet [NA-202]	USN VFA-94, NAS Lemoore, CA	
168492	Boeing F/A-18F Super Hornet [SD-125]	USN VX-23, NAS Patuxent River, MD	
168493	Boeing F/A-18F Super Hornet [AB-112]	USN VFA-11, NAS Oceana, VA	
168765	Boeing EA-18G Growler [NL-530]	USN VAQ-134, NAS Whidbey Island, WA	
168766	Boeing EA-18G Growler [NH-506]	USN VAQ-137, NAS Whidbey Island, WA	
168767	Boeing EA-18G Growler [NH-505]	USN VAQ-137, NAS Whidbey Island, WA	
168768	Boeing EA-18G Growler [NL-523]	USN VAQ-135, NAS Whidbey Island, WA	
168769	Boeing EA-18G Growler [NA-506]	USN VAQ-139, NAS Whidbey Island, WA	
168770	Boeing EA-18G Growler [502]	USN NAWDC, NAS Fallon, NV	
168771	Boeing EA-18G Growler [XE-555]	USN VX-9, NAWS China Lake, CA	
168772	Boeing EA-18G Growler [NJ-523]	USN VAQ-129, NAS Whidbey Island, WA	
168773	Boeing EA-18G Growler [NL-553]	USN VAQ-131, NAS Whidbey Island, WA	
168774	Boeing EA-18G Growler [NE-501]	USN VAQ-136, NAS Whidbey Island, WA	
168775	Boeing EA-18G Growler [AJ-501]	USN VAQ-142, NAS Whidbey Island, WA	
168776	Boeing EA-18G Growler [NL-544]	USN VAQ-132, NAS Whidbey Island, WA	
168865	Boeing F/A-18E Super Hornet [AC-405]	USN VFA-105, NAS Oceana, VA	
168866	Boeing F/A-18E Super Hornet [NA-301]	USN VFA-137, NAS Lemoore, CA	
168867	Boeing F/A-18E Super Hornet [NA-300]	USN VFA-137, NAS Lemoore, CA	
168868	Boeing F/A-18E Super Hornet [NG-203]	USN VFA-14, NAS Lemoore, CA	
168869	Boeing F/A-18E Super Hornet [NA-302]	USN VFA-137, NAS Lemoore, CA	
168870	Boeing F/A-18E Super Hornet [NA-303]	USN VFA-137, NAS Lemoore, CA	
168871	Boeing F/A-18E Super Hornet [NA-304]	USN VFA-137, NAS Lemoore, CA	
168872	Boeing F/A-18E Super Hornet [NA-305]	USN VFA-137, NAS Lemoore, CA	
168873	Boeing F/A-18E Super Hornet [NA-306]	USN VFA-137, NAS Lemoore, CA	
168874	Boeing F/A-18E Super Hornet [NA-307]	USN VFA-137, NAS Lemoore, CA	
168875	Boeing F/A-18E Super Hornet [NA-311]	USN VFA-137, NAS Lemoore, CA	

Notes	Serial	Type (code/other identity)	Owner/operator, location or fate
	168876	Boeing F/A-18E Super Hornet [NA-310]	USN VFA-137, NAS Lemoore, CA
	168877	Boeing F/A-18E Super Hornet [NA-411]	USN VFA-146, NAS Lemoore, CA
	168878	Boeing F/A-18E Super Hornet [NA-313]	USN VFA-137, NAS Lemoore, CA
	168879	Boeing F/A-18E Super Hornet [AG-401]	USN VFA-105, NAS Oceana, VA
	168880	Boeing F/A-18E Super Hornet [AG-402]	USN VFA-105, NAS Oceana, VA
	168881	Boeing F/A-18E Super Hornet [AG-403]	USN VFA-105, NAS Oceana, VA
	168882	Boeing F/A-18E Super Hornet	USN
	168884	Boeing F/A-18E Super Hornet [AG-404]	USN VFA-105, NAS Oceana, VA
	168885	Boeing F/A-18E Super Hornet [AG-405]	USN VFA-105, NAS Oceana, VA
	168886	Boeing F/A-18E Super Hornet [AG-406]	USN VFA-105, NAS Oceana, VA
	168887	Boeing F/A-18F Super Hornet [AB-113]	USN VFA-11, NAS Oceana, VA
	168888	Boeing F/A-18F Super Hornet [AC-104]	USN VFA-32, NAS Oceana, VA
	168889	Boeing F/A-18F Super Hornet [AG-103]	USN VFA-143, NAS Oceana, VA
	168890	Boeing F/A-18F Super Hornet [AJ-200]	USN VFA-213, NAS Oceana, VA
	168891	Boeing F/A-18F Super Hornet [AJ-204]	USN VFA-213, NAS Oceana, VA
	168892	Boeing F/A-18F Super Hornet [NF-116]	USN VFA-102, MCAS Iwakuni, Japan
	168893	Boeing EA-18G Growler [NF-500]	USN VAQ-141, MCAS Iwakuni, Japan
	168894	Boeing EA-18G Growler [NJ-556]	USN VAQ-129, NAS Whidbey Island, WA
	168895	Boeing EA-18G Growler [NJ-502]	USN VAQ-129, NAS Whidbey Island, WA
	168896	Boeing EA-18G Growler [AF-500]	USN VAQ-209, NAS Whidbey Island, WA
	168897	Boeing EA-18G Growler [NF-503]	USN VAQ-141, MCAS Iwakuni, Japan
	168898	Boeing EA-18G Growler [NF-504]	USN VAQ-141, MCAS Iwakuni, Japan
	168899	Boeing EA-18G Growler [NJ-505]	USN VAQ-129, NAS Whidbey Island, WA
	168900	Boeing EA-18G Growler [AG-500]	USN VAQ-140, NAS Whidbey Island, WA
	168901	Boeing EA-18G Growler {NF-506]	USN VAQ-141, MCAS Iwakuni, Japan
	168902	Boeing EA-18G Growler [NG-502]	USN VAQ-133, NAS Whidbey Island, WA
	168903	Boeing EA-18G Growler [NL-554]	USN VAQ-131, NAS Whidbey Island, WA
	168904	Boeing EA-18G Growler [NA-505]	USN VAQ-139, NAS Whidbey Island, WA
	168905	Boeing F/A-18E Super Hornet [NE-415]	USN VFA-192, NAS Lemoore, CA
	168906	Boeing F/A-18E Super Hornet [AB-206]	USN VFA-143, NAS Oceana, VA
	168908	Boeing F/A-18E Super Hornet [NH-206]	USN VFA-211, NAS Oceana, VA
	168909	Boeing F/A-18E Super Hornet [AG-300]	USN VFA-131, NAS Oceana, VA
	168910	Boeing F/A-18E Super Hornet [AJ-400]	USN VFA-87, NAS Oceana, VA
	168911	Boeing F/A-18E Super Hornet [AJ-401]	USN VFA-87, NAS Oceana, VA
	168912	Boeing F/A-18E Super Hornet [AJ-402]	USN VFA-87, NAS Oceana, VA
	168913	Boeing F/A-18E Super Hornet [NH-211]	USN VFA-211, NAS Oceana, VA
	168914	Boeing F/A-18E Super Hornet [NH-207]	USN VFA-211, NAS Oceana, VA
	168915	Boeing F/A-18E Super Hornet [NG-205]	USN VFA-14, NAS Oceana, VA
	168916	Boeing F/A-18E Super Hornet [AJ-406]	USN VFA-87, NAS Oceana, VA
	168917	Boeing F/A-18E Super Hornet [NE-311]	USN VFA-192, NAS Lemoore, CA
	168918	Boeing F/A-18E Super Hornet [AG-301]	USN VFA-131, NAS Oceana, VA
	168919	Boeing F/A-18E Super Hornet [AG-302]	USN VFA-131, NAS Oceana, VA
	168920	Boeing F/A-18E Super Hornet [NH-202]	USN VFA-211, NAS Oceana, VA
	168921	Boeing F/A-18E Super Hornet [AB-203]	USN VFA-143, NAS Oceana, VA
	168922	Boeing F/A-18E Super Hornet [AB-202]	USN VFA-143, NAS Oceana, VA
	168923	Boeing F/A-18E Super Hornet [NH-200]	USN VFA-211, NAS Oceana, VA
	168924	Boeing F/A-18E Super Hornet [AB-204]	USN VFA-143, NAS Oceana, VA
	168925	Boeing F/A-18E Super Hornet [AB-207]	USN VFA-143, NAS Oceana, VA
	168927	Boeing F/A-18E Super Hornet [NG-200]	USN VFA-14, NAS Oceana, VA
	168928	Boeing F/A-18F Super Hornet	USN
	168929	Boeing F/A-18F Super Hornet	USN
	168930	Boeing F/A-18F Super Hornet [AJ-213]	USN VFA-213, NAS Oceana, VA
	168931	Boeing EA-18G Growler [NL-512]	USN VAQ-138, NAS Whidbey Island, WA
	168932	Boeing EA-18G Growler [NF-500]	USN VAQ-141, MCAS Iwakuni, Japan
	168933	Boeing EA-18G Growler [NL-514]	USN VAQ-138, NAS Whidbey Island, WA
	168934	Boeing EA-18G Growler [AB-503]	USN VAQ-144, NAS Whidbey Island, WA
	168935	Boeing EA-18G Growler [NE-502]	USN VAQ-136, NAS Whidbey Island, WA
	168936	Boeing EA-18G Growler [NL-531]	USN VAQ-134, NAS Whidbey Island, WA
	168937	Boeing EA-18G Growler [NL-550]	USN VAQ-131, NAS Whidbey Island, WA
	168938	Boeing EA-18G Growler [NE-504]	USN VAQ-136, NAS Whidbey Island, WA
	168939	Boeing EA-18G Growler [NJ-567]	USN VAQ-129, NAS Whidbey Island, WA
	168940	Boeing EA-18G Growler [NG-505]	USN VAQ-133, NAS Whidbey Island, WA

Serial	Type (code/other identity)	Owner/operator, location or fate	Notes
168941	Boeing EA-18G Growler [DD-501]	USN VX-31, NAWS China Lake, CA	
168942	Boeing EA-18G Growler [AF-504]	USN VAQ-209, NAS Whidbey Island, WA	
169113	Boeing F/A-18E Super Hornet [AG-407]	USN VFA-105, NAS Oceana, VA	
169114	Boeing F/A-18E Super Hornet [AG-303]	USN VFA-131, NAS Oceana, VA	
169115	Boeing F/A-18E Super Hornet [NH-210]	USN VFA-211, NAS Oceana, VA	
169116	Boeing F/A-18E Super Hornet [AG-410]	USN VFA-105, NAS Oceana, VA	
169117	Boeing F/A-18E Super Hornet [AJ-102]	USN VFA-37, NAS Oceana, VA	
169118	Boeing F/A-18E Super Hornet [AG-304]	USN VFA-131, NAS Oceana, VA	
169119	Boeing F/A-18E Super Hornet [AG-305]	USN VFA-131, NAS Oceana, VA	
169120	Boeing F/A-18E Super Hornet [AG-310]	USN VFA-131, NAS Oceana, VA	
169121	Boeing F/A-18E Super Hornet [AG-311]	USN VFA-131, NAS Oceana, VA	
169122	Boeing F/A-18E Super Hornet [AG-312]	USN VFA-131, NAS Oceana, VA	
169123	Boeing F/A-18E Super Hornet [AG-314]	USN VFA-131, NAS Oceana, VA	
169124	Boeing EA-18G Growler [NH-503]	USN VAQ-137, NAS Whidbey Island, WA	
169125	Boeing EA-18G Growler [SD-525]	USN VX-23, NAS Patuxent River, MD	
169126	Boeing EA-18G Growler [DD-502]	USN VX-31, NAWS China Lake, CA	
169127	Boeing EA-18G Growler	USN	
169128	Boeing EA-18G Growler [NL-555]	USN VAQ-131, NAS Whidbey Island, WA	
169129	Boeing EA-18G Growler [AC-502]	USN VAQ-130, NAS Whidbey Island, WA	
169130	Boeing EA-18G Growler [NJ-515]	USN VAQ-129, NAS Whidbey Island, WA	
169131	Boeing EA-18G Growler [DD-503]	USN VX-31, NAWS China Lake, CA	
169132	Boeing EA-18G Growler [NA-506]	USN VAQ-139, NAS Whidbey Island, WA	
169133	Boeing EA-18G Growler [NJ-571]	USN VAQ-129, NAS Whidbey Island, WA	
169134	Boeing EA-18G Growler [NA-502]	USN VAQ-139, NAS Whidbey Island, WA	
169135	Boeing EA-18G Growler [NJ-566]	USN VAQ-129, NAS Whidbey Island, WA	
169136	Boeing EA-18G Growler [AG-503]	USN VAQ-140, NAS Whidbey Island, WA	
169137	Boeing EA-18G Growler [NG-500]	USN VAQ-133, NAS Whidbey Island, WA	
169138	Boeing EA-18G Growler [DD-506]	USN VX-31, NAWS China Lake, CA	
169139	Boeing EA-18G Growler	USN	
169140	Boeing EA-18G Growler [NA-505]	USN VAQ-139, NAS Whidbey Island, WA	
169141	Boeing EA-18G Growler [AJ-504]	USN VAQ-142, NAS Whidbey Island, WA	
169142	Boeing EA-18G Growler [NE-505]	USN VAQ-136, NAS Whidbey Island, WA	
169143	Boeing EA-18G Growler [SD-527]	USN VX-23, NAS Patuxent River, MD	
169144	Boeing EA-18G Growler [SD-529]	USN VX-23, NAS Patuxent River, MD	
169145	Boeing EA-18G Growler [NJ-500]	USN VAQ-129, NAS Whidbey Island, WA	
169146	Boeing EA-18G Growler [NF-505]	USN VAQ-141, MCAS Iwakuni, Japan	
169147	Boeing EA-18G Growler [AB-504]	USN VAQ-144, NAS Whidbey Island, WA	
169206	Boeing EA-18G Growler [AC-503]	USN VAQ-130, NAS Whidbey Island, WA	
169207	Boeing EA-18G Growler [NA-503]	USN VAQ-139, NAS Whidbey Island, WA	
169208	Boeing EA-18G Growler [506]	USN NAWDC, NAS Fallon, NV	
169209	Boeing EA-18G Growler [503]	USN NAWDC, NAS Fallon, NV	
169210	Boeing EA-18G Growler [NF-506]	USN VAQ-141, MCAS Iwakuni, Japan	
169211	Boeing EA-18G Growler [NE-503]	USN VAQ-136, NAS Whidbey Island, WA	
169212	Boeing EA-18G Growler [NF-507]	USN VAQ-141, MCAS Iwakuni, Japan	
169213	Boeing EA-18G Growler [XE-501]	USN VX-9, NAWS China Lake, CA	
169214	Boeing EA-18G Growler [XE—503]	USN VX-9, NAWS China Lake, CA	
169215	Boeing EA-18G Growler	USN	
169216	Boeing EA-18G Growler [NJ-503]	USN VAQ-129, NAS Whidbey Island, WA	
169217	Boeing EA-18G Growler [DD-507]	USN VX-31, NAWS China Lake, CA	
169218	Boeing EA-18G Growler [SD-531]	USN VX-23, NAS Patuxent River, MD	
169220	Boeing EA-18G Growler [SD-533]	USN VX-23, NAS Patuxent River, MD	
169395	Boeing F/A-18E Super Hornet [AJ-410]	USN VFA-87, NAS Oceana, VA	
169396	Boeing F/A-18E Super Hornet [AJ-411]	USN VFA-87, NAS Oceana, VA	
169397	Boeing F/A-18E Super Hornet [AJ-403]	USN VFA-87, NAS Oceana, VA	
169398	Boeing F/A-18E Super Hornet [AJ-404]	USN VFA-87, NAS Oceana, VA	
169399	Boeing F/A-18E Super Hornet [AG-400]	USN VFA-105, NAS Oceana, VA	
169400	Boeing EA-18G Growler [AG-502]	USN VAQ-140, NAS Whidbey Island, WA	
169401	Boeing EA-18G Growler	USN, stored, location unknown	
169402	Boeing EA-18G Growler	USN, stored, location unknown	
169403	Boeing EA-18G Growler	USN, stored, location unknown	
169404	Boeing EA-18G Growler	USN, stored, location unknown	
169405	Boeing EA-18G Growler	USN, stored, location unknown	

Notes	Serial	Type (code/other identity)	Owner/operator, location or fate
	169406	Boeing EA-18G Growler [NJ-536]	USN VAQ-129, NAS Whidbey Island, WA
	169641	Boeing F/A-18E Super Hornet [AC-300]	USN VFA-34, NAS Oceana, VA
	169642	Boeing F/A-18E Super Hornet [NH-302]	USN VFA-34, NAS Oceana, VA
	169643	Boeing F/A-18E Super Hornet [NH-303]	USN VFA-34, NAS Oceana, VA
	169644	Boeing F/A-18E Super Hornet [NH-304]	USN VFA-34, NAS Oceana, VA
	169645	Boeing F/A-18E Super Hornet [NH-305]	USN VFA-34, NAS Oceana, VA
	169646	Boeing F/A-18E Super Hornet [NH-301]	USN VFA-34, NAS Oceana, VA
	169647	Boeing F/A-18F Super Hornet [AC-104]	USN VFA-32, NAS Oceana, VA
	169648	Boeing F/A-18F Super Hornet [AC-103]	USN VFA-32, NAS Oceana, VA
	169649	Boeing F/A-18F Super Hornet [AC-102]	USN VFA-32, NAS Oceana, VA
	169650	Boeing F/A-18F Super Hornet [NH-105]	USN VFA-154, NAS Lemoore, CA
	169651	Boeing F/A-18F Super Hornet [NH-115]	USN VFA-154, NAS Lemoore, CA
	169652	Boeing F/A-18F Super Hornet [NH-102]	USN VFA-154, NAS Lemoore, CA
	169653	Boeing F/A-18F Super Hornet [NH-154]	USN VFA-154, NAS Lemoore, CA
	169654	Boeing F/A-18F Super Hornet [NH-103]	USN VFA-154, NAS Lemoore, CA
	169734	Boeing F/A-18E Super Hornet [NH-212]	USN VFA-211, NAS Oceana, VA
	169735	Boeing F/A-18E Super Hornet [NH-222]	USN VFA-211, NAS Oceana, VA
	169736	Boeing F/A-18E Super Hornet [NE-300]	USN VFA-192, NAS Lemoore, CA
	169737	Boeing F/A-18E Super Hornet [NE-301]	USN VFA-192, NAS Lemoore, CA
	169738	Boeing F/A-18E Super Hornet [NE-302]	USN VFA-192, NAS Lemoore, CA
	169739	Boeing F/A-18E Super Hornet [NE-303]	USN VFA-192, NAS Lemoore, CA
	169740	Boeing F/A-18E Super Hornet [NE-304]	USN VFA-192, NAS Lemoore, CA
	169741	Boeing F/A-18E Super Hornet [NE-305]	USN VFA-192, NAS Lemoore, CA
	169742	Boeing F/A-18E Super Hornet [NH-310]	USN VFA-34, NAS Oceana, VA
	169743	Boeing F/A-18E Super Hornet [NH-311]	USN VFA-34, NAS Oceana, VA
	169744	Boeing F/A-18E Super Hornet [NH-312]	USN VFA-34, NAS Oceana, VA
	169745	Boeing F/A-18E Super Hornet [NE-306]	USN VFA-192, NAS Lemoore, CA
	169746	Boeing F/A-18E Super Hornet [NE-307]	USN VFA-192, NAS Lemoore, CA
	169747	Boeing F/A-18E Super Hornet [NH-334]	USN VFA-34, NAS Oceana, VA
	169749	Boeing F/A-18F Super Hornet [NH-101]	USN VFA-154, NAS Lemoore, CA
	169750	Boeing F/A-18F Super Hornet [NH-100]	USN VFA-154, NAS Lemoore, CA
	169751	Boeing F/A-18F Super Hornet [DD-302]	USN VX-31, NAWS China Lake, CA
	169948	Boeing F/A-18E Super Hornet [XE-333]	USN VX-9, NAS Patuxent River, MD
	169949	Boeing F/A-18E Super Hornet [120]	USN NAWDC, NAS Fallon, NV
	169950	Boeing F/A-18F Super Hornet [122]	USN NAWDC, NAS Fallon, NV
	169951	Boeing F/A-18E Super Hornet [NE-200]	USN VFA-113, NAS Lemoore, CA
	169952	Boeing F/A-18E Super Hornet [NE-201]	USN VFA-113, NAS Lemoore, CA
	169953	Boeing F/A-18E Super Hornet [NH-400]	USN VFA-25, NAS Lemoore, CA
	169954	Boeing F/A-18E Super Hornet [NH-401]	USN VFA-25, NAS Lemoore, CA
	169955	Boeing F/A-18E Super Hornet [NH-402]	USN VFA-25, NAS Lemoore, CA
	169956	Boeing F/A-18E Super Hornet [NH-403]	USN VFA-25, NAS Lemoore, CA
	169957	Boeing F/A-18E Super Hornet [NH-404]	USN VFA-25, NAS Lemoore, CA
	169958	Boeing F/A-18E Super Hornet [NH-405]	USN VFA-25, NAS Lemoore, CA
	169959	Boeing F/A-18E Super Hornet [NH-406]	USN VFA-25, NAS Lemoore, CA
	169960	Boeing F/A-18E Super Hornet [NH-407]	USN VFA-25, NAS Lemoore, CA
	169961	Boeing F/A-18E Super Hornet [NE-202]	USN VFA-113, NAS Lemoore, CA
	169962	Boeing F/A-18E Super Hornet [NE-203]	USN VFA-113, NAS Lemoore, CA
	169963	Boeing F/A-18E Super Hornet [NE-204]	USN VFA-113, NAS Lemoore, CA
	169964	Boeing F/A-18E Super Hornet [NE-205]	USN VFA-113, NAS Lemoore, CA
	169965	Boeing F/A-18E Super Hornet [NE-206]	USN VFA-113, NAS Lemoore, CA
	169966	Boeing F/A-18E Super Hornet [NE-207]	USN VFA-113, NAS Lemoore, CA
	169967	Boeing F/A-18E Super Hornet [NE-210]	USN VFA-113, NAS Lemoore, CA
	169968	Boeing F/A-18E Super Hornet [NE-211]	USN VFA-113, NAS Lemoore, CA
	169969	Boeing F/A-18E Super Hornet [NH-410]	USN VFA-25, NAS Lemoore, CA
	169970	Boeing F/A-18E Super Hornet [NH-411]	USN VFA-25, NAS Lemoore, CA
	169971	Boeing F/A-18E Super Hornet [XE-360]	USN VX-9, NAWS China Lake, CA
	169972	Boeing F/A-18E Super Hornet [121]	USN NAWDC, NAS Fallon, NV
	169974	Boeing EA-18F Super Hornet [130]	USN NAWDC, NAS Fallon, NV
	169975	Boeing F/A-18F Super Hornet [XE-444]	USN VX-9, NAWS China Lake, CA
	169976	Boeing F/A-18F Super Hornet	USN (on order)
	169977	Boeing F/A-18F Super Hornet [131]	USN NAWDC, NAS Fallon, NV
	170297	Boeing F/A-18E Super Hornet [NA-206]	USN VFA-94, NAS Lemoore, CA

Serial	Type (code/other identity)	Owner/operator, location or fate	Notes
170298	Boeing F/A-18E Super Hornet	USN, stored, location unknown	
170299	Boeing F/A-18E Super Hornet	USN, stored, location unknown	
170300	Boeing F/A-18E Super Hornet [NA-200]	USN VFA-94, NAS Lemoore, CA	
170301	Boeing F/A-18E Super Hornet [NA-201]	USN VFA-94, NAS Lemoore, CA	
170302	Boeing F/A-18E Super Hornet [NA-202]	USN VFA-94, NAS Lemoore, CA	
170303	Boeing F/A-18E Super Hornet [NA-203]	USN VFA-94, NAS Lemoore, CA	
170304	Boeing F/A-18E Super Hornet [NA-204]	USN VFA-94, NAS Lemoore, CA	
170305	Boeing F/A-18E Super Hornet [NA-205]	USN VFA-94, NAS Lemoore, CA	
170306	Boeing F/A-18E Super Hornet [NA-405]	USN VFA-146, NAS Lemoore, CA	
170307	Boeing F/A-18E Super Hornet	USN (on order)	
170308	Boeing F/A-18E Super Hornet	USN (on order)	
170309	Boeing F/A-18E Super Hornet	USN (on order)	
170310	Boeing F/A-18E Super Hornet [NA-403]	USN VFA-146, NAS Lemoore, CA	
170311	Boeing F/A-18E Super Hornet [NA-211]	USN VFA-94, NAS Lemoore, CA	
170312	Boeing F/A-18E Super Hornet	USN (on order)	
170313	Boeing F/A-18E Super Hornet	USN (on order)	
170314	Boeing F/A-18E Super Hornet	USN (on order)	
170315	Boeing F/A-18F Super Hornet [132]	USN NAWDC, NAS Fallon, NV	
170316	Boeing F/A-18E Super Hornet	USN (on order)	
170317	Boeing F/A-18F Super Hornet	USN (on order)	
170318	Boeing F/A-18F Super Hornet	USN VX-23, NAS Patuxent River, MD	
170319	Boeing F/A-18F Super Hornet	USN (on order)	
170320	Boeing F/A-18F Super Hornet	USN (on order)	
170321	Boeing F/A-18E Super Hornet	USN (on order)	
170322	Boeing F/A-18E Super Hornet	USN (on order)	
170323	Boeing F/A-18E Super Hornet	USN (on order)	
170324	Boeing F/A-18E Super Hornet	USN (on order)	
170325	Boeing F/A-18E Super Hornet	USN (on order)	
170326	Boeing F/A-18E Super Hornet	USN (on order)	
170327	Boeing F/A-18E Super Hornet	USN (on order)	
170328	Boeing F/A-18E Super Hornet	USN (on order)	
170329	Boeing F/A-18E Super Hornet	USN (on order)	
170330	Boeing F/A-18E Super Hornet	USN (on order)	
170331	Boeing F/A-18E Super Hornet	USN (on order)	
170332	Boeing F/A-18E Super Hornet	USN (on order)	
170333	Boeing F/A-18E Super Hornet	USN (on order)	
170334	Boeing F/A-18E Super Hornet	USN (on order)	
170335	Boeing F/A-18E Super Hornet	USN (on order)	
170336	Boeing F/A-18E Super Hornet	USN (on order)	
170337	Boeing F/A-18E Super Hornet	USN (on order)	
170338	Boeing F/A-18E Super Hornet	USN (on order)	
170339	Boeing F/A-18F Super Hornet	USN (on order)	
170340	Boeing F/A-18F Super Hornet	USN (on order)	
170341	Boeing F/A-18F Super Hornet	USN (on order)	
170342	Boeing F/A-18F Super Hornet	USN (on order)	
170343	Boeing F/A-18F Super Hornet	USN (on order)	
170344	Boeing F/A-18F Super Hornet	USN (on order)	

Grumman C-20 Gulfstream

Serial	Type (code/other identity)	Owner/operator, location or fate	Notes
165094	Grumman NC-20G Gulfstream IV [BH-500]	USN VX-30, NAS Point Mugu, CA	
165152	Grumman C-20G Gulfstream IV	USMC VMR-Det, MCBH Kaneohe Bay, HI	
165153	Grumman C-20G Gulfstream IV	USMC VMR-Det, MCBH Kaneohe Bay, HI	

Bell/Boeing MV-22B Osprey

Serial	Type (code/other identity)	Owner/operator, location or fate	Notes
168280	Bell/Boeing MV-22B Osprey [01]	USMC HMX-1, Quantico, VA	
168284	Bell/Boeing MV-22B Osprey [02]	USMC HMX-1, Quantico, VA	
168289	Bell/Boeing MV-22B Osprey [03]	USMC HMX-1, Quantico, VA	
168292	Bell/Boeing MV-22B Osprey [04]	USMC HMX-1, Quantico, VA	
168297	Bell/Boeing MV-22B Osprey [05]	USMC HMX-1, Quantico, VA	
168302	Bell/Boeing MV-22B Osprey [06]	USMC HMX-1, Quantico, VA	
168306	Bell/Boeing MV-22B Osprey [07]	USMC HMX-1, Quantico, VA	
168324	Bell/Boeing MV-22B Osprey [08]	USMC HMX-1, Quantico, VA	

Notes	Serial	Type (code/other identity)	Owner/operator, location or fate
	168327	Bell/Boeing MV-22B Osprey [09]	USMC HMX-1, Quantico, VA
	168332	Bell/Boeing MV-22B Osprey [10]	USMC HMX-1, Quantico, VA
	168335	Bell/Boeing MV-22B Osprey [11]	USMC HMX-1, Quantico, VA
	168339	Bell/Boeing MV-22B Osprey [12]	USMC HMX-1, Quantico, VA
	168689	Bell/Boeing MV-22B Osprey [00]	USMC HMX-1, Quantico, VA
	168701	Bell/Boeing MV-22B Osprey [13]	USMC HMX-1, Quantico, VA

Cessna UC-35 Citation V

Notes	Serial	Type (code/other identity)	Owner/operator, location or fate
	165939	Cessna UC-35D Citation V	USMC H&HS Miramar, Miramar MCAS, CA
	166374	Cessna UC-35D Citation V	USMC H&HS Andrews, NAF Washington, MD
	166474	Cessna UC-35D Citation V	USMC H&HS Cherry Point, MCAS Cherry Point, NC
	166500	Cessna UC-35D Citation V	USMC H&HS Miramar, Miramar MCAS, CA
	166712	Cessna UC-35D Citation V	USMC H&HS Cherry Point, MCAS Cherry Point, NC
	166713	Cessna UC-35D Citation V	USMC H&HS Futenma, Futenma MCAS, Japan
	166714	Cessna UC-35D Citation V	USMC H&HS Andrews, NAF Washington, MD
	166715	Cessna UC-35D Citation V	USMC H&HS Cherry Point, MCAS Cherry Point, NC
	166766	Cessna UC-35D Citation V	USMC H&HS Futenma, Futenma MCAS, Japan
	166767	Cessna UC-35D Citation V [VM]	USMC H&HS Miramar, Miramar MCAS, CA

Gulfstream Aerospace C-37 Gulfstream 5

Notes	Serial	Type (code/other identity)	Owner/operator, location or fate
	166375	Gulfstream Aerospace C-37A Gulfstream V [365]	USN CFLSW Det, MCBH Kaneohe Bay, HI
	166376	Gulfstream Aerospace C-37B Gulfstream V [376]	USN VR-1, NAF Washington, MD
	166377	Gulfstream Aerospace C-37B Gulfstream V [377]	USN VR-1, NAF Washington, MD
	166378	Gulfstream Aerospace C-37B Gulfstream V [378]	USN VR-1, NAF Washington, MD
	166379	Gulfstream Aerospace NC-37B Gulfstream V [BH-100]	USN VX-30, NAS Point Mugu, CA

Boeing C-40A Clipper

Notes	Serial	Type (code/other identity)	Owner/operator, location or fate
	165829	Boeing C-40A Clipper (N1003N) [829]	USN VR-58, NAS Jacksonville, FL
	165830	Boeing C-40A Clipper (N1003M) [830]	USN VR-59, Fort Worth JRB, TX
	165831	Boeing C-40A Clipper (N1786B) [831]	USN VR-59, Fort Worth JRB, TX
	165832	Boeing C-40A Clipper (N1787B) [832]	USN VR-58, NAS Jacksonville, FL
	165833	Boeing C-40A Clipper [833]	USN VR-59, Fort Worth JRB, TX
	165834	Boeing C-40A Clipper [834]	USN VR-61, NAS Whidbey Island, WA
	165835	Boeing C-40A Clipper (N543BA) [835]	USN VR-57, NAS North Island, CA
	165836	Boeing C-40A Clipper [836]	USN VR-61, NAS Whidbey Island, WA
	166693	Boeing C-40A Clipper [693]	USN VR-51, MCBH Kaneohe Bay, Hawaii
	166694	Boeing C-40A Clipper [694]	USN VR-56, NAS Oceana, VA
	166695	Boeing C-40A Clipper (N1787B) [695]	USN VR-61, NAS Whidbey Island, WA
	166696	Boeing C-40A Clipper [696]	USN VR-59, Fort Worth JRB, TX
	168980	Boeing C-40A Clipper (N513NV) [980]	USN VR-58, NAS Jacksonville, FL
	168981	Boeing C-40A Clipper (N514NV) [981]	USN VR-59, Fort Worth JRB, TX
	169036	Boeing C-40A Clipper (N515NV) [036]	USN VR-61, NAS Whidbey Island, WA
	169792	Boeing C-40A Clipper (N1799B) [792]	USN VR-51, MCBH Kaneohe Bay, Hawaii
	169793	Boeing C-40A Clipper (N517NV) [793]	USN VR-57, NAS North Island, CA
	170041	Boeing C-40A Clipper (N743A) [041]	USMC VMR-1, Fort Worth JRB, TX
	170042	Boeing C-40A Clipper (N745A) [042]	USMC VMR-1, Fort Worth JRB, TX

Sikorsky VH-60N White Hawk

Notes	Serial	Type (code/other identity)	Owner/operator, location or fate
	163259	Sikorsky VH-60N White Hawk	USMC HMX-1, MCAS Quantico, VA
	163260	Sikorsky VH-60N White Hawk	USMC HMX-1, MCAS Quantico, VA
	163261	Sikorsky VH-60N White Hawk	USMC HMX-1, MCAS Quantico, VA
	163262	Sikorsky VH-60N White Hawk	USMC HMX-1, MCAS Quantico, VA
	163263	Sikorsky VH-60N White Hawk	USMC HMX-1, MCAS Quantico, VA
	163264	Sikorsky VH-60N White Hawk	USMC HMX-1, MCAS Quantico, VA
	163265	Sikorsky VH-60N White Hawk	USMC HMX-1, MCAS Quantico, VA
	163266	Sikorsky VH-60N White Hawk	USMC HMX-1, MCAS Quantico, VA
	165751	Sikorsky VH-60N White Hawk	USMC HMX-1, MCAS Quantico, VA

Lockheed C-130 Hercules

Notes	Serial	Type (code/other identity)	Owner/operator, location or fate
	162308	Lockheed KC-130T Hercules [BH-400]	USN VX-30, NAS Point Mugu, CA
	162309	Lockheed KC-130T Hercules [309]	USN VX-20, Patuxent River, MD
	162310	Lockheed KC-130T Hercules [310]	USN VX-20, Patuxent River, MD

Serial	Type (code/other identity)	Owner/operator, location or fate	Notes
162311	Lockheed KC-130T Hercules [BH-405]	USN VX-30, NAS Point Mugu, CA	
163310	Lockheed KC-130T Hercules [WB-X10]	USN VX-20, Patuxent River, MD	
163311	Lockheed KC-130T Hercules [RU-311]	USN VR-55, NAS Point Mugu, CA	
163591	Lockheed C-130T Hercules [RU-591]	USN VR-55, NAS Point Mugu, CA	
164105	Lockheed KC-130T Hercules [105]	USN VX-20, Patuxent River, MD	
164106	Lockheed KC-130T Hercules [RU-106]	USN VR-55, NAS Point Mugu, CA	
164180	Lockheed KC-130T Hercules [JW-180]	USN VR-62, NAS Jacksonville, FL	
164441	Lockheed KC-130T Hercules [JW-441]	USN VR-62, NAS Jacksonville, FL	
164597	Lockheed KC-130T-30 Hercules [BD-597] $	USN VR-64, McGuire AFB, NJ	
164598	Lockheed C-130T-30 Hercules [JW-598]	USN VR-62, NAS Jacksonville, FL	
164762	Lockheed C-130T Hercules [JW-762]	USN VR-62, NAS Jacksonville, FL	
164993	Lockheed C-130T Hercules [BD-993]	USN VR-64, McGuire AFB, NJ	
164994	Lockheed C-130T Hercules [CW-994]	USN VR-54, NAS New Orleans, LA	
164995	Lockheed C-130T Hercules [AX-995]	USN VR-53, NAF Washington, MD	
164996	Lockheed C-130T Hercules [RU-996]	USN VR-55, NAS Point Mugu, CA	
164997	Lockheed C-130T Hercules [AX-997]	USN VR-53, NAF Washington, MD	
164998	Lockheed C-130T Hercules [BD-998]	USN VR-64, McGuire AFB, NJ	
165158	Lockheed C-130T Hercules [CW-158]	USN VR-54, NAS New Orleans, LA	
165159	Lockheed C-130T Hercules [CW-159]	USN VR-54, NAS New Orleans, LA	
165160	Lockheed C-130T Hercules [CW-160]	USN VR-54, NAS New Orleans, LA	
165161	Lockheed C-130T Hercules [BD-161]	USN VR-64, McGuire AFB, NJ	
165313	Lockheed C-130T Hercules [AX-313]	USN VR-53, NAF Washington, MD	
165314	Lockheed C-130T Hercules [JW-314]	USN VR-62, NAS Jacksonville, FL	
165315	Lockheed KC-130T Hercules [AX-315]	USN VR-53, NAF Washington, MD	
165316	Lockheed KC-130T Hercules [BD-316]	USN VR-64, McGuire AFB, NJ	
165348	Lockheed C-130T Hercules [AX-348]	USN VR-53, NAF Washington, MD	
165349	Lockheed C-130T Hercules [AX-349]	USN VR-53, NAF Washington, MD	
165350	Lockheed C-130T Hercules [350]	USN VX-20, Patuxent River, MD	
165352	Lockheed KC-130T Hercules [BD-352]	USN VR-64, McGuire AFB, NJ	
165378	Lockheed C-130T Hercules [JW-378]	USN VR-62, NAS Jacksonville, FL	
165379	Lockheed C-130T Hercules [RU-379]	USN VR-55, NAS Point Mugu, CA	
165735	Lockheed KC-130J Hercules II [QB-735]	USMC VMGR-352, Miramar MCAS, CA	
165736	Lockheed KC-130J Hercules II [QB-736]	USMC VMGR-352, Miramar MCAS, CA	
165737	Lockheed KC-130J Hercules II [BH-737]	USMC VMGR-252, Cherry Point MCAS, NC	
165738	Lockheed KC-130J Hercules II [BH-738]	USMC VMGR-252, Cherry Point MCAS, NC	
165739	Lockheed KC-130J Hercules II [QB-739]	USMC VMGR-352, Miramar MCAS, CA	
165809	Lockheed KC-130J Hercules II [BH-809]	USMC VMGR-252, Cherry Point MCAS, NC	
165810	Lockheed KC-130J Hercules II [BH-810]	USMC VMGR-252, Cherry Point MCAS, NC	
165957	Lockheed KC-130J Hercules II [QD-957]	USMC VMGR-152, Iwakuni MCAS, Japan	
166380	Lockheed KC-130J Hercules II [QD-380]	USMC VMGR-152, Iwakuni MCAS, Japan	
166381	Lockheed KC-130J Hercules II [BH-381]	USMC VMGR-252, Cherry Point MCAS, NC	
166382	Lockheed KC-130J Hercules II [QB-382]	USMC VMGR-352, Miramar MCAS, CA	
166472	Lockheed KC-130J Hercules II [BH-472]	USMC VMGR-252, Cherry Point MCAS, NC	
166473	Lockheed KC-130J Hercules II [QH-473]	USMC VMGR-234, Fort Worth JRB, TX	
166511	Lockheed KC-130J Hercules II [BH-511]	USN VX-20, Patuxent River, MD	
166512	Lockheed KC-130J Hercules II [QH-512]	USMC VMGR-234, Fort Worth JRB, TX	
166513	Lockheed KC-130J Hercules II [BH-513]	USMC VMGR-252, Cherry Point MCAS, NC	
166514	Lockheed KC-130J Hercules II [BH-514]	Stored Abbotsford, BC, Canada	
166762	Lockheed KC-130J Hercules II [BH-762]	USMC VMGR-252, Cherry Point MCAS, NC	
166763	Lockheed KC-130J Hercules II [QH-763]	USMC VMGR-234, Fort Worth JRB, TX	
166764	Lockheed KC-130J Hercules II [QH-764]	USMC VMGR-234, Fort Worth JRB, TX	
167108	Lockheed KC-130J Hercules II [QB-108]	USMC VMGR-352, Miramar MCAS, CA	
167109	Lockheed KC-130J Hercules II [QD-109]	USMC VMGR-152, Iwakuni MCAS, Japan	
167110	Lockheed KC-130J Hercules II [QB-110]	USMC VMGR-352, Miramar MCAS, CA	
167111	Lockheed KC-130J Hercules II [QD-111]	USMC VMGR-152, Iwakuni MCAS, Japan	
167112	Lockheed KC-130J Hercules II [BH-112]	USMC VMGR-252, Cherry Point MCAS, NC	
167923	Lockheed KC-130J Hercules II [QD-923]	USMC VMGR-152, Iwakuni MCAS, Japan	
167924	Lockheed KC-130J Hercules II [QB-924]	USMC VMGR-352, Miramar MCAS, CA	
167925	Lockheed KC-130J Hercules II [QH-925]	USMC VMGR-234, Fort Worth JRB, TX	
167926	Lockheed KC-130J Hercules II [QD-926]	USMC VMGR-152, Iwakuni MCAS, Japan	
167927	Lockheed KC-130J Hercules II [QD-927]	USMC VMGR-152, Iwakuni MCAS, Japan	
167982	Lockheed KC-130J Hercules II [QD-982]	USMC VMGR-152, Iwakuni MCAS, Japan	

Notes	Serial	Type (code/other identity)	Owner/operator, location or fate
	167983	Lockheed KC-130J Hercules II [QD-983]	USMC VMGR-152, Iwakuni MCAS, Japan
	167984	Lockheed KC-130J Hercules II [QB-984]	USMC VMGR-352, Miramar MCAS, CA
	167985	Lockheed KC-130J Hercules II [QB-985]	USMC VMGR-352, Miramar MCAS, CA
	168065	Lockheed KC-130J Hercules II [QD-065]	USMC VMGR-152, Iwakuni MCAS, Japan
	168066	Lockheed KC-130J Hercules II [QD-066]	USMC VMGR-152, Iwakuni MCAS, Japan
	168067	Lockheed KC-130J Hercules II [QB-067]	USMC VMGR-352, Miramar MCAS, CA
	168068	Lockheed KC-130J Hercules II [QH-068]	USMC VMGR-234, Fort Worth JRB, TX
	168069	Lockheed KC-130J Hercules II [BH-069]	USMC VMGR-252, Cherry Point MCAS, NC
	168070	Lockheed KC-130J Hercules II [BH-070]	USMC VMGR-252, Cherry Point MCAS, NC
	168071	Lockheed KC-130J Hercules II [BH-071]	USMC VMGR-252, Cherry Point MCAS, NC
	168072	Lockheed KC-130J Hercules II [QB-072]	USMC VMGR-352, Miramar MCAS, CA
	168073	Lockheed KC-130J Hercules II [QB-073]	USMC VMGR-352, Miramar MCAS, CA
	168074	Lockheed KC-130J Hercules II [QD-074]	USMC VMGR-152, Iwakuni MCAS, Japan
	168075	Lockheed KC-130J Hercules II [QD-075]	USMC VMGR-152, Iwakuni MCAS, Japan
	169018	Lockheed KC-130J Hercules II [QH-018]	USMC VMGR-234, Fort Worth JRB, TX
	169225	Lockheed KC-130J Hercules II [QH-225]	USMC VMGR-234, Fort Worth JRB, TX
	169226	Lockheed KC-130J Hercules II [QB-226]	USMC VMGR-352, Miramar MCAS, CA
	169227	Lockheed KC-130J Hercules II [QD-227]	USMC VMGR-152, Iwakuni MCAS, Japan
	169228	Lockheed KC-130J Hercules II [QH-228]	USMC VMGR-234, Fort Worth JRB, TX
	169229	Lockheed KC-130J Hercules II [QH-229] $	USMC VMGR-234, Fort Worth JRB, TX
	169230	Lockheed KC-130J Hercules II [QB-230]	USMC VMGR-352, Miramar MCAS, CA
	169532	Lockheed KC-130J Hercules II [QD-532]	USMC VMGR-152, Iwakuni MCAS, Japan
	169533	Lockheed KC-130J Hercules II [QB-533]	USMC VMGR-352, Miramar MCAS, CA
	169534	Lockheed KC-130J Hercules II [BH-534]	USMC VMGR-252, Cherry Point MCAS, NC
	169535	Lockheed KC-130J Hercules II [QD-535]	USMC VMGR-152, Iwakuni MCAS, Japan
	169536	Lockheed KC-130J Hercules II [QB-536]	USMC VMGR-352, Miramar MCAS, CA
	170000	Lockheed C-130J Hercules II (N41030/ZH885)	USN *Blue Angels*, Pensacola, FL
	170037	Lockheed KC-130J Hercules II [KB-037]	USMC VMGR-153, MCBH Kaneohe Bay, Hawaii
	170038	Lockheed KC-130J Hercules II [BH-038]	USMC VMGR-252, Cherry Point MCAS, NC
	170039	Lockheed KC-130J Hercules II [KB-039]	USMC VMGR-153, MCBH Kaneohe Bay, Hawaii
	170040	Lockheed KC-130J Hercules II [BH-040]	USMC VMGR-252, Cherry Point MCAS, NC
	170271	Lockheed KC-130J Hercules II [BH-271]	USMC VMGR-252, Cherry Point MCAS, NC
	170272	Lockheed KC-130J Hercules II [KB-272]	USMC VMGR-153, MCBH Kaneohe Bay, Hawaii
	170273	Lockheed KC-130J Hercules II [KB-273]	USMC VMGR-153, MCBH Kaneohe Bay, Hawaii
	170274	Lockheed KC-130J Hercules II [BH-274]	USMC VMGR-252, Cherry Point MCAS, NC
	170275	Lockheed KC-130J Hercules II [QB-275]	USMC VMGR-352, Miramar MCAS, CA
	170276	Lockheed KC-130J Hercules II [BH-275]	USMC VMGR-252, Cherry Point MCAS, NC
	170277	Lockheed KC-130J Hercules II [QB-277]	USMC VMGR-352, Miramar MCAS, CA
	170278	Lockheed KC-130J Hercules II [QB-278]	USMC VMGR-352, Miramar MCAS, CA
	170279	Lockheed KC-130J Hercules II [BH-279]	USMC VMGR-252, Cherry Point MCAS, NC
	170280	Lockheed KC-130J Hercules II [KB-280]	USMC VMGR-153, MCBH Kaneohe Bay, Hawaii
	170281	Lockheed KC-130J Hercules II [KB-281]	USMC VMGR-153, MCBH Kaneohe Bay, Hawaii
	170282	Lockheed KC-130J Hercules II [BH-282]	USMC VMGR-252, Cherry Point MCAS, NC
	170283	Lockheed KC-130J Hercules II [QB-283]	USMC VMGR-352, Miramar MCAS, CA
	170284	Lockheed KC-130J Hercules II [KB-284]	USMC VMGR-153, MCBH Kaneohe Bay, Hawaii
	170285	Lockheed KC-130J Hercules II [QD-285]	USMC VMGR-152, Iwakuni MCAS, Japan
	170286	Lockheed KC-130J Hercules II [QB-286]	USMC (on order)
	170287	Lockheed KC-130J Hercules II	USMC (on order)

US-BASED US COAST GUARD AIRCRAFT

Serial	Type (code/other identity)	Owner/operator, location or fate	Notes
01	Gulfstream Aerospace C-37A Gulfstream V (N527GA)	USCG, Commandants Flt, Washington DC	
02	Gulfstream Aerospace C-37B Gulfstream V (N517GA)	USCG, Commandants Flt, Washington DC	
03	Gulfstream Aerospace C-37B Gulfstream V	USCG (on order)	
1701	Lockheed HC-130H Hercules	*USCG, stored USCGC Elizabeth City, NC*	
1702	Lockheed HC-130H Hercules	*USCG, stored USCGC Elizabeth City, NC*	
1703	Lockheed HC-130H Hercules	*USCG, stored USCGC Elizabeth City, NC*	
1704	Lockheed HC-130H Hercules	*USCG, stored USCGC Elizabeth City, NC*	
1707	Lockheed HC-130H Hercules	*USCG, stored USCGC Elizabeth City, NC*	
1711	Lockheed HC-130H Hercules	*USCG, stored USCGC Elizabeth City, NC*	
1712	Lockheed HC-130H Hercules	*USCG, stored USCGC Elizabeth City, NC*	
1715	Lockheed HC-130H Hercules	*USCG, stored USCGC Elizabeth City, NC*	
1716	Lockheed HC-130H Hercules	*USCG, stored USCGC Elizabeth City, NC*	
1718	Lockheed HC-130H Hercules	*USCG, stored USCGC Elizabeth City, NC*	
1720	Lockheed HC-130H Hercules	*USCG, stored USCGC Elizabeth City, NC*	
2001	Lockheed HC-130J Hercules II	USCG, USCGS Elizabeth City, NC	
2002	Lockheed HC-130J Hercules II	USCG, USCGS Barbers Point, HI	
2003	Lockheed HC-130J Hercules II	USCG, USCGS Kodiak, AK	
2004	Lockheed HC-130J Hercules II	USCG, USCGS Kodiak, AK	
2005	Lockheed HC-130J Hercules II	USCG, USCGS Kodiak, AK	
2006	Lockheed HC-130J Hercules II	USCG, USCGS Kodiak, AK	
2007	Lockheed HC-130J Hercules II	USCG, USCGS Barbers Point, HI	
2008	Lockheed HC-130J Hercules II	USCG, USCGS Barbers Point, HI	
2009	Lockheed HC-130J Hercules II	USCG, USCGS Barbers Point, HI	
2010	Lockheed HC-130J Hercules II	USCG, USCGS Elizabeth City, NC	
2011	Lockheed HC-130J Hercules II	USCG, USCGS Kodiak, AK	
2012	Lockheed HC-130J Hercules II	USCG, USCGS Barbers Point, HI	
2013	Lockheed HC-130J Hercules II	USCG, USCGS Elizabeth City, NC	
2014	Lockheed HC-130J Hercules II	USCG, USCGS Kodiak, AK	
2015	Lockheed HC-130J Hercules II	USCG, USCGS Elizabeth City, NC	
2016	Lockheed HC-130J Hercules II	USCG, USCGS Elizabeth City, NC	
2017	Lockheed HC-130J Hercules II	USCG, USCGS Elizabeth City, NC	
2018	Lockheed HC-130J Hercules II	LMTAS, Marietta, GA	

One of 2 squadrons operating the highly capable F-15E Strike Eagle from RAF Lakenheath, 01-2004 belongs to the 494th FS. *HJC*

Notes	Serial	Type (code/other identity)	Owner/operator, location or fate
	N67AU	Lockheed LM-100J Hercules II	Pallas Aviation, Fort Worth, TX
	N71KM	Lockheed LM-100J Hercules II	Pallas Aviation, Fort Worth, TX
	N85	Canadair CL.601 Challenger	Federal Aviation Administration, Oklahoma City, OK
	N86	Canadair CL.601 Challenger	Federal Aviation Administration, Oklahoma City, OK
	N87	Canadair CL.601 Challenger	Federal Aviation Administration, Oklahoma City, OK
	N88	Canadair CL.604 Challenger	Federal Aviation Administration, Oklahoma City, OK
	N89	Canadair CL.605 Challenger	Federal Aviation Administration, Oklahoma City, OK
	N90	Canadair CL.605 Challenger	Federal Aviation Administration, Oklahoma City, OK
	N91	Canadair CL.605 Challenger	Federal Aviation Administration, Oklahoma City, OK
	N91BU	Lockheed LM-100J Hercules II	Pallas Aviation, Fort Worth, TX
	N92	Canadair CL.605 Challenger	Federal Aviation Administration, Oklahoma City, OK
	N94	Canadair CL.605 Challenger	Federal Aviation Administration, Oklahoma City, OK
	N95	Canadair CL.605 Challenger	Federal Aviation Administration, Oklahoma City, OK
	N96MG	Lockheed LM-100J Hercules II	Pallas Aviation, Fort Worth, TX
	N139RB	Lockheed LM-100J Hercules II	Pallas Aviation, Fort Worth, TX

USAFE KC-135T 59-1464, based at RAF Mildenhall and seen here in the static at RIAT. *HJC*

The list below is not intended to be a complete list of military aviation sites on the Internet. The sites listed cover Museums, Locations, Air Forces, Companies and Organisations that are mentioned elsewhere in 'Military Aircraft Markings'. Sites listed are in English or contain sufficient English to be reasonably easily understood. Each site address was correct at the time of going to press. Additions are welcome, via the usual address found at the front of the book, or via e-mail to admin@aviation-links.co.uk. An up to date copy of this list is to be found at The 'Military Aircraft Markings' Web Site, http://www.militaryaircraftmarkings.co.uk/.

Name of Site	Web Address All prefixed 'http://')
MILITARY SITES-UK	
No 1 Sqn	www.raf.mod.uk/our-organisation/squadrons/1-f-squadron/
No 2 Sqn	www.raf.mod.uk/our-organisation/squadrons/ii-ac-squadron/
No 3 Sqn	www.raf.mod.uk/our-organisation/squadrons/3-f-squadron/
No 4 Sqn	www.raf.mod.uk/our-organisation/squadrons/iv-squadron/
No 6 Sqn	www.raf.mod.uk/our-organisation/squadrons/6-squadron/
No 7 Sqn	www.raf.mod.uk/our-organisation/squadrons/7-squadron/
No 8 Sqn	www.raf.mod.uk/our-organisation/squadrons/8-squadron/
No 9 Sqn	www.raf.mod.uk/our-organisation/squadrons/ix-b-squadron/
No 10 Sqn	www.raf.mod.uk/our-organisation/squadrons/10-squadron/
No 11 Sqn	www.raf.mod.uk/our-organisation/squadrons/xi-f-squadron/
No 12 Sqn	www.raf.mod.uk/our-organisation/squadrons/12-squadron/
No 13 Sqn	www.raf.mod.uk/our-organisation/squadrons/13-squadron/
No 14 Sqn	www.raf.mod.uk/our-organisation/squadrons/14-squadron/
No 16 Sqn	www.raf.mod.uk/our-organisation/squadrons/16-squadron/
No 17 Sqn	www.raf.mod.uk/our-organisation/squadrons/17-squadron/
No 18 Sqn	www.raf.mod.uk/our-organisation/squadrons/18-squadron/
No 22 Sqn	www.raf.mod.uk/our-organisation/squadrons/22-squadron/
No 24 Sqn	www.raf.mod.uk/our-organisation/squadrons/xxiv-squadron/
No 25 Sqn	www.raf.mod.uk/our-organisation/squadrons/xxv-f-squadron/
No 27 Sqn	www.raf.mod.uk/our-organisation/squadrons/27-squadron/
No 28 Sqn	www.raf.mod.uk/our-organisation/squadrons/28-squadron/
No 29 Sqn	www.raf.mod.uk/our-organisation/squadrons/29-squadron/
No 32 (The Royal) Sqn	www.raf.mod.uk/our-organisation/squadrons/32-squadron/
No 33 Sqn	www.raf.mod.uk/our-organisation/squadrons/33-squadron/
No 39 Sqn	www.raf.mod.uk/our-organisation/squadrons/39-squadron/
No 41 Sqn	www.raf.mod.uk/our-organisation/squadrons/41-squadron/
No 45 Sqn	www.raf.mod.uk/our-organisation/squadrons/45-squadron/
No 47 Sqn	www.raf.mod.uk/our-organisation/squadrons/47-squadron/
No 51 Sqn	www.raf.mod.uk/our-organisation/squadrons/51-squadron/
No 54 Sqn	www.raf.mod.uk/our-organisation/squadrons/54-squadron/
No 56 Sqn	www.raf.mod.uk/our-organisation/squadrons/56-squadron/
No 57 Sqn	www.raf.mod.uk/our-organisation/squadrons/lvii-squadron/
No 60 Sqn	www.raf.mod.uk/our-organisation/squadrons/60-squadron/
No 70 Sqn	www.raf.mod.uk/our-organisation/squadrons/lxx-squadron/
No 72 Sqn	www.raf.mod.uk/our-organisation/squadrons/72-squadron/
No 84 Sqn	www.raf.mod.uk/our-organisation/squadrons/84-squadron/
No 92 Sqn	www.raf.mod.uk/our-organisation/squadrons/92-squadron/
No 99 Sqn	www.raf.mod.uk/our-organisation/squadrons/99-squadron/
No 100 Sqn	www.raf.mod.uk/our-organisation/squadrons/100-squadron/
No 101 Sqn	www.raf.mod.uk/our-organisation/squadrons/101-squadron/
No 115 Sqn	www.raf.mod.uk/our-organisation/squadrons/115-squadron/
No 120 Sqn	www.raf.mod.uk/our-organisation/squadrons/120-squadron/
No 202 Sqn	www.raf.mod.uk/our-organisation/squadrons/202-squadron/
No 206 Sqn	www.raf.mod.uk/our-organisation/squadrons/206-squadron/
No 230 Sqn	www.raf.mod.uk/our-organisation/squadrons/230-squadron/
No 617 Sqn	www.raf.mod.uk/our-organisation/squadrons/617-squadron/
No 700X NAS	www.royalnavy.mod.uk/our-organisation/the-fighting-arms/fleet-air-arm/support-and-training/700x-naval-air-squadron
No 703 NAS	www.royalnavy.mod.uk/our-organisation/the-fighting-arms/fleet-air-arm/support-and-training/703-naval-air-squadron
No 705 NAS	www.royalnavy.mod.uk/our-organisation/the-fighting-arms/fleet-air-arm/support-and-training/705-naval-air-squadron
No 727 NAS	www.royalnavy.mod.uk/our-organisation/the-fighting-arms/fleet-air-arm/support-and-training/727-naval-air-squadron

Name of Site	Web Address All prefixed 'http://'
No 736 NAS	www.royalnavy.mod.uk/our-organisation/the-fighting-arms/fleet-air-arm/hawk-jets/736-naval-air-squadron
No 750 NAS	www.royalnavy.mod.uk/our-organisation/the-fighting-arms/fleet-air-arm/support-and-training/750-naval-air-squadron
No 809 NAS	www.royalnavy.mod.uk/our-organisation/the-fighting-arms/fleet-air-arm/future-aircraft/809-naval-air-squadron
No 814 NAS	www.royalnavy.mod.uk/our-organisation/the-fighting-arms/fleet-air-arm/helicopter-squadrons/merlin-mk2/814-naval-air-squadron
No 815 NAS	www.royalnavy.mod.uk/our-organisation/the-fighting-arms/fleet-air-arm/helicopter-squadrons/wildcat/815-naval-air-squadron
No 820 NAS	www.royalnavy.mod.uk/our-organisation/the-fighting-arms/fleet-air-arm/helicopter-squadrons/merlin-mk2/820-naval-air-squadron
No 824 NAS	www.royalnavy.mod.uk/our-organisation/the-fighting-arms/fleet-air-arm/helicopter-squadrons/merlin-mk2/824-naval-air-squadron
No 825 NAS	www.royalnavy.mod.uk/our-organisation/the-fighting-arms/fleet-air-arm/helicopter-squadrons/wildcat/825-naval-air-squadron
No 845 NAS	www.royalnavy.mod.uk/our-organisation/the-fighting-arms/fleet-air-arm/helicopter-squadrons/merlin-mk-4/845-naval-air-squadron
No 846 NAS	www.royalnavy.mod.uk/our-organisation/the-fighting-arms/fleet-air-arm/helicopter-squadrons/merlin-mk-4/846-naval-air-squadron
No 847 NAS	www.royalnavy.mod.uk/our-organisation/the-fighting-arms/fleet-air-arm/helicopter-squadrons/wildcat/847-naval-air-squadron
The Army Air Corps	www.army.mod.uk/who-we-are/corps-regiments-and-units/army-air-corps/
Fleet Air Arm	www.royalnavy.mod.uk/our-organisation/the-fighting-arms/fleet-air-arm
Ministry of Defence	www.gov.uk/government/organisations/ministry-of-defence
QinetiQ	www.qinetiq.com/
RAF Akrotiri	www.raf.mod.uk/our-organisation/stations/raf-akrotiri/
RAF Benson	www.raf.mod.uk/our-organisation/stations/raf-benson/
RAF Brize Norton	www.raf.mod.uk/our-organisation/stations/raf-brize-norton/
RAF College Cranwell	www.raf.mod.uk/our-organisation/stations/raf-college-cranwell/
RAF Coningsby	www.raf.mod.uk/our-organisation/stations/raf-coningsby/
Coningsby Aviation Site (unofficial)	milky01.co.uk/
RAF Cosford	www.raf.mod.uk/our-organisation/stations/raf-cosford/
RAF Leeming	www.raf.mod.uk/our-organisation/stations/raf-leeming/
RAF Lossiemouth	www.raf.mod.uk/our-organisation/stations/raf-lossiemouth/
RAF Marham	www.raf.mod.uk/our-organisation/stations/raf-marham/
RAF Mount Pleasant	www.raf.mod.uk/our-organisation/stations/raf-mount-pleasant/
RAF Northolt	www.raf.mod.uk/our-organisation/stations/raf-northolt/
RAF Odiham	www.raf.mod.uk/our-organisation/stations/raf-odiham/
RAF Scampton	www.raf.mod.uk/our-organisation/stations/raf-scampton/
RAF Shawbury	www.raf.mod.uk/our-organisation/stations/raf-shawbury/
RAF Syerston	www.raf.mod.uk/our-organisation/stations/raf-syerston/
RAF Valley	www.raf.mod.uk/our-organisation/stations/raf-valley/
RAF Waddington	www.raf.mod.uk/our-organisation/stations/raf-waddington/
RAF Wittering	www.raf.mod.uk/our-organisation/stations/raf-wittering/
RAF Woodvale	www.raf.mod.uk/our-organisation/stations/raf-woodvale/
RAF Wyton	www.raf.mod.uk/our-organisation/stations/raf-wyton/
Red Arrows	www.raf.mod.uk/display-teams/red-arrows/
Royal Air Force	www.raf.mod.uk/
University Air Squadrons	www.raf.mod.uk/our-organisation/university-air-squadrons/

MILITARY SITES-US

Air Combat Command	www.acc.af.mil/
Air Force Reserve Command	www.afrc.af.mil/
Air National Guard	www.ang.af.mil/
Aviano Air Base	www.aviano.af.mil/
Liberty Wing Home Page (48th FW)	www.lakenheath.af.mil/
NASA	www.nasa.gov/
Mildenhall	www.mildenhall.af.mil/
Ramstein Air Base	www.ramstein.af.mil/
Spangdahlem Air Base	www.spangdahlem.af.mil/
USAF	www.af.mil/

Name of Site	Web Address All prefixed 'http://')
USAF Europe	www.usafe.af.mil/
USAF World Wide Web Sites	www.af.mil/AF-Sites/
US Army	www.army.mil/
US Marine Corps	www.marines.mil/
US Navy	www.navy.mil/
US Navy Patrol Squadrons (unofficial)	www.vpnavy.com/

MILITARY SITES-ELSEWHERE

Armée de l'Air et de l'Espace	www.defense.gouv.fr/air/
Aeronautica Militare	www.aeronautica.difesa.it
Austrian Armed Forces (in German)	www.bundesheer.at/
Finnish Defence Force	puolustusvoimat.fi/en/frontpage
Força Aérea Portuguesa	www.emfa.pt/
German Marine	www.bundeswehr.de/en/organization/ navy/organization/naval-aviation-command
Hellenic Air Force	www.haf.gr/en/
Irish Air Corps	www.military.ie/en/who-we-are/air-corps/
Luftforsvaret	forsvaret.no/en/
Luftwaffe	www.luftwaffe.de
NATO	www.nato.int/
Royal Australian Air Force	www.airforce.gov.au/
Royal Canadian Air Force	www.airforce.forces.gc.ca/
Royal Danish Air Force	forsvaret.dk/en/organisation/airforce/
Royal Netherlands AF	www.defensie.nl/organisatie/luchtmacht
Royal New Zealand AF	www.nzdf.mil.nz/air-force/
Singapore Air Force	www.mindef.gov.sg/web/portal/rsaf/home/
South African AF Site (unofficial)	www.saairforce.co.za/
Swedish Air Force	www.forsvarsmakten.se/sv/var-verksamhet/verksamhetsomraden/flygvapnet/
Turkish Air Force	www.hvkk.tsk.tr/Portal/Page/HvkkEN

AIRCRAFT & AERO ENGINE MANUFACTURERS

Airbus Defence & Security	www.airbus.com/defence.html
BAE Systems	www.baesystems.com/
Beechcraft	beechcraft.txtav.com/
Bell	www.bellflight.com/
Boeing	www.boeing.com/
Bombardier	www.bombardier.com/
Britten-Norman	www.britten-norman.com/
Dassault	www.dassault-aviation.com/
Embraer	www.embraer.com/
General Electric	www.ge.com/
Grob Aircraft AG	grob-aircraft.com/en/
Gulfstream Aerospace	www.gulfstream.com/
Kaman Aerospace	www.kaman.com/
Leonardo	www.leonardocompany.com/
Lockheed Martin	www.lockheedmartin.com/
Rolls-Royce	www.rolls-royce.com/
Sikorsky	www.lockheedmartin.com/en-us/capabilities/sikorsky.html

UK AVIATION MUSEUMS

Army Flying Museum	www.armyflying.com/
Boscombe Down Aviation Collection, Old Sarum	www.boscombedownaviationcollection.co.uk/
Bournemouth Aviation Museum	www.bamhurn.org/
Brooklands Museum	www.brooklandsmuseum.com/
City of Norwich Aviation Museum	www.cnam.org.uk/
Cornwall Aviation Heritage Centre	cornwallaviationhc.co.uk/
de Havilland Aircraft Museum	www.dehavillandmuseum.co.uk/
Dumfries & Galloway Aviation Museum	www.dumfriesaviationmuseum.com/
Fleet Air Arm Museum	www.fleetairarm.com/
Gatwick Aviation Museum	www.gamc.org.uk/
IWM, Duxford	www.iwm.org.uk/visits/iwm-duxford
Imperial War Museum, Duxford (unofficial)	abetheaviator.wixsite.com/website/about

Name of Site	Web Address All prefixed 'http://')
The Jet Age Museum	jetagemuseum.org/
Lincs Aviation Heritage Centre	www.lincsaviation.co.uk/
Midland Air Museum	www.midlandairmuseum.co.uk/
Museum of Berkshire Aviation	www.museumofberkshireaviation.co.uk/
Museum of Science & Industry, Manchester	www.scienceandindustrymuseum.org.uk/
National Museum of Flight, East Fortune	www.nms.ac.uk/national-museum-of-flight
Newark Air Museum	www.newarkairmuseum.org/
North East Land, Sea & Air Museums	www.nelsam.org.uk/
RAF Museum, Cosford & Hendon	www.rafmuseum.org.uk/
Science Museum, South Kensington	www.sciencemuseum.org.uk/
South Wales Aviation Museum	www.swam.online/
South Yorkshire Aircraft Museum	www.southyorkshireaircraftmuseum.org.uk/
Wattisham Station Heritage Museum	www.wattishamstationheritage.org/
Yorkshire Air Museum, Elvington	www.yorkshireairmuseum.org/

AVIATION SOCIETIES

Air Britain	www.air-britain.com/
Air Yorkshire	www.airyorkshire.org.uk/
Aviation Heritage UK (was BAPC)	aviationheritageuk.org/
LAAS International	www.laasdata.com/
Military Aviation Review	militaryaviationreview.com/
Royal Aeronautical Society	www.aerosociety.com/
Scramble (Dutch Aviation Society)	www.scramble.nl/
Solent Aviation Society	www.solent-aviation-society.co.uk/
Spitfire Society	www.spitfiresociety.org/
The Aviation Society Manchester	www.tasmanchester.com/
Ulster Aviation Society	www.ulsteraviationsociety.org/
Wolverhampton Aviation Group	www.wolverhamptonaviationgroup.co.uk/

OPERATORS OF HISTORIC AIRCRAFT

The Aircraft Restoration Company	www.aircraftrestorationcompany.com/
B-17 Preservation Ltd.	www.sallyb.org.uk/
Battle of Britain Memorial Flight	www.raf.mod.uk/display-teams/battle-of-britain-memorial-flight/
The Catalina Society	www.catalina.org.uk/
Hangar 11 Collection	www.hangar11.co.uk/
Historic Helicopters	www.historichelicopters.com/
Navy Wings	www.navywings.org.uk/
The Fighter Collection	www.fighter-collection.com/
The Real Aeroplane Company	www.realaero.com/
The Shuttleworth Collection	www.shuttleworth.org/

SITES RELATING TO SPECIFIC TYPES OF MILITARY AIRCRAFT

The 655 Maintenance & Preservation Society	www.xm655.com/
B-24 Liberator	www.b24bestweb.com/
C-130 Hercules	www.c-130hercules.net/
EE Canberra	www.bywat.co.uk/
The Eurofighter site	www.eurofighter.com/
The ex FRADU Canberra Site	www.fradu-canberras.co.uk/
The ex FRADU Hunter Site	www.fradu-hunters.co.uk/
F-4 Phantom II Society	www.f4phantom.com/
F-16: The Complete Reference	www.f-16.net/
F-35 Lightning II	www.f35.com/
The Gripen	www.saab.com/products/air/fighter-systems
Jet Provost Heaven	www.jetprovosts.com
K5083 - Home Page (Hawker Hurricane)	www.k5083.mistral.co.uk/
Lockheed SR-71 Blackbird	www.wvi.com/~lelandh/sr-71~1.htm
The MiG-21 Page	www.topedge.com/panels/aircraft/sites/kraft/mig.htm
P-3 Orion Research Group	www.p3orion.nl/
Thunder & Lightnings (Postwar British Aircraft)	www.thunder-and-lightnings.co.uk/
UK Apache Resource Centre	ukapache.com/

Name of Site	Web Address All prefixed 'http://')
MISCELLANEOUS	
Aerodata Software Ltd.	www.aerodata.org/
AeroResource	www.aeroresource.co.uk/
The AirNet Web Site	www.aviation-links.co.uk/
ALAT.FR	www.alat.fr/
Aviation Databases	www.aviationdatabases.com/
Delta Reflex	www.deltareflex.com/forum
Demobbed - Out of Service British Military Aircraft	demobbed.org.uk/
Euro Demobbed	www.eurodemobbed.org.uk/
Fighter Control	fightercontrol.co.uk/
Freebird Aviation Database	www.freebirddb.com/
Iconic Aircraft	www.iconicaircraft.co.uk/
Joseph F. Baugher's US Military Serials Site	www.joebaugher.com/
The 'Military Aircraft Markings' Web Site	www.militaryaircraftmarkings.co.uk/
Pacific Aviation Database	www.gfiapac.org/
PlaneBaseNG	www.planebase.biz/
Thunder & Lightnings: Airfield Viewing Guides	www.thunder-and-lightnings.co.uk/spotting/
UK Airshow Review	www.airshows.co.uk/
UK Military Aircraft Serials Resource Centre	www.ukserials.com/

A sight that is unlikely to be repeated - a line-up of F-16s at Fairford 2024.

Serial	Type (other identity) [code]	Owner/operator, location or fate

OVERSEAS MILITARY MARKINGS

FRANCE
French Government

Serial	Type	Owner/operator
F-ZBQR	Airbus H.145D-3	Sécurité Civile
F-ZBQS	Airbus H.145D-3	Sécurité Civile
F-ZBQT	Airbus H.145D-3	Sécurité Civile (on order)
F-ZBQU	Airbus H.145D-3	Sécurité Civile (on order)
F-ZBQV	Airbus H.145D-3	Sécurité Civile (on order)

GERMANY
Luftwaffe, Marineflieger & Heeresfliegertruppe (Heer)

Serial	Type	Owner/operator
75+01	Airbus Helicopters H.145M (D-HADI)	Heer (on order)
75+02	Airbus Helicopters H.145M (D-HADV)	Heer (on order)
75+54	Airbus Helicopters H.145M (D-HBTA)	Heer IntHubschrAusbZ, Bückeburg
75+55	Airbus Helicopters H.145M (D-HBTP)	Heer (on order)
75+56	Airbus Helicopters H.145M (D-HBTT)	Heer IntHubschrAusbZ, Bückeburg